THE HANDBOOK OF
STRESS AND HEALTH

THE HANDBOOK OF STRESS AND HEALTH

A GUIDE TO RESEARCH AND PRACTICE

Edited by

Cary L. Cooper and James Campbell Quick

WILEY Blackwell

This edition first published 2017
© 2017 John Wiley & Sons Ltd.

Registered Office
John Wiley & Sons Ltd, The Atrium, Southern Gate, Chichester, West Sussex, PO19 8SQ, UK

Editorial Offices
350 Main Street, Malden, MA 02148-5020, USA
9600 Garsington Road, Oxford, OX4 2DQ, UK
The Atrium, Southern Gate, Chichester, West Sussex, PO19 8SQ, UK

For details of our global editorial offices, for customer services, and for information about how to apply for permission to reuse the copyright material in this book please see our website at www.wiley.com/wiley-blackwell.

The right of Cary L Cooper and James Campbell Quick to be identified as the authors of the editorial material in this work has been asserted in accordance with the UK Copyright, Designs and Patents Act 1988.

Library of Congress Cataloging-in-Publication Data applied for.
9781118993774 (hardback)

A catalogue record for this book is available from the British Library.

Cover image: ranplett/Gettyimages

Set in 10/12pt Times by Aptara Inc., New Delhi, India
Printed and bound in Malaysia by Vivar Printing Sdn Bhd

1   2017

Contents

Notes on Contributors

David A. Adler is a Professor of Medicine and Psychiatry, Tufts University School of Medicine and Sackler Graduate School of Biomedical Sciences, Senior Psychiatrist at Tufts Medical Center, and a mental health services researcher with a national reputation in depression research. As an integral member of the Program on Health, Work and Productivity, he has been involved in the design and implementation of many research projects across a broad array of psychiatric disorders conducted in both primary care and workplace settings.

Neal M. Ashkanasy is Professor of Management in the UQ Business School, University of Queensland. He studies emotion in organizations, leadership, culture, and ethical behavior. He has published in journals such as the *Academy of Management Journal and Review* and the *Journal of Applied Psychology*. He served as editor-in-chief of the *Journal of Organizational Behavior*, associate editor for the *Academy of Management Review*, and is currently series editor for *Research on Emotion in Organizations*.

Francisca Azocar is Vice President of Research and Evaluation of Behavioral Health Sciences at Optum Behavioral. Dr. Azocar has been at Optum for 17 years where she has created numerous research partnerships between academia, employers, and health plans. She has extensive experience conducting intervention research on workplace depression interventions, telephonic outreach and care management, patient-reported outcomes, dissemination of practice guidelines, and the impact of clinical interventions on utilization and costs.

Michelle Ball is a Senior Lecturer in Psychology at Victoria University, Melbourne. She completed training in clinical neuropsychology concurrent with her PhD, which investigated cognitive processing during sleep as applied to waking people up to their smoke alarm. She is currently the leader of a team at Victoria University that is studying the bidirectional influences of the brain–gut connection in people with a range of disorders, including myalgic encephalomyelitis/chronic fatigue syndrome and attention deficit hyperactivity disorder. In keeping with her training in neuropsychology, she is particularly interested in exploring gut dysbiosis and cognitive symptoms.

Julian Barling holds the Borden Chair of Leadership at the Queen's School of Business, Kingston, Ontario, and is author of *The Science of Leadership: Lessons from Research for Organizational Leaders* (2014). His research focuses on the effects of leaders' psychological well-being on the quality of their leadership behaviors, and the development of leadership behaviors. He is coeditor (with Christopher Barnes, Erica Carleton, and David Wagner) of *Work and Sleep: Research Insights for the Workplace* (2016).

Derrick A. Bennett obtained a PhD from the University of Manchester on the subject of psychosocial factors and eating disturbance in 1998. He joined the Clinical Trial Service Unit and Epidemiological Studies Unit, Nuffield Department of Population Health, University of Oxford, in 2004. Since then his main area of research has concentrated on the generation of reliable evidence from large-scale observational epidemiology and randomized trials of chronic disease.

Joel B. Bennett is President of Organizational Wellness and Learning Systems (OWLS), a consulting firm that specializes in evidence-based wellness and e-learning technologies to catalyze organizational health. Dr. Bennett first delivered stress management programming in 1985 and OWLS programs have since reached an estimated 50,000 workers across the United States and internationally. He is author of over 30 peer-reviewed articles and chapters and five books, including the most recent *Well-Being Champions: A Competency-Based Guidebook.* Dr. Bennett is on the board of directors for the National Wellness Institute.

Pernille E. Bidstrup has an MA in psychology and PhD in health science. She is a senior researcher and head of the research group Psychological and Behavioral Aspects of Cancer Survivorship at the Unit of Survivorship, Danish Cancer Society Research Center. Her research focuses primarily on psychological, physical, and health behavior aspects in cancer patients and their relatives. She has published 40 original papers in international peer-reviewed journals and contributed to three book chapters.

Amanda Biggs is a Lecturer in the Griffith Business School, Griffith University, Australia. Her research interests encompass the management of psychological and physical health at work, including work engagement, stress, bullying, healthy behaviours, and positive organizational cultures.

Bridget A. Blitz is a social worker with Optimizing Advanced Complex Illness Support (OACIS) at Lehigh Valley Health Network, Pennsylvania. She received her Master's degree at Rutgers University Graduate School of Social Work and has 20 years of experience in social work, including hospital case management, inpatient psychiatric and substance use treatment, and outpatient community health. At OACIS, she provides assessment, resources, and psychosocial support to home-based, palliative care patients and families.

Joyce E. Bono is the Walter J. Matherly Professor of Management at the University of Florida's Warrington College of Business Administration. She has a PhD in Organizational Behavior (minor in Personality and Social Psychology) from the University of Iowa. Her research focuses primarily on issues related to employees' quality of work life, including leadership, personality, work events, workplace relationships, affect, and motivation.

Christopher T. Boyko is a 50th Anniversary Lecturer in Design at Lancaster University, UK. His research involves human–environment interactions in the context of well-being, sustainability, and cities. He is currently leading research on the £6 million Liveable Cities project supported by the Engineering and Physical Sciences Research Council, examining the relationship between well-being, the built environment, and low-carbon living. This work builds on previous EPSRC projects, in which he investigated density within the planning process (Urban Futures) and mapped the urban design decision-making process (VivaCity2020).

Paula Brough is a Professor of Organizational Psychology in the School of Applied Psychology, Griffith University, Australia. Her research focuses on occupational stress, coping, the psychological health of high-risk workers (e.g., emergency service workers), work-life balance, and the effective measurement of psychological constructs. Professor Brough has published over 80 books, journal articles, and book chapters, and is the chief investigator on numerous national and international research grants.

Dorothy Bruck has particular expertise and interests in sleep/wake behaviour, mental health, chronic fatigue, arousal thresholds, and human behaviour in emergencies. Emeritus Professor Bruck has an international research reputation, with over 75 peer-reviewed full-length publications, some 800 citations and over $2 million in competitive grant income. Her research has been regularly featured in the media, including *Time Magazine* and *New Scientist*, and she is a founding Director of the Australian Sleep Health Foundation.

Donald Glenn Byrne is an Emeritus Professor of Clinical and Health Psychology at the Australian National University. He holds an honorary doctorate from the Norwegian University of Science and Technology, and serves on the boards of a number of scientific societies and centers. He has published widely on health and medical and clinical psychology.

Erica Carleton is an Assistant Professor at the Edwards School of Business at the University of Saskatchewan. She completed her PhD at the Smith School of Business, under the supervision of Julian Barling. Her research interests include leadership, sleep and well-being. She has received external government funding to conduct her PhD research examining sleep and its impact on leadership and well-being. Erica is also an editor of the 2016 book *Work and Sleep: Research Insights for the Workplace*.

Charles S. Carver is Distinguished Professor of Psychology at the University of Miami. His work spans the areas of personality psychology, social psychology, health psychology, and more recently experimental psychopathology. He served for six years as editor of the *Journal of Personality and Social Psychology*'s section on Personality Processes and Individual Differences and six years as an associate editor of *Psychological Review*.

Hong Chang is Statistician within the Tufts Medical Center Institute for Clinical Research and Health Policy Studies working with the Program on Health, Work and Productivity. He is an Assistant Professor of Medicine, Tufts University School of Medicine. Dr. Chang has been a key researcher involved in the development and testing of the Work Limitations Questionnaire (WLQ) and workplace health and productivity improvement interventions.

Peter Y. Chen is Professor of Psychology and a Fellow of the Society for Industrial and Organizational Psychology. He serves as editor of the *Journal of Occupational Health Psychology* and associate editor of the *Journal of Organizational Effectiveness: People and Performance*. Professor Chen was ranked twenty-ninth (2000–2004) based on Institute for Scientific Information citation impact in 30 management journals. He has written over 90 journal articles and book chapters.

Shoshi Chen received her PhD in Organizational Behavior from the Faculty of Management at Tel Aviv University, Israel. Her primary research interests are work and stress, preventive stress management, and training and learning in organizations. She is an organizational consultant and over the years has advised a number of large organizations on topics such as learning processes (both at the individual and the organizational level), training, job analysis, leaders and mangers training, mentoring, and team development.

Faye K. Cocchiara has a Ph.D. in organizational behavior and human resource management from the University of Texas at Arlington. She is a former Human Resource manager, responsible for diversity management programs, including designing and implementing corporate diversity training. Cocchiara's research interests focus on performance stereotypes, fairness in employment selection, and gender-related stress antecedents and effects. Her work appears in the *International Handbook of Work and Health Psychology* (3rd edition, 2009), in *Improving Employee Health and Well Being* (2014), and among a number of other management-related journals.

Cary L. Cooper, KBE, is 50th Anniversary Professor of Organizational Psychology and Health at Manchester Business School, University of Manchester, UK. He is also the President of the Chartered Institute of Personnel and Development, President of the British Academy of Management, and President of RELATE (the national relationship charity). He is the author or editor of over 150 books and over 350 scholarly articles, and a regular contributor to UK radio and TV. He was knighted by the Queen in 2014 for his contribution to the social sciences.

Rachel Cooper is Distinguished Professor of Design Management and Policy at Lancaster University where she is Director of ImaginationLancaster. Her research interests cover design management, design policy, new product development, design in the built environment, design against crime, and socially responsible design. She is currently coinvestigator of Liveable Cities, an ambitious, five-year program of research to develop a method of designing and engineering low-carbon, resource-secure, well-being-prioritized UK cities.

Tom Cox holds the Chair in Occupational Health Psychology and Management at Birkbeck, University of London, where he is Director of the Centre for Sustainable Working Life. He also holds an Honorary Chair in Psychosocial Oncology at the University of Aberdeen. His interests focus on the interplay of three areas: organizational psychology, occupational health and safety, and cancer survivorship and work engagement.

Marie P. Cross is a graduate student in Health Psychology at the University of California, Irvine. She is broadly interested in the connections between positive emotions and physical health. Her current research focuses on the associations between positive facial expressions and various indicators of physical health, including heart rate variability and self-reported health.

Susanne O. Dalton is currently working as Senior Researcher in Survivorship Unit, in the Danish Cancer Society Research Center. She heads the Research Group on Social Inequality in Survivorship, and conducts research that primarily focuses on social inequality in cancer and on the physical, psychological, and socioeconomic consequences of cancer. She has published 134 peer-reviewed papers in international scientific journals and has authored a number of book chapters.

Dennis Devine received his PhD in Industrial/Organizational Psychology from Michigan State University and is now an Associate Professor in I/O Psychology at Indiana University–Purdue University, Indianapolis. His research interests include group decision-making (particularly juries) and all aspects of team effectiveness. His work has appeared in *Personnel Psychology*, *Organizational Behavior and Human Decision Processes*, *Group Dynamics: Theory, Research, and Practice*, *Small Group Research*, and *Journal of Applied Social Psychology*. He is also the author of a book titled *Jury Decision Making: The State of the Science*.

Philip Dewe is an Emeritus Professor at Birkbeck, University of London. He has written extensively on work stress and coping.

Brian Jamel Dixon is a Board-Certified Adult, Child and Adolescent Psychiatrist who believes that reintegrating mental health into our modern lifestyle is crucial to well-being. His novel approach blending behavior modification, psychotherapy, and medication management empowers individuals to reach their full potential regardless of adversity. Exploring wellness and mental health is an exciting area for him and his private psychiatric practice based in Fort Worth, Texas. His services include public and private consultations with groups, schools, organizations, and businesses.

Marnie Dobson is an Adjunct Assistant Professor at the University of California, Irvine, Center for Occupational and Environmental Health, and the Associate Director of the Center for Social Epidemiology. She is a medical sociologist specializing in work stress research in occupational health, particularly work organization, cardovascular disease, obesity, and mental health. She has expertise in qualitative methods and participatory action research. She is coeditor of the book *Unhealthy Work: Causes, Consequences, Cures* (2009).

Cameron D. T. Dodd received his Master's from the University of Texas at Arlington in Quantitative Biology in 2015. His research interests lie in the treatment and prevention of common pathogens through the isolation of active sites in organic compounds.

Alexa Doerr is an Assistant Professor of Human Resources Development at Towson University. She has served in consulting positions at the Society for Human Resource Management and the American Institutes for Research. Her primary research interests include occupational health and safety, personnel selection, and testing. She has published a journal article in *The Industrial-Organizational Psychologist* and a book chapter in *Legal and Regulatory Issues in Human Resources Management* (2014).

Suzie Drummond recently completed her PhD in Organisational Psychology in the School of Applied Psychology, Griffith University, Australia. Her research focused on understanding future-oriented coping within the framework of the transactional model of stress and coping and its relationship with personality and individual and organizational well-being.

Geir Arild Espnes is a Professor of Health Psychology in Norwegian University of Science and Technology. He is Honorary Professor at Australian National University. He is Director of the NTNU Center for Health Promotion Research in Trondheim, has published widely, and is active as member and leader in a number of research societies.

Jane Fischer is a Research Fellow at the National Centre for Education and Training on Addiction, Flinders University, South Australia. She has been a quantitative public health researcher and educator in the substance use field for over 15 years, and was recently awarded a Doctorate of Philosophy from the University of Queensland for her dissertation, by publication, on the quality of life of substance users residing in community settings.

Trevor A. Foulk is a PhD student at the University of Florida's Warrington College of Business Administration. He holds a BBA (Summa Cum Laude) from the University of Massachusetts-Amherst. His research focuses primarily on negative behaviors in the workplace, power and influence, and the cognitive mechanisms underlying responses to workplace events.

Robert J. Gatchel is the Nancy P. and John G. Penson Endowed Professor of Clinical Health Psychology at the University of Texas at Arlington. He is also the Director of the Center for Excellence for the Study of Health and Chronic Illness there, as well as Director of Biopsychosocial Research, Osteopathic Research Center, University of North Texas Health Science Center. In addition, he is a Clinical Professor at the University of Texas Southwestern Medical Center at Dallas.

James Gerhart, PhD, is an Assistant Professor in the Department of Behavioral Sciences at Rush University Medical Center. His research focuses on the outcomes of traumatic stress and anger in the context of medical illness. In particular, he is interested in the ways that traumatic stress may manifest in impulsivity and hostility and impact medical care. He is currently evaluating programming to enhance resilience among medical providers who care for chronically ill and dying patients.

Elisabeth Gilbert is a PhD student at the University of Florida's Warrington College of Business Administration. She holds a BA from the University of North Carolina-Chapel Hill and an MBA from Rollins College. Her research focuses primarily on employee well-being and interpersonal influence in organizations.

Annabel Greenhill, MA, is a Research Associate at Tufts Medical Center. She provides support and consultation to the Evaluation Program in the Tufts Clinical and Translational Science Institute.

Bjørn Grinde received his education in natural sciences, psychology, and anthropology from the University of Oslo, being awarded a Dr. Scient. and Dr. Philos. in biology. He is presently Chief Scientist at the Division of Mental Health, Norwegian Institute of Public Health. Previously he served as a scientist and professor at leading universities in Norway, the United States, and Japan. He has written several books, including *Darwinian Happiness* (2012) and *The Evolution of Consciousness* (2016).

Gregory R. Harper is a retired oncologist who is certified by the American Board of Internal Medicine in both Medical Oncology and Hospice and Palliative Medicine. He holds an Emeritus appointment in the Department of Medicine at Lehigh Valley Health Network in Allentown, Pennsylvania, where he served as Physician in Chief of the John and Dorothy Morgan Cancer Center. Dr. Harper cared for adult cancer patients for 35 years, specializing in breast cancer and palliative care.

Meredith M. Hartzell has just finished her doctorate at the University of Texas at Arlington in Health Psychology. She studies the treatment of chronic pain patients and influential factors for pain severity, such as fear avoidance, depressive symptoms, and perceived disability. She has published widely on the topic of central sensitivity syndromes.

Juliet Hassard is Lecturer in Occupational Health Psychology at Birkbeck, University of London, where she is also Deputy Director of the Centre for Sustainable Working Life. Her research interests focus on best practice in health and safety management and, in particular, the nature and interplay of health and gender related issues.

Catherine A. Heaney is an Associate Professor (Teaching) in the Stanford Prevention Research Center, the Department of Psychology, and the interdisciplinary Program in Human

Biology at Stanford University. Dr. Heaney's primary research focus is work and health, collaborating with worksites and communities to develop and evaluate intervention strategies for restructuring physical, organizational, and social aspects of work to reduce sources of stress, build social support, enhance perceived control of work tasks, strengthen employee coping skills, improve employee health behaviors, and thereby promote workers' health.

Demetria F. Henderson is a doctoral candidate in the Department of Management at the University of Texas at Arlington. Her current research interests include diversity, positive organizational behavior, and career advancement. Prior to beginning her doctoral work, Demetria worked as a SAS programmer, utilizing her background in statistics. She holds a BS in Mathematics from Louisiana State University and an MS in Organization Development from the McColl School of Business at Queens University of Charlotte.

Stevan E. Hobfoll has published 12 books, and over 250 journal articles and book chapters. He is Presidential Professor and Chair of the Department of Behavioral Sciences at Rush Medical College in Chicago and Professor of Medicine and Preventive Medicine. He was a Senior Fellow of the Center for National Security Studies at the University of Haifa, Israel, and a Fulbright Senior Scholar. His framework for mass casualty intervention is the world standard.

Beverley Lim Høeg has a Master's degree in Psychology from the University of Copenhagen and is doing her doctoral research at the Unit of Cancer Survivorship, Danish Cancer Society Research Center. Her areas of research include stress and coping, bereavement, and return-to-work and follow-up treatment after cancer. She is also a counselor at the Danish Cancer Society's Counseling Center in Copenhagen, working with cancer patients and their caregivers.

Lucie Holmgreen is a postdoctoral fellow specializing in traumatic stress in the Department of Behavioral Sciences at Rush University Medical Center. Her research investigates the cognitive, emotional, and behavioral bases of the cyclical nature of trauma. Her work also examines institutional responses to traumatic stress as well as its pervasive physical health impacts.

Annekatrin Hoppe is a Professor for Occupational Health Psychology at Humboldt University of Berlin, Germany. Her research focuses on occupational health and ethnic health disparities, cultural diversity and well-being in teams, and the development and evaluation of resource-oriented interventions in the workplace.

Ning Hou is an Assistant Professor of Management at St. Cloud State University. She received her PhD in Industrial and Organizational Psychology, as well as an MS in Statistics. She has served as reviewer for Industrial and Organizational Psychology (SIOP) and Academy of Management (AOM) conferences. Her work has appeared in *Journal of Career Assessment*, *Journal of Beijing Jiaotong University* (Chinese), and *Railway Occupational Safety Health and Environmental Protection* (Chinese). She was awarded a SIOP Foundation Small Grant in 2013 as a Co-P.I., and was the winner of the Three Minute Thesis (3MT) competition in 2013.

Melinda L. Jackson is a Senior Research Fellow in the School of Health and Biomedical Sciences, RMIT University, Melbourne, and a psychologist specializing in behavioral treatment of sleep disorders. Her research interests span sleep and neuropsychology, with a particular focus on the role of sleep in mood disorders and other clinical conditions such as myalgic encephalomyelitis/chronic fatigue syndrome and obstructive sleep apnoea.

Christoffer Johansen is Head of Research in the Unit of Cancer Survivorship, one of seven units in the Danish Cancer Society Research Center. He is a Professor at the Oncology Clinic, Rigshospitalet, University of Copenhagen, with a focus on late effects in cancer. Professor Johansen has published more than 350 peer-reviewed publications, contributed to several books and authored three anthologies as well as coauthored one book – all on the topic of cancer and the mind, and psychological, social and late effects in relation to this disease. He is currently also Adjunct Professor at the Institute of Psychology, University of Copenhagen, Denmark, and at the Medical Faculty, University of Eppendorf, Hamburg, Germany.

Stina Johansson is Professor Emerita in Social Work at Umea University, Sweden. She received her doctorate in Sociology in 1986 and became Associate Professor in Sociology at Uppsala University in 1993. Her research interests are social care, social gerontology, gender, diversity, and comparative social policy. Stina Johansson has directed several research projects and has published together with researchers from the Scandinavian countries, China, and Australia. She coedited *Population Ageing from a Lifecourse Perspective* (2014).

Brandon A. Johnson completed his doctorate in Industrial/Organizational Psychology at Auburn University in Auburn, Alabama. As an active contributor in his field, he has conducted research and worked in various areas of the public and private sectors. His research interests include contemporary issues related to environmental stressors and workers' reactions to such stressors.

Morgan Jones is currently working in the private sector as a consultant for the pre-hire assessment company, FurstPerson. She received her MS in Industrial/Organizational Psychology at Indiana University–Purdue University, Indianapolis. Her research interests broadly include workplace mistreatment and the resulting organizational or health-related outcomes of such experiences.

Sandra Kiffin-Petersen is Assistant Professor at the University of Western Australia Business School where she teaches and consults in organizational behaviour, leadership, emotions, team effectiveness, trust, and negotiation. She has won Best Paper awards, and both published articles and presented numerous papers at conferences in Europe, United States, New Zealand, and Australia. She is a member of the Organisational Behaviour, and Managerial and Organizational Cognitions divisions of the Academy of Management (USA) and the Australian and New Zealand Academy of Management.

Victoria Kostadinov is a Research Officer at the National Centre for Education and Training on Addiction at Flinders University, South Australia. She holds a Master's degree in Organisational Psychology and Human Factors from the University of Adelaide. Her primary research interests lie in the social determinants of alcohol and drug use, and particularly the role of the workplace.

Paul Landsbergis is Associate Professor, Department of Environmental and Occupational Health Sciences, State University of New York–Downstate School of Public Health, Brooklyn, NY. He was a coeditor of *The Workplace and Cardiovascular Disease* (2000) and *Unhealthy Work* (2009), and a member of the National Research Council's Committee on the Health and Safety Needs of Older Workers. He is deputy editor of the *American Journal of Industrial Medicine*.

Michael P. Leiter is Professor of Psychology at Deakin University in Melbourne, Australia and an Adjunct Professor at Acadia University, Wolfville, Nova Scotia. He is internationally renowned for his work on job burnout and work engagement. His current initiative in research and consulting is CREW – Civility, Respect, and Engagement at Work – that improves collegiality within workgroups.

Debra Lerner is Senior Scientist within the Tufts Medical Center Institute for Clinical Research and Health Policy Studies, Director of the Program on Health, Work and Productivity and Professor of Medicine and Psychiatry, Tufts University School of Medicine and Sackler Graduate School of Biomedical Sciences. Dr. Lerner's research addresses the science and practice of employee health improvement with an emphasis on sustaining ability to function at work. She and her colleagues developed the widely used Work Limitations Questionnaire (WLQ).

Lennart Levi was Professor of Psychosocial Medicine (1978–95) and became Emeritus Professor in 1995, both at the Karolinska Institutet, Stockholm, Sweden. He was Founder and Director, National Swedish Institute for Psychosocial Medicine (1980–95); a member of the World Health Organization's Expert Panel on Mental Health (1973–96); temporary advisor/consultant to several UN Specialized Agencies, and Member of the Swedish Parliament 2006–2010. He was awarded the Royal Swedish Medal of Merit (2001), the NIOSH Career Achievement Award (2005) and the Compostela Prize (2014).

Donald P. Lewis is a medical physician with extensive specialist expertise in the assessment and treatment of myalgic encephalomyelitis/chronic fatigue syndrome. As the medical director at CFS Discovery Clinic in Melbourne, he has been dedicated to investigating this condition since 1985. Recognised as an international expert, Dr. Lewis's commitment to clinical research continues to enhance diagnostic and treatment outcomes for patients.

Luo Lu is currently the Distinguished Professor in National Taiwan University, Taiwan. Her major research interests include culture and self, subjective well-being, stress and adjustment, occupational health, and other Industrial/Organizational psychological topics. She has been awarded the Distinguished Research Award by the Taiwanese government. She has published extensively in journals and edited and authored books and book chapters.

Sara MacLennan is a Senior Lecturer in the Academic Urology Unit, University of Aberdeen, and Director of Operations for UCAN (a urological cancer charity). She is an Honorary Research Fellow at Birkbeck, University of London. She is a Registered Health Psychologist (Health and Care Professions Council). Her interests lie in the health psychology of cancer and, among other things, issues relating to survivorship and working life.

Wayne Martin, LCSW, is a psychophysiologist in private practice in Fort Worth, Texas, helping individuals and organizations learn to manage stress more successfully. He utilizes biofeedback, neurofeedback, clinical hypnosis, and mindfulness to facilitate the shift from surviving into fully thriving in this chaotic world. He keeps his balance by spending as much time as possible in the outdoors and sculpting meditation labyrinths.

Christina Maslach is a pioneering researcher on job burnout, and the author of the Maslach Burnout Inventory (MBI), the most widely used research measure in the burnout field. She has written numerous articles and books on this topic, several of which have received awards, and she is the founding coeditor, along with Michael Leiter, of the e-journal *Burnout Research*. She was recognized nationally as "Professor of the Year" for her outstanding research and teaching.

Gerald Matthews is a Research Professor at the Institute for Simulation and Training at the University of Central Florida. His research focuses on cognitive science models of personality, emotion, and human performance. Specific interests include the assessment of stress and fatigue states, models of personality and information-processing, emotional intelligence, and human factors applications of individual differences research. He has published 19 books and over 300 journal articles and chapters.

Samuel Melamed is Professor (Emeritus) of Occupational Health Psychology, School of Behavioral Sciences, the Academic College of Tel Aviv–Yaffo, and Sackler Faculty of Medicine, Tel Aviv University, Israel. His research is concerned with psychosocial factors at work, burnout, and health. He is the author and coauthor of over 150 scientific papers and book chapters and is the co-originator of the Shirom-Melamed Burnout Measure (SMBM).

Rebecca Michalak is Principal Consultant of Psychsafe Pty Ltd, which specializes in helping organizations maximize employee performance while minimizing exposure to psychosocial risks. A strategic human resources management and occupational health and safety expert, she combines organizational research with practice. She holds a PhD in Business from UQ Business School, University of Queensland; has both presented to and published in academic and industry-based channels; and is a member of various research and professional associations, including the Society for Industrial Organizational Psychology, the Australian Institute of Company Directors, and the Australian Human Resources Institute.

Unni Karin Moksnes holds a doctorate in Health Science, and is Associate Professor in Health Science at Norwegian University of Science and Technology. She is a Research Coordinator in the Center for Health Promotion Research in Trondheim, Norway. She has published widely and directed large research projects.

Fehmidah Munir is a Reader in Health Psychology in the School of Sport, Exercise and Health Sciences at Loughborough University, UK, and a Registered Health Psychologist (Health and Care Professions Council). Her expertise is in workplace health, particularly in preventing and managing long-term chronic health conditions in the workplace through research intervention.

Michael Neeper, Research Assistant with Organizational Wellness and Learning Systems (OWLS) since 2012, has worked on several projects, including an online system for teaching self-care with medical Qigong and an online version of the OWLS Team Awareness program for reducing workplace behavioral risks. Michael is doctoral candidate at the University of Texas at Arlington with a dissertation in the field of Organizational Wellness. His interests are wellness/fitness, training and development, statistics, and psychometrics.

Debra L. Nelson is the Spears School of Business Associates Chair and Professor of Management at Oklahoma State University. Her research focuses on positive organizational behavior, eustress at work, and identity management in the workplace. She is also a principal in Nelson Quick Group, specializing in executive coaching and leadership development.

Gianina-Ioana Postavaru is a postdoctoral researcher in the Centre for Sustainable Working Life at Birkbeck, University of London. Her research projects have mainly focused on breast cancer survivorship and treatment-related decisions in families with neoplastic children.

Sarah Pressman is an Associate Professor of Psychology and Social Behavior at the University of California, Irvine. Her research examines the associations between positive psychosocial factors, stress, and physical well-being, with a particular focus on the possible biological and behavioral pathways by which psychosocial factors "get under the skin" to influence health. She has published numerous papers in top psychology journals and her work has been cited extensively by the popular media.

James Campbell Quick holds the Goolsby–Fouse Endowed Chair at the University of Texas at Arlington and is Professor, Alliance Manchester Business School, University of Manchester, UK. He is a Fellow, American Psychological Association, and Fellow, Lancaster Leadership Centre, Lancaster University, UK. His awards include the Maroon Citation (Colgate University), the 2002 Harry and Miriam Levinson Award (American Psychological Foundation), and the Legion of Merit (United States Air Force). Jim is married to the former Sheri Grimes Schember. He is a partner in NelsonQuick Group, LLC.

Daniel E. Ray attended medical school at the Ohio State University and completed internal medicine and pulmonary/critical care training at Medical College of Wisconsin. He received a Robert Wood Johnson Foundation Grant for integrating palliative medicine in the intensive care unit at Lehigh Valley Health Network (LVHN). He is Chief of the Section of Palliative Medicine and Hospice, serves as medical director for OACIS and director for the Hospice and Palliative Medicine Fellowship program at LVHN.

Richard D. Roberts is Vice President and Chief Scientist, Center for Innovative Assessments, Professional Examination Service, New York. His main area of specialization is measurement, with a special emphasis on developing and researching innovative new items types for the assessment of both cognitive and noncognitive factors. Dr. Roberts has published over a dozen books, and about 200 peer-review articles/book chapters on these topics, with nearly 400 presentations across the globe.

Ann Roche is Director of the National Centre for Education and Training on Addiction, Flinders University. She holds a PhD in public health, and has worked for 30 years as a researcher, educator, policy analyst, and consultant to government and nongovernment bodies, including the World Health Organization. She has published over 100 peer-reviewed papers and several books and book chapters. She is a frequently invited speaker and media commentator, and a member of several national and international advisory bodies.

William H. Rogers is a Senior Statistician within the Tufts Medical Center Institute for Clinical Research and Health Policy Studies, primarily working with the Program on Health, Work and Productivity. He is nationally known expert in measuring depression and mental distress and analyzing treatment outcomes. He had a major role in developing the PC-SAD depression screener, the 36-Item Short Form Health Survey (SF-36), and the Work Limitations Questionnaire (WLQ). Dr. Rogers was chief statistician for the landmark Medical Outcomes Study.

Michael F. Scheier is Professor of Psychology at Carnegie Mellon University. His research falls at the intersection of personality, social psychology, and health psychology. His current work focuses on the effects of dispositional optimism on psychological and physical well-being, and on the health benefits of adaptive goal adjustment when confronting adversity. He is a fellow in Divisions 8 and 38 of the American Psychological Association, and has served as President of Division 38.

Peter Schnall is a Clinical Professor of Medicine at the University of California, Irvine, Division of Occupational and Environmental Medicine. He is a recognized expert on the role of occupational stress in causing hypertension and the lead editor of the standard text in this field, *The Workplace and Cardiovascular Disease* (2000). He also edited *Unhealthy Work: Causes, Consequences, Cures* (2009) and is Director of the Center for Social Epidemiology (www.unhealthywork.org).

Mim Senft is the President of Motivity Partnerships, Inc. Motivity provides wellness program evaluation and strategy design to businesses, as well as developing business to business relationships in the wellness and resilience space. Prior to starting Motivity Partnerships, Mim worked onsite at Goldman Sachs as a consultant in charge of wellness program strategy. She also worked at National Financial Partners, where she worked with more than 70 companies on wellness program and benefits design. She has more than 20 years of experience in the corporate world and has spoken at numerous conferences and roundtables on worksite wellness and benefits related topics. She currently serves on the Board of Directors for the National Wellness Institute and is Founding Member of Global Women 4 Wellbeing.

Catherine Serena is a core faculty member of the Division of Palliative Medicine, Lehigh Valley Health Network, in Allentown, PA, and has provided end-of-life care support through her 30-year career. She has a graduate degree in Social Work from Temple University, teaches college level death and dying courses, and continues to facilitate children's bereavement programming in the community while providing social work services for the inpatient team at Lehigh Valley Hospital.

Johannes Siegrist is Senior Professor of Work Stress Research at the University of Düsseldorf, Germany. Until 2012 he was Professor and Director of the Institute of Medical Sociology at that university. His main research fields are stressful work and health (being the author of the "effort–reward imbalance" model) and social inequalities in health, with over 300 scientific publications on these topics. He is a Fellow of Academia Europaea, London, and a Corresponding Fellow of the Heidelberg Academy of Sciences.

Maria Sjölund is Senior Lecturer in Social Work at Mid Sweden University. Her main research interests are social aspects of ageing and old age. Sjölund received her doctorate in Social Work at Umeå University, Sweden, 2012. Her PhD thesis, "Lived experiences of ageing," published in Swedish, contains notions and experiences of being and growing old.

Michael Sliter received his MA and PhD in Industrial/Organizational Psychology from Bowling Green State University under the supervisor of Steve Jex, PhD. Starting in academia at at Indiana University–Purdue University, Indianapolis, he has shifted to working in the field as a Senior Consultant at FurstPerson. His research focuses on workplace incivility/aggression, emotions, and workplace fitness, and has been published in top I/O journals, including

Journal of Applied Psychology, *Journal of Organizational Behavior*, and *Journal of Occupational Health Psychology*.

Ivalu Katajavaara Sørensen is a Master of Science in Public Health at the University of Copenhagen. Ivalu is an Assistant Research Scientist at the Unit of Cancer Survivorship, a part of the Danish Cancer Society Research Center. Her main focus of research is psychological stress and social relations. She is a coauthor of an ongoing systematic review and meta-analysis of psychological stress as a risk factor for cancer in collaboration with the Unit of Cancer Survivorship.

Donna Stevens is the program director for the Optimizing Advanced Complex Illness Support (OACIS) and Palliative Medicine programs at Lehigh Valley Health Network. These programs include inpatient consultation services, a nationally recognized and innovative home-based palliative care service, and an outpatient clinic. With a clinical background in occupational therapy, she had previously served as administrator in both psychiatry and skilled nursing. She serves on the Improving Outpatient Palliative Care Advisory Board of the Center to Advance Palliative Care.

Helen Thomas, LCSW, is a social worker focused on implementing best practice interventions for complex trauma affecting children, adolescents, and adults throughout our chaotic world. She understands and is passionate about assisting individuals and organizational systems recognize and treat the symptoms of trauma related to a powerful critical event and trauma related to repeated events such as domestic violence, abuse, neglect, and displacement due to war and disaster (complex trauma).

Vanessa Tirone is an Assistant Professor in the Department of Behavioral Sciences at Rush University Medical Center. Her research focuses on the impact of interpersonal violence on women's health, sexuality, and relationship functioning. She is currently developing a multidisciplinary trauma-sensitive intervention for women with chronic pelvic pain.

Sharon Toker is an Associate Professor and the head of the organizational consulting program at the Coller School of Management, Tel Aviv University, Israel. Professor Toker's research focuses on the effect of stress and burnout on physical and mental health. She is the author of more than 30 peer-reviewed papers and the recipient of the 2013 American Psychological Association and the National Institute of Occupational Safety and Health early career research award.

Amy Wallis is currently completing her Doctor of Philosophy degree at Victoria University, Melbourne, investigating the relationship between the gut and psychological symptoms in myalgic encephalomyelitis/chronic fatigue syndrome. In 2008, Amy completed her Master's in Psychology at Monash University. From her clinical experience working as a psychologist in educational, community and health settings, she is inspired to extend our current understanding of brain–gut interactions and use this knowledge to promote optimal health and well-being in the community.

Peter Warr is Emeritus Professor in the Institute of Work Psychology at the University of Sheffield, UK. He was for many years Director of the Social and Applied Psychology Unit at that university, and is an Honorary Fellow of the British Psychological Society, a Fellow of the International Association of Applied Psychology, and a Fellow of the Society for Industrial and Organizational Psychology. His research has examined psychological aspects of paid and other work, happiness and unhappiness, unemployment, aging, training, and social perception.

John Weaver, PsyD, is a licensed psychologist and director of the Healthy Thinking Initiative. John designed the Healthy Thinking Initiative and coordinates the efforts of the development team. He is a member of the steering committee for the Psychology in the Workplace Network of the American Psychological Association, and the author of *The Prevention of Depression: A Missing Piece in Wellness* and the lead author of *The Health Thinking Program* training manual. He lives and works in Waukesha, Wisconsin.

Mina Westman is a Professor Emeritus at the Faculty of Management, Tel Aviv University, and a Fellow of the Society for Industrial and Organizational Psychology (SIOP). Her research interests include job stress, work–family interchange, negative and positive crossover in the family and the workplace, the effects of vacation on stress and strain, and the impact of international assignments on the individual, the family, and the organization. She is the associate editor of *Stress and Health*.

Thomas A. Wright is the Felix E. Larkin Distinguished Professor in Management at Fordham University's Gabelli School of Business. He received his PhD from the University of California, Berkeley. A Fellow of the American Psychological Association, the Association for Psychological Science, and the Society for Industrial and Organizational Psychology, the highlight of his professional career has been publishing a number of articles on ethics with his father, Vincent P. Wright.

Moshe Zeidner is currently Professor of Educational Psychology at the University of Haifa, Israel, and founding Director and Head of the Center for Interdisciplinary Research on Emotions. He has conducted research in the area of personality and individual differences, with particular concern for the interface of personality and intelligence, emotions, emotional intelligence, and the stress and coping process. He is the author or coeditor of 10 books and author or coauthor of about 200 scientific papers and chapters.

Introduction

Cary L. Cooper and James Campbell Quick

The year 2015 marked the hundredth anniversary of Walter Bradford Cannon's seminal book *Bodily Changes in Pain, Hunger, Fear and Rage: An Account of Recent Researches into the Function of Emotional Excitement*, published originally in 1915 and revised several times. This work laid the contemporary cornerstone for our understanding of "the emergency response" as Cannon originally labeled it, later coming to term it the fight-or-flight response and the stress response. While Cannon charted primarily the sympathetic nervous system elements of the response, it was for Hans Selye (1976), who followed Cannon, to explore the endocrine (hormone) system elements of the response and connect stress to an array of diseases of adaptation. As physiologists and physicians, these two enabled us to understand how stress can make us ill, even contribute to premature death or disability. They revealed the stress–health link.

The intensive and extensive scientific research and clinical practice that occupied much of the subsequent decades of the twentieth century charted out the detailed role of stress in our health and our illnesses. Stress is directly or indirectly linked to seven of the ten leading causes of death in the United States, United Kingdom, and all developed nations (Cooper and Quick, 1999; Quick and Cooper, 2003). These seven are, in order: #1 – heart disease, #2 – cancer, #3 – stroke, #4 – injuries, #6 – suicide/homicide, #9 – chronic liver disease, and #10 – emphysema, chronic bronchitis. Therefore, stress plays a significant role in human mortality within the developed nations of the world.

In addition, stress is a major contributor to the burden of suffering in the developed nations (Macik-Frey, Quick, and Nelson, 2007); that is, stress is linked to a wide range of human morbidity. A number of the leading causes of death result from chronic health conditions, in contrast to infectious or contagious conditions, that are debilitating and cause extended suffering prior to death. These notably include heart disease, cancer, chronic liver disease, emphysema, and chronic bronchitis. Stress has been called both the spice of life and the kiss of death. Stress is an excellent rubric for a domain of knowledge and venue for clinical medical and psychological practice.

While the physiological and medical components of the stress response are foundational to the stress–health link, it was in the 1960s and 1970s that psychologists first began to make important contributions to our understanding of how stress and strain can lead to a variety of health disorders. Robert Kahn and his associates (1964) charted how organizational stress (i.e., psychosocial stress from being socially embedded in large industrial organizations) contributes to both individual and collective burdens of suffering. Cooper and Payne's (1978) research brought the stress concept and process squarely into work settings for a wide range of occupations. This era included the contribution of psychologist Richard Lazarus (1967), who placed the emphasis on the coping process. While coping is better than not coping, the concept does not quite go to the positive side of stress. Quick and Quick (1984) introduced the public health notions of prevention into the stress arena with their theory of preventive stress management, setting a framework for managing the chronic problem of stress in organizations.

However, as the twentieth century came to a close, the discovery and exploration of the positive aspect of stress came more to the fore. George Vaillant (1977) was the one who originally pointed out that successful adaptation to stress is what enables us to live, live abundantly, and to flourish. This left it for those who followed to explore the real positive dimensions of stress. Seligman (1990) really began that process with his charting of the science and practice of learned optimism, which laid the foundation for his emphasis on positive psychology during his presidency of the American Psychological Association at the end of that decade. The emphasis on human strengths, capacities, and potential moved us much closer to the positive side of stress.

Shelley Taylor and her colleagues (2000) made a major advance in stress research when they explored the architecture of the tend-and-befriend response under stressful conditions, a response significantly more hard-wired in women than in men. This life-saving response is one of the contributing factors to the greater life expectancy of women versus men. Another positive dimension of stress was advanced early in this century with the concept of challenge stress, in contrast to hindrance stress (Lepine, Podsakoff, and LePine, 2005). Challenge stress is positive stress because it enhances our strengths and develops our adaptive capacities, enabling us to live and flourish, as Vaillant might say.

These historical roots and foundations set the stage for the current scientific research and clinical practice in the nexus of stress and health. This comprehensive volume explores the up-to-date research on the link between stress and a variety of health outcomes, the theories and the processes, the moderating factors, and the intervention studies to improve health outcomes. Parts I–III explore the general theories linking stress to ill-health, summarize research for each of the health outcomes (e.g., heart disease, cancers, etc.) and then highlight some of the moderating factors (e.g. Type A behavior, locus of control). Parts IV–VI explore various intervention theories or models together with a review of interventions studies attempting to minimize the ill-health effects of stress. These additionally explore the preventive strategies to enhance well-being in a variety of contexts (e.g., the family, work, community).

Parts I–III focus on a range of stress theories and the linkages to ill-health outcomes. They include 20 chapters that address theories of stress and health processes, the set of illnesses where stress plays a direct or indirect causal role, and finally the moderating factors of the stress process.

Stress is a creatively ambiguous word without a universally agreed scientific definition. Therefore, Part I includes a set of chapters that put forth theoretical frameworks used throughout the field as organizing mechanisms: from Lennart Levi's demand–control–social support model to Johannes Siegrist's effort–reward imbalance model and Christina Maslach's classic burnout model.

As noted earlier, Hans Selye charted out the linkages of stress to a variety of diseases of maladaptation. Thus, Part II includes chapters addressing stress as a risk factor. Stress is directly or indirectly implicated in a range of human illnesses that contribute to both morbidity and mortality. Thus there are chapters on heart disease, cancer, mental health, chronic fatigue syndrome, burnout, endocrine diseases, musculoskeletal injuries, eating disorders, and caregiver fatigue.

Then Part III includes chapters on a host of moderating factors that influence the connection between stress and ill-health, such as locus of control, gender differences, personality predispositions, and socioeconomic status.

Parts IV–VI consist of 17 chapters focusing on theories of coping, prevention, and intervention research related to stress, the stress response, and the stress process. Part IV consists of a set of chapters on the coping process, and further chapters address intervention research and practice for a set of health disorders triggered or advanced by the experience of stress. Intervention research has lagged behind basic science related to the linkages between stress and ill-health. However, advances in the past several decades are turning the tide on the stress epidemic, and a range of evidence-based practices are integrating themselves into medical, psychological, and behavioral health practices.

Part V of the volume includes a set of chapters aimed at prevention, positive stress management, and enhanced well-being. Finally, Part VI concludes with four chapters aimed at preventive stress management and enhancing well-being from an organizational and community perspective.

References

Cannon, W. B. (1915). *Bodily Changes in Pain, Hunger, Fear and Rage: An Account of Recent Researches into the Function of Emotional Excitement*. New York: Appleton-Century-Crofts.

Cooper, C. L., and Payne, R. (1978). *Stress at Work*. New York: Wiley.

Cooper, C. L., and Quick, J. C. (1999). *Fast Facts: Stress and Strain*. Oxford: Health Press.

Kahn, R. L., Wolfe, D. M., Quinn, R. P., Snoek, J. D., and Rosenthal, R. A. (1964). *Organizational Stress: Studies in Role Conflict and Ambiguity*. New York: Wiley.

Lazarus, R. S. (1967). *Psychological Stress and the Coping Process*. New York: McGraw-Hill.

LePine, J. A., Podsakoff, N. P., and LePine, M. A. (2005). A meta-analytic test of the challenge stressor-hindrance stressor framework: An explanation for inconsistent relationships among stressors and performance. *Academy of Management Journal*, 48(5), 764–775.

Macik-Frey, M., Quick, J. C., and Nelson, D. L. (2007). Advances in occupational health: From a stressful beginning to a positive future. *Journal of Management*, *33*(6), 809–40.

Quick, J. C., and Cooper, C. L. (2003). *FAST FACTS: Stress and Strain*, 2nd edn. Oxford: Health Press.

Quick, J. C., and Quick, J. D. (1984). *Organizational Stress and Preventive Management*. New York: McGraw-Hill.

Seligman, M. E. P. (1990). *Learned Optimism*. New York: Knopf.

Selye, H. (1976). *Stress in Health and Disease*. Boston: Butterworth.

Taylor, S. E., Klein, L. C., Lewis, B. P., Gruenewald, T. L., Gurung, R. A. R., and Updegraff, J. A. (2000). Biobehavioral responses to stress in females: Tend-and-befriend, not fight-or-flight. *Psychological Review*, *107*(3), 411–429.

Vaillant, G. E. (1977). *Adaption to Life*. Boston: Little, Brown.

Part One

Theories

1

Bridging the Science–Policy and Policy–Implementation Gaps

A Crucial Challenge

Lennart Levi

"More, and better jobs." This is a cornerstone of the European Union's strategy for sustainable development for its 508 million inhabitants, and rightly so. But my own 60 years of active research and teaching and experience from my four years in the Swedish Parliament in this area, through countless conferences, speeches, publications, and discussions with fellow researchers, parliamentarians and cabinet ministers, have taught me that there is a rather long and deep *gap* between scientific knowledge on the one hand, and its translation into political decisions on the other. And between such policies and their successful implementation (cf. Levi, 2016).

These "science–policy and policy–implementation gaps" refer to the unnecessary delays and difficulties in turning scientific knowledge into policy and decision-making, and equally important, in *implementing* the decisions (and, eventually, in *evaluating* them).

It is widely accepted that a broad range of physical, biological, and chemical exposures can damage health and well-being – for example, bacteria, viruses, ionizing radiation, short asbestos fibers, lead, mercury, and organic solvents. It is harder but fully possible to demonstrate, and even find acceptance for, the notion that psychosocial influences brought about by social and economic conditions and conveyed by processes within the central nervous system or human behavior can have corresponding effects (Karasek and Theorell, 1990; Kompier and Levi, 1994; Levi, 1971; 1972; 1979; 1981; 2000a; 2000b; Levi and Andersson, 1974; Shimomitsu, 2000; Black, 2008; Government Office for Science, 2008).

Every day, everywhere, decisions are made concerning matters big and small, with direct or indirect effects on health and well-being. The decisions, or their absence, may concern

The Handbook of Stress and Health: A Guide to Research and Practice, First Edition.
Edited by Cary L. Cooper and James Campbell Quick.
© 2017 John Wiley & Sons, Ltd. Published 2017 by John Wiley & Sons, Ltd.

"diagnostic" procedures and/or various "therapeutic," "preventive," "promotive," and "pallia-tive" ones. A universal challenge is to conduct them in a humane, sustainable, integrated and evidence-based manner, in government as well as in management, on all levels. This can be very far from being the case, as illustrated by the following – historic – examples.

Famous Examples of Costly Gaps

Nearly two and a half millennia ago, Socrates came back from army service to report to his Greek countrymen that in one respect the Thracians were ahead of Greek civilization: They knew that the body could not be cured without the mind. "This," he continued, "is the rea-son why the cure of many diseases is unknown to the physicians of Hellas, because they are ignorant of the whole" (quoted by Dunbar, 1954, p. 3). About two millennia later Paracelsus emphasized that "true medicine only arises from the creative knowledge of the last and deepest powers of the whole universe" (1954, p. 3). Perhaps these assertions represent an early, intuitive understanding of what we today refer to as ecological, cybernetic, and systems approaches, and the idea of "health in all policies."

One of the well-documented examples of a very long and winding way to bridge a science–policy gap is given by Baron (2009) in his fascinating discussion of sailors' scurvy and options for its successful treatment and prevention, primarily by citrus fruits. For centuries, many sailors, some ships' doctors but few university-trained physicians cured and prevented scurvy with oranges and lemons. In 1753, James Lind described his prospective controlled therapeutic trial of 1747. Although not entirely reliable, his report stimulated Thomas Trotter and Gilbert Blane to persuade the British Navy in 1793 to abolish scurvy by compulsory lemon juice, only for it to reappear after 1860, when lime juice was substituted for lemon juice. This lack of awareness caused the unnecessary deaths of countless sailors during the centuries when long sea travels became both possible and common.

Additional examples are provided by the controversies between scientists (e.g., Galileo, Darwin) and the clergy, where the discoveries of the former were deemed heretical and were forbidden and even punished by the latter.

The very considerable difficulties in implementing existing evidence, even in more recent times, are provided by two examples (Schmitt, 1988). In 1929, Werner Forssmann, 25 years old, successfully applied *heart catheterization* – on himself. Encouraged by his success, he approached a world-famous surgeon, Professor Ferdinand Sauerbruch, proposing expanded research based on his discovery. To which the professor responded: "With such tricks you qualify yourself for a circus – not for a decent clinic." But Forssmann persisted and became one of the founders of modern cardiovascular diagnostics. He received the Nobel Prize in Physiology or Medicine in 1956.

In 1892, Carl Ludwig Schleich, 33 years old, presented his revolutionary discovery of *local anesthesia* at a surgical congress in Berlin, arguing: "So that I, with this harmless means at hand, for ideological, moral and legal reasons, can replace dangerous general anesthesia, when-ever the former is sufficient." His modest intervention triggered a storm of indignation from his audience. The chairman of his session turned to the audience: "Is anyone here convinced of the truth of what has just been hurled at us? If so, please raise your hand." No one reacted. Many years followed before Schleich's discovery was confirmed, appreciated – and implemented worldwide, to the great benefit of countless patients.

Obstacles

During the past century and the present one, we have relinquished as an ideal the mastery of the whole realm of human knowledge by one person, and replaced it by our training as specialists. This training has tended to keep each of us so closely limited by our own field that we have remained ignorant even of the fundamental principles in the fields outside our own, and of the total complex picture.

Superspecialization and fragmentation are becoming increasingly problematic against a background of ongoing rapid changes in public health conditions worldwide. Many of the major killers are now chronic, degenerative diseases. They are highly complex in their etiology, pathogenesis, manifestations, and effects. And they are not easily accessible to purely medical interventions (cf. Levi, 2009). At the same time, it seems likely that much of the morbidity and premature mortality is preventable. This, however, requires action beyond the health and health-care sector and may involve the empowerment of the grassroots. Sectors outside the traditional health and health-care field, but still of major importance for our health and well-being, include education, employment, work environment, economic resources, housing, transportation and communication, leisure and recreation, social relations, political resources, safety and security, and equality ("health in all policies").

What Was Known Regarding "Stress and Health" Half a Century Ago?

The author of the present chapter started working as a researcher in this field some 60 years ago. Already at that time, in the mid-1950s, there was much evidence for the health effects of social structures and processes (cf. Selye, 1950; Dunbar, 1954; Wolf and Goodell, 1968; Henry and Stephens, 1977). Some 15 years later, in order to summarize and promote implementation of what was known, I organized a series of five international, interdisciplinary one-week symposia for the World Health Organization and the University of Uppsala under the joint title "Society, Stress and Disease," bringing together leading scientists and some policy makers from all over the world. The focus was on social determinants of human health and disease, from the cradle to the grave. The symposia proceedings were published in five volumes (Levi, 1971; 1975; 1978; 1981; 1987), but also as five popular booklets (in Swedish), and further disseminated through daily, well-attended press conferences.

Subsequently, such issues were discussed, again, by the 27th World Health Assembly in Geneva in 1974, and by the European Union in Brussels in 1993 and in Helsinki in 2008 (European Pact for Mental Health and Well-Being, see below).

Invited by David A. Hamburg, President of the Institute of Medicine of the US National Academy of Sciences, I further prepared a chapter on "Psychosocial factors in preventive medicine" for the US Surgeon General's Report on Health Promotion and Disease Prevention, *Healthy People* (see Levi, 1979). Again at David A. Hamburg's invitation, Bertil Gardell, Marianne Frankenhaeuser and I prepared a chapter on "Work stress related to social structures and processes," for the volume *Stress and Human Health* (Elliot and Eisdorfer, 1982).

More than three decades ago, and following a series of preparatory meetings, the World Health Organization (WHO) and the International Labor Office (ILO) invited their joint ILO/WHO Committee on Occupational Health to prepare a report on "Identification and control of adverse psychosocial factors at work," meeting in Geneva on September 18–24, 1984. Dr. Alexander Cohen, Chief, Applied Psychology and Ergonomics Branch of the US National Institute for Occupational Safety and Health, was Chair and I was Vice-Chair of a group of 15 international experts, plus in-house experts from both organizations. Rapporteurs were Dr. Raija Kalimo of Finland and Dr. Noel Pardon of France. We all worked very hard for one full week, produced a report, signed it very solemnly, and submitted it to the Governing Body of the ILO and the Executive Board of the WHO. Both organizations endorsed the text, made it a joint, official document of both United Nations organizations, and distributed it to all member states around the world (Joint ILO/WHO Committee on Occupational Health, 1986).

Now, in 2016, we find that work-related stress, its causes and consequences, are still very common in the 28 European Union member states. Around half of EU workers consider stress to be common in their workplace, and it contributes to around half of all lost working days. Psychosocial risks arise from poor work design, organization and management, as well as a poor social context for work, and they may result in negative psychological, physical and social outcomes, such as work-related stress, burnout, depression, and cardiovascular and skeletomuscular morbidity. Common stressors include having excessive workloads, conflicting demands, job insecurity, psychological and sexual harassment, and low reward for invested effort (Eurofound and European Agency for Safety and Health at Work, 2014).

True, such a "causality" may imply a range of relationships. It can mean that a certain exposure is *necessary* – enough for a certain disease to develop (such as the exposure to lead causing lead poisoning). An exposure may also be *sufficient* – no additional influences or vulnerabilities are necessary. Or exposure may be *contributory* and neither necessary nor sufficient. The question also remains about whether an exposure really causes a specific disease or if it "just" *aggravates* it, accelerates its course, or triggers its symptoms. If we keep all these options in mind, it becomes clear that work-related exposures may very often be a prerequisite for the development of specific occupational diseases, as a *sine qua non*. On the other hand, it becomes equally clear that they may *contribute* to a wide variety of morbidity and mortality, a much wider spectrum than is usually realized.

Prevention

How, then, can such processes be prevented, and health and well-being promoted, at work and elsewhere? This could and should be achieved in accordance with principles spelled out in the EU Framework Directive on Safety and Health at Work (89/391/EEC), according to which employers have a "duty to ensure the safety and health of workers in *every* aspect related to the work" (emphasis added), on the basis of the following general principles of prevention:

- avoiding risks;
- evaluating the risks which cannot be avoided;
- combating the risks at source;
- adapting the work to the individual.

To implement this, strategies need to address the root causes (*primary* prevention), to reduce their effects on health (*secondary* prevention), and also to treat the resulting ill-health (*tertiary* prevention) (Quick, Quick, Nelson, and Hurrell, 1997). Accordingly, Article 152 of the

European Treaty of Amsterdam states that "a high level of human health protection shall be ensured in the definition and implementation of *all* Community policies and activities" (emphasis added).

As pointed out in the European Commission's Guidance on Work-Related Stress (Levi, 2000a), work-related disease prevention programs can aim at a variety of targets and be based on various philosophies. If the conditions at work – the "shoe" – do not "fit" the worker – the "foot" – one approach may be to urge the "shoe factories" to manufacture a wider variety of shoes in different sizes and configurations to fit every, or almost every, conceivable foot. Whenever possible, such instructions to the "shoe factories" should be *evidence-based* – in other words, based on measurements of a representative, random sample of all feet, all shoes, and of the existing fit. This is a first – diagnostic – step in a primary prevention approach on a *population* level.

Another approach, again based on primary prevention, aims at finding the right "shoe" for each individual "foot" – promoting "the right person in the right place."

A third, complementary approach is that the owner of each foot should have access to, and be encouraged to use, a "lasting device" to adjust available shoes to fit his or her feet. The emphasis here is on *empowerment* of active, responsible workers, able, willing, and encouraged to make adjustments to their working conditions, to improve the work–worker fit; and, of course, on a working life that allows such adjustments.

A fourth, very important approach can address the *inequity* of various feet in various shoes (cf. Marmot, 2004; 2015) – an impressive example of a successful bridging of the gap between knowledge and policy but unfortunately somewhat less so between policy and implementation. Marmot's research has been devoted to establishing the chain of disease causation from the social environment, through psychosocial influences, biological and behavioral pathways, to morbidity and mortality in a variety of physical and mental diseases. He had almost unbelievable success, convincing the leadership of the United Kingdom, the European Union and the WHO of the need to declare their support for his ideas and actual findings. Initiated by the WHO, a great number of heads of government, ministers and government representatives came together in Rio de Janeiro in 2011 and expressed – in the Rio Political Declaration on Social Determinants of Health – their determination to achieve social and health equity through action on social determinants of health and well-being by a comprehensive intersectoral approach (World Conference on Social Determinants of Health, 2011). The following year, the Sixty-Fifth World Health Assembly endorsed the Declaration and its many elaborate recommendations (WHO, 2012), predicting increased collaboration for this end with the United Nations and partner agencies and more support for member states to adopt an inclusive "health-for-all" approach.

Much Cry and Little Wool?

So far, in the EU and elsewhere, there is much talk about primary prevention and occupational health promotion, while most work-stress prevention approaches remain oriented toward secondary or tertiary prevention (Malzon and Lindsay, 1992). Most of the latter approaches involve, for example, the provision of on-site fitness facilities, smoking cessation programs, dietary control, relaxation and exercise classes, health screening, psychological counseling, or sometimes some combination of these packaged as a multimodular program available to employees (Cartwright, Cooper, and Murphy, 1995; Kompier and Cooper, 1999). This "band-aid" approach corresponds to just offering "corn plasters" to the owners of sore feet – or painkillers, tranquilizers, or psychotherapy to deal with the outcomes of the lack of fit between the worker and his or her conditions of work (cf. Levi, 2009).

This in no way implies a criticism against secondary and tertiary prevention approaches, particularly not as long as the latter constitute a part of a larger *package* that also includes primary prevention.

An obvious difficulty with primary prevention lies in the fact that "one size does not fit all." It follows that we need a multifaceted approach to stress prevention and to the promotion of healthy working in healthy companies. An attempt to design such an approach has been made by the US National Institute for Occupational Safety and Health (NIOSH) in its National Strategy for the Prevention of Work-Related Psychological Disorders (Sauter, Murphy, and Hurrell, 1990). It addresses:

- *Workload and work pace*   Avoiding both under- and overload, allowing recovery from demanding tasks and increasing control by workers over various work characteristics;
- *Work schedule*   Designing schedules to be compatible with demands and responsibilities outside the job and addressing flextime, job sharing, and rotating shifts;
- *Job future*   Avoiding ambiguity in opportunities for promotion and career or skill development and in matters pertaining to job security;
- *Social environment*   Providing opportunities for employee interaction and support; and
- *Job content*   Designing job tasks to have meaning, to provide stimulation, and to provide an opportunity to use existing skills and develop new ones.

All this was published 25 years ago. It was followed up by three additional publications from the US Department of Health and Human Services: *Stress … at Work* (NIOSH, 1999), *The Changing Organization of Work* (NIOSH, 2002), and *Worker Health Chartbook* (NIOSH, 2004). These were important texts but had only rather limited impact on the desired outcomes.

A key question, of course, concerns what is, indeed, *preventable* in terms of exposures and inequities in exposures to occupational stressors. Many tasks are intrinsically stressful but still need to be performed for the public good – for example, night work in an emergency ward. It can also be debated how much of the reaction to these stressors depends on excessive occupational demands and how much on individual vulnerabilities of the worker. In practice, however, there is an abundance of occupational exposure that the great majority of the labor force would experience as noxious and pathogenic. It is in the interest of all parties on the labor market to prevent, as far as possible, workers from being exposed to them. If, for one reason or another, this turns out not to be feasible, a complementary approach is to try to reduce exposure time or to buffer or otherwise decrease the noxious effects (cf. Levi, 2009).

Secondary or tertiary prevention can also involve improving the worker's *coping* repertoire. If "deep and troubled waters" cannot be eliminated, the attempt is to teach people to "swim" – that is, to cope. Coping is a cognitive and behavioral process of mastering, tolerating, or reducing internal and external demands (Lazarus and Folkman, 1984). It can be problem focused (trying to change the actual exposure), emotion focused (trying to modify the resulting emotions), or both.

European Union Initiatives

In 1993, the Belgian EU Presidency, the European Commission, and the European Foundation for the Improvement of Living and Working Conditions jointly organized a high-level conference on "Stress at work – a call for action." The conference highlighted the increasing impact of stress on the quality of working life, employees' health, and company performance (Eurofound, 1993). Special attention was devoted to stress monitoring and prevention at company, national, and European level. Instruments and policies for better stress prevention were presented and discussed. Finally, a roundtable on "Future perspectives on stress at work in the European Community" brought together representatives from national governments, the European Commission, the Union of Industrial and Employers' Confederations of Europe (UNICE, now BusinessEurope), the European Centre of Enterprises with Public Participation and of Enterprises of General Economic Interest (CEEP), the European Trade Union Confederation, and the European Foundation. Based on these deliberations, the European Commission created an ad hoc group to the Advisory Committee on Health and Safety on "Stress at work." The ad hoc group proposed and the Advisory Committee (1997) endorsed the preparation by the Commission of a "Guidance" in this field.

This Guidance (Levi, 2000a) reemphasizes that according to the EU Framework Directive, employers have a "duty to ensure the safety and health of workers in *every* aspect related to the work" (emphasis added). In addition, the Directive makes clear the employers' duty to develop "a coherent overall prevention policy." The Commission's Guidance provides a basis for such endeavors. Based on surveillance at individual workplaces and monitoring at national and regional levels, work-related stress should be prevented or counteracted by job redesign (e.g., by empowering the employees, and avoiding both over- and underload), by improving social support, and by providing reasonable reward for the effort invested by workers, as integral parts of the overall management system, also for small and medium-sized enterprises. And, of course, by adjusting occupational physical settings to the workers' abilities, needs, and reasonable expectations – all in line with the requirements of the EU Framework Directive and Article 152 of the Treaty of Amsterdam.

Supporting actions should include not only research but also adjustments of curricula in business schools, in schools of technology, medicine and behavioral and social sciences, and in the training and retraining of labor inspectors, occupational health officers, managers and supervisors, in line with such goals. This overall approach was further endorsed in the Swedish EU Presidency conclusions (European Council of Ministers, 2001) according to which employment not only involves focusing on more jobs, but also on better jobs. Increased efforts should be made to promote a good working environment for all, including equal opportunities for those with disabilities, gender equality, good and flexible work organization permitting better reconciliation of working and personal life, lifelong learning, health and safety at work, employee involvement and diversity in working life.

In 2004, a Framework Agreement on Work-Related Stress was signed by the four central partners on the EU labor market, with the aim of preventing, eliminating or reducing problems of work-related stress in the 160 million European workers covered by this agreement (ETUC, 2004).

Again, there remains long and deep gaps between the knowledge summarized above, and corresponding policies, actual implementations, and desired outcomes (European Social Partners, 2008).

The European Pact

In 2008, a European Pact for Mental Health and Well-Being was endorsed by a large number of high-ranking European decision-makers and scientists. With regard to occupational health, the Pact states:

> Employment is beneficial to physical and mental health. The mental health and well-being of the workforce is a key resource for productivity and innovation in the EU. The pace and nature of work is changing, leading to pressures on mental health and well-being. Action is needed to tackle the steady increase in work absenteeism and incapacity, and to utilize the unused potential for improving productivity that is linked to stress and mental disorders. The workplace plays a central role in the social inclusion of people with mental health problems.
>
> Policy makers, social partners and further stakeholders are invited to take action on mental health at the workplace including the following:

- Improve work organisation, organisational cultures and leadership practices to promote mental well-being at work, including the reconciliation of work and family life;
- Implement mental health and well-being programmes with risk assessment and prevention programmes for situations that can cause adverse effects on the mental health of workers (stress, abusive behaviour such as violence or harassment at work, alcohol, drugs) and early intervention schemes at workplaces;
- Provide measures to support the recruitment, retention or rehabilitation and return to work of people with mental health problems or disorders. (European Union, 2008)

Norms for Optimal Living and Working Conditions

But what level-of-living and quality of life levels should we aim at? According to UNICEF (2007), "the true measure of a nation's standing is how well it attends to its children – their health and safety, their material security, their education and socialization, and their sense of being loved, valued and included in the families and societies into which they are born." In its Declaration on Social Justice for a Fair Globalization, the International Labour Organization demanded "full and productive employment, and decent work for all" (ILO, 2008). With a focus on the other end of the life cycle, in 2014 the EuroHealthNet website set out impressive formulations about "healthy ageing," which means "optimizing opportunities for physical, social and mental health to enable older people to take an active part in society without discrimination, and to enjoy an independent and good quality of life. It means taking a holistic approach, taking into consideration the many different aspects of life which play a role." (See now EuroHealthNet, 2016.) The latter are reflected in nine points:

- Social inclusion and participation
- Physical activity
- Diet and nutrition
- Access to services
- Education and lifelong learning
- New technologies
- Employment and volunteering
- Environment and accessibility
- Long-term care

Briefly, then, responsible international stakeholders have, indeed, tried to bridge the science–policy gap by proposing the general content and goals of health and welfare policies, from the cradle to the grave. And these proposals and guidelines are generally based on reasonably solid scientific evidence.

It follows that a comprehensive approach is necessary in dealing with complex social and/or occupational environmental challenges. Such approaches meet obstacles in the form of routines regarding the design of parliamentary motions restricting their scope, and the mandate of the parliamentary committee or ministry dealing with it. Many rules and regulations remain based on a silo mentality, tunnel vision or tribalism. A comprehensive approach to complex issues is necessary because we may need packages of coordinated actions to deal with complex problems, across sectors and disciplines.

Factors Affecting Health

This is admirably envisaged in the British Government's summary of factors affecting health. It presents them in five categories:

1. The *fixed* factors, such as genes, sex and ageing
2. The *social and economic* ones, such as poverty, unemployment, and social exclusion
3. The *environmental* ones, such as air and water quality, housing, and the social environment
4. Next come *lifestyle factors*, such as physical activity, diet, smoking, alcohol and other "substances," sexual behavior
5. Fifth come *access to services*, such as the National Health Service, social services, education, transport and leisure. (Department of Health, 1998)

As repeatedly emphasized above, complex societal problems usually require a *systems* approach, a "whole-of-government" approach, in the analysis of etiology, pathogenesis, diagnosis, therapy, and prevention. Tunnel vision and silo approaches are very costly – and very inefficient.

Foresight Projects in the United Kingdom

An impressive example of such systems approaches to the compilation of knowledge concerning complex problems is provided by the British Government's "collection of foresight projects" (Government Office for Science, 2013). These projects are in-depth two-year studies which build a comprehensive evidence base on major issues, looking 20–80 years into the future. One of the crucially important projects concerned "Mental health and wellbeing: making the most of ourselves in the 21st century," with a final report based on more than 80 studies, involving some 400 scientists (Government Office for Science, 2008). Its key messages include: "If we are to prosper and thrive in our changing society and in an increasingly interconnected and competitive world, both our mental and material resources will be vital. Encouraging and enabling everyone to realise their potential through their lives will be crucial for our future prosperity and wellbeing."

An individual's mental capital and mental wellbeing crucially affect their path through life. Moreover, they are vitally important for the healthy functioning of families, communities and society. Together, they fundamentally affect behaviour, social cohesion, social inclusion, and our prosperity. A key conclusion of the Project is that mental capital and mental wellbeing are intimately linked: measures to address one will often affect the other. This argues for them to be considered together when developing policies and designing interventions.

The report comprises an impressive number of such proposals, covering the entire life span and taking into account a number of major challenges:

- The demographic age-shift;
- Changes in global economy and the world of work;
- The changing nature of UK society;
- Changing attitudes, new values and expectations of society;
- The changing nature of public services; and
- New science and technology.

Science and Government

One of the difficulties to overcome is that science and government usually have rather different priorities. Whereas science accepts probability, government usually expects certainty. Science is anticipatory, whereas government may think that time ends at the next election. Further, science is flexible and problem and discovery oriented, whereas government tends to be more rigid, and service and mission oriented. Failure and risk are accepted by science and often seen as intolerable by government. For science, innovation is prized, replication essential and the clientele diffuse, diverse, or not present, whereas for government, innovation is suspect, beliefs are situational, and the clientele is specific, immediate and insistent (Bradshaw and Borchers, 2000).

Which, then, is our situation in terms of psychosocially caused or triggered health problems in Europe (Eurofound and European Agency for Safety and Health at Work, 2014)?

According to the European Foundation's third European Quality of Life Survey (Eurofound, 2012b), unemployment, particularly if long-term, has a huge impact on subjective well-being. Women working full-time are more likely than men to report problems with work–life balance. Countries that report a better quality of life are those in the northern and western parts of the EU. Optimism about the future was expressed by fewer than 30 percent of people in Greece, Slovakia and Portugal, and by over 80 percent in Denmark and Sweden. The most vulnerable groups – the lowest income quartile, the unemployed, older people in central and eastern Europe – show the greatest decline in subjective well-being between Eurofound's surveys. There is a declining trust in public institutions, specifically in governments and parliaments at national level. There is an increased perception of rifts between racial and ethnic groups, and a growing proportion of people identify tensions between the rich and the poor. An increasing number of births occur outside marriage, and single parent households are shown to be disadvantaged in most domains of quality of life.

These findings indicate the very considerable gap between European goals, and recent outcomes.

Bridging the Gap

Logically, actions should be inclusive (e.g., work for all), sustainable (e.g., not pathogenic or only short-term), and life-friendly (salutogenic). Why so? Because in all democratic politics, it is desirable to give rational reasons for any given action likely to lead to a desired goal.

How can this be achieved? By (a) increasing the pull for evidence for outcomes as related to clearly formulated goals, and (b) by facilitating better evidence use (Sutcliffe and Court, 2005). Such evidence could carry different degrees of strength, such as case studies, expert statements, comparative studies, matched control groups, cohort and panel studies, randomized controlled studies, and systematic reviews (cf. Campbell Collaboration, 2016; Danish National Centre for Social Research, 2016). And evaluation of implemented policy results could include (a) effectiveness (did the intervention work as intended?), (b) appropriateness (was it acceptable to the consumers?), and (c) feasibility (cost, side effects, practice change?).

Any bridging of the science–policy gap should ideally involve

- Perception of a problem or a desired development;
- Search for and evaluation of the best available evidence and identification of knowledge gaps;
- Supplementary research to fill such gaps, identification of clear goals with a policy context;
- Forming the policy, finding funds and human resources;
- Realization of the policy;
- Evaluation of goal fulfillment and administrative procedures.

It is equally important to consider the *values* on which preventive and/or promotive action is based, such a democracy, equality, legality, objectivity, integrity, and freedom of opinion and information (Poznan Declaration, 2014).

Common obstacles to effective implementation of improvement policies are:

- Knowledge gaps
- Political considerations
- Lack of resources
- Effects of media intervention
- A nonlinear process, adjusted to a continuous modification of goals, different training and reward systems
- Communication problems
- Risk of oversimplification, different scale

Time to Implement

The conclusions concerning future action in the field of working conditions and environment, adopted by the International Labour Conference in June 1984, and several World Health Assembly resolutions recall that the improvement of working conditions and environment and the promotion of workers' health and well-being represent a positive contribution to national development and are part of the criteria for success of any economic and social policy. The conclusions from the report of the Joint ILO/WHO Committee on Occupational Health (1986) indicate that the following principles are fundamental in pursuing this objective:

- Work should take place in a safe and healthy working environment;
- Conditions of work should be consistent with workers' well-being and human dignity;
- Work should offer real possibilities for personal achievement, self-fulfillment and service to society;

- The improvement of working conditions and environment should be considered a global issue in which the many factors affecting the physical and mental well-being of the worker are closely interrelated;
- A global and multidisciplinary approach is therefore essential to the effective improvement of working conditions and environment, and to promoting workers' health and well-being.

As already mentioned, our report was submitted to both the Executive Board of the World Health Organization and the Governing Body of the International Labour Office. On behalf of both organizations our report was endorsed and distributed as their joint document to all governments of the world.

There it was probably placed on a bookshelf and later probably moved to an archive where it still remains. Instead, the wheel is reinvented, again and again, whereas implementation remains sluggish, insufficient and fragmented.

An example of this is provided by the Swedish Agency for Health Technology Assessment and Assessment of Social Services (2015), which recently reviewed all governmental attempts to improve national mental health during the period 1995–2015. It concludes that large challenges remain and new ones have appeared, in spite of all these attempts over a period of 20 years, and by a number of politically different governments The agency further concludes that in order to cope with this, the entire society needs to become involved, including municipalities, counties, authorities, schools, employers, and civil society.

Bradshaw and Borchers (2000) observe that

> conflict and indecision are hallmarks of … policy formulation. Some argue that the requisite information and certainty fall short of scientific standards for decision making; others argue that science is not the issue, and that indecisiveness reflects a lack of political willpower. One of the most difficult aspects of translating science into policy is scientific uncertainty. Whereas scientists are familiar with uncertainty and complexity, the public and policy makers often seek certainty and deterministic solutions. … The policies that best utilize scientific findings are defined here as those that accommodate the full scope of scientifically based predictions.

In an overview of the European Working Conditions Survey (Eurofound, 2012a), the authors conclude that

- Work intensity (tight deadlines at least a quarter of the time) varies widely, with Turkey, Cyprus and Germany ranking highest, with more than 70 percent of the labor force) and Portugal, Lithuania and Bulgaria being lowest (less than 50 percent).
- Ability to choose or change methods of work ("autonomy") is highest in Malta, Denmark, Norway and Sweden (>80 percent), and lowest in Bulgaria, Cyprus and Croatia (<60 percent).
- Work intensity is high and work autonomy low for plant and machine operators, and for transport and craft and trade workers, whereas managers, financial services and technicians rate high in both respects.
- Most frequent physical risks comprise repetitive hand or arm movements (>60 percent, increasing trend), heavy loads (>30 percent, decreasing trend), and tiring or painful positions (>40 percent, increasing trend).
- The percentage of workers thinking their health or safety is at risk because of their work is lowest in Denmark, the Netherlands, Ireland and Italy (<20 percent), and highest in Latvia, and Greece (>40 per cent).

- Among those working 48 hours or more per week, 38 percent reported problems with work–life balance, compared with 16 percent of those who worked less than 48 hours.
- Standard working time is the norm for the majority of workers, but 16 percent work long days (>5 times/month), 10 percent do night work (>3 times/month), 17 percent do shift work, 20 percent work on call.

According to the Sixth European Working Conditions Survey (Eurofound, 2015), more than 40 percent of all employees report working in painful or tiring positions more than a quarter of the time. One in three is working at high speed more than three-quarters of the time. About one in four is not learning new things. One in five do shift work, and 20 percent work on call. A majority have poor prospects for career advancement. One in six fears losing their job in the next six months. True, it has been worse and could be worse, but it is hardly something devoutly to be wished in view of the level of ambition of the stakeholders.

In their recent review of 94 psychosocial risks and mental health policies in the workplace in the European Union, Leka, Jain, Iavicoli, and Di Tecco (2015) reveal impact gaps between binding and nonbinding policies. In 2005 and again in 2010, every fourth worker believed that their health was at risk due to work-related stress. This is seen as a response people may have when presented with work demands and pressures that are not matched to their knowledge and abilities and which challenge their ability to cope. Even from early 2000, studies suggest that between 50 and 60 percent of all lost working days have some link to work-related stress, leading to significant financial costs to companies as well as society in terms of both human distress and impaired economic performance. The authors conclude that even though mental health and psychosocial risks in the workplace have been recognized as priorities in the European Union for at least two decades, and many policies have been introduced to this end, it is uncertain whether desired outcomes have been achieved in practice, since awareness in relation to mental health in the workplace and the importance of preventive action still seems to be lacking.

In their report on the implementation of the Framework Directive and other legally binding EU documents, Leka and Jain (2014) emphasize that

> workplace related mental health problems are currently one of the most serious workplace related health concerns, as reflected by an abundance of data (e.g., on absenteeism, long-term sick leave, work-related suicides), due to, inter alia, stress at work (itself the consequence of, e.g., new forms of work organisation, harassment and violence in the workplace, insecurity of tenure, exposure to a poor physical work environment) and depression.

In an evaluation report on policy and practice to promote mental health in the workplace in Europe, Leka et al. (2014) conclude that mental health has a profound impact on individuals, organizations and society, but awareness of the positive impact of good mental health also needs to be raised. They further conclude that the prevalence of mental ill-health in the workplace, including poor psychological well-being, is *widespread* across all countries in the European Union and the European Free Trade Association, and there are indications that this will only increase due to exposure to risk factors such as job insecurity, work intensification, and organizational restructuring. This is very likely to affect business performance as well, and also be costly at the society level. And these trends are projected to continue in the future, with most stakeholders turning a blind eye to the "significant and undisputed cost of inaction," which by far outweighs the cost of action.

Based on their thorough review of the European history of policy evolution in this field, the authors propose a series of actions, inter alia:

- Revisit the content of the Framework Directive to include clear reference to psychosocial risks and mental health in the workplace;
- Promote the interpretative document of the Directive to clarify legal requirements for employers and other key stakeholders in Europe;
- Promote the guidance document on how to implement a comprehensive approach for the promotion of mental health in the workplace.

Can Work-Related Stress Be Prevented?

Work-related stress can be approached on four levels – those of the individual worker, the work organization, the nation, and the European Union. Whatever the target(s), conditions are man-made and open to interventions by all relevant stakeholders. In all cases, there is a need to identify work-related stressors, stress reactions, and stress-related ill-health. As already emphasized, there are several reasons for doing this: stress is a problem for both the worker and his or her work organization, and for society; work stress problems are on the increase; it is a legal obligation under the EU Framework Directive on Safety and Health at Work; and many of the stressors and consequences are avoidable and can be adjusted by all three parties on the labor market if they act together in their own and mutual interests.

Thus, work-related stress may be prevented or counteracted by job redesign (e.g., by empowering the employees, and avoiding both over- and underload), by improving social support, and by promoting reasonable reward for the effort invested. And, of course, by adjusting occupational physical settings to the workers' abilities, needs, and reasonable expectations.

Approaches to be considered include participative management, flexible work schedules, and career development – all in line with the requirements of the EU Framework Directive and of Article 152 of the Treaty of Amsterdam.

Start Now

Does all this sound complicated or even utopian? It is not. It has been done in many enterprises, and with considerable success. The principles mentioned above are incorporated in the EU Framework Directive and in the Work Environment Acts of a number of European countries. True, it may take time and effort, but it can be done. And it is likely to be highly cost-effective.

Your first step? Consider the ILO's statement: "the future of work is what we will make it. The challenge is to make it the one we want" (ILO, 2015). The "right time" is now. It is likely to improve both working conditions and health, as well as your own, your company's and your country's output, creativity and competitiveness.

References

Advisory Committee for Safety, Hygiene and Health Protection at Work (1997). *22nd Annual Activity Report*. Doc. COM/98/0522. Luxembourg: European Commission.

Arbetsmiljöverket (2015). *Organisatorisk och social arbetsmiljö* [Organizational and social working environment regulations]. AFS 2015:4. Stockholm: Arbetsmiljöverket Författningssamling.

Baron, J. H. (2009). Sailors' scurvy before and after James Lind – a reassessment. *Nutrition Reviews*, *67*(6), 315–332.

Black, C. (2008). *Working for a Healthier Tomorrow*. London: Department for Health.

Bradshaw, G. A., and Borchers, J. G. (2000). Uncertainty as information: Narrowing the science–policy gap. *Conservation Ecology*, *4*(1), 7. At http://www.consecol.org/vol4/iss1/art7/ (accessed July 2016).

Campbell Collaboration (2016). Campbell systematic reviews. At http://www.campbellcollaboration.org/ (accessed July 2016).

Cartwright, S., Cooper, C. L., and Murphy, L. R. (1995). Diagnosing a healthy organization: A proactive approach to stress in the workplace. In L. R. Murphy, J. J. Hurrell, Jr., S. L. Sauter, and G. P. Keita (Eds.), *Job Stress Interventions* (pp. 217–233). Washington, DC: American Psychological Association.

Danish National Centre for Social Research (2016). Website at http://gl.sfi.dk/the_danish_national_centre_for_social_research-2631.aspx (accessed July 2016).

Department of Health (UK) (1998). *Our Healthier Nation. A Contract for Health*. Cm 3852. London: Stationery Office.

Dunbar, F. (1954). *Emotions and Bodily Changes*. New York: Columbia University Press.

Elliot, G. R., and Eisdorfer, C. (Eds.) (1982). *Stress and Human Health: Analysis and Implications of Research*. New York: Springer.

ETUC (European Trade Union Confederation) (2004). Framework agreement on stress at work. At http://www.worker-participation.eu/EU-Social-Dialogue/Interprofessional-ESD/Outcomes/Framework-agreements/Framework-agreement-on-stress-at-work-2004 (accessed July 2016).

Eurofound (1993). *European Conference on Stress at Work – A Call for Action: Proceedings*. Dublin: European Foundation for the Improvement of Living and Working Conditions.

Eurofound (2007). *Fourth European Survey on Working Conditions*. Dublin: European Foundation for the Improvement of Living and Working Conditions.

Eurofound (2012a). *Fifth European Working Conditions Survey*. Dublin: European Foundation for the Improvement of Living and Working Conditions.

Eurofound (2012b). *Quality of Life in Europe: Impacts of the Crisis*. Third European Quality of Life Survey. At http://www.eurofound.europa.eu/publications/htmlfiles/ef1264.htm (accessed July 2016).

Eurofound (2015). *First Findings: Sixth European Working Conditions Survey*. Dublin: European Foundation for the Improvement of Living and Working Conditions.

Eurofound and European Agency for Safety and Health at Work (2014). *Psychosocial Risks in Europe: Prevalence and Strategies for Prevention*. At https://osha.europa.eu/en/tools-and-publications/publications/reports/psychosocial-risks-eu-prevalence-strategies-prevention (accessed July 2016).

EuroHealthNet (2016). Healthy ageing: Resources. At http://www.healthyageing.eu/resources (accessed July 2016).

European Council of Ministers (2001). *Council Conclusions on Combating Stress and Depression-Related Problems*. At http://eur-lex.europa.eu/legal-content/EN/TXT/?uri=uriserv%3Ac11570a (accessed July 2016).

European Social Partners (2008). *Implementation of the European Autonomous Framework Agreement on Work-Related Stress*. At http://www.ueapme.com/IMG/pdf/Stress_Final_Implementation_report_231108.pdf (accessed July 2016).

European Union (2008). *European Pact for Mental Health and Well-Being*. At http://ec.europa.eu/health/ph_determinants/life_style/mental/docs/pact_en.pdf (accessed July 2016).

Government Office for Science (UK) (2008). *Mental Capital and Wellbeing: Making the Most of Ourselves in the 21st Century: Final Project Report*. London: Government Office for Science.

Government Office for Science (UK) (2013). Foresight projects. At https://www.gov.uk/government/collections/foresight-projects (accessed July 2016).

Henry, J. P., and Stephens, P. M. (1977). *Stress, Health and the Social Environment*. New York: Springer.

ILO (International Labour Organization) (2008). *ILO Declaration on Social Justice for a Fair Globalization*. Geneva: ILO.

ILO (International Labour Organization) (2015). *The Future of Work Centenary Initiative*. At http://www.ilo.org/wcmsp5/groups/public/@ed_norm/@relconf/documents/meetingdocument/wcms_369026.pdf (accessed July 2016).

Joint ILO/WHO Committee on Occupational Health (1986). *Report on Psychosocial Factors at Work: Recognition and Control*. Occupational Safety and Health Series No. 56. Geneva: International Labour Office.

Karasek, R., and Theorell, T. (1990). *Healthy Work: Stress, Productivity, and the Reconstruction of Working Life*. New York: Basic Books.

Kompier, M., and Cooper, C. (1999). *Preventing Stress, Improving Productivity: European Case Studies in the Workplace*. London: Routledge.

Kompier, M., and Levi, L. (1994). *Stress at Work: Causes, Effects, and Prevention: A Guide for Small and Medium Sized Enterprises*. Dublin: European Foundation for the Improvement of Living and Working Conditions.

Lazarus, R. S., and Folkman, S. (1984). *Stress, Appraisal, and Coping*. New York: Springer.

Leka, S., and Jain, A. (2014). *Interpretative Document of the Implementation of Council Directive 89/391/EEC in Relation to Mental Health in the Workplace*. Luxembourg: European Commission.

Leka, S., Jain, A., Houtman, I., McDaid, D., Park, A-La, De Broeck, V., and Wynne, R. (2014). *Evaluation of Policy and Practice to Promote Mental Health in the Workplace in Europe: Final Report*. Luxembourg: European Commission.

Leka, S., Jain, A., Iavicoli, S., and Di Tecco, C. (2015). *An Evaluation of the Policy Context on Psychosocial Risks and Mental Health in the Workplace in the European Union: Achievements, Challenges and the Future*. BioMed Research International. http://dx.doi.org/10.1155/2015/213089

Levi, L. (Ed.) (1971). *The Psychosocial Environment and Psychosomatic Diseases, vol. 1 of Society, Stress and Disease*. Oxford: Oxford University Press.

Levi, L. (1972). Stress and distress in response to psychosocial stimuli: Laboratory and real life studies on sympathoadrenomedullary and related reactions. *Acta Medica Scandinavica, 191, 528*, 1–166.

Levi, L. (Ed.) (1975). *Childhood and Adolescence, vol. 2 of Society, Stress and Disease*. Oxford: Oxford University Press.

Levi, L. (Ed.) (1978). *The Productive and Reproductive Age: Male/Female Roles and Relationships, vol. 3 of Society, Stress and Disease*. Oxford: Oxford University Press (1978).

Levi, L. (1979). Psychosocial factors in preventive medicine. In D. A. Hamburg, E. O. Nightingale, and V. Kalmar (Eds.), *Healthy People: The Surgeon General's Report on Health Promotion and Disease Prevention. Background Papers* (pp. 207–252). Washington, DC: US Government Printing Office.

Levi, L. (Ed.) (1981). *Working Life, vol. 4 of Society, Stress and Disease*. Oxford: Oxford University Press.

Levi, L. (Ed.) (1987) *Old Age, vol. 5 of Society, Stress and Disease*. Oxford: Oxford University Press.

Levi, L. (2000a). *Guidance on Work-Related Stress: Spice of Life or Kiss of Death?* Luxembourg: European Commission.

Levi, L. (2000b). Stress in the global environment. In J. Dunham (Ed.), *Stress in the Workplace: Past, Present and Future* (pp. 1–18). London: Whurr.

Levi, L. (2009). Foreword. In C. L. Cooper, J. C. Quick, and M. J. Schabracq (Eds.), *International Handbook of Work and Health Psychology*. Chichester, UK: Wiley-Blackwell.

Levi, L. (2016). Foreword. In J. Siegrist and M. Wahrendorf (Eds.), *Work Stress and Health in a Globalized Economy: The Model of Effort–Reward Imbalance*. Dordrecht: Springer.

Levi, L., and Andersson, L. (1974). *Population, Environment and Quality of Life: A Contribution to the United Nation's World Population Conference*. Stockholm: Royal Ministry of Foreign Affairs.

Malzon, R., and Lindsay, G. (1992). *Health Promotion at the Worksite: A Brief Survey of Large Organizations in Europe*. European Occupational Health Series No. 4. Copenhagen: WHO Regional Office for Europe.

Marmot, M. (2004). *Status Syndrome*. London: Bloomsbury.

Marmot, M. (2015). *The Health Gap*. London: Bloomsbury.

NIOSH (1999). *Stress … at Work*. NIOSH Publication No. 99-101. Washington, DC: National Institute for Occupational Safety and Health.

NIOSH (2002). *The Changing Organization of Work*. NIOSH Publication No. 2002-116. Washington, DC: National Institute for Occupational Safety and Health.

NIOSH (2004). *Worker Health Chartbook*. NIOSH Publication No. 2004-146. Washington, DC: National Institute for Occupational Safety and Health.

Poznan Declaration (2014). *Whole-of-University Promotion of Social Capital, Health and Development*. At http://qog.pol.gu.se/digitalAssets/1497/1497769_the-poznan-declaration.pdf (accessed July 2016).

Quick, J. C., Quick, J. D., Nelson, D. L., and Hurrell, J. J., Jr. (1997). *Preventive Stress Management in Organizations*. Washington, DC: American Psychological Association.

Sauter, S. L., Murphy, L. R., and Hurrell, J. J., Jr. (1990). Prevention of work-related psychological distress: A national strategy proposed by the National Institute for Occupational Safety and Health. *American Psychologist, 45*, 1146–1158.

Schmitt, W. (1988). Aphorismen, Sentenzen und anderes, nicht nur für Mediziner. Leipzig: Ambrosius Barth.

Selye, H. (1950). *The Physiology and Pathology of Exposure to Stress*. Montreal: Acta.

Shimomitsu, T. (2000). Work-related stress and health in three post-industrial settings: EU, Japan, and USA. *Journal of Tokyo Medical University, 58*, 327–469.

Sutcliffe, S., and Court, J. (2005). *Evidence-Based Policy Making*. London: Overseas Development Institute.

Swedish Agency for Health Technology Assessment and Assessment of Social Services (2015). *Mental Health – Joint Responsibility* [in Swedish]. Report No. 2015:10.

UNICEF (United Nations Children's Fund) (2007). *An Overview of Child Well-Being in Rich Countries*. Report Card 7. Florence: UNICEF/Innocenti Research Centre.

WHO (World Health Organization) (2012). World Health Assembly endorses the Rio Political Declaration on Social Determinants of Health. At http://www.who.int/sdhconference/background/en/ (accessed July 2016).

Wolf, S., and Goodell, H. (Eds.) (1968). *Harold G. Wolff's "Stress and Disease."* Springfield, IL: Charles C. Thomas.

World Conference on Social Determinants of Health (2011). *Rio Political Declaration on Social Determinants of Health*. Geneva: World Health Organization.

2

The Effort–Reward Imbalance Model

Johannes Siegrist

Introduction

The field of research on stress and health in human life is extremely broad and diverse. It covers a variety of scientific disciplines and combines information on distal and proximal natural and social environments with data on psychosocial and biological characteristics of people. Given this diversity of disciplines and this broad spectrum of topics, how is it possible to advance scientific knowledge? One answer to this challenge maintains that we need to develop and test theoretical models. A theoretical model offers at least three advantages. First, it reduces the complexity of phenomena under study by identifying a few general principles underlying this complexity. If successful, a model based on these principles provides an explanation or prediction of associations between the phenomena under study. To allow for an empirical test of these associations a theoretical model has to be measured by a standardized method. Thus, the accumulation of comparable information resulting from the recurrent empirical testing is considered a second advantage of a theoretical model. Third, if the explanations or predictions derived from the model are successful and provide a solid body of knowledge, the model can be used to guide plans and actions and to change specific aspects of our world.

In this chapter, one such model termed effort–reward imbalance is introduced, its measurement is discussed, and its contribution toward explaining associations between exposure to stressful social environments and adverse health outcomes is documented by reviewing evidence from observational and experimental research. Furthermore, the utility of knowledge derived from this model is demonstrated by pointing to selected applications, in particular the development of health-promoting working conditions at the level of organizations and at the level of national social and labor policies. Although the model was developed with

The Handbook of Stress and Health: A Guide to Research and Practice, First Edition.
Edited by Cary L. Cooper and James Campbell Quick.
© 2017 John Wiley & Sons, Ltd. Published 2017 by John Wiley & Sons, Ltd.

an explicit focus on paid work and employed populations, more recent extensions reveal its capacity to be applied to other types of costly social transactions, such as caring or volunteering. These extensions are briefly discussed in a final section with concluding remarks.

Theory

Theoretical models of stressful social environments and health often focus on work and employment.[1] This is due to the significance of work in adult life in modern societies. Having a job is a prerequisite for a continuous income and, more so than any other social circumstance, employment characteristics determine adult socioeconomic status. Beyond economic livelihood, a person's occupation is an important aim of long-term socialization, thus providing opportunities for personal growth and development. While a good quality of work, including stable employment, may contribute to employees' health and well-being, poor jobs and precarious work adversely affect their health. Traditionally, research on associations of work with health was the task of occupational medicine. Most often, noxious effects of physical, chemical, and biological hazards were analyzed. However, with the advent of advanced technologies, including automation, the growth of the service sector of employment, and the expansion of computer-based, information-processing jobs in postindustrial modern societies, the spectrum of occupational exposures with potential impact on health has changed rather dramatically. While traditional hazards still prevail in certain sectors of the labor market, the majority of employed people are now confronted with a variety of mental and emotional demands, threats, or conflicts, rather than with toxic substances and environments. This is exactly the place where stress concepts developed by social and behavioral sciences are needed to cope with this challenge. Effort–reward imbalance is one such concept identifying a stressful psychosocial work environment. The theoretical basis of this model is explained in two steps. The first step concerns its roots in sociological and social-psychological theory, whereas the second step addresses its roots in human stress theory.

Sociological and Social Psychological Theory

The "effort–reward imbalance" model is concerned with stressful features of the work contract, with a selective focus on the analytical notion of social reciprocity in costly transactions (Siegrist, 1996). Social reciprocity has been identified as a fundamental, evolutionary and stable principle of collaborative human exchange (Gouldner, 1960). According to this principle, any costly transaction provided by person A to person B that has some utility to B is expected to be returned by person B to A. Return expectancy does not implicate full identity of the service in return, but it is essential that this activity meets some agreed-upon standard of equivalence. Failed reciprocity results from situations where service in return is either denied or does not meet the agreed-upon level of equivalence. To secure equivalence of return in crucial types of costly transactions, social contracts have been established as a universal societal institution. The work contract (or contract of employment) is one such type where efforts are expected to be delivered by employees in exchange for rewards provided by the employer. Three basic types of rewards are transmitted in this case: salary or wage (financial reward), career promotion or job security (status-related reward), and esteem or recognition (socioemotional reward). Importantly, contracts of employment do not specify efforts and rewards in all details, but provide some room for flexibility and adaptation.

The model of effort–reward imbalance at work asserts that experiencing lack of reciprocity in terms of high cost spent and low gain received in turn elicits negative emotions of anger and frustration and associated bodily stress reactions, with adverse long-term consequences for health and well-being. Effort–reward imbalance at work occurs frequently under specific conditions. "Dependency" is one such condition, defined by situations where workers have no alternative choice in the labor market. For instance, unskilled or semiskilled workers, elderly employees, or those with restricted mobility or reduced work ability may be susceptible to an unfair contractual transaction. "Dependency" is relatively frequent in modern economies with a globalized labor market where parts of the workforce are exposed to job instability or job loss due to mergers, organizational downsizing, rapid technological change, and growing economic competition (Schnall, Dobson, and Rosskam, 2009). This latter observation points to a second condition of failed reciprocity at work, "strategic choice." Here, people accept the experience of "high cost/low gain" in their employment for a certain time, often without being forced to do so, because they may improve their chances of career promotion in a highly competitive job market.

The notion of effort at work implies both an extrinsic demand to which the working person responds, as well as a subjective motivation to match the demand. In most instances, matching the demands is part of the control structures established in organizations, thus leaving little room for variations of subjective motivation. Yet, demands are likely to be exceeded in situations of strong informal pressure exerted by a competing work team (e.g., group piece work). Similarly, demands are likely to be exceeded if people are characterized by a motivational pattern of excessive work-related "over-commitment." Consciously or unconsciously, they may strive toward continuously high achievement because of their underlying need for approval and esteem at work. This motivation contributes to "high cost/low gain" experience at work even in the absence of extrinsic pressure. To summarize, the model of effort–reward imbalance at work maintains that failed contractual reciprocity in terms of high cost and low gain is often experienced by people who have no alternative choice in the labor market, by those exposed to heavy job competition, and by those who are overcommitted to their work (see Figure 2.1).

In addition to its sociological basis of reciprocity in contractual exchange, the model of effort–reward imbalance builds on social-psychological equity theory as proposed by Adams (1965). According to this approach, there are two types of inequity of exchange which can be labeled "overfitting" and "underfitting." In the first case, the gains received outmatch the invested costs, whereas in the latter case, costs exceed the experienced gains. Equity theory posits that both states trigger some kind of inequity aversion that motivates people to reduce these discrepancies by behavioral or cognitive changes. Yet, a stronger motivation of change is expected in case of underfitting than in case of overfitting, given the powerful impact of loss experience. This basic assumption is valid in the effort–reward imbalance model as well. However, while Adams's main interest was to understand adaptive behavioral changes following perceived inequity rather than to explore potential effects on health and well-being, the latter model's distinct focus is put on the affective and bodily consequences of loss experiences. It thus explicitly links encounters in social life with psychobiological processes occurring in the human organism (see human stress theory in the next section). Moreover, whereas Adams's notion of inequity aversion does not distinguish between different types or degrees of relevance of social encounters, the current model is more restrictive as it focuses on contractual transactions embedded in core social roles, such as the work role.

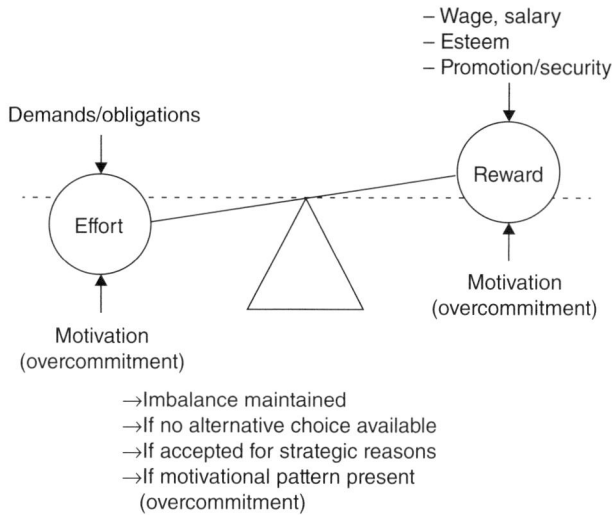

Figure 2.1 The model of effort–reward imbalance at work. *Source*: Modified from Siegrist (1996).

There is another, more subtle difference between social-psychological equity theory and the proposed sociological model. It concerns the distinction between distributive justice and justice of exchange. Inherent in the former concept is the notion of distributive justice (Greenberg, 2010). This results from the fact that balance, according to Adams, is not only contingent on the relation between "cost" (transferred from A to B) and "gain" (transferred from B to A) – that is justice of exchange – but is equally contingent on the fit of this balance with a comparable balance experienced by any member of a reference group (C) – that is, distributive justice. Distributive justice is given if each person of a group is expected to earn similar gain relative to the invested cost. Again, the effort–reward imbalance model's claim with its focus on justice of exchange is more restrictive than equity theory, which includes experiences of distributive justice in addition to those related to justice of exchange.

In conclusion, while "effort–reward imbalance" is expected to be an innovative theoretical approach to the field of stress and health, it nevertheless has its roots in distinct sociological and social-psychological theories.

Human Stress Theory

How is it possible that the recurrent experience of effort–reward imbalance at work triggers enhanced and intense stress reactions that ultimately result in adverse health outcomes? Obviously, successful performance on the job is a prerequisite for continued employment and associated material and nonmaterial benefits. Among these latter benefits the satisfaction of people's need for favorable experiences of self-efficacy and self-esteem matters most. Consider those situations where people are fully committed to meet the obligations and demands of their job, whether due to extrinsic pressure or due to intrinsic motivation, and where they fail to receive appropriate returns. For instance, their wages or salaries are reduced, or promised bonuses are not paid, due to heavy competition. Or, superiors are unwilling or unable to recognize and appreciate achievements based on the high performance of their subordinates. Even worse, reward frustration may occur as an unexpected life event where workers are laid off despite their long-standing contributions to the company's survival. These and related violations of trust, of fair and just exchange in a core social role, the work role, are expected to damage people's self-esteem and to evoke enhanced negative emotions of anger and disappointment. These negative emotions were shown to activate distinct areas in the brain reward circuits, including nucleus accumbens, anterior cingulated cortex, and insula (Schultz, 2006). This activation suppresses the production of dopamine and oxytocin, that is, neurotransmitters associated with pleasurable emotions and stress-buffering properties. Moreover, activation of the insula is associated with the experience of physical and emotional pain, and with strong visceral and somatic sensations (Baumgartner, Fischbacher, Feierabend, Lutz, and Fehr, 2009; Singer et al., 2004). Importantly, insula activation is modulated by the magnitude of loss following effort (Hernandez Lallement et al., 2014). It is conceivable that the brain's reward circuitry is sensitive to the experience of disadvantageous inequality in social exchange (Tricomi, Rangel, Camerer, and O'Doherty, 2010), thus lending some indirect support to the stress-theoretical assumption inherent in the effort–reward imbalance model.

Threat or loss of reward related to a person's core social role is associated with an extensive arousal of distinct stress axes within the organism, specifically the hypothalamic-pituitary-adrenocortical stress axis and the locus coeruleus-norepinephrine-autonomic system–adrenal medullary stress axis (Chrousos, 2009). Sustained activation of these stress axes in the organism may trigger states of allostatic load within several regulating systems of the body, and these states of allostatic load contribute to the onset of stress-related physical and mental disorders, such as coronary heart disease or depression (Kalia, 2005; McEwen, 1998; Steptoe and Kivimaki, 2012; Weiner, 1992).

"Threat or loss of reward" is not the only stress-theoretical approach toward studying health-adverse effects of work. "Threat or loss of control" is a further very important notion in this context, underlying the well-established job demand–control model (Karasek and Theorell, 1990). This model claims that stressful experience is elicited by jobs which fail to offer control and decision latitude to working people, especially so under conditions of high demands and work pressure. Lack of control threatens a person's sense of mastery and autonomy, thus evoking negative emotions of anger or anxiety and related psychobiological stress responses (Steptoe and Kivimaki, 2012). In conclusion, the two models of job demand–control and effort–reward imbalance complement each other, and their combined effects may adversely affect the working people's health (Siegrist, 2009).

Having explained the sociological, social psychological, and psychobiological basis of the model of effort–reward imbalance, information is now required on how to measure this construct.

Measurement

There are two major methods available in social science research to measure theoretical models: observation techniques and self-reported information obtained from interviews or from standardized questionnaires. Given the limitations of applying observation methods in large population studies, the use of psychometrically validated questionnaires has become a widely prevalent standard procedure. In the case of the effort–reward imbalance model, a questionnaire containing the following three scales with Likert-scaled items was developed: "effort"

(6 items), "reward" (11 items) and "over-commitment" (6 items). Given the three theoretical dimensions of the reward construct, the 11 items were assumed to represent the three factors "job promotion," "job security," and "esteem." By applying confirmatory factor analysis, a satisfactory fit between the theoretical model and the factorial structure of the scales was repeatedly observed, both in the original version of the questionnaire containing 23 items as well as in a short version containing 16 items that was developed subsequently (Leineweber et al., 2010; Siegrist et al., 2004).

To provide accurate data the scales have to meet defined quality criteria, such as a high degree of internal consistency (with Cronbach's alpha >0.70), of sensitivity to change, of discriminant validity, and of criterion validity. These criteria were tested in many studies, and extensive information on the psychometric properties of the questionnaire is documented on the effort–reward imbalance website at the University of Düsseldorf (2016). This website additionally provides the language versions of the questionnaire as far as validations in respective languages were performed.

Based on this method, the following core hypotheses derived from the model can be, and have been, tested in epidemiologic, experimental, and quasi-experimental studies: (1) Each of the three scales predicts a significantly elevated relative risk of developing a stress-related disorder, that is, scoring high on effort, low on reward, and high on over-commitment. (2) Combining scores of effort and reward by a ratio that quantifies the imbalance at individual level results in even higher predictions of relative risks compared to those derived from single scales. (3) The effect of effort–reward imbalance on the risk of stress-related disorder is magnified among people scoring high on the scale over-commitment.

Before reviewing selected empirical evidence along these lines, several limitations of this measurement approach must be mentioned. First, scales containing self-report data lack a calibration of measurement, thus compromising the comparability of data between different individuals. This basic problem can only partially be resolved, for example, by contrasting subjective information with objective data in cases where two complementary operational measures are available. Job insecurity provides an example where subjective evaluations of employees are compared with administrative data on the magnitude of downsizing and redundancy in respective organizations (Siegrist, Matschinger, Cremer, and Seidel, 1988). Some researchers claim that lack of calibration is not a major methodological problem in social and behavioral sciences research as long as the subjective data under study result in successful predictions of real events, such as the manifestation of a clinical disorder ("pragmatic utility"; Kampen and Swygedouw, 2000).

A second limitation concerns systematic measurement bias, for example, over- or underreporting due to distinct personality traits or due to contextual influences. In fact, bias control is an important challenge in this field of research. Therefore, the accuracy of findings is improved by adjusting for effects of reporting bias, for example, due to mood, negative affectivity, or mode of data collection (e.g., questionnaire filled in under controlled conditions). For instance, adjusting for the effect of negative affectivity resulted in a decrease of the originally observed effect size, but did not affect its statistical significance (Bosma, Peter, Siegrist, and Marmot, 1998). The construction of aggregate measures of individual-level reports of stressful work, for example, at the level of work units, provides a strong case of minimizing individual reporting bias, and this strategy has been successfully applied in recent research (Juvani et al., 2014; see below). A different approach toward increasing measurement accuracy concerns the application of a complementary method. Ecological momentary assessment is one such method where data are recorded in real time, at defined time intervals during a working day (Johnston, Jones, Charles, McCann, and McKee, 2013).

Empirical Evidence

Since its introduction to an international audience (Siegrist, 1996), the model has been extensively studied in a variety of research activities, resulting so far in more than 200 scientific publications. Two earlier reviews are now outdated (Tsutsumi and Kawakami, 2004; van Vegchel, Jonge, Bosma, and Schaufeli, 2005), and a recent book summarizing the evidence is restricted to the German language (Siegrist, 2015).[2] Therefore, information provided in the following paragraphs is far from being comprehensive. Rather than demonstrating variations of stressful work according to age, gender, socioeconomic position, occupational branch, or cultural context, the following selective review considers results on associations of stressful work with working people's health, based on two types of study designs, prospective cohort studies and experimental or quasi-experimental investigations.

Prospective cohort studies are considered a gold standard in this area of research, due to the fact that work stress is assessed at baseline in a population free from the disease under study. This working population is then followed up over a period of years, and the occurrence of new disease manifestations is analyzed in association with the exposure to stressful work measured at baseline. Elevated relative risks or odds ratios of disease incidence are calculated, adjusted for relevant confounders, such as, concurring risk factors of the disease under study, and the statistical significance of this elevated risk is calculated by comparing it to the risk in the group of workers who were free from stressful work. Available information on statistical associations needs to be complemented by data on mediating processes, that is on pathways documenting psychobiological and behavioral processes occurring between exposure to stressful work and the development of a stress-related mental or physical disorder. Depression and cardiovascular diseases, and more specifically ischemic heart diseases, are the two highly prevalent stress-related disorders that were most often studied in the field of work stress and health in general, and also with regard to this model. The methodological challenge of providing robust evidence on these pathways is tackled by experimental and quasi-experimental investigations.

Cohort Studies

Currently, the strongest evidence on associations of stressful work in terms of this model with adverse health is available from studies analyzing depression. At least ten prospective investigations demonstrate elevated odds ratios of depressive symptoms, including clinically relevant major depression, among employees exposed to effort–reward imbalance at work. The strength of associations varies across studies, but overall the relative risk of depression is elevated by about 80 percent among those experiencing stress at work compared to those who were free from it at study entry. These effects remain significant after adjusting for relevant confounders. These relationships are observed among men and women, in different age groups, different occupational groups, and different cultures, but several studies document particularly strong associations in working populations with low socioeconomic status, suggesting that this latter condition aggravates the effect of stressful work on depression (Rugulies et al., 2013; Siegrist, 2015).

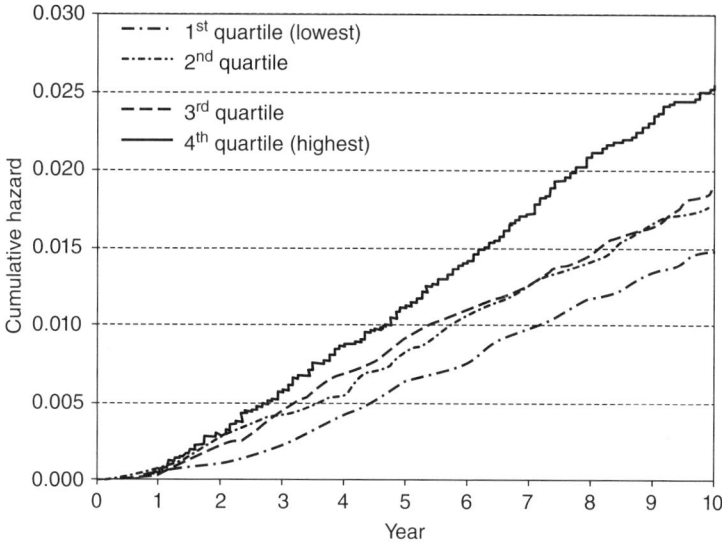

Figure 2.2 Cumulative hazard curves of disability pension due to depression by quartile of work unit-level effort–reward imbalance. *Source*: Juvani et al. (2014), with permission.

In Figure 2.2, the results of a large cohort study from Finland are displayed as an example of this line of research (Juvani et al., 2014). This study is remarkable in at least two regards. First, it uses disability pension due to depression as the relevant health outcome, analyzing the cumulative hazard of early exit from paid work due to this type of disability in a large cohort of more than 50,000 public-sector employees followed up over ten years. Thus, the study provides a strong empirical basis for testing a research hypothesis whose policy implications are evident. Second, the exposure measure, the ratio of the two scales "effort" and "reward," is assessed as an aggregate variable of individual data computed at work-unit level in order to reduce individual response bias (see the measurement section above). As demonstrated in Figure 2.2, a dose–response relationship is observed between the quartiles of the effort–reward ratio and the cumulative hazard of disability pension, leaving employees with work-unit scores in the highest quartile at highest risk.

Ischemic heart disease is the second main health outcome investigated in prospective studies. Although their number is smaller than in case of depression, the findings nevertheless confirm elevated risks of incident nonfatal or fatal events of ischemic heart disease among employees with a high level of work stress at baseline (Backé, Seidler, Latza, Rossnagel, and Schumann, 2012). Overall, odds ratios of about 1,4 are observed in these reports, indicating an elevated relative risk of 40 percent among exposed compared to nonexposed populations. It is of interest to note that these associations are not restricted to incident disease manifestations but hold equally true for recurrent coronary events among those who returned to work after survival of their first myocardial infarction (Li, Zhang, Loerbroks, Angerer, and Siegrist, 2015). In these reports, observed effects are commonly adjusted for the effects of major coronary risk factors in multivariate analysis, such as hypertension, atherogenic blood lipids, overweight, smoking, and lack of physical exercise. However, as some of these risk factors are influenced by stressful work as well, respective statistical adjustment may result in an underestimation of the "true" effect size. For instance, several studies indicate that effort–reward imbalance at work is associated with elevated blood pressure (Gilbert-Ouimet, Trudel, Brisson, Milot, and Vézina, 2014).

In a couple of cohort studies, health outcomes other than depression or ischemic heart disease were analyzed, such as type 2 diabetes, alcohol dependence, musculoskeletal disorders, or sleep disturbances. Although results often support the main research assumption, further replications of the findings are required (Siegrist, 2015). Finally, it should be noted that most studies so far tested either the first or the second hypothesis stated above, whereas the third hypothesis has been analyzed less frequently.

Experimental and Quasi-Experimental Studies

Experimental investigations provide a strong case for confirming or rejecting a research hypothesis, yet their external validity is often quite limited. Therefore, findings resulting from experimental studies complement rather than replace the knowledge obtained from research based on other study designs. Only a few studies transformed the model's basic assumption into an experimental procedure of unjust exchange. In one such study using a simple principal agent experiment, unfair pay was associated with reduced heart rate variability in a dose–response relationship (Falk, Menrath, Verde, and Siegrist, 2011). More often quasi-experimental or "naturalistic" study designs were applied to test associations of stressful work with one or several indicators of psychobiological processes that are assumed to link exposure experience with the development of a stress-elated disorder. A wide variety of psychobiological indicators has been studied with regard to effort–reward imbalance, most often in the context of everyday work environments (e.g., using ambulatory monitoring techniques). These indicators include systolic and diastolic blood pressure, heart rate and heart rate variability, stress hormones (e.g., saliva cortisol), and markers of the immune system (e.g., C-reactive protein, interleukin, counts of natural killer cells, etc.). Significant associations of these markers with single or combined scales of the effort–reward imbalance questionnaire were observed in a majority of these investigations (for review Siegrist, 2015).

Practical Implications

Solid scientific knowledge can be used to guide improvements in human living and working conditions. In this case, it is possible to identify and to reduce health-adverse psychosocial work environments by implementing health-conducive employment and working conditions. Despite the high economic costs produced by unhealthy work, enterprises and national labor policies in most countries so far have not yet addressed these challenges to a sufficient degree. To reduce the gap between available scientific evidence and its practical use, prevention efforts at two levels are needed.

The first level concerns worksite health promotion programs in companies that include improvements in organizational and personnel development. To strengthen justice of exchange at work, efforts should be balanced with equitable economic and noneconomic rewards, implementing fair wages and salaries, reducing excessive overtime work, developing appropriate promotion prospects, and strengthening participation and transformational leadership among managers, to mention just a few policy implications. Innovative theory-based intervention studies document improved mental health among employees in organizations that have been subject to distinct organizational changes instructed by leading work stress models (Bourbonnais, Brisson, and Vézina, 2011). Importantly, such measures should be extended from primary to secondary prevention to strengthen return to work and retaining one's job among people with chronic disease and disability.

At a second level, distinct national labor and social policies deserve further development. One such policy concerns the implementation of regulations dealing with monitoring and surveillance of work-related stress. This policy should be embedded in measures of social protection of vulnerable groups and in active labor market programs. Countries with a strong development of integrative employment policies, including continued education, benefit from significantly improved quality of work in their respective workforces, and improved quality of work contributes toward reducing the burden of work-related disease (Lunau, Wahrendorf, Dragano, and Siegrist, 2013; Wahrendorf and Siegrist, 2014).

Concluding Remarks

This chapter described the theoretical model of effort–reward imbalance at work, its sociological and social psychological basis, and its roots in human stress theory. Moreover, the measurement of this concept was discussed, and a selective review of evidence on its contribution toward explaining and predicting stress-related disorders was given. Finally, some policy implications of this new knowledge were highlighted. While several methodological improvements and further empirical support are expected from future research, it is instructive to conclude this chapter with some reflections on the advantage of a theoretical model.

Theories are considered useful because they offer explanations of phenomena under study, and they are judged successful to the extent that their explanations or predictions are confirmed by rigorous research. Moreover, the power of a theoretical model is contingent on the degree of generalization to which its explanations can be applied. As mentioned, the model of effort–reward imbalance was developed in the context of research on stressful work and employment and its effects on health. Is it possible to extend its basic notion of failed reciprocity in costly social transactions beyond this context of paid work? Can we explain elevated risks of stress-related disorders in other domains of role-based social exchange? In recent years, researchers set out to answer these questions. One such extension concerns volunteering, caring for a sick person, or providing informal help. Several studies document poor health functioning in association with the experience of "high cost" and "low gain" in these types of costly transactions (Wahrendorf, Ribet, Zins, Goldberg, and Siegrist, 2010). Housework and family work provides a second case where adverse effects on depression and anxiety disorders were reported in a large study of women with children (Sperlich, Arnhold-Kerri, Siegrist, and Geyer, 2013). More recently the model was applied to the school context among adolescents, and the recurrent experience of effort–reward imbalance at school was associated with elevated risks of reporting suicidal thoughts, especially so in a highly competitive educational context such as the one observed in urban settings in China (Shang, Li, Li, Wang, and Siegrist, 2014).

In conclusion, there is preliminary evidence that the theoretical model discussed in this chapter can be extended to types of costly social transactions other than paid work, thus offering a wider range of stress and health-related explanations. This conclusion may reflect the far-reaching significance of violations of an evolutionary old "grammar" of interpersonal transaction, the principle of social reciprocity.

Notes

1. Minor parts in this section are adapted from my chapter "Effort–reward imbalance model," in G. Fink (ed.), *Stress: Concepts, Cognition, Emotion, and Behavior* (Cambridge, MA: Academic Press, 2015).
2. However, see the recent publication, Siegrist and Wahrendorf (2016).

References

Adams, J. S. (1965). Inequity in social exchange. In Leonard Berkowitz (Ed.), *Advances in Experimental Social Psychology* (pp. 267–299). Cambridge, MA: Academic Press. At http://www.sciencedirect.com/science/article/pii/S0065260108601082 (accessed July 2016).

Backé, E.-M., Seidler, A., Latza, U., Rossnagel, K., and Schumann, B. (2012). The role of psychosocial stress at work for the development of cardiovascular diseases: A systematic review. *International Archives of Occupational and Environmental Health, 85*(1), 67–79. doi:10.1007/s00420-011-0643-6.

Baumgartner, T., Fischbacher, U., Feierabend, A., Lutz, K., and Fehr, E. (2009). The neural circuitry of a broken promise. *Neuron, 64*, 756–770.

Bosma, H., Peter, R., Siegrist, J., and Marmot, M. (1998). Two alternative job stress models and the risk of coronary heart disease. *American Journal of Public Health, 88*, 68–74.

Bourbonnais, R., Brisson, C., and Vézina, M. (2011). Long-term effects of an intervention on psychosocial work factors among healthcare professionals in a hospital setting. *Occupational and Environmental Medicine, 68*(7), 479–486.

Chrousos, G. P. (2009). Stress and disorders of the stress system. *Nature Reviews. Endocrinology, 5*(7), 374–381. doi:10.1038/nrendo.2009.106

Falk, A., Menrath, I., Verde, P., and Siegrist, J. (2011). Cardiovascular consequences of unfair pay. IZA Discussion Paper 5720. At http://papers.ssrn.com/sol3/papers.cfm?abstract_id=1855152 (accessed July 2016).

Gilbert-Ouimet, M., Trudel, X., Brisson, C., Milot, A., and Vézina, M. (2014). Adverse effects of psychosocial work factors on blood pressure: Systematic review of studies on demand-control-support and effort-reward imbalance models. *Scandinavian Journal of Work, Environment and Health, 40*(2), 109–132. doi:10.5271/sjweh.3390

Gouldner, A. W. (1960). The norm of reciprocity: A preliminary statement. *American Sociological Review, 25*(2), 161–178. doi:10.2307/2092623

Greenberg, J. (2010). Organizational injustice as an occupational health risk. *Academy of Management Annals, 4*, 205–243.

Hernandez Lallement, J., Kuss, K., Trautner, P., Weber, B., Falk, A., and Fliessbach, K. (2014). Effort increases sensitivity to reward and loss magnitude in the human brain. *Social Cognitive and Affective Neuroscience, 9*(3), 342–349. doi:10.1093/scan/nss147

Johnston, D. W., Jones, M. C., Charles, K., McCann, S. K., and McKee, L. (2013). Stress in nurses: Stress-related affect and its determinants examined over the nursing day. *Annals of Behavioral Medicine: A Publication of the Society of Behavioral Medicine, 45*(3), 348–356. doi:10.1007/s12160-012-9458-2

Juvani, A., Oksanen, T., Salo, P., Virtanen, M., Kivimaki, M., Pentti, J., and Vahtera, J. (2014). Effort–reward imbalance as a risk factor for disability pension: The Finnish Public Sector Study. *Scandinavian Journal of Work, Environment and Health, 40*(3), 266–277. doi:10.5271/sjweh.3402

Kalia, M. (2005). Neurobiological basis of depression: An update. *Metabolism, 54*, 24–27.

Kampen, J., and Swygedouw, M. (2000). The ordinal controversy revisited. *Quality and Quantity, 34*, 87–102.

Karasek, R., and Theorell, T. (1990). *Healthy Work: Stress, Productivity, and the Reconstruction of Working Life.* New York: Basic Books.

Leineweber, C., Wege, N., Westerlund, H., Theorell, T., Wahrendorf, M., and Siegrist, J. (2010). How valid is a short measure of effort–reward imbalance at work? A replication study from Sweden. *Occupational and Environmental Medicine, 67*(8), 526–531.

Li, J., Zhang, M., Loerbroks, A., Angerer, P., and Siegrist, J. (2015). Work stress and the risk of recurrent coronary heart disease events: A systematic review and meta-analysis. *International Journal of Occupational Medicine and Environmental Health, 28*, 8–19. doi:10.2478/s13382-014-0303-7

Lunau, T., Wahrendorf, M., Dragano, N., and Siegrist, J. (2013). Work stress and depressive symptoms in older employees: Impact of national labour and social policies. *BMC Public Health, 13*(1), 1086. doi:10.1186/1471-2458-13-1086

McEwen, B. (1998). Protective and damaging effects of stress mediators. *New England Journal of Medicine, 338*, 171–179.

Rugulies, R., Aust, B., Madsen, I. E. H., Burr, H., Siegrist, J., and Bultmann, U. (2013). Adverse psychosocial working conditions and risk of severe depressive symptoms: Do effects differ by occupational grade? *European Journal of Public Health, 23*, 415–420. doi:10.1093/eurpub/cks071

Schnall, P. L., Dobson, M., and Rosskam, E. (Eds.) (2009). *Unhealthy Work: Causes, Consequences, Cures.* Amityville, NY: Baywood.

Schultz, W. (2006). Behavioral theories and the neurophysiology of reward. *Annual Review of Psychology, 57*, 87–115.

Shang, L., Li, J., Li, Y., Wang, T., and Siegrist, J. (2014). Stressful psychosocial school environment and suicidal ideation in Chinese adolescents. *Social Psychiatry and Psychiatric Epidemiology, 49*, 205–210. doi:10.1007/s00127-013-0728-5

Siegrist, J. (1996). Adverse health effects of high effort–low reward conditions at work. *Journal of Occupational Health Psychology, 1*, 27–43.

Siegrist, J. (2009). Job control and reward: Effects on well-being. In S. Cartwright and C. L. Cooper (Eds.), *The Oxford Handbook of Organizational Well-Being* (pp. 109–132). Oxford: Oxford University Press.

Siegrist, J. (2015). *Arbeitswelt und stressbedingte Erkrankungen.* Munich: Elsevier.

Siegrist, J., Matschinger, H., Cremer, P., and Seidel, D. (1988). Atherogenic risk in men suffering from occupational stress. *Atherosclerosis, 69*(2–3), 211–218.

Siegrist, J., Starke, D., Chandola, T., Godin, I., Marmot, M., Niedhammer, I., and Peter, R. (2004). The measurement of effort–reward imbalance at work: European comparisons. *Social Science and Medicine, 58*(8), 1483–1499. doi:10.1016/S0277-9536(03)00351-4

Siegrist, J., and Wahrendorf, M. (Eds.) (2016). *Work Stress and Health in a Globalized Economy: The Model of Effort-Reward Imbalance.* New York: Springer International.

Singer, T., Seymour, B., O'Doherty, J., Kaube, H., Dolan, R., and Frith, C. D. (2004). Empathy for pain involves the affective but not sensory components of pain. *Science, 303*(5661), 1157–1162.

Sperlich, S., Arnhold-Kerri, S., Siegrist, J., and Geyer, S. (2013). The mismatch between high effort and low reward in household and family work predicts impaired health among mothers. *European Journal of Public Health, 23*, 893–898. doi:10.1093/eurpub/cks134

Steptoe, A., and Kivimaki, M. (2012). Stress and cardiovascular disease. *Nature Reviews. Cardiology, 9*(6), 360–370. doi:10.1038/nrcardio.2012.45

Tricomi, E., Rangel, A., Camerer, C. F., and O'Doherty, J. P. (2010). Neural evidence for inequality-averse social preferences. *Nature, 463*(7284), 1089–1091. doi:10.1038/nature08785

Tsutsumi, A., and Kawakami, N. (2004). A review of empirical studies on the model of effort–reward imbalance at work: Reducing occupational stress by implementing a new theory. *Social Science and Medicine, 59*(11), 2335–2359. doi:10.1016/j.socscimed.2004.03.030

University of Düsseldorf (2006). Effort–reward imbalance questionnaires. Institut für Medizinische Soziologie. At http://www.uniklinik-duesseldorf.de/unternehmen/institute/institut-fuer-medizinische-soziologie/forschung/the-eri-model-stress-and-health/eri-questionnaires/questionnaires-download/ (accessed July 2016).

van Vegchel, N., de Jonge, J., Bosma, H., and Schaufeli, W. (2005). Reviewing the effort–reward imbalance model: Drawing up the balance of 45 empirical studies. *Social Science and Medicine (1982), 60*(5), 1117–1131. doi:10.1016/j.socscimed.2004.06.043

Wahrendorf, M., Ribet, C., Zins, M., Goldberg, M., and Siegrist, J. (2010). Perceived reciprocity in social exchange and health functioning in early old age: Prospective findings from the GAZEL study. *Aging and Mental Health, 14*(4), 425–432. doi:10.1080/13607860903483102

Wahrendorf, M., and Siegrist, J. (2014). Proximal and distal determinants of stressful work: Framework and analysis of retrospective European data. *BMC Public Health, 14*(849).

Weiner, H. (1992). *Perturbing the Organism: The Biology of Stressful Experience.* Chicago: University of Chicago Press.

3

Understanding Burnout

New Models

Christina Maslach and Michael P. Leiter

Burnout first became the focus of social attention and research in the 1970s. Now, 40 years later, the phenomenon is recognized as a major problem in many workplaces around the world. The underlying imagery of "burnout" has an immediacy and accessibility which captures an increasingly common experience – something has gone wrong in people's relationship to their work. The basic narrative goes like this: People entered a job with positive expectations, enthusiasm, and the goal to be successful. Over time, things changed – and now people have a deep sense of exhaustion; feelings of frustration, anger, and cynicism; and a sense of ineffectiveness and failure. The initial flame has burned out. The experience impairs both personal and social functioning on the job, and thus carries some real costs for the individual worker, for the people affected by him or her, and for the organization as a whole. Although some people may quit the job as a result of burnout, others will stay but will only do the bare minimum rather than their very best. What emerges from this narrative is the centrality of people's motivation to achieve. They bring dedication, effort, and commitment to their work, and want to do well and to take pride in their accomplishments. The erosion of those noble qualities is what is represented by burnout.

Identifying the Burnout Phenomenon

Although the term "burnout" first became popular during the 1970s, it had several antecedents. Earlier writing, both fictional and nonfictional, described similar phenomena, including extreme fatigue and the loss of idealism and passion for one's job. Perhaps the clearest example is Grahame Greene's novel *A Burnt-Out Case* of 1961, in which a spiritually tormented and disillusioned architect quits his job and withdraws into the African jungle.

The Handbook of Stress and Health: A Guide to Research and Practice, First Edition.
Edited by Cary L. Cooper and James Campbell Quick.
© 2017 John Wiley & Sons, Ltd. Published 2017 by John Wiley & Sons, Ltd.

Another source was the illicit drug scene, where "burnout" referred to the physical effects of chronic drug abuse. Counselors and therapists who worked with drug addicts borrowed the term to describe their own psychological deterioration and stress (Freudenberger, 1974). Apparently this term spread to other health-care and social service fields, and the workers there used "burnout" to describe their psychological difficulties with their job (Maslach, 1976).

Contrary to other psychological concepts, burnout was not derived from some scholarly theory. Rather, it was more of a grass-roots phenomenon, in which many people found it to be a particularly apt description of what they were struggling to deal with at work. It was a very evocative term, and people could easily resonate to it. But that easy resonance posed a major challenge in that different people could have different meanings attributed to the term. Even if everybody was using the same word, it was not clear that they were using it to mean the same thing.

Burnout Definitions

Thus, establishing a clear and consensual definition of burnout was the first conceptual goal that needed to be achieved. The initial phase of this work involved a lot of exploratory, qualitative field research, which amassed many descriptions of the burnout phenomenon based on observations, interviews, case studies, and personal experience. A closer analysis of the varying perspectives emerging from these data revealed some common themes: burnout is a psychological experience involving feelings, attitudes, motives and expectations; and it is a negative experience for the individual, in that it concerns problems, distress, discomfort, dysfunction, and/or negative consequences.

What also emerged from this exploratory work were three basic dimensions of the burnout experience: an overwhelming exhaustion, feelings of cynicism and detachment from the job, and a sense of ineffectiveness and lack of accomplishment (see Maslach, 1993). These three dimensions appeared in many of the various definitions of burnout that were being proposed at that time. The exhaustion dimension was also described as wearing out, loss of energy, depletion, debilitation, and fatigue. The cynicism dimension was originally called depersonalization (given the nature of human services occupations), but was also described as negative or inappropriate attitudes, detached concern, irritability, loss of idealism, and withdrawal. The inefficacy dimension was originally called reduced personal accomplishment and was also described as reduced productivity or capability, low morale, and an inability to cope.

Burnout Measures

As the characteristics of burnout became more clearly identified, the next step was to develop measures that could assess them. Various measures were proposed, based on different assumptions about burnout, and many of them relied on the face validity of the measurement items or statements. The first burnout measure that was based on a comprehensive program of psychometric research was the Maslach Burnout Inventory (MBI; Maslach and Jackson, 1981; Maslach, Jackson, and Leiter, 1996). The MBI was specifically designed to assess the three dimensions of the burnout experience which had emerged from the earlier qualitative research; in contrast, other initial measures of burnout focused only on the dimension of exhaustion (e.g., Freudenberger and Richelson, 1980; Pines, Aronson, and Kafry, 1981).

This distinction between measures that assess several dimensions of burnout, and those that assess the sole dimension of exhaustion, continues to the present day, and reflects different conceptualizations of burnout. For example, the Bergen Burnout Inventory (BBI; Feldt et al., 2014) assesses three dimensions of burnout: exhaustion at work, cynicism toward the meaning of work, and sense of inadequacy at work. The Oldenburg Burnout Inventory (OLBI: Halbesleben and Demerouti, 2005) assesses the two dimensions of exhaustion and disengagement from work. Other burnout measures focus on exhaustion alone, although they differentiate between various aspects of exhaustion. For example, the Shirom-Melamed Burnout Questionnaire (SMBQ; Shirom and Melamed, 2005) distinguishes between physical fatigue, emotional exhaustion, and cognitive weariness; and the Copenhagen Burnout Inventory (CBI; Kristensen, Borritz, Villadsen, and Christensen, 2005) makes a distinction between physical and psychological exhaustion.

There have been other changes and modifications of burnout measures over the years. Because the initial concern about burnout emerged from caregiving occupations, such as health care and human services, the measures developed in the 1980s tended to reflect the experience of those professions. Later, however, other occupational groups became interested in the occurrence of burnout, but they had some difficulties in adapting the existing measures to their work situation. For the MBI, the solution was the development of a General Survey that could be used within any occupation (MBI-GS; Schaufeli, Leiter, Maslach, and Jackson, 1996). Not only were various items revised to be more "occupational-neutral," but the dimension of depersonalization (which was more specific to human services) was broadened to refer to a negative detachment from work and was renamed *cynicism*, and the dimension of personal accomplishment was broadened and renamed *professional efficacy*. More recent burnout measures utilized more occupational-neutral wording from the outset.

However, some measures also added some new dimensions to the concept of burnout. For example, the Spanish Burnout Inventory consists of four dimensions: enthusiasm toward the job, psychological exhaustion, indolence, and guilt (Gil-Monte and Figueiredo-Ferraz, 2013). Meanwhile, some researchers were concerned that the more neutral wording meant a loss of the specific interpersonal issues for human service workers, so they developed a new measure of interpersonal strain (Borgogni, Consiglio, Alessandri, and Schaufeli, 2012). It remains an open question whether these additional qualities are essential components of burnout, per se, or whether they assess experiences or conditions that often accompany the experience of burnout.

Research Assessments or Clinical Diagnosis

All of these burnout measures have been designed to enable researchers to obtain new evidence of the nature of the burnout phenomenon, and its causes and consequences. However, practitioners have been arguing that there is a growing need for a measure that provides a clinical diagnosis. In other words, what pattern of scores would indicate that a person is suffering from an extreme case of burnout, which would require some sort of treatment? Unfortunately, no clinical research has been done to establish that any particular score, or pattern of scores, is a meaningful indicator of serious problems in well-being or work performance. So what have been alternative strategies for assessing an individual diagnosis? Basically, there have been three approaches: (1) establish an arbitrary level of "high" scores on the research measures;

(2) establish a pattern of scores that is correlated with an independent clinical diagnosis of burnout; and (3) simplify the burnout phenomenon to a more easily diagnosed concept.

In the first approach, the distribution of scores on the research measures has been divided into thirds (high, average, and low), and individuals who score in the "high" third are assumed to be experiencing a strong case of burnout. In the second approach, patterns of scores were correlated with work-related neurasthenia, as the equivalent of clinical burnout (Schaufeli, Bakker, Hoogduin, Schaap and Kladler, 2001). The results established clinically validated cut-off scores for each of the three MBI scales, and led to the following decision rule: An individual is considered to be clinically burned-out when he or she has a "high" score on exhaustion in combination with a "high" score on either of the two remaining MBI dimensions (Roelofs, Verbraak, Keijsers, de Bruin, and Schmidt, 2005).

The third approach has been to simplify the burnout concept by reducing it to the single dimension of exhaustion. This is especially true in situations where the desire is to establish a medical diagnosis for burnout. For example, work-related neurasthenia has been largely reduced to the single dimension of exhaustion because its main characteristic is persistent fatigue and weakness. However, simplifying burnout by equating it to another known phenomenon begs the question of why the term "burnout" is even needed. There is no reason to rename exhaustion – to do so would invite the criticism of "putting old wine in new bottles." If exhaustion is all there is to burnout, then it should just be called "exhaustion" because the term "burnout" would not be adding any extra value. A more serious consequence of the "exhaustion only" argument is that it undermines our understanding of the original phenomenon, by ignoring the role of the linked dimension of cynicism, and the impact on professional efficacy (for a more complete discussion of these assessment issues, see Maslach, Leiter, and Schaufeli, 2009).

The effort to transform burnout into a medical diagnosis raises the question about whether or not burnout should be considered to be a mental illness. This question first appeared in the early stages of establishing a definition of burnout, given that it seemed to be related to anxiety and depression. Some argued that burnout was simply a form of depression, but subsequent empirical research established a clear distinction between burnout and depression (Bakker, Schaufeli, Demerouti, Janssen, Van der Hulst, and Brouwer, 2000; Glass and McKnight, 1996; Leiter and Durup, 1994). This research demonstrated that burnout is a problem that is more specific to the work context, in contrast to depression that tends to pervade every domain of a person's life. These findings lent empirical support to earlier claims that burnout is job-related and situation-specific, as opposed to depression, which is general and context-free (Freudenberger, 1983; Warr, 1987).

The link between job-related neurasthenia and burnout might support the argument that burnout is itself a form of mental illness. However, a more common assumption has been that burnout causes mental dysfunction – that is, it is a mediating state that precipitates negative effects in terms of mental health, such as anxiety, depression, drops in self-esteem, and so forth. Supportive evidence has come from research showing that burnout is predictive of depression (Greenglass and Burke, 1990; Schonfeld, 1989) and other emotional symptoms. A recent study found a reciprocal relationship between burnout and depression, with each predicting subsequent developments in the other. However, it was noteworthy that burnout fully mediated the relationship of workplace strains with depression: when problems at work contribute to depression, experiencing burnout is a step in the process (Ahola and Hakanen, 2007).

Engagement: The Positive Antithesis

An important development, at the beginning of the twenty-first century, has been that researchers have tried to broaden their understanding of burnout by extending their attention to its positive antithesis. This positive state has been identified as "engagement." Although there is general agreement that engagement with work represents a productive and fulfilling state within the occupational domain, there are differences in its definition. For some burnout researchers, engagement is considered to be the opposite of burnout and is defined in terms of the same three dimensions as burnout, but the positive end of those dimensions rather than the negative. From this perspective, engagement consists of a state of high energy, strong involvement, and a sense of efficacy (Leiter and Maslach, 1998). By implication, engagement is assessed by the opposite pattern of scores on the three MBI dimensions.

However, a different approach has defined work engagement as a persistent, positive affective-motivational state of fulfillment that is characterized by the three components of vigor, dedication, and absorption. In this view, work engagement is an independent and distinct concept, which is not the opposite of burnout (although it is negatively related to it). A new measure, the Utrecht Work Engagement Scale (UWES), was developed to assess this positive state (Schaufeli, Bakker, and Salanova, 2006), and extensive research has been carried out in the last decade (see the edited volume by Bakker and Leiter, 2010). The relationship between burnout and engagement continues to be debated, however, and a recent approach has been to use dialectical theory to synthesize conflicting views on the two constructs, and to develop an alternate model (Leon, Halbesleben, and Paustian-Underdahl, 2015).

Conceptual Models

Once the burnout phenomenon had been identified, the challenge was to identify existing concepts and theories that might help explain it. Because the earliest researchers came from social and clinical psychology, they gravitated toward relevant ideas from these fields. The social perspective utilized concepts involving interpersonal relationships; these included detached concern, dehumanization in self-defense, and attribution processes. It also brought in concepts of motivation and emotion (and especially coping with emotional arousal). The clinical perspective also dealt with motivation and emotion, but framed these more in terms of psychological disorders, such as depression. Subsequent researchers came from industrial-organizational psychology, and this perspective emphasized work attitudes and behaviors. It was also at this point that burnout was conceptualized as a form of job stress, although the primary focus was more on the context of the job environment, and less on the characteristics of the experienced stress.

Over the years, there have been a number of debates about key theoretical points. Some of these have focused on alternative views of the phenomenon itself, while others concern different proposals about its development over time, and its relationship to key causal factors.

Multidimensional vs. One-Dimensional Constructs

All theoretical perspectives on burnout have included exhaustion as a key defining dimension. The concept of exhaustion captures the basic stress experienced by an individual, as it refers to feelings of being overextended and depleted of one's emotional and physical resources. In the research literature on burnout, exhaustion is the most widely reported and the most thoroughly analyzed component of this syndrome. As mentioned earlier, some measures of burnout only assess exhaustion, and the underlying conceptual models point to exhaustion as the sole defining criterion. The strong identification of exhaustion with burnout has led some to argue that the other two aspects of the syndrome are incidental or unnecessary.

However, exhaustion is not all there is to burnout. It is a necessary criterion, but it is not sufficient. It reflects the strain dimension of burnout, thus identifying burnout as a stress phenomenon, but it does not capture the critical aspects of people's relationship to work. Rather, the cynicism dimension does that, by assessing people's negative, distancing response to their job and the individuals in it. It is these negative thoughts and behaviors that are considered "unprofessional" and thus are not often shared with others because of the stigma attached to them. Exhaustion, on the other hand, is usually not viewed as unprofessional; indeed, it can be a source of pride and a public bragging point of "how long and hard I have worked, and how committed I am," etc. But exhaustion can also prompt actions to distance oneself from one's work, presumably as a way to cope with work overload, and a consistent finding in burnout research, across a wide range of organizational and occupational settings, is that there is a strong relationship between exhaustion and cynicism.

The inclusion of distancing (cynicism) and discouragement (inefficacy) draws an important distinction between burnout and chronic exhaustion. People experiencing burnout are not simply fatigued or overwhelmed by their workload. They also have lost a psychological connection with their work that has implications for their motivation and their identity. If the only issue were exhaustion, the term "burnout" would add nothing beyond what is already and more straightforwardly captured by the term, chronic fatigue. Instead, the multidimensional model of burnout also captures a disaffection with work and a crisis in work-based efficacy expectations.

As a counterpoint to the more simplistic and exhaustion-centric view, recent research is restoring a major focus on the other dimensions of burnout. The basic proposal is that the use of multiple dimensions, rather than just a single one, will allow the identification of distinct patterns, or profiles, of burnout. For example, a full profile of Burnout would be indicated by the combination of exhaustion, cynicism, and inefficacy. But a Disengaged profile would reflect high scores on cynicism alone (and lower scores on the other two dimensions), and an Overextended profile would reflect high scores on exhaustion alone (and lower scores on the other two dimensions). In earlier longitudinal research, people with these latter two profiles were more likely to show changes in their level of burnout over the course of a year (Maslach and Leiter, 2008). A subsequent study demonstrated that the direction of that shift (toward more or less burnout) had implications for employees' long-term health (Leiter et al., 2013). Recent research has found that the Disengaged profile captures an experience that is closer to the full Burnout profile, while the Overextended profile is less negative (Leiter and Maslach, 2016). These findings provide further evidence that "exhaustion alone" is not a viable proxy for the phenomenon of burnout.

Another kind of strategy for studying burnout profiles is a person-centered approach that investigates different patterns of change over time. These patterns, or *trajectories*, capture the extent to which people are getting better or worse in terms of job well-being. In one study, people undergoing a long-term rehabilitation program were identified as displaying one of three trajectories: low burnout, high burnout–benefited, and high burnout–not benefited, which enabled the researchers to gain a better perspective on what factors promote burnout recovery (Hatinen et al., 2009).

The Development of Burnout over Time

Research has established that without definitive changes in work settings, burnout can remain fairly constant for long periods of time (Maslach, Schaufeli, and Leiter, 2001). This evidence aligns with a lot of the earliest qualitative studies of burnout, which often flagged chronic job stressors as the key causes. Clearly, this poses a challenge for any efforts to ameliorate or treat burnout, that is, to make positive, lasting changes, and so a better understanding of how burnout develops over time could be very helpful.

There have been various theoretical proposals about the developmental path of burnout. The earliest models took a sequential approach, on the assumption that there was an underlying set of stages to the growth of burnout. Later models were based on theories about job stress and the notion of imbalances leading to strain.

Sequential stages   The notion of a sequence of stages in burnout arose during the exploratory, qualitative interviews that took place with human service workers in the late 1970s (Maslach, 1982). What was often described was the following: First, people would experience an ever-growing and demanding workload that taxed their emotional resources, and so they experienced *emotional exhaustion*. To cope with this overload, people would begin to detach themselves from their work, develop negative reactions to the job, and treat people in callous and cynical ways – a response of *depersonalization*. If things did not get better over time, then people would begin to question their ability to do the job well, and would experience feelings of inadequacy and failure, or *reduced personal accomplishment*. The underlying assumption in this sequential process model is that the occurrence of one dimension precipitates the development of subsequent ones. The link between the first two dimensions has received more empirical support than the link between the second and third. Much of that research has relied primarily on cross-sectional studies and statistical causal models, but there have been some recent longitudinal studies that have provided empirical support for this process sequence (Bakker, Schaufeli, Sixma, Bosveld, and VanDierendonck, 2000; Leiter and Maslach, 2004; Toppinen-Tanner, Kalimo, and Mutanen, 2002).

A different sequential approach is the phase model, in which the three burnout dimensions are split into high and low categories, yielding eight different patterns, or phases, of burnout (Golembiewski and Munzenrider, 1988). The phase model has hypothesized that cynicism is the early minimum phase of burnout, followed by the additions of inefficacy, and finally by exhaustion.

An alternative sequential approach is a transactional model of burnout, which has three stages (Cherniss, 1980b). The first stage is an imbalance between work demands and individual resources (job stressors), the second stage involves an emotional response of exhaustion and anxiety (individual strain), and the third stage involves changes in attitudes and behavior, such as greater cynicism (defensive coping). Several studies have provided empirical support for this transactional model (Burke, Shearer, and Deszca, 1984; Burke and Greenglass, 1989).

Job stress and imbalance models   In the 1980s and 1990s, burnout got the attention of researchers in the areas of industrial-organizational psychology, as well as occupational health.

Much of this attention focused on *job stress*, which is a general rubric referring to the impact of external job demands (stressors) on the worker's internal experience (stress response), and to the subsequent outcomes of this process. A consistent theme throughout this research literature is the problematic relationship between the individual and the situation, which is often described in terms of imbalance or misalignment or misfit – for example, the demands of the job exceed the capacity of the individual to cope effectively, or the person's efforts are not reciprocated with equitable rewards. Some of the earliest models of organizational stress focused on this notion of job–person fit, which was assumed to predict less strain and better adjustment, and subsequent theorizing continued to highlight the importance of both individual and contextual factors (see Kahn and Byosiere, 1992).

The first burnout model to utilize this kind of framework was the Cherniss transaction model described earlier. The first stage of the transaction model is the imbalance between demands and resources. The second is the exhaustion stress response, which leads to cynicism and other changes. The identification of demands and resources as causal factors in burnout was incorporated into the process model for the MBI (Maslach et al., 1996; Maslach and Leiter, 1999) and in to other research on burnout (e.g., Aiken et al., 2001; Schaufeli and Bakker, 2004).

Further development of the concept of a demand–resource imbalance occurred in the conservation of resources model (COR; Hobfoll and Freedy, 1993). When individuals perceive that the resources they value are threatened, they strive to maintain those resources. The loss of resources or even the impending loss of resources may aggravate burnout. The COR model posits a fundamental motivation to conserve, recover, and acquire resources to maintain a capacity to address demands as they arise. In a well-resourced work environment, employees can accommodate more job demands through their access to job resources, moderating the effect of demands on their personal energy.

The next model to tackle the demand–resource imbalance was the job demands–resources model (JD-R; Demerouti, Bakker, Nachreiner, and Schaufeli, 2001). The JD-R model focuses on the notion that burnout arises when individuals experience incessant job demands and have inadequate resources available to address and to reduce those demands. People may call upon job resources to reduce the load on their personal resources, to augment the potential impact of those personal resources, or to replenish those resources after depletion. Job demands deplete resources, leading to burnout when left unattended; job resources supplement resources leading to work engagement when sustained. A recent meta-analysis has extended JD-R theory by pointing to a differentiation of challenge versus hindrance demands (Crawford, LePine, and Rich, 2010). Challenge demands were associated with increased engagement, while hindrance demands were associated with decreased engagement and increased burnout. Overall, both the JD-R and the COR theory of burnout development have received confirmation in research studies.

A different variation of an imbalance model of burnout is the areas of worklife model of burnout (AW; Maslach and Leiter, 1997; Leiter and Maslach, 2004), in which burnout mediates the impact of job stressors on individual outcomes. Like the transactional model, the AW model frames job stressors in terms of person–job imbalances, or mismatches, but identifies six key areas in which these imbalances take place: workload, control, reward, community, fairness, and values (see later section on causal factors). These stressors affect an individual's level of experienced burnout, and this level of burnout, in turn, determines various individual outcomes, such as work behaviors (e.g., performance, absenteeism), social behaviors (e.g., quality of home life), and personal health. The AW model proposes that the greater the

perceived incongruity, or mismatch, between the person and the job, the greater the likelihood of burnout; conversely, the greater the perceived congruity, the greater the likelihood of
engagement with work. Initial empirical support for this mediation model has been provided
by both cross-sectional and longitudinal analyses.

Causes and Consequences of Burnout

All of the models of burnout make explicit the causal theorizing that has always been implicit in
burnout research: Certain factors (both situational and individual) cause people to experience
burnout, and once burnout occurs, it causes certain outcomes (both situational and individual).
At first, these causal assumptions could not always be tested directly. Many studies on burnout
have involved cross-sectional designs or studies using statistical causal models. This correlational database has provided support for many of the hypothesized links between burnout
and its sources and effects, but it is unable to address the presumed causality of those linkages. The recent increase in longitudinal studies has begun to provide a better opportunity to
test sequential hypotheses, but stronger causal inferences will also require appropriate methodological designs (and these can be difficult to implement in applied settings). One other critical
constraint is that many of the variables have been assessed by self-report measures (rather than
other indices of behavior or health). Given these caveats, this section will provide an overview
of the major research findings on the predictors and outcomes of burnout.

Situational Predictors of Burnout

Over three decades of research on burnout have identified a plethora of organizational risk
factors across many occupations in various countries (see Maslach et al., 2001; Schaufeli and
Enzmann, 1998). In analyzing this research literature, Maslach and Leiter (1997; 1999) identified six key domains: workload, control, reward, community, fairness, and values. The first two
areas are reflected in the demand–control model of job stress (Karasek and Theorell, 1990),
and reward refers to the power of reinforcements to shape behavior. Community captures all
of the work on social support and interpersonal conflict, while fairness emerges from the literature on equity and social justice. Finally, the area of values picks up the cognitive-emotional
power of job goals and expectations.

Workload   A commonly discussed source of burnout is overload: job demands exceeding
human limits. People have to do too much in too little time with too few resources. Increased
workload has a consistent relationship with burnout, especially with the exhaustion dimension
(Cordes and Dougherty, 1993; Maslach et al., 2001; Schaufeli and Enzmann, 1998). Structural
models of burnout have shown that exhaustion then mediates the relationship of workload with
the other two dimensions of burnout (Lee and Ashforth, 1996; Leiter and Harvie, 1998). This
association reflects the relationship of work demands with occupational stress in the stress
and coping literature (Cox, Kuk, and Leiter, 1993). Both qualitative and quantitative work
overload contribute to exhaustion by depleting the capacity of people to meet the demands of
the job. The critical point occurs when people are unable to recover from work demands. That
is, acute fatigue resulting from an especially demanding event at work – meeting a deadline
or addressing a crisis – need not lead to burnout if people have an opportunity to recover
during restful periods at work or at home (Shinn, Rosario, Morch, and Chestnut, 1984). When

this kind of overload is a chronic job condition, not an occasional emergency, there is little opportunity to rest, recover, and restore balance. A manageable workload, in contrast, provides opportunities to use and refine existing skills as well as to become effective in new areas of activity (Landsbergis, 1988).

The distinction of challenge versus hindrance demands (Crawford, LePine, and Rich, 2010) has provided further evidence that exhaustion arises not simply from the quantity of demand but the quality of demands as well. Similarly, Semmer et al. (2010) have argued that demands that employees consider to be outside of the legitimate expectations for their jobs are more burdensome than are legitimate tasks. The central issue for both of these constructs is the extent of the match or mismatch of employees with workplace conditions.

Control   The demand–control theory of job stress (Karasek and Theorell, 1990) has made the case for the enabling role of control. This area includes employees' perceived capacity to influence decisions that affect their work, to exercise professional autonomy, and to gain access to the resources necessary to do an effective job. A major control problem occurs when people experience role conflict. Many burnout studies have found that greater role conflict is strongly and positively associated with greater exhaustion (Cordes and Dougherty, 1993; Maslach et al., 1996). Role conflict arises from multiple authorities with conflicting demands or incongruent values, and people in this situation cannot exercise effective control in their job. Role conflict is not simply an indicator of additional work demands, but is emotionally exhausting in itself (e.g., Siefert, Jayaratne, and Chess, 1991; Starnaman and Miller, 1992). Studies that examine role conflict usually also consider role ambiguity – the absence of direction in work. Generally, role ambiguity is associated with greater burnout, but the relationship is not nearly as consistent as that of role conflict (Cordes and Dougherty, 1993; Maslach et al., 1996). When people have more control in their work, their actions are more freely chosen, and this can lead to greater satisfaction with the job, and more commitment to it. Active participation in organizational decision-making has been consistently found to be associated with higher levels of efficacy and lower levels of exhaustion (Cherniss, 1980a; Lee and Ashforth, 1993; Leiter, 1992).

Control or autonomy at work takes many forms. Employees' skill and capacity to exercise time management skills have been shown to moderate the relationship of demands with burnout (Peeters and Rutte, 2005). Employees with greater "work self-determination" benefit greatly from additional autonomy, as they have shown even weaker relationships of demands with exhaustion when they were granted more decision-making authority (Fernet, Guay, and Senécal, 2004). Increasing control has been the focus of interventions designed to prevent burnout (Sonnentag, 2015).

Reward   The research literature on reward addresses the extent to which rewards – monetary, social, and intrinsic – are consistent with expectations. The results of various studies have shown that insufficient reward (whether financial, institutional, or social) increases people's vulnerability to burnout (e.g., Chappell and Novak, 1992; Glicken, 1983; Maslanka, 1996; Siefert et al., 1991). Lack of recognition from service recipients, colleagues, managers, and external stakeholders devalues both the work and the workers, and is closely associated with feelings of inefficacy (Cordes and Dougherty, 1993; Maslach et al., 1996). In contrast, consistency in the reward dimension between the person and the job means that there are both material rewards and opportunities for intrinsic satisfaction (Richardsen, Burke, and Leiter,

1992). Intrinsic rewards (such as pride in doing something of importance and doing it well) can be just as critical as extrinsic rewards, if not more so. What keeps work involving for most people is the pleasure and satisfaction they experience with the day-to-day flow of work that is going well (Leiter, 1992).

Recognition of employees' contributions has been identified as a direct, effective, and low-cost method for preventing burnout and increasing employees' engagement with their work (Day and Randell, 2014). The impact of rewards on employees' experience of workload is sensitive to the level of fairness that employees perceive in the allocation of rewards relative to the effort they contribute to their work (Hämmig, Brauchli, and Bauer, 2012).

Community   Community is the overall quality of social interaction at work, including issues of conflict, mutual support, closeness, and the capacity to work as a team. Burnout research has focused primarily on social support from supervisors, coworkers, and family members (Cordes and Dougherty, 1993; Greenglass, Fiksenbaum, and Burke, 1994; Greenglass, Pantony, and Burke, 1988; Maslach et al., 1996). Distinct patterns have been found for informal coworker support and supervisor support (Jackson, Schwab, and Schuler, 1986; Leiter and Maslach, 1988). Supervisor support has been more consistently associated with exhaustion, reflecting the supervisors' impact on staff members' workload. Coworker support is more closely related to accomplishment or efficacy, reflecting the value staff members put on expert evaluation by their peers. Regardless of its specific form, social support has been found to be associated with greater engagement (Leiter and Maslach, 1988; Schnorpfeil et al., 2002).

Research on the social context of burnout has also attended to the broader issues associated with a sense of community in an organization (Drory and Shamir, 1988; Farber, 1984; Royal and Rossi, 1996). A sense of community has been found to buffer the impact of feelings of inequity at work (Truchot and Deregard, 2001). Research on community orientation (Buunk and Schaufeli, 1993) provides a distinct but consistent perspective. However, when social relationships within the community become negative and even aggressive, burnout is the likely result (Deery, Walsh, and Guest. 2011; Dormann, and Zapf, 2004; Savicki, Cooley, and Gjesvold, 2003).

Research over the past decade on workplace incivility has also investigated the capacity of low-intensity negative social encounters to aggravate burnout among employees (Cortina, Magley, Williams, and Langhout, 2001). It has been proposed that the power of social encounters – even low-intensity, unintended slights – to undermine employees' sense of well-being reflects the centrality of workgroup social standing to employees' identity and self-concept (Leiter, 2012).

Fairness   Fairness is the extent to which decisions at work are perceived as being fair and equitable. Relevant research on procedural justice (e.g., Lawler, 1968; Tyler, 1990) has shown that people are more concerned with the fairness of the process (procedural) than with the favorableness of the outcome (distributive). This pattern is also seen in research on burnout (e.g., Lambert et al., 2010). People use the quality of the procedures, and their own treatment during the decision-making process, as an index of their place in the community. They will feel alienated from that community if they are subject to unfair, cursory, or disrespectful decision-making. In contrast, a fair decision is one in which people have an opportunity to present their arguments and in which they feel treated with respect and politeness. Thus, fairness shares some qualities with community, as well as with reward.

More recent research has differentiated among several forms of justice – substantive, distributive, and relational – to demonstrate the connection of injustice with the development of burnout and with subsequent behavior, such as job turnover (Campbell et al., 2013). The experience of injustice has a stronger association with the exhaustion and cynicism aspects of burnout than with efficacy (Jin, Zhang, and Wang, 2015). Reflecting the previously mentioned relevance of social encounters to burnout, research has confirmed that a perceived lack of reciprocity in working relationships was a major source of employees' experience of injustice at work (Moliner et al., 2013).

Fairness is central to equity theory (Walster, Berscheid, and Walster, 1973), which posits that perceptions of equity or inequity are based on people's determination of the balance between their inputs (i.e., time, effort, and expertise) and outputs (i.e., rewards and recognition). This core notion of inequity is also reflected in the effort–reward imbalance model (Siegrist, 1996). Research based on these theoretical frameworks has found that a lack of reciprocity, or imbalanced social exchange processes, is predictive of burnout (e.g., Bakker, Schaufeli, Sixma, Bosveld, and van Dierendonck, 2000; Schaufeli, van Dierendonck, and van Gorp, 1996). Fairness has also emerged as a critical factor in administrative leadership (e.g., White, 1987). It appears that employees value fairness in itself and consider it to be indicative of a genuine concern for the long-term good of the organization's staff, especially during difficult times.

Values   There has not been a lot of research on the impact of values for job stress, but current work suggests that it may play a key role in predicting levels of burnout and engagement (Leiter and Maslach, 2004). Values are the ideals and motivations that originally attracted people to their job, and thus they are the motivating connection between the worker and the workplace, which goes beyond the utilitarian exchange of time for money or advancement. When there is a values conflict in the job, and thus a gap between individual and organizational values, workers will find themselves making a trade-off between work they want to do and work they have to do. In some cases, people might feel constrained by the job to do things that are unethical and not in accord with their own values, or they may be caught between conflicting values of the organization (e.g., high quality service and cost containment do not always coexist). In other instances, there may be a conflict between personal career aspirations and organizational values, as when people realize that they entered an occupation with mistaken expectations. Studies have consistently found that value incongruence, along with work overload, is especially relevant to employees' experience of burnout (Brom et al., 2015; Leiter, Frank, and Matheson, 2009; Veage et al., 2014).

Integration of the six areas   It is not yet clear from the research whether some of these situational factors are more significant than others as predictors of burnout. The six areas are not independent of each other; indeed, problems in one area can be associated with problems in another area. For example, excessive workload often indicates problems in control and autonomy, because much of what people identify as excessive work demands are externally imposed tasks (rather than internally chosen ones). As another example, an organization that has a strong sense of community is likely to treat employees fairly and provide meaningful rewards.

However, recent research on the interrelationships of these six areas suggests that there is a consistent and complex pattern that predicts level of experienced burnout. Using the Areas of Worklife Scale (AWS) to assess person–job incongruities, or imbalances, in these six areas, Leiter and Maslach (2004) found that workload and control each play critical roles (thus replicating the demand–control model) but are not sufficient. Reward, community, and fairness add further power to predict values, which in turn was the critical predictor of the three dimensions of burnout. This structure has led to analyses that have argued for a two-process model of burnout (Leiter, Frank, and Matheson, 2009). First, in the Energy process, unmanageable workload aggravates exhaustion that in turn contributes to greater cynicism and reduced efficacy. Second, in the Values process, mismatches in various areas of worklife are consolidated as a mismatch of employees and their work setting regarding core values. This mismatch in values relates to all three aspects of burnout, being associated with reduced energy, involvement, and efficacy. Together, the two processes contribute to employees' experience of burnout.

Another possibility to consider in future research is whether the weighting of the importance of these six areas may reflect an important individual difference. For example, some people might place a higher weight on rewards than on values, and thus might be more distressed by insufficient rewards than by value conflicts.

Individual Predictors of Burnout

It is interesting to note that the empirical research on risk factors for burnout is far less for personal variables than for situational ones. This may reflect, to some extent, the theoretical orientations of the leading researchers in the field, but the pattern of findings suggests that personal factors play a less critical role as sources of burnout. Although some individual characteristics have been correlated with burnout, these relationships are not as great in size as those for situational factors, which implies that burnout is more of a social phenomenon than an individual one.

Several demographic variables have been studied in relation to burnout, but the studies are relatively few and the findings are not that consistent (see Schaufeli and Enzmann, 1998, for a review). Age is the one variable that shows a more consistent correlation with burnout. Among younger employees the level of burnout is reported to be higher than it is among those aged over 30 or 40 years. Age is confounded with work experience, so burnout appears to be more of a risk earlier in one's career, rather than later. The reasons for such an interpretation have not been studied very thoroughly. However, these findings should be viewed with caution because of the problem of survival bias – that is, those who burn out early in their careers are likely to quit their jobs, leaving behind the survivors, who consequently exhibit lower levels of burnout. The demographic variable of sex has not been a strong predictor of burnout. The one small but consistent sex difference is that males often score slightly higher on cynicism. There is also a tendency in some studies for women to score slightly higher on exhaustion. These results could be related to gender role stereotypes, but they may also reflect the confounding of sex with occupation (e.g., police officers are more likely to be male, nurses are more likely to be female). With regard to marital status, those who are unmarried seem to be more prone to burnout compared to those who are married, and singles seem to experience even higher burnout levels than those who are divorced (although, again, these variables are confounded with age). As for ethnicity, very few studies have assessed this demographic variable, so it is not possible to summarize any empirical trends.

Several personality traits have been studied in an attempt to discover which types of people may be at greater risk for experiencing burnout (see Schaufeli and Enzmann, 1998, for a review). As with demographic variables, there are some suggestive trends but not a large body of consistent empirical findings. Burnout tends to be higher among people who have low self-esteem, an external locus of control, low levels of hardiness, and a Type A behavior style. Those who are burned-out cope with stressful events in a rather passive, defensive way, whereas active and confronting coping is associated with less burnout. In particular, confronting coping is associated with the dimension of efficacy. More consistent findings have come from research on the Big Five personality dimensions, which has found that burnout is linked to the dimension of neuroticism (Deary et al., 1996; Hills and Norvell, 1991; Zellars, Perrewé, and Hochwarter, 2000). Neuroticism includes trait anxiety, hostility, depression, self-consciousness, and vulnerability; neurotic individuals are emotionally unstable and prone to psychological distress.

Outcomes of Burnout

Some of the research on burnout has viewed it as an important end-state in its own right, particularly when it has been considered to be a form of poor mental health and ineffective coping. However, the more common assumption is that the significance of burnout lies in its role as a mediator of other important outcomes. It is presumed that the person experiencing burnout will show a decline in job performance and an increase in job withdrawal (absenteeism, turnover). In addition, given that burnout is a stress phenomenon, the presumption is that it will also have important health outcomes for the individual, and may affect the person's home life as well. All of these outcomes have high costs not only for the individual and his or her personal life, but for the place where he or she works.

Work outcomes   Burnout has been frequently associated with various forms of negative responses to the job, including job dissatisfaction, low organizational commitment, absenteeism, intention to leave the job, and turnover (see Schaufeli and Enzmann, 1998, for a review). People who are experiencing burnout can have a negative impact on their colleagues, both by causing greater personal conflict and by disrupting job tasks. Thus, burnout can be "contagious" and perpetuate itself through social interactions on the job (Bakker, Le Blanc, and Schaufeli, 2005; González-Morales, Peiró, Rodríguez, and Bliese, 2012). Such findings suggest that burnout should be considered as a characteristic of workgroups rather than simply an individual syndrome.

Burnout can also have a negative "spillover" effect on workers' home life. Workers experiencing burnout were rated by their spouses in more negative ways (Jackson and Maslach, 1982; Zedeck, Maslach, Mosier, and Skitka, 1988), and they themselves reported that their work has a negative impact on their family and that their marriage is unsatisfactory (Burke and Greenglass, 1989; 2001).

A serious work outcome of burnout is poor job performance. For example, nurses experiencing higher levels of burnout were judged by their patients to be providing a lower level of patient care (Leiter, Harvie, and Frizzell, 1998; Vahey, Aiken, Sloane, Clarke, and Vargas, 2004), and the risk of patient mortality was higher when nurses had a higher patient workload and were experiencing greater burnout (Aiken, Clarke, Sloane, Sochalski and Silber, 2002). Burned-out police officers reported more use of violence against civilians (Kop, Euwema, and Schaufeli, 1999).

Health outcomes   Burnout has a complex pattern of relationships with physical and mental health in that poor health contributes to burnout and burnout contributes to poor health (Ahola and Hakanen, 2014). The general stress literature provides a clear theoretical basis for a relation between burnout and health. Of the three burnout dimensions, exhaustion is the closest to an orthodox stress variable, and therefore is more predictive of stress-related health outcomes than the other two dimensions. Exhaustion is typically correlated with such stress symptoms as headaches, chronic fatigue, gastrointestinal disorders, muscle tension, hypertension, cold/flu episodes, and sleep disturbances (e.g., Bhagat, Allie, and Ford, 1995; Burke and Deszca, 1986; Golembiewski and Munzenrider, 1988; Hendrix, Summers, Leap, and Steel, 1995; Jackson and Maslach, 1982; Kahill, 1988). These physiological correlates mirror those found with other indices of prolonged stress. A longitudinal study found that workload and exhaustion predicted the incidence of workplace injuries during the subsequent year (Leiter and Maslach, 2009). Some research has also found a link between burnout and lifestyle practices that carry health risks, such as smoking and alcohol use (e.g., Burke, Shearer, and Deszca, 1984) and psychotropic drug use (Leiter et al., 2013).

In terms of mental health, burnout has been predictive of depression (Greenglass and Burke, 1990; Schonfeld, 1989) and other emotional symptoms, such as anxiety and irritability. In analyses of a Finnish population, the rate of depression among people reporting severe burnout was 45 percent, while it was a much lower 11 percent among people with mild burnout, and only 3 percent among those showing no signs of burnout (Ahola, 2007). The importance of this relationship is emphasized by the recent report that the health problems with the greatest impact on quality of life in developed countries are heart disease, lower back pain, and major depressive disorders (Murray et al., 2012). Ahola (2007) also reported that a Finnish population study found that 90 percent of the respondents with severe burnout (i.e., daily occurrence of burnout symptoms) reported a physical or mental disease, with musculoskeletal pain and depression as the most common problems. Other Finnish research found that a one-unit increase in burnout score related to a 1.4 unit increase in risk for hospital admission for mental health problems, as well as a one-unit increase in risk for hospital admissions for cardiovascular problems (Ahola and Hakanen, 2014).

Other recent research is beginning to uncover the relationship of burnout to subsequent physical disease. For example, burnout predicted the emergence of cardiovascular problems among Israelis (Toker, Melamed, Berliner, Zeltser, and Shapira, 2012), while another Israeli study found links of burnout with the emergence of type 2 diabetes (Melamed, Shirom, Toker, and Shapira, 2006). Other research has identified the link of burnout to inflammation biomarkers, as well as to both physical and mental health problems (Toker, Shirom, Shapira, Berliner, and Melamed, 2005).

As noted above, the likely mechanism linking burnout with physical health problems, as well as with depression, is the exhaustion component of the syndrome. A chronic lack of energy could signal a diminished resistance to disease as well as vulnerability to experiencing accidents and injuries on the job. When exhaustion is combined with cynicism and inefficacy, people may be less committed to healthy lifestyles at work or at home. Despite this link between burnout and stress-related health behaviors, there has not yet been any research on relevant health outcomes, such as the utilization of health-care services or the filing of worker's compensation claims for stress.

Conclusion

A basic question has been whether burnout reflects something fundamental about a person, or whether a focus on the job environment in which the person operates is a better model for understanding burnout. Research provides more support for the latter approach, as the factors that disrupt people's relationship with their work are largely situated in the work environment. For example, several contextual themes underlie virtually all descriptions of the burnout experience. One has to do with imbalance, often between high demands and low or inadequate resources. Another has to do with the chronic nature of these job demands, or stressors; unlike acute crises, they are present on a continuing basis. Another theme concerns conflict – whether between people on the job (clients, colleagues, or managers), or between role demands, or between important values.

There is also an important cultural context for burnout, which has become more apparent in recent years, when there has been an upsurge in people's concern about what to do about burnout. In the past, burnout was largely identified as an occupational hazard for various people-oriented professions, such as health care, human services, and education. Now, as other occupations have become more oriented to "high-touch" customer service, and as global economic realities have changed organizations, the phenomenon of burnout has become relevant in these areas as well. What make so many of these jobs so stressful are various social, political, and economic factors that shape the work environment. For example, attempts to cut costs and increase profits have resulted in downsizing, so that fewer staff have to work harder to manage the same workload. Changes in public policy, as well as the rise of managed care, have strongly affected what services the staff can provide and what they cannot. In many professions, real wages have declined and job benefits have been cut back. The result has been a fundamental contradiction in the workplace. On the one hand, organizations increasingly need the creativity and involvement of their employees. On the other hand, organizations have been undertaking major changes that interfere with their employees' capacity to be engaged with their work. People often approach a job without fully appreciating the hazards within contemporary workplaces.

Significant progress in understanding burnout has been based on the development of new, rather than traditional, theoretical perspectives. The emphasis in theoretical formulations is, and needs to be, on what is unique about the burnout syndrome, and what distinguishes it from other types of job stress. Future progress will rest on the further elaboration of all three dimensions of burnout and on their relationship to the six areas of mismatch, or imbalance, between worker and workplace. This theoretical elaboration should generate better hypotheses about the causes and consequences linked to each of these dimensions, and should guide a more informed search for solutions to this important social problem.

References

Ahola, K. (2007). *Occupational Burnout and Health*. People and Work Research Reports 81. Helsinki: Finnish Institute of Occupational Health.

Ahola, K. and Hakanen, J. (2007). Job strain, burnout, and depressive symptoms: A prospective study among dentists. *Journal of Affective Disorders*, *104*, 103–110.

Ahola, K., and Hakanen, J. (2014). Burnout and health. In M. P. Leiter, A. B. Bakker, and C. Maslach (Eds.). *Burnout at Work: A Psychological Perspective* (pp. 10–31). London: Psychology Press.

Aiken, L. H., Clarke, S. P., Sloane, D. M., Sochalski, J. A., Busse, R., Clarke, H., ... Shamian, J. (2001). Nurses' reports on hospital care in five countries. *Health Affairs*, *20*, 43–53.

Aiken, L. H., Clarke, S. P., Sloane, D. M., Sochalski, J., and Silber, J. H. (2002). Hospital nurse staffing and patient mortality, nurse burnout, and job dissatisfaction. *Journal of the American Medical Association*, *288*, 1987–1993.

Bakker, A. B., Le Blanc, P. M., and Schaufeli, W. B. (2005). Burnout contagion among intensive care nurses. *Journal of Advanced Nursing*, *51*, 276–87.

Bakker, A. B., and Leiter, M. P. (Eds.) (2010). *Work Engagement: A Handbook of Essential Theory and Research*. New York: Psychology Press.

Bakker, A. B., Schaufeli, W. B., Demerouti, E., Janssen, P. M. P., Van der Hulst, R., and Brouwer, J. (2000). Using equity theory to examine the difference between burnout and depression. *Anxiety, Stress, and Coping, 13*, 247–68.

Bakker, A. B., Schaufeli, W. B., Sixma, H. J., Bosveld, W., Van Dierendonck, D. (2000). Patient demands, lack of reciprocity, and burnout: A five-year longitudinal study among general practitioners. *Journal of Organizational Behavior, 21*(4), 425–441.

Bhagat, R. S., Allie, S. M., and Ford, D. L., Jr. (1995). Coping with stressful life events: An empirical analysis. In R. Crandall and P. L. Perrewé (Eds.), *Occupational Stress: A Handbook* (pp. 93–112). Washington, DC: Taylor & Francis.

Borgogni, L., Consiglio, C., Alessandri, G., and Schaufeli, W. B. (2012). "Don't throw the baby out with the bathwater!" Interpersonal strain at work and burnout. *European Journal of Work and Organizational Psychology, 21*, 875–898.

Brom, S. S., Buruck, G., Horváth, I., Richter, P., and Leiter, M. P. (2015). Areas of worklife as predictors of occupational health: A validation study in two German samples. *Burnout Research, 2*, 60–70.

Burke, R. J., and Deszca, E. (1986). Correlates of psychological burnout phases among police officers. *Human Relations, 39*, 487–502.

Burke, R. J., and Greenglass, E. R. (1989). Psychological burnout among men and women in teaching: An examination of the Cherniss model. *Human Relations, 42*, 261–273.

Burke, R. J., and Greenglass, E. R. (2001). Hospital restructuring, work–family conflict and psychological burnout among nursing staff. *Psychology and Health, 16*, 83–94.

Burke, R. J., Shearer, J., and Deszca, G. (1984). Burnout among men and women in police work: An examination of the Cherniss model. *Journal of Health and Human Resources Administration, 7*, 162–188.

Buunk, B. P., and Schaufeli, W. B. (1993). Professional burnout: A perspective from social comparison theory. In W. B. Schaufeli, C. Maslach, and T. Marek (Eds.), *Professional Burnout: Recent Developments in Theory and Research* (pp. 53–69). Washington, DC: Taylor & Francis.

Campbell, N. S., Perry, S. J., Maertz, C. P., Allen, D. G., and Griffeth, R. W. (2013). All you need is … resources: The effects of justice and support on burnout and turnover. *Human Relations, 66*, 759–782.

Chappell, N. L., and Novak, M. (1992). The role of support in alleviating stress among nursing assistants. *Gerontologist, 32*(3), 351–359.

Cherniss, C. (1980a). *Professional Burnout in Human Service Organizations*. New York: Praeger.

Cherniss, C. (1980b). *Staff Burnout: Job Stress in the Human Services*. Beverly Hills: Sage.

Cordes C. L., and Dougherty, T. W. (1993). A review and an integration of research on job burnout. *Academy of Management Review, 18*, 621–656.

Cortina, L. M., Magley, V. J., Williams, J. H., and Langhout, R. D. (2001). Incivility in the workplace: Incidence and impact. *Journal of Occupational Health Psychology, 6*, 64–80.

Cox, T., Kuk, G., and Leiter, M. P. (1993). Burnout, health, work stress, and organizational healthiness. In W. Schaufeli, C. Maslach, and T. Marek (Eds.) *Professional Burnout: Recent Developments in Theory and Research* (pp. 177–193). Washington, DC: Taylor & Francis.

Crawford, E. R., LePine, J. A., and Rich, B. L. (2010). Linking job demands and resources to employee engagement and burnout: A theoretical extension and meta-analytic test. *Journal of Applied Psychology, 95*, 834.

Day, A., and Randell, D. (2014). Building a foundation for psychologically healthy workplaces and well-being. In A. Day, E. K. Kelloway, and J. J. Hurrel (Eds.) *Workplace Wellbeing: How to Build Psychologically Healthy Workplaces* (pp. 3–26). Chichester, UK: Wiley.

Deary, I. J., Blenkin, H., Agius, R. M., Endler, N. S., Zealley, H., and Wood, R. (1996). Models of job-related stress and personal achievement among consultant doctors. *British Journal of Psychology, 87*, 3–29.

Deery, S., Walsh, J., and Guest, D. (2011). Workplace aggression: The effects of harassment on job burnout and turnover intentions. *Work, Employment and Society, 25*, 742–759.

Demerouti, E., Bakker, A. B., Nachreiner, F., and Schaufeli, W. B. (2001). The job demands–resources model of burnout. *Journal of Applied Psychology, 86*, 499–512.

Dormann, C., and Zapf, D. (2004). Customer-related social stressors and burnout. *Journal of Occupational Health Psychology, 9*, 61–82.

Drory, A., and Shamir, B. (1988). Effects of organizational and life variables on job satisfaction and burnout. *Group and Organization Studies, 13*(4), 441–455.

Farber, B. A. (1984). Stress and burnout in suburban teachers. *Journal of Educational Research, 77*(6), 325–331.

Feldt, T., Rantanen, J., Hyvonen, K., Mäkikangas, A., Huhtala, M., Pihlajasaari, P., and Kinnunen, U. (2014). The 9-item Bergen Burnout Inventory: Factorial validity across organizations and measurements of longitudinal data. *Industrial Health, 52*, 102–112.

Fernet, C., Guay, F., and Senécal, C. (2004). Adjusting to job demands: The role of work self-determination and job control in predicting burnout. *Journal of Vocational Behavior, 65*, 39–56.

Freudenberger, H. J. (1974). Staff burn-out. *Journal of Social Issues, 30*(1), 159–165.

Freudenberger, H. J. (1983). Burnout: Contemporary issues, trends, and concerns. In B. A. Farber (Ed.), *Stress and Burnout in the Human Service Professions* (pp. 23–28). New York: Pergamon.

Freudenberger, H. J., and Richelson, G. (1980). *Burn-out: The High Cost of High Achievement.* Garden City, NY: Doubleday.

Gil-Monte, P. R., and Figueiredo-Ferraz, H. H. (2013). Psychometric properties of the "Spanish Burnout Inventory" among employees working with people with intellectual disability. *Journal of Intellectual Disability Research, 57*, 959–968.

Glass, D. C., and McKnight, J. D. (1996). Perceived control, depressive symptomatology, and professional burnout: A review of the evidence. *Psychology and Health, 11*, 23–48.

Glicken, M. D. (1983). A counseling approach to employee burnout. *Personnel Journal, 62*(3), 222–228.

Golembiewski, R. T., and Munzenrider, R. (1988). *Phases of Burnout: Developments in Concepts and Applications.* New York: Praeger.

González-Morales, M., Peiró, J. M., Rodríguez, I., and Bliese, P. D. (2012). Perceived collective burnout: A multilevel explanation of burnout. *Anxiety, Stress and Coping, 25*, 43–61.

Greenglass, E. R., and Burke, R. J. (1990). Burnout over time. *Journal of Health and Human Resources Administration, 13*, 192–204.

Greenglass, E. R., Fiksenbaum, L., and Burke, R. J. (1994). The relationship between social support and burnout over time in teachers. *Journal of Social Behavior and Personality, 9*, 219–230.

Greenglass, E. R., Pantony, K.-L., and Burke, R. J. (1988). A gender-role perspective on role conflict, work stress and social support. *Journal of Social Behavior and Personality, 3*, 317–328.

Halbesleben, J. B. R., and Demerouti, E. (2005). The construct validity of an alternative measure of burnout: Investigation of the English translation of the Oldenburg Burnout Inventory. *Work and Stress, 19*, 208–220.

Hämmig, O., Brauchli, R., and Bauer, G. F. (2012). Effort–reward and work–life imbalance, general stress and burnout among employees of a large public hospital in Switzerland. *Swiss Medical Weekly, 142*, 135–147.

Hatinen, M., Kinnunen, U., Mäkikangas, A., Kalimo, R., Tolvanen, A., and Pekkonen, M. (2009). Burnout during a long-term rehabilitation: Comparing low burnout, high burnout–benefited, and high burnout–not benefited trajectories. *Anxiety, Stress and Coping, 22*, 341–360.

Hendrix, W. H., Summers, T. P., Leap, T. L., and Steel, R. P. (1995). Antecedents and organizational effectiveness outcomes of employee stress and health. In R. Crandall and P. L. Perrewé (Eds.), *Occupational Stress: A Handbook* (pp. 73–92). Washington, DC: Taylor & Francis.

Hills, H., and Norvell, N. (1991). An examination of hardiness and neuroticism as potential moderators of stress outcomes. *Behavioral Medicine, 17*, 31–38.

Hobfoll, S. E., and Freedy, J. (1993). Conservation of resources: A general stress theory applied to burnout. In W. B. Schaufeli, C. Maslach, and T. Marek (Eds.), *Professional Burnout: Recent Developments in Theory and Research* (pp. 115–129). Washington, DC: Taylor & Francis.

Jackson, S. E., and Maslach, C. (1982). After-effects of job-related stress: Families as victims. *Journal of Occupational Behaviour, 3*, 63–77.

Jackson, S. E., Schwab, R. L., and Schuler, R. S. (1986). Toward an understanding of the burnout phenomenon. *Journal of Applied Psychology, 7*, 630–640.

Jin, W. M., Zhang, Y., and Wang, X. P. (2015). Job burnout and organizational justice among medical interns in Shanghai, People's Republic of China. *Advances in Medical Education and Practice, 6*, 539.

Kahill, S. (1988). Symptoms of professional burnout: A review of the empirical evidence. *Canadian Psychology, 29*, 284–297.

Kahn, R. L., and Byosiere, P. (1992). Stress in organizations. In M. D. Dunnette and L. M. Hough (Eds.), *Handbook of Industrial and Organizational Psychology*, vol. 3 (pp. 571–650). Palo Alto, CA: Consulting Psychologists Press.

Karasek, R., and Theorell, T. (1990). *Stress, Productivity, and the Reconstruction of Working Life.* New York: Basic Books.

Kop, N., Euwema, M., and Schaufeli, W. (1999). Burnout, job stress, and violent behaviour among Dutch police officers. *Work and Stress, 13*, 326–340.

Kristensen, T. S., Borritz, M., Villadsen, E., and Christensen, K. B. (2005). The Copenhagen Burnout Inventory: A new tool for the assessment of burnout. *Work and Stress, 19*, 192–207.

Lambert, E. G., Hogan, N. L., Jiang, S., Elechi, O., Benjamin, B., Morris, A., … Dupuy, P. (2010). The relationship among distributive and procedural justice and correctional life satisfaction, burnout, and turnover intent: An exploratory study. *Journal of Criminal Justice, 38*, 7–16.

Landsbergis, P. A. (1988). Occupational stress among health care workers: A test of the job demands–control model. *Journal of Organizational Behavior, 9*, 217–239.

Lawler, E. E., III (1968). Equity theory as a predictor of productivity and work quality. *Psychological Bulletin, 70*, 596–610.

Lee, R. T., and Ashforth, B. E. (1993). A longitudinal study of burnout among supervisors and managers: Comparisons between the Leiter and Maslach (1988) and Golembiewski et al. (1986) models. *Organizational Behavior and Human Decision Processes, 54*, 369–398.

Lee, R. T., and Ashforth, B. E. (1996). A meta-analytic examination of the correlates of the three dimensions of job burnout. *Journal of Applied Psychology, 81*, 123–133.

Leiter, M. P. (1992). Burnout as a crisis in professional role structures: Measurement and conceptual issues. *Anxiety, Stress, and Coping, 5*, 79–93.

Leiter, M. P. (2012). *Analyzing and Theorizing the Dynamics of the Workplace Incivility Crisis.* Amsterdam: Springer.

Leiter M. P., and Durup, J. (1994). The discriminant validity of burnout and depression: A confirmatory factor analytic study. *Anxiety, Stress and Coping, 7*, 357–373.

Leiter, M. P., Frank, E., and Matheson, T. J. (2009). Demands, values, and burnout: Their relevance for physicians. *Canadian Family Physician, 55*, 1224–1225, e1–e6.

Leiter, M. P., Hakanen, J., Toppinen-Tanner, S., Ahola, K., Koskinen, A., and Väänänen, A. (2013). Organizational predictors and health consequences of changes in burnout: A 12-year cohort study. *Journal of Organizational Behavior, 34*, 959–973.

Leiter, M. P., and Harvie, P. (1998). Conditions for staff acceptance of organizational change: Burnout as a mediating construct. *Anxiety, Stress and Coping, 11*, 1–25.

Leiter, M. P., Harvie, P., and Frizzell, C. (1998). The correspondence of patient satisfaction and nurse burnout. *Social Science and Medicine, 47*, 1611–1617.

Leiter, M. P., and Maslach, C. (1988). The impact of interpersonal environment on burnout and organizational commitment. *Journal of Organizational Behavior, 9*, 297–308.

Leiter, M. P., and Maslach, C. (1998). Burnout. In H. Friedman (Ed.), *Encyclopedia of Mental Health.* San Diego, CA: Academic Press.

Leiter, M. P., and Maslach, C. (2004). Areas of worklife: A structured approach to organizational predictors of job burnout. In P. L. Perrewé and D. C. Ganster (Eds.), *Research in Occupational Stress and Well Being*, vol. 3 (pp. 91–134). Oxford: Elsevier Science.

Leiter, M. P., and Maslach, C. (2009). Burnout and workplace injuries: A longitudinal analysis. In A. M. Rossi, J. C. Quick, and P. L. Perrewé (Eds.), *Stress and Quality of Working Life: The Positive and the Negative* (pp. 3–18). Greenwich, CT: Information Age.

Leiter, M. P., and Maslach, C. (2016). Latent burnout profiles: A new approach to understanding the burnout experience. *Burnout Research, 3*, 89–100.

Leon, M. R., Halbesleben, J. R. B., and Paustian-Underdahl, S. C. (2015). A dialectical perspective on burnout and engagement. *Burnout Research, 2*, 87–96.

Maslach, C. (1976). Burned-out. *Human Behavior, 5*, 16–22.

Maslach, C. (1982). *Burnout: The Cost of Caring.* Englewood Cliffs, NJ: Prentice Hall.

Maslach, C. (1993). Burnout: A multidimensional perspective. In W. B. Schaufeli, C. Maslach, and T. Marek (Eds.), *Professional Burnout: Recent Developments in Theory and Research* (pp. 19–32). Washington, DC: Taylor & Francis.

Maslach, C., and Jackson, S. E. (1981). The measurement of experienced burnout. *Journal of Occupational Behaviour, 2*, 99–113.

Maslach, C., Jackson, S. E., and Leiter, M. P. (1996). *The Maslach Burnout Inventory*, 3rd edn. Palo Alto, CA: Consulting Psychologists Press. [The MBI is now published and distributed by Mind Garden.]

Maslach, C., and Leiter, M. P. (1997). *The Truth about Burnout.* San Francisco: Jossey-Bass.

Maslach, C., and Leiter, M. P. (1999). Burnout and engagement in the workplace: A contextual analysis, *Advances in Motivation and Achievement, 11*, 275–302.

Maslach, C., and Leiter, M. P. (2008). Early predictors of job burnout and engagement. *Journal of Applied Psychology*, *93*, 498–512.

Maslach, C., Leiter, M. P., and Schaufeli, W. B. (2009). Measuring burnout. In C. L. Cooper and S. Cartwright (Eds.), *The Oxford Handbook of Organizational Well-Being* (pp. 86–108). Oxford: Oxford University Press.

Maslach, C., Schaufeli, W. B., and Leiter, M. P. (2001). Job burnout. *Annual Review of Psychology*, *52*, 397–422.

Maslanka, H. (1996). Burnout, social support and AIDS volunteers. *AIDS Care, 8*(2), 195–206.

Melamed, S., Shirom, A., Toker, S., and Shapira, I. (2006). Burnout and risk of type 2 diabetes: A prospective study of apparently healthy employed persons. *Psychosomatic Medicine*, *68*, 863–869.

Moliner, C., Martínez-Tur, V., Peiró, J. M., Ramos, J., and Cropanzano, R. (2013). Perceived reciprocity and well-being at work in non-professional employees: Fairness or self-interest? *Stress and Health, 29*, 31–39.

Murray, C. L., Vos, T., Lozano, R., Naghavi, M., Flaxman, A. D., Michaud, C., … Lopez, A. D. (2012). Disability adjusted life years (DALYs) for 291 diseases and injuries in 21 regions, 1990–2010: A systematic analysis for the Global Burden of Disease Study 2010. *Lancet*, *380*, 2197–2223.

Peeters, M. A., and Rutte, C. G. (2005). Time management behavior as a moderator for the job demand–control interaction. *Journal of Occupational Health Psychology*, *10*, 64.

Pines, A., Aronson, E., and Kafry, D. (1981). *Burnout: From Tedium to Personal Growth*. New York: Free Press.

Richardsen, A. M., Burke, R. J., and Leiter, M. P. (1992). Occupational demands, psychological burnout, and anxiety among hospital personnel in Norway. *Anxiety, Stress, and Coping*, *5*, 62–78.

Roelofs, J., Verbraak, M., Keijsers, G. P. J., de Bruin, M. B. N., and Schmidt, A. J. M. (2005). Psychometric properties of a Dutch version of the Maslach Burnout Inventory General Survey (MBI-DV) in individuals with and without clinical burnout. *Stress and Health*, *21*, 17–25

Royal, M. A., and Rossi, R. J. (1996). Individual level correlates of sense of community: Findings from workplace and school. *Journal of Community Psychology, 24*(4), 395–416.

Savicki, V., Cooley, E., and Gjesvold, J. (2003). Harassment as a predictor of job burnout in correctional officers. *Criminal Justice and Behavior*, *30*, 602–619.

Schaufeli, W. B., and Bakker, A. B. (2004). Job demands, job resources and their relationship with burnout and engagement: A multi-sample study. *Journal of Organizational Behavior, 25*(3), 293–315.

Schaufeli, W. B., Bakker, A. B., Hoogduin, K., Schaap, C., and Kladler, A. (2001). The clinical validity of the Maslach Burnout Inventory and the Burnout Measure. *Psychology and Health*, *16*, 565–582.

Schaufeli, W. B., Bakker, A. B., and Salanova, M. (2006). The measurement of work engagement with a brief questionnaire: A cross-national study. *Educational and Psychological Measurement*, *66*, 701–716.

Schaufeli, W. B., and Enzmann, D. (1998). *The Burnout Companion to Study and Practice: A Critical Analysis*. Washington, DC: Taylor & Francis.

Schaufeli, W. B., Leiter, M. P., Maslach, C., and Jackson, S. E. (1996). Maslach Burnout Inventory – General Survey (MBI–GS). In C. Maslach, S. E. Jackson, and M. P. Leiter, *MBI Manual*, 3rd edn. Palo Alto, CA: Consulting Psychologists Press. [The MBI is now published and distributed by Mind Garden.]

Schaufeli, W. B., van Dierendonck, D., and van Gorp, K. (1996). Burnout and reciprocity: Towards a dual-level social exchange model. *Work and Stress*, *10*, 225–237.

Schnorpfeil, P., Noll, A., Wirtz, P., Schulze, R., Ehlert, U., Frey, K., and Fischer, J. E. (2002). Assessment of exhaustion and related risk factors in employees in the manufacturing industry – a cross-sectional study. *International Archives of Occupational and Environmental Health*, *75*, 535–540.

Schonfeld, I. S. (1989). Psychological distress in a sample of teachers. *Journal of Psychology*, *124*, 321–338.

Semmer, N. K., Tschan, F., Meier, L. L., Facchin, S., and Jacobshagen, N. (2010). Illegitimate tasks and counterproductive work behavior. *Applied Psychology*, *59*, 70–96.

Shinn, M., Rosario, M., Morch, H., and Chestnut, D. E. (1984). Coping with job stress and burnout in the human services. *Journal of Personality and Social Psychology*, *46*, 864–876.

Shirom, A., and Melamed, S. (2005). Does burnout affect physical health? A review of the evidence. In A. S. G. Antoniou and C. L. Cooper (Eds.), *Research Companion to Organizational Health Psychology* (pp. 599–622). Cheltenham, UK: Edward Elgar.

Siefert, K., Jayaratne, S., and Chess, W. A. (1991). Job satisfaction, burnout, and turnover in health care social workers. *Health and Social Work, 16*(3), 193–202.

Siegrist, J. (1996). Adverse health effects of high-effort/low-reward conditions. *Journal of Occupational Health Psychology*, *1*, 27–41.

Sonnentag, S. (2015). Wellbeing and burnout in the workplace: Organizational causes and consequences. In *International Encyclopedia of the Social and Behavioral Sciences*, 2nd edn, vol. 25 (pp. 537–540). Oxford: Elsevier.

Starnaman, S. M., and Miller, K. I. (1992) A test of a causal model of communication and burnout in the teaching profession. *Communication Education, 41*(1), 40–53.

Toker, S., Melamed, S., Berliner, S., Zeltser, D., and Shapira, I. (2012). Burnout and the risk of coronary heart disease: A prospective study of 8838 employees. *Psychosomatic Medicine, 74*, 840–847.

Toker, S., Shirom, A., Shapira, I., Berliner, S., and Melamed, S. (2005). The association between burnout, depression, anxiety, and inflammation biomarkers: C-reactive protein and fibrinogen in men and women. *Journal of Occupational Health Psychology, 10*, 344–362.

Toppinen-Tanner, S., Kalimo, R., and Mutanen, P. (2002). The process of burnout in white-collar and blue-collar jobs: An eight-year prospective study of exhaustion. *Journal of Organizational Behavior, 23*, 555–570.

Truchot, D., and Deregard, M. (2001). Perceived inequity, communal orientation and burnout: The role of helping models. *Work and Stress, 15*, 347–356.

Tyler, T. R. (1990). *Why People Obey the Law*. New Haven: Yale University Press.

Vahey, D. C., Aiken, L. H., Sloane, D. M., Clarke, S. P., and Vargas, D. (2004). Nurse burnout and patient satisfaction. *Medical Care, 24*(2), 57–66.

Veage, S., Ciarrochi, J., Deane, F. P., Andresen, R., Oades, L. G., and Crowe, T. P. (2014). Value congruence, importance and success in the workplace: Links with well-being and burnout amongst mental health practitioners. *Journal of Contextual Behavioral Science, 3*(4), 258–264.

Walster, E., Berscheid, E., and Walster, G. W. (1973). New directions in equity research. *Journal of Personality and Social Psychology, 25*, 151–176.

Warr, P. B. (1987). *Work, Unemployment and Mental Health*. Oxford: Clarendon Press.

White, S. L. (1987). Human resource development: The future through people. *Administration in Mental Health, 14*(3–4), 199–208.

Zedeck, S., Maslach, C., Mosier, K., and Skitka, L. (1988). Affective response to work and quality of family life: Employee and spouse perspectives. *Journal of Social Behavior and Personality, 3*, 135–157.

Zellars, K. L., Perrewé, P. L., and Hochwarter, W. A. (2000). Burnout in health care: The role of the five factors of personality. *Journal of Applied Social Psychology, 30*, 1570–1598.

4

Happiness and Mental Health

A Framework of Vitamins in the Environment and Mental Processes in the Person

Peter Warr

The constructs of mental health and happiness overlap with each other to a substantial degree. Positive or negative feelings are intrinsic to each, and the constructs, although distinct, have partly similar causes and consequences. The vitamin model summarized here originated primarily as a perspective on mental health (Warr, 1987) but has since been applied mainly to happiness or unhappiness in settings such as paid work, unemployment and retirement (e.g., Warr, 2007). This chapter also focuses on happiness and unhappiness; it outlines main aspects of the framework as modified over several years.

Conceptual Starting Points

Building on a wide range of earlier perspectives, the vitamin model seeks to be distinctive in three principal respects. First it aims for comprehensiveness in outlook and content, bringing together themes and research findings from diverse models, focusing on sources from within the person as well as from the environment, and including many mental processes beyond conventional types of appraisal. The framework also explicitly addresses different levels of scope, embracing processes in a person's life as a whole, within separate domains (family life, a social institution, paid work, unemployment, and so on), and also as part of attitudes to particular things, events or ideas. These three levels of scope may be referred to as "context-free," "domain-specific" and "facet-specific" respectively.

Many approaches to this area are stress-oriented, being focused explicitly and entirely on harmful aspects of the environment and ways to cope with those. That immediately cuts out huge sections of experience, and generates a particular set of orienting concepts and research

The Handbook of Stress and Health: A Guide to Research and Practice, First Edition.
Edited by Cary L. Cooper and James Campbell Quick.
© 2017 John Wiley & Sons, Ltd. Published 2017 by John Wiley & Sons, Ltd.

methods which necessarily exclude other ways of thinking. Schaubroeck (2012) has drawn attention to dangers arising from overreliance on any theoretical framework: "(a) restricting the boundaries of the phenomena that are considered relevant, (b) introducing barriers to changing or supplanting theories, (c) biasing estimation of relationships due to omitted variables, (d) encouraging authors to exclude contrary evidence and insights from their narratives, and (e) limiting how scholars evaluate theoretical contributions" (p. 86). The vitamin model seeks to minimize those kinds of constraint. Although the framework inevitably creates its own conceptual template, that is intended to be less restrictive than others.

Second, the model does not follow the common practice of conceptualization in terms of mutually exclusive categories of elements, such as "resources" as a group or in terms of sets of stressors which are designated as one or other of "challenges" or "hindrances." Such approaches are fraught with problems of definition and boundary-setting, and can lead to simplifying empirical or conceptual generalizations about categories as a whole, whereas diverse category components in fact have multiply contrasting characteristics and operating mechanisms; components require to be treated separately (e.g., Halbesleben, Neveu, Paustian-Underhahl, and Westman, 2014). The vitamin framework is instead concerned with single features of the environment, each with its own sources and consequences.

A third notable aspect of the model is its divergence from the standard assumption that features in the environment are consistently either positive (e.g., always a desirable resource) or negative (e.g., always a harmful stressor). Instead, it is argued that many environmental features can be either affectively positive or negative depending on their level. The notion that different forms of the same element can be evaluated in contrasting ways leads in turn to an emphasis on environment–outcome relationships which are nonlinear rather than linear as is generally presumed.

In overview, the vitamin framework offers an alternative way of thinking about environments and their impact, building on themes from established models and seeking to minimize the conceptual restrictions which are necessarily created by a theoretical structure. For exposition it is presented here in four sections, first addressing types of outcome and then moving on to sources in the environment, sources in the person and outcomes arising jointly from a person and an environment.

Components of Mental Health and Happiness

First, what outcomes need to be considered? Drawing on work by Jahoda (1982) and others, Warr (1987) characterized mental health in terms of five broad components: affective well-being, competence, autonomy, aspiration, and integrated functioning. Poor mental health almost always embodies negative feelings (low affective well-being) as well as impaired functioning in one or more of the other ways listed above. Thus, in addition to affective well-being which is low, a person with poor mental health may be unable to cope with interpersonal or other conditions (being low in competence), feel excessively constrained in thought or action (low autonomy), or disengage from a situation or life in general (low aspiration). The final component of mental health, labeled in the model as integrated functioning, concerns the person as a whole, often through combinations of the other elements. It has been treated in varying ways by different theoreticians and taken to imply different procedures for therapeutic intervention.

Unhappiness and happiness are also characterized in those multiple ways, involving both affective well-being and a number of functional elements. The beyond-well-being aspects of happiness have been interpreted in different ways and with diverse labels, often described overall as "eudaimonic" in contrast with hedonic experiences in terms of positive or negative affect (e.g., Waterman, 1993). The notion of eudaimonia originated in the discussion by Aristotle (384–322 BCE) of the good or worthwhile life, and has more recently been modified and articulated in terms of "flourishing" (e.g., Keyes, 2002; Waterman, 1993). That construct, as well as others in this field, has been treated in dissimilar ways by different authors, but a primary feature is a person's experience of meaningfulness or identity-linked purpose (e.g., Baumeister, Vohs, Aaker, and Garbinsky, 2013; McGregor and Little, 1998). Additional eudaimonic components of happiness (of different salience in different models) have included a person's engagement in the world ("aspiration" above), feeling able to achieve personally important goals ("competence" above), being able to influence one's life ("autonomy" above), having vitality, and interacting positively with other people (e.g., Huppert, 2014; Seligman, 2011; Warr, forthcoming). Eudaimonic themes tend to emphasize the functioning rather than affective elements introduced above.

Although functioning has been examined variously in models of mental health, happiness studies have focused almost entirely on the other component – a person's hedonic state. Referred to above as affective well-being, this takes a variety of overlapping forms. For example, core affect can be described in terms of two axes – feeling bad to feeling good (valence, from displeasure to pleasure) and also low versus high activation or arousal, a state of mental or physical readiness for energy expenditure (e.g., Watson and Tellegen, 1985; Yik, Russell, and Steiger, 2011). Treating the two axes as orthogonal to each other permits the identification of four conceptual segments which may be labeled as feelings of anxiety (high activation, low pleasure), enthusiasm (both high), calmness (low activation, high pleasure), and depression (both low) (Warr, 1990; 2007; 2012). Positive or negative feelings can be measured through several combinations of these affects (e.g., Madrid and Patterson 2014; Warr, Bindl, Parker, and Inceoglu, 2014), and there is evidence that axes from depression to enthusiasm and from anxiety to calmness (characterizing processes of approach and avoidance respectively) are based on separate neurophysiological systems (Carver, 2001; Posner, Russell, and Peterson, 2005). Furthermore, particular environmental factors can influence feelings of these several kinds in different ways (Warr, 2007), and experienced activation and valence themselves predict different aspects of motivation (Seo, Bartunek, and Feldman-Barrett, 2010).

In addition to these forms of core affect, hedonic happiness has also been examined in terms of cognitive-affective syndromes which incorporate not only feelings but also explicit or implicit recollections, anticipations and social comparisons. For example, reports of satisfaction with a job or with one's life as a whole are based on a wide range of retrospective, current, and future considerations. And, as with feelings alone, happiness syndromes of these kinds can also be viewed in terms of activation as well as valence (Warr and Inceoglu, 2012).

Influences from the Environment

Table 4.1 points to 12 primary environmental features that have been found in empirical research of many kinds to be associated with positive well-being (e.g., Crawford, LePine, and Rich, 2010; Humphrey, Nahrgang, and Morgensen, 2007; Luchman and Gonzáles-Morales, 2013; Warr, 1987; 2007). The table is constructed so that feelings in any life context can depend on the first nine aspects. For example, the opportunity for personal control (E1) is essential in any setting for meeting personal goals, for sustaining a sense of personal agency, and for

Table 4.1 Principal environmental characteristics affecting happiness or unhappiness, with investigated themes in job settings

Environmental feature	Investigated components in paid work
E1 Opportunity for personal control	Personal influence, autonomy, discretion, decision latitude, participation
E2 Opportunity for skill use and acquisition	A setting's potential for applying and developing expertise and knowledge
E3 Externally generated goals	External demands, challenge, workload, underload and overload, competition from others, task identity, role conflict, work–home conflict, required emotional labor
E4 Variety	Variability in task content and social contact, varied work location
E5 Environmental clarity	Predictable outcomes of action, clear requirements, role clarity, task feedback, low future ambiguity
E6 Contact with others	Quality of social interaction and relationships, quantity of social contact, interdependence with others, team working
E7 Availability of money	Income received, pay level, payment for results
E8 Physical security	Working conditions, degree of hazard, quality of equipment
E9 Valued social position	Significance of a task or role, position in valued groups, contribution to society
E10 Supportive supervision	Sympathetic consideration by bosses, fair treatment by supervisor, concern for one's welfare, effective supervisory behavior
E11 Career outlook	Job security, the opportunity to gain promotion or shift to other roles
E12 Equity	Justice within one's organization, fairness in the organization's relations with society

reducing feelings of helplessness. Environmental clarity (E5) is essential to reduce anxiety about an ambiguous future and to make it possible to plan, initiate and regulate actions; and the nature of interpersonal contact (E6) can contribute to both health and well-being (Uchino, 2006). In addition to these everywhere-important features (E1 to E9), other influential aspects of the environment are specific to particular domains. In the present case, features E10 to E12 are identified as additionally important in the domain of jobs, and job-related components of each one are illustrated in the second column. As indicated earlier, the model is applicable to many other kinds of setting, allowing for additional factors specific to a particular domain beyond the everywhere-important first nine.

Nonlinear Associations and the Vitamin Analogy

The importance of these environmental features or their components has been demonstrated by research in many countries, almost always envisaging a linear relationship between levels of well-being and the feature. However, it is more likely that the level of an environmental characteristic is associated with happiness or mental health in a nonlinear fashion, specifically in a pattern analogous to the effect of vitamins on bodily condition. Vitamins are important for physical health up to but not beyond a certain level. At low levels of intake, vitamin deficiency gives rise to physiological impairment and ill-health, but after a moderate level has been reached (the "recommended, or guideline, daily allowance") there is no benefit from additional

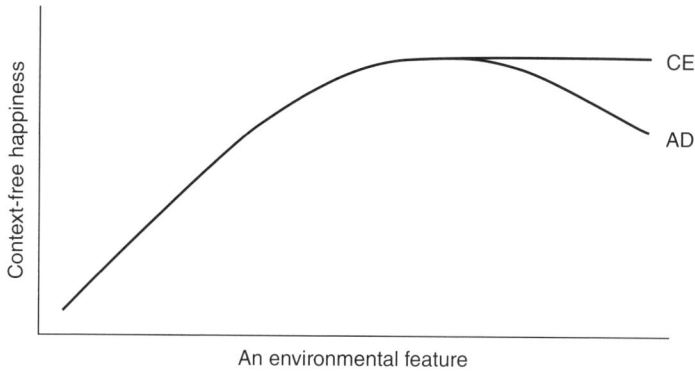

Figure 4.1   The vitamin analogy: proposed "additional decrement" (AD) and "constant effect" (CE) relationships between environmental features and context-free happiness

quantities. In a similar manner, it may be that the absence or near-absence of a primary environmental characteristic leads to negative psychological conditions, but that its presence beyond a certain level does not further improve those conditions.

In addition, some vitamins become toxic in very large quantities, so that the association between increased vitamin intake and physical health becomes negative above moderate amounts. This pattern may also occur for certain aspects of the environment, particularly with respect to context-free happiness rather than a more restricted form; many aspects of life are affectively positive until very high levels are reached. This "too much of a good thing" possibility is summarized in Figure 4.1, where low ("deficiency") values of an environmental feature are depicted as particularly harmful to happiness and mental health and those in the middle range are shown as having a constant beneficial effect. A second, smaller decrement is proposed at particularly high ("toxic") values for certain environmental features (labeled as "AD") but not for others ("CE").

Those two labels are also based on abbreviations in the vitamin analogy. There are no toxic consequences from very high intakes of certain vitamins: deficiency causes ill-health, but additional doses beyond a moderate amount have a constant effect. Vitamins C and E are of that kind. The abbreviation "CE" in Figure 4.1 reflects this pattern, and can also stand for "constant effect" in the present model. On the other hand, vitamins A and D are toxic at very high levels, and "AD" in the figure may be read as an "additional decrement."

The environmental section of the vitamin model suggests that six of the primary environmental features considered so far may be viewed as analogues of vitamins A and D, and that the other six instead parallel vitamins C and E. Suggested AD vitamins are E1 to E6 in Table 4.1: opportunity for personal control, opportunity for skill use and acquisition, externally generated goals, variety, environmental clarity, and contact with others. The CE features thought to have a constant effect beyond moderate levels are E7 to E9 for life in general: availability of money, physical security and valued social position. In addition, for the specific domain of paid work, E10 to E12 are also likely to take the CE form: supportive supervision, career outlook, and equity (Warr, 2007).

Why should certain features of the environment (E1 to E6), desirable at moderate levels, become harmful when at extremely high levels? The curvilinear pattern seems likely for both intrinsic reasons and because of associated effects from other features. Very high levels of some environmental characteristics can become punishing in themselves, and they are likely also to be accompanied by extremely high levels of other features that themselves yield an additional decrement.

Thus features identified as "opportunities" (for control and for skill use; E1 and E2) are expected to yield decrements at the extreme right-hand side of Figure 4.1 as the "opportunity" becomes an "unavoidable requirement" at very high levels; behavior is then constrained and coerced rather than being encouraged or facilitated. For example, environments that call for unremitting control (a very high level of feature E1) through extremely difficult autonomous decision-making and sustained personal responsibility, or which demand continuous use of extremely complex skills (E2), can give rise to overload problems as very high demands exceed personal capabilities (e.g., Burger, 1989). In part, those problems of excessive control arise from an associated shift to a particularly high level of externally generated goals (E3). When imposed goals become extremely difficult and/or numerous, multiple demands may also become internally contradictory, beyond a person's ability to cope (e.g., Warr, 2007, ch. 6).

Extremely high variety in the environment (E4) requires constant switching of attention and activity, with resulting low concentration and limited attainment of single goals; conflict between contradictory goals and entailed actions may then be present (an aspect of E3), and extreme diversity may prohibit the sustained use of skills (E2). Environmental clarity (E5) appears also to be of this "additional decrement" kind. At extremely high levels, there is no uncertainty about the future, events are entirely predictable and never novel, and a fixed set of role requirements permits no new experiences. Such settings prevent risk-taking, contain little potential for skill development, and provide no opportunity to expand one's control over the environment.

A similar downturn of the happiness curve is expected at very high levels of contact with other people (E6). Extremely large social inputs can impair well-being through overcrowding and absence of privacy in high-density situations or through a lack of personal control, frequent interruptions, and the prevention of valued activities because of other people's continuing demands. Behavioral procedures and physical structures to prevent excessive social contact have been created in cultures of all kinds.

Several environmental features are thus assumed to be of the "additional decrement" kind, with their positive association with happiness not only leveling off across the moderate to high range but also becoming reversed at very high levels; research evidence from the domain of jobs will be illustrated below. Harmful effects at very high "toxic" levels are likely to be less severe than at very low levels, since deficiencies in a feature (at the left of Figure 4.1) carry particularly negative implications for the person; and even high levels that are excessive retain some of the benefits provided in the moderate range.

The average pattern for context-free happiness in Figure 4.1 is likely to be slightly different for more narrow forms – domain-specific or facet-specific happiness. The relationship between *context-free* happiness (e.g., life satisfaction) and an environmental feature is determined simultaneously by a wide range of features, so that multiple aspects of life (e.g., family, social and job domains) cumulatively bear upon context-free happiness in different ways for different people and with potentially inconsistent or conflicting impacts. Average happiness that is context-free is thus created in many different ways. However, more focused forms of happiness (such as job satisfaction rather than life satisfaction) are less subject to influences from other domains, and the mid-range plateau in Figure 4.1 is expected to be progressively shorter as consideration moves from context-free to more focused experiences, with environment–happiness associations at the facet-specific level tending to be most linear; see Warr (2007, ch. 4).

The vitamin model also proposes that, across all their higher range, differences in the other six features in Table 4.1 (E7 to E12) are then uncorrelated with happiness, exhibiting a "constant effect" in that range (CE in Figure 4.1). Although extremely high levels of these features can be linked to unhappiness in particular cases, on average across people in general further increases in the high to very high range are not likely to have a negative effect. The high-range negative impact proposed for additional-decrement features (above) was suggested to arise from two sources: each one's inherent harmful impact at very high levels, and associated harm from other variables. Neither of those impacts is expected on average for high levels of the identified constant effect features. Instead, it is assumed that high to very high values of those characteristics are on average accompanied by similar levels of well-being.

In all cases, a nonlinear association between the level of an environmental feature and people's happiness is thus proposed for people in general. Environmental increments of a certain size at lower values are suggested to give rise to greater increases in happiness than do increments of the same magnitude at moderate to high values. Some nonlinearity of this kind appears to be logically necessary, since feelings are inherently limited in their intensity; it is not possible for them to continue to increase at the same rate without limit. Between-person variation around this average pattern will be considered later.

To what extent have research findings been consistent with these proposals? Only a tiny proportion of studies have examined possible departures from linearity, and many of those are unsuitable for the task since their environmental (e.g., job) scores are restricted in range and do not extend fully from very low to very high levels. Linked to that, research into several characteristics has intentionally focused on only a limited section of high or low scores (only underload or overload, for example).

Empirical evidence about Figure 4.1 relationships is thus both scarce and often methodologically inadequate. However additional decrements, as proposed for the first six "vitamins," have been observed in several studies of job-related well-being. In respect of E1 (opportunity for personal control), Baltes, Bauer, Bajdo, and Parker (2002) recorded an AD pattern for job satisfaction; the negative impact of very difficult decisions was demonstrated by Anderson (2003) and Burger (1989); and a leveling off beyond medium levels was present in studies reviewed by Warr (2007). In respect of E2 (opportunity for skill use and acquisition), research extending across a very wide range is not available in job settings, but overlaps of that feature with the curvilinear E1 and E3 suggest that a similar pattern is present.

For externally generated goals (E3), occupational research restricted to merely low or high demands has shown that well-being is, as expected, associated in opposite directions at the two extremes of the horizontal axis in Figure 4.1. Across a more comprehensive range of load, additional-decrement patterns have been demonstrated in jobs by, for instance, Karasek (1979) and Warr (1990); and for role clarity (an aspect of E5), significant nonlinearity with a decrement at highest levels was observed in job settings by Baltes et al. (2002).

In respect of social contact (E6), research has examined both quantity and quality. In terms of quantity, very low social density can of course yield feelings of loneliness and personal isolation; and very high levels of input from other people have been shown to be undesirable in work settings through studies of open-plan offices (e.g., Brennan, Chugh, and Kline, 2002). An experiment by Deelstra et al. (2003) arranged for workers in a simulated office setting to

receive instrumental assistance from a coworker, who was in fact a confederate of the investi-
gators. Extremely large amounts of social support of this kind led to a downturn in affect as in
Figure 4.1. That pattern was also observed in an organizational sample by De Jonge, Reuvers,
Houtman, Bongers, and Kompier (2000).

For the other environmental features in Table 4.1 even fewer studies have examined possible nonlinearity. However, stabilization of association after moderate quantities has frequently
been demonstrated in respect of income (E7) and context-free happiness. A standard increment
in income, which can provide a major benefit to people in poverty, yields a smaller benefit to
happiness in the wealthy. This constant-effect pattern has been found in comparisons between
individuals within a single country (e.g., Diener, Sandvik, Seidlitz, and Diener, 1993) and in
terms of average scores for entire nations (e.g., Diener and Seligman, 2004). Examining variation in considerate supervisor behavior (E10), nonlinearity at the work-group level (rather
than in respect of individuals themselves) was observed by Fleishman and Harris (1962) in a
study of subordinates' grievances and turnover. For equity (E12), Schaufeli's (2006) review
identified nonlinear patterns in several occupational studies. This constant-effect (CE) pattern
appears likely on conceptual grounds to be widely found: above a moderate level of CE features E7 to E12, further gains (important at low levels) are expected to be of little average
consequence.

In some cases, environmental features may combine with each other in an interactive manner, yielding nonlinear patterns only in certain combinations. For example, Chung-Yan (2010)
found an inverted-U relationship between job complexity and job satisfaction for workers
whose job autonomy was low but not for workers with higher autonomy: the tipping point
at which additional complexity became undesirable to a job-holder was lower when the freedom to handle that complexity was also low.

In overview, the environmental section of the vitamin model proposes average nonlinearity
of association between a situation and happiness or unhappiness, with different forms of nonlinearity in two sets of features. Additionally but not detailed here because of space limitations,
the model contains different predictions for different forms of affective well-being as introduced above. For example, job demands that are very high are expected and found to have a
particularly negative impact in respect of feelings in terms of job-related anxiety–contentment
rather than for those along an axis from depression to enthusiasm (Warr, 2007). Another implication of this nonlinear account concerns between-study differences. If an examined sample is
mainly to the right of Figure 4.1 in, say, externally generated demands (E3), a negative association between that feature and happiness is expected. However, if the sample happens to be
more widely spread or located mainly in the middle of the range, a correlation around zero is
likely (e.g., Luchman and Gonzáles-Morales, 2013). Observed demands–happiness patterns
are thus expected to vary systematically between investigations, and that is indeed the case in
occupational research (Crawford et al., 2010, p. 836; Warr, 2007).

Principal Sources within the Person

The vitamin model also addresses the ways in which happiness or mental health derive from
within a person himself or herself. Two kinds of within-person sources are important: longer-
term characteristics, such as dispositional or demographic features, and an individual's way
of attending to and thinking about particular situations as they are experienced. In the former
respect, personality traits such as neuroticism, extraversion and conscientiousness have been

Table 4.2 Situation-based mental processes (not always in current awareness) with implications for happiness or unhappiness

Type of mental process	Illustrative self-questions
J1 Comparisons with other people	J1 "How does my situation compare with that of another individual/group or people in general?"
J2 Comparisons with other situations	
J2A Previously expected situation	J2A "How does my situation compare with the situation I expected?"
J2B Counterfactual situation(s)	J2B "How might the situation have developed in other ways?"
J3 Comparisons with other times	
J3A Previous trend	J3A "Up to now, has the situation deteriorated, improved, or remained unchanged?"
J3B Expected future trend	J3B "From now on, is the situation likely to deteriorate, improve, or remain unchanged?"
J4 Assessment of self-efficacy	J4 "How effective was/is my performance in this situation?"
J5 Assessment of novelty or familiarity	J5 "To what extent is the situation unusual or previously experienced?"
J6 Assessment of personal salience/value	
J6A Rated importance/evaluation of role membership	J6A "How much do I want to be in this role?"
J6B Rated importance/evaluation of a role characteristic	J6B "How much do I value this feature?"
J6C Rated attractiveness of core tasks in the role	J6C "How much do I like the things I have to do?"

shown to be significantly related to many happiness indicators (e.g., Friedman and Kern, 2014; Inceoglu and Warr, 2011; Judge, Heller, and Mount, 2002; Steel, Schmidt, and Shultz, 2008), as are scales of self-esteem and self-efficacy (Chang, Ferris, Johnson, Rosen, and Tan, 2012). Demographic features such as age (e.g., Blanchflower and Oswald, 2008; Clark, Oswald, and Warr, 1996; Stone, Schwartz, Broderick, and Deaton, 2010) and gender (e.g., Rosenfield and Mouzon, 2013) are also significantly related to some forms of happiness or mental health. In regard to shorter-term processes, feelings are partly a function of several comparative judgments, concerned with where one has been, where one now might be instead, how the future might develop, and assessments of self-efficacy, novelty and personal salience (Warr, 2006). Representing this section of the vitamin model, ten explicit or underlying judgments of those kinds are summarized in Table 4.2 together with questions that people might ask themselves in respect of each one. Sometimes their operation is outside conscious awareness.

In respect of judgment J1 in the table, it is regularly found that "downward" comparisons with other people (i.e., judgments made relative to people who are worse off in the relevant respect) tend to enhance a person's own happiness (e.g., Wheeler, 2000). Some studies in employment settings have adopted the framework of equity theory to examine social comparisons of several kinds, finding that perceived input–output ratios in comparison with other people's ratios affect feelings; happiness can depend in part on perceptions of fairness in relation to other people. For example, satisfaction with level of pay has been shown to depend on perceived comparisons with other people's level relative to their effort, skill and other "inputs" (e.g., Adams, 1965) or with income within the local community (Hagerty, 2000). Schaufeli (2006) has documented similar themes in respect of social exchange in organizations, and social-comparative cognitive processes of this kind are likely in respect of several other environmental contributors in Table 4.1

Comparisons with other situations (J2 in Table 4.2) can be of two kinds – in relation to situations that were expected (J2A), or relative to those that otherwise might have occurred (J2B). In the first case, laboratory studies and everyday experience have confirmed that events that are unexpected have a greater impact on happiness or unhappiness than do those that were expected. The J2B comparison involves consideration of either poorer or better counterfactual alternatives, those which are contrary to the facts. People may focus attention on other ways in which their current situation might instead have developed, for example judging that the situation could be a lot worse or better than it is. Upward counterfactual judgments (relative to a more attractive possibility) tend to evoke unpleasant feelings, whereas downward comparisons (which consider possible alternatives which are worse than reality) can increase happiness (Olson, Buhrman, and Roese, 2000). The process was illustrated by Medvec, Madey and Gilovich (1995) in a study of Olympic medalists. Those receiving silver medals for achieving second place tended to be less happy with their position than were bronze medalists in third place. Many second-place winners appeared to base their feelings in part on upward counterfactual comparisons ("I failed to be the best"), whereas athletes in third place were more likely to make downward comparisons, being pleased to have reached the medal positions ("I did better than all the rest").

Third in Table 4.2 are assessments of previous and likely future trends (J3). For example (J3A), has this stressful situation been getting better or worse? Have I moved adequately towards a goal? Given that goals may be defined as "internal representations of desired states" (Austin and Vancouver, 1996), good progress toward a goal (a "desired state") is generally associated with better well-being, and low or negative progress gives rise to reduced well-being (e.g., Lyubomirsky, Sheldon, and Schkade, 2005).

Table 4.2 also draws attention to the possible impact on well-being of expectations about a future trend (J3B). This has sometimes been examined as perceived probability of success, and positive expectancies of that kind are significantly associated with affective well-being (e.g., Emmons, 1986). Furthermore, in settings of multiple objectives, both expectancy and perceived proximity to attainment contribute to the allocation of effort to certain goals more than to others (Louro, Pieters, and Zeelenberg, 2007). One implication is that in stressful situations unhappiness is expected in part to be a function of expected future levels of that stress (Meurs and Perrewé, 2011; Warr, 2006). Examining the extent to which employees mentally "switch off" after a working day, Sonnentag and Bayer (2005) concluded that it is not only the amount of time pressure that one has faced at work that makes psychological detachment difficult, but also the anticipation that time pressure will continue during the working days to come.

The mental processes reviewed so far (J1 to J3) have their impact on happiness or unhappiness through comparisons with reference standards that are external to the person. J4 to J6 in Table 4.2 operate instead in relation to a person's own benchmarks, in terms of self-efficacy, novelty and personal salience.

Self-efficacy (J4 in Table 4.2) reflects a person's perception that he or she is competent in relation to present or expected demands. Both retrospective and prospective judgments about situation-related self-efficacy are likely to influence happiness. In the first case, recent behavior is compared against one's benchmark level of competence: have I coped well or poorly? For example, recognition that one has failed to prevent a controllable negative event might give rise to even more unhappiness. Scheck and Kinicki (2000) found that employees' positive assessments of their self-efficacy during an organizational change were linked to lower perceptions of threat and potential harm. In addition, future-oriented beliefs about one's personal efficacy in a situation (such as "I'm going to be able to handle this" or "I'm not going to cope") are expected to influence current happiness, even when a perceived ability to exercise control over that situation is in fact illusory (e.g., Bandura and Locke, 2003).

Also important are a person's assessments of the novelty or familiarity of a current situation (J5 in Table 4.2). Continued exposure to a situation tends to reduce its affective potential, either negative or positive, so that more familiar inputs come to generate feelings that are less intense. In part, you evaluate your position in terms of what you are used to; the same environmental input can be evaluated differently after a period of adaptation.

Biological and psychological processes of habituation have been widely observed, when responses to a stimulus become diminished after repeated presentation of that stimulus. Such a change may be viewed in terms of a raised comparison level, when exposure to earlier stimuli establishes a higher standard against which later stimuli are judged. Over time, instances of a particular stimulus have to exceed that increased threshold in order to influence well-being to the same degree. For example, judgmental thresholds may be indexed as the average pleasantness of recent experiences (Parducci, 1995). An increase across time in this average pleasantness implies that a later event or situation has to be still more pleasurable (exceeding the raised judgmental standard) before it has the same impact on well-being.

Much research has demonstrated that positive feelings in response to a constant or repeated environmental stimulus can gradually become reduced or even give way to indifference. For example, Brickman, Coates, and Janoff-Bulman (1978) reported adaptation across time in people who had won large sums of money in a state lottery, and also found that victims of serious accidents did not appear as unhappy as might have been expected (see also Oswald and Powdthavee, 2008). Brickman and colleagues drew attention to a common perceptual error, when observers see victims of misfortune as more distressed than do those people themselves.

Forms of hedonic adaptation have also been illustrated in several projects in organizations. Boswell, Boudreau, and Tichy (2005) studied well-being changes longitudinally among employees voluntarily moving into a new job. Overall job satisfaction was found to increase immediately after entry into a new position, but in subsequent years it declined significantly as individuals became adapted to the realities of their role. Daniels and Guppy (1997) examined employees' strain as a function of particular environmental stressors, finding that experienced strain was less from those stressors that had previously been encountered. In that respect, everyday experience suggests that the capacity to manage a substantial level of demand often becomes ratcheted up after a period of coping with increased pressure; demands that initially caused difficulties and strain can more easily be handled after a person has become adapted to the high demands. A reverse form of habituation is through affective contrast. When a new stimulus is substantially less or more attractive or painful than the one immediately preceding it, it can be experienced as markedly pleasant or unpleasant. Rather than always being fixed, the affective consequences of an environment can depend in part on variables within the person.

Adaptation can operate through other judgments in the framework. For example, changes in J1 and J2B (comparisons with other people and with other possible situations) can contribute to adaptation, as people over time come to reinterpret their situation through new social comparisons or by emphasizing different counterfactual possibilities. In addition, adaptation can give rise to psychological changes in relation to environmental features. For example, environmental clarity (E5 in Table 4.1) can increase as knowledge develops, and contact with other people (E6) may be modified as mutual learning occurs between an individual and people in his or her setting. Adjustment to a situation may also involve shifts in related goals (E3), as different activities are undertaken or a person's ability to attain particular objectives becomes enhanced or reduced.

The happiness or unhappiness of people whose situation has improved or deteriorated is for these reasons likely to return toward an equilibrium level, perhaps being held under personal homeostatic control (Cummins, 2000). The "dynamic equilibrium model" of Headey and Wearing (1992) proposes that each person has a customary level of well-being, and that changes from that level are likely to be only temporary as subsequent adaptation occurs. Headey and Wearing observed this pattern in a community sample across a six-year period. The longitudinal pattern reported for job-changers by Boswell et al. (2005) (above) also illustrates a return to baseline happiness levels after a temporary increase. Within banking organizations, Griffin (1991) found that, although the content of employees' jobs remained enhanced for several years after job redesign, their overall job satisfaction increased only temporarily after a change before falling back to its earlier level. This tendency for happiness and unhappiness to stabilize around a person's "set point" is reflected in significant associations with personality traits (illustrated above) and in the high consistency of affective states across time (e.g., Trzesniewski, Donnellan, and Robins, 2003).

Finally in Table 4.2 appear judgments about the personal salience of an environmental feature (J6); these are likely to have a moderating influence on happiness in many domains of life. Table 4.2 points out that relevant themes may be viewed at three levels of generality – concerned with the value attached to role membership (J6A) (for example, the strength of one's commitment to having a job), the salience of role characteristics (J6B) (e.g., how much one values personal autonomy in a job), or the personal value of core tasks (J6C) (for instance, how much one is attracted to playing football or working with animals) (e.g., Warr, 2007). Given limited space, discussion in the next section will be restricted to J6B, concerned with the role of personal values.

Environmental and Personal Influences in Combination

In bringing together perspectives that are environment-centered and person-centered, joint operation of several forms can be envisaged. For example, the two kinds of variable might have a moderating impact on each other, with one's association depending on the level of the other; or mutual impact can develop across time, for example as individuals' cognitive, physical or personality attributes encourage a transition into or out of certain environments or a concentration on certain activities. Joint operation of those kinds can involve personal variables that are either relatively long-term (e.g., dispositional traits) or shorter-term and possibly fluctuating (e.g., situation-specific judgments).

Longer-Term Personal Influences

Mediation of a personality–happiness link has been illustrated in occupational research by Judge, Bono, and Locke (2000) and Grant and Langan-Fox (2007), and evidence is growing about the moderation of associations by relevant aspects of personality; environmental features can have either more or less impact depending on certain dispositional traits. For example, Kahn, Wolfe, Quinn, and Snoek (1964) and Keenan and McBain (1979) showed that the correlation of role ambiguity with aspects of happiness differed between workers with low and high ambiguity tolerance. Personality moderation has also been reported by, for example, Vroom (1959), Rogelberg, Leach, Warr, and Burnfield (2006), Bond, Flaxman, and Bunce (2008), Rego, Souto, and Cunha (2009), and Van Doorn and Hülsheger (2015).

Moderation of this kind has also been demonstrated in respect of workers' continuing value preferences for particular job features. Individuals who more value a particular job characteristic are more likely to be affected by the degree to which it is present or absent. Much research has confirmed that correlations between relevant job features and job satisfaction are greater for workers who more strongly value the features (e.g., Loher, Noe, Moeller, and Fitzgerald, 1985). However, observed person–situation interactions are not always statistically significant, and an additional, higher-order, moderator is required to account for this variation between studies. Warr and Inceoglu (2015) have suggested a possible explanation in terms of an environmental feature's "affective strength" – the degree to which assessments are evaluatively similar between people.

Personal dispositions are expected also to influence the nonlinearity of associations, being associated with lower or higher tipping points. For example, substantial task demands can sooner overload workers who are less able, while their more competent colleagues cope with those demands and may seek still more challenge. Greater demands are thus expected to give rise to a leveling off and downturn in well-being at more moderate levels for less able individuals than for those who can cope. Similarly, low scorers on a particular personality trait will sooner reach a tipping point for trait-relevant environmental features; they do not want still higher levels of those features in the way that high-trait individuals do. Rego et al. (2009) found that workers with a lower need to belong showed greater nonlinearity in the association between degree of social support and affective well-being than did high-need workers; for individuals with a lower need for interpersonal input, high levels of support more readily yielded decrements beyond the tipping point than for workers who more sought that support. Between-person differences in tipping point of this kind are also expected in respect of traits such as (for example) optimism, perfectionism and neuroticism.

Shorter-Term Personal Influences

In these ways environmental features are associated with happiness or unhappiness to different degrees and in different ways according to characteristics of an individual. This pattern is likely to be linked to disposition-related differences in ways of thinking and feeling about one's environment, and mental processes of that kind (see Table 4.2) require inclusion in studies and models of well-being.

A key research requirement is for the creation of robust measures of thought processes that can be incorporated in such studies. There are undoubtedly problems in the measurement of mental activity, and the reliability and validity of some retrospective self-reports is open to question. Nevertheless, given that observed correlations between environmental features and outcome indicators are often only moderate and that causal mechanisms can depend on the mental processes involved, it is essential that empirical research in this area includes measures of at least some of the judgments in Table 4.2. For example, the nature of a person's social or counterfactual comparisons (J1 and J2B) should be recorded, and job-content preferences (J6B) should routinely be examined within studies of environmental characteristics and their outcomes. Given that the degree of discrepancy between job content and a worker's preference for that content is in general linked to job-related well-being (e.g., Ostroff and Judge, 2007), more research into specific forms of misfit and different aspects of well-being would now be valuable (Warr and Inceoglu, 2012). It is also important to learn about factors linked to the occurrence or non-occurrence of each type of Table 4.2 judgment. Their prevalence, and thus relative priority and potential impact, is likely to be associated with factors such as the nature of a setting, personality traits, age and gender, and differences in cognitive emphasis are also likely to depend in part on local norms in a group or wider culture (Warr, 2006).

Interventions to Enhance Happiness

In addition to environment-and-person studies that examine together the two kinds of variable (above), a third combined approach is through individual-level interventions to enhance happiness or mental health. Counseling procedures to reduce strain in a particular setting often seek to encourage relaxation, meditation, stress awareness, more appropriate assertiveness, or improved time management and goal-setting. Some programs have applied themes from cognitive behavioral therapy, in which a trainer and a client work together to identify a person's negative thoughts and seek to replace those by more constructive routines. Between-person variations in the process and outcome of intervention now deserve additional investigation.

In employment settings, strain management programs have proved to be effective across at least several subsequent weeks (e.g., Richardson and Rothstein, 2008), especially for workers with high initial levels of distress (Flaxman and Bond, 2010). Positive findings in non-job settings have been brought together by Sin and Lyubomirsky (2009) and applied to happiness at work by Warr and Clapperton (2010). Systematic person-centered studies of this kind, introducing and monitoring change and individual variation, are in effect experiments into the impact of potentially important cognitive and affective variables. They take us more directly to potential within-person causal explanations, and are thus desirable for both practical and theoretical reasons – both to reduce strain and also to develop and test models about underlying person-level processes in particular environmental conditions.

Overview and Future Directions

This chapter and its underlying model have emphasized that, in order to understand and enhance mental health and happiness, it is essential to bring together aspects of the person and features of an environment, rather than examining the environment or the person alone. Within that overall need we should explore the presence of nonlinear relationships between environmental features and different outcomes, and examine how nonlinearity may vary between individuals with different characteristics. More developed understanding of mental processes of the kind illustrated in Table 4.2 is also required, to move beyond the limited notion of primary appraisal of stressors which is common in this area (e.g., Webster, Beehr, and Love, 2011). In addition, research into happiness needs to extend beyond the traditional emphasis only on affective well-being to also consider eudaimonic themes (at present more common in mental health perspectives), and cyclical processes across time clearly require more extensive investigation.

The vitamin model is an overarching framework which is open to more detailed specification in particular settings. Broad frameworks of this comprehensive kind aim to provide a theoretical fabric and set of constructs within which particular micromodels of component processes may be investigated. Theories are always open to development and adjustment, and it is essential that research moves to and fro between broad framework construction as here and the targeted empirical examination of more limited models.

References

Adams, J. S. (1965). Inequity in social exchange. In L. Berkowitz (Ed.), *Advances in Experimental Social Psychology* (pp. 267–299). San Diego, CA: Academic Press.

Anderson, C. J. (2003). The psychology of doing nothing: Forms of decision avoidance result from reason and emotion. *Psychological Bulletin*, *129*, 139–167.

Austin, J. T., and Vancouver, J. B. (1996). Goal constructs in psychology: Structure, process, and content. *Psychological Bulletin*, *120*, 338–375.

Baltes, B. B., Bauer, C. C., Bajdo, L. M., and Parker, C. P. (2002). The use of multitrait-multimethod data for detecting non-linear relationships: The case of psychological climate and job satisfaction. *Journal of Business and Psychology*, *17*, 3–17.

Bandura, A., and Locke, E. A. (2003). Negative self-efficacy and goal effects revisited. *Journal of Applied Psychology*, *88*, 87–99.

Baumeister, R. F., Vohs, K. D., Aaker, J. L., and Garbinsky, E. N. (2013). Some key differences between a happy life and a meaningful life. *Journal of Positive Psychology*, *8*, 505–516.

Blanchflower, D. G., and Oswald, A. J. (2008). Is well-being U-shaped over the life cycle? *Social Science and Medicine*, *66*, 1733–1749.

Bond, F. W., Flaxman, P. E., and Bunce, D. (2008). The influence of psychological flexibility on work redesign: Mediated moderation of a work reorganization intervention. *Journal of Applied Psychology*, *93*, 645–654.

Boswell, W. R., Boudreau, J. W., and Tichy, J. (2005). The relationship between employee job change and job satisfaction: The honeymoon-hangover effect. *Journal of Applied Psychology*, *90*, 882–892.

Brennan, A., Chugh, J. S., and Kline, T. (2002). Traditional versus open office design: A longitudinal field study. *Environment and Behavior*, *34*, 279–299.

Brickman, P., Coates, D., and Janoff-Bulman, R. (1978). Lottery winners and accident victims: Is happiness relative? *Journal of Personality and Social Psychology*, *36*, 917–927.

Burger, J. M. (1989). Negative reactions to increases in perceived personal control. *Journal of Personality and Social Psychology*, *56*, 246–256.

Carver, C. S. (2001). Affect and the functional bases of behavior: On the dimensional structure of affective experience. *Personality and Social Psychology Review*, *5*, 345–356.

Chang, C.-H., Ferris, D. L., Johnson, R. E., Rosen, C. C, and Tan, J. A. (2012). Core self-evaluations: A review and evaluation of the literature. *Journal of Management*, *38*, 81–128.

Chung-Yan, G. A. (2010). The nonlinear effects of job complexity and autonomy on job satisfaction, turnover, and psychological well-being. *Journal of Occupational Health Psychology*, *15*, 237–251.

Clark, A. E., Oswald, A., and Warr, P. B. (1996). Is job satisfaction U-shaped in age? *Journal of Occupational and Organizational Psychology*, *69*, 57–81.

Crawford, E. R., LePine, J. A., and Rich, B. L. (2010). Linking job demands and resources to employee engagement and burnout: A theoretical extension and meta-analytic test. *Journal of Applied Psychology*, *95*, 834–848.

Cummins, R. A. (2000). Objective and subjective quality of life: An interactive model. *Social Indicators Research*, *52*, 55–72.

Daniels, K., and Guppy, A. (1997). Stressors, locus of control, and social support as consequences of affective psychological well-being. *Journal of Occupational Health Psychology*, *2*, 156–174.

Deelstra, J. T., Peeters, M. C. W., Schaufeli, W. B., Stroebe, W., Zijlstra, F. R. H., and van Doornen, L. P. (2003). Receiving instrumental support at work: When help is not welcome. *Journal of Applied Psychology*, *88*, 324–331.

De Jonge, J., Reuvers, M. M. E. N., Houtman, I. L. D., Bongers, P. M., and Kompier, M. A. J. (2000). Linear and non-linear relations between psychosocial job characteristics, subjective outcomes, and sickness absence: Baseline results from SMASH. *Journal of Occupational Health Psychology*, *5*, 256–268.

Diener, E., Sandvik, E., Seidlitz, L, and Diener, M. (1993). The relationship between income and subjective well-being: Relative or absolute? *Social Indicators Research*, *28*, 195–223.

Diener, E. and Seligman, M. E. P. (2004). Beyond money. *Psychological Science in the Public Interest*, *5*, 1–31.

Emmons, R. A. (1986). Personal strivings: An approach to personality and subjective well-being. *Journal of Personality and Social Psychology*, *51*, 1058–1068.

Flaxman, P. E., and Bond, F. W. (2010). Worksite stress management training: Moderated effects and clinical significance. *Journal of Occupational Health Psychology*, *15*, 347–358.

Fleishman, E. A., and Harris, E. F. (1962). Patterns of leadership behavior related to employee grievances and turnover. *Personnel Psychology*, *15*, 43–56.

Friedman, H. S., and Kern, M. L. (2014). Personality, well-being, and health. *Annual Review of Psychology*, *65*, 719–742.

Grant, S., and Langan-Fox, J. (2007). Personality and the occupational stressor-strain relationship: The role of the Big Five. *Journal of Occupational Health Psychology*, *12*, 20–33.

Griffin, R. W. (1991). Effects of work redesign on employee perceptions, attitudes, and behaviors: A long-term investigation. *Academy of Management Journal*, *34*, 425–435.

Hagerty, M. R. (2000). Social comparisons of income in one's community. *Journal of Personality and Social Psychology*, *78*, 764–771.

Halbesleben, J. R. B., Neveu, J.-P., Paustian-Underhahl, S. C., and Westman, M. (2014). Getting to the "COR": Understanding the role of resources in conservation of resources theory. *Journal of Management*, *40*, 1334–1364.

Headey, B., and Wearing, A. (1992). *Understanding Happiness: A Theory of Subjective Well-Being*. Melbourne: Longman Cheshire.

Humphrey, S. E., Nahrgang, J. D., and Morgensen, F. P. (2007). Integrating motivational, social, and contextual work design features: A meta-analytic summary and theoretical extension of the work design literature. *Journal of Applied Psychology*, *92*, 1332–1356.

Huppert, F. A. (2014). The state of wellbeing science. In F. A. Huppert and C. L. Cooper (Eds.), *Interventions and Policies to Enhance Wellbeing*. Chichester, UK: Wiley.

Inceoglu, I., and Warr, P. B. (2011). Personality and job engagement. *Journal of Personnel Psychology*, *10*, 177–181.

Jahoda, M. (1982). *Employment and Unemployment: A Social-Psychological Analysis*. Cambridge: Cambridge University Press.

Judge, T. A., Bono, J. E., and Locke, E. A. (2000). Personality and job satisfaction: The mediating role of job characteristics. *Journal of Applied Psychology*, *85*, 237–249.

Judge, T. A., Heller, D., and Mount, M. K. (2002). Five-factor model of personality and job satisfaction: A meta-analysis. *Journal of Applied Psychology*, *87*, 530–541.

Kahn, R. L., Wolfe, D. M., Quinn, R. P., and Snoek, J. D. (1964). *Organizational Stress: Studies in Role Conflict and Ambiguity*. New York: Wiley.

Karasek, R. A. (1979). Job demands, job decision latitude, and mental strain: Implications for job design. *Administrative Science Quarterly*, *24*, 285–308.

Keenan, A., and McBain, G. D. M. (1979). Effects of Type A behaviour, intolerance of ambiguity, and locus of control on the relationship between role stress and work-related outcomes. *Journal of Occupational Psychology*, *52*, 277–285.

Keyes, C. L. M. (2002). The mental health continuum: From languishing to flourishing in life. *Journal of Health and Social Research*, *43*, 207–222.

Loher, B. T., Noe, R. A., Moeller, N. L., and Fitzgerald, M. P. (1985). A meta-analysis of the relation of job characteristics to job satisfaction. *Journal of Applied Psychology*, *70*, 280–289.

Louro, M. J., Pieters, R., and Zeelenberg, M. (2007). Dynamics of multiple goal pursuit. *Journal of Personality and Social Psychology*, *93*, 174–193.

Luchman, J. N., and González-Morales, M. G. (2013). Demands, support, and control: A meta-analytic review of work characteristics relationships. *Journal of Occupational Health Psychology*, *18*, 37–52.

Lyubomirsky, S., Sheldon, K. M., and Schkade, D. (2005). Pursuing happiness: The architecture of sustainable change. *Review of General Psychology*, *9*, 111–131.

Madrid, H., and Patterson, M. G., (2014). Measuring affect at work based on the valence and arousal circumplex model. *Spanish Journal of Psychology*, *17*, 1–12.

McGregor, I., and Little, B. R., (1998). Personal projects, happiness, and meaning: On doing well and being yourself. *Journal of Personality and Social Psychology*, *74*, 494–512.

Medvec, V. H., Madey, S. F., and Gilovich, T. (1995). When less is more: Counterfactual thinking and satisfaction among Olympic athletes. *Journal of Personality and Social Psychology, 69*, 603–610.

Meurs, J. A., and Perrewé, P. L. (2011). Cognitive activation theory of stress: An integrative theoretical approach to work stress. *Journal of Management, 37*, 1043–1068.

Olson, J. M., Buhrman, O., and Roese, N. J. (2000). Comparing comparisons: An integrative perspective on social comparison and counterfactual thinking. In J. Suls and L. Wheeler (Eds.), *Handbook of Social Comparison: Theory and Research* (pp. 379–398). New York: Kluwer/Plenum.

Ostroff, C., and Judge, T. A. (Eds.) (2007). *Perspectives on Organizational Fit*. New York: Erlbaum.

Oswald, A. J., and Powdthavee, N. (2008). Does happiness adapt? A longitudinal study of disability with implications for economists and judges. *Journal of Public Economics, 92*, 1061–1077.

Parducci, A. (1995). *Happiness, Pleasure, and Judgment*. Mahwah, NJ: Erlbaum.

Posner, J., Russell, J. A., and Peterson, B. S. (2005). The circumplex model of affect: An integrative approach to affective neurosciences, cognitive development, and psychopharmacology. *Development and Psychopathology, 17*, 715–734.

Rego, A., Souto, S., and Cunha, M. P. (2009). Does the need to belong moderate the relationship between perceptions of spirit of camaraderie and employees' happiness? *Journal of Occupational Health Psychology, 14*, 148–164.

Richardson, K. M., and Rothstein, H. R. (2008). Effects of occupational stress management intervention programs: A meta-analysis. *Journal of Occupational Health Psychology, 13*, 69–93.

Rogelberg, S. G., Leach, D. J., Warr, P. B., and Burnfield, J. (2006). "Not another meeting!" Are meeting time demands related to employee well-being? *Journal of Applied Psychology, 91*, 83–96.

Rosenfield, S., and Mouzon, D. (2013). Gender and mental health. In C. S. Aneshensel, J. C. Phelan, and A. Bierman (Eds.), *Handbook of the Sociology of Mental Health* (pp. 277–296). Amsterdam: Springer.

Schaubroeck, J. M. (2012). Pitfalls of appropriating prestigious theories to frame conceptual arguments. *Organizational Psychology Review, 3*, 86–97.

Schaufeli, W. B. (2006). The balance of give and take: Toward a social exchange model of burnout. *Revue Internationale de Psychologie Sociale, 19*, 87–131.

Scheck, C. L., and Kinicki, A. (2000). Identifying the antecedents of coping with an organizational acquisition: A structural assessment. *Journal of Organizational Behavior, 21*, 627–648.

Seo, M.-G., Bartunek, J. M., and Feldman-Barrett, L. (2010). The role of affective experience in work motivation: Test of a conceptual model. *Journal of Organizational Behavior, 31*, 951–968.

Seligman, M. E. P. (2011). *Flourish*. London: Nicholas Brealey.

Sin, N. L., and Lyubomirsky, S. (2009). Enhancing well-being and alleviating depressive symptoms with positive psychology interventions: A practice-friendly meta-analysis. *Journal of Clinical Psychology, 65*, 467–487.

Sonnentag, S., and Bayer, U.-V. (2005). Switching off mentally: Predictors and consequences of psychological detachment from work during off-job time. *Journal of Occupational Health Psychology, 10*, 393–414.

Steel, P., Schmidt, J., and Shultz, J. (2008). Refining the relationship between personality and subjective well-being. *Psychological Bulletin, 134*, 138–161.

Stone, A. A., Schwartz, J. E., Broderick, J. E., and Deaton, A. (2010). A snapshot of the age distribution of psychological well-being in the United States. *Proceedings of the National Academy of Sciences in the United States of America, 107*, 9985–9990.

Trzesniewski, K. H., Donnellan, M. B., and Robins, R. W. (2003). Stability of self-esteem across the life-span. *Journal of Personality and Social Psychology, 84*, 205–220.

Uchino, B. N. (2006). Social support and health: A review of physiological processes potentially underlying links to disease outcomes. *Journal of Behavioral Medicine, 29*, 377–387.

Van Doorn, R. R. A., and Hülsheger, U. R. (2015). What make employees resilient to job demands? The role of core self-evaluations in the relationship between job demands and strain reactions. *European Journal of Work and Organizational Psychology, 24*, 76–87.

Vroom, V. H. (1959). Some personality determinants of the effects of participation. *Journal of Abnormal and Social Psychology, 59*, 322–327.

Warr, P. B. (1987). *Work, Unemployment, and Mental Health*. Oxford: Oxford University Press.

Warr, P. B. (1990). Decision latitude, job demands and employee well-being. *Work and Stress, 4*, 285–294.

Warr, P. B. (2006). Differential activation of judgments in employee well-being. *Journal of Occupational and Organizational Psychology, 79*, 225–244.

Warr, P. B. (2007). *Work, Happiness, and Unhappiness*. Mahwah, NJ: Erlbaum.

Warr, P. B. (2012). How to think about and measure psychological well-being. In M. Wang, R. R. Sinclair, and L. E. Tetrick (Eds.), *Research Methods in Occupational Health Psychology*. New York: Routledge.

Warr, P. B. (forthcoming). *Journal of Occupational Health Psychology*, in press.

Warr, P. B., Bindl, U., Parker, S., and Inceoglu, I. (2014). Four-quadrant investigation of job-related affects and behaviours. *European Journal of Work and Organizational Psychology*, *23*, 342–363.

Warr, P. B., and Clapperton, G. (2010). *The Joy of Work? Jobs, Happiness, and You*. New York: Routledge.

Warr, P. B., and Inceoglu, I. (2012). Job satisfaction, job engagement, and contrasting associations with person–job fit. *Journal of Occupational Health Psychology*, *17*, 129–138.

Warr, P. B., and Inceoglu, I. (2015). Job features, job values, and affective strength. *European Journal of Work and Organizational Psychology*, *24*, 101–112.

Waterman, A. S. (1993). Two conceptions of happiness: Contrasts of personal expressiveness (eudaimonia) and hedonic enjoyment. *Journal of Personality and Social Psychology*, *64*, 678–691.

Watson, D., and Tellegen, A. (1985). Toward a consensual structure of mood. *Psychological Bulletin*, *98*, 219–235.

Webster, J. R., Beehr, T. A., and Love, K. (2011).Extending the challenge-hindrance model of occupational stress: The role of appraisal. *Journal of Vocational Behavior*, *79*, 505–516.

Wheeler, L. (2000). Individual differences in social comparison. In J. Suls and L. Wheeler (Eds.), *Handbook of Social Comparison: Theory and Research* (pp. 141–158). New York: Kluwer/Plenum.

Yik, M., Russell, J. A., and Steiger, J. H. (2011). A 12-point circumplex structure of core affect. *Emotion*, *11*, 705–731.

5

Understanding the Connections between Positive Affect and Health

Marie P. Cross and Sarah D. Pressman

It is now firmly established that positive affect (PA) is tied to better physical health. Studies have connected PA with various health benefits such as greater longevity (e.g., Kawamoto and Doi, 2002; Ostir, Markides, Black, and Goodwin, 2000), lower rates of illness onset (e.g., Boehm and Kubzansky, 2012; Cohen, Doyle, Turner, Alper, and Skoner, 2003), and reduced reports of symptoms and pain (e.g., Sullivan, LaCroix, Russo, and Walker, 2001; Zautra, Johnson, and Davis, 2005). Although there are many hypothesized pathways that explain how PA is connected to physical wellness, researchers are still attempting to pinpoint the underlying mechanisms of this association. This chapter will provide a brief review of the known connections between PA and physical health (for a comprehensive review, see Pressman and Cohen, 2005), as well as a discussion of future directions for research in this area. We begin, however, with a short overview of important issues in the fields of affect and health.

Important Issues in the Study of Affect and Health

Measurement of Affect

Affect is typically divided into two time-based categories: short-lasting state affect (transient emotion and mood) versus long-lasting trait affect. For example, a person may feel transient anger at getting a traffic ticket (state), but this same person may be generally happy in his or her daily life (trait). State and trait affect are highly correlated because reports of state affect often reflect underlying trait affect. Conceptually, it makes more sense to examine trait affect when examining health outcomes given the expected longer lasting effects of a disposition on wellness (i.e., impacts on physiology and behavior *every day*); however, researchers often include measures of state affect (e.g., Steptoe and Wardle, 2011), which has similar predictive

The Handbook of Stress and Health: A Guide to Research and Practice, First Edition.
Edited by Cary L. Cooper and James Campbell Quick.
© 2017 John Wiley & Sons, Ltd. Published 2017 by John Wiley & Sons, Ltd.

abilities. That being said, any benefit of state affect on long-term future health is likely due to state affect picking up on the disposition of the subject.

Beyond timing, there are also many different positive emotion *types* to consider. One method for differentiating types of emotion is to map them on conceptual dimensions of affect features like valence (positive/negative) and arousal/activation (Russell, 1980). This form of emotion differentiation is particularly appealing and important to health research since arousal may map onto physiological arousal (e.g., elevated stress hormones, heart rate alteration), which may in turn influence physical health. Unfortunately, two common self-report adjective checklist measurement tools in health research – the Positive and Negative Affect Schedule (PANAS; Watson, Clark, and Tellegen, 1988) and the Profile of Mood States (POMS; McNair, Lorr, and Droppleman, 1971) – both focus on high arousal emotion (e.g., vigor). This focus has resulted in an incomplete understanding of the role of low arousal PA (e.g., calm) in a large swath of medical work. Researchers are beginning to address this problem by using scales that include low arousal PA, such as a variant on the POMS that includes a low arousal dimension (Cohen, et al., 2003; Marsland, Cohen, Rabin, and Manuck, 2001) or the expanded version of the PANAS, the PANAS-X (Watson and Clark, 1991), which includes a serenity dimension that taps feelings of being at ease and relaxed (e.g., Moreno et al., 2016). Most frequent, however, are studies that utilize mixed arousal levels of PA via multi-item and multi-arousal scales (e.g., overall PA from the POMS, the positive items from the CES-D depression scale (Radloff, 1977; Sheehan, Fifield, Reisine, and Tennen, 1995), single items assessing specific positive emotions such as "happiness" (e.g., J. E. Brown, Butow, Culjak, Coates, and Dunn, 2000)).

Another critical measurement issue is the connection between PA and negative affect (NA). PA and NA can be highly correlated, but can also be independent of one another. This relationship depends on factors like the adjectives and time periods used in scales, as well as the intensity of the experienced emotions (Diener and Emmons, 1984; Diener, Larsen, Levine, and Emmons, 1985; Watson, 1988; Watson et al., 1988). Since NA has established detrimental effects on physical health (T. Q. Miller, Smith, Turner, Guijarro, and Hallet, 1996; Suls and Bunde, 2005), researchers often question whether PA benefits are simply the *opposite* of NA detriments. Because of this, PA researchers are frequently required to control for the effects of NA in studies of health to prove that this effect occurs over and above the effects of NA, which is frequently the case (e.g., Gil et al., 2004; Pressman and Cohen, 2012; Pressman, Gallagher, and Lopez, 2013; Ostir, Markides, Peek, and Goodwin, 2001). Interestingly, while most researchers now control for NA in PA-health analyses, *how* researchers control for NA varies. Multicollinearity between PA and NA in many emotion scales is an issue, which results in the effects of *both* PA and NA being wiped out when simultaneously included in the same analysis. In an effort to avoid this, some researchers utilize different negativity measures as covariates (such as depression) instead of NA (e.g., Moreno et al., 2016; Moskowitz, 2003). While helpful in dealing with collinearity issues, depression is conceptually different from NA, and frequently includes a variety of non-affect items (see the Beck Depression Inventory (Beck, Shaw, Rush, and Emery, 1979) or the CES-D (Radloff, 1977) for examples). There is no clear, perfect solution to this problem; therefore, science would benefit if researchers opted to report the health and physiological associations of *both* PA and NA in their analyses so that researchers can disentangle whether some health outcomes are disproportionately influenced by one valence over another.

It is also important to note that not all positive psychological measures are equal. PA is distinct from similar constructs such as life satisfaction, optimism, and subjective well-being.

Although these constructs are also important for health (e.g., Creswell et al., 2005; Rasmussen, Scheier, and Greenhouse, 2009; Strine, Chapman, Balluz, Moriarty, and Mokdad, 2008), they may have different health implications and influence health through different pathways. For example, extraversion includes social components that PA does not include, and optimism is a cognitive expectation of good things to come in the future. PA does not tap these critical components, so it may operate on health via different pathways. At the same time, it is known that these variables overlap, and it could be the case that some of their effects on health happen *via* influences on PA, although this remains an open and relatively unstudied question. Therefore, investigators need to think carefully about which positive construct they should assess and not equate all variables as though they are the same.

Finally, there is an overdependence on participant self-report when measuring affect in health studies. This is problematic because self-report can be influenced by social desirability and self-presentation desires (e.g., participants may be self-conscious about reporting low PA). A perfect example of this was illustrated in a recent study that found the *opposite* of the typically observed (self-report) happiness bias in conservatives when examining non self-report methods (Wojcik, Hovasapian, Graham, Motyl, and Ditto, 2015). To circumvent this type of concern, researchers have started exploring alternative emotion measurement techniques in health and health-relevant studies. Some of these techniques include using computer programs to code affective words in writing (e.g., Eichstaedt et al., 2015; Pennebaker, Francis, and Booth, 2001; Pressman and Cohen, 2007), coding smiling as an outward expression of positive emotionality (Harker and Keltner, 2001; Seder and Oishi, 2011), and using informants to gauge positive feelings of others (e.g., Friedman et al., 1993), although recent work has indicated that this methodology may not always be accurate (e.g., López-Pérez and Wilson, 2015). While these alternative techniques may have interpretation issues of their own and are not equivalent to self-report (Harker and Keltner, 2001; Kolar, Funder, and Colvin, 1996; Pennebaker, Mehl, and Niederhoffer, 2003), these methods do not fall prey to the same biases as self-report and provide options for researchers to supplement their self-report data and add generalizability to their findings.

Health Measurement

It is important for studies investigating the connections between PA and health to have a measure of physical health at baseline (i.e., to use a prospective design). This helps address the possible confound of happy people being healthier at study start and allows for a study of change in health over time. Measures of health can be subjective (self-report) or objective, with different resulting interpretations. Subjective health is typically assessed through single items (e.g., "How would you rate your health over the past year?") or via symptom checklists such as the Cohen-Hoberman Inventory of Physical Symptoms (CHIPS; Cohen and Hoberman, 1983). Critically, subjective health is an important future health predictor (e.g., Cesari et al., 2008; Miilunpalo, Vuori, Oja, Pasanen, and Urponen, 1997), and sometimes a stronger predictor of longevity than medical records (e.g., Idler and Benyamini, 1997). One explanation for this is that subjective health captures something not tapped by standard medical tests and histories, such as pre-illness physiological dysfunction and/or minor but currently undiagnosed disease. Problematic with these measures, however, is that they are intricately linked with PA. Some self-rated health measures, such as the Short Form Health Survey (SF-36; Ware and Sherbourne, 1992), include items that could be interpreted (and are sometimes measured) as

PA. Furthermore, when individuals *feel* healthier (i.e., are not actively ill) they also feel psychologically better, resulting in close ties between PA and self-reported health.

Objective health is typically assessed with physician reports, in-person physical assessments, or medical records of disease. If a person has a medical condition, it might also be tapped by medication usage or certain physiological parameters (e.g., viral load or T cell counts in HIV-positive patients). It is important to note that while somewhat objective, psychosocial factors can contaminate these measures as well. For example, medical records are only valuable if individuals *go* to the doctor to get diagnosed with a disorder and this doctor is the one who provides the records for the study. Another issue is that medical care may not be comparable across subjects because of factors such as socioeconomic status. Thus, the gold standard is a physical exam conducted at the start of the study by a medical professional.

Causality Issues

One important question is whether the presence or lack of PA actually *causes* the development of certain diseases. Causation is impossible to ascertain without experimental design, and this is rare in the medical literature since it is unethical to randomly expose individuals to illness and dangerous health behaviors. That being said, there has been some experimental work done on minor and acute illnesses like the common cold and flu, as demonstrated in the landmark studies conducted by Cohen and colleagues (2003; Cohen, Alper, Doyle, Treanor, and Turner, 2006) discussed later. Chronic diseases that develop over the course of the lifespan, on the other hand, cannot be experimentally manipulated. Thus, investigators instead conduct prospective longitudinal studies (controlling for baseline health and physiology) over months or years in an attempt to determine what factors may predict the development of chronic disease and whether there are findings that are consistent with a causal effect.

Similarly, there are experimental and intervention studies that manipulate PA and then examine subsequent health and physiological changes. With proper controls and designs, these studies can give us some confidence that it is PA that *leads* to better health. Although the bulk of this work is on short-term biological change (e.g., changes in immune and heart function) as opposed to objective health outcomes, this is changing with growing interest in positive psychology interventions (see the section on positivity interventions below).

Distinguishing between Health and Physiology

A final point to consider in the health psychology literature is that changes in physiological function and symptoms are not equivalent to changes in *health*. For example, experimentally induced increases in blood pressure are not equivalent to the presence or absence of hypertension. However, physiological measurements can be used as a proxy for health-relevant functionality and can be predictive of future health (e.g., Matthews et al., 2004; G. E. Miller and Blackwell, 2006; Sephton, Sapolsky, Kraemer, and Spiegel, 2000). Physiological indicators (e.g., immune function, cortisol levels, cardiovascular activity) also serve as plausible underlying mechanisms that connect affect to better or worse health, which will be discussed later in this chapter. However, it is still important to remember that a small change in immune function may *not* be clinically meaningful, and similar alterations in related physical function measurement (e.g., cortisol, heart rate) should not be presumed to be *equivalent* to health.

Review of PA and Physical Health

Although the connections between PA and physical health have been investigated in a wide range of health domains, we focus on four key outcomes: longevity, morbidity, survival, and self-reported health outcomes (e.g., symptoms and pain).

Longevity

Prospective longitudinal designs of mortality involve assessing baseline health, then following participants for months or years to determine who is still living at the end of the study (mortality rate). Most studies that investigate PA and longevity have been conducted with samples of healthy, community-residing elderly adults. Overall, there have been approximately 35 studies conducted in this population, many of which have found connections between PA and reduced mortality rates (see reviews by Chida and Steptoe, 2008; Diener and Chan, 2011; Pressman and Cohen, 2005). An example of a typical study of this type is work by Kawamoto and Doi (2002) of 2,274 community-dwelling older adults (ages 65–98). They found that baseline self-rated happiness was higher in those still living during a three-year follow-up. Similarly, a study of older Mexican American adults (ages 65–99) showed increased longevity two years later for those reporting higher PA at baseline (Ostir et al., 2000). Findings such as these have also been replicated in studies with even longer follow-up periods (e.g., ten years; Blazer and Hybels, 2004) and, in many studies, PA benefits remain after controlling for critical baseline variables discussed earlier like baseline health and NA (e.g., Ostir et al., 2000).

Interestingly, several researchers have also broached this topic using non self-report methodologies to tap PA. In one creative study, nuns in their early twenties wrote short auto-biographical sketches of their lives, which were later coded for positive and negative emotion word usage. Fifty years later, researchers found that those who used more positive emotion words in their writing lived almost 11 years longer than those who used the fewest positive emotion words (Danner, Snowdon, and Friesen, 2001). This effect was replicated by Pressman and Cohen (2012), who used writing samples of famous deceased psychologists. They found that individuals writing with more frequent high arousal positive words (e.g., vigor) gained approximately six extra years of life versus those who did not use these types of words as often. In both of these studies, PA-related benefits were independent from those of NA. Another non self-report measure of emotion is affect displayed in the face. While this method has rarely been used in health research, Abel and Kruger (2010) found in the first study of its kind that baseball players who smiled more intensely on their Major League Baseball cards lived longer than those who did not smile. Thus, these studies add confidence that this effect is not driven by a self-report bias in the more common self-reported PA studies; generally, across different measurement types, PA is beneficial for long life. There is clearly important health-relevant information to be gained when utilizing some of these more novel, non self-report indicators of emotion.

It is also important to note that there are some studies that have not found a benefit of PA for life span. For example, studies investigating PA in less healthy populations of residents in nursing homes have shown that PA is sometimes connected with an *increased* risk of mortality (Janoff-Bulman and Marshall, 1982; Stones, Dornan, and Kozma, 1989). For example, a small study of 25 elderly residents of a nursing home found that residents with higher baseline well-being scores were *more* likely to have died over a 30-month follow-up period (Janoff-Bulman and Marshall, 1982). Why is there PA-related harm in this sample? One possibility is that PA in ill individuals is correlated with behaviors and cognitions not conducive to living longer. For example, positive individuals may be less likely to report new symptoms and seek medical care when facing a health burden (see self-reported health outcomes section). This may result in caretakers missing important changes in health, which could lead to earlier death; however, future research is necessary to test this hypothesis. PA may also lead individuals to be overly optimistic about their illness and not adhere to their treatment regimens (as discussed in Pressman and Cohen, 2005). Finally, another possibility, which we raise in the disease survival section of this chapter, is that individuals in nursing homes may have illnesses that are simply too far along to be influenced by pathways altered by PA. For example, if an individual has end-stage renal failure, having higher levels of happiness cannot cure a non-functioning kidney. For this reason, it is critical to consider the mechanisms by which PA influences wellness and the physical health context of the individuals in the study.

Another study with surprising reverse effects of PA investigated whether *childhood* PA is beneficial across the life span. Friedman and colleagues (1993) found that teacher- or parent-rated childhood cheerfulness (at a mean age of 11) was associated with dying sooner over a 65-year follow up. Why might childhood PA lead to a shorter life in this sample? One possibility is that individuals who are rated as more cheerful at younger ages might also be more outgoing, energetic, and adventurous (since PA here indicates outward expressions of positivity). This may be tied to differences in health behaviors at younger adult ages, openness to experiences that put them in danger, or even poorer health behaviors because they are less concerned about things that could go wrong with their bodies (Martin et al., 2002). It is also possible that since this study did not rely on self-report or a measure of the participant directly (such as their own writing or facial expressions), PA reports were not accurately capturing how participants felt and are not interchangeable with the self-reports of the children themselves (Eiser and Morse, 2001). Future studies on the health correlates of informant-reported PA are needed to determine the replicability of this sample, especially given its non-generalizability to other samples (it was a sample of highly gifted, primarily Caucasian young children).

Thus, while there are some rare exceptions, PA is generally connected with lower rates of mortality in healthy samples of community-residing elderly adults. A meta-analysis supported this conclusion; the authors found that positive psychological well-being was connected with lower rates of mortality in both healthy (combined hazard ratio (HR) = 0.82) and ill (combined HR = 0.98) populations (Chida and Steptoe, 2008). However, it is important to note that PA may not always have beneficial effects on mortality rates, and researchers should continue to investigate this association in a variety of populations in order to determine for whom PA is most beneficial in the context of longevity.

Morbidity

Morbidity is the incidence of a diseased state; studies investigating the connections between PA and morbidity have looked at a wide variety of outcomes such as stroke incidence (Ostir et al., 2001) and coronary heart disease (Kubzansky and Thurston, 2007). These studies typically recruit healthy participants at baseline and then follow them over time to determine who develops the illness of interest. Although most of these studies are longitudinal, a handful of notable studies in this literature are experimental (Cohen et al., 2003; 2006). Participants in these seminal studies completed a battery of psychosocial questionnaires, including emotional styles, health practices, and many other sociodemographic measures. They were then exposed to a novel common cold virus and quarantined for five days. Those with higher levels of PA were less likely to develop an objective cold, as determined by objective indicators of illness such as mucus weight in used tissues and cold virus replication (Cohen et al., 2003; 2006). These results were also replicated with experimental exposure to an influenza A virus (Cohen et al., 2006), suggesting that PA may be important in decreasing the risk of catching acute, contagious diseases.

Although the Cohen and colleagues studies are the only experimental studies in this literature, there are also many well-designed longitudinal studies that provide almost unanimous support that PA is connected with less risk of illness and injury across a wide range of outcomes and age groups (Pressman and Cohen, 2005). For example, one study that examined male high school hockey players revealed that levels of vigor (i.e., high activation PA) before the start of the season were associated with fewer future injuries (Smith et al., 1997). PA may also be helpful for morbidity in older age groups; in a study of elderly patients hospitalized for a hip fracture, higher baseline PA was associated with better overall functioning at each follow-up point (up to two years post-hospitalization; Fredman, Hawkes, Black, Bertrand, and Magaziner, 2006). Although these results would benefit from replications, the range of benefits of PA in slowing or preventing illness across the lifespan is notable.

Within the morbidity literature, likely the most studied and replicated disease findings have been within the cardiovascular disease (CVD) literature, especially if we consider positive constructs more broadly (e.g., including measures like optimism). As shown in a recent review, positive psychological well-being (broadly defined) consistently protects against CVD, independent of known coronary risk factors and NA (Boehm and Kubzansky, 2012). Designs of these studies typically assess healthy individuals (or those with a moderate CVD risk) at baseline and follow them for occurrence of CVD related events, or alternatively, follow individuals with existing CVD for future related events. One example of this is in a study of 121 CVD patients (ages 55 and up) where participants who reported higher PA about their current circumstances were less likely to be readmitted to the hospital over a 90-day follow up (Middleton and Byrd, 1996). NA was not reported in this study, however, leaving some open questions about the extent to which this effect may be driven by a lack of negative experiences and feelings. Another study found that emotional vitality (characterized by effective emotion regulation, positive energy, and positive well-being) in a large, nationally representative sample predicted lower risk of developing coronary heart disease 15 years later (Kubzansky and Thurston, 2007). While there are many studies of stroke and CVD, one complication within this literature is that well-being is a broad construct assessed in numerous ways, such as energy/vitality, positive expectations, positive feelings about something specific, hope, optimism, and more (e.g., Leedham, Meyerowitz, Muirhead, and Frist, 1995; Scheier et al., 1989). The use of such differing measures convolutes the literature because PA may have different effects on CVD versus other positive constructs that may tap into stable personality traits or cognitive expectations. Thus, it makes it difficult for interventionists, researchers, and practitioners to know what types of positive skills and experiences to focus on, since the active positive ingredients remain unclear. Standardized emotion measurement tools utilized across studies would help greatly in this vein. Also problematic is the vast literature on NA components and cardiovascular disorder (e.g., hostility, depression, anxiety; T. Q. Miller et al., 1996; Suls and Bunde, 2005). Given the known risks tied to these negative feelings, studies must be diligent in separating out the effects of known risks from the positive measures so that researchers can better understand whether these effects are independent, interactive, or overlapping.

Survival

Survival studies of PA are conducted with individuals who have serious, often fatal, illnesses. Researchers take baseline assessments in already diagnosed patients, and then follow them over time (over the course of months or years) to determine whether PA leads to a longer lifespan. Overall, this literature is more mixed than the longevity and morbidity literatures, although this may be related to the sometime use of weak PA measures (single item questions; e.g., Scherer and Herrmann-Lingen, 2009), few replications of the same illness, and a lack of consideration for *when* and *how* PA might be helpful (e.g., in what types of diseases and at what stage of disease). When considering the latter, that is, characteristics of the disease, Pressman and Cohen (2005) noted that PA seems to be most helpful in early stages of disease and for illnesses with better prognoses. For example, individuals with diabetes (Moskowitz, Epel, and Acree, 2008), HIV-positive women (Ickovics et al., 2006), and outpatients with heart disease (Hoen, Denollet, de Jonge, and Whooley, 2013) have all been found to have longer survival when reporting higher PA at the baseline of the study, even after accounting for a host of disease-related covariates (e.g., illness severity, medication, physiological function). A strong example of this type of finding is a study by Moskowitz (2003) who showed that HIV-positive men with high PA at baseline had a lower risk of mortality over a 7.5 year follow-up, even after controlling for NA and critical health covariates.

The influence of PA on advanced diseases is more mixed. Some studies have found PA to be detrimental to survival (e.g., Devins et al., 1990), whereas others have found some positive emotions to be beneficial. For example, Levy, Lee, Bagley, and Lippman (1988) found that in recurrent breast cancer patients with an average survival time of two years, only the joy subscores from the Affect Balance Scale predicted longer survival as compared to overall PA or NA. It has also been shown that certain high arousal positive emotions like vigor and pep are more helpful for advanced diseases like congestive heart failure and end-stage renal disease (e.g., Kalantar-Zadeh, Kopple, Block, and Humphreys, 2001; Konstam et al., 1996; Parkerson and Gutman, 2000). While few studies have examined the effects of specific positive emotions on survival, we advocate for studies to take greater pains in examining the "active ingredients" of positive constructs in future studies so that health-promoting interventions in these samples can be better targeted at the specific emotions that will make a difference in patient wellness. This issue will be further pursued in the future directions section of this chapter.

High PA may also be specifically harmful for those with "end-stage" diseases that have high short-term mortality rates because the affect type does not match the needs of the situation. High PA in the face of a life-threatening disease may indicate that individuals are taking their disease less seriously, which may result in less adherence to suggested treatments, decreased frequency of doctor visits, and/or less attention to changing health symptoms. However, PA may be helpful for individuals with diseases that have longer-term expectations for living, since behavioral factors influenced by PA such as sleep, exercise, and adherence to medical regimen play a larger role in these diseases (e.g., Ickovics et al., 2006; Moskowitz, 2003; van Domburg, Pedersen, van den Brand, and Erdman, 2001). Furthermore, slight alterations in stress, immune, and cardiovascular function known to occur with heightened state PA may serve some benefit (see review by Pressman and Cohen, 2005).

Given the complex interplay between disease course, type of PA, stress, and numerous other factors, future theory-based work on the connections between PA, adherence, and health behaviors of diseased populations is warranted, as is work that replicates findings within diseases. It will only be with thoughtful work in this vein that we will be able to truly unpack when PA is helpful versus harmful and how to take advantage of this information to maximize health in these ill samples.

Self-Reported Health Outcomes

PA has consistently been connected with reduced reports of symptoms and better self-reported health (e.g., Pettit, Kline, Gencoz, Gencoz, and Joiner, 2001). These effects have been replicated across a variety of disease populations, including patients with coronary artery disease (Sullivan et al., 2001) and upper respiratory infection (Cohen et al., 2003). There is also evidence that patients who report less PA report more medically unexplained symptoms, or symptoms that cannot be explained by health-care professionals (De Gucht, Fischler, and Heiser, 2004). In addition to generalized symptoms, both state and trait PA have been associated with lower levels of self-reported pain, in both diseased and healthy populations. One study conducted with women with osteoarthritis and/or fibromyalgia (two conditions characterized by chronic pain) found that higher levels of PA predicted lower levels of pain in following weeks. PA also resulted in less NA both directly and in interaction with pain and stress (Zautra et al., 2005). Furthermore, a daily diary study of 41 adults with sickle-cell disease determined that PA was associated with lower levels of pain, both on the same day and subsequent day (Gil et al., 2004). PA also appears to mediate the relationship between resiliency and pain catastrophizing (i.e., an exaggerated response to actual or anticipated pain), such that experiences of positive emotion by resilient individuals result in lower daily pain catastrophizing (Ong, Zautra, and Reid, 2010). While clearly there are strong ties between PA and pain, one of the concerns with these types of studies is that symptoms and pain are solely measured through subjective self-report, which can be confounded with personality traits such as neuroticism (Okun, 1984). Thus, these findings may not reflect objective physiologically based differences. Studies investigating the effects of PA on self-reported health outcomes must therefore be careful to control for factors such as these and should interpret their findings with caution. That being said, there are plausible biological mechanisms for these differences (e.g., differences in endorphins or opioid levels). Future research should try to extricate the subjective from the objective effects of PA on health in this literature.

Possible Pathways

Although it is evident that PA influences health in many different domains, the pathways through which this occurs are still unclear. There are currently two models that attempt to explain the underlying pathways between PA and health: the main effect hypothesis and the stress-buffering hypothesis (Pressman and Cohen, 2005). Both of these models include direct and indirect effects of emotion on health.

The main effect hypothesis posits that PA directly influences health through many pathways, the first being physiological via health-altering systems (e.g., immune, cardiovascular, endocrine; Pressman and Cohen, 2005). For example, greater trait PA has been associated with lower levels of IL-6, a proinflammatory cytokine connected with inflammation that can be harmful to health at high levels (Stellar et al., 2015). PA has also been tied to higher levels of beneficial antioxidants (Boehm and Kubzansky, 2012), lower blood pressure (Steptoe and Wardle, 2005), and reduced levels of potentially damaging stress hormones like cortisol (Jacobs et al., 2007; Steptoe, O'Donnell, Badrick, Kumari, and Marmot, 2008).

The main effect hypothesis also proposes that PA influences health via indirect behavioral pathways, such as social processes and health behaviors. Individuals who report higher levels of PA also report more and stronger social ties (Diener and Seligman, 2002; Lyubomirsky, King, and Diener, 2005) and specific positive emotions like gratitude may be especially beneficial in the context of relationships (Algoe, Gable, and Maisel, 2010; Algoe, Haidt, and Gable, 2008). Findings such as these support the broaden-and-build theory, which hypothesizes that PA can both broaden an individual's thinking and build personal resources (like relationships) which may in turn benefit future health (Fredrickson, 1998; 2001). Since social relationships are closely tied to physical wellness (Holt-Lunstad, Smith, and Layton, 2010), this becomes a likely pathway to better health for those high in PA. Beyond relationships, PA has also been shown to positively influence a variety of health behaviors, such as medication adherence (Ogedegbe et al., 2012), sleep (Ong et al., 2013), and physical activity (Garcia, Archer, Moradi, and Andersson-Arntén, 2012). It is of course well established that engaging in better health behaviors can lead directly to improved physical health, providing another likely connecting path between PA and better health.

Stress-altering effects are the second likely pathway connecting PA to health. This stress-buffering hypothesis states that PA may be *most* effective in stressful circumstances because it can decrease the negative psychological, physiological, and health consequences of stress (Pressman and Cohen, 2005). A recent example of this is a study of parents of children with developmental disorders (a high-stress sample), which found that those with higher PA had lower allostatic load (a measure of accumulated "wear and tear" across multiple systems in the body; Song et al., 2014). Similarly, PA may "undo" the negative effects of NA, such as leading to faster cardiovascular recovery after stress (Fredrickson and Levenson, 1998). For example, one study found that positive films shown after a fear-inducing film returned heightened cardiovascular arousal levels toward baseline more rapidly than neutral or sad films (Fredrickson and Levenson, 1998). Similarly, simply smiling during stress (a known positive emotion induction) can have similar cardiovascular recovery benefits (Kraft and Pressman, 2012). In addition to merely "undoing" negative effects of NA, Salovey and colleagues (2000) suggested that PA may actually allow individuals to build resources under stress, including resilience and endurance, potentially protecting them against future stressors. There is currently evidence for both the main effect and the stress-buffering hypotheses, and it is likely that both operate in tandem to influence health.

Future Directions

Although the broad connections between PA and health have been more widely researched in recent years, there are many exciting future directions for research on this topic.

Emotion Subtypes

Each emotion has a specific arousal level associated with it. For example, feeling excited and enthusiastic (high arousal PA) is associated with increased heart rate activity, while feeling peaceful and calm (low arousal PA) has the opposite effect (Pressman and Cohen, 2005; Shiota, Neufeld, Yeung, Moser, and Perea, 2011; Witvliet and Vrana, 1995). Most emotion research to date operates under the assumption that *any* type of PA can benefit any stressful context or stimuli, or a "one size fits all" main effect model. However, a handful of studies in health psychology have distinguished between the effects of high vs. low arousal emotions. One study investigated the effects of excitement induction or hypnosis (i.e., inducing a relaxed state) in patients with irritable bowel syndrome and found that excitement increased colon activity (harmful to those with this disorder), whereas hypnosis was associated with lower colon activity (Whorwell, Houghton, Taylor, and Maxton, 1992). On the other hand, arousal-based emotions were shown to be *helpful* to those with diabetes, but not for those with heart disease (Shirom, Toker, Jacobson, and Balicer, 2010). Given that high arousal PA is frequently measured in studies of health via the PANAS, and given that many studies have found it to be generally beneficial for health and longevity (Cohen et al., 2003; Pressman and Cohen, 2012), it is important for researchers to better understand when high activation PA is a healthful emotional state.

Beyond activation distinctions, there is also growing work examining specific positive emotions and physiological functioning. Most positive health research equates all positive emotion types as equal, but a recent study determined that there are different autonomic activation profiles for each of five distinct positive emotions: anticipatory enthusiasm, attachment love, nurturant love, amusement, and awe (Shiota et al., 2011). There are also a host of other positive emotions that are rarely studied in the context of health and physiology such as gratitude, elevation, inspiration, curiosity, and compassion. This leaves many open questions for researchers to test on the health impact of specific positive feelings.

Balancing PA and NA Ratios in Emotion Research

Researchers have long searched for the "magic" PA to NA ratio that allows individuals to lead overall happy lives. The 3:1 ratio posited by Fredrickson and Losada (2005) was long considered the "positivity ratio" that characterized when individuals were in flourishing mental health. However, the advanced math behind this ratio has recently come under scrutiny (N. J. L. Brown, Sokal, and Friedman, 2013), making the value and impact of the ratio approach unclear. Despite the controversy over the original work, the idea of an ideal PA to NA ratio is intriguing and echoes the non-benefits of PA during negative experiences. That is, in stressful contexts, it may be important to have some adaptive amount of negativity experienced alongside a healthy amount of positivity. Thus, we feel that it is warranted that researchers continue to measure both PA and NA in their studies, including a possible exploration of whether certain forms and amounts of affect balance serve greater benefits.

Cultural Differences and Affect Preferences

Most research on emotion and health has been conducted in industrialized, Western countries, leaving some question as to whether the effects of PA on health are universal. One recent study examined that question and indeed found that PA and NA exhibited unique, moderate effects on self-reported health in almost 150 different countries (Pressman et al., 2013). Interestingly, while PA was universally beneficial, the magnitude of the effect varied by country wealth such that PA–health connections were strongest in low-GDP countries. In a response to this work,

Curhan and colleagues (2014) raised the issue of considering culture in global studies of emotion and health. They found that NA more strongly predicted poor health in the United States as compared to Japan, possibly because NA is more acceptable in Japanese culture. Unfortunately, PA effects were not reported, and when examined in a larger sample, this effect was not replicated (Pressman, Gallagher, Lopez, and Campos, 2014). What did emerge, however, was that effect sizes for the association between PA and self-reported health were fairly stable across countries, including those with known differences in affect valuations (Pressman et al., 2014). Given the wide variability in how individuals want to feel across cultures (e.g., differences in ideal affect; Tsai, 2007), and the little work examining culture by emotion interactions in the context of health, future work needs to pay attention to this important and potentially critical difference.

A small body of work on the culturally influenced variable of ideal affect (i.e., the affect you *want* to feel) has indicated that it may also be important to health. For example, self-rated physical health was associated with values of ideal positive low-arousal affect over and above levels of actual affect, although this effect was not found for ideal preferences of positive high-arousal affect (Scheibe, English, Tsai, and Carstensen, 2013). Ideal affect may also influence health-care preferences. Sims and colleagues (2014) found that those who idealize and want to feel high arousal positive states are more likely to select a high arousal positive physician, and those who prefer low arousal positive feelings are more likely to select a calm practitioner. Actual affect, on the other hand, did not predict physician preference (Sims, Tsai, Koopmann-Holm, Thomas, and Goldstein, 2014). While physician preference is not a health outcome on its own, individuals who better like their physicians may be more likely to go to the doctor and engage in preventive care. Thus, there are many interesting pathways by which idealized affective states could play a role in health. It may be that wanting to feel a certain way alters the meaning and thus the influence of emotion on health, or alternatively, that desired emotions alter our behaviors and choices. Either way, this area of ideal affect and cultural differences in affect and affect preference is an interesting new direction for the field.

Direct Effects of Smiling

Another important area for research on PA and health is the connections between positive facial expressions and health. Smiling is commonly understood as an expression of experienced PA and has been utilized as a non self-report indicator of PA in past health studies (e.g., Fredrickson and Levenson, 1998). Interestingly, one theory takes the opposite view; the facial feedback hypothesis proposes that merely making a facial expression is enough to *create or alter* emotion (Tourangeau and Ellsworth, 1979). This finding has been utilized in a health context by manipulating smiling in the context of stress. Individuals did not know that they were smiling (they were told a cover story and held chopsticks in their mouths to activate the correct position), yet smilers had faster post-stress heart rate recovery versus non-smilers (Kraft and Pressman, 2012). While emotion induction may have been the pathway at play here (i.e., PA induction counteracted the effects of stress), this study found minimal emotional change, raising the question of whether the effect was due to direct facial muscle to heart pathways, such as the oculocardiac reflex (Tyrrell, Thayer, Friedman, Leibowitz, and Francis, 1995). This physiological finding has since been replicated in a study of needle injection pain (Pressman, Acevedo, Aucott, and Kraft, 2016), and researchers additionally found an over 40 percent reduction in self-reported needle pain when individuals were smiling. While provocative, a meta-analysis of the connections between various PA induction methods and self-reported moods suggested that facial expression was the weakest manipulation (Westermann, Spies, Stahl, and Hesse, 1996). Thus, benefits may be due to direct physiological pathways from facial muscle activity that work in tandem with more subtle emotional changes. Mechanistic studies using techniques like fMRI would be helpful in unpacking some of the subtleties of this emerging literature.

Hedonia vs. Eudaimonia

Philosophers since the time of Aristotle have distinguished between two "types" of well-being: hedonia and eudaimonia. Hedonia is more state-like and is the sum of positive experiences in the moment. Eudaimonia, on the other hand, is more trait-like and focuses on a deeper sense of well-being, such as purpose in life (Ryan and Deci, 2001; Waterman, 1993). Researchers have recently begun to investigate the connections between eudaimonic and hedonic well-being and health. For example, a recent review found that cardiovascular health is more consistently associated with hedonic well-being (Boehm and Kubzansky, 2012). However, Ryff and colleagues (2004) found the opposite: that eudaimonic, and *not* hedonic, well-being was connected with lower cardiovascular risk and daily salivary cortisol. Similarly, a recent study found that eudaimonia was connected with favorable gene-expression profiles in immune cells, but hedonia was not (Fredrickson et al., 2013), although the validity of this finding has been questioned (N. J. L. Brown, MacDonald, Samanta, Friedman, and Coyne, 2014), and there is ongoing debate (e.g., Cole and Fredrickson, 2014). Conflicting findings such as these may be due to the high correlations between eudaimonic and hedonic well-being, providing evidence that they are not distinct concepts and may in fact operate together (e.g., Kashdan, Biswas-Diener, and King, 2008). In addition, because of the ever growing number of positive variables in these areas, some call for parsimony in the measurement of well-being and even argue for a single, common calculation of subjective well-being (i.e., Sheldon, 2013), compatible with the model of Diener (1984), which has rarely been utilized in health research (see Xu and Roberts, 2010, for an exception).

Positivity Interventions

Largely due to the recent positive psychology movement (Seligman and Csikszentmihalyi, 2000), positivity focused interventions have become popular in order to achieve a variety of outcomes, including greater PA, reduced depressive symptoms, and even improvements in physical health. A meta-analysis of 51 positive psychology interventions found that, overall, the interventions were effective at increasing well-being and decreasing depressive symptoms (Sin and Lyubomirsky, 2009). Although there are many different kinds of positivity interventions, one of the largest literatures in the health arena examines benefits of various kinds of meditation in healthy and ill populations (e.g., Carlson, Speca, Patel, and Goodey, 2003). The goal of most forms of meditation (e.g., the popular Mindfulness Based Stress Reduction (MBSR) technique; Kabat-Zinn, 1982) is to relax and be fully present in the moment, which may include the induction of low arousal emotions such as calm, although this is rarely assessed. Thus, it is currently unclear whether meditation interventions are beneficial for health *because* of increases in PA or due to other mechanisms (e.g., reductions in NA or stress, activation of the parasympathetic nervous system). While MBSR does not purposely seek to increase

PA, another form of meditation, loving-kindness, specifically does (i.e., the focus is to increase warmth and caring for self and others). Critically, this technique has been shown to reduce pain, anger, and psychological distress in chronic low back pain patients (Carson et al., 2005) and depressive symptoms in healthy adults (Fredrickson, Cohn, Coffey, Pek, and Finkel, 2008). Furthermore, increases in PA from this technique predict increased vagal tone, an index of parasympathetic nervous system health (Kok and Fredrickson, 2010).

Aside from meditation, there are many other innovative interventions geared at increasing positivity such as well-being therapy (e.g., Fava and Ruini, 2003), expressive writing about past and current stresses (e.g., Broderick, Junghaenel, and Schwartz, 2005; Petrie, Fontanilla, Thomas, Booth, and Pennebaker, 2004), and writing about positive experiences (e.g., Burton and King, 2004). At this point in the field, these studies primarily focus on mental health outcomes or behavioral and self-reported health outcomes (e.g., health center visits, self-reported pain or sleep; Burton and King, 2004; Emmons and McCullough, 2003). PA interventions have also mostly been conducted in healthy populations; thus, there is a long way to go before this work can be fully implemented into medical practice. Researchers are beginning to design specific positivity-focused interventions to combat negative effects of illness (Moskowitz et al., 2012) and are developing sophistication in intervention implementation (Schueller, 2010). At this point, however, we know little about what type of PA is most beneficial for health and even less about whether certain types of PA might be most helpful for certain diseases and/or at certain points in a disease course. Thus, while this is an exciting future direction for the field, researchers should proceed with caution and pay attention to subtle nuances that may determine effects of PA-enhancing activities.

Technology, PA, and Health

Technology can provide researchers with unique methodologies for investigating the connections between PA and health. One methodology is ecological momentary assessment (EMA), which allows multiple precise measures of emotion across the course of a day and over extended periods of time. This methodology utilizes digital devices like cell phones or tablets so that participants can be alerted to fill out questionnaires repeatedly. One advantage of this method is that participants can make precise PA assessments in their natural environments as opposed to in a laboratory setting (Stone and Shiffman, 1994). It also allows for an examination of affect variability, which is connected to psychological health (e.g., Gruber, Kogan, Quoidbach, and Mauss, 2013). The downside is that EMA studies are sometimes viewed as annoying and intrusive because of the time commitment and repeated measurements. Another method has therefore emerged to try to deal with this problem: the electronically activated recorder (EAR). The EAR unobtrusively records snippets of sounds from participants' environments (Mehl, Pennebaker, Crow, Dabbs, and Price, 2001), which can then be analyzed in numerous ways. For PA assessment, researchers can code positive words or even positive behaviors like laughing. Both EMA and the EAR provide opportunities for researchers to gain better insight into the daily emotions of participants, and may even result in more accurate health predictions as compared to one-time in lab assessments.

Finally, there is growing interest in utilizing "big data" from websites such as Twitter and Facebook to investigate the connections between psychology and health. One PA-relevant study analyzed Twitter data and found that positive emotion words were protective against atherosclerotic heart disease at the community level (Eichstaedt et al., 2015). "Big data" methods such as these may be able to provide useful information across many health-relevant domains; thus, it will be interesting to see how this literature emerges over time as techniques to explore these public data sets become simple and accessible.

Conclusion

PA is beneficial across many different health domains, with only some exceptions, but there are still many unanswered questions. Researchers must move beyond simple tests of the connections between PA and health and consider more difficult designs and interpretations that can deal with issues of culture, positive measure type and method, stress context, and disease type. Researchers should also continue to play close attention to methodological concerns and criticisms in the study of affect and health, such as accurate measurement of PA, controlling for NA in analyses, and ensuring appropriate baseline assessments of health and PA-relevant covariates in their studies. In order to supplement self-report data, studies should consider the use of different measures of positive emotion such as facial expressions or language analysis, or even incorporate new technologies such as the EAR. By investigating PA and health in different domains, while also continuing to replicate past results, researchers can build a deeper understanding of when, for whom, and how PA is beneficial. This will not only advance the science of the field, but could also lead to targeted and effective PA-related interventions that improve the health of the populace in the not too distant future.

References

Abel, E. L., and Kruger, M. L. (2010). Smile intensity in photographs predicts longevity. *Psychological Science*, *21*(4), 542–544.

Algoe, S. B., Gable, S. L., and Maisel, N. C. (2010). It's the little things: Everyday gratitude as a booster shot for romantic relationships. *Personal Relationships*, *17*(2), 217–233.

Algoe, S. B., Haidt, J., and Gable, S. L. (2008). Beyond reciprocity: Gratitude and relationships in everyday life. *Emotion*, *8*(3), 425–429.

Beck, A. T., Shaw, B. F., Rush, A. J., and Emery, G. (1979). *Cognitive Therapy of Depression*. New York: Guilford Press.

Blazer, D. G., and Hybels, C. F. (2004). What symptoms of depression predict mortality in community-dwelling elders? *Journal of the American Geriatrics Society*, *52*(12), 2052–2056.

Boehm, J. K., and Kubzansky, L. D. (2012). The heart's content: The association between positive psychological well-being and cardiovascular health. *Psychological Bulletin*, *128*(4), 655–691.

Broderick, J. E., Junghaenel, D. U., and Schwartz, J. E. (2005). Written emotional expression produces health benefits in fibromyalgia patients. *Psychosomatic Medicine*, *67*(2), 326–334.

Brown, J. E., Butow, P. N., Culjak, G., Coates, A. S., and Dunn, S. M. (2000). Psychosocial predictors of outcome: Time to relapse and survival in patients with early stage melanoma. *British Journal of Cancer*, *83*(11), 1448–1453.

Brown, N. J. L., MacDonald, D. A., Samanta, M. P., Friedman, H. L., and Coyne, J. C. (2014). A critical reanalysis of the relationship between genomics and well-being. *Proceedings of the National Academy of Sciences*, *111*(35), 12705–12709.

Brown, N. J. L., Sokal, A. D., and Friedman, H. L. (2013). The complex dynamics of wishful thinking: The critical positivity ratio. *American Psychologist*, *68*(9), 801–813.

Burton, C. M., and King, L. A. (2004). The health benefits of writing about intensely positive experiences. *Journal of Research in Personality*, *38*(2), 150–163.

Carlson, L. E., Speca, M., Patel, K. D., and Goodey, E. (2003). Mindfulness-based stress reduction in relation to quality of life, mood, symptoms of stress, and immune parameters in breast and prostate cancer outpatients. *Psychosomatic Medicine*, *65*(4), 571–581.

Carson, J. W., Keefe, F. J., Lynch, T. R., Carson, K. M., Goli, V., Fras, A. M., and Thorp, S. R. (2005). Loving-kindness meditation for chronic low back pain: Results from a pilot trial. *Journal of Holistic Nursing, 23*(3), 287–304.

Cesari, M., Onder, G., Zamboni, V., Manini, T., Shorr, R. I., Russo, A., … Landi, F. (2008). Physical function and self-rated health status as predictors of mortality: Results from longitudinal analysis in the ilSIRENTE study. *BMC Geriatrics, 8*(34).

Chida, Y., and Steptoe, A. (2008). Positive psychological well-being and mortality: A quantitative review of prospective observational studies. *Psychosomatic Medicine, 70*(7), 741–756.

Cohen, S., Alper, C. M., Doyle, W. J., Treanor, J. J., and Turner, R. B. (2006). Positive emotional style predicts resistance to illness after experimental exposure to rhinovirus or influenza A virus. *Psychosomatic Medicine, 68*(6), 809–815.

Cohen, S., Doyle, W. J., Turner, R. B., Alper, C. M., and Skoner, D. P. (2003). Emotional style and susceptibility to the common cold. *Psychosomatic Medicine, 65*(4), 652–657.

Cohen, S., and Hoberman, H. (1983). Positive events and social supports as buffers of life change stress. *Journal of Applied Social Psychology, 13*(2), 99–125.

Cole, S. W., and Fredrickson, B. L. (2014). Errors in the Brown et al. critical analysis. *Proceedings of the National Academy of Sciences, 111*(35), E3581.

Creswell, J. D., Welch, W. T., Taylor, S. E., Sherman, D. K., Gruenewald, T. L., and Mann, T. (2005). Affirmation of personal values buffers neuroendocrine and psychological stress responses. *Psychological Science, 16*(11), 846–851.

Curhan, K. B., Sims, T., Markus, H. R., Kitayama, S., Karasawa, M., Kawakami, N., … Ryff, C. D. (2014). Just how bad negative affect is for your health depends on culture. *Psychological Science, 25*(12), 2777–2280.

Danner, D. D., Snowdon, D. A., and Friesen, W. V. (2001). Positive emotions in early life and longevity: Findings from the nun study. *Journal of Personality and Social Psychology, 80*(5), 804–813.

De Gucht, V., Fischler, B., and Heiser, W. (2004). Neuroticism, alexithymia, negative affect, and positive affect as determinants of medically unexplained symptoms. *Personality and Individual Differences, 36*(7), 1655–1667.

Devins, G. M., Mann, J., Mandin, H., Paul, L. C., Hons, R. B., Burgess, E. D., … Buckle, S. (1990). Psychosocial predictors of survival in end-stage renal disease. *The Journal of Nervous and Mental Disease, 178*(2), 127–133.

Diener, E. (1984). Subjective well-being. *Psychological Bulletin, 95*(3), 542–575.

Diener, E., and Chan, M. Y. (2011). Happy people live longer: Subjective well-being contributes to health and longevity. *Applied Psychology: Health and Well-Being, 3*(1), 1–43.

Diener, E., and Emmons, R. A. (1984). The independence of positive and negative affect. *Journal of Personality and Social Psychology, 47*(5), 1105–1117.

Diener, E., Larsen, R. J., Levine, S., and Emmons, R. A. (1985). Intensity and frequency: Dimensions underlying positive and negative affect. *Journal of Personality and Social Psychology, 48*(5), 1253–1265.

Diener, E., and Seligman, M. E. (2002). Very happy people. *Psychological Science, 13*(1), 81–84.

Eichstaedt, J. C., Schwartz, H. A., Kern, M. L., Park, G., Labarthe, D. R., Merchant, R. M., … Seligman, M. E. P. (2015). Psychological language on Twitter predicts county-level heart disease mortality. *Psychological Science, 26*(2), 159–169.

Eiser, C., and Morse, R. (2001). Can parents rate their child's health-related quality of life? Results of a systematic review. *Quality of Life Research, 10*(4), 347–357.

Emmons, R. A., and McCullough, M. E. (2003). Counting blessings versus burdens: An experimental investigation of gratitude and subjective well-being in daily life. *Journal of Personality and Social Psychology, 84*(2), 377–389.

Fava, G. A., and Ruini, C. (2003). Development and characteristics of a well-being enhancing psychotherapeutic strategy: Well-being therapy. *Journal of Behavior Therapy and Experimental Psychiatry, 34*(1), 45–63.

Fredman, L., Hawkes, W. G., Black, S., Bertrand, R. M., and Magaziner, J. (2006). Elderly patients with hip fracture with positive affect have better functional recovery over 2 years. *Journal of the American Geriatrics Society, 54*(7), 1074–1081.

Fredrickson, B. L. (1998). What good are positive emotions? *Review of General Psychology, 2*(3), 300–319.

Fredrickson, B. L. (2001). The role of positive emotions in positive psychology: The broaden-and-build theory of positive emotions. *American Psychologist, 56*(3), 218–226.

Fredrickson, B. L., Cohn, M. A., Coffey, K. A., Pek, J., and Finkel, S. M. (2008). Open hearts build lives: Positive emotions, induced through loving-kindness meditation, build consequential personal resources. *Journal of Personality and Social Psychology, 95*(5), 1045–1062.

Fredrickson, B. L., Grewen, K. M., Coffey, K. A., Algoe, S. B., Firestine, A. M., Arevalo, J. M. G., … Cole, S. W. (2013). A functional genomic perspective on human well-being. *Proceedings of the National Academy of Sciences*, *110*(33), 13684–13689.

Fredrickson, B. L., and Levenson, R. W. (1998). Positive emotions speed recovery from the cardiovascular sequelae of negative emotions. *Cognition and Emotion*, *12*(2), 191–220.

Fredrickson, B. L., and Losada, M. F. (2005). Positive affect and the complex dynamics of human flourishing. *American Psychologist*, *60*(7), 678–686.

Friedman, H. S., Tucker, J. S., Tomlinson-Keasey, C., Schwartz, J. E., Wingard, D. L., and Criqui, M. H. (1993). Does childhood personality predict longevity? *Journal of Personality and Social Psychology*, *65*(1), 176–185.

Garcia, D., Archer, T., Moradi, S., and Andersson-Arntén, A. C. (2012). Exercise frequency, high activation positive affect, and psychological well-being: Beyond age, gender, and occupation. *Psychology*, *3*(4), 328–336.

Gil, K. M., Carson, J. W., Porter, L. S., Scipio, C., Bediako, S. M., and Orringer, E. (2004). Daily mood and stress predict pain, health care use, and work activity in African American adults with sickle-cell disease. *Health Psychology*, *23*(3), 267–274.

Gruber, J., Kogan, A., Quoidbach, J., and Mauss, I. B. (2013). Happiness is best kept stable: Positive emotion variability is associated with poorer psychological health. *Emotion*, *13*(1), 1–6.

Harker, L., and Keltner, D. (2001). Expressions of positive emotion in women's college yearbook pictures and their relationship to personality and life outcomes across adulthood. *Journal of Personality and Social Psychology*, *80*(1), 112–124.

Hoen, P. W., Denollet, J., de Jonge, P., and Whooley, M. A. (2013). Positive affect and survival in patients with stable coronary heart disease: Findings from the Heart and Soul Study. *Journal of Clinical Psychiatry*, *74*(7), 716–722.

Holt-Lunstad, J., Smith, T. B., and Layton, J. B. (2010). Social relationships and mortality risk: A meta-analytic review. *PLoS Medicine*, *7*(7), e1000316.

Ickovics, J. R., Milan, S., Boland, R., Schoenbaum, E., Schuman, P., and Vlahov, D. (2006). Psychological resources protect health: 5-year survival and immune function among HIV-infected women from four US cities. *AIDS*, *20*(14), 1851–1860.

Idler, E. L., and Benyamini, Y. (1997). Self-rated health and mortality: A review of twenty-seven community studies. *Journal of Health and Social Behavior*, *38*(1), 21–37.

Jacobs, N., Myin-Germeys, I., Derom, C., Delespaul, P., van Os, J., and Nicolson, N. A. (2007). A momentary assessment study of the relationship between affective and adrenocortical stress responses in daily life. *Biological Psychology*, *74*(1), 60–66.

Janoff-Bulman, R., and Marshall, G. (1982). Mortality, well-being, and control: A study of a population of institutionalized aged. *Personality and Social Psychology Bulletin*, *8*(4), 691–698.

Kabat-Zinn, J. (1982). An out-patient program in behavioral medicine for chronic pain patients based on the practice of mindfulness meditation: Theoretical considerations and preliminary results. *General Hospital Psychiatry*, *4*(1), 33–47.

Kalantar-Zadeh, K., Kopple, J. D., Block, G., and Humphreys, M. H. (2001). Association among SF36 quality of life measures and nutrition, hospitalization, and mortality in hemodialysis. *Journal of the American Society of Nephrology*, *12*(12), 2797–2806.

Kashdan, T. B., Biswas-Diener, R., and King, L. A. (2008). Reconsidering happiness: The costs of distinguishing between hedonics and eudaimonia. *Journal of Positive Psychology*, *3*(4), 219–233.

Kawamoto, R., and Doi, T. (2002). Self-reported functional ability predicts three-year mobility and mortality in community-dwelling older persons. *Geriatrics and Gerontology International*, *2*(2), 68–74.

Kok, B. E., and Fredrickson, B. L. (2010). Upward spirals of the heart: Autonomic flexibility, as indexed by vagal tone, reciprocally and prospectively predicts positive emotions and social connectedness. *Biological Psychology*, *85*(3), 432–436.

Kolar, D. W., Funder, D. C., and Colvin, C. R. (1996). Comparing the accuracy of personality judgments by the self and knowledgeable others. *Journal of Personality*, *64*(2), 311–337.

Konstam, V., Salem, D., Pouleur, H., Kostis, J., Gorkin, L., Shumaker, S., … Yusuf, S. (1996). Baseline quality of life as a predictor of mortality and hospitalization in 5,025 patients with congestive heart failure. *American Journal of Cardiology*, *78*(8), 890–895.

Kraft, T. L., and Pressman, S. D. (2012). Grin and bear it: The influence of manipulated positive facial expression on the stress response. *Psychological Science*, *23*(11), 1372–1378.

Kubzansky, L. D., and Thurston, R. C. (2007). Emotional vitality and incident coronary heart disease. *Archives of General Psychiatry*, *64*(12), 1393–1401.

Leedham, B., Meyerowitz, B. E., Muirhead, J., and Frist, W. H. (1995). Positive expectations predict health after heart transplantation. *Health Psychology*, *14*(1), 74–79.

Levy, S. M., Lee, J., Bagley, C., and Lippman, M. (1988). Survival hazards analysis in first recurrent breast cancer patients: Seven-year follow-up. *Psychosomatic Medicine*, *50*(5), 520–528.

López-Pérez, B., and Wilson, E. L. (2015). Parent–child discrepancies in the assessment of children's and adolescents' happiness. *Journal of Experimental Child Psychology*, *139*, 249–255.

Lyubomirsky, S., King, L., and Diener, E. (2005). The benefits of frequent positive affect: Does happiness lead to success? *Psychological Bulletin*, *131*(6), 803–855.

Marsland, A. L., Cohen, S., Rabin, B. S., and Manuck, S. B. (2001). Associations between stress, trait negative affect, acute immune reactivity, and antibody response to Hepatitis B injection in healthy young adults. *Health Psychology*, *20*(1), 4–11.

Martin, L. R., Friedman, H. S., Tucker, J. S., Tomlinson-Keasey, C., Criqui, M. H., and Schwartz, J. E. (2002). A life course perspective on childhood cheerfulness and its relation to mortality risk. *Personality and Social Psychology Bulletin*, *28*(9), 1155–1165.

Matthews, K. A., Katholi, C. R., McCreath, H., Whooley, M. A., Williams, D. R., Zhu, S., and Markovitz, J. H. (2004). Blood pressure reactivity to psychological stress predicts hypertension in the CARDIA study. *Circulation*, *110*(1), 74–78.

McNair, D. M., Lorr, M., and Droppleman, L. F. (1971). *Profile of Mood States*. San Diego, CA: Educational and Industrial Testing Service.

Mehl, M. R., Pennebaker, J. W., Crow, D. M., Dabbs, J., and Price, J. H. (2001). The electronically activated recorded (EAR): A device for sampling naturalistic daily activities and conversations. *Behavior Research Methods, Instruments, and Computers*, *33*(4), 517–523.

Middleton, R. A., and Byrd, E. K. (1996). Psychosocial factors and hospital readmission status of older persons with cardiovascular disease. *Journal of Applied Rehabilitation Counseling*, *27*(4), 3–10.

Miilunpalo, S., Vuori, I., Oja, P., Pasanen, M., and Urponen, H. (1997). Self-rated health status as a health measure: The predictive value of self-reported health status on the use of physician services and on mortality in the working-age population. *Journal of Clinical Epidemiology*, *50*(5), 517–528.

Miller, G. E., and Blackwell, E. (2006). Turning up the heat: Inflammation as a mechanism linking chronic stress, depression, and heart disease. *Current Directions in Psychological Science*, *15*(6), 269–272.

Miller, T. Q., Smith, T. W., Turner, C. W., Guijarro, M. L., and Hallet, A. J. (1996). Meta-analytic review of research on hostility and physical health. *Psychological Bulletin*, *119*(2), 322–348.

Moreno, P. I., Moskowitz, A. L., Ganz, P. A., and Bower, J. E. (2016). Positive affect and inflammatory activity in breast cancer survivors: Examining the role of affective arousal. *Psychosomatic Medicine*, *78*(5), 532–41.

Moskowitz, J. T. (2003). Positive affect predicts lower risk of AIDS mortality. *Psychosomatic Medicine*, *65*(4), 620–626.

Moskowitz, J. T., Epel, E. S., and Acree, M. (2008). Positive affect uniquely predicts lower risk of mortality in people with diabetes. *Health Psychology*, *27*(1 Suppl.), S73–82.

Moskowitz, J. T., Hult, J. R., Duncan, L. G., Cohn, M. A., Maurer, S., Bussolari, C., and Acree, M. (2012). A positive affect intervention for people experiencing health-related stress: Development and non-randomized pilot test. *Journal of Health Psychology*, *17*(5), 676–692.

Ogedegbe, G. O., Boutin-Foster, C., Wells, M. T., Allegrante, J. P., Isen, A. M., Jobe, J. B., and Charlson, M. E. (2012). A randomized controlled trial of positive-affect intervention and medication adherence in hypertensive African Americans. *Archives of Internal Medicine*, *172*(4), 322–326.

Okun, M. A. (1984). Physician- and self-ratings of health, neuroticism and subjective well-being among men and women. *Personality and Individual Differences*, *5*(5), 533–539.

Ong, A. D., Exner-Cortens, D., Riffin, C., Steptoe, A., Zautra, A., and Almeida, D. M. (2013). Linking stable and dynamic features of positive affect to sleep. *Annals of Behavioral Medicine*, *46*(1), 52–61.

Ong, A. D., Zautra, A. J., and Reid, M. C. (2010). Psychological resilience predicts decreases in pain catastrophizing through positive emotions. *Psychology and Aging*, *25*(3), 516–523.

Ostir, G. V., Markides, K. S., Black, S. A., and Goodwin, J. S. (2000). Emotional well-being predicts subsequent functional independence and survival. *Journal of the American Geriatrics Society*, *48*(5), 473–478.

Ostir, G. V., Markides, K. S., Peek, M. K., and Goodwin, J. S. (2001). The association between emotional well-being and the incidence of stroke in older adults. *Psychosomatic Medicine*, *63*(2), 210–215.

Parkerson, G. R., and Gutman, R. A. (2000). Health-related quality of life predictors of survival and hospital utilization. *Health Care Financing Review*, *21*(3), 171–184.

Pennebaker, J. W., Francis, M. E., and Booth, R. J. (2001). *Linguistic Inquiry and Word Count (LIWC): LIWC2001.* Mahwah, NJ: Erlbaum.

Pennebaker, J. W., Mehl, M. R., and Niederhoffer, K. G. (2003). Psychological aspects of natural language use: Our words, our selves. *Annual Review of Psychology, 54*(1), 547–577.

Petrie, K. J., Fontanilla, I., Thomas, M. G., Booth, R. J., and Pennebaker, J. W. (2004). Effect of written emotional expression on immune function in patients with human immunodeficiency virus infection: A randomized trial. *Psychosomatic Medicine, 66*(2), 272–275.

Pettit, J. W., Kline, J. P., Gencoz, T., Gencoz, F., and Joiner, T. E., Jr. (2001). Are happy people healthier? The specific role of positive affect in predicting self-reported health symptoms. *Journal of Research in Personality, 35*(4), 521–536.

Pressman, S. D., Acevedo, A. M., Aucott, K., and Kraft, T. L. (2016). Reducing needle pain with facial expressions. MS under review.

Pressman, S. D., and Cohen, S. (2005). Does positive affect influence health? *Psychological Bulletin, 131*(6), 925–971.

Pressman, S. D., and Cohen, S. (2007). Use of social words in autobiographies and longevity. *Psychosomatic Medicine, 69*(3), 262–269.

Pressman, S. D., and Cohen, S. (2012). Positive emotion word use and longevity in famous deceased psychologists. *Health Psychology, 31*(3), 297–305.

Pressman, S. D., Gallagher, M., and Lopez, S. J. (2013). Is the emotion–health connection a "first world problem"? *Psychological Science, 24*(4), 544–549.

Pressman, S. D., Gallagher, M., Lopez, S. J., and Campos, B. (2014). Incorporating culture into the study of affect and health. *Psychological Science, 25*(12), 2281–2283.

Radloff, L. S. (1977). The CES-D scale: A self-report depression scale for research in the general population. *Journal of Applied Psychological Measurement, 1*(3), 385–401.

Rasmussen, H. N., Scheier, M. F., and Greenhouse, J. B. (2009). Optimism and physical health: A meta-analytic review. *Annals of Behavioral Medicine, 37*(3), 239–256.

Russell, J. A. (1980). A circumplex model of affect. *Journal of Personality and Social Psychology, 39*(6), 1161–1178.

Ryan, R. M., and Deci, E. L. (2001). On happiness and human potentials: A review of research on hedonic and eudaimonic well-being. *Annual Review of Psychology, 52*(1), 141–166.

Ryff, C. D., Singer, B. H., and Love, G. D. (2004). Positive health: Connecting well-being with biology. *Philosophical Transactions of the Royal Society B: Biological Sciences, 359*(1449), 1383–1394.

Salovey, P., Rothman, A. J., Detweiler, J. B., and Steward, W. T. (2000). Emotional states and physical health. *American Psychologist, 55*(1), 110–121.

Scheibe, S., English, T., Tsai, J. L., and Carstensen, L. L. (2013). Striving to feel good: Ideal affect, actual affect, and their correspondence across adulthood. *Psychology and Aging, 28*(1), 160–171.

Scheier, M. F., Matthews, K. A., Owens, J. F., Magovern, G. J., Lefebvre, R. C., Abbott, R. A., and Carver, C. S. (1989). Dispositional optimism and recovery from coronary artery bypass surgery: The beneficial effects on physical and psychological well-being. *Journal of Personality and Social Psychology, 57*(6), 1024–1040.

Scherer, M., and Herrmann-Lingen, C. (2009). Single item on positive affect is associated with 1-year survival in consecutive medical inpatients. *General Hospital Psychiatry, 31*(1), 8–13.

Schueller, S. M. (2010). Preferences for positive psychology exercises. *Journal of Positive Psychology, 5*(3), 192–203.

Seder, J. P., and Oishi, S. (2011). Intensity of smiling in Facebook photos predicts future life satisfaction. *Social Psychological and Personality Science, 3*(4), 407–413.

Seligman, M. E. P., and Csikszentmihalyi, M. (2000). Positive psychology: An introduction. *American Psychologist, 55*(1), 5–14.

Sephton, S. E., Sapolsky, R. M., Kraemer, H. C., and Spiegel, D. (2000). Diurnal cortisol rhythm as a predictor of breast cancer survival. *Journal of the National Cancer Institute, 92*(12), 994–1000.

Sheehan, T. J., Fifield, J., Reisine, S., and Tennen, H. (1995). The measurement structure of the Center for Epidemiologic Studies Depression Scale. *Journal of Personality Assessment, 64*(3), 507–521.

Sheldon, K. M. (2013). Individual daimon, universal needs, and subjective well-being: Happiness as the natural consequence of a live well lived. In A. S. Waterman (ed.), *The Best within Us: Positive Psychology Perspectives on Eudaimonia (119–137)*. Washington, DC: American Psychological Association.

Shiota, M. N., Neufeld, S. L., Yeung, W. H., Moser, S. E., and Perea, E. F. (2011). Feeling good: Autonomic nervous system responding in five positive emotions. *Emotion, 11*(6), 1368–1378.

Shirom, A., Toker, S., Jacobson, O., and Balicer, R. D. (2010). Feeling vigorous and the risks of all-cause mortality, ischemic heart disease, and diabetes: A 20-year follow-up of healthy employees. *Psychosomatic Medicine*, *72*(8), 727–733.

Sims, T., Tsai, J. L., Koopmann-Holm, B., Thomas, E. A. C., and Goldstein, M. K. (2014). Choosing a physician depends on how you want to feel: The role of ideal affect in health-related decision making. *Emotion*, *14*(1), 187–192.

Sin, N. L., and Lyubomirsky, S. (2009). Enhancing well-being and alleviating depressive symptoms with positive psychology interventions: A practice-friendly meta-analysis. *Journal of Clinical Psychology*, *65*(5), 467–487.

Smith, A. M., Stuart, M. J., Wiese-Bjornstal, D. M., and Gunnon, C. (1997). Predictors of injury in ice hockey players. a multivariate, multidisciplinary approach. *American Journal of Sports Medicine*, *25*(4), 500–507.

Song, J., Mailick, M. R., Ryff, C. D., Coe, C. L., Greenberg, J. S., and Hong, J. (2014). Allostatic load in parents of children with developmental disorders: Moderating influence of positive affect. *Journal of Health Psychology*, *19*(2), 262–272.

Stellar, J. E., John-Henderson, N., Anderson, C. L., Gordon, A. M., McNeil, G. D., and Keltner, D. (2015). Positive affect and markers of inflammation: Discrete positive emotions predict lower levels of inflammatory cytokines. *Emotion*, *15*(2), 129–133.

Steptoe, A., O'Donnell, K., Badrick, E., Kumari, M., and Marmot, M. G. (2008). Neuroendocrine and inflammatory factors associated with positive affect in healthy men and women: Whitehall II study. *American Journal of Epidemiology*, *167*(1), 96–102.

Steptoe, A., and Wardle, J. (2005). Positive affect and biological function in everyday life. *Neurobiology of Aging*, *26*(1), 108–112.

Steptoe, A., and Wardle, J. (2011). Positive affect measured using ecological momentary assessment and survival in older men and women. *Proceedings of the National Academy of Sciences*, *108*(45), 18244–18248.

Stone, A. A., and Shiffman, S. (1994). Ecological momentary assessment (EMA) in behavioral medicine. *Annals of Behavioral Medicine*, *16*(3), 199–202.

Stones, M. J., Dornan, B., and Kozma, A. (1989). The prediction of mortality in elderly institution residents. *Journals of Gerontology*, *44*(3), P72–P79.

Strine, T. W., Chapman, D. P., Balluz, L. S., Moriarty, D. G., and Mokdad, A. H. (2008). The associations between life satisfaction and health-related quality of life, chronic illness, and health behaviors among US community-dwelling adults. *Journal of Community Health*, *33*(1), 40–50.

Sullivan, M. D., LaCroix, A. Z., Russo, J. E., and Walker, E. A. (2001). Depression and self-reported physical health in patients with coronary disease: Mediating and moderating factors. *Psychosomatic Medicine*, *63*(2), 248–256.

Suls, J., and Bunde, J. (2005). Anger, anxiety, and depression as risk factors for cardiovascular disease: The problems and implications of overlapping affective dispositions. *Psychological Bulletin*, *131*(2), 260–300.

Tourangeau, R., and Ellsworth, P. C. (1979). The role of facial response in the experience of emotion. *Journal of Personality and Social Psychology*, *37*(9), 1519–1531.

Tsai, J. (2007). Ideal affect: Cultural causes and behavioral consequences. *Perspectives on Psychological Science*, *2*(3), 242–259.

Tyrrell, R. A., Thayer, J. F., Friedman, B. H., Leibowitz, H. W., and Francis, E. L. (1995). A behavioral link between the oculomotor and cardiovascular systems. *Integrative Physiological and Behavioral Science*, *30*(1), 46–67.

van Domburg, R. T., Pedersen, S. S., van den Brand, M. J. B. M., and Erdman, R. A. M. (2001). Feelings of being disabled as a predictor of mortality in men 10 years after percutaneous coronary transluminal angioplasty. *Journal of Psychosomatic Research*, *51*(3), 469–477.

Ware, J. E., and Sherbourne, C. D. (1992). The MOS 36-item short-form health survey (SF-36): I. Conceptual framework and item selection. *Medical Care*, *30*, 473–483.

Waterman, A. S. (1993). Two conceptions of happiness: Contrasts of personal expressiveness (eudaimonia) and hedonic enjoyment. *Journal of Personality and Social Psychology*, *64*(4), 678–691.

Watson, D. (1988). The vicissitudes of mood measurement: Effects of varying descriptors, time frames, and response formats on measures of positive and negative affect. *Journal of Personality and Social Psychology*, *55*(1), 128–141.

Watson, D., and Clark, L. A. (1991). Preliminary manual for the Positive and Negative Affect Schedule (Expanded Form). MS, Southern Methodist University, Dallas, Texas.

Watson, D., Clark, L. A., and Tellegen, A. (1988). Development and validation of brief measures of positive and negative affect: The PANAS scales. *Journal of Personality and Social Psychology*, *54*(6), 1063–1070.

Westermann, R., Spies, K., Stahl, G., and Hesse, F. W. (1996). Relative effectiveness and validity of mood induction procedures: A meta-analysis. *European Journal of Social Psychology*, *26*(4), 557–580.

Witvliet, C. V., and Vrana, S. R. (1995). Psychophysiological responses as indices of affective dimensions. *Psychophysiology*, *32*(5), 436–443.

Whorwell, P. J., Houghton, L. A., Taylor, E. E., and Maxton, D. G. (1992). Physiological effects of emotion: Assessment via hypnosis. *Lancet*, *340*(8811), 69–72.

Wojcik, S. P., Hovasapian, A., Graham, J., Motyl, M., and Ditto, P. H. (2015). Conservatives report, but liberals display, greater happiness. *Science*, *347*(6227), 1243–1246.

Xu, J., and Roberts, R. E. (2010). The power of positive emotions: It's a matter of life or death – subjective well-being and longevity over 28 years in a general population. *Health Psychology*, *29*(1), 9–19.

Zautra, A. J., Johnson, L. M., and Davis, M. C. (2005). Positive affect as a source of resilience for women in chronic pain. *Journal of Consulting and Clinical Psychology*, *73*(2), 212–220.

Part Two

Impact of Stress on Health

6

Work, Stress, and Cardiovascular Disease

Peter L. Schnall, Marnie Dobson, and Paul Landsbergis

Introduction

In this chapter, we explore the relationship between work stress and cardiovascular disease (CVD) and CVD risk factors, with an emphasis on hypertension. First, we provide an overview of the epidemiology of CVD and CVD risk factors, highlighting their relationship to evolving forms of modern production and work organization. We then discuss the concept of work stress, including possible physiological mechanisms which may explain how work stressors lead to CVD. We review the large body of research linking work stressors to CVD and its risk factors. We also include a brief discussion of the changing nature of work resulting from globalization processes, including increases in precarious work and job insecurity, and review the evidence that links these work stressors to CVD (see Figure 6.1). Lastly, we examine strategies for the prevention and management of CVD at the workplace, including programs for risk assessment (e.g., surveillance), management of CVD (e.g., return to work programs) and reduction in CVD risk factors (worksite health promotion), as well as primary prevention efforts, including job redesign and legislation, to prevent work stressors.

The Epidemiology of CVD

CVD accounts for about 30 percent of all global deaths and is the leading cause of morbidity and mortality in all developing regions of the world, with one exception – sub-Saharan Africa, where CVD is the leading cause of death in people over 45 years (Gaziano and Gaziano, 2012; Gaziano et al., 2010). In the United States, CVD results in the loss, on average, of seven years of life expectancy (R. N. Anderson, 1999). In China, a rapidly developing middle-income country, CVD, which accounted for only 12 percent of all deaths in 1957, accounted for 40 percent in 2012 (European Society of Cardiology, 2012; L. Liu, 2007). Hypertension, the number one risk

The Handbook of Stress and Health: A Guide to Research and Practice, First Edition.
Edited by Cary L. Cooper and James Campbell Quick.
© 2017 John Wiley & Sons, Ltd. Published 2017 by John Wiley & Sons, Ltd.

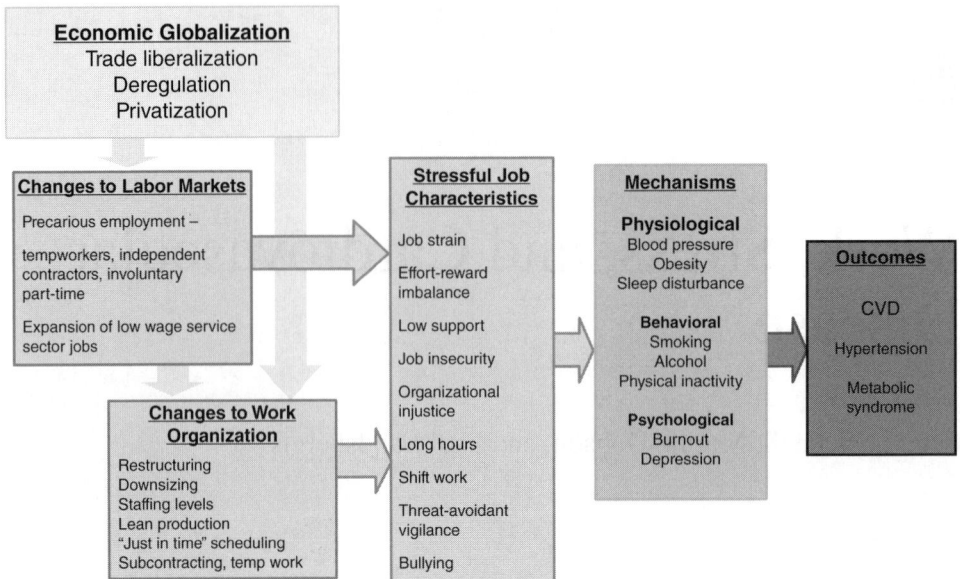

Figure 6.1 Work, psychosocial stressors, and CVD. *Source*: Adapted from Landsbergis et al. (2011); NIOSH (2002).

factor for CVD, affects more than 1 billion adults (26 percent of the world's adult population). Hypertension prevalence is steadily increasing in both developed and developing countries, with a projected worldwide prevalence of 1.56 billion adults (29 percent) by 2025 (Kearney et al., 2005).

CVD and its risk factors, including hypertension, obesity, diabetes and metabolic syndrome, have become global epidemics increasing in tandem with rapid urbanization, industrialization, and economic globalization (Gaziano and Gaziano, 2012; Gaziano et al., 2010). Economic globalization is characterized by profound changes in labor markets and work organization (Moutsatsos, 2009), including increases in work-related psychosocial stressors (Johnson, 2007; 2009).

Origins of Psychosocial Work Stress Models

Our understanding of the importance of occupational stress in the etiology of CVD took an important step forward when, in 1976, Robert Karasek combined two research traditions: (a) a focus on environmental demands that came from research on the health impacts of stressful life events (Holmes and Rahe, 1967), and (b) industrial/organizational (I/O) psychology's focus on the motivating effects of job characteristics, such as autonomy and variety (Hackman and Lawler, 1971). Karasek's model of stress at work combined high psychological work demands with low job decision latitude or control, into a concept he called "job strain" (Karasek and Theorell, 1990). Further progress in identifying work-related stress factors occurred in the 1990s when Johannes Siegrist developed the effort–reward imbalance (ERI) model (Siegrist, 1996), which defines deleterious job conditions as a mismatch between high efforts spent and low rewards received (Siegrist et al., 2004). "Reward" includes concepts such as income, "esteem reward" (respect, support), and "status control" (promotion prospects, job security). Along with job strain and ERI, the most widely studied models of work stress in relationship to CVD are shift work, long work hours, support/isostrain, job insecurity/precariousness, threat-avoidant vigilant work, and organizational justice. Several other sources of stress at work, including work–family imbalance/spillover and emotional labor, have not yet been studied extensively in relationship to CVD but they may also play a role.

Physiological Mechanisms

Most psychosocial work stressors incorporate some version of "control" as a constituent variable. For example, the job strain model measures decision latitude over work tasks such as control over work pace and the use of skills on the job, while in the ERI model, control is operationalized as "status control," including job security and advancement opportunities.

There are now several theories supported by substantial research, including laboratory studies, shedding light on the potential physiological mechanisms by which the above-mentioned work stressors affect the body and health. Frankenhaeuser and colleagues, building on the work of Henry and Stephens (1977), provided evidence that two neuroendocrine systems were part of the biological stress response – the sympathoadrenal medullary system (SMS, which secretes catecholamines, epinephrine and norepinephrine), and the hypothalamic-pituitary-adrenal cortical system (HPA axis, which secretes corticosteroids, such as cortisol). Under conditions of high demand over which organisms cannot exert control, analogous to "job strain," both epinephrine and cortisol levels are elevated. Under demanding conditions where organisms can exert control, epinephrine levels increase but cortisol levels do not (Frankenhaeuser and Johansson, 1986). In the short term, raised levels of cortisol and adrenaline play an important and helpful role in coping with stressful situations. However, chronic exposure to elevated levels of catecholamines and cortisol has severe consequences, including promoting blood pressure levels, dyslipidemia, and myocardial pathology (Schnall, Belkić, Landsbergis, and Baker, 2000). Repetitive and machine-paced jobs, and excessive overtime, tend to prolong "unwinding," the return of neuroendocrine levels to baseline.

Sterling and Eyer developed the term "allostasis" in 1988 and expanded theories of stress to include the physiological consequences of chronic exposure (Sterling and Eyer, 1988). The concept of allostasis was broadened by McEwen and Stellar to include "allostatic load," which describes the "wear and tear on the body" of being exposed to the physiological consequences of chronic exposure to stress, including heightened and fluctuating neural mechanisms and neuroendocrine responses (Schnorpfeil et al., 2003; McEwen, 1998; McEwen and Stellar, 1993). Allostasis – the idea that stressful environmental conditions can cause sustained physiological arousal – captures the observed relationship between stressful work exposures such as job strain, ERI, and job insecurity and heightened signs of arousal assessed by elevations of blood pressure or cortisol. The allostasis model does not explicitly focus on control over the environment and thus is less consistent than the aforementioned model put forth by Marianne Frankenhaeuser that examines the job demands–control (job strain) model of work stress and other work stress models with a focus on "control." However, the allostasis model has contributed to our understanding of the consequences of prolonged physiological arousal, which include chronic changes in human physiology (hypertension) and anatomic changes such as hypertrophy of artery walls (Devereux, 1989; Devereux and Pickering, 1991; Devereux et al., 1983), as well as atherosclerosis and CVD.

Literature Review

Work Stressors and CVD

Job strain   The most frequently studied work stressor in relationship to CVD for the past 30 years has been job strain. Most reviews and meta-analyses show evidence of a strong, positive relationship (Belkić, Landsbergis, Schnall, and Baker, 2004; Kivimäki et al., 2006b; Backé et al., 2012), particularly among men. In a 2012 review of 13 cohort studies, seven showed a significant effect of job strain on CVD risk (Backé et al., 2012). In a pooled individual-participant data (IPD) meta-analysis of 13 European cohort studies representing 197,473 participants, a hazard ratio of 1.23 for job strain and incident coronary heart disease was observed after adjustment for age and sex (Kivimäki et al., 2012). However, this finding is likely an underestimate of the true risk due to the existence of several biases toward the null in many of the studies included (Choi et al., 2015).

An additional IPD meta-analysis, including cohorts from the US and Australia as well as Europe, also found a significant effect of job strain on incident ischemic stroke (hazard ratio (HR) 1.24; 95% confidence interval (CI) 1.05–1.47), although the effect was slightly lower after adjusting for socioeconomic status (SES) (HR 1.18; CI 1.00–1.39) (Fransson et al., 2015). Steptoe and Kivimäki report in a recent review article a 1.3 fold excess risk of CVD for job strain (also likely to be an underestimate of the true risk) and they argued that "adverse metabolic changes are one of the underlying plausible mechanisms" (Steptoe and Kivimäki, 2013).

In general, the few studies of job strain and CVD that have examined interaction with SES have found more consistent and stronger associations among blue-collar workers (Johnson and Hall, 1988; Theorell et al., 1998), with risk ratios as high as 10 (Hallqvist et al., 1998). Findings have varied for men and women, however; in the recent IPD meta-analysis (Kivimäki et al., 2012), the authors found no significant effect modification of the job strain–CVD association by gender or SES.

Effort–reward imbalance   Although there are fewer studies to date of the ERI model than job strain, ERI has consistently been associated with CVD. In 2005, a systematic review of 11 prospective studies concluded that workers with ERI were twice as likely to suffer from incident CVD (Siegrist, 2005). Evidence was stronger for men than for women. Backé et al. (2012) found that all reviewed papers, including three published prospective cohort studies of ERI and CVD, had statistically significant associations. In one study examining an ERI–SES interaction, the authors found that the combination of ERI and lower SES was more strongly associated with CVD than the combination of ERI and higher SES (Kuper, Singh-Manouz, Siegrist, and Marmot, 2002).

Social support   Lack of social support and absence of social networks are both established independent risk factors for CVD in men and women, although support is conceptualized and measured in different ways in this literature (Lett et al., 2005). The concept of "isostrain" – work characterized by the presence of job strain (high demands and low control) coupled with low levels of supervisor and/or coworker support, was introduced by Jeffrey Johnson in the late 1980s (Johnson and Theorell, 1987). The combination of job strain and social isolation among Swedish working men was associated with CVD morbidity and mortality with an age-adjusted prevalence ratio (PR) of 1.77, while among blue-collar workers the PR was 2.04 (Johnson and Hall, 1988; Johnson, Hall, and Theorell, 1989). A review of studies of isostrain and CVD conducted in 2004 generally found, compared to job strain alone, that workers with low support at work and job strain were at a further increased risk (Belkić et al., 2004). Recent reviews reached the same conclusions (Eller et al., 2009; Pejtersen et al., 2015). During the past decade, studies of isostrain have tended to focus less on CVD and more on possible mediating outcomes of CVD such as sleep disturbances (Chazelle, Chastang, and Niedhammer, 2015), exhaustion (Lindeberg et al., 2011), and the metabolic syndrome (Chandola, Brunner, and Marmot, 2006). Unfortunately, it appears that the use of social support as an exposure/moderator variable in studies of CVD has been on the wane in recent years despite what appears to be a consistently positive set of findings.

Organizational justice   A recently introduced work stress concept, organizational justice has not yet been extensively investigated in relationship to CVD. Various definitions have been advanced including "whether or not decision-making procedures (in the workplace) are consistently applied, correctable, ethical, and include input from affected parties (procedural justice). It also refers to respectful, considerate and fair treatment of people by supervisors (relational justice)" (Muntaner et al., 2006). Several studies have examined organizational justice and CVD (Elovainio, Leino-Arjas, Vahtera, and Kivimäki, 2006b; De Vogli et al., 2007; Kivimäki et al., 2005) and cardiovascular reactivity (Elovainio et al., 2006a). In a prospective cohort study of 800 Finnish factory workers, with a mean follow-up of 25 years, Elovainio et al. (2006b) found that, after adjusting for standard risk factors and other work stress factors, employees reporting high justice at work had a 45 percent lower risk of CVD mortality than those with low or intermediate justice. In the British Whitehall study, those with higher levels of unfairness were more likely to experience an incident coronary event (HR 1.55, CI 1.11 to 2.17) (De Vogli et al., 2007), and in another Whitehall analysis, "relational justice" (the presence of primarily supervisor support) was associated with reduced risk of CVD (Kivimäki et al., 2005). This is a promising concept worthy of further research.

Threat-avoidant vigilant work   TAV (Belkić et al., 1992) involves an individual continuously maintaining a high level of vigilance in order to avoid disaster, such as loss of human life, and is a feature of a number of occupations at high risk for CVD, for example urban mass transit operators, truck drivers, air traffic controllers, and sea pilots. The strongest evidence for this risk factor comes from studies of single occupations, where professional drivers, particularly urban transit operators, emerge as the occupation with the most consistent evidence of elevated risk of hypertension and CVD (Belkić, Emdad, and Theorell, 1998; Tuchsen, 2000; Davila et al., 2012).

Long work hours   "Karoshi" is the term coined by Japanese researchers for CVD death due to long hours of demanding work and is a well recognized entity in Japan (Shimomitsu and Odagiri, 2000), also becoming acknowledged elsewhere, including in China (Oster, 2014). Previous research suggested working more than 60 hours per week may increase risk of heart disease (Y. Liu and Tanaka, 2002; Sokejima and Kagamimori, 1998; Virtanen et al., 2010);

however, more recent and robust studies have shown effects on CVD at 55 or even 50 hours per week.

A 2012 IPD meta-analysis (including one cross-sectional, seven case control, and four prospective studies) showed an adjusted relative risk of 1.8 (CI 1.42–2.29) for "long work hours" (ranging from >40 to >65 hours/week) and coronary heart disease (CHD) (Virtanen et al., 2012). In a subgroup analysis of the IPD data, those working over 50 hours/week or >10 hours/day had a relative risk (RR) of 2.37 (CI 1.56–3.59) compared to those working less than 50 hours/week or 10 hours/day (RR 1.41, CI 1.14–1.74) (Virtanen et al., 2012). In 2015, two meta-analytic studies using cohorts with individual-participant data from Europe, US and Australia showed significant associations between long work hours (>55 hours/week) and CHD (RR 1.13, CI 1.02–1.26), incident stroke (RR 1.33, CI 1.11–1.61) and diabetes (RR 1.29, CI 1.06–1.57), particularly within low SES groups (Kivimäki et al., 2015a; Kivimäki et al., 2015b). Little is known yet about prolonged exposure to stressful working conditions; individuals in jobs with both long work hours and exposure to work stressors such as job strain may experience greater accelerated disease processes (Michie and Cockcroft, 1996; Belkić, Schnall, Savic, and Landsbergis, 2000).

Shift work   Work schedules involving irregular hours compared to those of normal daytime work hours, referred to as "shift work," can involve night work, as well as rotating work schedules that can vary week to week or day to day. Night shift work is implicated in CVD risk; shift workers had an estimated 40 percent increased CVD risk compared to day workers (Boggild and Knutsson, 1999). A 2011 review concluded that there was moderate evidence for, but not "conclusive evidence" of an association between shift work and CVD (Wang et al., 2011). Similarly, a recent meta-analysis of 34 studies showed moderate and significant associations between shift work and myocardial infarction (RR 1.23, CI 1.15–1.31), ischemic stroke (RR 1.05, CI 1.01–1.09), and coronary events (RR 1.24, CI 1.10–1.39) (Vyas et al., 2012).

Work stressors and recurrent CVD   A recent meta-analysis found a significant association between work stress measured by "job strain" and recurrent coronary heart disease, with a hazard ratio of 1.65 (CI 1.23–2.22) (Li et al., 2014). The meta-analysis included four prospective studies from Sweden and Canada and was based on the demand–control model (Theorell et al., 1991; Orth-Gomer et al., 2000; Aboa-Éboulé et al., 2007; Laszlo et al., 2010) and the effort–reward imbalance model (Aboa-Éboulé et al., 2011). For example, a four-year prospective study showed that workers returning to work after a myocardial infarction (heart attack) who returned to jobs with high ERI (HR 1.75, CI 0.99–3.08) or low reward (HR 1.77, CI 1.16–2.71) were at increased risk of a second heart attack (Aboa-Éboulé et al., 2011).

Work Stressors and Hypertension

Raised blood pressure at work is a mechanism that can at least partly explain the relationship between workplace stressors and CVD. Evidence for such a mechanism began accumulating in the early 1980s, when ambulatory blood pressure (ABP) monitoring showed that BP is higher at work compared to hours not at work (Pickering et al., 1982; Pieper, Schnall, Warren, and Pickering, 1993; del Arco-Galan, Suarez-Fernandez, and Gabriel-Sanchez, 1994). Subsequently it was learned that ABP is a much better predictor of target organ damage (Verdecchia et al., 1999; Sega et al., 2001) and incident CVD (Pierdomenico et al., 2005; Ohkubo et al., 2005) compared to casual clinic BP.

Job strain   The New York City Worksite Blood Pressure Study began in 1985 and followed participants for ten years measuring job strain and ABP. Men at entry to the study with job strain (Time 1), compared to men with no job strain, had higher levels of work, home, *and* sleep ABP and increases in the size of their heart's left ventricle (a sign of damage to the heart), after adjusting for other risk factors including, age, race, and body mass index (BMI) (Schnall et al., 1990; Schnall et al., 1992; Landsbergis et al., 1994). Three years later (Time 2), men facing job strain at both Time 1 and Time 2 (i.e., cumulative exposure) had an 11–12 mm Hg higher systolic and 6–9 mm Hg higher diastolic work ABP than men having no job strain at both times. Men reporting job strain at Time 1 but no job strain at Time 2 showed a drop in systolic ABP of 5.3 mm Hg at work and 4.7 mm Hg at home (Schnall et al., 1998), perhaps showing a benefit of leaving a job characterized as having job strain.

Recently, we conducted a systematic review and meta-analysis of job strain and ABP which included 22 cross-sectional studies as well as several other studies (one case–control study, three studies of cumulative exposure to job strain, and three longitudinal studies) (Landsbergis, Dobson, Koutsouras, and Schnall, 2013). A one-time exposure to job strain in the cross-sectional studies was associated with higher work systolic ABP (3.43 mm Hg, CI 2.02–4.84) and diastolic ABP (2.07 mm Hg, CI 1.17–2.97). Stronger associations were observed in population-based studies than in white-collar only studies (presumably due to a greater range of work exposures in the population-based studies), and no significant association was observed in single occupation studies (due most likely to lack of variation of the exposure variables in single occupations). Biases toward the null were far more common than biases away from the null, suggesting that the findings were underestimates of the true associations.

After publication of the meta-analysis, a new prospective study of white-collar workers from Quebec, Canada (Trudel et al., 2013) found a stronger association between men in active (high demand–high control) jobs and ABP than men in high strain jobs for contemporaneous exposure. Past job strain exposure was not significantly associated with ABP and there was no association for women. It is unclear what characteristics of the study population (white-collar workers from three public insurance institutions in Quebec), in addition to the likely restriction of variance in work exposures, may account for these findings. The nature of "active" jobs in these institutions needs further exploration.

Despite the many limitations of casual clinic BP (CBP), such as low reliability and poor predictive validity compared to ABP (Landsbergis et al., 2013; Landsbergis et al., 2008), in a systematic review which included 26 cross-sectional and 6 prospective studies of BP and job strain, Gilbert-Ouimet et al. (2014) found that 12/22 studies showed a significant association between job strain and BP in men and only 4/14 in women. 3/3 prospective CBP studies showed significant associations for men, 1/3 for women. All the prospective ABP studies (3/3) showed significant associations with job strain. However, only two out of four prospective studies showed significant results for women. Studies with better methodological quality tended to show stronger associations. An interaction between job strain and low SES was also observed for BP among New York City men (Landsbergis et al., 2003) and men and women in the Framingham Offspring Study (Landsbergis et al., 2005).

Effort–reward imbalance   Gilbert-Ouimet and colleagues (2014) also reviewed 11 cross-sectional and one prospective study of ERI and BP, finding nine studies with a significant association with either BP or hypertension. The only prospective study of ERI and ABP published to date was of white-collar workers in Quebec, which showed a significant impact of ERI on ABP in younger women and increased risk of hypertension in older women. Results were not significant for male white-collar workers (Gilbert-Ouimet et al., 2012). In this same population, over three exposure periods over seven years, past ERI exposure (top vs. bottom tertile) was associated with higher systolic ABP (2.4 mm Hg) and diastolic ABP (1.72 mm Hg) in men and systolic ABP (1.53 mm Hg) and diastolic ABP (1.2 mm Hg) in women (Trudel et al., 2013).

Threat-avoidant vigilant work   Occupations involving threat-avoidant vigilance, such as urban transit operators and protective service workers (firefighters and police), have higher prevalence and elevated risk of hypertension (Davila et al., 2012; Greiner Krause, Ragland, and Fisher, 2004).

Long work hours   Only one study (from Japan) examined ABP and found evidence linking working >55 hours/week and ABP among men (Hayashi, Kobayashi, Yamaoka, K. and Yano, 1996). Self-report data from California indicated that employees working >50 hours/week had a 29 percent increased risk of hypertension compared to those working 11–39 hours/week (Yang et al., 2006). A study of female physicians found an association between a clinical diagnosis of hypertension (based upon several measures of casual clinic BP) and Occupational Stress Index high demand scores and several of its elements, especially long work hours (Nedic, Belkić, Filipović, Jocić, 2010). However, a 2014 review article on long working hours and BP did not find a consistent relationship (Bannai and Tamakoshi, 2014).

Work Stressors and Diabetes/Metabolic Syndrome

Job strain   There is growing evidence that job strain is also a risk factor for diabetes and the metabolic syndrome. Insulin resistance represents a possible biological mechanism between stress at work and the development of type 2 diabetes, as Brunner and Kivimäki (2013) argue: "[cortisol] stimulates glucose production in the liver and antagonizes the action of insulin in peripheral tissues." Those reporting high stress at work show evidence of higher cortisol secretion after waking (Brunner and Kivimäki, 2013). Most prospective cohort studies or IPD meta-analyses of job strain and diabetes show a strong, positive relationship (Leynen et al., 2003; Nyberg et al., 2013; Huth et al., 2014; Eriksson, Van Den Donk, Hilding, and Östenson, 2013), and the effect was even larger when measuring cumulative exposure to job strain in one study of the metabolic syndrome (Chandola et al., 2006).

Effort–reward imbalance   In a cross-sectional study of 4,000 German industrial workers, a weak association was found between ERI and the metabolic syndrome (odds ratio (OR) 1.14, CI 1.03–1.26) (Schmidt et al., 2015).

Long work hours   In an IPD meta-analysis of long work hours and incident diabetes in 19 European cohorts, Kivimäki et al. (2015b) found a moderate association in low SES workers (OR 1.29, CI 1.06–1.57).

Work Stressors, Depression, and CVD

There is a growing literature showing a link between depression and the development of CVD (Musselman, Evans, and Nemeroff, 1998; Nicholson, Kuper, and Hemingway, 2006; Russ et al., 2012; Rugulies, 2002). The mechanism through which depression and depressive symptoms could act on CVD is theorized to be associated with the activation of the hypothalamic-pituitary-adrenal axis, lower heart rate variability (HRV), ventricular instability and myocardial ischemia in reaction to mental stress, and in alterations in platelet receptors and/or reactivity (Russ et al., 2012; Musselman et al., 1996; Musselman et al., 1998). There is also a large literature with evidence of a strong relationship between job strain, ERI, job insecurity and depression or depressive symptoms (Clays et al., 2007; LaMontagne et al., 2008; Netterstrom et al., 2008; Siegrist, 2008; Bonde, 2008; LaMontagne, Sanderson, and Cocker, 2010; Stansfeld, Fuhrer, Shipley, and Marmot, 1999; Stansfeld and Candy, 2006). The relationship between work stressors and depression may also be partly mediated by unhealthy behaviors (CVD risk factors), including smoking, alcohol, or lack of exercise (Stansfeld and Candy, 2006). Work-related burnout (a prelude to depression) is related to work stressors (Borritz et al., 2005) and is also associated with CVD and cardiovascular reactivity (Melamed, Ben-Avi, and Green, 1992; Melamed et al., 2006; Shirom et al., 2009).

Work Stressors and Behavioral CVD Risk Factors

There is accumulating evidence that work stressors may also contribute to CVD by influencing behavioral variables such as alcohol use, weight and obesity, and physical (in)activity, already identified as risk factors for heart disease.

Smoking and alcohol

Job strain   In workers with job strain there is some evidence for a greater risk of smoking and alcohol consumption (Heikkilä et al., 2012a; Heikkilä et al., 2012b; Schnall et al., 1992; Hellerstedt and Jeffery, 1997). Nyberg et al. (2013), in an IPD meta-analysis including eight studies and 47,000 participants, found a cross-sectional association between job strain and smoking (OR 1.14; CI 1.08–1.20) and job strain and high alcohol use (OR 1.06; CI 0.99–1.13). Baseline smokers with job strain were 9 percent less likely to give up smoking at follow-up compared to those with no job strain in a longitudinal analysis from the same European cohorts (six studies, 42,000 participants) (Heikkilä et al., 2012a). In a longitudinal study of Danish nurses (n = 12,980), among baseline smokers, the odds of quitting smoking at six-year follow-up were higher in those with physical job demands, job control, and day shift work (Sanderson et al., 2005).

Effort–reward imbalance   Although there are only two published studies, strong positive associations were found between ERI and smoking intensity, although these differed by gender. Partial support for ERI and demands/control and heavy alcohol consumption was found in four of six longitudinal studies (Siegrist and Rodel, 2006).

Physical inactivity, BMI/obesity

Sedentary labor reduces caloric expenditure and may play a role in the development of obesity; the more hours of sedentary work, the greater the risk of obesity (Choi et al., 2009a). There is growing evidence in cross-sectional studies of a positive relationship between psychosocial work stressors and higher BMI. However, there are few quality longitudinal studies of work stressors and obesity (Solovieva et al., 2013). The main mechanisms by which work stressors may impact weight gain include behaviors such as stress-induced eating, sedentary behavior at work (Solovieva et al., 2013; Pandalai, Schulte, and Miller, 2013;, Choi et al., 2011; Choi et al., 2009a, Choi et al., 2009b), and less leisure-time physical activity (Choi et al., 2010; Fransson et al., 2012; Church et al., 2011). Work stress may also have a direct effect on weight through circadian rhythm disturbance (e.g., sleep disturbances due to shift work) or hyperactivation of the hypothalamic-pituitary-adrenocortical (HPA) axis and metabolic changes (neuroendocrine pathway) (Solovieva et al., 2013; Choi et al., 2011).

Job strain   Some positive relationships between psychosocial work factors and weight have been found in a recent review (over half of 36 studies), particularly strong in men with long work hours (Solovieva et al., 2013). Positive cross-sectional associations between job strain and BMI or obesity were found in European IPD meta-analyses; however, longitudinal results were less convincing (Nyberg et al., 2013; Nyberg et al., 2012). A change from no job strain at baseline to job strain at follow-up was related to non-obesity at baseline and obesity at follow-up. These recent studies suggest there may be a U-shaped relationship between BMI and job strain, with job strain prevalence highest in underweight and obese groups (Nyberg et al., 2012; Kivimäki et al., 2006a). Possible explanations include a divided response to stress, with some people eating more under stress while others eat less (Stonea and Brownell, 1994). Such a hypothesis needs attention in future studies.

Leisure-time physical activity and job strain have shown some associations in several recent studies. Nyberg et al. (2013) found that compared to those with no job strain, those with high strain were significantly more likely to be physically inactive (OR 1.43, CI 1.36–1.51). In a prospective IPD meta-analysis of European cohort studies, Fransson et al. (2012) found that among the physically active at baseline, the odds of becoming physically inactive at follow-up were 21 percent higher for those with high strain (OR 1.21, 1.11–1.32). Choi et al. (2010) found that among middle-aged US workers, those with active and low-strain jobs compared to passive jobs had greater odds of active leisure-time physical activity.

Effort–reward imbalance   ERI was related to higher BMI in two cross-sectional studies, while weight increase was evident in one longitudinal study (Siegrist and Rodel, 2006).

Long work hours and shift work   Positive associations are evident in recent studies of shift work, long work hours, and obesity (Nyberg et al., 2012; Solovieva et al., 2013). Longitudinal evidence of relationships between work factors (overtime) and unhealthy behaviors found overtime to be associated with lower physical activity and less fruit and vegetable consumption, but not with smoking, alcohol use, or BMI (Taris et al., 2011).

Globalization, the Changing Nature of Work, and Work Stressors

Evidence for a relationship between work stressors and CVD has been accumulating over several decades. Recent research findings indicate that the changes brought about by economic globalization are impacting the global CVD epidemic. There is now evidence that the changes brought about by globalization that influence labor markets as well as the organization of work are intensifying work stressors.

The pattern of CVD incidence is linked to a country's stage of economic development (IOM, 2010; Gaziano et al., 2010; Gaziano and Gaziano, 2012), which for many developing countries means profound changes in rates of disease as a consequence of economic globalization. The rise in CVD risk factors and the CVD epidemic since World War II in the developing world mirror the same trends that occurred in conjunction with industrialization and urbanization in developed countries over the past 150 years. For example, in India, hypertension prevalence rose from 1–3 percent in 1950 to 10–30 percent in 2000 (Greenberg, Raymond, and Leeder, 2005). China has also seen dramatic increases in hypertension occurring concurrently with rapid industrialization, with 20.5 percent of adults (153 million adults) affected in 2010 (Tao et al., 1995; W. J. Ma et al., 2012), and a higher prevalence in urban areas (25 percent) compared to rural areas (16 percent) (He et al., 1991). In 2005, 2.3 million CVD deaths (out of 3.1 million) were attributed to hypertension in China (Hu et al., 2012; He et al., 2009). Other CVD risk factors are also on the rise in developing countries, including smoking, increased sedentary labor, obesity, and diabetes. In China, 54 percent of men smoked cigarettes in 2012 and 33 percent of all Chinese adults are overweight. Type 2 diabetes prevalence has increased in China to nearly 10 percent of adults in 2007 (Greenberg et al., 2005; B.-Q. Liu et al., 1998).

The transformation of economies impacts wealth and income distribution (Sandle, 2015; Milanovic, 2012), as well as labor markets and work organization. In the US and Europe, there have been numerous changes to methods of production, including outsourcing to developing markets and enhanced technologies requiring fewer workers. This has led to mass layoffs, restructuring, and downsizing of more expensive labor pools, and a decline in union membership and labor protections in developed countries (Johnson, 2007; 2009; Moutsatsos, 2009; Aldersen and Nielsen, 2002; Kalleberg, 2011; Kwon and Pontusson, 2006).

Part of this transformation of work is in response to increased global competition, to enhance "efficiency," productivity, and profitability. Employers in the private and, more recently, the public sector (e.g., health care, social services, and government services) (Carter et al., 2011) are implementing new "lean" systems of work organization or "lean production," "total quality management" or "just-in-time management," modern versions of scientific management or "Taylorism" originally developed at Toyota (Landsbergis, Cahill, and Schnall, 1999; Adler, 1995). While some tasks and responsibilities are transferred to teams of workers and may include job rotation and "multiskilling," which are claimed to ease the stress of mass-production assembly lines (Womack, 1996), studies have shown that workers frequently experience tighter supervision, surveillance, multitasking (rather than multiskilling), no increase in job control, and increased stress (Landsbergis et al., 1999; Toivanen and Landsbergis, 2013).

This transformation of work in developed countries has led to a higher prevalence of precarious work, increased job insecurity, time pressure, and work intensification (Benach et al., 2014; Kalleberg, 2011; Quinlan, Mayhew, and Bohle, 2001). For example, in Europe "time constraints" rose between 1977 and 1996 (Eurofound, 1997), and in the US the proportion reporting "never enough time to get everything done on my job" increased from 40 to 60 percent between 1977 and 1997 (Bond, Galinsky, and Swanberg, 1998). European surveys show a continuing rise in job demands between 1990 and 2005, but no change or slight declines in job control or autonomy since 1995 (Eurofound, 2006), suggesting an increase in the prevalence of job strain.

Declining work hours in other developed countries have led to annual US work hours becoming the longest in the developed world, about 8–10 more working weeks per year than workers in Western Europe (Mishel and Bernstein, 2006). One survey found that full-time and salaried Americans work well over 40 hours per week (average is 47 hours), with 25 percent of salaried workers saying they work 50 or more hours (Saad, 2014).

Precarious employment and job insecurity   While flexible work hours and telecommuting may have some benefits for working people, there has also been an increase in involuntary part-time work, temporary contracts, and "independent contractors," which increases vulnerability and is associated with greater job stress such as job insecurity, work intensification, and lower control (Quinlan et al., 2001; Eurofound, 2006). Since the 2008 financial crisis, an increase in layoffs, restructuring, and downsizing has led to anticipatory job loss and greater job demands among remaining workers or those who are working on temporary contracts alongside per-manent workers as they compete for potentially full-term permanent contracts (Benach et al., 2014; Quinlan and Mayhew, 2000; Louie et al., 2006; Benach and Muntaner, 2007; Vives et al., 2010).

Perceived job insecurity, a central construct in "precarious employment" (Vives et al., 2010), is thought to act as a chronic stressor, giving rise to adverse health outcomes. Research in Europe on workforce reductions shows a doubling of the risk of CVD mortality (Vahtera et al., 2004) among Finnish public employees, partly mediated by higher levels of physical demands, job insecurity, and decreased levels of skill discretion and participation (Kivimäki et al., 2000). In an IPD meta-analysis and systematic review including 13 European cohort studies (174,438 participants, mean follow-up of 9.7 years) the age-adjusted relative risk for high vs. low job insecurity and CHD was 1.32 (CI 1.09–1.59) and 1.19 after adjusting for SES and other risk factors(Virtanen et al., 2013). Another recent review article by Benach et al. (2014) investi-gating precarious employment and health outcomes including CVD concludes that there is a modest effect between job insecurity and CHD. However, most studies have not yet taken into account changes in employment status across the life course.

Population Attributable Risk (PAR)

A number of work stressors appear to play an important role in the etiology of CVD and CVD risk factors, particularly hypertension. However, it is not clear that all the identified psychosocial work stressors will qualify as independent risk factors for CVD. For example, some exposures such as job strain and ERI have overlapping dimensions that tap into shared constructs such as "work demands" or "control." Few studies of CVD incorporate and test multiple psychosocial variables at the same time, as they are primarily designed to establish the role of a particular variable while also avoiding the problems raised by multiple hypothesis testing. Studies exploring multiple exposures and their relationships to each other and health outcomes are needed.

In March 2013, the Sixth International Conference on Work Environment and Cardiovas-cular Diseases, under the auspices of the International Commission on Occupational Health (ICOH) Scientific Committee on Cardiology in Occupational Health, met in Tokyo, Japan and adopted a statement – the Tokyo Declaration (ICOH, 2013) – following publication of the IPD work group results on the PAR% of job strain and CVD in *The Lancet* (Kivimäki et al., 2012). The Tokyo Declaration concluded that 80 percent of CVD mortality would be preventable if existing knowledge were effectively applied and that "according to research data about 10 to 20% of all causes of CVD deaths among working age populations can be attributed to work, i.e., are work-related" (p. 4). Given the PAR of 10–20% and the general agreement that work factors play an important role in the development of CVD, it is reasonable to conclude that the workplace and the organization of work should be a target of primary prevention of CVD and CVD risk factors.

Work Stress and the Prevention of CVD

Given the evidence that work stressors are related to CVD and its risk factors, the workplace has been proposed as a location in which public health programs can address CVD prevention and reduce health care costs (Goh, Pfeffer, and Zenios, 2015a; 2015b). A primary prevention public health approach is needed to address work stressors and work organization to improve the cardiovascular health of working people, in concert with secondary prevention and disease management.

Currently, treatment of CVD risk factors, such as hypertension and cholesterol, with medication is the dominant approach to reducing CVD morbidity and mortality. Providing drug treatment for individuals with CVD risk factors is important, yet it represents a very costly approach in terms of drug treatment side-effects and decreased quality of life, as well as economic costs. Currently 1 in 6 US health dollars are spent on CVD, and costs for CVD are predicted to increase in the US to $818 billion by 2030 (Heidenreich et al., 2011). Given that 80 percent of the burden of CVD deaths now occurs in developing countries (Gaziano, 2005), medicating 1.5 to 2 billion people with hypertension or with abnormal lipid levels to prevent CVD does not appear to be a feasible solution in lower-income developing countries.

Workers with chronic illnesses contribute to rising health-care premiums, disability, and workers' compensation costs for US employers (Goetzel et al., 2004; Leigh et al., 2004; Leigh and Robbins, 2004). They may work at a reduced level (presenteeism) and/or will be more likely to have more absenteeism, sick leave, and worker compensation claims (Jauregui and Schnall, 2009). A relationship between psychosocial work factors and these productivity outcomes has been demonstrated (Goh et al., 2015b; Mäntyniemi, 2012; Laine et al., 2009; Rugulies et al., 2007; Virtanen et al., 2001). A 2015 meta-analysis by researchers at Stanford and Harvard of 228 studies assessing ten workplace stress exposures and four health outcomes found that high job demands raised the odds of a diagnosed illness by 35 percent, and that long work hours increased mortality by almost 20 percent (Goh et al., 2015b). A follow-up publication by these same researchers estimated the excess mortality and health-care costs associated with these ten workplace exposures, including job demands, job control, job insecurity, low social support at work, long work hours, and shift work, as well as unemployment and lack of health insurance (Goh et al., 2015a). The authors conservatively estimated more than 120,000 deaths each year, and 5–8 percent of health-care costs may be attributable to "how US companies manage their work force." With US health-care costs hitting $3 trillion in 2014, 6 percent of these costs represent $180 billion dollars.

Return to Work after Cardiac Events

Work stress should be a consideration, in addition to physical fitness, when cardiologists judge the cardiovascular fitness of patients who have suffered a cardiac event in determining whether their patient may return to work. This is particularly crucial for those people in jobs in which public safety could be compromised if a worker were to experience a reoccurrence of a cardiac event (deGaudemaris, 2000). These jobs, however, are also unfortunately characterized by high exposure to work stressors (e.g., urban transit operators, air traffic controllers) (Fisher and Belkić, 2000). Identifying potentially modifiable stressors in a person's work environment and formulating a plan for a safe return to work is an important goal in partnership with clinicians. See the work of Dr. Belkić (2003) for case examples. This is especially important given the increased risk of recurrent heart disease among heart attack patients who return to work to stressful jobs (Li et al., 2014).

Workplace Health Promotion

Nearly 50 percent of all medium/large businesses in the United States have implemented workplace health promotion programs to reduce individual CVD risk factors and behaviors such as smoking, overeating, and lack of exercise. However, these programs have met with limited success (L. M. Anderson et al., 2009; Goetzel, 2001; Wilson, 1996; Caloyeras et al., 2014). One limitation is a general failure to address the work environment as a source of the stress which promotes CVD risk factors. The National Institute for Occupational Safety and Health (NIOSH) recommends to businesses a Total Worker Health™ (TWH) approach to integrate health promotion and disease management aimed at individuals, with "health protection" (occupational health), addressing both the work environment and psychosocial stressors (NIOSH, 2012). A TWH approach also has the potential to enhance employee participation in health promotion (Sorensen et al., 1998; Sorensen, Barbeau, Hunt, and Emmons, 2004; Sorensen et al., 2005; Sorensen et al., 2011; McLellan, Harden, Markkanen, and Sorensen, 2012); however, TWH in practice has also been criticized for failing to live up to its promise (Lax, 2016).

Stress and its health consequences are not preventable nor fully treatable by taking an individual or medical approach. Prevention of stress needs to include a broader public health approach, including changes to work organization to reduce work stressors.

Job Stress Interventions and CVD

While the evidence for the effectiveness of work organization interventions in reducing CVD risk factors and improving worker health is growing (LaMontagne and Keegel, 2012; LaMontagne, Noblet, and Landsbergis, 2012; Sorensen et al., 2011; Landsbergis, 2009; LaMontagne et al., 2007; Anger et al., 2014), more research is needed. Efforts to increase employee participation and job control, social support, and moderate job demands hold great promise in improving employee health (Lindstrom, Schrey, Ahonen, and Kaleva, 2000; Bond and Bunce, 2001; Eklof, Ingelgard, and Hagberg, 2004; Bourbonnais, Brisson, and Vézina, 2011).

However, to date, we are aware of only two work organization intervention studies that *assess cardiovascular outcomes*. One program initiated by the Stockholm municipal transit agency reduced traffic congestion and improved passenger service. During planning, there was interest by the municipal workers' union and researchers to also study job stress and the health of bus drivers (Rydstedt, Johansson, and Evans, 1998). Bus routes were changed; the number and length of bus lanes were increased; automatic green lights were provided for buses; bus stops were moved and rebuilt; and a computerized passenger information system was provided on the bus and at bus stops. As a result, on "intervention" bus routes, drivers reported fewer job "hassles" and less distress after work compared to workers on other routes that were not changed. There was objective evidence for reduced hassles such as fewer illegally parked cars, fewer delays due to passenger obstruction or information requests, and less risky behaviors by pedestrians/cyclists. Finally, there was a large decline in the systolic blood pressure of drivers in the intervention group (−10.7 mm Hg), larger than the decline among bus drivers on control routes (–4.3 mm Hg). The BP decline in controls may have been due to a 5 percent reduction in traffic passing through the city center of Stockholm during the study, which affected both study groups (Rydstedt et al., 1998).

The second study, an intervention among Swedish office workers, involved individual stress management (relaxation training) and worker committees which developed and helped carry out "action plans" to reduce sources of stress at work. Compared to a control group, the intervention group reported increases in work challenge and autonomy over eight months, increases in supervisor support, and improvements in their lipid profile (cholesterol), a change not explained by changes in diet, exercise, smoking, or weight (Orth-Gomer et al., 1994).

Unfortunately, intervention studies at the workplace are very difficult and expensive to mount. They require extensive funding, the active cooperation of management and workers, sufficient numbers of participants, and long follow-ups to allow time for organizational interventions aimed at targeted populations to have sufficient power to detect changes in cardiovascular risk factors.

National Surveillance of Work Stressors and CVD

Better national surveillance data are needed to determine the magnitude and distribution of unhealthy working conditions in the US and their association with chronic illnesses. While Europe has extensive national data on psychosocial working conditions, in the US, national surveillance data such as the National Health and Nutrition Examination Survey (NHANES) and the National Health Interview Survey (NHIS) have little consistent data on work stressors. A short occupational health supplement to the NHIS was included in 1988, 2010, and 2015, and NIOSH conducted the national Quality of Worklife Surveys in 2002, 2006, 2010, and 2014. However, due to limited budgets, results about psychosocial stressors from these surveys are not readily available and have not been routinely analyzed and reported.

Legislative and Regulatory Approaches to Work Stressors

In Northern and Western Europe, there has been a concerted effort to reduce and prevent workplace psychosocial stressors, including the Swedish Work Environment Act, No. 677, amended in 1991 (Government Offices of Sweden, 1991), and the European Framework for Psychosocial Risk Management–PRIMA-EF. Arguably, this may account for a lower prevalence of job strain and other job stressors in some European countries and their recent decline in prevalence (Leka and Cox, 2008; Leka, Jain, Cox, and Kortum, 2011). For example, Denmark, Norway, and the Netherlands displayed a significantly lower prevalence of exposure to four psychosocial factors or more (such as job strain, bullying, work–family imbalance, long work hours, job insecurity, and effort–reward imbalance), while some Southern and Eastern countries, especially the Czech Republic, Greece, Lithuania, and Turkey, had a higher prevalence (Niedhammer et al., 2012). In the Nordic countries, in 2005, the prevalence of job strain was well below the European Union average of 26.9 percent and the prevalence of ERI was well below the EU average of 20.4 percent (Niedhammer et al., 2014).

The US has not yet enacted similar legislation (Weinberg, 1996; Wolff, 1995), with the exception of some state laws banning mandatory overtime or mandating adequate staffing levels for nurses (Aiken et al., 2010).

Conclusion

CVD is a global epidemic that is continuing to increase in size, health consequences, and economic cost, paralleling increased industrialization and urbanization in developing countries. In economically more developed countries, the age-adjusted prevalence of hypertension is still increasing (Mozaffarian et al., 2015), while the decline in CVD mortality rates is slowing (J. Ma, Ward, Siegel, and Jemal, 2015), paralleling increasing economic insecurity and inequality, a weakened labor movement, and lean production practices. A strong body of evidence from prospective studies in Europe and North America shows that stressful work factors, including demands, control, job strain, effort–reward imbalance, job insecurity, and long work hours, play a substantial role in the etiology of CVD and contribute to many of the standard CVD risk factors.

Given the many consequences – the loss of years of life and decreased health and quality of life for individuals, as well as the high costs of medical treatment and the economic costs to employers of ill-health, lost productivity, and sickness absence – it is in the interest of all to improve work organization. These improvements should parallel those made in Europe, including the passage of regulations and laws defining psychosocial stressors as a workplace hazard and setting standards limiting excessive work hours and repetitive work, inter alia, and encouraging employers to provide for, and employees to take paid vacation time.

Given the scientific evidence of the important role of work and work stressors in relationship to CVD and CVD risk factors, public health professionals and all those people concerned with the prevention of chronic illnesses need to work together to educate the general public, as well as public policy makers, about the necessity of improving work organization and reducing psychosocial work stressors. Changes at the workplace to reduce work stressors can be an important part of preventing the global chronic disease epidemics, while offering workers improved health and quality of life.

References

Aboa-Éboulé, C., Brisson, C., Maunsell, E., Bourbonnais, R., Vézina, M., Milot, A., and Dagenais, G. (2011). Effort–reward imbalance at work and recurrent coronary heart disease events: A 4-year prospective study of post-myocardial infarction patients. *Psychosomatic Medicine*, *73*, 436–447.

Aboa-Éboulé, C., Brisson, C., Maunsell, E., Mâsse, B., Bourbonnais, R., Vézina, M., ... Dagenais, G. (2007). Job strain and risk of acute recurrent coronary heart disease events. *JAMA*, *298*, 1652–1660.

Adler, P. (1995). "Democratic Taylorism": The Toyota production system at Nummi. In S. Babson (Ed.), *Lean Work: Empowerment and Exploitation in the Global Auto Industry*. Detroit: Wayne State University Press.

Aiken, L. H., Sloane, D. M., Cimiotti, J. P., Clarke, S. P., Flynn, L., Seago, J. A., ... Smith, H. L. (2010). Implications of the California nurse staffing mandate for other states. *Health Services Research*, *45*(4), 904–921. doi:10.1111/j.1475-6773.2010.01114.x

Aldersen, A., and Nielsen, F. (2002). Globalization and the great U-turn: Income inequality trends in 16 OECD countries. *American Journal of Sociology*, *107*, 1244–1299.

Anderson, L. M., Quinn, T. A., Glanz, K., Ramirez, G., Kahwati, L. C., Johnson, D. B., ... Katz, D. L. (2009). The effectiveness of worksite nutrition and physical activity interventions for controlling employee overweight and obesity: A systematic review. *American Journal of Preventive Medicine*, *37*, 340–357.

Anderson, R. N. (1999). *US Decennial Life Tables for 1989–91*, *1*(4), *United States Life Tables Eliminating Certain Causes of Death*, Table 22. Centers for Disease Control and Prevention, National Center for Health Statistics.

Anger, W. K., Elliot, D. L., Bodner, T., Olson, R., Rohlman, D. S., Truxillo, D. M., ... Montgomery, D. (2014). Effectiveness of total worker health interventions. *Journal of Occupational Health Psychology*, *20*(2), 226–247. http://dx.doi.org/10.1037/a0038340

Backé, E.-M., Seidler, A., Latza, U., Rossnagel, K. and Schumann, B. (2012). The role of psychosocial stress at work for the development of cardiovascular diseases: A systematic review. *International Archives of Occupational and Environmental Health, 85,* 67–79.

Bannai, A., and Tamakoshi, A. (2014). The association between long working hours and health: A systematic review of epidemiological evidence. *Scandinavian Journal of Public Health, 40,* 5–18.

Belkić, K. (2003). *The Occupational Stress Index: An Approach Derived from Cognitive Ergonomics and Brain Research for Clinical Practice.* Cambridge: Cambridge International Science.

Belkić, K., Emdad, R., and Theorell, T. (1998). Occupational profile and cardiac risk: Possible mechanisms and implications for professional drivers. *International Journal of Occupational Medicine and Environmental Health, 11,* 37–57.

Belkić, K., Landsbergis, P., Schnall, P., and Baker, D. (2004). Is job strain a major source of cardiovascular disease risk? *Scandinavian Journal of Work, Environment and Health, 30,* 85–128.

Belkić, K., Savic, C., Djordjevic, M., Ugljesic, M., and Mickovic, L. (1992). Event-related potentials in professional city drivers: Heightened sensitivity to cognitively relevant visual signals. *Physiology and Behavior, 52,* 423–427.

Belkić, K., Schnall, P., Savic, C., and Landsbergis, P. A. (2000). Multiple exposures: Toward a model of total occupational burden. *Occupational Medicine: State-of-the-Art Reviews, 15,* 94–98.

Benach, J., and Muntaner, C. (2007). Precarious employment and health: Developing a research agenda. *Journal of Epidemiology and Community Health, 61,* 276–277.

Benach, J., Vives, A., Amable, M., Vanroelen, C., Tarafa, G., and Muntaner, C. (2014). Precarious employment: Understanding an emerging social determinant of health. *Annual Review of Public Health, 35,* 229–253.

Boggild, H., and Knutsson, A. (1999). Shift work, risk factors, and cardiovascular disease. *Scandinavian Journal of Work, Environment and Health, 25,* 85–89.

Bond, F., and Bunce, D. (2001). Job control mediates change in a work reorganization intervention for stress reduction. *Journal of Occupational Health Psychology, 6,* 290–302.

Bond, J. T., Galinsky, E., and Swanberg, J. E. (1998). *The 1997 National Study of the Changing Workforce.* New York: Families and Work Institute.

Bonde, J. P. (2008). Psychosocial factors at work and risk of depression: A systematic review of the epidemiological evidence. *Occupational and Environmental Medicine, 65,* 438–445.

Borritz, M., Bültmann, U., Rugulies, R., Christensen, K., Villadsen, E., and Kristensen, T. (2005). Psychosocial work environment factors as predictors for burnout: Prospective findings from 3-year follow-up of the PUMA study. *Journal of Occupational and Environmental Medicine, 47,* 1015–1025.

Bourbonnais, R., Brisson, C., and Vézina, M. (2011). Long-term effects of an intervention on psychosocial work factors among healthcare professionals in a hospital setting. *Occupational and Environmental Medicine, 68,* 479–486.

Brunner, E., and Kivimäki, M. (2013). Work-related stress and the risk of type 2 diabetes mellitus. *Nature Reviews. Endocrinology, 9,* 449–450.

Caloyeras, J. P., Liu, H., Exum, E., Broderick, M., and Mattke, S. (2014). Managing manifest diseases, but not health risks, saved PepsiCo money over seven years. *Health Affairs, 33,* 124–131.

Carter, B., Danford, A., Howcroft, D., Richardson, H., Smith, A., and Taylor, P. (2011). "All they lack is a chain": Lean and the new performance management in the British civil service. *New Technology, Work and Employment, 26,* 83–97.

Chandola, T., Brunner, E., and Marmot, M. (2006). Chronic stress at work and the metabolic syndrome: Prospective study. *British Medical Journal, 332,* 521.

Chazelle, E., Chastang, J., and Niedhammer, I. (2015). Psychosocial work factors and sleep problems: Findings from the French national SIP survey. *International Archives of Occupational and Environmental Health.* Epub ahead of print.

Choi, B., Schnall, P., Dobson, M., Israel, L., Landsbergis, P., Galassetti, P., … Baker, D. (2011). Exploring occupational and behavioral risk factors for obesity in firefighters: A theoretical framework and study design. *Safety and Health at Work, 2,* 301–312.

Choi, B., Schnall, P., Landsbergis, P., Dobson, M., Ko, S., Gómez-Ortiz, V., … Baker, D. (2015). Recommendations for individual participant data meta-analyses on work stressors and health outcomes: Comments on IPD-Work Consortium papers. *Scandinavian Journal of Work, Environment and Health, 41,* 299–311.

Choi, B., Schnall, P., Yang, H., Dobson, M., Landsbergis, P., Israel, L., … Baker, D. (2009a). Sedentary work, low physical job demand, and obesity in US workers. *International Journal of Occupational and Environmental Health, 22*(suppl.), 42.

Choi, B., Schnall, P., Yang, H., Dobson, M., Landsbergis, P., Israel, L., et al. (2009b). Work stress, overeating coping, and obesity in the US workforce. Paper for the 8th International Conference on Occupational Stress and Health, San Juan, Puerto Rico.

Choi, B., Schnall, P. L., Yang, H., Dobson, M., Landsbergis, P., Israel, L., … Baker, D. (2010). Psychosocial working conditions and active leisure-time physical activity in middle-aged US workers. *International Journal of Occupational Medicine and Environmental Health, 23*, 239–253.

Church T. S., Thomas, D. M., Tudor-Locke, C., Katzmarzyk, P. T., Earnest, C. P., Rodante, R. Q., … Bouchard, C. (2011). Trends over 5 decades in US occupation-related physical activity and their associations with obesity. *PLoS ONE, 6*(5), e19657. doi:10.1371/journal.pone.0019657

Clays, E., De Bacquer, D., Leynen, F., Kornitzer, M., Kittel, F., and De Backer, G. (2007). Job stress and depression symptoms in middle-aged workers: Prospective results from the Belstress study. *Scandinavian Journal of Work, Environment and Health, 33*, 252–259.

Davila, E. P., Kuklina, E. V., Valderrama, A. L., Yoon, P. W., Rolle, I., and Nsubuga, P. (2012). Prevalence, management, and control of hypertension among US workers: Does occupation matter? *Journal of Occupational and Environmental Medicine, 54*, 1150–1156.

De Vogli, R., Ferrie, J. E., Chandola, T., Kivimäki, M., and Marmot, M. G. (2007). Unfairness and health: Evidence from the Whitehall II study. *Journal of Epidemiology and Community Health, 61*, 513–518.

Degaudemaris, R. (2000). Clinical issues: Return to work and public safety. *Occupational Medicine: State of the Art Reviews, 15*, 223–230.

del Arco-Galan, C., Suarez-Fernandez, C., and Gabriel-Sanchez, R. (1994). What happens to blood pressure when on-call? *American Journal of Hypertension, 7*, 396–401.

Devereux, R. B. (1989). Importance of left ventricular mass as a predictor of cardiovascular morbidity in hypertension. *American Journal of Hypertension, 2*, 650–654.

Devereux, R. B., and Pickering, T. G. (1991). Relationship between the level, pattern and variability of ambulatory blood pressure and target organ damage in hypertension. *Journal of Hypertension: Supplement, 9*, S34–8.

Devereux, R. B., Pickering, T. G., Harshfield, G. A., Kleinert, H. D., Denby, L., Clark, L., … Laragh, J. H. (1983). Left ventricular hypertrophy in patients with hypertension: Importance of blood pressure response to regularly recurring stress. *Circulation, 68*, 476–479.

Eklof, M., Ingelgard, A., and Hagberg, M. (2004). Is participative ergonomics associated with better working environment and health? A study among Swedish white-collar VDU users. *International Journal of Industrial Ergonomics, 34*, 355–366.

Eller, N., Netterstrøm, B., Gyntelberg, F., Kristensen, T., Nielsen, F., Steptoe, A., and Theorell, T. (2009). Work-related psychosocial factors and the development of ischemic heart disease: A systematic review. *Cardiology Review, 17*, 83–97.

Elovainio, M., Kivimäki, M., Puttonen, S., Lindholm, H., Pohjonen, T., and Sinervo, T. (2006a). Organisational injustice and impaired cardiovascular regulation among female employees. *Occupational and Environmental Medicine, 63*, 141–144.

Elovainio, M., Leino-Arjas, P., Vahtera, J., and Kivimäki, M. (2006b). Justice at work and cardiovascular mortality: A prospective cohort study. *Journal of Psychosomatic Research, 61*, 271–274.

Eriksson, A., Van Den Donk, M., Hilding, A., and Östenson, C. (2013). Work stress, sense of coherence, and risk of type 2 diabetes in a prospective study of middle-aged Swedish men and women. *Diabetes Care, 36*, 2683–2689.

Eurofound (1997). *Time Constraints and Autonomy at Work in the European Union.* Dublin: European Foundation for the Improvement of Living and Working Conditions.

Eurofound (2006). *Fifteen Years of Working Conditions in the EU: Charting the Trends.* Dublin: European Foundation for the Improvement of Living and Working Conditions.

European Society of Cardiology (2012). One CVD death in China every 10 seconds. *Science Daily*, Oct. 11.

Fisher, J., and Belkić, K. (2000). A public health approach in clinical practice. In P. Schnall et al. (Eds.), *The Workplace and Cardiovascular Disease.* Philadelphia: Hanley & Belfus.

Frankenhaeuser, M., and Johansson, G. (1986). Stress at work: Psychobiological and psychosocial aspects. *International Review of Applied Psychology, 35*, 287–299.

Fransson, E. I., Heikkilä, K., Nyberg, S. T., Zins, M., Westerlund, H., Westerholm, P., … Kivimäki, M. (2012). Job strain as a risk factor for leisure-time physical inactivity: An individual-participant meta-analysis of up to 170,000 men and women: The IPD-Work Consortium. *American Journal of Epidemiology, 176*, 1078–1089.

Fransson, E. I., Nyberg, S. T., Heikkilä, K., Alfredsson, L., Bjorner, J. B., Borritz, M., … Kivimäki, M. (2015). Job strain and the risk of stroke: An individual-participant data meta-analysis. *Stroke, 46*(2), 557–559.

Gaziano, T. (2005). Cardiovascular disease in the developing world and its cost-effective management. *Circulation*, *112*, 3547–3553.

Gaziano, T., Bitton, A., Anand, S., Abrahams-Gessel, S., and Murphy, A. (2010). Growing epidemic of coronary heart disease in low- and middle-income countries. *Current Problems in Cardiology*, *35*, 72–115.

Gaziano, T., and Gaziano, J. (2012). Global burden of cardiovascular disease. In R. Bonow, D. Mann, D. Zipes, and P. Libby (Eds.), *Brunwald's Heart Disease: A Textbook of Cardiovascular Medicine*, 9th edn. Philadelphia: Elsevier.

Gilbert-Ouimet, M., Brisson, C., Vézina, M., Milot, A., and Blanchette, C. (2012). Repeated exposure to effort–reward imbalance, increased blood pressure, and hypertension incidence among white-collar workers: Effort–reward imbalance and blood pressure. *Journal of Psychosomatic Research*, *72*, 26–32.

Gilbert-Ouimet, M., Trudel, X., Brisson, C., Milot, A., and Vézina, M. (2014). Adverse effects of psychosocial work factors on blood pressure: Systematic review of studies on demand–control–support and effort–reward imbalance models. *Scandinavian Journal of Work, Environment and Health*, *40*, 109–132.

Goetzel, R. Z. (2001). The financial impact of health promotion and disease prevention programs – why is it so hard to prove value? *American Journal of Health Promotion*, *15*, 277–280.

Goetzel, R. Z., Long, S. R., Ozminkowski, R. J., Hawkins, K., Wang, S. and Lynch, W. (2004). Health, absence, disability, and presenteeism cost estimates of certain physical and mental health conditions affecting US employers. *Journal of Occupational and Environmental Medicine*, *46*, 398–412.

Goh, J., Pfeffer, J., and Zenios, S. A. (2015a). The relationship between workplace stressors and mortality and health costs in the United States. *Management Science*, *62*(2).

Goh, J., Pfeffer, J., and Zenios, S. A. (2015b). Workplace stressors and health outcomes: Health policy for the workplace. *Behavioral Science and Policy*, *1*, 43–52.

Government Offices of Sweden (1991). Work Environment Act, No. 677/91, amending Work Environment Act, No. 1160 of 1977. *Svensk Författningssamling*, No. 677, June 17, p. 115. At http://www.ilo.org/dyn/natlex/docs/webtext/37339/64925/e91swe02.htm (accessed July 2016).

Greenberg, H., Raymond, S., and Leeder, S. (2005). Cardiovascular disease and global health: Threat and opportunity. *Health Affairs*, *55*(3), 259. doi:10.1377/hlthaff.W5.31

Greiner, B., Krause, N., Ragland, D. and Fisher, J. (2004). Occupational stressors and hypertension: A multi-method study using observer-based job analysis and self-reports in urban transit operators. *Social Science and Medicine*, *59*, 1081–1094.

Hackman, J. R., and Lawler, E. E. (1971). Employee reactions to job characteristics. *Journal of Applied Psychology*, *55*, 259–286.

Hallqvist, J., Diderichsen, F., Theorell, T., Reuterwall, C., Ahlbom, A., and Sheep Study Group (1998). Is the effect of job strain on myocardial infarction due to interaction between high psychological demands and low decision latitude? Results from Stockholm Heart Epidemiology Program (SHEEP). *Social Science and Medicine*, *46*, 1405–1415.

Hayashi, T., Kobayashi, Y., Yamaoka, K., and Yano, E. (1996). Effect of overtime work on 24-hour ambulatory blood pressure. *Journal of Occupational and Environmental Medicine*, *38*, 1007–1011.

He, J., Gu, D., Chen, J., Wu, X., Kelly, T., Huang, J., … Klag, M. (2009). Premature deaths attributable to blood pressure in China: A prospective cohort study. *Lancet*, *374*, 1765–1772.

He, J., Klag, M. J., Whelton, P. K., Chen, J. Y., Mo, J. P., Qian, M. C., … He, G. Q. (1991). Migration, blood pressure pattern, and hypertension: The Yi Migrant study. *American Journal of Epidemiology*, *134*, 1085–1101.

Heidenreich, P. A., Trogdon, J. G., Khavjou, O. A., Butler, J., Dracup, K., Ezekowitz, M. D., … Interdisciplinary Council on Quality of Care and Outcomes Research (2011). Forecasting the future of cardiovascular disease in the United States: A policy statement from the American Heart Association. *Circulation*, *123*, 933–944.

Heikkilä, K., Nyberg, S. T., Fransson, E. I., Alfredsson, L. and Bacquer, D. D., Bjorner, J. B., … IPD-Work Consortium (2012a). Job strain and tobacco smoking: An individual-participant data meta-analysis of 166,130 adults in 15 European studies. *Plos One*, *7*, e35463.

Heikkilä, K., Nyberg, S. T., Fransson, E. I., Alfredsson, L., Bacquer, D. D., Bjorner, J., … IPD-Work Consortium (2012b). Job strain and alcohol intake: A collaborative meta-analysis of individual-participant data from 140,000 men and women. *Plos One*, *7*, e40101.

Hellerstedt, W. L., and Jeffery, R. W. (1997). The association of job strain and health behaviours in men and women. *International Journal of Epidemiology*, *26*, 575–583.

Henry, J. P., and Stephens, P. M. (1977). *Stress, Health and the Social Environment: A Sociobiologic Approach to Medicine*. New York: Springer.

Holmes, T. H., and Rahe, R. H. (1967). The social readjustment rating scale. *Journal of Psychosomatic Research, 11*, 213–218.

Hu, S. S., Kong, L. Z., Gao, R. L., Zhu, M. L., Wang, W., Wang, Y. J., … Liu, M. B. (2012). Outline of the report on cardiovascular disease in China, 2010. *Biomedicine and Environmental Science, 25*, 251–256.

Huth, C., Thorand, B., Baumert, J., Kruse, J., Thwing Emeny, R., Schneider, A., … Ladwig, K. (2014). Job strain as a risk factor for the onset of type 2 diabetes mellitus: Findings from the MONICA/KORA Augsburg cohort study. *Psychosomatic Medicine, 76*(7), 562–568.

ICOH (International Commission on Occupational Health) (2013). Tokyo Declaration on Prevention and Management of Work-Related Cardiovascular Disorders. Adopted by the Plenary of the Sixth ICOH International Conference on Work Environment and Cardiovascular Diseases under the auspices of the ICOH Scientific Committee on Cardiology in Occupational Health in Tokyo, Japan on 30 March 2013. *ICOH Newsletter, 11*(2–3), 4–6.

IOM (Institute of Medicine) (2010). *Promoting Cardiovascular Health in the Developing World: A Critical Challenge to Achieve Global Health*, ed. V. Fuster and B. B. Kelly. Washington, DC: National Academies Press.

Jauregui, M., and Schnall, P. (2009). Work, psychosocial stressors and the bottom line. In P. Schnall et al. (Eds.), *Unhealthy Work: Causes, Consequences and Cures*. Amityville, NY: Baywood.

Johnson, J. V. (2007). Globalization, workers' power, and the psychosocial work environment: Is the demand–control–support model still useful in a neoliberal era? *Scandinavian Journal of Work, Environment and Health, 34*, 15–21.

Johnson, J. V. (2009). The growing imbalance. In P. Schnall et al. (Eds.), *Unhealthy Work: Causes, Consequences and Cures*. Amityville, NY: Baywood.

Johnson, J. V., and Hall, E. M. (1988). Job strain, workplace social support, and cardiovascular disease: A cross-sectional study of a random sample of the Swedish working population. *American Journal of Public Health, 78*, 1336–1342.

Johnson, J. V., Hall, E. M., and Theorell, T. (1989). Combined effects of job strain and social isolation on cardiovascular disease morbidity and mortality in a random sample of the Swedish male working population. *Scandinavian Journal of Work, Environment and Health, 15*, 271–279.

Johnson, J. V., and Theorell, T. (1987). The effect of work strain and social isolation on cardiovascular disease risk. Paper presented at Annual Meetings of the American Public Health Association, New Orleans.

Kalleberg, A. (2011). *Good Jobs, Bad Jobs: The Rise of Polarized and Precarious Employment Systems in the United States, 1970s to 2000s. American Sociological Association's Rose Series in Sociology*. New York: Russell Sage Foundation.

Karasek, R., and Theorell, T. (1990). *Healthy Work: Stress, Productivity, and the Reconstruction of Working Life*. New York: Basic Books.

Kearney, P., Whelton, M., Reynolds, K., Muntner, P., Whelton, P., and He, J. (2005). Global burden of hypertension: Analysis of worldwide data. *Lancet, 365*, 217–223.

Kivimäki, M., Ferrie, J., Brunner, E., Head, J., Shipley, M., Vahtera, J., and Marmot, M. (2005). Justice at work and reduced risk of coronary heart disease among employees: The Whitehall II study. *Archives of Internal Medicine, 165*, 2245–2251.

Kivimäki, M., Ferrie, J. E., Shipley, M. J., Brunner, E., Vahtera, J., and Marmot, M. G. (2006a). Work stress, weight gain and weight loss: Evidence for bidirectional effects of job strain on body mass index in the Whitehall II study. *International Journal of Obesity, 30*, 982–987.

Kivimäki, M., Jokela, M., Nyberg, S. T., Singh-Manoux, A., Fransson, E. I., Alfredsson, L., … IPD-Work Consortium (2015a). Long working hours and risk of coronary heart disease and stroke: A systematic review and meta-analysis of published and unpublished data for 603,838 individuals. *Lancet, 386*(10005), 1739–1946. http://dx.doi.org/10.1016/S0140-6736(15)60295-1

Kivimäki, M., Nyberg, S. T., Batty, G. D., Fransson, E. I., Heikkilä, K., Alfredsson, L., … IPD-Work Consortium (2012). Job strain as a risk factor for coronary heart disease: A collaborative meta-analysis of individual participant data. *Lancet, 380*, 1491–1497.

Kivimäki, M., Vahtera, J., Pentti, J., and Ferrie, J. E. (2000). Factors underlying the effect of organisational downsizing on health of employees: Longitudinal cohort study. *British Medical Journal, 320*(7240), 971–975.

Kivimäki, M., Virtanen, M., Elovainio, M., Kouvonen, A., Vaananen, A., and Vahtera, J. (2006b). Work stress in the etiology of coronary heart disease: A meta-analysis. *Scandinavian Journal of Work, Environment and Health, 32*, 431–442.

Kivimäki, M., Virtanen, M., Kawachi, I., Nyberg, S. T., Alfredsson, L., Batty, G. D., … Jokela, M. (2015b). Long working hours, socioeconomic status, and the risk of incident type 2 diabetes: A meta-analysis of published and unpublished data from 222,120 individuals. *Lancet Diabetes Endocrinology, 3*, 27–34.

Kuper, H., Singh-Manouz, A., Siegrist, J., and Marmot, M. (2002). When reciprocity fails: Effort–reward imbalance in relation to coronary heart disease and health functioning in the Whitehall II study. *Occupational and Environmental Medicine, 59*, 777–784.

Kwon, H., and Pontusson, J. (2006). *Globalization, union decline and the politics of social spending growth in OECD countries, 1962–2000*. Yale University.

Laine, S., Gimeno, D., Virtanen, M., Oksanen, T., Vahtera, J., Elovainio, … Kivimäki, M. (2009). Job strain as a predictor of disability pension: The Finnish Public Sector Study. *Journal of Epidemiology and Community Health, 63*, 24–30.

LaMontagne, A., Keegel, T., Louie, A., Ostry, A., and Landsbergis, P. (2007). A systematic review of the job stress intervention evaluation literature: 1990–2005. *International Journal of Occupational and Environmental Health, 13*, 268–280.

LaMontagne, A., Keegel, T., Vallance, D., Ostry, A., and Wolfe, R. (2008). Job strain-attributable depression in a sample of working Australians: Assessing the contribution to health inequalities. *BMC Public Health, 8*, 181.

LaMontagne, A. D., and Keegel, T. G. (2012). *Reducing Stress in the Workplace: An Evidence Review: Full Report*. Melbourne: Victorian Heath Promotion Foundation (VicHealth).

LaMontagne, A. D., Noblet, A. J., and Landsbergis, P. A. (2012). Intervention development and implementation: Understanding and addressing barriers to organizational-level interventions. In C. Biron, M. Karanika-Murray, and C. L. Cooper (Eds.), *Improving Organizational Interventions for Stress and Well-Being: Addressing Process and Context* (pp. 21–38). New York: Routledge.

LaMontagne, A. D., Sanderson, K., and Cocker, F. (2010). *Estimating the Economic Benefits of Eliminating Job Strain as a Risk Factor for Depression*. Melbourne: Victorian Heath Promotion Foundation (VicHealth).

Landsbergis, P. (2009). Interventions to reduce job stress and improve work organization and worker health. In P. Schnall et al. (Eds.), *Unhealthy Work: Causes, Consequences and Cures*. Amityville, NY: Baywood.

Landsbergis, P., Cahill, J., and Schnall, P. (1999). The impact of lean production and related new systems of work organization on worker health. *Journal of Occupational Health Psychology, 4*(2), 108–130.

Landsbergis, P., Dobson, M., Koutsouras, G., and Schnall, P. (2013). Job strain and ambulatory blood pressure: A meta-analysis and systematic review. *American Journal of Public Health, 103*, e61–e71.

Landsbergis, P., Schnall, P., Belkić, K., Schwartz, J., Baker, D., and Pickering, T. (2008). Work conditions and masked (hidden) hypertension: Insights into the global epidemic of hypertension. *Scandinavian Journal of Work, Environment and Health, Supplement 2008* (6), 41–51.

Landsbergis, P., Schnall, P., Chace, R., Sullivan, L., and D'Agostino, R. (2005). Psychosocial job stressors and cardiovascular disease in the Framingham Offspring Study: A prospective analysis. Poster, 4th ICOH Conference on Work Environment and Cardiovascular Disease, Newport Beach, CA.

Landsbergis, P., Schnall, P., Pickering, T., Warren, K., and Schwartz, J. (2003). Lower socioeconomic status among men in relation to the association between job strain and blood pressure. *Scandinavian Journal of Work, Environment and Health, 29*, 206–215.

Landsbergis, P. A., Schnall, P. L., Warren, K., Pickering, T. G., and Schwartz, J. E. (1994). Association between ambulatory blood pressure and alternative formulations of job strain. *Scandinavian Journal of Work, Environment and Health, 20*, 349–363.

Landsbergis, P. A., Sinclair, R., Dobson, M., Hammer, L. B., Jauregui, M., LaMontagne, A. D., … Warren, N. (2011). Occupational health psychology. In D. Anna (Ed.), *The Occupational Environment: Its Evaluation, Control, and Management*, 3rd edn (pp. 1086–1130). Fairfax, VA: American Industrial Hygiene Association.

Laszlo, K., Ahnve, S., Hallqvist, J., Ahlbom, A., and Janszky, I. (2010). Job strain predicts recurrent events after a first acute myocardial infarction: The Stockholm Heart Epidemiology Program. *Journal of Internal Medicine, 267*, 599–611.

Lax, M. (2016). The perils of integrating wellness and safety and health and the possibility of a worker-oriented alternative. *New Solutions, 26*(1), 11–39.

Leigh, J. P. P., and Robbins, J. A. (2004). Occupational disease and workers' compensation: Coverage, costs, and consequences. *Milbank Quarterly, 82*, 689–722.

Leigh, J. P. P., Waehrer, G. P., Miller, T. R. P., and Keenan, C. (2004). Costs of occupational injury and illness across industries. *Scandinavian Journal of Work, Environment and Health, 30*, 199–205.

Leka, S., and Cox, T. (Eds.) (2008). *The European Framework for Psychosocial Risk Management: PRIMA-EF*. Nottingham, UK: Institute of Work, Health and Organisations.

Leka, S., Jain, A., Cox, T., and Kortum, E. (2011) The development of the European Framework for Psychosocial Risk Management: PRIMA-EF. *Journal of Occupational Health, 53*(2), 137–143.

Lett, H., Blumenthal, J., Babyak, M., Strauman, T., Robins, C., and Sherwood, A. (2005). Social support and coronary heart disease: Epidemiologic evidence and implications for treatment. *Psychosomatic Medicine, 67*, 869–878.

Leynen, F., Moreau, M., Pelfrene, E., Clays, E., De Backer, G., and Kornitzer, M. (2003). Job stress and prevalence of diabetes: Results from the Belstress study. *Archives of Public Health, 61*, 75–90.

Li, J., Zhang, M., Loerbroks, A., Angerer, P., and Siegrist, J. (2014). Work stress and the risk of recurrent coronary heart disease events: A systematic review and meta-analysis. *International Journal of Occupational Medicine and Environmental Health*. Epub ahead of print.

Lindeberg, S., Rosvall, M., Choi, B., Canivet, C., Isacsson, S. Q., Karasek, S. O., and Ostergren, P. O. (2011). Psychosocial working conditions and exhaustion in a working population sample of Swedish middle-aged men and women. *European Journal of Public Health, 21*, 190–196.

Lindstrom, K., Schrey, K., Ahonen, G., and Kaleva, S. (2000). The effects of promoting organisational health on worker well-being and organisational effectiveness in small and medium-sized enterprises. In L. R. Murphy and C. Cooper (Eds.), *Healthy and Productive Work: An International Perspective*. London: Taylor & Francis.

Liu, B.-Q., Peto, R., Chen, Z.-M., Boreham, J., Wu, Y.-P., Li, J.-Y., … Chen, J.-S. (1998). Emerging tobacco hazards in China: 1. Retrospective proportional mortality study of one million deaths. *British Medical Journal, 317*, 1411–1422.

Liu, L. (2007). Cardiovascular diseases in China. *Biochemistry and Cell Biology, 85*, 157–63.

Liu, Y., and Tanaka, H. (2002). Overtime work, insufficient sleep, and risk of nonfatal acute myocardial infarction in Japanese men (the Fukuoka Heart Study Group). *Occupational and Environmental Medicine, 59*, 447–451.

Louie, A., Ostry, A., Quinlan, M., Keegel, T., Shoveller, J., and Lamontagne, A. (2006). Empirical study of employment arrangements and precariousness in Australia. *Relations Industrielles/Industrial Relations, 61*, 465–489.

Ma, J., Ward, E. M., Siegel, R. L., and Jemal, A. (2015). Temporal trends in mortality in the United States, 1969–2013. *JAMA, 314*, 1731–1739.

Ma, W. J., Tang, J. L., Zhang, Y. H., Xu, Y. J., Lin, J. Y., Li, J. S., … Yu, T. (2012). Hypertension prevalence, awareness, treatment, control, and associated factors in adults in southern China. *American Journal of Hypertension, 25*, 590–596.

Mäntyniemi, A., Oksanen, T., Salo, P., Virtanen, M., Sjösten, N., Pentti, J., et al. (2012). Job strain and the risk of disability pension due to musculoskeletal disorders, depression or coronary heart disease: A prospective cohort study of 69,842 employees. *Occupational and Environmental Medicine, 69*, 574–581.

McEwen, B. S. (1998). Protective and damaging effects of stress mediators. *New England Journal of Medicine, 338*, 171–179.

McEwen, B., and Stellar, E. (1993). Stress and the individual: Mechanisms leading to disease. *Archives of Internal Medicine, 153*, 2093–3101.

McLellan, D., Harden, E., Markkanen, P., and Sorensen, G. (2012). *SafeWell Practice Guidelines: An Integrated Approach to Worker Health / Version 1.0*. Harvard School of Public Health, Center for Work, Health and Well-Being.

Melamed, S., Ben-Avi, I., and Green, M. S. (1992). The effects of monotony at work on psychological distress and cardiovascular risk factors among males and females in the Chordis study. In G. Puryear Keita and S. L. Sauter (Eds.), *Stress in the 90's: A Changing Workforce in a Changing Workplace*. Washington DC: American Psychological Association and National Institute for Occupational Safety and Health.

Melamed, S., Shirom, A., Toker, S., Berliner, S., and Shapira, I. (2006). Burnout and risk of cardiovascular disease: Evidence, possible casual paths, and promising research directions. *Psychological Bulletin, 132*, 327–353.

Michie, S., and Cockcroft, A. (1996). Overwork can kill: Especially if combined with high demand, low control, and poor social support. *British Medical Journal, 312*, 921–922.

Milanovic, B. (2012). *Global Income Inequality by the Numbers: In History and Now – An Overview*. Policy Research Working Paper Series 6259. Washington, DC: World Bank.

Mishel, L., and Bernstein, J. (2006). *The State of Working America*. Washington, DC: Economic Policy Institute.

Moutsatsos, C. (2009). Economic globalization and its effects on labor. In P. Schnall, M. Dobson, and E. Rosskam (Eds.), *Unhealthy Work: Causes, Consequences, Cures*. Amityville, NY: Baywood.

Mozaffarian, D., Benjamin, E. J., Go, A. S., Arnett, D. K., Blaha, M. J., Cushman, M., … Turner, M. B. (2015). Heart disease and stroke statistics – 2015 update: A report from the American Heart Association. *Circulation, 131*(4), e29–322.

Muntaner, C., Benach, J., Hadden, W., Gimeno, D., and Benavides, F. (2006). A glossary for the social epidemiology of work organisation: Part 1, Terms from social psychology. *Journal of Epidemiology and Community Health, 60*, 914–916.

Musselman, D. L., Evans, D. L., and Nemeroff, C. B. (1998). The relationship of depression to cardiovascular disease: Epidemiology, biology, and treatment. *Archives of General Psychiatry*, *55*, 580–592.

Musselman, D. L., Tomer, A., Manatunga, A. K., Knight, B. T., Porter, M. R., Kasey, S., … Nemeroff, C. B. (1996). Exaggerated platelet reactivity in major depression. *American Journal of Psychiatry*, *153*, 1313–1317.

Nedic, O., Belkić, K., Filipović, D., and Jocić, N. (2010). Job stressors among female physicians: Relation to having a clinical diagnosis of hypertension. *International Journal of Occupational and Environmental Health*, *16*(3), 330–340.

Netterstrom, B., Conrad, N., Bech, P., Fink, P., Olson, O., Rugulies, R., and Stansfeld, S. (2008). The relation between work-related psychosocial factors and the development of depression. *Epidemiologic Reviews*, *30*, 118–132.

Nicholson, A., Kuper, H., and Hemingway, H. (2006). Depression as an aetiologic and prognostic factor in coronary heart disease: A meta-analysis of 6362 events among 146 538 participants in 54 observational studies. *European Heart Journal*, *27*, 2763–2774.

Niedhammer, I., Sultan-Taieb, H., Chastang, J. F., Vermeylen, G., and Parent-Thirion, A. (2012). Exposure to psychosocial work factors in 31 European countries. *Occupational Medicine (London)*, *62*, 196–202.

Niedhammer, I., Sultan-Taieb, H., Chastang, J. F., Vermeylen, G., and Parent-Thirion, A. (2014). Fractions of cardiovascular diseases and mental disorders attributable to psychosocial work factors in 31 countries in Europe. *International Archives of Occupational and Environmental Health*, *87*, 403–11.

NIOSH (National Institute for Occupational Safety and Health) (2002). *The Changing Organization of Work and the Safety and Health of Working People*. Report No. 2002-116. Cincinnati: NIOSH.

NIOSH (National Institute for Occupational Safety and Health) (2012). *The Research Compendium: The NIOSH Total Worker Health*[TM] *Program: Seminal Research Papers* 2012. Washington, DC: US Department of Health and Human Services.

Nyberg, S. T., Fransson, E. I., Heikkilä, K., Alfredsson, L., Casini, A., Clays, E., … Kivimäki, M. (2013). Job strain and cardiovascular disease risk factors: Meta-analysis of individual-participant data from 47,000 men and women. *PLoS One*, *8*, e67323.

Nyberg, S. T., Heikkilä, K., Fransson, E. I., Alfredsson, L., De Bacquer, D., Bjorner, J. B., … Kivimäki, M. (2012). Job strain in relation to body mass index: Pooled analysis of 160,000 adults from 13 cohort studies. *Journal of Internal Medicine*, *272*(1), 65–73.

Ohkubo, T., Kikuya, M., Metoki, H., Asayama, K., Obara, T., Hashimoto, J., … Imai, Y. (2005). Prognosis of masked hypertension and white coat hypertension detected by 24-h ambulatory blood pressure monitoring. *Journal of the American College of Cardiology*, *46*, 508–515.

Orth-Gomer, K., Eriksson, I., Moser, V., Theorell, T., and Fredlund, P. (1994). Lipid lowering through work stress reduction. *International Journal of Behavioral Medicine*, *1*, 204–214.

Orth-Gomer, K., Wamala, S. P., Horsten, M., Schenck-Gustafsson, K., Schneiderman, N., and Mittleman, M. A. (2000). Marital stress worsens prognosis in women with coronary heart disease. *Journal of the American Medical Association*, *284*, 3008–3014.

Oster, S. (2014). In China, 1,600 People die every day from working too hard. *Bloomberg Businessweek*, July 3.

Pandalai, S., Schulte, P., and Miller, D. (2013). Conceptual heuristic models of the interrelationships between obesity and the occupational environment. *Scandinavian Journal of Work, Environment and Health*, *39*, 221–232.

Pejtersen, J. H., Burr, H., Hannerz, H., Fishta, A., and Eller, N. H. (2015). Update on work-related psychosocial factors and the development of ischemic heart disease: A systematic review. *Cardiology in Review*, *23*, 94–98.

Pickering, T., Harshfield, G., Kleinert, H., Blank, S., and Laragh, J. (1982). Blood pressure during normal daily activities, sleep, and exercise: Comparison of values in normal and hypertensive subjects. *JAMA*, *247*, 992–996.

Pieper, C., Schnall, P. L., Warren, K., and Pickering, T. G. (1993). A comparison of ambulatory blood pressure and heart rate at home and work on work and non-work days. *Journal of Hypertension*, *11*, 177–183.

Pierdomenico, S., Lapenna, D., Bucci, A., Di Tommaso, R., Di Mascio, R., Manente, B., … Mezzetti, A. (2005). Cardiovascular outcome in treated hypertensive patients with responder, masked, false resistant, and true resistant hypertension. *American Journal of Hypertension*, *18*, 1422–1428.

Quinlan, M., and Mayhew, C. (2000). Precarious employment, work re-organisation and the fracturing of OHS management. In K. Frick, P. L. Jensen, M. Quinlan, and T. Wilthagen (Eds.), *Systematic Occupational Health and Safety Management: Perspectives on an International Development*. New York: Pergamon.

Quinlan, M., Mayhew, C., and Bohle, P. (2001). The global expansion of precarious employment, work disorganization, and consequences for occupational health: A review of recent research. *International Journal of Health Services*, *31*, 335–414.

Rugulies, R. (2002). Depression as a predictor for coronary heart disease: A review and meta-analysis. *American Journal of Preventive Medicine, 23*, 51–61.

Rugulies, R., Christensen, K., Borritz, M., Villadsen, E., Bultmann, U., and Kristensen, T. (2007). The contribution of the psychosocial work environment to sickness absence in human service workers: Results of a 3-year follow-up study. *Work and Stress, 21*, 293–311.

Russ, T., Stamatakis, E., Hamer, M., Starr, J., Kivimäki, M., and Batty, G. (2012). Association between psychological distress and mortality: Individual participant pooled analysis of 10 prospective cohort studies. *British Medical Journal, 345*, e4933.

Rydstedt, L. W., Johansson, G., and Evans, G. W. (1998). The human side of the road: Improving the working conditions of urban bus drivers. *Journal of Occupational Health Psychology, 3*, 161–171.

Saad, L. (2014). The "40-hour" workweek is actually longer – by seven hours. Gallup Annual Work and Education Survey. At http://www.gallup.com/poll/175286/hour-workweek-actually-longer-seven-hours.aspx (accessed July 2016).

Sanderson, D. M., Ekholm, O., Hundrup, Y. A., and Rasmussen, N. K. (2005). Influence of lifestyle, health, and work environment on smoking cessation among Danish nurses followed over 6 years. *Preventive Medicine, 41*, 757–760.

Sandle, P. (2015). Richest 1 percent will own more than the rest by 2016: Oxfam. Reuters.

Schmidt, B., Bosch, J., Jarczok, M., Herr, R., Loerbroks, A., Van Vianen, A., and Fischer, J. (2015). Effort–reward imbalance is associated with the metabolic syndrome: Findings from the Mannheim Industrial Cohort Study (MICS). *International Journal of Cardiology, 178*, 24–28.

Schnall, P. L., Belkić, K., Landsbergis, P., and Baker, D. (2000). The workplace and cardiovascular disease. *Occupational Medicine, 15*, 1–322.

Schnall, P. L., Landsbergis, P. A., Schwartz, J., Warren, K., and Pickering, T. G. (1998). A longitudinal study of job strain and ambulatory blood pressure: Results from a three-year follow-up. *Psychosomatic Medicine, 60*, 697–706.

Schnall, P. L., Pieper, C., Schwartz, J. E., Karasek, R. A., Schlussel, Y., Devereux, R. B., ... Pickering, T. G. (1990). The relationship between "job strain," workplace diastolic blood pressure, and left ventricular mass index: Results of a case-control study [published erratum appears in *JAMA*, 267(9) (1992), 1209]. *Journal of the American Medical Association, 263*, 1929–1935.

Schnall, P. L., Schwartz, J. E., Landsbergis, P. A., Warren, K., and Pickering, T. G. (1992). Relation between job strain, alcohol, and ambulatory blood pressure. *Hypertension, 19*, 488–494.

Schnorpfeil, P., Noll, A., Schulze, R., Ehlert, U., Frey, K., and Fischer, J. E. (2003). Allostatic load and work conditions. *Social Science and Medicine, 57*(4), 647–656.

Sega, R., Trocino, G., Lanzarotti, A., Carugo, S., Cesana, G., Schiavina, R., ... Mancia, G. (2001). Alterations of cardiac structure in patients with isolated office, ambulatory, or home hypertension: Data from the general population: Pressione Arteriose Monitorate e Loro Associazioni (PAMELA) study. *Circulation, 104*, 1385–1392.

Shimomitsu, T., and Odagiri, Y. (2000). Working life in Japan. *Occupational Medicine: State of the Art Reviews, 15*, 280–281.

Shirom, A., Armon, G., Berliner, S., Shapira, I., and Melamed, S. (2009). The effects of job strain on risk factors for cardiovascular disease. In C. L. Cooper, J. Quick, and M. J. Schabracq (Eds.), *International Handbook of Work and Health Psychology*, 3rd edn (pp. 49–76). Oxford: Wiley-Blackwell.

Siegrist, J. (1996). Adverse health effects of high-effort/low-reward conditions. *Journal of Occupational Health Psychology, 1*, 27–43.

Siegrist, J. (2005). Social reciprocity and health: New scientific evidence and policy implications *Psychoneuroendocrinology, 30*, 1033–1038.

Siegrist, J. (2008). Chronic psychosocial stress at work and risk of depression: Evidence from prospective studies. *European Archives of Psychiatry and Clinical Neuroscience, 258*(suppl. 5), 115–119.

Siegrist, J., and Rodel, A. (2006). Work stress and health risk behavior. *Scandinavian Journal of Work, Environment and Health, 32*, 473–481.

Siegrist, J., Starke, D., Chandola, T., Godin, I., Marmot, M., Niedhammer, I., and Peter, R. (2004). The measurement of effort–reward imbalance at work: European comparisons. *Social Science and Medicine, 58*, 1483–1499.

Sokejima, S., and Kagamimori, S. (1998). Working hours as a risk factor for acute myocardial infarction in Japan: Case-control study. *British Medical Journal, 317*, 775–780.

Solovieva, S., Lallukka, T., Virtanen, M., and Viikari-Juntura, E. (2013). Psychosocial factors at work, long work hours, and obesity: A systematic review. *Scandinavian Journal of Work, Environment and Health, 39*, 241–258.

Sorensen, G., Barbeau, E., Hunt, M. K., and Emmons, K. (2004). Reducing social disparities in tobacco use: A social-contextual model for reducing tobacco use among blue-collar workers. *American Journal of Public Health*, *94*(2), 230–239.

Sorensen, G., Barbeau, E., Stoddard, A. M., Hunt, M. K., Kaphingst, K., and Wallace, L. (2005). Promoting behavior change among working-class, multiethnic workers: results of the healthy directions–small business study. *American Journal of Public Health*, *95*, 1389–95.

Sorensen, G., Landsbergis, P., Hammer, L., Amick, B. C., III, Linnan, L., Yancey, A., ... Pratt, C. (2011). Preventing chronic disease in the workplace: A workshop report and recommendations. *American Journal of Public Health*, *101*(suppl. 1), S196–S207.

Sorensen, G., Stoddard, A., Hunt, M. K., Hebert, J. R., Ockene, J. K., Avrunin, J. S., ... Hammond, S. K. (1998). The effects of a health promotion–health protection intervention on behavior change: The WellWorks study. *American Journal of Public Health*, *88*, 1685–90.

Stansfeld, S., and Candy, B. (2006). Psychosocial work environment and mental health: A meta-analytic review. *Scandinavian Journal of Work, Environment and Health*, *32*, 443–462.

Stansfeld, S., Fuhrer, R., Shipley, M., and Marmot, M. (1999). Work characteristics predict psychiatric disorders: Prospective results from the Whitehall II study. *Occupation and Environmental Medicine*, *56*, 302–307.

Steptoe, A., and Kivimäki, M. (2013). Stress and cardiovascular disease: An update on current knowledge. *Annual Reviews of Public Health*, *34*, 337–54.

Sterling, P., and Eyer, J. (1988). Allostasis: A new paradigm to explain arousal pathology. In S. Fisher and J. T. Reason (Eds.), *Handbook of Life Stress, Cognition, and Health*. Hoboken, NJ: Wiley.

Stonea, A. A., and Brownell, K. D. (1994). The stress-eating paradox: Multiple daily measurements in adult males and females. *Psychology and Health*, *9*, 425–436.

Tao, S., Wu, X., Duan, X., Fang, W., Hao, J., Fan, D., ... Li, Y. (1995). Hypertension prevalence and status of awareness, treatment and control in China. *Chinese Medical Journal (English)*, *108*, 483–489.

Taris, T. W., Ybema, J. F., Beckers, D. G. J., Verheijden, M. W., Geurts, S. A. E., and Kompier, M. A. J. (2011). Investigating the associations among overtime work, health behaviors, and health: A longitudinal study among full-time employees. *International Journal of Behavioral Medicine*, *18*, 352–360.

Theorell, T., Perski, A., Orth-Gomer, K., Hamsten, A., and De Faire, U. (1991). The effects of the strain of returning to work on the risk of cardiac death after a first myocardial infarction before age 45. *International Journal of Cardiology*, *30*, 61–67.

Theorell, T., Tsutsumi, A., Hallqvist, J., Reuterwall, C., Hogstedt, C., Fredlund, P., ... Johnson, J. V. (1998). Decision latitude, job strain and myocardial infarction: a study of working men in Stockholm. *American Journal of Public Health*, *88*, 382–388.

Toivanen, S., and Landsbergis, P. (2013). Lean och arbetstagarnas hälsa [Lean and worker health]. In P. Sederblad and L. Abrahamsson (Eds.), *Lean i arbetslivet [Lean in working life]*. Stockholm: Liber.

Trudel, X., Brisson, C., Milot, A., Masse, B., and Vézina, M. (2013). Psychosocial work environment and ambulatory blood pressure: Independent and combined effect of demand–control and effort–reward imbalance models. *Occupational and Environmental Medicine*, *70*, 815–822.

Tuchsen, F. (2000). High-risk occupations for cardiovascular disease. In P. Schnall et al. (Eds.), *The Workplace and Cardiovascular Disease*. Philadelphia: Hanley & Belfus.

Vahtera, J., Kivimäki, M., Pentti, J., Linna, A., Virtanen, M., Virtanen, P., and Ferrie, J. E. (2004). Organisational downsizing, sickness absence, and mortality: 10-town prospective cohort study. *British Medical Journal*, *328*, 555.

Verdecchia, P., Clement, D., Fagard, R., Palatini, P., and Parati, G. (1999). Task force III: Target-organ damage, morbidity and mortality. *Blood Pressure Monitoring*, *4*, 303–317.

Virtanen, M., Ferrie, J. E., Singh-Manoux, A., Shipley, M. J., Vahtera, J., Marmot, M. G., and Kivimäki, M. (2010). Overtime work and incident coronary heart disease: The Whitehall II prospective cohort study. *European Heart Journal*, *31*, 1737–1744.

Virtanen, M, Heikkilä, K., Jokela, M., Ferrie, J. E., Batty, G. D., Vahtera, J., and Kivimäki, M. (2012). Long working hours and coronary heart disease: A systematic review and meta-analysis. *American Journal of Epidemiology*, *176*, 586–596.

Virtanen, M., Kivimäki, M., Elovainio, M., Vahtera, J., and Cooper, C. (2001). Contingent employment, health and sickness absence. *Scandinavian Journal of Work, Environment and Health*, *27*, 365–372.

Virtanen, M., Nyberg, S. T., Batty, G. D., Jokela, M., Heikkila, K., Fransson, E. I., ... Kivimäki, M. (2013). Perceived job insecurity as a risk factor for incident coronary heart disease: Systematic review and meta-analysis. *British Medical Journal*, *347*, f4746.

Vives, A., Amable, M., Ferrer, M., Moncada, S., Llorens, C., Muntaner, C., … Benach, J. (2010). The Employment Precariousness Scale (EPRES): Psychometric properties of a new tool for epidemiological studies among waged and salaried workers. *Occupational and Environmental Medicine*, *67*, 548–555.

Vyas, M., Garg, A., Iansavichus, A., Costella, J., Donner, A., Laugsand, L., … Hackam, D. G. (2012). Shift work and vascular events: Systematic review and meta-analysis. *British Medical Journal*, *345*, e4800.

Wang, X.-S., Armstrong, M. E. G., Cairns, B. J., Key, T. J., and Travis, R. C. (2011). Shift work and chronic disease: The epidemiological evidence. *Occupational Medicine*, *61*, 78–89.

Weinberg, D. (1996). A brief look at postwar US income inequality. *Current Population Reports*. US Census Bureau,.

Wilson, M. G. (1996). A comprehensive review of the effects of worksite health promotion on health-related outcomes: An update. *American Journal of Health Promotion*, *11*, 107–108.

Wolff, E. (1995). *Top Heavy: A Study of Wealth Inequality in America*. New York: Twentieth Century Fund Press.

Womack, J. P. (1996). The psychology of lean production. *Applied Psychology: An International Review*, *45*, 119–152.

Yang, H., Schnall, P., Jauregui, M., Su, T., and Baker, D. (2006). Work hours and self-reported hypertension among working people in California. *Hypertension*, *48*, 744–750.

7

Stress and Cancer

Christoffer Johansen, Ivalu Katajavaara Sørensen, Beverley Lim Høeg,
Pernille E. Bidstrup, and Susanne O. Dalton

Stress has become a metaphor for being a part of the emerging human being who is constantly interactive and accessible through the internet. Whether this is at your work, your home, in a hotel, or on vacation in remote places, you are able to take a call, write a text message, respond to an email, send a photo, and download huge files of information. The interactive platform connects instruments for both work and spare-time activities, and boundaries between work and leisure time are challenged. It is the same platform and almost the same commands, whatever the platform, which are used in reading the news, checking your bank account, analyzing data, or ordering a flight ticket for a summer holiday. The human being may feel stressed because of this constant accessibility.

To be stressed is a condition which may be used more or less correctly, but certainly differently by different people. Stress is a reaction to pressure and, in principle, to the unknown. It involves unknown factors which may be perceived as a threat, and also phenomena inside ourselves that pose a risk for reactions which we cannot foresee, whether these are cognitive, behavioral, or emotional – or a mixture of these dimensions of the human capacity for dealing with stress. A stressor is what may cause you to become stressed, which can be more precisely termed a stressful event, an experience of exposure that is well defined.

We have always been stressed and worried about the unknown and the current situation is as unpredictable as the situation experienced by the Stone Age man looking for food, constantly snacking on nuts, small berries, and overlooked green leaves, and drinking water from the melted glacier.

For centuries stress has been considered a cause of disease. And even today stress is feared and deemed unhealthy. Look around you and listen to the debate about why people imagine they become ill, ask both lay persons and health professionals what they believe causes diseases, and a majority will probably rate stress as quite an important risk factor for most acute and chronic diseases. Numerous studies conducted all over the world and published in high-ranking international peer-reviewed scientific journals support this idea and nourish our understanding of a mind–body relationship.

The idea that stress causes cancer goes back far in time. Galen, a second-century Greek surgeon, believed, as did Hippocrates, that cancer (which he termed *oncos*, Greek for swelling) was caused by an imbalance in the humoral fluids, with an excess of black bile, and he specifically also noted that women with breast cancer were more often melancholic than sanguine women. This idea that certain personality traits or ways of coping with the challenges of everyday life may cause cancer has played a major role in the understanding of what causes cancer through history. Nowadays, it still seems to play a role among patients, who try to bring some kind of order to the chaos surrounding their disease, even if it was actually caused or partly caused by infection or associated with other environmental or behavioral exposure.

Seen from a scientific point of view, one can investigate if stress *causes* cancer, how stress may *predict* a cancer prognosis, and how being diagnosed with cancer *influences* the level of stress. Finally, one can also study interventions to relieve stress in cancer patients and investigate the effect of such interventions on levels of stress.

However, before giving some examples from the scientific literature, a few points about methods for studying the association between stress and cancer would be appropriate. The first question which always arises is how to measure stress exposure. Major life events, depression, or certain personality traits may impose stress on an individual mainly due to the change in their entire equilibrium. The stressors may include internal as well as external sources but they may all be identified by the low degree of predictability, the low possibility of control, the low degree of meaning, and the difficulty of relating the stressor to the individual's life in general. Stress may be a constant factor which influences the level of physical, psychological, and social functioning. It may influence hormonal functioning in terms of estrogen, prolactin, and other well-known hormones; it may affect the output of adrenalin and noradrenalin (fight or flight substances) from the medulla (center) of the adrenal glands. People under stress may act more aggressively in social circumstances, and stress may influence the quality of contact between parents and children, between partners, and at the workplace.

In the last century, Holmes and Rahe (1967) constructed a scale measuring stressors – events which make you stressed. Based on interviews with a relatively high number of people, they wanted to clarify what people actually agreed upon as the most severe events that could be experienced, and which in broad terms would potentially influence a person's health status. They created a major life event scale based on the responses. As the top three most important events, Holmes and Rahe ranked the death of a spouse, the death of a child, or a severe, life-threatening disease in a close relative.

The next methodological issue is related to the design of a scientific study. You will not find many authors discussing the pros and cons of a given design for a study. Scientists and clinicians only rarely dwell on such issues and many try to indirectly hide important study information. By the term "design" we are referring to the issues of how data collection is organized with regard to timing in relation to exposure to stress, and the outcomes to be measured and thus studied. But it also concerns the ways of selecting and inviting both cases (patients with cancer) and controls (persons without cancer). This latter population serves as a comparison group for any given case group. Many designs have been developed to investigate any hypothesis and each of them have their advantages and limitations. To be able to establish causality, the optimal design is the experimental randomized controlled study, where participants are allocated by random to exposure or lack of exposure (i.e., given a placebo or usual care). This is often not possible to do when studying stress in terms of exposure to disease, and thus we must use observational designs. In short, prospective cohort studies which include healthy persons who are asked for information about exposure (questionnaire, interview, sometimes also blood samples and tissue biopsies) and who are followed over time until disease occurs provide the next best design after the randomized controlled trial. Ranking third is the case-control design where persons with cancer are compared with persons without cancer; this design will always be limited by the fact that people will remember and answer differently according to whether they are sick or not. There follows the cross-sectional design where data are collected at a single point in time. Finally, at the lowest rank, there is the case study, a description of a patient story or a number of stories, which are even less reliable in determining if stress influences the development of cancer. The literature on stress and cancer has only included this rather important discussion to a limited degree in the reporting of findings from studies.

Stress as a Risk Factor for Cancer

No consensus has been reached on whether or not stress affects the incidence of cancer, or on what pathway might explain such a relationship. Thus, several reviews have been carried out of the studies that have been made, but the evidence is still inconsistent, with discrepancies between the different conclusions. Potential explanations are different inclusion criteria, study populations, study design, ways of defining and measuring stress, length of follow-up, and different cancer diseases as outcomes. The discrepancies could also to some extent be attributed to the backgrounds of the various authors and their accompanying scientific perspectives. Authors working mainly with epidemiology may view the stress–cancer relationship differently than authors working directly with cancer patients who may often consider that stress could have been a contributing factor to the onset of their cancer (Bleiker and van der Ploeg, 1999; McKenna, Zevon, Corn, and Rounds, 1999). It could be hypothesized that these environmental circumstances might affect the way in which a clinician regarded his or her findings compared to an epidemiologist evaluating the same findings. Furthermore, clinicians and epidemiologists sometimes have different criteria for evaluating when a statistical effect size is of clinical importance (Coyne, Ranchor, and Palmer, 2010).

The examined evidence indicates that a possible association between stress and cancer has not been established, and that discrepancies still exist among researchers in the field. The majority of the reviews conclude that there were either no or only weak causal associations between stress and cancer incidence (Bleiker and van der Ploeg, 1999; Butow et al., 2000; Dalton, Boesen, Ross, Schapiro, and Johansen, 2002; Duijts, Zeegers, and Borne, 2003; Garssen, 2004; Nielsen and Gronbaek, 2006; Santos et al., 2009). Petticrew, Fraser, and Regan (1999) found a possible relationship when using the random effects model in their meta-analysis, but pointed out that the quality of the included studies varied, causing possible bias when they were pooled. Because of that, subgroup analyses were conducted on the studies with the highest methodological quality. The results of these analyses showed no statistical association. Butow et al. (2000) found a weak relationship and recommended that future studies of greater methodological rigor should be conducted. In addition they pointed out that many studies included small sample sizes and that some studies combined cases and controls from different sources. Duijts et al. (2003) found a modest association between death of a spouse and the risk of development of breast cancer after controlling for homogeneity and publication bias. Both Dalton et al. (2002) and Nielsen and Gronbaek (2006) concluded that stressful life events did not seem to increase the risk of incidence of breast cancer. Dalton et al. criticized the studies included in the review for being of poor methodological quality, possibly affecting study results, while Nielsen et al. found some sign of heterogeneity in their obtained results. A meta-analysis by Santos et al. (2009) found a borderline association between high-intensity stress and breast cancer.

The latest review including all cancer types presented by Chida, Hamer, Wardle, and Steptoe (2008) found an association between stress-related psychosocial factors and cancer incidence and survival. Several points of critique can be mentioned regarding this review (Coyne et al., 2010). It included a large number of studies and thus observations, which automatically heightens the chance of a statistically significant result. Making causal assumptions on the basis of the p-values is therefore not the most valid way of evaluating the results of an analysis. Rather, conclusions should be drawn on the basis of the measure of association and the corresponding confidence intervals (Coyne et al., 2010). Arriving at a conclusion on the basis of statistical significance is especially a problem when studies with little statistical strength are included. These studies have an increased risk not only of type II error but also type I error, should the null hypothesis be rejected (Christley, 2010). In their criticism, Coyne et al. point out that the quality of some of the covered studies was poor, which in turn affects the quality of the review including them. Chida et al. (2008) included the same samples several times while treating them as independent cohorts. This method increases the risk of making less valid analyses and this is worsened because the authors did not conduct sensitivity analyses, in which for example only the best quality studies are included. Possible recall bias is also introduced into the estimates presented by Chida et al. because of the inclusion of both sick and healthy populations, making it hard to determine possible temporality between the exposure to stress and the diagnosis of cancer.

An overall tendency in the reviews is to mention studies that lack methodological rigor, evidently affecting the quality of the review itself. By including retrospective and/or quasi-prospective studies, reviewers encounter problems with determining temporality and the possible underlying causality. Several reviews also found possible publication bias in the review literature, indicating a tendency to publish "positive" results supporting the notion that stress can cause cancer. A general problem mentioned in many of the reviews is the lack of adequate adjustment for confounders in some of the included studies, lowering the validity of the findings. Looking at the presented reviews, the existing knowledge in this field of research needs to be summarized by reviews where the paramount focus is on including studies with high methodological quality.

Stress as a Prognostic Factor in Cancer

How do cancer patients cope with the stress related to diagnosis, treatment, and a changed perspective on life? What is the impact of psychological stress on survival? What does it mean to think positively? These and other questions all reflect the popular idea that psychological factors such as coping style may influence survival from cancer. It is our belief that this idea became prevalent in the population partly based on a small study published in 1979 by Greer, Morris, and Pettingale (1979). In this study it was observed that women who used "fighting spirit" as their coping style lived longer compared to women who used other coping styles. On the other hand, and in support of that finding, other studies have reported that 'helplessness/hopelessness' predicted a poorer outcome. It is, of course, very important to investigate to what degree coping style influences the outcome following a cancer diagnosis. First, patients might benefit from becoming more focused on their ways of coping with life as a cancer patient. Secondly, psychological interventions are currently implemented that aim at changing and enhancing the use of certain means of coping with cancer – and there is a strong support among patients, their families, and also among professionals for the idea that this kind of coping training is of benefit to the patient. Some studies investigating this issue were initially identified for a review that we published in 2002 (Ross, Boesen, Dalton, and Johansen, 2002). More reviews have been published since (Chow, Tsao, and Harth, 2004; Coyne, Lepore, and Palmer, 2006; Faller et al., 2013; Galway et al., 2012; Hersch, Juraskova, Price, and Mullan, 2009; Hoon, Chi Sally, and Hong-Gu, 2013), but in principle they did not change the overall conclusion that we do not know if psychological and/or other stress-reducing interventions impact on survival and/or well-being

Distress

The stress that people may experience in connection with the disease of cancer can be captured in the construct of distress, which may be simply defined as the experience of significant emotional upset, and which arises from various psychological and psychiatric conditions (Carlson et al., 2004; Carlson et al., 2010). It is a common but treatable complication of cancer, and it can present at any stage in the cancer pathway (Fallowfield, Ratcliffe, Jenkins, and Saul, 2001). It may consist predominantly of depression, anxiety or anger, or present as a mixed, broadly defined state (Graves et al., 2007). In recent work, the prevalence of distress was 30–50 percent, depending on the method of assessment (Mitchell, 2007). Using distress as the key emotional, patient-reported outcome measure rather than depression has the advantage of lower perceived stigma and broad acceptability to patients; the disadvantage is that distress is poorly operationalized, and there is therefore a risk of categorizing patients who have short-lived, "normal" emotional responses to cancer as ill (Mulder, 2008). The National Comprehensive Cancer Network (2007) has proposed a distress term, while other bodies prefer the term "adjustment disorder," or a psychiatric disorder from the *International Classification of Diseases*, 10th edition, or the *Diagnostic and Statistical Manual of Mental Disorders*, 4th edition.

For the purposes of deciding when to offer professional help, it is useful to attempt to grade distress: for example, into minimal, mild, moderate, or severe, with no, slight, moderate, or moderate to severe functional impairment, respectively. Accumulating evidence suggests that the presence of distress is associated with reduced health-related quality of life (Shim et al., 2006), poor satisfaction with medical care (von Essen, Larsson, Oberg, and Sjoden, 2002), and possibly reduced survival after cancer (Faller, Bulzebruck, Drings, and Lang, 1999). The finding in a large nationwide, population-based cohort study in Denmark that the risk for admission with an affective disorder was significantly increased up to ten years after a cancer diagnosis (Dalton, Laursen, Ross, Mortensen, and Johansen, 2009) illustrates the possible serious evolution of distress.

According to the National Comprehensive Cancer Network, distress should be recognized and monitored through screening and treated promptly at all stages of the disease (Holland et al., 2010). Distress in cancer patients is, however, often overlooked (Fallowfield et al., 2001) and thus frequently untreated. Most physicians working with cancer patients do not use a screening instrument to identify those with mood disorders, including depression. For example, 90 percent of 226 health professionals working in cancer care in the United Kingdom reported that they did not use a validated instrument to identify mood disorders among their patients (Mitchell, Kaar, Coggan, and Herdman, 2008). So the question is, how do cancer patients then cope with the distress of cancer?

Coping with the Stress of Cancer

The handling of everyday problems that people face does not initiate coping efforts and may be looked upon as a continuous row of more mechanical/instrumental solutions –behavioral, emotional, and/or cognitive. In contrast, people confronted with stressful events need to mobilize resources in order to cope with these major problems. A cancer diagnosis can be considered very stressful because it is interpreted as a threat to the individual person and to social life. Many scientific studies have focused on the association between ways of coping and the prognosis of patients diagnosed with cancer. Stressors demand certain specific coping skills in order to be mastered, and in this context it seems reasonable to include the concept of coping.

How do people cope with serious stressors? A number of research studies have investigated this topic and a classic division of these theoretical approaches distinguishes between a situational and a more personality-driven coping style as the two main perspectives involved in the explanation of the nature of coping. The situational approach was identified by Lazarus, who illustrate his idea by dividing the coping process in two separate, though integrated parts (Lazarus, 1966). In a first step, the individual realizes the size and impact of the stressor, evaluates possible solutions, and reflects these "observations" in an integrated manner, leading to a decision about how to cope with a particular problem. The exact solution or coping approach is determined by the social context in which the threat appeared, depending on experience with a way of coping, on personality, and possibly also on gender, age, and socioeconomic parameters. However, this completely integrated model makes it difficult to distinguish various parts of each problem, and measurement becomes a very complex matter. Another interesting theory in this area of research uses a more personality focused approach and was initially defined by Haan (Haan and Lykken, 2013). In this interpretation of the coping process, personality characteristics are defined as more important compared to the situational perspective. The idea is based on a psychoanalytic approach, and Haan defined coping as the healthy person's most developed response, followed by defense behavior, and lastly, a loss of ego function or fragmentation. It seems reasonable to anticipate that coping is influenced by personal and social circumstances, and further, that ways of coping are also influenced by the situation and experiences with different ways of coping containing all three of emotional, behavioral, and cognitive elements.

By definition, coping is a response to stress. In one of his final writings, Lazarus wrote, "Coping is the effort to manage *psychological* stress." Stress was initially studied as a physiological *response* based on animal models (Selye, 1956), and later was seen as a *stimulus* in the form of life events that were considered stressors (Holmes and Rahe, 1967). Lazarus (1966) moved beyond these response and stimulus-based conceptualizations by proposing a more dynamic transactional framework. He believed that stress did not exist in a single event, but rather was a result of transactions between a person and his or her environment. This model was expanded into Lazarus and Folkman's highly influential transactional model of stress and coping (1984). Unlike other models, Lazarus and Folkman's model explicitly defines the act of coping. What, then, accounts for this variation in how different people cope with particular stressful conditions? Here, Lazarus and Folkman (1984) proposed that cognitive appraisal played the primary role of mediator in the person–environment transaction model. This conceptualization of appraisal became one of the most important contributions to our current understanding of the coping process (Lyon, 2000).

Lazarus and Folkman (1984) defined coping as "constantly changing cognitive and behavioral efforts to manage specific external and/or internal demands that are appraised as taxing or exceeding the resources of the person." In a later definition, they added that these cognitive and behavioral efforts are constantly changing "as a function of continuous appraisals and reappraisals of the person–environment relationship" (Folkman and Lazarus, 1991). This definition delineates several aspects of coping, namely: (1) coping is process oriented, not a trait or an outcome; (2) the act of coping is not to be confounded with the outcome of coping; (3) coping involves all efforts to manage stress, and is not equated with mastery; and (4) it requires cognitive appraisal of the person's environment and resources, thus limiting coping to psychological stress, and excludes automatized behaviors (Lyon, 2000).

In this chapter, "coping" is defined as a response to psychological stress, a response that takes place in a process that is dynamic and embedded in situational and individual context. Coping is not synonymous with a positive outcome – a definition often used in mainstream literature (Kleinke, 2007) – and neither is it fixed, as coping acts and thoughts may change as the stressful encounter unfolds (Lazarus and Folkman, 1984). This distinction has not always been made. In traditional, physiological-behavioral models of stress, coping was synonymous with the positive outcome of mastering the environment (Lyon, 2000). This shifted with the psychoanalytic ego psychology model, which placed more emphasis on cognitive processes in solving problems and reducing stress (Lazarus and Folkman, 1984). However, coping was still equated with more mature ego processes (e.g., sublimation, humor or altruism), while less adaptive mechanisms (e.g., denial of external reality, distortion, or projection) were called immature defenses (Lazarus and Folkman, 1991). Distinguishing between the process of coping and its outcome (whether it is positive or negative) removes the confusion that can arise due to the confounding of the two constructs. In order to study the relationship between the process of coping with the outcome of coping, the two must be kept independent (Lazarus and Folkman, 1991).

So how does research introduce coping into the field of cancer? Most of the early studies divided coping into "coping styles" and asked cancer patients about their coping attitudes in relation to known problems. Information seeking, denial, or hopelessness were categories chosen to describe the ways patients coped with the disease (Watson, Haviland, Greer, Davidson, and Bliss, 1999). This has now almost been abandoned, and the focus is more on actually overcoming the problems that patients face when they are diagnosed with cancer. The emphasis is not so much on coping as on supporting various behavioral and psychological techniques and interventions (which, of course, are coping techniques in more pragmatic terms), turning away from the entire area of coping with the stress of being a cancer survivor. One of the reasons behind this is also the difficulty of measuring the concept of coping in a meaningful way.

These interventions in behavior mostly follow the recommendations of the *World Cancer Report*, asking cancer survivors to live their lives as citizens who are cancer free, in order to avoid a recurrence: to eat a diet low in fat, keep to low amounts of alcohol, abstain from smoking, and ensure daily physical activity (IARC, 2003). Beside this quite simple advice, easier to state than to follow, there is a growing interest in mindfulness and other psychological techniques that emphasize reflection and time for silent prayer or meditation. This compares to the techniques used during the last two decades of the last century, which focused on communicating with other patients and self-realization in groups of peers. Coping with cancer is a cultural phenomenon which follows the trends in a society always looking for new ways of handling life.

There has been a great deal of interest in the idea that psychology alone is able to reduce stress after cancer and thereby improve survival. In our opinion, the effect of psychological interventions on the survival of cancer patients, which has been debated for the past 20 years, does not seem to be such a strong factor as originally anticipated, as indicated by the contradictory findings in the studies published so far. Several reviews have been published, almost all of them criticizing the methods used in the studies. After reviewing the literature and applying measures to gauge the strength of the evidence for enhanced survival after participation in psychosocial interventions, the results are quite negative. In our view, although areas such as quality of life may be improved through psychotherapeutic interventions, the hypothesis that psychotherapy alone enhances survival should be abandoned: the evidence to date points instead to a need to investigate the interactions between the medical, psychological, social, and health behavior components of intervention programs, as recently published studies indicate reduced mortality among patients who engage in physical activity and change to a healthier diet.

References

Bleiker, E. M., and van der Ploeg, H. M. (1999). Psychosocial factors in the etiology of breast cancer: Review of a popular link. *Patient Education and Counseling*, *37*(3), 201–214.

Butow, P. N., Hiller, J. E., Price, M. A., Thackway, S. V., Kricker, A., and Tennant, C. C. (2000). Epidemiological evidence for a relationship between life events, coping style, and personality factors in the development of breast cancer. *Journal of Psychosomatic Research*, *49*(3), 169–181.

Carlson, L. E., Angen, M., Cullum, J., Goodey, E., Koopmans, J., Lamont, L., … Bultz, B. D. (2004). High levels of untreated distress and fatigue in cancer patients. *British Journal of Cancer*, *90*(12), 2297–2304.

Carlson, L. E., Clifford, S. K., Groff, S. L., Maciejewski, O., and Bultz, B. (2010). Screening for depression in cancer care. In A. J. Mitchell and J. C. Coyne (Eds.), *Screening for Depression in Clinical Practice* (pp. 265–298). Oxford: Oxford University Press.

Chida, Y., Hamer, M., Wardle, J., and Steptoe, A. (2008). Do stress-related psychosocial factors contribute to cancer incidence and survival? *Nature Reviews Clinical Oncology*, *5*(8), 466–475. doi:10.1038/ncponc1134

Chow, E., Tsao, M. N., and Harth, T. (2004). Does psychosocial intervention improve survival in cancer? A meta-analysis. *Palliative Medicine*, *18*(1), 25–31.

Christley, R. (2010). Power and error: Increased risk of false positive results in underpowered studies. *Open Epidemiology Journal*, *3*(1), 16–19.

Coyne, J. C., Lepore, S. J., and Palmer, S. C. (2006). Efficacy of psychosocial interventions in cancer care: Evidence is weaker than it first looks. *Annals of Behavioral Medicine*, *32*(2), 104–110. doi:10.1207/s15324796abm3202_5

Coyne, J. C., Ranchor, A. V., and Palmer, S. C. (2010). Meta-analysis of stress-related factors in cancer. *Nature Reviews Clinical Oncology*, *7*(5). doi:10.1038/ncponc1134-c1; author reply, doi:10.1038/ncponc1134-c210.1038/ncponc1134-c1

Dalton, S. O., Boesen, E. H., Ross, L., Schapiro, I. R., and Johansen, C. (2002). Mind and cancer: Do psychological factors cause cancer? *European Journal of Cancer*, *38*(10), 1313–1323.

Dalton, S. O., Laursen, T. M., Ross, L., Mortensen, P. B., and Johansen, C. (2009). Risk for hospitalization with depression after a cancer diagnosis: A nationwide, population-based study of cancer patients in Denmark from 1973 to 2003. *Journal of Clinical Oncology*, *27*(9), 1440–1445.

Duijts, S. F., Zeegers, M. P., and Borne, B. V. (2003). The association between stressful life events and breast cancer risk: A meta-analysis. *International Journal of Cancer*, *107*(6), 1023–1029. doi:10.1002/ijc.11504

Faller, H., Bulzebruck, H., Drings, P., and Lang, H. (1999). Coping, distress, and survival among patients with lung cancer. *Archives of General Psychiatry, 56*(8), 756–762.

Faller, H., Schuler, M., Richard, M., Heckl, U., Weis, J., and Kuffner, R. (2013). Effects of psycho-oncologic interventions on emotional distress and quality of life in adult patients with cancer: Systematic review and meta-analysis. *Journal of Clinical Oncology, 31*(6), 782–793. doi:10.1200/jco.2011.40.8922

Fallowfield, L., Ratcliffe, D., Jenkins, V., and Saul, J. (2001). Psychiatric morbidity and its recognition by doctors in patients with cancer. *British Journal of Cancer, 84*(8), 1011–1015.

Folkman, S., and Lazarus, R. S. (1991). Coping and emotion. In A. Monat and R. S. Lazarus (Eds.), *Stress and Coping: An Anthology*. New York: Columbia University Press.

Galway, K., Black, A., Cantwell, M., Cardwell, C. R., Mills, M., and Donnelly, M. (2012). Psychosocial interventions to improve quality of life and emotional wellbeing for recently diagnosed cancer patients. *Cochrane Database of Systematic Reviews, 11*, CD007064. doi:10.1002/14651858.CD007064.pub2

Garssen, B. (2004). Psychological factors and cancer development: Evidence after 30 years of research. *Clinical Psychology Review, 24*(3), 315–338. doi:10.1016/j.cpr.2004.01.002

Graves, K. D., Arnold, S. M., Love, C. L., Kirsh, K. L., Moore, P. G., and Passik, S. D. (2007). Distress screening in a multidisciplinary lung cancer clinic: Prevalence and predictors of clinically significant distress. *Lung Cancer, 55*(2), 215–224.

Greer S., Morris, T., and Pettingale, K. W. (1979). Psychological response to breast cancer: Effect on outcome. *Lancet, 2*(8146), 785–787.

Haan, N., and Lykken, D. T. (2013). *Coping and Defending: Processes of Self-Environment Organization*. Amsterdam: Elsevier Science.

Hersch, J., Juraskova, I., Price, M., and Mullan, B. (2009). Psychosocial interventions and quality of life in gynaecological cancer patients: A systematic review. *Psycho-oncology, 18*(8), 795–810. doi:10.1002/pon.1443

Holland, J. C., Breitbart, W., Dudley, M. M., Fulcher, C., Greiner, C. B., and Hoofring, L. (2010). Distress management: Clinical practice guidelines in oncology. *Journal of the National Comprehensive Cancer Network, 8*, 448–485.

Holmes, T. H., and Rahe, R. H. (1967). The social readjustment rating scale. *Journal of Psychosomatic Research, 11*(2), 213–218. http://dx.doi.org/10.1016/0022-3999\05067\05190010-4

Hoon, L. S., Chi Sally, C. W., and Hong-Gu, H. (2013). Effect of psychosocial interventions on outcomes of patients with colorectal cancer: A review of the literature. *European Journal of Oncology Nursing, 17*(6), 883–891. doi:10.1016/j.ejon.2013.05.001

IARC (International Agency for Research on Cancer) (2003). *World Cancer Report 2003*, ed. B. W. Stewart and P. Kleihues. Lyon: IARC.

Kleinke, C. L. (2007). What does it mean to cope? In A. Monat (Ed.), *The Praeger Handbook on Stress and Coping* (pp. 289–308). Westport, CT: Praeger.

Lazarus, R. S. (1966). *Psychological Stress and the Coping Process*. New York: McGraw-Hill.

Lazarus, R. S., and Folkman, S. (1984). *Stress, Appraisal, and Coping*. Dordrecht: Springer.

Lazarus, R. S., and Folkman, S. (1991). The concept of coping. In A. Monat and R. S. Lazarus (Eds.), *Stress and Coping: An Anthology* (pp. 189–206). New York: Columbia University Press.

Lyon, B. L. (2000). Stress, coping, and health: A conceptual overview. In V. H. Rice (Ed.), *Handbook of Stress, Coping, and Health: Implications for Nursing Research, Theory, and Practice*. London: Sage.

McKenna, M. C., Zevon, M. A., Corn, B., and Rounds, J. (1999). Psychosocial factors and the development of breast cancer: A meta-analysis. *Health Psychology, 18*(5), 520–531.

Mitchell, A. J. (2007). Pooled results from 38 analyses of the accuracy of distress thermometer and other ultra-short methods of detecting cancer-related mood disorders. *Journal of Clinical Oncology, 25*(29), 4670–4681.

Mitchell, A. J., Kaar, S., Coggan, C., and Herdman, J. (2008). Acceptability of common screening methods used to detect distress and related mood disorders – preferences of cancer specialists and non-specialists. *Psycho-oncology, 17*(3), 226–236.

Mulder, R. T. (2008). An epidemic of depression or the medicalization of distress? *Perspectives in Biology and Medicine, 51*(2), 238–20.

National Comprehensive Cancer Network (2007). NCCN clinical practice guidelines in oncology distress management 1. At https://www.nccn.org/professionals/physician_gls/f_guidelines.asp (accessed July 2016).

Nielsen, N. R., and Gronbaek, M. (2006). Stress and breast cancer: A systematic update on the current knowledge. *Nature Clinical Practice. Oncology, 3*(11), 612–620. doi:10.1038/ncponc0652

Petticrew, M., Fraser, J. M., and Regan, M. F. (1999). Adverse life-events and risk of breast cancer. *British Journal of Health Psychology*, *4*(1), 1–17.

Ross, L., Boesen, E. H., Dalton, S. O., and Johansen, C. (2002). Mind and cancer: Does psychosocial intervention improve survival and psychological well-being? *European Journal of Cancer*, *38*(11), 1447–1457.

Santos, M. C., Horta, B. L., Amaral, J. J., Fernandes, P. F., Galvao, C. M., and Fernandes, A. F. (2009). Association between stress and breast cancer in women: A meta-analysis. *Cadernos de Saúde Pública*, *25*, suppl. 3, S453–463.

Selye, H. (1956). *The Stress of Life*. New York: McGraw-Hill.

Shim, E. J., Mehnert, A., Koyama, A., Cho, S. J., Inui, H., Paik, N. S., and Koch, U. (2006). Health-related quality of life in breast cancer: A cross-cultural survey of German, Japanese, and South Korean patients. *Breast Cancer Research and Treatment*, *99*(3), 341–350.

von Essen, L., Larsson, G., Oberg, K., and Sjoden, P. O. (2002). "Satisfaction with care": Associations with health-related quality of life and psychosocial function among Swedish patients with endocrine gastrointestinal tumours. *European Journal of Cancer Care (Engl.)*, *11*(2), 91–99.

Watson, M., Haviland, J. S., Greer, S., Davidson, J., and Bliss, J. M. (1999). Influence of psychological response on survival in breast cancer: A population-based cohort study. *Lancet*, *354*(9187), 1331–1336.

8

Stress and Chronic Fatigue Syndrome

Bjørn Grinde

Introduction

Chronic fatigue syndrome (CFS), also referred to as myalgic encephalomyelitis (ME), is characterized by a severe, debilitating fatigue lasting for at least six months (for reviews see Devanur and Kerr, 2006; Prins, van der Meer, and Bleijenberg, 2006; Sanders and Korf, 2008). Unlike other forms of fatigue, the condition is not due to exertion, nor relieved by rest, and it is not caused by known medical conditions. Additional symptoms vary, but typically include muscle and joint pain, sore throat, tender lymph nodes, malaise upon exertion, headache, and cognitive difficulties. Patients with the worst forms of CFS may be locked in bed for years, often in darkness and silence due to hypersensitivity to external signals. The condition may lead to premature death (Jason et al., 2006). On the other hand, quite a few patients recover, partly or completely, even after many years of disease.

Reported prevalences show considerable variation, depending on diagnostic criteria, availability of health services, and urban versus rural setting (Reeves et al., 2007; Brurberg et al., 2013; Johnston, Brenu, Staines, and Marshall-Gradisnik, 2013). Typical data suggest that anywhere from 0.2 to 2 percent of the adult population suffers; with the least strict diagnostic criteria the prevalence may rise to several percent. The condition is more common among women compared to men, low in children, but surprisingly high in adolescents (Lievesley, Rimes, and Chalder, 2014).

Interestingly, there have been several apparent "outbreaks" of CFS in the form of clustering of cases geographically and within families (Afari and Buchwald, 2003). The epidemiology appears to be relevant, and suggestive of an infectious cause, although it is difficult to distinguish between real outbreaks and clustering due to heightened awareness of the disorder.

There are no obvious clinical signs or laboratory abnormalities, so diagnosis, or case definition, relies on self-reported information. The patients report as to whether they experience

The Handbook of Stress and Health: A Guide to Research and Practice, First Edition.
Edited by Cary L. Cooper and James Campbell Quick.
© 2017 John Wiley & Sons, Ltd. Published 2017 by John Wiley & Sons, Ltd.

Table 8.1 Symptoms and findings associated with CFS in addition to fatigue; in order to be relevant for diagnostics the symptoms should be persistent

Core symptoms (CDC)	Other common complaints	Physiological correlates
Impaired memory and concentration	Mental "fog"	Aberrations in hypothalamic-pituitary-adrenal axis and stress hormones
Sore throat	Balance problems, dizziness, nausea	Infections
Tender lymph nodes	Chronic pain	Irregular blood pressure
Aching or stiff muscles	Symptoms associated with irritable bowel syndrome	Irregular body temperature
Multijoint pain	Night sweats or chills	Inflammation
Headaches	Sensitivity to light	Autoimmunity
Unrefreshing sleep	Depression	Other aberrations in immune functioning
Postexertional malaise	Allergy	Increased oxidative stress
	General malaise	Morphometric changes in central nervous system
	Sleep problems	

various symptoms, and the diagnosis depends on how the individual scores on these criteria. For example, the Centers for Disease Control (CDC) in the United States operate with a list of eight criteria (in addition to the chronic fatigue), for which a positive on four is required to define a case (Table 8.1, first column) (CDC, 2016). The heterogeneity of the patients necessarily depends on the formulation of the criteria, and the number of manifestations required. Research has been hampered by the fact that the case definition differs between countries and health institutions (Brurberg et al., 2013). Moreover, part of the diagnostic procedure is to rule out alternative explanations for the fatigue, which include disorders such as cancer, hypothyroidism, anemia, diabetes, mononucleosis, and borreliosis. There are attempts at obtaining more objective diagnostic tools in the form of biomarkers (Fischer et al., 2014). If relevant tools had been available, CFS patients would perhaps have been divided into separate disorders (Jason et al., 2005).

In this chapter, I shall focus first on the pathology (in the meaning of how the disease manifests itself), and then on the etiology (that is, what factors trigger and perpetuate the condition).

Pathology: Onset and Manifestations

Onset

The majority of CFS cases start unexpectedly; that is, without previous tendencies toward fatigue (Salit, 1997). Surprisingly often the victims are young and active, with considerable mental resources. In many cases the precipitating factor appears to be an acute infection, typically in the form of a "flu-like" condition (Afari and Buchwald, 2003; Lievesley et al., 2014). In fact, the association with contagious diseases is sufficiently strong to have warranted some scientists to refer to the condition as "post-infective fatigue syndrome" (Hickie et al., 2006). Then again, a significant proportion of cases start in connection with, or soon after, the patients have experienced severe mental stress (Theorell, Blomkvist, Lindh, and Evengård, 1999; Hatcher and House, 2003).

Mental and Somatic Symptoms

As to clinical observations, it is difficult to distinguish between symptoms directly associated with CFS, and what may constitute either comorbidity or secondary consequences of the fatigue. Many patients suffer from other (more or less unrelated) conditions; moreover, the details as to how CFS affects the central nervous system (CNS) may explain the heterogeneity of reported morbidity. The list of CFS-associated symptoms does, nevertheless, shed some light as to the nature of the disorder (Table 8.1).

The primary cognitive symptoms are deficits in concentration and attention, as well as in memory and reaction time (Cockshell and Mathias, 2010). Typical deficits are in the range of 0.5 to 1.0 standard deviation below normal values. The measured deficiencies are generally consistent with what patients report, and are of a magnitude that easily explains reduced functioning. Yet, perceptual abilities, language, motor speed, and intelligence do not appear to be significantly compromised.

Other complaints typically revolve around pain, sleep problems, and other consequences of a considerably reduced general fitness. In addition to the self-reported symptoms there are a range of suggestive clinical findings; the more prominent involves the immune system and infections. However, these markers are all restricted to subsets of patients. Some studies find anatomical abnormalities in the brain (de Lange et al., 2005; Okada et al., 2004). Other common observations include dysregulation of blood pressure and body temperature (Wyller et al., 2007a; Wyller, Saul, Amlie, and Thaulow, 2007b), and dysfunctional changes in the hypothalamic-pituitary-adrenal (HPA) axis in relation to stress hormones (Van Houdenhove, Van Den Eede, and Luyten, 2009).

There is often an increased inflammatory tendency, as well as general immune activation or suppression; but again the observations are not consistent (Lyall, Peakman, and Wessely, 2003; Appel, Chapman, and Shoenfeld, 2007). The immunological changes are not restricted to the blood, relevant immunological factors can also be traced in the spinal fluid.

Functioning

The functional capacity of CFS patients varies considerably (Ross et al., 2004). Some persons lead reasonably normal lives, while others stay in bed most of the time and are more or less unable to care for themselves. In severe cases the condition causes more manifest malady – both in regard to functional level and quality of life – than most major medical disorders, including multiple sclerosis and heart failure (Komaroff et al., 1996). Most patients experience periods of remission to be followed by recurrence of symptoms. When a patient feels better he or she may take the opportunity to be particularly active, which again may trigger a worsening of the condition.

Etiology: Causal Factors

Mental Stress

The various factors implicated as either precipitating or perpetuating causes of CFS are outlined in Table 8.2. Stress is here understood as external or internal factors that affect resilience. The factors include the pressures of everyday life such as workload, personal expectations as to performance, psychosocial conflicts, and lack of resources; but also the mental effects of health problems.

Table 8.2 Possible etiological factors: a subjective evaluation as to whether the factors are likely to either cause or maintain CFS is suggested

Main factor	Subtypes	Precipitate	Perpetuate	Comments
Stress and related mental factors	General stress	++	+	Reasonable evidence for a contributing role, but not in all cases
	Trauma	+	?	
	Depression/anxiety	(+)	?	
Immune system aberrations	Inflammation	?	(+)	Possible secondary consequences of CFS, but may play a role
	Autoimmunity	(+)	(+)	
	General immune activation		(+)	
	Oxidative stress	(+)	(+)	
Infections	Flu or related agents	+	−	Strong evidence for a potential triggering role, likely theoretical candidates for maintaining the condition
	Epstein-Barr virus	++	?	
	Other herpesviruses	(+)	?	
	Enteroviruses	(+)		
	Anellovirus	?	?	
Neurological anomaly		−	(+)	Unlikely to trigger CFS, but a neurological correlate is obvious and could help perpetuate the condition
Genetics		(+)	(+)	A general inheritance of susceptibility is likely, but a particular genetic requirement is unlikely

Stress has been increasingly recognized as important in the etiology of CFS (Nater, Maloney, Heim, and Reeves, 2011). Besides being commonly reported as a pre-onset condition in patients, various studies report that people diagnosed with CFS experienced more stressful life events than controls in the year prior to onset of illness (Masuda et al., 2002; Faulkner and Smith, 2008). That is, both occurrence of stressful events and chronic stress levels appear to be increased. The point is substantiated by the observation that a considerable fraction of people with CFS are also diagnosed with posttraumatic stress disorder, a condition that reflects aberrant response to extreme stress (Nater et al., 2009). Yet, it should be pointed out that the majority of people who develop posttraumatic stress disorder, or experience other forms of severe stress, do not have CFS.

Whether or not stress alone can cause the syndrome, it seems reasonably well documented that it can aggravate the condition (Oka et al., 2013). For example, one study found that the physical symptoms of CFS were exacerbated in patients who experienced Hurricane Andrew in Florida (Lutgendorf et al., 1995).

It should be pointed out that living with this condition is a substantial stressor by itself. To the extent that stress is an etiological factor, this would suggest a negative feedback loop where the condition gets worse due to the consequence of having the disorder. The notion may help explain the cycling nature of symptoms, where people tend to get worse, partly recover, only then to be dragged down again. The point is underlined by research indicating that stress management can mitigate the condition (Lattie et al., 2012; Hall et al., 2014)

The presumed main mediator of stress is the hypothalamic-pituitary-adrenal (HPA) axis. Stress leads to altered release of corticotrophin-releasing hormone (CRH), cortisol, as well as other related hormones. Extensive research has focused on the role of the HPA axis and cortisol in CFS (Papadopoulos and Cleare, 2011). Cortisol is primarily known for its role in reducing inflammation, but it also activates antistress pathways. Many CFS patients produce lower levels of cortisol compared to healthy people, which may aggravate both stress and inflammatory processes. Aberrations in the *cortisol awakening response* (the hormonal increase typically observed in the morning) have stood out as a marker of endocrine dysregulation in connection with fatigue, and are therefore particularly relevant in CFS (Hall et al., 2014). There are two main problems as to the role of the HPA axis in the etiology of CFS. For one, the observed aberrations could be secondary effects of CFS, or due to comorbidity with other disorders; and two, only a subfraction of patients display measurable deviation in hormonal stress response.

A variety of stressors have been linked to CFS. At least in younger patients, there is an association with conscientiousness and high expectations as to achievement (Lievesley et al., 2014). Although these personality factors suggest a resourceful person, they may also be a cause of stress. Another observation is the considerable psychiatric comorbidity, particularly in the form of anxiety and depression, in people with CFS (Lievesley et al., 2014). These disorders may act as stressors, but as most studies only look at associations, it is not obvious whether they help precipitate CFS or are secondary consequences.

The association between stress and CFS has led some practitioners to suggest that the condition is solely due to psychological factors, and thus should be labeled as a psychiatric disorder. Although mental issues are relevant in connection with chronic fatigue, it seems likely that the extreme state observed in typical CFS patients has a more distinct cause. Moreover, most patients dispute the idea of CFS as a psychiatric disorder, perhaps sometimes to the effect that the patients are unwilling to try out potentially beneficial mental therapies.

One pertinent question is whether the stress might act as a trigger for events that are the real key to understanding CFS. As pointed out above, stress will impact on the immune system, and thus on processes related to inflammation, autoimmunity, and infections. Stress also has both direct and indirect (e.g., through the immune system) effects on the CNS. It seems relevant to examine these perspectives.

Immunology

It is well known that the brain and the immune system influence each other, particularly via the HPA axis and in the sympathetic nervous system. The stress response can, by way of changing the level of immunological factors in the blood, result in neurological symptoms due to the effect of these factors on neurotransmitter systems.

Besides the potential for direct effects on nerve circuits, altered immune functioning may trigger an autoimmune response. A substantial fraction of CFS patients have signs of autoimmunity (Morris, Berk, Galecki, and Maes, 2014).

Many patients display a more or less chronic inflammation, or other forms of aberrant activity of the immune system (Afari and Buchwald, 2003; Appel et al., 2007; Lattie et al.,

2012). These conditions are reflected in altered immune parameters such as cytokine profile (high level of proinflammatory cytokines and dysregulation of anti-inflammatory cytokines), decreased function of natural killer cells, and a reduced response of T cells. Oxidative stress has been suggested as a possible explanation for immune activation (Morris and Maes, 2014). Oxidative stress implies an increase in free radicals that may induce cellular injury, and thus either inflammation or autoimmunity.

None of the immunological parameters are consistently associated with CFS. Moreover, various immune-related therapies have been investigated, but so far with limited success, suggesting that although changes in immunological parameters may be relevant, they are unlikely to play a key role in CFS.

Infections

Arguably the hottest topic in relation to research on CFS has been the potential involvement of infectious agents. Although substantial research has been carried out, and a range of associations found, there is so far no conclusive evidence for a required role of microorganisms in either triggering or maintaining the condition. Outbreaks of CFS (or CFS-related disorders) have been described suggesting that infections play a part in the etiology (Jenkins, 1991; Afari and Buchwald, 2003; Chia, 2005). Moreover, many patients report the onset to be connected with either mononucleosis or a flu-like illness (Devanur and Kerr, 2006; Lievesley, Rimes, and Chalder, 2014). The viruses responsible for mononucleosis, either Epstein Barr virus (EBV) or cytomegalovirus (CMV), cause persistent infections. This would fit with a role in the etiology, but direct evidence is lacking. As these viruses are present in most people, it is not possible to hold them responsible simply because they can be found in patients.

It is generally assumed that to the extent infections are involved, the more likely candidates are viruses. If bacteria or other cellular agents were responsible, the association would presumably have been easier to demonstrate. Yet a few cellular agents have been suggested, particularly *Coxiella burnetii* and *Chlamydia pneumoniae* (Devanur and Kerr, 2006). One possible scenario is that a variety of agents may be responsible; the shared etiological feature could be a low-grade infection of the CNS. It is well known that an infection with certain viruses, including herpesviruses such as EBV, and Ross River virus (an alphavirus), can lead to a postinfective condition that at least partly meets the criteria for CFS. Individuals who had severe symptoms in the primary infection are more likely to later develop fatigue. Besides the above mentioned viruses, other herpesviruses, enteroviruses and parvoviruses have been implicated (Devanur and Kerr, 2006).

Among the suggested viruses, the herpesviruses are particularly interesting because they tend to cause lifelong infections, and are associated with the CNS. They are reactivated on a recurrent basis, for example as a consequence of stress (Grinde, 2013). Although there is considerable evidence associating EBV with the onset of CFS, at least in a subset of patients, the evidence as to maintaining the conditions is lacking. Obviously their universal presence complicates this line of research.

Another complicating factor is that viral activity will tend to increase in individuals with decreased immune surveillance (Moen et al., 2003). The stress associated with the initiation of CFS may cause an increase in viral titer, and so may the stress of having CFS. In both cases viruses are more likely to be detected in patients as opposed to healthy controls, which may lead to falsely accusing particular viruses of being responsible for the disease.

One hypothesis is that CFS is caused by a virus that is chronically present in most people, but normally benign (Grinde, 2008). The causative event could then be either a triggering of viral replication due to reduced immune surveillance as a consequence of stress; or that the stress (or other factors) allowed a virus that is normally present in the blood to establish a CNS infection. The following observations support this hypothesis.

Certain viruses that only occasionally penetrate into the brain, including hepatitis C virus (Tillmann, 2004; Forton, Thomas, and Taylor-Robinson, 2004) and Nipah virus (Ng, Lim, Yeoh, and Lee, 2004), have been reported to cause chronic or disabling fatigue in select patients. However, these two viruses are unlikely candidates as to most cases of CFS, as hepatitis C is rare except in drug abusers, and Nipah virus is a rare zoonotic agent. Moreover, if CFS had been a normal consequence of the infection of one or a few rare viruses, one would expect a different epidemiological pattern. That is, the cases should cluster along possible infectious pathways. Most cases do not. The epidemiology does, however, fit with the notion that the event leading to the disease is an unexpected crossing of the blood–brain barrier of a virus present in most people. On the other hand, if it had been one of the viruses investigated in relation to CFS, one would expect the culprit(s) to be found.

The above reasoning leaves one tantalizing possibility. The responsible agent is either a totally unknown virus (which there are good reasons to believe exists), or a known virus, but one that has not been thoroughly investigated. The lack of a positive result may be due to several factors. For one, the heterogeneity, or low titer, of the virus causes it to evade standard methods of detection; two, its presence in most people makes a positive finding meaningless; or three, it has not been looked into simply because it is not considered pathogenic. Note that most viral diagnostics deal with blood samples rather than spinal fluids because the latter are more difficult to obtain.

There are viruses that fit the above description; most notably members of the related families of *Circoviridae* and *Anelloviridae* (previously combined under the name circoviruses), but to some extent also polyomaviruses. These viruses are normally associated with other parts of the body, yet can penetrate the brain and replicate there (Maggi et al., 2001; Doerries, 2006; Smits et al., 2013; Tan et al., 2013). While polyomaviruses are known to cause clinical symptoms in the brain (Doerries, 2006), *Circoviridae* and *Anelloviridae* have no known pathogenicity in humans, but have been observed in spinal fluid of patients with CNS manifestations. Moreover, animal circoviruses can infect the brain and cause disease, for example postweaning, multisystemic wasting syndrome in pigs, a condition with certain similarities to CFS (Seeliger et al., 2007).

The observation that CFS is typically preceded by an acute systemic infection, or by severe stress, fits the above hypothesis. These conditions may cause a virus normally present in the blood to enter the CNS, either due to increased titer as a result of suppressed immune function, or by weakening the blood–brain barrier. Circoviruses have been shown to increase drastically in titer upon immunosuppression (Moen et al., 2003).

Viruses affecting the CNS are difficult to diagnose. Even in cases of encephalitis or meningitis where there is reasonable evidence to suggest a viral etiology, specific agents are often not found. The problem may be partly related to not testing for the right virus, but can also be due to a low-grade infection. Viruses belonging to the *Circoviridae* or *Anelloviridae* have, to the author's knowledge, never been tested in connection with CFS; and they are designed by evolution to yield low-grade, chronic infections, and are thus difficult to detect. There are markers suggestive of infection in the spinal fluid of CFS patients (Natelson, Weaver, Tseng, and Ottenweller, 2005), and treatment with the broad-spectrum antiviral agents interferon and Ribavirin has been reported to improve the condition (Chia, 2005).

Another interesting observation is that mothers of adolescents with CFS more often display related symptoms than do the fathers (van de Putte et al., 2006). This could be explained by the transfer of certain strains of virus during pregnancy or birth, which presumably happens in the case of anelloviruses, circoviruses, and polyomaviruses. It is conceivable that certain strains of these viruses are more likely to result in CFS; and that the particular symptoms experienced are to some extent strain specific.

It is worth noting that the presence of EBV has been shown to stimulate the replication of anelloviruses obtained from the brain of a patient with multiple sclerosis (Borkosky et al., 2012). Multiple sclerosis has a certain resemblance with CFS. A possible scenario could be that stress lowers the viral defense and thus allows EBV to be more active; EBV promotes the replication of anelloviruses, which again cause the neurological alterations responsible for CFS.

Neurology

The World Health Organization classifies CFS as a nervous system disease. Whether it is considered a psychiatric disorder or an infection, there is necessarily a neurobiological correlate. Yet, it seems unlikely that neurobiological events are the sole, or primary, cause of CFS.

Certain neurological abnormalities, as revealed by brain scans, have been associated with CFS (Schwartz et al., 1994), as have changes in the serotonin signaling pathways (Cleare, Messa, Rabiner, and Grasby, 2005). Although direct neural damage due to stress has been proposed as part of the etiology (Tanaka, Ishii, and Watanabe, 2013), so far there is no obvious correlates in the brain that match a majority of patients. A reasonable explanation is that the disease is due to subtle changes in nerve circuits.

Genetics

Although genetic constitution most likely is relevant for the development of CFS (Afari and Buchwald, 2003; Crawley and Smith, 2007; Lievesley, Rimes, and Chalder, 2014), there is no strong case for the involvement of particular genes. Nevertheless, weak associations have been found for genes involved in the HPA axis, neuroendocrine functions, apoptosis, and metabolism (Whistler, Unger, Nisenbaum, and Vernon, 2003; Goertzel et al., 2006; Smith et al., 2006).

Even in conditions with a relatively high hereditability, genome-wide associations studies typically fail to pinpoint mutations accounting for more than a small percentage of the estimated inheritance. Often, though, one does find rare mutations that cause the condition with a high penetrance, as exemplified by the genes responsible for familial breast cancer or type 1 diabetes. In the case of CFS, the lack of more direct evidence for genetic causes suggests that to the extent that susceptibility is inheritable, it is a question of various constellations of a large number of alleles. It should also be mentioned that certain chronic viruses are transmitted in utero, including anelloviruses and polyomaviruses, meaning that particular strains will run in the family. An involvement of these viruses would tend to exaggerate the heritability estimates.

Discussion

Despite a considerable effort, we still have limited knowledge as to what causes CFS. It may be a combination of several factors, and the factors may differ between the somewhat heterogeneous patients. The lack of understanding is a serious hindrance to both prevention and treatment.

If there should prove to be one primary factor responsible for all, or a majority, of cases, I believe the more likely candidate would be a virus. A viral etiology is compatible with the pathological symptoms and observations described in this chapter. It offers an explanation for the role of stress and other infections; and if the virus impacts on the hypothalamus, an effect on the HPA axis would be expected. If the culprit proved to be an anellovirus, it would also justify the particular association with EBV (Borkosky et al., 2012). Moreover, a viral etiology does not demand other precipitating events, which is congruent with the observation that the various associations outlined only hold for subsets of patients.

If aberrations in the HPA axis or immune function were the primary culprits, one might expect the etiology to be worked out. On the other hand, the involvement of a low-grade infection with either unknown or rarely studied viruses is more difficult to identify. The apparently never-ending discovery of novel human viruses testifies to the difficulty involved in detecting them. It gets even more complicated if pathology requires a particular strain of virus, perhaps in combination with particular host genotypes.

It is becoming increasingly evident that most viral infections, even in the case of potentially pathogenic agents such as the enteroviruses, can replicate in the body without causing symptoms (Witsø et al., 2006). When they do cause a disease, it probably reflects a detrimental blend of host and viral factors. This may also be the case in CFS. As to anelloviruses, the importance of immune function for viral activity has been demonstrated (Moen et al., 2003). The modulating effect of the immune system means that elucidating the etiological role of viruses in stress-related diseases is particularly challenging. An association may simply imply an increase in viral titer due to secondary consequences of the diseases.

The more common, pathogenic infections in the CNS manifest as acute inflammation and are referred to as *encephalitis*. Typical symptoms include headache, fever, confusion, drowsiness, and fatigue. The common causes are either viral or bacterial infections. More chronic, low-grade infections of the CNS (e.g., caused by spirochetes such as syphilis and borreliosis, or viruses such as HIV and herpes viruses) cause less inflammation and fever, but are often associated with fatigue, and may have more specific manifestations ranging from pain to hallucinations. The nature of the manifestations typically varies between patients. Based on this description, a viral cause of CFS fits the general picture.

The notion of a highly prevalent, but normally benign, virus as the core etiological factor is particularly attractive. The rare event of gaining access to the CNS would then be the precipitator. The hypothesis is also compatible with the epidemiology; CFS clusters in families, and shows occasional geographically defined outbreaks. The familial clustering could be due to a combination of shared viral strains and shared genetics.

The situation would be a parallel to the observation that the more severe viral diseases (e.g., HIV, Ebola, SARS, and avian influenza) are caused by zoonotic agents. Viruses with a long-term relationship with a host – or, in this case, certain host organs – generally develop a benevolent profile, but when given the opportunity to infect a novel host species – or organ – pathogenicity is more likely to follow.

So far CFS is diagnosed based on manifestations, rather than on a causative agent. This means it may include patients with a completely different etiology, but also exclude patients with the same etiology and different manifestations. In other words, the chronic fatigue that is essential for a CFS diagnosis may not be universally present in all patients harboring the same causative agent. Fibromyalgia, for example, is a related disorder, but the diagnosis focuses on pain rather than on fatigue. Otherwise the symptoms overlap; even the hormonal abnormalities are quite similar (Papadopoulos and Cleare, 2011). The same agent could cause fibromyalgia, and the differences simply reflect the precise neurological structures affected.

References

Afari, N., and Buchwald, D. (2003). Chronic fatigue syndrome: A review. *American Journal of Psychiatry*, *160*(2), 221–236.

Appel, S., Chapman, J., and Shoenfeld, Y. (2007). Infection and vaccination in chronic fatigue syndrome: Myth or reality? *Autoimmunity*, *40*(1), 48–53.

Borkosky, S. S., Whitley, C., Kopp-Schneider, A., zur Hausen, H., and de Villiers, E. M. (2012). Epstein-Barr virus stimulates torque teno virus replication: A possible relationship to multiple sclerosis. *PLoS One*, *7*(2), e32160.

Brurberg, K. G., Fønhus, M. S., Larun, L., Flottorp, S., and Malterud, K. (2013). Case definitions for chronic fatigue syndrome/myalgic encephalomyelitis (CFS/ME): A systematic review. *BMJ Open*, *4*(2), e003973. doi:10.1136/bmjopen-2013-003973

CDC (Centers for Disease Control and Prevention) (2016). Chronic fatigue syndrome (CFS): General information. At http://www.cdc.gov/cfs/general/index.html (accessed July 2016).

Chia, J. K. S. (2005). The role of enterovirus in chronic fatigue syndrome. *Journal of Clinical Pathology*, *58*, 1126–1132.

Cleare, A. J., Messa, C., Rabiner, E. A., and Grasby, P. M. (2005). Brain 5-HT1A receptor binding in chronic fatigue syndrome measured using positron emission tomography and [11C]WAY-100635. *Biological Psychiatry*, *57*(3), 239–246.

Cockshell, S. J., and Mathias, J. L. (2010). Cognitive functioning in chronic fatigue syndrome: A meta-analysis. *Psychological Medicine*, *40*(8), 1–15.

Crawley, E., and Smith, G. D. (2007). Is chronic fatigue syndrome (CFS/ME) heritable in children, and if so, why does it matter? *Archives of Disease in Childhood*, *92*, 1058–1061.

de Lange, F. P., Kalkman, J. S., Bleijenberg, G., Hagoort, P., van der Meer, J. W., and Toni, I. (2005). Gray matter volume reduction in the chronic fatigue syndrome. *NeuroImage*, *26*(3), 777–781.

Devanur, L. D., and Kerr, J. R. (2006). Chronic fatigue syndrome. *Journal of Clinical Virology*, *37*, 139–150.

Doerries, K. (2006). Human polyomavirus JC and Bk persistent infection. *Advances in Experimental Medicine and Biology*, *577*, 102–116.

Faulkner, S., and Smith, A. (2008). A longitudinal study of the relationship between psychological distress and recurrence of upper respiratory tract infections in chronic fatigue syndrome. *British Journal of Health Psychology*, *13*(pt 1), 177–186.

Fischer, D. B., William, A. H., Strauss, A. C., Unger, E. R., Jason, L., Marshall, G. D., and Dimitrakoff, J. D. (2014). Chronic fatigue syndrome: The current status and future potentials of emerging biomarkers. *Fatigue*, *2*(2), 93–109.

Forton, D. M., Thomas, H. C., and Taylor-Robinson, S. D. (2004). Central nervous system involvement in hepatitis C virus infection. *Metabolic Brain Disease*, *19*, 383–391.

Goertzel, B. N., Pennachin, C., de Souza-Coehlo, L., Gurbaxani, B., Maloney, E. M., and Jones, J. F. (2006). Combinations of single nucleotide polymorphisms in neuroendocrine effector and receptor genes predict chronic fatigue syndrome. *Pharmacogenomics*, *7*(3), 475–483.

Grinde, B. (2008). Is chronic fatigue syndrome caused by a rare brain infection of a common, normally benign virus? *Medical Hypotheses*, *71*, 270–274.

Grinde, B. (2013). Herpesviruses: Latency and reactivation viral strategies and host response. *Journal of Oral Microbiology*, *5*, e22766.

Hall, D. L., Lattie, E. G., Antoni, M. H., Fletcher, M. A., Czaja, S., Perdomo, D., and Klimas, N. G. (2014). Stress management skills, cortisol awakening response, and post-exertional malaise in chronic fatigue syndrome. *Psychoneuroendocrinology*, *49*, 26–31.

Hatcher, S., and House, A. (2003). Life events, difficulties and dilemmas in the onset of chronic fatigue syndrome: A case-control study. *Psychological Medicine, 33*(7), 1185–1192. doi:10.1017/S0033291703008274

Hickie, I., Davenport, T., Wakefield, D., Vollmer-Conna, U., Cameron, B., Vernon, S. D., ... Lloyd, A. (2006). Post-infective and chronic fatigue syndromes precipitated by viral and non-viral pathogens: Prospective cohort study. *British Medical Journal, 333*(7568), 575. doi:10.1136/bmj.38933.585764.AE

Jason, L. A., Corradi, K., Torres-Harding, S., Taylor, R. R., and King, C. (2005). Chronic fatigue syndrome: The need for subtypes. *Neuropsychological Review, 15*(1), 29–58.

Jason, L. A., Corradi, K., Gress, S., Williams, S., and Torres-Harding, S. (2006). Causes of death among patients with chronic fatigue syndrome. *Health Care for Women International, 27*, 615–626.

Jenkins, R. (1991). Epidemiology: Lessons from the past. *British Medical Bulletin, 47*, 952–965.

Johnston, S., Brenu, E. W., Staines, D., and Marshall-Gradisnik, S. (2013). The prevalence of chronic fatigue syndrome/myalgic encephalomyelitis: A meta-analysis. *Clinical Epidemiology, 5*, 105–110.

Komaroff, A. L., Fagioli, L. R., Doolittle, T. H., Gandek, B., Gleit, M. A., Guerriero, R. T., ... Bates, D. W. (1996). Health status in patients with chronic fatigue syndrome and in general population and disease comparison groups. *American Journal of Medicine, 101*, 281–290.

Lattie, E. G., Antoni, M. H., Fletcher, M. A., Penedo, F., Czaja, S., Lopez, C., ... Klimas, N. (2012). Stress management skills, neuroimmune processes and fatigue levels in persons with chronic fatigue syndrome. *Brain, Behavior, and Immunity, 26*(6), 849–858.

Lievesley, K., Rimes, K. A., and Chalder, T. (2014). A review of the predisposing, precipitating and perpetuating factors in chronic fatigue syndrome in children and adolescents. *Clinical Psychology Review, 34*, 233–248.

Lutgendorf, S. K., Antoni, M. H., Ironson, G., Fletcher, M. A., Penedo, F., Baum, A., ... Klimas, N. (1995). Physical symptoms of chronic fatigue syndrome are exacerbated by the stress of Hurricane Andrew. *Psychosomatic Medicine, 57*(4), 310–323.

Lyall, M., Peakman, M., and Wessely, S. (2003). A systematic review and critical evaluation of the immunology of chronic fatigue syndrome. *Journal of Psychosomatic Research, 55*(2), 79–90.

Maggi, F., Fornai, C., Vatteroni, M. L., Siciliano, G., Menichetti, F., Tascini, C., ... Bendinelli, M. (2001). Low prevalence of TT virus in the cerebrospinal fluid of viremic patients with central nervous system disorders. *Journal of Medical Virology, 65*, 418–422.

Masuda, A., Munemoto, T., Yamanaka, T., Takei, M., and Tei, C. (2002). Psychosocial characteristics and immunological functions in patients with postinfectious chronic fatigue syndrome and noninfectious chronic fatigue syndrome. *Journal of Behavioral Medicine, 25*(5), 477–485.

Moen, E. M., Sagedal, S., Bjøro, K., Degre, M., Opstad, P. K., and Grinde, B. (2003). Effect of immune modulation on TT virus (TTV) and TTVlike-mini-virus (TLMV) viremia. *Journal of Medical Virology, 70*, 177–182.

Morris, G., and Maes, M. (2014). Oxidative and nitrosative stress and immune-inflammatory pathways in patients with myalgic encephalomyelitis (ME)/chronic fatigue syndrome (CFS). *Current Neuropharmacology, 12*(2), 168–185.

Morris, G., Berk, M., Galecki, P., and Maes, M. (2014). The emerging role of autoimmunity in myalgic encephalomyelitis/chronic fatigue syndrome (ME/CFS). *Molecular Neurobiology, 49*(2), 741–756.

Natelson, B. H., Weaver, S. A., Tseng, C.-L., and Ottenweller, J. E. (2005). Spinal fluid abnormalities in patients with chronic fatigue syndrome. *Clinical and Diagnostic Laboratory Immunology, 12*, 52–55.

Nater, U. M., Lin, J.-M., Maloney, E., Jones, J. F., Tian, H., Raison, C. L., ... Heim, C. (2009). Psychiatric comorbidity in persons with chronic fatigue syndrome in the general population of Georgia. *Psychosomatic Medicine, 71*(5), 557–565.

Nater, U. M., Maloney, E., Heim, C., and Reeves, W. C. (2011). Cumulative life stress in chronic fatigue syndrome. *Psychiatry Research, 189*(2), 318–320.

Ng, B. Y., Lim, C. C., Yeoh, A., and Lee, W. L. (2004). Neuropsychiatric sequelae of Nipah virus encephalitis. *Journal of Neuropsychiatry and Clinical Neuroscience, 16*, 500–504.

Oka, T., Kanemitsu, Y., Sudo, N., Hayashi, H., and Oka, K. (2013). Psychological stress contributed to the development of low-grade fever in a patient with chronic fatigue syndrome: A case report. *BioPsychoSocial Medicine, 7*(7), 1–7.

Okada, T., Tanaka, M., Kuratsune, H., Watanabe, Y., and Sadato, N. (2004). Mechanisms underlying fatigue: A voxel-based morphometric study of chronic fatigue syndrome. *BMC Neurology, 4*(1), 14. doi:10.1186/1471-2377-4-14

Papadopoulos, A. S., and Cleare, A. J. (2011). Hypothalamic-pituitary-adrenal axis dysfunction in chronic fatigue syndrome. *Nature Reviews Endocrinology 8*(1), 22–32.

Prins, J. B., van der Meer, J. W. M., and Bleijenberg, G. (2006). Chronic fatigue syndrome. *Lancet, 367*, 346–355.

Reeves, W. C., Jones, J. F., Maloney, E., Heim, C., Hoaglin, D. C., Boneva, R. S., ... Devlin, R. (2007). Prevalence of chronic fatigue syndrome in metropolitan, urban, and rural Georgia. *Population Health Metrics, 5*. doi:10.1186/1478-7954-5-5

Ross, S. D., Estok, R. P., Frame, D., Stone, L. R., Ludensky, V., and Levine, C. B. (2004). Disability and chronic fatigue syndrome: A focus on function. *Archives of Internal Medicine, 164*(10), 1098–1107.

Salit, I. E. (1997). Precipitating factors for the chronic fatigue syndrome. *Journal of Psychiatric Research, 31*(1), 59–65.

Sanders, P., and Korf, J. (2008). Neuroaetiology of chronic fatigue syndrome: An overview. *World Journal of Biological Psychiatry, 9*(3), 165–171.

Schwartz, R. B., Garada, B. M., Komaroff, A. L., Tice, H. M., Gleit, M., Jolesz, F. A., and Holman, B. L. (1994). Detection of intracranial abnormalities in patients with chronic fatigue syndrome: Comparison of MR imaging and SPECT. *American Journal of Roentgenology, 162*(4), 935–941.

Seeliger, F. A., Brügmann, M. L., Krüger, L., Greiser-Wilke, I., Verspohl, J., Segalés, J., and Baumgärtner, W. (2007). Porcine circovirus type 2-associated cerebellar vasculitis in postweaning multisystemic wasting syndrome (PMWS)-affected pigs. *Veterinary Pathology, 44*, 621–634.

Smith, A. K., White, P. D., Aslakson, E., Vollmer-Conna, U., and Rajeevan, M. S. (2006). Polymorphisms in genes regulating the HPA axis associated with empirically delineated classes of unexplained chronic fatigue. *Pharmacogenomics, 7*(3), 387–394.

Smits, S. L., Zijlstra, E. E., van Hellemond, J., Schapendonk, C., Bodewes, R., Schürch, A. C., … Osterhaus, A. D. (2013). Novel cyclovirus in human cerebrospinal fluid, Malawi, 2010–2011. *Emerging Infectious Diseases, 19*(9). doi:10.3201/eid1909.130404

Tan, Le V., van Doorn, H. R., Nghia, H. D., Chau, T. T., Tu, Le T. P., de Vries, M., … de Jong, M. D. (2013). Identification of a new cyclovirus in cerebrospinal fluid of patients with acute central nervous system infections. *mBio, 4*(3), e00231-13. doi:10.1128/mBio.00231-13

Tanaka, M., Ishii, A., and Watanabe, Y. (2013). Neural mechanisms underlying chronic fatigue. *Reviews in Neuroscience, 24*(6), 617–628.

Theorell, T., Blomkvist, V., Lindh, G., and Evengård, B. (1999). Critical life events, infections, and symptoms during the year preceding chronic fatigue syndrome (CFS): An examination of CFS patients and subjects with a nonspecific life crisis. *Psychosomatic Medicine, 61*(3), 304–310.

Tillmann, H. L. (2004). Hepatitis C virus infection and the brain. *Metabolic Brain Disease, 19*, 351–356.

van de Putte, E. M., van Doornen, L. J., Engelbert, R. H., Kuis, W., Kimpen, J. L., and Uiterwaal, C. S. (2006). Mirrored symptoms in mother and child with chronic fatigue syndrome. *Pediatrics, 117*, 2074–2079.

Van Houdenhove, B., Van Den Eede, F., and Luyten, P. (2009). Does hypothalamic-pituitary-adrenal axis hypofunction in chronic fatigue syndrome reflect a "crash" in the stress system? *Medical Hypotheses, 72*(6), 701–705.

Whistler, T., Unger, E. R., Nisenbaum, R., and Vernon, S. D. (2003). Integration of gene expression, clinical, and epidemiologic data to characterize chronic fatigue syndrome. *Journal of Translational Medicine, 1*(1), 10. doi:10.1186/1479-5876-1-10

Witsø, E., Palacios, G., Cinek, O., Stene, L. C., Grinde, B., Janowitz, D., … Rønningen, K. S. (2006). High prevalence of human enterovirus A infections in natural circulation of human enteroviruses. *Journal of Clinical Microbiology, 44*(11), 4095–4100.

Wyller, V. B., Godang, K., Mørkrid, L., Saul, J. P., Thaulow, E., and Walløe, L. (2007a). Abnormal thermoregulatory responses in adolescents with chronic fatigue syndrome: Relation to clinical symptoms. *Pediatrics, 120*, e129–137.

Wyller, V. B., Saul, J. P., Amlie, J. P., and Thaulow, E. (2007b). Sympathetic predominance of cardiovascular regulation during mild orthostatic stress in adolescents with chronic fatigue. *Clinical Physiology and Functional Imaging, 27*, 231–238.

9

The Double Burden of Work Stress and Depression

A Workplace Intervention

Debra Lerner, David A. Adler, William H. Rogers, Hong Chang, Annabel Greenhill, and Francisca Azocar

Introduction

The Status of Work Stress Intervention

It is hard to imagine a person who has not experienced work stress at some time in his or her career. According to the United States Centers for Disease Control and Prevention, work stress (also referred to as "job stress") is "the harmful physical and emotional responses that occur when the requirements of the job do not match the capabilities, resources, or needs of the worker" (NIOSH, 1999). In a recent national survey, one out of every five US workers reported high daily work stress and another 52 percent reported moderate daily work stress (American Psychological Association, 2011). A 2014 national probability sample in the US found that 60 percent of respondents regarded work as a "very" or "somewhat" significant stressor in their lives, making it second only to finances (American Psychological Association, 2015).

Simply on the basis of the human suffering it involves, work stress is a cause for concern. But its near-term harm is only part of the story. Work stress has the added impact of increasing vulnerability to physical and mental health problems, many of which take a further toll on quality of life (Michie and Williams, 2003; Sapolsky, 2004). Additionally, the direct and indirect costs of work stress in the US are staggering, costing business more than $300 billion a year in absenteeism, employee turnover, diminished productivity, and medical, legal and insurance costs (Rosch, 2001).

The Handbook of Stress and Health: A Guide to Research and Practice, First Edition.
Edited by Cary L. Cooper and James Campbell Quick.
© 2017 John Wiley & Sons, Ltd. Published 2017 by John Wiley & Sons, Ltd.

Yet, the US (the context discussed in this chapter) has no national strategy to tackle work stress. In fact, in contrast to public health initiatives for other health risk factors such as tobacco use, substance abuse and obesity, there are no national surveillance efforts of either work stress or its contributing psychosocial work conditions (NIOSH, 2002; Landsbergis, Grzywacz, and LaMontagne, 2011). Absent are broad-based educational campaigns, screening initiatives and/or prevention efforts. Even the US Occupational Safety and Health Administration, the leading workplace health and safety regulatory agency, has not established standards related to work stress, limiting its role to providing information about stress for critical incident occupations and workplace violence (OSHA, 2015). The US Centers for Disease Control and Prevention, within which the National Institute for Occupational Safety and Health (NIOSH) operates (the agency responsible for occupational health research), primarily serves as an information resource, disseminating facts about work stress and employer best practice recommendations for work stress prevention.

The absence of national or state policies does not that mean work stress is perceived as unimportant to business and organized labor. In fact, many such organizations are concerned about stress at work and home and its impact on employee health, work performance and productivity. Employers regard work stress as a costly problem that hurts the bottom line by increasing health-care costs, reducing productivity and threatening their ability to attract and retain talented employees (National Business Group on Health, 2015). For organized labor, work stress is a worrisome health and safety issue particularly within industries such as health care, human services and education (American Federation of Teachers, 2015; AFL-CIO America's Unions, 2000).

Billions of dollars have been spent on worker stress prevention and management programs, most of which are subsidized by employers or their health insurance plans. A 2012 RAND employer survey found that 51 percent of all US employers with at least 50 employees offered a wellness program, of which 77 percent offered lifestyle management programs. Among employers offering lifestyle interventions, 52 percent offered stress management programs (Mattke et al., 2015). A 2010 survey of mainly large employers which are members of a health benefits research organization reported that 60 percent offered stress management programs (Integrated Benefits Institute, 2010).

The many available worker stress prevention and management programs overwhelmingly fall into the category of individual-level interventions rather than organizational-level ones, and emphasize secondary prevention among individuals who are at high risk of stress or already stressed. While variation in stress reduction program methods makes it difficult to generalize, a common intervention aim is to enable workers to recognize stressors and apply more appropriate coping skills (Spangler, Koesten, Fox, and Radel, 2012; Giga, Cooper, and Faragher, 2003). Programs may offer training in the use of cognitive-behavioral strategies, problem-solving techniques, relaxation, meditation and mindfulness. In addition, Employee Assistance Programs (EAPs) often provide stress management services, including short-term one-on-one psychological counseling, referrals to supportive resources, group-level stress management programs and crisis intervention. EAPs are relatively widely available, being offered by 29 percent of all US firms that provide health benefits to their employees, but 79 percent of large companies (Kaiser Family Foundation and Health Research and Educational Trust, 2014). Finally, some employers wishing to promote primary stress prevention have initiated programs such as worker resiliency training.

While US companies have relied heavily on individual-level interventions, such approaches are often criticized for neglecting the critical (and evidenced-based) part that characteristics of work organization play in generating work stress, and for placing too much of the responsibility for change on workers instead of the company (Noblet and LaMontagne, 2006). However, for a variety of reasons, organizational-level stress interventions have not caught on. Neither have programs combining organizational and individual level interventions, though they have some support from scientific studies (Bond and Bunce, 2000; Bunce, 1997) and mental health professional organizations (Spangler, 2007). Thus, in the US, the breadth and depth of awareness and acceptance of work stress as a health problem is paradoxical given the relatively narrow range of solutions.

The Double Burden of Work Stress and Major Illness

One troubling aspect of conceptualizing work stress as an occupational problem of individual workers is its segregation from the person's total health. This fragmentation of occupational and nonoccupational aspects of health and health services was one of the factors motivating NIOSH to advance its Total Worker Health initiative, which is aimed at integrating occupational health services and workplace health promotion and wellness initiatives (Hammer and Sauter, 2013).

This chapter is concerned with a group of workers that has been overlooked in service delivery settings and intervention research: those who have the double burden of both work stress and one or more major illnesses (physical and/or mental). Major illnesses are defined as chronic and/or limiting diseases and disorders. In 2005, 133 million US residents had at least one chronic condition and 63 million had more than one (CDC, 2015a). About 25 million people, nearly one in ten, are estimated to suffer from major limitations in activities of daily living due to chronic health problems (CDC, 2015b). Because population aging is partly responsible for these rates, the size of the chronically ill population is projected to grow at least through 2030.

Alarmingly little is known about workers who have both work stress and major illness concurrently. Yet, many workers are likely to be shouldering this double burden. This is partly because stress and illness are often related: work stress can be both a "cause" of some illnesses (i.e., increasing risk of illness) and a consequence. The stress–illness relationship suggests that some workers who have a major illness may be vulnerable to work stress as well as having had some significant past and/or recent exposure to work stress. In fact, major illness often requires people to make significant adjustments, such as avoiding symptom flare-ups, adhering to medication regimens, compensating for changes in abilities, managing interpersonal relationships and dealing with stigma, which can be particularly difficult to manage when working (Munir et al., 2007).

This chapter will review ongoing efforts to improve the health and work outcomes of working adults with depression as an example, and as part of a larger effort to reduce the adverse impact of physical and mental health problems on working people and their employers. This new depression program was developed in order to enable workers to perform their jobs more effectively and productively (Lerner et al., 2012; Lerner et al., 2015). As program testing advanced, it became evident that some workers with depression also were experiencing work stress. The aims of this chapter are to (1) describe a novel intervention for improving the health and work outcomes of employees with depression and work stress; (2) using data from a recent intervention trial, identify the prevalence of work stress among employees who have depression and enumerate the types of stressors they report; and (3) report on the intervention's effectiveness for workers with depression and work stress.

Magnitude and Nature of the Depression and Work Stress Problem

Depression is a relatively common health problem within the employed population. With a one-year prevalence rate of 7 percent in employed adults (Center for Behavioral Health Statistics and Quality, 2005; 2010), depression is often chronic, recurring in 50 percent of cases, and often deprives people of the opportunity to lead satisfying and productive lives (Pratt and Brody, 2008). In the United States, major depression ranks fifth in the number of disability-adjusted life-years – years of life lost and years lived with disability – resulting from illness (Murray and Lopez, 2013) and costs an estimated $44 billion annually in lost work productivity (Stewart, Ricci, Chee, Hahn, and Morganstein, 2003; Murray and Lopez, 2013; Lerner and Henke, 2008).

Many epidemiological studies have quantified the probability of developing depression after exposure to work stress but only a few large-scale studies, including studies in the United Kingdom, Canada, and the US, have estimated the number of employed adults with both depressive symptoms and work stress concurrently.

First, Stansfeld, North, White, and Marmot (1995) reported cross-sectional findings from the Whitehall II study for psychiatric disorders (i.e., anxiety and depression) and work stress, which was measured according to the job strain model (Karasek and Theorell, 1992). Whitehall II classified the study participants' jobs in terms of their control (decision authority and skill discretion), psychological demands, and social supports, hypothesizing that workers in high strain jobs (low control and high psychological demands) would have the most psychiatric morbidity. Among men in high strain jobs, 36.5 percent had probable psychiatric disorder (anxiety and/or depression) compared to 15.7 percent in low strain jobs. Among women, the rates were 40.8 percent vs. 20.3 percent, respectively. In another cross-sectional study conducted in 2002, 3.4 percent of men and 6.0 percent of women had major depression. Within these groups, 5.6 percent and 7.7 percent were classified as having high strain jobs (Blackmore et al., 2007). Finally, in a 2002 US national survey (Lerner, Rogers, Bungay, Chang, and Massagli, 2004b), a sample of 1,168 employed respondents completed a validated NIOSH quality of working life survey (NIOSH, 2013) which included a single-item assessment of work stress and, in a separate survey administration, the Patient Health Questionnaire (PHQ)-9 for depression (Kroenke and Spitzer, 2002). Thirty percent of this employed sample had high work stress, 45 percent had moderate work stress, and 25 percent had little or no work stress. The corresponding prevalence rates for depression were approximately 14 percent, 9 percent, and 4 percent, respectively. Conversely, among the 9.2 percent in this sample classified as having depression, 45 percent had high stress.

Issues Pertaining to Depression Care

In the US as well as other nations, ensuring that people with depression are adequately diagnosed and treated is a persistent and formidable public health challenge (Pratt and Brody, 2008). Due to a host of issues, including stigma, access barriers, unmet needs for provider training and support, affordability of care, and medication concerns, less than half of the adults diagnosed with depression also receive care, while, among those who do, more than half receive care that is considered suboptimal (US Preventive Services Task Force, 2009; see also, for the United Kingdom, NICE, 2009). To improve mental health care in the US, several initiatives have been undertaken, including health insurance parity legislation (US Department of Labor, 2015), the development of medical practice guidelines defining quality for mental health diagnosis and treatment in primary care (US Preventive Services Task Force, 2009), workplace depression awareness and screening campaigns (Partnership for Workplace Mental Health, 2015), programs to combat stigma, and various cost and quality management initiatives. Despite gains, high quality care still does not reach most of those who need it or want it. This situation has left many people vulnerable to undiagnosed and/or untreated depression as well as improperly treated depression and related functional consequences that take a toll on ability to work.

Generally speaking, depression care (diagnosis and treatment), even within the newer collaborative care paradigm, does not involve explicit assessment of or intervention for work stress. Instead it consists of providing prescription antidepressant medication, psychotherapy, or both. Treatment is aimed at reducing symptoms (e.g., depressed mood, loss of interest, fatigue, and difficulty concentrating), which is assumed to restore ability to perform activities of daily living and social roles, including employment. Far outside the realm of occupational health services, most depression care is provided by primary care professionals, with psychiatrists and other masters level behavioral health clinicians a distant second (Olfson and Klerman, 1992).

While providing high quality depression care improves depression and employment outcomes relative to usual care (Rush et al., 2006), including reducing unemployment, job loss, absenteeism, and at-work performance deficits known as "presenteeism" (Rost, Smith, and Dickinson, 2004; Rost, Fortney, and Coyne, 2005; Schoenbaum et al., 2002), evidence suggests that the care does not go far enough to address the needs of working people. First, studies indicate that many individuals, including those who have received high quality care and have had their symptoms improve, still exhibit residual limitations that interfere with working (Hirschfeld et al., 2002; Judd et al., 2000; Lerner et al., 2011; Buist-Bouwman, Ormel, de Graaf, and Vollebergh, 2004). For example, a major clinical trial, STAR*D (Sequenced Treatment Alternatives to Relieve Depression), found that patients who responded to first-line antidepressants had become less limited in their ability to work, but patients whose symptoms did not respond to initial treatment failed to regain their ability to work even when second-line antidepressants eventually reduced their symptoms (Trivedi et al., 2013). Second, a systematic review of interventions for reducing work absences due to depression, which examined the effectiveness of several types of interventions, found that enhancing the quality of primary care did not reduce absences, and that different antidepressants were similar in effectiveness to each other. In contrast, when work-directed interventions were added to clinical interventions (e.g., light duty, graded work exposure, or enhancing coping in the workplace), outcomes improved (Nieuwenhuijsen et al., 2014). Finally, studies suggest that standards of improvement in medical care are not necessarily aligned with those operating in the workplace. A longitudinal observational study compared two cohorts of working adults; a group that screened-in for depression, and a group that did not meet screening criteria for depression and had no other major illnesses (Lerner et al., 2011). Six months after baseline, 17 percent of the depression group did well by clinical standards; they were either in remission or had a clinically significant improvement in depression symptoms. Moreover, health-related productivity loss in this improved depression group declined an average of 2 percent (from approximately 9 to 7 percent output loss). However, the productivity of the improved group was still five points lower than the rate of nondepressed control workers. Eighteen months after baseline, this productivity gap between initially depressed workers and those without depression had not closed. Thus, a clinical success may not be commensurate with a successful work outcome.

Making Work Considerations a Dimension of Treatment

Work stress may play a part in explaining why initially some workers with depression will experience work limitations before they are treated and why after treatment some will have persistent work limitations. In the observational study cited previously, the outcomes of depressed workers within different types of jobs were compared. Those in psychologically demanding and/or low control jobs had significantly more difficulty functioning at work than depressed workers in less demanding, higher control positions (Lerner et al., 2010). Also, depressed workers who had jobs involving high demands for interpersonal interactions at work and requirements for judgment and decision-making had significantly more work limitations than depressed workers in jobs involving lesser amounts of these demands (Lerner et al., 2004a).

Currently, the impact of work stressors on the employment outcomes of individuals with depression has not received a great deal attention in either research or service settings. Depression treatment, which takes place mainly in primary care rather than behavioral health care settings, remains primarily based on the biomedical model, emphasizing health mechanisms internal to the person. This is not the situation for other areas of mental health care. In fact, chronically and severely mentally ill individuals (e.g., those with schizophrenia) are more likely than individuals with major depression to receive interventions such as supported employment programs and vocational rehabilitation which address work conditions (Becker et al., 2007). These interventions are based on a disability model in which full participation in social roles is seen as influenced by the person–environment fit. Until now, generally, a similar perspective has not been applied to people with depression.

Creating a New Intervention Model

Since 2004, a series of studies has been testing a program for currently employed workers with depression. This program was intended to provide multifaceted services in a manner that is accessible to working adults, private (not requiring any disclosure to employers about the illness), and coordinated with (not replacing) medical, psychiatric or behavioral care. Using three integrated service modalities, the intervention involves assessment of adaptive challenges present at work and barriers to effective functioning, as well as the use of tailored strategies to address these. It is referred to as the Work-Focused Intervention (WFI).

To join the program, an anonymous online screening survey which assesses mental health and related work limitations must be completed by the candidate. The screening survey is made available from any computer with an internet connection. The screening survey includes validated measures to identify individuals who meet criteria for either major depressive disorder (MDD) and/or persistent depressive disorder (PDD) and have work limitations.

Eligible individuals may enroll in the WFI either online or by telephone. Once enrolled, a designated WFI coach (called an "Advocate") provides individualized care. The care is provided by telephone and at times deemed mutually convenient, including before, during and after work hours. The WFI program includes eight, 50-minute sessions at two-week intervals. WFI Advocates have Masters' degrees in social work or psychology and work experience in an EAP or other workplace health program. Advocates receive training in the WFI protocols and participate in weekly supervision with a multidisciplinary team including a psychiatrist, clinical psychologist and a work sociologist. In eight WFI sessions over four months, Advocates provide the following services: (1) care coordination; (2) training in cognitive-behavioral therapy (CBT) strategies; and (3) work coaching. All care is documented in an electronic record and is monitored continually.

Care coordination addresses barriers to functional improvement related to gaps in the worker's knowledge of depression and its treatment, as well as failure to include restoration of work function in the medical treatment plan. Psycho-education is important both because of the degree of misinformation about depression and the fact that many people with depression are unaware of depression's symptoms or its adverse functional impact. Three-way communication between the Advocate, the worker, and his or her medical provider (usually a primary care physician) is arranged because physicians and patients often do not discuss work as a routine part of depression care. To facilitate this three-way interaction, the Advocate performs a monthly assessment of the worker's depression symptoms and related work limitations and shares the results with the worker and provider. In addition, the Advocate employs motivational enhancement techniques to help the worker actively participate in care and stay goal-oriented.

The next WFI component is aimed at helping workers to develop cognitive and behavioral skills to combat thoughts, feelings and behaviors that interfere with functioning effectively at work (Beck, 1979; Lewinsohn, Antonuccio, Steinmetz, and Teri, 1984). This component is based on CBT principles, which have been shown to be effective for either depression or work stress (van der Klink, Blonk, Schene, and van Dijk, 2001; Wang et al., 2007). A workbook is used to provide a series of specific homework exercises, which are designed to help the worker identify emotional, cognitive and behavioral responses that are making it difficult to work, and develop new coping strategies.

The third component, known as work coaching, addresses aspects of work routines and the work environment that make it difficult for the person to perform his or her work. This WFI component includes both a structured assessment to identify environmental barriers to functioning effectively, and guidance on adjustments and compensatory strategies. Small, sometimes subtle changes are recommended so that they do not require the worker to disclose his or her illness at work nor introduce additional stress. The Advocates can access the WFI's online library, Tools and Tips, which includes ideas culled from diverse fields including disability management, vocational rehabilitation, supported employment and business management.

The initial assessment of the worker's functional problems is based on the Work Limitations Questionnaire (WLQ) (Lerner et al., 2001; Lerner et al., 2003), which addresses health-related difficulties in the following areas: time management, physical tasks, mental and interpersonal tasks, and output tasks. Next, work stressors are assessed using an open-ended procedure, which is guided by the list of common work stressors (Box 9.1) (Leka, Griffiths, and Cox, 2003; Leka and Jain, 2010). Following this work coaching assessment, the Advocates generally recommend changes to one or more aspects of work. These are organized into the Five T's (Box 9.2). The specific interventions chosen will vary with individual worker, his or her specific work difficulties and the characteristics of the work situation. As workers attempt to make changes, the Advocate monitors the situation closely for signs of adverse effects (including increased distress).

Box 9.1   Common work stressors

Job-level problems

- *Job content*   Underuse of skills, repetitive work/lack of variety, fragmented or meaningless work
- *Role in organization*   Role clarity/role ambiguity, role conflict, responsibility for
  people
- *Workload and work pace*   Work underload or overload (physically, psychologically or
  emotionally demanding), machine pacing, time pressures, deadlines
- *Work schedule*   Shift work, night work, etc., inflexible work schedules, unpredictable
  hours, long or unsociable hours
- *Control/autonomy*   Little opportunity to participate in decision-making, lack of control
  over workload, pacing, etc.
- *Career development*   Career stagnation, uncertainty about future, underpromotion or
  overpromotion, poor pay, job insecurity, low social value to work
- *Environment and equipment*   Inadequate space, light, etc., poorly maintained or otherwise inadequate space and equipment
- *Interpersonal relationships at work*   Social or physical isolation, poor relationships
  with supervisors, interpersonal conflict, lack of social support, bullying, harassment
- *Organizational culture and function*   Poor communication, low levels of support for
  problem-solving and personal development, poor commitment to worker safety and
  health, discrimination, unfair treatment, ethical issues, lack of definition of or agreement on organizational objectives
- *Home–work interface/balance*   Conflicting demands, low support at home, dual career
  problems

Worker-level problems

- Competencies (knowledge and skills mismatched to job), training and experience (e.g.,
  outdated knowledge), physical abilities (strength, energy, endurance, etc.), cognitive
  skills, social skills, ethical conflicts, emotional resiliency and coping, motivation/sense
  of purpose and meaning (intrinsic rewards)

Box 9.2   Five T's: the Work-Focused Intervention targets for change

- Work **T**asks and responsibilities: psychological and physical work demands,
  autonomy
- Work **T**iming: timing and sequence of tasks, deadlines, work schedule, hours, shift
- Work **T**echniques: work procedures including use of technology
- Work **T**eam: interpersonal relationships with supervisors, coworkers, customers; team-
  work and communications
- Work **T**urf: physical and social environment

To illustrate the range of possible options, consider a worker who is having difficulty staying mentally engaged with work. He reports that his mind is wandering and assignments are not being completed. Depending on a number of considerations, including the worker's preferences, the Advocate may consider one or more of the following solutions: create and use a customized self-monitoring procedure involving a task checklist with scheduled check-ins; break down larger tasks into smaller steps and monitor where in the process he veers off course; program a computer or phone to emit sounds periodically to restore attention; identify acceptable time-saving shortcuts to limit requirements for prolonged attention; learn skills to negotiate with a manager to schedule certain tasks when attention is optimal; and build in microbreaks to reenergize and reorient to the task. There is no single recipe for change and several different techniques may be tried until one or more of the best options are identified. At the last WFI session, the worker and Advocate codevelop a self-care plan. This plan highlights the strategies found to be most effective during WFI treatment.

Research Methods

Intervening to Improve Ability to Function at Work

This chapter characterizes the double burden of work stress and depression and how the WFI was helpful to workers who had both depression and work stress. This topic is addressed using data from a randomized controlled trial (RCT) in which employed adults with depression were randomly assigned to the WFI group or a usual care group. Study participants were employed, age 45 or older, met screening criteria for MDD or PDD or both (double depression), and had work limitations. The National Institute on Aging of the US National Institutes of Health sponsored this trial (Clinical Trials registration number, NCT01163890).

Screening for depression and work limitations was conducted on a privacy-protected study website in 13 private-sector employers, six public-sector employers and five organizations serving employed populations (for example, employee benefits organizations). The screening process was voluntary, anonymous and provided immediate personalized electronic feedback about the screened person's depression symptom severity and work limitations. [1] If, during screening, suicidal thoughts were reported, a pop-up message offered confidential assistance.

Each worker assigned to the WFI was informed that a program Advocate would call within two business days to initiate the eight-session cycle. [2] Each worker assigned to usual care was advised to contact a health-care provider (for example, primary care physician, psychiatrist, or behavioral health specialist) and, when available, an employer-sponsored EAP. The study provided no direct care to the usual care group. In addition, all study participants were given intranet links to depression information and care resources.

During the study, participants were not restricted from using any other services. Because this was a nonblinded study, WFI Advocates were prohibited from providing care to any members of the usual care group and study participants were unaware of which questions specifically measured the study's endpoints. In addition, to minimize a socially desirable response set, there was minimal interaction between the researchers who were evaluating the program and those involved in providing the WFI.

Study participants completed assessments preintervention and postintervention. The follow-up was obtained four months after baseline; a time aligned with the end of the acute phase of depression. Assessments were based on questionnaires consisting of validated self-report survey instruments. Among these were the WLQ (measuring limitations in four dimensions of work performance, including time management, physical task performance, performance of mental and interpersonal tasks and performance of output-related tasks). The WLQ also generates a productivity loss score. This score is computed by an algorithm developed empirically in research on the relationship of the scale scores to objectively measured work productivity (Lerner et al., 2003). It reflects the difference between the subject's work productivity (output) compared to a healthy workers. The WLQ productivity loss score can be monetized to dollars by multiplying the score by job earnings.

Also included was the PHQ-9 for depression (Kroenke and Spitzer, 2002). Additionally, the assessment (baseline only) included portions of the Job Content Questionnaire, previously adapted for administration in a national survey of adults in US households, including psychological demands, physical demands, autonomy and support (Lerner, Levine, Malspeis, and D'Agostino, 1994). Also obtained were extensive data on demographic, health and work characteristics, as well as use of supplemental programs and services.

Results

Participant Characteristics

Over 30 months 18,102 workers were screened of whom 1,227 (7 percent) were eligible for the study. Of these 431 (35 percent) consented to participate and 12 percent left the study before follow-up. The mean age of study participants was 54.7 (SD (standard deviation) = 6.1), 72 percent were female, 88 percent were white non-Hispanic, and 68 percent had earned a bachelor's degree or higher (see Table 9.1). Annual median earnings were US$63,000 (interquartile range (IQR) = US$39,536). Most (88 percent) worked full-time and had white-collar occupations (72 percent). The mean number of weekly hours worked was 42.1 (SD = 10.9). More than half (59 percent) had held their jobs for five years or longer, 27 percent had union positions, and 6 percent were self-employed.

Based on the preintervention WLQ, work limitations affecting time management were present 42.7 percent of the time on average (SD = 22.0) in the two weeks prior to baseline. Limitations in physical task performance were occurring 22.3 percent of the time on average (SD = 20.2). Limitations performing mental and interpersonal work tasks were present 38.1 percent of the time on average (SD = 17.3). Limitations affecting output requirements were occurring an average of 42.3 percent of the time (SD = 23.5). These combined to reduce productivity while on the job by (presenteeism) by mean 10.3 percent (SD = 4.4). By comparison, the US norm for at-work productivity loss due to health problems is 2.7 percent. Also, in the two weeks prior to baseline, participants had mean 1.6 days of sickness absence (SD = 2.2), or 14.6 percent lost productivity due to missed work time (SD = 18.8).

Work Stress

The total sample was classified according to their baseline psychological job demands, physical demands, control and social support scores by dividing each score into high vs. low groups. Each variable was dichotomized as high or low using the US median as the cut-point (50th percentile for workers age 45 years or older). A high score was set at or above the median; low was set at below the median.

Table 9.1 Baseline characteristics of employed adults randomized to the Work-Focused Intervention (WFI) or usual care for depression

Characteristic	Total (N = 431) N	%	Work-Focused Intervention (N = 217) N	%	Usual care (N = 214) N	%	Analysis p
Age (M ± SD)	54.7 ± 6.1		54.6 ± 6.1		54.8 ± 6.1		0.78
Female	309	72	149	69	160	75	0.16
White non-Hispanic	378	88	193	89	185	87	0.51
Married	223	52	99	46	124	58	0.01
No. of comorbidities (M ± SD)	2.9 ± 1.9		2.7 ± 1.9		3.2 ± 1.9		<0.01
Education							
Less than high school	2	0.5	1	0.5	1	0.5	
High school graduate	26	6	12	6	14	7	
Some college, no degree	75	17	27	12	48	22	
Associate's degree	34	8	18	8	16	8	
Bachelor's degree	130	30	74	34	56	26	
Post-bachelor's degree	164	38	85	39	79	37	
Annual income (Median ± IQR)	63000 ± 39536		61783 ± 39000		64000 ± 39000		0.66
Weekly work hours (M ± SD)	42.1 ± 10.9		41.7 ± 11.1		42.4 ± 10.7		0.49
Occupation							0.30
White collar	309	72	162	75	147	69	
Blue collar	21	5	11	5	10	5	
Sales, support and service	101	23	44	20	57	27	
In job ≥ 5 years	253	59	131	60	122	57	0.48
Union member	115	27	64	30	51	24	0.19
Self-employed	25	6	16	7	9	4	0.16
Job strain and support[a]							
Psychological demands (M ± SD)	64.0 ± 19.6		63.5 ± 20.2		64.5 ± 18.9		0.606
Control (M ± SD)	44.1 ± 21.3		44.8 ± 22.0		43.3 ± 20.7		0.446
Physical demands (M ± SD)	29.6 + 23.6		29.5 ± 24.6		29.7 ± 22.6		0.937
Supervisor support (M ± SD)	49.1 ± 31.3		49.2 ± 31.3		49.1 ± 31.5		0.965
Coworker support (M ± SD)	59.0 ± 26.7		59.1 ± 27.7		58.8 ± 25.7		0.895
Subgroups[b]							
High psychological demands	333	77.3	161	74.2	172	80.4	0.126
High physical demands	279	64.7	130	59.9	149	69.6	**0.035**
Low job control	343	79.6	170	78.3	173	80.8	0.521
Low supervisor support	255	59.3	131	60.4	124	58.2	0.651
Low coworker support	189	44.1	94	43.5	95	44.6	0.822
Job strain[c]							
High strain	264	61.3	123	56.7	141	65.9	0.19
Active	69	16.0	38	17.5	31	14.5	0.19
Low strain	19	4.4	9	4.1	10	4.7	0.19
Passive	79	18.3	47	21.7	32	15.0	0.19

(continued)

Table 9.1   (*Continued*)

Characteristic	Total (N = 431)		Work-Focused Intervention (N = 217)		Usual care (N = 214)		Analysis
	N	%	N	%	N	%	p
Presenteeism (M ± SD)[d]							
Percent at-work productivity loss[c]	10.3 ± 4.4		10.2 ± 4.3		10.4 ± 4.5		0.75
Percent time with at-work limitations by task							
Time management	42.7 ± 22.0		43.7 ± 21.8		41.7 ± 22.1		0.35
Physical tasks	22.3 ± 20.2		22.0 ± 20.1		22.6 ± 20.4		0.75
Mental-interpersonal tasks	38.1 ± 17.3		37.6 ± 17.0		38.6 ± 17.6		0.55
Output tasks	42.3 ± 23.5		42.1 ± 23.3		42.5 ± 23.8		0.86
Absences due to health or medical care (M ± SD)[e]							
Days missed per 2 weeks	1.6 ± 2.2		1.5 ± 2.1		1.6 ± 2.3		0.55
Percent productivity loss due to absence	14.6 ± 18.8		14.2 ± 18.4		15.0 ± 19.2		0.65

M ± SD = mean plus or minus standard deviation; IQR = interqartile range.

[a]Based on a modified version of the Job Content Questionnaire. Scores range from 0 (lowest amount) to 100 (greatest amount).

[b]The cut-point for defining high was at or above the median US score and low was below the median US score for employed adults in US households 45 years of age and older.

[c]Job strain categories were created by cross-classifying psychological demands and job control variables. Each variable was dichotomized into a high or low category for cross-classification.

[d]Based on responses to the Work Limitations Questionnaire (WLQ). Scale scores indicate the percent of time limited in the past two weeks in ability to perform job tasks (e.g., time management). Possible scale scores range from 0 to 100, with higher scores indicating greater percentage of time limited in the past two weeks in ability to perform job tasks. Possible productivity loss scores range from 0 to 27, with higher scores indicating greater productivity loss.

[e]Based on responses to the WLQ Time Loss Module. Productivity loss is the mean percentage of hours missed in the past two weeks divided by the total number of hours usually worked in that time period. Possible days missed range from 0 to 14. Possible percent productivity loss due to absenteeism ranges from 0 to 100, with higher scores indicating greater productivity loss.

In comparison to the US norm, a considerably higher percentage of workers in this sample had poor work conditions. Instead of 50 percent of the sample, more than three-quarters (77.3 percent) had high psychological demands, 64.7 percent had high physical demands (with a significantly higher rate among usual care participants), 79.6 percent had low control, 59.3 percent had low supervisor support, and 44.1 percent had low coworker support. Additionally, based on the cross-classification of the dichotomized psychological demands and control variables, 61.3 percent of the participants had high strain jobs (high demands/low control), 16.0 percent had active jobs (high demands/high control), 4.4 percent had low strain jobs (low demands/high control), and 18.3 percent had passive jobs (low demands/low control).

During the WFI intervention sessions, the Advocates had the opportunity to obtain more detailed information about the nature of the participants' work stressors (see Table 9.2). There was no significant association of the job strain and support variables with depression severity, gender or occupation (data not shown). Using the taxonomy shown in Box 9.1 for those participants who reported one or more stressors, the rates for three of the identified stressors

Table 9.2 Work stressors identified during intervention based on Work-Focused Intervention Advocate documentation

	Reporting ≥ 1 work problem (N = 163)	
	N	%
Job content	25	15.3
Role in organization	19	11.7
Workload, work pace	68	41.7
Control over work schedule, hours	16	9.8
Job autonomy	8	4.9
Career development	40	24.5
Environmental conditions, tools and equipment	0	0.0
Interpersonal problems	76	46.6
Organizational culture and behavior	23	14.1
Personal competency for job	78	47.9
Other	46	28.2
Work and home interface	34	20.9
No. work problems (mean, SD)	1.2	2.7

were relatively high. Almost half (46.6 percent) were interpersonal stressors (e.g., conflicts with supervisors), 47.9 percent were competency-related stressors (e.g., insufficient training and job preparation), and 41.7 percent were stressors related to work overload (e.g., excessive amount of work) and work pace. Roughly 20 to 30 percent were stressors related to career development opportunities (24.5 percent), work–home spillover or imbalance issues (20.9 percent), and stressors not otherwise classified (28.2 percent). Between 10 and 19 percent were stressors related to job content (15.3 percent), which included psychologically demanding work, organization-level issues (14.1 percent), and the person's role in the organization (11.7 percent), which included role ambiguity and role conflict. Other work stressors occurred to a lesser extent.

The distribution of the stressors occupationally and demographically identified few significant subgroup differences (data not shown). Stratified by white collar vs. all other occupations, 21.6 percent of blue collar and sales, service and support workers had poor control over work scheduling compared to 6.5 percent in white-collar occupations (p = 0.005). Comparing hourly to salaried workers, problems related to competency for the job were present for 34.1 percent of hourly workers vs. 50.4 percent of salaried workers, but the difference did not reach statistical significance (p = 0.063). Comparing genders, 24.8 percent of female workers had problems with work–home spillover or imbalance vs. 10.9 percent of male workers (p = 0.034). The mean number of stressors identified was 2.6 (including participants reporting zero stressors).

Intervention Results

At the close of the intervention period, four months after baseline, the WFI intervention group had fared considerably better than the usual care group.[3] In the WFI group, work limitations had declined significantly and each pre- to postintervention improvement in that group was significantly greater in magnitude than the change observed for the usual-care group (see

Table 9.3). WFI group at-work productivity loss improved 44 percent (p < 0.001) compared with 13 percent (p < 0.001) in the usual-care group (p < 0.001 for the difference in change). Additionally, absences declined by 44 percent in the WFI group (p < 0.001) versus 13 percent in the usual-care group (p = 0.31) (p < 0.001 for the difference in change). Absence-related productivity loss improved in the WFI group by 49 percent (p < 0.001) versus 43 percent (p = 0.35) in the usual-care group (p < 0.01 for the difference in change). Finally, mean depression symptom severity scores fell by 51 percent (p < 0.001) in the WFI group (similar to findings in RCTs designed to treat MDD) versus 26 percent (p < 0.001) in the usual-care group (p < 0.001 for the difference in change).

Next, given the relatively high prevalence of work stress in this sample, the analysis explored the extent to which having a high strain job modified the WFI's effects. Conceivably, the WFI and/or usual care could have been less effective (or more effective) in some work stress subgroups than in others. This analysis tested whether the difference in the change in outcomes discussed previously is related to the main effects of intervention, treating the work stress indicators separately as well as their interactions.

As shown in the graphs (see Figure 9.1), the WFI was similarly effective for most of the workers' stress subgroups. However, analyses of subgroups defined by social support and physical demands indicated some exceptions applied. Workers in the WFI group who had low coworker support at baseline vs. high coworker support had a significantly greater improvement in their ability to perform mental and interpersonal tasks and output tasks (measured with the WLQ). A similar pattern occurred in the usual care group. However, the magnitude of the change was much larger (and positive) in the WFI group. Further, in the WFI group only, workers starting out with low coworker support vs. high support also had the greatest reductions in their depression symptom severity (measured with the PHQ-9). Also, workers who had physically demanding jobs vs. jobs low in physical demands had greater improvements in one key outcome. With the WFI, their limitations in ability to perform physical work tasks (measured with the WLQ) improved to a significantly greater degree. Finally, workers in usual care who had low supervisor support at baseline had significantly poorer outcomes than those starting out with high supervisor support. In this low support subgroup, both the number of absence days and depression symptom severity worsened.

Discussion

While common sense tells us that some workers, particularly those with chronic or severe work stress, will have depression and that some workers with depression will have work stress, this doubly burdened group has been neglected in both intervention research and service delivery settings. One of the reasons for this gap is that occupational health, on the one hand, and primary care and behavioral health, on the other, historically have operated independently of each other with little coordination between them.

In recent years, occupational health has begun to embrace a more holistic view of health and particularly the interconnections between behavioral, biomedical, and environmental risk factors with illness and injury. Similarly, the psychosocial and behavioral dimensions of health have taken on a larger role in the diagnosis and treatment of chronic illnesses and aging populations. Both the aging of the workforce and the projected need for adults to increase the duration of employment into the later years of life provide a strong rationale for adopting a more holistic view of worker health and safety, including taking seriously the need to minimize the burden of work stress and chronic medical or psychiatric conditions.

Table 9.3 Mixed effects models for three outcomes in the Work-Focused Intervention (WFI) and usual care[a]

	Work-Focused Intervention						Usual Care						Difference in Change Scores			
	Baseline N = 217		Follow-up N = 190		Change Mean	Effect Size	Baseline N = 214		Follow-up N = 190		Change Mean	Effect Size	Change Mean	95% CI	Effect Size[e]	p
	Mean	SD	Mean	SD			Mean	SD	Mean	SD						
Presenteeism[b]																
% At-work productivity loss	10.2	4.3	5.7	4.3	−4.5	−1.05	10.4	4.5	9.0	5.1	−1.4	−0.31	−3.2	−4.2 to −2.3	−0.72	<0.001
% Time with at-work limitations by task																
Time management	43.7	21.8	24.5	20.7	−19.2	−0.88	41.7	22.1	39.1	23.5	−2.6	−0.12	−15.6	−20.2 to −11.0	−0.67	<0.001
Physical tasks	22.0	20.1	12.2	18.7	−9.8	−0.49	22.6	20.4	21.0	21.3	−1.7	−0.08	−7.1	−11.3 to −2.9	−0.37	<0.001
Mental-interpersonal tasks	37.6	17.0	20.3	16.3	−17.3	−1.02	38.6	17.6	31.7	19.0	−6.9	−0.39	−11.1	−14.8 to −7.5	−0.63	<0.001
Output tasks	42.1	23.3	22.3	21.6	−19.8	−0.85	42.5	23.8	36.5	25.3	−6.0	−0.25	−14.0	−18.9 to −9.1	−0.61	<0.001
Absences due to health or treatment[c]																
Days missed	1.5	2.1	0.8	1.4	−0.8	−0.38	1.6	2.3	1.4	2.7	−0.2	−0.09	−0.8	−1.3 to −0.4	−0.31	<0.001
% Productivity loss due to absence	14.2	18.4	7.4	15.2	−6.9	−0.38	15.0	19.2	13.4	23.7	−1.7	−0.09	−6.4	−10.4 to −2.4	−0.30	<0.01
Depression[d]																
Symptom severity	14.4	5.2	7.1	6.1	−7.3	−1.40	14.3	4.9	10.6	5.6	−3.7	−0.76	−3.7	−4.8 to −2.5	−0.60	<0.001

[a]Models are adjusted for study site, baseline mean age, percent male, percent white, percentage married, percentage white collar occupation, mean number of comorbidities, percentage full-time employed, and mean scores of model dependent variable. All significance tests were conducted using the chi-square test with a degree of freedom of 1.

[b]Based on the Work Limitations Questionnaire (WLQ). Scale scores indicate the percent of time limited in the past two weeks in ability to perform job tasks (e.g., time management). The percent at-work productivity loss variable is the mean percent difference in productivity compared to an external healthy benchmark employee norm. Possible scale scores range from 0 to 100, with higher scores indicating greater percentage of time limited in the past two weeks in ability to perform job tasks. Possible productivity loss scores range from 0 to 27, with higher scores indicating greater productivity loss.

[c]Based on the WLQ Time Loss Module. Productivity loss is the mean percentage of hours missed in the past two weeks divided by the total number of hours usually worked in that time period. Possible days missed range from 0 to 14. Possible percent productivity loss due to absenteeism ranges from 0 to 100, with higher scores indicating greater productivity loss.

[d]Depression symptom severity is the mean Patient Health Questionnaire (PHQ-9) score. Possible scores range from 0 to 27. Higher scores indicate more severe depressive symptoms.

[e]Effect size was computed as the ratio of the difference of change score and the pooled standard deviation of baseline scores for both groups.

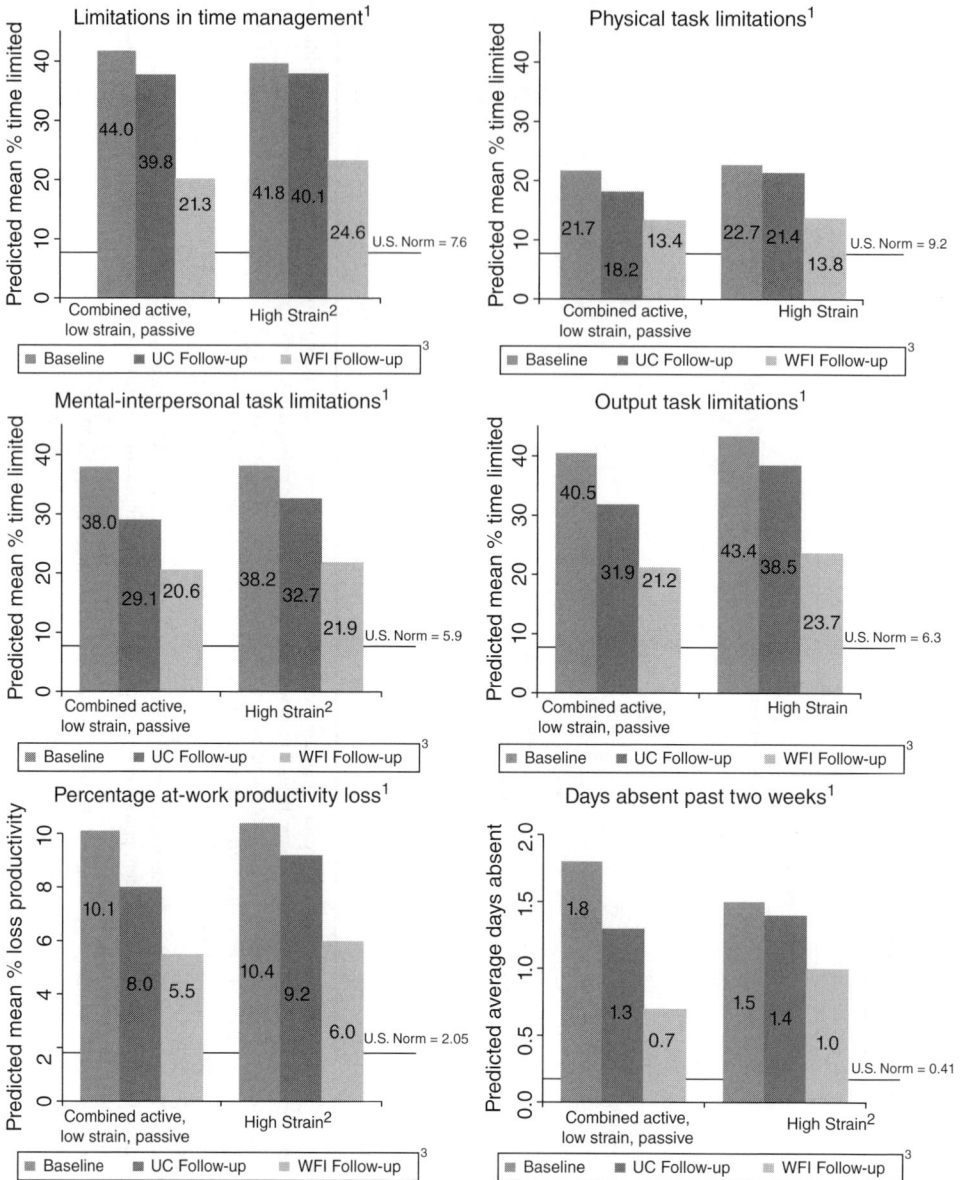

Figure 9.1 High strain job as an intervention effect modifier of Work-Focused Intervention (WFI) and usual care (UC).

[1]Change in time management physical tasks, mental-interpersonal tasks, output tasks and at-work productivity loss were measured with the Work Limitations Questionnaire (WLQ). Changes in work absences were measured with the WLQ Time Loss Module. Change in depression severity was measured with the PHQ-9. The US norm reflects estimates from the 2002 national WLQ norming survey.

[2]Control ≤61.5 = low and psychological demands ≥49.5 = high.

[3]Baseline n = 167 for active, low strain and passive groups; n = 264 for high strain group. Within usual care, follow-up n = 73 for active, low strain and passive groups; n = 141 for high strain groups. Within the WFI group, follow-up n = 94 for active low strain, passive group; n = 123 for high strain group.

In the group of workers studied here, the majority met the specific criteria for defining unhealthy levels of psychological demands and low control as well as high strain work. Generally, these individuals would not be considered to have comorbid mental health problems because work stress is not classified as a diagnosis. However, at best, addressing one and not the other is short-sighted. At worst, it can result in disaster for these individuals and others at home and in the workplace.

The intervention described in this chapter, the WFI program, had several unique features. It applied a boundary-spanning approach to care, which bridged the workplace and the health-care system, used both work-directed and clinical intervention methods, and was structured to offer a high degree of accessibility so workers are able to get care when and where they want it. While the WFI was implemented as a workplace program, it can be accessed anywhere there is a computer and a telephone. Thus, it could have just as easily been offered through a health-care provider's office, clinic or community-based program. Importantly, its interventions were tailored to the worker's situation and preferences. This is important partly because change may be stress-inducing.

The WFI program was limited in several respects. The most obvious deficiency is that it did not address workplace conditions at a system level. Nor did it provide primary prevention services. It also did not include services for those workers who have already left the labor market because they feel they are no longer able to work.

The encouraging news is that this study of depressed workers found that the WFI was as or more effective for those who also had work stress. In most instances, job strain did not influence the treatment effect. In a few instances, adverse work characteristics such as low coworker support improved the treatment effect even further, though this may partly reflect regression to the mean.

While the results regarding the effectiveness of the WFI were positive for individuals with work stress, they may be subject to some biases. A limiting factor was that the sample was obtained during a depressive episode and regression to the mean is possible for the outcomes. In addition, duration of follow-up was restricted to the immediate postintervention period and no longer. With regard to stress measurement, the study did not include external measures of work conditions and work stress, all data were self-report, and measures were taken only at the preintervention stage, when everyone was depressed. Postintervention stress measures would have better addressed the actual change in the relevant variables.

The potential for bias in self-reported data on stress at work is a concern of many work stress researchers (Frese and Zapf, 1988). In the analyses conducted here, the severity of the depression symptoms was unrelated to the degree of measures of psychological and physical work demands, control, and supervisor and coworker support. This lack of association suggests that, within this sample of depressed individuals, the portion with relatively more severe illness reported about the same amount of work stress as others whose illnesses were less severe. However, another potential type of bias was identified, which is that depression may have contributed to perceptions of the source of the stress. Specifically, the study found that there was a relatively high frequency, among all of the different work stressors, of lacking job competence. This perception could reflect the tendency among depressed individuals toward self-blame and negative self-evaluations.

Despite certain limitations, this study's results suggest that the WFI could be an effective method for reducing the double burden of depression and work stress. Along with continued efforts to make the work environment less stressful and improve the quality of work life, this individualized, work-directed approach could be beneficial. Given the ongoing impact of stress on worker health, well-being and productivity, and the enormous amount of time and money being invested in intervention programs that lack a strong evidence base, new approaches are needed. Despite certain limitations, study results suggest that the WFI could be an effective method for reducing the double burden of depression and work stress. It may also serve as a model for workers with conditions other than depression. Along with the challenge of making work and work organizations less stressful and providing all who work a good quality of working life, this individualized, work-directed approach is both practical and beneficial.

Notes

1. The 11 Advocates were employed by Optum EAP, Eden Prairie, Minnesota. Study personnel provided them with 2.5 days of in-person WFI training. Fidelity to the intervention was supported by weekly group supervision by telephone and individualized support. In addition, the Advocates were required to document all WFI care in the study's electronic information system, and supervisors reviewed this information regularly.
2. A screening diagnosis of major depression requires meeting criteria of a certain number of depressive symptoms in the past two weeks. Persistent depressive disorder is chronic in nature and requires the severity of certain depressive symptoms lasting two years or longer. The indication for major depression was a Patient Health Questionnaire–9 (PHQ-9) score of five of nine symptoms at qualifying levels (Kroenke and Spitzer, 2002). For persistent depressive disorder, it was a score of at least two of six symptoms on the Primary Care Screener for Affective Disorder (Rogers, Wilson, Bungay, Cynn, and Adler, 2002). Work limitations were signified by an at-work productivity loss score of 5% on the Work Limitations Questionnaire (WLQ) (Lerner et al., 2001; Lerner et al., 2003). All questionnaires have been validated for depressed groups (Kroenke and Spitzer, 2002; Despiegel, Danchenko, Francois, Lensberg, and Drummond, 2012; Sanderson, Tilse, Nicholson, Oldenburg, and Graves, 2007). The study excluded individuals with psychosis, bipolar disorder, current alcohol abuse or dependence (which the WFI does not address), inability to speak English, and severe physical limitations.
3. A full description of the methods used in the randomized trial of the WFI is published in Lerner et al. (2015), which includes a detailed methods supplement.

References

AFL-CIO America's Unions (2000). New findings on working women's irregular hours help explain stresses in balancing work and family. At http://www.aflcio.org/Press-Room/Press-Releases/New-Findings-on-Working-Women-s-Irregular-Hours-He (accessed July 2016).

American Federation of Teachers (2015). Quality of worklife survey. At http://www.aft.org/sites/default/files/worklifesurveyresults2015.pdf (accessed July 2016).

American Psychological Association (2011). Stress in the workplace: Survey summary. At https://www.apa.org/news/press/releases/phwa-survey-summary.pdf (accessed July 2016).

American Psychological Association (2015). Stress in America: Paying with our health. At http://www.apa.org/news/press/releases/stress/2014/financial-stress.aspx (accessed July 2016).

Beck, A. T. (1979). *Cognitive Therapy and the Emotional Disorders*. New York: International University Press.

Becker, D. R., Baker, S. R., Carlson, L., Flint, L., Howell, R., Lindsay, S., … Drake, R. E. (2007). Critical strategies for implementing supported employment. *J Vocat Rehabil*, 27, 13–20.

Blackmore, E. R., Stansfeld, S. A., Weller, I., Munce, S., Zagorski, B. M., and Stewart, D. E. (2007). Major depressive episodes and work stress: Results from a national population survey. *Am J Public Health*, 97, 2088–2093.

Bond, F. W., and Bunce, D. (2000). Mediators of change in emotion-focused and problem-focused worksite stress management interventions. *J Occup Health Psychol*, 5, 156–163.

Buist-Bouwman, M. A., Ormel, J., de Graaf, R., and Vollebergh, W. A. (2004). Functioning after a major depressive episode: Complete or incomplete recovery? *J Affect Disord, 82*, 363–371.

Bunce, D. (1997). What factors are associated with the outcome of individual-focused worksite stress management interventions? *J Occup Organ Psychol, 70*, 1–17.

CDC (Centers for Disease Control and Prevention) (2015a). Chronic disease overview. At http://www.cdc.gov/chronicdisease/overview/ (accessed July 2016).

CDC (Centers for Disease Control and Prevention) (2015b). Chronic disease prevention and health promotion. At http://www.cdc.gov/chronicdisease/index.htm (accessed July 2016).

Center for Behavioral Health Statistics and Quality (2005). National survey on drug use and health, 2005. At http://www.icpsr.umich.edu/icpsrweb/ICPSR/series/64 (accessed July 2016).

Center for Behavioral Health Statistics and Quality (2010). National survey on drug use and health, 2010. At http://www.icpsr.umich.edu/icpsrweb/ICPSR/series/64 (accessed July 2016).

Despiegel, N., Danchenko, N., Francois, C., Lensberg, B., and Drummond, M. F. (2012). The use and performance of productivity scales to evaluate presenteeism in mood disorders. *Value Health, 15*, 1148–1161.

Frese, M., and Zapf, D. (1988). Methodological issues in the study of work stress: Objective vs subjective measurement of work stress and the question of longitudinal studies. In C. L. Cooper and R. Payne (Eds.), *Causes, Coping and Consequences of Stress at Work* (pp. 375–411). New York: Wiley.

Giga, S., Cooper, C. L., and Faragher, B. (2003). The development of a framework for a comprehensive approach to stress management interventions at work. *Int J Stress Managt, 10*, 280–296.

Hammer, L. B., and Sauter, S. (2013). Total worker health and work–life stress. *J Occup Environ Med, 55*, S25–S29.

Hirschfeld, R. M., Dunner, D. L., Keitner, G., Klein, D. N., Koran, L. M., Kornstein, S. G., … Markowitz, J. C. (2002). Does psychosocial functioning improve independent of depressive symptoms? A comparison of nefazodone, psychotherapy, and their combination. *Biol Psychiatry, 51*, 123–133.

Integrated Benefits Institute (2010). *More Than Health Promotion: How Employers Manage Health and Productivity* San Francisco, CA: Integrated Benefits Institute.

Judd, L., Akiskal, H., Zeller, P., Paulus, M., Leon, A., Maser, J. … Endicott, J. (2000). Psychosocial disability during the long-term course of unipolar major depressive disorder. *Arch Gen Psychiatry, 57*, 375–380.

Kaiser Family Foundation and Health Research and Educational Trust (2014). Employer health benefits: 2014 annual survey. At https://kaiserfamilyfoundation.files.wordpress.com/2014/09/8625-employer-health-benefits-2014-annual-survey6.pdf (accessed July 2016).

Karasek, R. A., and Theorell, T. (1992). *Healthy Work: Stress, Productivity, and the Reconstruction of Working Life*. New York: Basic Books.

Kroenke, K., and Spitzer, R. L. (2002). The PHQ-9: A new depression diagnostic and severity measure. *Psychiatr Ann, 32*, 509–515.

Landsbergis, P. A., Grzywacz, J. G., and LaMontagne, A. D. (2011). Work organization, job insecurity, and occupational health disparities. Issue paper for discussion at the Eliminating Health and Safety Disparities at Work Conference, Sept. 14 and 15.

Leka, S., Griffiths, A., and Cox, T. (2003). *Work Organization and Stress*. Geneva: World Health Organization.

Leka, S., and Jain, A. (2010). *Health Impact of Psychosocial Hazards at Work: An Overview*. Geneva: World Health Organization.

Lerner, D., Adler, D. A., Chang, H., Berndt, E. R., Irish, J. T., Lapitsky, L., … Hood, M. Y. (2004a). The clinical and occupational correlates of work productivity loss among employed patients with depression. *J Occup Environ Med, 46*, S46–S55.

Lerner, D., Adler, D. A., Hermann, R. C, Chang, H., Ludman, E., Greenhill, A., … Perch, K. (2012). Impact of a work-focused intervention on the productivity and symptoms of employees with depression. *J Occup Environ Med, 54*, 128–135.

Lerner, D., Adler, D. A., Hermann, R. C., Rogers, W. H., Chang, H., Thomas, P., … Greenhill, A. (2011). Depression and work performance: The work and health initiative study. In I. Z. Schultz and E. S. Rogers (Eds.), *Work Accommodation and Retention in Mental Health* (pp. 103–120). New York: Springer.

Lerner, D., Adler, D. A., Rogers, W. H., Chang, H., Greenhill, A., Cymerman, E., and Azocar, F. (2015). A randomized clinical trial of a telephone depression intervention to reduce employee presenteeism and absenteeism. *Psychiatr Serv, 66*(6), 570–577.

Lerner, D., Adler, D. A., Rogers, W. H., Chang, H., Lapitsky, L., McLaughlin, T., … Reed, J. (2010). Work performance of employees with depression: The impact of work stressors. *Am J Health Promot, 24*, 205–213.

Lerner, D., Amick, B. C., III, Lee, J. C., Rooney, T., Rogers, W. H., Chang, H., ... Berndt, E. R. (2003). Relationship of employee-reported work limitations to work productivity. *Med Care, 41*, 649–659.

Lerner, D., Amick, B. C., III, Rogers, W. H., Malspeis, S., Bungay, K., and Cynn, D. (2001). The work limitations questionnaire. *Med Care, 39*, 72–85.

Lerner, D., and Henke, R. (2008). What does research tell us about depression, job performance and work productivity? *J Occup Environ Med, 50*, 401–410.

Lerner, D. J., Levine, S., Malspeis, S., and D'Agostino, R. B. (1994). Job strain and health-related quality of life in a national sample. *Am J Public Health, 84*, 1580–1585.

Lerner, D., Rogers, W. H., Bungay, K., Chang, H., and Massagli, M. (2004b). *Improving Work Productivity Data Quality: A Study to Norm the Leading Indicators.* Boston: Health Institute, Institute for Clinical Research and Health Policy Studies, Tufts Medical Center.

Lewinsohn, P. M., Antonuccio, D. A., Steinmetz, J., and Teri, L. (1984). *The Coping with Depression Course: A Psychoeducational Intervention for Unipolar Depression.* Eugene, OR: Castalia Press.

Mattke, S., Liu, H., Caloyeras, J. P., Huang, C. Y., Van Busum, K. R., Khodyakov, D., ... Shier, V. (2015). *Workplace Wellness Programs Study.* US Department of Labor, US Department of Health and Human Services, RAND Health.

Michie, S.; and Williams, S. (2003). Reducing work related psychological ill health and sickness absence: A systematic literature review. *Occup and Env Med, 60*, 3–9.

Munir, F., Yarker, J., Haslam, C., Long, H., Leka, S., Griffiths, A., ... Cox, S. (2007). Work factors related to psychological and health-related distress among employees with chronic illnesses. *J Occup Rehabil, 17*, 259–277.

Murray, C. J., and Lopez, A. D. (2013). Measuring the global burden of disease. *N Engl J Med, 369*, 448–457.

National Business Group on Health (2015). Managing stress: Employer strategies and interventions. At http://www.businessgrouphealth.org/toolkits/et_stress.cfm (accessed July 2016).

NICE (National Institute for Health and Care Excellence) (2009). Depression in adults: Recognition and management. Updated at https://www.nice.org.uk/guidance/CG90 (accessed July 2016).

Nieuwenhuijsen, K., Faber, B., Verbeek, J. H., Neumeyer-Gromen, A., Hees, H. L., Verhoeven, A. C., ... van der Feltz-Cornelis, C. M. (2014). Interventions to improve return to work in depressed people. *Cochrane Database Syst Rev, 12*, CD006237.

NIOSH (National Institute for Occupational Safety and Health) (1999). Stress ... at work. At http://www.cdc.gov/niosh/docs/99-101/ (accessed July 2016).

NIOSH (National Institute for Occupational Safety and Health) (2002). The changing organization of work and the safety and health of working people: knowledge gaps and research directions. At http://stacks.cdc.gov/view/cdc/6460 (accessed July 2016).

NIOSH (National Institute for Occupational Safety and Health) (2013). Quality of worklife questionnaire. At http://www.cdc.gov/niosh/topics/stress/qwlquest.html}overview (accessed July 2016).

Noblet, A., and LaMontagne, A. D. (2006). The role of workplace health promotion in addressing job stress. *Health Promot Int, 21*, 346–353.

Olfson, M., and Klerman, G. L. (1992). The treatment of depression: Prescribing practices of primary care physicians and psychiatrists. *J Fam Pract, 35*, 627–635.

OSHA (Occupational Safety and Health Administration) (2015). Critical incident stress guide. At https://www.osha.gov/SLTC/emergencypreparedness/guides/critical.html (accessed July 2016).

Partnership for Workplace Mental Health (2015). Right Direction. Initiative of the American Psychiatric Association Foundation and Employers Health Coalition. At http://www.rightdirectionforme.com/ (accessed July 2016).

Pratt, L. A., and Brody, D. J. (2008). *Depression in the United States Household Population, 2005–2006.* At http://www.cdc.gov/nchs/products/databriefs/db07.htm (accessed July 2016).

Rogers, W. H., Wilson, I. B., Bungay, K. M., Cynn, D. J., and Adler, D. A. (2002). Assessing the performance of a new depression screener for primary care (PC-SAD). *J Clin Epidemiol, 55*, 164–175.

Rosch, P. J. (2001). The quandary of job stress compensation. *Health and Stress*, No. 3, 1–4.

Rost, K., Fortney, J., and Coyne, J. (2005). The relationship of depression treatment quality indicators to employee absenteeism. *Ment Health Serv Res, 7*, 161–169.

Rost, K., Smith, J. L., and Dickinson, M. (2004). The effect of improving primary care depression management on employee absenteeism and productivity: A randomized trial. *Med Care, 42*, 1202–1210.

Rush, A. J., Trivedi, M. H., Wisniewski, S. R., Nierenberg, A. A., Stewart, J. W., Warden, D., ... Niederehe, G. (2006). Acute and longer-term outcomes in depressed outpatients requiring one or several treatment steps: A STAR*D report. *Am J Psychiatry, 163*, 1905–1917.

Sanderson, K., Tilse, E., Nicholson, J., Oldenburg, B., and Graves, N. (2007). Which presenteeism measures are more sensitive to depression and anxiety? *J Affect Disord*, *101*, 65–74.

Sapolsky, R. M. (2004). Organismal stress and telomeric aging: An unexpected connection. *Proc Natl Acad Sci U.S A*, *101*, 17323–17324.

Schoenbaum, M., Unutzer, J., McCaffrey, D., Duan, N., Sherbourne, C., and Wells, K. B. (2002). The effects of primary care depression treatment on patients' clinical status and employment. *Health Serv Res*, *37*, 1145–1158.

Spangler, N. (2007). US and Canadian employers urged to help close research gaps in workplace mental health. *Mental HealthWorks*, fourth quarter.

Spangler, N. W., Koesten, J., Fox, M. H., and Radel, J. (2012). Employer perceptions of stress and resilience intervention. *J Occup.Environ Med, 54*, 1421–1429.

Stansfeld, S. A., North, F. M., White, I., and Marmot, M. G. (1995). Work characteristics and psychiatric disorder in civil servants in London. *J Epidemiol Community Health, 49*, 48–53.

Stewart, W. F., Ricci, J. A., Chee, E., Hahn, S. R., and Morganstein, D. (2003). Cost of lost productive work time among US workers with depression. *JAMA, 289*, 3135–3144.

Trivedi, M. H., Morris, D. W., Wisniewski, S. R., Lesser, I., Nierenberg, A. A., Daly, E., … Kurian, B.T. (2013). Increase in work productivity of depressed individuals with improvement in depressive symptom severity. *Am J Psych, 170*, 633–641.

US Department of Labor (2015). Mental health and substance use disorder parity. At http://www.dol.gov/ebsa/ mentalhealthparity/ (accessed July 2016).

US Preventive Services Task Force (2009). Screening for depression in adults: Recommendation statement. Agency for Healthcare Research and Quality (AHRQ) Publication No.10-05143-EF-2.At http://www.uspreventiveservices taskforce.org/uspstf09/adultdepression/addeprrs.htm#rationale (accessed July 2016).

van der Klink, J. J., Blonk, R. W., Schene, A. H., and van Dijk, F. J. (2001). The benefits of interventions for work-related stress. *Am J Public Health, 91*, 270–276.

Wang, P. S., Simon, G. E., Avorn, J., Azocar, F., Ludman, E. J., McCulloch, J., … Petukhova, M. Z. (2007). Telephone screening, outreach, and care management for depressed workers and impact on clinical and work productivity outcomes: A randomized controlled trial. *JAMA, 298*, 1401–1411.

10

Stress, Recovery, Sleep, and Burnout

Sharon Toker and Samuel Melamed

Burnout, a chronic affective state, has been shown to result in severe negative consequences for individuals' functioning, sleep, health and well-being. Its development is often precipitated by insufficient recovery from work stress, namely an inability to replenish lost resources and gain new ones. We review studies that associated a need for recovery with burnout, and link long work hours and lack of boundaries between work and nonwork, with impeded recovery processes. We then review possible moderators such as engagement in active leisure activities, short-term respite from work, and taking vacations and conclude with promising interventions.

Conceptual and Operational Definitions of Burnout

Over the last decades burnout has been conceptualized in several ways. Maslach and Jackson (1981) defined burnout as a syndrome that develops in response to chronic occupational stress in human service occupations and that comprises emotional exhaustion, depersonalization, and reduced personal accomplishment (measured by the Maslach Burnout Inventory, MBI). Later, the conceptualization of burnout was modified to apply to people in all occupations, and it included the following three dimensions: exhaustion, cynicism, and lack of professional efficacy (measured by the Maslach Burnout Inventory–General Survey, MBI-GS; Schaufeli et al., 1996). In both conceptualizations, exhaustion (i.e., feeling depleted of one's emotional resources) is considered the core component of burnout, and has been shown to precede cynicism and lack of professional efficacy (Taris, LeBlanc, Schaufeli, and Schreurs, 2005).

Shirom (2003) proposes another conceptualization of burnout, based on the premises of conservation of resources theory (COR, discussed further below). Specifically, he defines burnout as an affective state comprising emotional exhaustion, physical fatigue, and cognitive weariness that develops in response to cumulative and chronic exposure to work and life stress

The Handbook of Stress and Health: A Guide to Research and Practice, First Edition.
Edited by Cary L. Cooper and James Campbell Quick.
© 2017 John Wiley & Sons, Ltd. Published 2017 by John Wiley & Sons, Ltd.

(Hobfoll and Shirom, 2000). The Shirom-Melamed Burnout Measure (SMBM) was constructed on the basis of this conceptualization (Melamed et al., 1999). The SMBM consists of three facets: physical fatigue (i.e., a feeling of tiredness and low energy), emotional exhaustion (i.e., a lack of energy to display empathy to others), and cognitive weariness (i.e., one's feeling of reduced mental agility); able to be gauged by a single burnout score.

Although additional scales have been developed for measuring burnout, including the Burnout Measure (BM, Pines, Aronson, and Kafry, 1981), the Copenhagen Burnout Inventory (Kristensen, Borritz, Villadsen, and Christensen, 2005), and the Oldenburg Burnout Inventory (Demerouti, Bakker, Vardakou, and Kantas, 2003), the MBI/MBI-GS and the SMBM are the scales that are currently used most frequently in studies investigating the association between burnout and health (Bianchi, Schonfeld, and Laurent, 2015).

Consequences of Burnout

Empirical data show that, in the absence of intervention, the state of burnout is remarkably stable over time, even over time intervals extending up to eight years (Melamed et al., 2006). Furthermore, as noted by Maslach, Schaufeli, and Leiter (2001), it has a potential impact on variety of important outcomes. The breadth of these outcomes, documented in the literature, is illustrated below.

Health-related outcomes   Accumulated evidence, mostly from prospective studies, points to an association between burnout and risk to physical health. This association is manifested both in transient health problems, such as recurring common infections, as well as in chronic health problems such as cardiovascular diseases (CVD), diabetes, musculoskeletal pain, poor self-rated health, sleep problems, accelerated rate of biological aging, and ultimately in early mortality (for reviews, see Shirom, 2010; Melamed et al., 2006; Ahola and Hakanen, 2014).

Cognitive and emotional outcomes   Both self-report based and neuropsychological studies have established associations between burnout and cognitive impairments, including concentration problems (Deligkaris, Panagopoulou, Montgomery, and Masoura, 2014; Diestel, Cosmar, and Schmidt, 2013). In addition, prospective studies have indicated that burnout is related to the development of mood disturbance (Hillhouse, Adler, and Walters, 2000), depressive and anxiety symptoms (Ahola and Hakanen, 2014; Toker and Biron, 2012) and health complaints (Kim, Ji, and Kao, 2011). These outcomes are likely to impair functioning at work and reduce work ability.

Work disability and organizational outcomes   Burnout has been shown to affect individuals' work ability, as exemplified by multiple indicators: low work ability index (Glise, Hadzibajramovic, and Josdottir, 2010), sickness absence, intention to leave work, early retirement, and increased risk of requiring a disability pension (for reviews, see Ahola and Hakanen, 2014; Swider and Zimmerman, 2010). Additional evidence points to negative organizational outcomes of burnout, such as impaired productivity, reduced in-role performance, lower levels of organizational citizenship behavior, low work engagement, and reduced customer satisfaction (Swider and Zimmerman, 2010; Taris, 2006; Cole, Walter, Bedeian, and O'Boyle, 2012).

Antecedents of Burnout

As indicated above, burnout develops as a result of exposure to chronic stressors. Examples of chronic work stressors that have been extensively studied include work overload, role conflict, work–home conflict, compensation inequity, job insecurity, role ambiguity, and job complexity (Wheaton, 1999). These chronic work stressors are embedded in several theoretical models of work stress, which focus on health-related outcomes of stress. These models include, for instance the job demand–control model (JDC; Karasek, 1979), and its extended version, the job demand–control–support model (JDCS; Karasek and Theorell, 1990). Both models incorporate job demands – referring primarily to workload – and job control, which primarily reflects the freedom permitted the worker in deciding how to meet his job requirements; the JDCS also includes social support, which refers to "helpful social interaction available on the job from both co-workers and supervisors" (Karasek and Theorell, 1990, p. 69). Various hypotheses propose different relationships between strain (burnout) and the components of these models: The iso-strain hypothesis proposes that strain is a result of additive (main) deleterious effects of high job demands, low control, and low social support), whereas the buffer hypothesis proposes that strain results from moderating or buffering effects of control and support on the workload–strain association (van der Doef and Maes, 1998). The iso-strain hypothesis is more firmly grounded in empirical evidence and has been associated with burnout in both cross-sectional and longitudinal studies (Melamed, Armon, Shirom, and Shapira, 2011; Van der Doef and Maes, 1999).

Inspired by the dominant JDCS model, Dutch researchers have developed the job demands–resources (JD-R) model (Demerouti, Bakker, Nachreiner, and Schaufeli, 2001; Schaufeli and Bakker, 2004). The central proposition of the JD-R model is that job demands and job resources evoke two psychological processes. The first process, referred to as the health impairment process, results from chronic job demands (e.g., workload and organizational demands), which require sustained effort that over time exhausts employees' resources. This depletion of resources leads to energy depletion, burnout, and health deterioration (Schaufeli and Bakker, 2004; Xanthopoulou, Bakker, Demerouti, and Schaufeli, 2007). The second process, referred to as the motivational process, begins with the presence of suitable job resources (e.g., social support and instrumental support) that increase employee motivation, leading to job engagement and positive work outcomes (Schaufeli and Bakker, 2004). Empirical research has found strong main effects of job demands on burnout and weaker main effects of low job resources on burnout (Schaufeli and Bakker, 2004; Schaufeli, Bakker, and Van Rhenen, 2009), in addition to a moderating effect of job resources on the association between job demands and burnout (Bakker, Demerouti, and Euwema, 2005). Another model, the effort–reward imbalance (ERI) model (Siegrist, 1996), assumes that job strain and burnout stem from an imbalance between effort (extrinsic job demands and intrinsic motivation to meet these demands) and reward (in terms of salary, esteem, rewards, job security and career opportunities). The basic assumption of this model is that a lack of reciprocity between effort and reward (i.e., high effort coupled with low reward conditions) leads to arousal and stress, which in turn may lead to cardiovascular risks and other strain reactions. The combination of high effort and low reward at work has indeed been found to predict job burnout and health outcomes, including cardiovascular diseases, subjective impaired health, and mild psychiatric disorders (Kivimäki et al., 2006b; van Vegchel, de Jonge, Bosma, and Schaufeli, 2005).

COR theory is a leading theory associated with burnout. This theory suggests that people are motivated to retain, protect and foster resources that they value, and to acquire new resources. These resources include objects, personal characteristics, conditions or energies (Hobfoll, 1989). People experience stress when the resources that they value are lost or threatened, or when initial resource investment does not beget future resource gain. These situations lead individuals to engage in coping efforts, aimed at averting further losses or replenishing lost resources. Failure to cope successfully with resource loss or threat may lead to psychological distress, impaired functioning, and illness. Hobfoll and Shirom (2000) apply these notions to burnout, arguing that individuals experience burnout when they perceive a net loss of physical, emotional, or cognitive energy resources. Any effort to replenish these lost resources by using existing resources may exacerbate loss by triggering an escalating loss spiral. Loss spirals are especially likely to happen in situations characterized by chronic stress. Specifically, constant exposure to stressors intensifies the saliency of actual or anticipated resource loss, and results in actual resource loss, leading to a state of burnout (i.e., emotional, physical and cognitive resource depletion; Hobfoll and Shirom, 2000).

Possible Moderators of the Stressor–Burnout Relationship

Despite the common belief that burnout and chronic exposure to stressors are closely related, meta-analytic studies involving large numbers of participants show that chronic stress and burnout are only moderately correlated, with metacorrelations mostly ranging in the 0.40s (Alarcon, 2011). These moderate metacorrelations indicate that moderators are likely to be present. Research has identified several potential moderators of the stressor–burnout relationship, including successful coping strategies (Shin et al., 2014), personality variables (Alarcon, Eschleman, and Bowling, 2009), personal resources (Nagel and Sonnentag, 2013), and job resources (Bakker et al., 2005). Another important moderator is postwork recovery from stress (Geurts and Sonnentag, 2006; Geurts, Beckers, and Tucker, 2014). As chronic exposure to work stressors demands resource investment (time, energy, etc.; Hobfoll and Shirom, 2000), individuals are motivated to protect their resource levels by gaining new resources or replenishing threatened or lost ones (Sonnentag and Fritz, 2007; Zijlstra, Cropley, and Rydstedt, 2014). The process of replenishing one's resource reservoir is referred to as *recovery* and includes cognitive as well as psychophysiological processes that most often run in parallel (Zijlstra et al., 2014). As we will argue, burnout develops as an outcome of a complex interplay between exposure to work (and life) stressors and insufficient recovery processes that take place, partially during work but mainly outside work, as well as during sleep.

Recovery from Work Stress

Sonnentag and Geurts (2009) define recovery from stress, in terms of stress physiology, as the process whereby psychophysiological systems that were activated during exposure to stressors return to and stabilize at baseline levels after the stressor has been removed, and no special demands are made on the individual (i.e., the individual is not exposed to additional stressors). Following the process of recovery, individuals feel regenerated not only at the physiological level but also at the cognitive and affective levels, owing to the restoration of impaired mood or the reduction of psychological strain (Geurts and Sonnentag, 2006). Incomplete recovery, however, can lead to sustained sympathetic and neuroendocrine activation and to depletion of energetic resources, resulting in feelings of fatigue, burnout and other symptoms of psychological strain, including poor sleep (Geurts and Sonnentag, 2006). Various longitudinal studies have substantiated these long-term adverse health effects of incomplete day-to- day recovery (see Geurts, 2014, for a review).

A more recent conceptualization of recovery from work stress (Zijlstra et al., 2014) views recovery as a dynamic process of self-regulation, in which a person needs to actively regulate their energy level throughout the day. For example, the availability of energetic resources is in part dependent on circadian rhythm; thus, at a given time of day, an individual's level of physiological activation or arousal may not be sufficiently high in order for them to meet their job demands. In such situations, the person aims to adjust their psychophysiological state to the demands facing them, by "up regulating" their arousal level. Although this up-regulation process enables the individual to exert more efforts, it also consumes energetic resources that will later need to be restored. Thus, such up-regulation takes a toll on the individual's ability to recover. For recovery, a process of "down regulation" is needed. Furthermore, in order to fall asleep, the individual must use self-regulation and "wind down" the system in the evening (i.e., lower their arousal levels). If this process fails, and arousal levels remain high, for example due to high pressure during the day, working late, or an inability to detach from work-related issues, sleep may be impaired, and the restoration process that occurs during sleep cannot take place. If an extended period of time passes in which an individual's psychophysiological state is not down-regulated – implying that a high level of arousal or activation is sustained – then he may experience allostatic load consequences (McEwen, 1998), discussed below.

Insufficient physiological recovery   Two main psychophysiological stress systems have been implicated in individuals' responses to potential threat: the sympathetic-adrenal-medullary (SAM) system and the hypothalamic-pituitary-adrenal (HPA) axis activation system. The SAM system enables the body and mind to expend effort when needed (e.g., in the presence of a stressor, or while performing physical activity) through the production of catecholamines (adrenaline and noradrenaline). These catecholamines accelerate heart rate and elevate blood pressure, thus instantly providing the brain and muscles with energy. The HPA-axis activation system also affects physiological functionality but is more strongly linked to stressful experiences. In response to the presence of a stressor, the body releases cortisol, a stress hormone that triggers an increase in blood sugar, suppresses the immune system, and has additional energetic effects (Black and Garbutt, 2002; Tsigos and Chrousos, 2002).

In the presence of an acute stressor, the body exerts efforts to cope with it through activation of the stress systems. Generally, the stress responses of both the SAM and HPA-axis systems are meant to be acute or at least of limited duration., The time-limited nature of this process renders its accompanying antianabolic, catabolic and immunosuppressive effects temporarily beneficial and with no adverse consequences (Tsigos and Chrousos, 2002). However, with exposure to chronic or recurrent stressors, an individual's psychophysiological stress reactions may be prolonged, and recovery is impaired (i.e., the body does not return to baseline conditions). Recent evidence suggests that the prolongation of physiological stress responses to a stressor (manifested in prolonged neuroendocrine activation and delayed cardiovascular recovery) is predictive of ill-health (Geurts, 2014).

McEwen (1998) proposes a process by which prolonged activation of stress response may lead to ill-health. Specifically, he introduces the concept of *allostasis*, defined as achieving stability through change. Adaptation to the challenges of daily life is mediated by allostatic systems such as the HPA axis, the autonomic nervous system, the metabolic system, and the immune system. McEwen maintains that ongoing overactivation or dysregulation of the HPA axis (i.e., allostatic response) that is not followed by sufficient recovery plays a significant role in the cascade of events leading to pathological changes. This proposition is based on the core assumption that chronic activation of initially protective allostatic systems (the SAM system, HPA axis, and immune system) results in so-called *allostatic load*, a term that refers to either overactivity or inactivity of allostatic systems. Allostatic load, in turn, is manifested in chronic sleep problems, burnout, and accelerated disease processes (McEwen, 1998; Ganster and Rosen, 2013). A number of studies have demonstrated a link between burnout and allostatic load score (Bellingrath, Weigl, and Kudielka, 2009; Juster et al., 2011; Kakiashvili, Leszek, and Rutkowski, 2013), while other studies were unable to establish such a link (e.g., Langelaan et al., 2007; Sjors, Jansson, Eriksson, and Jonsdottir, 2013). The differences between the findings of the two sets of studies may be partially attributable to differences in the manner in which they defined and measured allostatic load.

Need for Recovery, Burnout and Health

Expressed need for recovery (NFR) is the most commonly used measure of subjective experience of insufficient recovery. It refers to a subjective experience of longing for temporary relief from exposure to stressors and for having some time that allows for low baseline activity, in order to replenish resources (Sonnentag and Zijlstra, 2006). NFR is typically measured by questionnaire items, such as "At the end of the working day I am really worn-out," and "I find it hard to relax at the end of working day" (Sluiter, de Croon, Meijman, and Frings-Dresen, 2003). Agreement with such statements is often accompanied by feelings of overload, irritability, social withdrawal, lack of energy for investing new effort, and impaired performance, which can be observed during the last hours of work or immediately after work (van Veldhoven and Broersen, 2003).

Although NFR was initially assumed to be a transient state, affected by daily changes in work demands (Sluiter et al., 2003), it has been shown to be stable over a two-year interval, in work environments that have relatively stable levels of demands (de Croon, Sluiter, and Frings-Dresen, 2006). Individuals who chronically experience NFR may be subject to substantial health consequences (van Veldhoven, 2008), and indeed, studies on the relationship between psychosocial work characteristics and work-related health problems have considered NFR as a mediating variable (Sluiter et al., 2003). Several studies have confirmed the role of NFR in predicting poor well-being and risk of adverse health effects, such as subjective health complaints in different occupational groups (Sluiter, et al., 2003) and elevated levels of psychological distress (Devereux, Rydstedt, and Cropley, 2011). NFR was also associated with morbidity, as manifested in increased risk of CVD (van Amelsvoort, Kant, Bultmann, and Swaen, 2003), as well as CVD mortality (Kivimäki, et al., 2006a). Interestingly, in most of these studies, NFR or incomplete recovery were stronger predictors of impaired health compared with psychosocial work characteristics, thus supporting the assertion that a lack of recovery from exposure to stressors is a stronger predictor of impaired health compared with the exposure itself (Zijlstra and Sonnentag, 2006).

The putative association between insufficient recovery and burnout has been supported in a number of cross-sectional studies. High levels of NFR have been closely associated with burnout and emotional exhaustion (Sonnentag and Fritz, 2007; 2014; Sonnentag, Kuttler, and Fritz, 2010b), suggesting that NFR may have a moderating role in the relatively weak relationship between burnout and exposure to stressors. Moreover, the association between burnout and NFR, coupled with the finding that NFR remains relatively stable over time and possesses risk to health, suggest that NFR might have a moderating role in the link between burnout and impaired health. Longitudinal studies in which burnout, NFR and health outcomes are simultaneously examined over time can provide direct confirmation of this assertion.

Sleep and Recovery

Sleep plays an essential role in recovery processes: it constitutes the recuperative process of the central nervous system, restores brain physiology to normal levels and restores abilities such as alertness and memory capacity, as well as mood (Åkerstedt, Nilsson, and Kecklund, 2009). In addition, during sleep, peripheral anabolic processes such as secretion of growth hormone and testosterone are enhanced, while catabolic processes such as secretion of cortisol and catecholamines are suppressed (Åkerstedt, Nilsson, and Kecklund, 2009). Thus, sleep is crucial for maintaining one's energy levels, renewing personal resources, and consequently preserving and improving physical health and mental well-being (Nagel and Sonnentag, 2013). Correspondingly, sleep disturbances have been shown to pose a health threat. Prolonged sleep curtailment (including insomnia) contributes to depression, type 2 diabetes, obesity, cardiovascular diseases and mortality (e.g., Åkerstedt, Nilsson, and Kecklund, 2009; Porkka-Heiskanen, Zitting, and Wigren, 2013).

   Much evidence points to a strong link between insomnia and stress, including stress induced by exposure to work stressors (Jansson and Linton, 2006). In fact, stress is often considered to be the primary cause of persistent psychophysiologic insomnia, with hyperarousal fulfilling a mediating role (for a review, see Bonnet and Arand, 2010). As indicated above, in order to be able to fall asleep, an individual must engage in self-regulation and "wind down" the system in the evening. Exposure to work-related stressors such as high work pressure, long working hours, inability to detach from work-related issues and work-related rumination may cause arousal levels to stay high, and thus to interfere with sleep (Zijlstra et al., 2014). Disturbed sleep was also shown to be associated with subjective feelings of insufficient recovery, as indicated by self-reports of NFR (Sluiter et al., 2003; van Veldhoven and Sluiter, 2009).

Burnout and Impaired Sleep

Findings from studies based on self-reports of sleep problems show that burnout is positively associated with poor quality of sleep, nonrestorative sleep, a sensation of not feeling refreshed on awakening, and the presence of sleepiness and/or fatigue during the day (Åkerstedt, Anund, Axelsson, and Kecklund, 2014; Nordin, Åkerstedt, and Nordin, 2013). These self-report based observations have been corroborated by objective data: Evidence derived from objective polysomnographic recordings points to an association between burnout and sleep disturbances, particularly chronic insomnia. The latter data show that burned-out individuals experience more sleep disturbance than others do: they have higher frequency of arousal during sleep; their sleep is fragmented; and they experience lower sleep efficiency, less slow-wave sleep, less rapid eye movement (REM) sleep, and lower delta power density (Ekstedt, Soderstrom, and Åkerstedt, 2009; Soderstrom et al., 2004). Furthermore, in the study by Soderstrom et al. (2004), individuals who scored high on burnout not only experienced more arousals during sleep and more sleepiness during working days (compared with individuals who scored lower on burnout) but also were unable to recover during days off. Other studies have repeatedly shown that insomnia and fragmented sleep are related to daytime sleepiness and impaired cognitive performance (Fortier-Brochu, Beaulieu-Bonneau, Ivers, and Morin, 2012; Liu et al., 2014). Thus, the insomnia and nonrefreshing sleep observed among burned-out persons may partly explain the chronic physical and mental fatigue as well as the cognitive dysfunction characterizing such persons.

Bidirectional Association between Burnout and Insomnia

As discussed above, burnout has been associated with allostatic load, while allostatic load, in turn, is associated with chronic sleep problems (McEwen, 1998; Ganster and Rosen, 2013). Thus, one might expect burnout to predict the development of insomnia over time. On the other hand, on the basis of COR theory, it can be also hypothesized that insomnia predicts the development of burnout over time. In the latter case, the linkage between burnout and insomnia may constitute a variant of an escalating spiral of losses, in which insomniacs' disturbed sleep prevents the replenishment of depleted coping resources, which may lead to burnout. Taken together, these hypotheses suggest that the association between burnout and insomnia is bidirectional, that is, burnout and insomnia recursively predict each other's development over time.

To date, three studies have prospectively examined the bidirectional association between burnout and insomnia (Armon, 2009; Armon, Shirom, Shapira, and Melamed, 2008; Jansson-Fröjmark and Lindblom, 2010). While Armon et al. (2008) observed a bidirectional association, Jansson-Fröjmark and Lindblom (2010) found that insomnia predicted new onset of burnout but not vice versa. In both studies, the association between burnout and insomnia remained significant even after controlling for depression. Findings in Armon's study (2009) reconfirmed the reciprocal association between burnout and insomnia. That study further showed that the relationship between burnout and insomnia over time holds when both depression and job strain exposure are controlled for (Armon, 2009).

The long-term reciprocal association between burnout and insomnia, uncovered in the studies cited above, may partly explain the observed chronicity of burnout symptoms. Exposure to chronic work and life stressors, without opportunities for recovery (discussed below), may result in depletion of energetic resources, culminating in a state of burnout. Burned-out individuals who also experience sleep disturbance are further prevented from replenishing lost resources, and this, in turn, exacerbates the symptoms of burnout. This vicious cycle of resource loss may perpetuate the symptoms of burnout for years. Findings from two studies support this contention: Soderstrom et al. (2012) found that insufficient sleep predicts clinical burnout, while Sonnenschein et al. (2007) found that impaired sleep recovery may prevent improvement of treated burnout, independently of depressed mood.

Factors That Hinder or Facilitate Recovery Processes and Their Influence on Fatigue and Burnout

Thus far we have discussed the conceptualization and different dimensions of recovery from work stress, and presented evidence indicating that insufficient recovery, most notably gauged by expressed NFR, is associated with increased risk of developing a state of burnout. Below we review factors that have been proposed to hinder or facilitate recovery processes. Many of the studies in this vein focus on associations between specific factors and recovery complaints (i.e., expressed NFR), while others test how various factors relate to fatigue (one facet of burnout), emotional exhaustion, or burnout.

Lack of boundaries between work and nonwork and long working hours   Developments in information and communication technology (ICT) have eliminated the physical constraints that once limited working hours, and employees, business partners and customers can now be reached – and in many cases are expected to be available – anywhere and at any time. As a result, for many employees, work is no longer spatially, temporally, or socially distinct from nonwork (Kompier, 2006), and it has become more common for employees to work in their free time in order to meet job demands. Likewise, some companies extend their working hours to maintain a competitive edge, thereby cutting into the time available for employees to recover from job demands (Härmä, 2006). Notably, workers who work longer hours are also more likely to work outside their working hours (Eurofound, 2012). A recent study by Barber and Santuzzi (2014) points to potential negative outcomes associated with these phenomena, showing that workplace telepressure (the combination of preoccupation and the urge to immediately respond to work-related ICT messages) predicts burnout, low sleep quality, and absenteeism.

As argued above, individuals' capacity to recover from work is related to their ability to regulate their effort investment and their psychophysiological states (Zieltra et al., 2014). Understandably, an individual's capacity to engage in self-regulation depends on the availability of time to do so. Long working hours and the spillover of work into nonwork time may seriously hamper people's ability to self-regulate their effort, thereby impairing their capacity to recover from work and to unwind after work (Rissler, 1977). One study identified a positive relationship between working overtime and NFR (Sonnentag and Zijlstra, 2006), whereas another study identified such a relationship only among workers employed in high-strain jobs (van der Hulst, Van Veldhoven, and Beckers, 2006). Accumulating evidence suggests that long working hours inflict an undesirable cost: A systematic review (Bannai and Tamakoshi, 2014) has shown that individuals who work longer hours are more likely to experience a depressive state, anxiety, sleep disturbance, and CVD.

Empirical evidence shows that NFR, health, fatigue, and well-being are associated not only with negative job characteristics (Sonnentag and Zijlstra, 2006; Kraaijeveld et al., 2014; Sluiter et al., 2003) but also with the extent to which employees carry out job-related activities outside of work. Specifically, Sonnentag and Zijlstra (2006) found that pursuing work-related activities during off-job time is positively related to NFR and fatigue. This association might result from the fact that, in order to carry out such job-related activities, employees must draw on resources similar to those already called upon during working time, thereby increasing resource loss.

Work–family dynamics   Drawing upon COR theory, Grandey and Cropanzano (1999) discuss work–family dynamics as the interplay between gains and losses in both work and family domains. Work stressors that consume or threaten resources and thus interfere with resource investment at home may exacerbate work–home interference, which has been associated with burnout. For example, in a longitudinal study, Demerouti, Bakker, and Bulters (2004) uncovered a reciprocal association between work–home interference and emotional exhaustion. Likewise, familial conditions that demand resource investment leave fewer resources for investment at work and lead to family role stress and home–work interference. Indeed, in a longitudinal study, Demerouti, Taris, and Bakker (2007) found a negative reciprocal association over time between home–work interference and NFR, suggesting that these two states may create a negative spiral in the home domain that can easily intrude into the work domain. Specifically, the authors propose that because of depleted individual resources, people feel that they are not sufficiently recovered, and they lack the energy to participate in family life and meet home demands. (For a comprehensive review of family and job responsibilities that constrain recovery processes, see Sonnentag and Braun, 2013.)

Opportunities for recovery   To prevent exhaustion of their resources, people have to find opportunities to replenish their resources. These opportunities may occur within the context of work (internal recovery), as well as outside work (external recovery) (Geurts and Sonnentag, 2006; van Veldhoven and Sluiter, 2009). Internal recovery opportunities include work characteristics that allow workers to take breaks, to interrupt task performance at will, and to adjust their work strategies in accordance with their current need for recovery. These work characteristics can be considered as a subdimension of job control (van Veldhoven and Sluiter, 2009). Several studies have identified an association between a lack of work-related recovery opportunities (such as the ability to determine when the work day begins and ends or to take breaks during the work day) and NFR, sleep disturbances, and health complaints (e.g., van Veldhoven and Sluiter, 2009).

External opportunities for recovery are those that occur during off-job time. Opportunities for short respite (days off, weekends) and longer respite (vacations) and involvement in absorbing leisure-time activities not only can replenish resources, diminish accumulated strain and lead to recovery from work-related efforts (Geurts and Sonnentag, 2006; van Veldhoven and Sluiter, 2009) but also lead to resource gain (Westman et al., 2004). Such opportunities for respite have been found to alleviate symptoms of burnout and fatigue. In particular, the ability to recover during weekends may have a protective effect on health (Kivimäki et al., 2006a). In addition, one study shows that engaging in a short weekend respite is associated with lower burnout and higher vigor levels compared with taking two days off midweek (Drach-Zahavy and Marzuq, 2013). Yet, an important aspect that should be taken into consideration is the way people use their off-job time. A study by Fritz and Sonnentag (2005), for example, showed that negative weekend experiences (such as nonwork hassles and low social activity) predicted post-weekend burnout and poor general well-being. A complementary finding was obtained in a study that recorded employees' off-job activities over a two-week period. Burned-out employees who spent time on job-related activities during their respite did not recover, while non burned-out employees did report experiencing a state of physical strength, cognitive liveliness and feeling recovered following a similar respite (Oerlemans and Bakker, 2014).

Vacation   Westman et al. (2004) suggested that vacation may have a beneficial effect on stress and burnout, as a vacation allows a person to be distant from their job, thus halting the resources loss cycle. Yet a meta-analysis on vacation effects (de Bloom et al., 2009) shows that vacation has only a small positive effect on health and well-being, and that these effects soon fade away. Furthermore, research indicates that the nature of an individual's experiences during their vacation plays a significant moderating role. In a study by Westman and Eden (1997), for example, participants who were satisfied with their vacation reported greater burnout relief compared with others who were dissatisfied. In a similar manner, de Bloom, Geurts, and Kompier (2012) found that vacations that included experiences of relaxation and detachment from work (concepts that are further discussed below) positively influenced health and well-being, while the experience of working during vacation time negatively influenced these factors. Finally, a longitudinal study of faculty members found that during a sabbatical leave, life satisfaction increased more and feelings of burnout declined more among participants who detached from their work than among those who could not mentally disengage from work (Davidson et al., 2010).

Physical activity and other leisure-time activities   Physical activity has been shown to yield substantial benefits in terms of enhancing physical and mental well-being. Several mechanisms may explain the contribution of physical activity to recovery processes. First, from a COR perspective (Hobfoll, 1989), physical activity can be seen as a recovery mechanism that halts the downward spiral in which exposure to stressors leads to an escalation of energy depletion; such activity allows employees to be temporarily relieved of job burnout in order to replenish the resources needed to once again face job demands (e.g., Sonnentag and Zijlstra, 2006). Second, the biological changes induced by physical activity may reduce individuals' physiological sensitivity to stress, such that among people who engage in such activity, psychological stress is less likely to lead to cardiovascular symptoms (Forcier et al., 2006). Last, physical activity, as well as other absorbing leisure activities, may be viewed as behavioral distractions that take people's minds off stressful situations and thus reduce the psychological impact of these situations (e.g., Altshuler and Ruble, 1989; Sonnentag and Zijlstra, 2006). Indeed, a study by Oerlemans and Bakker (2014) found that the amount of time spent on physical activities had a positive effect on recovery for burned-out employees, regardless of differences in the initial level of burnout. Winwood, Bakker, and Winefield (2007) found that employees in diverse occupations who reported higher levels of specific types of activities during their off-job time – active leisure activities, exercise, and creative (hobby) social activities – also reported better sleep, recovery between work periods, and lower chronic maladaptive fatigue symptomatology. In a similar vein, Sonnentag and Zijlstra (2006) found that the amount of time spent on active types of activities (social and physical activities), but not passive types of activities (e.g., watching TV), is negatively related to NFR and, in turn, to fatigue level.

Psychological detachment from work   Sonnentag and colleagues offer a complementary psychological view on the factors that promote recovery from work stress. The basic tenet of their approach is that it is not the specific activity per se that helps the individual to recover; rather, it is the underlying attributes of the activity, including relaxation, mastery, control and psychological detachment from work-related issues (Sonnentag and Fritz, 2007). Of these attributes, psychological detachment has been shown to be the core factor contributing to the recovery experience (Siltaloppi, Kinnunen, and Feldt, 2009; Sonnentag and Fritz, 2007, 2014).

Psychological detachment from work during one's afterwork hours means refraining from job-related activities and mentally disengaging from work ("switching off"). Such detachment involves not only letting go of work-related thoughts and activities but also being mentally involved in other content areas, such as those mentioned above (hobbies, sports, joint activities with others; Sonnentag and Fritz, 2014; Sonnentag et al., 2010b). A number of studies have identified benefits of psychological detachment, including positive associations with work and life satisfaction, positive affect, professional efficacy and work engagement (Siltaloppi et al., 2009; Sonnentag and Fritz, 2014). Conversely, poor psychological detachment from work has been associated with insufficient recovery from stress, as indicated by high levels of NFR. It has also been related to high levels of psychosomatic symptoms, fatigue, sleep problems, burnout and emotional exhaustion (Sonnentag and Fritz, 2007; 2014; Sonnentag, Binnewies, and Mojza, 2010a). A longitudinal study showed that a lack of psychological detachment from work was associated with increased emotional exhaustion one year later (Sonnentag et al., 2010a).

Additional studies have shown that psychological detachment from work may have a moderating effect on the stressor–strain relationship, such that it attenuates the impact of exposure to job stressors on strain. For example, Moreno-Jiménez, Rodríguez-Muñoz, Sanz-Vergel, and Garrosa (2012) found that psychological detachment attenuated the relationship between role conflict and anxiety. In a longitudinal study, psychological detachment moderated the relationship between quantitative job demands and psychosomatic complaints as well as low work engagement (Sonnentag et al., 2010a). Derks and Bakker (2014) found an interaction effect between frequency of employer-provided smartphone use and detachment. Employees who frequently used their smartphones experienced a high level of work–home inference and burnout on days when their detachment level was low. In most of these studies, stressors were more strongly related to indicators of strain and poor well-being when psychological detachment was low. These findings suggest that psychological detachment can provide a mental break from job stressors and thereby reduce their negative impact. The moderating effect of psychological detachment lends support to the basic tenet of this chapter, namely, that the impact of work stressors on employee outcomes, including burnout, may be buffered by recovery experiences, particularly those that facilitate psychological detachment from work.

Implications for Interventions and Strategies for Prevention

In light of the adverse consequences of burnout for individuals' health and well-being, as well as for organizational outcomes, various intervention programs have been designed to combat burnout. These interventions are mostly targeted at the individual level (i.e., relaxation training, cognitive behavioral therapy), whereas few are targeted at the organizational level (e.g., job redesign), or at a combination of both (Awa, Plaumann, and Walter, 2010). Insights gained from the evidence reviewed above suggest that in order to combat burnout, it is important to come up with interventions and strategies that promote recovery from work (and home) stressors. One example of such an intervention is relaxation training; indeed, a recent meta-analysis of interventions concluded that cognitive-behavioral interventions and interventions based on relaxation techniques are effective at reducing emotional exhaustion (a core component of burnout; Maricuţoiu, Sava, and Butta, 2014). Below we present a few additional suggestions.

Setting boundaries between work time and nonwork time   In order to set boundaries between work and nonwork domains, legislation or declared policy changes are often needed (e.g., labor agreements signed in France limit email traffic after 6 p.m.). Another step that organizations can take is to help employees to allocate their vacation time. As the effect of respites tends to fade away upon the employee's return to work (Kühnel and Sonnentag, 2011), researchers suggest that taking frequent short respites (e.g., once a month) is effective in enhancing well-being (de Bloom et al., 2012), and may be more effective in reducing burnout, compared with taking long infrequent respites (e.g., a long vacation, once a year; de Bloom, Geurts, and Kompier, 2010).

Enhancing recovery experiences Above, we presented evidence of the potential moderating effect of recovery experiences, particularly psychological detachment from work, on the stressor–strain (burnout) relationship. Two pioneering studies have shown that the ability to achieve psychological detachment and enhance one's recovery experiences can be acquired through training, but that the impact of this ability on burnout is somewhat limited. In the first study (Hahn, Binnewies, Sonnentag, and Moza, 2011), psychological detachment training had a beneficial effect, over time, on recovery-related self-efficacy, sleep quality and well-being, but not on emotional exhaustion. In the second study (Siu, Cooper, and Philips, 2014), improvement of recovery experiences led to reduction in burnout levels among health-care workers, but not among teachers. Further studies should test ways to teach skills of psychological detachment from work and facilitate recovery, in order to reduce the risk of burnout.

Improving sleep quality and treating disturbed sleep Evidence suggests that good sleep quality enhances the effectiveness of various factors that reduce strain and promote recovery. For example, longer sleep duration was shown to enhance the beneficial effect of exercise on renewing personal resources and reducing emotional exhaustion (Nagel and Sonnentag, 2013). In another study, sleep quality was found to moderate the association between work–home interference and psychological strain (Sanz-Vergel, Demerouti, Mayo, and Moreno-Jiménez, 2011). Sleep hygiene measures that workers might adopt to improve their sleep quality (and thus enjoy its beneficial effects) include going to bed at regular times, or not drinking alcohol or caffeinated beverages before going to sleep (see, e.g., Mastin, Bryson, and Corwyn, 2006). Furthermore, in light of the reciprocal association between insomnia and burnout, it seems theoretically plausible that treating either condition could potentially reduce the symptoms associated with the other condition. To our knowledge, to date, only one direction of influence has been examined; specifically, initial evidence suggests that a reduction in burnout levels leads to improved sleep physiology (Eksted et al., 2009). Therefore, it seems worthwhile to examine whether treating insomnia might also lead to a reduction in burnout symptoms. To our knowledge, to date, such a possibility has not been tested.

Conclusions

The state of burnout resulting from prolonged exposure to work stressors (in addition to stressors outside work) has been found to be remarkably stable over time and to have severe negative consequences for individuals' functioning, health and well-being, as well as for organizational outcomes. The stressor–burnout relationship has been shown to be moderated by recovery processes; viewed from the perspective of COR theory, such processes enable the worker to replenish energetic resources, halt resource loss and gain new resources. Development of burnout has been shown to stem from insufficient recovery, manifested in recovery complaints (NFR) and in physiological indicators of lack of recovery, including disturbed and nonrefreshing sleep. Recovery from stress may occur partly during work, but it is most likely to occur after work and during sleep. Long work hours, a lack of boundaries between work and nonwork time, and home requirements have been found to impede recovery processes and to increase the risk of fatigue and burnout. Engagement in active leisure activities, short-term respite from work (e.g., during weekends) and taking vacations have been shown to reduce symptoms of strain and burnout, especially among individuals who are able to psychologically detach themselves from work. Future studies that focus on the antecedents of burnout would benefit greatly from taking into account recovery processes as possible moderators of stressor–burnout relationships. Furthermore, research should explore ways to enhance the effectiveness of interventions designed to combat burnout and its adverse consequences. One promising direction is to focus on interventions designed to promote recovery processes (e.g., interventions that teach skills of psychological detachment from work or improving sleep quality).

References

Ahola, K., and Hakanen, J. (2014). Burnout and health. In M. P. Leiter, A. B. Bakker, and C. Maslach (Eds.), *Burnout at Work: A Psychological Perspective* (pp. 10–31). New York: Psychology Press.

Åkerstedt, T., Anund, A., Axelsson, J., and Kecklund, G. (2014). Subjective sleepiness is a sensitive indicator of insufficient sleep and impaired waking function. *Journal of Sleep Research, 23*(3), 242–254.

Åkerstedt, T., Nilsson P. M., and Kecklund, G. (2009) Sleep and recovery. In S. Sonnentag, P. L. Perrewé, and D. C. Ganster (Eds.), *Current Perspectives on Job-Stress Recovery: Research in Occupational Stress and Well-Being*, vol. 7 (pp. 205–247). Bradford, UK: Emerald Group.

Alarcon, G. M. (2011). A meta-analysis of burnout with job demands, resources, and attitudes. *Journal of Vocational Behavior, 79*, 549–562.

Alarcon, G., Eschleman, K. J., and Bowling, N. A. (2009). Relationships between personality variables and burnout: A meta-analysis. *Work and Stress, 23*(3), 244–263.

Altshuler, J. L., and Ruble, D. N. (1989). Developmental changes in children's awareness of strategies for coping with uncontrollable stress. *Child Development, 60*, 1337–1349.

Armon, G. (2009). Do burnout and insomnia predict each other's levels of change over time independently of the job demand control–support (JDC–S) model?. *Stress and Health, 25*(4), 333–342.

Armon, G., Shirom, A., Shapira, I., and Melamed, S. (2008). On the nature of burnout–insomnia relationships: A prospective study of employed adults. *Journal of Psychosomatic Research, 65*(1), 5–12.

Awa, W. L., Plaumann, M., and Walter, U. (2010). Burnout prevention: A review of intervention programs. *Patient Education and Counseling, 78*, 184–190.

Bakker, A. B., Demerouti, E., and Euwema, M. C. (2005). Job resources buffer the impact of job demands on burnout. *Journal of Occupational Health Psychology, 10*(2), 170.

Bannai, A., and Tamakoshi, A. (2014). The association between long working hours and health: A systematic review of epidemiological evidence. *Scandinavian Journal of Work, Environment and Health, 40*(1), 5–18.

Barber, L. K., and Santuzzi, A. M. (2014). Please respond ASAP: Workplace telepressure and employee recovery. *Journal of Occupational Health Psychology*. Epub ahead of print.

Bellingrath, S., Weigl, T., and Kudielka, B. (2009). Chronic work stress and exhaustion is associated with higher allostatic load in female school teachers. *Stress, 12*(1), 37–48.

Bianchi, R., Schonfeld, I. S., and Laurent, E. (2015). Burnout–depression overlap: A review. *Clinical Psychology Review, 36*, 28–41.

Black, P. H., and Garbutt, L. D. (2002). Stress, inflammation and cardiovascular disease. *Journal of Psychosomatic Research, 52*(1), 1–23.

Bonnet, M. H., and Arand, D. L. (2010). Hyperarousal and insomnia: State of the science. *Sleep Medicine Reviews, 14*(1), 9–15.

Cole, M. S., Walter, F., Bedeian, A. G., and O'Boyle, E. H. (2012). Job burnout and employee engagement: A meta-analytic examination of construct proliferation. *Journal of Management, 38*(5), 1550–1581

Davidson, O. B., Eden, D., Westman, M., Cohen-Charash, Y., Hammer, L. B., Kluger, A. N., ... Spector, P. E. (2010). Sabbatical leave: Who gains and how much? *Journal of Applied Psychology, 95*, 953–964.

de Bloom, J., Geurts, S., and Kompier, M. (2010). Vacation from work as prototypical recovery opportunity. *Gedrag en Organisatie, 23*(4), 333.

de Bloom, J., Geurts, S. A., and Kompier, M. A. (2012). Effects of short vacations, vacation activities and experiences on employee health and well-being. *Stress and Health, 28*(4), 305–318.

de Bloom, J., Kompier, M., Geurts, S., de Weerth, C., Taris, T., and Sonnentag, S. (2009). Do we recover from vacation? Meta-analysis of vacation effects on health and well-being. *Journal of Occupational Health, 51*(1), 13–25.

de Croon, E. M., Sluiter, J. K., and Frings-Dresen, M. H. W. (2006). Psychometric properties of the need for recovery after work scale: Test-retest reliability and sensitivity to detect change. *Occupational and Environmental Medicine*, *63*, 202–206.

Deligkaris, P., Panagopoulou, E., Montgomery, A. J., and Masoura, E. (2014). Job burnout and cognitive functioning: A systematic review. *Work and Stress*, *28*(2), 107–123.

Demerouti, E., Bakker, A. B., and Bulters, A. J. (2004). The loss spiral of work pressure, work–home interference and exhaustion: Reciprocal relations in a three-wave study. *Journal of Vocational Behavior*, *64*(1), 131–149.

Demerouti, E., Bakker, A. B., Nachreiner, F., and Schaufeli, W. B. (2001). The job demands–resources model of burnout. *Journal of Applied Psychology*, *86*(3), 499.

Demerouti, E., Bakker, A.B., Vardakou, I., and Kantas, A. (2003). The convergent validity of two burnout instruments. *European Journal of Psychological Assessment*, *19*(1), 12–23.

Demerouti, E., Taris, T. W., and Bakker, A. B. (2007). Need for recovery, home–work interference and performance: Is lack of concentration the link? *Journal of Vocational Behavior*, *71*(2), 204–220.

Derks, D., and Bakker, A. B. (2014). Smartphone use, work–home interference, and burnout: A diary study on the role of recovery. *Applied Psychology*, *63*(3), 411–440.

Devereux, J. J., Rydstedt, L. W., and Cropley, M. (2011). Psychosocial work characteristics, need for recovery and musculoskeletal problems predict psychological distress in a sample of British workers. *Ergonomics*, *54*(9), 840–848.

Diestel, S., Cosmar, M., and Schmidt, K. H. (2013). Burnout and impaired cognitive functioning: The role of executive control in the performance of cognitive tasks. *Work and Stress*, *27*(2), 164–180.

Drach-Zahavy, A., and Marzuq, N. (2013). The weekend matters: Exploring when and how nurses best recover from work stress. *Journal of Advanced Nursing*, *69*(3), 578–589.

Ekstedt, M., Soderstrom, M., and Åkerstrom, T. (2009). Sleep physiology in recovery from burnout. *Biological Psychology*, *82*, 267–273.

Eurofound (2012). *Fifth European Working Conditions Survey*. European Foundation for the Improvement of Living and Working Conditions. Luxembourg: Publication Office of the European Union.

Forcier, K., Stroud, L. R., Papandonatos, G. D., Hitsman, B., Reiches, M., Krishnamoorthy, J., and Niaura, R. (2006). Links between physical fitness and cardiovascular reactivity and recovery to psychological stressors: A meta-analysis. *Health Psychology*, *25*(6), 723.

Fortier-Brochu, É., Beaulieu-Bonneau, S., Ivers, H., and Morin, C. M. (2012). Insomnia and daytime cognitive performance: A meta-analysis. *Sleep Medicine Reviews*, *16*(1), 83–94.

Fritz, C., and Sonnentag, S. (2005). Recovery, health, and job performance: Effects of weekend experiences. *Journal of Occupational Health Psychology*, *10*(3), 187.

Ganster, D. C., and Rosen, C. C. (2013). Work stress and employee health: A multidisciplinary review. *Journal of Management*, *39*(5), 185–1122.

Geurts, S. A. (2014). Recovery from work during off-job time. In G. F. Bauer and O. Hämmig (Eds.), *Bridging Occupational, Organizational and Public Health* (pp. 193–208). Amsterdam: Springer.

Geurts, S. A. E., Beckers, D. G. J., and Tucker, P. (2014). Recovery from demanding work hours. In M. C. W. Peeters, J. deJonge, and T. W. Taris (Eds.), *An Introduction to Contemporary Work Psychology* (pp. 197–219). Chichester, UK: Wiley.

Geurts, S. A. E., and Sonnentag, S. (2006). Recovery as an exploratory mechanism in the relation between acute stress reactions and chronic health impairment. *Scandinavian Journal of Work, Environment and Health*, *32*, 482–492.

Glise, K., Hadzibajramovic, E., and Josdottir, I. H. (2010). Self-reported exhaustion: A possible indicator of reduced work ability and increased risk of sickness absence among human service workers. *International Archives of Occupational and Environmental Health*, *83*, 511–520.

Grandey, A. A., and Cropanzano, R. (1999). The conservation of resources model applied to work–family conflict and strain. *Journal of Vocational Behavior*, *54*(2), 350–370.

Hahn, V.C., Binnewies, C., Sonnentag, S., and Moza, E. (2011). Learning how to recover from job stress: Effects of a recovery training program on recovery, recovery-related self-efficacy and well-being. *Journal of Occupational Health Psychology*, *16*(2), 202–216.

Härmä, M. (2006). Work hours in relation to work stress, recovery and health. *Scandinavian Journal of Work, Environment and Health*, *32*, 502–514.

Hillhouse, J. J., Adler, C. M., Walters, D. N. (2000). A simple model of stress, burnout and symptomatology in medical residents: A longitudinal study. *Psychology, Health and Medicine*, *5*, 63–73.

Hobfoll, S. E. (1989). Conservation of resources: A new attempt at conceptualizing stress. *American Psychologist*, *44*(3), 513.

Hobfoll, S. E., and Shirom, A. (2000). Conservation of resources theory: Applications to stress and management in the workplace. In R. T. Golembiewski (Ed.), *Handbook of Organizational Behavior* (pp. 57–81). New York: Dekker.

Jansson, M., and Linton, S. J. (2006). Psychosocial work stressors in the development and maintenance of insomnia: A prospective study. *Journal of Occupational Health Psychology, 11*(3), 241.

Jansson-Fröjmark, M., and Lindblom, K. (2010). Is there a bidirectional link between insomnia and burnout? A prospective study in the Swedish workforce. *International Journal of Behavioral Medicine, 17*(4), 306–313.

Juster, R.-P., Sindi, S., Marin, M.-F., Perna, A., Hashemi, A., Pruessner, J. C., and Lupin, S. J. (2011). A clinical allostatic load index is associated with burnout symptoms and hypocortisolemic profiles in healthy workers. *Psychoneuroendocrinology, 36*, 797–805.

Kakiashvili, T., Leszek, J., and Rutkowski, K. (2013). The medical perspective on burnout. *International Journal of Occupational Medicine and Environmental Health, 26*(3), 401–412.

Karasek, R. A. (1979). Job demands, job decision latitude, and mental strain: Implications for job redesign. *Administrative Science Quarterly, 24*, 285–308.

Karasek, R., and Theorell, T. (1990). *Healthy Work: Stress, Productivity, and the Reconstruction of Working Life.* New York: Basic Books.

Kim, H., Ji, J., and Kao, D. (2011). Burnout and physical health among social workers: A three-year longitudinal study. *Social Work, 56*(3), 258–268.

Kivimäki, M., Leino-Arjas, P., Kaila-Kangas, L., Luukkonen, R.,Vahtera, J., Elovainio, M., Härmä, M., and Kirjonen, J. (2006a). Is incomplete recovery from work a risk marker of cardiovascular death? Prospective evidence from industrial employees. *Psychosomatic Medicine, 68*, 402–407.

Kivimäki, M., Virtanen, M., Elovainio, M., Kouvonen, A., Vaananen, A., and Vahtera, J. (2006b). Work stress in the etiology of coronary heart disease – a meta-analysis. *Scandinavian Journal of Work, Environment and Health, 32*, 431–442.

Kompier, M. A. (2006). New systems of work organization and workers' health. *Scandinavian Journal of Work, Environment and Health, 32*, 421–430.

Kraaijeveld, R. A., Huysmans, M. A., Hoozemans, M. J., Van der Beek, A. J., and Speklé, E. M. (2014). The influence of psychosocial work characteristics on the need for recovery from work: A prospective study among computer workers. *International Archives of Occupational and Environmental Health, 87*(3), 241–248.

Kristensen, T. S., Borritz, M., Villadsen, E., and Christensen, K. B. (2005). The Copenhagen Burnout Inventory: A new tool for the assessment of burnout. *Work and Stress, 19*, 192–207.

Kühnel, J., and Sonnentag, S. (2011). How long do you benefit from vacation? A closer look at the fade-out of vacation effects. *Journal of Organizational Behavior, 32*(1), 125–143.

Langelaan, S., Bakker, A. B., Schaufeli, W. B., van Rhenen, W., and van Doornen, L. J. (2007). Is burnout related to allostatic load? *International Journal of Behavioral Medicine, 14*(4), 213–221.

Liu, H., Wang, D., Li, Y., Zhang, Y., Lei, F., Du, L., and Tang, X. (2014). Examination of daytime sleepiness and cognitive performance testing in patients with primary insomnia. *PloS One, 9*(6), e100965.

Maricuţoiu, L. P., Sava, F. A., and Butta, O. (2014). The effectiveness of controlled interventions on employees' burnout: A meta-analysis. *Journal of Occupational and Organizational Psychology.* Epub ahead of print.

Maslach, C., and Jackson, S. E. (1981). The measurement of experienced burnout. *Journal of Organizational Behavior, 2*(2), 99–113.

Maslach, S., Schaufeli, W. B., and Leiter, M. P. (2001). Job burnout. *Annual Review of Psychology, 52*, 397–422.

Mastin, D. F., Bryson, J., and Corwyn, R. (2006). Assessment of sleep hygiene using the sleep hygiene index. *Journal of Behavioral Medicine, 29*, 223–227.

McEwen, B. S. (1998). Stress adaptation, and disease: Allostasis and allostatic load. *Annals of the New York Academy of Sciences, 840*, 33–44.

Melamed, S., Armon, G., Shirom, A., and Shapira, I. (2011). Exploring the reciprocal causal relationship between job strain and burnout: A longitudinal study of apparently healthy employed persons. *Stress and Health, 27*(4), 272–281.

Melamed, S., Shirom, A., Toker, S., Berliner, S., and Shapira, I. (2006). Burnout and risk of cardiovascular disease: Evidence, possible causal paths, and promising research directions. *Psychological Bulletin, 132*(3), 327.

Melamed, S., Ugarten, U., Shirom, A., Kahana, L., Lerman, Y., and Froom, P. (1999). Chronic burnout, somatic arousal and elevated salivary cortisol levels. *Journal of Psychosomatic Research, 46*(6), 591–598.

Moreno-Jiménez, B., Rodríguez-Muñoz, A., Sanz-Vergel, A. I., and Garrosa, E. (2012). Elucidating the role of recovery experiences in the job demands-resources model. *Spanish Journal of Psychology, 15*(2), 659–669.

Nagel, I. J., and Sonnentag, S. (2013). Exercise and sleep predict personal resources in employees' daily life. *Applied Psychology: Health and Well-Being, 5*(3), 348–368.

Nordin, M., Åkerstedt, T., and Nordin, S. (2013). Psychometric evaluation and normative data for the Karolinska Sleep Questionnaire. *Sleep and Biological Rhythms*, *11*(4), 216–226.

Oerlemans, W. G., and Bakker, A. B. (2014). Burnout and daily recovery: A day reconstruction study. *Journal of Occupational Health Psychology*, *19*(3), 303.

Pines, A. M., Aronson, E., and Kafry, D. (1981). *Burnout: From Tedium to Personal Growth*. New York: Free Press.

Porkka-Heiskanen, T., Zitting, K. M., and Wigren, H. K. (2013). Sleep, its regulation and possible mechanisms of sleep disturbances. *Acta Physiologica*, *208*(4), 311–328.

Rissler, A. (1977). Stress reactions at work and after work during a period of quantitative overload. *Ergonomics*, *20*(5), 577–580.

Sanz-Vergel, A. N., Demerouti, E., Mayo, M., and Moreno-Jiménez, B. (2011). Work–home interaction and psychological strain: The moderating role of sleep quality. *Applied Psychology: An International Review*, *60*(2), 210–230.

Schaufeli, W. B., and Bakker, A. B. (2004). Job demands, job resources, and their relationship with burnout and engagement: A multi-sample study. *Journal of Organizational Behavior*, *25*(3), 293–315.

Schaufeli, W. B., Bakker, A. B., and Van Rhenen, W. (2009). How changes in job demands and resources predict burnout, work engagement, and sickness absenteeism. *Journal of Organizational Behavior*, *30*(7), 893–917.

Schaufeli, W. B., Leiter, M. P., Maslach, C., and Jackson, S. E. (1996). The Maslach Burnout Inventory – General Survey. In C. Maslach, S. E. Jackson, and M. P. Leiter (Eds.), *Maslach Burnout Inventory: Manual*, 3rd edn. (pp. 19–26). Palo Alto, CA: Consulting Psychologists Press.

Shin, H., Park, Y. M., Ying, J. Y., Kim, B., Noh, H., and Lee, S. M. (2014). Relationships between coping strategies and burnout symptoms. *Professional Psychology: Research and Practice*, *45*(1), 44–56.

Shirom, A. (2003). Job-related burnout: A review. In J. C. Quick and L. Tetrick (Eds.), *Handbook of Occupational Health Psychology* (pp. 245–264). Was hington, DC: American Psychological Association.

Shirom, A. (2010). Employee burnout and health: Current knowledge and future research paths. In J. Houdmunt and S. Leka (Eds)., *Contemporary Health Psychology: Global Perspectives in Research and Practice*, vol. 1. Chichester, UK: Wiley-Blackwell.

Siegrist, J. (1996). Adverse health effects of high-effort/low-reward conditions. *Journal of Occupational Health Psychology*, *1*(1), 27.

Siltaloppi, M., Kinnunen, U., and Feldt, T. (2009). Recovery experiences as moderators between psychosocial work characteristics and occupational well-being. *Work and Stress*, *23*(4), 330–348.

Siu, O. L., Cooper, C. L., and Philips, D. R. (2014). Intervention studies on enhancing work well-being, reducing burnout, and improving recovery experiences among Hong Kong health care workers and teachers. *International Journal of Stress Management*, *21*(1), 69–84.

Sjors, A., Jansson, P.-A., Eriksson, J. W., and Jonsdottir, I. H. (2013). Increased insulin secretion and decreased glucose concentrations, but not allostatic load, are associated with stress-related exhaustion in clinical patient population. *Stress*, *16*(1), 224–233.

Sluiter, J. K., de Croon, E. M., Meijman, T. F., and Frings-Dresen, M. H. W. (2003). Need for recovery from work related fatigue and its role in the development and prediction of subjective health complaints. *Occupational and Environmental Medicine*, *60*(suppl. 1), i62–i70.

Soderstrom, M., Ekstedt, M., Åkerstedt, T., Nilsson, J., and Axelsson, J. (2004). Sleep and sleepiness in young individuals with high burnout scores. *Sleep*, *27*, 1369–1378.

Soderstrom, M., Jeding, K., Exstedt, M., Perski, A., and Akerstedt, T. (2012). Insufficient sleep predicts clinical burnout. *Journal of Occupational Health Psychology*, *17*(2), 175–183.

Sonnenschein, M., Sorbi, M. J., van Doornen, L. J. P., Schaufeli, W. B., and Maas, C. J. M. (2007). Evidence that impaired sleep recovery may complicate burnout improvement independently of depressed mood. *Journal of Psychosomatic Research*, *62*, 487–494.

Sonnentag, S., Binnewies, C., and Mojza, E. J. (2010a). Staying well and engaged when demands are high: The role of psychological detachment. *Journal of Applied Psychology*, *95*(5), 965.

Sonnentag, S., and Braun, I. (2013). Not always a sweet home: Family and job responsibilities constrain recovery processes. In J. G. Grzywacz and E. Demerouti (Eds.), *New Frontiers in Work and Family Research: Current Issues in Work and Organizational Psychology* (pp. 71–92). New York: Psychology Press.

Sonnentag, S., and Fritz, C. (2007). The recovery experience questionnaire: Development and validation of a measure for assessing recuperation and unwinding from work. *Journal of Occupational Health Psychology*, *12*(3), 204–221.

Sonnentag, S., and Fritz, C. (2014). Recovery from job stress: The stressor-detachment model as an integrative framework. *Journal of Organizational Behavior*. Epub ahead of print.

Sonnentag, S., and Geurts, S. A. (2009). Methodological issues in recovery research. *Current Perspectives on Job-Stress Recovery, 7,* 1–46.

Sonnentag, S., Kuttler, I., and Fritz, C. (2010b). Job stressors, emotional exhaustion, and need for recovery: A multi-source study on the benefits of psychological detachment. *Journal of Vocational Behavior, 76*(3), 355–365.

Sonnentag, S., and Zijlstra, F. R. H. (2006). Job characteristics and off-job activities as predictors of need for recovery, well-being, and fatigue. *Journal of Applied Psychology, 9*(2), 330–350.

Swider, B. W., and Zimmerman, R. D. (2010). Born to burnout: A meta-analytic path model of personality, job burnout, and work outcomes. *Journal of Vocational Behavior, 76*(3), 487–506.

Taris, T. W. (2006). Is there a relationship between burnout and objective performance? A critical review of 16 studies. *Work and Stress, 20*(4), 316–334.

Taris, T. W., LeBlanc, P. M., Schaufeli, W. B., and Schreurs, P. J. (2005). Are there causal relationships between the dimensions of the Maslach Burnout Inventory? A review and two longitudinal tests. *Work and Stress, 19,* 238–255.

Toker, S., and Biron, M. (2012). Job burnout and depression: Unraveling their temporal relationship and considering the role of physical activity. *Journal of Applied Psychology, 97*(3), 699.

Tsigos, C., and Chrousos, G. P. (2002). Hypothalamic–pituitary–adrenal axis, neuroendocrine factors and stress. *Journal of Psychosomatic Research, 53*(4), 865–871.

van Amelsvoort, L. G. P. M., Kant, I. J., Bultmann, U., and Swaen, G. M. H. (2003). Need for recovery after work and the subsequent risk of cardiovascular disease in a working population. *Occupational and Environmental Medicine, 60*(suppl. 1), i83–i87.

van der Doef, M., and Maes, S. (1998). The job demand–control (–support) model and physical health outcomes: A review of the strain and buffer hypotheses. *Psychology and Health, 13*(5), 909–936.

van der Doef, M., and Maes, S. (1999). The job demand–control (–support) model and psychological well-being: A review of 20 years of empirical research. *Work and Stress, 13*(2), 87–114.

van der Hulst, M., Van Veldhoven, M., and Beckers, D. (2006). Overtime and need for recovery in relation to job demands and job control. *Journal of Occupational Health, 48*(1), 11–19.

van Vegchel, N., de Jonge, J., Bosma, H., and Schaufeli, W. B. (2005). Reviewing the effort–reward imbalance model: Drawing up the balance of 45 empirical studies. *Social Science and Medicine, 60,* 1117–1131.

van Veldhoven, M. (2008). Need for recovery after work: An overview of construct, measurement and research. In J. Houdmont and S. Leka (Eds), *Occupational Health Psychology: European Perspectives on Research, Education and Practice* (pp. 1–25). Nottingham: Nottingham University Press.

van Veldhoven, M., and Broersen, S. (2003). Measurement quality and validity of the "need for recovery scale." *Occupational and Environmental Medicine, 60*(suppl. 1), i3–i9.

van Veldhoven, M. J., and Sluiter, J. K. (2009). Work-related recovery opportunities: Testing scale properties and validity in relation to health. *International Archives of Occupational and Environmental Health, 82*(9), 1065–1075.

Westman, M., and Eden, D. (1997). Effects of vacation on job stress and burnout: Relief and fade-out. *Journal of Applied Psychology, 82,* 516–527.

Westman, M., Hobfoll, S. E., Chen, S., Davidson, R., and Lasky, S. (2004). Organizational stress through the lens of conservation of resources (COR) theory. In P. Perrrewé and D. Ganster (Eds.), *Research in Occupational Stress and Well-Being,* vol. 5 (pp. 167–220). Oxford: JAI Press/Elsevier Science.

Wheaton, B. (1999). Social stress. In C. S. Aneshensel (Ed.), *Handbook of the Sociology of Mental Health* (pp. 277–300). New York: Springer.

Winwood, P. C., Bakker, A. B., and Winefield, A. H. (2007). An investigation of the role of non–work-time behavior in buffering the effects of work strain. *Journal of Occupational and Environmental Medicine, 49*(8), 862–871.

Xanthopoulou, D., Bakker, A. B., Demerouti, E., and Schaufeli, W. B. (2007). The role of personal resources in the job demands–resources model. *International Journal of Stress Management, 14*(2), 121.

Zijlstra, F. R. H., Cropley, M., and Rydstedt, L. W. (2014). From recovery to regulation: An attempt to reconceptualize "recovery from work." *Stress and Health, 30*(3), 244–252.

Zijlstra, F. R., and Sonnentag, S. (2006). After work is done: Psychological perspectives on recovery from work. *European Journal of Work and Organizational Psychology, 15*(2), 129–138.

11

Stress and Eating Disturbed Behavior

Derrick A. Bennett

Introduction

Although there has been a large body of literature (that includes prospective observational and experimental studies) on the risk and maintenance factors for eating pathology, this literature has not been critically reviewed or synthesized for the independent role of stress in eating pathology. Several reviews have concentrated on the interplay between stress, coping styles, social support availability, and personality factors (Aime, Sabourin, and Ratte, 2006; Bardone-Cone et al., 2007; Bennett and Cooper, 1999; Troop, Holbrey, and Treasure, 1998). Other studies have examined the role of stress and eating disorders in specific populations such as dancers (Arcelus, Witcomb, and Mitchell, 2014) or athletes (Coelho, Gomes, Ribeiro, and Soares, 2014). This chapter aims to evaluate and critically appraise the current epidemiological evidence on the relationship between life stress with anorexia nervosa (AN), bulimia nervosa (BN), and the partial syndromes of these two eating disorders. The first aim of this chapter is bring together the quantitative and qualitative evidence on the role played by different types of life stress in eating pathology in order to better understand the etiological and maintenance processes involved. The second aim of this chapter is to discuss the associations found as well as the methodological weaknesses of the evidence in order to assess how robust these findings are. This chapter is split into four sections. First, a brief overview of how "eating disturbed behavior" is defined in this context, along with details of how it is assessed. Second, the hypothesized role of life stress in determining eating behavior is outlined. Third, the evidence from the contemporary literature for specific models of stress and "eating disturbed behavior," with the associated limitations, is summarized. Fourth, a summary and conclusion is provided based on the current best qualitative and quantitative evidence for the role played by stress (in the form of stressful or adverse life events) in eating disturbance pathology.

The Handbook of Stress and Health: A Guide to Research and Practice, First Edition.
Edited by Cary L. Cooper and James Campbell Quick.
© 2017 John Wiley & Sons, Ltd. Published 2017 by John Wiley & Sons, Ltd.

Definition and Assessment of "Eating Disturbance"

For the purpose of this chapter we use the term "eating disturbance" to encompass the clinically diagnosed eating disorders as well as eating disorder symptoms that are assessed using standardized validated screening questionnaires designed to ascertain eating disorder psychopathology but not eating disorders diagnosis according to established criteria. These are now described in more detail.

Diagnostic Criteria for Eating Disorders

Anorexia nervosa is a syndrome in which the individual maintains a low weight as a result of a preoccupation with body weight, construed either as a fear of fatness or pursuit of thinness. Box 11.1 outlines the four key diagnostic criteria that are based on the *Diagnostic and Statistical Manual of Mental Disorders*, fourth edition (DSM-IV-TR) criteria (American Psychiatric Association Task Force on DSM-IV, 2000). Bulimia nervosa is characterized by recurrent episodes of binge eating and secondly by compensatory behavior (vomiting, purging, fasting or exercising or a combination of these) in order to prevent weight gain. Binge eating is accompanied by a subjective feeling of loss of control over eating. Self-induced vomiting and excessive exercise, as well as the misuse of laxatives, diuretics, thyroxine, amphetamine or other medication, may occur. As in AN, self-evaluation is unduly influenced by body shape and weight, and prior to the onset of their bulimia there may have been an earlier episode of anorexia nervosa (Box 11.1). Finally, there are eating disorders that closely resemble AN and BN, but which are considered atypical (Box 11.1), as they do not meet the precise diagnostic criteria for these conditions (Fairburn and Harrison, 2003). In Europe, these are often termed "atypical eating disorders," the equivalent American term being "eating disorders not otherwise specified" (EDNOS) (Fairburn and Harrison, 2003; Treasure, Claudino, and Zucker, 2010; Yates, Sweat, Yau, Turchiano, and Convit, 2012).

Box 11.1   Diagnostic criteria for eating disorders according to DSM-IV-TR (American Psychiatric Association, 2000)

Anorexia Nervosa (AN)

A. Refusal to maintain body weight at or above a minimally normal weight for age and height (e.g., weight loss leading to maintenance of body weight less than 85% of that expected; or failure to make expected weight gain during period of growth, leading to body weight less than 85% of that expected).
B. Intense fear of gaining weight or becoming fat, even though underweight.
C. Disturbance in the way in which one's body weight or shape is experienced, undue influence of body weight or shape on self-evaluation, or denial of the seriousness of the current low body weight.
D. In postmenarcheal females, amenorrhea, i.e., the absence of at least three consecutive menstrual cycles. (A woman is considered to have amenorrhea if her periods occur only following hormone, e.g. estrogen, administration.)

Specify type:

Restricting type: during the current episode of Anorexia Nervosa, the person has not regularly engaged in binge-eating or purging behavior (i.e. self-induced vomiting or the misuse of laxatives, diuretics, or enemas).

Binge-eating/Purging type: during the current episode of Anorexia Nervosa, the person has regularly engaged in binge-eating or purging behavior (i.e. self-induced vomiting or the misuse of laxatives, diuretics, or enemas).

Bulimia Nervosa (BN)

A. Recurrent episodes of binge eating. An episode of binge eating is characterized by both of the following:
   1. eating in a discrete period of time (e.g., within any 2-hour period), an amount of food that is definitely larger than what most people would eat during a similar period of time and under similar circumstances.
   2. a sense of lack of control over eating during the episode (i.e., a feeling that one cannot stop eating or control what or how much one is eating).
B. Recurrent inappropriate compensatory behavior in order to prevent weight gain, such as self-induced vomiting; misuse of laxatives, diuretics, enemas, or other medications; fasting; or excessive exercise.
C. The binge eating and inappropriate compensatory behaviors both occur, on average, at least twice a week for 3 months.
D. Self-evaluation is unduly influenced by body shape and weight.
E. The disturbance does not occur exclusively during episodes of Anorexia Nervosa.

Specify type:

Purging type: during the current episode of Bulimia Nervosa, the person has regularly engaged in self-induced vomiting or the misuse of laxatives, diuretics, or enemas

Nonpurging type: during the current episode of Bulimia Nervosa, the person has used other inappropriate compensatory behaviours, such as fasting or excessive exercise, but has not regularly engaged in self-induced vomiting or the misuse of laxatives, diuretics, or enemas.

Eating disorder not otherwise specified (EDNOS)

1. For females, all of the criteria for Anorexia Nervosa are met except for the fact that the individual has regular menses.
2. All of the criteria for Anorexia Nervosa are met except that, despite substantial weight loss, the individual's current weight is in the normal range.
3. All of the criteria for Bulimia Nervosa are met except that the binge eating and inappropriate compensatory mechanisms occur at a frequency of less than twice a week or for a duration of less than 3 months.

4. The regular use of inappropriate compensatory behavior by an individual of normal body weight after eating small amounts of food (e.g., self-induced vomiting after the consumption of two cookies).
5. Repeated chewing and spitting out, but not swallowing, of large amounts of food.
6. Binge eating disorder: recurrent episodes of binge eating in the absence of the regular use of inappropriate compensatory behaviors characteristic of Bulimia Nervosa.

Reproduced with permission of the American Psychiatric Association (received June 2016).

The American Psychiatric Association diagnostic criteria have been updated to DSM-5 (American Psychiatric Association, 2013). Hebebrand and Bulik (2011) comprehensively discuss the rationale behind the revised criteria, highlighting the reframing of psychological symptoms so that some pejorative attitudes are removed and other criteria are redefined to reflect the evidence. The main classifications of eating disorders according to DSM-5 are AN, BN, binge eating disorder (BED), and other specified feeding or eating disorders (OSFED) (American Psychiatric Association, 2013). Due to the very recent introduction of DSM-5 this chapter will only discuss diagnosed eating disorders based on the DSM-IV-TR criteria (American Psychiatric Association Task Force on DSM-IV, 2000) or earlier.

The main way of applying these diagnostic criteria is via a semistructured interview process. One such semistructured interview is designed to assess psychopathology associated with AN and BN is the Eating Disorder Examination (EDE) (E, Zhang, Zhou, and Wang, 2014; Sharma and Ebadi, 2014). The EDE assesses two behavioral indices, overeating and methods of extreme weight control, as well as four subscales (restraint, eating concern, shape concern, and weight concern). The EDE is an investigator-based interview, in which the interviewer, not the participant, rates the severity of symptoms. This is particularly important in rating episodes of binge eating, because the term "binge" appears to be defined differently by laypersons and professionals. Another semistructured interview is the Interview for the Diagnosis of Eating Disorders–IV (IDEDIV) (Malviya et al., 2013) that was developed for the purpose of differential diagnosis using DSM-IV criteria, including AN and BN as well as BED and other subthreshold syndromes currently categorized under EDNOS.

Screening Instruments for Eating Disorder Pathology

It is not always possible to diagnose an eating disorder but it is possible to screen for an eating disorder. When screening for the presence of eating disorders, it is not necessary to determine an exact diagnosis or obtain detailed patterns of problematic symptoms. The main purpose of the screening process is to identify individuals who are likely to have significant levels of eating pathology and need further assessment (Treasure et al., 2010). The screening measures employed for this purpose are usually brief, self-report inventories with a recommended cut-off score to indicate clinical levels of psychopathology. Three of the most common tests are now briefly described. The Eating Attitudes Test (Jacobi, Abascal, and Taylor, 2004a) is a 40-item self-report inventory originally designed to measure symptoms of AN. A modified version, the EAT-26, was developed after factor analysis which found 14 items of the original EAT were redundant and thus could be omitted (Sachs-Ericsson et al., 2012). Although the EAT was designed to identify individuals with AN-like symptoms, it is best conceptualized as a measure of general eating disorder pathology. The Bulimia Test–Revised (BULIT-R) (Skinner et al., 2013) is a 28-item questionnaire designed to measure the DSM-III-R symptoms of BN (American Psychiatric Association, 1987). A more detailed review of diagnostic questionnaires and other screening tools that are psychometrically robust instruments are reviewed in detail elsewhere (Surgenor and Maguire, 2013).

The etiology of eating disorders (in common with most other psychiatric disorders) is generally considered to be multifactorial; no single etiological factor in isolation can account for the development of the disorder in an individual, nor can it be seen to account for the variation among individuals (Fairburn and Harrison, 2003; Treasure et al., 2010). Whether or not a person develops disturbed eating behavior will depend on their individual vulnerability (Lilenfeld, 2011) consequent on the presence of biological or other predisposing factors, their exposure to particular provoking risk factors, and on the operation of protective factors. One such factor is stress, and the postulated role of stress in general eating behavior as well as eating disturbed behavior is now summarized.

Introduction to Stress and Eating Behavior

The term "stress" refers to processes involving perception, appraisal, and response to noxious events or stimuli (Karatsoreos and McEwen, 2011). Stress experiences can be emotionally (e.g., interpersonal conflict, loss of loved ones, unemployment) or physiologically (e.g., food deprivation, illness, drug withdrawal states) challenging. In addition, regular and binge use of addictive substances may serve as pharmacological stressors. Acute stress (e.g. possibly severe but short-term stressors) activates adaptive responses, but prolonged stress (e.g. possibly less severe but long-term stressors) leads to "wear-and-tear" (also known as allostatic load) of the regulatory systems, resulting in biological alterations that weaken stress-related adaptive processes and increase disease susceptibility (McEwen, 2008). Thus, mildly challenging stimuli limited in duration can be "good stress" or "eustress" and may increase motivation to achieve goal-direct outcomes and homeostasis – this is hypothesized to result in a sense of mastery and accomplishment, and can be perceived as positive and exciting (Selye, 1955). However, the more prolonged and more intense the stressful situation, the lower the sense of mastery and adaptability and thus the greater the stress response and risk for persistent homeostatic dysregulation (Selye, 1955). The perception and appraisal of stress relies on specific aspects of the presenting external or internal stimuli and may be moderated or mediated by personality traits, emotional state, and physiological responses that together contribute to the experience of distress (Herrman et al., 2011).

Stress and Eating Disturbed Behavior

A recent review of human and nonhuman studies show that chronic stress exposure increases consumption of palatable food (Dallman, 2010). There is good evidence that following laboratory exposure to ego threats, people exhibiting high negative affect or greater cortisol reactivity eat more sweet and high fat food (Karwautz, Wober-Bingol, and Wober, 1993; Scott, 1995). Dietary restraint involves efforts to control food intake for the purpose of weight loss or maintenance. However, people endorsing higher levels of dietary restraint show little difference in calorie intake compared to people with low restraint, or in food intake when in a controlled laboratory setting (Stice, Sysko, Roberto, and Allison, 2010) and in a free-living population setting (Stice, Fisher, and Lowe, 2004). It has also been suggested that some types of dietary restraint are more effective than others with "flexible restraint" (which may prevent excessive consumption of palatable nonnutritious food), being better than "rigid restraint" (which may eventually lead to overeating) (Groesz et al., 2012).

Multiple quantitative studies and narrative reviews have claimed that stress is associated with an increased risk of eating disturbed behavior. The observed associations between stress and eating disturbance could be either causal, due to confounding, or spurious due to methodological weaknesses. If causal, these associations might be of great importance for public health given the substantial global burden of these diseases (Whiteford et al., 2013). It is also possible, however, that some of the claimed associations could be caused by biases in the literature, in particular selective reporting biases favoring the publication of significant associations (Easterbrook, Gopalan, Berlin, and Matthews, 1991) and causing either false positives or inflated estimates of association (Ioannidis, 2005).

Assessment of the Evidence of Stress and Eating Disturbed Behavior

This chapter aims to understand the strength of evidence and extent of potential biases in the claimed associations between stress and risk of developing eating disturbed behavior. In order to achieve this goal an "umbrella review" was performed in order to appraise the contemporary evidence across published meta-analyses or systematic reviews conducted since the start of the twenty-first century. Several models have been proposed to explain the connection between stressful life events and eating disturbance and have been comprehensively summarized by Sharpe, Ryst, Hinshaw, and Steiner (1997). A "cumulative stressor model" suggests that individuals who experience a large number of relatively small but regular stressful events may be at risk for eating disturbance. The "traumatic life events" model posits that unusually severe or adverse life events play a direct role in the development of eating disturbance. Finally, a "normative stressor model" proposes eating-disturbed and non eating-disturbed individuals may experience similar life events but the individual perception of these events are what determines whether an individual goes on to develop an eating disturbance or not (Sharpe et al., 1997). The next section describes how the evidence was gathered on the main types of eating disturbed behavior that have been studied to assess their association with aforementioned different models of stress. The evidence is summarized by describing the magnitude, direction, and interpretation of the observed associations; reporting whether there are hints of biases in this evidence and how they manifest; and finally which are the most robust associations without potential biases.

Literature Search

The electronic databases PubMed, Embase, PsychInfo, and Medline were searched from January 2000 to the end of January 2015 for qualitative systematic reviews or quantitative meta-analyses of epidemiological studies investigating the association between stress and eating disturbed behavior using the following search terms: "(anorexia OR bulimia OR binge eating disorder OR eating disturbance) AND (stress OR life events OR psychosocial factors OR life stress OR perceived stress OR daily hassles) AND (meta-analysis OR systematic review)." A manual review of reference lists from the eligible studies was also performed. The titles, abstracts, and full texts of the resulting papers were examined in detail. The search strategy was limited to reports from the start of this century and to stress in general (rather than specific types of stressor such as bereavement), in order to keep the review manageable, and the aim was to provide an overview of the evidence based on the contemporary literature on this topic.

Eligibility Criteria and Data Extraction

Articles were eligible if the authors had performed a systematic search to identify pertinent studies. We included only English-language publications of meta-analyses or systematic reviews of epidemiological studies in humans. Systematic reviews that present either qualitative or quantitative findings were included. If an article presented separate results for models for different aspects of stress, these were assessed separately. From each eligible narrative, systematic review information was extracted on first author, year of publication, outcome examined, number of included studies, and the reported qualitative information was summarized.

For the studies that included a quantitative meta-analysis, information was extracted on the study design, the number of cases and controls (if applicable) or the number of cases and population participants (in cohort studies), and the maximally adjusted risk ratio for cohort studies (reported as odds ratio (OR) for case-control studies) and the associated 95 percent confidence intervals (CIs). A value of 1 for the odds ratio or risk ratio indicates that there is no association with the specified risk (that is, the event or disease is equally likely in the high- and low-risk groups); as the value of odds ratio or risk ratio increases or decreases away from 1, the association grows increasingly stronger (Bland and Altman, 2000). It is well known that, under certain circumstances (low population rates of "cases" <10 percent) and with specific study designs (case-control studies), the odds ratio provides a good approximation to a risk ratio (Bland and Altman, 2000). In classical epidemiological studies an odds ratio of <1.5 is considered small, while an odds ratio of >5 is considered to be large (H. Chen, Cohen, and Chen, 2010). Quantitative meta-analyses in psychological research often assess the association of factors with a particular outcome using correlations as the measure of effect size. A rough guide as to what constitute small, medium and large effect sizes in terms of correlations (r) are given as $r > 0.10$, $r > 0.30$ and $r > 0.50$, respectively (Cohen, 1992; Rosenthal, 1991). These rules are applied throughout this chapter in order to provide the reader with some guidance in terms of interpretation of the findings of the quantitative meta-analyses that involve correlations. Information was also extracted on whether heterogeneity between studies was assessed. If there is a large amount of heterogeneity in the meta-analysis then it could mean that combining the studies may be unreasonable or highly suspect (Bennett and Emberson, 2009). Finally, information was also extracted on whether publication or small study bias (that is, if small studies tend to give higher risk estimates than large studies) was assessed. Small study effects can indicate publication and other reporting biases, but they can also reflect genuine heterogeneity, chance, or other reasons for differences between small and large studies (Sterne, Gavaghan, and Egger, 2000).

Summary of the Evidence for Stress and Eating Disturbance

In total there were 12 reports that provided an overview of published information on the association of stress and eating disturbance (Figure 11.1). These 12 reports were comprised of seven qualitative systematic reviews and five quantitative meta-analyses. These 12 studies reported

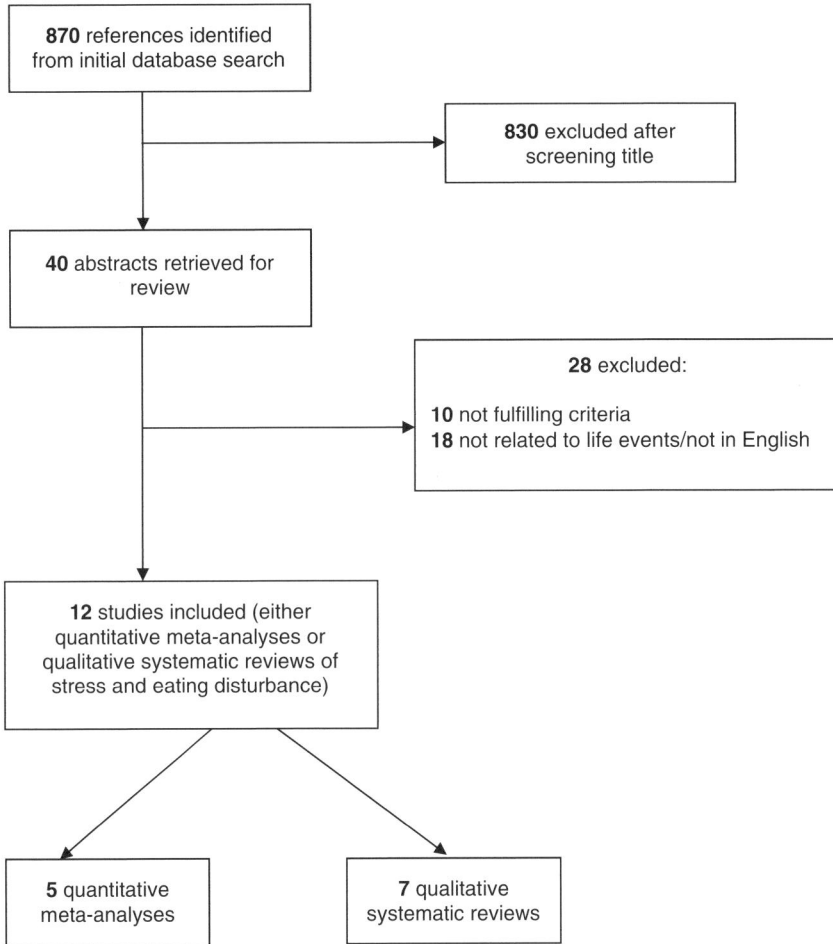

Figure 11.1   Screening and selection of included studies in stress and eating disturbance review.

on several different aspects of stress that could influence eating disturbed behavior under certain types of stressor model. The evidence for each of these stressor models reported in these included studies is now described in more detail.

Evidence for the Cumulative Stressor Model

A *cumulative stressor model* suggests that individuals who experience a large number of relatively normative and/or nonnormative stressors may be at risk for eating disturbed behavior. It has been suggested that cumulative stress may stem from such areas as family or caregiver conflict or dysfunction, puberty or early menarche, peer conflict and academic challenges (Sharpe et al., 1997). There were five reports that investigated the role played by cumulative stressors in eating disturbance (Table 11.1).

Table 11.1 Evidence for the cumulative stressor model and eating disturbance

Report	Type of systematic review	Type of stressor	Type of eating disturbed behavior[1]	Reported number of studies	Reported number of people	Measure of effect	Magnitude or direction of effect size	Evidence of heterogeneity	Evidence of publication bias
Holtom-Viesel, A	Qualitative	Family environment: general family functioning	AN	2	NR	NR	Lower family functioning than controls	NR	NR
Holtom-Viesel, A	Qualitative	Family environment: general family functioning	Any ED	2	NR	NR	Lower family functioning than controls	NR	NR
Jacobi, C	Qualitative	Family environment	Any ED	4	NR	NR	Positively associated	NR	NR
Vince, E	Quantitative	Family environment	Any ED	27	3,984	correlation	0.13	Yes	Yes
Vince, E	Quantitative	Family environment	AN	4	162	correlation	0.09	Yes	No
Vince, E	Quantitative	Family environment	BN	9	743	correlation	0.2	No	No
Vince, E	Quantitative	Family environment: poor caregiver relationship	Any ED	13	1,256	correlation	0.3	Yes	No
Vince, E	Quantitative	Family environment: poor caregiver relationship	AN	4	245	correlation	0.27	Yes	No
Vince, E	Quantitative	Family environment: poor caregiver relationship	BN	4	199	correlation	0.4	Yes	No
Klump, KL	Qualitative	Puberty and early menarche	Females: Diagnosed AN	8	NR	NR	Increased prevalence of AN	NR	NR
Klump, KL	Qualitative	Puberty and early menarche	Females: Diagnosed BN	13	NR	NR	Positively associated with early puberty	NR	NR
Klump, KL	Qualitative	Puberty and early menarche	Females: Diagnosed AN & BN	4	NR	NR	Positively associated with advanced pubertal status	NR	NR

Klump, KL	Qualitative	Puberty and early menarche	Females: Diagnosed EDNOS	1	NR	NR	Positively associated with advanced pubertal status	NR	NR
Klump, KL	Qualitative	Puberty and early menarche	Males: Diagnosed AN	1	NR	NR	Not associated with early pubertal timing	NR	NR
Klump, KL	Qualitative	Puberty and early menarche	Males: Diagnosed BN	2	NR	NR	Inconclusive as one study associated early pubertal timing, the other study not associated with advanced puberty	NR	NR
Klump, KL	Qualitative	Puberty and early menarche	Females: Any ED symptoms (global measure)	18	NR	NR	Mostly positively associated with early puberty and advanced pubertal status	NR	NR
Klump, KL	Qualitative	Puberty and early menarche	Males: Any ED symptoms (global measure)	2	NR	NR	Inconclusive as some studies associated, others not associated	NR	NR
Jacobi, C	Qualitative	Puberty and early menarche	Any ED	NR	NR	NR	No clear evidence of an association	NR	NR
Stice, E	Quantitative	Puberty and early menarche	Any ED	5	8,790	correlation	0.04	No	NR

[1] AN: anorexia nervosa; Any ED: any eating disturbance; BN: bulimia nervosa; NR: not reported.

Family environment

Historically, the role of dysfunctional family interaction styles was put forward in theories on the development of eating disorders (Bruch, 1973; Lacey and Price, 2004; Minuchin, Rosman, and Baker, 1978). Characteristics of the patient–family relationships of patients with eating disturbance include problematic family structures, interaction or communication styles (e.g., overprotection, enmeshment), and attachment styles.

Qualitative evidence for association of family environment with eating disturbed behavior

Jacobi, Hayward, de Zwaan, Kraemer, and Agras (2004b) performed a narrative systematic review that investigated the role of family environment as part of a wider review of risk factors for eating disturbance. The authors reported that in the majority of studies anorexic and bulimic patients describe different aspects of their family structure as more disturbed, having more conflict, or dysfunctional than do controls across different family assessment measures. The authors also made a point that the key limitation of these studies is that temporal sequence cannot be ascertained as these studies were mainly cross-sectional in nature. They also note that some studies included in their review commented that issues with family relationships occur in non eating-disturbed populations, indicating a possible non-specific nature of these family-related issues. The authors reviewed three case-control studies that assessed family relationships prior to the onset of eating disturbance and found that some parental variables (high expectations, low contact, and critical comments about weight and shape by the family) were found to be specifically predictive for bulimia nervosa when compared with the psychiatric comparison group (Jacobi et al., 2004b). The authors also summarized the findings of four longitudinal studies that investigated family structure or family functioning as potential risk factors for later eating problems. In three of the studies, family relationship issues did not contribute further to the prediction of eating disturbance several years later. One study found moderate associations between family environment and eating disturbance several years later, but initial eating disturbances levels were not controlled for in the analyses. The report authors noted that based on the findings of their narrative review, the evidence for the association of family environment is relatively weak (Jacobi et al., 2007). The report by Holtom-Viesel and Allan (2014) found that general family functioning was worse in the family containing an individual with an eating disturbance compared to control families that did not contain a person with an eating disturbance. This was also the case when they compared families with an individual with anorexic type eating disturbance to control families. The authors reported that there was little evidence for a typical pattern of family dysfunction.

Quantitative evidence for association of family environment with eating disturbed behavior

Vince and Walker (2007) investigated the role of general family environment with eating disturbed behavior, and found that there was a small association overall ($r = 0.13$) between eating disturbance and family environment, but there was substantial heterogeneity in the effect sizes observed. The report contained a sensitivity analysis that stratified by age; the heterogeneity could be explained by one larger study in older subjects reporting a negative correlation compared to the positive correlation observed in the studies that involved younger subjects. In this meta-analysis only small effects were observed when investigating the specific associations for AN and BN with family environment ($r = 0.09$, $r = 0.20$, respectively). Although the BN studies appeared to be consistent, the AN studies were heterogeneous, and the authors suggested that difference in age was the most likely cause of the heterogeneity as after the exclusion of the study in older subjects most of the heterogeneity was removed.

The meta-analysis by Vince and Walker (2007) also investigated the quality of the fundamental relationship with the primary caregiver: attachment style and perceived parental bonding. The studies that were included were cross-sectional, included data on female participants that were at least 13 years old, and were presented using correlations. The overall analysis found a moderate association (r = 0.30) between general eating disturbance and poor caregiver relationship, but the effect sizes varied. Separate analyses of AN and BN subjects found that both groups reported more maladaptive relationships with their caregivers (r = 0.26, r = 0.40, respectively). However, these analyses found that there was heterogeneity in effect sizes; particularly for the BN analyses, the authors found that the effect sizes were larger for the most recent studies. Overall, this meta-analysis indicated that women displaying eating disturbed behaviors, especially the clinical variants of AN and BN, are more likely than control women to report dysfunctional relationships with their primary caregivers.

Puberty or early menarche

It has long been suggested that early pubertal development fosters body image and eating disturbances in females (Rierdan and Koff, 1991). This has been attributed to the fact that early menarche leads to increased adipose tissue, and in particular it moves girls away from the normative body shape of adolescents and the current thin ideal, which theoretically increases body dissatisfaction and consequent dieting and eating disturbances (Rierdan and Koff, 1991).

Qualitative studies for association of puberty or early menarche with eating disturbed behavior   In a narrative systematic review by Klump (2013), the researcher reported that most studies have found significant effects of both pubertal status and timing on global as well as specific eating disturbance symptoms. She noted that many reports tend to find higher levels of eating disturbance symptoms in girls at more advanced stages of pubertal development, especially when comparisons were made between pre–early puberty to mid–late puberty. The systematic review commented that there have been some prospective and retrospective studies that have observed that there are pubertal timing effects in late and middle adulthood. However, the author notes that of the few prospective studies of pubertal status that have been conducted, it has been found that advanced pubertal development at the time of initial assessment predicted eating disturbed symptoms eight months to three years later (Klump, 2013). The author concluded that overall, the majority of the evidence available suggests that puberty is likely to play a much larger role in clinical eating disorder risk in girls than boys and that sex-specific processes during puberty may differentially contribute to eating disturbances in females versus males.

Jacobi and colleagues (2004b) have pointed out that it is not clear whether the association between eating disturbance symptoms and sexual maturation is a function of increasing body mass index (BMI) at puberty or other aspects of puberty. This is due to the fact that sexual maturation and BMI are highly positively correlated, and it is thus difficult to separate out their respective independent contributions. Jacobi et al. (2004b) also remark that puberty appears to be weakly associated with eating disturbance symptoms after adjustment for important confounders in multivariable regression models. They suggest that perhaps the best way to regard the role of pubertal status in relation to risk of eating disturbed behavior is that "pubertal status is more related to when symptoms develop rather than whether symptoms develop" (p. 49). It was also remarked that in terms of pubertal timing, these effects are often confounded with pubertal status effects in cross-sectional studies that only include a limited age range. In addition, even though all girls pass through puberty, the age at which puberty begins varies considerably. The association between early pubertal timing and eating disturbed symptomatology as well as diagnosis has been observed in three studies included in the review (Jacobi et al., 2004b). One of these studies included girls currently in the pubertal transition, and the other two studies were samples where all girls had completed puberty and had retrospectively assessed whether higher rates of eating disturbance where present in those with early puberty compared with their peers. This review found that in the five longitudinal studies in which different indicators of pubertal timing were assessed, it was not associated with subsequent eating disturbances.

Quantitative reviews for association of puberty and early menarche with eating disturbed behavior   Stice (2002) reports details of a meta-analysis of longitudinal studies (with a range of follow-up between 24 and 96 months) that assessed whether early menarche was associated with increased eating pathology. The authors reported that the effect of early menarche on eating pathology was significant, but very small, in the five studies that reported an association (overall effect $r = 0.04$), and there was no significant heterogeneity in the effect sizes observed. One of the studies was conducted in adults, three of the studies were in adolescents, and one study involved children. The authors suggest that the weak results could be explained by the fact that the "adverse effects of early menarche are developmentally localized and only occur during the period in which youth are developmentally deviant (i.e., during early adolescence)" (Stice, 2002, p. 839). They go on further to suggest that longitudinal studies should therefore examine the effects of early menarche in subjects in early adolescence in order to reliably detect any associations.

Evidence for the Traumatic Stressor Model

According to a traumatic stressor model, unusually severe life stressors play a direct role in the development of eating disturbance (Degortes et al., 2014; Pike et al., 2006). Traumatic life events include such experiences as general, sexual, physical or psychological abuse, total neglect or abandonment in childhood, and loss of a loved one (Cattanach, Malley, and Rodin, 1988). There were ten reports that investigated the role of traumatic stressors with eating disturbance (Table 11.2).

General abuse

There was no qualitative evidence identified from the search strategy for the association of general abuse with eating disturbed behavior. One study was identified that provided some quantitative evidence for association of general abuse with eating disturbed behavior. This meta-analysis by Vince and Walker (2007) of cross-sectional studies of female participants who were at least 13 years old investigated whether women who have suffered abuse in general are more likely to display eating disturbances. Abuse, in general, was related to eating disturbance with a small effect size ($r = 0.19$). A disorder-specific analysis demonstrated a small–medium association ($r = 0.26$) between BN and general abuse.

Table 11.2 Evidence for the traumatic stressor model and eating disturbance

Report	Type of systematic review	Type of stressor	Type of eating disturbed behavior[1]	Reported number of studies	Reported number of people	Measure of effect	Magnitude or direction of effect size	Evidence of heterogeneity	Evidence of publication bias
Bundock, L	Qualitative	Physical abuse: IPV	AN	2	3,047	prevalence	Associated with increased prevalence of lifetime IPV in men (25%) and women (19%)	NR	NR
Vince, E	Quantitative	General abuse	AN	6	634	correlation	0.26	No	No
Vince, E	Quantitative	General abuse	Any ED	18	2,792	correlation	0.19	No	No
Carr, C	Qualitative	Physical abuse	Any ED	4	NR	NR	Positively associated	NR	NR
Mitchison, D	Qualitative	Physical abuse	Any ED	12	NR	NR	All studies showed a positive association	NR	NR
Bundock, L	Qualitative	Physical abuse: IPV	BN	4	3,256	prevalence	Associated with increased prevalence of lifetime IPV in men (67%) and women (35%–40%)	NR	NR
Bundock, L	Qualitative	Physical abuse: IPV	BED	1	7,393	prevalence	Associated with increased prevalence of lifetime IPV in men (19%) and women (12.5%)	NR	NR
Vince, E	Quantitative	Physical abuse	Any ED	3	837	correlation	0.12	No	No
Bundock, L	Quantitative	Physical abuse: IPV	Female: EDNOS	1	7,393	odds ratios	5.4 (95% CI: 3.3, 8.0)	NR	NR
Bundock, L	Quantitative	Physical abuse: IPV	Male: EDNOS	1	7,393	odds ratios	2.8 (95% CI: 0.9, 8.0)	NR	NR
Carr, C	Qualitative	Sexual abuse	Any ED	8	NR	NR	Positively associated	NR	NR
Mitchison, D	Qualitative	Sexual abuse	Any ED	14	NR	NR	Majority of studies showed a positive association	NR	NR

(continued)

Table 11.2 (Continued)

Report	Type of systematic review	Type of stressor	Type of eating disturbed behavior[1]	Reported number of studies	Reported number of people	Measure of effect	Magnitude or direction of effect size	Evidence of heterogeneity	Evidence of publication bias
Jacobi, C	Qualitative	Sexual abuse	Any ED	10	NR	NR	Positively associated with onset of ED	NR	NR
Smolak, L and Murnen, SK	Quantitative	Childhood sexual abuse	Any ED	53	41,304	correlation	0.101	Yes	NR
Chen, LP	Quantitative	Sexual abuse	Any ED	11	7,468	odds ratios	2.72 (95% CI: 2.04, 3.63)	Yes	No
Vince, E	Quantitative	Sexual abuse	Any ED	14	2,128	correlation	0.2	No	No
Carr, C	Qualitative	Emotional abuse	Any ED	2	NR	NR	Positively associated	NR	NR
Carr, C	Qualitative	Physical neglect	Any ED	1	NR	NR	Positively associated	NR	NR
Carr, C	Qualitative	Emotional neglect	Any ED	2	NR	NR	Positively associated	NR	NR
Mitchison, D	Qualitative	Physical neglect	Any ED	7	NR	NR	Evidence of a positive association	NR	NR
Mitchison, D	Qualitative	Emotional neglect	Any ED	1	NR	NR	Some evidence of a positive association	NR	NR
Quick, VM	Qualitative	Chronic illness	Any ED	NR	NR	NR	Positively associated	NR	NR
Krug, I	Quantitative	Obstetric complications (instrumental delivery)	Any ED	5	NR	odds ratios	1.06 (95% CI: 0.69, 1.65)	Yes	NR
Krug, I	Quantitative	Obstetric complications (premature delivery)	Any ED	5	NR	odds ratios	1.17 (95% CI: 0.91, 1.52)	No	NR
Hall, KS	Qualitative	Posttraumatic stress disorder	BED	9	27,818	NR	Inconclusive as some studies associated, others not associated	NR	NR
Mitchison, D	Qualitative	Adverse life events	Any ED	10	NR	NR	Some evidence of a positive association	NR	NR
Jacobi, C	Qualitative	Adverse life events	Any ED	6	NR	NR	No clear evidence of an association	NR	NR

[1] AN: anorexia nervosa; Any ED: any eating disturbance; BED: binge-eating disorder; BN: bulimia nervosa; EDNOS: eating disorders not otherwise specified; IPV: intimate partner violence; NR: not reported.

Physical abuse

Abuse during childhood has long been hypothesized to be a risk factor for the development of eating disturbances. Abuse can cause intolerable emotions and undermine identity (Rayworth, Wise, and Harlow, 2004). It has been suggested that eating disturbed behavior can serve as an attempt to regulate negative affect (Polivy and Herman, 2002; Schmidt, Humfress, and Treasure, 1997).

Qualitative evidence for association of physical abuse with eating disturbed behavior
The narrative review by Bundock et al. (2013) investigated the prevalence of intimate partner violence (IPV) among people with eating disturbance. Four studies included in their review reported on BN in women and found that the lifetime prevalence of physical IPV in these individuals ranged from 22.7 to 40 percent. The review also included a single study based on a nationally representative household survey of BN in men, and this study found that the lifetime prevalence of physical IPV was 67 percent. The review by Bundock et al. (2013) also reported on the lifetime prevalence of IPV in participants with AN, BED, or any eating disturbance, based on a study that used nationally representative data. They found that the lifetime prevalence of physical IPV in subjects with AN was 25 percent for men and 19 percent for women; for BED the prevalence of lifetime IPV among women was 19 percent and among men 13 percent, and for any eating disturbance the lifetime prevalence was around 60 percent for women and 30 percent for men. The review also reported the increased odds ratios for lifetime IPV of 5.4 (95% CI: 3.3, 8.0) and 2.8 (95% CI: 0.9, 8.0) for women and men respectively with EDNOS compared with women and men without an eating disturbance. This is a strong effect size for women and a moderate effect size for men based on the criteria described in the eligibility criteria and data extraction section of this chapter. Although lifetime prevalence of IPV appeared to be high for eating disturbed individuals, the review highlights that evidence is lacking on the association of eating disturbance with IPV in the past year and on whether the associations between eating disturbance and IPV vary by type of IPV, and temporality (Bundock et al., 2013).

Quantitative evidence for the association of physical abuse with eating disturbed behavior
The meta-analysis by Vince and Walker (2007) also investigated whether women who have been physically abused were more likely to have eating disturbance. This meta-analysis found a modest association between physical abuse and eating disturbance (r = 0.12); however, the authors report that this result could have been affected by publication or small study bias.

Sexual abuse

It has been argued that childhood sexual abuse is a risk factor for the development of eating disorders (Wonderlich, Wilsnack, Wilsnack, and Harris, 1996). It has been suggested that childhood sexual abuse might lead to poor coping styles (Perry, Pollard, Blakley, Baker, and Vigilante, 1995) or that it may manifest itself as binge eating. It has also been suggested that childhood sexual abuse may lead to poor self-esteem or the individual may feel that they lack control of their life and so control of their eating behavior may allow them to take control of their life (Smolak and Murnen, 2002). This section looks at the contemporary evidence on sexual abuse in general that may also include childhood sexual abuse.

Qualitative evidence for the association of sexual abuse with eating disturbed behavior
The systematic review by Jacobi et al. (2004b) conducted in the early part of the twenty-first century concluded that in the five studies that investigated any form of sexual abuse (two community samples and three clinical samples) the evidence suggested that the sexual abuse had taken place prior to the onset of the eating disturbance. However, the authors note that in the studies that had reported precedence, the evidence was stronger for BN than AN (Jacobi et al., 2004b). A more recent review by Carr, Martins, Stingel, Lemgruber, and Juruena (2013) reported that childhood sexual abuse was associated with eating disturbance in general, as well as other forms of self-destructive behavior. A qualitative systematic review by Mitchison and Hay (2014) reported that 10 studies out of the 14 included in their review reported an association between being a victim of sexual abuse and eating disturbed behavior.

Quantitative evidence for the association of sexual abuse with eating disturbed behavior
The review by Vince and Walker (2007) found that sexual abuse only had a modest association with eating disturbance (r = 0.20). Similarly an earlier meta-analysis of 53 studies found only a weak association (r = 0.10) between childhood sexual abuse and eating disturbance (Smolak and Murnen, 2002). However, Smolak and Murnen noted that there was considerable heterogeneity due to methodological differences between the studies included in the meta-analysis (such as different comparison groups and measurement instruments). A more recent meta-analysis by L. P. Chen and colleagues (2010) that investigated the association of sexual abuse with psychiatric disorders in general found that there was almost a threefold association between past sexual abuse and a lifetime diagnosis of an eating disorder (OR, 2.72; 95% CI: 2.04, 3.63). This moderate effect size was based on 11 studies (seven case-control and four cohort studies) that included ~7,000 participants, and there was no evidence of publication bias or heterogeneity in the findings (L. P. Chen et al., 2010). Both the quantitative and qualitative evidence on physical abuse and sexual abuse have the same shortcomings. The main problem is that the details are not given on the perpetrator and his or her age difference from the victim, or an age cut-off for the abuse, and very few make an attempt to separate out abuse that occurred before the onset of the eating disturbed behavior, or give any information on the severity of the abuse included.

Emotional abuse, emotional neglect, and physical neglect

The systematic review by Carr et al. (2013) found that emotional abuse was associated with eating disturbance in two studies and suggested that it may be predictive of more severe eating disturbance in bulimic individuals. One of the studies included in this review provided evidence of a positive association between emotional and physical neglect in eating disturbed individuals (Becker and Grilo, 2011). A review by Mitchison and Hay (2014) found a positive association between child neglect and eating disturbed behavior in the single study that met their inclusion criteria. There were no quantitative meta-analyses identified by the literature search on this topic.

Adverse life events and posttraumatic stress disorder (PSTD)

In the systematic review by Jacobi et al. (2004b), the authors conclude that there is some evidence that eating disturbed individuals experience more adverse life events prior to the onset of eating disturbed behavior than healthy control subjects. Mitchison and Hay (2014) report that having experienced significant stress in general was associated with greater eating disturbed behavior prevalence. Jacobi et al. (2004b) make the important point that the increased number of adverse life events experienced is not specific to eating disturbed individuals but is also the case for other psychiatric disorders. The systematic review by Hall, Hoerster, and Yancy (2015) identified nine published observational studies that reported the associations between PTSD and eating behaviors, all of which were conducted over the last two decades. Six of the nine studies examined the associations between PTSD and binge eating disorder and reported conflicting results. Three of these studies reported no significant differences in the prevalence of PTSD between patients with and without binge eating disorder, while two studies reported significant associations between PTSD and binge eating disorder. There were no quantitative meta-analyses identified by the literature search on this topic.

Chronic illness and obstetric complications

The review by Quick, Byrd-Bredbenner, and Neumark-Sztainer (2013) reported the prevalence of eating disturbed behavior in young adults with selected diet-related chronic health conditions (DRCHCs). There was some weak evidence that the prevalence of eating disturbed behavior was higher in those with DRCHCs compared with the general population. The overall findings suggested that young people with DRCHCs may be at increased risk of endorsing eating disturbed behavior over the course of the treatment for their chronic illness (Quick et al., 2013). Krug, Taborelli, Sallis, Treasure, and Micali (2013) investigated the role of obstetric complications (OCs) and the development of eating disturbed behavior. Of the six included studies, five reported on the same OCs, namely vaginal instrumental delivery and prematurity. The authors reported a nonsignificant association of instrumental delivery with an OR of 1.06 (95% CI: 0.69, 1.65) and for prematurity an OR of 1.17 (95% CI: 0.91, 1.52) with diagnosed AN. They concluded that the evidence on OCs and eating disturbance is inconclusive due to methodological limitations.

Evidence for the Normative Stressor Model

A *normative stressor model* proposes that eating disturbed and non eating-disturbed individuals do not necessarily differ in the number of objectively defined stressors that they encounter. Rather, it may be the individuals' perceptions of these events that are the critical factors with regard to pathology (Byrne, 1984). Experiences such as growing up and associating with peers and sociocultural pressures may be viewed by eating disturbed individuals as particularly stressful (Rutter, 1981). Two reports investigated the role played by normative stressors in eating disturbance (Table 11.3).

Sociocultural pressures

The sociocultural model of eating pathology posits that social pressure to be thin fosters an internalization of the thin ideal and body dissatisfaction, which in turn place individuals at risk for dieting, negative affect, and eating pathology (Benowitz-Fredericks, Garcia, Massey, Vasagar, and Borzekowski, 2012). Pressure to be thin from family, peers, and the media theoretically contributes to an internalization of the thin ideal and a generalized overvaluation of

Table 11.3 Evidence for the normative stressor model and eating disturbance

Report	Type of systematic review	Type of stressor	Type of eating disturbed behavior[1]	Reported number of studies	Reported number of people	Measure of effect	Magnitude or direction of effect size	Evidence of heterogeneity	Evidence of publication bias
Stice, E	Quantitative	Sociocultural pressure: perceived pressure to be thin	Any ED	5	7,895	correlation	0.12	NR	NR
Stice, E	Quantitative	Sociocultural pressure: internalisation of the thin ideal	Any ED	4	15,128	correlation	0.08	Yes	NR
Vince, E	Quantitative	Sociocultural pressure: internalisation of the thin ideal	Any ED	8	1,606	correlation	0.11	Yes	Yes
Vince, E	Quantitative	Sociocultural pressure: media influence	Any ED	6	811	correlation	0.14	Yes	Yes
Vince, E	Quantitative	Sociocultural pressure: teasing about weight from family friends	Any ED	4	287	correlation	0.6	Yes	No
Vince, E	Quantitative	Irrational cognitions	Any ED	17	1,969	correlation	0.4	Yes	Yes
Vince, E	Quantitative	Irrational cognitions	AN	5	329	correlation	0.62	Yes	Yes
Vince, E	Quantitative	Irrational cognitions	BN	8	537	correlation	0.61	Yes	Yes

[1] AN: anorexia nervosa; Any ED: any eating disturbance; BN: bulimia nervosa; NR: not reported.

the importance of appearance (Field et al., 2001). Elevated pressure to be thin is also thought to lead to body dissatisfaction, as repeated messages that an individual is not thin enough is most likely to lead to discontent with their own body. Furthermore, pressure to be thin may directly promote dieting in the absence of body dissatisfaction because people might believe that this would reduce social pressures to be thin.

Evidence for the association of sociocultural pressures with eating disturbed behavior
There was no qualitative evidence in the form of a systematic review identified by the literature search on sociocultural pressures and eating disturbed behavior. Stice (2002) reported that the average effect of perceived pressure to be thin on effect on eating pathology was small ($r = 0.12$). Stice did note that effect sizes were larger for studies that used reliable and validated measures compared to those studies that did not. Stice (2002) also reported that the observed effect sizes were also significantly larger ($z = 3.99$, $p < 0.001$) for studies that examined adolescents (mean $r = 0.19$) versus pre-adolescents (mean $r = 0.05$). He suggested that this may be because studies examining adolescents had greater power to detect effects because this is the developmental period during which eating disturbances typically emerge (Stice, Killen, Hayward, and Taylor, 1998). Vince and Walker (2007) conducted a meta-analysis that investigated multiple risk factors for eating disturbance in females aged over 13 years of age. In order to accommodate the multifaceted concept of sociocultural pressure it was broken down into three areas: internalization of the thin ideal, the influence of the media, and peer and family teasing/pressure. For eight studies included in the analysis there was a weak association found between internalization and disturbed eating ($r = 0.11$), although a sensitivity analysis showed that two larger studies with negative correlations had influenced the effect seen overall by attenuating the medium association seen in the six smaller studies (mean $r = 0.37$).

In their quantitative review, Vince and Walker (2007) found a strong, robust association ($r = 0.60$) between eating disturbance and teasing about weight and shape by family and friends, with varied effect sizes noted. They noted that one of two studies which found a much smaller effect size ($r = 0.16$) compared women with high Bulimia Test (BULIT) scale scores to those with low scores, potentially resulting in the control group having a higher degree of disturbed eating than the control groups of all the other studies, which included only women from the general population. Stice (2002) reported that perceived pressure to be thin was a non-statistically significant maintenance factor for bulimic pathology (though this effect was moderate). He went on to conclude that the pattern of effects suggested that perceived pressure to be thin might play a more important role in fostering eating pathology than in maintaining it.

Irrational cognitions

There was no qualitative evidence for this topic ascertained from the literature search. In their quantitative review, Vince and Walker (2007) found an association ($r = 0.40$) between general eating disturbance and irrational cognitions (a commonly used term to encompass negative self-beliefs/core beliefs or dysfunctional cognitions and underlying assumptions regarding eating, weight and body shape seen in people with eating disturbance). They reported that the effect sizes ranged from very weak ($r = 0.05$) to very strong ($r = 0.89$), with 14 out of the 17 studies reporting an effect size of 0.28 or greater. Exploration of the heterogeneity found that studies using eating-specific measures of irrational cognitions found the strongest associations. A stratified analysis based on measurement scale used was conducted to explore this further.

Although all the eating-specific measures found associations between irrational cognitions and disturbed eating, only the Dysfunctional Attitudes Scale (DAS) resulted in homogeneous effect sizes. The authors suggested that although the DAS's conceptualization of dysfunctional attitudes may differ from that of the beliefs assessed in the other measures, their findings suggest that choice of measurement scale was not solely responsible for the initial effect size heterogeneity (Vince and Walker, 2007). The analyses for the specific diagnosed eating disturbances of AN and BN produced results similar to the overall analysis ($r = 0.62$, $r = 0.61$, respectively). Overall, their analyses appeared to demonstrate that women with disturbed eating, and AN and BN specifically, show higher levels of irrational cognitions than do women with no eating disturbances, although there was substantial heterogeneity in the strength of this finding. When cognitions are assessed by the DAS, the relationship appeared to be more robust than when measured with other relevant measures (Vince and Walker, 2007).

Summary and Conclusions

The aim of this review was to summarize the findings from systematic reviews and meta-analyses published over the last 15 years in order to identify associations based on different models of stress and eating disturbed behavior. There are several limitations of this review. Even though different models of stress were covered, the review focused on systematic reviews or meta-analyses that investigated stressors that were considered relevant to these models and eating disturbed behavior rather than specific aspects of stress or specific stressors. The review was also restricted to the last 15 years in order to utilize information from DSM-IV so as to avoid the evidence being affected by changes in diagnostic classification systems over time (as there have been slight changes to the criteria for AN and BN, and the introduction of BED). A further limitation was that data were extracted by one author only, the search did not include "gray" literature (i.e., unpublished papers or papers in the pipeline for publication), and non-English language publications were excluded.

Despite these limitations in the conduct of the review, based on the summary of the evidence the strongest and most consistent associations identified were between history of sexual abuse, sociocultural pressures, irrational cognitions, and eating disturbed behavior. Although these associations were consistent between qualitative and quantitative reviews, the majority of the quantitative meta-analyses were based on cross-sectional data and thus presented correlations, or presented odds ratios based on case-control data. Due to a lack of associations obtained from prospective cohort studies, it is therefore not possible to make a reliable assessment of whether these associations are causal for the onset of eating disturbed behavior. The review of the evidence identified that the most suitable study population for these prospective investigations is a predominantly female adolescent population as the onset of puberty is a high risk period for the development of symptoms of eating disturbance. In order for this area of research to advance, there is a need for more well-conducted prospective studies that can identify the specific stressors that may have occurred prior to the onset of disturbed eating behavior and thus enable more reliable assessment of causality.

References

Aime, A., Sabourin, S., and Ratte, C. (2006). The eating disturbed spectrum in relation with coping and interpersonal functioning. *Eat Weight Disord*, *11*(2), 66–72.

American Psychiatric Association (1987). *Diagnostic and Statistical Manual of Mental Disorders*, 3rd edn. rev. Arlington, VA: American Psychiatric Association.

American Psychiatric Association Task Force on DSM-IV (2000). *Diagnostic and Statistical Manual of Mental Disorders: DSM-IV-TR*. Washington, DC: American Psychiatric Association.

American Psychiatric Association (2013). *Diagnostic and Statistical Manual of Mental Disorders*, 5th edn. Arlington, VA: American Psychiatric Association.

Arcelus, J., Witcomb, G. L., and Mitchell, A. (2014). Prevalence of eating disorders amongst dancers: A systemic review and meta-analysis. *Eur Eat Disord Rev*, 22(2), 92–101. doi:10.1002/erv.2271

Bardone-Cone, A. M., Wonderlich, S. A., Frost, R. O., Bulik, C. M., Mitchell, J. E., Uppala, S., and Simonich, H. (2007). Perfectionism and eating disorders: Current status and future directions. *Clin Psychol Rev*, 27(3), 384–405. doi:10.1016/j.cpr.2006.12.005

Becker, D. F., and Grilo, C. M. (2011). Childhood maltreatment in women with binge-eating disorder: Associations with psychiatric comorbidity, psychological functioning, and eating pathology. *Eat Weight Disord*, 16(2), e113–120.

Bennett, D. A., and Cooper, C. L. (1999). Eating disturbance as a manifestation of the stress process: A review of the literature. *Stress Medicine*, 15(3), 167–182. doi:10.1002/(sici)1099-1700(199907)15:3<167::aid-smi812>3.0.co; 2-7

Bennett, D. A., and Emberson, J. R. (2009). Stratification for exploring heterogeneity in systematic reviews. *Evid Based Med*, 14(6), 162–164. doi:10.1136/ebm.14.6.162-a

Benowitz-Fredericks, C. A., Garcia, K., Massey, M., Vasagar, B., and Borzekowski, D. L. G. (2012). Body image, eating disorders, and the relationship to adolescent media use. *Pediatr Clin of North Am*, 59(3), 693–704. doi:http://dx.doi.org/10.1016/j.pcl.2012.03.017

Bland, J. M., and Altman, D. G. (2000). Statistics notes. The odds ratio. *BMJ*, 320(7247), 1468.

Bruch, H. (1973). Thin fat people. *J Am Med Womens Assoc*, 28(4), 187–188.

Bundock, L., Howard, L. M., Trevillion, K., Malcolm, E., Feder, G., and Oram, S. (2013). Prevalence and risk of experiences of intimate partner violence among people with eating disorders: A systematic review. *J Psychiatr Res*, 47(9), 1134–1142. doi:10.1016/j.jpsychires.2013.04.014

Byrne, D. G. (1984). Personal assessments of life-event stress and the near future onset of psychological symptoms. *Br J Med Psychol*, 57(pt 3), 241–248.

Carr, C. P., Martins, C. M. S., Stingel, A. M., Lemgruber, V. B., and Juruena, M. F. (2013). The role of early life stress in adult psychiatric disorders: A systematic review according to childhood trauma subtypes. *J Nerv Ment Dis*, 201(12), 1007–1020. doi:10.1097/nmd.0000000000000049

Cattanach, L., Malley, R., and Rodin, J. (1988). Psychologic and physiologic reactivity to stressors in eating disordered individuals. *Psychosom Med*, 50(6), 591–599.

Chen, H., Cohen, P., and Chen, S. (2010). How big is a big odds ratio? Interpreting the magnitudes of odds ratios in epidemiological studies. *Communications in Statistics – Simulation and Computation*, 39(4), 860–864. doi:10.1080/03610911003650383

Chen, L. P., Murad, M. H., Paras, M. L., Colbenson, K. M., Sattler, A. L., Goranson, E. N., … Zirakzadeh, A. (2010). Sexual abuse and lifetime diagnosis of psychiatric disorders: Systematic review and meta-analysis. *Mayo Clin Proc*, 85(7), 618–629. doi:10.4065/mcp.2009.0583

Coelho, G. M. d. O., Gomes, A. I. d. S., Ribeiro, B. G., and Soares, E. d. A. (2014). Prevention of eating disorders in female athletes. *Open Access Journal of Sports Medicine*, 5, 105–113. doi:10.2147/oajsm.s36528

Cohen, J. (1992). A power primer. *Psychol Bull*, 112(1), 155–159. doi:10.1037/0033-2909.112.1.155

Dallman, M. F. (2010). Stress-induced obesity and the emotional nervous system. *Trends Endocrinol Metab*, 21(3), 159–165. doi:10.1016/j.tem.2009.10.004

Degortes, D., Santonastaso, P., Zanetti, T., Tenconi, E., Veronese, A., and Favaro, A. (2014). Stressful life events and binge eating disorder. *Eur Eat Disord Rev*, 22(5), 378–382. doi:10.1002/erv.2308

E, Z. G., Zhang, Y. P., Zhou, J. H., and Wang, L. (2014). Mini review roles of the bZIP gene family in rice. *Genet Mol Res*, 13(2), 3025–3036. doi:10.4238/2014.April.16.11

Easterbrook, P. J., Gopalan, R., Berlin, J. A., and Matthews, D. R. (1991). Publication bias in clinical research. *Lancet*, 337(8746), 867–872. doi:http://dx.doi.org/10.1016/0140-6736(91)90201-Y

Fairburn, C. G., and Harrison, P. J. (2003). Eating disorders. *Lancet*, 361(9355), 407–416. doi:10.1016/S0140-6736(03)12378-1

Field, A. E., Camargo, C. A., Taylor, C. B., Berkey, C. S., Roberts, S. B., and Colditz, G. A. (2001). Peer, parent, and media influences on the development of weight concerns and frequent dieting among preadolescent and adolescent girls and boys. *Pediatrics*, 107(1), 54–60. doi:10.1542/peds.107.1.54.

Groesz, L. M., McCoy, S., Carl, J., Saslow, L., Stewart, J., Adler, N., … Epel, E. (2012). What is eating you? Stress and the drive to eat. *Appetite*, 58(2), 717–721. doi:10.1016/j.appet.2011.11.028

Hall, K. S., Hoerster, K. D., and Yancy, W. S., Jr. (2015). Post-traumatic stress disorder, physical activity, and eating behaviors. *Epidemiol Rev*, *37*(1), 103–115. doi:10.1093/epirev/mxu011

Hebebrand, J., and Bulik, C. M. (2011). Critical appraisal of the provisional DSM-5 criteria for anorexia nervosa and an alternative proposal. *Int J Eat Disord*, *44*(8), 665–678. doi:10.1002/eat.20875

Herrman, H., Stewart, D. E., Diaz-Granados, N., Berger, E. L., Jackson, B., and Yuen, T. (2011). What is resilience? *Can J Psychiatry*, *56*(5), 258–265.

Holtom-Viesel, A., and Allan, S. (2014). A systematic review of the literature on family functioning across all eating disorder diagnoses in comparison to control families. *Clin Psychol Rev*, *34*(1), 29–43. doi:10.1016/j.cpr.2013.10.005

Ioannidis, J. P. A. (2005). Why most published research findings are false. *PLoS Med*, *2*(8), e124. doi:10.1371/journal.pmed.0020124

Jacobi, C., Abascal, L., and Taylor, C. B. (2004a). Screening for eating disorders and high-risk behavior: Caution. *Int J Eat Disord*, *36*(3), 280–295. doi:10.1002/eat.20048

Jacobi, C., Hayward, C., de Zwaan, M., Kraemer, H. C., and Agras, W. S. (2004b). Coming to terms with risk factors for eating disorders: Application of risk terminology and suggestions for a general taxonomy. *Psychol Bull*, *130*(1), 19–65. doi:10.1037/0033-2909.130.1.19

Jacobi, C., Morris, L., Beckers, C., Bronisch-Holtze, J., Winter, J., Winzelberg, A. J., and Taylor, C. B. (2007). Maintenance of internet-based prevention: A randomized controlled trial. *Int J Eat Disord*, *40*(2), 114–119. doi:10.1002/eat.20344

Karatsoreos, I. N., and McEwen, B. S. (2011). Psychobiological allostasis: Resistance, resilience and vulnerability. *Trends in Cogn Sci*, *15*(12), 576–584. http://dx.doi.org/10.1016/j.tics.2011.10.005

Karwautz, A., Wober-Bingol, C., and Wober, C. (1993). [Idiopathic headache in childhood and adolescence.] *Nervenarzt*, *64*(12), 753–765.

Klump, K. L. (2013). Puberty as a critical risk period for eating disorders: A review of human and animal studies. *Horm Behav*, *64*(2), 399–410. doi:10.1016/j.yhbeh.2013.02.019

Krug, I., Taborelli, E., Sallis, H., Treasure, J., and Micali, N. (2013). A systematic review of obstetric complications as risk factors for eating disorder and a meta-analysis of delivery method and prematurity. *Physiol Behav*, *109*, 51–62. doi:10.1016/j.physbeh.2012.11.003

Lacey, J. H., and Price, C. (2004). Disturbed families, or families disturbed? *Br J Psychiatry*, *184*(3), 195–196.

Lilenfeld, L. R. (2011). Personality and temperament. *Curr Top Behav Neurosci*, *6*, 3–16. doi:10.1007/7854_2010_86

Malviya, S. A., Kelly, S. D., Greenlee, M. M., Eaton, D. C., Duke, B. J., Bourke, C. H., and Neigh, G. N. (2013). Estradiol stimulates an anti-translocation expression pattern of glucocorticoid co-regulators in a hippocampal cell model. *Physiol Behav*, *122*, 187–192. doi:10.1016/j.physbeh.2013.03.018

McEwen, B. S. (2008). Central effects of stress hormones in health and disease: Understanding the protective and damaging effects of stress and stress mediators. *Eur J Pharmacol*, *583*(2–3), 174–185. doi:10.1016/j.ejphar.2007.11.071

Minuchin, S., Rosman, B., and Baker, L. (1978). *Psychosomatic Families: Treating Anorexia in Context*. Cambridge, MA: Harvard University Press.

Mitchison, D., and Hay, P. J. (2014). The epidemiology of eating disorders: Genetic, environmental, and societal factors. *Clin Epidemiol*, *6*, 89–97. doi:10.2147/CLEP.S40841

Perry, B. D., Pollard, R. A., Blakley, T. L., Baker, W. L., and Vigilante, D. (1995). Childhood trauma, the neurobiology of adaptation, and "use-dependent" development of the brain: How "states" become "traits." *Infant Ment Health J*, *16*(4), 271–291. doi:10.1002/1097-0355(199524)16:4<271::aid-imhj2280160404>3.0.co;2-b

Pike, K. M., Wilfley, D., Hilbert, A., Fairburn, C. G., Dohm, F.-A., and Striegel-Moore, R. H. (2006). Antecedent life events of binge-eating disorder. *Psychiatry Res*, *142*(1), 19–29. doi:10.1016/j.psychres.2005.10.006

Polivy, J., and Herman, C. P. (2002). Causes of eating disorders. *Annu Rev Psychol*, *53*(1), 187–213. doi:10.1146/annurev.psych.53.100901.135103

Quick, V. M., Byrd-Bredbenner, C., and Neumark-Sztainer, D. (2013). Chronic illness and disordered eating: A discussion of the literature. *Adv Nutr*, *4*(3), 277–286. doi:10.3945/an.112.003608

Rayworth, B. B., Wise, L. A., and Harlow, B. L. (2004). Childhood abuse and risk of eating disorders in women. *Epidemiology*, *15*(3), 271–278. doi:10.1097/01.ede.0000120047.07140.9d

Rierdan, J., and Koff, E. (1991). Depressive symptomatology among very early maturing girls. *J Youth Adolesc*, *20*(4), 415–425. doi:10.1007/Bf01537183

Rosenthal, R. (1991). Meta-analysis: A review. *Psychosom Med*, *53*(3), 247–271.

Rutter, M. (1981). Stress, coping and development: Some issues and some questions. *J Child Psychol Psychiatry*, *22*(4), 323–356.

Sachs-Ericsson, N., Keel, P. K., Holland, L., Selby, E. A., Verona, E., Cougle, J. R., and Palmer, E. (2012). Parental disorders, childhood abuse, and binge eating in a large community sample. *Int J Eat Disord*, *45*(3), 316–325. doi:10.1002/eat.20938

Schmidt, U., Humfress, H., and Treasure, J. (1997). The role of general family environment and sexual and physical abuse in the origins of eating disorders. *Eur Eat Disord Rev*, *5*(3), 184–207. doi:10.1002/(sici)1099-0968(199709)5:3<184::aid-erv203>3.0.co;2-b

Scott, J. (1995). Psychotherapy for bipolar disorder. *Br J Psychiatry*, *167*(5), 581–588.

Selye, H. (1955). Stress and disease. *Science*, *122*(3171), 625–631. doi:10.1126/science.122.3171.625

Sharma, S., and Ebadi, M. (2014). Significance of metallothioneins in aging brain. *Neurochem Int*, *65*, 40–48. doi:10.1016/j.neuint.2013.12.009

Sharpe, T. M., Ryst, E., Hinshaw, S. P., and Steiner, H. (1997). Reports of stress: A comparison between eating disordered and non-eating disordered adolescents. *Child Psychiatry Hum Dev*, *28*(2), 117–132.

Skinner, T., McNeil, L., Olaithe, M., Eastwood, P., Hillman, D., Phang, J., … Bucks, R. S. (2013). Predicting uptake of continuous positive airway pressure (CPAP) therapy in obstructive sleep apnoea (OSA): a belief-based theoretical approach. *Sleep Breath*, *17*(4), 1229–1240. doi:10.1007/s11325-013-0828-1

Smolak, L., and Murnen, S. K. (2002). A meta-analytic examination of the relationship between child sexual abuse and eating disorders. *Int J Eat Disord*, *31*(2), 136–150. doi:10.1002/eat.10008

Sterne, J. A. C., Gavaghan, D., and Egger, M. (2000). Publication and related bias in meta-analysis: Power of statistical tests and prevalence in the literature. *J Clin Epidemiol*, *53*(11), 1119–1129. doi:http://dx.doi.org/10.1016/S0895-4356(00)00242-0

Stice, E. (2002). Risk and maintenance factors for eating pathology: A meta-analytic review. *Psychol Bull*, *128*(5), 825–848.

Stice, E., Fisher, M., and Lowe, M. R. (2004). Are dietary restraint scales valid measures of acute dietary restriction? Unobtrusive observational data suggest not. *Psychol Assess*, *16*(1), 51–59. doi:10.1037/1040-3590.16.1.51

Stice, E., Killen, J. D., Hayward, C., and Taylor, C. B. (1998). Support for the continuity hypothesis of bulimic pathology. *J Consult Clin Psychol*, *66*(5), 784–790.

Stice, E., Sysko, R., Roberto, C. A., and Allison, S. (2010). Are dietary restraint scales valid measures of dietary restriction? Additional objective behavioral and biological data suggest not. *Appetite*, *54*(2), 331–339. doi:10.1016/j.appet.2009.12.009

Surgenor, L., and Maguire, S. (2013). Assessment of anorexia nervosa: An overview of universal issues and contextual challenges. *J Eat Disord*, *1*(1), 29.

Treasure, J., Claudino, A. M., and Zucker, N. (2010). Eating disorders. *Lancet*, *375*(9714), 583–593. doi:10.1016/S0140-6736(09)61748-7

Troop, N. A., Holbrey, A., and Treasure, J. L. (1998). Stress, coping, and crisis support in eating disorders. *Int J Eat Disord*, *24*(2), 157–166.

Vince, E., and Walker, I. (2007). A set of meta-analytic studies on the factors associated with disordered eating. *Internet Journal of Mental Health*, *5*(1).

Whiteford, H. A., Degenhardt, L., Rehm, J., Baxter, A. J., Ferrari, A. J., Erskine, H. E., … Vos, T. (2013). Global burden of disease attributable to mental and substance use disorders: Findings from the Global Burden of Disease Study 2010. *Lancet*, *382*(9904), 1575–1586. doi:http://dx.doi.org/10.1016/S0140-6736(13)61611-6

Wonderlich, S. A., Wilsnack, R. W., Wilsnack, S. C., and Harris, T. R. (1996). Childhood sexual abuse and bulimic behavior in a nationally representative sample. *Am J Public Health*, *86*(8), 1082–1086.

Yates, K. F., Sweat, V., Yau, P. L., Turchiano, M. M., and Convit, A. (2012). Impact of metabolic syndrome on cognition and brain: A selected review of the literature. *Arterioscler Thromb Vasc Biol*, *32*(9), 2060–2067. doi:10.1161/ATVBAHA.112.252759

12

Stress and Musculoskeletal Injury

Meredith M. Hartzell, Cameron D. T. Dodd, and Robert J. Gatchel

Introduction

Prevalence and Costs of Musculoskeletal Injury

Pain may account for up to 80 percent of all physician visits (Gatchel, Peng, Peters, Fuchs, and Turk, 2007), and musculoskeletal pain from overuse injuries affects 33 percent of adults and accounts for 29 percent of lost workdays due to illness (US Bureau of Labor Statistics, 2011; IASP, 2009). In the United States, occupational musculoskeletal injuries are highly prevalent and account for higher costs to the health-care system than any other type of occupational disorder (Hernandez and Peterson, 2012). The Department of Labor reported 34 cases of musculoskeletal disorders per 10,000 full-time workers in 2010. It is estimated that the costs associated with health-care utilization, lost work days and compensation for occupational musculoskeletal disorders is approximately $100 billion per year (Gatchel, McGeary, McGeary, and Lippe, 2014).

Stress

One of the factors that can exacerbate the symptoms of musculoskeletal injury, and prolong recovery time, is stress. Stress is an inherently ambiguous term, applying to any disturbance of homeostasis. Contrary to popular belief, stress does not necessarily have to be negative; it is just, by definition, change. Positive change is called eustress, while negative stress is called distress. However, both forms of stress include a process of stimuli, appraisal, and response. The stimuli are anything perceived as harmful or requiring excessive exertion. Appraisal is when the threat is analyzed and evaluated, taking into account the stimuli, context, mitigating factors, and personality, to determine if or how strong a response is required (Lazarus, 1993). Mitigating factors alter the individual's emotional state. For example, isolation can increase the strength of the stress response (Detillion, Craft, Glasper, Prendergast, and DeVries, 2004).

The Handbook of Stress and Health: A Guide to Research and Practice, First Edition.
Edited by Cary L. Cooper and James Campbell Quick.
© 2017 John Wiley & Sons, Ltd. Published 2017 by John Wiley & Sons, Ltd.

After a stimulus has been appraised as a threat, the sympathetic nervous system (SNS) is activated, initiating a "fight or flight" response. Blood is diverted from the digestive, integumentary, and reproductive systems to the larger skeletal muscles. In addition, heart rate, blood pressure, and respiration increase, to distribute nutrients and oxygen to the muscles in preparation for immediate action.

The SNS can be broken down into two main mechanisms. First, there is a very fast, but short-lived response via direct synaptic transmission, and then a second response that maintains elevated levels of activity (i.e., heart and respiration rate) through the endocrine system. Epinephrine is released from the adrenal and sympathetic neurons, causing a slower, but often more powerful response through receptor binding. Second, the SNS response is supported by the hypothalamic-pituitary-adrenocortical (HPA) axis response, which is activated at the same time, but takes up to half an hour to be effective. The HPA response is marked by the release of corticotrophin-releasing hormones that eventually release corticosteroids (also known as cortisol), which is an anti-inflammatory with lasting metabolic effects. Both the SNS and the HPA axis provide skeletal muscles with as much oxygen and glucose as possible in complementary and redundant systems.

An acute stress response is favorable in natural selection, allowing for increased survival rates. In humans, short-term stress can even have some health benefits. The Yerkes–Dodson Law states that performance in tasks is improved by moderate levels of stress; however, when stressed too much, efficiency declines (Yerkes and Dodson, 1908). Optimal stress levels differ among individuals, and are adjusted based on the appraisal process, the resources/coping techniques possessed, and even personality. For instance, it appears that extraverts are more likely to require additional SNS activation than introverts (Adler, 1991).

Chronic stress has several deleterious effects. For instance, in an emergency, the anti-inflammatory properties of cortisol are important; it maintains blood flow through the body, decreasing the likelihood of blood collecting in injured areas, and increases mobility by reducing swelling in the joints. This is accomplished by immune suppression and the decrease of cytokines that cause swelling by dilating blood vessels and recruiting additional immune cells. In the short term, immune suppression is unimportant, but in the long term, consistently high levels of cortisol (i.e., chronic stress) cause higher rates of disease and infection (Cohen, 1995) and slower rates of wound healing, due to less blood and oxygen at the injury site (Finestone, Alfeeli, and Fisher, 2008). Stress can affect injury frequency and duration (Jacobs, Hincapie, and Cassidy, 2012), and moderate to high stress was indicated as a risk factor for musculoskeletal injury (Rice, Mays, and Gable, 2009). High levels of distress are also a risk factor for higher pain intensity (Egwu and Nwuga, 2008) and pain without a known origin (Lampe et al., 1998).

These long stretches of immobilization can lead to "deconditioning syndrome," or a physical and psychological loss of fitness (Mayer and Gatchel, 1988). If muscles go unused, they lose the calcium required to maintain muscle contractions and the nitrogen necessary to build proteins integral to muscle mass. Capillary and mitochondrial density decreases as well, in as few as 15 days of immobility, meaning that there is lower blood flow and, subsequently, fewer nutrients to convert and utilize as energy (Holloszy, 1975; Houston, Bentzen, and Larsen, 1979). These factors combine to show dramatic results: 37 percent of muscle mass is lost by the time a person has been inactive for three months (Staron, Hagerman, and Hikida, 1981). Perhaps even more startling is that, in an attempt to be efficient, the brain goes through synaptic pruning, removing unused synaptic connections meant for muscle activation and generally decreasing neuromuscular coordination (Cassisi, Robinson, O'Conner, and MacMillan, 1993; Danneels et al., 2002).

Other consequences of prolonged stress include fatigue, caused by the constant activation of the SNS and HPA axis, which consumes energy; and elevated cardiovascular and cardiopulmonary pressures, caused by the increased heart rate induced by the SNS and cortisol, which can lead to heart disease. Because blood flow is diverted away from the digestive tract and reproductive organs, constriction of the blood vessels may lead to stomach ulcers, suppression of ovulation, impotency, and loss of libido (Sapolsky, 1992). All of these factors can add up. It was estimated that the cost of stress upon employers alone was £370 million, or roughly US$555 million, in 2003 (Johnson and Cooper, 2003).

Specific Stressors Related to Musculoskeletal Injury

Workplace Stressors

There are many workplace risk factors that exacerbate the connection between musculoskeletal injuries and stress. The first is burnout, a result of chronic job stress. Burnout increases muscle tension, providing a direct link from workplace stress to musculoskeletal injury, although it is also associated with a number of negative work outcomes, including poor work quality and exhaustion. Especially in blue-collar employment, poor work quality and fatigue can easily lead to an increased propensity for injury (Liao, Arvey, Butler, and Nutting, 2001). Twenty-nine percent of Americans reported being very sleepy or actually having fallen asleep at work in the past month (National Sleep Foundation, 2008), which increases the risk for occupational accidents and injuries (Åkerstedt, Fredlund, Gillberg, and Jansson, 2002; Nakata et al., 2005; Simpson, Wadsworth, Moss, and Smith, 2005). Workers report feeling more at risk for workplace hazards when they are burnt out and exhausted (Leiter and Robichaud, 1997).

Many other stressful situations also exist in the workplace, such as role ambiguity (e.g., not having clearly delineated tasks), role conflict (e.g., having orders that are in direct opposition to each other), interpersonal conflict, and high workload (DeArmond and Chen, 2009). Lack of work–life balance can be stressful as well, and the effects of burnout can spill over into home life (Johnson et al., 2009; Maslach, 2004), causing additional interpersonal stress. In the same vein, high levels of workplace aggression, both physical and psychosocial, are associated with increased risk for musculoskeletal injury (Zhou, Yang, and Spector, 2015).

Some jobs are more stressful than others. Emergency services, teaching, social services, customer service, and prison guarding are among the most stressful jobs, in part because they require "emotional labor" (Zapf, 2002), have the threat of violence, or lack control (Johnson et al., 2009). Workloads also play a role in stress: those with high workloads experience higher cortisol levels (DeArmond and Chen, 2009). Having a higher socioeconomic status is also a risk factor for increased fatigue and stress (Schneider and Stone, 2014).

Other labor factors play a role in the development of musculoskeletal injury. Jobs that involve lifting, twisting, and bending are more likely to cause injuries, and people with previous injuries are more likely to reinjure themselves (Bigos et al., 1986), perhaps because of a "damaged goods" perception (Barnes, 1991). Experience on the job is another significant factor: the less time on the job, and the lower the supervisor performance rating of the employee, the higher the risk for occupational musculoskeletal injury (Barnes, 1991). Amount of travel is also influential, with those who travel more having increased likelihood of back injuries

(Biering-Sørensen and Thomsen, 1986), perhaps in part due to the high stress involved in commuting. Other workplace environmental factors, such as noise levels, lighting quality, and perceiving the job as repetitive or boring (Frymoyer and Cats-Baril, 1987) can also increase the prevalence of musculoskeletal injury through a stress pathway.

Obesity

Those who are obese may experience more stress, as stress can influence eating choices (Wardle, Steptoe, Oliver, and Lipsey, 2000). In addition, intra-abdominal fat stores can increase the release of glucocorticoids (Schulte et al., 2007), presenting a cause-or-effect issue. Obesity increases the risk of occupational musculoskeletal injury, particularly vibration-induced injury. This may be because safety equipment is often limited in large sizes (Schulte et al., 2007; Wearing, Henning, Byrne, Steele, and Hills, 2006), or has not been tested effectively for heavier body weights (Hsiao, Bradtmiller, and Whitestone, 2003; Ilmarinen, Lindholm, Koivistoinen, and Helistén, 2004). Obesity is also associated with other musculoskeletal disorders, such as carpal tunnel syndrome and osteoarthritis. Lastly, those who are obese may experience discrimination, both social and occupational, based on their weight (Schulte et al., 2007), which could lead to higher levels of interpersonal workplace and social stress, and may influence eating choices, creating a vicious cycle.

Catastrophic Events and Trauma

Previous research demonstrates that catastrophic events increase stress levels, which can exacerbate musculoskeletal injury recovery. For instance, one of the main symptoms of the Three Mile Island nuclear meltdown was noted as psychosocial stress (Baum, Gatchel, Fleming, and Lake, 1981; Bromet, 1980). It has also been found that large-scale disasters (such as the terrorist attacks on 9/11) may increase pain on a community level (Polatin, Young, Mayer, and Gatchel, 2005), especially when the media constantly replay the incident, creating effects similar to posttraumatic stress disorder (PTSD).

Other traumatic events do not necessarily take place on such large a scale. For instance, motor vehicle accidents are typically personal rather than widespread. Being at fault for causing the incident, blaming others, receiving injury compensation, and avoidance of distressing thoughts can lead to increased stress and emotional disturbance (Littleton et al., 2011; Littleton et al., 2012; Rosenbloom, Khan, McCartney, and Katz, 2013). Those with prior anxiety disorders, rumination about the trauma, lack of social support, and higher perceived threat to life were more likely to develop PTSD after a motor vehicle accident (Heron-Delaney, Kenardy, Charlton, and Matsuoka, 2013).

Psychosocial Stressors

It is generally accepted that chronic stress has an impact on mental well-being and physical health. Higher rates of psychopathology are found in chronic pain populations (Dersh et al., 2007a; Dersh, Gatchel, Polatin, and Mayer, 2002; Dersh et al., 2007b), with 39 percent diagnosed prior to their pain condition. A number of other psychosocial problems can exacerbate both the musculoskeletal injury experience and the stress component, including personality factors, depressive symptoms, and social factors. One study found that self-reported stress levels alone were risk factors for musculoskeletal injury symptoms interfering with job capacity (Rice et al., 2009), and another study found that psychosocial stress is much higher in dancers at risk for a musculoskeletal injury (Air, 2013).

Personality factors may influence either stress or musculoskeletal injury. In particular, having neuroticism and disconnection to reality were associated with higher job stress (Gramstad, Gjestad, and Haver, 2013), and low novelty-seeking was also indicative of high stress (Tyrka et al., 2007). Personality disorders may also interfere with treatment for musculoskeletal injury, causing noncompliance, negative interactions with health-care providers, and an unwillingness to change behavior (Wesley, Polatin, Gatchel, and Gatchel, 2000).

Depressive symptoms are another stressor that can influence musculoskeletal injury progression In pain patients, symptoms such as disturbed sleep, worry, and low energy are particularly common (Rush, Polatin, and Gatchel, 2000). Depressive symptoms can influence how much pain interferes with daily function and mobility, and the frequency of pain intrusion/breakthrough pain (Von Korff and Simon, 1996). Expectations after a musculoskeletal injury influence how severe future symptoms will be (Ferrari and Russell, 2010). Therefore, a patient with depressive symptoms who is demonstrating Beck's "cognitive triad" of negative thinking will likely have longer recovery times than those who are optimistic. Rectifying these cognitive errors may be particularly difficult because coping with chronic pain takes additional resources (Wesley et al., 2000). Stressed patients may focus on the negative aspects only, overgeneralize their negative experiences to other areas of their lives, and feel personally responsible for negative occurrences, all of which can delay musculoskeletal injury recovery (Lefebvre, 1981). One recent study found that having depressive symptoms alone is enough to increase stress levels (Phillips, Carroll, and Der, 2015).

Overall dissatisfaction with social relationships (Magora, 1973), especially family stress (Payne and Norfleet, 1986), are linked to low back pain. Examples of stress at home may include home life: instability, interference with work, familial problems, and lack of coping skills (Fan, Blumenthal, Watkins, and Sherwood, 2015). Stress can also influence financial planning, with those under more stress taking excessive risks, which can cause additional problems (Robinson, Bond, and Roiser, 2015). Particularly stressful, however, is intimate partner violence. To begin with, physical violence can cause musculoskeletal injury, especially of the head and neck. Recent literature, therefore, implores musculoskeletal clinicians to educate themselves and their patients, and to screen for domestic abuse (Sprague et al., 2013). There is also a link between nonphysical abuse and musculoskeletal injury: health-care workers who were verbally abused were more likely to have musculoskeletal injury (Sabbath et al., 2014). In addition, the link between central sensitivity syndromes, many of which have a musculoskeletal component, and abuse is well known for exacerbating the progression of illness (Häuser, Kosseva, Üceyler, Klose, and Sommer, 2011; Seth and Teichman, 2008; Wilson, 2010). There is also evidence to suggest that those who had early childhood abuse of any sort are more predisposed to psychosocial distress and disability, and are less likely to return to work after musculoskeletal injury (McMahon, Gatchel, Polatin, and Mayer, 1997).

Secondary Gain

Secondary gain, or the benefits one receives from an injury, is composed of both social and economic factors. Social factors include people paying more attention to an injured person, or completing undesirable tasks for the injured person; having more time to spend on pleasurable activities; and increased feelings of safety, security, or dependence (Leeman, Polatin,

Gatchel, and Kishino, 2000). Economic and occupational factors are more likely in patients who were injured at work, and may either compound social issues or be individual problems. These secondary gain factors include anger at the employer; lower motivation to return to work; tax-free temporary income benefits, protection from legal obligations such as alimony, court appearances, and parole/probation demands; the ability to redirect careers through job retraining (Leeman et al., 2000); and waiver of mortgages and other loans (Polatin and Gatchel, 1997). Secondary gain, therefore, presents a balance in competing personal goals (Crombez, Eccleston, Van Damme, Vlaeyen, and Karoly, 2012). For example, they may be debating the "perks" of their injury, such as increased attention and care, with the negative factors, such as increased pain severity and disability.

Assessment of Stress in a Musculoskeletal Population

There are a number of different ways to assess stress, but they fall into two main categories: physiological biomarkers for stress, and psychosocial self-report questionnaires. Observable physiological biomarkers of stress include increased heart rate, sweating, rapid breathing, pupil dilation, and involuntary muscle contraction (spasms). Blood can also be tested for levels of cortisol and its predecessors, cytokines, epinephrine, norepinephrine, or growth hormone. Epinephrine and norepinephrine can also be found in saliva or urine (Baum, Grunberg, and Singer, 1982). When stressed, cortisol levels increase due to activation of the HPA axis, and cytokine concentrations drop due to higher levels of cortisol. Levels of epinephrine and norepinephrine increase due to the activation of the SNS. Growth hormone concentrations increase during periods of stress to increase the amount of available energy to fuel stress responses.

Typically, self-report questionnaires are more cost-effective than laboratory studies, although they are not as objective (Solivan, Xiong, Harville, and Buekens, 2015). Musculoskeletal injury and stress-specific questionnaires include the Impact of Events Scale (IES) and the Distress Risk Assessment Method. The IES was designed specifically to combine musculoskeletal injury and posttraumatic stress aspects together, and includes elements of cognitive and emotional stress (Brunet, St-Hilaire, Jehel, and King, 2003; Sullivan et al., 2009). The Distress Risk Assessment Method questionnaire measures psychosocial distress in orthopedic patients (Carragee, Alamin, Miller, and Carragee, 2005; Daubs et al., 2010; Trief, Grant, and Fredrickson, 2000). It is also important to assess pain behaviors in person, which will provide information on potential secondary gain issues that may delay treatment. Pain behaviors can include groaning, making grimacing faces, guarding the body part or holding it rigid, limping, rubbing painful body parts, asking for assistance, and using unnecessary assistive devices or using the devices excessively (Leeman et al., 2000).

The next set of self-report questionnaires for stress could be adapted to musculoskeletal injury populations with little difficulty. To address occupational stress in the workplace, use of An Organizational Stress Screening Tool (ASSET) is recommended. ASSET measures employees' exposure to stress and recognizes factors such as job satisfaction, organizational commitment, work–life balance, job overload, and communication that may modulate the stress experience. ASSET also has subscales for psychosocial well-being and physical health (Cartwright and Cooper, 2002; Johnson and Cooper, 2003). Another questionnaire developed for occupational stress is the Occupational Stress Indicator (OSI). However, the OSI works better for white-collar or management positions (Cooper, Sloan, and Williams, 1988).

In clinical health-care populations, not specific to musculoskeletal injury, other questionnaires are used. The Perceived Stress Scale (PSS) (Cohen, Kamarck, and Mermelstein, 1983) assesses event-related stress; feeling out of control or rushed; and stress reactions. Another useful measure is the Depression Anxiety Stress Scales (DASS) (Gomez, Summers, Summers, Wolf, and Summers, 2014; Lovibond and Lovibond, 1995), with the subscales of stress, depression, and anxiety. The stress scale includes questions on tension, impatience, overreactivity, irritability/agitation, and difficulty relaxing. Stress can also be assessed in a daily diary format, with Likert scales measuring stress levels at a given period of time (Schneider and Stone, 2014).

Treatment

Preventative Occupational Treatment

There are many preventative approaches that decrease the likelihood of musculoskeletal injury occurrence or exacerbation in the workplace, such as changing employee posture; the work performed (either type or variety); the equipment used; or the layout of the work area (Denis, St-Vincent, Imbeau, Jetté, and Nastasia, 2008). One study found that an ergonomics intervention, including work station assessment and stretching exercises, was effective in decreasing pain, job stress, and functional limitations (Feuerstein et al., 2004). Another found that muscle biofeedback during daily tasks preventatively decreases muscle tension (Faucett, Garry, Nadler, and Ettare, 2002).

Stress-Specific Treatment

After a catastrophic/traumatic event, it is important to complete critical incident stress debriefing, which is when victims are allowed to share observations, facts, and emotional reactions about the event to help minimize development of stress reactions (Sattler, Boyd, and Kirsch, 2014). It is also important to plan ahead for traumatic events, identifying populations that may have higher stress reaction risk and setting aside resources for credible risk communication. Patients may believe that their level of danger is much higher than the reality, which can increase stress and anxiety levels (Gray and Ropeik, 2002; Mullin, 2002) and burdens both the physical and mental health-care systems. People may be more likely to become stressed if they are unsure of the situation, feel that the risk is personal (i.e., believe that it could happen to them) or new, or if they feel they cannot control the situation. Credible risk communication addresses these problems, especially when education is lacking (Gray and Ropeik, 2002). Both health-care professionals and the media can provide support.

Other stress interventions include self-guided interventions. Web-based interventions are typically popular, cost-effective, and have high efficacy. One study found that a self-guided treatment for stress delivered by smartphone and/or computer decreased symptoms of stress and increased work and social functioning (Proudfoot et al., 2013). Another effective treatment for stress and pain is Mindfulness-Based Stress Reduction (MBSR) therapy. MBSR focuses attention on the present moment through a variety of exercises and meditations to reduce stress, anxiety, and depression (Serpa, Taylor, and Tillisch, 2014).

Medical Management for Musculoskeletal Injury

The first line of treatment for musculoskeletal injury is primary rehabilitation, which controls pain and prepares the body for proper healing. Therapy includes over-the-counter analgesics, muscle relaxants/opioids in rare cases, and physical agents such as ultrasound, heat, cold, or electrical stimulation. If patients are unresponsive, or the injury is particularly severe, patients proceed to secondary rehabilitation. The goals of secondary rehabilitation include prevention of physical deconditioning, medication habituation, and adverse psychosocial reactions. It also includes mobilization and strengthening of the injured area and restoration of function. If secondary rehabilitation is unsuccessful, then tertiary rehabilitation takes place (Mayer and Polatin, 2000).

The most effective tertiary intervention is interdisciplinary treatment. Interdisciplinary treatment follows the biopsychosocial model, which treats the biological, psychological, and social components of injury (Gatchel and Okifuji, 2006; Gatchel et al., 2014). One specific interdisciplinary program is functional restoration, which focuses on return to function rather than pain reduction. Functional restoration consists of a medically supervised, quantitatively directed exercise progression combined with a multimodal disability management program (MDMP). The components of MDMP include cognitive-behavioral therapy (CBT), stress management/biofeedback training, education, and vocational reintegration (Gatchel, 2005; Mayer and Gatchel, 1988). CBT and vocational reintegration should address any secondary gain factors involved. The stress management component of CBT can include many different factors. Goal-setting can be a particularly useful technique, as it can help patients develop positive social support and a perception of control. It has been found that perceived control decreases stress perception, arousal level, and pain sensation when undergoing experimental shock (Geer, Davison, and Gatchel, 1970).

There are also a number of relatively new techniques that may be useful in musculoskeletal injury patients with high stress. Current evidence points to the use of vitamin D to help maintain optimal muscle function and to reduce inflammation, pain, and myopathy (Shuler, Wingate, Moore, and Giangarra, 2012). Another recent treatment is hyperbaric oxygen therapy. Injuries may progress from acute to chronic because of insufficient oxygen early in the healing process, potentially caused by lack of inflammation due to elevated cortisol levels associated with stress (Finestone et al., 2008) or by hyperventilation (Schleifer, Ley, and Spalding, 2002). Hyperbaric oxygen therapy supplies wounds with enough oxygen to ameliorate the detrimental side-effects of stress and normalizes healing rates (Gajendrareddy, Sen, Horan, and Marucha, 2005).

Conclusions

Musculoskeletal injuries are widespread and quite costly, both to the individual and to society. Although it is widely recognized that stress can significantly impact the progression of a musculoskeletal injury from acute to chronic, and can decrease the chances of effective rehabilitation, few studies actually look at the direct effects of perceived stress on musculoskeletal injury, or even the biological process of how stress might influence musculoskeletal injury recovery. It is clear, however, that stresses from the workplace, home life, interpersonal relationships, personality characteristics, and mental disorders all play a role in the prevalence and treatment of musculoskeletal injury. Finally, many of the biopsychosocial factors discussed in the present chapter are more thoroughly reviewed by Gatchel and Shultz (2014).

References

Adler, G. (1991). [The hyperarousal hypothesis: New aspects of a neurophysiologic concept of endogenous psychoses.] *Fortschritte der Neurologie-Psychiatrie*, *59*(6), 203–206.

Air, M. E. (2013). Psychological distress among dancers seeking outpatient treatment for musculoskeletal injury. *Journal of Dance Medicine and Science, 17*(3), 115–125.

Åkerstedt, T., Fredlund, P., Gillberg, M., and Jansson, B. (2002). A prospective study of fatal occupational accidents – relationship to sleeping difficulties and occupational factors. *Journal of Sleep Research, 11*(1), 69–71.

Barnes, D. (1991). Social factors affecting back pain. In T. G. Mayer, V. Mooney and R. J. Gatchel (Eds.), *Contemporary Conservative Care for Painful Spinal Disorders* (pp. 143–148). Philadelphia: Lea & Febiger.

Baum, A., Gatchel, R. J., Fleming, R., and Lake, C. R. (1981). *Chronic and Acute Stress Associated with the Three Mile Island Accident and Decontamination: Preliminary Findings of a Longitudinal Study.* Technical report submitted to the U.S. Nuclear Regulatory Commission. Washington, DC: Government Printing Office.

Baum, A., Grunberg, N. E., and Singer, J. E. (1982). The use of psychological and neuroendocrinological measurements in the study of stress. *Health psychology, 1*(3), 217.

Biering-Sørensen, F., and Thomsen, C. (1986). Medical, social and occupational history as risk indicators for low-back trouble in a general population. *Spine, 11*(7), 720–725.

Bigos, S. J., Spengler, D. M., Martin, N. A., Zeh, J., Fisher, L., Nachemson, A., and Wang, M. H. (1986). Back injuries in industry: A retrospective study. II. Injury factors. *Spine, 11*(3), 246–251.

Bromet, E. (1980). *Preliminary Report on the Mental Health of Three Mile Island Residents.* Pittsburgh: Western Psychiatric Institute.

Brunet, A., St-Hilaire, A., Jehel, L., and King, S. (2003). Validation of a French version of the impact of event scale-revised. *Canadian Journal of Psychiatry/Revue Canadienne de Psychiatrie, 48*(1), 56–61.

Carragee, E. J., Alamin, T. F., Miller, J. L., and Carragee, J. M. (2005). Discographic, MRI and psychosocial determinants of low back pain disability and remission: A prospective study in subjects with benign persistent back pain. *Spine Journal, 5*(1), 24–35.

Cartwright, S., and Cooper, C. L. (2002). *ASSET: An Organisational Stress Screening Tool: The Management Guide.* Manchester, UK: RCL Ltd.

Cassisi, J. E., Robinson, M. E., O'Conner, P., and MacMillan, M. (1993). Trunk strength and lumbar paraspinal muscle activity during isometric exercise in chronic low-back pain patients and controls. *Spine, 18*(2), 245–251.

Cohen, S. (1995). Psychological stress and susceptibility to upper respiratory infections. *American Journal of Respiratory and Critical Care Medicine, 152*(4), S53–S58.

Cohen, S., Kamarck, T., and Mermelstein, R. (1983). A global measure of perceived stress. *Journal of Health and Social Behavior, 24*(4), 385–396.

Cooper, C. L., Sloan, S. J., and Williams, S. (1988). *Occupational Stress Indicator Management Guide.* Windsor, UK: NFER-Nelson.

Crombez, G., Eccleston, C., Van Damme, S., Vlaeyen, J. W. S., and Karoly, P. (2012). Fear-avoidance model of chronic pain: The next generation. *Clinical Journal of Pain, 28*(6), 475–483.

Danneels, L. A., Coorevits, P. L., Cools, A. M., Vanderstraeten, G. G., Cambier, D. C., Witvrouw, E. E., and De, C. H. J. (2002). Differences in electromyographic activity in the multifidus muscle and the iliocostalis lumborum between healthy subjects and patients with sub-acute and chronic low back pain. *European Spine Journal, 11*(1), 13–19.

Daubs, M. D., Patel, A. A., Willick, S. E., Kendall, R. W., Hansen, P., Petron, D. J., and Brodke, D. S. (2010). Clinical impression versus standardized questionnaire: The spinal surgeon's ability to assess psychological distress. *Journal of Bone and Joint Surgery. American Volume, 92*(18), 2878–2883.

DeArmond, S., and Chen, P. Y. (2009). Occupational stress and workplace sleepiness. In A. M. Rossi, J. C. Quick and P. L. Perrewé (Eds.), *Stress and Quality of Working Life: The Positive and Negative* (pp. 41–65). Charlotte, NC: Information Age.

Denis, D., St-Vincent, M., Imbeau, D., Jetté, C., and Nastasia, I. (2008). Intervention practices in musculoskeletal disorder prevention: A critical literature review. *Applied Ergonomics, 39*(1), 1–14.

Dersh, J., Gatchel, R. J., Polatin, P., and Mayer, T. (2002). Prevalence of psychiatric disorders in patients with chronic work-related musculoskeletal pain disability. *Journal of Occupational and Environmental Medicine/American College of Occupational and Environmental Medicine, 44*(5), 459–468.

Dersh, J., Mayer, T., Gatchel, R., Towns, B., Theodore, B., and Polatin, P. B. (2007a). Do psychiatric disorders affect functional restoration outcomes in chronic disabling occupational spinal disorders? *Spine, 32,* 1045–1051.

Dersh, J., Mayer, T., Gatchel, R. J., Towns, B., Theodore, B., and Polatin, P. (2007b). Psychiatric comorbidity in chronic disabling occupational spinal disorders has minimal impact on functional restoration socioeconomic outcomes. *Spine, 32*(17), 1917–1925.

Detillion, C. E., Craft, T. K. S., Glasper, E. R., Prendergast, B. J., and DeVries, A. C. (2004). Social facilitation of wound healing. *Psychoneuroendocrinology*, *29*(8), 1004–1011.

Egwu, M. O., and Nwuga, V. C. B. (2008). Relationship between low back pain and life-stressing events among Nigerian and Caucasian patients. *Physiotherapy*, *94*(2), 133–140.

Fan, L., Blumenthal, J. A., Watkins, L. L., and Sherwood, A. (2015). Work and home stress: Associations with anxiety and depression symptoms. *Occupational Medicine (Oxford)*, *65*(2), 110–116.

Faucett, J., Garry, M., Nadler, D., and Ettare, D. (2002). A test of two training interventions to prevent work-related musculoskeletal disorders of the upper extremity. *Applied Ergonomics*, *33*(4), 337–347.

Ferrari, R., and Russell, A. S. (2010). Correlations between coping styles and symptom expectation for whiplash injury. *Clinical Rheumatology*, *29*(11), 1245–1249.

Feuerstein, M., Nicholas, R. A., Huang, G. D., Dimberg, L., Ali, D., and Rogers, H. (2004). Job stress management and ergonomic intervention for work-related upper extremity symptoms. *Applied Ergonomics*, *35*(6), 565–574.

Finestone, H. M., Alfeeli, A., and Fisher, W. A. (2008). Stress-induced physiologic changes as a basis for the biopsychosocial model of chronic musculoskeletal pain: A new theory? *Clinical Journal of Pain*, *24*(9), 767–775.

Frymoyer, J. W., and Cats-Baril, W. (1987). Predictors of low back pain disability. *Clinical Orthopaedics and Related Research*, No. *221*, 89–98.

Gajendrareddy, P. K., Sen, C. K., Horan, M. P., and Marucha, P. T. (2005). Hyperbaric oxygen therapy ameliorates stress-impaired dermal wound healing. *Brain, Behavior, and Immunity*, *19*(3), 217–222.

Gatchel, R. J. (2005). *Clinical Essentials of Pain Management*. Washington, DC: American Psychological Association.

Gatchel, R. J., McGeary, D. D., McGeary, C. A., and Lippe, B. (2014). Interdisciplinary chronic pain management: Past, present, and future. *American Psychologist*, *69*(2), 119–130.

Gatchel, R. J., and Okifuji, A. (2006). Evidence-based scientific data documenting the treatment and cost-effectiveness of comprehensive pain programs for chronic nonmalignant pain. *Journal of Pain*, *7*(11), 779–793.

Gatchel, R. J., Peng, Y. B., Peters, M. L., Fuchs, P. N., and Turk, D. C. (2007). The biopsychosocial approach to chronic pain: Scientific advances and future directions. *Psychological Bulletin*, *133*(4), 581–624.

Gatchel, R. J., and Schultz, I. (2014). *Handbook of Musculoskeletal Pain and Disability Disorders in the Workplace*. New York: Springer.

Geer, J. H., Davison, G. C., and Gatchel, R. I. (1970). Reduction of stress in humans through nonveridical perceived control of aversive stimulation. *Journal of Personality and Social Psychology*, *16*(4), 731–738.

Gomez, R., Summers, M., Summers, A., Wolf, A., and Summers, J. (2014). Depression Anxiety Stress Scales-21: Measurement and structural invariance across ratings of men and women. *Assessment*, *21*(4), 418–426.

Gramstad, T. O., Gjestad, R., and Haver, B. (2013). Personality traits predict job stress, depression and anxiety among junior physicians. *BMC Medical Education*, *13*, 150.

Gray, G. M., and Ropeik, D. P. (2002). Dealing with the dangers of fear: The role of risk communication. *Health Affairs (Project Hope)*, *21*(6), 106–116.

Häuser, W., Kosseva, M., Üceyler, N., Klose, P., and Sommer, C. (2011). Emotional, physical, and sexual abuse in fibromyalgia syndrome: A systematic review with meta-analysis. *Arthritis Care and Research*, *63*(6), 808–820.

Hernandez, A. M., and Peterson, A. L. (2012). Work-related musculoskeletal disorders and pain. In R. J. Gatchel, and I. Z. Schultz (Eds.), *Handbook of Occupational Health and Wellness* (pp. 63–86). New York: Springer.

Heron-Delaney, M., Kenardy, J., Charlton, E., and Matsuoka, Y. (2013). A systematic review of predictors of post-traumatic stress disorder (PTSD) for adult road traffic crash survivors. *Injury*, *44*(11), 1413–1422.

Holloszy, J. O. (1975). Adaptation of skeletal muscle to endurance exercise. *Medicine and Science in Sports*, *7*(3), 155–164.

Houston, M. E., Bentzen, H., and Larsen, H. (1979). Interrelationships between skeletal muscle adaptations and performance as studied by detraining and retraining. *Acta Physiologica Scandinavica*, *105*(2), 163–170.

Hsiao, H., Bradtmiller, B., and Whitestone, J. (2003). Sizing and fit of fall-protection harnesses. *Ergonomics*, *46*(12), 1233–1258.

IASP (International Association for the Study of Pain) (2009). Musculoskeletal pain. At http://www.iasp-pain.org/files/Content/ContentFolders/GlobalYearAgainstPain2/MusculoskeletalPainFactSheets/MusculoskeletalPain_Final.pdf (accessed July 2016).

Ilmarinen, R., Lindholm, H., Koivistoinen, K., and Helistén, P. (2004). Physiological evaluation of chemical protective suit systems (CPSS) in hot conditions. *International Journal of Occupational Safety and Ergonomics: JOSE*, *10*(3), 215–226.

Jacobs, C. L., Hincapie, C. A., and Cassidy, J. D. (2012). Musculoskeletal injuries and pain in dancers: A systematic review update. *Journal of Dance Medicine and Science*, *16*(2), 72–84.

Johnson, S., and Cooper, C. (2003). The construct validity of the ASSET stress measure. *Stress and Health*, *19*(3), 181–185.

Johnson, S., Cooper, C., Cartwright, S., Donald, I., Taylor, P., and Cook, C. (2009). The experience of work-related stress across occupations. In A. M. Rossi, J. C. Quick and P. L. Perrewé (Eds.), *Stress and Quality of Working Life: The Positive and Negative* (pp. 67–77). Charlotte, NC: Information Age.

Lampe, A., Söllner, W., Krismer, M., Rumpold, G., Kantner-Rumplmair, W., Ogon, M., and Rathner, G. (1998). The impact of stressful life events on exacerbation of chronic low-back pain. *Journal of Psychosomatic Research*, *44*(5), 555–563.

Lazarus, R. S. (1993). From psychological stress to the emotions: A history of changing outlooks. *Annual Review of Psychology*, *44*, 1–21.

Leeman, G., Polatin, P., Gatchel, R., and Kishino, N. (2000). Managing secondary gain in patients with pain-associated disability: A clinical perspective. *Journal of Workers Compensation*, *9*(4), 25–44.

Lefebvre, M. F. (1981). Cognitive distortion and cognitive errors in depressed psychiatric and low back pain patients. *Journal of Consulting and Clinical Psychology*, *49*(4), 517–525.

Leiter, M. P., and Robichaud, L. (1997). Relationships of occupational hazards with burnout: An assessment of measures and models. *Journal of Occupational Health Psychology*, *2*(1), 35–44.

Liao, H., Arvey, R. D., Butler, R. J., and Nutting, S. M. (2001). Correlates of work injury frequency and duration among firefighters. *Journal of Occupational Health Psychology*, *6*(3), 229–242.

Littleton, S. M., Cameron, I. D., Poustie, S. J., Hughes, D. C., Robinson, B. J., Neeman, T., and Smith, P. N. (2011). The association of compensation on longer term health status for people with musculoskeletal injuries following road traffic crashes: Emergency department inception cohort study. *Injury*, *42*(9), 927–933.

Littleton, S. M., Hughes, D. C., Poustie, S. J., Robinson, B. J., Neeman, T., Smith, P. N., and Cameron, I. D. (2012). The influence of fault on health in the immediate post-crash period following road traffic crashes. *Injury*, *43*(9), 1586–1592.

Lovibond, S. H., and Lovibond, P. F. (1995). *Manual for the Depression Anxiety Stress Scales*. Sydney: Psychology Foundation.

Magora, A. (1973). Investigation of the relation between low back pain and occupation. V. Psychological aspects. *Scandinavian Journal of Rehabilitation Medicine*, *5*(4), 191–196.

Maslach, C. (2004). Understanding burnout: Work and family issues. In D. F. Halpern and S. G. Murphy (Eds.), *Changing the Metaphor: From Work–Family Balance to Work–Family Interaction* (pp. 99–114). Mahwah, NJ: Lawrence Erlbaum.

Mayer, T. G., and Gatchel, R. J. (1988). *Functional Restoration for Spinal Disorders: The Sports Medicine Approach*. Philadelphia: Lea & Febiger.

Mayer, T. G., and Polatin, P. B. (2000). Tertiary nonoperative interdisciplinary programs: The functional restoration variant of the outpatient chronic pain management program. In T. G. Mayer, R. J. Gatchel, and P. B. Polatin (Eds.), *Occupational Musculoskeletal Disorders* (pp. 639–649). Philadelphia: Lippincott Williams & Wilkins.

McMahon, M. J., Gatchel, R. J., Polatin, P. B., and Mayer, T. G. (1997). Early childhood abuse in chronic spinal disorder patients: A major barrier to treatment success. *Spine*, *22*, 2408–2415.

Mullin, S. (2002). Public health and the media: The challenge now faced by bioterrorism. *Journal of Urban Health*, *79*(1), 12–12.

Nakata, A., Ikeda, T., Takahashi, M., Haratani, T., Fujioka, Y., Fukui, S., … Araki, S. (2005). Sleep-related risk of occupational injuries in Japanese small and medium-scale enterprises. *Industrial Health*, *43*(1), 89–97.

National Sleep Foundation (2008). *2008 Sleep in America Poll: Summary of Findings*. Washington, DC: Sleep Foundation.

Payne, B., and Norfleet, M. A. (1986). Chronic pain and the family: A review. *Pain*, *26*(1), 1–22.

Phillips, A. C., Carroll, D., and Der, G. (2015). Negative life events and symptoms of depression and anxiety: Stress causation and/or stress generation. *Anxiety, Stress, and Coping*, *28*(4), 357–371.

Polatin, P., and Gatchel, R. (1997). Psychosocial factors in spinal disorders. In *Orthopaedic Knowledge Update: Spine* (pp. 149–152). Rosemont, IL: American Academy of Orthopaedic Surgeons.

Polatin, P. B., Young, M., Mayer, M., and Gatchel, R. (2005). Bioterrorism, stress, and pain: The importance of an anticipatory community preparedness intervention. *Journal of Psychosomatic Research*, *58*(4), 311–316.

Proudfoot, J., Clarke, J., Birch, M., Whitton, A. E., Parker, G., Manicavasagar, V., … Hadzi-Pavlovic, D. (2013). Impact of a mobile phone and web program on symptom and functional outcomes for people with mild-to-moderate depression, anxiety and stress: A randomised controlled trial. *BMC Psychiatry*, *13*, 312–312.

Rice, V. J. B., Mays, M. Z., and Gable, C. (2009). Self-reported health status of students in-processing into military medical advanced individual training. *Work*, *34*(4), 387–400.

Robinson, O. J., Bond, R. L., and Roiser, J. P. (2015). The impact of stress on financial decision-making varies as a function of depression and anxiety symptoms. *PeerJ*, *3*, e770–e770.

Rosenbloom, B. N., Khan, S., McCartney, C., and Katz, J. (2013). Systematic review of persistent pain and psychological outcomes following traumatic musculoskeletal injury. *Journal of Pain Research*, *6*, 39–51.

Rush, A. J., Polatin, P., and Gatchel, R. J. (2000). Depression and chronic low back pain: Establishing priorities in treatment. *Spine*, *25*(20), 2566–2571.

Sabbath, E. L., Hurtado, D. A., Okechukwu, C. A., Tamers, S. L., Nelson, C., Kim, S., … Sorenson, G. (2014). Occupational injury among hospital patient-care workers: What is the association with workplace verbal abuse? *American Journal of Industrial Medicine*, *57*(2), 222–232.

Sapolsky, R. M. (1992). Neuroendocrinology of the stress-response. In J. B. Becker, S. M. Breedlove and D. Crews (Eds.), *Behavioral Endocrinology* (pp. 287–324). Cambridge, MA: MIT Press.

Sattler, D. N., Boyd, B., and Kirsch, J. (2014). Trauma-exposed firefighters: Relationships among posttraumatic growth, posttraumatic stress, resource availability, coping and critical incident stress debriefing experience. *Stress and Health*, *30*(5), 356–365.

Schleifer, L. M., Ley, R., and Spalding, T. W. (2002). A hyperventilation theory of job stress and musculoskeletal disorders. *American Journal of Industrial Medicine*, *41*(5), 420–432.

Schneider, S., and Stone, A. A. (2014). Distinguishing between frequency and intensity of health-related symptoms from diary assessments. *Journal of Psychosomatic Research*, *77*(3), 205–212.

Schulte, P. A., Wagner, G. R., Ostry, A., Blanciforti, L. A., Cutlip, R. G., Krajnak, K. M., … Miller, D. B. (2007). Work, obesity, and occupational safety and health. *American Journal of Public Health*, *97*(3), 428–436.

Serpa, J. G., Taylor, S. L., and Tillisch, K. (2014). Mindfulness-based stress reduction (MBSR) reduces anxiety, depression, and suicidal ideation in veterans. *Medical Care*, *52*(12), S19–S24.

Seth, A., and Teichman, J. M. H. (2008). Differences in the clinical presentation of interstitial cystitis/painful bladder syndrome in patients with or without sexual abuse history. *Journal of Urology*, *180*(5), 2029–2033.

Shuler, F. D., Wingate, M. K., Moore, G. H., and Giangarra, C. (2012). Sports health benefits of vitamin D. *Sports Health*, *4*(6), 496–501.

Simpson, S. A., Wadsworth, E. J. K., Moss, S. C., and Smith, A. P. (2005). Minor injuries, cognitive failures and accidents at work: Incidence and associated features. *Occupational Medicine (Oxford)*, *55*(2), 99–108.

Solivan, A. E., Xiong, X., Harville, E. W., and Buekens, P. (2015). Measurement of perceived stress among pregnant women: A comparison of two different instruments. *Maternal and Child Health Journal*, *19*(9), 1910–1915.

Sprague, S., Madden, K., Dosanjh, S., Godin, K., Goslings, J. C., Schemitsch, E. H., and Bhandari, M. (2013). *Intimate Partner Violence and Musculoskeletal Injury: Bridging the Knowledge Gap in Orthopaedic Fracture Clinics*. London: BioMed Central.

Staron, R. S., Hagerman, F. C., and Hikida, R. S. (1981). The effects of detraining on an elite power lifter: A case study. *Journal of the Neurological Sciences*, *51*(2), 247–257.

Sullivan, M. J. L., Thibault, P., Simmonds, M. J., Milioto, M., Cantin, A., and Velly, A. M. (2009). Pain, perceived injustice and the persistence of post-traumatic stress symptoms during the course of rehabilitation for whiplash injuries. *Pain*, *145*(3), 325–331.

Trief, P. M., Grant, W., and Fredrickson, B. (2000). A prospective study of psychological predictors of lumbar surgery outcome. *Spine*, *25*(20), 2616–2621.

Tyrka, A. R., Wier, L. M., Anderson, G. M., Wilkinson, C. W., Price, L. H., and Carpenter, L. L. (2007). Temperament and response to the trier social stress test. *Acta Psychiatrica Scandinavica*, *115*(5), 395–402.

US Bureau of Labor Statistics (2011). Nonfatal occupational injuries and illnesses requiring days away from work, 2010. News release. At http://www.bls.gov/news.release/archives/osh2_11092011.pdf (accessed July 2016).

Von Korff, M., and Simon, G. (1996). The relationship between pain and depression. *British Journal of Psychiatry, Supplement*, No. *30*, 101–108.

Wardle, J., Steptoe, A., Oliver, G., and Lipsey, Z. (2000). Stress, dietary restraint and food intake. *Journal of Psychosomatic Research*, *48*(2), 195–202.

Wearing, S. C., Henning, E. M., Byrne, N. M., Steele, J. R., and Hills, A. P. (2006). Musculoskeletal disorders associated with obesity: A biomechanical perspective. *Obesity*, *7*, 239–250.

Wesley, A. L., Polatin, P. B., Gatchel, R. J., and Gatchel, R. J. (2000). Psychosocial, psychiatric, and socioeconomic factors in chronic occupational musculoskeletal disorders. In T. G. Mayer, R. J. Gatchel, and P. B. Polatin (Eds.), *Occupational Musculoskeletal Disorders* (pp. 577–586). Philadelphia: Lippincott Williams & Wilkins.

Wilson, D. R. (2010). Health consequences of childhood sexual abuse. *Perspectives in Psychiatric Care*, *46*(1), 56–64.

Yerkes, R. M., and Dodson, J. D. (1908). The relation of strength of stimulus to rapidity of habit-formation. *Journal of Comparative Neurology and Psychology*, *18*(5), 459–482.

Zapf, D. (2002). Emotion work and psychological well-being: A review of the literature and some conceptual considerations. *Human Resource Management Review*, *12*(2), 237.

Zhou, Z. E., Yang, L. Q., and Spector, P. E. (2015). Political skill: A proactive inhibitor of workplace aggression exposure and an active buffer of the aggression–strain relationship. *Journal of Occupational Health Psychology*, *20*(4), 405–419.

13

Managing the Impact of Advanced Complex Illness on Family Caregiver and Professional Caregiver Stress

A Role for Palliative Care

Gregory R. Harper, Bridget Blitz, Catherine Serena, Donna Stevens, and Daniel E. Ray

Introduction

Population trends in Western countries demonstrate an increase in median age. Between 2005 and 2030 in the United States, for example, the number of adults age 65 and older will nearly double from 37 million to more than 70 million, representing an increase from 12% to almost 20% of the US population (Institute of Medicine, 2008). Persons aged 65 and older have more complex health-care needs and utilize more health-care services than younger persons. In the US, these older Americans account for 26% of physician visits, 35% of all hospital stays, 38% of emergency medical service responses, and 34% of all prescriptions. Older persons occupy 90% of nursing home beds. More than 60% of older persons with disabilities obtain long-term services, such as help with personal care and household chores. Unpaid family or informal caregivers provide as much as 90% of this in-home long-term care (Adelman, Tmanova, Delgado, Dion, and Lachs, 2014). The majority of caregivers are women who take care of either a relative (86%) or a friend (14%), spending an average of 20.5 hours per week providing care. The economic value of this care for persons with dementia is estimated to be $56,290 annually (Hurd, Martorell, Delavande, Mullen, and Langa, 2013). In 32% of

The Handbook of Stress and Health: A Guide to Research and Practice, First Edition.
Edited by Cary L. Cooper and James Campbell Quick.
© 2017 John Wiley & Sons, Ltd. Published 2017 by John Wiley & Sons, Ltd.

caregivers, measures of caregiver burden were considered at a high level based on amount of time spent providing care and the recipient's degree of dependency (National Alliance for Caregiving and AARP, 2009). Compared to an adult child caring for a parent, spousal caregivers face greater challenges because they are likely to live with the recipient of their care, have little choice in taking on the caregiver role, and are potentially more vulnerable because of their own age and associated illnesses. Risk factors for caregiver burden include being female, having low educational attainment, living with the care recipient, the presence of depression, social isolation, financial stress, high number of hours in the caregiver role, and lack of choice in being a caregiver (Adelman et al., 2014). These risks are especially high in the presence of the challenging care needs of persons with dementia, decreased functional status (e.g., neurological disorders), cancer, and end-of-life care. Of particular concern is the lack of effective interaction with the caregiver by the attending physician and other members of the health-care team.

The first step in addressing caregiver stress among informal caregivers is the assessment of caregiver burden. In 2005, the Family Caregiver Alliance convened the National Consensus Development Conference for Caregiver Assessment, at which the following recommendations for assessment and intervention were proposed: (1) identification of primary and additional caregivers; (2) incorporation of the needs and preferences of both the care recipient (referred to as "patient centeredness") and the caregiver in care planning; (3) improvement of caregivers' understanding of their role and teaching skills necessary to the tasks required; and (4) recognition of the need for periodic assessments of both ongoing burden and outcomes of interventions undertaken (Family Caregiver Alliance, 2006). Discussion opportunities with caregivers can be facilitated by asking questions directed at caregiver health, quality of life, support, and what the caregivers' expectations are if an emergency arises. In their review of caregiver burden, Adelman et al. (2014) have summarized suggested practical interventions to reduce caregiver burden (Table 13.1).

In the face of the increasing health-care needs of an aging population, the current health-care workforce in the United States is neither large enough nor sufficiently trained to meet older patients' needs. Health-care workers with special training in geriatrics are especially scarce, and shortages exist for nursing assistants, who provide 70 to 80 percent of direct-care hours; physician assistants, who provide medical care for one-third of outpatient visits by older persons; and social workers trained in geriatrics, who currently account for only about 4 percent of all social workers (Institute of Medicine, 2008).

The two most common causes of death in the US are cardiovascular disease and cancer. Despite consistent reductions in cardiovascular deaths, it was estimated that over 1.6 million new cancer cases would be diagnosed in the United States in 2014, and nearly 600,000 Americans would die of the disease (American Cancer Society, 2014). In the face of an increase in both the number of new cancers and the number of cancer survivors, the American Society of Clinical Oncology (ASCO) estimates that, by 2025, demand for oncology services will grow by 42 percent, while the supply of oncologists will grow by only 28 percent (Yang et al., 2014). Exacerbating this shortfall is the high level of oncologist distress manifesting as symptoms of burnout, such as emotional exhaustion, depersonalization, and low sense of personal accomplishment on the Maslach Burnout Inventory (Maslach, Jackson, and Leiter, 1996). Among 1,117 responding US oncologists surveyed by ASCO between October 2012 and March 2013, 44.7 percent were burned out on the emotional exhaustion and/or depersonalization domains (Shanafelt et al., 2014).

Table 13.1 Practical interventions to reduce caregiver burden

Intervention	Discussion
Encourage participation of caregiver as member of the care team	Physicians and other providers assess both caregiver and recipient at clinic and home visits
Encourage self-care for the caregiver	Caregivers should continue to meet their own health-care needs, but may require supportive measures at home (food delivery, respite care) for the caregiver to engage in self-care
Provide education, information	Educate and inform caregivers about the nature of the recipient's illness and care needs, expectations about the benefits of treatment, prognosis, hospice and end-of-life care, advance care planning
Use supportive technology	Emergency response systems, mobility trackers for patients who wander, home monitoring systems, internet-based face-to-face communication (e.g., Skype)
Coordinate and refer for assistance services	Alzheimer's Association, Meals on Wheels, home safety modification, home health care, physical therapy, day care
Respite care	Explore availability of respite services such as day care, hospice volunteer services or respite admission

Source: Adapted from Adelman et al. (2014).

Stress and burnout is prevalent among health-care providers in the United States. Among US physicians, the rate of reported symptoms of burnout is 46 percent (Shanafelt et al., 2012). The rate among internal medicine subspecialists is 44 percent, lower than rates observed in general internists (54 percent). The rate of burnout among US oncologists is about 45 percent, consistent with other US physicians, with the principal risk factor among oncologists being the number of hours per week spent seeing patients. Older oncologists were at less risk for burnout than younger physicians, while added hours during the week for attending to administrative tasks increased the risk.

Caregiver stress and burnout has been reported in oncology physicians and nurses not only in the US, but also in Canada, Great Britain, and Japan (Sherman, Edwards, Simonton, and Mehta, 2006). In a systematic review of burnout in palliative care providers, dealing with death and dying, team conflict, time pressures, increasing responsibilities, and excessive bureaucracy were risk factors for emotional exhaustion. Team conflict, interpersonal pressures, insufficient education, patient avoidance, and the absence of supportive team strategies contributed to depersonalization. However, in almost every study reviewed, the presence of individual as well as team support, available time to spend with patients and families, and effective communication strategies for patients, families and providers provided protection from burnout (Pereira, Fonseca, and Carvalho, 2011).

Caregiver stress, therefore, is a challenge for both family and informal caregivers who provide the bulk of caregiver work at home, as well as for members of the health-care team responsible for the medical care of the increasing numbers of patients with advanced complex illnesses who need care, both in health-care settings and at home. This chapter will describe the approach taken at the Lehigh Valley Health Network (LVHN) in Allentown, Pennsylvania to manage stress experienced by informal caregivers (predominantly family or recipient partners) as well as by the health-care providers challenged by caring for patients with advanced complex illness. The approach is grounded in palliative medicine principles, is dependent on effective teamwork, and is based on developing an increased role for palliative care providers who work in partnership with both home-based caregivers and health-care providers – physicians, advanced practice clinicians (physician assistants, nurse practitioners), nurses, social workers, and others – in providing care and support for the patient and caregivers. Two clinical case examples will describe how this approach can be successful and, in addition, illustrate the limitations and challenges faced by caregivers and providers.

Palliative Medicine at LVHN

History

In early 2006, LVHN held a Future Search meeting (Future Search, 2003), bringing together a broad range of stakeholders – physicians, nurses, allied health professionals, patients, families, administrators, network leaders, payor organizations, and community agencies – to assess the status of chronic illness care in the community and create a shared vision of optimal health care for patients with serious and chronic illness. The culmination of these efforts resulted in a network strategic initiative that created one platform for the delivery of palliative care. The service was named Optimizing Advanced Complex Illness Support (OACIS).

Initially, OACIS provided access to palliative care through two service branches: an inpatient consultation service and a home-based consultation service. Administratively, the program was housed in the division of Home Health Services, which fostered a shared understanding of the scope of practice among palliative medicine, home care, and hospice services. The establishment of a hospice and palliative medicine fellowship program, accredited by the Accreditation Council for Graduate Medical Education, created an opportunity to align the medical and home-based palliative care services under the section of Palliative Medicine and Hospice within the LVHN Department of Medicine. In 2012, a palliative care outpatient clinic (PCOC) was established in LVHN's cancer center to promote greater integration of oncology and palliative care. Ongoing development of OACIS and palliative medicine at LVHN has been informed by (1) the National Consensus Project for Quality Palliative Care guidelines (NCP, 2013); (2) the Chronic Illness Collaborative, part of the Institute for Healthcare Improvement's breakthrough series (IHI, 2003); (3) the Medicare Innovations Collaborative (Leff et al., 2012); and (4) ongoing technical support and access to tools and resources made available from the Center to Advance Palliative Care (CAPC, 2015).

Team and Operations

Palliative care, also known as palliative medicine, is specialized medical care for people living with serious illnesses. It is focused on providing patients with relief from the symptoms and stress of a serious illness – whatever the diagnosis. The goal is to improve quality of life for both patients and their caregivers. Palliative care is provided by a team of doctors, nurses, and other specialists who work with a patient's primary and other specialty physicians to provide an extra layer of support. Palliative care is appropriate at any age and at any stage in a serious illness, and can be provided together with curative treatment (CAPC, 2015).

The creation of OACIS at LVHN involved not only the clinical branches of palliative medicine, but also required culture change in the network to organize service delivery around the needs of patients across the continuum of care – not just when the patient was in the hospital. This change required both community and physician engagement as well as an understanding of the business culture within the network, which was oriented primarily toward inpatient hospital services. The OACIS program is also responsible for culture change aimed at increasing the utilization of advance care planning both within the network and in the community (Faulkner, Rockwell, Stevens, and Ray, 2015). The availability of specialty palliative care services in the home for patients with advanced complex illness is rare. OACIS represents an innovative home-based health service delivery model that links specialty palliative care services provided by hospice and palliative care–Certified Registered Nurse Practitioners (CRNPs) to both primary and specialty physicians. In addition to providing palliative care in the home, the CRNPs support physicians by co-managing a complex patient population that, while placing significant demands on providing physicians, may constitute a small percentage of their overall patient population.

The OACIS/Palliative Medicine team comprises doctors, CRNPs, social workers, registered nurses, and clinical support staff, as well as administrative support. It is one team with three clinical services, including inpatient, clinic, and home-based. The clinical providers bill for services, covering between 40 and 50 percent of their cost, which is supplemented by network support. Outcome results include significant decreases in hospitalizations and the cost of subsequent hospitalizations (Lukas, Foltz and Paxton, 2013).

The team approach in palliative medicine is well suited to the care of patients with advanced complex illness. The OACIS team not only is involved in the care of patients and their families, but also is a platform for support of the professional caregivers who work in palliative medicine. Education sessions are used strategically to convene the team and provide a format for connection and meaningful interchange. Sessions begin with a "check-in" question; all members, regardless of role, are encouraged to attend. Self-care efforts are frequently incorporated: formally, in regular rounding and telling the patient story, and informally, with individual recognition through staff meeting "pats on the back" to validate specific contributions to each other and recognition of accomplishments and milestones. Regular retreats are held to decompress and problem-solve issues, giving attention to the individual needs of each member. Part of the culture is validation from leadership staff, who recognize the difficult emotions that the team members encounter in patient care.

Additional sources of provider support include the Palliative Medical Scholars (PalMS) program (Hirschmann, Ray, and Foster, 2011) and Schwartz Rounds (Schwartz Center, 2015). PalMS was implemented in 2008 as a strategic initiative to foster education on palliative care principles and to provide a vehicle to both connect and support all levels of staff providing patient care. A connection was formed among inpatient providers, dieticians, social workers, nurses, physical therapists, unit clerks, etc., around the needs of the very sick patients. The regularly scheduled Schwartz Rounds emphasize provider self-care in the setting of the inherent emotional difficulties in taking care of patients.

Clinical Cases

Two cases are presented to illustrate both the successes and challenges inherent in providing effective medical and palliative care for patients with advanced complex illness. In addition, we outline the strategies employed to manage the caregiver stress experienced by both informal and professional health-care caregivers. Names and identifying personal health information have been altered to protect patient confidentiality.

Case 1 V was a 34-year-old married Hispanic female professional in a high-level position and the mother of three children when she was diagnosed with a relatively advanced high-risk breast cancer. In addition, she was positive for the breast cancer susceptibility gene BRCA2, inherited from one of her parents. Cared for by one of the authors (GH), her initial treatment plan was designed to reduce the risks of recurrence and included removal of the affected breast, chemotherapy, radiation therapy, bilateral oophorectomy (removal of both ovaries), and anti-estrogen therapy. Despite comprehensive initial treatment, her cancer recurred three and a half years later. She subsequently underwent multiple additional treatments with chemotherapy, anti-estrogen therapy, radiation therapy, and investigational therapy at a US National Cancer Institute–designated comprehensive cancer research center. The principal sites of metastases were her bones, causing significant pain, as well as skin, liver, and lung metastases. In the course of nearly five years of treatment, she experienced ten hospital admissions as well as eight additional emergency room visits that did not result in admission. Six of the hospital stays, most of them pain-related, were in her last 18 months of life.

In addition to V's hospital admissions, she was seen multiple times in the office by her oncologist for anxiety, pain and symptom management. Her care was a significant challenge to her oncology care team because she experienced both a highly symptomatic disease course exacerbated by significant pain, as well as extreme anxiety about the course of her disease, her prognosis and the knowledge that she would ultimately succumb to her cancer. Her anxiety was fueled primarily by concern for the care of her children, resulting in an extraordinary desire to try "anything" that might keep her alive a little longer. Despite multiple approaches to treatment, lack of significant improvement was frequent, and achieving lasting palliation of her pain from bone metastases proved difficult, causing frustration for both her oncologist and the oncology care team. In addition, the oncology team responded to frequent calls and requests for unscheduled office visits to address her anxiety about new symptoms, some of which were the result of anxiety, but many of which were disease-related symptoms reflecting the worsening of her cancer. Moreover, her treating oncologist of more than four years retired from practice about six months before she died, resulting in additional stress and anxiety associated with the transition to a new physician.

The OACIS Palliative Medicine program was initially consulted 14 months after V's disease recurrence, primarily to assist the oncology care team with symptom management but also to facilitate a realistic conversation with the patient about her overall goals of care in the setting of incurable, metastatic breast cancer. Because the OACIS program provides services in multiple settings, V received these services in the hospital, the palliative care outpatient clinic, and in her home. The PCOC, staffed by a CRNP and located in the cancer center, provided the opportunity to better integrate both palliative and oncology care plans. It was clear through the duration of her care that V consciously tried to reduce the strain on her family, especially on her parents, who had moved from their own out-of-state home into V's home to assist with her children. Efforts by the OACIS team to incorporate additional services to ease the stress within the home were met with hesitance, as her family viewed privacy as paramount. Respecting the patient's and family's wishes for privacy and their desire to maintain as normal a routine as possible meant that the team had to accept consistent rejection of these services. Clinical visits in the home were conditional on the patient being able to fully engage and maintain some control in decision-making. Conversely, visits by the inpatient OACIS team in the hospital where she had limited control were more readily accepted by the patient.

Gaining and maintaining trust and rapport were challenging, as V was seen by the OACIS CRNP and social worker in all three settings (home, hospital, and the palliative care outpatient clinic). Other challenges faced by the team stemmed from the language barrier of V's parents as well as the patient and family's ongoing preference for privacy. In particular, the treating oncologist was especially challenged in explaining – in the presence of V, her parents (V could not bring herself to tell her parents on her own), and a medical interpreter – the role that her inherited BRCA2 gene played in causing her breast cancer.

V wanted to maintain responsibility for her three children, and protect them, not only from strangers but from the implications of her disease itself. While her husband continued to work outside the home and provide for his family in that regard, V reserved her right to shelter her children lovingly, again not allowing for extended outside support beyond OACIS services. As V's disease process progressed, both her family and the professional caregivers grew increasingly weary of trying to maintain normalcy and order within the home while the patient adjusted to a new oncologist and started to come to terms with the prognosis of her fatal disease. This clearly had an impact, not only on V but on her entire family. The children consistently attended school and/or work and V's relatives surrounded her with loving attention and assistance. Home-based OACIS services and traditional home care, when possible, continued. Support directed toward the patient's symptom management was rendered frequently via telephone. V often declined home visits as her condition progressed, consistent with her wishes for privacy at such an intimate time.

Consistent with US national trends, V resisted transition to the care of the hospice until just a few days before her death, and her family, despite efforts by OACIS and hospice caregivers and in keeping with the family's previous wishes for privacy, declined offers of bereavement support both before and after V's death.

Specific challenges to managing stress in the family caregivers were (1) the strong cultural and personal preferences for privacy that limited offered interventions; (2) language differences that prevented effective communication with the parents and husband, resulting in all communication being filtered through the patient; and (3) the delay in accepting referral to hospice services. The principal challenge to the oncology and palliative care providers, aside from medical management, was the characteristic behavior of the patient concerning her prognosis. Despite the presence of metastatic disease and the reality of incurability, the patient approached each new treatment as a chance for "cure," or, at least, long-term remission. The disassociation between patients' understanding of treatment goals (cure versus palliative) has been well documented – nearly two-thirds of patients receiving either palliative chemotherapy (Weeks et al., 2012) or radiation (Chen et al., 2013), when asked, believe that they are receiving "curative" treatment. This "disconnect," often existing in the patient undergoing palliative cancer treatment, creates a tension between the patient and family and the health-care team that is endeavoring to maintain patient confidence and satisfaction while also striving to educate both patient and family in the realities of the disease and prepare them for the ultimate outcome of the patient's death. This tension results in an inverse relationship between patient satisfaction and the degree of hopefulness for cure expressed by the oncologist, complicating efforts to better educate patients regarding the relative benefits and risks of palliative cancer treatment that is not curative. In addition, it takes its toll on the provider care team, potentially leading to patient and family dissatisfaction with the providers' care. Moreover, despite recommendations from ASCO (Partridge et al., 2014) and the Institute of Medicine (Foley and Gelband, 2001) that cancer care be better integrated with palliative care, there exist patient, regulatory, and financial barriers in the United States to doing so. Patients and families, even when able to reconcile their prognosis and the need for palliation of their symptoms, experience appointment fatigue, scheduling conflicts and, in addition, insurance coverage barriers, which include additional co-pays and lack of reimbursement for co-management by oncology and palliative care providers. All of these barriers frustrated efforts of the palliative care team to better integrate V's care with the oncology care team.

Finally, while the death of a loved one certainly "leaves a hole in your heart" for family, nurses and other professionals grieve also. In addition, while professional caregivers are trained to not shrink away from the indignities of death, they may try to "shield everyone else from any ugliness" that could occur (Zurlinden, 2000). In our patient's circumstances, the OACIS clinicians involved in caring for her wanted the very best for her family and benefited from professional support at regular OACIS team meetings. In fact, it may have been the professional caregivers themselves who struggled more with the pending and actual loss, projecting their anticipatory grief onto the family. Mary L. S. Vachon (1995) reported that staff stress in palliative care has been shown to be less than initially anticipated, but still requires some intervention and continued monitoring. Despite the patient-imposed limitations and barriers to providing optimal palliative care, good team communication, team building and team support proved to be essential underpinnings to the palliative care that V did receive and, especially, to the support of her professional caregivers.

Case 2   K is a 48-year-old married mother who has lived with secondary, progressive multiple sclerosis (MS) for 15 years. Her care is managed by a home-based CRNP and a social worker. The CRNP sees K every four weeks to monitor her medical needs and help maintain her comfort, focusing primarily on the medical problems arising from her MS – dysphagia; chronic, plaque-induced gingivitis; urinary urgency; stage one pressure ulcer; and the palliative care needs for her disease burden. The social worker provides home visits to assist the family with in-home care, which the patient's husband and son had been providing prior to OACIS involvement. Complicating K's care needs is her husband's chronic medical issue that requires treatment three times weekly, during which he is away from the home for up to six hours, including travel time to and from his care. The couple's son had moved in from out of town to help provide care, but was exhausted from working nights and providing care during the day. He also had been driving his father to and from treatment, leaving his mother vulnerable because of her inability to stand, pivot or call for help on the phone if needed. Meeting repeatedly with the family at home, the social worker was able to assess the emotional impact of long-term caregiving on the family. Exhaustion from constant caregiving affected both husband and son. Although they expressed love and devotion to K, they were unable to provide enough help for her in the home. The OACIS team also witnessed feelings of isolation and sadness resulting from the lack of help or visits from other family members. Her husband barely had time to tend to his own serious medical condition and continually worried about his wife not having the necessary help while he was in treatment. He openly grieved for the life they had before K, at a relatively young age, became virtually unable to move more than her face and hands.

The OACIS social worker was able to organize several interventions:

1. Referral to the National MS Society, which granted the family 80 hours of complimentary in-home care (by aides) to be used for K's bathing, dressing, household chores, laundry and other tasks;
2. Completion of the process to apply for long-term, in-home care through the Pennsylvania Independent Enrollment Broker and local Public Assistance office waiver program;

3. Referral to Community Exchange, a time bank of volunteers within LVHN, which provided volunteers up to three days a week for much of the duration of K's husband's treatments so that her son could sleep and rest for his night job;
4. Eventually, successful application to the state to pay K's son to provide daytime care for his mother, permitting him to quit his overnight job and focus on his mother's needs as well as his own self-care.

K's husband admits that his wife's rapid physical decline at her young age – she has become almost unable to speak and requires full care – has been profoundly emotionally challenging for him and his family. With his own medical needs and the likelihood of requiring another surgery in the near future, respite care became necessary for the family, made possible through the state-provided care management company Abilities in Motion. The company's care managers ensure that K is receiving an appropriate amount of in-home care, supervise the state expenditures for her care, and review the paid care provided for her by her son.

The nurse practitioner continues to see K monthly and the social worker provides as-needed support in person or by phone. All services, whether provided directly by OACIS or arranged through community resources, have been sources of heretofore unavailable support for the family. Though the ultimate course of K's MS will be a continuing decline, she and her family will benefit from reliable, long-term OACIS support, including the inevitable future transition to hospice care.

Figved, Myhr, Larsen, and Aarsland (2007) wrote that care providers for spouses with MS report higher levels of caregiver distress than other caregiver groups (e.g., close friends). With MS, as with other debilitating diseases, the authors found a high correlation between the patient's disability, cognition and neuropsychiatric symptom measures and caregiver distress, although the psychological symptoms created more caregiver impact than physical disability. Many spouses will share with palliative care team members how painful it is to watch loved ones physically weaken and struggle. Watching loved ones *mentally* weaken and struggle, however, appears to cause even more pain among spouses. Figved and colleagues (2007) noted that caring for a spouse with MS often pushes the caregiver into a parental role, which may dilute the marriage bond or change the dynamics. Buchanan, Radin, and Huang (2011) state that being a male caregiver of a female patient creates a higher caregiver burden. Interestingly, simple factors that can reduce the impact on caregivers of those with MS are (1) treating bladder dysfunction, and (2) connecting a family to respite services, both of which have been shown to lower caregiver burden and improve caregiver mental health (Buchanan et al., 2011). Managing these simple needs can bring new energy to a family experiencing caregivers' exhaustion.

Some of the incredible burden of MS comes from its effect on so many aspects of the patient's physical and cognitive self (Holland, Schneider, Rapp, and Kalb, 2011). Much of the strain on these patients and their caregivers stems from receiving diagnoses at young ages when they are still busy raising young children, working, and managing a home while their physical selves are starting to experience a drastic reduction in abilities. Holland and colleagues (2011) found feelings of guilt in caregivers related to their own self-care or for taking time away from the intense care of a loved one. To help mitigate this guilt, palliative health-care workers can encourage caregivers to take time for themselves – an important first step. However, by reinforcing this encouragement with a respite alternative that fills in the care "gap," caregivers can then, without regret, free up the time necessary for their own well-being.

Despite the findings by some authors that male caregivers caring for female loved ones experience higher burden (Buchanan et al., 2011; Bevans and Sternberg, 2012), William Breitbart (2004), caregiver and author, was able to find and celebrate deep personal meaning from his wife's journey with MS through the love and caring of professional and informal caregivers. In his story about his wife's 20-year journey with MS and his corresponding experiences as her caregiver, he related that there are vital healing powers inherent in love from family and friends as well as from health-care providers. As palliative care providers, it may be easy to forget how great the impact of our daily interactions with patients and family members is on them. Many patients and family members report developing a strong bond with professional caregivers who have helped provide valuable medical intervention and psychosocial support during a particularly challenging and frightening time for them. Perhaps the professional is one of the few consistently positive forces in a patient's life; hence, the number of lives that are touched by palliative caregivers cannot be overestimated.

Discussion

For the coming decades, an aging US population will challenge family and informal caregivers of patients with advanced complex illness who will require in-home care during the course of their illness. Health-care professionals tasked with providing care to these patients face shortfalls in workforce numbers and complexities in patient care management within a health-care system that remains highly fragmented, as well as the ongoing burden of work–life balance characterized by time constraints inherent in juggling patient care, administrative and bureaucratic demands. It follows that mitigating stress will continue to be a challenge for both family and professional caregivers. This chapter described two cases that illustrate patients with advanced complex illnesses – one with cancer and one with multiple sclerosis – and the challenges faced by their families and professional caregivers. Both patients were also cared for by a novel outpatient palliative care program developed by the authors' hospital network for optimizing advanced chronic illness support (OACIS). The outpatient OACIS team of nurse practitioners, social workers and support staff not only coordinate the care of patients at home, but also intercede to identify and reduce stress in the family and informal caregivers. Whereas the social worker involved in the care of the patient with MS was able to intercede with referrals to community and state resources to assist both the husband and son in caring for her, OACIS team members were less successful with efforts to provide additional support for the patient with cancer, who regularly resisted initiatives for additional support for her husband and children. Nevertheless, the OACIS team did partially bridge the care and coordination gap that often arises between the specialty physician (the oncologist in this case) and the patient's primary care physician.

While both patients benefited from the home-based palliative care that OACIS provides, the program is also an essential platform for professional caregiver support. Weekly educational and case management conferences serve to educate and support members of the care team, as well as to coordinate care plans for the patients under their care. The PalMS program provides both an infrastructure and educational culture to provide palliative care providers with knowledge of procedures and principles of palliative medicine. "Pats on the back" for good work, regular program retreats, and the interdisciplinary nature of the team create an environment in which all team members are valued for their contributions, and each team member is able to both witness and receive support from colleagues. Participating in Schwartz Center Rounds

(Schwartz Center, 2015) fosters increased communication, teamwork and provider support (Lown and Manning, 2010), but these outcomes depend on regular participation by providers who have difficulty finding additional time in their schedules for these activities.

Whereas the OACIS and palliative medicine caregivers meet regularly, there remains a significant challenge to integrating palliative care with the care provided by specialty services, such as oncology. Both infrastructure and reimbursement barriers limit the ability of the oncologist and the palliative care team to co-manage the patient. Patient care demands (office hours and hospital consultations) on the oncologist's time do not permit regular participation with OACIS or palliative care providers in team meetings. Care coordination, then, is too often limited to phone calls or progress notes posted to the medical record or sent back and forth between the providers. The palliative care outpatient clinic, while deliberately located in the LVHN cancer center, is nevertheless a separate operational entity in space, providers, and billing. Despite the call for better integration of oncology and palliative care (Partridge et al., 2014), appointment fatigue by the patient and family, along with operational silos complicated by the lack of aligned office schedules between oncology and palliative care providers, limit face-to-face meetings to chance encounters and make real-time co-management and coordination of care a near impossibility. An increasing emphasis on palliative care by the Institute of Medicine, ASCO, and American College of Surgeons (Partridge et al., 2014) may contribute to necessary changes in both culture and infrastructure to achieve both improved integration of palliative care for the cancer patient, as well as support for professional caregivers as they confront an increasing burden of palliative care for their patients.

The future role of palliative care for patients with advanced complex illness is likely to lie with the integration of primary palliative care with the ongoing care provided by the principal physician responsible for the treatment of the patient (Weissman and Meier, 2011). For the oncology patient, the oncologist will continue to provide primary palliative care, directing and managing the day-to-day symptoms and complications encountered by patients as a result of either their disease or their treatment. Secondary palliative care consultations with palliative medicine specialists will still be required when symptom management and care coordination, especially in the home setting, becomes too challenging for the oncology care team, or when changes in goals of care for patients with incurable disease or at end of life lead to increasing distress in the family or conflict with the treating physician. However, this model faces numerous obstacles, including the need for cultural and paradigmatic change by oncologists providing care to overcome the prevailing perception of the cure/care dichotomy and to recognize that palliative care belongs throughout the continuum of care (Partridge et al., 2014). Programs like OACIS can be platforms for coordinating the palliative care of patients with advanced complex illness, and serve as interdisciplinary vehicles for improved caregiver support.

Note

The authors thank Jacqueline Grove for her editorial expertise, and Elke H. Rockwell, PhD, for her assistance in preparing this manuscript.

References

Adelman, R. D., Tmanova, L. L., Delgado, D., Dion, S., and Lachs, M. S. (2014). Caregiver burden: A clinical review. *JAMA, 311*(10), 1052–1060.

American Cancer Society (2014). *Cancer Facts and Figures 2014*. No. 500814. Atlanta: American Cancer Society.

Bevans, M., and Sternberg, E. M. (2012). Caregiving burden, stress, and health effects among family caregivers of adult cancer patients. *JAMA*, *307*(4), 398–403.

Breitbart, W. (2004). Living with multiple sclerosis: A spiritual journey of loss. *Palliative and Supportive Care*, *2*(3), 319–320.

Buchanan, R. J., Radin, D., and Huang, C. (2011). Caregiver burden among informal caregivers assisting people with multiple sclerosis. *International Journal of MS Care*, *13*(2), 76–83.

CAPC (Center to Advance Palliative Care) (2015). About palliative care. At https://www.capc.org/about/palliative-care/ (accessed July 2016).

Chen, A., Cronin, A., Weeks, J., Chrischilles, E., Malin, J., Hayman, J., and Schrag, D. (2013). Expectations about the effectiveness of radiation therapy among patients with incurable lung cancer. *Journal of Clinical Oncology*, *31*(21), 2730–2735. doi:10.1200/JCO.2012.48.5748

Family Caregiver Alliance (2006). Caregivers count too! An online toolkit to help practitioners assess the needs of family caregivers. At http://caregiver.org/caregivers-count-too-toolkit (accessed July 2016).

Faulkner, D. L., Rockwell, E., H., Stevens, D., and Ray, D. E. (2015). Innovation in palliative care delivery: A historical case study yields key drivers of successful implementation. *Nursing in the 21st Century*, No. 4: New Conversations in End-of-Life Care. Hudson Whitman Excelsior College Press.

Figved, N., Myhr, K. M., Larsen, J. P., and Aarsland, D. (2007). Caregiver burden in multiple sclerosis: The impact of neuropsychiatric symptoms. *Journal of Neurology, Neurosurgery and Psychiatry*, *78*(10), 1097–1102.

Foley, K. M., and Gelband, H. (Eds.) (2001). *Improving Palliative Care for Cancer*. Washington, DC: National Academies Press.

Future Search (2003). Future search methodology. At http://www.futuresearch.net/method/methodology/index.cfm (accessed July 2016).

Hirschmann, K. M., Ray, D., and Foster, E. (2011). "When we're all together, the patient knows it": Creating an interdisciplinary learning community in palliative medicine. Poster presented at the national seminar of the Center to Advance Palliative Care, San Diego, CA, Nov.

Holland, N. J., Schneider, D. M., Rapp, R., and Kalb, R. C. (2011). Meeting the needs of people with primary progressive multiple sclerosis, their families, and the health-care community. *International Journal of MS Care*, *13*(2), 65–74.

Hurd, M. D., Martorell, P., Delavande, A., Mullen, K. J., and Langa, K. M. (2013). Monetary costs of dementia in the United States. *New England Journal of Medicine*, *368*(14), 1326–1334.

IHI (Institute for Healthcare Improvement) (2003). *The Breakthrough Series: IHI's Collaborative Model for Achieving Breakthrough Improvement*. IHI Innovation Series white paper. Boston: IHI.

Institute of Medicine (2008). *Retooling for an Aging America: Building the Health Care Workforce*. Washington, DC: National Academies Press.

Leff, B., Spragens, L. H., Morano, B. Powell, J., Bickert, T., Bond, C., ... Siu, A. L. (2012). Rapid reengineering of acute medical care for Medicare beneficiaries: The Medicare Innovations Collaborative. *Health Affairs*, *31*(6), 1204–1215.

Lown, B. A., and Manning, C. F. (2010). The Schwartz Center Rounds: Evaluation of an interdisciplinary approach to enhancing patient-centered communication, teamwork, and provider support. *Academic Medicine*, *85*(6), 1073–1081.

Lukas, L., Foltz, C., and Paxton, H. (2013) Hospital outcomes for a home-based palliative medicine consulting service. *Journal of Palliative Medicine*, *16*(2), 179–184.

Maslach, C., Jackson, S., and Leiter, M. (1996). *Maslach Burnout Inventory Manual*, 3rd edn. Palo Alto, CA: Consulting Psychologists Press.

National Alliance for Caregiving and AARP (2009). Caregiving in the United States 2009. At http://www.caregiving.org/data/Caregiving_in_the_US_2009_full_report.pdf (accessed July 2016).

NCP (National Consensus Project for Quality Palliative Care) (2013). *Clinical Practice Guidelines for Quality Palliative Care*, 3rd edn, ed. C. Dahlin. Pittsburgh: National Consensus Project. At http://www.nationalconsensusproject.org/guidelines_download2.aspx (accessed July 2016).

Partridge, A. H., Seah, D. S. E., King, T., Leighl, N. B., Hauke, R., Wollins, D. S., and Von Roenn, J. H. (2014). Developing a service model that integrates palliative care throughout cancer care: The time is now. *Journal of Clinical Oncology*, *32*(29), 3330–3336.

Pereira, S. M., Fonseca, A. M., and Carvalho, A. S. (2011). Burnout in palliative care: A systematic review. *Nursing Ethics*, *18*(3), 317–326.

Schwartz Center (2015). Schwartz Center Rounds®. At http://www.theschwartzcenter.org/supporting-caregivers/schwartz-center-rounds/ (accessed July 2016).

Shanafelt, T. D., Boone, S., Tan, L., Dyrbye, L. N., Sotile, W., Satele, D., … Oreskovich, M. R. (2012). Burnout and satisfaction with work–life balance among US physicians relative to the general US population. *Archives of Internal Medicine*, *172*(18), 1377–1385.

Shanafelt, T. D., Gradishar, W.J., Kosty, M., Satele, D., Chew, H., Horn, L., … Raymond, M. (2014). Burnout and career satisfaction among US oncologists. *Journal of Clinical Oncology*, *32*(7), 678–686.

Sherman, A. C., Edwards, D., Simonton, S., and Mehta, P. (2006). Caregiver stress and burnout in an oncology unit. *Palliative and Supportive Care*, *4*(1), 65–80.

Vachon, M. L. (1995). Staff stress in hospice/palliative care: A review. *Palliative Medicine*, *9*(2), 91–122.

Weeks, J., Catalano, P., Cronin, A., Finkelman, M., Mack, J., Keating, N., and Schrag, D. (2012). Patients' expectations about effects of chemotherapy for advanced cancer. *New England Journal of Medicine*, *367*(17), 1616–1625. doi:10.1056/NEJMoa1204410

Weissman, D. E., and Meier, D. E. (2011). Identifying patients in need of a palliative care assessment in the hospital setting. *Journal of Palliative Medicine*, *14*(1), 1–7.

Yang, W., Williams, J. H., Hogan, P. F., Bruinooge, S. S., Rodriguez, G. I., Kosty, M. P., … Goldstein, M. (2014). Projected supply of and demand for oncologists and radiation oncologists through 2025: An aging, better-insured population will result in shortage. *Journal of Oncology Practice*, *10*(1), 39–45.

Zurlinden, J. (2000). How we nurses grieve. *Nursing Spectrum*, *10*, 9.

14

Crossover of Burnout and Engagement from Managers to Followers

The Role of Social Support

Mina Westman and Shoshi Chen

Stress, Burnout and Engagement in the Workplace

Work-related stress is estimated to be the second largest problem related to the working environment. It represents a huge cost in terms of both adverse human health effects and impaired economic performance. Studies suggest that between 50 and 60 percent of all lost working days in Europe have some link to work-related stress (European Agency for Safety and Health at Work, 2009). As for the United States, findings from the 2014 *Stress in America*™ survey show that work is the second most commonly reported significant source of stress (60 percent) (APA, 2015).

Job stressors are caused by various demands such as overload, noise, time pressure, physically demanding work, or interruptions and a high risk of errors (Beehr, 1998). Empirical data indicate that leaders can have a significant impact on employee health and well-being, not only as the cause of psychological distress and other negative outcomes such as burnout (e.g., Skogstad, Einarsen, Torsheim, Aasland, and Hetland, 2007), but also by enhancing general psychological well-being and fostering a positive state of mind, especially engagement (e.g., Arnold, Turner, Barling, Kelloway, and McKee, 2007).

In the next section we discuss the importance of resources in general, and social support in particular, for preventing stress and enhancing well-being in the workplace. We begin by reviewing the role of resources for employees' well-being and then focus on the various functions played by social support, one of the most important resources.

The Handbook of Stress and Health: A Guide to Research and Practice, First Edition.
Edited by Cary L. Cooper and James Campbell Quick.
© 2017 John Wiley & Sons, Ltd. Published 2017 by John Wiley & Sons, Ltd.

The Role of Resources: Focusing on Social Support

According to conservation of resources (COR) theory (Hobfoll, 2002), resources are defined as "those entities that either are centrally valued in their own right (e.g., self-esteem, close attachments, health, and inner peace), or act as means to obtain centrally valued ends (e.g., money, social support, and credit)" (p. 307). COR theory argues that individuals strive to protect their own interests and attain pleasure. Schaufeli and Bakker (2004) indicated that job resources refer to those physical, psychological, social, or organizational aspects of the job that either (1) reduce job demands and the associated physiological and psychological costs; (2) are functional in achieving work goals; or (3) stimulate personal growth, learning and development. According to Hobfoll (2002), resources are not only necessary to deal with job demands and to "getting things done," but also are instrumental in people's efforts "to protect against resource loss, recover from losses and gain resources" (p. 349), implying that an individual's resources reduce their vulnerability to the effects of threatened or actual future resource loss. This principle highlights the significance of proactive resource investment for preventive purposes and has important implications for stress prevention.

The accumulation of resources is also likely to result in positive emotional states and attitudes. Social support is one such resource; as it accumulates, it can broaden an individual's resource pool and replace or reinforce other resources that are lacking (Hobfoll, 1985). Social support resources lead individuals to feel more confident about their ability to successfully accomplish their role-related goals and meet expectations in both the work and family domains.

Therefore, COR theory views social support as a robust type of resource and one of the main routes for expanding resources available to the individual to meet environmental demands and achieving personal goals (Hobfoll, 2002; Hobfoll, Lilly, and Jackson, 1992; Vaux, 1992).

Social Support

One of the most frequently researched job resources is social support (Gorgievski, Halbesleben, and Bakker, 2011), which is embedded in the personal aspects of work and the social environment, respectively (Tims, Bakker, and Derks, 2012). Social support is defined as a relationship: the interactions between individuals and their environments for the purpose of extending or obtaining behavioral or emotional assistance (Hobfoll, Parris, and Stephens, 1990; Vaux, 1988). Social support also indicates that others care for or empathize with someone or are willing and able to provide important information and material aid to that person (Winnubst, 1993).

Social support includes instrumental aid, emotional concern, provision of information, and appraisals. House (1981) distinguished between four main forms of social support: emotional concern, instrumental aid, provision of information, and appraisal, all of which are intended to enhance the well-being of the recipient. He further maintained that social support may originate from various sources such as supervisors, coworkers, or family and friends. Hobfoll (2001) identified several such social support resources in the work and family domains, such as "support from coworkers" and "understanding from my employer/boss" in the workplace, along with family-based resources such as "help with chores at home."

Various sources of support may have varying effects on stress and individual outcomes. In a meta-analysis of 103 studies of social support, Halbesleben (2006) found that work-related sources of support were more strongly negatively associated with employee burnout than non work-related sources of support. He interpreted these findings as evidence that colleagues at work were in a better position to provide more effective support.

In a similar vein, Kossek, Colquitt, and Noe (2011) found that a specific kind of social support, supervisory work–family support, is likely to be a more useful resource for managing work–family stressors, such as time, strain, or behavior-based conflicts, than general workplace social support. They maintain that supervisory work–family support provides employees with additional resources to cope with the negative effects of high workloads, and the ability to jointly manage work and family demands. Thus, when a supportive supervisor demonstrates understanding and empathy toward employees' family-related obligations, such support boosts the psychological resources available to an individual to deal with related stress, thus reducing distress and conflict with work demands. Through such support from their manager, employees effectively gain new resources to help them juggle their work and family demands.

Recently, Goh, Ilies, and Wilson (2015) demonstrated that supervisory work–family support moderated the relationship between daily workload and work–family conflict, attesting to the importance of supervisory support in reducing interference between work and family. This finding among others supports the claim that different forms of support satisfy different functions and that specific support is usually more beneficial that general support.

Direct effects of social support have been documented by several researchers. Kahn and Byosiere (1992), who reviewed the social support literature, concluded that the majority of studies found evidence of a main effect of social support on levels of well-being. Similarly, a meta-analysis by Viswesvaran, Sanchez, and Fisher (1999) found a mitigating effect (negative relationship) of supervisor support on various stressors and demonstrated that direct effects yielded stronger results than moderating effects.

Social Support: The Buffering Hypothesis

Cohen and Wills (1985) distinguished between social support's main effects and buffering effects on stress, and this distinction has since played a foundational role in shaping social support theory and research. Social support is usually regarded as a moderating variable in the relationship between stress and strain (Beehr, Farmer, Glazer, Gudanowski, and Nair, 2003; Viswesvaran et al., 1999). The buffering model proposes that social support protects individuals against the adverse effects of stress. Evidence for stress buffering is indicated when the link between stress and strain is stronger for people with low social support than for people with high social support.

According to the buffering hypothesis, the amount of social support an individual receives can influence their appraisal of stressful situations, that is, potential stressors are appraised as more manageable and less threatening when individuals perceive high levels of social support (Cohen and Wills, 1985). The social support buffering model has been thoroughly developed and has dominated social support research. Nearly all research on social support is guided by the assumption that social support's link to health reflects stress buffering.

While main effects of perceived social support on health are more consistent, only a few studies supported the social support buffering model. House and Wells (1978) found that social support buffered the negative effects of work stressors on psychological and physiological well-being. Similarly, LaRocco, House, and French (1980) found evidence for the buffering model of social support on well-being but not on job satisfaction. Terry, Nielsen, and Perchard

(1993) demonstrated that availability of a supervisor's work-related support buffered the negative effects of role conflict and work overload.

Cohen and Wills (1985) label this critical problem with the social support buffering hypothesis as the stress–support matching hypothesis, and posit that buffering effects will be observed when the support functions measured are those that are most relevant for the stressors faced by the person. Beehr et al. (2003) attributed the paucity of empirical support for the buffering hypothesis to a lack of "source congruence," or the lack of identity or at least similarity between the source of a stressor and the source of support in the studies. On this view, buffering is most likely to occur when the moderators are specific to, or match, the stressors being investigated. When it comes to job stressors, support from a supervisor or colleague would be more of a match than support from family and friends. Supervisors have more power to change certain aspects of work demands than peers or others.

In summary, social support is an important resource that can reduce stress and strain and buffer the relationship between them when source congruence exists. Furthermore, social support in the work environment may affect the target individual as well as others, through spillover from domain to domain and crossover between people.

Spillover and Crossover

Leaders have an impact on their followers' stress and strain as well as their well-being. One way leaders have a negative or positive impact is by transmitting emotions and experiences to their followers. Crossover and spillover are two ways in which stress or strain is carried over within and across individuals and domains (Bolger, DeLongis, Kessler, and Wethington, 1989). *Spillover* is the within-person transdomain transmission of experiences, from work to home and from home to work for the same individual (Eby, Casper, Lockwood, Bordeaux, and Brinley, 2005). In contrast, *crossover* is defined as the interpersonal process that occurs when job stress or psychological strain experienced by one person affects the level of strain of another person in the same social environment (Bolger et al., 1989). Several studies have recently demonstrated that resources such as self-efficacy and self-esteem may also cross over from leaders to followers (e.g., Ten Brummelhuis, Haar, and Roche, 2014). In order to explore this issue, we first describe the crossover model (Westman, 2001) and specifically discuss crossover from leaders to followers.

The Crossover Model

Westman (2001) developed a conceptual crossover model based on role theory (Katz and Kahn, 1978), which extended previous approaches by adding an interpersonal focus of analysis, specifically the dyad. The crossover model describes a mechanism by which experiences, emotions, and resources are transferred within social and organizational contexts. The model identifies specific perceptions of stress, strain, and positive experiences as antecedent influences of the crossover process, and posits interpersonal (social support, undermining) and individual variables as possible moderators of the crossover process. The model posits that one person's stress or strain has an impact on close others in different settings, reflecting a complex causal relationship between stress and strain in the individual arena and between stress and strain of dyads and later in teams. The model shows that one person's experienced stress and strain may directly induce strain in the other individual.

Westman (2001) proposed three mechanisms – direct crossover, indirect crossover, and common stressors to explain the crossover process. In the first mechanism, *direct crossover*, experiences, emotions, and states are transmitted between the partners via empathy. The basis for this view is the finding that crossover effects appear between closely related partners who care for each other and share the greater part of their lives. Lazarus (1991) defined empathy as "sharing another's feelings by placing oneself psychologically in that person's circumstances" (p. 287). The core relational theme for empathy implies a sharing of another person's emotional state, distressed or otherwise. Accordingly, an individual's strain produces an empathic reaction in the partner that increases the partner's strain through what may be called *empathic identification*. If individuals pay close attention to others, and if they construe themselves as interrelated to others, direct crossover between partners is highly likely.

The second mechanism, indirect crossover, posits that crossover of emotions occurs through moderating variables. Coping mechanisms such as social support and undermining have been widely identified as mediators and moderators of stress and strain responses (Coyne and Downey, 1991; Pearlin, 1989). Individuals may respond to stress by engaging in undermining behavior, such as actions that undermine the partner's sense of self-worth by displaying negative affect or negatively evaluating the target person (Demerouti, Bakker, and Schaufeli, 2005). Such behavior is a stressor for the target person, impairing their psychological well-being (Vinokur and Van Ryn, 1993). Another form of coping in the crossover process is reduced social support, implying that burned-out individuals are unable to provide their partner with adequate social support. Eventually, the lack of social support increases the partner's stress (Hobfoll and London, 1986).

In the third proposed mechanism, *common stressors* affecting both partners will impact the strain of both partners, and the similarity in the strain will appear as crossover. Thus, Westman and Vinokur (1998) suggest that common stressors in a shared environment that increase both partners' strain should be considered a spurious case of crossover. These mechanisms have been tested and supported by findings of several studies (Howe, Levy, and Caplan, 2004; Song, Foo, Uy, and Sun, 2011; Westman and Vinokur, 1998).

Studies of crossover processes between partners have initially focused on the crossover of job stressors and psychological strain from the individual to stress and strain of the partner (Westman, 2001), finding evidence of the crossover of stress and psychological strains such as anxiety (Westman, Etzion, and Horovitz, 2004a), burnout (e.g., Bakker and Schaufeli, 2000), distress (Ten Brummelhuis, Haar, and van der Lippe, 2010), depression (Howe et al., 2004; Song et al., 2011), work–family conflict (e.g., Hammer, Allen, and Grigsby, 1997; Westman and Etzion, 2005), and marital dissatisfaction (Westman, Vinokur, Hamilton, and Roziner, 2004b).

Westman (2001) proposed that crossover mechanisms (direct, indirect, and common experiences) are equally applicable to negative and positive crossover. Westman argued that just as stressful job demands have a negative impact on the partner's well-being, positive feelings following positive job or home events may also cross over to and have a positive effect on partner's well-being. There are many positive instances, such as enjoyable experiences in one's job (reaching sales targets, getting a promotion, getting positive feedback), that lead to the crossover of job satisfaction and engagement to one's partner. Just as strain in one partner may produce an empathetic reaction in the other, which increases the recipient's strain, work engagement expressed by one partner may fuel the partner's engagement. Furthermore, crossover of positive emotions may occur indirectly, following an interaction between the partners. Positive events at work spill over to the home domain and lead to positive interactions at home such as social support, which lead to positive crossover for the partner.

The investigation of the crossover of positive emotions is in line with the growing interest in positive psychology (e.g., Seligman and Csikszentmihalyi, 2000) and with Fredrickson's (2001) broaden-and-build theory, which postulates that positive emotions broaden individuals' thought–action repertoires, prompting them to pursue a wider range of thoughts and actions than they typically use. Burns et al. (2008) and Tugade, Fredrickson, and Feldman (2004) demonstrated that positive emotions can improve our ability to cope with stress, which subsequently enhances our resilience. Such feelings may facilitate positive crossover via empathy.

Most studies that have demonstrated positive crossover focused on the crossover of engagement or its components (e.g., Bakker and Xanthopoulou, 2009; Demerouti, Bakker, and Schaufeli, 2005; Westman, Etzion, and Chen, 2009). Schaufeli and Bakker (2004) defined *work engagement* as a positive and fulfilling work-related state of mind characterized by vigor, dedication, and absorption (see also Schaufeli, Salanova, González-Romá, and Bakker, 2002). Rather than a momentary and specific state, engagement refers to a more persistent and pervasive affective-cognitive state that is not focused on any specific object, event, individual, or behavior. Engaged employees have a sense of energetic and effective connection with their work activities, and they perceive themselves as able to handle the demands of their job satisfactorily. The engagement literature identifies job resources (e.g., performance feedback, job autonomy, and supervisor support) and personal resources (e.g., self-efficacy, self-esteem) that predict individual engagement (Schaufeli and Bakker, 2004). This accretion of resources may, in turn, increase the likelihood that they will participate in other roles, such as providing support to partners and coworkers. Engaged individuals are less likely to withdraw from social interactions and to engage in undermining behaviors, while being more likely to engage in supportive behavior (Bakker et al., 2009).

Bakker, Demerouti, and Schaufeli (2005) provided evidence for the crossover of engagement among partners. Their results revealed that positive feelings of vigor and dedication expressed by one partner influenced the other partner, even after controlling for relevant aspects of the work and home environment. Similarly, Bakker and Xanthopoulou (2009) found a crossover of daily work engagement, but only on days when employees interacted more frequently than usual within a dyad. These findings suggest a process in which one partner who feels engaged as a result of the resources available at work is likely to express this engagement in their interactions with their partner. The partner is influenced by this positive emotional state and begins to feel the same way, that is, engaged.

The Spillover–Crossover Model

Westman's (2001) argument that spillover is a necessary but insufficient condition for crossover was a trigger for the development of the spillover–crossover model (SCM) by Bakker and Demerouti (2013), who aimed to gain a better understanding of the processes that link work and family domains. While spillover researchers have generally neglected to examine the impact of employees' experiences at work on partners' well-being at home, crossover researchers have generally ignored the work-related links of the employees' experiences at work on their experiences and outcomes at home. By integrating both literatures, better insight is gained into the processes that link the work and family domains.

According to the SCM, experiences built up at work first spill over to the employee's home domain, influencing their behavior at home, and then cross over to influence the partner's well-being. Evidence for this "double transmission" of experiences has been found in several studies. For example, Bakker, Demerouti, and Dollard (2008) found that job demands were positively related to the focal individuals' own work–family conflict (spillover), which led to their partner's exhaustion (crossover). Furthermore, social undermining mediated the relationship between individuals' work–family conflict (WFC) and their partners' home demands. Thus, as employees' work overload increased, their work began to interfere with family life, resulting in undermining their partners. This behavior increased the partners' home demands, resulting in high levels of partners' exhaustion (indirect crossover via undermining).

The SCM was also supported by the results of Shimazu, Bakker, and Demerouti (2009) that demonstrated that job demands were related to work–family conflict and poor relationship quality (spillover) and to partners' depressive symptoms and physical complaints (crossover). Focusing on positive outcomes, Bakker et al. (2011) found in a longitudinal study that work engagement was positively related to work–family facilitation (spillover), which, in turn, also predicted own and partner's life satisfaction a year later (crossover). In the same vein, Rodríguez-Muñoz, Sanz-Vergel, and Demerouti (2014) found in a diary study that daily work engagement has a direct effect on daily happiness (spillover). Furthermore, employees' daily work engagement influenced their partners' daily happiness through the employees' own daily happiness (crossover). The findings demonstrate the bidirectional crossover of daily happiness between both partners and confirm that the positive effects of work engagement extend beyond the work setting and beyond the individual employee.

Crossover of Resources

A new topic of research that has emerged is the crossover of resources. Recently Neff, Sonnentag, Niessen, and Unger (2012; 2013a; 2013b) demonstrated the crossover of resources (self-esteem and self-efficacy) from one partner to another, suggesting that one partner can act as a source of positive work-related resources to the other partner. The researchers based this line of research on self-expansion theory (Aron et al., 2005) and on the assumption that in the course of an intimate relationship, individuals increasingly incorporate their partners' resources, perspectives, and identities into their own self. Aron et al. (2005) proposed that "the evaluative and affective responses to another's acquisition and loss of resources … are to some extent the same as if the acquisition or loss was with regard to one's own resources" (p. 210).

Neff et al. (2012) showed in a diary study that day-performance self-esteem experienced by one partner after work crossed over to the other partner in the evening. Neff et al. (2013b) further examined the crossover of performance self-esteem longitudinally and demonstrated that an actor's self-esteem at Time 1 predicted changes in the partner's performance self-esteem at Time 2. Furthermore, they found that the actor's performance self-esteem was related to the partner's work engagement at Time 2 through indirect crossover of self-esteem.

The authors proposed that one partner's day-specific self-esteem perceptions trigger social comparison processes within the other partner, especially when the partner reported low self-esteem and high empathic concern. They argued that due to the intimacy of couples, witnessing a partner's self-esteem in the evening can cause similar self-evaluations to the other partner, enhancing the crossover of self-esteem. This finding is in line with the proposed direct crossover mechanism and with the role of crossover as a reflection of direct empathic reaction (Westman, 2001).

Neff et al. (2013a) also found that job-related self-efficacy crossed over to the partner's job-related self-efficacy. They found that crossover of self-efficacy occurred when both partners talk about their jobs and become aware of how the other partner copes with difficult situations. Thus, a person brings home job-related self-efficacy beliefs, and thereby affects the partner via crossover processes. Speaking about one's own accomplishments can additionally enhance the partner's job-related self-efficacy beliefs. They also showed that the crossover of job-related self-efficacy was linked to the partner's perceived work engagement (indirect crossover).

The partner's work engagement was also enhanced by the transfer of self-esteem and self-efficacy from one partner to another, creating a potential spiral of gains that illustrates how resource caravans (Hobfoll, 2011) are transmitted to partners. The finding that high job-related self-efficacy is not only beneficial for the individual's outcomes (Abele and Spurk, 2009; Stajkovic and Luthans, 1998), but also affects the partner via crossover processes, has practical implications for couples, team members, manager–subordinate dyads and teams, and organizations. Supporting employees' job-related self-efficacy at work might positively affect employees and their partners via crossover processes, which may, in turn, positively affect the partner's work engagement, ultimately leading to improved performance. Replicating these findings could lead to investigation of the crossover of social support in the family and at the workplace. Crossover of resources in general and of social support in particular may contribute to a more resilient family, more resilient and productive workplace, and healthier organizations in society.

In the next section we integrate the literature on spillover, crossover and social support to suggest that social support contributes to the crossover process between leaders and followers.

Leaders, Followers, and Social Support

Leadership is defined by Yukl (2010) as "the process of influencing others to understand and agree about what needs to be done and how to do it, and the process of facilitating individual and collective efforts to accomplish shared objectives" (p. 8). Most accepted definitions of leadership indicate that the key component of leadership is influence, or the ability to motivate people to perform tasks.

Yukl (2010) called for more concentrated efforts to understand mediators that link leadership behaviors to follower outcomes. One far-reaching outcome is employee stress and well-being. Research has concluded that many stress-related symptoms and illnesses arise when a relationship between employees and leaders is perceived as psychologically unhealthy (Cooper and Payne, 1991: Landeweerd and Boumans, 1994; Tepper, 2000).In contrast, leader support and empowering behaviors, and a good relationship between leaders and their employees, are recognized as leader behaviors that may reduce stress and improve well-being among employees (Bass and Avolio, 1990; Schaufeli and Enzmann, 1998; Yukl, 2010). Three theories have been proposed to explain leaders' ability to impact their followers' outcomes, and the mechanisms underlying such effects: leader–member exchange (LMX) theory (Graen and Uhl-Bien, 1995), the full range of leadership model (Bass, 1998), and the crossover model (Westman, 2001). These models are discussed below.

Leadership Styles and Employee Well-Being

An emerging body of research has identified a link between leadership styles and employee well-being (Kuoppala, Lamminpää, Liira, and Vainio, 2008; Shieh, Mills, and Waltz, 2001;

Van Dierendonck, Haynes, Borril, and Stride, 2004). In particular, transformational leadership styles have been negatively linked to outcomes such as job stress and burnout (Sosik and Godshalk, 2000). Seltzer and Numerof (1988) examined the relationship between supervisory consideration and subordinate burnout. They found that subordinates reported less burnout when their supervisors provided a higher amount of consideration behaviors and less structure. Thomas and Lankau (2009) found that employees benefit from high-quality relationships with their supervisors, and that individuals who reported higher-quality relationships with their supervisors were better socialized and experienced lower role stress.

One way leaders influence their followers' stress and strain is through their impact on the employees' psychological resource pool. Leader–member exchange theory (Graen and Uhl-Bien, 1995) sheds some light on how leadership styles affect followers' resource pools and well-being through an exchange of important resources (such as social support) with subordinates that assist the latter in completing their work. According to LMX theory, leaders develop different forms of exchange relationships with their subordinates such that subordinates who maintain good exchange relationships receive more resources than others (Graen and Uhl-Bien, 1995). LMX theory suggests that a positive and high-quality social exchange between managers and employees is vital for individual, group, and organizational outcomes (Gerstner and Day, 1997; Graen and Uhl-Bien, 1995). For example, Thomas and Lankau (2009) found that high-LMX supervisors and nonsupervisory mentors serve as resources that minimize emotional exhaustion through increased socialization and decreased role stress.

Cullen (2014) tested how supervisors' burnout affects their subordinates' burnout, directly and indirectly, through their leader–member exchange relationships. Consistent with context theory and role theory (Katz and Kahn, 1978), employees interpret cues from their social environment to inform their behavior at work. Accordingly, supervisors appear most prominently to act as transmitters of burnout. As supervisors control employees' resources and interactions, they have more opportunities to express and transmit their burnout. When supervisors begin to experience depersonalization, a component of burnout, they manifest negative behavior, such as criticism (Dean, Brandes, and Dharwadkar, 1998). These behaviors are associated with reduced emotional attachment to others (Naus, van Iterson, and Roe, 2007), expressions of negative emotions, and reduced social support to employees (Kirkpatrick and Locke, 1991). Supervisors experiencing depersonalization begin to conserve their own resources in an effort to reduce furthering of their own burnout and withdraw from investing in their employees, thus resulting in lower-quality LMX relationships. In such cases, subordinates begin perceiving that their investments of resources are likely to be followed by a lack of resource gain and that their supervisor lacks concern for them, resulting in diminished perceptions of their LMX relationship. In contrast, high-quality LMX supervisors provide their subordinates with social support through extensive attention and interaction that convey their interpersonal concerns. Subordinates who receive such attention and social support experience less job burnout.

Leaders may also impact employee's outcomes by affecting their resources, as indicated by Bass's (1998) full range of leadership model. This leadership style expands employees' resource pool by creating new resources for employees (objects, psychological, feedback, money, self-esteem, social support, etc.), yet depletes the leaders' own resource pool as transactional leadership requires investment of resources (effort, time. knowledge).

According to Bass (1998), transformational leaders appeal to the motivational, emotional, and developmental needs of their subordinates. Transformational leadership is characterized by four elements: inspirational motivation, idealized influence, individualized support, and intellectual stimulation. Transformational leaders inspire subordinates to higher levels of effort and commitment by empowering them through emotional appeals (Yukl, 2010) and by reframing stressful situations as opportunities for growth, while providing the necessary social support throughout the process (Bass, 1998; Sosik and Godshalk, 2000).

Transformational leaders may influence subordinates' stress appraisals because of the support, encouragement, and emotional involvement that characterize their daily interactions with employees. Transformational leadership behaviors may also be related to positive affective well-being. Previous research has found that transformational leaders are more optimistic than others (Spreitzer and Quinn, 1996) and tend to interpret their surroundings more positively. Indeed, McColl-Kennedy and Anderson (2002) found that transformational leadership style was positively associated with followers' optimism. Through idealized influence, leaders enact what is right, and employees who see their leaders doing the right thing will trust and respect them and have positive perceptions. Finally, through individualized consideration, leaders show concern for their employees through listening and being compassionate, thus providing social support. Such a close relationship between leader and follower may increase employees' sense of well-being (Sivanathan, Arnold, Turner, and Barling, 2004).

An additional possible mechanism through which transformational leaders influence subordinates' outcomes is based on the crossover model (Westman, 2001), which predicts that the crossover of stress and strain occurs when a leader's mood is "contagious" or crosses over from managers to followers. Sy, Cote, and Saavedra (2005) demonstrated the effects of leaders' mood on individuals. They found that when leaders were in a positive mood, in comparison to a negative mood, individual group members experienced more positive and less negative mood, and groups had a more positive and a less negative affective tone. The authors also found that groups with leaders in a positive mood exhibited more coordination and expended less effort than did groups with leaders in a negative mood. Support for the crossover effect also was found in a study by Glasø and Einarsen (2006), who found that managers and employees shared emotions during interactions: When managers showed positive emotions, such as feeling respected, wanted, and confident, so did employees. Similarly, Sutherland and Davidson's (1993) qualitative study showed that managers' job dissatisfaction was related to employees' relationship issues. Thus, leaders high in positive moods and emotions may influence their followers' moods and emotions through a contagion process (Bakker, Westman, and Van Emmerik, 2009). This line of research may suggest that leaders' stress levels and affective well-being have an impact on the stress and affective well-being of employees.

The Impact of Managers' Work–family Interface on Their Employees

While studies based on the SCM focused on spillover from work to home, several studies, focusing on managers, demonstrated a complementary process, spillover from the manager's home to work (e.g., work–family conflict/work–family enrichment leads to manager's burnout/engagement), and subsequently cross over from the manager to employees.

Managers' work–family conflict (WFC) and work–family enrichment (WFE) can also cross over directly to their employees. As part of the social environment at work, employees may take cues from their managers regarding the prioritization of the work domain in relation to the family domain. For example, if a manager displays to employees that his or her work responsibilities conflict with family responsibilities, the employees may interpret that they too should put work before family responsibilities, thereby leading to their own work–family conflict.

The same process may unfold when managers display ways in which their work enhances their family life.

To illustrate, Ten Brummelhuis et al. (2014) investigated whether leaders' WFC and WFE influenced their own well-being at work (i.e., job burnout and work engagement) and consequently influenced the well-being of their followers due to crossover processes (indirect crossover). They found that leaders' burnout was negatively related to leaders' supportive behavior, indirectly increasing burnout among followers. Followers rated burnt-out leaders as being less supportive to them. Thus, leaders' reduced provision of support exacerbated feelings of burnout in their followers. To provide support, leaders must focus on followers' needs, an act that requires resources (energy, involvement). Burnt-out leaders are lacking in these resources and therefore are unable provide support to their followers. On the other hand, leaders who experienced high levels of WFE were more enthusiastic, vigorous and dedicated at work. These leaders transferred these positive feelings to their followers, supporting them and boosting their work engagement. These findings support the spillover–crossover model; leaders' family matters first spill over to the work domain, affecting leaders' well-being, and these outcomes cross over to the followers. Their results underscored that leaders' family life affects work, influencing not only their own well-being but also how they motivate and support their followers, and ultimately influences their followers' burnout or engagement as well.

Management support is an important precondition for a personal and team's high performance. These findings indicate that the various forms of support provide employees with necessary psychological and utilitarian support during the work process, form an important social interaction process, and promote a harmonious atmosphere.

Summary

Leaders play an important role in defining an environment in which employees can thrive and experience well-being (Nielsen, Yarker, Brenner, Randall, and Borg, 2008; Rasulzada, Dackert, and Johansson, 2003). A particular behavior by a leader or a component of a particular leadership style can be either inherently stressful or positive for employees, and consequently influence their stress and affective well-being. The crossover effect between leaders and followers is an important process as leaders function as role models and can influence their employees' well-being (Salanova and Schaufeli, 2008).

In this chapter, we demonstrated how leadership styles are related to employee outcomes by integrating three bodies of knowledge: theories and research related to crossover, resources, and leadership. We elaborated three mechanisms through which this process operates: LMX, transformational leadership and the crossover model. We focused on social support as an important resource in the process, discussing its main and buffering effects, its importance in the crossover process in general, and its role in the crossover from leaders to followers in particular.

Studies highlight the critical nature of social support in both the work and family realms. Employees who enjoy supportive relationships both in and out of work are likely to be more satisfied with various aspects of their lives than those who are relatively isolated. Social support at work and especially from leaders is very instrumental to employees' well-being and performance and should be developed.

Employees' burnout is an important concern for organizations because of its links to costly outcomes (Cordes and Dougherty, 1993). Understanding the role of the supervisor in the subordinates' burnout process may help organizations develop leadership practices that reduce and eliminate burnout's prevalence in the workplace. Managers have a very important role in achieving the organizations goals. They also have a key role in developing the human resources. Due to their positions within organizations, supervisors may influence their subordinates' critical job resources such as lack of social support, which may lead to employee burnout. Therefore, understanding the way they impact their employees' well-being can help to improve employee well-being and organizational performance. There are many managerial development programs, but few focus on this issue.

Unlike other resources that influence individual responses to stress, social support may be initiated by management and can potentially serve as an important preventive intervention measure (Quick, Quick, Nelson, and Hurrell, 1997). Therefore, organizations that create and maintain supportive work cultures may reap the rewards in the form of a more satisfied and productive workforce.

References

Abele, A. E., and Spurk, D. (2009). The longitudinal impact of self-efficacy and career goals on objective and subjective career success. *Journal of Vocational Behavior, 74*, 53–62.

APA (American Psychological Association) (2015). *Stress in America^TM: Paying with Our Health*. At http://www.apa.org/news/press/releases/stress/2014/stress-report.pdf (accessed July 2016).

Arnold, K. A., Turner, N., Barling, J., Kelloway, E. K., and McKee, M. C. (2007). Transformational leadership and psychological well-being: The mediating role of meaningful work. *Journal of Occupational Health Psychology, 12*, 193–203. doi:10.1037/1076-8998.12.3.193

Aron, A., Mashek, D., McLaughlin-Volpe, T., Wright, S., Lewandowski, G., and Aron, E. N. (2005). Including close others in the cognitive structure of the self. In M. W. Baldwin (Ed.), *Interpersonal Cognition* (pp. 206–232). New York: Guilford Press.

Bakker, A. B., and Demerouti, E. (2013). The spillover-crossover model. In J. Grzywacs and E. Demerouti (Eds.), *New Frontiers in Work and Family Research* (pp. 54–70). Hove, UK: Psychology Press.

Bakker, A. B., Demerouti, E., and Dollard, M. F. (2008). How job demands affect partners' experience of exhaustion: Integrating work–family conflict and crossover theory. *Journal of Applied Psychology, 93*, 901–911. doi:10.1037/0021-9010.93.4.901

Bakker, A. B., Demerouti, E., and Schaufeli, W. B. (2005). The crossover of burnout and work engagement among working couples. *Human Relations, 58*, 661–689. doi:10.1177/0018726705055967

Bakker, A. B., and Schaufeli, W. B. (2000). Burnout contagion processes among teachers. *Journal of Applied Social Psychology, 30*, 2289–2308. doi:10.1111/j.1559-1816.2000.tb02437.x

Bakker, A. B., Shimazu, A., Demerouti, E., Shimada, K., and Kawakami, N. (2011). Crossover of work engagement among Japanese couples: Perspective taking by both partners. *Journal of Occupational Health Psychology, 16*, 112–125. doi:10.1016/j.socscimed.2011.05.049

Bakker, A.B., Westman, M., and Van Emmerik, I. J. H. (2009). Advancements in crossover theory. *Journal of Managerial Psychology, 24*, 206–219. doi:10.1108/02683940910939304

Bakker, A. B., and Xanthopoulou, D. (2009). The crossover of daily work engagement: Test of an actor–partner interdependence model. *Journal of Applied Psychology, 94*, 1562–1571. doi:10.1037/a0017525

Bass, B. (1998). *Transformational Leadership: Industrial, Military, and Educational Impact*. Mahwah, NJ: Erlbaum.

Bass, B., and Avolio, B. (1990). *Transformational Leadership Development: Manual for the Multifactor Leadership Questionnaire*. Palo Alto, CA: Consulting Psychologists Press.

Beehr, T. (1998). An organizational psychology meta-model of occupational stress. In C. L. Cooper (Ed.), *Theories of Organizational Stress* (pp. 6–27). Oxford: Oxford University Press.

Beehr, T. A., Farmer, S. J., Glazer, S., Gudanowski, D. M., and Nair, V. N. (2003). The enigma of social support and occupational stress: Source congruence and gender role effects. *Journal of Occupational Health Psychology, 8*, 220–231. doi:10.1037/1076-8998.8.3.220

Bolger, N., DeLongis, A., Kessler, R. C., and Wethington, E. (1989). The contagion of stress across multiple roles. *Journal of Marriage and the Family, 51*, 175–183. doi:10.2307/352378.

Burns, A. B., Brown, J. S., Sachs-Ericsson, N., Ashby Plant, E., Thomas Curtis, J., Fredrickson, B. L., and Joiner, T. E. (2008). Upward spirals of positive emotion and coping: Replication, extension, and initial exploration of neurochemical substrates. *Personality and Individual Differences*, 44, 360–370.

Cohen, S., and Wills, T. A. (1985). Stress, social support, and the buffering hypothesis. *Psychological Bulletin*, 98, 310–357. doi:10.1037/0033-2909.98.2.310

Cooper, C. L., and Payne, R. E. (1991). *Personality and Stress: Individual Differences in the Stress Process*. New York: Wiley.

Cordes, C. L., and Dougherty, T. W. (1993). A review and an integration of research on job burnout. *Academy of Management Review*, 18, 621–656. doi:10.5465/AMR.1993.9402210153

Coyne, J. C., and Downey, G. (1991). Social factors and psychopathology: Stress, social support, and coping processes. *Annual Review of Psychology*, 42, 401–425. doi:10.1146/ 42.020191.002153

Cullen, L. (2014). How does supervisor burnout affect leader–member exchange? A dyadic perspective. *International Business and Economic Research Journal*, 13, 1113–1125.

Dean, J. W., Brandes, P., and Dharwadkar, R. (1998). Organizational cynicism. *Academy of Management Review*, 23, 341–352. doi:10.5465/533230

Demerouti, E., Bakker, A. B., and Schaufeli, W. B. (2005). Spillover and crossover of exhaustion and life satisfaction among dual-earner parents. *Journal of Vocational Behavior*, 67, 266–289.

Eby, L. T., Casper, W. J., Lockwood, A., Bordeaux, C., and Brinley, A. (2005). Work and family research in IO/OB: Content analysis and review of the literature (1980–2002). *Journal of Vocational Behavior*, 66, 124–197.

EU-OSHA (European Agency for Safety and Health at Work) (2009). *OSH in Figures: Stress at Work – Facts and Figures*. At https://osha.europa.eu/en/tools-and-publications/publications/reports/TE-81-08-478-EN-C_OSH_in_figures_stress_at_work (accessed July 2016).

Fredrickson, B. L. (2001). The role of positive emotions in positive psychology: The broaden-and-build theory of positive emotions. *American Psychologist*, 56, 218–226. doi:10.1037/0003-066X.56.3.218

Gerstner, C. R., and Day, D. V. (1997). Meta-analytic review of leader–member exchange theory: Correlates and construct issues. *Journal of Applied Psychology*, 82, 827–844. doi:10.1037/0021-9010.82.6.827

Glasø, L., and Einarsen, S. (2006). Experienced affects in leader–subordinate relationships. *Scandinavian Journal of Management*, 22, 49–73.

Goh, Z., Ilies, R., and Wilson, K. S. (2015). Supportive supervisors improve employees' daily lives: The role supervisors play in the impact of daily workload on life satisfaction via work–family conflict. *Journal of Vocational Behavior*, 89, 65–73.

Gorgievski, M. J., Halbesleben, J. R., and Bakker, A. B. (2011). Expanding the boundaries of psychological resource theories. *Journal of Occupational and Organizational Psychology*, 84, 1–7. doi:10.1111/j.2044-8325.2010.02015.x

Graen, G. B., and Uhl-Bien, M. (1995). Relationship-based approach to leadership: Development of leader–member exchange (LMX) theory of leadership over 25 years: Applying a multi-level multi-domain perspective. *Leadership Quarterly*, 6, 219–247. doi:10.1016/1048-9843(95)90036-5

Halbesleben, J. R. (2006). Sources of social support and burnout: a meta-analytic test of the conservation of resources model. *Journal of Applied Psychology*, 91, 1134–1145. doi:10.1037/0021-9010.91.5.1134

Hammer, L. B., Allen, E., and Grigsby, T. D. (1997). Work–family conflict in dual-earner couples: Within-individual and crossover effects of work and family. *Journal of Vocational Behavior*, 50, 185–203. doi:10.1006.1557

Hobfoll, S. E. (1985). The limitations of social support in the stress process. In I. G. Sarason and B. R. Sarason (Eds.), *Social Support: Theory, Research, and Application* (pp. 391–414). The Hague: Nijhoff.

Hobfoll, S. E. (2001). The influence of culture, community, and the nested-self in the stress process: Advancing conservation of resources theory. *Applied Psychology*, 50, 337–421. doi:10.1111/1464-0597.00062

Hobfoll, S. E. (2002). Social and psychological resources and adaptation. *Review of General Psychology*, 6, 307–324. doi:10.1037/1089-2680.6.4.307

Hobfoll, S. E. (2011). Conservation of resources theory: Its implication for stress, health, and resilience. In S. Folkman (Ed.), *The Oxford Handbook of Stress, Health, and Coping*. Oxford: Oxford University Press.

Hobfoll, S. E., Lilly, R. S. and Jackson, A. P. (1992). Conservation of social resources and the self. In H. O. Veiel, and U. Baumann (Eds.), *The Meaning and Measurement of Social Support* (pp. 125–141). Washington, DC: Hemisphere.

Hobfoll, S. E., and London, P. (1986). The relationship of self-concept and social support to emotional distress among women during war. *Journal of Social and Clinical Psychology*, 4, 189–203.

Hobfoll, S. E., Parris, M., and Stephens, A. (1990). Social support during extreme stress: Consequences and intervention. In B. R. Sarason, I. G. Sarason, and G. R. Pierce (Eds.), *Social Support: An Interactional View* (pp. 454–481). New York: Wiley.

House, J. S. (1981). *Work Stress and Social Support*. Reading, MA: Addison-Wesley.

House, J. S., and Wells, J. A. (1978). Occupational stress, social support and health. In A. McLean, G. Black, and M. Colligan (Eds.), *Reducing Occupational Stress: Proceedings of a Conference*, HEW Publication No. 78-140 (pp. 8–29). Washington, DC: US Government Printing Office.

Howe, G. W., Levy, M. L., and Caplan, R. D. (2004). Job loss and depressive symptoms in couples: Common stressors, stress transmission, or relationship disruption? *Journal of Family Psychology*, 18, 639–650. doi:10.1037/0893-3200.18.4.639

Kahn, R. L, and Byosiere, P. (1992). Stress in organizations. In M. D. Dunnette and L. M. Hough (Eds.), *Handbook of Industrial and Organizational Psychology*, vol. 3, 2nd edn. (pp. 571–650). Palo Alto, CA: Consulting Psychologists Press.

Katz, D., and Kahn, R. L. (1978). *The Social Psychology of Organizations*, 2nd edn. New York: Wiley.

Kirkpatrick, S. A., and Locke, E. A. (1991). Leadership: Do traits matter? *The Executive*, 5, 48–60. doi:10.5465/.4274679

Kossek, E. E., Colquitt, J. A., and Noe, R. A. (2011). Caregiving decisions, well-being, and performance: The effects of place and provider as a function of dependent type and work-family climates. *Academy of Management Journal*, 44, 29–44. doi:10.2307/3069335

Kuoppala, J., Lamminpää, A., Liira, J., and Vainio, H. (2008). Leadership, job well-being, and health effects: A systematic review and a meta-analysis. *Journal of Occupational and Environmental Medicine*, 50, 604–915. doi:10.1097/ 013e31817e918d

Landeweerd, J. A., and Boumans, N. P. (1994). The effect of work dimensions and need for autonomy on nurses' work satisfaction and health. *Journal of Occupational and Organizational Psychology*, 67, 207–217. doi:10.1111/j.2044-8325.1994.tb00563.x

LaRocco, J. M., House, J. S., and French, J. R., Jr. (1980). Social support, occupational stress, and health. *Journal of Health and Social Behavior*, 21, 202–218. doi:10.2307/2136616

Lazarus, R. S. (1991). *Emotion and Adaptation*. Oxford: Oxford University Press.

McColl-Kennedy, J. R., and Anderson, R. D. (2002). Impact of leadership style and emotions on subordinate performance. *Leadership Quarterly*, 13, 545–559. doi:10.1016/S1048-9843(02)00143-1

Naus, F., Van Iterson, A., and Roe, R. (2007). Organizational cynicism: Extending the exit, voice, loyalty, and neglect model of employees' responses to adverse conditions in the workplace. *Human Relations*, 60, 683–718. doi:10.1177/0018726707079198

Neff, A., Niessen, C., Sonnentag, S., and Unger, D. (2013a). Expanding crossover research: The crossover of job-related self-efficacy within couples. *Human Relations*, 66, 803–827. doi:10.1177/0018726712465095

Neff, A., Sonnentag, S., Niessen, C., and Unger, D. (2012). What's mine is yours: The crossover of day-specific self-esteem. *Journal of Vocational Behavior*, 81, 385–394.

Neff, A., Sonnentag, S., Niessen C., and Unger, D. (2013b). The crossover of self-esteem: A longitudinal perspective. *European Journal of Work and Organizational Psychology*, 23, 1–14. doi:10.1080/1359432X.2013.856298

Nielsen, K., Yarker, J., Brenner, S. O., Randall, R., and Borg, V. (2008). The importance of transformational leadership style for the well-being of employees working with older people. *Journal of Advanced Nursing*, 63, 465–475. doi:10.1111/j.1365-2648.2008.04701.x

Pearlin, L. I. (1989). The sociological study of stress. *Journal of Health and Social Behavior*, 30, 241–256. doi:10.2307/2136956

Quick, J. C., Quick, J. D., Nelson, D. L., and Hurrell J. J. (1997). *Preventive Stress Management in Organizations*. Washington, DC: American Psychological Association.

Rasulzada, F., Dackert, I., and Johansson, C. R. (2003). Employee wellbeing in relation to organizational climate and leadership style. In *Proceedings of the Fifth European Conference of the European Academy of Occupational Health Psychology* (pp. 220–224). Nottingham, UK: Institute of Work Health and Organizations, University of Nottingham.

Rodríguez-Muñoz, A., Sanz-Vergel, A. I., Demerouti, E., and Bakker, A. B. (2014). Engaged at work and happy at home: A spillover-crossover model. *Journal of Happiness Studies*, 15, 271–283. doi:10.1007/s10902-013-9421-3

Salanova, M., and Schaufeli, W. B. (2008). A cross-national study of work engagement as a mediator between job resources and proactive behaviour. *International Journal of Human Resource Management*, 19, 116–131. doi:10.1080/09585190701763982

Schaufeli, W. B., and Bakker, A. B. (2004). Job demands, job resources, and their relationship with burnout and engagement: A multi-sample study. *Journal of Organizational Behavior*, 25, 293–315. doi:10.1002/job.248

Schaufeli, W., and Enzmann, D. (1998). *The Burnout Companion to Study and Practice: A Critical Analysis*. Washington, DC: Taylor & Francis.

Schaufeli, W. B., Salanova, M., González-Romá, V., and Bakker, A. B. (2002). The measurement of engagement and burnout: A two sample confirmatory factor analytic approach. *Journal of Happiness Studies*, *3*, 71–92. doi:10.1023/A:1015630930326

Seligman, M. E., and Csikszentmihalyi, M. (2000). Positive psychology: An introduction. *American Psychologist*, *55*, 5–14. doi:10.1037//0003-066X.55.1.5

Seltzer, J., and Numerof, R. E. (1988). Supervisory leadership and subordinate burnout. *Academy of Management Journal*, *31*, 439–446. doi:10.2307/256559

Shieh, H.-L., Mills, M. E., and Waltz, C. E. (2001). Academic leadership style predictors for nursing faculty job satisfaction in Taiwan. *Journal of Nursing Education*, *40*, 203–209.

Shimazu, A., Bakker, A. B., and Demerouti, E. (2009). How job demands affect an intimate partner: A test of the spillover-crossover model in Japan. *Journal of Occupational Health*, *51*, 239–248. doi:10.1539/L8160

Sivanathan, N., Arnold, K.A., Turner, N. and Barling, J. (2004). Leading well: Transformational leadership and well-being. In P. A. Linley and S. Joseph (Eds.), *Positive Psychology in Practice* (pp. 241–255). New York: Wiley.

Skogstad, A., Einarsen, S., Torsheim, T., Aasland, M. S., and Hetland, H. (2007). The destructiveness of laissez-faire leadership behavior. *Journal of Occupational Health Psychology*, *12*, 80–92. doi:10.1037/1076-8998.12.1.80

Song, Z., Foo, M. D., Uy, M. A., and Sun, S. (2011). Unraveling the daily stress crossover between unemployed individuals and their employed spouses. *Journal of Applied Psychology*, *96*, 151–168. doi:10.1037/a0021035

Sosik, J., and Godshalk, V. (2000). Leadership styles, mentoring functions received, and job-related stress: A conceptual model and preliminary study. *Journal of Organizational Behavior*, *21*, 365–390.

Spreitzer, G. M., and Quinn, R. E. (1996). Empowering middle managers to be transformational leaders. *Journal of Applied Behavioral Science*, *32*, 237–261. doi:10.1177/0021886396323001

Stajkovic, A. D., and Luthans, F. (1998). Self-efficacy and work-related performance: A meta-analysis. *Psychological Bulletin*, *124*, 240–261. doi:10.1037/0033-2909.124.2.240

Sutherland, V., and Davidson, M. J. (1993). Using a stress audit: The construction site manager experience in the UK. *Work and Stress*, *7*, 273–286. doi:10.1080/02678379308257067

Sy, T., Cote, S., and Saavedra, R. (2005). The contagious leader: Impact of the leader's mood on the mood of group member, group affective tone, and group processes. *Journal of Applied Psychology*, *90*, 295–305. doi:10.1037/0021-9010.90.2.295

Ten Brummelhuis, L. L., Haar, J. M., and Roche, M. (2014). Does family life help to be a better leader? A closer look at crossover processes from leaders to followers. *Personnel Psychology*, *67*, 917–949.

Ten Brummelhuis, L. L., Haar, J. M., and van der Lippe, T. (2010). Crossover of distress due to work and family demands in dual-earner couples: A dyadic analysis. *Work and Stress*, *24*, 324–341. doi:10.1080/02678373.2010.533553

Tepper, B. J. (2000). Consequences of abusive supervision. *Academy of Management Journal*, *43*, 178–190. doi:10.2307/1556375

Terry, D. J., Nielsen, M., and Perchard, L. (1993). Effects of work stress on psychological well-being and job satisfaction: The stress-buffering role of social support. *Australian Journal of Psychology*, *45*, 168–175. doi:10.1080/00049539308259135

Thomas, C. H., and Lankau, M. J. (2009). Preventing burnout: the effects of LMX and mentoring on socialization, role stress, and burnout. *Human Resource Management*, *48*, 417–432.

Tims, M., Bakker, A. B., and Derks, D. (2012). Development and validation of the job crafting scale. *Journal of Vocational Behavior*, *80*, 173–186. doi:10.1016/j.jvb.2011.05.009

Tugade, M. M., Fredrickson, B. L., and Feldman Barrett, L. (2004). Psychological resilience and positive emotional granularity: Examining the benefits of positive emotions on coping and health. *Journal of Personality*, *72*, 1161–1190. doi:10.1111/j.1467-6494.2004.00294.x

Van Dierendonck, D., Haynes, C., Borrill, C., and Stride, C. (2004). Leadership behavior and subordinate well-being. *Journal of Occupational Health Psychology*, *9*, 165–175. doi:10.1037/1076-8998.9.2.165

Vaux, A. (1988). *Social Support: Theory, Research, and Intervention*. New York: Praeger.

Vaux, A. (1992). Assessment of social support. In H. Veiel and U. Baumann (Eds.), *The Meaning and Measurement of Social Support* (pp. 193–216). New York: Hemisphere.

Vinokur, A. D., and Van Ryn, M. (1993). Social support and undermining in close relationships: Their independent effects on the mental health of unemployed persons. *Journal of Personality and Social Psychology*, *65*, 350–359. doi:10.1037/0022-3514.65.2.350

Visweswaran, C., Sanchez, J. I., and Fisher, J. (1999). The role of social support in the process of work stress: A meta-analysis. *Journal of Vocational Behavior*, *54*, 314–334.

Westman, M. (2001). Stress and strain crossover. *Human Relations*, *54*, 557–591. doi:10.1177/0018726701546002

Westman, M., and Etzion, D. (2005). The crossover of work–family conflict from one spouse to the other. *Journal of Applied Social Psychology*, *35*, 1936–1957. doi:10.1111/j.1559-1816.2005.tb02203.x

Westman, M., Etzion, D., and Chen, S. (2009). The crossover of exhaustion and vigor between international business travelers and their spouses. *Journal of Managerial Psychology*, *24*, 269–284. doi:10.1002/.4030160207

Westman, M., Etzion, D., and Horovitz, S. (2004a). The toll of unemployment does not stop with the unemployed. *Human Relations*, *57*, 823–844. doi:10.1177/0018726704045767

Westman, M., and Vinokur, A. D. (1998). Unraveling the relationship of distress levels within couples: Common stressors, empathic reactions, or crossover via social interaction? *Human Relations*, *51*, 137–156. doi:10.1023/A:1016910118568

Westman, M., Vinokur, A. D., Hamilton, V. L., and Roziner, I. (2004b). Crossover of marital dissatisfaction during military downsizing among Russian army officers and their spouses. *Journal of Applied Psychology*, *89*, 769–779. doi:10.1037/0021-9010.89.5.769.

Winnubst, J. (1993). Organizational structure, social support and burnout. In W. B. Schaufeli, C. Maslach, and T. Marek (Eds.), *Professional Burnout: Recent Developments in Theory and Research* (pp. 151–162). New York: Taylor & Francis.

Yukl, G. A. (2010). *Leadership in Organizations*, 7th edn. Englewood Cliffs, NJ: Prentice Hall.

15

Stress and Addiction

Ann Roche, Victoria Kostadinov, and Jane Fischer

Introduction and Background

Defining Stress

The scientific conceptualization of stress is over a century old, and was originally based on physiological studies of feedback. In recent years, there have been major advances that have led to a reconceptualization of the definition of stress and that now incorporate an understanding of the role of epigenetics and the importance of gender differences and stressor specificity.

Sinha (2008) defines stress as processes that involve perception, appraisal, and responses to harmful, threatening or challenging stimuli. Stress experiences can be emotionally or physiologically challenging, and can activate stress responses and adaptive processes to regain homeostasis.

Exposure to stress is integral to life (Keyes, Hatzenbuehler, and Hasin, 2011). Further, not all stress is perceived to be bad, negative or deleterious to an organism. The concept of "eustress" or positive reactions to stressors has been widely acknowledged. Selye (1976), acclaimed as the father of stress research, identified individual differences in stress reactivity which included "distress" and "eustress," or positive reactions. That is, mild to moderate levels of stress, within a person's coping range, can ultimately produce positive outcomes. However, stress that exceeds one's coping capacity can result in threats to physical and psychological well-being.

Several different types of stressors have been identified:

1. Emotional stressors, such as interpersonal conflict, loss of relationship, death of a close family member or spouse, loss of a child
2. Physiological stressors, such as hunger or food deprivation, sleep deprivation or insomnia, extreme hyper- or hypothermia, drug withdrawal states
3. Pharmacological stressors, such as regular and binge use of various psychoactive drugs (Sinha, 2008)

The Handbook of Stress and Health: A Guide to Research and Practice, First Edition.
Edited by Cary L. Cooper and James Campbell Quick.
© 2017 John Wiley & Sons, Ltd. Published 2017 by John Wiley & Sons, Ltd.

Conceptualizing stress in this way allows for separate consideration of (1) internal and external events or stimuli that exert demands or load on the organism; (2) the neural processes that evaluate the demands and assess availability of adaptive resources to cope with the demands; (3) the subjective, behavioral, and physiological activity that signals stress to the organism; (4) neuroadaptations in emotional and motivational brain systems associated with chronic stress; and (5) behavioral, cognitive, and physiological adaptation in response to stressors (Sinha, 2008).

Defining Addiction

Although this chapter is framed in terms of the role that stress plays in "addiction," it is helpful to take a wider conceptualization of the contributory role of stress in any form of problematic alcohol and other drug (AOD) use. That is, various forms of problematic AOD use can cause considerable harm and distress to the individual or individuals involved or to society in general, but may not necessarily fall within the traditional definitions of addiction. For example, "binge drinking" may result from exposure to current or previous life stressors without constituting an addiction.

The recent *DSM-5* criteria for alcohol and drug use disorders substantially redefine the narrower, traditional perspective of addiction (American Psychiatric Association, 2013; Helzer, Bucholz, and Gossop, 2007). However, many of the studies drawn upon here to establish the evidence base for the role played by stress applied earlier *DSM* criteria, and thereby may differ in the parameters used.

Understanding the relationship between stress and AOD use draws on various disciplines, including epidemiology, physiology, pharmacology, psychology, and psychiatry. Different disciplines apply different lenses through which investigations and examinations have been undertaken, and understandably can draw different and at times contrasting and even conflicting conclusions. Indeed, much of the literature in this area is characterized by inconsistency. However, there are some key findings that provide a firm evidence base from which reasonably robust conclusions can be drawn.

The relationship between stress and the use of alcohol, and more latterly other psychoactive substances, entails numerous components and facets. These components and facets will be examined throughout the chapter. Traditionally, research in this area has focused on individuals. More recently, however, greater attention has been directed toward populations as a whole, and subgroups within populations. These broadened perspectives offer new insights into stress and its potential impacts and appropriate responses.

Which Drugs?

The types of substances that are likely to be implicated in stress relationships have important ramifications for future clinical and treatment interventions, as well as prevention strategies and approaches.

Research to date has largely concentrated on the relationship between stress and alcohol. However, there is growing interest in the use of other psychoactive substances in relation to stress, including tobacco smoking (Bruijnzeel, 2012; Hiscock, Bauld, Amos, Fidler, and Munafo, 2012; Lindstrom, Moden, and Rosvall, 2013) and cannabis use (Hyman and Sinha, 2009; Temple, Driver, and Brown, 2014), with particular emphasis currently focused on stimulants such as methamphetamine.

In addition, there are a number of other drugs with potential addictive properties such as benzodiazepines and prescribed opioids. In the case of the latter, these drugs have now overtaken all combined illicit drugs in the United States in terms of potential harms and cause of death (Dart et al., 2015; C. M. Jones, Mack, and Paulozzi, 2013; SAMHSA, 2012). The growing use of, and dependence on, prescribed opioids has generated considerable attention. Reasons for growth in the use of prescribed opioids and subsequent development of dependence in a large proportion of users has resulted in speculation about causal relationships. Such speculation has included the role of chronic pain and associated physical and mental stress.

It is also noted that in addition to the psychoactive drugs identified above, there is also a range of other appetitive or excessive behaviors (Orford, Copello, Velleman, and Templeton, 2010) that have potential for the development of dependence and that may similarly result from stress exposures. These include gambling, hypersexuality, dysfunctional internet use, and eating (Lemieux and al'Absi, 2015). However, these behaviors are out of scope in the current context.

Beyond Traditional Reactive Perspectives

A common initial perspective is to conceptualize the relationship between stress and AOD use as the use of various psychoactive substances in *response* to various stressors. However, as we shall see, this is only one potential direction and form in which this complex and multifaceted relationship can manifest.

Bidirectional relationships between stress and AOD use are common. For example, alcohol or drugs may be initially taken to alleviate, for instance, job stress and pressures, but subsequently result in the emergence of greater stress through the negative effects of the drug on performance and functionality through cognitive impairment, as well as through the emergence of mental health problems such as paranoia and psychosis.

The development of regular patterns of use and dependence[1] similarly brings with it a range of new and additional stressors. Moreover, exposure to stressors of particular sorts is likely to induce a lapse or a relapse in a drug-dependent person. The use of alcohol or drugs can also render an individual vulnerable to situations that are conducive to stressful life events: sometimes termed "reverse causation." Mechanisms underlying the stress–AOD use relationship are discussed in greater detail below.

Dimensions of Stress

The subjective experience of stress and related AOD use (whether preceding, concurrent, or subsequent) may vary considerably depending on both the type of stressor and its characteristics.

Stressor *type* is relatively simple to conceptualize, and several taxonomies have been proposed. Particularly pertinent is Keyes et al.'s (2011) categorization, which classifies stressors relevant to AOD use into four categories:

1. Life stressors (e.g., divorce, job loss)
2. Catastrophic/fateful stress (e.g., acts of terrorism, major disasters)
3. Childhood maltreatment
4. Minority stress (including gender and race/ethnicity)

We have reconceptualized and expanded this typology in the following way, to incorporate 10 categories:

1. Generic life stressors (e.g., bereavement, divorce, financial struggles)
2. Work-related stressors (e.g., within-work stressors, retirement)
3. Traumatic events (e.g., violent crime, accidents)
4. Physical and mental health (e.g., chronic pain, depression, anxiety)
5. Insecure housing (i.e., primary, secondary, or tertiary)
6. Catastrophic/fateful stress (e.g., major disasters, war)
7. Childhood maltreatment (e.g., neglect, abuse)
8. Gender-specific stressors (e.g., sexual assault, domestic violence, pregnancy/childbirth/ child rearing, single parenthood)
9. Racial/ethnic minority stressors (e.g., racism, discrimination)
10. Gender identification/sexual orientation stressors (e.g., discrimination against lesbian, gay, bisexual, transgender, or intersex individuals)

In our typology of stressors we have created a separate category for workplace stress given the expanding knowledge base that has addressed this issue and the greater awareness of work and workplace factors and their impact on wellbeing. We also consider it inappropriate to conflate "minorities" and women, who comprise more than 50 percent of most populations. Hence, we have created a separate category for gender, or more specifically "femaleness," to address the unique experiences encountered by women in their life that are frequently the source of substantial stress.

Stressors within each of the categories can additionally be classed according to their *characteristics*. These characteristics interplay with stressor type, individual attributes, and AOD use to form a complex, multidirectional relationship. Keyes et al. (2011) proposed six salient stress characteristics (see Figure 15.1):

1. How severe the stress is
2. When in the life course it occurs

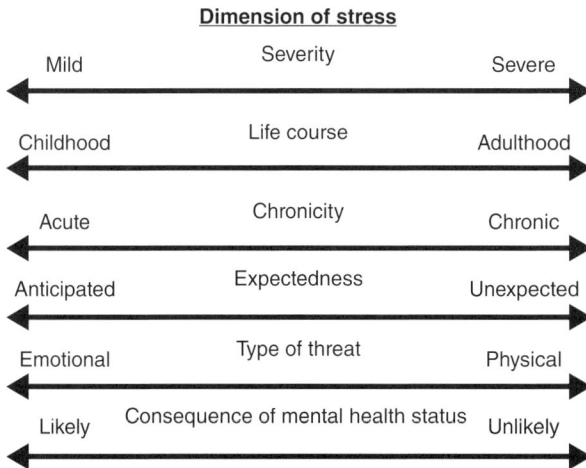

Dimension of stress

Mild	Severity	Severe
Childhood	Life course	Adulthood
Acute	Chronicity	Chronic
Anticipated	Expectedness	Unexpected
Emotional	Type of threat	Physical
Likely	Consequence of mental health status	Unlikely

Figure 15.1   Characteristics of stressful experiences (derived from Keyes et al., 2011).

3. Whether it is acute or chronic
4. Whether it is expected or unexpected
5. Whether it relates to an emotional or physical threat
6. Whether or it is a cause or consequence of mental health status (including AOD use)

Mechanisms underlying the Stress–Addiction Relationship

Stress has long been recognized as a factor in the development of drug dependence (Haass-Koffler and Bartlett, 2012; Koob, 2013). One explanation for the high concordance between stress and drug addiction is the self-medication hypothesis, which suggests that drugs are used to cope with tension or to relieve anxiety or depression symptoms resulting from a traumatic event (Goeders, 2007). An important distinction in this common phenomenon is the difference identified by Lemieux and al'Absi (2015), who distinguished the initial lived, phenomenological experience of stress from the subsequent "stress response" that occurs through various physiological and neurophysiological changes that accompany the stress experience.

There is a substantial literature on the significant association between acute and chronic stress and the motivation[2] to use and/or abuse addictive substances. Converging lines of research evidence point to the critical role that stress plays in increasing vulnerability to the development of addiction (Sinha, 2008). An extensive literature has shown that addictive drugs affect the systems that govern reward pathways (mesolimbic dopaminergic systems), learning and memory (hippocampus), emotion (amygdala), and cognitive functions (prefrontal cortex) (Haass-Koffler and Bartlett, 2012).

The neural circuitry underlying responses to stress intersects with those that promote drug reward. Functional magnetic imagery (MRI) studies indicate that stress and drug exposure lead to activation of similar brain regions, including the mesolimbic and mesocortical dopamine projection regions. Acute drug administration and acute stress exposure also elicit a similar enhancement in excitatory synaptic strength in the ventral tegmental areas (VTA) (Briand and Blendy, 2010).

Appetitive behaviors are under significant regulatory control by the hypothalamic-pituitary-adrenal (HPA) and hypothalamic-pituitary gonadal (HPG) axes (Hildebrandt and Greif, 2013). Recent research has begun to examine how these systems interact to cause and maintain poor regulation of appetitive behaviors and influence motivation–reward processes. A range of genetic, molecular, neuroendocrine, and hormonal mechanisms are involved that may explain individual differences.

Stress and the neurobiology of the stress response play multiple roles in relation to AOD use, including:

- AOD use initiation
- Maintenance
- Relapse (Lemieux and al'Absi, 2015)

Complex interactions between biological mediators of the stress response and the dopaminergic reward system, and mediators of the stress response and other systems that are crucial in moderating the key addiction-related behaviors such as the endogenous opioids, the sympathetic-adrenal-medullary system, and endocannabinoids (Lemieux and al'Absi, 2015).

Early research by Selye (1976) identified the general adaption syndrome (GAS), comprised of alarm, resistance, and exhaustion. In the resistance phase an organism seeks to reduce or eradicate the source of stress that initiates the GAS. Attempts to cope with or eliminate stressors can include AOD use. When coping fails, the glucocorticoid production persists, due to failure of the negative feedback regulation of the system, until physiological and emotional exhaustion occurs. The HPA and GAS systems work in a highly complex central nervous system (CNS) of dynamic interactions.

Subsequent research examined the sympathetic-adrenal-medullary (SAM) axis that stimulates the production of the neurotransmitters norepinephrine and epinephrine, and the physiological consequences of emotion-induced sympathetic nervous system (SNS) arousal and negative emotional states, with speculation of differential catecholamine profiles in stress and addiction (Lemieux and al'Absi, 2015).

Other work has focused on the hypothalamic-pituitary-adrenal (HPA axis. The hypothalamic-pituitary-adrenal neuroendocrine stress axis is the mechanism by which stressors trigger the release of hormones in the brain that result in increased levels of cortisol (the stress hormone) (Anthenelli, 2010). Prolonged stress produces a cascade of events starting with the production of corticotropin-releasing factor (CRF). CRF has been shown to induce various behavioral changes related to adaption to stress (Haass-Koffler and Bartlett, 2012). Drugs of abuse mediate CRF activity and correspondingly changes in CRF mediate drug taking and reward (Briand and Blendy, 2010).

For example, early studies found that acute cocaine and morphine administration leads to alterations in the HPA axis that are dependent on CRF (Sarnyai et al., 1995), with chronic opioid administration leading to development of tolerance to the HPA-activating effects of the drug (el Daly, 1996). Nicotine has been demonstrated to activate the HPA axis via hypothalamic CRF activity (Matta, Beyer, McAllen, and Sharp, 1987). Acute alcohol and cannabinoid administration has been shown to increase adrenocorticotropic hormone (ACTH) and corticosterone (Rodriguez de Fonseca et al., 1996).

Although substances with abuse potential have different mechanisms of action, repeated exposure has been shown to lead to similar neural adaptations (Haass-Koffler and Bartlett, 2012).

Overall, the key neurotransmitter systems with circumscribed neurocircuitry that mediate behavioral responses to stressors include:

- Glucocorticoids
- Corticotropin-releasing factor (CRF)
- Norepinephrine
- Dynorphin (opioid peptides)

The key neurotransmitter systems that act in opposition to the brain stress systems include:

- Neuropeptide Y
- Nociception
- Endocannabinoids

The two brain stress systems that play particularly salient roles in the development of addiction are CRF and dynorphin.

Many of the major theories of addiction identify an important role of stress in addiction processes. These range from psychological models of addiction that view drug use and abuse as a coping strategy to deal with stress, reduce tension, self-medicate, and decrease withdrawal-related distress, to neurobiological models that propose incentive sensitization and stress allostasis[3] concepts to explain how neuroadaptations in reward, learning and stress pathways may enhance craving, loss of control, and compulsion. The latter are the key elements in the transition from casual AOD use to the inability to stop chronic use despite adverse consequences – a defining feature of addiction.

Koob et al. (2014) have hypothesized that the development of addiction produces aversive or stress-like states via two mechanisms: direct activation of stress-like, fear-like states in the extended amygdala (CRF), and indirect activation of a depression-like state by suppressing dopamine.

Addiction has also been characterized as a *stress surfeit disorder* (Koob et al., 2014), wherein drug taking alleviates negative emotional states. The negative emotional states (stress) that drive such negative reinforcement[4] (drug use) are derived from dysregulation of key neurochemical elements in the brain stress system within the frontal cortex, ventral striatum, and extended amygdala. Specific neurochemicals involved include CRF in the extended amygdala as well as the dynorphin-*K* opioid aversive systems in the frontal cortex. The engagement of these brain stress systems is speculated to occur early in the process of the development of addiction as well as subsequently (see Table 15.1).

There is also mounting evidence that genetic or epigenetic effects can help explain risk or resilience to the development of drug dependence (Butelman, Yuferov, and Kreek, 2012). The direct effect of gonadal hormones on motivation and reward has also become an area of significant development, largely because of the growing research documenting gender differences in relation to AOD use disorders (Lemieux and al'Absi, 2015; Wetherington, 2010). For example, women evidence an enhanced HPA-axis response to cocaine (Evans and Foltin, 2010) and observed increased escalation of use (Anker and Carroll, 2011).

Table 15.1 Recruitment of the brain stress systems in the development of dependence

Initial use	Impulsive use	Compulsive use
Characterized by activation of the hypothalamic-pituitary-adrenal axis to drive the binge/intoxication stage.	Characterized by prefrontal cortex dysfunction with activation of corticotropin-releasing factor (CRF), *y*-aminobutyric acid (GABA), and possibly dynorphin in the prefrontal cortex and subsequent disinhibition of the nucleus accumbens and extended amygdala that, in turn, drives increases in dynorphin in the nucleus accumbens and CRF in the extended amygdala.	Involves a pronounced activation of CRF in the extended amygdala, dynorphin-induced decreases in dopamine in the nucleus accumbens, and a pronounced loss of executive function in the prefrontal cortex, all leading to the spiraling distress and loss of control associated with full-blown dependence mediated by negative reinforcement.

Source: Derived from Koob et al. (2014).

Thus, while our understanding of the exact mechanisms underlying the stress–AOD use relationship remains incomplete, it is clear that these neurobiological effects play an important role. The following section of this chapter examines the different types of stressors which can trigger or interact with these physiological pathways to shape AOD use behaviors.

Types of Stressors and Their Relationship with Addiction

This section provides an overview of the evidence regarding the relationship between the 10 identified stressor types (see dimensions of stress, above) and AOD use. However, while the categories are presented here as discrete phenomena, in reality there is a large degree of overlap and interrelation between them. For example, experiencing one type of stressor (e.g., physical or mental health issues) may interact with and increase the likelihood of other stressors (e.g., work difficulties, and subsequent financial hardship), in turn influencing patterns of AOD use in unique ways. Thus, the relationship between stress and AOD use may be more complex and reciprocal than presented below.

Generic Life Stressors

Generic life stressors include events that many people will experience at some point during their lives. While they are typically acute and may be relatively mild compared to other categories of stressor, they can nevertheless cause a large degree of stress and distress. Examples of generic life stressors include:

- Bereavement
- Relationship breakup
- Financial difficulties
- Changing employment status
- Family member in poor health
- Legal difficulties
- Interpersonal difficulties
- Being victim of a crime

The relationship between AOD use and generic life stressors is particularly circuitous. AOD use may both result from and contribute to the development of many of these stressors (Boden, Fergusson, and Horwood, 2014; Catalano, Dooley, Wilson, and Hough, 1993; Garland, Pettus-Davis, and Howard, 2013; Giskes, Turrell, Bentley, and Kavanagh, 2011; Pilling, Thege, Demetrovics, and Kopp, 2012; Rodriguez, Neighbors, and Knee, 2014; Veenstra et al., 2006), making the interpretation of temporal and causal associations especially fraught. In addition, research regarding generic stressors typically involves checklists, with participants reporting whether or not they experienced each stressor on the list within a given time frame. However, this method does not take into account the subjective meaning associated with the events. For example, job loss may be an inconvenience for some but devastating for others, while a relationship breakup may at times be perceived as positive (Keyes et al., 2011).

Recent reviews by Keyes and colleagues (Keyes, Hatzenbuehler, Grant, and Hasin, 2012a; Keyes et al., 2011) have examined the association between generic life stressors and AOD use, but note the lack of large-scale epidemiological studies. These reviews found that the number of stressful life events experienced is positively associated with problematic alcohol consumption, although the long-term impact of stressful events remains inconclusive. There is also evidence that the relationship between life stressors and AOD use is modified by both genetic factors and sex. Men and women tend to report experiencing different stressors, with women typically reporting a greater number of stressors than men. However, it remains an open question whether stressful events are more likely to result in AOD use for women or men.

Certain population groups are at increased risk of experiencing generic life stressors and associated harms. For example, individuals with lower socioeconomic status are more likely to encounter social and financial difficulties. They may also not have sufficient resources to either ameliorate the stressor or apply constructive coping strategies, potentially resulting in AOD use (Roche et al., 2015a). Furthermore, disadvantaged groups may be unwilling or unable to access treatment for AOD problems, worsening the associated stressors and perpetuating the cycle. Thus, among vulnerable populations, common life stressors and associated AOD use may escalate into extreme difficulties relatively quickly. Generic stressors (e.g., job loss) may also lead to and interact with other stressor types (e.g., insecure housing, mental/physical health problems), compounding problems and associated AOD use.

Other groups at particular risk of experiencing stressful life events include members of minority groups,[5] older individuals, and those living in rural or remote locations. For older people, stressors related to new patterns of socializing, retirement, bereavement, social isolation, and poor health can elevate risk of AOD use (Hunter, Lubman, and Barratt, 2011; Wadd, Lapworth, Sullivan, Forrester, and Galvani, 2011). Similarly, individuals living in remote areas are subject to unpredictable socioeconomic and ecological circumstances, social isolation, and limited infrastructure (Vines, 2011), which may increase stress and promote risky AOD use.

Individuals who are subject to multiple forms of disadvantage (e.g., members of minority groups with low socioeconomic status) are at particular risk of experiencing numerous severe life stressors (as well as other types of stressors discussed below). It is imperative that sufficient and appropriate services are available to support these vulnerable populations to implement constructive coping strategies and manage AOD use, in order to prevent the escalation of problems.

Work-Related Stressors

Work-related stress refers to "psychological, physical and behavioral responses to work-related demands over a discrete or short-term period" (Dollard, Winefield, and Winefield, 2003). Applying a workforce development approach (Roche and Skinner, 2005), work-related stress can derive from four different domains:

- Systems (e.g., legislation, regulations, funding)
- Organizations (e.g., work conditions, resources)
- Teams (e.g., support, supervision, cohesion)
- Individual (e.g., motivation, skill, rewards)

A large body of literature has identified work-related stress as a precursor to risky alcohol consumption (Battams et al., 2014; Roche et al., 2015b; Virtanen et al., 2015) and tobacco smoking (Heikkilä et al., 2012). Increasingly work-related stress has also been implicated in both cannabis and prescription drug use and misuse (Maier and Schaub, 2015).

Recent international systematic reviews (Roche et al., 2015b; Virtanen et al., 2015) have identified a number of work-related stressors which can increase the risk of employee AOD use. Roche et al. (2015b) broadly categorized these stressors as:

- Demographic factors (e.g., being younger, male, less educated)
- Individual factors (e.g., job dissatisfaction, minimal external support)
- Social norms at work
- Team environment
- Work conditions (e.g., high demands, job insecurity, low skill discretion and control)
- Work–home interference
- Structural/socioeconomic factors (e.g. manual, blue-collar work)

The relationship between work-related stressors and AOD use is complex. Evidence suggests that employee AOD use is the consequence of a combination of stressors. Broadly, employees with excessive job demands, low job control, and long work hours and/or problems with managers or coworkers may use alcohol in risky ways (Keyes et al., 2011; Virtanen et al., 2015; Roche et al., 2015b) or smoke more cigarettes (Heikkilä et al., 2012) as a coping mechanism. Alternatively, alcohol and tobacco may be used to build and maintain social relationships with colleagues.

Several industries and occupations have been identified which involve particularly stressful working conditions (both mental and physical) and have correspondingly high rates of worker AOD use. These include:

- Males employed in male-dominated industries (e.g., construction and transport) (Battams et al., 2014; Roche et al., 2015b; Virtanen et al., 2015)
- Emergency response personnel (e.g., police, fire officers, paramedics) (Archer, Williams, Sofianopoulos, and Thompson, 2012; Chopko, Palmieri, and Adams, 2013; Harvey et al., 2015; E. C. Meyer et al., 2012)
- Military personnel (Kok, Herrell, Thomas, and Hoge, 2012; Lane, Hourani, Bray, and Williams, 2012; Marmar et al., 2015)
- Health and human service workers (e.g., alcohol and other drug workers, social workers, nurses) (Ewer, Teesson, Sannibale, Roche, and Mills, 2015; Mark and Smith, 2012; Rössler, 2012)

There is also evidence that young adults first beginning work are at particular risk of experiencing work-related stress and AOD use (Gibb, Fergusson, and Horwood, 2012; Pidd, Roche, and Fischer, 2015; Pidd, Roche, and Kostadinov, 2014). The transition from late adolescence to early adulthood (i.e., "emerging adulthood") is a particularly important life stage where individuals engage in behaviors and form long-term beliefs and attitudes that are influential in their ongoing development. Emerging adulthood is also associated with AOD use, more so than any other age group. Thus, new workers are both particularly likely to experience stress and use alcohol and other drugs, and to carry these behaviors forward into later work roles.

Traumatic Events

A traumatic event can be understood as a situation in which life or safety is at serious risk. The event may be either directly experienced or witnessed, and isolated or ongoing (Mills et al.,

2011). Examples include accidents leading to disablement or death, violent crime, physical or sexual abuse.

Individuals' responses to traumatic stressors vary (Wiechelt and Straussner, 2015). However, while many individuals will experience a traumatic stressor during their lifetime, few develop debilitating responses, such as AOD use disorders, posttraumatic stress, or other related disorders (Kessler, Sonnega, Bromet, and Hughes, 1995). This seems partly due to a combination of personal "resilience" (Keyes et al., 2011) and the mediating effect of pre-trauma sociodemographic characteristics (Straussner and Calnan, 2014).

When debilitating responses do eventuate, comorbidity (e.g., both substance misuse and posttraumatic stress disorder (PTSD)) is common (Debell et al., 2014; Grant et al., 2016; Mills et al., 2011; Wiechelt and Straussner, 2015). For example, in a recent population-based study, participants with a substance use disorder (SUD) were 60 percent more likely to have both a SUD and PTSD than participants without a SUD (Grant et al., 2016).

AOD use may be related to traumatic events in two ways. First, acute changes in AOD use may occur in the aftermath of a traumatic event. Increases in AOD use at this time are "reactional" or a form of "self-medication" (Haller and Chassin, 2014; Mills et al., 2011). These reactional changes may be a consequence of conscious and unconscious physical responses, changes in thinking, emotional reactions, and behavioral patterns (Mills et al., 2011).

Second, AOD use associated with trauma may develop into dependence. This appears to involve a complex interplay between the acute traumatic stress itself and pharmacological components of the substances used (Debell et al., 2014; Fu et al., 2007; Mills et al., 2011; Wiechelt and Straussner, 2015). In these circumstances, people who have experienced a traumatic event need to increase the amount and/or frequency of their AOD use in order to achieve the same effect (Debell et al., 2014; Mills et al., 2011) and to manage withdrawal symptoms.

Physical and Mental Health

Physical and mental health conditions such a chronic pain, depression and anxiety can be the source of enormous physiological and psychological stress. It is therefore unsurprising that problematic AOD use often co-occurs with physical and mental health problems. Indeed, comorbid conditions are often reported by health-care professionals to be the expectation rather than the exception (Merkes, Lewis, and Canaway, 2010). Problematic AOD use may be comorbid with physical health conditions, mental health conditions, or both.

In terms of physical health, there is an association between chronic pain and AOD use. While a proportion of individuals who are prescribed opioids for pain management may subsequently develop dependence (both on opioids and other drugs) (Edlund et al., 2007), chronic pain may also be more prevalent in those with a history of AOD use (Warner, 2012). However, the causal pathway for these relationships remains unclear, and it is likely that the high rate of mental health disorders among individuals with chronic pain plays a mediating role. Heavy AOD users are also likely to develop physical health issues as a direct result of their substance use, which can compound preexisting stressors and complicate treatment options (Keaney et al., 2011).

In terms of mental health, a large body of international evidence demonstrates the very high prevalence of comorbid AOD use and mood/anxiety disorders. A recent systematic review of 22 studies found that people with an alcohol use disorder were 2.1 times more likely to have an anxiety disorder, and 3.1 times more likely to have major depression, compared to those without alcohol disorders (Lai, Cleary, Sitharthan, and Hunt, 2015).

The relationship between health stressors and AOD use is complex. AOD use may be either a cause and/or a consequence of health problems (Conner, Pinquart, and Gamble, 2009; Jane-Llopis and Matytsina, 2006). In some instances, one condition may directly cause the other (e.g., alcohol-related depression). Alternatively, the relationship may be indirect. For example, stress and distress may result from a preexisting health condition, leading to the use of alcohol or drugs in an attempt to self-medicate. AOD use itself can also place individuals at risk of stressful life circumstances that may cause or exacerbate physical or mental health problems. Finally, health problems and AOD use may both arise from the same underlying cause (e.g., genetic predisposition, life circumstances, previous trauma) (Lai et al., 2015).

From a neurological perspective, it has been noted that individuals with alcohol use disorders and those suffering from depression or PTSD display similar alterations in HPA-axis function, leading to higher cortisol levels (Anthenelli, 2010). Similarly, there is emerging evidence that both pain and addiction share a common neurobiological foundation (Elman and Borsook, 2016), and that alcohol consumption causes metabolic changes that can increase the risk of depression (Boden and Fergusson, 2011). While large knowledge gaps remain, it is likely that such physiological processes also play a role in the relationship between health conditions and AOD use.

Insecure Housing

While individuals who are without adequate shelter or housing are commonly referred to as "homeless," there is no widely accepted definition of homelessness. The Australian Bureau of Statistics (Chamberlain and Mackenzie, 2008) differentiates between primary, secondary, and tertiary homelessness:

- Primary homelessness: lacking conventional accommodation (e.g., living on the streets, in cars, in derelict buildings)
- Secondary homelessness: moving frequently from one form of temporary shelter to another (e.g., emergency or transitional accommodation, boarding houses, other households)
- Tertiary homelessness: long-term (more than 12 weeks) use of accommodation that doesn't meet the minimum community standard of a small self-contained flat (e.g., boarding houses)

The term *insecure housing* is used here to encompass all three levels of homelessness.

Due to logistical challenges and the use of inconsistent definitions, it is difficult to firmly establish how many people live in insecure housing at any given time. However, there is a well-established relationship between insecure housing and AOD use (SAMHSA, 2013). Youth are at particular risk, with research indicating that up to 90 percent of insecurely housed young people use alcohol and/or drugs problematically (Edidin, Ganim, Hunter, and Karnik, 2012).

Personal, situational, and economic factors converge and interact to promote both insecure housing and problematic AOD use (Kulik, Gaetz, Crowe, and Ford-Jones, 2011). Thus, AOD use may be both a cause and a consequence of insecure housing. For example, AOD use may contribute to insecure housing through job loss, income displacement, exacerbating other contributory factors (e.g. mental health problems), and/or the loss of social ties (Roche et al., 2015a). The extreme stress associated with insecure housing can also lead to AOD use as a coping mechanism. In addition, persons who are insecurely housed are likely to have high rates of AOD use within their social networks, further increasing the likelihood of use (Edidin et al.,

2012). Compounding this, many programs and services for insecurely housed populations will not accept participants with AOD use problems, making it more difficult for individuals to reestablish themselves in stable accommodation.

In addition to the direct risks of AOD use, individuals who are insecurely housed and use alcohol or drugs are at high risk of comorbid mental health problems and other risky behaviors (Edidin et al., 2012; Kulik et al., 2011; Salkow and Fichter, 2003). Despite this, insecurely housed populations are often reluctant or unable to access treatment services. Barriers to treatment may be financial, structural, or personal, and include:

- Few appropriate services available
- Lack of knowledge about available services
- Shame or embarrassment
- Lack of health insurance
- Lack of transport
- Need to spend time looking for food and shelter
- Real or perceived discrimination by health-care providers (Edidin et al., 2012; Kulik et al., 2011; Medlow, Klineberg, and Steinbeck, 2014)

These factors can make it difficult for insecurely housed people who use alcohol and other drugs to access treatment and support services, thus perpetuating the stress, AOD use, insecure housing cycle.

Catastrophic/Fateful Stressors

Catastrophic or fateful stress stems from events experienced by an entire population or community. These events may be natural (e.g., flood, tsunami, hurricane, earthquake, fire, famine), man-made (e.g., mass shootings, nuclear accidents, transport accidents), or political (e.g., terrorism, war, civil unrest/disturbance). According to Keyes et al. (2011), these ostensibly random events typically lie on the more extreme end of the severity continuum and involve both a physical and emotional threat.

Goldmann and Galear (2014) categorized catastrophic stressors associated with psychopathology according to the temporality of the risk in relation to the disaster. The three categories of stressor they proposed are pre-disaster, peri-disaster, and post-disaster. This approach is useful in disentangling catastrophic-related risk factors for AOD use, and is applied here.

Pre-disaster experiences of psychosocial stress increase risk of post-disaster AOD use. Psychosocial stressors include low socioeconomic status, low social support, or poor relationships (Norris et al., 2002). Specific demographic characteristics also increase the risk of post-disaster AOD use. Populations at greater risk are youth (Goldmann and Galea, 2014; Norris et al., 2002; Peters et al., 2010) and women (Vetter, Rossegger, Rossler, Bisson, and Endrass, 2008). Prior psychological distress, particularly among people with mental health conditions, has also been associated with AOD use after disasters (Goldmann and Galea, 2014). People who have an alcohol use disorder are particularly vulnerable to relapse subsequent to a catastrophic stressor (Goldmann and Galea, 2014; Keyes et al., 2011; North, Ringwalt, Downs, Derzon, and Galvin, 2011; Welch et al., 2014).

The extent of *peri-disaster* exposure is also a risk factor for later AOD use. Research increasingly recognizes the multidimensional nature of exposure to traumatic events. While previously measurement was binomial, it now often comprises a series of "experience" sub-domains, assessed with Likert scales or similar (Fergusson, Horwood, Boden, and Mulder, 2014; Turner, Alderman, Huang, and Tong, 2013; Vetter et al., 2008; Welch et al., 2014). There is also an apparent dose–response relationship between the number of traumatic experiences and AOD use frequency, particularly risky drinking, tobacco smoking and other drug use, such as medications (Fergusson et al., 2014; Turner et al., 2013; Welch et al., 2014). For example, in New Zealand, exposure to recent earthquakes resulted in statically significant linear increases in the rates of nicotine dependence, alcohol abuse/dependence, and illicit drug abuse/dependence (Fergusson et al., 2014).

Changes in life circumstance *post-disaster* are also a risk factor for AOD use, specifically alcohol consumption. Alcohol may be used as a coping strategy in response to events related to the disaster, such as job loss, property damage, marital stress, physical health conditions, displacement, and diminished social support (Fergusson et al., 2014; Goldmann and Galea, 2014; North et al., 2011). Alcohol and tobacco may also be used as forms of self-medication to manage symptoms of PTSD that arise as a result of the catastrophic event (Fergusson et al., 2014; Haller and Chassin, 2014; Welch, Jasek, Caramanica, Chiles, and Johns, 2015).

However, the etiology of the relationship between catastrophic/fateful stress and AOD use is still not well understood. Strong evidence generally remains unavailable, particularly in relation to illicit drugs and medication use (Keyes et al., 2011). Further research is required to examine this issue.

Childhood Maltreatment

Childhood maltreatment includes a range of potential adverse events or exposures such as trauma; sexual, emotional, and/or physical abuse; and neglect. There is growing recognition and understanding of the long-term impact that such experiences may have on an individual. It is speculated that such childhood events may act as contributory or causal factors in a wide range of stress-related adult psychopathology, including problematic AOD use (Afifi et al., 2008; Green et al., 2010).

A number of factors may influence whether a child who is mistreated will subsequently develop AOD-related problems. Most salient of these is the degree of chronicity and severity of the traumatic event(s) experienced. In addition, exposure to one type of childhood stressor increases the likelihood that other stressors will also be experienced; this in turn increases the risk of later poor outcomes. The temporal relationship between childhood traumatic events and the development of AOD problems is also often more protracted than for other sources of stress. As a result, early identification and intervention before problems become established is a priority.

Maltreatment is also more likely to occur among children of alcohol- or drug-dependent parents (Kuntsche, Rehm, and Gmel, 2004; Redelinghuys and Dar, 2008; Solis, Shadur, Burns, and Hussong, 2012). Not only does parental AOD use increase the risk of poor and potentially harmful parenting practices, but there is speculation about the possible transmission of genotypes that may increase the probability of that child also developing AOD-related problems. Thus, the nature and specificity of the relationship between childhood maltreatment and AOD use are particularly complex.

In addition to abuse and neglect (Butt, Chou, and Browne, 2011; Herrenkohl, Seunghye, Klika, Herrenkohl, and Russo, 2013; Maniglio, 2011), other adverse childhood events associated with increased risk of later AOD use include parental divorce (Hayatbakhsh, Najman, Jamrozik, Mamun, and Alati, 2006; Waldron et al., 2014); death of a parent (Otowaa, York, Gardner, Kendler, and Hettema, 2014); and involvement with the child welfare system (Braciszewski and Stout, 2012; Traube, James, Zhang, and Landsverk, 2012). There is also preliminary evidence that certain genetic variants can interact with the experience of child-hood maltreatment to predict later AOD use (Keyes et al., 2012a; Keyes et al., 2011). Simi-larly, recent research has identified that childhood maltreatment is associated with changes to brain structures, which may also contribute to increased risk of AOD use later in life (Teicher, Andersen, Ohashi, and Polcari, 2014).

On balance, the evidence appears to support an interaction effect where early exposure to maltreatment and subsequent development of problematic AOD use is mediated by the home environment and genetic vulnerability.

Gender-Specific Stressors

Previous typologies have included gender-specific sources of stress as part of broader catego-rizations such as "minorities." However, we maintain that the nature and extent of stressors exclusively or primarily experienced by women warrant a category of their own.

Biological and psychosocial variables interact to shape how women experience and respond to stress. Cultural and gender norms dictate the type of social, professional, and familial experiences women encounter, associated stressors, and their reactions (including AOD use). In general, women are more likely than men to encounter discrimination, to be victims of domestic and sexual violence, to be single parents, and to bear the largest burden of house-hold/caring duties (Aassve, Fuochi, and Mencarini, 2014; Carter, 2015; Yavorsky, Kamp Dush, and Schoppe-Sullivan, 2015). These factors are both important stressors in their own right and the antecedents to further stressors, including poverty and unhealthy aging. Furthermore, women typically have less access to information, care, services and resources that can act as buffers against the negative consequences of stress (WHO, 2010).

The significant and ongoing stressors faced by women are discussed in more detail below. These stressors contribute to women's higher incidence of depression, anxiety, and psycho-logical distress (McLean, Asnaani, Litz, and Hofmann, 2011; Van de Velde, Bracke, and Levecque, 2010). Rates of AOD use among women in developed countries are also esca-lating (WHO, 1997), with rates of alcohol consumption among women and men beginning to approach parity (Roche and Deehan, 2002). This may constitute a coping strategy on the part of women to ameliorate the stress and distress arising from the factors discussed below (WHO, 1993; 2000). However, according to the "convergence hypothesis," this trend may also reflect the slowly equalizing relative status of women in society, and the relaxing of "mascu-line" vs. "feminine" behavior norms. This is supported by research showing that the higher the position of women in society, the smaller the difference in men and women's drinking rates (Rahav, Wilsnack, Bloomfield, Gmel, and Kuntsche, 2006; Roche and Deehan, 2002; Schmitt, Branscombe, Postmes, and Garcia, 2014).

Discrimination and sexism   In most societies globally, men have historically dominated in political, economic, and legal institutions. Patriarchal legacies continue today, with women typically occupying lower status positions, holding relatively limited power, earning less, and being subject to discrimination and sexism (Lee, Fiske, and Glick, 2010). These conditions constitute important and ubiquitous stressors facing women throughout the world, including in developed countries. Sexism may take different forms, including not only overt negative conceptions of women, but also condescending stereotypes of women as nurturers in need of protection (Glick and Fiske, 2001). The prevalence of such attitudes and their detrimental impact upon women's mental health and life circumstances (e.g., employment opportunities) can result in extreme and ongoing stress.

Violence and sexual assault   Violence against women (both by their partners and by men not known to them) remains unacceptably and appalling high (Devries et al., 2014; Garcia-Moreno et al., 2013). As would be expected, violence and sexual assault are associated with severe stress and ongoing physical and mental health issues (Garcia-Moreno et al., 2013; Howard, Oram, Galley, Trevillion, and Feder, 2013). Considerably more research examining the relationship between violence and AOD use exists compared to other stressors experienced by women. There is a well-established association between men consuming alcohol and subsequently committing violence against their partner (Abramsky et al., 2011; Devries et al., 2014; Salom, Williams, Najman, and Alati, 2015). Women may also drink alcohol in order to self-medicate the traumatic sequelae of abuse, or conversely men may attempt to use women's alcohol consumption as a justification for violence (Devries et al., 2014).

Reproduction   Even in developed countries, women do not have free and unlimited access to safe, effective and affordable methods of fertility regulation. The autonomy of women in regard to decisions concerning childbearing, contraception, and abortion is far from complete (WHO, 1993; 2000). The stress associated with this diminished control (and its physical, mental, and social consequences) should not be underestimated. In addition, women are far more likely than men to be single parents, placing them (and their children) at risk of stress and lower well-being (Hayatbakhsh et al., 2013; Östberg and Hagekull, 2013). Pregnancy and motherhood are major life events and are often stressful even in "ideal" circumstances, as evidenced by the high rate of postnatal depression (Leahy-Warren and McCarthy, 2007). Single mothers must additionally cope with the combined stressors of childbearing, child rearing, and employment/financial issues, often with limited support and while experiencing loneliness and isolation (WHO, 2000).

Employment   Women in the paid workforce are systemically disadvantaged compared to employed men. Women employed in the same jobs as men typically earn less, and the lowest paid and most "insecure" jobs (e.g., causal work) usually have higher proportions of women (WHO, 2000). Furthermore, research demonstrates that women spend significantly more time engaged in housework and child-care duties than men, even when both partners are employed full-time (Aassve et al., 2014; Yavorsky et al., 2015). This not only contributes to stress and burnout, but disproportionately limits women's ability to engage in self-care activities, or devote the necessary time to moving up the professional ladder (WHO, 1993; 2000). As a result, women have a substantially reduced capacity to amass savings or superannuation. They also may be financially dependent upon men, creating power imbalances and potentially trapping women in unhappy or dangerous relationships (Devries et al., 2014; Matjasko, Niolon, and Valle, 2013; Regan and Durvasula, 2015).

Financial hardship and poverty   In part due to the stressors discussed above, many women experience severe financial hardship and/or live below the poverty line. Poverty reduces autonomy, constrains decision-making, limits access to support systems, and often necessitates exposure to dangerous environments. It is associated with feelings of frustration, fear, powerlessness, and worthlessness (WHO, 2000). As a result, poverty is considered a severe stressor in its own right. In addition, poor women (particularly those belonging to minority groups) are at high risk of experiencing other resultant stressors such as violence, homelessness, and mental health issues. Healthy coping behaviors to mitigate these risks (e.g., counseling, accessing support services, nutritious food, regular exercise) necessitate resources (e.g., time, energy, money, knowledge, alternative options) that are often beyond the scope of disadvantaged women (WHO, 1993; 2000).

Aging   Women in developed countries generally have a longer life-expectancy and tend to marry at a younger age than men (Mathers, Stevens, Boerma, White, and Tobias, 2015). As a result, a large proportion of older women are widowed. For many elderly women, this leads to substantial stress associated with bereavement, failing health, and living alone with few social supports and little financial security. These stressors may in part account for the increasing rates of AOD use reported among older age groups in recent years (Caputo et al., 2012; Gossop et al., 2007; Nicholas and Roche, 2014).

Racial/Ethnic Minority Stressors

It is well-established that individuals from racial and ethnic minority groups are often subject to numerous stressors. These include social disadvantage (e.g., lower socioeconomic status, neighborhood poverty) and stressors related to acculturation, stigma and discrimination (Chartier, Vaeth, and Caetano, 2013).

Discrimination can manifest in a multitude of ways, including:

- Individual racism (actions of a personal, degrading nature that promote inferiority beliefs about minority individuals)
- Cultural racism (beliefs of the dominant group are regarded as superior to those of the subordinate group)
- Institutionalized racism (systematic inequality based on race that is reinforced by differential access to societal resources, services, and opportunities)
- Collective racism (members of the dominant group work to restrict or deny basic rights and privileges of minority group members) (Clark, Salas-Wright, Vaughn, and Whitfield, 2015; J. M. Jones, 1997)

Research demonstrates that there is a positive association between the experience of discrimination and levels of AOD use, and that the former typically precedes the latter (Clark, 2014; Clark et al., 2015; Paradies, 2006; Priest et al., 2013; Unger, Schwartz, Huh, Soto, and Baezconde-Garbanati, 2014). Furthermore, the type of discrimination experienced may influence AOD use patterns. For example, Clark et al. (2015) found that a combination of discriminatory experiences across multiple domains placed individuals at greatest risk of AOD use.

Many minority groups additionally experience disproportionately high alcohol- and drug-related harms, relative to their level of consumption (Keyes, Liu, and Cerda, 2012b). This may be further influenced by structural and cultural factors such as greater neighborhood availability of alcohol and drugs, reduced health-care and treatment access/utilization, and preference for stronger alcohol beverages (Chartier et al., 2013, Roche et al., 2015a).

It has been suggested by some researchers that discrimination can lead to severe psychological distress, which results in the use of alcohol and/or drugs in order to emotionally regulate (Clark et al., 2015). Similarly, in the stress-coping model, discrimination is said to deplete coping resources and encourage avoidant coping strategies (e.g., anger, frustration, sadness, depression) (Clark, 2014). This in turn may lead to AOD use in an attempt to self-medicate. Alternatively, minorities may feel unwelcome and unaccepted by the mainstream population when they are discriminated against, leading to the adoption of "oppositional identities" which may include AOD use (Unger et al., 2014).

It is important to note, however, that genetic, historical, social, and cultural heterogeneity exists both between and within ethnic groups (Szapocznik, Prado, Burlew, Williams, and Santisteban, 2007). Thus, AOD use behaviors and intervention efforts should not be generalized as valid for all minority groups.

Gender Identification/Sexual Orientation Stressors

Lesbian, gay, bisexual, transgender, and intersex (LGBTI) individuals have an elevated prevalence of AOD use compared with heterosexual populations (K. E. Green and Feinstein, 2012; Roxburgh, Lea, de Wit, and Degenhardt, 2015). The higher frequency of AOD use most commonly occurs among adolescent and young adult LGBTI individuals (Blosnich, Lee, and Horn, 2013; Goldbach, Tanner-Smith, Bagwell, and Dunlap, 2014; K. E. Green and Feinstein, 2012; Keyes et al., 2011; McCabe, Bostwick, Hughes, West, and Boyd, 2010; Roxburgh et al., 2015). The dominant explanation for higher rates of AOD use among LGBTI people is *minority stress* (Goldbach et al., 2014; I. H. Meyer, 2003).

Minority stress is defined as the exposure of LGBTI individuals to multiple, chronic, and persistent stressors due to their sexual orientation or gender identity (Jabson, Farmer, and Bowen, 2014; Keyes et al., 2011; I. H. Meyer, 2003). Systematic reviews (Goldbach et al., 2014; Keyes et al., 2011; I. H. Meyer, 2003) have identified an array of interrelated social and psychological stressors associated with increased AOD use in these populations. These stressors can be categorized as social, individual, or institutional.

LGBTI people experience *social stressors* as a consequence of persistent negative social attitudes toward their sexual orientation/gender identity (Lea, de Wit, and Reynolds, 2014; I. H. Meyer, 2003). These include negative reactions to disclosure from family, friends and the wider community, and pressure to change "nonconforming" behaviors (Blosnich et al., 2013; Goldbach et al., 2014; Rosario et al., 2014). Social stressors are demonstrated in prejudice (I. H. Meyer, 2003), victimization (Collier, van Beusekom, Bos, and Sandfort, 2013), and verbal and physical abuse (Goldbach et al., 2014; Ignatavicius, 2013).

Many LGBTI people experience internalized, or *individual* stressors. These include stigmatization and discrimination from the wider community, psychological stress, and "internalized homophobia" (Goldbach et al., 2014; Lea et al., 2014). Internalized homophobia is a process of inwardly directing familial and societal negative attitudes toward LGBTI. However, the way in which internalized homophobia is expressed differs between different age groups and subpopulations (Goldbach et al., 2014; Lea et al., 2014).

Societies institutionalize prevailing norms and values (Hatzenbuehler, 2014) to the detriment of LGBTI people, resulting in *institutional* stressors. These stressors are macroforms of stigma which disadvantage stigmatized individuals (Hatzenbuehler, 2014). This is illustrated in discriminatory legislation, such as institutional bans on "gay marriage" (Hatzenbuehler, 2014; McCabe et al., 2010), and the illegality of alternative sexual preferences/orientations in many countries. Involvement with the policy and social persecution of "criminal" behaviors and penalties incurs substantial stress.

Treatment and Prevention Implications

Early Intervention and Prevention

There is increasing recognition and understanding of the role played by stress in relation to AOD use, and the multiple levels and stages at which this association can occur. It is also evident from this review that there are many life domains across which stress may manifest as problematic AOD use. Here we have identified 10 such domains, and there may indeed be others.

There is now also greater understanding of the role played by secure attachments and their association with increased resilience in the face of stress, accompanied by less reactive reward responding, that is, increased resilience against addiction. The development of strong social attachments, including parent–offspring and adult pair bonds, may protect against abuse and stress effects (Tops, Koole, Ijzerman, and Buisman-Pijlman, 2014). While the behavioral aspects of the reciprocal relations between social attachment, stress and substance abuse have been well documented, the understanding of the neural mechanisms involved remains incomplete and sketchy (Tops et al., 2014).

Stress-strain-coping-support (SSCS) models have also been developed which recognize that substance misuse issues in families may also constitute a form of stressful life circumstance which is often long-standing and which puts affected family members at risk of experiencing strain in the form of physical and/or psychological ill-health (Orford et al., 2010).

Improved understanding of these issues leaves greater scope for intervention at a primary or secondary prevention level. For example, screening and assessment repertoires increasingly address current and previous life stress, and incorporate strategies to mediate potential effects. Similarly, where PTSD and AOD use problems co-occur, treatment guidelines now suggest that careful histories of *both* potential conditions are taken where either condition has been detected (Debell et al., 2014), and that alcohol problems should be addressed before tackling PTSD (NICE, 2005).

Relapse Prevention

A critical problem in addiction is relapse. This is where an addicted individual returns to compulsive AOD use after a period of prolonged withdrawal or cessation. Koob et al. (2014) maintain that the mechanisms operating here are a drug-, cue-, and stress-induced reinstatement of neurocircuits that are driven by a hypofunctioning prefrontal system. In this situation, the hypofunctioning cortical system fails to inhibit the subcortical structures that drive addiction.

Thus, the hypothesized allostatic, dysregulated reward and sensitized stress state produces motivational symptoms of acute withdrawal and protracted abstinence, and provides the basis by which priming, drug cues, and acute stressors acquire even more power to elicit drug-seeking behavior (Vendruscolo et al., 2012).

The neurobiological framework for understanding animal reinstatement models for human relapse to addiction has explicated mechanisms ranging from neuroanatomical pathways to neurotransmitters to intraneuronal messengers and the associated gene activations indicated by acute and chronic drug self-administration (Kosten, 2011).

Treatment aimed at reducing stress may therefore be therapeutically effective in preventing addiction and/or relapse. Elucidating the molecular mechanisms underlying the interactions between stress and AOD use is critical to the development of such therapies and central to current and emerging research (Briand and Blendy, 2010). Therapy that aims to reduce the stress component of addiction may lead to more effective solutions for treatment programs and the development of subsequently targeted pharmacological interventions. Similarly, mindfulness therapies for addiction may also prove to be increasingly effective when targeting stress and pain etiologies (Garland, 2013).

Easing stress-induced AOD seeking may help reduce relapse and facilitate the formation of memories with less deleterious behavioral consequences (Haass-Koffler and Bartlett, 2012). As the addictive process progresses over time, the initial positive reinforcing, pleasurable drug effects are augmented by negatively reinforcing relief from a negative emotional state. The neuroadaptation that encompasses the recruitment of the extrahypothalamic CRF and dynorphin brain stress systems are central to this shift.

Future Research Directions

While there is a growing evidence base regarding AOD use and stress, substantial work remains to be undertaken in this area. Little is known about the epigenetics of potentiating stress events. Greater refinement of the measures and concepts used, and untangling of reverse causation, are also required. In addition, issues of individual differences and vulnerabilities, personality differences, and resilience require further investigation. Population-wide studies of stress levels at the community and collective levels have important prevention implications and are also needed.

Emerging research addressing the mechanisms by which particular hormones sensitize target neurons or neurocircuits may help explain gender differences in stress-induced appetitive behaviors and also the specificity of types of addiction (e.g., food vs. drugs) (Hildebrandt and Greif, 2013). Such research may also help to develop more targeted interventions and identify robust biomarkers for risk and resilience to a range of addictions.

Repeated use of drugs with dependence-producing potential leads to attempts by the brain's stress systems at the molecular, cellular and neurocircuitry levels to maintain stability or an allostatic state. This involves recruitment of antireward systems and consequent chronic decreased function of reward circuits, both of which lead to compulsive drug seeking and loss of control over intake (Koob et al., 2014). The questions of how these systems are modulated by other known brain emotional systems, how frontal cortex dysregulations in the cognitive domain linked to impairments in executive function contribute to the dysregulation of the extended amygdala, and how individuals differ at the molecular-genetic level remain a challenge for future research (Koob et al., 2014).

Conclusions

As problems associated with AOD use and addiction continue to plague most societies, improved understanding of the mechanisms and associations with stress are increasingly important (Briand and Blendy, 2010). The story is far from complete. It is evident that stress modulates the acquisition of AOD use, the transition to addiction, as well as relapse to AOD seeking. Behavioral, molecular, and genetic approaches have helped to identify the stress reward circuits, which appear to be important in both drug reward and reinstatement as well as in stress responsivity (Briand and Blendy, 2010). Efforts are increasingly directed to modulating the CRF system as a possible therapeutic strategy for treating dysregulation of emotional behaviors, including addiction (Haass-Koffler and Bartlett, 2012). Research to identify causal pathways and efficacious interventions, while currently incomplete, is nevertheless encouraging.

Notes

1. Note that the terms "dependence" and "addiction" are used here interchangeably in line with the recent *DSM-5* criteria and definitions (American Psychiatric Association, 2013).
2. Motivation is the state that involves arousal, emotion, and expectation, all of which direct behavior. Motivation has been inextricably linked to hedonic, affective, or emotional states in addiction.
3. Allostasis is the process by which individuals adjust to the continually changing demands that are put upon somatic activity by salient events.
4. Negative reinforcement is defined as the process by which removal of an aversive stimulus or state increases the probability of a response. Positive reinforcement is the process by which presentation of stimulus increases the probability of a response.
5. The unique stressors associated with ethnic/racial minorities, lesbian, gay, bisexual, transgender and intersex individuals, and women are discussed in greater detail in later sections.

References

Aassve, A., Fuochi, G., and Mencarini, L. (2014). Desperate housework: Relative resources, time availability, economic dependency, and gender ideology across Europe. *Journal of Family Issues, 35*(8), 1000–1022.

Abramsky, T., Watts, C. H., Garcia-Moreno, C., Devries, K., Kiss, L., Ellsberg, M., … Heise, L. (2011). What factors are associated with recent intimate partner violence? Findings from the WHO multi-country study on women's health and domestic violence. *BMC Public Health, 11*(1), 109.

Afifi, T. O., Enns, M. W., Cox, B. J., Asmundson, G. J., Stein, M. B., and Sareen, J. (2008). Population attributable fractions of psychiatric disorders and suicide ideation and attempts associated with adverse childhood experiences. *American Journal of Public Health, 98*, 946–952.

American Psychiatric Association (2013). *Diagnostic and Statistical Manual of Mental Disorders: DSM-5.* Washington, DC: American Psychiatric Association.

Anker, J. J., and Carroll, M. E. (2011). Females are more vulnerable to drug abuse than males: Evidence from preclinical studies and the role of ovarian hormones. *Current Topics in Behavioral Neurosciences, 8*, 73–96.

Anthenelli, R. M. (2010). Comorbid mental health disorders. *Alcohol Research and Health, 33*(1–2), 109–117.

Archer, F., Williams, B., Sofianopoulos, S., and Thompson, B. (2012). The exploration of physical fatigue, sleep and depression in paramedics: A pilot study. *Australasian Journal of Paramedicine, 9*(1), 3.

Battams, S., Roche, A. M., Fischer, J. A., Lee, N., Cameron, J., and Kostadiniov, V. (2014). Workplace risk factors in male-dominated industries: A systematic review. *Health Psychology and Behavioral Medicine, 2*(1), 983–1008.

Blosnich, J., Lee, J. G., and Horn, K. (2013). A systematic review of the aetiology of tobacco disparities for sexual minorities. *Tobacco Control, 22*(2), 66–73.

Boden, J. M., and Fergusson, D. M. (2011). Alcohol and depression. *Addiction*, *106*(5), 906–914. doi: 10.1111/j.1360-0443.2010.03351.x

Boden, J. M., Fergusson, D. M., and Horwood, L. J. (2014). Associations between exposure to stressful life events and alcohol use disorder in a longitudinal birth cohort studied to age 30. *Drug and Alcohol Dependence*, *142*, 154–160. doi:10.1016/j.drugalcdep.2014.06.010

Braciszewski, J. M., and Stout, R. L. (2012). Substance use among current and former foster youth: A systematic review. *Children and Youth Services Review*, *34*(12), 2337–2344. doi:10.1016/j.childyouth.2012.08.011

Briand, L. A., and Blendy, J. A. (2010). Molecular and genetic substrates linking stress and addiction. *Brain Research*, 1314, 219–234.

Bruijnzeel, A. W. (2012). Tobacco addiction and the dysregulation of brain stress systems. *Neuroscience and Biobehavioral Reviews*, *36*(5), 1418–1441.

Butelman, E. R., Yuferov, V., and Kreek, M. J. (2012). Kappa-opioid receptor/dynorphin system: Genetic and pharmacotherapeutic implications for addiction. *Trends in Neuroscience*, *35*(10), 587–596.

Butt, S., Chou, S. N., and Browne, K. (2011). A rapid systematic review on the association between childhood physical and sexual abuse and illicit drug use among males. *Child Abuse Review*, *20*(1), 6–38. doi:10.1002/car.1100

Caputo, F., Vignoli, T., Leggio, L., Addolorato, G., Zoli, G., and Bernardi, M. (2012). Alcohol use disorders in the elderly: A brief overview from epidemiology to treatment options. *Experimental gerontology*, *47*(6), 411–416.

Carter, J. (2015). Patriarchy and violence against women and girls. *Lancet*, *385*(9978), e40–e41.

Catalano, R., Dooley, D., Wilson, G., and Hough, R. (1993). Job loss and alcohol abuse – a test using data from the epidemiologic catchment-area project. *Journal of Health and Social Behavior*, *34*(3), 215–225. doi:10.2307/2137203

Chamberlain, C., and Mackenzie, D. (2008). *Australian Census Analytic Program: Counting the Homeless 2006*. No. 2050.0. Canberra: Australian Bureau of Statistics.

Chartier, K. G., Vaeth, P. A. C., and Caetano, R. (2013). Ethnicity and the social and health harms from drinking. *Alcohol Research: Current Reviews*, *35*(2), 229–237.

Chopko, B. A., Palmieri, P. A., and Adams, R. E. (2013). Associations between police stress and alcohol use: Implications for practice *Journal of Loss and Trauma*, *18*(5), 482–497.

Clark, T. T. (2014). Perceived discrimination, depressive symptoms, and substance use in young adulthood. *Addictive Behaviors*, *39*, 1021–1025.

Clark, T. T., Salas-Wright, C. P., Vaughn, M. G., and Whitfield, K. E. (2015). Everyday discrimination and mood and substance use disorders: A latent profile analysis with African Americans and Caribbean Blacks. *Addictive Behaviors*, *40*, 119–125. doi:10.1016/j.addbeh.2014.08.006

Collier, K. L., van Beusekom, G., Bos, H. M., and Sandfort, T. G. (2013). Sexual orientation and gender identity/expression related peer victimization in adolescence: A systematic review of associated psychosocial and health outcomes. *Journal of Sex Research*, *50*(3–4), 299–317.

Conner, K. R., Pinquart, M., and Gamble, S. A. (2009). Meta-analysis of depression and substance use among individuals with alcohol use disorders. *Journal of Substance Abuse Treatment*, *37*, 127–137.

Dart, R. C., Bronstein, A. C., Spyker, D. A., Cantilena, L. R., Seifert, S. A., Heard, S. E., and Krenzelok, E. P. (2015). Poisoning in the United States: 2012 Emergency Medicine report of the national poison data system. *Annals of Emergency Medicine*, *65*(4), 416–422.

Debell, F., Fear, N., Head, M., Batt-Rawden, S., Greenberg, N., Wessely, S., and Goodwin, L. (2014). A systematic review of the comorbidity between PTSD and alcohol use. *Social and Psychiatry and Psychiatric Epidemiology*, *49*, 1401–1425.

Devries, K. M., Child, J. C., Bacchus, L. J., Mak, J., Falder, G., Graham, K., … Heise, L. (2014). Intimate partner violence victimization and alcohol consumption in women: A systematic review and meta-analysis. *Addiction*, *109*(3), 379–391.

Dollard, M. F., Winefield, A. H., and Winefield, H. R. (2003). *Occupational Stress in the Service Professions*. London: Taylor & Francis.

Edidin, J. P., Ganim, Z., Hunter, S. J., and Karnik, N. S. (2012). The mental and physical health of homeless youth: A literature review. *Child Psychiatry and Human Development*, *43*(3), 354–375. doi:10.1007/s10578-011-0270-1

Edlund, M., Sullivan, M., Steffick, D., Harris, K., B., K., and Wells, K. (2007). Do users of regularly prescribed opioids have higher rates of substance use problems than nonusers? *Pain Medicine*, *8*, 647–656.

el Daly, E. S. (1996). Influence of acute and chronic morphine or stadol on the secretion of adrenocorticotrophin and its hypothalamic releasing hormone in the rat. *Life Science*, *59*, 1881–1890.

Elman, I., and Borsook, D. (2016). Common brain mechanisms of chronic pain and addiction. *Neuron*, *89*, 11–38.

Evans, S. M., and Foltin, R. W. (2010). Does the response to cocaine differ as a function of sex or hormonal status in human and non-human primates? *Hormones and Behavior*, *58*(1), 13–21.

Ewer, P. L., Teesson, M., Sannibale, C., Roche, A., and Mills, A. (2015). The prevalence and correlates of secondary traumatic stress among alcohol and other drug workers in Australia. *Drug and Alcohol Review*, *34*, 252–258.

Fergusson, D. M., Horwood, L. J., Boden, J. M., and Mulder, R. T. (2014). Impact of a major disaster on the mental health of a well-studied cohort. *JAMA Psychiatry*, *71*(9), 1025–1031.

Fu, S. S., McFall, M., Saxon, A. J., Beckham, J. C., Carmody, T. P., Baker, D. G., and Joseph, A. M. (2007). Posttraumatic stress disorder and smoking: A systematic review. *Nicotine and Tobacco Research*, *9*(11), 1071–1084. doi:10.1080/14622200701488418

Garcia-Moreno, C., Pallitto, C., Devries, K., Stockl, H., Watts, C., and Abrahams, N. (2013). *Global and Regional Estimates of Violence against Women: Prevalence and Health Effects of Intimate Partner Violence and Non-partner Sexual Violence*. Geneva: World Health Organization.

Garland, E. L. (2013). *Mindfulness-Oriented Recovery Enhancement for Addiction, Stress, and Pain*. Washington, DC: NASW Press.

Garland, E. L., Pettus-Davis, C., and Howard, M. O. (2013). Self-medication among traumatized youth: Structural equation modeling of pathways between trauma history, substance misuse, and psychological distress. *Journal of Behavioral Medicine*, *36*(2), 175–185. doi:10.1007/s10865-012-9413-5

Gibb, S. J., Fergusson, D. M., and Horwood, L. J. (2012). Working hours and alcohol problems in early adulthood. *Addiction*, *107*(1), 81–88.

Giskes, K., Turrell, G., Bentley, R., and Kavanagh, A. (2011). Individual and household-level socioeconomic position is associated with harmful alcohol consumption behaviours among adults. *Australian and New Zealand Journal of Public Health*, *35*(3), 270–277.

Glick, P., and Fiske, S. T. (2001). An ambivalent alliance: Hostile and benevolent sexism as complementary justifications for gender inequality. *American Psychologist*, *56*(2), 109–118.

Goeders, N. E. (2007). The hypothalamic-pituitary-adrenal axis and addiction. In M. al'Absi (Ed.), *Stress and Addiction: Biological and Psychological Mechanisms*. Cambridge: Academic Press.

Goldbach, J. T., Tanner-Smith, E. E., Bagwell, M., and Dunlap, S. (2014). Minority stress and substance use in sexual minority adolescents: A meta-analysis. *Prevention Science*, *15*(3), 350–363.

Goldmann, E., and Galea, S. (2014). Mental health consequences of disasters. *Annual Review of Public Health*, *35*, 169–183.

Gossop, M., Neto, D., Radovanovic, M., Batra, A., Toteva, S., Musalek, M., ... Goos, C. (2007). Physical health problems among patients seeking treatment for alcohol use disorders: A study in six European cities. *Addiction Biology*, *12*(2), 190–196. doi:10.1111/j.1369-1600.2007.00066.x

Grant, B. F., Tulshi, D. S., Ruan, J., Goldstein, R. B., Chou, P., Jung, J., ... Hasin, D. S. (2016). Epidemiology of DSM-5 drug use disorder results from the National Epidemiologic Survey on Alcohol and Related Conditions-III. *JAMA Psychiatry*, *73*(1), 39–47.

Green, J. G., McLaughlin, K. A., Berglund, P. A., Gruber, M. J., Sampson, N. A., Zaslavsky, A. M., and Kessler, R. C. (2010). Childhood adversities and adult psychiatric disorders in the national comorbidity survey replication I: Associations with first onset of DSM-IV disorders. *Archives of General Psychiatry*, *67*, 113–123.

Green, K. E., and Feinstein, B. A. (2012). Substance use in lesbian, gay, and bisexual populations: An update on empirical research and implications for treatment. *Psychology of Addictive Behaviors*, *26*(2), 265–278.

Haass-Koffler, C. K., and Bartlett, S. E. (2012). Stress and addiction: Contribution of the corticotropin releasing factor (CRF) system in neuroplasticity. *Frontiers in Molecular Neuroscience*, *5*(91).

Haller, M., and Chassin, L. (2014). Risk pathways among traumatic stress, posttraumatic stress disorder symptoms, and alcohol and drug problems: A test of four hypotheses. *Psychology of Addictive Behaviors*, *28*(3), 841–851. doi:10.1037/a0035878

Harvey, S. B., Milligan-Saville, J. S., Paterson, H. M., Harkness, E. L., Marsh, A. M., Dobson, M., ... Bryant, R. A. (2015). The mental health of fire-fighters: An examination of the impact of repeated trauma exposure. *Australian and New Zealand Journal of Psychiatry*, 1–10. doi:0.1177/0004867415615217

Hatzenbuehler, M. L. (2014). Structural stigma and the health of lesbian, gay, and bisexual populations. *Current Directions in Psychological Science*, *23*(2), 127–132.

Hayatbakhsh, R., Clavarino, A. M., Williams, G. M., Bor, W., O'Callaghan, M. J., and Najman, J. M. (2013). Family structure, marital discord and offspring's psychopathology in early adulthood: A prospective study. *European Child and Adolescent Psychiatry*, *22*(11), 693–700.

Hayatbakhsh, M. R., Najman, J. M., Jamrozik, K., Mamun, A. A., and Alati, R. (2006). Do parents' marital circumstances predict young adults' DSM-IV cannabis use disorders? A prospective study. *Addiction, 101*, 1778–1786.

Heikkilä, K., Nyberg, S. T., Fransson, E. I., Alfredsson, L., De Bacquer, D., Bjorner, J. B., … Casini, A. (2012). Job strain and tobacco smoking: An individual-participant data meta-analysis of 166 130 adults in 15 European studies. *PloS One, 7*(7), e35463.

Helzer, J. E., Bucholz, K. K., and Gossop, M. (2007). A dimensional option for the diagnosis of substance dependence in DSM-V. *International Journal of Methods in Psychiatric Research, 16*(S1), S24–S33.

Herrenkohl, T. I., Seunghye, H., Klika, J. B., Herrenkohl, R. C., and Russo, M. J. (2013). Developmental impacts of child abuse and neglect related to adult mental health, substance use, and physical health. *Journal of Family Violence, 28*, 191–199.

Hildebrandt, T., and Greif, R. (2013). Stress and addiction. *Psychoneuroendocrinology, 38*, 1923–1927.

Hiscock, R., Bauld, L., Amos, A., Fidler, J. A., and Munafo, M. (2012). Socioeconomic status and smoking: A review. *Annals of the New York Academy of Sciences, 1248*(1), 107–123.

Howard, L. M., Oram, S., Galley, H., Trevillion, K., and Feder, G. (2013). Domestic violence and perinatal mental disorders: A systematic review and meta-analysis. *PloS One, 7*(12). doi:10.1371/journal.pone.0051740

Hunter, B., Lubman, D., and Barratt, M. (2011). Alcohol and drug misuse in the elderly. *Australian and New Zealand Journal of Psychiatry, 45*(4), 343–343.

Hyman, S. M., and Sinha, R. (2009). Stress-related factors in cannabis use and misuse: Implications for prevention and treatment. *Journal of Substance Abuse Treatment, 36*(4), 400–413. doi:10.1016/j.jsat.2008.08.005

Ignatavicius, S. (2013). Stress in female-identified transgender youth: A review of the literature on effects and interventions. *Journal of LGBT Youth, 10*(4), 267–286.

Jabson, J. M., Farmer, G. W., and Bowen, D. J. (2014). Stress mediates the relationship between sexual orientation and behavioral risk disparities. *BMC Public Health, 14*, 401. doi:10.1186/1471-2458-14-401

Jane-Llopis, E., and Matytsina, I. (2006). Mental health and alcohol, drugs and tobacco: A review of the comorbidity between mental disorders and the use of alcohol, tobacco and illicit drugs. *Drug and Alcohol Review, 25*, 515–536.

Jones, C. M., Mack, K. A., and Paulozzi, L. J. (2013). Pharmaceutical overdose deaths, United States, 2010. *JAMA, 309*(7), 657–659.

Jones, J. M. (1997). *Prejudice and Racism*. New York: McGraw-Hill.

Keaney, F., Gossop, M., Dimech, A., Guerrini, I., Butterworth, M., Al-Hassani, H., and Morinan, A. (2011). Physical health problems among patients seeking treatment for substance use disorders: A comparison of drug dependent and alcohol dependent patients. *Journal of Substance Use, 16*(1), 27–37. doi:10.3109/14659890903580474

Kessler, R. C., Sonnega, A., Bromet, E., and Hughes, E. N., C. (1995). Posttraumatic stress disorder in the national comorbidity survey. *Archives of General Psychiatry, 52*, 1048–1060.

Keyes, K., Hatzenbuehler, M., Grant, B. F., and Hasin, D. S. (2012a). Stress and alcohol: Epidemiologic evidence. *Alcohol Research: Current reviews, 34*(4), 391.

Keyes, K. M., Hatzenbuehler, M. L., and Hasin, D. S. (2011). Stressful life experiences, alcohol consumption, and alcohol use disorders: The epidemiologic evidence for four main types of stressors. *Psychopharmacology, 218*(1), 1–17.

Keyes, K. M., Liu, X. C., and Cerda, M. (2012b). The role of race/ethnicity in alcohol-attributable injury in the United States. *Epidemiologic Reviews, 34*(1), 89–102. doi:10.1093/epirev/mxr018

Kok, B. C., Herrell, R. K., Thomas, J. L., and Hoge, C. W. (2012). Posttraumatic stress disorder associated with combat service in Iraq or Afghanistan: Reconciling prevalence differences between studies. *Journal of Nervous and Mental Disease, 200*(5), 444–450.

Koob, G. F. (2013). Addiction is a reward deficit and stress surfeit disorder. *Frontiers in Psychiatry, 4*(72).

Koob, G. F., Buck, C. L., Cohen, A., Edwards, S., Park, P. E., Schlosburg, J. E., … George, O. (2014). Addiction as a stress surfeit disorder. *Neuropharmacology, 76*, 370–382.

Kosten, T. R. (2011). Stress and addiction. *American Journal of Psychiatry, 168*(6), 566–568.

Kulik, D. M., Gaetz, S., Crowe, C., and Ford-Jones, E. (2011). Homeless youth's overwhelming health burden: A review of the literature. *Paediatrics and Child Health, 16*(6), E43–E47.

Kuntsche, E., Rehm, J., and Gmel, G. (2004). Characteristics of binge drinkers in Europe. *Social Science and Medicine, 59*(1), 113–127.

Lai, H. M. X., Cleary, M., Sitharthan, T., and Hunt, G. E. (2015). Prevalence of comorbid substance use, anxiety and mood disorders in epidemiological surveys, 1990–2014: A systematic review and meta-analysis. *Drug and Alcohol Dependence, 154*, 1–13. doi:10.1016/j.drugalcdep.2015.05.031

Lane, M. E., Hourani, L. L., Bray, R. M., and Williams, J. (2012). Prevalence of perceived stress and mental health indicators among reserve-component and active-duty military personnel. *American Journal of Public Health*, *102*(6), 1213–1220. doi:10.2105/AJPH.2011.300280

Lea, T., de Wit, J., and Reynolds, R. (2014). Minority stress in lesbian, gay, and bisexual young adults in Australia: Associations with psychological distress, suicidality, and substance use. *Archives of Sexual Behavior*, *43*(8), 1571–1578. doi:10.1007/s10508-014-0266-6

Leahy-Warren, P., and McCarthy, G. (2007). Postnatal depression: Prevalence, mothers' perspectives, and treatments. *Archives of Psychiatric Nursing*, *21*(2), 91–100.

Lee, T. L., Fiske, S. T., and Glick, P. (2010). Next gen ambivalent sexism: Converging correlates, causality in context, and converse causality, an introduction to the special issue. *Sex Roles*, *62*(7–8), 395–404. doi:10.1007/s11199-010-9747-9

Lemieux, A., and al'Absi, M. (2015). Stress psychobiology in the context of addiction medicine: From drugs of abuse to behavioral addictions. *Progress in Brain Research*. Early online view. doi: 10.1016/bs.pbr.2015.08.001

Lindstrom, M., Moden, B., and Rosvall, M. (2013). A life-course perspective on economic stress and tobacco smoking: A population-based study. *Addiction*, *108*, 1305–1314.

Maier, L. J., and Schaub, M. P. (2015). The use of prescription drugs and drugs of abuse for neuroenhancement in Europe. *European Psychologist*, *20*(3), 155–166. doi:10.1027/1016-9040/a000228

Maniglio, R. (2011). The role of child sexual abuse in the etiology of substance-related disorders. *Journal of Addictive Diseases*, *30*(3), 216–228. doi:10.1080/10550887.2011.581987

Mark, G., and Smith, A. P. (2012). Occupational stress, job characteristics, coping, and the mental health of nurses. *British Journal of Health Psychology*, *17*(3), 505–521.

Marmar, C. R., Schlenger, W., Henn-Haase, C., Qian, M., Purchia, E., Li, M., … Karstoft, K. I. (2015). Course of posttraumatic stress disorder 40 years after the Vietnam War: Findings from the National Vietnam Veterans Longitudinal Study. *JAMA Psychiatry*, *72*(9), 875–881.

Mathers, C. D., Stevens, G. A., White, R. A., and Tobias, M. I. (2015). Causes of international increases in older age life expectancy. *Lancet*, *385*(9967), 540–548.

Matjasko, J. L., Niolon, P. H., and Valle, L. A. (2013). The role of economic factors and economic support in preventing and escaping from intimate partner violence. *Journal of Policy Analysis and Management*, *32*(1), 122–128.

Matta, S. G., Beyer, H. S., McAllen, K. M., and Sharp, B. M. (1987). Nicotine elevates rat plasma ACTH by a central mechanism. *Journal of Pharmacology and Experimental Therapeutics*, *243*, 217–226.

McCabe, S. E., Bostwick, W. B., Hughes, T. L., West, B. T., and Boyd, C. J. (2010). The relationship between discrimination and substance use disorders among lesbian, gay, and bisexual adults in the United States. *American Journal of Public Health*, *100*(10), 1946–1952.

McLean, C. P., Asnaani, A., Litz, B. T., and Hofmann, S. G. (2011). Gender differences in anxiety disorders: Prevalence, course of illness, comorbidity and burden of illness. *Journal of Psychiatric Research*, *45*(8), 1027–1035.

Medlow, S., Klineberg, E., and Steinbeck, K. (2014). The health diagnoses of homeless adolescents: A systematic review of the literature. *Journal of Adolescence*, *37*(5), 531–542. doi:10.1016/j.adolescence.2014.04.003

Merkes, M., Lewis, V., and Canaway, R. (2010). Supporting good practice in the provision of services to people with comorbid mental health and alcohol and other drug problems in Australia: Describing key elements of good service models. *Health Services Research*, *10*, 325. doi:10.1186/1472-6963-10-325

Meyer, E. C., Zimering, R., Daly, E., Knight, J., Kamholz, B. W., and Gulliver, S. B. (2012). Predictors of posttraumatic stress disorder and other psychological symptoms in trauma-exposed firefighters. *Psychological Services*, *9*(1), 1–15.

Meyer, I. H. (2003). Prejudice, social stress, and mental health in lesbian, gay, and bisexual populations: Conceptual issues and research evidence. *Psychological Bulletin*, *129*(5), 674–697.

Mills, K., Ewer, P., Marel, C., Baker, A., Teesson, M., Dore, G., … Trimingham, T. (2011). *Trauma and Substance Use*. Sydney: National Drug and Alcohol Research Centre, University of New South Wales.

NICE (National Institute for Health and Care Excellence) (2005). *Post-traumatic Stress Disorder: Management*. London: National Institute for Health and Care Excellence.

Nicholas, R., and Roche, A. M. (2014). *Alcohol and Other Drug Use and Healthy Ageing: Patterns of Use and Harm among Older Australians*. Information Sheet 2. Adelaide: National Centre for Education and Training in Addiction.

Norris, F. H., Friedman, M. J., Watson, P. J., Byrne, C. M., Diaz, E., and Kaniasty, K. (2002). 60,000 disaster victims speak: Part I. An empirical review of the empirical literature, 1981–2001. *Psychiatry Research*, *65*(3), 207–239.

North, C. S., Ringwalt, C. L., Downs, D., Derzon, J., and Galvin, D. (2011). Postdisaster course of alcohol use disorders in systematically studied survivors of 10 disasters. *Archives of General Psychiatry*, *68*(2), 173–180.

Orford, J., Copello, A., Velleman, R., and Templeton, L. (2010). Family members affected by a close relative's addiction: The stress-strain-coping-support model. *Drugs: Education, Prevention and Policy*, *17*(S1), 36–43.

Östberg, M., and Hagekull, B. (2013). Parenting stress and external stressors as predictors of maternal ratings of child adjustment. *Scandinavian Journal of Psychology*, *54*(3), 213–221.

Otowaa, T., York, T. P., Gardner, C. O., Kendler, K. S., and Hettema, J. M. (2014). The impact of childhood parental loss on risk for mood, anxiety and substance use disorders in a population-based sample of male twins. *Psychiatry Research*, *220*, 404–409.

Paradies, Y. (2006). A systematic review of empirical research on self-reported racism and health. *International Journal of Epidemiology*, *35*(4), 888–901. doi:10.1093/ije/dyl056

Peters, R. J., Meshack, A., Amos, C., Scott-Gurnell, K., Savage, C., and Ford, K. (2010). The association of drug use and post-traumatic stress reactions due to Hurricane Ike among Fifth Ward Houstonian youth. *Journal of Ethnicity in Substance Abuse*, *9*(2), 143–151.

Pidd, K., Roche, A., and Fischer, J. (2015). A recipe for good mental health: A pilot randomised controlled trial of a psychological wellbeing and substance use intervention targeting young chefs. *Drugs: Education, Prevention and Policy*, *22*(4), 1–10.

Pidd, K., Roche, A., and Kostadinov, V. (2014). Trainee chefs' experiences of alcohol, tobacco and drug use. *Journal of Hospitality and Tourism Management*, *21*, 108–115.

Pilling, J., Thege, B. K., Demetrovics, Z., and Kopp, M. S. (2012). Alcohol use in the first three years of bereavement: A national representative survey. *Substance Abuse Treatment Prevention and Policy*, *7*. doi:10.1186/1747-597x-7-3

Priest, N., Paradies, Y., Trenerry, B., Truong, M., Karlsen, S., and Kelly, Y. (2013). A systematic review of studies examining the relationship between reported racism and health and wellbeing for children and young people. *Social Science and Medicine*, *95*, 115–127. doi:10.1016/j.socscimed.2012.11.031

Rahav, G., Wilsnack, R., Bloomfield, K., Gmel, G., and Kuntsche, S. (2006). The influence of societal level factors on men's and women's alcohol consumption and alcohol problems. *Alcohol and Alcoholism*, *41*(suppl. 1), i47–i55.

Redelinghuys, J., and Dar, K. (2008). A survey of parents receiving treatment for substance dependence: The impact on their children. *Journal of Substance Use*, *13*(1), 37–48.

Regan, P. C., and Durvasula, R. S. (2015). A brief review of intimate partner violence in the United States: Nature, correlates, and proposed preventative measures. *Interpersona: An International Journal on Personal Relationships*, *9*(2), 127–134.

Roche, A., and Deehan, A. (2002). Women's alcohol consumption: Emerging patterns, problems and public health implications. *Drug and Alcohol Review*, *21*, 169–178.

Roche, A., Kostadinov, V., Fischer, J., Nicholas, R., O'Rourke, K., Pidd, K., and Trifonoff, A. (2015a). Addressing inequities in alcohol consumption and related harms. *Health Promotion International*, *30*(S2), ii20–ii35.

Roche, A. M., Lee, N. K., Battams, S., Fischer, J. A., Cameron, J., and McEntee, A. (2015b). Alcohol use among workers in male-dominated industries: A systematic review of risk factors. *Safety Science*, *78*, 124–141.

Roche, A. M., and Skinner, N. (2005). An introduction to workforce development. In N. Skinner, A. M. Roche, J. O'Connor, Y. Pollard and C. Todd (Eds.), *Workforce Development TIPS (Theory into Practice Strategies): A Resource Kit for the Alcohol and Other Drugs Field*. Adelaide: National Centre for Education and Training on Addiction (NCETA), Flinders University.

Rodriguez, L. M., Neighbors, C., and Knee, C. R. (2014). Problematic alcohol use and marital distress: An interdependence theory perspective. *Addiction Research and Theory*, *22*(4), 294–312. doi:10.3109/16066359.2013.841890

Rodriguez de Fonseca, F., Rubio, P., Menzaghi, F., Merlo-Pich, E., Rivier, J., Koob, G. F., and Navarro, M. (1996). Corticotropin-releasing factor (CRF) antagonist [D-Phe12,Nle21,38,C alpha MeLeu37] CRF attenuates the acute actions of the highly potent cannabinoid receptor agonist HU-210 on defensive-withdrawal behavior in rats. *Journal of Experimental and Clinical Pharmacology*, *276*, 56–64.

Rosario, M., Reisner, S. L., Corliss, H. L., Wypij, D., Calzo, J., and Austin, S. B. (2014). Sexual-orientation disparities in substance use in emerging adults: A function of stress and attachment paradigms. *Psychology of Addictive Behaviors*, *28*(3), 790–804. doi:10.1037/a0035499

Rössler, W. (2012). Stress, burnout, and job dissatisfaction in mental health workers. *European Archives of Psychiatry and Clinical Neuroscience*, *262*(2), 65–69.

Roxburgh, A., Lea, T., de Wit, J., and Degenhardt, L. (2015). Sexual identity and prevalence of alcohol and other drug use among Australians in the general population. *International Journal of Drug Policy*. doi:10.1016/j.drugpo.2015.11.005

Salkow, K., and Fichter, M. (2003). Homelessness and mental illness. *Current Opinion in Psychiatry*, *16*(4), 467–471. doi:10.1097/01.yco.0000079207.36371.29

Salom, C. L., Williams, G. M., Najman, J. M., and Alati, R. (2015). Substance use and mental health disorders are linked to different forms of intimate partner violence victimisation. *Drug and Alcohol Dependence*, *151*, 121–127.

SAMHSA (Substance Abuse and Mental Health Services Administration) (2012). *Results from the 2011 National Survey on Drug Use and Health: Summary of National findings*. Rockville, MD: Substance Abuse and Mental Health Services Administration.

SAMHSA (Substance Abuse and Mental Health Services Administration) (2013). *Behavioral Health Services for People Who Are Homeless*. Treatment Improvement Protocol (TIP) Series 55. HHS Publication No. (SMA) 13-4734. Rockville, MD: Substance Abuse and Mental Health Services Administration.

Sarnyai, Z., Biro, E., Gardi, J., Vecsernyes, M., Julesz, J., and Telegdy, G. (1995). Brain corticotropin-releasing factor mediates "anxiety-like" behavior induced by cocaine withdrawal in rats. *Brain Research*, *675*, 89–97.

Schmitt, M. T., Branscombe, N. R., Postmes, T., and Garcia, A. (2014). The consequences of perceived discrimination for psychological well-being: A meta-analytic review. *Psychological Bulletin*, *140*(4), 921–948. doi:10.1037/a0035754

Selye, H. (1976). 40 years of stress research: Principal remaining problems and misconceptions. *Canadian Medical Association Journal*, *115*(1), 53–56.

Sinha, R. (2008). Chronic stress, drug use, and vulnerability to addiction. *Annals of the New York Academy of Sciences*, *1141*, 105–130.

Solis, J. M., Shadur, J. M., Burns, A. R., and Hussong, A. M. (2012). Understanding the diverse needs of children whose parents abuse substances. *Current Drug Abuse Reviews*, *5*(2), 135–147.

Straussner, S. L. A., and Calnan, A. J. (2014). Trauma through the life cycle: A review of current literature. *Clinical Social Work Journal*, *42*(4), 323–335.

Szapocznik, J., Prado, G., Burlew, A. K., Williams, R. A., and Santisteban, D. A. (2007). Drug abuse in African American and Hispanic adolescents: Culture, development, and behavior. In *Annual Review of Clinical Psychology*, vol. 3 (pp. 77–105). Palo Alto, CA: Annual Reviews.

Teicher, M. H., Andersen, S. L., Ohashi, K., and Polcari, A. (2014). Childhood maltreatment: Altered network centrality of cingulate, precuneus, temporal pole and insula. *Biological Psychiatry*, *76*(4), 297–305.

Temple, E. C., Driver, M., and Brown, R. F. (2014). Cannabis use and anxiety: Is stress the missing piece of the puzzle? *Frontiers in Molecular Psychiatry*, *5*(168).

Tops, M., Koole, S. L., Ijzerman, H., and Buisman-Pijlman, F. T. A. (2014). Why social attachment and oxytocin protect against addiction and stress: Insights from the dynamics between ventral and dorsal corticostriatal systems. *Pharmacology, Biochemistry, and Behavior*, *119*, 39–48.

Traube, D. E., James, S., Zhang, J., and Landsverk, J. (2012). A national study of risk and protective factors for substance use among youth in the child welfare system. *Addictive Behaviors*, *37*, 641–650.

Turner, L. R., Alderman, K., Huang, C., and Tong, S. (2013). Impact of the 2011 Queensland floods on the use of tobacco, alcohol and medication. *Australian and New Zealand Journal of Public Health*, *37*(4), 396–396.

Unger, J. B., Schwartz, S. J., Huh, J., Soto, D. W., and Baezconde-Garbanati, L. (2014). Acculturation and perceived discrimination: Predictors of substance use trajectories from adolescence to emerging adulthood among Hispanics. *Addictive Behaviors*, *39*(9), 1293–1296. doi:10.1016/j.addbeh.2014.04.014

Van de Velde, S., Bracke, P., and Levecque, K. (2010). Gender differences in depression in 23 European countries: Cross-national variation in the gender gap in depression. *Social Science and Medicine*, *71*(2), 305–313.

Veenstra, M. Y., Lemmens, P., Friesema, I. H. M., Garretsen, H. F. L., Knottnerus, J. A., and Zwietering, P. J. (2006). A literature overview of the relationship between life-events and alcohol use in the general population. *Alcohol and Alcoholism*, *41*(4), 455–463. doi:10.1093/alcalc/ag1023

Vendruscolo, L. F., Barbier, E., Schlosburg, J. E., Misra, K. K., Whitfield, T., Jr., Logrip, M. L., ... Koob, G. F. (2012). Corticosteroid-dependent plasticity mediates compulsive alcohol drinking in rats. *Journal of Neuroscience*, *32*(22), 7563–7571.

Vetter, S., Rossegger, A., Rossler, W., Bisson, J. I., and Endrass, J. (2008). Exposure to the tsunami disaster, PTSD symptoms and increased substance use: An internet based survey of male and female residents of Switzerland. *BMC Public Health*, *8*(1), 92. doi:10.1186/1471-2458-8-92

Vines, R. (2011). Equity in health and wellbeing: Why does regional, rural and remote Australia matter? *InPsych*, *33*(5), 8–11.

Virtanen, M., Jokela, M., Nyberg, S. T., Madsen, I. E., Lallukka, T., Ahola, K., ... Burr, H. (2015). Long working hours and alcohol use: Systematic review and meta-analysis of published studies and unpublished individual participant data. *British Medical Journal*, *350*, g7772.

Wadd, S., Lapworth, K., Sullivan, M., Forrester, D., and Galvani, S. (2011). *Working with Older Drinkers*. Bedford: Tilda Goldberg Centre, University of Bedfordshire.

Waldron, M., Grant, J. D., Bucholz, K. K., Lynskey, M. T., Slutske, W. S., Glowinski, A. L., … Heath, A. C. (2014). Parental separation and early substance involvement: Results from children of alcoholic and cannabis dependent twins. *Drug and Alcohol Dependence*, *134*, 78–84.

Warner, E. A. (2012). Opioids for the treatment of chronic noncancer pain. *American Journal of Medicine*, *125*(12), 1155–1161.

Welch, A. E., Caramanica, K., Maslow, C. B., Cone, J. E., Farfel, M. R., Keyes, K. M., … Hasin, D. S. (2014). Frequent binge drinking five to six years after exposure to 9/11: Findings from the World Trade Center Health Registry. *Drug and Alcohol Dependence*, *140*, 1–7.

Welch, A. E., Jasek, J. P., Caramanica, K., Chiles, M. C., and Johns, M. (2015). Cigarette smoking and 9/11-related posttraumatic stress disorder among World Trade Center Health Registry enrollees, 2003–12. *Preventive Medicine*, *73*, 94–99.

Wetherington, C. L. (2010). Sex differences and gonadal hormone influences in drug addiction and sexual behavior: Progress and possibilities. *Hormones and Behavior*, *58*(1), 2–7.

WHO (World Health Organization) (1993). *Psychosocial and Mental Health Aspects of Women's Health*. Geneva: World Health Organization.

WHO (World Health Organization) (1997). *Nations for Mental Health: A Focus on Women*. Geneva: World Health Organization.

WHO (World Health Organization) (2000). *Women's Mental Health: An Evidence Based Review*. Geneva: World Health Organization.

WHO (World Health Organization) (2010). *Social and Gender Inequalities in Environment and Health*. Geneva: World Health Organization.

Wiechelt, S. A., and Straussner, S. L. A. (2015). Introduction to the special issue: Examining the relationship between trauma and addiction. *Journal of Social Work Practice in the Addictions*, *15*(1), 1–5.

Yavorsky, J. E., Kamp Dush, C. M., and Schoppe-Sullivan, S. J. (2015). The production of inequality: The gender division of labor across the transition to parenthood. *Journal of Marriage and Family*, *77*(3), 662–679.

Part Three

Personality, Demographics, and Stress

16

Locus of Control

Ning Hou, Alexa Doerr, Brandon A. Johnson, and Peter Y. Chen

The focus of the current chapter is to review the moderating role of locus of control on the relationship between job stressors and health/illness. The latter consists of mental and physical health. The chapter consists of four main sections. First, we review the construct, dimensionality, and domain of locus of control. Next, we define and distinguish job stressors and job strains, and describe the relationship between job stressor and strain based on job demands–resources theory (Bakker and Demerouti, 2014). Then, we review research that has examined if locus of control moderates the relationship of job stressors with mental and physical health. Lastly, we discuss implications of the current review with regard to future research and practice.

Locus of Control

Broadly speaking, control can be thought of both as a circumstantial condition denoting one's actual ability to do something, and as a perceptual construction of those conditions (Eatough and Spector, 2014). Perceptually constructed control refers to the belief that one can attain desired outcomes and circumvent undesirable ones (Thompson, 2009). Both perceived control and actual control over one's situation have been found to play a substantial role in shaping one's confidence to deal with aversive events. According to the minimax hypothesis (Miller, 1979), control affords a person the ability to minimize the maximum discomfort or danger of a situation. Miller further explains that a person with control can attribute the cause of protection from the aversive event to a secure internal origin, the self, rather than a less stable external origin. The perception of control permits greater confidence that the harshness of an aversive event can be kept within bearable confines.

In relation to perceptually constructed control, the term locus of control (LOC) has been used to describe how inclined someone is to believe they have control over their life circumstances (Eatough and Spector, 2014). LOC has been at the heart of psychological research since it was first introduced by Rotter in 1966. For instance, Judge, Erez, Bono, and Thoresen (2002)

The Handbook of Stress and Health: A Guide to Research and Practice, First Edition.
Edited by Cary L. Cooper and James Campbell Quick.
© 2017 John Wiley & Sons, Ltd. Published 2017 by John Wiley & Sons, Ltd.

found 13,428 articles listing locus of control as a keyword in their review. Particular topics of interest include the implications of locus of control may have for the decisions we make, the lifestyles we lead, and the way we cope with and manage stressful events.

The construct of LOC arose from the social learning theory advanced by Rotter (1954). According to social learning theory, behavior potential is conveyed as a function of expectancy and reinforcement value, where expectancy refers to the subjective probability that a particular behavior will lead to a certain outcome, and the reinforcement value refers to the attractiveness of that outcome. In relation to reinforcement, people with high internal locus of control believe that they have considerable personal control over the events in their life, and tend to perceive outcomes as the result of their own characteristics. In contrast, people with high external locus of control believe that luck, fate, or powerful others are more frequently the source of control in their life (Rotter, 1966).

Empirical studies have conveyed the beneficial effects of internal controls and detrimental effects of external controls on numerous health outcomes, such as depression (Gray-Stanley et al., 2010), burnout (Caron, Corcoran, and Simcoe, 1983), physical health (Muhonen and Torkelson, 2004), psychological and physiological distress (Leung, Siu, and Spector, 2000), psychological disorders (Cohen and Edwards, 1986), job strains (e.g., job dissatisfaction, symptoms, and emotional distress; Spector,1986) and well-being (Spector et al., 2002).

Dimensionality and Domain of Locus of Control

In his conceptualization of the construct, Rotter (1966) viewed LOC as a unidimensional continuum whereby an increase in internal orientation is accompanied by a decrease in external orientation. Yet, some researchers advocate LOC as a multidimensional construct (e.g., Ashkanasy, 1985; Levenson, 1973; Montag and Comrey, 1987). For instance, Levenson conceptualized LOC as consisting of three unique dimensions – chance, powerful others, and internal. The first dimension, chance, represents how much an individual attributes their outcomes to chance or fate. The second dimension, powerful others, represents how much an individual attributes their outcomes to the actions of powerful other people in their lives. The third dimension, internal, represents how much an individual attributes their outcomes to internal factors.

The concept of LOC can be expanded into specific domains to achieve greater prediction for behavior in certain situations (Rotter, 1975). Based on Rotter's (1966) unidimensional conceptualization, Spector (1988) developed a work locus of control scale to assess a person's beliefs about control in their work environment. Similarly, Wallston, Wallston, and DeVellis (1978) developed a multidimensional health LOC scale to assess a person's beliefs that the source of reinforcements for **health**-related behaviors is predominantly internal, a matter of chance, or under the **control** of powerful others.

Job Stressor–Strain Relationships

Job stressors are conditions in the work environment that can be expected to lead to adverse behavioral, physical, or psychological reactions (Spector, Chen, and O'Connell, 2000). Job stressors can be classified as task-related stressors (e.g., work overload, work complexity), role stressors (e.g., role ambiguity, role conflict), interpersonal or social stressors (e.g., incivility, interpersonal conflict), and so on (Kahn and Byosiere, 1992; Sonnentag and Frese, 2012).

Job stressors can also be classified based on single incidents (i.e., acute stressors), or events over extended periods of time (i.e., chronic stressors). Furthermore, job stressors have been classified into one of three situations: regulation uncertainty, regulation obstacles, and over-taxing regulations (Frese and Zapf, 1994). Regulation uncertainty occurs when a person does not know how to achieve goals or what actions or feedback should be taken. Role stressors fall into this category. In the context of regulation obstacles, job conditions interfere with some-one's ability to achieve their goals, and employees have to exert more efforts/energies to reach their goals. An example of regulation obstacles is when employees are asked to meet the quar-terly sales goal yet quality of product has been inconsistent. Finally, overtaxing regulations are circumstances in which employees need to work quickly or work with great intensity.

Job strains are considered an individual's reactions to job stressors, and have been fur-ther delineated in Beehr and Newman's (1978) seminal article on behavioral, physical, and psychological strains. Behavioral strains (e.g., absenteeism) are actions in response to job stressors. For example, an employee may stay home from work after having had an argu-ment with a coworker. Physical strains are physiological responses to stressors (e.g., increase of epinephrine excretion of blood pressure). Psychological strains are affective reactions in response to stressors (e.g., negative mood). Individuals who experience such psychological strains may report increased frustration, depression, or anxiety.

While defining job stressors, we indicated that job stressors might be acute or chronic. This classification is relevant for describing strain responses to either acute or chronic job stressors. Specifically, strain responses may persist after job stressors have been reduced or eliminated. For example, individuals may experience frustration or anxiety regarding a work argument, even though they are at home and no longer experiencing the job stressor. If job stressors persist over extended periods of time, strain responses might become chronic and subsequently impact health outcomes and/or lead to burnout (Bakker, Demerouti, and Verbeke, 2004). The total experience of such stressors ultimately may lead to an overall decreased perception of well-being (Sonnentag and Fritz, 2014). It should be noted that, although job strains are defined as reactions to stressors, the causal relationship between job stressors and job strains is complex, as concluded by Spector, Dwyer and Jex (1988).

Moderating Role of Locus of Control on the Job Stressor–Health/Illness Relationship

As postulated by job demands–resources theory (Bakker and Demerouti, 2014), both job demands and job resources contribute to the complexities of the work environment (Crawford, LePine, and Rich, 2010). Job demands refer to the physical, social, organizational, or psy-chological components of the job that require sustained physical and/or mental effort and may incur physiological or psychological tolls (Demerouti, Bakker, Nachreiner, and Schaufeli, 2001). Examples of such demands include job stressors reviewed earlier and stressors result-ing from the interface between work and family. Like job demands, job resources also involve the physical, social, organizational, and psychological components of the job, and these com-ponents may help to achieve work goals, reduce job demands, or facilitate personal growth, learning, and development (Bakker and Demerouti, 2007).

Research has shown that job demands may continue to elicit strain reactions even when all job-related resources have been made readily available (van Doorn and Hülsheger, 2015), and that effective resource management differs among individuals (Heckhausen and Schulz,

1995; Hockey, 1997). The difference among individuals on resource management suggests the important role of individual differences, such as locus of control, in coping with job demands. Aneshensel (1992) and King and King (1991) further argue that a sense of control as a resistance resource may protect people against psychological strain. As previously mentioned, internals who tend to believe that they have control over events such as job stressors are more likely to take actions and put effort into coping with the stressors and/or reduce adverse effects of job stressors. In contrast, externals believe luck, fate, or powerful others are the main source of control in their life (Rotter, 1966). Specifically, people who consider job stressors as uncontrollable are less likely to take actions to cope with job stressors or mitigate adverse effects of the job stressors, which then make them more vulnerable to stressor-led health problems.

According to conservation of resources theory, personal characteristics such as locus of control are resources that may have instrumental value to assist people to resist stressors/strains (Hobfoll, 1989; 2011). Specifically, psychological and social resources may benefit people through confronting and coping with job stressors (Lin, 1986). Ensel and Lin (1991; 2004) suggested that resources play two functions – deterring and coping. The deterring function implies that resources would reduce strain outcomes, while the coping function suggests the moderating effect of resources on the stressor–strain relationship.

With regard to the deterring function of locus of control, past research has shown that internals tend to successfully adapt to stressful work setting (Parkes, 1986), compared to externals. Spector (1988) has reported that compared to individuals with external work locus of control, individuals with internal work locus of control tend to be more content with their jobs, view their supervisors as higher on consideration and initiating structure (where the leader defines the roles and actions of the group), report fewer role stressors, recognize more autonomy and control, and enjoy longer occupational tenure. Additional positive outcomes of internal locus of control have been reported in prior literature (e.g., Caron et al., 1983; Cohen and Edwards, 1986; Gray-Stanley et al., 2010; Leung et al., 2000; Muhonen and Torkelson, 2004; Spector et al., 2002).

With regard to the coping function of locus of control, researchers have shown that locus of control plays a crucial role in mitigating the effect of stressors on health outcomes (e.g., Schmitz, Neumann, and Oppermann, 2000; Gray-Stanley et al., 2010; Muhonen and Torkelson, 2004). For instance, Schmitz et al. (2000) reported that the relationship between stressors and burnout increased among nurses with low internal locus of control (i.e., externals). Similarly, Muhonen and Torkelson (2004) showed that the positive relationship between job stressors and health symptoms increased among female employees with high external work locus of control.

Although we have attempted to align the current review with topics covered in Part II of this volume, we did not identify articles that examine if locus of control moderates the relationship of job stressors with cancer, chronic fatigue syndrome, gastrointestinal disorders, eating disorders, drug/alcohol misuses, infectious disease, or posttraumatic stress (PTS).

Among articles we identified based on keywords (e.g., job stress, stressor, various health outcomes, etc.), we retained articles based on the following criteria. First, constructs such as perceived control and personal control are included because of their conceptual similarity with locus of control, as noted in Rotter's (1966) conceptualization of the generalized expectation of events that occur due to different attributions. However, studies mainly focusing on job control or job autonomy (e.g., Schaubroeck and Merritt, 1997) are excluded from the review because these studies do not address generalized expectation nor are they considered as a personal resource.

Second, we excluded studies using a composite of multiple scales including locus of control. For instance, Tang and Hammontree (1992) did not find a significant buffering effect of hardiness on the relationship between police stress and physical illness. Yet, the relationship between police stress and absenteeism was moderated by hardiness. The hardiness measure chosen in the study is a composite score of five scales, including alienation from self, alienation from work, and Rotter, Seeman, and Liverant's (1962) Locus of Control Scale. Although locus of control was available in the study, there was no moderated analysis conducted based on locus of control.

Third, in some instances, the interaction of locus of control and other variables such as job control or social support were investigated together (Meier, Semmer, Elfering, and Jacobshagen, 2008; Parkes, 1991). Although the three-way interaction among job stressors, locus of control, and other variables is by itself interesting, the current review only focuses on two-way interaction between locus of control and job stressors. Finally, studies assessing stress level based on a combination of life and job events (e.g., Holmes's schedule of recent experience used by Lawler and Schmied, 1987; 1992) don't specifically focus on job stressors. Thus, these studies are also excluded from the present review.

Mental Health

Among the retained articles, we have identifies studies examining if locus of control affects the relationship of job stressors with various mental health outcomes, including burnout, depression, psychological distress, psychological strain, psychological anxiety, and psychiatric symptomatology. In addition to the following review, a brief description of these studies is summarized in Table 16.1.

Burnout   Chronic exposure to job stressors has been found to be associated with burnout (Cherniss, 1980). Etzion and Westman (1994) examined the moderating role of sense of control on the relationship of burnout with job stressors such as overload and conflicting demands among male career officers in the Israeli armed forces. Sense of control is viewed as an individual's belief in changing the environment effectively (Greenberger and Strasser, 1986). Results supported their hypotheses that sense of control served as a resistance resource (Aneshensel, 1992; King and King, 1991) which attenuates the adverse impact of job stressors on burnout. Specifically, the stressor–burnout relationship is strong among officers with low sense of control. In contrast, the relationship diminishes among officers with high sense of control.

Rahim (1995) also investigated the moderating effect of locus of control on the relationship between job stressors and burnout among entrepreneurs and managers. They found locus of control buffered the stressor–burnout relationship only among the manager sample. However, the moderating results are not consistent. For instance, Koeske and Kirk (1995) did not find the moderating effect on the relationship between role conflict and emotional exhaustion (a component of burnout) in either mental health professionals or intensive case managers.

Depression   There were relatively fewer studies examining the moderating role of locus of control on the relationship between job stressors and depression, compared to early research focusing on the relationship between life stressors and depression (Johnson and Sarason,

Table 16.1 Moderating role of locus of control on job stressor–mental health relationship

Mental health	Study	Sample (N)	Stressor measure	LOC measure	Outcome measure
Burnout	Etzion & Westman, 1994	Male career military officers ($n = 101$)	11-item self-report job stress questionnaire	Sense of control: 7 items selected from the perceived stress scale (PSS; Cohen et al., 1983)	21-item burnout measure (Pines et al., 1981), including physical, emotional, and mental exhaustion dimensions
	Rahim, 1995	Entrepreneurs ($n = 238$) and managers ($n = 288$)	25-item Occupational Stress Inventory (OSI; Osipow & Spokane, 1983), including role conflict, role ambiguity, role overload, and role insufficiency dimensions	8-item internal locus of control subscale (Levenson, 1973)	21-item tedium measure (Pines et al., 1981), including physical, emotional, and mental exhaustion dimensions
Depression	Gray-Stanley et al., 2010	US DSPs from community-based organizations ($n = 323$)	26-item measure including work overload (Caplan, 1971), role ambiguity (Rizzo et al., 1970), role conflict (1970), lack of involvement in decision-making (Vroom, 1960), and client disability dimensions (Hester Adrian Research Centre, 1999)	8-item Ross's locus of control scale (Ross & Mirowsky, 1989)	10-item version of the Centers for Epidemiologic Studies (CES-D) scale (Radloff, 1977; Cole et al., 2004)

Psychological distress	Krause & Stryker, 1984	Middle-aged men from national longitudinal survey (n = 2090)	6-item index of job and economic-related events	11-item short version of Rotter (1966) internal-external locus of control scale	7-item psychophysiological distress (Langner, 1962)
	Leung et al., 2000	University teachers from Hong Kong (n = 106)	24 items modified from the sources of stress scale of the Occupational Stress Indicator-2 (OSI-2; Cooper & Williams, 1996)	16-item work locus of control (WLOC; Spector, 1988)	13-item psychological distress (Siu & Cooper, 1998), including physical ill-health, mental ill-health, and depressive symptoms dimensions
Others (psychological strain, psychological anxiety, and psychiatric symptomatology)	Dijkstra et al., 2011	Members of the nursing and ancillary staff of an institution for disabled people (n = 744)	8-item intragroup conflict scale (Pearson et al., 2002), including task conflict and relational conflict dimensions	5-item internality, Dutch adaptation of the locus of control scale of the Occupational Stress Indicator (Evers et al., 2000)	13-item Dutch adaptation of the Occupational Stress Indicator by Evers et al. (2000).
	Rahim, 1997	Entrepreneurs (n = 238); managers (n = 288) or 526 members of the Chamber of Commerce in a southern state	25-item Occupational Stress Inventory (OSI; Osipow & Spokane, 1983)	8-item internal locus of control subscale (Levenson, 1973)	29-item of the Psychiatric Symptoms Index (PSI; Ilfeld, 1976), including depression, anxiety, cognitive disturbance, and anger.

LOC = locus of control; DSP = direct support professional. Only studies with significant moderation effects are presented in the table.

1978; Lefcourt, Martin, and Saleh, 1984; Sandler and Lakey, 1982). With regard to the job stressor–depression relationship, Gray-Stanley et al. (2010) conducted a survey in a sample of direct support professionals who serve adults with intellectual and developmental disabilities in community-based organizations. Among five types of job stressors, they only found support for locus of control buffering the relationship between work overload (one of the five job stressors) and depression. The moderating result suggests that internals are more active in addressing work overload, which in turn reduces the adverse effect of work overload. Fusilier, Ganster, and Mayes (1987) conducted a study investigating the moderating role of locus of control between job stressors (i.e., role conflict and ambiguity) and depression among police officers and firefighters, yet the result was not supported by the data.

Psychological distress   The stressor–distress relationship has attracted researchers' interests as well. Krause and Stryker (1984) analyzed data of the National Longitudinal Survey of middle-aged men from 1969 and 1971. They first categorized samples into groups based on internal and external locus of control beliefs. Results showed that men in the internal locus of control group experienced significantly lower levels of psychophysiological distress resulting from stressful events. It should be emphasized that items in the psychophysiological distress measure consist of a mix of mental and physical health problems: pain, tiring easily, lack of strength, aches, fainting, anxiety, and shortness of breath.

Krause and Stryker (1984) further divided the groups into moderate internal, extreme internal, moderate external, and extreme external groups. Interestingly, men with moderate internal locus of control showed the greatest buffering effect and the most effective coping for stressful events, whereas men with moderate external locus of control beliefs were shown to be most vulnerable to the job stressors. It was contended that extreme internals may not cope effectively because they strongly feel that they are responsible for the occurrence of the initial stressful events. Following similar rationale, the authors reasoned that extreme externals likely adapt better than moderate externals because the former do not regard themselves as responsible for what happened.

Leung et al. (2000) also investigated whether work locus of control moderated the job stressors–psychological distress relationships. Among six types of job stressors, locus of control only moderates the relationship between perceived organizational practices (e.g., conflicting demand, inadequate guidance) and psychological distress. The positive relationship was stronger for people with external locus of control. Similar to Krause and Stryker (1984), the psychological distress measure employed in the study by Leung et al. (2000) consisted of a mixture of mental and physical health items (i.e., five items measuring physical ill-health, five items assessing mental ill-health, and three items measuring depressive symptoms). Leung et al. (2000) did not provide different analyses to examine each of these distress categories.

Others   There are several studies reporting outcome variables that do not fall into the categories described above. These outcome variables include psychological strain (e.g., feeling miserable, panicky, upset, and worried; Dijkstra, Beersma, and Evers, 2011), psychological anxiety (Perrewé, 1986), and psychiatric symptomatology (psychiatric symptom indicators such as depression, anxiety, cognitive disturbance, and anger; Rahim, 1997). Among four types of job stressors, role conflict, role ambiguity, role overload, and role insufficiency, Rahim (1997) found that the relationships of role ambiguity and role overload with psychiatric symptoms were significantly higher for managers with external locus of control than for managers with internal locus of control. Similarly, Dijkstra et al. (2011) found that the relationship between workplace conflict and psychological strain was stronger among health-care workers with external locus of control than their counterparts. However, Perrewé (1986) did not find support for a moderating effect on the relationship between job demand and psychological anxiety.

Physical Health

In addition to the mitigating role of locus of control on job stressor–mental health relationships studied in the literature, past studies have examined a similar role in the relationship between job stressor and physical health, which include somatic complaints (e.g., headaches, nausea, or sweaty palms), illness/symptoms, and physiological distress/strain. Similar to the prior section, a brief description of these studies is summarized in Table 16.2.

Somatic complaints   Fusilier et al. (1987) examined the moderating role of locus of control on the relationship between job stressors (i.e., role conflict and ambiguity) and somatic complaints. They found that the relationship between role conflict and somatic complaints varied and was contingent upon type of locus of control. Specifically, role conflict was positively related to somatic complaints among externals. In contrast, the relationship decreased and was not significant among internals.

Illness/symptoms   Muhonen and Torkelson (2004) reported a significant buffering effect of locus of control on the job stressor–symptom relationship among female employees in a Swedish telecom company. However, a similar result was not found among male employees. To explain the different results found, Muhonen and Torkelson argued that females may have more externality tendencies, and may be more vulnerable to health problems when they experience a high level of job stressors.

Physiological distress/strain   As noted earlier, both Krause and Stryker (1984) and Leung et al. (2000) used a psychological distress measure that consists of a mixture of mental and physical health items. To assess physiological strain, Fusilier et al. (1987) measured epinephrine excretion to gauge the level of physiological responses toward environmental demand or threat. However, they did not find a significant moderating effect of locus of control on the relationship between job stressors (i.e., role conflict and ambiguity) and physiological distress.

Conclusion and Future Directions

Overall, empirical evidence generally supports the relationships of locus of control with mental and physical health. Nonetheless, the presumed linear relationship between locus of control and health may require further investigation. According to Rotter (1966), people with an intermediate level of internality might be healthier than people with an extreme level of internality, due to different defensive tendencies (Efran, 1963), different motivations in achievement situations (Rotter and Mulry, 1965), and different values of reinforcement for skills and chance. Schorr and Rodin (1984) also contended that people with an internal locus of control tend

Table 16.2 Moderating role of locus of control on job stressor–physical health relationship

Physical health	Study	Sample (N)	Stress measure	LOC measure	Outcome measure
Somatic complaints	Fusilier et al., 1987	Police officers and firefighters (n = 312)	Work role conflict and ambiguity stress scales (Rizzo et al., 1970)	16-item Levenson (1973) locus of control scale	17-item of somatic complaints symptoms, such as headaches, nausea, and sweaty palms
Illness/symptoms	Muhonen & Torkelson, 2004	Employees in a Swedish telecom company (n = 422)	11-item sources of stress at work	16-item Swedish version (Muhonen, 1999) of Spector's (1988) work locus of control (WLCS)	25-item ill-health by the Hopkins Symptom Checklist-25 (HSCL-25; Derogatis et al., 1974).
Physiological distress/strain	Krause & Stryker, 1984	Middle-aged men from national longitudinal survey (n = 2090)	6-item index of job and economic-related events	11-item short version of Rotter (1966) internal-external locus of control scale	7-item psychophysiological distress from Langner (1962)
	Leung et al., 2000	University teachers from Hong Kong (n = 106)	24-item modified from the sources of stress scale of the Occupational Stress Indicator-2 (OSI-2; Cooper & Williams, 1996)	16-item work locus of control (WLOC; Spector, 1988)	5-item measuring physical ill-health (Siu & Cooper, 1998)
	Fusilier et al., 1987	Police officers and firefighters (n = 312)	Work role conflict and ambiguity stress scales (Rizzo et al., 1970)	16-item Levenson (1973) locus of control scale	Physiological strain using epinephrine levels from urine samples

LOC = locus of control. Only studies with significant moderation effects are presented in the table.

to prefer control-relevant options more than externals do. This argument assumes that internals have stronger motivation for control than externals have. Those internals who are strongly motivated to have control (Schorr and Rodin, 1984) may run the risk of self-blame, loss of self-esteem, and frustration, particularly under harsh environments (Caron et al., 1983; Koeske and Kirk, 1995; Reid, 1984; Wagener and Taylor, 1986). This argument may explain why the previously reviewed buffering effects of internal locus of control at the moderate level benefited people more than at the extreme level (Krause and Stryker, 1984). More research in work contexts is needed to examine the potential hindrance effects on mental and physical health between people with an extreme level of internality and those with an intermediate level of internality.

However, results of the buffering effect of locus of control on job stressor–health relationships are not consistent, particularly for physical health outcomes. A caveat regarding this review is that the majority of included studies were self-reported with cross-sectional design. Past research (e.g., Dijkstra et al., 2011; Ross and Mirowsky, 1989) has often contented that internals are more likely to cope actively to reduce health problems, yet this proposition has rarely been tested with adequate research designs. The current review suggests that there is a gap of understanding underlying mechanisms that explain the relationships among locus of control, job stressors, and health.

The moderating effects of locus of control seem to be inconsistent between male and female samples. Among research focusing on the life stressors–health relationship, some studies showed a significant buffering effect in male compared to female samples (e.g., Johnson and Sarason, 1978; Lefcourt, 1982). Yet, other studies revealed a significant buffering effect in female samples (e.g., Husaini, Neff, Newbrough, and Moore, 1982). Similarly, among studies focusing on the job stressor–health relationship, Muhonen and Torkelson (2004) reported significant buffering effects of work locus of control in their female sample but not in their male sample, yet Etzion and Westman (1994) reported the significant buffering effect in male officers. In the study by Fusilier et al. (1987), 80 percent of 312 fire fighters and police were males. They did not find any significant moderating effect of locus of control on the relationship of role conflict and ambiguity with depression and physiological distress, yet the moderating effect was significant in the relationship between role conflict and somatic complaints. The above review suggests future research needs to investigate why the moderating effects are not consistent across gender.

The present review further revealed that moderating effects of locus of control are not consistent across different job stressors (e.g., Fusilier et al., 1987; Gray-Stanley et al., 2010; Leung et al., 2000; Rahim, 1997). This observation suggests an additional need in this line of literature to articulate what aspect of locus of control is congruent with job stressors. This is in line with Hobfoll's (1989) suggestion to consider the ecology of job stressors.

Gray-Stanley et al. (2010) reported that locus of control mitigated the detrimental effect of work overload on depression, but primarily found this relationship in workers with a lower level of work overload. Thus, they argued that perhaps in overwhelmed working contexts, personal resources are not sufficient. This proposition suggests the importance of considering external resources such as social support that may enhance the buffering effect of locus of control. For instance, Sandler and Lakey (1982) reported that social support significantly moderated the relationship between life stressors and psychological disorder among internals, but not externals. Kobasa and Puccetti's (1983) results showed that under high-stress contexts, social support had buffering effects when coupled with sense of control.

However, the role of social support in the buffering effect of locus of control has not been fully understood in past literature, and requires further investigation. Some researchers have argued that social support may reciprocally promote locus of control because of the power of support to encourage sense of control (Nelson and Quick, 1991; Wethington and Kessler 1986; Lefcourt, 1982; Sandler and Lakey, 1982; Ganellen and Blaney, 1984). Yet, other researchers have argued that social support may detract from control because it limits autonomy and fosters dependence (Mirowsky and Ross, 1984; Mutran and Reitzes 1984; Kessler and McLeod 1984; Pearlin and Schooler, 1978).

In addition to the above suggestions for future research, we also conclude that the reviewed studies strongly advocate that employees' psychological and physical health could be improved through an increase in personal control. If personal control could be boosted, even steadily, interventions could be used to develop and promote workers' internal control beliefs in their work environment (Schieman and Turner 1998; Jang, Haley, Small, and Mortimer, 2002). To date, some initial evidence has supported the proposition that control could be developed and promoted (e.g., Spence, 1994; Schmitz et al., 2000; Sharp et al., 1997; Diamond and Shapiro, 1973). Interventions with the goal of enhancing internal locus of control may prove to be a promising direction in mitigating or buffering the relationship between life or job stressors and mental and physical health. However, this domain of research could benefit from greater study, with the ultimate goal of understanding where and why inconsistencies exist across gender, stressors, and mental and physiological symptoms.

References

*Empirical studies. †Reference for the measure in the empirical studies.

Aneshensel, C. S. (1992). Social stress: Theory and research. *Annual Review of Sociology*, *18*, 15–38.
Ashkanasy, N. M. (1985). Rotter's internal–external scale: Confirmatory factor analysis and correlation with social desirability for alternative scale formats. *Journal of Personality and Social Psychology*, *48*, 1328–1340.
Bakker, A. B., and Demerouti, E. (2007). The job demands–resources model: State of the art. *Journal of Managerial Psychology*, *22*, 309–328.
Bakker, A. B., and Demerouti, E. (2014). Job demands–resources theory. In P. Y. Chen and C. L. Cooper (Eds.), *Wellbeing: A Complete Reference Guide*, vol. 3: *Work and Wellbeing* (pp. 37–64). Chichester, UK: Wiley.
Bakker, A. B., Demerouti, E., and Verbeke, W. (2004). Using the job–demands resources model to predict burnout and performance. *Human Resource Management*, *43*, 83–104.
Beehr, T. A., and Newman, J. E. (1978). Job stress, employee health, and organizational effectiveness: A facet analysis, model, and literature review. *Personnel Psychology*, *31*, 665–699.
†Caplan, R. D. (1971) Organizational stress and individual strain: A social psychological study of risk factors in coronary heart disease among administrators, engineers, and scientists. Thesis, University of Michigan.
Caron, C., Corcoran, K. J., and Simcoe, F. (1983). Intrapersonal correlates of burnout: The role of locus of control in burnout and self-esteem. *Clinical Supervisor*, *1*, 53–62.
Cherniss, C. (1980). *Staff Burnout: Job Stress in the Human Services*. Beverly Hills, CA: Sage.
Cohen, S., and Edwards, J. R. (1986). Personality characteristics as moderators of the relationship between stress and disorder. In R. W. J. Neufeld (Ed.), *Advances in the Investigation of Psychological Stress*. New York: Wiley.
†Cohen, S., Kamarck, T., and Mermelstein, R. (1983). A global measure of perceived stress. *Journal of Health and Social Behavior*, *24*, 385–396.
†Cole, J. C., Rabin, A. S., Smith, T. L. and Kaufman, A. S. (2004). Development and validation of a Rasch-derived CES-D short form. *Psychological Assessment*, *16*, 360–72.
†Cooper, C. L., and Williams, S. (1996). *Occupational Stress Indicator: Version 2*. Harrogate: RAD Ltd.
Crawford, E. R., LePine, J. A., and Rich, B. L. (2010). Linking job demands and resources to employee engagement and burnout: A theoretical extension and meta-analytic test. *Journal of Applied Psychology*, *95*, 834–848.

Demerouti, E., Bakker, A. B., Nachreiner, F., and Schaufeli, W. B. (2001). The job demands–resources model of burnout. *Journal of Applied Psychology, 86,* 499–512.

Derogatis L. R., Lipman, R. S., Rickels, K., Uhlenhuth, E. H., and Covi, L. (1974). The Hopkins symptom checklist (HSCL): A self-report symptom inventory. *Behavioral Science, 19,* 1–15.

*Dijkstra, M. T., Beersma, B., and Evers, A. (2011). Reducing conflict-related employee strain: The benefits of an internal locus of control and a problem-solving conflict management strategy. *Work and Stress, 25,* 167–184.

Diamond, M. J., and Shapiro, J. L. (1973). Changes in locus of control as a function of encounter group experiences: A study and replication. *Journal of Abnormal Psychology, 82,* 514–518.

Eatough, E. M., and Spector, P. E. (2014). The role of workplace control in positive health and wellbeing. In P. Y. Chen and C. L. Cooper (Eds.), *Wellbeing: A Complete Reference Guide, vol. 3: Work and Wellbeing* (pp. 91–109). Chichester, UK: Wiley.

Efran, J. S. (1963). Some personality determinants of memory for success and failure. Dissertation, Ohio State University.

Ensel, W. M., and Lin, N. (1991). The life stress paradigm and psychological distress. *Journal of Health and Social Behavior, 32,* 321–341.

Ensel, W. M., and Lin, N. (2004). Physical fitness and the stress process. *Journal of Community Psychology, 32,* 81–101.

*Etzion, D., and Westman, M. (1994). Social support and sense of control as moderators of the stress–burnout relationship in military careers. *Journal of Social Behavior and Personality, 9,* 639–656.

†Evers, A., Frese, M., and Cooper, C. L. (2000). Revisions and further developments of the Occupational Stress Indicator: LISREL results from four Dutch studies. *Journal of Occupational and Organizational Psychology, 73,* 221–240.

Frese, M., and Zapf, D. (1994). Methodological issues in the study of work stress: Objective vs subjective measurement of work stress and the question of longitudinal studies. In C. L. Cooper, R. Payne, C. L. Cooper, and R. Payne (Eds.), *Causes, Coping and Consequences of Stress at Work* (pp. 375–411). New York: Wiley.

*Fusilier, M. R., Ganster, D. C., and Mayes, B. T. (1987). Effects of social support, role stress, and locus of control of health. *Journal of Management, 13,* 517.

Ganellen, R. J., and Blaney, P. H. (1984). Hardiness and social support as moderators of the effects of life stress. *Journal of Personality and Social Psychology, 47,* 156–163.

*Gray-Stanley, J. A., Muramatsu, N., Heller, T., Hughes, S., Johnson, T. P., and Ramirez-Valles, J. (2010). Work stress and depression among direct support professionals: The role of work support and locus of control. *Journal of Intellectual Disability Research, 54,* 749–761.

Greenberger, D. G., and Strasser, S. (1986). Development and application of a model of personal control in organizations. *Academy of Management Review, 11,* 164–177.

Heckhausen, J., and Schulz, R. (1995). A life-span theory of control. *Psychological Review, 102,* 284–304.

†Hester Adrian Research Centre (1999). *Survey on Working in Services for People with Learning Disabilities.* Manchester: Hester Adrian Research Centre.

Hobfoll, S. E. (1989). Conservation of resources: A new attempt at conceptualizing stress. *American Psychologist, 44,* 513–524.

Hobfoll, S. E. (2011). Conservation of resource caravans and engaged settings. *Journal of Occupational and Organizational Psychology, 84,* 116–122.

Hockey, G. R. J. (1997). Compensatory control in the regulation of human performance under stress and high workload: A cognitive-energetical framework. *Biological Psychology, 45,* 73–93.

Husaini, B., Neff, J., Newbrough, J. R., and Moore, M. C. (1982). The stress-buffering role of social support and personal competence among the rural unmarried. *Journal of Community Psychology, 10,* 409–426.

†Ilfeld, F. W., Jr. (1976). Further validation of a psychiatric symptom index in a normal population. *Psychological Reports, 39,* 1215–1228.

Jang, Y., Haley, W. E., Small, B. J., and Mortimer, J. A. (2002). The role of mastery and social resources in the associations between disability and depression in later life. *Gerontologist, 42,* 807–13.

Johnson, J. H., and Sarason, I. (1978). Moderator variables in life stress research. In I. G. Sarason and C. D. Spielberger (Eds.), *Stress and Anxiety,* vol. 6. New York: Wiley.

Judge, T. A., Erez, A., Bono, J. E., and Thoresen, C. J. (2002). Are measures of self-esteem, neuroticism, locus of control, and generalized self-efficacy indicators of a common core construct? *Journal of Personality and Social Psychology, 83,* 693–710.

Kahn, R. L., and Byosiere, P. (1992). Stress in organizations. In M. D. Dunnette and L. M. Hough (Eds.), *Handbook of Industrial and Organizational Psychology*, 2nd edn., vol. 3 (pp. 571–650). Palo Alto, CA: Consulting Psychologists Press.

Kessler, R. C., and McLeod, J. D. (1984). Sex differences in vulnerability to undesirable life events. *American Sociological Review*, *49*, 620–631.

King, L. A., and King, D. W. (1991). Role conflict and role ambiguity: A critical assessment of construct validity. *Psychological Bulletin*, *107*, 48–64.

Kobasa, S. C., and Puccetti, M. C. (1983). Personality and social resources in stress resistance. *Journal of Personality and Social Psychology*, *45*, 839.

Koeske, G. F., and Kirk, S. A. (1995). Direct and buffering effects of internal locus of control among mental health professionals. *Journal of Social Service Research*, *20*(3–4), 1–28.

*Krause, N., and Stryker, S. (1984). Stress and well-being: The buffering role of locus of control beliefs. *Social Science and Medicine*, *18*, 783–790.

†Langner, T. A. (1962). Twenty-two item screening score of psychiatric symptoms indicating impairment. *Journal of Health and Social Behavior*, *3*, 269–276.

Lawler, K. A., and Schmied, L. A. (1987). The relationship of stress, Type A behavior and powerlessness to physiological responses in female clerical workers. *Journal of Psychosomatic Research*, *31*, 555–566.

Lawler, K. A., and Schmied, L. (1992). A prospective study of women's health: The effects of stress, hardiness, locus of control, Type A behavior, and physiological reactivity. *Women and Health*, *19*, 27–41.

Lefcourt, H. M. (1982). *Locus of Control*. New York: Academic Press.

Lefcourt, H. M., Martin, R. A., and Saleh, W. E. (1984). Locus of control and social support: Interactive moderators of stress. *Journal of Personality and Social Psychology*, *47*, 378–389.

*Leung, T.-W., Siu, O.-L., and Spector, P. E. (2000). Faculty stressors, job satisfaction, and psychological distress among university teachers in Hong Kong: The role of locus of control. *International Journal of Stress Management*, *7*, 121–138.

Levenson, H. (1973). Multidimensional locus of control in psychiatric patients. *Journal of Consulting and Clinical Psychology*, *41*, 397–404.

Lin, N. (1986). Conceptualizing social support. In N. Lin, A. Dean, and W. Ensel (Eds.), *Social Support, Life Events, and Depression* (pp. 17–30). New York: Academic Press.

Meier, L. L., Semmer, N. K., Elfering, A., and Jacobshagen, N. (2008). The double meaning of control: Three-way interactions between internal resources, job control, and stressors at work. *Journal of Occupational Health Psychology*, *13*, 244.

Miller, S. M. (1979). Controllability and human stress: Method, evidence and theory. *Behaviour Research and Therapy*, *17*, 287–304.

Mirowsky, J., and Ross, C. E. (1984). Mexican culture and its emotional contradictions. *Journal of Health and Social Behavior*, *25*, 2–13.

Montag, I., and Comrey, A. L. (1987). Internality and externality as correlates of involvement in fatal driving accidents. *Journal of Applied Psychology*, *72*, 339–343.

†Muhonen, T. (1999). Women, career, and family: A study among managers in four different branches. Doctoral thesis, Department of Psychology, Lund University (in Swedish with English summary).

*Muhonen, T., and Torkelson, E. (2004). Work locus of control and its relationship to health and job satisfaction from a gender perspective. *Stress and Health*, *20*, 21–28.

Mutran, E., and Reitzes, D. C. (1984). Intergenerational support activities and well-being among the elderly: A convergence of exchange and symbolic interaction perspectives. *American Sociological Review*, *49*, 117–130.

Nelson, D. L., and Quick, J. C. (1991). Social support and newcomer adjustment in organizations: Attachment theory at work? *Journal of Organizational Behavior*, *12*, 543–554.

†Osipow, S.H., and Spokane, A. R. (1983). *Occupational Stress Inventory: Manual*. Odessa, FL: Psychological Assessment Resources.

Parkes, K. R. (1986). Coping in stressful episodes: The role of individual differences, environmental factors, and situational characteristics. *Journal of Personality and Social Psychology*, *51*, 1277–1292.

Parkes, K. R. (1991). Locus of control as moderator: An explanation for additive versus interactive findings in the demand–discretion model of work stress? *British Journal of Psychology*, *82*, 291–312.

Pearlin, L. I., and Schooler, C. (1978). The structure of coping. *Journal of Health and Social Behavior*, *19*, 2–21.

†Pearson, W. A., Ensley, M. D., and Amason, A. C. (2002). An assessment and refinement of Jehn's Intragroup Conflict Scale. *International Journal of Conflict Management*, *13*, 110–126.

Perrewé, P. L. (1986). Locus of control and activity level as moderators in the quantitative job demands–satisfaction/psychological anxiety relationship: An experimental analysis. *Journal of Applied Social Psychology*, 16, 620–632.

†Pines, A. M., Aronson, E., and Kafey, D. (1981). *Burnout: From Tedium to Personal Growth*. New York: Free Press.

†Radloff L. S. (1977) The CES-D scale: A self-report depression scale for research in the general population. *Applied Psychological Measurement*, 1, 385–401.

*Rahim, M. A. (1995). A comparative study of entrepreneurs and managers: Stress, burnout, locus of control, and social support. *Journal of Health and Human Services Administration*, 18, 68–89.

*Rahim, M. A. (1997). Relationships of stress, locus of control, and social support to psychiatric symptoms and propensity to leave a job: A field study with managers. *Journal of Business and Psychology*, 12, 159–174.

Reid, D. W. (1984). Participatory control and the chronic-illness adjustment process. In H. M. Lefcourt (Ed.), *Research with the Locus of Control Construct*, vol. 3 (pp. 361–389). Orlando, FL: Academic Press.

†Rizzo, J., House, R. J., and Lirtzman, S. I. (1970). Role conflict and ambiguity in complex organizations. *Administrative Science Quarterly*, 15, 150–63.

Ross, C. E., and Mirowsky, J. (1989). Explaining the social patterns of depression: Control and problem solving – or support and talking? *Journal of Health and Social Behavior*, 30, 206–219.

Rotter, J. B. (1954). *Social Learning and Clinical Psychology*. New York: Prentice Hall.

Rotter, J. B. (1966). Generalized expectancies for internal versus external control of reinforcement. *Psychological Monographs*, 80, 1–28.

Rotter, J.B. (1975). Some problems and misconceptions related to the construct of internal versus external control of reinforcement. *Journal of Consulting and Clinical Psychology*, 43, 56–67.

Rotter, J. B., and Mulry, R. C. (1965). Internal versus external control of reinforcement and decision time. *Journal of Personality and Social Psychology*, 2, 598–604.

Rotter, J. B., Seeman, M., and Liverant, S. (1962). Internal versus external control of reinforcement: A major variable in behavior theory. *Decisions, Values, and Groups*, 2, 473–516.

Sandler, I. N., and Lakey, B. (1982). Locus of control as a stress moderator: The role of control perceptions and social support. *American Journal of Community Psychology*, 10, 65–80.

Schaubroeck, J., and Merritt, D. E. (1997). Divergent effects of job control on coping with work stressors: The key role of self-efficacy. *Academy of Management Journal*, 40, 738–754.

Schieman, S., and Turner, H. A. (1998). Age, disability, and sense of mastery. *Journal of Health and Social Behavior*, 39, 169–86.

Schmitz, N., Neumann, W., and Oppermann, R. (2000). Stress, burnout and locus of control in German nurses. *International Journal of Nursing Studies*, 37, 95–99.

Schorr, D., and Rodin, J. (1984). Motivation to control one's environment in individuals with obsessive-compulsive, depressive, and normal personality traits. *Journal of Personality and Social Psychology*, 46, 1148.

Sharp, C., Hurford, D. P., Allison, J., Sparks, R., and Cameron, B. P. (1997). Facilitation of internal locus of control in adolescent alcoholics through a brief biofeedback-assisted autogenic relaxation training procedure. *Journal of Substance Abuse Treatment*, 14, 55–60.

†Siu, O.-L., and Cooper, C. L. (1998). A study of occupational stress, job satisfaction and quitting intention in Hong Kong firms: The role of locus of control and organizational commitment. *Stress Medicine*, 14, 55–66.

Sonnentag, S., and Fritz, C. (2014). Recovery from job stress: the stressor-detachment model as an integrative framework. *Journal of Organizational Behavior*, 36, 72–103.

Sonnentag, S., and Frese, M. (2012). Stress in organizations. In N. W. Schmitt, and S. Highhouse (Eds.), *Handbook of Psychology, vol. 12: Industrial and Organizational Psychology*, 2nd edn. (pp. 560–592). Hoboken, NJ: Wiley.

Spector, P. E. (1986). Perceived control by employees: A meta-analysis of studies concerning autonomy and participation at work. *Human Relations*, 39, 1005–1016.

Spector, P. E. (1988). Development of the work locus of control scale. *Journal of Occupational Psychology*, 61, 335–340.

Spector, P. E., Chen, P. Y., and O'Connell, B. J. (2000). A longitudinal study of relations between job stressors and job strains while controlling for prior negative affectivity and strains. *Journal of Applied Psychology*, 85, 211–218.

Spector, P. E., Cooper, C. L., Sanchez, J. I., O'Driscoll, M., Sparks, K., Bernin, P., … Yu, S. (2002). Locus of control and well-being at work: How generalizable are Western findings? *Academy of Management Journal*, 45, 453–466.

Spector, P. E., Dwyer, D. J., and Jex, S. M. (1988). Relation of job stressors to affective, health, and performance outcomes: A comparison of multiple data sources. *Journal of Applied Psychology*, 73, 11–19.

Spence, S. H. (1994) Practitioner review: cognitive therapy with children and adolescents: From theory to practice. *Journal of Child Psychology and Psychiatry and Allied Disciplines*, *35*, 1191–228.

Tang, T. L. P., and Hammontree, M. L. (1992). The effects of hardiness, police stress, and life stress on police officers' illness and absenteeism. *Public Personnel Management*, *21*, 493–493.

Thompson, S. C. (2009). The role of personal control in adaptive functioning. In C. R. Snyder and S. J. Lopez (Eds.), *Oxford Handbook of Positive Psychology*, 2nd edn. (pp. 271–278). New York: Oxford University Press.

van Doorn, R. R., and Hülsheger, U. R. (2015). What makes employees resilient to job demands? The role of core self-evaluations in the relationship between job demands and strain reactions. *European Journal of Work and Organizational Psychology*, *24*, 76–87.

† Vroom V. H. (1960). *Some Personality Determinants of the Effects of Participation*. Englewood Cliffs, NJ: Prentice Hall.

Wagener, J. J., and Taylor, S. E. (1986). What else could I have done? Patients' responses to failed treatment decisions. *Health Psychology*, *5*, 481–496.

Wallston, K. A., Wallston, B. S., and DeVellis, R. (1978). Development of the Multidimensional Health Locus of Control (MHLC) scales. *Health Education Monographs*, *6*, 160–170.

Wethington, E., and Kessler, R. C. (1986). Perceived support, received support, and adjustment to stressful life events. *Journal of Health and Social Behavior*, *27*, 78–89.

17

The Type A Behavior Pattern

Geir Arild Espnes, Unni Karin Moksnes, and Donald Glenn Byrne

The development of coronary heart disease (CHD) has long been thought of as connected to stress and anger. In Norwegian folklore tales we hear stories of trolls who get so angry when Askeladden (the youngest and most charming lad in the family) teases the others that the trolls' hearts quite simply crack from stress caused by anger.

The history of the psychology behind CHD carries the same theme. When Ray Rosenman and Meyer Friedman started their work on the Type A Behavior Pattern, the same pragmatic origin emerged. They themselves tell of the upholsterer who repaired the furniture in their waiting room. He noted how stressed their patients must have been since it was only the front edges of the chairs that showed signs of wear. That made the two insightful cardiologists curious about the behaviors of their patients and instigated both a discussion to conceptualize the nature of those behaviors and, eventually, a program of research to determine whether the speculation – for that is what it initially was – had any validity (M. Friedman and Rosenman, 1974). And from small beginnings, it was the motivation for the iconic Western Collaborative Group Study (WCGS), a large study to reveal if there was a common behavioral pattern among persons in danger of suffering a clinical event of CHD.

The study concluded, on the basis of incontestable evidence, that there were indeed similarities in the behavior of those at risk of CHD, and the behavioral pattern that emerged was named Type A Behavior Pattern (TABP). The WCGS was the first study to conceptualize and investigate behavior patterns as risks for heart attacks. Some 3,524 men aged 39–59 and employed in the San Francisco Bay or Los Angeles areas were enrolled in 1960 and 1961. In addition to determinations of behavior pattern, the initial examination assessed the person's medical and family history, with a raft of medical and biomedical tests. And the evidence of and eight-year follow-up supported the conclusion that Type A behavior was indeed a very significant risk factor for the development of CHD.

In just a few years, through the 1950s and 1960s, Friedman and Rosenman's TABP became well known, if controversial, and became recognized as *the* "coronary prone behavior" pattern

The Handbook of Stress and Health: A Guide to Research and Practice, First Edition.
Edited by Cary L. Cooper and James Campbell Quick.
© 2017 John Wiley & Sons, Ltd. Published 2017 by John Wiley & Sons, Ltd.

(M. Friedman and Rosenman, 1974). The overall hypothesis, that a distinct pattern of behavioral characteristics could be an independent risk factor for CHD development (Rosenman et al., 1964; M. Friedman and Rosenman, 1974; Rosenman et al., 1975), was based partly on their creative intellectual curiosity (seen in the story of the upholsterer), and partly on much earlier observations asserting psychological factors in CHD development (e.g. Osler, 1897; Menninger and Menninger, 1936; Kemple, 1945; Gildea, 1949).

The Framingham Heart Study persuasively confirmed the finding – people with the TABP showed a relative risk of 2.9 among white-collar workers, and 2.1 in women working outside the home, for developing a CHD, other risk factors having been taken into account (Haynes, Feinleib, and Kannel, 1980). So, both these major studies supported the hypothesis that there was a cluster of recognizable behaviors which increased the probability of CHD onset. Both studies concluded that the pattern of characteristics (the TABP) was an independent risk factor for CHD development, and that it was as strong a predictor of CHD as the rest of the known risk factors combined. This led the American National Lung and Blood Institute review panel, in a rather momentous step, to conclude without equivocation that the TABP is associated with increased risk of clinically apparent CHD in employed, middle-aged US citizens (Review Panel, 1981), with TABP broadly defined as referring to any person who "is involved in an aggressive and incessant struggle to achieve more and more in less and less time" (M. Friedman and Rosenman, 1974).

Both clinicians and researchers worldwide rapidly expressed confidence in the TABP, and its ability to predict future cardiac problems. And, by extension, that modifications to this behavior pattern through psychological interventions could have the capacity to prevent the development of CHD in men to the same extent as the modification of smoking behavior, elevated cholesterol, or high blood pressure would be expected to achieve.

The Role of Stress in the Understanding of the TABP and CHD

Coincidentally, researchers had been studying stress and its impact on psychological and physical health for many decades. Historical research has linked stress to more diseases than any other biopsychological factor in the published literature, and not surprisingly, stress has long been connected to the development of CHD. A widely used definition of stressful situations is one in which the demands of the situation threaten to exceed the resources of the individual to cope (Lazarus and Folkman 1984). It is clear that all of us are exposed to stressful situations at the societal, community, and interpersonal levels (Monroe, 2008). Acute stress responses in healthy individuals may be adaptive and typically do not impose a health burden. However, if the threat is persistent, the long-term effects of stressors can damage health. The relationship between psychosocial stressors and disease (in this context, CHD) is thus affected by the nature, number, and persistence of the stressors, as well as by the individual's biological vulnerability, psychosocial resources, personality (e.g. Type A behavior pattern), and learned patterns of coping (Monroe, 2008). This is particularly the case if the person has few psychosocial resources and poor coping skills. Stress experiences thus have a major influence upon mood, our sense of well-being, behavior, and health.

Assessment of the TABP: Measures and Their Relative Usefulness

The capacity of the TABP to predict future CHD rests heavily on the psychometric integrity of the instruments developed to measure that construct. Over the past five decades, the use of many instruments has been reported in this context, some simply modifications of existing psychometric scales and others developed for the express purpose of measuring the TABP. Only three have really met the criteria of specificity (to explicitly measure the TABP) and empirical validity (demonstrated statistical links either with clinical CHD events or aspects of coronary artery pathology).

The structured interview (SI) developed for the WCGS by Rosenman et al. (1966) combined direct questions eliciting self-reports of Type A behaviors, with deliberate behavioral challenges designed to elicit observable instances of Type A behavior recorded and rated by trained interviewers. The SI has long been considered the benchmark of Type A measures (Chesney, Eagleston, and Rosenman, 1980) and its predictive capacity in regard to CHD incidence in the WCGS was remarkable (Rosenman, Brand, Sholtz, and Friedman, 1976). However, for greater convenience in large sample studies, the purely self-report Jenkins Activity Survey (JAS) was developed by Jenkins, Zyzanski, and Rosenman (1971) to complement the SI where the use of interviewers was not possible. The JAS was also found to be predictive of future CHD in the WCGS (Rosenman et al., 1976), and has been used over many years now as the instrument of choice in a multitude of well-designed and largely positive studies linking the TABP with CHD.

Neither the SI nor the JAS was specifically used in the Framingham study, but a measure of Type A behavior was retrospectively constructed from existing psychosocial items in the Framingham database. This scale too was longitudinally predictive of CHD using Framingham data (Haynes et al., 1980), but not consistently across genders or age groups. The scale was, importantly, later validated against the JAS (Suls and Marco, 1990).

Byrne, Rosenman, Schiller, and Chesney (1985) published a comparative study of several specific and generic Type A measures in a large nonclinical sample, noting that most related strongly to one another. They concluded that the thematic content of most scales reflected a significant overlap of behavioral domains, the single one lacking, however, being that of experienced emotions. And as this review will go on to note, this has been a serious flaw in both the conceptualization and measurement of the TABP.

Historical Research on the TABP and CHD

The TABP in the 1980s

A meta-analytic report by Booth-Kewley and Friedman in 1987 found as its most important conclusion that Type A behavior is modestly but reliably related to CHD (and other occlusive diseases), but that the true picture seems to be one of a person with one or more negative emotions: perhaps someone who is depressed, aggressively competitive, easily frustrated, anxious, angry or some combination (H. S. Friedman and Booth-Kewley, 1987, pp. 789–791; see also Espnes 1996; Espnes and Opdahl, 1999).

The role of negative emotions in relation to CHD has been tested in a number of studies, but the results are contradictory (e.g. Espnes and Opdahl, 1999; Todaro, Shen, Niaura, Spiro, and Ward, 2003), and it is impossible presently to draw clear conclusions. One of the reasons may well be the lack of a "solid" operational definition of which feelings or other psychological constructs should be included in "negative emotions."

In 1988 Karen Matthews wrote a commentary on the Friedman and Booth-Kewley studies, noting that meta-analyses may be flawed by the subjectivity of rating, and by the inclusion of both prospective and retrospective studies in the same analysis. She further reminds the reader that two independent epidemiological studies (Cohen and Reed, 1985; Johnston, Cook, and Shaper, 1987) have found significant relationships between TABP and CHD in prospective studies, but not in cross-sectional ones. Friedman and Booth-Kewley addressed Matthews's (1988) comments, underlining in their response that "the construct of coronary prone behavior and its incarnation as the Type A behavior pattern have been defined in so many ways and assessed so unsystematically that some authors throw up their hands and conclude that the whole matter is not worthy of attention" (H. S. Friedman and Booth-Kewley, 1988, p. 381).

What Friedman and Booth-Kewley were stressing here is obviously an important point. There is simply no other way to compare the predictive strength of the TABP for CHD for the present population than to follow the line of research that used the SI (see earlier section on the measures to assess the TABP) to obtain data.

Krantz, Contrada, Hill, and Friedler's (1988) review also (inter alia) examined the (then) current status of the TABP, overviewing the landmark prospective studies – the WCGS, the Framingham study, the Belgian-French Collaborative Heart Study (see, e.g., Kornitzer, Kittel, De Backer, and Dramaix, 1981), and the Recurrent Coronary Prevention Project (M. Friedman et al., 1982) which marked the TABP as *the* "coronary-prone behavior." Results from last of these showed that the TABP could be altered by behavior intervention treatment, to prevent recurrent CHD. Krantz et al. (1988) also offered four possible explanations for the paucity of existing positive findings relating the TAPB and CHD. First, they suggested that global TABP is not a simple risk factor for CHD. And secondly, they noted that the positive findings in the Recurrent Coronary Prevention Project might have been caused by the nonspecific stress reducing effects of the intervention, or effects of social support. They pointed to the fact (citing Blumenthal and Emery, 1988) that there had been a number of studies supporting the view that more global stress-reducing interventions promote better clinical outcomes. Thirdly, they underlined that most of the studies of the era were designed as treatment trials to evaluate the efficacy of either drugs or behavior modification techniques to reduce CHD risk, and participation in such projects may alter aspects of TABP or modify its pathogenic qualities. And finally, they noted that TABP may be so common among CHD patients that it could therefore be an insensitive predictor of subsequent clinical outcomes (Krantz et al., 1988).

Further systematic database searches to the end of the 1980s reveal a number of articles on Type A and CHD, but these appear not to have introduced new data but to be papers simply reviewing previous work with the TABP, and often employing instruments not validated against the benchmarks of the SI or JAS (Leon, Finn, Murray, and Bailey 1988). These papers rarely dealt with the major criticisms of the predictive validity of the TABP for CHD development, but appear, in fact, to follow two parallel lines of thought: those publishing on Type A behavior pattern as if it had not conceptually moved from its origins in the 1960s, and those heavily attacking Type A for lack of predictive value.

The TABP toward the New Millennium

Clearly, some researchers had still strong belief in the TABP at the beginning of the 1990s (e.g. Craig and Weiss, 1990; Zapotoczky and Wenzel, 1990; Strube, 1991; Monat and Lazarus, 1991; Snyder and Forsyth, 1991; Spielberger, Sarason, Kulcsar, and Van Heck, 1991; Cooper and Payne, 1991; Byrne, 1992; Goldberger and Breznitz, 1993; Siegman and Smith, 1994; Carey and McDevitt, 1994; M. Friedman, Fleischmann, and Price, 1996; Low, 1991; Gross, 1994; and Hirschfield, 1995). But this did not mirror the enthusiasm of the previous three decades.

Examination of work from 1990 to the change of the millennium can fittingly start with a paper by one of the fathers of the concept, Ray Rosenman (1990). In a comprehensive and scholarly review, Rosenman highlights inconsistent conceptualizations and measures of the TABP as strong candidates to explain equivocal results. He notes the undue emphasis on studies of cardiovascular reactivity but with few studies with hard CHD outcome data. He also directs attention to the emerging evidence on hostility and competitiveness – both prominent components of the TABP – as clear predictors of CHD. And he makes it clear that the inclusion of papers based on methodological flaws is at the root of many negative reviews of the TABP and its capacity to predict CHD. Importantly, Rosenman foreshadows that while the focus of the TABP remains on behaviors, there is now a place for the emotions as well. In essence, Rosenman signals a transition from a monolithic notion of the TABP to one which recognizes its uniquely cardiotoxic subcomponents (see, e.g., Williams et al., 1980).

In 1991 a new meta-analysis was published to reexamine both Booth-Kewley and Friedman's (1987) and Matthews's (1988) conclusions (Miller, Turner, Tindale, Posavac, and Dugoni, 1991) on the trend toward null findings in research attempting to link the TABP and CHD. These authors also point to the fact that even over this period, there had been studies where earlier findings of positive prediction had been replicated. Based on earlier publications (Matthews, 1988; Pearson, 1984; Pickering, 1985), Miller et al. (1991) offered a possible – and interesting – explanation for the null findings, which they name disease-based spectrum bias (DBS). This is present in studies where subjects are directed into or excluded from a sample according to their disease status (see Miller, Turner, Tindale, and Posavac, 1988).

Evidence suggests that the *global* measure of TABP might also not be the most profitable strategy to use in the prediction of CHD incidence (Edwards and Baglioni, 1991; Räikkönen, 1992). Räikkönen (1992) goes on to state that the many differing operational definitions of Type A have resulted both in conceptual confusion, and in confusion with regard to the nature of the Type A risk, emphasizing that TABP should now be treated as a multidimensional construct, with some aspects playing a more important role than others in linking the TABP with CHD. Edwards and Baglioni (1991) compared the global and component measures of TABP, and concluded that component TABP analyses showed predictive advantages over global TABP measures. They suggest that effort should be made to construct good component measurements, and note that in their study, the behavioral entities that showed clearest relationship with the CHD were those reflecting speed and time pressure.

A new meta-analysis of data linking the TABP to cardiovascular reactivity was published by Lyness in 1993. Based on information from a total of 99 studies, Lyness concludes that Type A persons showed greater stress reactivity that did the Type Bs, even if the effect is small. She also argues that the difference in reactivity between the As and the Bs may actually be larger than found in this meta-analysis, making reference to the fact that recent studies (Chesney, Hecker, and Black, 1988; Ganster, Schaubroeck, Sime, and Mayes, 1991; Williams and Barefoot, 1988) have gone into finer detail concerning pathogenic components of the Type A behavior patterns, such as hostility, anger suppression, or speech characteristics, and their relationship to cardiovascular reactivity (Lyness, 1993). Myrtek's (1995) meta-analysis of more recent studies on the TABP and cardiovascular reactivity essentially mirrors these conclusions.

While most studies of the early 1990s reported negative results (e.g., Edwards and Baglioni, 1991; Greenglass and Julkunen, 1991; Räikkönen, 1992) their focus was largely on the TABP as a global construct. As the decade progressed, however, greater attention appeared to emerge on studies of component TABP, for example anger and aggression, hostility, irritability, suspicion, frustration and guilt (see e.g. Kopper, 1993; Weekes and Waterhouse, 1991;

Eriksen, 1994; Hill, Kelleher and Shumaker, 1991). While definitions and conceptualizations of component TABP here too were often not precise, a finer level of definition was becoming apparent.

Publications at that time quite often jointly addressed both psychosocial risk factors for CHD development, and the personality characteristics in persons who had suffered CHD, and did not take sufficient care that risk factors for a first clinical event of CHD and a recurrent attack might well be partly, if not totally, different things (e.g., Espnes 1996).

Based on the history of the TABP to date, and the contrary and inconclusive findings, Byrne (1996) looked at a reconceptualization of the TABP as coronary-prone behavior. His attempt to resolve the issue was to fit the new information into a model of how the TABP could explain both benign and pathological outcomes with CHD. Byrne argued that it was crucial to reveal the uniquely toxic components of TABP (see, e.g., Williams et al., 1980; Shekelle, Gale, Ostfeld, and Paul, 1983; Barefoot, Dahlstrom, and Williams, 1983; Byrne and Rosenman, 1990), and in this light, he suggested a model of the psychopathological paths which the TAPB follows to "produce" CHD risk (Byrne, 1996, p. 234). In his view, competitiveness as a "global motivational predisposition to behavior" ranked high among the several characteristics of the TABP (goal oriented, achievement oriented, control oriented, time urgent, job involved and acquisitive) as a potential precursor of CHD. He argued that it is the way in which the Type A individual solves ongoing behavioral demands, and whether that pattern of behavior leads to expression or frustration of Type A attributes, that decides whether the likelihood of CHD risk is elevated or not. If the psychosocial situation allows expression of the TABP, what follows will be emotional equilibrium and satisfaction, and the CHD risk will not rise above the age-standard risk. However, if the psychosocial context causes frustration of Type A behaviors in individuals characterized by the TABP, what follows will be emotional distress and dissatisfaction, and a potentially elevated level of coronary risk.

Byrne's (1996) argument was meant as a way of reconceptualizing future research on the TABP and CHD. Unfortunately, this reconceptualization the did not lead to major new studies, perhaps due to a now rapidly declining interest in the whole notion of Type A behavior and CHD. In publications after 1996 the TABP as measured with the original SI was reported in only one study (Markovitz, Matthews, Kiss, and Smitherman, 1996), and even here, the SI was used merely as a psychologically stressful task (together with one other cognitive task) to elicit the physiological effects of a mental stressor. This study did, however, reveal encouragingly positive results in regard to the TABP and CHD.

But the idea of a need to reconceptualize the TABP was more recently taken up. As part of the large longitudinal Normative Aging Study in Boston (Kawachi et al., 1998), the authors conclude of the TABP that rather than abandon the TABP concept in the face of negative findings, we need to search for the sources of disagreement between studies and find whether the problem lies in the concept itself or in the methods used to measure it; and further, Kawachi et al. (1998) concur with Matthews (1988) that occurrence of some failures to replicate does not justify abandoning the concept

Just a small cohort of papers at the close of the twentieth century related the TABP to left ventricular hypertrophy in male patients with essential hypertension (Munakata et al., 1999), and some subcomponents of the TABP to measures of total cholesterol and low density lipoprotein (Richards, Hof, and Alvarenga, 2000) – though the direction of the findings did not recommend simple interpretations, and the measure of the TABP was not a standard one (Forgays, Forgays, Bonaiuto, and Wresniewski, 1993).

Research on the TABP in the Twenty-First Century

In 2000, Elianne Riska published a paper in which she claims that the fall of Type A man started when researchers moved to viewing the Type A concept more as a personality type than a straightforward description of overt patterns of behaviors. This was, of course, a position strongly espoused by Rosenman (1990). The conceptual importance of Riska's assertion lies with the questions it poses on the evolution and decline of a once strong and widely accepted construct. Had the TABP construct become out of date, had scientific research shown it to be seriously flawed, either conceptually or in definition, or had those contributing to the scientific evidence underlying the acquisition of CHD risk research simply forgotten about it?

Riska's (2000) paper comprehensively sums up the TABP research domain, and seeks to delineate what happened to a concept, leading then to a description of a pattern of behavior, the possession of which endowed a conspicuous risk to health. One clear conclusion emerged from her conceptual analysis; the problem appeared to arise when the TABP evolved from a simple behavioral typology into a more complex psychological or personality "type." While originally only the surface of the Type A man was mapped by means of behavioral typing, now the exploration of the interior of the Type A man had begun. Where physicians saw behaviors, psychologists looked for inner reasons – and sought to redesign the TABP in line with their conceptual predispositions. In a review of Riska's article (2000), Goldstein (2006), concluded that Riska had shown that TABP and related concepts "medicalized" manás suffering in ways that denied the important role of social position.

Riska's paper is interesting for many reasons; it presents an alternative way to evaluate the evolution of the Type A construct, but it is also consistent with the critical comments often leveled at the two originators of the TABP, Rosenman and Friedman. Friedman and Rosenman were themselves quite often critical of the approach that psychologists took to the whole concept, and Rosenman more than once expressed the view that "I know nothing about personality and personality traits, I only know that this behavior pattern as we have described shows with great certainty who is going to suffer a cardiac attack" (Rosenman, 1997). Friedman similarly criticized psychologists and the way they treated the TABP (M. Friedman and Ulmer 1984). Another veteran of the Type A conceptual debate, Virginia Price, was also critical but from a different perspective. She wrote: "In fact, the failure to develop a conceptual model of Type A grounded in contemporary psychology seems to be responsible for the rather slow accumulation of generalizable and replicable findings in Type A research" (Price, 1982).

Some of this understanding is also voiced by Myrtek (2001), where the descriptor "TAPB" is replaced in the title, by Type A personality. It is quite clear, then, from a conceptual perspective that it is the Type A "personality" he wants to explore, and not the TABP, employing only the keywords "Type A personality" and "coronary heart disease" in his literature search (to reveal 559 published studies used in a subsequent meta-analysis of Type A personality, hostility, and CHD). By doing so he falls into the same trap as others; he mixes different concepts in the analyses without realizing that semantic or superficial relationships between the concepts used (the TABP, Type A personality, and simply Type A), with their varying meanings and definitions, do not allow research outcomes to be directly comparable to one another.

The Fukuoka Heart Study Group (Yoshimasu et al., 2002) reports a retrospective study of Type A behavior patterns and job-related psychological factors as risks for myocardial infarction in a small clinical sample. Here yet another scale, the Tokai Activity Survey (Maeda, 1991) was used, rendering direct comparison with studies impossible.

In an attempt to establish a national consensus of psychosocial risk factors for CHD, the *Medical Journal of Australia* a decade ago published a national position statement on "stress" and coronary heart disease (Bunker et al., 2003). In this statement it is conceded that the TABP, while promising in early studies, has not continued that promise in more recent times.

Gallacher, Sweetnam, Yarnell, Elwood, and Stansfeld (2003) reported on a large investigation into whether the TABP acts as a trigger for clinical events of CHD. In this study the TABP was assessed by three different self-report instruments; the Jenkins Activity Survey, the Bortner scale, and the Framingham scale. Interestingly, the most important finding from the study was that while there was no difference in Type A scores between those who suffered a clinical event and those who did not, the TABP was strongly associated with the timing of the event.

Williams, Barefoot, and Schneiderman (2003) discussed the relationship between behaviors believed to be related to the development of CHD and behaviors making up the TABP complex. They concluded that both hostility and time urgency, both well-known behavioral characteristics of the TABP, had been closely related to CHD development in published studies. And while Oshi (2003) supported the continuing relevance of the TABP based on a review of the reported effects on CHD of modifying the behavior pattern, Amelang and Schmidt-Rathjens (2003), in another review of contemporary evidence, concluded that research on TABP and similar variables in relation to CHD risk has decreased over time, while biomedical variables and their links to CHD remain widely researched.

An evidence-based paper from the Framingham Offspring Study (Eaker, Sullivan, Kelley-Hayes, D'Agostino, and Benjamin, 2004) concluded that anger and hostility appear to be more relevant to the study of CHD mortality and risk of arrhythmias than is TABP as a global construct. In this light, Matthews (2005) underscored the timeliness of constructing a new and comprehensive model for understanding the psychosocial contributors to CHD risk that broadly integrates socioeconomic status, environmental stress, and person-level factors from a life-span perspective.

From around 2006 onward there have been few studies specifically focusing on the TABP and its relation to CHD. Rebollo and Boomsma (2006) scrutinized the hereditary impact on TABP as a risk factor for CHD development, concluding that research has now changed from looking at global TABP and CHD risk, to risk related more to emotional components like anger. However, a single empirical study reported that year showed that the TABP was a risk factor for arteriosclerosis (as indicated by brachial-ankle pulse) and also may increase the risk of later cardiovascular disease related to arteriosclerosis (H. Liu et al., 2006).

Of more anecdotal value are two interesting (but peripheral) studies on TABP having outcome focuses other than CHD. One examined the TABP in relation to risk of road traffic accidents (Nabi et al., 2005), concluding that those with the TABP had an increased risk of being involved in road traffic accidents. The other related scores on the Jenkins Activity Survey (JAS-C) as a measure of the TABP to mood, finding that the construct distinguished depressed unipolar people from depressed bipolar II patients (Wang et al., 2011).

During 2007 two further and important studies were published on TABP in relation to CHD. The Cardiovascular Risk in Young Finns Study (Keltikangas-Järvinen et al., 2007) examined the relation of TABP to adult carotid artery intima-media thickness (IMT) and concluded that there was a significant effect of the eagerness-energy component in TABP on IMT, and that this component is a robust predictor of the biomedical risk marker. The other focused on whether diet was a potent way of mediating the association between TABP and CHD. However, the researchers were led to conclude that the association between Type A behavior and CHD is unlikely to be mediated by diet (Appleton et al., 2007). Two book chapters on TABP were also published in 2007, but both were historical overviews of the Type A behavior research and contributed little that was new to the debate.

One single journal article was found for 2008 (Ikeda, Hiroyasu, Kawashi, Inoue, and Tsugane, 2008), reporting on a prospective study of TABP in a very large population (N = 86,361) and with a CHD incidence of 669 cases at follow-up. TABP was measured with use of a self-made questionnaire based on the Framingham Type A scale and the MMPI-2 Type A scale. The findings were clear-cut, that TABP does not predict CHD onset in a Japanese population; however, the authors suggests that the cardiotoxic effect from TABP is both gender specific and culturally contingent.

In 2009 and 2010, no articles with significant information for the TABP/CHD debate were found. For the following two years, only one article on TABP and its relation to CHD (T. Liu, Deng, Zhang, and Jing, 2012) was published, but also a further article on the TABP and its relationship to Type D personality (the tendency to accumulate repressed (or denied) negative emotion) (Zhao, Bai, Li, and Xu, 2011), which also has attracted attention as a CHD-prone characteristic in the research in the area. These, together with a book chapter by Robert Allan in *Heart and Mind: The Practice of Cardiac Psychology* in 2012, are the last publications on TABP elicited by the present review.

Conclusions

It is quite clear from the evidence presented above that many studies of Type A behavior published in the last 20 years have suffered from (1) poor and imprecise operationalization of the theoretical concepts; (2) the use of a number of different but poorly validated scales and instruments to assess TAPB, or related concepts too often confused with the TABP; (3) a focus on groups and samples – namely those with existing CHD, or those at high risk of a recurrent attack – in which the links between the TAPB and CHD have not been reported for almost 40 years; (4) poor, inaccurate, or vague definitions of the TAPB or its related constructs (e.g., Type A personality), so mitigating against the possibility of comparing studies across the field, or of reexamining them; and (5) a focus of recent research on Eastern cultures with little in common with the cultural characteristics implicit to the original construct, and that research, incidentally, suffering from many of the methodological and conceptual problems outlined above. On these grounds, while there is clearly a need to critically consider both the concept of the TABP and the evidence linking it with CHD, caution is needed lest we abandon the construct too quickly and throw out the baby with the bathwater.

Large cohort prospective studies of the TABP and CHD have not been entirely abandoned. And on balance, the emerging evidence indicates to us that completely discarding the TABP would at this point be premature. A better integration of demographic and cultural factors into predictive equations, and the commitment to undertake the "definitive" epidemiological study with sufficient statistical power, where the TABP is the major focus of interest (a new WCGS, perhaps), would effectively address the controversy once and for all. And so a final "burial" of the construct is not yet indicated – the promise is still there.

References

Allan, R. (2012). Type A behavior pattern. In R. Allan and J. Fisher (Eds.), *Heart and Mind: The Practice of Cardiac Psychology*, 2nd edn. (pp. 287–290). Washington DC: American Psychological Association.

Amelang, M., and Schmidt-Rathjens, C. (2003). Persönlichkeit, krebs und koronare herzerkrankungen: Fiktionen und fakten in der ätiologieforschung [Personality cancer and coronary heart disease: Fictions and facts in the etiological research]. *Psychologische Rundschau, 54,* 12–23.

Appleton, K. M., Woodside, J. V., Yarnell, J. W. G., Arveiler, D., Haas, B., Amouyel, P., ... Evans, A. (2007). Depressed mood and dietary fish intake: Direct relationship or indirect relationship as a result of diet and lifestyle? *Journal of Affective Disorders, 104*(1–3), 217–223.

Barefoot, J. C., Dahlstrom, W. G., and Williams, R. B. (1983). Hostility, CHD incidence and total mortality. *Psychosomatic Medicine, 45,* 59–64.

Blumenthal, J. A., and Emery, C. F. (1988). Rehabilitation of patients following myocardial infarction. *Journal of Consulting and Clinical Psychology, 56,* 374–381.

Booth-Kewley, S., and Friedman, H. S. (1987). Psychological predictors of heart disease: A quantitative review. *Psychological Bulletin, 101,* 343–62.

Bunker, S. J., Colquhoun, D. M., Esler, M. D., Hickie, I. B., Hunt, D., Jelinek, V. M., ... Tonkin, A. M. (2003). "Stress" and coronary heart disease: Psychosocial risk factors. *Medical Journal of Australia, 178,* 272–276.

Byrne, D. G. (1992). The Type A behavior pattern and coronary heart disease. In D. G. Byrne and G. R. Caddy (Eds.), *Behavioral Medicine: International Perspectives,* vol. 1 (pp. 63–92). Norwood, NJ: Ablex.

Byrne, D. G. (1996). Type A behavior, anxiety, and neuroticism: Reconceptualizing the pathophysiological paths and boundaries of coronary-prone behavior. *Stress Medicine, 12,* 227–238.

Byrne, D. G., and Rosenman, R. H. (1990). *Anxiety and the Heart.* New York: Hemisphere.

Byrne, D. G., Rosenman, R. H., Schiller, E., and Chesney, M. (1985). Consistency and variation among instruments purporting to measure the Type A behaviour pattern. *Psychosomatic Medicine, 47,* 242–261.

Carey, W. B., and McDevitt, S. C. (1994). Prevention and early intervention: Individual differences as risk factors for the mental health of children. In W. B. Carey and S. C. McDevitt (Eds.), *Prevention and Early Intervention: Individual Differences as Risk Factors for the Mental Health of Children: A Festschrift for Stella Chess and Alexander Thomas.* New York: Brunner Mazel.

Chesney, M. A., Eagleston, J. R., and Rosenman, R. H. (1980). The Type A structured interview: A behavioural assessment in the rough. *Journal of Behaviour Assessment, 2,* 255–272.

Chesney, M. A., Hecker, M. H. L., and Black, G. W. (1988). Coronary-prone components of Type A behavior in the WCGS: A new methodology. In B. K. Houston and C. R. Snyder (Eds.), *Type A Behavior Pattern: Research, Theory, and Intervention* (pp. 168–188). New York: Wiley.

Cohen, J. B., and Reed, D. (1985). The Type A behavior pattern and coronary heart disease among Japanese men in Hawaii. *Journal of Behavioral Medicine, 8,* 343–352.

Cooper, C. L., and Payne, R. (1991). *Personality and Stress: Individual Differences in the Stress Process.* New York: Wiley.

Craig, K. D., and Weiss, S. M. (1990). *Health Enhancement, Disease Prevention, and Early Intervention: Biobehavioral Perspectives.* Conference proceedings based on the 18th Banff International Conference on Behavioral Sciences, Banff, Alberta, Canada, 1986.

Eaker E. D., Sullivan, L. M., Kelley-Hayes, M., D'Agostino, R. B., and Benjamin, E. J. (2004). Does job strain increase the risk for coronary heart disease or death in men and women? The Framingham Offspring Study. *American Journal of Epidemiology, 159*(10), 950–958.

Edwards, J. R., and Baglioni, A. J. (1991). Relationship between Type A behavior pattern and mental and physical symptoms: A comparison of global and component measures: Correction. *Journal of Applied Psychology, 76,* 643.

Eriksen, W. (1994). The role of social support in the pathogenesis of coronary heart disease: A literature review. *Family Practice, 11,* 201–209.

Espnes, G. A. (1996). The Type 2 construct and personality traits: Aggression, hostility, anxiety and depression. *Personality and Individual Differences, 20,* 641–48.

Espnes, G. A., and Opdahl, A. (1999). Associations among behavior, personality, and traditional risk factors for coronary heart disease: A study at a primary health care center in mid-Norway. *Psychological Reports, 85,* 505–517.

Forgays, D. K., Forgays, D. G., Bonaiuto, P., and Wrezsniewski, K. (1993). Measurement of the Type A behaviour pattern from adolescence through midlife: Further development of the Adolescent/Adult Type A Behavior Scale (AATABS). *Journal of Behavioral Medicine, 16,* 64–77.

Friedman, H. S., and Booth-Kewley, S. (1987). Personality, Type A behavior, and coronary heart disease: The role of emotional expression. *Journal of Personality and Social Psychology, 53,* 783–792.

Friedman, H. S., and Booth-Kewley, S. (1988). Validity of the Type A construct: A reprise. *Psychological Bulletin*, *104*, 381–384.

Friedman, M., Fleischmann, N., and Price, V. (1996). Diagnosis of Type A behavior pattern. In R. Allan and S. Scheit (Eds.), *Heart and Mind: The Practice of Cardiac Psychology* (p. 179–196). Washington, DC: American Psychological Association.

Friedman, M., and Rosenman, R. H. (1974). *Type A Behavior and Your Heart*. New York: Knopf.

Friedman, M., Thoresen, C. E., Gill, J. J., Ulmer U., Thompson L., Powell, L., … Tasto, D. L. (1982). Feasibility of altering Type A behavior pattern after myocardial infarction: Recurrent Coronary Prevention Project Study: Methods, baseline results and preliminary findings. *Circulation*, *66*, 83–92.

Friedman, M., and Ulmer, D. (1984). *Treating Type A Behavior and Your Heart*. New York: Knopf.

Gallacher, J. E. J., Sweetnam, P. M., Yarnell, J. W. G., Elwood, P. C., and Stansfeld, S. A. (2003). Is Type A behavior really a trigger for coronary heart disease events? *Psychosomatic Medicine*, *65*, 339–346.

Ganster, D. C., Schaubroeck, J., Sime, W. E., and Mayes, B. T. (1991). The nomological validity of the Type A personality among employed adults. *Journal of Applied Psychology*, *76*, 143–168.

Gildea, E. (1949). Special features of personality, which are common to certain psychosomatic disorders. *Psychosomatic Medicine*, *11*, 273–77.

Goldberger, L., and Breznitz, S. (1993). *Handbook of Stress: Theoretical and Clinical Aspects*, 2nd edn. New York: Free Press.

Goldstein, M. S. (2006). Masculinity and men's health: Coronary heart disease in medical and public discourse. *International Journal of Men's Health*, *5*(1), 107–108.

Greenglass, E. R., and Julkunen, J. (1991). Cook-Medley hostility, anger, and the Type A behavior pattern in Finland. *Psychological Reports*, *68*, 1059–1066.

Gross, R. E., Jr. (1994). The relation of psychological type, hostility level, and Type A behavior pattern to coronary heart disease. *Dissertation Abstracts International: Section B: The Sciences and Engineering*, *55*(4-B).

Haynes, S. G., Feinleib, M., and Kannel W. B. (1980). The relationship of psychosocial factors to coronary heart disease in the Framingham study, III. Eight-year incidence of coronary heart disease. *American Journal of Epidemiology*, *3*, 37–58.

Hill, D. R., Kelleher, K., and Shumaker, S. A. (1991). Psychosocial interventions in adult patients with coronary heart disease and cancer: A literature review. *General Hospital Psychiatry*, *14*, 28–42.

Hirschfield, R. J. (1995). Type A behavior, self-efficacy, and performance in small business firms. *Dissertation Abstracts International*, *55*(9-A).

Ikeda, A., Hiroyasu, I., Kawashi, I., Inoue, M., and Tsugane, S. (2008). Type A behaviour and risk of coronary heart disease: The JPHC Study. *International Journal of Epidemiology*, *37*, 1395–1405.

Jenkins, C. D., Zyzanski, S. J., and Rosenman, R. H. (1971). Progress toward validation of a computer scored test for the Type A coronary prone behavior pattern. *Psychosomatic Medicine*, *33*, 193–202.

Johnston, D. W., Cook, D. G., and Shaper, A. G. (1987). Type A behaviour and ischemic heart disease in middle aged British men. *British Medical Journal*, *295*, 86–89.

Kawachi, I., Sparrow, D., Kubzansky, L. D., Spiro, A., Vokonas, P. S., and Weiss, S. T. (1998). Prospective study of a self-report Type A scale and risk of coronary heart disease: Test of the MMPI-2 Type A scale. *Circulation*, *98*, 405–412.

Keltikangas-Järvinen, L., Hintsa, T., Kivimäki, M., Puttonen, S., Juonala, M., Viikari, J. S. A., and Raitakari, O. T. (2007). Type A eagerness-energy across developmental periods predicts adulthood carotid intima-media thickness: The Cardiovascular Risk in Young Finns Study. *Arteriosclerosis, Thrombosis, and Vascular Biology*, *27*, 1638–1644.

Kemple, C. (1945). Rorschach method and psychosomatic diagnosis: Personality traits of patients with rheumatic disease, hypertension, cardiovascular disease, coronary occlusion and fracture. *Psychosomatic Medicine*, *7*, 85–89.

Kopper, B. A. (1993). Role of gender, sex role identity, and Type A behavior in anger expression and mental health functioning. *Journal of Counseling Psychology*, *40*, 232–237.

Kornitzer, M., Kittel, F., De Backer, G., and Dramaix M. (1981). The Belgian Heart Disease Prevention Project: Type "A" behavior pattern and the prevalence of coronary heart disease. *Psychosomatic Medicine*, *43*, 133–145.

Krantz, D. S., Contrada, R. J., Hill. D. R., and Friedler, E. (1988). Environmental stress and biobehavioral antecedents of coronary heart disease. *Journal of Consulting and Clinical Psychology*, *56*, 333–341.

Lazarus, R. S., and Folkman, S. (1984). *Stress, Appraisal, and Coping*. New York: Springer.

Leon, G. R., Finn, S. E., Murray, D., and Bailey, J. M. (1988). Inability to predict cardiovascular disease from hostility scores or MMPI items related to Type A behavior. *Journal of Consulting and Clinical Psychology*, *56*, 597–600.

Liu, H., Saijo, Y., Zhang, X., Shiraishi, Y., Luo, Y., Maruyama, M., ... Yambe, T. (2006). Impact of Type A behavior on brachial-ankle pulse wave velocity in Japanese. *Tohoku Journal of Experimental Medicine, 209,* 15–21.

Liu, T., Deng, G.-h., Zhang, L.-y., and Jing, M. (2012). Effect of the Type A behaviour pattern on the heart autonomic nerve activity in healthy males. *Chinese Journal of Clinical Psychology, 20,* 301–304.

Low, K. G. (1991). Psychosocial variables, Type A behavior pattern, and coronary heart disease in women. *Dissertation Abstracts International, 52*(1-A), 85.

Lyness, S. A. (1993). Predictors of differences between Type A and B individuals in heart rate and blood pressure reactivity. *Psychological Bulletin, 114,* 266–295.

Maeda, S. (1991). Application of a brief questionnaire for the behaviour pattern survey. *Taipu A, 2,* 33–40.

Markovitz, J. H., Matthews, K. A., Kiss, J., and Smitherman, T. (1996). Effects of hostility on platelet reactivity to psychological stress in coronary heart disease patients and in healthy controls. *Psychosomatic Medicine, 58,* 143–149.

Matthews, K. A. (1988). Coronary heart disease and Type A behaviors: Update on and alternative to the Booth-Kewley and Friedman (1987) quantitative review. *Psychological Bulletin, 104,* 373–380.

Matthews, K. A. (2005). Psychological perspectives on the development of coronary heart disease. *American Psychologist, 60,* 783–796.

Menninger, K. A., and Menninger, W. C. (1936). Psychoanalytic observations in cardiac disorders. *American Heart Journal, 11,* 10–26.

Miller, T. Q., Turner, C. W., Tindale, R. S., and Posavac, E. J. (1988). Disease-based spectrum bias in referred samples and the relationship between Type A behavior and atherosclerosis. *Journal of Clinical Epidemiology, 41,* 1139–1149.

Miller, T. Q., Turner, C. W., Tindale, R. S., Posavac, E. J., and Dugoni, B. L. (1991). Reasons for the trend toward null findings in research on Type A behavior. *Psychological Bulletin, 110,* 469–485.

Monat, A., and Lazarus, R. S. (1991). *Stress and Coping: An Anthology.* New York: Columbia University Press.

Monroe, S. M. (2008). Modern approaches to conceptualizing and measuring human life stress. *Annual Review of Clinical Psychology, 4,* 33–52.

Munakata, M., Hiraizumi, T., Nunokawa, T., Ito, N., Taguchi, F., Yamauchi, Y., and Yoshinaga, K. (1999). Type A behavior is associated with an increased risk of left ventricular hypertrophy in male patients with essential hypertension. *Journal of Hypertension, 17,* 115–120.

Myrtek, M. (1995). Type A behavior pattern, personality factors, disease, and physiological reactivity: A meta-analytic update. *Personality and Individual Differences, 18,* 491–502.

Myrtek, M. (2001). Meta-analyses of prospective studies on coronary heart disease, Type A personality, and hostility. *International Journal of Cardiology, 79,* 245–251.

Nabi, H., Consoli, S. M., Chastang, J.-F., Chiron, M., Lafont, S., and Lagarde, E. (2005). Type A behavior pattern, risky driving behaviors, and serious road traffic accidents: A prospective study of the GAZEL cohort. *American Journal Epidemiology, 161,* 864–870.

Oshi, O. (2003). A review of the psychological interventions for the modification of Type A behavior pattern. *Japanese Journal of Counseling Science, 36,* 175–186.

Osler, W. (1897). *Lectures on Angina Pectoris and Allied States.* New York: D. Appleton.

Pearson, T. A. (1984). Coronary arteriography in the study of the epidemiology of coronary heart disease. *Epidemiological Reviews, 6,* 140–166.

Pickering, T. G. (1985). Should studies of patients undergoing angiography be used to evaluate the role of behavioral risk factors for coronary heart disease. *Journal of Behavioral Medicine, 8,* 203–213.

Price, V. A. (1982) *Type A Behavior Pattern: A Model for Research and Practice.* New York: Academic Press.

Raïkkönen, K. (1992). Modern views on the concept of Type A behavior. *Psychiatria Fennica, 23,* 89–94.

Rebollo, I., and Boomsma, D. I. (2006). Genetic analysis of anger: Genetic dominance or competitive sibling interaction. *Behavior Genetics, 36,* 216–228.

Review Panel on Coronary-Prone Behavior and Coronary Heart Disease (1981). Coronary-prone behavior and coronary heart disease: A critical review. *Circulation, 63,* 1199–1215.

Richards, J. C., Hof, A., and Alvarenga, M. (2000). Serum lipids and their relationships with hostility and angry affect and behaviors in men. *Health Psychology, 19,* 393–398.

Riska, E. (2000). The rise and fall of Type A man. *Social Science and Medicine, 51,* 1665–1674.

Rosenman, R. H. (1990). Type A behavior pattern: A personal overview. *Journal of Social Behavior and Personality, 5,* 1–24.

Rosenman, R. H. (1997). Lecture given at 14th World Congress of Psychosomatic Medicine Aug. 31–Sept. 5.

Rosenman, R. H., Brand, R. J., Jenkins, C. D., Friedman, M., Straus, R., and Wurm, M. (1975). Coronary heart disease in the Western Collaborative Group Study: Final follow-up experience of $8\frac{1}{2}$ years. *JAMA, 233,* 420–425.

Rosenman, R. H., Brand, R. J., Sholtz, R. I., and Friedman, M. (1976). Multivariate prediction of coronary heart disease during the 8.5 year follow-up in the Western Collaborative Group Study. *American Journal of Cardiology, 37,* 903–910.

Rosenman, R. H., Friedman, M., Straus, R., Wurm, M,. Kositchek, R., Hahn, W., and Werthessen, N. (1964). A predictive study of coronary heart disease: The Western Collaborative Group Study. *JAMA, 189,* 15–26.

Rosenman, R. H., Friedman, M., Straus, R., Wurm, M., Jenkins, C. D., Harley B., and Messinger, H. B. (1966). Coronary heart disease in the Western Collaborative Group Study: A follow-up experience of two years. *JAMA, 195*(2), 86–92.

Shekelle, R. B., Gale, M., Ostfeld, A. M., and Paul, O. (1983). Hostility, risk of coronary heart disease, and mortality. *Psychosomatic Medicine, 45,* 109–114.

Siegman, A. W., and Smith, T. W. (1994). *Anger, Hostility, and the Heart.* Mahwah, NJ: Lawrence Erlbaum Associates.

Snyder, C. R., and Forsyth, D. R. (1991). *Handbook of Social and Clinical Psychology: The Health Perspective.* Oxford: Pergamon.

Spielberger, C. D., Sarason, I. G., Kulcsar, Z., and Van Heck, G. L. (Eds.) (1991). *Stress and Emotion: Anxiety, Anger, and Curiosity,* vol. 14. New York: Hemisphere.

Strube, M. J. (1991). *Type A Behavior.* Thousand Oaks, CA: Sage.

Suls, J., and Marco, C. A. (1990). Relationship between the JAS and FTAS-TABP and non-CHD illness: A prospective study controlling for negative affectivity. *Health Psychology, 9,* 479–492.

Todaro, J. F., Shen, B.-J., Niaura, R., Spiro, A., III, and Ward, K. D. (2003). Effect of negative emotions on frequency of coronary heart disease (the Normative Aging Study). *American Journal of Cardiology, 92,* 901–906.

Wang, Y., Terao, T., Hoaki, N., Goto, S., Tsuchiyama, K., Iwata, N., ... Nakamura, J. (2011). Type A behavior pattern and hyperthymic temperament: Possible association with bipolar IV disorder. *Journal of Affective Disorders, 133,* 22–28.

Weekes, B. S., and Waterhouse, I. K. (1991). Hostile attitudes and the coronary prone personality. *Australian Psychologist, 26,* 33–36.

Williams, R. B., Jr., and Barefoot, J. C. (1988). Coronary-prone behavior: The emerging role of the hostility complex. In B. K. Houston and C. R. Snyder (Eds.), *Type A Behavior Pattern: Research, Theory, and Intervention* (pp. 189–211). New York: Wiley.

Williams, R. B., Jr., Barefoot, J. C., and Schneiderman, N. (2003). Psychosocial risk factors for cardiovascular disease: More than one culprit at work. *JAMA, 290,* 2190–2192.

Williams, R. B., Jr., Janey, T. L., Kee, K. L., Kong, Y., Blumenthal, J. A., and Whalen, R. E. (1980). Type A behavior, hostility, and coronary atherosclerosis. *Psychosomatic Medicine, 42,* 539–49.

Yoshimasu, K., Washio, M., Tokunaga, S., Tanaka, K., Liu, Y., Kodama, H., ... Takeshita, A. (2002). Relation between Type A behavior pattern and the extent of coronary atherosclerosis in Japanese women. *International Journal of Behavioral Medicine, 9,* 77–93.

Zapotoczky, H.-G., and Wenzel, T. (1990). The scientific dialogue: From basic research to clinical intervention. In *Annual Series of European Research in Behavior Therapy,* vol. 5. Conference proceedings from 19th Annual Congress of the European Association of Behavior Therapy, Vienna.

Zhao, X.-r., Bai, J.-y., Li, N., and Xu, X.-f. (2011). Two year follow-up on the psychosocial factors influencing the prognosis of the patients with coronary heart disease. *Chinese Journal of Clinical Psychology, 19,* 106–109.

18

Emotional Intelligence, Health, and Stress

Gerald Matthews, Moshe Zeidner, and Richard D. Roberts

Affective science increasingly focuses on the interplay between health and emotion, as well as the role of its cognitive, social, and physiological concomitants. A recent review (DeSteno, Gross, and Kubzansky, 2013) distinguishes direct effects of emotion, mediated by physiology, such as psychoneuroimmunological factors, and indirect effects mediated by processes such as health behaviors and coping with stress. There is also a dynamic reciprocal influence of health on emotion as the person strives to maintain health and manage disease. Thus, it is important to identify individual differences in emotional functioning that may impinge on health. For example, the neuroticism personality trait is associated with vulnerability to both mental and physical disorders (Matthews, Deary, and Whiteman, 2009). However, standard personality factors may not pick up abilities for understanding and regulating emotion that may also have ramifications for health. In this chapter we address the role in health of emotional intelligence (EI), which refers to the set of aptitudes, competencies, and skills used for managing emotion and emotive encounters (Zeidner, Matthews, and Roberts, 2009).

Measures of EI are positively associated with a range of mental and physical health outcomes, but the present contribution to health psychology of EI studies is limited in several respects (Zeidner, Matthews, and Roberts, 2012). The construct is often poorly defined and there is no accepted "gold standard" test for assessment. Questionnaire scales tend to be confounded with standard personality traits. Indeed, the jury is still out on whether EI constitutes a major dimension of individual differences on a par with cognitive ability and the Big Five personality traits (Matthews, Zeidner, and Roberts, 2002; 2012). Most studies use self-report measures of health, which are of questionable validity. It is more common to use samples of predominantly healthy students than to investigate patient groups, although a literature on EI in psychiatric disorder is emerging (Matthews et al., 2012). Perhaps most concerningly, the EI literature makes only limited contact with contemporary perspectives on individual differences

The Handbook of Stress and Health: A Guide to Research and Practice, First Edition.
Edited by Cary L. Cooper and James Campbell Quick.
© 2017 John Wiley & Sons, Ltd. Published 2017 by John Wiley & Sons, Ltd.

in health which also emphasize the social context. For example, Friedman and Kern (2014) advocate studying patterns of living over extended periods that may promote or injure health. Determining the role of EI in the health process over the life span requires a more strongly theory-driven approach than has typically been the case.

The present review is structured as follows. First, we review the definition and assessment of EI. Second, we provide a brief review of the correlational evidence linking EI to health criteria, including studies of mental disorder. Third, we consider the physiological, emotional, cognitive and social processes to which EI may be linked. A process-based account of EI and health is critical for further progress, although current evidence is not yet sufficient for detailed theory building. We will conclude by looking at applications of research for health psychology, and challenges for research and practice.

What Is Emotional Intelligence?

There is much debate over how EI should be conceptualized but no general consensus on definition (Matthews et al., 2002; 2012). Two schemas may be useful for understanding the broad domain. First, we can view the facets of EI from an information-processing perspective. The emotionally intelligent person encodes emotive stimuli accurately (perception and attention), analyzes and understands their significance (working memory and problem-solving), and acts effectively and constructively within emotional encounters (response selection and execution). Second, EI has both intra- and interpersonal aspects, as expressed in multiple intelligence theory (Gardner, 2006). Emotionally intelligent people are skilled both in understanding and regulating their own emotions, and in reading and managing the emotions of others.

Beyond these general views, the field has fractured sharply into two camps. The first sees EI as a true ability such that the emotionally intelligent person is objectively superior in processing emotional stimuli (Mayer, Caruso and Salovey, 1999). Thus, EI should be measurable using tests with objective right-or-wrong answers. The second perspective is that EI is a set of personality traits that promote effective personality functioning, and so can be measured by self-report (Petrides, Furnham, and Mavroveli, 2007). In fact, measures of the two variants are typically poorly intercorrelated, suggesting they measure separate constructs (Joseph and Newman, 2010; Zeidner et al., 2009). Both forms of EI are said to promote social-emotional functioning, but they should be distinguished from one another, as we will do next.

The Ability Model of Emotional Intelligence

The best-known ability model was advanced by Mayer, Caruso, and Salovey (e.g., 1999). Their four-branch model discriminates four aspects of EI compatible with an information-processing perspective. The first two branches – emotion perception and assimilation of emotion into thought – are foundational, somewhat intuitive, abilities described as "experiential EI." The other two branches, emotion understanding and emotion management, are more dependent on explicit cognitive processes, and are grouped together as "strategic EI." Mayer, Salovey, and Caruso's (2012) test of EI, the Mayer-Salovey-Caruso Emotional Intelligence Test (MSCEIT), comprises eight subtests that measure the four branches, experiential and strategic EI, and overall ability. Subtest content is quite diverse, ranging from identification of facial emotion (emotion perception) to evaluating possible responses to emotional events (emotion management). For the most part, the MSCEIT meets conventional psychometric criteria such as internal consistency of scores (Mayer et al., 2012). As required for an intelligence test, scores tend to correlate with conventional cognitive ability (Mayer et al., 2012).

The MSCEIT predicts various indicators of well-being, social competency, and relationship satisfaction (Rivers, Brackett, Salovey, and Mayer, 2007). Scoring objective tests for emotional functioning is problematic because there is often no clear standard for establishing correct answers for items (Matthews et al., 2002). In addition, validity coefficients are often modest (Matthews et al., 2012). The MSCEIT is also a rather weak predictor of job performance, though it is more predictive for jobs requiring emotional labor than those that do not (Joseph and Newman, 2010). Most of the validation studies use self-report outcomes so that it is difficult to build a theory of how ability EI stems from individual differences in cognitive and neural processes (Fiori, 2009; Matthews, Zeidner and Roberts, 2004).

Other approaches to measuring EI as an ability include several language-based tests which assess the person's ability to use complex emotion language or their ability to integrate emotional information into reasoning (see Matthews et al., 2002). Computer analysis of emotional language use may be especially relevant to health; there is consistent evidence that expressive emotional writing, for example about traumatic events, produces lasting benefits to both mental and physical health (Pennebaker and Ferrell, 2013). Another objective approach is the use of Situation Judgment Tests (SJTs), which require the person to choose between response alternatives to emotional scenarios, using either text or multimedia materials (MacCann, Lievens, Libbrecht, and Roberts, 2015). SJTs of these kinds for EI converge with the MSCEIT and predict relevant criteria such as life satisfaction and adaptive coping (MacCann et al., 2015).

The Personality Trait Model of Emotional Intelligence

EI is also seen as an aspect of personality, but this perspective may be problematic in the health context. Personality research has already furnished quite a detailed account of the roles of various traits in both emotion and health. Lahey's (2009) review concluded that neuroticism is implicated in numerous mental and physical disorders, as well as usage of health services. Neuroticism may have direct effects on physiology (in part associated with genetic antecedents) as well as indirect effects associated with poorer social support and maladaptive coping with stressors. Friedman and Kern (2014) argued that another Big Five factor, conscientiousness, is a more reliable predictor of overall mortality, likely because of its role in health behaviors and associations with more supportive social contexts. Thus, any attempt to advance EI-as-personality in this domain must focus sharply on whether any influence of EI on health is distinct from those of other traits.

Petrides et al. (2007) argued that what they called "trait EI" properly belongs in the personality domain because the subjective nature of emotional experience precludes objective assessment. They list 15 constructs that delineate the "sampling domain" of trait EI, assessed by their Trait Emotional Intelligence Questionnaire (TEIQue). Factor analysis suggests four distinct subfactors of emotionality, self-control, sociability, and well-being, as well as a general factor. Petrides et al. (2007) cite studies that show that TEIQue scores predict a variety of criteria for well-being and social functioning. There are numerous other questionnaire measures of EI that also predict relevant outcomes (see Zeidner et al., 2009). Some are more narrowly focused. For example, the Trait Meta-Mood Scale (TMMS: Salovey et al., 1995) measures dimensions of attention to emotions, clarity of emotions, and mood repair.

Taken in isolation, the evidence on validity of the TEIQue and similar scales is persuasive, but the problem of confounding with standard personality domains remains (Zeidner et al., 2009). A fairly large-scale study (Vernon, Villani, Schermer and Petrides, 2008) showed that overall trait EI correlates at −0. 61 with neuroticism, 0.51 with extraversion, 0.47 with conscientiousness, and 0.32 with both agreeableness and openness. In fact, Petrides et al. (2007) estimate that there is about 65 percent overlap in variance between trait EI and the Big Five; the confounding of the construct with low neuroticism and conscientiousness is a particular problem for health researchers. It may be preferable to work with subfactors; the emotionality subfactor, in particular, is relatively distinct from the Big Five. (The factor name is confusing: it refers more to self-rated emotion perception and regulation than to emotional responsiveness). Working with subfactors also counters the criterion contamination problem that traits associated with the well-being subfactor, such as happiness, overlap with criterion measures commonly used in health research. The validity of trait EI as a predictor of health outcomes is, not surprisingly, much reduced if criterion contamination is controlled (Zeidner et al., 2012). Nevertheless, various studies show modest incremental prediction of well-being outcomes for trait EI scales with the Big Five controlled, suggesting that such scales may be useful for researching the role of personality in health (Keefer, Parker, and Saklofske, 2009).

Does Emotional Intelligence Correlate with Health Outcomes?

Several reviews (Keefer et al., 2009; Martins, Ramalho, and Morin, 2010; Zeidner et al., 2012) have concluded that EI is quite consistently correlated with health outcomes, including lower levels of stress symptoms. Martins et al. (2010) conducted a meta-analysis that distinguished trait and ability EI. In all cases, health measures were largely self-report. Estimated correlations between trait EI and physical, mental and psychosomatic indicators of health were 0.27, 0.36, and 0.33, suggesting a consistent medium effect size. Martins et al. (2010) located fewer studies of ability EI, but they estimated a smaller 0.17 effect for its association with mental health.

Applied studies also suggest that EI is typically associated with higher well-being and lower stress (Zeidner et al., 2009). For example, EI predicts self-reports of lower job stress, although evidence for EI effects on objective occupational outcomes is weak (Zeidner et al., 2009). Examples of the role of EI in occupational stress come from studies of health workers. Zeidner, Hadar, Matthews, and Roberts (2013a) examined burnout in samples of Israeli mental health and medical practitioners working with trauma patients. Both trait EI and emotion management, a facet of ability EI, were independently associated with lower burnout, and specifically with its compassion fatigue component. Problem-focused coping mediated the impact on burnout of trait EI, but not of emotion management. There is also a growing literature showing that EI may protect against stress in nurses and student nurses (Smith, Profetto-McGrath, and Cummings, 2009). EI may be especially important in managing the emotional labor of signaling empathic concern and support to patients (Karimi et al., 2014). The social context is important; emotional demands on nurses increase with stress factors such as hospital restructuring and unmet patient care needs, potentially leading to emotional exhaustion (Smith et al., 2009).

Personality as a Confound of Trait EI

Associations between trait EI and health are expected given the overlap between this variant of EI and the Big Five personality traits. Some studies have shown modest incremental validity for trait EI (Keefer et al., 2009). For example, in a study of 499 adolescents, Davis and Humphrey (2012) showed that the Big Five explained 18 percent of the variance in a regression model for depression as a criterion, and trait EI added a further 8 percent to the variance. However, studies working with global assessments of trait EI may miss differential associations between health and the various facets of trait EI. More fine-grained assessment of trait EI is important for two reasons. First, different facets of trait EI show different levels of confounding with personality (e.g., Vernon et al., 2008); a facet-level approach may be necessary to determine what is truly unique about questionnaire scales for EI. Second, the more fine-grained approach may also address the issue of criterion contamination; for instance, trait EI scales may include items for outcomes such as happiness, producing spurious correlations with similar health measures.

One of the larger studies in the field (Greven, Chamorro-Premuzic, Arteche, and Furnham, 2008) shows the utility of a finer grained approach. In a sample of 1,038 university students, these authors distinguished the four TEIQue factors (well-being, self-control, emotionality, and sociability) as predictors of self-reported general health. The strongest correlation was found for the well-being factor ($r = -0.56$). However, this factor is the one most vulnerable to criterion contamination, as it assesses qualities such as general mood, and it is also strongly associated with low neuroticism ($r = -0.61$ in Greven et al., 2008). A reanalysis of these data (Zeidner et al., 2012) found that well-being was the only one of the four TEIQue factors to show incremental validity over the Big Five in predicting general health. In this study, at least, incremental validity may be an artifact of criterion contamination. However, future research may clarify the role of specific trait EI facets in health, over and above the Big Five.

The limitations of cross-sectional, correlational studies can be countered by adopting experimental studies that have investigated individual differences in response to stress manipulations. For example, Mikolajczak et al. (2007) showed that trait EI predicted emotional and physiological responsivity to stress over and above the Big Five. Studies of this kind have been reviewed by Keefer et al. (2009), who arrived at three main conclusions. First, higher EI individuals are typically already in a better mood when they begin the experiment, so that investigations of stress response must control for baseline variation. Second, effects of EI on mood response are rather mixed, and individual difference factors other than EI may be more important. Third, EI appears to have more consistent effects on recovery from induced distress, consistent with the notion that EI is associated with more effective emotion-regulation strategies, such as mood repair (Salovey et al., 1995).

Emotional Intelligence in Clinical Disorder

The Martins et al. (2010) meta-analysis showed a rather modest association between ability EI and effect size. The MSCEIT is also a rather weak predictor of stress response in experimental studies (Matthews et al., 2006). However, ability EI may come into its own when we turn to externalizing rather than internalizing disorders (Davis and Humphrey, 2012). Davis and Humphrey cite evidence that the MSCEIT predicts substance abuse, as well as deviant and disruptive behaviors. Their study of adolescents showed that both ability and trait EI added to the prediction of disruptive behavior (conduct and oppositional defiant disorder symptoms), but the variance increments with the Big Five controlled were small (<2 percent in each case). Poor self-control, lack of empathy and distorted, hostile perceptions of others might contribute to an association between EI and externalizing disorders (Matthews et al., 2012).

A final source of evidence comes from clinical studies of mental disorder. Matthews et al. (2012) have reviewed these studies: we offer a brief precis here. As expected, levels of both trait EI and ability EI are typically, though not invariably, lower in patients with various emotional disorders. EI overlaps with alexithymia, a clinical construct that refers to deficits in recognizing, understanding and verbalizing emotional states. Such deficits may also contribute to vulnerability to disorder, although one of the few longitudinal studies of EI in the clinical context found that lower EI seemed to be more a consequence than a cause of clinical depression (Hansenne and Bianchi, 2009). Lower EI may also be a feature of disorders characterized by social disconnection and impairments in social skill, including schizophrenia and autism.

Why Should Emotional Intelligence Predict Health?

EI is prone to be an over-inclusive concept that can mean all things to all people (Matthews et al., 2002), so it is important that research on EI, health and stress is based on a sound conceptual platform. In fact, models for individual differences in health outcomes are prone to complexity, and must accommodate physiological, psychological, and social processes, as well as their dynamic interaction.

A transactional perspective on health changes over the life span recognizes both internal and external factors, and their interaction (Lazarus, 1999; Matthews et al., 2009). Vulnerability to illness in part reflects internal structural weaknesses, such as genetic predispositions and physiological characteristics. It also reflects external psychosocial conditions such as stressful life circumstances and availability of social support (Friedman and Kern, 2014). In fact, stress might impair emotional competency; for example, fatigue is associated with impairments in perceiving and attending to facial emotion (Matthews et al., 2015). Psychological processes such as emotion-regulation and coping may mediate the interplay between internal and external factors. For example, a person with genetic predispositions toward anxiety and toward finding that opiate drugs are reinforcing (structural weaknesses) may live in a poor neighborhood in which living is stressful and drug dealers are easy to access (psychosocial conditions). If the person chooses to cope with stressors through drug use there will be a harmful and synergistic effect of internal and external factors leading to addiction and the further stresses that may ensue from participation in criminal activities. The emotionally intelligent individual may avoid addiction through various aspects of the process, including a calm temperament (internal), the availability or construction of a supportive social network (external), and finding alternative strategies for regulating negative emotional responses to stressful events (transactional). Research may be directed toward establishing links between EI and specific factors of these kinds, but the ultimate though unrealized goal is to understand the role of EI within the transactional process as it unfolds over the life span.

We should also distinguish mental and physical health. Various psychological constructs influence vulnerability to mental disorders and allied subclinical conditions such as dysthymia and distress (Wells and Matthews, 2015). Meta-analyses show large to moderate effect sizes for associations between neuroticism and various Axis I and Axis II disorders (Lahey, 2009); cognitive ability plays a small but substantiated role in vulnerability to emotional disorder (Austin et al., 2011). Thus, studies of EI can be integrated into this existing work.

The role of psychological factors in physical health remains more controversial. For example, high neuroticism individuals may be more prone to complaining about health than to actual medical illness. Furthermore, some aspects of neuroticism may be beneficial, such as maintaining vigilance for symptoms (Friedman and Kern, 2014). On the other hand, there is growing evidence from prospective studies for an etiological role for neuroticism in a range of conditions, including medical conditions such as cardiovascular disease (Lahey, 2009; Matthews et al., 2009). Affective science provides the necessary foundation for theory-driven EI research, and we will distinguish several types of influence on health which may be linked to EI, although detailed theoretical models are lacking.

Physiological Influences

Personality studies provide paradigms for linking individual difference factors to physiological influences on health. There is considerable overlap between genes associated with emotional disorders and those associated with neurotic personality (Hettema, Prescott and Kendler, 2004). There is also a substantial genetic correlation between trait EI and low neuroticism, estimated at -0.80 by Vernon et al. (2008), suggesting that genes for low trait EI are likely to also confer liability to emotional disorder. Neuroticism is largely independent of ability EI, however (Zeidner et al., 2009). Genes in turn influence the multitude of brain systems that may influence vulnerability to mental disorder. Possible mechanisms are too numerous to mention but we will give two illustrations. First, genes influence the development of brain systems that control stress vulnerability such as the hypothalamo-pituitary-adrenal (HPA) axis. Low EI – especially low trait EI – may be associated with biological vulnerability factors of this kind, to the extent that its effects can be differentiated from those of neuroticism.

Second, reduced serotonergic functioning encourages impulsive response to strong emotive cues, with diminished reflection (Carver, Johnson, and Joormann, 2013). Lack of control under emotional provocation is emotionally unintelligent, and associated with externalizing disorders, and so it may be worth investigating the role of serotonin in EI, although evidence is currently lacking. It is unclear whether EI can be differentiated from conscientiousness in this context. Somewhat confusingly, Carver et al. (2013) also link serotonergic functioning to depression, suggesting a further direction for EI research.

Similar mechanisms might generate associations between EI and physical health: both immunological impairments associated with stress and poor impulse control (Friedman and Kern, 2014) are likely to increase mortality. Indeed, mental disorders may impinge on physical illness. Depression is a risk factor for cardiac disease (Compare et al., 2013). These authors list several possible direct mechanisms, including inflammatory and immune processes, increased activity of the sympathoadrenal and pituitary-adrenal axes, hormonal effects, and others. Indirect factors associated with unhealthy lifestyles may also play a role.

Evidence on how EI might relate to relevant physiological mechanisms is limited, other than via its overlap with standard personality traits. Several studies demonstrate the potential for research on this topic. Mikolajczak et al. (2007) conducted an experimental study of individual differences in response to a public-speaking stressor. Individuals high in trait EI showed a reduced cortisol response to the stressor, as well as reduced mood response. These findings were maintained with the Big Five personality traits controlled. Cortisol is associated with HPA; prolonged cortisol response may lead to physical disease. Individual differences in mood-regulation traits assessed by Salovey et al.'s (1995) TMMS have also been linked to reduced cortisol response (Ruiz-Robledillo and Moya-Albiol, 2014). Tolegenova, Kustubayeva, and Matthews (2014) found that the TMMS predicted higher electroencephalogram (EEG) theta and gamma power when participants watched a fear-inducing movie clip, a pattern of response linked to emotion regulation. The association between the TMMS and EEG was highest when participants were instructed to use reappraisal as a strategy for regulation.

Costa, Petrides, and Tillmann (2014) secured TEIQue scores from a sample of adults diagnosed with a range of inflammatory diseases such as rheumatoid arthritis and multiple sclerosis. Stress and negative emotions may play a role in these diseases, mediated by over-activation and dysregulation of the hypothalamus-pituitary-Adrenal axis. In fact, Costa et al. (2014) did not find any overall differences in trait EI between disease groups and a healthy control group. However, individuals with rheumatoid arthritis reported lower levels of well-being and sociability than healthy controls. The direction of causality between trait EI and the disease condition is open to question.

Psychological Factors

Another rationale for linking EI to health centers on individual differences in emotional and stress processing. On the one hand, emotionally intelligent individuals may be able to appraise life events constructively, supporting personal development and happiness (Epstein, 1998). Positive emotions may have direct benefits for health (DeSteno et al., 2013), although adaptive patterns of living and social interaction that produce happiness as a byproduct may be better for health than positive emotion per se (Friedman and Kern, 2014). On the other hand, emotionally intelligent individuals may have superior skills in coping with threatening events, either through direct management of stressors, or through finding opportunities for personal growth and learning in adverse circumstances (Zeidner et al., 2009). We will briefly review some of the possible pathways for psychological impacts on health and the evidence for a role for EI.

Emotion regulation Broadly, emotion regulation refers to efforts to monitor and shape one's emotions according to some preference, most often to improve mood. Models of emotion regulation have become increasingly elaborate in recent years (e.g., DeSteno et al., 2013) and here we must perforce work with a simplified account. One important conceptual issue is how to distinguish emotion regulation from the related construct of coping, referring to active management of potentially stressful encounters (Lazarus, 1999). Emotion regulation is broader in referring to positive as well as to negative emotions. Current models (e.g., DeSteno et al., 2013) also encroach increasingly on the traditional territory of coping by including situation selection and modification as forms of regulation. Here we will define emotion regulation rather more narrowly as strategies that have the goal of changing emotional state directly. For example, Salovey et al. (1995) list attention to emotions, clarity of emotions, and mood repair as dimensions of regulation. Cognitive reappraisal of events and suppression of unwanted emotional responses are other relevant aspects of emotion regulation (DeSteno et al., 2013). Emotion-focused coping in the Lazarus (1999) stress model overlaps with these constructs, although it also includes coping with a wider focus than emotion change, for example striving to find opportunities for self-improvement.

Generally, those high in EI should be superior both at monitoring and understanding their affective state, and at exerting control over emotions (Salovey et al., 1995). Control implies calibrating emotions to current needs; for example, sometimes positive emotions should be down-regulated to maintain task focus. Dysfunctional emotion regulation may contribute to mental disorder (Wells and Matthews, 2015). There are also possible impacts on physical health.

DeSteno et al. (2013) consider two emotion-regulation strategies. They state that reappraisal is associated with reduced autonomic nervous system activation and inflammation, whereas suppression is associated with the reverse outcomes, suggesting it may be a risk factor for heart disease.

Peña-Sarrionandia, Mikolajczak, and Gross (2015) reported a meta-analysis of associations between EI and various aspects of emotion regulation, as defined broadly. Limitations of the article include lack of control for personality confounds of trait EI, and a reliance on self-report criteria for emotion regulation, but findings are informative. Trait EI is reliably and substantially associated with greater use of reappraisal and less of suppression strategies; no studies of ability IE and these dimensions exist. Both trait and ability EI are also related to self-efficacy, though this should properly be seen as an aspect of self-knowledge that may feed into choice of regulatory strategy, rather than an emotion-regulation strategy per se.

Coping   Models of coping discriminate multiple strategies for managing adverse events (Carver and Connor-Smith, 2010; Lazarus, 1999). Strategies associated with direct, problem-focused coping and active engagement with the stressor are considered more effective than avoidance of threatening situations (Carver and Connor-Smith, 2010). Emotion-focused coping tends to be identified with maladaptive strategies such as self-criticism and rumination on problems, although emotion focus can be constructive when directed toward coming to terms with events. However, coping strategies are typically not intrinsically adaptive or maladaptive; flexible matching of strategies to the specific demands of the stressful situation may determine whether or not coping is successful (Zeidner et al., 2012).

Research on trait EI and coping stands in the long shadow cast by extensive existing research on personality traits. Reviews (Carver and Connor-Smith, 2010; Matthews et al., 2009) have concluded that extraversion and conscientiousness tend to relate modestly to the use of strategies deemed more adaptive, such as problem-focus and engagement, whereas neuroticism is associated with counterproductive strategies such as self-criticism and avoidance. Thus, given that trait EI overlaps substantially with traits linked to more adaptive coping, it is no surprise that trait EI correlates similarly with coping. The Peña-Sarrionandia et al. (2015) meta-analysis found that trait EI is strongly associated with reported use of problem-focused strategies, and, to a lesser degree, with lower use of rumination and avoidance. Trait EI is also related to greater use of presumably maladaptive emotion-focused coping strategies (Saklofske, Austin, Galloway and Davidson, 2007). By contrast, evidence from studies of ability EI is more equivocal. MSCEIT scores tend to correlate with a broadly adaptive style of coping, associated with higher problem-focus, lower emotion-focus, and lower avoidance, but results are somewhat inconsistent across studies (Zeidner et al., 2012; Zeidner, Matthews, and Shemesh, 2015).

Low EI may also be implicated in psychological vulnerability factors for emotional disorders associated with counterproductive efforts at coping. Such factors include dysfunctional styles of emotion regulation and lack of insight into mental events (e.g., Wells and Matthews, 2015). For example, fruitless rumination on personal problems is a vulnerability factor for emotional disorder, and may reflect dysfunctional styles of metacognition that lead to excessive attention to negative thoughts and images (Wells and Matthews, 2015). Lanciano et al. (2012) found quite a strong negative association between the MSCEIT and dysfunctional rumination, although, again, low EI may overlap with neuroticism and cognate traits.

Social factors   Social functioning is also important for health, as evidenced by the role of social support in well-being and in physical health (Taylor, 2011). Both trait and ability EI are fairly consistently correlated with a range of measures of social competence and functioning (Rivers et al., 2007; Zeidner et al., 2009), but there are several possible mechanisms through which those high in EI may enjoy the benefits of higher social engagement (Zeidner et al., 2015). First, EI, especially ability EI, may be associated with objectively greater social skills. For example, there is evidence that others perceive high scorers on the MSCEIT as being more socially competent (Brackett et al., 2006). Second, EI may be associated with greater availability of social support as well as with higher satisfaction in social support received (Zeidner et al., 2015). Social support is shown to mediate affective benefits of trait EI (Kong, Zhao, and You, 2012). Zeidner et al. (2015) found that the MSCEIT may be more strongly related to social support than to coping.

Third, EI may be associated with elevated perceptions of personal social competence, irrespective of objective social skills. In a study of marital satisfaction, Zeidner, Kloda and Matthews (2013b) found that high trait and ability EI both conferred personal satisfaction and perceptions of enhanced dyadic coping, but had no impact on the partner's perceptions of the marriage. In this case, EI appeared to be associated with benign illusions rather than actual quality of dyadic partner interactions. Similarly, perceived social support brings health benefits over and above objective support (Taylor, 2011).

Fourth, associations between EI, social functioning and health might be understood at a societal rather than an individual level, consistent with life-span perspectives. Community-level perspectives on well-being (Helliwell, 2012) suggest that EI might be a collective attribute of emotionally supportive groups. Conversely, social factors such as poverty, communal strife and poor education may contribute to life-span trajectories that stunt development of emotional competencies within the communities concerned.

Health behaviors   Finally, EI might have indirect effects through behaviors that are supportive or damaging to health. Keefer et al.'s (2009) review identifies some possible mechanisms of this type. Those high in EI may be generally better at taking good care of themselves, through engaging in physical exercise, eating a healthy diet, sleeping well, and managing illnesses more effectively, for example through complying with treatments. Conversely, lower EI may be associated with damaging behaviors such as self-harm, reckless driving, and abuse of alcohol and other substances.

While the evidence is somewhat mixed (Keefer et al., 2009; Zeidner et al., 2009), it is sufficient to suggest that further research on health behaviors is warranted. For example, Saklofske et al. (2007) found that trait EI was significantly but modestly ($rs < 0.2$) associated with self-report measures of exercise, healthy diet, and doctor visits. The latter metric was interpreted as an index of proactive health management rather than sickness. A recent review (Laborde, Dosseville, and Allen, 2015) has substantiated associations between EI, physical activity, and positive attitudes toward activity. Trait EI has also been linked to lower alcohol consumption, eating more fruits and vegetables, and using protection during sex (Lana, Baizán, Faya-Ornia, and López, 2015).

A recent large-scale study in Belgium (Mikolajczak et al., 2015) investigated relationships between trait EI, health behaviors, and objective measures of health service utilization, including physician consultations and hospitalizations. The study confirmed significant though small associations between EI and objective indicators such as days spent in hospital ($r = -0.08$).

The study presented a multivariate model in which the impact of EI on health service utilization was partly mediated by social support, health behaviors, and lower negative affect. There was also a direct path from EI to outcome. The study also found moderator effects such that high EI may mitigate the impacts of risk factors.

Conclusions: Is Emotional Intelligence Useful to Health Psychology Practitioners?

From an affective science standpoint, EI remains a promising construct whose true importance for health psychology has yet to be determined. A major obstacle to progress is lack of agreement on definition and measurement of the construct, exemplified by the schism between ability and trait EI researchers. Ability EI represents the more novel approach, but at best it is only a modest predictor of health and stress criteria. The role of ability EI in seeking and utilizing social support is one of the more promising research directions we have reviewed. Trait EI overlaps substantially with the standard Big Five personality traits, and so it is no surprise that it correlates the similar health criteria to low neuroticism and additional dimensions. However, some facets of trait EI, especially those associated with emotion-regulation strategies, may add to existing personality models. Most empirical studies are methodologically limited, with an overreliance on cross-sectional studies using self-report health criteria.

Clear demarcation of novel elements of trait EI is necessary to make further progress. Both ability and trait EI perspectives are limited by their neglect of the theoretical underpinnings of the constructs concerned. However, research is emerging that may allow a better understanding of the role of these constructs in the intra- and interpersonal processes that shape health trajectories over the life span. We have reviewed evidence that EI may be associated with individual differences in physiological functioning, emotion regulation, coping with life events, building supportive relationships, and health behaviors. Until such time as theory is considerably further advanced, we do not see current work on EI as having compelling implications for health practitioners. However, there are several applications for which the construct has potential, and we will conclude with a brief survey of these.

Evaluation and diagnosis   Psychometric tests of various kinds are traditionally seen as valuable in determining personal characteristics that are relevant to formal diagnosis of disorders, understanding the client in more depth, and suggesting treatment options (Austin et al., 2011). Measures of ability and trait EI may play an adjunct role in assessment, though they are unlikely to supplant existing measures. The task of EI researchers is to determine which personal characteristics are uniquely identified by EI test scores. What can the EI test tell us that no other standard test can? Current research provides only limited clues. For example, there may be some nexus of low ability EI, substance abuse, poor social skills, and lack of social support. Perhaps low EI substance abusers should be taught emotion-regulation skills or social skills, or guided toward more supportive social networks. Research on such issues has some way to go before practical recommendations of these kinds may be made.

In the case of trait EI, the question is complicated by overlap with personality. Given that finer-grained facet-level personality assessments are typically more predictive than broad personality dimensions, it is no surprise that aspects of trait EI on occasion show incremental validity over the Big Five. What is needed is an elaboration of standard personality models to identify novel facets, such as those for emotion regulation, so that health-relevant facets of trait EI can be assessed within some more comprehensive psychometric model.

Guiding the treatment regime   Practitioners may both treat disorders and encourage healthy lifestyles in nonclinical groups. In both cases, it is important to ensure the cooperation and compliance of the individual. Existing psychometric tests can be used for such purposes; for example, low conscientiousness might suggest a need for close monitoring of compliance (Austin et al., 2011; Friedman and Kern, 2014). The links between EI and health behaviors (Keefer et al., 2009) suggest the potential for using trait and ability EI scales for a similar purpose. Again, the onus is on researchers to show that EI measures provide information on client response to treatment not available from other sources.

Changing emotional intelligence   It is increasingly recognized that social-emotional skills are trainable (Matthews et al., 2012). Such interventions have the potential to produce a range of health benefits, most obviously in relation to mitigating maladaptive behaviors such as substance abuse and reckless externalizing behaviors. Enhanced emotion-regulation, effective stress management, and experience of positive emotions may also confer psychological and physiological benefits (DeSteno et al., 2013). A meta-analysis of 213 school-based social and emotional (SEL) programs (Durlak et al., 2011) found that they produced substantial, practically meaningful improvements in a range of relevant skills, as well as in attitudes and positive social behavior. Specific programs vary in outcome, but the factors that determine success are becoming clearer (Matthews et al., 2012).

The malleability of social-emotional functioning should encourage practitioners to consider interventions adapted to their particular needs. However, it remains an open question whether SEL programs are really changing EI in some global sense, as opposed to training specific skills such as saying no to drugs or resolving interpersonal conflicts. If we want people to take more exercise or to adopt healthy diets, it may be better to train the requisite skills directly, rather than seek to change the rather more nebulous characteristic of EI. Again, a more fine-grained approach might be of value. Training people in emotion-regulation techniques that can be applied to a variety of contexts might have advantages over both training in specific skills and attempts at general personality change; indeed current cognitive-behavioral therapies may do just this in training techniques for mitigating anxiety (Wells and Matthews, 2015). Once again, a stronger theoretical understanding of EI is necessary to understand which of its facets might be trained to enhance health.

Community interventions   The transactional, life-span perspective on health implies that it is important to consider environmental factors that impact emotional functioning as much as the personal qualities of the individual. Helliwell (2012) advocates for the importance of the social context in designing social and health policy interventions. Generally, there is a positive feedback loop linking social engagement and support, happiness and health outcomes, which interventions should support. Helliwell does not mention EI but its potential relevance is clear. Training EI at an individual level might enhance social engagement, but so too might enhancements to the social environment that facilitate constructive interpersonal emotional relationships. For example, interventions to boost social trust within troubled communities might enhance collective EI. Friedman and Kern (2014) point out that low conscientiousness often coexists with environmental factors such as poor education, unstable marriages, substance abuse, and poor work performance, all of which promote ill-health. Thus, tackling the associated health problems may require a focus on changing the social environment, for example to promote stable employment and relationships, as much as in training EI in individuals.

References

Austin, E. J., Boyle, G. J., Groth-Marnat, G., Matthews, G., Saklofske, D. H., Schwean, V. L., and Zeidner, M. (2011). Integrating intelligence and personality: Theory, research and implications for clinical assessment. In G. Groth-Marnat (Ed.), *Integrative Assessment of Adult Personality*, 3rd edn. (pp. 119–151). New York: Guilford.

Brackett, M. A., Rivers, S. E., Shiffman, S., Lerner, N., and Salovey, P. (2006). Relating emotional abilities to social functioning: A comparison of self-report and performance measures of emotional intelligence. *Journal of Personality and Social Psychology, 91*, 780–795.

Carver, C.S., and Connor-Smith, J. (2010). Personality and coping. *Annual Review of Psychology, 61*, 679–704.

Carver, C. S., Johnson, S. L., and Joormann, J. (2013). Major depressive disorder and impulsive reactivity to emotion: Toward a dual-process view of depression. *British Journal of Clinical Psychology, 52*, 285–299.

Compare, A., Zarbo, C., Manzoni, G. M., Castelnuovo, G., Baldassari, E., Bonardi, A. ... and Romagnoni, C. (2013). Social support, depression, and heart disease: A ten year literature review. *Frontiers in Psychology, 4*, 384.

Costa, S., Petrides, K. V., and Tillmann, T. (2014). Trait emotional intelligence and inflammatory diseases. *Psychology, Health and Medicine, 19*, 180–189.

Davis, S. K., and Humphrey, N. (2012). Emotional intelligence predicts adolescent mental health beyond personality and cognitive ability. *Personality and Individual Differences, 52*, 144–149.

DeSteno, D., Gross, J. J., and Kubzansky, L. (2013). Affective science and health: The importance of emotion and emotion regulation. *Health Psychology, 32*, 474–486.

Durlak, J. A., Weissberg, R. P., Dymnicki, A. B., Taylor, R. D., and Schellinger, K. B. (2011). The impact of enhancing students' social and emotional learning: A meta-analysis of school-based universal interventions. *Child Development, 82*, 405–432.

Epstein, S. (1998). *Constructive Thinking: The Key to Emotional Intelligence*. Westport, CT: Praeger.

Fiori, M. (2009). A new look at emotional intelligence: A dual-process framework. *Personality and Social Psychology Review, 13*, 21–44.

Friedman, H. S., and Kern, M. L. (2014). Personality, well-being, and health. *Annual Review of Psychology, 65*, 719–742.

Gardner, H. (2006). *Multiple Intelligences: New Horizons*. New York: Basic Books.

Greven, C., Chamorro-Premuzic, T., Arteche, A., and Furnham, A. (2008). A hierarchical integration of dispositional determinants of general health in students: The Big Five, trait emotional intelligence and humour styles. *Personality and Individual Differences, 44*, 1562–1573.

Hansenne, M., and Bianchi, J. (2009). Emotional intelligence and personality in major depression: Trait versus state effects. *Psychiatry Research, 166*, 63–68.

Helliwell, J. F. (2012). Understanding and improving the social context of well-being. NBER Working Paper No. 18486. Cambridge, MA: National Bureau of Economic Research.

Hettema, J. M., Prescott, C. A., and Kendler, K. S. (2004). Genetic and environmental sources of covariation between generalized anxiety disorder and neuroticism. *American Journal of Psychiatry, 161*, 1581–1587.

Joseph, D. L., and Newman, D. A. (2010). Discriminant validity of self-reported emotional intelligence: A multitrait-multisource study. *Educational and Psychological Measurement, 70*, 672–694.

Karimi, L., Leggat, S. G., Donohue, L., Farrell, G., and Couper, G. E. (2014). Emotional rescue: The role of emotional intelligence and emotional labour on well-being and job-stress among community nurses. *Journal of Advanced Nursing, 70*, 176–186.

Keefer, K. V., Parker, J. D. A., and Saklofske, D. H. (2009). Emotional intelligence and physical health. In C. Stough, D. H. Saklofske and J. D. A. Parker (Eds.), *Assessing Emotional Intelligence: Theory, Research, Applications* (pp. 191–218). New York: Springer.

Kong, F., Zhao, J., and You, X. (2012). Social support mediates the impact of emotional intelligence on mental distress and life satisfaction in Chinese young adults. *Personality and Individual Differences, 53*, 513–517.

Laborde, S., Dosseville, F., and Allen, M. S. (2015). Emotional intelligence in sport and exercise: A systematic review. *Scandinavian Journal of Medicine and Science in Sports*. Epub ahead of print.

Lahey, B. B. (2009). Public health significance of neuroticism. *American Psychologist*, *64*, 241–256.

Lana, A., Baizán, E. M., Faya-Ornia, G., and López, M. L. (2015). Emotional intelligence and health risk behaviors in nursing students. *Journal of Nursing Education*, *54*, 464–467.

Lanciano, T., Curci, A., Kafetsios, K., Elia, L., and Zammuner, V. L. (2012). Attachment and dysfunctional rumination: The mediating role of emotional intelligence abilities. *Personality and Individual Differences*, *53*, 753–758.

Lazarus, R. S. (1999). *Stress and Emotion: A New Synthesis*. New York: Springer.

MacCann, C., Lievens, F., Libbrecht, N., and Roberts, R. D. (2015). Differences between multimedia and text-based assessments of emotion management: An exploration with the multimedia emotion management assessment (MEMA). *Cognition and Emotion*. Epub ahead of print.

Martins, A., Ramalho, N., and Morin, E. (2010). A comprehensive meta-analysis of the relationship between emotional intelligence and health. *Personality and Individual Differences*, *49*, 554–564.

Matthews, G., Deary, I. J., and Whiteman, M. C. (2009). *Personality Traits*, 3rd edn. Cambridge: Cambridge University Press.

Matthews, G., Emo, A. K., Funke, G., Zeidner, M., Roberts, R. D., Costa, P. T., Jr., and Schulze, R. (2006). Emotional intelligence, personality, and task-induced stress. *Journal of Experimental Psychology: Applied*, *12*, 96–107.

Matthews, G., Pérez-González, J.-C., Fellner, A. N., Funke, G. J., Emo, A. K., Zeidner, M., and Roberts, R. D. (2015). Individual differences in facial emotion processing: Trait emotional intelligence, cognitive ability or transient stress? *Journal of Psychoeducational Assessment*, *33*, 68–82.

Matthews, G., Zeidner, M., and Roberts, R. D. (2002). *Emotional Intelligence: Science and Myth*. Cambridge, MA: MIT Press.

Matthews, G., Zeidner, M., and Roberts, R. D. (2004). Seven myths of emotional intelligence. *Psychological Inquiry*, *15*, 179–196.

Matthews, G., Zeidner, M., and Roberts, R. D. (2012). *Emotional Intelligence 101*. New York: Springer.

Mayer, J. D., Caruso, D. R., and Salovey, P. (1999). Emotional intelligence meets traditional standards for an intelligence. *Intelligence*, *27*, 267–298.

Mayer, J. D., Salovey, P., and Caruso, D. R. (2012). The validity of the MSCEIT: Additional analyses and evidence. *Emotion Review*, *4*, 403–408.

Mikolajczak, M., Avalosse, H., Vancorenland, S., Verniest, R., Callens, M., Van Broeck, N. … and Mierop, A. (2015). A nationally representative study of emotional competence and health. *Emotion*, *15*, 653–667.

Mikolajczak, M., Roy, E., Luminet, O., Fillée, C., and de Timary, P. (2007). The moderating impact of emotional intelligence on free cortisol responses to stress. *Psychoneuroendocrinology*, *32*, 1000–1012.

Peña-Sarrionandia, A., Mikolajczak, M., and Gross, J. J. (2015). Integrating emotion regulation and emotional intelligence traditions: A meta-analysis. *Frontiers in Psychology*, *6*, 160.

Pennebaker, J. W., and Ferrell, J. D. (2013). Can expressive writing change emotions? An oblique answer to the wrong question. In D. Hermans, B. Rim, and B. Mesquita (Eds.), *Changing Emotions* (pp. 183–186). New York: Psychology Press.

Petrides, K. V., Furnham, A., and Mavroveli, S. (2007). Trait emotional intelligence: Moving forward in the field of EI. In G. Matthews, M. Zeidner, and R. D. Roberts (Eds.), *The Science of Emotional Intelligence: Knowns and Unknowns* (pp. 151–166). New York: Oxford University Press.

Rivers, S. E., Brackett, M. A., Salovey, P., and Mayer, J. D. (2007). Measuring emotional intelligence as a set of mental abilities. In G. Matthews, M. Zeidner, and R. D. Roberts (Eds.), *The Science of Emotional Intelligence: Knowns and Unknowns* (pp. 230–257). New York: Oxford University Press.

Ruiz-Robledillo, N., and Moya-Albiol, L. (2014). Emotional intelligence modulates cortisol awakening response and self-reported health in caregivers of people with autism spectrum disorders. *Research in Autism Spectrum Disorders*, *8*, 1535–1543.

Saklofske, D. H., Austin, E. J., Galloway, J., and Davidson, K. (2007). Individual difference correlates of health-related behaviours: Preliminary evidence for links between emotional intelligence and coping. *Personality and Individual Differences*, *42*, 491–502.

Salovey, P., Mayer, J. D, Goldman, S., Turvey, C., and Palfai, T. (1995). Emotional attention, clarity, and repair: Exploring emotional intelligence using the Trait Meta-Mood Scale. In J. W. Pennebaker (Ed.), *Emotion, Disclosure, and Health* (pp. 125–154). Washington, DC: American Psychological Association.

Smith, K. B., Profetto-McGrath, J., and Cummings, G. G. (2009), Emotional intelligence and nursing: An integrative literature review. *International Journal of Nursing Studies*, *46*, 1624–1636.

Taylor, S. (2011). Social support: A review. In H. Friedman (Ed.), *Oxford Handbook of Health Psychology* (pp. 189–214). New York: Oxford University Press.

Tolegenova, A. A., Kustubayeva, A. M., and Matthews, G. (2014).Trait meta-mood, gender and EEG response during emotion-regulation. *Personality and Individual Differences*, *65*, 75–80.

Vernon, P. A., Villani, V. C., Schermer, J. A., and Petrides, K. V. (2008). Phenotypic and genetic associations between the big five and trait emotional intelligence. *Twin Research and Human Genetics*, *11*, 524–530.

Wells, A., and Matthews, G. (2015). *Attention and Emotion: A Clinical Perspective* (Classic edn). New York: Psychology Press.

Zeidner, M., Hadar, D., Matthews, G., and Roberts, R. D. (2013a). Personal factors related to compassion fatigue in health professionals. *Anxiety, Stress and Coping*, *26*, 595–609.

Zeidner, M., Kloda, I., and Matthews, G. (2013b). Does dyadic coping mediate the relationship between emotional intelligence (EI) and marital quality? *Journal of Family Psychology*, *27*, 795–805.

Zeidner, M., Matthews, G., and Roberts, R. D. (2009). *What We Know about Emotional Intelligence: How It Affects Learning, Work, Relationships, and Our Mental Health*. Cambridge, MA: MIT Press.

Zeidner, M., Matthews, G., and Roberts, R. D. (2012). The emotional intelligence, health, and well-being nexus: What have we learned and what have we missed? *Applied Psychology: Health and Well-being*, *4*, 1–30.

Zeidner, M., Matthews, G., and Shemesh, D. O. (2015). Cognitive-social sources of wellbeing: Differentiating the roles of coping style, social support and emotional intelligence. *Journal of Happiness Studies* (Dec.). doi:10.1007/s10902-015-9703-z

19

Gender, Workplace Stress, and Coping

Faye K. Cocchiara

Introduction

Today's workplace has become a breeding ground of conflicting job demands that, unless properly addressed, can lead to negative stress or strain. According to the National Institute for Occupational Safety and Health, high levels of job stress have become the rule rather than the exception. One quarter of employees consider their jobs to be the number one source of stress in their lives, with work problems having a stronger association with health complaints than any other life stressor (NIOSH, 1999). More recently, an American Psychological Association survey found that one in three workers in the United States experience chronic work stress. The same survey found that women reported experiencing more acute stress than men (APA, 2013). That women report that they are more stressed out than men is especially troubling, given that women make up more than half of the labor force in the US (e.g., US Bureau of Labor Statistics, 2014) and in 12 European countries (e.g., Kindergan, 2014).

Researchers have devoted a great deal of attention to understanding the stress response and the role it plays in workplace performance and well-being for both men and women (Quick, Quick, Nelson, and Hurrell, 1997). For instance, Davidson and Cooper (1984) investigated the relationship between occupational stressors and manifestations of stress for 696 women managers representing four management levels in a variety of industries. Gyllensten and Palmer (2005) conducted a systematic review of cross-cultural studies investigating the role of gender in the workplace. The purpose of this chapter is to review the extant research on gender and workplace stress to gain a better understanding of the differential experiences that women face in the workplace and their usage of problem-focused and behavioral-focused actions as effective coping strategies. I begin with a review of stressors that women tend to face in the

The Handbook of Stress and Health: A Guide to Research and Practice, First Edition.
Edited by Cary L. Cooper and James Campbell Quick.
© 2017 John Wiley & Sons, Ltd. Published 2017 by John Wiley & Sons, Ltd.

workplace. Next, I discuss commonly used appraisal and coping strategies, both cognitive and behavioral. I conclude the chapter with a review of the preventive stress management framework and suggested preventive stress measures to ensure employee well-being and organizational performance.

Women's Workplace Stressors

Work/Life Balance

Workplace demands, concerns about the economy, family-related problems, financial challenges, and illness all contribute to increased workplace stress. The role of working women has shifted remarkably, with more women taking on positions traditionally held by men. This shift in roles has made women susceptible to the same occupational stressors (prolonged exposure to stressful working conditions) as men. Yet, working women are exposed to a number of workplace stressors that are unique to them. Many of these stressors stem from attempts to achieve balance between multiple and conflicting roles. Indeed, working women have made great strides in this area over the past decades. Marissa Mayer, President and CEO of Yahoo, appears to have mastered the work and family dilemma since announcing her pregnancy with twins and electing to take very little time off and work throughout her maternity leave – as she did during her first pregnancy several years ago (e.g., Bellstrom, 2015). Despite Mayer's apparent success, the fact remains that women continue to experience a heavier burden than men when it comes to balancing work and family.[1] A recent Pew Research study found that mothers with children aged 18 and under were three times as likely as fathers to report that being a working parent made it more difficult for them to advance on the job (Parker, 2015). Groysberg and Abrahams (2014) consider work/life balance an elusive ideal at best and a complete myth at worst.

One of the primary reasons why working women seek balance in their lives is inter-role conflict. Nelson and Quick (2015) define inter-role conflict as "opposing expectations related to two separate roles assumed by the same individual" (p. 105). Therefore, a sick child presents the working mother with a conflict between her role as a mother and caregiver and that of an employee. It is clear that the more roles a person takes on, the higher the potential for stress (Langan-Fox, 1998). Interestingly, having a spouse or partner who also works tends to have little or no effect on a woman's experiences with role conflict (Cleveland, Cordeiero, Fisk, and Mulvaney, 2006). And while men's work consists primarily of paid employment, women's work tends to be diffused between paid work, child care, and housework (e.g., Krantz, Berntsson, and Lundberg, 2005). This diffusion has had a detrimental effect on women's health in the form of increased exhaustion, heart disease, depression, anxiety, and increased and sustained stress (Cocchiara and Bell, 2009).

Multiple roles for women, though challenging, are not entirely harmful. Ruderman, Ohlott, Panzer, and King (2002) found positive outcomes for working women when multiple roles accumulated in such a way that their personal roles benefited their professional ones. For example, the planning skills women managers used to juggle familial responsibilities at home served as good practice for managing multiple responsibilities in the workplace. Ruderman et al. (2002) agree that while fewer roles are better than many, multiple roles can contribute to rather than interfere with good performance of women managers.

Career Progress

A perceived lack of progress toward achieving their career goals presents another source of strain for many working women (Gyllensten and Palmer, 2005; Nelson, Quick, Hitt, and Moesel, 1990). Despite having similar credentials, women managers fail to move up corporate hierarchies as quickly as men managers (Stroh, Brett, and Reilly, 1992). How does failing to achieve one's career goals translate into negative stress? The process begins with one's appraisal of a demand. When a worker is presented with a particular demand (career mobility in this instance) and she perceives that giving in to the demand outweighs the rewards, stress is often the result. For many working women, engaging in what they believe are all the "right" behaviors to achieve higher organizational levels yet failing to achieve a level representative of their efforts can result in frustration and distress. Men also experience frustration and become distressed when they fail to achieve desired organizational levels. However, women tend to face a more challenging organizational climate in the form of glass ceilings and social isolation.

Glass ceilings describe the largely invisible barriers that limit career advancement for women, particularly in large organizations and in male-dominated professions such as engineering and medicine (e.g., Cocchiara and Bell, 2009). This issue goes beyond the notion that fewer women are represented at all levels of management; the term "glass ceiling" suggests that women face increasingly more difficulty gaining access to organizational positions that represent "real" power (Wright and Baxter, 2000). Though invisible, glass ceilings are obvious to the women who experience them and have genuine effects on their career mobility and, consequently, their mental state.

There is sufficient evidence to indicate that even when women reach the highest rungs of leadership in organizations, they are often the first or only ones in their positions, resulting in limited opportunities to form interpersonal relationships or receive the kinds of subtle and informal cues necessary to advance. In essence, these women become statistical "tokens," with their actions (whether positive or negative) being scrutinized more than those in the majority and their personal characteristics contrasted more carefully (Cocchiara and Bell, 2009). Researchers have found a persistent link between social isolation and psychological health, finding that the effect of workplace exclusion on work attitudes and psychological health depended on employee gender. Men were affected more negatively at high levels of workplace exclusion than women at the same levels (Hitlan, Cliffton, and DeSoto, 2006).

Discrimination and Stereotyping

Closely related to the lack of career progress for working women are the issues of discrimination and gender stereotyping. Perceived discrimination has been linked to a variety of outcomes, including psychological distress (e.g., Fischer and Holz, 2007). Being the object of discrimination (perceived or actual) is harmful in many ways. When women perceive they are the object of sex discrimination, they tend to have more negative views of themselves as individuals and as members of the group (Fischer and Holz, 2007). Such negative views can lead to increased psychological distress and feelings of worthlessness, which can lead to reduced performance (e.g., Gaumer, Shah, and Ashley-Cotleur, 2005).

Gender stereotyping is another stressor that affects working women, particularly women leaders. Women in leadership positions often find themselves in a bit of a quandary regarding how they *should* behave in the workplace (Cocchiara and Bell, 2009). Ann Hopkins, a highly successful business manager with Price Waterhouse, is a good example. Hopkins amassed more billable hours than any other prospective partner, bringing in $25 million in new business. Yet, Hopkins was denied partnership on the basis that she wasn't feminine enough (cf. Ryan and Haslam, 2007). However, a woman who is caring, cries, or otherwise shows her "feminine" side is deemed as not possessing the traits associated with being an effective leader (Cocchiara and Bell, 2009). This difference equates to a perceived deficiency in leadership, with the result being discrimination, although sometimes at a subconscious level. When actual behaviors are at odds with expected behaviors that stem from stereotypes, the result can be undue stress for individuals at the center of the conflict.

There is evidence of the difficulties that women in general face with being accepted as leaders and into informal networks in corporate environments. Much less is known about the experiences of women of color and any difficulties that they may experience as a result of the "double-bind" that many women of color experience in organizational environments. For instance, do race and gender intersect to result in higher levels of job stress? Might the experiences of women of color have differential effects on their stress outcomes? Because there is such limited research on this specific topic, I extrapolate from comparable research on minorities to speculate on potential stress outcomes. Indeed, one relevant study found that while half of all black women surveyed reported that they felt accepted as an organizational member, 80 percent of white women felt the same way (Bell and Nkomo, 2001). Gender stereotypes that negatively affect the perceived suitability of women as leaders combine with cultural stereotypes that plague minority women. Perceptions that black women will miss work more often because they are single parents or that Latinas have lower levels of commitment to their organizations due to their familial responsibilities are inaccurate, yet these perceptions can form barriers to their acceptance (Cocchiara, Bell, and Berry, 2006). A recent study investigating the connections between race, gender, and stress on research productivity found that stress due to subtle discrimination had a particularly negative effect for men and women faculty of color on the quality and quantity of scholarly research (Eagan and Garvey, 2015).

Experiencing discrimination and being the object of gender stereotypes are common stressors for many working women. However, it should be pointed out that unhealthy job stress is not an inevitable outcome of workplace pressures for women. Women who work generally experience fewer health-related illnesses such as cardiovascular disease and enjoy increased emotional well-being through challenging jobs, emotional support and encouragement than do unemployed women (Nelson and Burke, 2000). When women are successful at negotiating personal roles, it may lead to positive crossover benefits in the ways that they handle their professional roles, and vice versa (Ruderman et al., 2002).

Demand Appraisal and Coping

Prior to 1995, the samples used in compiling stress research were comprised of only 17 percent females (Taylor et al., 2000). As a result, much of what we know about responding to stress is based on evidence using male samples (Taylor et al., 2000). As discussed earlier and as studies on stress have found, the health risks for working men and women are not evenly distributed between the sexes (Abdel-Khalek, and Maltby, 2009). What is clear from a preponderance of evidence is that there are differences in the coping strategies that men and women use.

Shelley Taylor's research on females' stress responses demonstrated that women are, by design, better equipped for the physical and emotional challenges of life (Taylor et al., 2000). As a result, American women outlive their male counterparts by over half a decade. The female tend-and-befriend capacity provides significant protective armor against the physical and psychological threats that lead to emotional suffering, one key manifestation of distress (Cocchiara, Gavin, Gavin, and Quick, 2014). Whereas males tend to respond to stress and pressures by fighting or fleeing, the female response to stress is much less aggressive and is geared to nurturing and protecting. Taylor et al. (2000) confirms that the female physiology differs from that of males. That physiological difference manifests itself behaviorally as well. In the face of constant stress, females will release high levels of oxytocin, an estrogen-enhanced hormone associated with relaxation and sedation. When men have a particularly stressful day at work, they may withdraw (or "flee") from their families. While the fight-or-flight stress response quickly mobilizes bodily organs to react to stress, it can cause significant damage when the stress is chronic (Parker-Pope, 2007). The response for women is markedly different. Women appear to be at their most nurturing and caring (especially with their family members) on their most stressful days. This "reaching out" behavior by women (tend-and-befriend) under stress extends to relationships outside the immediate family. According to Taylor et al. (2000), women are more likely than men to maintain relationships with other women and seek out support from those relationships, particularly in times of distress. Women derive numerous social benefits by simply living with and caring for others. These benefits do not disappear when women are faced with stress. Rather, they become more essential.

Lazarus and Folkman (1984) developed a widely supported model of stress and coping. Their transactional model proposes an ongoing cognitive appraisal consisting of three processes that take place on the way to the stress outcome, whether detrimental or advantageous. Each process can be regarded as a *pathway*. The first process includes the primary appraisal of the stressor, whether the stressor constitutes a hindrance or a challenge (demand – primary appraisal pathway). Next is a secondary appraisal of the stressor. The secondary appraisal considers the availability and likely success of coping strategies (primary appraisal – secondary appraisal pathway). The final process consists of selecting and deploying the chosen coping strategy (secondary appraisal – coping pathway). See Figure 19.1 for an illustration of the demand–appraisal process.

A recent study tested this stress coping process and found that, as predicted, women differed from men in their perceptions of stress. The women in the study perceived the demand as stressful immediately after their primary appraisal, while the men tended to experience stress once they had evaluated the feasibility of available coping resources for reducing negative stress outcomes (e.g., Watson, Goh, and Sawang, 2011). The researchers noted that the retrospective nature of reporting during the study might have influenced these results and suggested that the women were perhaps more inclined than men to report their initial feelings as they reflected on the stressor. Nevertheless, the combination of primary and secondary appraisals of job demands is crucial for triggering the appropriate coping behaviors (Johnstone and Feeney, 2015).

Two types of coping strategies are available to individuals when faced with demands, problem focused and emotion focused. For instance, an individual who perceives a stressor to be overwhelming and believes she does not have the necessary resources to cope will be more likely to use emotion-focused behaviors that manage the response to the demand. On the other hand, individuals may use problem-focused coping behaviors to manage the demand itself.

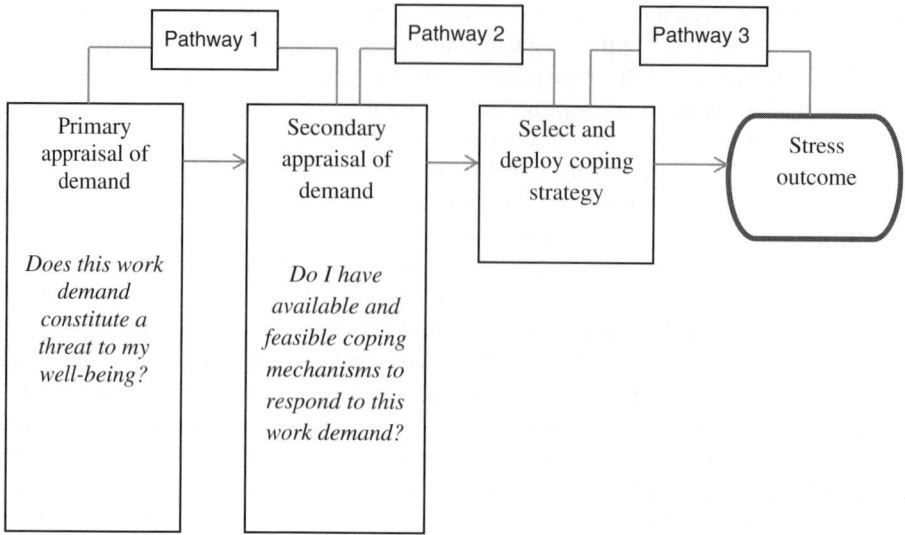

Figure 19.1 Transactional model of stress (based on Lazarus and Folkman, 1984).

This strategy is feasible when an individual appraises the stressor as controllable. Many of the coping strategies that working men and women use were developed early on in life, with women using more emotion-focused coping strategies (e.g., expressing feelings, seeking emotional support, and positive reframing) compared to men (e.g., Davies et al., 2000). However, many working women use problem-focused strategies to cope with their unique workplace demands, including reducing work hours, taking time off from work, telecommuting, and hiring live-in nannies or seeking alternate sources of support. For example, some women executives have even chosen to forgo marriage and children to avoid the pressures of balancing work and family (Groysberg and Abrahams, 2014). See Table 19.1 for sample problem-focused and emotion-focused behaviors that executive women use to manage workplace demands.

Table 19.1 Sample coping strategies for working women

	Problem-focused	Emotion-focused
Behavioral	• Work harder to achieve goals • Seek help from friends and family members • Hire nanny or other caregiver • Limit business travel • Leave the organization	• Vent frustrations to trusted colleagues • Seek professional counseling
Cognitive	• (Re)Prioritize work and nonwork activities • Practice self-motivation • Seek additional strategies for achieving success • Decide when to "unplug" from technology	• Assign special significance to a particular nonwork metric • Redefine professional success • Look for the positive in the current workplace situation

Though some of these strategies have proven beneficial for helping women cope with the immediate stressor, many women report that using these strategies had unintended effects on their careers. A recent Pew Research study found that among women who reduced their work hours to care for a child or another family member, women were twice as likely to say that reducing their hours hurt their career overall. One out of three women who took significant time off from work said that doing so hurt their career also (Parker, 2015). Executive women who have forgone having children or getting married may also experience negative consequences, but not necessarily in the form of career stagnation. For instance, Harvard researchers studied nearly 4,000 high-ranking men and women executives over the course of five years and surveyed 82 executives in a Harvard Business School leadership course to gauge their perceptions about work/life balance relative to their personal and professional success (Groysberg and Abrahams, 2014). One executive, when asked about the sacrifices she made to achieve balance between her work and family, revealed that she made a conscious decision to neither get married nor have children. The repercussions she suffered took another form. Regarding her decision and the aftermath, the leader stated: "People assume that if you don't have kids, then you either can't have kids or else you're a hard-driving bitch. So I haven't had any negative career repercussions, but I've probably been judged personally." As Groysberg and Abrahams (2014) suggest, deliberate choices designed to balance work and family do not guarantee control. Often, the choices that executive women make about their careers are made in concert with a partner or other family members.

Organizational Prevention

Workplace characteristics have an important impact on the types and amount of stress experienced by employees, with negative effects not only on the employees themselves, but also on organizational competitiveness (e.g., Gaumer et al., 2005). Organizational leaders have a responsibility to cultivate and maintain low-stress environments where employees can thrive. Yet, when asked about the level of support their organizations provided them with to help manage stress, just 36 percent of workers felt their organizations provided sufficient resources. Forty-four percent of employees felt their organizations met their mental health needs. With nearly two-thirds of US adults citing work as a significant source of stress, and 35 percent saying they typically feel stressed during the workday, it is in organizations' best interests to provide sufficient resources to help employees face these challenges. According to Norman B. Anderson, then CEO of the American Psychological Association, helping employees deal with workplace stress "isn't just an HR or management issue. The well-being of an organization's workforce is a strategic business imperative that is linked to its performance and success" (APA, 2013).

The work/life balance, limited opportunities, discrimination, and career frustrations discussed earlier have led many women to leave the organizational situation and pursue entrepreneurship. In 2014, nearly 30 percent of all new businesses were women-owned, growing at one and a half times the rate of other small business owners (Center for Women in Business, 2014). Many women have left corporate careers because they feel they've been "pushed out" and believe their talents can best be used (and appreciated) elsewhere (Cocchiara and Bell, 2009). Consider Erica Nicole, who left the corporate world to start *YFS Magazine* – for the "young, fabulous, and self-employed." According to Nicole, "The glass ceiling that once limited a woman's career path has paved a new road towards business ownership, where women can utilize their sharp business acumen while building strong family ties" (MacNeil, 2012). When large proportions of women leave organizations, it not only disrupts their careers, it creates gaps in available talent.

There are many methods that organizations can use to prevent such gaps in human talent. One such method is preventive stress management. Preventive stress management is a philosophy that assigns mutual responsibility to organizations and individuals for promoting health and preventing distress and strain among employees. The preventive stress management framework got its origins from public health practices used in preventive medicine and includes three stages of prevention: primary, secondary, and tertiary (Nelson and Quick, 2015). Primary prevention is designed to eliminate organizational stressors and mitigate the risks of harm from work demands. One of the most challenging aspects of managing work and family is prioritizing among the resources required to perform the different roles for which employees, particularly women, are responsible. Ensuring that roles are clarified and that employees have the ability to negotiate their roles is a primary preventive measure that can have positive results. Allowing flexible work schedules is another primary preventive stress measure that can help workers navigate among numerous and often conflicting roles. Secondary prevention is directed at modifying the individual's or organization's response to the stressors. Women leaders who are in token leadership roles in organizations may benefit from team-building experiences whereby members of the leadership team, both men and women, openly discuss relational issues and concerns that could have a negative impact on organizational and/or unit performance. Tertiary prevention is directed at the symptom. Once the individual is experiencing negative stress outcomes, tertiary preventive measures are designed to "heal" the disease. Many organizations have called on chaplains as spiritual advisors, not to proselytize or push their own religious beliefs, but rather to comfort and provide emotional support. Several years ago, Tyson Foods employed 120 chaplains to serve its 117,000 employees. Tyson executives believed that the services chaplains provided helped reduce employee turnover (Shellenbarger, 2010). Support networks made up of trusted colleagues may also prove invaluable resources during times of emotional crises and help employees weather the difficult times and return to normal functioning.

Summary

Work pressures are quite common in today's workplaces. The fact that 33 percent of employees report experiencing chronic work-related stress is alarming (e.g., APA, 2013) and should serve as a call to action for employers. Chronic stress reduces mental clarity, affecting short-term memory, decision-making, and moods – all necessary for increased productivity (cf. Weber and Shellenbarger, 2013). Though men are certainly not devoid of work-related pressures, women feel especially stuck in organizational situations characterized by increased role conflicts and limited opportunities for advancement. Thirty-two percent of women believe their employers neither appreciate what they do nor provide them with sufficient opportunities to grow in their careers (APA, 2013). Beliefs that their career trajectories are stunted despite increased investments in education and experience only increase perceptions that they are undervalued and underappreciated. Gender stereotypes and discrimination often affect perceptions of women's ability to lead. Viewing women as "not being tough enough to lead" or "too emotional to lead" is not only erroneous but can lead to undue stress for individuals and limited productivity for organizations.

It is well documented that women differ from men in their responses to workplace stress and deploy a variety of coping strategies to respond to the challenges they face, both inside and outside the workplace. It is important that they continue to do so. It is also important that organizations take the necessary actions to mitigate potential stressors on the job. Adopting primary preventive stress management measures to proactively address work demands before they become asymptomatic is one such action.

Note

1. Verizon agreed to pay nearly $5 billion to acquire Yahoo's core assets. At the time of this writing, Mayer had agreed to remain at Yahoo at least through the transition (Fitzpatrick, 2016).

References

Abdel-Khalek, A. M., and Maltby, J. (2009). Differences in anxiety scores of college students from Germany, Spain, the United Kingdom, and the USA. *Psychological Reports, 104*, 624–626.

APA (American Psychological Association) (2013). APA survey finds US employers unresponsive to employee needs. At http://www.apa.org/news/press/releases/2013/03/employee-needs.aspx (accessed July 2016).

Bell, E. L. J. E., and Nkomo, S. M. (2001). *Our Separate Ways: Black and White Women and the Struggle for Professional Identity*. Boston: Harvard Business School Press.

Bellstrom, K. (2015). Marissa can parent however she wants – as long as she sends one message to employees. Fortune.com. At http://fortune.com/2015/09/02/marissa-parent-reassure-employees/ (accessed July 2016).

Center for Women in Business (2014). Women-owned businesses: Carving a new American business landscape. US Chamber of Commerce Foundation. At https://www.uschamber.com/sites/default/files/documents/files/CCFWIB_report_design_final2.pdf (accessed July 2016).

Cleveland, J. N., Cordeiro, B., Fisk, G., and Mulvaney, R. H. (2006). The role of person, spouse, and organizational climate on work-family perceptions. *Irish Journal of Management, 27*(2), 229–253.

Cocchiara, F. K., and Bell, M. P. (2009). Gender and work stress: Unique stressors, unique responses. In C. L. Cooper, J. C. Quick, and M. J. Schabracq (Eds.), *International Handbook of Work and Health Psychology*, 3rd ed. Chichester, UK: Wiley.

Cocchiara, F. K., Bell, M. P., and Berry, D. P. (2006). Latinas and black women: Key factors for a growing proportion of the US workforce. *Equal Opportunities International, 25*, 272–284.

Cocchiara, F. K., Gavin, D. J., Gavin, J. H., and Quick, J. C. (2014). The "right" tools: Stress response lessons from the opposite sex. In A. M. Rossi, J. A. Meurs, and P. L. Perrewé (Eds.), *Improving Employee Health and Well-Being*. Charlotte, NC: Information Age.

Davies, J., McCrae, B. P., Frank, J., Dochnahl, A., Pickering, T., Harrison, B., Zakrzewski, J., and Wilson, K. (2000). Identifying male college students' perceived health needs, barriers to seeking help, and recommendations to help men adopt healthier lifestyles. *Journal of American College Health, 48*(6), 259–267.

Davidson, M. J., and Cooper, C. L. (1984). Occupational stress in female managers: A comparative study. *Journal of Management Studies, 21*, 185–205.

Eagan, M. K., Jr. and Garvey, J. C. (2015). Stressing out: Connecting race, gender, and stress with faculty productivity. *Journal of Higher Education, 86*(6), 923–954.

Fischer, A. R., and Holz, K. B. (2007). Perceived discrimination and women's psychological distress: The roles of collective and personal self-esteem. *Journal of Counseling Psychology, 54*, 154–164.

Fitzpatrick, A. (2016). Marissa Mayer staying at Yahoo despite Verizon takeover. *Time.com, July 25*, 1.

Gaumer, C. J., Shah, A. J., and Ashley-Colteur, C. (2005). Enhancing organizational competitiveness: Causes and effects of stress on women. *Journal of Workplace Behavioral Health, 21*, 31–43.

Groysberg, B., and Abrahams, R. (2014). Manage your work, manage your life. *Harvard Business Review, 92*(3), 58–66.

Gyllensten, K., and Palmer, S. (2005). The role of gender in workplace stress: A critical literature review. *Health Education Journal, 64*, 271–288.

Hitlan, R. T., Cliffton, R. J., and DeSoto, M. (2006). Perceived exclusion in the workplace: The moderating effects of gender on work-related attitudes and psychological health. *North American Journal of Psychology*, *8*(2), 217–236.

Johnstone, M., and Feeney, J. A. (2015). Individual differences in responses to workplace stress: The contribution of attachment theory. *Journal of Applied Social Psychology*, *45*, 412–424.

Kindergan, A. (2014). The participation gap. *TheFinancialist*. Credit Suisse. At https://www.thefinancialist.com/the-participation-gap/ (accessed July 2016).

Krantz, G., Berntsson, L., and Lundberg, U. (2005). Total workload, work stress and perceived symptoms in Swedish male and female white-collar employees. *European Journal of Public Health*, *15*(2), 209–214.

Langan-Fox, J. (1998). Women's careers and occupational stress. *International Review of Industrial and Organizational Psychology*, *13*, 273–302.

Lazarus, R. S., and Folkman, S. (1984). *Stress, Appraisal, and Coping*. New York: Springer.

MacNeil, N. (2012). Entrepreneurship is the new women's movement. Forbes.com. At http://www.forbes.com/sites/work-in-progress/2012/06/08/entrepreneurship-is-the-new-womens-movement/ (accessed July 2016).

Nelson, D. L., and Burke, R. J. (2000). Women executives: Health, stress, and success. *Academy of Management Review*, *10*, 206–218.

Nelson, D. L., and Quick, J. C. (2015). *ORGB 4*. Stamford, CT: Cengage Learning.

Nelson, D. L., Quick, J. C., Hitt, M. A., and Moesel, D. (1990). Politics, lack of career progress, and work/home conflict: Stress and strain for working women. *Sex Roles*, *23*, 169–183.

NIOSH (National Institute for Occupational Safety and Health) (1999). *Stress … at Work*. DHHS Publication No. 99-101. At http://www.cdc.gov/niosh/docs/99-101/default.html (accessed July 2016).

Parker, K. (2015). Despite progress, women still bear heavier load than men in balancing work and family. Pew Research Center. At http://www.pewresearch.org/fact-tank/2015/03/10/women-still-bear-heavier-load-than-men-balancing-work-family/ (accessed July 2016).

Parker-Pope, T. (2007). The man problem. *Wall Street Journal*, Apr. 24, D1–D3.

Quick, J. C., Quick, J. D., Nelson, D. L., and Hurrell, J. J., Jr. (1997). *Preventive Stress Management in Organizations*, Washington, DC: American Psychological Association.

Ruderman, M. N., Ohlott, P. J., Panzer, K., and King, S. N. (2002). Benefits of multiple roles for managerial women. *Academy of Management Journal*, *45*(2), 369–386.

Ryan, M. R., and Haslam, S. A. (2007). The glass cliff: Exploring the dynamics surrounding the appointment of women to precarious leadership positions. *Academy of Management Review*, *32*, 549–572.

Shellenbarger, S. (2010). Praying with the office chaplain. *Wall Street Journal*, June 23. At http://www.wsj.com/articles/SB10001424052748704853404575322742500015642 (accessed July 2016).

Stroh, L. K., Brett, J. J., and Reilly, A. H. (1992). All the right stuff: A comparison of female and male managers' career progression. *Journal of Applied Psychology*, *77*, 251–260.

Taylor, S. E., Klein, L. C., Lewis, B. P., Gruenewald, T. L., Gurung, R. A. R., and Updegraff, J. A. (2000). Biobehavioral responses to stress in females: Tend-and-befriend, not fight-or-flight. *Psychological Review*, *107*, 411–429.

US Bureau of Labor Statistics (2014). Women in the labor force: A databook. Report 1049. At http://www.bls.gov/opub/reports/cps/womenlaborforce_2013.pdf (accessed July 2016).

Watson, S. B., Goh, Y. W., and Sawang, S. (2011). Gender influences on the work-related stress-coping process. *Journal of Individual Differences*, *32*(1), 39–46.

Weber, L., and Shellenbarger, S. (2013). Office stress: His vs. hers. *Wall Street Journal*, Mar. 5. At http://www.wsj.com/articles/SB10001424127887324678604578340332290414820 (accessed July 2016).

Wright, E. O., and Baxter, J. (2000). The glass ceiling hypothesis: A reply to critics. *Gender and Society*, *14*, 814–821.

20

Socioeconomic Inequities in Health

The Power of Social Relationships

Catherine A. Heaney and Annekatrin Hoppe

Introduction

Lower socioeconomic status (SES) has been consistently associated with poor health (Adler and Rehkopf, 2008). Initial explanations for this association focused on the negative health effects of material deprivation. However, as it became clear that the association between SES and health was a linear dose-response gradient rather than solely an effect of poverty, psychosocial explanations for the relationship were posited (Siegrist and Marmot, 2004).

One such explanation has been put forth by Gallo and her colleagues (Gallo, 2009; Matthews, Gallo, and Taylor, 2010) as the reserve capacity model. This model suggests that people with lower SES experience poorer health because they are likely to experience high levels of psychosocial stress and to have few psychosocial resources at their disposal to enable effective coping and successful prevention of subsequent stress. In this model, resources are conceptualized as both intrapersonal psychological factors (e.g., self-esteem, self-efficacy, optimism, control perceptions) and interpersonal social factors (e.g., supportive social relationships, opportunities to participate in decision-making or exercise control). This model has its intellectual roots in conservation of resources theory (Hobfoll, 1988), which posits that people "strive to obtain and protect their personal and social resources and that they experience stress when circumstances threaten or result in loss of these valued states" (Hobfoll, Freedy, Lane, and Geller, 1990, p. 466).

Research that has explicitly tested the reserve capacity model has tended to look at an aggregate of personal and social resources (Matthews and Gallo, 2011). However, understanding the role of specific resources and identifying those that are most likely to effectively reduce socioeconomic health inequities could greatly aid the development of evidence-based interventions. According to Hobfoll et al. (1990), social support can contribute to one's reservoir

The Handbook of Stress and Health: A Guide to Research and Practice, First Edition.
Edited by Cary L. Cooper and James Campbell Quick.
© 2017 John Wiley & Sons, Ltd. Published 2017 by John Wiley & Sons, Ltd.

of resources in two important ways: (1) by enhancing an individual's personal resources of self-esteem, mastery or control over important life events and transitions, and a view of oneself as deserving of love and care, and (2) by allowing individuals to acquire new resources through resource passageways – the routes through which resources flow between individuals. Indeed, a large literature describes the role of social relationships in promoting good health and protecting against the deleterious effects of stress on health (Berkman and Glass, 2000). In addition, there are various potential points of intervention for improving social relationships to make them more health promoting (Heaney and Israel, 2008), and many of the strategies for improving social relationships are highly accessible to low SES communities. Thus, supportive social relationships are an excellent candidate as a resource that might play an important role in reducing socioeconomic health inequities.

In this chapter we will:

1. Set forth a conceptual framework for studying SES, social relationships and health;
2. Review the evidence for an association between SES and social relationships;
3. Assess the extent to which social relationships play a role in the association between SES and health;
4. Present a case example of how social relationships can positively impact the health and well-being of immigrant low-wage workers and potentially reduce health inequities experienced by these workers; and
5. Suggest future directions for research and intervention.

Conceptual Framework

The conceptual framework presented in Figure 20.1 is deceptively simple. It suggests that SES influences health both directly and indirectly through its effects on social relationships. The

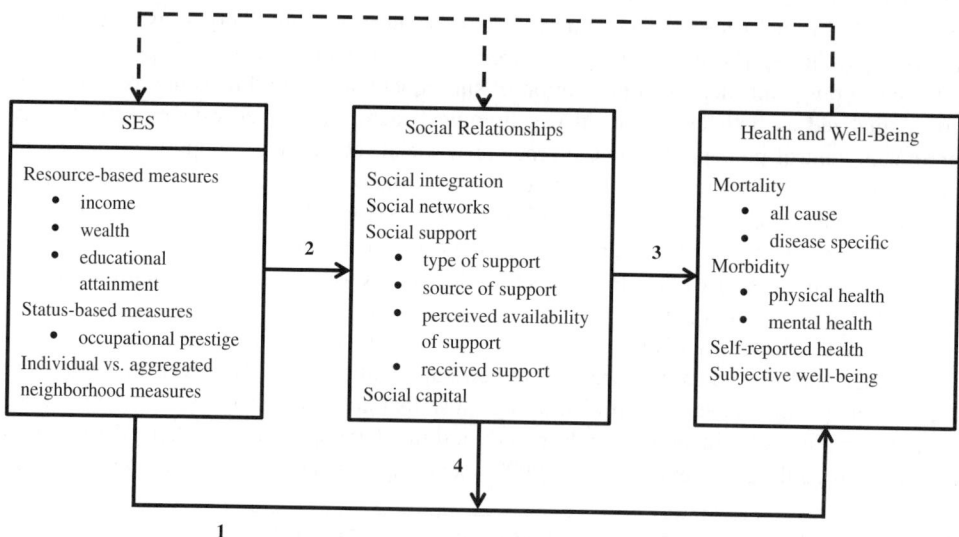

Figure 20.1 Conceptual framework linking SES, social relationships, and health.

complexity of the framework lies in the multiple concepts and indicators within each of the overarching concepts.

Socioeconomic status   Socioeconomic status refers to an individual's or group's position within a hierarchical social structure. Sometimes one's position in the hierarchy is resource based and measured by income, wealth, or educational attainment. Other times, status in the hierarchy is based on prestige or the extent to which others value and admire your position. Measures of occupational prestige are a good example of this type of indicator of SES (Fujishiro, Xu, and Gong, 2010). Resource-based indicators of SES can be measured objectively (e.g., how much money is in your bank account, how many years of schooling you have completed, or what your salary is) or subjectively (e.g., personal perceptions of economic deprivation). Prestige or status based measures can be measured through one's own perceptions (e.g., where you think you stand in the social hierarchy) or through the aggregated perceptions of others (e.g., what value or status others assign to your occupation). The MacArthur SES Ladder Scale is an example of a measure of an individual's personal assessment of his or her own social status (Operario, Adler, and Williams, 2004).

In addition to an individual's social standing, the SES of their neighborhood or community can be assessed. Neighborhood SES can have effects on health in various ways, including influencing opportunities to purchase healthy foods, engage in physical activity, and navigate one's community safely (Diez Roux and Mair, 2010). A low SES individual might live in a more affluent neighborhood. Research has explored the interaction of individual SES with neighborhood SES, addressing the question of whether low SES individuals in higher SES neighborhoods experience better health and well-being than do low SES individuals in low SES neighborhoods (see, e.g., Stafford and Marmot, 2003). Although there is ample evidence that various measures of SES are only moderately correlated and cannot be used interchangeably (Braveman et al., 2005; Geyer, Hemstrom, Peter, and Vagero, 2006), there has been little systematic consideration of when and why particular indicators should be prioritized over others.

Social relationships   Several key terms have been used in studies of the potential health-enhancing components of social relationships (Berkman and Glass, 2000). The term *social integration* has been used to refer to the existence of social relationships and to indicate the extent to which an individual is integrated into the social fabric of their community. The term *social network* refers to the web of social relationships within which individuals live. Social networks can be described in terms of the characteristics of specific social ties (e.g., the extent to which a relationship is characterized by emotional closeness (intensity or strength) or the extent to which resources and support are both given and received in a relationship (reciprocity)) and in terms of the characteristics of the network as a whole (e.g., the extent to which network members are similar in terms of demographic characteristics such as age, race, and socioeconomic status (homophily), or the extent to which network members know and interact with each other (density)) (Heaney and Israel, 2008; Smith and Christakis, 2008). The term *social capital* focuses on the value of social networks, taking into account the benefits that arise from the trust and reciprocity found within social networks (Kawachi, Subramanian, and Kim, 2008).

Many social processes unfold through social networks, including the provision of *social support*. Social support has been defined in many ways. According to the classic typology first put forth by sociologist James House (1981), social support refers to four categories of supportive behaviors: *emotional support*, which involves the provision of empathy, love, trust, and caring; *instrumental support*, which involves the provision of tangible aid and services; *informational support*, which is the provision of advice, suggestions, and information; and *appraisal support*, which involves the provision of information that is useful for self-evaluation purposes (i.e., constructive feedback and affirmation). These types of support can be provided by different sources (e.g., family, friends, supervisors, and formal helpers). Research has suggested that the actual provision (or receipt) of social support can be differentiated from the perceived availability of support and may have somewhat different effects on health and well-being (Wethington and Kessler, 1986).

Health and well-being   Many indicators of health have been shown to be associated with SES. All-cause mortality, cause-specific mortality (such as deaths related to cardiovascular disease), and the incidence, prevalence and severity of certain diseases (both physical ailments and mental disorders) have all been linked with SES (Adler and Rehkopf, 2008; Muntaner, Eaton, Miech, and O'Campo, 2004). Even though the World Health Organization's definition of health as "a state of complete physical, mental and social well-being and not merely the absence of disease or infirmity" was first put forward nearly 70 years ago (WHO, 2006, preamble), much of the research in this arena has focused on mortality and disease-related outcomes. However, some studies have examined (and found) associations between SES and measures of health that do not rely on the presence or absence of disease. For example, self-rated health (Ahnquist, Wamala, and Lindstrom, 2012; Fujishiro et al., 2010) and subjective overall health functioning as assessed by the SF-36 questionnaire (Marmot, Bosma, Hemingway, Brunner, and Stansfeld, 1997) or the GHQ-12 (Ahnquist et al., 2012) have been associated with an individual's SES.

Let us return to Figure 20.1. For our purposes, the direct effect (arrow #1) represents any association between SES and health that is not explained by some aspect of social relationships. Thus, this arrow includes the influence of material resources, psychosocial stress, and the loss or gain of resources other than those provided through social relationships. The indirect relationship of SES on health suggests that people of different SES vary in terms of the quantity or quality of their social relationships (arrow #2) and that by meeting basic human needs for companionship, intimacy, a sense of belonging, and reassurance of one's worth as a person, as well as providing important tangible and instrumental resources for living, these social relationships influence health and well-being (arrow #3). The combination of arrow #2 and arrow #3 at least partially explains (or mediates) the overall association between SES and health.

Social relationships may also moderate the association between SES and health (arrow #4). One explanation for this effect relies on the strong evidence for the importance of social relationships in buffering the negative effect of stress on health (Cohen and Wills, 1985; Thoits, 2011). Some research suggests that people of low SES experience higher levels of psychosocial stress than do those with high SES (see, e.g., Lantz, House, Mero, and Williams, 2005). Thus, it is a small step forward to suggest that social relationships may be a more important protective factor against poor health for those of lower SES because it is needed to help buffer against the excess stress being experienced. Another explanation for a potential moderating effect of social relationships is that people with lower SES do not have access to other types of resources (e.g., money to prevent or solve a problem) or opportunities (e.g., opportunities to participate in work-related decisions or to set community agendas) that might help reduce stress or the negative effects of stress on health. Thus, the resource of social relationships may be of particular importance to those with low SES.

SES and Social Relationships

There are various explanations for why the quantity and quality of people's social relationships may vary across social economic strata. The economic deprivation perspective suggests that a scarcity of resources leads to a lesser availability of social support and other social network resources. In this perspective, lower SES individuals are engaged in trying to "make ends meet" and may have less time and fewer opportunities to cultivate strong social relationships. Within a low SES community, scarce resources may get depleted and social network members cannot mobilize in response to an individual member's need (Mickelson and Kubzansky, 2003). On the other hand, socially disadvantaged groups may place strong emphasis on providing support to kin and other close associates because more formal sources of support are not available.

In the United States, immigrants and members of ethnic or racial minorities tend to be overrepresented among those with lower SES (Bureau of Labor Statistics, 2014). A cultural perspective suggests that the cultures of these low SES immigrants and minorities may highly value certain types of social relationships (Mickelson and Kubzansky, 2003). For example, there is some evidence that Mexican immigrants to the US tend to have large family networks through which much social support is exchanged (Almeida, Molnar, Kawachi, and Subramanian, 2009).

In a recent review of social relations and health, J. B. Turner and Turner (2013) state that the evidence for the social patterning of social support is "sparse and variable" (p. 347). However, in general, the evidence supports the notion that people of lower SES are likely to have smaller social networks that provide less social support than do those of people with higher SES. For example, among a sample of adults in Canada, a positive linear relationship was found between SES and perceived social support aggregated across various sources of support (R. J. Turner and Marino, 1994). In Finland, adults in manual occupations (considered to be lower status occupations) were less likely to be satisfied with the social support available to them than were adults in nonmanual occupations (Huurre, Eerola, Rahkonen, and Aro, 2007). And in a large study in France, income level was associated with several indicators of social isolation and lack of social integration. Those with less income were more likely to have felt alone on the previous day, have no friends, not be a member of a club, and to live alone than were those with more income (Heritage, Wilkinson, Grimaud, and Pickett, 2008).

Some studies found that the social patterning of social relationships differed depending on the social relationship concept measured and/or the indicator of SES used. In one US study, social support from friends was higher in high SES groups but support from family did not differ by SES (Almeida et al., 2009). In another US study, education and social support were positively related, but income and social support were not significantly related (Ross and Mirowsky, 1989).

In some of the studies that found a relationship between SES and social relationships, a threshold association was found, with the lowest SES group differing from all other groups. For example, among adults in a US national representative sample, those who earned less than $20,000 a year (in 1990–2) reported having less contact with friends, receiving less social support, and experiencing more negative social interactions than did members of all other income groups (Mickelson and Kubzansky, 2003). Other studies have found a more linear gradient (see, e.g., Heritage et al., 2008; R. J. Turner and Marino, 1994). In one German study, both types of associations were found, with the shape of the association (threshold versus linear) varying across the social relationship concepts being measured and SES indicators used (i.e., income versus education) (Weyers et al., 2008). When education was used as the SES indicator, people in the lowest educational attainment group were more likely to experience a lack of instrumental support and a lack of emotional support than were those in the highest educational attainment group. People in the middle two educational groups did not differ from the high educational group, thus indicating a threshold effect. However, when income was used as the SES indicator, a linear gradient relationship was found between SES and these two types of support. A measure of social integration reflected a threshold effect across both educational strata and income strata, with members of the lowest groups more likely to be socially isolated than those in the highest SES groups.

The associations between SES and social relationships also vary across demographic subgroups defined by gender or ethnicity. In the Whitehall II study of civil service workers in the United Kingdom, men exhibited a consistent positive relationship between occupational rank and various indicators of frequency of contact with social network members, social support, and fewer negative social interactions. Women, on the other hand, did not experience any differences in emotional support or in negative social interactions across occupational ranks. And women in the lower ranks were more likely to be married and reported receiving *more* instrumental support than did women in the higher occupational ranks (Stringhini et al., 2012). A US study found differences based on ethnicity and race. Latinos of higher SES reported less familial support than their lower SES counterparts, but this was not true for African Americans, Caucasians, or Asian Americans (Almeida et al., 2009).

To summarize, the literature describes a complex relationship between SES and social relationships. As stated previously, people of lower SES tend to be less socially integrated (and more prone to social isolation) and to be less satisfied with the social support that is available to them. However, the magnitude and direction of these associations vary across study populations, indicators of SES, and aspects of social relationships being investigated. This variation across study results suggests that different underlying mechanisms or explanations for associations between SES and social relationships may be at work.

SES, Social Relationships, and Health

Mediating Effects

Given the variations found in the results linking SES and aspects of social relationships, it is not surprising that we find similar inconsistencies in the results of analyses exploring a potential mediating role for social relationships in the association between SES and health. Matthews et al. (2010) reviewed ten studies examining this mediating effect. Four studies found no effects. Six studies found some mediating effects, but with results varying across health outcomes, types of social relationship measures, and sociodemographic groups. For example, in one study social support reduced the association between SES and the incidence of coronary heart disease for men but increased it for women (Marmot et al., 1997). The strength of the mediation effect across studies varied, with social relationships reducing the association between SES and the health outcome by 14–37 percent (Matthews et al., 2010). The studies utilized various health outcomes but are too few in number to discern a pattern or to identify health outcomes for which the association with SES might be more strongly influenced by social relationship factors.

Other relevant studies not included in the review described above also show inconsistent results. Using data from the Whitehall II cohort study, Stringhini et al. (2012) found that marital status and the frequency of contact with social network members explained 27 percent of the association between SES and all-cause mortality among men in the study. However, similar patterns were not found among the women. In a longitudinal study investigating the relationship between SES and depression, little evidence was found for a mediating effect of social relationships (Huurre et al., 2007). In a longitudinal study conducted in Germany, the odds ratios for experiencing poor or very poor self-rated health across SES groups were reduced by between 2 and 27 percent when social relationships were added to regression models using SES indicators to predict self-reported health (Vonneilich et al., 2012). All of the odds ratios across the SES groups remained significant even after all of the measures of aspects of social relationships (social integration, instrumental support, and emotional support) were included in the models, indicating that mediation was only partial at best. The magnitude of the mediating effects varied depending on the measures of SES and social relationships being entered into the models. The biggest decreases in the odds of reporting poor health when social relationship variables were included in the models were found among those in the lowest SES group (Vonneilich et al., 2012).

Moderating Effects

While the evidence for mediational effects is far from consistent, aspects of social relationships do appear to moderate the effect of SES on health. Among the six studies reviewed, five found that people in low SES groups and with low social support (or poorer social integration) were consistently at the greatest risk for poor health (Ahnquist et al., 2012; Heritage et al., 2008; Huurre et al., 2007; Sun, Rehnberg, and Meng, 2009; Vonneilich et al., 2011). The interactions of SES and social relationships were not always statistically significant, but were consistently indicating that poor social relationships were more strongly associated with poor health outcomes among those of lower SES. For example, Huurre et al. (2007) found that dissatisfaction with the social support provided to them was more strongly associated with depression among women in lower status occupations as compared to women in higher status occupations. As another example, Heritage et al. (2008) found that feeling lonely increased the likelihood of reporting being in poor health to a greater extent among those with low incomes as compared to those with higher incomes. And in a Swedish study, those who experienced economic deprivation and experienced low social participation were at significantly higher risk of poor health than would be expected from simply the additive effects of each predictor (Ahnquist et al., 2012).

The exception to this pattern stems from a prospective analysis of a French cohort of employees in a large utility company (Melchior, Berkman, Niedhammer, Chea, and Goldberg, 2003). In this study, the effect of low social support on self-reported health was strongest among men in high status occupations rather than in low status occupations. Among women, the effect of social support on health did not differ across occupational status groups.

Case example: Supervisor Support among Low-Wage Immigrant Workers

The literature summarized above suggests the potential importance of narrowly defining the study population and carefully choosing the indicators of SES and the measures of social relationships when investigating the associations among SES, social relationships, and health. In this section, we will present a case example of how social support can positively impact the health and well-being of a low status group, namely low-wage immigrant workers. We focus on a specific context, the work setting, and on social support from one source, the supervisor.

By definition, low-wage workers occupy low socioeconomic positions by virtue of their low incomes. They also tend to have lower educational attainment than higher paid workers (Capps, Fortuny, and Fix, 2007). In addition, a large proportion of low-wage workers in developed countries are immigrants (Bureau of Labor Statistics, 2014; Gautie and Schmitt, 2010), and immigrant workers often have lower social status compared to their native-born counterparts (Hoppe, Heaney, and Fujishiro, 2010; Bureau of Labor Statistics, 2015). Ridgeway (1991) explains these differences in social status as follows: If groups are distinguished by nominal features (e.g., ethnicity or being an immigrant) and if one group has better access to resources than others (e.g., Caucasians in the US or the dominant racial/ethnic group in any society), then the defining feature of the group (e.g., Caucasian) becomes a status marker.

A core social resource in the work setting is supervisor support (Luchman and González-Morales, 2013). While the specific behaviors and characteristics of supportive supervisors are still being identified, supervisors who help employees accomplish their tasks (instrumental support) and who listen to employees' concerns and issues (emotional support) are important social resources for employees. Low-wage workers tend to experience less supervisor support than do higher SES workers (Huurre et al., 2007; Morris, Conrad, Marcantonio, Marks, and Ribisl, 1999; Sundquist, Östergren, Sundquist, and Johansson, 2003). More specifically, the Sundquist et al. (2003) study revealed that within the same occupational category of low-wage workers, the lower status group of immigrant workers experienced less supervisor support than did workers who were native Swedes. Although not all studies demonstrate a relationship between being a low-wage worker and experiencing low levels of supervisor support (Simmons and Swanberg, 2009), many compelling, well-conducted studies have consistent results supporting this association.

While supervisor support may be less available to low-wage immigrant workers, several studies have shown that it is a job resource of particular benefit for this group (Hoppe, 2011; Hoppe et al., 2010). For example, in a study of Latino and white low-wage warehouse workers in the United States, supervisor support buffered the negative effect of work stressors on well-being among the Latino immigrant workers, but not among the white workers (Hoppe et al., 2010). Likewise, supervisor support helped immigrant workers in Germany to cope with work stressors and reduce the negative effect of these stressors on well-being. This buffering function of supervisor support was significantly stronger for the immigrants than for the native German employees (Hoppe, 2011). Finally, the same protective function of supervisor support was found among Russian immigrant workers in Israel; the positive effect of supervisor support on well-being was stronger for immigrant workers than for native Israeli employees who worked in similar jobs (Toker, Hoppe, Schachler, and Ziegler, 2015). These consistent findings of stronger direct and moderating effects of supervisor support among immigrant workers across countries and occupations give us reason to believe that supervisor support is an important resource for maintaining health and well-being among immigrant workers of low socioeconomic status.

The protective function of supervisor support for the well-being of low-wage immigrant workers may be key for designing health-promoting and stress-reducing interventions for these workers. According to Hobfoll et al. (1990), social relationships are continuously developing and can be changed for the better. Furthermore, designing interventions for the workplace can be especially valuable for immigrant low-wage workers who are a population generally hard to reach. Given that workers spend many of their waking hours at the workplace, the workplace provides a high impact lever for change (Stokols, 1996).

Interventions to enhance supervisor support should focus on training health-promoting supervisor behaviors that cover the four types of social support (Heaney, 2014): (1) providing positive feedback when appropriate (appraisal support), (2) offering assistance and guidance when needed (instrumental support), (3) communicating information that is important for the job (informational support), and (4) showing care and concern for employee well-being (emotional support). In addition, the specific cultural norms of the workplace and the employees need to be taken into consideration as supervisors attempt to engage in more supportive behavior. Whereas some employees will appreciate a supervisor who asks about and listens to their personal problems, others may consider this to be intrusive and inappropriate. In some cultures keeping distance from one's supervisor or clearly separating work and private work life is the preferred norm (Uhlmann, Heaphy, Ashford, Zhu, and Sanchez-Burks, 2013).

Future Directions

In their 2010 review of the extent to which psychosocial factors mediate the association between SES and health, Matthews et al. (2010) expressed surprise about "how much there is yet to be learned" (p. 168). Our more focused review of the role of social relationships in understanding SES health disparities lends itself to similar surprise. While general theories such as the reserve capacity model (Gallo, 2009) or conservation of social resources theory (Hobfoll et al., 1990) offer guidance in positing hypotheses about associations among SES, social relationships, and health, each of the three concepts is so highly complex and multifaceted that it is likely that different mechanisms are operating in different contexts and with different study populations.

One implication is that measures of SES and of structural and functional aspects of social relationships should be selected and interpreted in concert with posited, plausible underlying mechanisms or explanatory pathways for the context and population being studied. Given the importance of subjective assessments of SES in predicting health (Adler and Rehkopf, 2008; Operario et al., 2004), the associations between more objective measures of SES and subjective social status measures should be further explored in order to identify conditions under which income, educational attainment, and occupation have varying magnitudes of influence on subjective assessments of status.

Another implication of the context-specific results in the literature is that we should revisit the question first posed by James House (1981) in thinking about the potential health-promoting roles of social relationships: *Who should provide what to whom (and when)?* The case example of the immigrant low-wage workers is illustrative here. Supervisor support, an important social resource for workers in general, was frequently found to be (1) less often experienced or received by low-wage immigrant workers and (2) more strongly associated with health and well-being for these workers than for their native-born counterparts. Thus, a specific source of support, the supervisor, has been identified that is likely to be an effective target of intervention for reducing health disparities. Identifying the structural and functional aspects of social relationships that are lacking or scarce among members of specific low SES groups and assessing the potential health-promoting role of these social relationship characteristics if they are more adequately available will enhance our understanding of how social relationships can help to reduce SES-related health disparities.

Lastly, there is a dearth of rigorous intervention research targeting the social networks of low SES communities or subgroups. Only through the development and evaluation of evidence-based social network interventions will we be able to fully assess the extent to which enhanced social relationships can reduce SES-related health disparities.

References

Adler, N. E., and Rehkopf, D. H. (2008). US disparities in health: Descriptions, causes, and mechanisms. *Annual Review of Public Health, 29*, 235–252. doi:10.1146/annurev.publhealth.29.020907.090852

Ahnquist, J., Wamala, S. P., and Lindstrom, M. (2012). Social determinants of health: A question of social or economic capital? Interaction effects of socioeconomic factors on health outcomes. *Social Science and Medicine, 74*(6), 930–939. doi:10.1016/j.socscimed.2011.11.026

Almeida, J., Molnar, B. E., Kawachi, I., and Subramanian, S. V. (2009). Ethnicity and nativity status as determinants of perceived social support: Testing the concept of familism. *Social Science and Medicine, 68*(10), 1852–1858. doi:10.1016/j.socscimed.2009.02.029

Berkman, L. F., and Glass, T. (2000). Social integration, social networks, social support, and health. In B. L.F. and K. I. (Eds.), *Social Epidemiology* (pp. 137–173). New York: Oxford University Press.

Braveman, P. A., Cubbin, C., Egerter, S., Chideya, S., Marchi, K. S., Metzler, M., and Posner, S. (2005). Socioeconomic status in health research: One size does not fit all. *Journal of the American Medical Association, 294*(22), 2879–2888. doi:10.1001/jama.294.22.2879

Bureau of Labor Statistics (2014). Employed persons by occupation, race, Hispanic or Latino ethnicity, and sex. US Department of Labor. At www.bls.gov/cps/cpsaat11.htm (accessed July 2016).

Bureau of Labor Statistics (2015). Labor force characteristics of foreign-born workers summary. US Department of Labor. At http://www.bls.gov/news.release/forbrn.nr0.htm (accessed July 2016).

Capps, R., Fortuny, K., and Fix, M. (2007). Trends in the low-wage immigrant labor force, 2000–2005. At http://www.urban.org/research/publication/trends-low-wage-immigrant-labor-force-2000-2005 (accessed July 2016).

Cohen, S., and Wills, T. A. (1985). Stress, social support, and the buffering hypothesis. *Psychological Bulletin, 98*(2), 310–357.

Diez Roux, A. V., and Mair, C. (2010). Neighborhoods and health. *Annals of the New York Academy of Sciences, 1186*, 125–145. doi:10.1111/j.1749-6632.2009.05333.x

Fujishiro, K., Xu, J., and Gong, F. (2010). What does "occupation" represent as an indicator of socioeconomic status? Exploring occupational prestige and health. *Social Science and Medicine, 71*(12), 2100–2107. doi:10.1016/j.socscimed.2010.09.026

Gallo, L. C. (2009). The reserve capacity model as a framework for understanding psychosocial factors in health disparities. *Applied Psychology: Health and Well-Being, 1*(1), 62–72. doi:10.1111/j.1758-0854.2008.01000.x

Gautie, J., and Schmitt, J. (2010). *Low-Wage Work in the Wealthy World*. New York: Russell Sage Foundation.

Geyer, S., Hemstrom, O., Peter, R., and Vagero, D. (2006). Education, income and occupational class cannot be used interchangeably in social epidemiology: Empirical evidence against a common practice. *Journal of Epidemiology and Community Health, 60*, 804–810.

Heaney, C. A. (2014). Social relationships: Harnessing their potential to promote health. In M. P. O'Donnell (Ed.), *Health Promotion in the Workplace*, 4th edn. (pp. 615–634). Troy, MI: American Journal of Health Promotion.

Heaney, C. A., and Israel, B. (2008). Social networks and social support. In K. Glanz, B. K. Rimer, and K. Viswanath (Eds.), *Health Behavior and Health Education: Theory, Research and Practice*, 4th edn. (pp. 189–210). San Francisco: Jossey-Bass.

Heritage, Z., Wilkinson, R., Grimaud, O., and Pickett, K. (2008). Impact of social ties on self-reported health in France: Is everyone affected equally? *BMC Public Health*, *8*(1), 243–250. doi:10.1186/1471-2458-8-243

Hobfoll, S. E. (1988). *The Ecology of Stress*. New York: Hemisphere.

Hobfoll, S. E., Freedy, J., Lane, C., and Geller, P. (1990). Conservation of social resources: Social support resource theory. *Journal of Social and Personal Relationships*, *7*(4), 465–478. doi:10.1177/0265407590074004

Hoppe, A. (2011). Psychosocial working conditions and well-being among immigrant and German low wage workers. *Journal of Occupational Health Psychology*, *16*(2), 187–201. doi:10.1037/a0021728

Hoppe, A., Heaney, C. A., and Fujishiro, K. (2010). Stressors, resources, and well-being among Latino and white warehouse workers in the United States. *American Journal of Industrial Medicine*, *53*(3), 252–263. doi:10.1002/ajim.20752

House, J. S. (1981). *Work Stress and Social Support*. Reading, MA: Addison-Wesley.

Huurre, T., Eerola, M., Rahkonen, O., and Aro, H. (2007). Does social support affect the relationship between socioeconomic status and depression? A longitudinal study from adolescence to adulthood. *Journal of Affective Disorders*, *100*(1–3), 55–64. doi:10.1016/j.jad.2006.09.019

Kawachi, I., Subramanian, S. V., and Kim, D. (2008). *Social Capital and Health: A Decade of Progress and Beyond*. New York: Springer.

Lantz, P. M., House, J. S., Mero, R. P., and Williams, D. R. (2005). Stress, life events, and socioeconomic disparities in health: Results from the Americans' Changing Lives Study. *Journal of Health and Social Behavior*, *46*(3), 274–288. doi:10.1177/002214650504600305

Luchman, J. N., and González-Morales, M. G. (2013). Demands, control, and support: A meta-analytic review of work characteristics interrelationships. *Journal of Occupational Health Psychology*, *18*(1), 37–52. doi:10.1037/a0030541

Marmot, M. G., Bosma, H., Hemingway, H., Brunner, E., and Stansfeld, S. (1997). Contribution of job control and other risk factors to social variations in coronary heart disease incidence. *Lancet*, *350*, 235–239.

Matthews, K. A., and Gallo, L. C. (2011). Psychological perspectives on pathways linking socioeconomic status and physical health. *Annual Review of Psychology*, *62*, 501–530. doi:10.1146/annurev.psych.031809.130711

Matthews, K. A., Gallo, L. C., and Taylor, S. E. (2010). Are psychosocial factors mediators of socioeconomic status and health connections? *Annals of the New York Academy of Sciences*, *1186*, 146–173.

Melchior, M., Berkman, L. F., Niedhammer, I., Chea, M., and Goldberg, M. (2003). Social relations and self-reported health: A prospective analysis of the French Gazel cohort. *Social Science and Medicine*, *56*(8), 1817–1830. doi:10.1016/S0277-9536(02)00181-8

Mickelson, K. D., and Kubzansky, L. D. (2003). Social distribution of social support: The mediating role of life events. *American Journal of Community Psychology*, *32*(3–4), 265–281. doi:10.1023/B:AJCP.0000004747.99099.7e

Morris, W. R., Conrad, K. M., Marcantonio, R. J., Marks, B. A., and Ribisl, K. M. (1999). Do blue-collar workers perceive the worksite health climate differently than white-collar workers? *American Journal of Health Promotion*, *13*(6), 319–324. http://dx.doi.org/10.4278/0890-1171-13.6.319

Muntaner, C., Eaton, W. W., Miech, R., and O'Campo, P. (2004). Socioeconomic position and major mental disorders. *Epidemiologic Reviews*, *26*, 53–62. doi:10.1093/epirev/mxh001

Operario, D., Adler, N. E., and Williams, D. R. (2004). Subjective social status: Reliability and predictive utility for global health. *Psychology and Health*, *19*(2), 237–246.

Ridgeway, C. (1991). The social construction of status value: Gender and other nominal characteristics. *Social Forces*, *70*, 367–386.

Ross, C. E., and Mirowsky, J. (1989). Explaining the social patterns of depression: Control and problem solving – or support and talking? *Journal of Health and Social Behavior*, *30*, 206–219.

Siegrist, J., and Marmot, M. (2004). Health inequalities and the psychosocial environment – two scientific challenges. *Social Science and Medicine*, *58*(8), 1463–1473.

Simmons, L. A., and Swanberg, J. E. (2009). Psychosocial work environment and depressive symptoms among US workers: Comparing working poor and working non-poor. *Social Psychiatry and Psychiatric Epidemiology*, *44*(8), 628–635. http://dx.doi.org/10.1007/s00127-008-0479-x

Smith, K. P., and Christakis, N. A. (2008). Social networks and health. *Annual Review of Sociology*, *34*, 405–429. doi:10.1146/annurev.soc.34.040507.13460

Stafford, M., and Marmot, M. (2003). Neighbourhood deprivation and health: Does it affect us all equally? *International Journal of Epidemiology*, *32*, 357–366. doi:10.1093/ije/dyg084

Stokols, D. (1996). Translating social ecological theory into guidelines for community health promotion. *American Journal of Health Promotion*, *10*(4), 282–298.

Stringhini, S., Berkman, L., Dugravot, A., Ferrie, J. E., Marmot, M., Kivimäki, M., and Singh-Manoux, A. (2012). Socioeconomic status, structural and functional measures of social support, and mortality: The British Whitehall II cohort study, 1985–2009. *American Journal of Epidemiology*, *175*(12), 1275–1283. doi:10.1093/aje/kwr461

Sun, X., Rehnberg, C., and Meng, Q. (2009). How are individual-level social capital and poverty associated with health equity? A study from two Chinese cities. *International Journal for Equity in Health*, *8*(2). doi:10.1186/1475-9276-8-2

Sundquist, J., Östergren, P. O., Sundquist, K., and Johansson, S. E. (2003). Psychosocial working conditions and self-reported long-term illness: A population-based study of Swedish-born and foreign-born employed persons. *Ethnicity and Health*, *8*(4), 307–317. doi:10.1080/1355785032000163939

Thoits, P. A. (2011). Mechanisms linking social ties and support to physical and mental health. *Journal of Health and Social Behavior*, *52*, 145–161. doi:10.1177/0022146510395592

Toker, S., Hoppe, A., Schachler, V., and Ziegler, M. (2015). Change in job control and supervisor support on change in cognitive and physical vigor: Differential effects for immigrant and native employees in Israel. Paper presented at the 36th Conference of the Stress and Anxiety Research Society, Tel Aviv, Israel.

Turner, J. B., and Turner, R. J. (2013). Social relations, social integration, and social support. In C. S. Aneshensel, J. C. Phelan, A. Bierman, C. S. Aneshensel, J. C. Phelan, and A. Bierman (Eds.), *Handbook of the Sociology of Mental Health*, 2nd edn. (pp. 341–356). New York: Springer Science + Business Media.

Turner, R. J., and Marino, F. (1994). Social support and social structure: A descriptive epidemiology. *Journal of Health and Social Behavior*, *35*(3), 193–212. doi:10.2307/2137276

Uhlmann, E. L., Heaphy, E., Ashford, S. J., Zhu, L., and Sanchez-Burks, J. (2013). Acting professional: An exploration of culturally bounded norms against nonwork role referencing. *Journal of Organizational Behavior*, *34*(6), 866–886.

Vonneilich, N., Jockel, K.-H., Erbel, R., Klein, J., Dragano, N., Siegrist, J., and von dem Knesebeck, O. (2012). The mediating effect of social relationships on the association between socioeconomic status and subjective health: Results from the Heinz Nixdorf Recall cohort study. *BMC Public Health*, *12*. doi:10.1186/1471-2458-12-285

Vonneilich, N., Jockel, K.-H., Erbel, R., Klein, J., Dragano, N., Weyers, S., … von dem Knesebeck, O. (2011). Does socioeconomic status affect the association of social relationships and health? A moderator analysis. *International Journal for Equity in Health*, *10*. doi:10.1186/1475-9276-10-43

Wethington, E., and Kessler, R. C. (1986). Perceived support, received support, and adjustment to stressful life events. *Journal of Health and Social Behavior*, *27*(78–89).

Weyers, S., Dragano, N., Mobus, S., Beck, E.-M., Stang, A., Mohlenkamp, S., … Siegrist, J. (2008). Low socio-economic position is associated with poor social networks and social support: Results from the Heinz Nixdorf Recall Study. *International Journal for Equity in Health*, *7*, 13–19. doi:10.1186/1475-9276-7-13

WHO (World Health Organization) (2006). Constitution of the World Health Organization. At http://www.who.int/governance/eb/who_constitution_en.pdf (accessed July 2016).

Part Four
Coping with Stress

21

Lazarus and Folkman's Psychological Stress and Coping Theory

Amanda Biggs, Paula Brough, and Suzie Drummond

Introduction

Psychological stress is a complex phenomenon and numerous theoretical models have attempted to explain its etiology. These theoretical explanations can be categorized according to their primary conceptualization of the stress experience: stress as an external *stimulus*; stress as a *response*; stress as an individual/environmental *interaction*; and stress as an individual/environmental *transaction* (Brough, O'Driscoll, Kalliath, Cooper, and Poelmans, 2009; Cox and Griffiths, 2010). Transactional explanations of stress emphasize the cognitive-phenomenological processes that enable individuals to attribute meaning to their environment, emphasizing the relational, dynamic nature of the transaction in which stress may arise (Lazarus, 1966; Lazarus and Folkman, 1984). Inherent within the transactional approach is the bidirectional nature of the transactions between an individual and their environment; therefore, it is neither the individual nor the environment alone that produces stress but a complex transaction between the two (Folkman, 1984; Lazarus and Folkman, 1984).

The transactional theory of stress and coping, developed by Lazarus and Folkman (Lazarus, 1966; Lazarus and Folkman, 1984), has been particularly instrumental in shaping stress and coping research over the past five decades. This chapter provides an overview of the original theory, in addition to the more recent revisions made by Susan Folkman to more effectively consider the positive, as well as negative, emotions that arise during the stress process. The predominant coping taxonomy proposed by the theory will be presented, followed by a review of some pertinent critiques of coping conceptualizations. Finally, we discuss the theoretical

The Handbook of Stress and Health: A Guide to Research and Practice, First Edition.
Edited by Cary L. Cooper and James Campbell Quick.
© 2017 John Wiley & Sons, Ltd. Published 2017 by John Wiley & Sons, Ltd.

refinements and suggest future research directions inspired by the transactional theory of stress and coping.

Key Concepts of the Transactional Theory

According to Lazarus and Folkman's transactional theory of stress and coping, individuals are constantly appraising stimuli within their environment. This appraisal process generates emotions, and when stimuli are appraised as threatening, challenging, or harmful (i.e., stressors), the resultant distress initiates coping strategies to manage emotions or attempt to directly address the stressor itself. Coping processes produce an outcome (i.e., a change to the person–environment relationship), which is reappraised as favorable, unfavorable, or unresolved. Favorable resolution of stressors elicit positive emotions, while unresolved or unfavorable resolutions elicit distress, provoking the individual to consider further coping options to attempt to resolve the stressor (Folkman, 1997; Folkman and Lazarus, 1985; Folkman and Lazarus, 1988; Lazarus, 1990; Lazarus, DeLongis, Folkman, and Gruen, 1985; Lazarus and Folkman, 1984). According to this perspective, stress is defined as exposure to stimuli appraised as harmful, threatening, or challenging, that exceeds the individual's capacity to cope (Lazarus and Folkman, 1984). As noted, the primary features of the original theory are (a) *cognitive appraisal*, and (b) *coping*.

Cognitive Appraisal

Transactional theory proposes that the intensity of a stress reaction is influenced by the mediating role of appraisal, the cognitive process through which meaning is ascribed to events/stimuli (Boyd, Lewin, and Sager, 2009; Dewe and Cooper, 2007; Lazarus and Folkman, 1984; Oliver and Brough, 2002). According to Lazarus (1991), appraisals of individual/environmental transactions integrate two sets of forces: (a) an individual's personal agenda, including their values, goals, and beliefs, and (b) environmental factors, such as demands and resources. The variation in individual agendas and the complex and ambiguous nature of external environmental contexts explain the "great variation in the appraisals people make in the same environmental context" (Lazarus, 1991, p. 6). The importance placed on appraisal in the transactional theory of stress and coping emphasizes that it is the perception that the event is stressful, rather than the event itself, that determines whether coping strategies are initiated and whether the stressor is ultimately resolved (Lazarus, 1991; 1999). Lazarus and Folkman (1984) described two core forms of appraisal: *primary appraisal* and *secondary appraisal*.

Primary appraisal ascribes meaning to a specific individual/environmental transaction, and determines the significance of that transaction to an individual's well-being (Folkman, 1984; Lazarus and Folkman, 1984). The transaction may be deemed as benign-positive (exerting a positive effect on one's well-being), irrelevant (of no significance to one's well-being), or stressful (event could signify harm/loss, threat, or challenge). In the original transactional theory of stress and coping, the first two categories do not evoke negative emotions or the need for subsequent coping actions; rather, it is the third category, stressful transactions, that is of primary interest. Stressful transactions may further be appraised as producing substantial harm/loss, threatened harm/loss, or challenge (Oliver and Brough, 2002). Threat and harm appraisals refer to transactions that have the potential to harm or damage, and provoke negative emotions. Challenge appraisals differ from harm/threat appraisals, as they entail the potential for rewards and growth when sufficient coping resources are available, and are characterized by positive emotions (Hobfoll, 1989; Lazarus, 1991).

While primary appraisal determines the meaning and significance of a transaction to well-being, secondary appraisal determines what can be done to manage the stressor and its resultant distress (Dewe and Cooper, 2007). Secondary appraisal is enacted when a specific transaction is deemed to be stressful, and involves a cognitive process through which the individual identifies and evaluates their coping resources (e.g., self-efficacy), situational variables (e.g., job control), and coping styles (i.e., the manner in which the individual has coped with similar events in the past; Dewe and Cooper, 2007; Folkman, 1984). The interaction between these factors determines the coping actions enacted to "shape, manage, or resolve the event" (Dewe and Cooper, 2007, p. 144). It is important to clarify that the use of the word 'secondary' does not imply that secondary appraisal is of less importance, or that primary and secondary appraisals are independent, sequential processes. Rather, an individual's stress reactions are influenced by a complex, dynamic process involving the simultaneous interchange between primary and secondary appraisal (Dewe and Cooper, 2007).

Research evidence generally supports the mediating role of cognitive appraisal occurring between situational/individual resources and coping, and the mediating role of coping occurring between individual resources and outcomes. For example, Jerusalem (1993) found support for the mediating role of stress appraisals between both situational conditions (employment status and housing conditions) and personal resources (self-efficacy and optimism) and emotional coping and subjective health. More recently, Nicholls, Polman, and Levy (2012) demonstrated support for the relationships between threat and challenge appraisals and unpleasant and pleasant emotions respectively, and these associations in turn impacted upon coping and performance satisfaction outcomes. The vast literature referring to the transactional theory largely concurs that an individual's appraisal of the situation greatly influences their resultant emotions, coping strategies, and subsequent outcomes (e.g., Brough et al., 2009).

Problem-Focused and Emotion-Focused Coping

When a situation is appraised as stressful (primary appraisal) and requiring efforts to manage or resolve the event (secondary appraisal), coping actions are enacted (Folkman and Lazarus, 1988). According to the transactional theory, coping involves "constantly changing cognitive and behavioral efforts to manage external and/or internal demands that are appraised as taxing or exceeding the resources of a person" (Lazarus and Folkman, 1984, p. 141). According to their perspective, coping is process-oriented and dynamic, rather than trait-based (Brough, O'Driscoll, and Kalliath, 2005a; 2005b), and involves conscious, purposeful actions employed when an individual appraises a situation as stressful (Lazarus and Folkman, 1984). Within this theory, coping strategies aim to either directly manage the stressor (*problem-focused coping*, PFC) or regulate emotions arising as a consequence of the stressful encounter (*emotion-focused coping*, EFC; Lazarus and Folkman, 1984).

The outcome of coping efforts, accompanied with new information from the environment, result in a process of *cognitive reappraisal*, whereby the situation is reappraised to determine whether coping efforts have been successful, or to determine if the nature of the situation has changed from stressful to irrelevant or benign-positive (Lazarus and Folkman, 1984). Although positive affect may occur as a result of successful adaptation, unsuccessful adaptation may initiate further coping strategies, with continued failure resulting in negative affect and physiological disturbances (Edwards, 1992). Overall, Lazarus and Folkman's (1984) stress and coping theory emphasizes that the stress process is a *continuous cycle* of transactions between the individual and environment, experienced as disruptions to equilibrium and adaptive processes enacted to resolve this disequilibrium.

Coping Effectiveness

A frequent discussion within the coping literature is the comparative effectiveness of two PFC and EFC strategies. Most broadly, EFC is regarded as maladaptive and ineffective, with research associating EFC with negative outcomes, while less consistent, albeit generally positive effects have been associated with PFC (Folkman and Moskowitz, 2004; O'Driscoll, Brough, and Kalliath, 2009; Taylor and Stanton, 2007). For example, Graven et al. (2014) conducted a systematic review of the relationships between coping and health-related outcomes for cardiac patients. PFC was generally associated with improved psychological well-being, self-care, and health-related quality of life, while EFC was associated with poorer psychological well-being and health-related quality of life, and a higher risk of mortality. Boyd et al. (2009) also demonstrated that EFC was associated with adverse outcomes such as increased anxiety, emotional exhaustion, and dissatisfaction, while PFC was associated with lower levels of emotional exhaustion.

While EFC is often cited as a maladaptive coping strategy, many researchers have argued against generalizing the effects of PFC and EFC in this simplistic way (e.g., Dewe and Guest, 1990). The persistent notion that EFC strategies are maladaptive is due in part to the negative labeling of EFC reactions (e.g., escape and avoidance; Dewe and Cooper, 2007), as well as the tendency for EFC to be significantly associated with adverse outcomes (Folkman and Moskowitz, 2004). However, Lazarus and Folkman's (1984) transactional theory of stress and coping suggested that neither coping strategy is inherently effective or ineffective. Instead, the effectiveness of a given coping strategy is dependent on how well the coping strategy corresponds with appraisals and situational conditions (Cummings and Cooper, 1998; Dewe and Cooper, 2007; Folkman and Moskowitz, 2004). Therefore, the crucial components determining coping effectiveness are *fit* and *context*.

For example, EFC is generally described as exerting short-term adaptive effects when appraisals generate intense emotional distress, when stressors are appraised as being uncontrollable, and when existing resources are insufficient to support PFC strategies. According to Folkman and Moskowitz (2004), the need for coping arises in intensely emotional environments, and an initial function of coping "is to down-regulate negative emotions that are stressful in and of themselves and may be interfering with instrumental forms of coping" (p. 747). The short-term adoption of EFC may, therefore, be *adaptive* when stressors are appraised as being uncontrollable and when insufficient resources exist, allowing individuals to amalgamate the resources required to engage in future PFC strategies (Ben-Zur, 2009; Terry, 1994).

Nonetheless, the sole and persistent reliance on EFC or avoidance strategies over long periods of time is not considered to be beneficial. EFC behaviors encourage individuals to disconnect from the problem, and this in turn prevents further attempts to cope and contributes minimally to directly addressing the stressor (Ben-Zur, 2009; Semmer, 2006). Avoidance coping, for example, has been associated with lower adherence to treatment regimens (Taylor and Stanton, 2007). A training simulation study investigating the effect of different coping styles in relation to posttraumatic stress disorder (PTSD) symptoms, stress responses (anxiety, heart rate, and salivary cortisol levels), and performance within a sample of police recruits found that avoidance coping was related to positive short-term effects (lowered anxiety) but adverse long-term effects (e.g., increased salivary cortisol and PTSD symptoms; LeBlanc, Regehr, Jelley, and Barath, 2008). Thus, EFC and avoidance coping strategies may initially be adaptive because they enable individuals to avoid intensely emotional reactions to their work situations, but continual reliance on these strategies is maladaptive.

Unfortunately, few studies allow for genuine evaluations of coping effectiveness as they fail to simultaneously consider situational characteristics, personal characteristics, and outcomes (Boyd et al., 2009; Dewe and Cooper, 2007). Studies adopting a longitudinal research design are scarce, despite recognition of the necessity for these designs in order to accurately assess the evolving stress process, including the extent to which multiple coping strategies are implemented and interchanged (Brough et al., 2005a; Semmer, 2006). Additionally, coping effectiveness has primarily been evaluated in relation to negative outcomes: EFC behaviors have more consistently been related to these outcomes (e.g., psychological strain), while mixed findings have generally been produced for PFC (Folkman and Moskowitz, 2004; Taylor and Stanton, 2007). Taylor and Stanton argued that PFC is likely to have more persistent effects on positive outcomes (e.g., well-being), which are generally less frequently studied. Coping effectiveness can, therefore, be usefully conceptualized as strategies that reduce negative outcomes and increase positive outcomes (Dewe and Cooper, 2007).

Coping Taxonomy Critiques

The theoretical distinction between PFC and EFC "provides a useful way of talking about many kinds of coping in broad brushstrokes" (Folkman and Moskowitz, 2004, p. 751) and, as noted above, this coping dichotomy has been highly influential within the broader coping literature. Nonetheless, this dual coping taxonomy has been criticized primarily for both its theoretical and its methodological flaws (Brough et al., 2005a). One common criticism is that the PFC and EFC dichotomy provides only a surface explanation of coping and fails to adequately differentiate between the conceptual complexities of these coping responses (Dewe and Guest, 1990; Folkman and Moskowitz, 2004; Skinner, Edge, Altman, and Sherwood, 2003). For example, Latack and Havlovic (1992) observed that the PFC and EFC taxonomy is "insufficiently specific to capture the various sub-dimensions that have emerged in coping research" (Latack and Havlovic, 1992, p. 492). More specifically, the PFC–EFC dichotomy provides an inadequate categorization for the subdivisions of coping strategies; masks important differences within categories; and is neither mutually exclusive nor exhaustive, given that some strategies can be classified as both PFC and EFC (e.g., support seeking; Folkman and Moskowitz, 2004; Latack and Havlovic, 1992). Skinner et al. (2003) emphasized that coping taxonomies need to be *conceptually clear*, *mutually exclusive*, and *exhaustive*. As we will discuss, the PFC and EFC taxonomy generally does not meet these conceptual characteristics.

Conceptually clear taxonomies are those in which coping behaviors and strategies clearly align with a higher-order category of coping and can be precisely and unambiguously assigned (Skinner et al., 2003). For example, seeking information about the problem, brainstorming solutions, and making plans to address the problem are behaviors or strategies that are focused on the problem, and could, therefore, be categorized as "approach" coping. However, in terms of the PFC and EFC taxonomy, the inclusion of behaviors and strategies is less clear. Emotion-focused coping in particular is an ambiguous construct and is defined in research investigations by an extraordinarily wide variety of coping behaviors, including active attempts to calm one-self, venting and panic, exercise, positive reinterpretation, and acceptance (Jerusalem, 1993; Stanton, Danoff-Burg, Cameron, and Ellis, 1994). This ambiguity of what exactly consti-tutes EFC, in particular, is cited as evidence that this categorization is not at all conceptually clear.

Mutually exclusive taxonomies include coping reactions that are described in one single cat-egory (Skinner et al., 2003). For example, a coping response such as "making a plan" directly contributes to problem-solving but can also calm emotions, thereby enabling it to be classified as both a PFC and an EFC response. Similarly, seeking social support may be classified as a PFC strategy if it relates to seeking support about the problem; alternatively, seeking social support can also be described as EFC if the purpose is venting emotions (Pargament, Koenig, Tarakeshwar, and Hahn, 2004; Stanton et al., 2000). Hence the conceptual overlap between the PFC and EFC classifications is evident and weakens empirical evidence supporting the stress and coping theory.

Exhaustive or comprehensive taxonomies are those in which the core coping methods are fully included within the described categories (Skinner et al., 2003). This is unfortunately not the case for PFC and EFC behaviors because they do not encompass *all* coping behaviors. For example, the use of avoidance coping is not fully encompassed by the PFC and EFC taxonomy because avoidance coping (e.g., denial, escapism) does not purely focus on the problem or the emotions. Consequentially, avoidance coping is commonly included as an additional category in coping assessments based on the EFC–PFC taxonomy (Folkman and Moskowitz, 2004; Williams, Hundt, and Nelson-Gray, 2014).

The categorical assessment of behaviors as either PFC or EFC is, therefore, highly prob-lematic. Lazarus (1996) acknowledged this issue and suggested that "any coping thought or act can serve both or perhaps many other functions" (p. 293). Despite this theoretical lim-itation, coping research has, in the vast majority of cases, overlooked the limitations of the EFC–PFC taxonomy and descriptions of coping responses as a dual dichotomy using this tax-onomy remain prolific.

Alternative Coping Taxonomies

As an alternative to the PFC–EFC dichotomy, other coping taxonomies have been proposed that purport to explain coping responses more accurately. One such multifaceted coping tax-onomy, for example, was developed by Edwards and Baglioni (1993; 2000) and is based on *cybernetic theory*. The cybernetic theory (Edwards, 1992) defines coping as a reaction to min-imize symptoms of strain, modify perceptions of desired and actual mental states, and resolve discrepancies between perceived and desired states via five coping mechanisms. Consistent with the PFC strategies, direct coping actions may be made to actively *change the situation*. Alternatively, if the situation is perceived as being uncontrollable, or if previous coping efforts have failed, indirect attempts to minimize the symptoms of ill-health may be enacted (*symp-tom reduction*). An individual may repress undesirable aspects of a stressor (*avoidance*), adjust their own desires so they are better aligned with the perceived situation (*accommodation*), or minimize the importance of the discrepancy (*devaluation*; Edwards and Baglioni, 1993; 2000). One of the strengths of this cybernetic theory of coping is that it contains multiple forms of EFC strategies (Dewe and Guest, 1990). An empirical evaluation of this cybernetic coping taxonomy has been conducted and evidence noted for the strength of its psychometric properties – a point on which the Ways of Coping instrument commonly used to assess Lazarus and Folkman's (1984) EFC–PFC coping taxonomy has been criticized (e.g., Brough et al., 2005a; 2005b; Guppy et al., 2004).

Another classification of coping behaviors was suggested by Skinner et al. (2003), who classified coping into three categories according to its *adaptive function*. That is, adaptive processes that coordinate an individual's actions with the contingencies in the environment (*competence*); adaptive processes that coordinate the individual's reliance on others with the social resources in the environment (*relatedness*); and adaptive processes that coordinate an individual's preferences with the options available in the environment (*autonomy*). Each adaptive process is made up of four types or "families" of coping (i.e., 12 coping dimensions in total) that represent a higher-order category of coping, such as *problem-solving* or *information seeking*. Each coping family describes specific coping behaviors or strategies, such as *planning* or *asking others*. By first asking what the adaptive process is, and then asking what the function is within that adaptive process, Skinner et al. (2003) suggested that it is possible to categorize specific coping behaviors.

Duhachek and Oakley (2007) empirically assessed Skinner et al.'s (2003) three-stage coping taxonomy by developing items to assess the 12 dimensions. Their results across two studies supported the validity of the 12 coping dimensions. Support for Skinner et al.'s model was also produced by Webster, Brough, and Daly (2014), who used the framework to classify qualitative data on the ways of coping with toxic leadership, and by Didymus and Fletcher (2014), who also found support for these 12 coping dimensions system in a sample of athletes. These studies provide promising support for this classification of coping across different contexts, and further research utilizing this will be valuable for increasing our understanding of the taxonomy of coping.

Folkman's Revised Transactional Theory

Lazarus and Folkman's (1984) transactional theory of stress and coping, described above, focuses on coping processes that directly modify stressors and mitigate emotional distress arising from negative individual/environmental transactions. Subsequent research demonstrating the *simultaneous* existence of positive and negative emotions in the stress process, even during the direst circumstances, indicated a need to revise the theory to account for the role of coping in facilitating positive emotions (Folkman and Moskowitz, 2004). As a result, Folkman (1997) described two key areas to be developed: the need to better understand (a) the function of positive emotions within the stress and coping process, and (b) the role of coping processes in facilitating positive emotions during intensely stressful events.

In the original theoretical explanation (Lazarus and Folkman, 1984), cognitive reappraisal determined whether coping efforts were successful or unsuccessful. Successful outcomes led to positive emotions, while failure to successfully resolve the situation produced distress, which initiated further appraisal and coping attempts. However, the revised theory proposed that unsuccessful coping and its resultant distress may actually trigger *meaning-focused coping*, particularly when stressors are perceived to be overwhelmingly aversive and uncontrollable (Folkman, 1997; 2008). Meaning-focused coping involves drawing on one's values, beliefs, and goals to reorder life priorities, ascribe positive meaning to ordinary events, and to find and remind oneself of the benefits of stress (Carver and Connor-Smith, 2010; Folkman, 2008). Meaning-focused coping in turn elicits positive emotions, which restore the resources that influence cognitive appraisals, sustain coping efforts over time, and provide relief from distress (Folkman, 2008). Thus, there are two feedback loops from unfavorable outcomes and distress, one characterized by positive emotions, and the second characterized by negative emotions.

Future Directions

There are a number of promising avenues for future research that are likely to improve the theoretical explanations proposed by the transactional theory of stress and coping. As discussed previously, the additions of meaning-focused coping and positive emotions to the transactional theory are two valuable contributions focused specifically upon positive outcomes. We suggest that two other valuable research contributions are *future-oriented coping*, and the use of *ecological momentary assessments*, which offer further advancements to the transactional process of stress and coping. In this final section of the chapter, we summarize the key research within these two areas.

Future-Oriented Coping

The vast majority of coping research has focused on how people cope with past stressors and/ or stressors occurring in the present. However, the experiences of coping with *potential future stressors*, known broadly as *future-oriented coping*, has increasingly been acknowledged (Folkman and Moskowitz, 2004). Thus, some stressors are anticipated before they occur (e.g., birth of a new baby, intensive workload, bereavement), and the consequent coping behaviors can also be planned in advance to varying extents. Schwarzer (2000) proposed four categories of coping depending on the temporal location of the (potential) stressor and the degree of certainty with which it would occur: *reactive*, *anticipatory*, *preventive*, and *proactive coping*. Greenglass, Schwarzer, and colleagues also developed an empirical instrument to assess both future-oriented coping and avoidance coping, the *Proactive Coping Inventory* (PCI; Greenglass, Schwarzer, Jakubiec, Fiksenbaum, and Taubert, 1999a; Greenglass, Schwarzer and Taubert, 1999b). This measure, therefore, assesses future-oriented coping from a trait perspective.

Reactive coping is undertaken to deal with the harm or loss that has already been experienced, thereby situating it in the past and as having certainly occurred. The majority of coping research to date, including that described by Lazarus and Folkman's (1984) transactional theory of stress and coping, consists of reactive coping. *Anticipatory coping* is enacted in response to a recognized upcoming event of likely certainty in the short-term future. An example is preparing for an upcoming exam or performance appraisal assessment occurring within the next few weeks. The focus, therefore, is on managing known risks and utilizing resources to reduce the stressor or maximize anticipated benefits (Schwarzer and Taubert, 2002). *Preventive coping* is utilized to deal with potential future stressors that are possible, although their eventual occurrence is uncertain, and reflects efforts aimed at accumulating resources to assist in reducing the severity of the stressor. An example might be preparing a survival kit and emergency plan in case of a house fire or a severe weather event sometime in the future. It is akin to risk management in a broad sense of preparing resources "just in case." Due to its emphasis on preventing or reducing the impact of negative outcomes, preventive coping is primarily driven by threat appraisals (Schwarzer and Knoll, 2003).

Finally, *proactive coping* focuses on the accumulation of resources to enhance one's potential and opportunities for personal growth (Schwarzer, 2000). It is typically enacted for events
that are highly likely to occur in the future. An example of proactive coping is actively attending professional development workshops to enhance one's chances of a job promotion due to
increased knowledge, skills, and performance. It is, therefore, akin to goal management rather
than risk management, and is primarily driven by challenge appraisals (Schwarzer and Knoll,
2003).

Of these four types of coping, proactive coping has received the most research attention,
followed by preventive coping. Research has supported the mediating role of proactive coping
between stressors and a variety of health and work-related outcomes. For example, Angelo and
Chambel (2012) demonstrated that proactive coping significantly mediated the relationships
between job demands and both psychological burnout and work engagement for a sample
of firefighters. That is, when proactive coping was enacted the subsequent health and work
outcomes for the firefighters were improved. Similarly, Nizielski, Hallum, Schütz, and Lopes
(2013) reported that proactive coping significantly mediated the relationship between emotion-
appraisal and psychological burnout, such that levels of burnout were again reduced when
proactive coping occurred. The mediating impacts of both preventive and proactive coping
were also demonstrated between stressors and student engagement by Gan, Yang, Zhou, and
Zhang (2007), supporting the beneficial effects of these types of coping on individual well-
being outcomes.

Future-Oriented Coping and the Transactional Theory

Research has employed the theoretical framework of the transactional theory of stress and
coping, to assess relationships between future-oriented coping with research variables such as
cognitive appraisal, personality, support, and outcomes (e.g., Drummond, 2014). This research
revealed that future-oriented coping demonstrated significant relationships with cognitive
appraisal, work-related support, personality, and psychological strain, in accordance with the
propositions of the transactional theory. Further support that proactive coping operates as
a mediator of personality and support in predicting health and work-related outcomes was
demonstrated by Drummond and Brough (2016a), who found support for proactive coping
as a mediator between personality (optimism, goal orientation, and future and past orientation) and psychological strain. Similarly, Angelo and Chambel (2012) also demonstrated that
both colleague support and supervisor support predicted work engagement through proactive
coping. More research, however, is needed to understand the role of preventive coping as a
mediator between personality and support on health and work-related outcomes.

Preventive coping has been investigated in terms of its application to interventions aimed at
improving health. For example, Thoolen, de Ridder, Bensing, Gorter, and Rutten (2009) implemented an intervention based on preventive coping and self-regulation principles to improve
self-care behaviors in adults with newly diagnosed type 2 diabetes, showing that the intervention was successful in improving health-related behaviors and reducing weight over 12 months.
Similarly, Vinkers, Adriaanse, Kroese, and de Ridder (2014) conducted an intervention for
weight control in overweight and obese adults using preventive coping principles, and found
the experimental groups reduced their body mass index compared to a control group who
did not. These researchers also developed a tool to assess situation-specific (i.e., state-based)
preventive coping, referring to it as the *Proactive Competence Scale* (PCS; Bode, de Ridder,

Kuijer, and Bensing, 2007). The PCS assesses state-based skills or competencies to engage in proactive/preventive coping behaviors. Therefore, the PCS could be used in conjunction with proactive and preventive coping measures to assess the tendency and ability to engage in proactive and preventive coping and the impacts these have on health and work-related outcomes. This suggested approach reflects the *transaction* between the person and their environment in the prediction of outcomes, as suggested by the transactional theory.

Sohl and Moyer (2009) conducted such a study in which they tested whether the proactive coping competencies mediated the relationship between proactive and preventive coping and well-being after controlling for the effects of optimism and pessimism. Their results revealed that proactive coping predicted two of the four proactive competencies scales (use of resources and realistic goal setting), which in turn predicted improved well-being. Interestingly, this mediation effect was not significant for preventive coping, which Sohl and Moyer explained was due to a large proportion of its variance being shared with proactive coping. Drummond and Brough (2016b) demonstrated proactive and preventive coping are distinct constructs, however, future research investigating these relationships in more detail is required to specifically identify how future-oriented coping interacts with environmental factors in predicting health and work-related outcomes.

Overall, the impact of both preventive coping and proactive coping in improving the associations between a stressor and a psychological health/work outcome (via mediation) replicates the evidence for the more widely reported mediating role of *reactive* (past) coping in these stressor–outcomes associations. It is valuable to note that regardless of the past/future orientation of coping behaviors, these responses successfully reduce the impact of stressors on individual-level health and attitudinal outcomes. Theoretical explanations of stress–coping–outcomes relationships, therefore, appear applicable to *both* past and future-orientated coping responses.

Ecological Momentary Assessments

A final important area for future coping research is the measurement of the coping process. One promising application is the use of *ecological momentary assessments* (EMA), a research method which assesses behavioral and cognitive processes within their natural environments. Stone and Shiffman (1994) proposed four qualities that define EMAs: (a) assessments are made as they occur, (b) assessments are carefully timed, (c) repeated observations are often made, and (d) assessments occur in the participant's environment. According to Gunthert and Wenze (2012), EMA studies represent intensive research designs in which respondents are usually prompted to report multiple times per day. This is contrasted to their definition of *diary studies*, in which respondents are generally required to report only once per day. The primary value of EMA is the use of repeated measures to assess respondents' experience of stress and coping in real time, thereby offering greater insight of the actual unfolding stress and coping process.

These types of repeated assessments have been employed within the stress and coping field to assess cognitive appraisals and coping efforts. For example, Clarkson and Hodgkinson (2007) required participants to complete a critical incident diary over five consecutive days in which they recorded their self-identified critical incidents that triggered stress and their reactions to it, including thoughts, feelings, perception of its consequences, and coping strategies. Daniels and Harris (2005) employed a similar diary method but instead of having respondents

write freely about their experiences, they required respondents to fill out a diary of questionnaires twice each day for two weeks to gain insight into stressors (work demands), coping
efforts, goals, and affect.

Although these methods have been utilized in research for over 25 years, recent advancements in technology, such as the widespread use of smartphones, have enabled researchers
to assess thoughts and behaviors in real time with relatively little difficulty for participants.
For example, Daniels, Beesley, Cheyne, and Wimalasiri (2008) assessed problem-solving
demands, coping, and well-being four times per day using personal digital assistants (PDAs)
for five consecutive days. Similarly, Khor, Melvin, Reid, and Gray (2014) employed a mobile
phone application to assess stress and coping strategies four times per day for two weeks.

The benefits of these electronic methods is that they can provide time and date stamps that
are useful to identify if assessments were taken at the appropriate time, and also how long
participants took to respond, which can be important for assessing respondent burden and data
quality (Iida, Shrout, Laurenceau, and Bolger, 2012). The recorded data can also be directly
downloaded into statistical software programs for increased ease and accuracy of analyses
(Iida et al., 2012). Future research employing these research methods is considered to be highly
beneficial for progressing our knowledge of the dynamic coping process.

Conclusion

In this chapter we have reviewed the key components of Lazarus and Folkman's (1984) transactional theory of stress and coping, and focused specifically on the effectiveness of the PFC and
EFC taxonomy. The influence of this theoretical explanation of the stress and coping process is
striking; a June 2015 search of Google Scholar produced over 54,000 "hits" for the search term
transactional theory of stress and coping and over 20,000 results each for *problem-focused
coping* and *emotion-focused coping*, which attests to the quantity of citations of these terms.
Thirty years on from its publication, this theory remains the cornerstone of psychological stress
and coping research across multiple fields and disciplines.

Recent developments, specifically with the new waves of research exploring the future-
oriented coping processes, are refreshing and have rescued coping research from the "stagnation" of knowledge which the field had been generally experiencing (e.g., Brough et al.,
2005a). Improving planned coping responses to manage anticipated future stressors offers significant potential for both improving individuals' behaviors and performance, and increasing
our knowledge of the specific inherent processes of the stress and coping dynamic. Technological improvements in stress and coping measurement ensure that this field will remain research
active for the foreseeable future. Stress and coping research over the next decades will of
course be keenly observed, to determine how influential the theoretical explanations offered
by Lazarus and Folkman remain.

References

Angelo, R. P., and Chambel, M. J. (2012). The role of proactive coping in the job demands–resources model: A
cross-section study with firefighters. *European Journal of Work and Organizational Psychology, 23*, 203–216.
doi:10.1080/1359432X.2012.728701

Ben-Zur, H. (2009). Coping styles and affect. *International Journal of Stress Management, 16*(2), 87–101.
doi:10.1037/a0015731

Bode, C., de Ridder, D. T. D., Kuijer, R. G., and Bensing, J. M. (2007). Effects of an intervention promoting proactive coping competencies in middle and late adulthood. *Gerontologist*, *47*, 42–51. doi:10.1093/geront/47.1.42

Boyd, N. G., Lewin, J. E., and Sager, J. K. (2009). A model of stress and coping and their influence on individual and organizational outcomes. *Journal of Vocational Behavior*, *75*, 197–211. doi:10.1016/j.jvb.2009.03.010

Brough, P., O'Driscoll, M., and Kalliath, T. (2005a). Confirmatory factor analysis of the cybernetic coping scale. *Journal of Occupational and Organizational Psychology*, *78*(1), 53–61. doi:10.1348/096317904X23754

Brough, P., O'Driscoll, M., and Kalliath, T. (2005b). Evaluating the criterion validity of the cybernetic coping scale: Cross-lagged predictions of psychological strain, job and family satisfaction. *Work and Stress*, *19*(3), 276–292. doi:10.1080/02678370500287507

Brough, P., O'Driscoll, M., Kalliath, T., Cooper, C. L., and Poelmans, S. (2009). *Workplace Psychological Health: Current Research and Practice*. Cheltenham, UK: Edward Elgar.

Carver, C. S., and Connor-Smith, J. (2010). Personality and coping. *Annual Review of Psychology*, *61*, 679–704. doi:10.1146/annurev.psych.093008.100352

Clarkson, G. P., and Hodgkinson, G. P. (2007). What can occupational stress diaries achieve that questionnaires can't? *Personnel Review*, *36*, 684–700. doi:10.1108/00483480710773990

Cox, T., and Griffiths, A. (2010). Work-related stress: A theoretical perspective. In S. Leka and J. Houdmont (Eds.), *Occupational Health Psychology* (pp. 31–56). Hoboken, NJ: Wiley-Blackwell.

Cummings, T. G., and Cooper, C. L. (1998). A cybernetic theory of organizational stress. In C. L. Cooper (Ed.), *Theories of Organizational Stress* (pp. 101–121). New York: Oxford University Press.

Daniels, K., Beesley, N., Cheyne, A., and Wimalasiri, V. (2008). Coping processes linking the demands–control–support model, affect and risky decisions at work. *Human Relations*, *61*, 845–874. doi:10.1177/0018726708093543

Daniels, K., and Harris, C. (2005). A daily diary study of coping in the context of the job demands–control–support model. *Journal of Vocational Behavior*, *66*, 219–237. doi:10.1016/j.jvb.2004.10.004

Dewe, P., and Cooper, C. L. (2007). Coping research and measurement in the context of work related stress. In G. P. Hodgkinson and J. K. Ford (Eds.), *International Review of Industrial and Organizational Psychology*, vol. 22 (pp. 141–191). Chichester, UK: John Wiley & Sons.

Dewe, P., and Guest, D. E. (1990). Methods of coping with stress at work: A conceptual analysis and empirical study of measurement issues. *Journal of Organizational Behavior*, *11*(2), 135–150. doi:10.1002/job.4030110205

Didymus, F. F., and Fletcher, D. (2014). Swimmers' experiences of organizational stress: Exploring the role of cognitive appraisal and coping strategies. *Journal of Clinical Sport Psychology*, *8*, 159–183. doi:10.1123/jcsp.2014-0020

Drummond, S. (2014). Being proactive about proactive coping: Exploring future-oriented coping and appraisal within a transactional framework. Doctoral dissertation. Griffith University, Brisbane, Australia.

Drummond, S., and Brough, P. (2016a). Future-orientated coping and personality. In A.-S. Antoniou and C. L. Cooper (Eds.), *Coping, Personality and the Workplace: Responding to Psychological Crisis and Critical Events*. Abingdon, UK: Routledge.

Drummond, S., and Brough, P. (2016b). Proactive coping and preventive coping: Evidence for two distinct constructs? *Personality and Individual Differences*, *92*, 123–127. doi:10.1016/j.paid.2015.12.029

Duhachek, A., and Oakley, J. L. (2007). Mapping the hierarchical structure of coping: Unifying empirical and theoretical perspectives. *Journal of Consumer Psychology*, *17*, 218–233. doi:10.1016/S1057-7408(07)70030-X

Edwards, J. R. (1992). A cybernetic theory of stress, coping, and well-being in organizations. *Academy of Management Review*, *17*(2), 238–274. doi:10.5465/AMR.1992.4279536

Edwards, J. R., and Baglioni, A. J., Jr. (1993). The measurement of coping with stress: Construct validity of the ways of coping checklist and the cybernetic coping scale. *Work and Stress*, *7*(1), 17–31. doi:10.1080/02678379308257047

Edwards, J. R., and Baglioni, A. J., Jr. (2000). Empirical versus theoretical approaches to the measurement of coping: A comparison using the ways of coping questionnaire and the cybernetic coping scale. In P. Dewe, M. Leiter and T. Cox (Eds.), *Coping, Health and Organizations* (pp. 29–50). London: Taylor & Francis.

Folkman, S. (1984). Personal control and stress and coping processes: A theoretical analysis. *Journal of Personality and Social Psychology*, *46*(4), 839–852. doi:10.1037/0022-3514.46.4.839

Folkman, S. (1997). Positive psychological states and coping with severe stress. *Social Science and Medicine*, *45*(8), 1207–1221. doi:10.1016/S0277-9536(97)00040-3

Folkman, S. (2008). The case for positive emotions in the stress process. *Anxiety, Stress, and Coping*, *21*(1), 3–14. doi:10.1080/10615800701740457

Folkman, S., and Lazarus, R. S. (1985). If it changes it must be a process: Study of emotion and coping during three stages of a college examination. *Journal of Personality and Social Psychology*, *48*, 150–170. doi:10.1037/0022-3514.48.1.150

Folkman, S., and Lazarus, R. S. (1988). Coping as a mediator of emotion. *Journal of Personality and Social Psychology*, *54*(3), 466–475. doi:10.1037/0022-3514.54.3.466

Folkman, S., and Moskowitz, J. T. (2004). Coping: Pitfalls and promise. *Annual Review of Psychology*, *55*, 745–774. doi:10.1146/annurev.psych.55.090902.141456

Gan, Y., Yang, M., Zhou, Y., and Zhang, Y. (2007). The two-factor structure of future-oriented coping and its mediating role in student engagement. *Personality and Individual Differences*, *43*, 851–863. doi:0.1016/j.paid.2007.02.009

Graven, L. J., Grant, J. S., Vance, D. E., Pryor, E. R., Grubbs, L., and Karioth, S. (2014). Coping styles associated with heart failure outcomes: A systematic review. *Journal of Nursing Education and Practice*, *4*, 227–242. doi:10.5430/jnep.v4n2p227

Greenglass, E., Schwarzer, R., Jakubiec, D., Fiksenbaum, L., and Taubert, S. (1999a). The Proactive Coping Inventory (PCI): A multidimensional research instrument. Paper presented at the 20th International Conference of the Stress and Anxiety Research Society, Krakow, Poland.

Greenglass, E., Schwarzer, R., and Taubert, S. (1999b). The Proactive Coping Inventory (PCI): A multidimensional research instrument. At http://userpage.fu-berlin.de/~health/greenpci.htm (accessed July 2016).

Gunthert, K. C., and Wenze, S. J. (2012). Daily diary methods. In M. R. Mehl and T. S. Conner (Eds.), *Handbook of Research Methods for Studying Daily Life* (pp. 144–159). New York: Guilford Press.

Guppy, A., Edwards, J. A., Brough, P., Peters-Bean, K. M., Sale, C., and Short, E. (2004). The psychometric properties of the short version of the Cybernetic Coping Scale: A multigroup confirmatory factor analysis across four samples. *Journal of Occupational and Organizational Psychology*, *77*, 39–62. doi:10.1348/096317904322915900

Hobfoll, S. E. (1989). Conservation of resources: A new attempt at conceptualizing stress. *American Psychologist*, *44*, 513–524. doi:10.1037/0003-066X.44.3.513

Iida, M., Shrout, P. E., Laurenceau, J.-P., and Bolger, N. (2012). Using diary methods in psychological research. In H. Cooper (Gen. Ed.), *APA Handbook of Research Methods in Psychology, vol. 1: Foundations, Planning, Measures, and Psychometrics* (pp. 277–305). Washington, DC: American Psychological Association.

Jerusalem, M. (1993). Personal resources, environmental constraints, and adaptational processes: The predictive power of a theoretical stress model. *Personality and Individual Differences*, *14*, 15–24. doi:10.1016/0191-8869(93)90170-8

Khor, A. S., Melvin, G. A., Reid, S. C., and Gray, K. M. (2014). Coping, daily hassles and behavior and emotional problems in adolescents with high-functioning Autism/Asperger's Disorder. *Journal of Autism Developmental Disorders*, *44*, 593–608. doi:10.1007/s10803-013-1912-x

Latack, J. C., and Havlovic, S. J. (1992). Coping with job stress: A conceptual evaluation framework for coping measures. *Journal of Organizational Behavior*, *13*, 479–508.

Lazarus, R. S. (1966). *Psychological Stress and the Coping Process*. New York: McGraw Hill.

Lazarus, R. S. (1990). Theory-based stress measurement. *Psychological Inquiry*, *1*, 3–13. doi:10.1207/s15327965pli0101_1

Lazarus, R. S. (1991). *Emotion and Adaptation*. Oxford: Oxford University Press.

Lazarus, R. S. (1996). The role of coping in the emotions and how coping changes over the life course. In C. Magai and S. H. McFadden (Eds.), *Handbook of Emotion, Adult Development, and Aging* (pp. 289–306). New York: Academic Press.

Lazarus, R. S. (1999). *Stress and Emotion: A New Synthesis*. New York: Springer.

Lazarus, R. S., DeLongis, A., Folkman, S., and Gruen, R. (1985). Stress and adaptational outcomes: The problem of confounded measures. *American Psychologist*, *40*, 770–779. doi:10.1037/0003-066X.40.7.770

Lazarus, R. S., and Folkman, S. (1984). *Stress, Appraisal, and Coping*. New York: Springer.

LeBlanc, V. R., Regehr, C., Jelley, R. B., and Barath, I. (2008). The relationship between coping styles, performance, and responses to stressful scenarios in police recruits. *International Journal of Stress Management*, *15*(1), 76–93. doi:10.1037/1072-5245.15.1.76

Nicholls, A. R., Polman, R. C. J., and Levy, A. R. (2012). A path analysis of stress appraisals, emotions, coping, and performance satisfaction among athletes. *Psychology of Sport and Exercise*, *13*, 263–270. doi:10.1016/j.psychsport.2011.12.003

Nizielski, S., Hallum, S., Schütz, A., and Lopes, P. N. (2013). A note on emotion appraisal and burnout: The mediating role of antecedent-focused coping strategies. *Journal of Occupational Health Psychology*, *18*, 363–369. doi:10.1037/a0033043

O'Driscoll, M., Brough, P., and Kalliath, T. (2009). Stress and coping. In S. Cartwright and C. Cooper (Eds.), *The Oxford Handbook of Organizational Well-Being* (pp. 237–266). Oxford: Oxford University Press.

Oliver, J., and Brough, P. (2002). Cognitive appraisal, negative affectivity and psychological well-being. *New Zealand Journal of Psychology*, *31*, 2–7.

Pargament, K. I., Koenig, H. G., Tarakeshwar, N., and Hahn, J. (2004). Religious coping methods as predictors of psychological, physical and spiritual outcomes among medically ill elderly patients: A two-year longitudinal study. *Journal of Health Psychology*, *9*, 713–730. doi:10.1177/1359105304045366

Schwarzer, R. (2000). Manage stress at work through preventive and proactive coping. In E. A. Locke (Ed.), *The Blackwell Handbook of Principles of Organizational Behavior* (pp. 342–355). Oxford: Blackwell.

Schwarzer, R., and Knoll, N. (2003). Positive coping: Mastering demands and searching for meaning. In S. J. Lopez and C. R. Snyder (Eds.), *Positive Psychological Assessment: A Handbook of Models and Measures* (pp. 393–409). Washington, DC: American Psychological Association.

Schwarzer, R., and Taubert, S. (2002). Tenacious goal pursuits and striving toward personal growth: Proactive coping. In E. Frydenberg (Ed.), *Beyond Coping: Meeting Goals, Visions and Challenges* (pp. 19–35). Oxford: Oxford University Press.

Semmer, N. K. (2006). Personality, stress, and coping. In M. E. Vollrath (Ed.), *Handbook of Personality and Health* (pp. 73–113). Chichester, UK: John Wiley & Sons.

Skinner, E. A., Edge, K., Altman, J., and Sherwood, H. (2003). Searching for the structure of coping: A review and critique of category systems for classifying ways of coping. *Psychological Bulletin*, *129*, 216–269. doi:10.1037/0033-2909.129.2.216

Sohl, S. J., and Moyer, A. (2009). Refining the conceptualization of a future-oriented self-regulatory behavior: Proactive coping. *Personality and Individual Differences*, *47*, 139–144. doi:10.1016/j.paid.2009.02.013

Stanton, A. L., Danoff-Burg, S., Cameron, C. L., Bishop, M., Collins, C. A., Kirk, S. B., … Twillman, R. (2000). Emotionally expressive coping predicts psychological and physical adjustment to breast cancer. *Journal of Consulting and Clinical Psychology*, *68*, 875–882. doi:10.1037//0022-006X.68.5.875

Stanton, A. L., Danoff-Burg, S., Cameron, C. L., Ellis, A. P. (1994). Coping through emotional approach: Problems of conceptualization and confounding. *Journal of Personality and Social Psychology*, *66*, 350–362. doi:10.1037/0022-3514.66.2.350

Stone, A. A., and Shiffman, S. (1994). Ecological momentary assessment (EMA) in behavioral medicine. *Annals of Behavioral Medicine*, *16*(3), 199–202.

Taylor, S. E., and Stanton, A. L. (2007). Coping resources, coping processes, and mental health. *Annual Review of Clinical Psychology*, *3*, 377–401. doi:10.1146/annurev.clinpsy.3.022806.091520

Terry, D. J. (1994). Determinants of coping: The role of stable and situational factors. *Journal of Personality and Social Psychology*, *66*(5), 895–910.

Thoolen, B. J., de Ridder, D., Bensing, J., Gorter, K., and Rutten, G. (2009). Beyond good intentions: The role of proactive coping in achieving sustained behavioural change in the context of diabetes management. *Psychology and Health*, *24*, 247–254. doi:10.1080/08870440701864504

Vinkers, C. D. W., Adriaanse, M. A., Kroese, F. M., and de Ridder, D. T. D. (2014). Efficacy of a self-management intervention for weight control in overweight and obese adults: A randomized controlled trial. *Journal of Behavioural Medicine*, *37*, 781–792. doi:10.1007/s10865-013-9530-9

Webster, V., Brough, P., and Daly, K. (2014). Fight, flight or freeze: Common responses for follower coping with toxic leadership. *Stress and Health*. Epub ahead of print. doi:10.1002/smi.2626

Williams, A. M., Hundt, N. E., and Nelson-Gray, R. (2014). BIS and cognitive appraisals in predicting coping strategies. *Personality and Individual Differences*, *59*, 60–64. doi:10.1016/j.paid.2013.11.006

22

Coping with Interpersonal Mistreatment

Not a Case of "Either Or," but Rather "It Depends"

Rebecca Michalak, Sandra Kiffin-Petersen, and Neal M. Ashkanasy

> Life is not what it's supposed to be. It is what it is. The way you cope with it is what makes the difference.
>
> Virginia Satir, American psychologist and educator, 1916–1988

Poor interpersonal relationships are oft-cited sources of workplace stress (e.g., Kelloway, Teed, and Kelley, 2008; Redfern, Rees and Rowlands, 2008), which has in turn been linked to negative individual outcomes such as depression (Shields, 2006). According to a plethora of studies crossing cultures and countries (e.g., see meta-analyses by Alarcon, 2011; Podsakoff, LePine, and LePine, 2007; Schyns and Schilling, 2013), these adverse consequences are not only ubiquitous, but also universally costly from an economic point of view. The European Agency for Safety and Health at Work (EU-OSHA, 2009), for example, reported that 50 to 60 percent of absenteeism costs (€20 billion per annum) relate to stress at work. In Australia, workplace stress is estimated to cost $14.81 billion each year, with a direct cost to employers of $10.11 billion just in stress-related absenteeism and presenteeism (Medibank, 2011).

A problem, however, is that we still have little understanding of the underlying processes that determine employees' responses to stressful events, and how these responses may influence both employee well-being and job performance outcomes. In this chapter, we seek to address this problem by focusing on the potentially stressful effects of interpersonal mistreatment in the workplace. We do so through the dual lens of affective events theory (AET: Weiss and

The Handbook of Stress and Health: A Guide to Research and Practice, First Edition.
Edited by Cary L. Cooper and James Campbell Quick.
© 2017 John Wiley & Sons, Ltd. Published 2017 by John Wiley & Sons, Ltd.

Cropanzano, 1996) and the transactional theory of psychological stress (TTPS: Lazarus, 1966; 1981; Lazarus and Folkman, 1984).

According to Harlos and Axelrod (2005), a potential source of stress within contemporary workplaces is the experience of interpersonal mistreatment by a colleague or supervisor. In this respect, we adopt Cortina and Magley's (2003) definition of interpersonal mistreatment (herein referred to as "mistreatment") as "a specific, antisocial variety of organizational deviance, involving a situation in which at least one organizational member takes counter normative negative actions – or terminates normative positive actions – against another member" (p. 247). Mistreatment is viewed by Robinson and Bennett (1995) as a particular variety of interpersonal deviance, and encompasses a wide range of deviant organizational behavior, from minor infractions, including disrespect and general incivility, to more severe forms of mistreatment such as sexual harassment and aggressive acts (Lim and Cortina, 2005). As such, mistreatment behaviors are generally intended to intimidate, to humiliate, to obstruct, and/or to undermine the victim (Harlos and Axelrod, 2005).

Importantly, mistreatment can have serious consequences for individuals and organizations. Interpersonal deviance, for example, has been shown to be related to turnover intentions and poor physical health (Lim, Cortina, and Magley, 2008), low job satisfaction, job withdrawal, and psychological distress (Cortina, Magley, Williams, and Langhout, 2001), declines in performance (Caza and Cortina, 2007), posttraumatic stress (Nielsen, Matthiesen, and Einarsen, 2008), physical symptoms (Djurkovic, McCormack, and Casimir, 2004), psychological ill-health (Zapf, Knorz, and Kulla, 1996), absenteeism, chronic disease rates, and high body mass indices (Kivimäki, Elovainio, and Vahtera, 2000), decreases in organizational commitment and physical/mental health (Willness, Steel, and Lee, 2007), drinking behavior (Bacharach, Bamberger, and Sonnenstuhl, 2002), and negative changes in victim attitudes and performance (O'Leary-Kelly, Bowes-Sperry, Bates, and Lean, 2009). In one of the few studies to examine mistreatment per se, Deitch et al. (2003) found that mistreatment relates to lowered job satisfaction and poor emotional and physical well-being. Harlos and Axelrod (2005) found similarly that mistreatment is negatively related to well-being, satisfaction, and commitment; and positively related to intention to leave.

Indeed, how employees cope with mistreatment and its stressful consequences is a continuing source of intrigue in organizational behavior research (Chan and McAllister, 2014), especially in view of the high costs associated with stress-related illnesses and the potential legal implications for organizations (EU-OSHA, 2009; Medibank, 2011). A conundrum exists, however, in that scholars have yet to develop a comprehensive model of the processes and causal relationships that underlie the mistreatment phenomenon (Ganster and Rosen, 2013). To address this issue, we integrate AET and TTPS with research on emotions, stress, coping, mistreatment, job performance, and interpersonal deviance to propose a dual theory, process-and-variance model of mistreatment and its effects in organizations.

In developing our model, we also address two particular criticisms of stress and coping research raised by Lazarus (2006), whereby researchers have failed to consider concomitantly (1) the individual engaging in appraisal and coping, and (2) the context in which the stressor, appraisal, and coping occurs. These omissions have led to a misinterpretation and misapplication of the emotion-focused and problem-focused coping terms. This misinterpretation and misapplication has then resulted in coping choices being erroneously considered "either or" when, in fact, a more accurate assessment of what constitutes an effective coping style is "it depends" (Lazarus, 1981, p. 179; Sideridis, 2006). Our main contribution, therefore, lies in explicating the individual appraisal and coping strategies that might arise in response to the stress of mistreatment. We also examine how these internal processes combine to affect a victim's psychological health, well-being, and behavior relevant to job performance.

We illustrate our dual theory process-and-variance model of mistreatment in Figure 22.1. Grounded in principles of AET and the TTPS, we first outline the antecedents to mistreatment, which we refer to as "precipitating environments" and "probable targets." These represent the workplace context and individual differences variables (i.e., as per AET) that influence an individual's perception that they have been mistreated. Note we consider mistreatment "to lie in the eyes of the beholder" and deliberately refrain from differentiating between behaviors *perceived* to be mistreatment and behavior *objectively measured* as mistreatment. We proceed from an initial analysis of the mistreatment episode (the affective event) to discuss the role of stress theory (TTPS, the microstructure), including the potential individual and organizational impacts of primary, secondary, and (what we refer to as) tertiary appraisal processes, as well as different coping strategies, in determining mistreatment's effects within organizations.

Macrostructure: Affective Events Theory

We argue that AET (Weiss and Cropanzano, 1996) is an appropriate framework for exploring the causes and outcomes of affective workplace experiences (for examples of recent applications of AET, see Ashkanasy and Humphrey, 2011; Glasø, Vie, Holmdal, and Einarsen, 2011; Wegge, van Dick, Fisher, West, and Dawson, 2006). According to Weiss and Cropanzano (1996), events that occur in the workplace environment can "generate an emotional reaction or mood change in people" (p. 31). These changes in emotional states then lead to a variety of both "affect-driven" and "judgment-driven" (p. 13) behaviors. Affect-driven behavior is closely and temporally linked to emotional states, whereas judgment-driven behavior is related to more stable attitudes regarding the job or organization, with attitudes influenced (but not directly driven) by emotions.

Support for the main suppositions of AET are plentiful (see Weiss and Beal, 2005), with studies indicating that affect and job satisfaction are related but not equivalent constructs; and that emotions can lead to both pro- and anti-organizational behavior and outcomes. For example, positive affective experiences relate to affective commitment and helping behavior (Fisher, 2002), and turnover intentions have been found to be predicted by attitudes (rather than affective reactions per se; Weiss and Beal, 2005). Holtom, Burton, and Crossley (2012) also used an AET framework to examine how negative shocks (an affective event), job embeddedness, and dispositional influences combine to influence employee behaviors. We stress, however, that AET was never intended to be an explanatory model, but rather that it is a framework to study the antecedents and effects of emotional experiences (Weiss and Beal, 2005; Weiss and Cropanzano, 1996). Consistent with this idea, we argue that AET acts, in effect, as a macrostructure for our model, which also requires the support of a microstructure such as the TTPS to flesh out and to explain the proposed relationships more fully.

Microstructure: The Transactional Theory of Psychological Stress

Transactional stress theory, also known as the cognitive phenomenological theory of psychological stress (TTPS), is a process-based theory in which appraisal and coping serve as mediators of person–environment interactions. Therefore, appraisal and coping can have

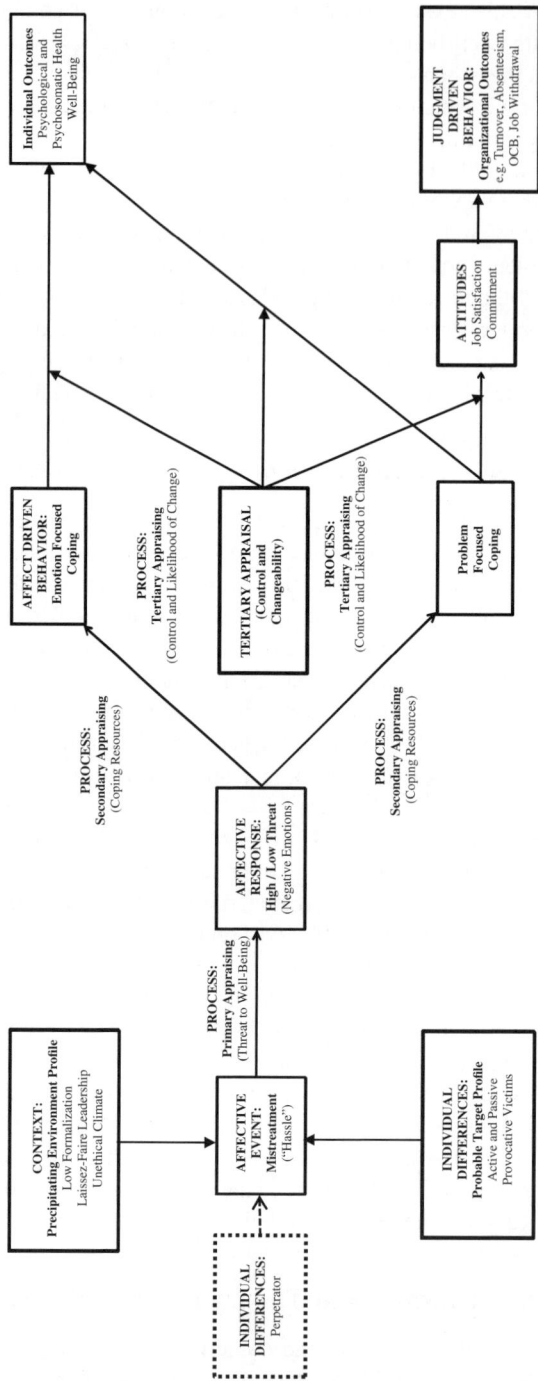

Figure 22.1 A dual theory, process-and-variance model of interpersonal mistreatment.

an impact on both long-term and short-term outcomes (Lazarus, 1981; 1991; Lazarus and Folkman, 1984). TTPS focuses on cognitive appraisal processes, coping and adaptation, with the latter either adaptive or maladaptive in well-being terms. As such, the theory differs from alternative stress process theories such as the allostatic load model (ALM; McEwen and Seeman, 1999), which focuses on the primary and secondary physiological processes that influence within-person allostatic mechanisms.

Folkman, Lazarus, Gruen, and DeLongis (1986) define coping as an individual's "cognitive and behavioral efforts to manage (reduce, minimize, master or tolerate) the internal and external demands of the person–environment transaction that is appraised as taxing or exceeding the person's resources" (p. 572). Lazarus and Folkman (1984) note in particular that coping follows the cognitive process of appraisal, wherein individuals initially evaluate whether an environmental stimulus is likely to cause harm to their well-being or thwart attainment of personal goals. Lazarus (2006) summarizes appraisal as the process that enables individuals to determine "the significance of what is happening in the person–environmental relationship, the most important aspect of which is interpersonal" (p. 12).

Lazarus and Folkman (1984) argue that it is a person's *interpretation* of an event that shapes their emotional and behavioral responses in the *primary* stage of appraisal; and the more (potentially or actually) harmful an event is perceived to be, the more likely it is that the individual will develop a state of *distress*. An assessment of threat to well-being then triggers a negative emotional response, including emotions such as fear and anxiety. In contrast, an appraisal of the event as a challenge or resulting in the achievement of important goals can lead to positive affect, and have a more motivating *eustress* effect.

The *secondary* stage of the appraisal process occurs when the individual assesses what emotion-focused or problem-focused coping potential or capabilities they might have, which in turn should influence whether the outcome of the event is negative or positive (Lazarus, 1991). In short, secondary appraisal intervenes between threat assessment (arising from primary appraisal) and the coping process (Lazarus, 1966). Smith and Lazarus (1993) argue further that secondary appraisal can be broken into four components: (1) availability of problem-focused coping options, (2) availability of emotion-focused coping options, (3) accountability (who is responsible for the situation and, therefore, should be the target of any subsequent coping efforts), and (4) future expectancy (likelihood of change). The last two derive from notions of whether the individual believes the situation to be within or outside their control, and the stressor is either amenable vs. refractory to change (Lazarus, 1966; 1991).

This four-component view presents a complex theoretical issue in terms of secondary appraisal, which has traditionally been thought of as a *mediator* in the stressor–coping process. An alternative possibility is that accountability and future expectancy act as *moderators* of the relationship between coping strategies (problem-focused, emotion-focused, or both) and their outcomes, potentially serving an evaluative function in the person's assessment of the suitability of their coping choice. Because these latter two components potentially have a differing function, we argue for them to be included in a separate category that we will refer to as *tertiary* appraisal.

Precipitators of Mistreatment

The initial components of our model refer to the precipitators of mistreatment, including the nature of the environment where the mistreatment takes place, and the characteristics of the target of mistreatment.

Precipitating Environments

In AET, Weiss and Cropanzano (1996) posit that the environment plays a central role in determining whether an affective event occurs in the first instance. Vardi and Weitz (2004) suggest similarly that organizations themselves provide an opportunity for individuals to misbehave; and that certain organizational factors may encourage or deter misbehavior within the workplace. The notion of organizational influences links to Bono and Judge's (2004) argument that organizations possess a strong situational strength that can provoke or dissuade behaviors. Likewise, Olson-Buchanan and Boswell (2008) assert that characteristics of the situation act as potential triggers, which can be perceived by the individual as mistreatment, or otherwise. In this section of our analysis, therefore, we explore organizational climate, formalization, and leadership style as critical environmental factors that may serve as a precipitating environment for mistreatment.

Organizational climate, defined as the "environmental description of an organization's practices and procedures" (Ashkanasy, 2008, p. 1028), is part of our precipitating environment profile based on Hoel and Salin's (2003) suggestion that climate is an antecedent to workplace bullying. A negative or "bullying" climate is characterized by both an absence of measures to prevent employees from being mistreated and a lack of punishment when mistreatment does occur. Similarly, an organizational climate of tolerance for sexual harassment (Willness et al., 2007; Fitzgerald, Swan, and Fischer, 1995) may inadvertently convey to employees that such behavior is acceptable. Targets of workplace harassment have, therefore, been known to blame the organization's culture and climate for their experiences (Bowling and Beehr, 2006).

Different types of climate, particularly ethical climates, theoretically and empirically relate to supervisory and employee behavior, including various forms of interpersonal deviance (e.g., see Appelbaum, Deguire, and Lay, 2005; Bulutlar and Oz, 2008; Peterson, 2002; Wimbush and Shepard, 1994; Wimbush, Shepard, and Markham, 1997). While the ethical climate of an organization has been defined as "the shared perceptions of what is ethically correct behavior and how ethical issues should be handled in the organization" (Victor and Cullen, 1987, pp. 51–52), Key (1999) argues that the ethical climate perceptions of individuals in a given organization are, by definition, individually constructed, and may not constitute a shared phenomenon. We consider mistreatment to be an unethical behavior insomuch as mistreatment does not conform to accepted standards of behavior and is morally wrong (O'Reilly and Aquino, 2011). As a result, we focus on (perceived un)ethical climate as a specific form of organizational climate anticipated to relate positively to perceived instances of mistreatment occurring.

Formalization is the second construct in the precipitating environment profile. The term can be broadly defined as the extent to which the organization has written documentation of rules, procedures, and policies to guide behavior and decision-making (Wood et al., 2013). There are mixed views on whether formalization deters (e.g., Salin, 2003; Vardi and Weitz, 2004) or encourages (e.g., Einarsen and Skogstad, 1996; Glendinning, 2001) poor interpersonal behavior. Consistent with Bowling and Beehr's (2006) position, we argue in favor of formalization being a deterrent. Victims may attribute or blame the workplace harassment on the organization because the organization is responsible for selecting, training, and rewarding/punishing perpetrators – all of which are human resources practices that fall within the formalization domain. Thus, we propose that employees in organizations with more formalized control processes will experience fewer instances of perceived mistreatment.

Leadership, or more specifically laissez-faire leadership (Bass, 1997) is the third component of our precipitating environment profile. The decision to include laissez-faire leadership in our model is based on research findings that show that this style of leadership is linked to different forms of interpersonal deviance (e.g., Cogin and Fish, 2007; O'Moore and Lynch, 2007; O'Moore, Seigne, McGuire, and Smith, 1998). These findings are consistent with Skogstad, Einarsen, Torsheim, Aasland, and Hetland's (2007) view that laissez faire leadership can be destructive, rather than merely a failure to lead. For example, a helpless or uninterested manager is one of several key organizational factors in the development of bullying (Leymann, 1996). Therefore, it is possible that laissez-faire leadership indirectly contributes to bullying by conveying the impression that bullying is acceptable behavior (Hoel and Salin, 2003). Abusive leadership is also positively associated with experiences of gender harassment and unwanted sexual attention (Cogin and Fish, 2007).

Based on the foregoing discussion and consistent with AET (i.e., environments have an indirect influence on affective experiences by rendering certain events more or less likely to occur), we argue that, *ceteris paribus*, individuals in precipitating environments for mistreatment (characterized by an unethical climate, low levels of formalization, and high levels of laissez-faire leadership) perceive more mistreatment events directed at themselves than do individuals in environments with ethical climates, high levels of formalization, and low levels of laissez-faire leadership.

Victim Individual Differences

In the next component of our model, we explore the characteristics of the target of mistreatment and propose that individuals with a particular combination of personal characteristics are more likely to be targeted than other individuals; which we term the "probable target." While many studies have been conducted on perpetrator characteristics (e.g., see Bolin and Heatherly, 2001; Judge, Scott, and Ilies, 2006; Lee and Allen, 2002; Mount, Ilies, and Johnson 2006; Seigne, Coyne, Randall, and Parker, 2007; South, Oltmanns, and Turkheimer, 2003), the characteristics of the victims of workplace mistreatment appear to have been neglected. This lack of attention has likely arisen because including target characteristics as possible antecedents to mistreatment may be viewed as victim-blaming. We argue, however, that the victim is central to our model given our specific interest in how victims cope with perceived mistreatment episodes (Aquino and Byron, 2002). In using the term "probable targets," we acknowledge however that we are adopting an external, interactional view of mistreatment (i.e., how the perpetrator may perceive the target).

Personality traits have dominated the sparse literature on targets for mistreatment, with the Big Five appearing most often (e.g., see Coyne, Seigne, and Randall, 2000; Milam, Spitzmueller, and Penney, 2009). Results have largely been inconsistent however, and seem to vary depending on the type of interpersonal deviance studied. In addition, while trait negative affect and interpersonal deviance appear to be uniformly negatively related (e.g., Bowling and Beehr, 2006) and trait negative affect is found in other victim profiles (e.g., abusive supervision victims; Tepper, Duffy, Henle, and Lambert, 2006), the direction of causality is unclear (Aquino and Thau, 2009). As efforts to understand the victim increase, researchers have been encouraged to select traits for examination based on sound theoretical grounds, given the sheer number that could be explored (Griffin and Lopez, 2005).

At this point, we argue that gaining insight into how a victim may inadvertently influence the occurrence of mistreatment events actually requires viewing mistreatment through a fundamentally different theoretical lens. Thus, rather than embracing the popular bad barrel (environment) and bad apples (perpetrator) perspective (Dunlop and Lee, 2004; O'Boyle, Forsyth, and O'Boyle, 2011), we follow Sandberg and Alvesson's (2011) recommendation to problematize our review of the literature by adopting a victimology approach. Victimology, the study of victimization, includes (but is not limited to) intertwined relationships between victims, offenders, and systems (Karmen, 2003), which we deem equivalent to targets, perpetrators, and the organizational context.

According to victimology literature, a victim's contribution to a crime occurring (or in the present case, the target's role in ostensibly causing mistreatment) is known as "victim precipitation" (Elias, 1986; Landau and Freeman-Longo, 1990). These authors suggest victim precipitation can be classified into five levels. Levels 3 to 5 ("moderate," "high," "maximal") are particularly relevant to our provocative victim argument. This is because these three levels respectively represent situations in which victimization could probably have been preventable, could clearly have been avoidable, or never would have occurred, had the victim's characteristics or behavior been different.

While typically excluded from studies of mistreatment and interpersonal deviance in general, victim precipitation is not a new idea. For example, as stated by Zapf et al. (1996), "it is often argued that it is the fault of the victims themselves when they are harassed because of their socially incompetent behavior, low achievement, or pathological personalities" (p. 219). Even some physicians treating "mobbing" (group-bullying) victims have argued that victims themselves are the cause of the behavior (Zapf, 1999).

In line with the foregoing arguments, we contend that some victims precipitate mistreatment by virtue of their personal characteristics and behavior. More specifically, we propose that such individuals are in effect provocative victims, and are therefore probable targets for mistreatment. A contentious notion from its inception to the present day, the term "provocative victim" was originally coined by Olweus (1978) to describe highly aggressive persons who display provocative, hostile or threatening behaviors that invite retaliatory responses from others. Levinson (1978) described these individuals as having an "abrasive personality" (p. 101). Olweus (1978) used the separate term "submissive victims" to characterize potential victims who were overly passive, hesitant to defend themselves, extremely sensitive and quiet, and with a tendency to hold negative self-views and adopt an accommodating conflict style.

More recently researchers have tended to group provocative and submissive victim profiles under one umbrella term "provocative victim," referring to any individual who is more likely to be a target of an interpersonally deviant behavior than other individuals. For example, Matthiesen and Einarsen (2007) differed from Olweus (1978) in arguing that a provocative victim for bullying might unintentionally create a hostile environment in which others feel uncomfortable, and show a general inability to function well in social situations, thus leading to an increased likelihood of being targeted. These authors defined the provocative victim as an individual with low self-esteem, high social anxiety, and trait aggressiveness.

Although examples of research in interpersonal deviance conducted in organizational settings that incorporate victim precipitation or a provocative victim aspect are rare (for notable exceptions, see Aquino and Byron, 2002; Henle and Gross, 2014), the research from more general (especially schoolyard) perspectives is compelling. Therefore, we feel it is appropriate to expect that a probable target for mistreatment profile includes both active and passive provocative victim characteristics. In other words, *ceteris paribus*, individuals who show characteristics of a provocative victim (the "probable target") are more likely to self-report experiencing mistreatment than other individuals.

Primary and Secondary Appraisal

Having discussed the characteristics of the precipitating environment and the probable target of mistreatment, we now move on to examine the process of appraisal. As we discussed earlier, the Lazarus and Folkman (1984) model based in TTPS theory, which includes primary and secondary appraisal, is traditionally invoked in this regard. Note that in a subsequent section of our chapter we adopt an alternative view on traditional secondary appraisal, and introduce a third form of appraisal, which we term "tertiary appraisal."

Primary Appraisal

At this point, we address the internal processes underlying the target's perceived experience of mistreatment. In this respect, Weiss and Cropanzano (1996) theorized in AET that an individual assesses the relevance of affective events in terms of how they correspond to their personal goals; or the degree to which the event is congruent or in conflict with the individual's desires. It appears that this assessment arises from an appraisal process. In this case, TTPS (i.e., the microstructure), wherein primary appraisal is the process through which individuals assess whether an event is likely to threaten their well-being, becomes relevant. In this regard, it is important to encompass appraisal process components within our model to understand the mechanisms by which environmental and individual factors combine to influence individual responses to mistreatment events.

Frijda (1988) pointed out that appraisal begins when the individual experiences a negative response to an event "point(ing) to the presence of some concern" (p. 351), and seeks to evaluate the probability of resultant harm. This evaluation then results in an affective response; for example, negative affect (e.g., fear) when the event is appraised to be a threat. In the context of our theorizing, mistreatment can be construed as an affective event that triggers primary appraisal. In support of this idea, in an AET-based study of bullying, Glasø et al. (2011) found that employees reported experiencing negative affect in direct response to their mistreatment. Similarly, in a study of incivility, Cortina and Magley (2009) found that appraisals of incivility experiences were generally negative (as measured by negative emotions such as feeling annoyed). On the basis of this evidence, it is logical to suggest, via the primary appraisal process, that a mistreatment event is likely to be perceived to be a stressor (threat), which results in the victim experiencing a negative affective response.

Secondary Appraisal

Lazarus and Folkman (1984) posit secondary appraisal as the set of processes underlying the individual's choice of coping strategy, which can be problem-focused, emotion-focused, or a combination of the two. Based on AET, we previously proposed that mistreatment events generate a negative emotional response. The addition of TTPS to the AET framework makes the role of target secondary appraisal clearer; it is the process that influences what coping strategies (or combination of strategies) the target chooses to adopt to cope with their emotional reaction.

According to Smith and Lazarus (1993), in TTPS, secondary appraisal involves assessing the availability of coping resources. To this end, the key components of the secondary appraisal process that directly influence coping choices are twofold: (1) the individual's perceived emotion-focused options, and (2) their perceived problem-focused options. It seems reasonable to conclude that if, on the one hand, an individual first appraises an event to be highly stressful (high threat) and determines emotion-focused coping strategies are available, they are more likely to deploy emotion-focused coping. If, on the other hand, the event has been appraised as low threat, the affective response is unlikely to be intensely negative. In this latter case, if secondary appraisal assesses problem-focused strategies to be available, the target is likely to choose these. These ideas collectively suggest a *mediatory* relationship between the event, the affective response, and coping choices, underpinned by primary and (partial) secondary appraisal processes. In other words, a target's negative affective response mediates the relationship between their perceived experience of mistreatment and the coping strategy or strategies (problem vs. emotion focused) they adopt.

Despite evidence of a potential relationship between emotion valence and subsequent behaviors (e.g., negative and positive emotions, and engaging in avoidance and helping behavior; Barclay and Kiefer, 2012), few researchers to date have examined this process in detail. An exception is a study by Scheck and Kinicki (2000), who used Lazarus and Folkman's (1984) TTPS to look at the antecedents of coping, and in particular to explore the role of negative emotion arising out of primary appraisals of a threatening situation. Scheck and Kinicki found that employees' ability to focus on positive, problem-solving alternatives appears to be impeded when they experience strong negative affect (e.g., anger) in response to an organizational change initiative.

Indeed, mistreatment, when appraised as a potentially harmful event, may increase a target's anxiety and fear to a point where they have difficulty accessing information from the cerebral cortex (Perry, Pollard, Blakley, Baker, and Vigilante, 1995). Such "emotional flooding" (Jones and Bodtker, 2001, p. 218) affects the individual's ability to function and think effectively (see also Gooty, Gavin, Ashkanasy, and Thomas, 2014).

There is also evidence that emotion activation levels influence whether a target engages in emotion- or problem- focused coping. At the discrete level, negative emotions sit on a bipolar continuum ranging from high to low activation. Emotions such as feeling frightened, angry, and agitated are considered high activation; embarrassed and dissatisfied are medium activation, and sad, miserable and depressed are low activation (Morgan and Heise, 1988).

Emotions categorized as medium to high activation typically lead to *hot cognition* behavior (Mandler, 1982), which is behavior primarily influenced by emotion (Abelson, 1963; Kunda, 1999). Aligned with the concepts of emotional flooding (Gooty et al., 2014; Jones and Bodtker, 2001; Perry et al., 1995) and the infusion-into-judgment continuum in the affect infusion model (AIM; Forgas, 1995; Forgas and George, 2001), hot cognition is a rapid and automatic response driven by high-activation emotions which make it difficult for the target to process or analyze information in a rational manner, thus leading to biased and low-quality decision-making. In contrast, low arousal negative emotions represent *cold cognition*, which, typically, leads to more rational behavior (Kunda, 1999). Based in this reasoning, we contend that a target who experiences negative affect in response to mistreatment is likely to engage in emotion- or problem-focused coping depending on the intensity of the experienced affect, such that higher intensity affect is more likely to lead to emotion-focused coping, while lower intensity affect is more likely to lead to problem-focused coping.

Coping as a Mediator of the (Negative) Affect–Outcome Relationship

So far, we have argued that mistreatment is likely to be appraised as a stressor and thus to lead to a negative affective response, which in turn elicits emotion- or problem-focused coping. We have also suggested that, in cases where the (di)stress reaction is high, and where a secondary appraisal process determines that emotion-focused coping is available, individuals are more likely to select emotion-focused than problem-focused coping. This brings us to how coping strategies mediate between stress reactions and individual and organizational outcomes.

As we have outlined already, organizational mistreatment researchers have not yet included the roles of the stressor, appraisal processes, coping *and* outcomes (adaptation), nor have they adopted an AET framework. Hence, while it is clear that various forms of mistreatment have negative consequences, both for the individual victim and their organization, research has largely failed to identify how or why these outcomes manifest. Ineffective coping may well be an explanation for the relationships between stressors (such as perceived mistreatment) and negative outcomes, such as diminished individual health and well-being. Moreover, and as Lazarus (2006) points out, researchers have failed to consider the individual engaging in appraisal and coping, and the context in which the stressor, appraisal, and coping occurs. In this case, there would appear to be an imperative to challenge the notions that coping is a case of "either or" and that problem-focused coping is more effective in reducing the impact of stressful experiences (cf. Gooty et al., 2014).

In reference to what type of coping works best in a particular situation, Skinner, Edge, Altman, and Sherwood (2003) preempted Lazarus (2006) in stating, "Any arguments about the 'right' or 'wrong' way to cope are pointless. If the ways that an individual copes are assembled based on the specific stressor(s) and situational constraints, then any way of coping can be locally adaptive" (2003, p. 231).

Differing opinions as to the effectiveness of the two categories of coping may exist, however. In part, this is because of the expression of emotional distress and self-deprecation in some measures of emotion-focused coping (e.g., see Austenfeld and Stanton, 2004), rather than an actual assessment of the impact of coping on negative outcomes; the latter is rarely (if ever) studied in context. In addition, although van Rhenen, Blonk, Schaufeli, and van Dijk (2007) found that problem-focused coping is more effective than emotion-focused coping in reducing absences due to illness, they neglected the role of appraisal, the individual, and the situational context. Aquino and Thau (2009) and Gooty et al. (2014) go as far as to say that in certain circumstances some problem-focused coping strategies (e.g., confronting the perpetrator) may even make the situation worse.

Sideridis (2006) found, in particular, that while combining both categories of coping can lead to significantly less stress, each coping style might be unrelated to stress when considered on its own. Similarly, Boyd, Lewin, and Sager (2009) found that emotion-focused and problem-focused coping together affect psychological outcomes, which, in turn, affect job-related outcomes, such as job satisfaction and intention to withdraw. As such, it seems that the effectiveness of any coping strategy will depend on a variety of different factors, including the type of stressor, the context in which it occurs, characteristics of the individual, and appraisal of the event. *Inter alia*, coping may not be a case of simply "either or," but rather "it depends."

We argue here that inclusion of TTPS within an AET framework facilitates consideration of all these major factors, and thus our model represents an effort to address the concerns regarding coping research raised by Lazarus (1981; 1991; 2006). We also seek to put to rest the ill-informed debate over the effectiveness of emotion-focused versus problem-focused coping in terms of adaptation by proposing that *both* emotion-focused and problem-focused coping mediate the relationship between a victim's negative affective response and individual outcomes of psychological and psychosomatic well-being.

Work Attitudes and Judgment-Driven Behavior

Earlier, we suggested that emotion-focused coping is primarily influenced by negative emotions; hence, emotion-focused coping is representative of affect-driven behavior. We now return to the core tenets of AET to discuss judgment-driven behavior (Weiss and Cropanzano, 1996). Weiss and Cropanzano define this form of behavior as behavior that arises from attitudes. Unlike affect-driven behavior, judgment-driven behavior is not normally associated with a particular emotional state; it is the consequence of a careful decision-making process influenced by the person's evaluation of their job. An employee's intention to leave the organization, for example, is a cognitively driven behavior that Fisher (2002) found to be predicted by job satisfaction. In an early meta-analysis, Mathieu and Zajac (1990) found both job satisfaction and organizational commitment predicted job performance and turnover intentions. Likewise, Jaramillo, Mulki, and Marshall (2005) found a positive relationship between organizational commitment and job performance. Note, however, that we do not imply that no affective process is involved in the cognitive route to employee behavior, but rather that the relative weight and importance of affect will differ (Wegge et al., 2006).

Moving on now to consider the effects of mistreatment, we see that negative organizational behaviors such as turnover (Djurkovic et al., 2004; Lim et al., 2008), withdrawal (Cortina et al., 2001), performance decline (Caza and Cortina, 2007), absenteeism (Kivimäki et al., 2000), and job withdrawal (O'Leary-Kelly et al., 2009) are all associated with experiences of interpersonal mistreatment. On the other hand, positive behaviors such as individually directed organizational citizenship behavior (OCBI; Aquino and Bommer, 2003), organizational citizenship behavior (OCB; Zellars, Tepper, and Duffy, 2002), and expressions of organizational commitment (Willness et al., 2007) have been found to be negatively related to mistreatment. What is missing from these studies, however, is a potential mediating role of appraisal and coping.

As we noted earlier, judgment-driven behaviors, which include both in-role (e.g., job performance, see Petty, McGee, and Cavender, 1984) and extra-role behaviors such as OCB (see, e.g., LePine, Erez, and Johnson, 2002), link to attitudes, and play an essential role in organizational productivity and effectiveness. Based on TTPS and AET, we therefore conclude that in situations where the target selects problem-focused coping, this form of coping should serve as a mediator between the affective responses and attitudes, with attitudes then influencing judgment-driven behavior. This double-mediation effect essentially means problem-focused coping mediates the effect of negative affective responses on work attitudes such as organizational commitment and job satisfaction that, in turn, determine judgment-driven behaviors such as organizational citizenship, turnover intentions, and absenteeism.

With all major notions of AET now discussed, the final step is to discuss the moderation effects of what we term "tertiary appraisal." This requires a revisiting of TTPS or, more specifically, the role of the third and fourth component of "traditional" secondary appraisal (Smith and Lazarus, 1993) in influencing individual and organizational outcomes of stress.

"Tertiary Appraisal" as a Moderator of the Coping–Outcome Relationship

As we previously argued, and according to TTPS, secondary appraisal mediates the stressor–outcome relationship. We now introduce the other two components of TTPS: future expectancy (likelihood of change) and accountability (whether the individual has control over the outcome of the situation, see Smith and Lazarus, 1993). These components derive from the notion of a stressor being either amenable or refractory to change (Lazarus, 1991) and the degree to which the individual feels the situation is within or outside their control (Lazarus, 1966). Smith and Lazarus's resulting four-component view of the secondary appraisal process presents a complex issue in terms of the traditional view that secondary appraisal serves as a mediator in the stressor–coping process. It is possible that accountability and future expectancy might affect outcomes via an alternative process, which we refer to as "tertiary appraisal," to distinguish these two components from other appraisal processes.

We propose that the tertiary appraisal process potentially serves an evaluative function in assessing the suitability of coping choices based on control and likelihood of change. Specifically, we argue that the degree of control (i.e., accountability) an actor perceives herself or himself to have over the outcomes of a situation, and the assessment of whether the situation is amenable or refractory to change, plays a moderating role in the coping–outcome relationship. Our assertion is in line with van Rhenen and colleagues (2007), who argue that problem-focused coping is more suitable in situations where the individual feels a degree of control over the stressor. In other words, we argue that tertiary appraisal moderates the relationship between (1) emotion-focused coping and individual outcomes; and (2) problem-focused coping and attitude formation and individual outcomes. Critically, we posit further that tertiary appraisal takes place *after* coping strategies are selected and deployed.

Our rationale for the foregoing assertion is based on the literature on stress and coping that makes multiple references to the role of perceptions of control and likelihood of change in the secondary appraisal process. When we apply TTPS as a microstructure to support the AET macrostructure, however, we argue that coping choices are fully explained based on two key factors. These are (a) the need to deal with affective reactions to an event (the AET argument); and (b) perceptions of the availability of emotion-focused and problem-focused coping resources that occur as part of the assessment process, which directly inform the selection of coping strategies (the TTPS argument). On this basis, the role of accountability and future expectancy may constitute a process subsequent to secondary appraisal, perhaps more relevant to evaluating the suitability of coping strategy choices.

In support of this notion, and with specific reference to accountability, Smith and Lazarus (1993) argue that the secondary appraisal process determines who will receive credit or blame for the outcome of the event. Moreover, this determination refers to whether the outcome is motivationally congruent or incongruent with an individual's goals or desires. Recall that the primary appraisal process refers to the degree to which the individual deems the (affective) event consistent or inconsistent with their goals or desires, resulting in an assessment of an event as being irrelevant (no further action required), positive (preserves or improves the actor's situation, potentially leading to positive emotions), or stressful (e.g., a threat to well-being, leading to a negative emotional response; see Lazarus and Folkman, 1984).

In our model, an assessment of threat (i.e., leading to distress and negative emotions) leads to secondary appraisals of the coping options available, followed by deployment of emotion-focused and/or problem-focused strategies. If effective, coping (regardless of whether it is problem or emotion focused) should result in a motivationally congruent outcome. The stressor impact should reduce so that the individual is likely to feel that the threat or challenge to their goals no longer exists. Thus, if the concept of control or accountability refers to allocation of credit or blame for the outcome, it logically follows that the progress toward the outcome (i.e., adaptation) must have already commenced or been achieved. This approach would make accountability a *post-coping strategy deployment evaluation process*, rather than a direct process affecting coping choices (as traditionally theorized).

In sum, we argue that this approach suggests the presence of an appraisal process beyond the traditional secondary appraisal process. We thus refer to this as the *tertiary appraisal process*. In other words, we contend that an individual chooses a coping style to address a stressor (based on an assessment of the coping options available to them, and their affective reactions to the stimuli). The individual then evaluates the degree of accountability for the outcomes and the extent to which the situation is amenable vs. refractory to change. These evaluations represent an additional appraisal process, which then serves to moderate the relationship between both types of coping and their eventual outcomes.

With perceptions of control and changeability varying depending on the situation and individual, we argue that tertiary appraisal of control and the likelihood of change moderates the relationship between emotion-focused coping and well-being, such that the relationship is stronger when the individual deems the situation to be out of control and refractory to change. We also contend tertiary appraisal moderates the relationships between problem-focused coping and psychological health and well-being outcomes, and between problem-focused coping and attitudes, such that these two relationships are stronger when the individual deems the situation to be in control and amenable to change.

Boundary Conditions

Our model has four important boundary conditions: (1) focusing on mistreatment as a harmful or threatening event; (2) omission of the potential influence of individual differences in abilities on the appraisal and coping process; (3) assumption of a one-way process; and (4) modeling based on a single mistreatment event when the form, frequency, and duration of the experience may all play a role in determining outcomes. While full development of these issues is beyond the scope of our model, it is appropriate to discuss each issue, and provide some points for future research in these respects.

Mistreatment as a Negative Affective Event

The first boundary to our theorizing arises because the microstructures embedded within our model are derived from an appraisal process that elicits an increase in negative emotions, such as anger or anxiety, in response to the perception of being mistreated (e.g., Glasø et al., 2011; Grandey, Tam, and Brauberger, 2002). In bullying situations, Glasø and his colleagues found that not only do negative emotions arise, but also positive emotions can be reduced. Notwithstanding this, the asymmetry effect whereby negative emotions tend to be recalled more easily than positive emotions (Dasborough, 2006) suggests that in mistreatment situations, negative emotions will be more salient. Because two distinct mechanisms are involved in generating positive and negative affect in response to specific events (Gable, Reis, and Elliot, 2000), we have dealt with the relationships between threat-based appraisals, negative emotions, and the coping strategies deployed in response to mistreatment.

Ignoring Individual Differences in Abilities

A second boundary relates to the potential role of individual differences in abilities in the appraisal and coping processes, such as emotional intelligence (EI) (Mayer and Salovey, 1997) and problem-solving ability (Heppner, 1988). Emotional intelligence abilities may influence a number of the relationships proposed in our model. EI can play a role in moderating the effects of stress for some individuals (Gohm, Corser, and Dalsky, 2005). The ability to manage our own emotions (Mayer and Salovey, 1997) could be useful in terms of using emotion-focused coping strategies to regulate emotions. As Salovey (2001) notes, both expressing and suppressing negative emotions can negatively impact health. In this regard, emotion management is the ability to determine when expression vs. suppression is more appropriate. In line with this, Stanton and Low (2012) argue that emotion-focused coping in the form of expressing emotions in stressful situations can be beneficial or maladaptive. Similarly, Lawrence, Troth, Jordan, and Collins (2011) also argue that, depending on a number of conditions, emotional intelligence and emotion expression displays can lead to both functional and dysfunctional outcomes.

Moreover, emotional suppression may sometimes have negative consequences (e.g., see Antonakis in Antonakis, Ashkanasy, and Dasborough, 2009). Butler et al. (2003) found that suppressing negative emotions led to raised blood pressure (in both the regulators and their counterpart), disturbed communication, reduced rapport, and inhibited relationship formation, suggesting suppression is maladaptive and leads to poor social outcomes. The emotional regulation strategy of reappraisal may be a more effective way of managing emotions than suppression (Gross, 2002; Gross and John, 2003).

Assuming a Linear Process

In line with cognitive appraisal theory, we have assumed that a person's appraisal of mistreatment elicits negative emotions (Lazarus, 1982). An employee's emotion may also affect their appraisal of a given situation (Izard, 2009). Based on Forgas's (1995) AIM, actors' emotional state can influence everyday judgments about an event, particularly when a complex or unusual situation requires substantial information processing. In this instance, emotions can affect the information the person recalls and interprets, upon which they base their judgment about how to respond. Given the close relationship between emotion and cognition, it is possible there is a complex, reciprocal relationship between the event, appraisal, and emotion. In line with this idea, Fugate, Harrison, and Kinicki (2011) identified a synchronous relationship between negative appraisal, negative emotions, and coping in response to an organizational change initiative in a large public company. Emotion and cognition may continually and dynamically interact to influence a person's choice of coping strategy and subsequent behavior in response to perceived mistreatment in organizations. Lazarus and Folkman (1984) clearly stated that primary and secondary appraisals do not necessarily operate independently; they can interact, co-occur, and occur more than once. Hence, though our model implies a linear process, it is possible that appraisal processes do not operate independently but can co-occur, and recursively reoccur.

Impact of Form, Frequency, and Duration

Finally we note that, in developing our model, we focused on the dynamic nature of the cognitive appraisal and coping strategies that a person might use to manage mistreatment (Lazarus and Folkman, 1984; Folkman and Lazarus, 1985). We acknowledge, however, that mistreatment can, by definition, be either an isolated incident or a number of incidents, and that mistreatment is but one form of interpersonal deviance. Although beyond the scope of our theorizing in this chapter, a potential addition to our model may therefore be a feedback loop from coping to primary appraisal of an initial mistreatment event as harmful or threatening, as well as a feedback loop that accounts for subsequent mistreatment experiences. This would also allow for the possibility that a person may (re)appraise either the initial or subsequent (repeated) acts of mistreatment as more, or less, threatening depending on the relative adaptive success of problem-focused or emotion-focused coping strategies (Folkman et al., 1986).

Evidence also suggests that, in contrast to perpetrators, victim accounts of perpetration (interpersonal conflict) are likely to accumulate, where the targets' emotional response (e.g., anger) builds up over time as a consequence of repeated experiences (Baumeister, Stillwell, and Wotman, 1990). As a result, the appraisal–emotion relationship may strengthen or weaken over time based on the frequency with which mistreatment events occur. Klarner, By, and Diefenbach (2011) suggest that emotions experienced during an organizational change process can impact on the appraisal process triggered by a subsequent change, given that threat appraisals can also be anticipatory (Lazarus an Folkman, 1984). Similarly, modeling the appraisal of and responses to different forms of interpersonal deviance such as bullying (which occurs not only on a systematic (frequent) basis, but also for an extended period of time; Quine, 1999) would need to account for both the frequency of the experience and the duration of time over which the experiences occurred. Testing such a model would require multiple assessments at different time points, that is, a longitudinal, time-lagged design, to understand how appraisal and coping change as subsequent events occur (Lazarus and Folkman, 1984).

Implications

Implications for Theory

Our primary aim in this chapter has been to deal with the problem that, to date, we lack a well-developed theory of the processes underlying employees' responses to stressful events. To solve this problem, we have set forth a dual theory process-and-variance model of mistreatment to explain, in part, the causes and consequences of mistreatment at work. We argue that our model has potential to contribute to our understanding of the antecedents of interpersonal mistreatment, as well as how individuals cope with their emotional reaction to mistreatment events. In particular, our model, if supported, should have clear implications for both theory and practice.

In the first instance, while previous research has shown a link between deviance and individual/organizational outcomes, a problem exists insofar as researchers into organizational mistreatment have largely failed to explain how and why relationships between mistreatment behaviors and various negative individual and organizational outcomes exist. In using AET as a macrostructure and TTPS as a microstructure, we further develop the conceptual work of researchers such as Ashkanasy, Ashton-James, and Jordan (2004) and Ashton-James and

Ashkanasy (2005) to offer an explanation of how and why negative outcomes may manifest. We also address the call of AET theorists, such as Weiss and Cropanzano (1996) and Weiss and Beal (2005), to add further explanatory power to the AET framework. We acknowledge that our model is complex, but this very complexity is what will enable exploration and explanation of what is a complicated, but currently oversimplified, organizational behavior phenomenon.

A further theoretical contribution of our model is embedded in our idea that the traditional four-component approach to secondary appraisal adopted by Smith and Lazarus (1993) is potentially better separated, such that accountability and future expectancy form a tertiary appraisal process. In this case, tertiary appraisal serves to evaluate the suitability of the coping strategy decision, which is arguably best determined by a combination of the affective reaction to the event, and an appraisal of the availability of problem-focused and emotion-focused coping options. Based on this premise, tertiary appraisal plays a moderating, rather than a mediating role in influencing outcomes of stressful events. We argue that this is a new perspective on a long-standing concept that warrants further examination.

In summary, we posit that our model and its associated propositions contribute to management scholarship in three important ways. First, by adopting the victim's subjective perspective, we address the imbalance between victim and perpetrator research. Second, we have problematized the existing "causal" literature by adopting a victimology lens, and sought to develop a profile of precipitating environments and probable targets, rather than exploring only one or the other group of antecedents in isolation, as previous research has tended to do (e.g., Olson-Buchanan and Boswell, 2008). Third, we have heeded Lazarus's (1981; 1991; 2006) calls to take into account the complex nature of the mistreatment phenomenon throughout the entire process from antecedents to outcomes. In particular, the failure of the extant research to adopt a holistic perspective has been an important shortcoming of the ill-informed problem-focused versus emotion-focused coping debate.

Implications for Practice

Our model also has potential managerial implications for practice. As can be seen in Figure 22.1, our model concludes with individual and organizational outcomes, both of which are widely acknowledged to influence organizational effectiveness. Thus, while there are multiple categories of organizational effectiveness, including financial performance, customer satisfaction, internal business processes, learning and growth (Kaplan and Norton, 1992), effectiveness can be more broadly defined as the achievement of organizational goals (Robertson, Callinan, and Bartram, 2002). The issue is that regardless of where in the world an organization operates – be it Europe, Asia-Pacific, or elsewhere – low levels of job performance and organizational citizenship behavior, decreased employee emotional, psychological, and physical wellbeing and high job withdrawal, turnover, and absenteeism, can thwart organizational goal achievement. We argue that mistreatment in the workplace is likely to affect each of these outcomes, albeit via different processes.

In exploring the organizational environment that may lead to mistreatment and organizational outcomes, we have focused on human resources and organizational management practices. If supported by empirical research, our model should be of critical relevance to the business domain for two key reasons: first, we emphasize in our model the need to foster an environment that does not implicitly legitimize mistreatment, and that actively assists in its prevention; and second, we highlight the potential for reduced organizational effectiveness owing to turnover, decreases in employee satisfaction, commitment and well-being, and withdrawal of beneficial extra-role behaviors when mistreatment does occur.

References

Abelson, R. P. (1963). Computer simulation of "hot cognition." In S. Tomkins and S. Messick (Eds.), *Computer Simulation and Personality: Frontier of Psychological Theory* (pp. 277–298). New York: Wiley.

Alarcon, G. M. (2011). A meta-analysis of burnout with job demands, resources, and attitudes. *Journal of Vocational Behavior, 79,* 549–562.

Antonakis, J., Ashkanasy, N. M., and Dasborough, M. T. (2009). Does leadership need emotional intelligence? *Leadership Quarterly, 20,* 247–261.

Appelbaum, S. H., Deguire, K. J., and Lay, M. (2005). The relationship of ethical climate to deviant workplace behavior. *Corporate Governance, 5,* 4–55.

Aquino, K., and Bommer, H. (2003). Preferential mistreatment: How victim status moderates the relationship between organizational citizenship behavior and workplace victimization. *Organization Science, 14,* 274–285.

Aquino, K., and Byron, K. (2002). Dominating interpersonal behavior and perceived victimization in groups: Evidence for a curvilinear relationship. *Journal of Management, 28,* 69–87.

Aquino, K., and Thau, S. (2009). Workplace victimization: Aggression from the target's perspective. *Annual Review of Psychology, 60,* 717–741.

Ashkanasy, N. M. (2008). Organizational climate. In S. R. Clegg and J. R. Bailey (Eds.), *International Encyclopedia of Organization Studies,* vol. 3 (pp. 1028–1030). Thousand Oaks, CA: Sage.

Ashkanasy, N. M., Ashton-James, C. E., and Jordan, P. J. (2004). Performance impacts of appraisal and coping with stress in workplace settings: The role of affect and emotional intelligence. *Research in Occupational Stress and Well Being, 3,* 3–43.

Ashkanasy, N. M., and Humphrey, R. H. (2011). Current research on emotion in organizations. *Emotion Review, 3,* 214–224

Ashton-James, C. E., and Ashkanasy, N. M. (2005). What lies beneath? A process analysis of affective events theory. *Research on Emotion in Organizations, 1,* 23–46.

Austenfeld, J., and Stanton, A. (2004). Coping through emotional approach: A new look at emotion, coping, and health-related outcomes. *Journal of Personality, 72,* 1335–1363.

Bacharach, S. B., Bamberger, P., and Sonnenstuhl, W. J. (2002). Driven to drink: Managerial control, work related risk factors and employee drinking behavior. *Academy of Management Journal, 45,* 637–658.

Barclay, L. J., and Kiefer, T. (2012). Approach or avoid? Exploring overall justice and the differential effects of positive and negative emotions. *Journal of Management.* Epub ahead of print. doi:10.1177/0149206312441833

Bass, B. M. (1997). Does the transactional-transformational leadership paradigm transcend organizational and national boundaries? *American Psychologist, 52*(2), 130–139.

Baumeister, R. F., Stillwell, A., and Wotman, S. R. (1990). Victim and perpetrator accounts of interpersonal conflict: Autobiographical narratives about anger. *Journal of Personality and Social Psychology, 59,* 994–1005.

Bolin, A., and Heatherly, L. (2001). Predictors of employee deviance: The relationship between bad attitudes and bad behavior. *Journal of Business and Psychology, 15,* 405–418.

Bono, J. E., and Judge, T. A. (2004). Personality and transformational and transactional leadership: A meta-analysis. *Journal of Applied Psychology, 89,* 901–910.

Bowling, N. A., and Beehr, T. A. (2006). Workplace harassment from the victim's perspective: A theoretical model and meta-analysis. *Journal of Applied Psychology, 91,* 988–1012.

Boyd, N. G., Lewin, J. E., and Sager, J. K. (2009). A model of stress and coping and their influence on individual and organizational outcomes. *Journal of Vocational Behavior, 75,* 197–211.

Bulutlar, F. S., and Oz, E. U. (2008). The effects of ethical climates on bullying behavior in the workplace. *Journal of Business Ethics, 86,* 273–295.

Butler, E. A., Egloff, B., Wilhelm, F. H., Smith, N. C., Erickson, E. A. and Gross, J. J. (2003). The social consequences of expressive suppression. *Emotion, 3*(1), 48–67.

Caza, B., and Cortina, L. (2007). From insult to injury: Explaining the impact of incivility. *Basic and Applied Social Psychology, 29,* 335–350.

Chan, M. E., and McAllister, D. (2014). Abusive supervision though the lens of employee state paranoia. *Academy of Management Review, 39*, 44–66.

Cogin, J., and Fish, A. (2007). Managing sexual harassment more strategically: An analysis of environmental causes. *Asia Pacific Journal of Human Resources, 45*, 333–350.

Cortina, L. M., and Magley, V. J. (2003). Raising voice, risking retaliation: Events following interpersonal mistreatment in the workplace. *Journal of Occupational Health Psychology, 8*, 247–265.

Cortina, L. M., and Magley, V. J. (2009). Patterns and profiles of response to incivility in the workplace. *Journal of Occupational Health Psychology, 14*, 272–288.

Cortina, L. M., Magley, V. J., Williams, J. H., and Langhout, R. D. (2001). Incivility in the workplace: Incidence and impact. *Journal of Occupational Health Psychology, 6*, 64–80.

Coyne, I., Seigne, E., and Randall, P. (2000). Predicting workplace victim status from personality. *European Journal of Work and Organizational Psychology, 9*, 335–349.

Dasborough, M. T. (2006). Cognitive asymmetry in employee emotional reactions to leadership behaviors. *Leadership Quarterly, 17*, 163–178.

Deitch, E., Barsky, A., Butz, A., Chan, R., Breif, S., and Bradley, A. (2003). Subtle yet significant: The existence and impact of everyday racial discrimination in the workplace. *Human Relations, 56*, 1299–1324.

Djurkovic, N., McCormack, D., and Casimir, G. (2004). The physical and psychological effects of workplace bullying and their relationship to intention to leave: A test of the psychosomatic and disability hypotheses. *International Journal of Organization Theory and Behavior, 7*, 469–497.

Dunlop, P. D., and Lee, K. (2004). Workplace deviance, organizational citizenship behavior, and business unit performance: The bad apples do spoil the whole barrel. *Journal of Organizational Behavior, 25*, 67–80.

Einarsen, S., and Skogstad, A. (1996). Bullying at work: Epidemiological findings in public and private organizations. *European Journal of Work and Organizational Psychology, 5*(2), 185–201.

Elias, R. (1986). *The Politics of Victimization: Victims, Victimology, and Human Rights*. New York: Oxford University Press.

EU-OSHA (European Agency for Safety and Health at Work) (2009). *OSH in Figures: Stress at Work – Facts and Figures*. At https://osha.europa.eu/en/node/6862/file_view (accessed July 2016).

Fisher, C. D. (2002). Antecedents and consequences of real-time affective reactions at work. *Motivation and Emotion, 26*(1), 3–30.

Fitzgerald, L. F., Swan, S., and Fischer, K. (1995). Why didn't she just report him? The psychological and legal implications of women's responses to sexual harassment. *Journal of Social Issues, 51*, 117–138.

Folkman, S., and Lazarus, R. S. (1985). If it changes it must be a process: Study of emotion and coping during three stages of a college examination. *Journal of Personality and Social Psychology, 48*, 150–170.

Folkman, S., Lazarus, R. S., Gruen, R. J., and DeLongis, A. (1986). Appraisal, coping, health status, and psychological symptoms. *Journal of Personality and Social Psychology, 50*, 571–579.

Forgas, J. P. (1995). Mood and judgment: The affect infusion model (AIM). *Psychological Bulletin, 117*, 39–66.

Forgas, J. P., and George, J. M. (2001). Affective influences on judgments and behavior in organizations: An information processing perspective. *Organizational Behavior and Human Decision Processes, 86*, 3–34.

Frijda, N. H. (1988). The laws of emotion. *American Psychologist, 43*(5), 349–358.

Fugate, M., Harrison, S., and Kinicki, A. J. (2011). Thoughts and feelings about organizational change: A field test of appraisal theory. *Journal of Leadership and Organizational Studies, 18*, 421–437.

Gable, S. L., Reis, H. T., and Elliot, A. J. (2000). Behavioral activation and inhibition in everyday life. *Journal of Personality and Social Psychology, 78*(6), 1135–1149.

Ganster, D. C., and Rosen, C. C. (2013). Work stress and employee health: A multidisciplinary review. *Journal of Management, 39*, 1085–1122

Glasø, L., Vie, T. L., Holmdal, G. R., and Einarsen, S. (2011). An application of affective events theory to workplace bullying: The role of emotions, trait anxiety, and trait anger. *European Psychologist, 16*, 198–208.

Glendinning, P. (2001). Workplace bullying: Curing the cancer of the American workplace. *Public Personnel Management, 30*(3), 269–286.

Gohm, C. L., Corser, G. C., and Dalsky, D. J. (2005). Emotional intelligence under stress: Useful, unnecessary, or irrelevant? *Personality and Individual Differences, 39*, 1017–1028.

Gooty, J., Gavin, M., Ashkanasy, N. M., and Thomas, J. S. (2014). The wisdom of letting go: Emotions and performance at work. *Journal of Occupational and Organizational Psychology, 87*, 392–413.

Grandey, A. A., Tam, A. P., and Brauberger, A. L. (2002). Affective states and traits in the workplace: Diary and survey data from young workers. *Motivation and Emotion, 34*, 31–55.

Griffin, R. W., and Lopez, Y. P. (2005). "Bad behavior" in organizations: A review and typology for future research. *Journal of Management, 31*, 988–1005.

Gross, J. J. (2002). Emotion regulation: Affective, cognitive, and social consequences. *Psychophysiology, 39*, 281–291.

Gross, J. J., and John, O. P. (2003). Individual differences in two emotion regulation processes: Implications for affect, relationships, and well-being. *Journal of Personality and Social Psychology, 85*(2), 348–362.

Harlos, K. P., and Axelrod, L. J. (2005). Investigating hospital administrators' experience of workplace mistreatment. *Canadian Journal of Behavioral Science, 37*, 262–272.

Henle, C. A., and Gross, M. A. (2014). What have I done to deserve this? Effects of employee personality and emotion on abusive supervision. *Journal of Business Ethics, 122*, 461–474.

Heppner, P. P. (1988). *The Problem Solving Inventory: Manual.* Palo Alto, CA: Consulting Psychologists Press.

Hoel, H., and Salin, D. (2003). Organizational antecedents of workplace bullying. In E. Einarsen, D. Zapf, H. Hoel, and C. L. Cooper (Eds.), *Bullying and Emotional Abuse in the Workplace: International Perspectives in Research and Practice.* New York: Taylor & Francis.

Holtom, B. C., Burton, J. P., and Crossley, C. D. (2012). How negative affectivity moderates the relationship between shocks, embeddedness and worker behaviors. *Journal of Vocational Behavior, 80*(2), 434–443.

Hoppe, A., Toker, S., Schachler, V., and Ziegler, M. (2016). The effect of change in supervisor support and job control on change in vigor: Differential relationships for immigrant and native employees in Israel. *Journal of Organizational Behavior*, online. doi:10.1002/job.2151

Izard, C. E. (2009). Emotion theory and research: Highlights, unanswered questions, and emerging issues. *Annual Review of Psychology, 60*, 1–25.

Jaramillo, F., Mulki, J. P., and Marshall, G. W. (2005). A meta-analysis of the relationship between organizational commitment and salesperson job performance: 25 years of research. *Journal of Business Research, 58*, 705–714.

Jones, T. S., and Bodtker, A. (2001). Mediating with heart in mind: Addressing emotion in mediation practice. *Negotiation Journal, 17*(3), 207–244.

Judge, T. A., Scott, B. A., and Ilies, R. (2006). Hostility, job attitudes, and workplace deviance: Test of a multilevel model. *Journal of Applied Psychology, 91*, 126–138.

Kaplan, R. S., and Norton, D. P. (1992). The balanced scorecard: Measures that drive performance. *Harvard Business Review* (Jan.–Feb.), 71–79.

Karmen, A. (2003). *Crime Victims: An Introduction to Victimology.* Belmont, CA: Wadsworth.

Kelloway, K., Teed, M., and Kelley, E. (2008). The psychosocial environment: Towards an agenda for research. *International Journal of Workplace Health Management, 11*, 50–64.

Key, S. (1999). Organizational ethical climate: Real or imagined? *Journal of Business Ethics, 20*, 217–225.

Kivimäki, M., Elovainio, M., and Vahtera, J. (2000). Workplace bullying and sickness absence in hospital staff. *Occupational and Environmental Medicine, 57*, 650–660.

Klarner, P., By, R. T., and Diefenbach, T. (2011). Employee emotions during organizational change: Towards a new research agenda. *Scandinavian Journal of Management, 27*, 332–340.

Kunda, Z. (1999). *Social Cognition: Making Sense of People.* Cambridge, MA: MIT Press.

Landau, S. F., and Freeman-Longo, R. E. (1990). Classifying victims: A proposed multi-dimensional victimological typology. *International Review of Victimology, 1*, 267–286.

Lawrence, S. A., Troth, A. C., Jordan, P. J., and Collins, A. L. (2011). A review of emotion regulation and development of a framework for emotion regulation in the workplace. In P. L. Perrewé and D. C. Ganster (Eds.), *The Role of Individual Differences in Occupational Stress and Well Being* (pp. 197–263). Bingley, UK: Emerald.

Lazarus, R. (1966). Some principles of psychological stress and their relation to dentistry. *Journal of Dental Research, 45*, 1620–1626.

Lazarus, R. S. (1981). The stress and coping paradigm. In C. Eisdorfer, D. Cohen, A. Kleinman, and P. Maxim (Eds.), *Models for Clinical Psychopathology* (pp. 174–214). New York: Spectrum.

Lazarus, R. (1982). Thoughts on the relations between emotion and cognition. *American Psychologist, 37*, 1019–1024.

Lazarus, R. (1991). *Emotion and Adaptation.* New York: Oxford University Press.

Lazarus, R. (2006). Emotions and interpersonal relationships: Towards a person-centered conceptualization of emotions and coping. *Journal of Personality, 74*, 9–46.

Lazarus, R., and Folkman, S. (1984). *Stress, Appraisal and Coping.* New York: Springer.

Lee, K., and Allen, N. J. (2002). Organizational citizenship behavior and workplace deviance: The role of affect and cognition. *Journal of Applied Psychology, 87*, 131–142.

LePine, J. A., Erez, A., and Johnson, D. E. (2002). The nature and dimensionality of organizational citizenship behavior: A critical review and meta-analysis. *Journal of Applied Psychology, 87*, 52–65.

Levinson, H. (1978). The abrasive personality. *Harvard Business Review, 56*(3), 86–94.

Leymann, H. (1996). The content and development of mobbing at work. *European Journal of Work and Organizational Psychology, 5*, 165–184.

Lim, S., and Cortina, L. M. (2005). Interpersonal mistreatment in the workplace: The interface and impact of general incivility and sexual harassment. *Journal of Applied Psychology, 90*, 483–496.

Lim, S., Cortina, L. M., and Magley, V. J. (2008). Personal and workgroup incivility: Impact on work and health outcomes. *Journal of Applied Psychology, 93*, 95–107.

Mandler, G. (1982). Stress and thought processes. In L. Goldberger and S. Breznitz (Eds.), *Handbook of Stress: Theoretical and Clinical Aspects* (pp. 88–104). New York: Free Press.

Mathieu, J. E., and Zajac, D. (1990). A review and meta-analysis of the antecedents, correlates, and consequences of organizational commitment. *Psychological Bulletin, 108*, 171–194.

Matthiesen, S. P., and Einarsen, S. P. (2007). Perpetrators and targets of bullying at work: Role stress and individual differences. *Violence and Victims, 22*, 735–753.

Mayer, J. D., and Salovey, P. (1997). What is emotional intelligence? In P. Salovey and D. J. Sluyter (Eds.), *Emotional Development and Emotional Intelligence*. New York: Basic Books.

McEwen, B. S., and Seeman, T. E. (1999). Protective and damaging effects of mediators of stress. In N. E. Adler, M. Marmot and B. S. McEwen (Eds.), *Socioeconomic Status and Health in Industrial Nations: Social, Psychological and Biological Pathways* (pp. 30–47). New York: Academic Sciences

Medibank (2011). Sick at work: The cost of presenteeism to your business and the economy. At http://www.medibank.com.au/Client/Documents/Pdfs/sick_at_work.pdf (accessed July 2016).

Milam, A. C., Spitzmueller, C., and Penney, L. M. (2009). Investigating individual differences among targets of workplace incivility. *Journal of Occupational Health Psychology, 14*, 58–69.

Morgan, R. L., and Heise, D. (1988). Structure of emotions. *Social Psychology Quarterly, 51*(1), 19–31.

Mount, M., Ilies, R., and Johnson, E. (2006). Relationship of personality traits and counterproductive work behaviors: The mediating effects of job satisfaction. *Personnel Psychology, 59*, 591–622.

Nielsen, M. B., Matthiesen, S. B., and Einarsen, S. (2008). Sense of coherence as a protective mechanism among targets of workplace bullying. *Journal of Occupational Health Psychology, 13*, 128–136.

O'Boyle, E. H., Forsyth, D. R., and O'Boyle, A. S. (2011). Bad apples or bad barrels: An examination of group- and organizational-level effects in the study of counterproductive work behavior. *Group and Organization Management, 36*(1), 39–69.

O'Leary-Kelly, A., Bowes-Sperry, L., Bates, C., and Lean, E. (2009). Sexual harassment at work: A decade (plus) of progress. *Journal of Management, 35*, 503–536.

Olson-Buchanan, J., and Boswell, W. (2008). An integrative model of experiencing and responding to mistreatment at work. *Academy of Management Review, 33*(1), 76–96.

Olweus, D. (1978). *Aggression in the Schools: Bullies and Whipping Boys*. Washington, DC: Hemisphere.

O'Moore, A. M., and Lynch, J. (2007). Leadership, working environment and workplace bullying. *International Journal of Organization Theory and Behavior, 10*, 95–117.

O'Moore, A. M., Seigne, E., McGuire, L., and Smith, M. (1998). Victims of bullying at work in Ireland. *Journal of Occupational Health and Safety, 14*, 569–574.

O'Reilly, J., and Aquino, K. (2011). A model of third parties' morally motivated responses to mistreatment in organizations. *Academy of Management Review, 36*, 526–543.

Perry, B. D., Pollard, R. A., Blakley, T. L., Baker, W. L., and Vigilante, D. (1995). Childhood trauma, the neurobiology of adaptation, and "use-dependent" development of the brain: How "states" become "traits." *Infant Mental Health Journal, 16*(4), 271–291.

Peterson, D. K. (2002). Deviant workplace behavior and the organization's ethical climate. *Journal of Business and Psychology, 17*, 47–61.

Petty, M. M., McGee, G. W., and Cavender, J. W. (1984). A meta-analysis of the relationships between individual job satisfaction and individual performance. *Academy of Management Review, 9*, 712–721.

Podsakoff, N. P., LePine, J. A., and LePine, M. A. (2007). Differential challenge stressor–hindrance stressor relationships with job attitudes, turnover intentions, turnover, and withdrawal behavior: A meta-analysis. *Journal of Applied Psychology, 92*(2), 438–454.

Quine, L. (1999). Workplace bullying in the NHS community trust: Staff questionnaire survey. *British Medical Journal, 318*, 228–232.

Redfern, D., Rees, C., and Rowlands, K. (2008). Occupational stress: Consensus or divergence? A challenge for training and development specialists. *Industrial and Commercial Training*, *40*, 287–294.

Robertson, I. T., Callinan, M., and Bartram, D. (Eds.) (2002). *Organizational Effectiveness: The Role of Psychologists*. Chichester, UK: Wiley.

Robinson, S. L., and Bennett, R. J. (1995). A typology of deviant workplace behaviors: A multidimensional scaling study. *Academy of Management Journal*, *38*, 555–572.

Salin, D. (2003). Ways of explaining workplace bullying: A review of enabling, motivating and precipitating structures and processes in the work environment. *Human Relations*, *56*, 1213–1232.

Salovey, P. (2001). Applied emotional intelligence: Regulating emotions to become healthy, wealthy, and wise. In J. Ciarrochi, J. P. Forgas, and J. D. Mayer (Eds.), *Emotional Intelligence in Everyday Life: A Scientific Inquiry* (pp. 168–215). Philadelphia: Psychology Press.

Sandberg, J., and Alvesson, M. (2011). Ways of constructing research questions: Gap-spotting or problematization? *Organization, 18*(1), 23–44.

Scheck, C., and Kinicki, A. (2000). Identifying the antecedents of coping with an organizational acquisition: A structural assessment. *Journal of Organizational Behavior*, *21*, 627–648.

Schyns, B., and Schilling, J. (2013). How bad are the effects of bad leaders? A meta-analysis of destructive leadership and its outcomes. *Leadership Quarterly, 24*(1), 138–158.

Seigne, E., Coyne, I., Randall, P., and Parker, J. (2007). Personality traits of bullies as a contributory factor in workplace bullying: An exploratory study. *International Journal of Organization Theory and Behavior*, *10*, 118–132.

Shields, M. (2006). Stress and depression in the employed population. *Health Reports*, *174*, 11–29.

Sideridis, G. (2006). Coping is not an "either" "or": The interaction of coping strategies in regulating affect, arousal and performance. *Stress and Health*, *22*, 315–327.

Skinner, E. Edge, K., Altman, J., and Sherwood, H. (2003). Searching for the structure of coping: A review and critique of category systems for classifying ways of coping. *Psychological Bulletin*, *129*, 216–269.

Skogstad, A., Einarsen, S., Torsheim, T., Aasland, M. S., and Hetland, H. (2007). The destructiveness of laissez-faire leadership behavior. *Journal of Occupational Health Psychology*, *12*, 80–92.

Smith, C. A., and Lazarus, R. S. (1993). Appraisal components, core relational themes, and the emotions. *Cognition and Emotion*, *7*, 233–269.

South, S. C., Oltmanns, T. F., and Turkheimer, E. (2003). Personality and the derogation of others: Descriptions based on self and peer report. *Journal of Research in Personality*, *37*, 16–33.

Stanton, A. L., and Low, C. A. (2012). Expressing emotions in stressful contexts: Benefits, moderators, and mechanisms. *Current Directions in Psychological Science, 21*(2), 124–128.

Tepper, B. J., Duffy, M. K., Henle, C. A., and Lambert, L. S. (2006). Procedural injustice, victim precipitation, and abusive supervision. *Personnel Psychology*, *59*, 101–123.

van Rhenen, W., Blonk, R. W. B., Schaufeli, W. B., and van Dijk, F. J. H. (2007). Can sickness absence be reduced by stress reduction programs: On the effectiveness of two approaches. *International Archives of Occupational and Environmental Health*, *80*, 505–515.

Vardi, Y., and Weitz, E. (2004). *Misbehavior in Organizations: Theory, Research and Management*. Mahwah, NJ: Lawrence Erlbaum.

Victor, B., and Cullen, J. (1987). A theory and measure of ethical climate in organizations. In W. C. Frederick (Ed.), *Research in Corporate Social Performance and Policy: Empirical Studies of Business Ethics and Values* (pp. 51–71). Greenwich, CT: JAI Press.

Wegge, J., van Dick, R., Fisher, G. L., West, M. A., and Dawson, J. F. (2006). A test of basic assumptions of affective events theory (AET) in call centre work. *British Journal of Management*, *17*, 237–254.

Weiss, H. M., and Beal, D. J. (2005). Reflections on affective events theory. *Research on Emotion in Organizations*, *1*, 1–21.

Weiss, H. M., and Cropanzano, R. (1996). Affective events theory: A theoretical discussion of the structure, causes, and consequences of affective experiences at work. *Research in Organizational Behavior*, *18*, 1–74.

Willness, C., Steel, P., and Lee, K. (2007). A meta-analysis of the antecedents and consequences of workplace sexual harassment. *Personnel Psychology*, *60*, 127–162.

Wimbush, J. C., and Shepard, J. C. (1994). Toward an understanding of ethical climate: Its relationship to ethical behavior and supervisory influence. *Journal of Business Ethics*, *13*, 637–647.

Wimbush, J. C., Shepard, J. M., and Markham, S. E. (1997). An empirical examination of the relationship between ethical climate and ethical behavior from multiple levels of analysis. *Journal of Business Ethics*, *16*, 1705–1716.

Wood, J. M., Zeffane, R. M., Fromholtz, Wiesner, M., Morrison, R., and Seet, P. (2013). *Organisational Behaviour: Core Concepts and Applications*, 3rd edn. Chichester, UK: John Wiley & Sons.

Zapf, D. (1999). Organizational, work group related and personal causes of mobbing/bullying at work. *International Journal of Manpower*, *20*, 70–85.

Zapf, D., Knorz, C., and Kulla, M. (1996). On the relationship between mobbing factors, and job content, social work environment, and health outcomes. *European Journal of Work and Organizational Psychology*, *5*, 215–237.

Zellars, K., Tepper, B., and Duffy, M. (2002). Abusive supervision and subordinates' organizational citizenship behavior. *Journal of Applied Psychology*, *87*, 1068–1076.

23

Creating Well-Being among Older People

An Eastern Perspective

Luo Lu

Population aging is undoubtedly one of the most challenging issues of the twenty-first century, facing both developed and developing countries worldwide. In the developed world, there has already been a substantial amount of research on aging, both biomedical and psychosocial, to help understand the difficulties and potential of older age. There is an emerging view toward maintaining ability, developing potential, and continued competence (Ross, 2010). Aging is an even more pressing problem for developing countries such as the Chinese societies of main-land China and Taiwan. In Taiwan, for instance, advances in medical science and technology, successful promotion of health care, material prosperity, coupled with the gradual demise of Chinese family values and lifestyle (e.g., large extended family living together), have sent the birth rate into a steady decline, but life expectancy to a steady increase. Consequently, as early as September 1993, Taiwan was officially an "aging society" as the proportion of those aged over 65 had exceeded 7 percent of the country's population (Lin, 2002). However, systematic research on aging topics in Taiwan is still in its infancy and relies heavily upon Western theories and findings. Furthermore, most research efforts have been devoted to medical gerontology and other aging-related medical care topics, while psychosocial issues of normative aging are generally overlooked. Although there has been some research pointing out the beneficial effects of social support for Chinese older people in Taiwan (Hu, 1992; Lu and Hsieh, 1997), other psychosocial correlates of well-being (WB) in later years, such as active participation in life (e.g., leisure), have been largely overlooked. Furthermore, older people's self-definition and perception of aging have been ignored. The purpose of this chapter, therefore, is twofold: First, to critique and rethink a basic issue in social gerontology from older people's point of view: what are the constituting elements of "positive aging" as a representation of the avowed positive experience for older people? Second, in addition to the known protectors of WB in older age, does participation in leisure have a role to play in ensuring positive aging?

In developing this chapter, I have not attempted to review all of the research on aging and WB conducted in the West, as there are extensive reviews available. Instead, I have decided to review studies set in a different cultural context: Taiwan, a society which combines traditional Chinese cultural values and contemporary work and family arrangements. Taiwan is a new democracy with a full-bloom market economy, and is also proud of being a stronghold for preserving the Confucian heritage. Empirical research has confirmed that Taiwan is the "most traditional Chinese society" compared to Mainland China and Hong Kong, reporting the highest level of endorsement of traditional Chinese values (Leung and Bond, 2004; Lu, Kao, Chang, Wu, and Zhang, 2008). Thus, using Taiwan as an exemplar should better serve my purpose of bringing out the cultural thrust in the aging and WB research.

Conceptualizing Well-Being in Older Age: Positive Aging Revisited

Well-being defined in ethical, theological, political, economic, and psychological terms has been studied in a large number of disciplines over many centuries, and has generated increasing interest among researchers and practitioners involved in caring for older people (Gentile, 1991). Well-being is the result of a person's comprehensive appraisal of life against individual and social goals, and four sectors comprising "the good life" have been proposed: behavioral competence, psychological well-being, perceived quality of life, and objective environment (Lawton, 1983). This demarcation of sectors is in broad agreement with the objective/subjective distinction in the tradition of WB research (Gentile, 1991; Arnold, 1991; Bowling and Gabriel, 2004; Rioux, 2005). Objective indicators of WB are those that exist outside the body of the person, such as economic resources, health functioning, and social contact (Arnold, 1991), while subjective indicators of WB are those that are perceived, experienced, and evaluated by the human mind, such as life satisfaction, happiness, morale, and positive outlook (Gentile, 1991). Mirroring the trend in generic WB research, far more efforts have been expended on looking for "objective" external rather than subjective psychological indicators of WB for older people, as the former are relatively easy to define and assess (Arnold, 1991). Another characteristic of the WB research is its focus on sick and frail older people rather than normal and healthy older adults in the community (Lawton, 1983). As noted by Bowling and Gabriel (2004), people of different ages, health status, and residence arrangements may have different priorities when judging their WB. Fry (2000) further suggested that personal mastery, autonomy, self-sufficiency, lifestyle choices, and privacy are the most important indicators of quality of life (QOL, synonymous with WB) for older people residing in the community. All of these are subjective indicators. A recent Taiwanese study corroborates the Western view, confirming that a healthy body, a sense of self-worth, companionship, living environment and leisure facilities, social contacts with friends and relatives, and joy are all important aspects of QOL for older people in Taiwan (Hsieh, 2004). The fact that, even for older people with disabilities involved in this study, subjective QOL is as relevant as objective indicators serves to underline the necessity of more emphasis on psychological aspects of WB in gerontological research. So far, the positive outlook of older age is a largely neglected topic in the WB research.

   In addition to the objective/subjective distinction underlying various constructs and definitions of WB, another dimension contrasts end-state vs. process. The MacArthur Foundation
offered a pioneering set of studies on successful aging. In summarizing the findings, Rowe
and Kahn's (1987; 1998) model provided scientifically grounded parameters for understanding health across the life course. Successful aging is defined as the avoidance of disease and
disability, as well as the maintenance of physical and cognitive functions and engagement
in social and productive activities. Clearly depicting a desirable state of WB with measurable
(objective) indicators, Rowe and Kahn's model has become the most influential framework for
promoting successful aging and WB interventions. The World Health Organization's earlier
definition of "healthy aging" (WHO, 1990) as a complete state of physiological, psychological, and social well-being, too, relies heavily on objective indicators (lack of disease and disability) to depict a desirable end-state for human existence. However, in a more recent report
(WHO, 2002), the term has been replaced by "active aging," accompanied with a shift from
the end-state to a more fluid and dynamic process: active aging is the process of optimizing
opportunities for health, participation, and security in order to enhance quality of life as people
age (p. 12). Baltes and Baltes (1990) also conceptualized "successful aging" as a process comprising three identifiable stages: selection, optimization, and compensation (SOC). The SOC
model emphasizes human agency and behavioral plasticity, advocating the human potential
in self-regulation to achieve a better adjustment to the changing environment. In other words,
aging is a continuous process of adaptation: the better the adaptation, the more successful the
aging. Figure 23.1 shows an organization of these influential definitions of WB in older age in
the extant literature.
   Influential as they are, the above notions of WB and aging are not without criticism. Rowe
and Kahn's (1998) model has been criticized for its neglect of spirituality as a major construct
relating to health outcomes (Crowther, Parker, Achenbaum, Larimore, and Koenig, 2002).
Well-being as conceptualized in the process models is difficult to assess, and hard to generate across different contexts (social and cultural). For instance, a recent Taiwanese qualitative

		Subjective	Objective
Defining feature	End-state	**Positive aging** (this chapter)	**Successful aging** (Rowe & Kahn, 1998) **Healthy aging** (WHO, 1990)
	Process	**Successful aging (SOC model)** (Baltes & Baltes, 1990)	**Active aging** (WHO, 2002)

Assessment index

Figure 23.1   A theoretical organization of well-being constructs for older people and/or ideals for
normal aging.

study on successful aging found that the SOC concepts were quite alien to Chinese older people (Chen, Chang, Kao and Lu, 2013). This is because selection (of goals) has to emanate from a crystalized sense of self-understanding in terms of personal needs, wants, competencies, etc., which is not encouraged and developed for a traditional Chinese person. Thus, it seems that a feasible strategy to approach the WB construct in older age is to conceptualize it as a relatively stable end-state while taking into consideration older people's subjective evaluations (the top-left cell of Figure 23.1).

Specifically, I propose that well-being in older age may be conceptualized from a psychological perspective with the following basic propositions. First, well-being is the result of the positive evaluation of the lived experiences of aging. Similar to that in the life course, the defining feature of WB is its subjective nature: feeling good about one's life is a state of mind largely independent of objective circumstances (Kahneman, Diener, and Schwarz, 1999). It is a well-established fact that a collection of objective indicators of life circumstances has a rather limited contribution to avowed WB of people of all ages, both in the West (Kahneman et al., 1999) and in the East (Lu, 2010b). The same is true for older people, Western and Eastern (Freund and Smith, 1999; Hsieh, 2004).

Second, well-being is a coherent multifaceted construct encompassing elements of the basic psychological process. These constituting aspects are clearly defined, measurable, and interrelated indicators of WB. As in the case of subjective well-being (SWB), the constituting aspects encompass both the affective (positive affect, lack of negative affect) and the cognitive (life satisfaction) psychological processes, which are pancultural and stable (Kahneman et al., 1999; Lu, 2005). Such conceptual coherence and empirical convergence can then provide a solid basis for concerted research to generate compatible findings. The same is desirable for the WB construct in older age: a comprehensive yet stable conceptualization to organize empirical findings and to promote interventions.

To this end, I argue that *well-being in older age is the result of a global, positive evaluation of one's own aging experience.* The subjective judgment is based on the cognitive, affective, and self-evaluative processes, which collectively represent a positive state of mind. Specifically, I propose that WB for older people is indexed by a sense of meaning in life (cognitive), happiness and peace of mind (affective), as well as a positive aging self-perception (self-evaluative). Meaning in life (MIL) is derived from the belief that a person is realizing important values in life, and actively committed to the relevant goals (Battista and Almond, 1973). Happiness defined as SWB encompasses positive affect, lack of negative affect, and a global conviction of life satisfaction (Diener, Suh, Lucas, and Smith, 1999). Peace of mind (POM) emphasizes a harmonious inner state of balance and calm, which is in contrast to elated emotions often used to indicate hedonic pleasure (Lee, Lin, Huang, and Fredrickson, 2013). The construct of POM is rooted in the Confucian tradition of self-cultivation in striving for moderation and an internal state of peacefulness. Thus, happiness/SWB and POM complement each other and in combination encompass affective WB valued both in the West and the East. Aging self-perception (ASP) is an integral part of the self-definition for older people basing on their lived experiences of aging. To borrow from the theoretical framework of attitudes toward older people (Lu and Kao, 2009a), aging self-perception is formed with self-evaluations along four dimensions, drawing information from a person's own aging experience. These self-evaluative dimensions are: appearance and physical characteristics; psychological and cognitive characteristics; interpersonal relations and social participation; and work and economic security. A positive ASP denotes a self-affirming state of mind, and such positivity is observed among the older adults both in the West, and recently in the East. Items used for assessing ASP are listed in Box 23.1, which shows the Older People Scale discussed below.

As part of the Berlin Aging Study, Freund and Smith (1999) collected spontaneous self-definitions in a heterogeneous sample of 516 participants (aged 70–103 years). The content of the self-definitions revealed that these older adults still viewed themselves as active and present-oriented, and overall, there were more positive than negative self-evaluations. More importantly, perhaps, positive emotional well-being was associated with naming more and richer self-defining domains. In Taiwan, social gerontological research on self-perceptions of older people or normative aging experiences is very rare. However, Lee (1999) surveyed a nationally representative sample of Taiwanese for the general impression of life in middle to late adulthood, and found that although people tended to perceive old age rather negatively, they nonetheless acknowledged some positive aspects of aging. Specifically, positive attitudes and traits pertaining to psychological and cognitive aspects of aging, such as rich experiences, wisdom, and authoritative status, were attributed to older persons. More encouragingly, recent studies revealed that older people reported more positive attitudes toward their own aging experiences than those projected by non-old adults in Taiwan, especially those pertaining to cognitive and psychological aspects of aging (Lee, 1999; Lu and Kao, 2009a). One Taiwanese study (Lu, Kao, and Hsieh, 2010) found that older people living in the community reported a positive perception of aging in general, disregarding sex, age (young old vs. old old), and living arrangement (with family vs. alone).

In sum, I believe that the constellation of meaning in life, happiness, peace of mind, and a positive aging self-perception, resulting from the basic cognitive, affective, and self-evaluative psychological processes of human functioning, encompasses the essence of a desirable state of human existence. In the context of aging and adaptation, the four facets represent the construct of "positive aging". In a recent two-wave panel study of Taiwanese older adults, positive aging has been validated as a second-order factor (with four constituting indicators) in confirmatory factor analysis with data at both time points (Chen and Lu, 2015). Moreover, as theorized, the four first-order factors of meaning in life, happiness, peace of mind, and aging self-perception had consistently high interrelations among one another (all $rs > 0.80$) across two data points. The preliminary empirical evidence supports the notion that positive aging can be indexed with stable and coherent subjective indicators of WB.

Further evidence can be drawn from the extant literature. One study in the West found that when defining "old," older people focused less on appearance or body image, and more on health status and psychological factors such as loss of autonomy (Logan, Ward, and Spitze, 1992). In other words, frailty and disability may not be the most psychologically salient experiences of aging for older people. Earlier, Lu and Chang (1998) argued that aging is not an inevitably negative experience, even for those with compromised health. Although participants in the study (aged 65–90 years) all had at least one chronic medical condition, the authors observed that they nonetheless maintained good functioning in daily activities, perceived little interference by illnesses with their normal life, and reported fairly good psychological health and optimistic outlooks in life.

In another series of studies in Taiwan (Lu, 2010a; 2012; Lu and Kao, 2009a; 2010; Lu et al., 2010; Lu, Kao, and Hsieh, 2011), researchers used the Older People Scale (OPS) (see Box 23.1) developed specifically for Chinese people, to assess attitudes toward older people (responses from non-old participants), and aging self-perception (responses from older participants). With each item rated on a 7-point scale (1 = strongly disagree, 7 = strongly agree),

Box 23.1   Attitudes towards Older People Scale (OPS, 22-item version)

The items below are to understand your impression and opinions about *older adults aged 65 and above in general*. Please rate each item on a 1–7 scale.

Overall, I think older adults aged 65 and above are …

Dimensions	Item #	Items
Appearance and physical ability (5 items)	1	Vigorous and energetic
	2	Healthy
	3	Not likable (−)
	4	Frail with lots of illnesses (−)
	5	Less energetic (−)
Psychological and cognitive abilities (7 items)	6	Compassionate
	7	Happy
	8	Have problem-solving abilities
	9	Open-minded
	10	Pessimistic and gloomy (−)
	11	Hard to communicate with (−)
	12	Full of regrets (−)
Interpersonal relationships and social engagement (7 items)	13	Obliging and accommodating
	14	Easy-going
	15	A burden for family or society (−)
	16	Nagging (−)
	17	Disconnected from the society (−)
	18	Taking advantage of being old (−)
	19	Selfish (−)
Employment and financial security (3 items)	20	In poverty and distress (−)
	21	Stingy (−)
	22	Inefficient (−)

Note: (−) are reverse-coded items.

a higher score indicated more positive attitudes toward older people or aging. The consistent finding was that older people reported high item means for the aggregated score on OPS (4.74) and on its four subscales measuring the four facets of ASP delineated earlier (4.61, 4.81, 4.72, 4.89). All five mean scores were not only in the positive ranges of the scale, but also statistically significant from the mid-point of 4 on the 1–7 scale. Furthermore, older people's own perception of aging was significantly more positive than the projections of them by a broad section of population in Taiwan, including college students, company managers, and workers. These results are encouraging when interpreted as one indicator of positive aging: Taiwanese older people not only view aging more positively than their younger counterparts, they remain optimistic in all aspects of the aging process, physical, psychological, social, and financial.

Adopting a different research paradigm, a qualitative research study reported 22 in-depth interviews with community older adults in Taiwan (Lu and Chen, 2002). Researchers noted that many of their interviewees held rather positive self-perceptions of their family roles in later life. Such decidedly positive self-evaluations and confidence were rooted in rich life experiences, in the belief that they could teach, guide and help their children and grandchildren, and in the prevailing societal value of respecting the old and ascribing authority to the old in the family. Unlike in the work domain upon retirement, there is no discontinuity or role diminishment for Chinese older people in family life. Instead, the patriarchal family institution, the filial piety cultural value, and the close intergenerational relations grant older people continuity in active participation in family life, as a sage, a counsel, a helper, an investor, a figurehead, or in some other productive role. The rich personal accounts of productive aging firmly rooted in active and meaningful participation in the family gave researchers the optimism to conclude that, health and financial security permitting, Taiwanese older people possessed generally positive aging perceptions and were able to perform their family roles with confidence and satisfaction.

Synthesizing these strands of research, I believe that aging can be experienced positively in a Chinese culture. At the society level, the prevailing social value of filial piety and the social norm of respecting the old in Chinese society help to strengthen the status and prestige of older people both in and beyond the family domain (Lee, 1999; Lu and Chen, 2002). At the individual level, the possibility of maintaining a positive outlook for old age and experiencing aging positively is supported by a theoretical perspective emphasizing life-course development (Erikson, 1982). From the perspective of life-span development, there still exist opportunities for positive change and personal growth in later years, and staying positive is pivotal to successful adaptation. This is exactly what has been revealed in a Taiwanese community study: for older people, more positive aging perception was related to higher happiness and fewer depressive symptoms (Lu et al., 2010). Moreover, these effects on well-being persisted even after controlling for the effects of social support and community participation. To reiterate, conceptualizing *positive aging* as a successful state of human adjustment in later years, characterized by meaning in life, happiness, peace of mind, and a positive aging self-perception, can complete the theoretical map (Figure 23.1) and provide a set of coherent, measurable and reliable indicators of WB for older people, while respecting their subjectively lived aging experiences.

Creating Well-Being: Leisure Participation as a Means to Positive Aging

A basic tenet of the WHO (2002) agenda for "active aging" is to encourage older people to stay active and engaged in various roles and activities in diverse life domains. Well documented in the Western literature and supported by findings reviewed above for Chinese older people, the beneficial effects of family participation and social integration for positive aging are unequivocal. However, other domains of active participation in life, especially subjective experiences of leisure, have so far largely been ignored. Below I will theorize possible mechanisms linking meaningful leisure experiences in older age to well-being, and present empirical evidence supporting the beneficial effects of leisure over and beyond those of known protectors such as physical health, financial security, and social embeddedness, both in the West and in Taiwan.

In a recent study, Bowling (2008) interviewed 337 British older adults living at home, and found that 43 percent regarded having/maintaining physical health and 34 percent regarded participating in leisure and social activities as elements of active aging. It is rather encouraging to note that a third rated themselves as aging "very actively" and almost half as "fairly actively."

This research provides an empirical basis for the notion of active aging as "engagement with life," including role participation with work, family, friends, community, and leisure (Rundek and Bennett, 2006; WHO, 2002).

Time being one of the most available assets in older age, leisure can serve a key role in creating well-being and can be a constructive way of engaging with life. One recent study found that Australian older people spent 4.5 hours a day on solitary leisure and 2.7 hours a day on social leisure (McKenna, Broome, and Liddle, 2007). Although there are no data on time use of Taiwanese older adults, Chen (2003) did find that participation in various leisure activities was positively related to increased life satisfaction for older people.

More striking evidence came from a ten-year study with a nationally representative sample of older people in Sweden (Silverstein and Parker, 2002). Researchers found that those increasing their leisure activity participation across domains perceived an improvement in their life conditions. Another study found that for Japanese older men, less interaction with neighbors, society, and friends was strongly associated with depressed mood, while for women, engaging in various types of activities related to community, leisure, and children/grandchildren was associated with less depressed mood (Arai et al., 2007).

Various leisure theories have provided us with frameworks to understand the benefits of leisure for WB. For instance, Beard and Ragheb (1980) suggested that leisure could gratify basic human needs and generate satisfaction pertaining to six aspects: psychological (e.g., interesting activities), social (e.g., getting to know people), physical (e.g., getting exercise, keeping fit), educational (e.g., learning new things), relaxation (e.g., unwinding), and aesthetic (e.g., beautiful surroundings). Existing leisure research has confirmed that various leisure activities can indeed generate short-term benefits, including positive mood, physical fitness, and immediate satisfaction, as well as long-term effects of happiness, mental health, physical health, and social integration (Argyle, 1996; Lu and Hu, 2005). Interview studies with older Taiwanese people further revealed that they often use leisure to structure time and keep a desirable flow of events in daily life (Chen et al., 2013; Lu and Chen, 2002). Since older adults have ample time to spend, Western research has found that leisure is especially important for older people (Argyle, 1996).

A recent study (Pressman et al., 2009) has shown that among a large sample of American adults (1,399, aged 19–89 years), leisure participation in aggregate was associated with lower blood pressure, lower level of cortisol, smaller waist circumference, lower body mass index, and perceptions of better physical function. These associations withstood controlling for demographic measures. Leisure participation also correlated with higher levels of positive psychosocial states and lower levels of depression and negative affect. It seems that leisure activities are associated with both psychological and physical outcomes. A large-scale Taiwanese study with a national representative sample (2,147, aged 20–96 years) also found that leisure participation in aggregate across 13 common activities was associated with higher satisfaction (Lu and Kao, 2009b). There is thus empirical evidence that Taiwanese people generally feel happy about their leisure and may indeed gain benefits from this particular aspect of life.

One possible mechanism of leisure participation in enhancing WB for older people may be through social support and social engagement, as many activities are conducted with family and friends (Arai et al., 2007; Fu, Lu, and Chen, 2009). Joining in activities with others reflects the social organization of leisure, strengthens interpersonal relationships, and enhances a sense of belonging among the participants (Cheek and Burch, 1976). Leisure-related social support has indeed been found to buffer the stress–illness relationship for Americans (Iso-Ahola and Park, 1996).

Moreover, leisure has the potential to go beyond social engagement or social support. The aforementioned Swedish study (Silverstein and Parker, 2002) revealed that the beneficial effects of increased leisure participation were particularly strong among older adults who became widowed, developed functional impairments, and had relatively low contact with family. These results suggest that maximizing leisure participation is an adaptive strategy taken by older adults to compensate for social and physical losses in later life.

Yet another possible mechanism of leisure participation in enhancing WB in older age may be through cognitive stimulation of the brain. Leisure activities may help brain function and protect against cognitive deterioration. Longitudinal data have allowed for exploration of the effects of social network, physical leisure, and nonphysical activity on cognition and dementia (Fratiglioni, Paillard-Borg, and Winblad, 2004). For all three lifestyle components (social, physical, and mental), a beneficial effect on cognition and a protective effect against dementia are suggested. Evidence further showed that cognitively stimulating leisure activities are protective against cognitive decline in older people, while passive activities such as watching TV may actually damage more than protect cognitive functioning (Rundek and Bennett, 2006).

So far, it seems that participation in leisure activities may facilitate WB partly via its instrumental gains in enabling people to join and maintain social networks, to stimulate brain function, and partly via enjoyment of leisure per se. An Australian study (Sellar and Boshoff, 2006) found that for older people, relaxation and being engrossed were commonly expressed experiences while engaging in leisure. Such subjective experiences were different from, yet complementary to those derived from social support, such as care and respect.

One pioneering Taiwanese study (Lu, 2011) explored older people's subjective leisure experiences, and further examined associations of such experiences with their depressive symptoms in a national representative sample of older people in the community (1,308, aged 65+). Known correlates of depression such as demographics, physical health, and social support were taken into account. Face-to-face interviews were conducted to collect high quality data. A checklist of ten leisure activities was provided, including TV/radio, reading newspaper/magazine, playing chess/board games/cards, visiting relatives/friends/neighbors, PC/internet, gardening/plants, interests/hobbies, attending concerts/plays, movies/shopping, and walking/exercising. Results showed that after controlling for effects of demographics, physical health, and social support, perceived meaningfulness of leisure encompassing aspects of psychological, social, physical, educational, and relaxation experiences was independently related to fewer depressive symptoms. Thus the benefits of meaningful leisure pursuits as a subjective human experience for WB were clearly demonstrated over and beyond known protectors for Taiwanese older people living in community.

Conclusion

The purpose of this chapter was twofold: to reconceptualize WB in the context of normal aging, especially for those living in a developing Chinese society, Taiwan, and to further examine whether leisure pursuits are instrumental in creating WB in later years. On the first front, in Figure 23.1 I have organized some of the most influential definitions of WB in older age along two axes: end-state vs. process, objective vs. subjective. I have argued that WB can be fruitfully approached from a psychological standpoint, respecting older people's subjective judgment of their own lived experiences based on cognitive, affective, and self-evaluative processes. Specifically, I argue that *well-being in older age is the result of a global, positive evaluation of one's own aging experience. Positive aging* as a successful state of human adjustment in later years is characterized by *meaning in life, happiness, peace of mind, and a positive aging self-perception*. I presented preliminary evidence supporting such a four-facet construct of WB from a two-wave community study in Taiwan. Although this new construct awaits more support for its validity, unequivocal evidence from concerted research efforts demonstrates that notwithstanding challenges and losses in older age, aging is still experienced positively by many, both in the developed West and the developing East. Positive aging is a meaningful theoretical construct with real-life relevance. Positive aging need not remain an ideal; it is humanly possible and socially responsible. More concerted efforts of research and intervention should be invested to ensure and enhance this subjective aspect of WB for older adults.

On the second front, I have presented unequivocal evidence from several large scale studies examining leisure as a psychosocial correlate of WB for Taiwanese older people, along with other known factors. The most striking evidence presented is that leisure pursuits in older age are related to emotional well-being (depressive symptoms), even after controlling for effects of demographics, physical health/disability, and social support. Although leisure experiences may not be the strongest predictors, their potential for creating WB and maintaining a meaningful engagement in life should not be overlooked. In fact, crafting leisure as a means to strengthen social support and community integration, to organize personal and family life, and to protect physical mobility and cognitive functioning opens doors for effective intervention to improve WB for older people. Looking ahead, in a fast-changing developing society, health care, financial planning, social integration, and active participation in life are all integral aspects of a high quality of life in later years. Individuals, family, organizations, and society at large need to join hands to ensure positive experiences in the these aspects of living.

"Do not go gentle into that good night" (Dylan Thomas).

Note

In writing up this chapter, the author was supported by a grant from the Ministry of Science and Technology, Taiwan, MOST 105-2420-H-002-020-MY3.

References

Arai, A., Ishida, K., Tomimori, M., Katsumata, Y., Grove, J. S., and Tamashiro, H. (2007). Association between lifestyle activity and depressed mood among home-dwelling older people: A community-based study in Japan. *Aging and Mental Health*, *11*(5), 547–555.

Argyle, M. (1996). *The Social Psychology of Leisure*. London: Penguin Books.

Arnold, S. B. (1991). The measurement of quality of life in the frail elderly. In J. E. Birren, J. E. Lubben, J. C. Rowe, and D. E. Deutchman (Eds.), *The Concept and Measurement of Quality of Life in the Frail Elderly* (pp. 50–74). San Diego, CA: Academic Press.

Baltes, P. B., and Baltes, M. M. (1990). *Successful Aging: Perspectives from the Behavioral Sciences*. Cambridge: Cambridge University Press.

Battista, J., and Almond, R. (1973). The development of meaning in life. *Psychiatry*, *36*, 409–427.

Beard, J. G., and Ragheb, M. G. (1980). Measuring leisure satisfaction. *Journal of Leisure Research*, *12*(1), 20–33.

Bowling, A. (2008). Enhancing later life: How older people perceive active ageing? *Aging and Mental Health*, *12*(3), 293–301.

Bowling, A., and Gabriel, Z. (2004). An integrational model of quality of life in older age. *Social Indicator Research*, *69*(1), 1–36.

Cheek, N. H., and Burch, W. R. (1976). *The Social Organization of Leisure in Human Society*. New York: Harper and Row.

Chen, C. N. (2003). Older people's leisure and quality of life in Taiwan. *Journal of Population Studies, 26*, 96–136.

Chen, F. M., and Lu, L. (2015, March). Towards positive aging: Key factors of positive aging and situational effects. Paper presented at the 2015 Annual Conference of Taiwan Association of Gerontology, Taipei, Taiwan.

Chen, J. W., Chang, Y. Y., Kao, S. F., and Lu, L. (2013). Getting old is terrible? The process of optimal aging among Taiwanese older people. *Indigenous Psychological Research in Chinese Societies, 40*, 87–140.

Crowther, M. R., Parker, M. W., Achenbaum, W. A., Larimore, W. L., and Koenig, H. G. (2002). Rowe and Kahn's model of successful aging revisited: Positive spirituality, the forgotten factor. *Gerontologist, 42*(5), 613–620.

Diener, E., Suh, E. M., Lucas, R. E., and Smith, H. L. (1999). Subjective well-being: Three decades of progress. *Psychological Bulletin, 125*, 276–302.

Erikson, E. H. (1982). *The Life Circle Completed*. New York: Norton.

Fratiglioni, L., Paillard-Borg, S., and Winblad, B. (2004). An active and socially integrated lifestyle in late life might protect against dementia. *Lancet. Neurology, 3*(6), 343–353.

Freund, A. M., and Smith, J. (1999). Content and function of the self-definition in old and very old age. *Journals of Gerontology, Series B: Psychological Sciences and Social Sciences, 54*(1), P55–P67.

Fry, P. S. (2000). Guest editorial: Aging and quality of life (QOL) – the continuing search for quality of life indicators. *International Journal of Aging and Human Development, 50*(4), 245–61.

Fu, Y. C., Lu, L., and Chen, S. Y. (2009). Differentiating personal facilitators of leisure participation: Socio-demographics, personality traits, and the need for sociability. *Journal of Tourism and Leisure Studies, 15*, 187–212.

Gentile K. M. (1991). A review of the literature on interventions and quality of life in the frail elderly. In J. E. Birren, J. E. Lubben, J. C. Rowe, and D. E. Deutchman (Eds.), *The Concept and Measurement of Quality of Life in the Frail Elderly* (pp. 75–90). San Diego, CA: Academic Press.

Hsieh, M. O. (2004). Related factors of living arrangements and quality of life among disabled elderly: A quantitative exploration. *Social Policy and Social Work, 8*(1), 1–49.

Hu, Y. H. (1992). Gender and caring for the old. *Quarterly Journal of Community Development, 58*, 170–183.

Iso-Ahola, S. E., and Park, C. J. (1996). Leisure-related social support and self-determination as buffers of stress–illness relationship. *Journal of Leisure Research, 28*(3), 169–187.

Kahneman, D., Diener, E., and Schwarz, N. (Eds.) (1999). *Well-Being: The Foundations of Hedonic Psychology*. New York: Russell Sage Foundation.

Lawton, M. P. (1983). Environment and other determinants of well-being in older people. *Gerontologist, 23*, 349–357.

Lee, L. J. (1999). Adults' perceived images of life experience and personality traits of middle-aged and older adults. *Bulletin of National Chengchi University, 78*, 1–54.

Lee, Y. C., Lin, Y. C., Huang, C. L., and Fredrickson, B. L. (2013). The construct and measurement of peace of mind. *Journal of Happiness Studies, 14*, 571–590.

Leung, K., and Bond, M. H. (2004). Social axioms: A model for social beliefs in multicultural perspective. *Advanced Experimental Social Psychology, 36*, 119–197.

Lin, W. Y. (2002). Family changes and family policy in Taiwan. *Journal of NTU Social Work, 6*, 35–88.

Logan, J. R., Ward, R., and Spitze, G. (1992). As old as you feel: Age identity in middle and later life. *Social Forces, 71*(2), 451–467.

Lu, L. (2005). In pursuit of happiness: The cultural psychological study of SWB [subjective well-being]. *Chinese Journal of Psychology, 47*, 99–112.

Lu, L. (2010a). Attitudes towards older people and coworkers' intention to work with older employees: A Taiwanese study. *International Journal of Ageing and Human Development, 71*, 305–322.

Lu, L. (2010b). Who is happy in Taiwan? The demographic classifications of the happy person. *Psychologia, 53*, 55–67.

Lu, L. (2011). Leisure experiences and depressive symptoms among Chinese older people: A national survey in Taiwan. *Educational Gerontology, 37*(9), 753–771.

Lu, L. (2012). Attitudes towards aging and older people's intentions to continue working: A Taiwanese study. *Career Development International, 17*, 83–98.

Lu, L., and Chang, C. J. (1998). Health and satisfaction among the elderly with chronic conditions: Demographic differentials. *Kaohsiung Journal of Medical Sciences, 14*, 139–149.

Lu, L., and Chen, H. H. (2002). An exploratory study on role adjustment and intergenerational relationships among the elderly in the changing Taiwan. *Research in Applied Psychology, 14,* 221–249.

Lu, L., and Hsieh, Y. H. (1997). Demographic variables, control, stress, support and health among the elderly. *Journal of Health Psychology, 2,* 97–106.

Lu, L., and Hu, C. H. (2005). Personality, leisure experiences and happiness. *Journal of Happiness Studies, 6,* 325–342.

Lu, L., and Kao, S. F. (2009a). Attitudes towards old people in Taiwan: Scale development and preliminary evidence of reliability and validity. *Journal of Education and Psychology, 32,* 147–171.

Lu, L., and Kao, S. F. (2009b). Direct and indirect effects of personality traits on leisure satisfaction: Evidence from a national probability sample in Taiwan. *Social Behavior and Personality, 37,* 191–192.

Lu, L., and Kao, S. F. (2010). Attitudes towards old people and their relation to career choices among Taiwanese university students. *Journal of Education and Psychology, 33,* 33–54.

Lu, L., Kao, S. F., and Hsieh, Y. H. (2010). Positive attitudes towards older people and well-being among Chinese community older adults. *Journal of Applied Gerontology, 29,* 622–639.

Lu, L., Kao, S. F., and Hsieh, Y. H. (2011). Attitudes towards older people and managers' intention to hire older workers: A Taiwanese study. *Educational Gerontology, 37,* 835–853.

Lu, L., Kao, S. F., Chang, T. T., Wu, H. P., and Zhang, J. (2008). The individual- and social-oriented Chinese bicultural self: A sub-cultural analysis contrasting mainland Chinese and Taiwanese. *Social Behavior and Personality, 36,* 337–346.

McKenna, K., Broome, K., and Liddle, J. (2007). What older people do: Time use and exploring the link between role participation and life satisfaction in people aged 65 years and over. *Australian Occupational Therapy Journal, 54*(4), 273–284.

Pressman, S. D., Matthews, K. A., Cohen, S., Martire, L. M., Scheier, M., Baum, A., and Schulz, R. (2009). Association of enjoyable leisure activities with psychological and physical well-being. *Psychosomatic Medicine, 71*(7), 725.

Rioux, L. (2005). The well-being of aging people living in their own homes. *Journal of Environmental Psychology, 25*(2), 231–243.

Ross, D. (2010). Ageing and work: An overview. *Occupational Medicine, 60,* 169–171.

Rowe, J. W., and Kahn, R. L. (1987). Human aging: Usual and successful. *Science, 237,* 143–149.

Rowe, J. W., and Kahn, R. L. (1998). *Successful Aging.* New York: Random House.

Rundek, T., and Bennett, D. A. (2006). Cognitive leisure activities, but not watching TV, for future brain benefits. *Neurology, 66*(6), 794–795.

Sellar, B., and Boshoff, K. (2006). Subjective leisure experiences of older Australians. *Australian Occupational Therapy Journal, 53*(3), 211–219.

Silverstein, M., and Parker, M. G. (2002). Leisure activities and quality of life among the oldest old in Sweden. *Research on Aging, 24*(5), 528–547.

WHO (World Health Organization) (1990). *Healthy Ageing.* Geneva: World Health Organization.

WHO (World Health Organization) (2002). *Ethical Choices in Long-Term Care: What Does Justice Require?* Geneva: World Health Organization.

24

Optimism, Coping, and Well-Being

Charles S. Carver and Michael F. Scheier

Optimists are people who expect good things to happen to them; pessimists are people who expect bad things to happen to them. This difference among people has been recognized for a long time. Research over the past three decades suggests that it is a difference that matters. This rather simple difference – anticipating good outcomes versus bad ones – is linked to key motivational processes underlying behavior. How these people differ in their approaches to the world, following from these motivational processes, has substantial impact on their lives.

Background

Scientific definitions of optimism and pessimism focus on expectancies for the future. This focus links these ideas to a long history of expectancy–value models of motivation in psychology. Expectancy–value theories hold that behavior reflects the pursuit of goals: desired states or activities. The more important a given goal is to the person, the greater its *value* (Austin and Vancouver, 1996; Carver and Scheier, 1998; Higgins, 2006). The other part of this motivational model is *expectancy* – confidence that the goal can be reached. If people doubt they can reach a goal, they withdraw effort. They may stop prematurely, or they may never really start. People who are confident about reaching an outcome will persevere even in the face of great adversity.

The expectancy construct can be applied at many levels. Confidence and doubt can pertain to quite narrow contexts (e.g., the ability to cross a street unaided), to moderately broad contexts (e.g., the ability to navigate an unfamiliar city), and to even broader contexts (e.g., the ability to develop a good reputation in one's profession). Optimism is a generalized version of confidence; it is confidence pertaining to life, rather than to just a specific context (Scheier and Carver, 1992). Thus, optimists should tend to be confident and persistent in the face of diverse life challenges (even when progress is difficult or slow). Pessimists should be more doubtful and hesitant in such situations. These differences in how people confront adversity

The Handbook of Stress and Health: A Guide to Research and Practice, First Edition.
Edited by Cary L. Cooper and James Campbell Quick.
© 2017 John Wiley & Sons, Ltd. Published 2017 by John Wiley & Sons, Ltd.

have implications for success in goal-directed behavior. They also have implications for how people cope with stress.

Measurement Issues

There are at least two ways to think about these generalized expectancies and how to measure them. One might measure them directly, asking people whether they expect outcomes in their lives to be good or bad (Scheier and Carver, 1992). This is reflected in the Life Orientation Test (LOT) and its successor the Life Orientation Test-Revised (LOT-R; Scheier, Carver, and Bridges, 1994). This is the measure we use in our own work. It consists of a set of statements (e.g., "I'm always optimistic about my future," "I rarely count on good things happening to me" (reverse coded)) to which people indicate their degree of agreement or disagreement (other measures of this trait have also been created with a similar structure, e.g., Dember, Martin, Hummer, Howe, and Melton, 1989).

A different approach rests on the idea that people's expectancies for the future stem from their interpretations of the past (Peterson and Seligman, 1984). If past failures reflect stable causes, future failure will also be expected, because the cause (which is relatively permanent) is likely to remain in place. If past failures reflect unstable causes, the future may be brighter, because the cause may no longer be present. Following this reasoning, some assess optimism and pessimism as patterns of attributions about the causes of events (e.g., Peterson and Seligman, 1984), and infer that the attributions ultimately yield expectancies. Somewhat surprisingly, however, stable attributions for negative events are only modestly correlated with direct measures of generalized expectancies (Ahrens and Haaga, 1993; Peterson and Vaidya, 2001). Thus, despite the fact that the measures relate to conceptually similar outcomes, they can not be considered interchangeable.

Each measurement approach yields a continuous distribution of scores. Although it is common to refer to optimists and pessimists as distinct categories of people, this is generally a verbal convenience. People almost never are placed into two groups. People range from very optimistic to very pessimistic, with most being somewhere between. On the other hand, if one were to identify those who are optimistic or pessimistic in an absolute sense, because they agree with optimistic items (e.g., "In uncertain times, I usually expect the best") and disagree with pessimistic items (e.g., "If something can go wrong for me, it will"), pessimists would be a minority. Most people are optimistic, but to varying degrees (Segerstrom, 2006a).

Further Issues

Optimism is a trait, and test–retest correlations have generally been relatively high, ranging from 0.58 to 0.79 over periods of a few weeks to three years (Atienza, Stephens, and Townsend, 2004; Lucas, Diener, and Suh, 1996; Scheier and Carver, 1985; Scheier et al., 1994). Even across a long time period (10.4 years), Matthews, Räikkönen, Sutton-Tyrrell, and Kuller (2004) found a correlation of 0.71 in a group of middle-aged women. On the other hand, one ten-year test–retest correlation was only 0.35 (Segerstrom, 2007). It is of interest that most change in that study was in the optimistic direction and was predicted by increases in social resources.

Where does this trait come from? One project found a heritability estimate for optimism of approximately 25 percent (Plomin et al., 1992). This is lower than many personality traits, but still indicates a substantial genetic influence. Other evidence points to childhood environment, in the form of resources such as parental warmth and financial security, as a predictor of adult optimism (Heinonen, Räikkönen, and Keltikangas-Järvinen, 2005; Heinonen et al., 2006).

Another issue that bears mention is that there has been some controversy about whether the construct should be seen as a single bipolar dimension or whether two separable dimensions exist, one pertaining to affirmation of optimism, the other pertaining to affirmation of pessimism. There have been cases in which separating the qualities has led to better prediction of outcomes (Marshall, Wortman, Kusulas, Hervig, and Vickers, 1992; Robinson-Whelen, Kim, MacCallum, and Kiecolt-Glaser, 1997) but that has not always been the case. A number of studies trying to settle the issue have reached opposite conclusions. Some hold that a unidimensional view is accurate (Rauch, Schweizer, and Moosbrugger, 2007), others that there are two dimensions (Herzberg, Glaesmer, and Hoyer, 2006).

The issue seems to be that people respond differently to positively worded items than to negatively worded items. The question is whether this difference (which is quite common for measures with that structure) reflects method variance or substantive variance. At present this remains unresolved.

For the sake of simplicity, we treat optimism–pessimism here as one dimension. Keep in mind, however, that in some studies what mattered most was whether people endorsed versus rejected a pessimistic outlook; in other studies what mattered most was whether people endorsed versus rejected an optimistic outlook. In yet other studies, the issue did not matter at all.

In the sections that follow we describe some ways in which individual differences in optimism versus pessimism, measured as expectations for one's future, relate to other aspects of life (see also Carver and Scheier, 2014; Segerstrom, 2006a). We address five manifestations of optimism: subjective well-being, coping, fostering and interfering with well-being, physical health, and socioeconomic and social resources.

Optimism and Subjective Well-Being

A straightforward effect of optimism and pessimism is on how people feel when they encounter problems. When things get difficult, people's emotions range from enthusiasm and eagerness to anger, anxiety, and depression. The balance among feelings relates to variation in optimism. Optimists expect good outcomes, even when things are hard. This yields a relatively positive mix of feelings. Pessimists, expecting bad outcomes, have more negative feelings – anxiety, anger, sadness, even despair (Carver and Scheier, 1998; Scheier and Carver, 1992).

Relations between optimism and distress have been examined in a wide range of contexts, including students starting college (Aspinwall and Taylor, 1992; Brissette, Scheier, and Carver, 2002); survivors of missile attacks (Zeidner and Hammer, 1992); cancer caregivers (Given et al., 1993); Alzheimer's caregivers (Hooker, Monahan, Shifren, and Hutchinson, 1992; Shifren and Hooker, 1995); and people dealing with stresses of childbirth (Carver and Gaines, 1987), coronary artery bypass surgery (Fitzgerald, Tennen, Affleck, and Pransky, 1993; Scheier et al., 1989), failed attempts at in vitro fertilization (Litt, Tennen, Affleck, and Klock, 1992), bone marrow transplantation (Curbow, Somerfield, Baker, Wingard, and Legro, 1993), cancer (Carver et al., 1993; Friedman et al., 1992), and the progression of AIDS (Taylor et al., 1992).

The studies vary in complexity. Some are cross-sectional, showing that lower optimism relates to reports of more distress in some difficult situation. What those studies *cannot* show is whether less optimistic people had more distress even prior to the adversity. Other studies assess people at multiple time points. These give a better picture of how distress shifts over time and circumstances, and allow controls for initial levels of distress.

A very early study examined the development of depressed feelings after childbirth (Carver and Gaines, 1987). Women completed the LOT and a depression scale in the last third of their pregnancy. They completed the depression scale again three weeks after delivery. Optimism related to lower depression symptoms at initial assessment and also predicted lower depression post-partum, controlling for initial levels. Thus optimism appeared to confer resistance to postpartum depressive symptoms.

Medical Contexts

A good deal of the research on optimism and emotional well-being has been done in medical settings. Several projects have studied people having coronary artery bypass surgery. One assessed people a month beforehand and eight months afterward (Fitzgerald et al., 1993). Optimists had less distress beforehand, and (controlling for presurgical life satisfaction) had more life satisfaction after surgery. Optimism about life appeared to lead to a specific optimism about the surgery, and from there to satisfaction with life. A similar study by Scheier and colleagues (1989) found that optimists retained a higher quality of life even up to five years after the surgery.

In another health context, treatment for breast cancer (Carver et al., 1993), women were interviewed at diagnosis, on the day before surgery, a few days after surgery, and 3, 6, and 12 months later. Optimism predicted less distress over time, controlling for earlier distress. Thus, optimism conferred resilience against distress during the full year. A study of head and neck cancer patients yielded similar results (Allison, Guichard, and Gilain, 2000). Although it has been suggested that optimism might set people up for disappointment (Schwarzer, 1994; Tennen and Affleck, 1987), this has really not been found.

Yet another context in which effects of optimism have been studied is treatment for ischemic heart disease. In this project (Shnek, Irvine, Stewart, and Abbey, 2001), lower optimism related to more symptoms of depression shortly after hospitalization. Lower optimism also predicted more symptoms of depression at a one-year follow-up, after controlling for earlier depression and a variety of other variables.

Other Settings

Medical conditions are not the only sources of stress. Caregiving is also highly stressful. One project studied cancer patients and their caregivers (Given et al., 1993). Caregivers' optimism predicted less depression and less of an adverse impact of caregiving on their physical health. Similar results have been found among caregiver spouses of Alzheimer's patients (Hooker et al., 1992; Shifren and Hooker, 1995).

Other studies have examined events that are challenging, but far less severe. For example, starting college is a stressful time, and at least two studies have examined optimism among students adjusting to their first semester (Aspinwall and Taylor, 1992; Brissette et al., 2002). Optimism and other variables were assessed when they arrived on campus, and well-being was measured at semester's end. Higher optimism predicted less distress.

Also challenging is the simple process of late-life aging. A Dutch study of elderly men examined the role of personality at an initial assessment as a predictor of depression across a 15-year follow-up (Giltay, Zitman, and Kromhout, 2006). Optimism predicted significantly lower cumulative incidence of depression symptoms.

Optimism and Coping

If optimists have less distress than pessimists under adversity, is it just because they are cheerful people? That apparently is not all of it, because differences often remain when controls are included for prior distress. This section considers another path to differences in well-being: differences in coping. The ways in which optimists and pessimists differ in coping resemble the differences in broad behavioral tendencies discussed earlier in the chapter. That is, people who are confident about eventual success continue trying, even when the going is hard. People who are doubtful try to escape by wishful thinking or temporary distractions that don't help solve the problem, and they sometimes even stop trying.

Support for this picture has been found in a number of studies (for detailed review and meta-analysis see Solberg Nes and Segerstrom, 2006). Early studies examined student reports of situational coping responses and general coping styles (e.g., Scheier, Carver, and Bridges, 2001), finding that optimists appear generally to be approach copers, and pessimists appear to be avoidant copers. Conceptually similar results have followed repeatedly.

Indeed, several of the studies described earlier, in the context of well-being, also looked at coping. In their study of coronary artery bypass surgery, Scheier et al. (1989) assessed attentional-cognitive strategies as ways of coping with the experience. Before surgery, optimists reported making plans for their future and setting goals for recovery more than did pessimists. They also focused less on negative aspects of the experience – distress and symptoms. Once surgery was past, optimists were more likely than pessimists to report seeking out information about what they would be required to do in the months ahead, and they were less likely to say they were suppressing thoughts about their symptoms.

Relations between optimism and coping also have been examined among cancer patients in several studies. Stanton and Snider (1993) found that pessimistic women used more cognitive avoidance in coping with an upcoming biopsy than optimists. Cognitive avoidance before the biopsy predicted distress afterward among women with cancer diagnoses.

Another study of cancer patients mentioned earlier (Carver et al., 1993) examined how women coped with treatment for breast cancer during the first year after diagnosis. Both before and after surgery, optimism related to coping that involved accepting the reality of the situation, placing as positive a light on it as possible, and using humor to cope. Pessimism related to overt denial (trying to push the reality of the situation away) and to giving-up tendencies at each time point. The coping responses that were related to optimism were also related to distress. The effect of optimism on distress was largely indirect through coping, particularly at postsurgery.

Another study of coping among women under treatment for breast cancer (Schou, Ekeberg, and Ruland, 2005) focused on two coping responses: fighting spirit (confronting the cancer and trying to beat it), and hopelessness/helplessness (feeling a sense of giving up). These responses mediated the relationship between optimism and quality of life a year after diagnosis. The greater fighting spirit of optimists (assessed before diagnosis) predicted better quality of life at one-year follow-up.

Categories of Coping

As reflected in the preceding paragraphs, there are many ways to cope (Compas, Connor-Smith, Saltzman, Thomsen, and Wadsworth, 2001; Folkman and Moskowitz, 2004; Skinner, Edge, Altman, and Sherwood, 2003) and many ways to categorize coping responses (Carver and Connor-Smith, 2010; Skinner et al., 2003). One distinction, made early in the analysis of coping, divides problem-focused coping – doing something about the stressor to blunt its impact – from emotion-focused coping – soothing distress (Lazarus and Folkman, 1984). A particularly important distinction is between engagement or approach coping – dealing with the stressor or emotions stemming from it – and disengagement or avoidance coping – escaping the stressor or emotions stemming from it (e.g., Roth and Cohen, 1986; Skinner et al., 2003).

Solberg Nes and Segerstrom (2006) crossed these two distinctions in their meta-analysis of optimism and coping, fitting particular coping responses into the four categories. Optimism was positively associated with measures of engagement coping, and with both subsets of engagement coping: those that are problem focused (e.g., planning, seeking instrumental support) and those that are emotion focused (e.g., cognitive restructuring, acceptance). Furthermore, optimists were responsive to what sort of stressor was being confronted. They used more problem-focused coping for controllable stressors (e.g., academic demands) and more emotion-focused coping for uncontrollable stressors (e.g., trauma). Thus, optimism predicted active attempts to both change and accommodate to stressful circumstances, in ways that reflect flexible engagement.

For disengagement coping, the pattern was opposite to that for engagement coping. Optimism related inversely to disengagement coping, and to both subsets of disengagement: problem-focused (e.g., behavioral disengagement) and emotion-focused (e.g., denial, wishful thinking). As would be expected from the expectancy–value viewpoint, then, the relationship of optimism to coping differed far more substantially between engagement and disengagement than between problem focus and emotion focus.

In sum, optimists differ from pessimists in stable coping tendencies and in coping responses that emerge when confronting stressful situations (Solberg Nes and Segerstrom, 2006). Particularly noteworthy may be the contrast between acceptance and active denial. Denial (refusing to accept the reality of the situation) means trying to maintain a worldview that no longer applies. Acceptance means restructuring perceptions to come to grips with the situation.

We stress that acceptance here does not mean giving up. Resignation to illness may hasten death (Greer, Morris, Pettingale, and Haybittle, 1990; Reed, Kemeny, Taylor, Wang, and Visscher, 1994). Acceptance of the reality of the diagnosis has different effects. Accepting that life is compromised (but not over) lets people develop adaptive parameters within which to live the time left to them. Acceptance may actually serve the purpose of keeping the person goal-engaged, and indeed "life-engaged" (Scheier and Carver, 2001).

Health Promoting and Damaging Behaviors

The concept of coping has been extended to what has been called preventive or proactive coping (Aspinwall and Taylor, 1997), processes that promote good health and well-being rather than reacting to adversity. Optimists expect positive outcomes in their future, and maybe they take active steps to ensure those outcomes. This would resemble problem-focused coping, except that it is intended to prevent a stressor from arising.

Health Promotion

Health promotion might occur in many ways. An example is seeking knowledge about potential risk. Some people might expect that adults who are optimistic would not make much effort to learn about risks related to heart attacks. One study investigated this question in a group of middle-aged adults (Radcliffe and Klein, 2002). Those high in dispositional optimism actually knew more about the risk factors than those who were less optimistic.

Proactive efforts have also been examined among patients in cardiac rehabilitation (Shepperd, Maroto, and Pbert, 1996). Optimists were more successful in lowering saturated fat, body fat, and an index of overall coronary risk. Optimism also related to increases in exercise. Another study of the lifestyles of coronary artery bypass patients five years after surgery found optimists more likely than pessimists to be taking vitamins, eating low-fat foods, and to be enrolled in a cardiac rehabilitation program (Scheier and Carver, 1992).

Other proactive health-related behaviors concern management of HIV risk. By avoiding certain sexual practices (e.g., sex with unknown partners), people can reduce risk of infection. One study of HIV-negative gay men found that optimists reported fewer anonymous sexual partners than pessimists (Taylor et al., 1992), suggesting that optimists were making efforts to safeguard their health.

In sum, optimists do not stick their heads in the sand and ignore threats to well-being. Rather, they seem to take action to minimize health risks. They attend to risks, but selectively. They focus on risks that relate to potentially serious health problems and apply to them (Aspinwall and Brunhart, 1996). If the potential problem is minor, or if it doesn't bear on them, they are not especially vigilant. Optimists appear to scan for threats to well-being but save their behavioral responses for meaningful threats.

It might seem surprising that people who expect good things to happen take active steps to make sure good things *do* happen. Presumably experience teaches people that their own efforts play an important part in many kinds of life outcomes. Optimists may be more confident than pessimists that their efforts will be successful. For that reason, they are quicker to engage those efforts when there is a need for them.

Health-Defeating Behaviors

We have said that optimists are persistent in trying to reach goals and pessimists are more likely to give up. Some of the giving-up tendencies among pessimists represent health-defeating behaviors. For example, giving up may underlie excessive alcohol use, which is often seen as an escape from problems. Pessimists are more prone to this than optimists.

One study of women with a family history of alcoholism found that pessimists were more likely than optimists to report drinking problems (Ohannessian, Hesselbrock, Tennen, and Affleck, 1993). In another study, people who had been treated for alcohol abuse were more likely to drop out of an aftercare program and return to drinking than optimists (Strack, Carver, and Blaney, 1987). Another study (Park, Moore, Turner, and Adler, 1997) found that optimistic women were less likely to engage in substance abuse during their pregnancies than pessimistic women.

A more recent study examined giving up in terms of the disruption of normal activities. In this study, breast cancer patients reported illness-related disruption of social activities after treatment (Carver, Lehman, and Antoni, 2003). At each assessment, pessimism predicted more disruption (along with distress and fatigue). Thus, when confronted with a health threat, pessimism led to a withdrawal from the social activities that support a normal life.

In sum, evidence indicates that pessimism can lead people into self-defeating patterns. The result can be less persistence, more avoidance coping, and various kinds of health-damaging behavior. Without confidence about the future, it is hard to remain engaged in life.

Optimism and Physical Health

The sections on subjective well-being and coping included frequent mention of medical problems. As that implies, much of the research on optimism has been in health psychology. Some of that research has examined optimism and physical well-being. The general line of thinking behind this research is that optimists may be less reactive than pessimists to the stresses of life; the lower physiological stress responses may (over many years) result in less physical wear and tear on the body; the end result may be better physical health and even greater longevity. This section describes a few examples of this research (for broader treatment see Rasmussen, Scheier, and Greenhouse, 2009).

Carotid intima thickness is a physical marker of the development of heart disease. In one study of physical well being, intima thickness was measured among middle-aged women at a baseline assessment and at three-year follow-up (Matthews et al., 2004). Greater pessimism at the first assessment predicted increases in intima thickness at follow-up. Optimists experienced almost no increase over the three-year period.

Another project concerning cardiovascular health examined patterns of rehospitalization after coronary artery bypass surgery (Scheier et al., 1999). Rehospitalization after bypass is quite common. In this study, optimism predicted significantly less likelihood of rehospitalization and a longer time before it occurred. Interestingly, the effects of optimism were independent of self-esteem, depression, and neuroticism.

Perhaps the most compelling evidence on optimism and cardiovascular disease comes from the Women's Health Initiative (WHI), a large-scale project studying quality of life, chronic disease, morbidity and mortality across time among American women. Using WHI participants, Tindale et al. (2009) studied over 95,000 women across an eight-year period. All were free of cancer and cardiovascular disease at study entry. Optimists were less likely than pessimists to develop coronary heart disease (CHD), were less likely to die from CHD-related causes, and had lower total mortality across the eight years of study. The advantage due to optimism ranged from 9 percent for incident cases of CHD to 30 percent for CHD-related mortality.

Healing and immunity have also been examined. In one study, men received a biopsy and were followed through healing (Ebrecht et al., 2004). The sample was split into "slow healers" and "fast healers." Slow healers were lower in optimism than fast healers. In another study, older adults received an influenza vaccine; optimism predicted a better immune response two weeks later (Kohut, Cooper, Nickolaus, Russell, and Cunnick, 2002). Other research has found, however, that under very high challenge, optimism related to lower, rather than higher, immune responses (Segerstrom, 2005; 2006b). It was suggested that the reduction under high challenge may reflect greater behavioral engagement with the challenge, which can suppress immune responses so as to conserve energy.

The physiological stress responses and physical health outcomes that relate to optimism also suggest additional pathways by which optimism might influence mental health. For example, substrates of stress such as norepinephrine and corticotrophin releasing hormone are implicated in anxiety disorders (Brunello et al., 2003; Dunn and Berridge, 1990). Myocardial infarction greatly increases the risk for major depressive disorder (Lesperance, Frasure-Smith, and Talajic, 1996). Thus, differences in physiological reactivity to stress may themselves result in differences in vulnerability to psychological problems.

To sum up, research suggests that optimism is relevant to physical health. Relations between optimism and physical health clearly deserve more study in future work.

Optimism and Resources

Optimism and Socioeconomic Status

Health psychology and subjective well-being have been the main arenas for studying effects of optimism and pessimism, but not all research on this trait has had this focus. Optimists' tendency toward persistent goal pursuit and their active coping with stressors may also make it possible for them to translate short-term tendencies toward approach (rather than withdrawal) into long-term resources. Available evidence points toward correlations of optimism with two indicators of socioeconomic status: education and income.

Dispositional optimism before starting college was associated with a higher probability of returning the second year (Solberg Nes, Evans, and Segerstrom, 2009). Pessimists had a dropout rate of about 30 percent, roughly twice that for very optimistic students. In a sample of law students, optimism before starting school predicted higher income ten years later (Segerstrom, 2007).

Socioeconomic resources are also linked to the development of optimism over time. In a study we alluded to earlier, Heinonen et al. (2006) assessed parental socioeconomic status (SES; an aggregate of education level, occupational class, and employment status) of a group of children who were either three or six years of age. They were assessed again 21 years later when they were 24 and 27 years old. There was a positive association between initial parental SES and adult optimism 21 years later, even when their own adult SES was controlled. Thus, a poor childhood SES breeds pessimism later in life.

Optimism and Social Resources

Optimism also serves well in the social domain. For example, a study described earlier examined how students coped with the challenge of starting college (Brissette et al., 2002). This study also found that optimists had greater increases in their social networks across the first semester than did pessimists.

Earlier we said that pessimistic women under treatment for breast cancer were more likely to report withdrawing from their social activities because of their treatment than were more optimistic women (Carver et al., 2003). This is a problem, because social networks are very important to well-being (Taylor, 2007). There is recent evidence that social networks and optimism have mutually reinforcing effects: Segerstrom (2007) found that developing larger social networks over a ten-year period predicted increases in optimism over that same period.

A number of people have by now come to characterize optimism as a positive resource for relationships, both general social networks and also close relationships. Why? One reason is that optimists are easier to like than pessimists. People are more accepting of someone who voices positive expectations for the future and more rejecting of someone expressing negative expectations (Carver, Kus, and Scheier, 1994; Helweg-Larsen, Sadeghian, and Webb, 2002). Actual social interactions with optimistic people are also more positive (Räikkönen, Matthews, Flory, Owens, and Gump, 1999). In yet another study, pessimism among men about to undergo coronary artery bypass surgery predicted reports of higher caregiver burden from their wives 18 months later (Ruiz, Matthews, Scheier, and Schulz, 2006).

Better social relations may also follow from the fact that optimists tend to see things in the best light, including things pertaining to their relationships. This might make the optimist more satisfied in the relationship even if things are not perfect. A recent study found that optimists had higher relationship satisfaction than pessimists, a difference that was mediated by perceptions of the relative supportiveness of their partners (Srivastava, McGonigal, Richards, Butler, and Gross, 2006). Evidence that optimists perceive greater social support than pessimists also comes from other sources (e.g., Abend and Williamson, 2002; Trunzo and Pinto, 2003).

Yet another reason why optimism represents a resource for relationships may be that optimists work harder (or more effectively) at their relationships. This would be consistent with their greater engagement with high priority tasks (Geers, Wellman, and Lassiter, 2009). In a study bearing on this question (Srivastava et al., 2006), relationship partners had a lab conversation about the topic of their greatest disagreement. The couples then rated both their behavior and their partner's behavior during that conversation, yielding an index of positive engagement (being a good listener, not criticizing, etc.). A week later, the couples were asked how well the conflict had been resolved by that time. Optimism predicted perceptions of more supportiveness from the partner, which predicted more positive engagement in the conflict discussion. The latter predicted better conflict resolution a week later. These effects emerged in the individual's own reports, and also in the reports made by partners. The beneficial effect of optimism on conflict resolution was partially mediated by perceptions of supportiveness and by positive engagement.

One year later the couples were contacted and were asked about the relationship. About a third of the couples had broken up by then. Men's optimism (but not women's) was a predictor of the relationship's survival, and again there was partial mediation by perceptions of partner supportiveness.

Just as optimists use problem-focused coping when under stress, they may also excel in problem solving in relationships. Assad, Donnellan, and Conger (2007) studied married couples across a two-year span. All completed measures of cooperative problem solving, and discussed their relationship. Raters coded the discussion for relationship quality and negative interactions. Optimism was related to better relationship quality, fewer negative interactions, and higher levels of cooperative problem solving. Two years later, women's optimism (but not men's) predicted relationship survival. Among those still married, optimism at time 1 also predicted relationship quality, even controlling for earlier relationship quality.

In sum, although there are relatively few studies of the role of optimism in relationships, what evidence does exist is consistent in indicating that pessimists have a harder road than do optimists. This is yet one more area in which the optimist appears to have an advantage.

Does Optimism Have a Downside?

The evidence reviewed here suggests that optimists have the keys to a happy and fulfilling life. Compared to pessimists, they are less distressed when they encounter adversity. They cope with difficulty by remaining engaged in the goals and activities that are being threatened. They engage in problem-focused coping when there is something to be done, and accommodative coping when the adversity has to be endured. Perhaps via these differences in coping, they also have better health-related outcomes and better social connections. These properties sound quite adaptive.

However, some have asked whether optimism can lead to problems in certain contexts. One is problem gambling. Gibson and Sanbonmatsu (2004) reasoned that gambling is a context in which confidence and persistence might be counterproductive. They found that optimists had more positive expectations for gambling than did pessimists, and were less likely to reduce their bets after poor outcomes. These people did not have actual gambling problems, but this pattern suggests the possibility that optimists may be vulnerable to such problems.

Other studies ask whether the persistence of optimists can create problems because they fail to recognize what they cannot accomplish. Optimists may not know when to quit. Certainly people sometimes have to recognize that goals are lost, and that the adaptive course is to give up on them (Wrosch, Scheier, Carver, and Schulz, 2003). Does optimism prevent that from occurring?

One project on this question stemmed from the reasoning that persistence should lead to greater goal conflict, because commitment to many goals makes people spread resources thinner (Segerstrom and Solberg Nes, 2006). Two studies (one prospective) found that optimism did relate to greater goal conflict. However, the conflict had no adverse consequences. Evidence from the second study suggested that optimists balanced expectancy, value, and cost of goal pursuit more effectively than pessimists. Optimists were committed to more mutually demanding goals, but they were better at managing the conflict.

Other research (Aspinwall and Richter, 1999) examined people's willingness to quit tasks on which they were failing (the task actually was impossible). For some, there was no alternative task to turn to; for others, there was an alternative. When there was no alternative task, everyone persisted at the impossible task. When there was another task, optimists turned to it faster than pessimists. In effect, optimists gave up on a task they could not master in order to turn to a similar task that they *could* perhaps master. Indeed, when they had been led to think that the other task measured a somewhat different skill, they even outperformed the less optimistic people on it.

These results parallel associations reported by others (Rasmussen, Wrosch, Scheier, and Carver, 2006). When their goals are perceived to be unattainable, optimists do not find it easier to disengage from those goals than pessimists. They do report, however, that it is easier for them to find new goals to value and pursue (see also Duke, Leventhal, Brownlee, and Leventhal, 2002).

In sum, there do appear to be some cases in which optimism has drawbacks. It is not clear how rare these cases are, or whether there are moderators that serve to limit the range of the problems. This doubtless will remain a topic for future work.

Concluding Comment

A large literature shows that people with positive expectations for the future respond to difficulty and adversity in more adaptive ways than those with negative expectations. Indeed, optimism seems to confer benefits in both intrapersonal and interpersonal domains, even in the absence of stress. Expectancies influence how people approach both threats and opportunities, and they influence the success with which people deal with them. There are some ways in which the focused efforts and persistence of optimists can go awry, but these cases are infrequent compared to the benefits that optimism seems to confer.

Optimism has been linked to better emotional well-being, more effective coping, and even to better outcomes in several aspects of physical health. The advantages of optimism also seem to carry into interpersonal relationships: optimists are better liked than pessimists, they benefit from their tendency to see things in the best light, and they appear to engage more productive effort in the sorts of problem solving that keep relationships alive and vibrant. Given the evidence, it is clear that this variable plays a central role in human experience.

References

Abend, T. A., and Williamson, G. M. (2002). Feeling attractive in the wake of breast cancer: Optimism matters, and so do interpersonal relationships. *Personality and Social Psychology Bulletin, 28*, 427–436.

Ahrens, A. H., and Haaga, D. A. F. (1993). The specificity of attributional style and expectations to positive and negative affectivity, depression, and anxiety. *Cognitive Therapy and Research, 17*, 83–98.

Allison, P. J., Guichard, C., and Gilain, L. (2000). A prospective investigation of dispositional optimism as a predictor of health-related quality of life in head and neck cancer patients. *Quality of Life Research, 9*, 951–960.

Aspinwall, L. G., and Brunhart, S. N. (1996). Distinguishing optimism from denial: Optimistic beliefs predict attention to health threats. *Personality and Social Psychology Bulletin, 22*, 993–1003.

Aspinwall, L. G., and Richter, L. (1999). Optimism and self-mastery predict more rapid disengagement from unsolvable tasks in the presence of alternatives. *Motivation and Emotion, 23*, 221–245.

Aspinwall, L. G., and Taylor, S. E. (1992). Modeling cognitive adaptation: A longitudinal investigation of the impact of individual differences and coping on college adjustment and performance. *Journal of Personality and Social Psychology, 61*, 755–765.

Aspinwall, L. G., and Taylor, S. E. (1997). A stitch in time: Self-regulation and proactive coping. *Psychological Bulletin, 121*, 417–436.

Assad, K. K., Donnellan, M. B., and Conger, R. D. (2007). Optimism: An enduring resource for romantic relationships. *Journal of Personality and Social Psychology, 93*, 285–297.

Atienza, A. A., Stephens, M. A. P., and Townsend, A. L. (2004). Role stressors as predictors of changes in women's optimistic expectations. *Personality and Individual Differences, 37*, 471–484.

Austin, J. T., and Vancouver, J. B. (1996). Goal constructs in psychology: Structure, process, and content. *Psychological Bulletin, 120*, 338–375.

Brissette, I., Scheier, M. F., and Carver, C. S. (2002). The role of optimism in social network development, coping, and psychological adjustment during a life transition. *Journal of Personality and Social Psychology, 82*, 102–111.

Brunello, N., Blier, P., Judd, L.L., Mendlewicz, J., Nelson, C.J., Souery, D., ... Racagni, G. (2003). Noradrenaline in mood and anxiety disorders: Basic and clinical studies. *International Clinical Psychopharmacology, 18*, 191–202.

Carver, C. S., and Connor-Smith, J. (2010). Personality and coping. *Annual Review of Psychology, 61*, 679–704.

Carver, C. S., and Gaines, J. G. (1987). Optimism, pessimism, and postpartum depression. *Cognitive Therapy and Research, 11*, 449–462.

Carver, C. S., Kus, L. A., and Scheier, M. F. (1994). Effects of good versus bad mood and optimistic versus pessimistic outlook on social acceptance versus rejection. *Journal of Social and Clinical Psychology, 13*, 138–151.

Carver, C. S., Lehman, J. M., and Antoni, M. H. (2003). Dispositional pessimism predicts illness-related disruption of social and recreational activities among breast cancer patients. *Journal of Personality and Social Psychology, 84*, 813–821.

Carver, C. S., Pozo, C., Harris, S. D., Noriega, V., Scheier, M.F., Robinson, D. S., ... Clark, K. C. (1993). How coping mediates the effect of optimism on distress: A study of women with early stage breast cancer. *Journal of Personality and Social Psychology, 65*, 375–390.

Carver, C. S., and Scheier, M. F. (1998). *On the Self-Regulation of Behavior*. New York: Cambridge University Press.

Carver, C. S., and Scheier, M. F. (2014). Dispositional optimism. *Trends in Cognitive Sciences, 18*, 293–299.

Compas, B. E., Connor-Smith, J. K., Saltzman, H., Thomsen, A. H., and Wadsworth, M. E. (2001). Coping with stress during childhood and adolescence: Problems, progress, and potential in theory and research. *Psychological Bulletin, 127*, 87–127.

Curbow, B. Somerfield, M. R., Baker, F. Wingard, J. R., and Legro, M. W. (1993). Personal changes, dispositional optimism, and psychological adjustment to bone marrow transplantation. *Journal of Behavioral Medicine, 16*, 423–443.

Dember, W. M., Martin, S. H., Hummer, M. K., Howe, S. R., and Melton, R. S. (1989). The measurement of optimism and pessimism. *Current Psychology: Research and Reviews, 8*, 102–119.

Duke, J., Leventhal, H., Brownlee, S., and Leventhal, E. A. (2002). Giving up and replacing activities in response to illness. *Journals of Gerontology, Series B, Psychological Sciences and Social Sciences, 57*, P367–P376.

Dunn, A. J., and Berridge, C. W. (1990). Physiological and behavioral responses to corticotropin-releasing factors administration: Is CRF a mediator of anxiety or stress responses? *Brain Research Reviews, 15*, 71–100.

Ebrecht, M., Hextall, J., Kirtley, L.-G., Taylor, A. M. Dyson, M., and Weinman, J. (2004). Perceived stress and cortisol levels predict speed of wound healing in healthy male adults. *Psychoneuroendrocrinology, 29*, 798–809.

Fitzgerald, T. E., Tennen, H., Affleck, G., and Pransky, G. S. (1993). The relative importance of dispositional optimism and control appraisals in quality of life after coronary artery bypass surgery. *Journal of Behavioral Medicine, 16*, 25–43.

Folkman, S., and Moskowitz, J. T. (2004). Coping: Pitfalls and promise. *Annual Review of Psychology, 55*, 745–774.

Friedman, L. C., Nelson, D. V., Baer, P. E., Lane, M., Smith, F. E., and Dworkin, R. J. (1992). The relationship of dispositional optimism, daily life stress, and domestic environment to coping methods used by cancer patients. *Journal of Behavioral Medicine, 15*, 127–141.

Geers, A. L., Wellman, J. A., and Lassiter, G. D. (2009). Dispositional optimism and engagement: The moderating influence of goal prioritization. *Journal of Personality and Social Psychology, 96*, 913–932.

Gibson, B., and Sanbonmatsu, D. M. (2004). Optimism, pessimism, and gambling: The downside of optimism. *Personality and Social Psychology Bulletin, 30*, 149–160.

Giltay, E. J., Zitman, F. G., and Kromhout, D. (2006). Dispositional optimism and the risk of depressive symptoms during 15 years of follow-up: The Zutphen Elderly Study. *Journal of Affective Disorders, 91*, 45–52.

Given, C. W., Stommel, M., Given, B., Osuch, J., Kurtz, M. E., and Kurtz, J. C. (1993). The influence of cancer patients' symptoms and functional states on patients' depression and family caregivers' reaction and depression. *Health Psychology, 12*, 277–285.

Greer, S., Morris, T., Pettingale, K. W., and Haybittle, J. L. (1990). Psychological response to breast cancer and 15-year outcome. *Lancet, 335*(8680), 49–50.

Heinonen, K., Räikkönen, K., and Keltikangas-Järvinen, L. (2005). Dispositional optimism: Development over 21 years from the perspectives of perceived temperament and mothering. *Personality and Individual Differences, 38*, 425–435.

Heinonen, K., Räikkönen, K., Matthews, K. A., Scheier, M. F., Raitakari, O. T., Pulkki, L., and Keltikangas-Järvinen, L. (2006). Socioeconomic status in childhood and adulthood: Associations with dispositional optimism and pessimism over a 21-year follow-up. *Journal of Personality, 74*, 1111–1126.

Helweg-Larsen, M., Sadeghian, P., and Webb, M. S. (2002). The stigma of being pessimistically biased. *Journal of Social and Clinical Psychology, 21*, 92–107.

Herzberg, P. Y., Glaesmer, H., and Hoyer, J. (2006). Separating optimism and pessimism: A robust psychometric analysis of the revised Life Orientation Test (LOT–R). *Psychological Assessment, 18*, 433–438.

Higgins, E. T. (2006). Value from hedonic experience *and* engagement. *Psychological Review, 113*, 439–460.

Hooker, K., Monahan, D., Shifren, K., and Hutchinson, C. (1992). Mental and physical health of spouse caregivers: The role of personality. *Psychology and Aging, 7*, 367–375.

Kohut, M. L., Cooper, M. M., Nickolaus, M. S., Russell, D. R., and Cunnick, J. E. (2002). Exercise and psychosocial factors modulate immunity to influenza vaccine in elderly individuals. *Journals of Gerontology, Series A, Biological Sciences and Medical Sciences, 57*, M557–M562.

Lazarus, R. S., and Folkman, S. (1984). *Stress, Appraisal, and Coping*. New York: Springer.

Lesperance, F., Frasure-Smith, N., and Talajic, M. (1996). Major depression before and after myocardial infarction: Its nature and consequences. *Psychosomatic Medicine, 58*, 99–110.

Litt, M. D., Tennen, H., Affleck, G., and Klock, S. (1992). Coping and cognitive factors in adaptation to *in vitro* fertilization failure. *Journal of Behavioral Medicine, 15*, 171–187.

Lucas, R. E., Diener, E., and Suh, E. (1996). Discriminant validity of well-being measures. *Journal of Personality and Social Psychology, 71*, 616–628.

Marshall, G. N, Wortman, C. B., Kusulas, J. W., Hervig, L. K., and Vickers, R. R., Jr. (1992). Distinguishing optimism from pessimism: Relations to fundamental dimensions of mood and personality. *Journal of Personality and Social Psychology, 62*, 1067–1074.

Matthews, K. A., Räikkönen, K., Sutton-Tyrrell, K., and Kuller, L. H. (2004). Optimistic attitudes protect against progression of carotid atherosclerosis in healthy middle-aged women. *Psychosomatic Medicine, 66*, 640–644.

Ohannessian, C. M., Hesselbrock, V. M., Tennen, H., and Affleck, G. (1993). Hassles and uplifts and generalized outcome expectancies as moderators on the relation between a family history of alcoholism and drinking behaviors. *Journal of Studies on Alcohol, 55*, 754–763.

Park, C. L., Moore, P. J., Turner, R. A., and Adler, N. E. (1997). The roles of constructive thinking and optimism in psychological and behavioral adjustment during pregnancy. *Journal of Personality and Social Psychology, 73*, 584–592.

Peterson, C., and Seligman, M. E. P. (1984). Causal explanations as a risk factor for depression: Theory and evidence. *Psychological Review, 91*, 347–374.

Peterson, C., and Vaidya, R. S. (2001). Explanatory style, expectations, and depressive symptoms. *Personality and Individual Differences, 31*, 1217–1223.

Plomin, R., Scheier, M. F., Bergeman, C. S., Pedersen, N. L., Nesselroade, J. R., and McClearn, G. E. (1992). Optimism, pessimism, and mental health: A twin/adoption analysis. *Personality and Individual Differences, 13*, 921–930.

Radcliffe, N. M., and Klein, W. M. P. (2002). Dispositional, unrealistic, and comparative optimism: Differential relations with the knowledge and processing of risk information and beliefs about personal risk. *Personality and Social Psychology Bulletin, 28*, 836–846.

Räikkönen, K., Matthews, K. A., Flory, J. D., Owens, J. F., and Gump, B. B. (1999). Effects of optimism, pessimism, and trait anxiety on ambulatory blood pressure and mood during everyday life. *Journal of Personality and Social Psychology, 76*, 104–113.

Rasmussen, H. N., Scheier, M. F., and Greenhouse, J. B. (2009). Optimism and physical health: A meta-analytic review. *Annals of Behavioral Medicine, 37*, 239–256.

Rasmussen, H. N., Wrosch, C., Scheier, M. F., and Carver, C. S. (2006). Self-regulation processes and health: The importance of optimism and goal adjustment. *Journal of Personality, 74*, 1721–1747.

Rauch, W. A., Schweizer, K., and Moosbrugger, H. (2007). Method effects due to social desirability as a parsimonious explanation of the deviation from unidimensionality in LOT-R scores. *Personality and Individual Differences, 42*, 1597–1607.

Reed, G. M., Kemeny, M. E., Taylor, S. E., Wang, H.-Y. J., and Visscher, B. R. (1994). Realistic acceptance as a predictor of decreased survival time in gay men with AIDS. *Health Psychology, 13*, 299–307.

Robinson-Whelen, S., Kim, C., MacCallum, R. C., and Kiecolt-Glaser, J. K. (1997). Distinguishing optimism from pessimism in older adults: Is it more important to be optimistic or not to be pessimistic? *Journal of Personality and Social Psychology, 73*, 1345–1353.

Roth, S., and Cohen, L. J. (1986). Approach, avoidance, and coping with stress. *American Psychologist, 41*, 813–819.

Ruiz, J. M., Matthews, K. A., Scheier, M. F., and Schulz, R. (2006). Does who you marry matter for your health? Influence of patients' and spouses' personality on their partners' psychological well-being following coronary artery bypass surgery. *Journal of Personality and Social Psychology, 91*, 255–267.

Scheier, M. F., and Carver, C. S. (1985). Optimism, coping, and health: Assessment and implication of generalized outcome expectancies. *Health Psychology, 4*, 219–247.

Scheier, M. F., and Carver, C. S. (1992). Effects of optimism on psychological and physical well-being: Theoretical overview and empirical update. *Cognitive Therapy and Research, 16*, 201–228.

Scheier, M. F., and Carver, C. S. (2001). Adapting to cancer: The importance of hope and purpose. In A. Baum and B. L. Andersen (Eds.), *Psychosocial Interventions for Cancer* (pp. 15–36). Washington, DC: American Psychological Association.

Scheier, M. F., Carver, C. S., and Bridges, M. W. (1994). Distinguishing optimism from neuroticism (and trait anxiety, self-mastery, and self-esteem): A reevaluation of the Life Orientation Test. *Journal of Personality and Social Psychology, 67*, 1063–1078.

Scheier, M. F., Carver, C. S., and Bridges, M. W. (2001). Optimism, pessimism, and psychological well-being. In E. C. Chang (Ed.), *Optimism and Pessimism: Implications for Theory, Research, and Practice* (pp. 189–216). Washington, DC: American Psychological Association.

Scheier, M. F., Matthews, K. A., Owens, J. F., Magovern, G. J., Lefebvre, R. C., Abbott, R. A., and Carver, C. S. (1989). Dispositional optimism and recovery from coronary artery bypass surgery: The beneficial effects on physical and psychological well-being. *Journal of Personality and Social Psychology, 57*, 1024–1040.

Scheier, M. F., Matthews, K. A., Owens, J. F., Schulz, R., Bridges, M. W., Magovern, G. J., Sr., and Carver, C. S. (1999). Optimism and rehospitalization following coronary artery bypass graft surgery. *Archives of Internal Medicine*, *159*, 829–835.

Schou, I., Ekeberg, O., and Ruland, C. M. (2005). The mediating role of appraisal and coping in the relationship between optimism-pessimism and quality of life. *Psycho-Oncology*, *14*, 718–727.

Schwarzer, R. (1994). Optimism, vulnerability, and self-beliefs as health-related cognitions: A systematic overview. *Psychology and Health*, *9*, 161–180.

Segerstrom, S. C. (2005). Optimism and immunity: Do positive thoughts always lead to positive effects? *Brain, Behavior, and Immunity*, *19*, 195–200.

Segerstrom, S. C. (2006a). *Breaking Murphy's Law*. New York: Guilford.

Segerstrom, S. C. (2006b). How does optimism suppress immunity? Evaluation of three affective pathways. *Health Psychology*, *25*, 653–657.

Segerstrom, S. C. (2007). Optimism and resources: Effects on each other and on health over 10 years. *Journal of Research in Personality*, *41*, 772–786.

Segerstrom, S. C., and Solberg Nes, L. (2006). When goals conflict but people prosper: The case of dispositional optimism. *Journal of Research in Personality*, *40*, 675–693.

Shepperd, J. A., Maroto, J. J., and Pbert, L. A. (1996). Dispositional optimism as a predictor of health changes among cardiac patients. *Journal of Research in Personality*, *30*, 517–534.

Shifren, K., and Hooker, K. (1995). Stability and change in optimism: A study among spouse caregivers. *Experimental Aging Research*, *21*, 59–76.

Shnek, Z. M., Irvine, J., Stewart, D., and Abbey, S. (2001). Psychological factors and depressive symptoms in ischemic heart disease. *Health Psychology*, *20*, 141–145.

Skinner, E. A., Edge, K., Altman, J., and Sherwood, H. (2003). Searching for the structure of coping: A review and critique of category systems for classifying ways of coping. *Psychological Bulletin*, *129*, 216–269.

Solberg Nes, L., Evans, D. R., and Segerstrom, S. C. (2009). Optimism and college retention: Mediation by motivation, performance, and adjustment. *Journal of Applied Social Psychology*, *39*, 1887–1912.

Solberg Nes, L., and Segerstrom, S. C. (2006). Dispositional optimism and coping: A meta-analytic review. *Personality and Social Psychology Review*, *10*, 235–251.

Srivastava, S., McGonigal, K. M., Richards, J. M., Butler, E. A., and Gross, J. J. (2006). Optimism in close relationships: How seeing things in a positive light makes them so. *Journal of Personality and Social Psychology*, *91*, 143–153.

Stanton, A. L., and Snider, P. R. (1993). Coping with breast cancer diagnosis: A prospective study. *Health Psychology*, *12*, 16–23.

Strack, S., Carver, C. S., and Blaney, P. H. (1987). Predicting successful completion of an aftercare program following treatment for alcoholism: The role of dispositional optimism. *Journal of Personality and Social Psychology*, *53*, 579–584.

Taylor, S. E. (2007). Social support. In H. S. Friedman and R. C. Silver (Eds.), *Foundations of Health Psychology* (pp. 145–171). New York: Oxford University Press.

Taylor, S. E., Kemeny, M. E., Aspinwall, L. G., Schneider, S. G., Rodriguez, R., and Herbert, M. (1992). Optimism, coping, psychological distress, and high-risk sexual behavior among men at risk for acquired immunodeficiency syndrome (AIDS). *Journal of Personality and Social Psychology*, *63*, 460–473.

Tennen, H., and Affleck, G. (1987). The costs and benefits of optimistic explanations and dispositional optimism. *Journal of Personality*, *55*, 377–393.

Tindale, H. A., Chang, Y., Kuller, L. H., Manson, J. E., Robinson, J. G., Rosal, M. C., ... Matthews, K. A. (2009). Optimism, cynical hostility, and incident coronary heart disease and mortality in the Women's Health Initiative. *Circulation*, *120*, 656–662.

Trunzo, J. J., and Pinto, B. M. (2003). Social support as a mediator of optimism and distress in breast cancer survivors. *Journal of Consulting and Clinical Psychology*, *4*, 805–811.

Wrosch, C., Scheier, M. F., Carver, C. S., and Schulz, R. (2003). The importance of goal disengagement in adaptive self-regulation: When giving up is beneficial. *Self and Identity*, *2*, 1–20.

Zeidner, M., and Hammer, A. L. (1992). Coping with missile attack: Resources, strategies, and outcomes. *Journal of Personality*, *60*, 709–746.

25

Seligman's Positive Psychology

Past, Present and Future Connections with Organizational Research

Thomas A. Wright

> A wise man should consider that health is the greatest of human blessings, and learn how by his own thought to derive benefit from his illnesses.
>
> Hippocrates, *Regimen in Health*, Book 9

It is hard to believe that it has already been over 15 years since the genesis of the Positive Psychology Movement. It was the result of a "meeting of the minds" in the Yucatan in early 1998 initiated by Martin Seligman with his close associates, Mihaly Csikszentmihalyi and Raymond Fowler (Seligman, 2002). At the end of this working vacation, these three pioneers had agreed upon a master plan for positive psychology, including plan content, method and infrastructure. To that end, the stated mission of positive psychology was, and still is, to help shift the focus of psychology away from a focus on pathology, victimology and mental illness (the "disease model") to the creation of a "health model" (Cooper, Dewe, and O'Driscoll, 2001; Macik-Frey, Quick, and Nelson, 2007; Quick, Wright, Adkins, Nelson, and Quick, 2013; Seligman and Csikszentmihalyi, 2000; Wright and Quick, 2009a; 2009b). In addition, a second overarching goal was proposed of having a movement built upon the foundations of rigorous science. In particular, Seligman and Csikszentmihalyi (2000) were adamant that positive psychology would not follow the humanism of the 1960s and become overly dedicated to "crystal healing, aromatherapy, and reaching the inner child ..." (p. 7).

Infused with the very competent help of such luminaries as Ed Diener, the late Chris Peterson, George Valliant, Kathleen Hall Jamieson, the late Robert Nozick and Peter Schulman, positive psychology's three content pillars were identified as positive emotion, positive character and positive institutions. This chapter will provide an overview of positive

The Handbook of Stress and Health: A Guide to Research and Practice, First Edition.
Edited by Cary L. Cooper and James Campbell Quick.
© 2017 John Wiley & Sons, Ltd. Published 2017 by John Wiley & Sons, Ltd.

psychology's three content pillars. In particular, I will highlight the past, present and possible future contributions of positive psychology within the context of organizational research. I begin with a brief description of these three pillars.

The Three Pillars of Positive Psychology

At least early on in the movement, happiness and well-being were used interchangeably "as overarching terms to describe the goals of the whole Positive Psychology enterprise" (Seligman, 2002, p. 261). However defined, positive emotions (including well-being and happiness) have typically been divided into three types, those directed toward the past (satisfaction, contentment, pleased, and lucky); the future (optimism, hope, confidence, inspiration, and faith); and present (warmhearted, enthusiastic, cheerful, and interested). Considered within the framework of positive psychology, one leads a *pleasant life* when one is able to successfully pursue various positive emotions associated with aspects of not only the past, but also the present and future. However, the primary goal of positive psychology, happiness or well-being, is clearly not limited to the achievement of momentary pleasure.

In his best-selling book *Authentic Happiness*, Seligman discusses at length the need to be authentic and genuine. However, authenticity does not come from the sole pursuit of momentary pleasure, but from the pursuit and attainment of one's signature strengths of character, the second pillar of positive psychology (Seligman, 2002; Wright and Goodstein, 2007). In fact, one only achieves the *good life* through the effective implementation of our signature character strengths in our life pursuits, whether this pursuit is obtained through work, family, or love. Finally, what Seligman (2002) termed the *meaningful life* adds an additional aspect to the good life, the use of these signature strengths in the service of someone or something much larger than oneself (Pillar III). I next provide a brief historical overview of past attempts to include the current, basic precepts of positive psychology in organizational scholarship.

The Basis for a Positive Psychology in Organizational Research

While possibly surprising to many, the basic tenets of many aspects of positive psychology have roots that run deep in early organizational and applied research (Wright, 2006). Perhaps positive psychology's first systematic linkage with the past involved the work of Rexford B. Hersey, professor at the University of Pennsylvania Wharton Business School. Incorporating rigorous, longitudinal field research, Hersey (1932) gathered a wide range of data on various feelings of employees, including well-being and happiness, as well as productivity and efficiency, in an impressive attempt "to obtain a complete picture of their whole life" (p. 459). Certainly one of Hersey's contributions to positive psychology was his path-breaking work on identifying possible emotional cycles in male workers.

Repeatedly interviewing male workers (and their wives if available) over time at both work and their home, Hersey (1932) created a 13-point emotion-based scale ranging from worried (−6) through neutral (+0) to elated (+6). Examining these workers over time afforded Hersey the opportunity to observe a comprehensive pattern of mood variation. Quite prescient when taken in conjunction with the later work of Csikszentmihalyi (1991; 1997) on flow and Fredrickson's positivity ratio (Fredrickson, 2001; Fredrickson and Losada, 2005), Hersey found different mood cycles across respondents. Understandably enthused by these findings, Hersey spent the next 30 years examining the value of cyclic patterns of human behavior until his death in 1965. Perhaps because of possible perceived connections to the discredited field of astrology, coupled with the sad fact that we often fail to credit our academic pioneers, Hersey's work (and that of such other early scholars as Kornhauser, 1933; Mayo, 1924; Pennock, 1930; Putnam, 1930; and Snow, 1923) has gone largely uncredited in the positive psychology, positive organizational behavior and positive organizational scholarship movements.

Drawing on the early momentum created by positive psychology (Diener, 2000; Seligman and Csikszentmihalyi, 2000), a number of organizational scholars noted similar needs for a more positive and proactive approach to organizational research. This approach has been termed positive organizational behavior (POB) (Luthans, 2002a; 2002b; Nelson and Cooper, 2007; Wright, 2003) and positive organizational scholarship (POS) (Cameron, Dutton, and Quinn, 2003; Pratt and Ashforth, 2003; Wrzesniewski, 2003). Focused more on such temporary or state-like characteristics as confidence, resiliency, and optimism, POB is concerned with psychological and behavioral processes more conducive to immediate or short-term change strategies. Alternatively, when compared with POB, POS is more concerned with psychological and behavioral processes considered to be more stable or trait-like in nature. While not tied to a specific theory, POS has tended to focus on dynamics that are typically described by such words as excellence, thriving, flourishing, abundance, or virtuousness (Wright and Quick, 2009a, p. 148; 2009b). With that distinction noted, there are several significant inroads of positive psychology into positive organizational research at each of the three pillar levels.

Positive Psychology Meets Positive Organizational Research: Pillar I

Building upon the work of Hersey (1929; 1932), Mayo (1924), Kornhauser (1933), Bales (1950), Bradburn (1969) and Berkman (1971), the most well-known Pillar I concept from positive psychology to make significant inroads in organizational research has been Barbara Fredrickson's (2009) positivity ratio. The positivity ratio premise is simple and straightforward. Given that such positive feelings as joy, interest, amusement, serenity, enthusiasm, excitement, and interest are beneficial to the attainment of individual betterment and achievement, the question becomes whether an optimal positive to negative ratio or "tipping point" exists which allows individuals to "flourish" in their life pursuits.

To test this thesis, in their widely cited article (1,813 citations as of August 26, 2016, according to Google Scholar), Fredrickson and Losada (2005) incorporated a mathematical model based upon nonlinear dynamics (cf., Lorenz, 1963; 1993) and reported finding two critical positivity ratio values. The first was a minimum threshold ratio of 2.9013 and the second involved a maximum positivity ratio of 11.6346 (Wright, 2014). Extending their claims further, Fredrickson and Losada (2005) proposed that individuals who score between these two critical values will "flourish," while those falling outside this range will "languish." Later, in her best-selling book, Fredrickson (2009) was so moved to remark that "The consistency here is extraordinary. For individuals, marriages, and business teams, flourishing – or doing remarkably well – comes with positivity ratios above 3 to 1 ..." (p. 133). Fredrickson went even further in noting that she could not "help wondering whether human flourishing at still larger scales – in organizations like schools and companies, in governing bodies like the U.S Congress and the United Nations, or in vehicles of culture like television and the Internet – will also obey this apparent law for the positivity ratio tipping point" (p. 134). Unfortunately, Brown, Sokal, and Friedman (2013; 2014) provide highly compelling evidence refuting these critical lower and upper limits. As a result, the *American Psychologist* was forced to formally withdraw the mathematical modeling component (Fredrickson and Losada, 2005) as invalid (Fredrickson and Losada, 2013).

While clearly a setback, in the long run this public retraction could very well be a blessing in disguise for the positive psychology, positive organizational behavior and positive organizational scholarship movements. Why so? Let us revisit our discussion of the work of Rexford B. Hersey for guidance. Like Fredrickson and Losada (2005), Hersey (1932) proposed to test a theory articulating psychological processes occurring within employees and across time. To that end, Hersey correctly tested his within-person across-time theory with data collected from individuals over multiple time points. However, Fredrickson and Losada (2005), while also proposing a within-person across-time model, inappropriately tested their model relying solely on a within-time across-person methodology (Nickerson, 2014). Fredrickson (2013) only implicitly acknowledged this failure after the fact in noting the need for "longitudinal field studies and experiments that use densely repeated measures of emotions and relevant outcomes" (p. 820). With this caveat in mind, Fredrickson's (1998; 2003) main theoretical contribution to positive psychology, called the "broaden-and-build model," provides us with invaluable insight into how theory *and* methodology can be effectively used in providing direction into one of organizational behavior's "Holy Grails," the pursuit of the happy-productive worker thesis (Wright and Cropanzano, 2000).

"Broaden-and-Build" Meets "The Happy-Productive Worker Thesis"

Since at least the time of the seminal Hawthorne experiments (Roethlisberger and Dickson, 1939), organizational scholars have diligently worked to demonstrate that "happy" workers are more productive than "unhappy" ones (Brief, 1998; Wright and Doherty, 1998). Early on, this hypothesis was usually operationalized through the association of job satisfaction with supervisory ratings of performance (Wright and Cropanzano, 2000). More recently, this line of research has been expanded to include measures of psychological well-being (for a review, see Wright, 2014). Wright and Cropanzano (2000) provided the first comparative test of the relative contributions of job satisfaction and psychological well-being as predictors of employee performance. Extending the extant body of knowledge, Fredrickson's (2001; 2003) broaden-and-build model provided the necessary theoretical basis for the long-standing belief that such positive feelings as psychological well-being may have a moderating effect on the job satisfaction–job performance relationship (Kornhauser and Sharp, 1932; Pennock, 1930).

According to the broaden-and-build model, such positive emotions as psychological well-being have the capacity to broaden an individual's momentary thought–action repertoires through the possible expansion of the obtainable array of potential thoughts and actions that come readily to mind (see Fredrickson and Branigan, 2001; Wright, 2005). More specifically, compared to neutral feeling states, positive feelings broaden or expand upon these possible thought and action repertories, while negative emotions have the adverse effect. That is, negative feelings tend to narrow or constrict one's potential array of thoughts and actions (Fredrickson, 2000; Fredrickson and Levenson, 1998). As a result, such positively based emotions as joy, excitement and psychological well-being can play significant roles in an employee's cognitive and social development (Wright and Wright, 2002).

But that is not all. In addition, continued attention further develops, expands and builds on these positive urges, creating an "upward spiral" capable of encouraging employee character development, which in turn helps build one's individual resources, whether psychological, intellectual, social or physical in nature (Hobfoll, 1998; Wright and Hobfoll, 2004). As a consequence, through the impetus provided by these positive emotions, Wright and Wright (2002) proposed that individuals are more easily able to transform themselves and become more creative, resilient, socially connected, and physically and mentally healthy. In particular, Wright and his colleagues incorporated the use of multiple field studies to examine the broaden-and-build capabilities of positive well-being as a moderator of the job satisfaction/job performance (Wright, Cropanzano, and Bonett, 2007) and job satisfaction and employee retention relationships (Wright and Bonett, 2007). Consistent with Fredrickson's model, Wright et al. (2007, p. 93) found that performance was highest when employees scored high on both positive well-being *and* job satisfaction. Interestingly, and by way of further clarification, job satisfaction was only predictive of performance if the employee manifested high positive well-being. This moderating effect of positive well-being undoubtedly explains the inconsistent findings over the years involving the job satisfaction–job performance relationship (Judge, Thoresen, Bono, and Patton, 2001).

Fredrickson's model is also illuminating in explaining Wright and Bonett's (2007) finding that positive well-being and job satisfaction interact to predict whether or not employees will stay on the job. As hypothesized, the relation between job satisfaction and employee voluntary retention was stronger for employees exhibiting high positive well-being. One important conclusion is that employees exhibiting positive well-being are more likely to remain on the job, regardless of their level of job satisfaction. Considered together, the broaden-and-build model has provided the theoretical support for the long assumed belief that high positive employee well-being is a consequential factor in better understanding such individual and organizational outcome variables as job satisfaction and employee retention decisions.

The work of Wright and his colleagues (Wright and Bonett, 2007; Wright et al., 2007) provided strong support for their hypothesis using a within-time across-employee methodology. Research is now needed which not only replicates their findings, but also extends their work by incorporating a within-person across-time design. For example, and reminiscent of the work of Hersey (1929; 1932), what pattern(s) of well-being responses do particular employees exhibit both over time and across context? The investigation of these types of distinctions will be highly beneficial in helping us better understand and predict such employee behaviors as absenteeism, tardiness, turnover, and job performance.

I next discuss the second pillar of positive psychology by focusing on two prominent research streams. First, highlighting the work of Fred Luthans and his colleagues (Luthans, Avolio, Avey, and Norman, 2007a; Luthans and Youssef, 2007; Luthans, Youssef, and Avolio, 2007b), the development, assessment and implementation of psychological capital is discussed. The second approach engages the chapter audience with an overview of the work on strengths of character.

Positive Psychology Meets Positive Organizational Research: Pillar II

> There is no attribute of the superior man greater than his helping men to practice virtue.
>
> Mencius, *Works*, Book 2, 1:8.5

A recent addition to the happiness and flourishing literature is the construct of psychological capital (PsyCap) developed by Luthans and his colleagues (Luthans et al., 2007a; Luthans and

Youssef, 2007; Luthans et al., 2007b). PsyCap is suggested as a general capacity to triumph over obstacles and provide the essential motivational skills to foster one's desire to flourish and prosper. Luthans et al. (2007b) have succinctly defined PsyCap in this way:

> PsyCap is an individual's positive psychological state of development and is characterized by: (1) having confidence (self-efficacy) to take on and put in the necessary effort to succeed at challenging tasks; (2) making a positive attribution (optimism) about succeeding now and in the future: (3) persevering toward goals and, when necessary, redirecting paths to goals (hope) in order to succeed; and (4) when beset by problems and adversity, sustaining and bouncing back and even beyond (resiliency) to attain success. (p. 3)

Luthans et al. (2007a) have empirically demonstrated that PsyCap is a second-order, core construct consisting of the following four positive psychological resources: hope, resiliency, efficacy, and optimism. Considered as a second-order, core construct, these four resources reflect "one's positive appraisal of circumstances and probability for success based on motivated effort and perseverance" (p. 550). Avey, Reichard, Luthans, and Mhatre (2011) demonstrated the predictive ability of PsyCap across a wide range of individual and organizational outcomes, including job satisfaction, organizational commitment, turnover intentions, organizational citizenship behavior, psychological well-being and various self, subjective, and objective measures of performance (for additional evidence, see Luthans and Youssef, 2007).

PsyCap is undoubtedly the most widely cited organizational-based concept with strong roots in positive psychology. For example, in just 2015 alone, Fred Luthans garnered an incredible 5,772 citations (Google Scholar), with the majority of these citations derived from his work on PsyCap. What makes PsyCap such an interesting concept in the present discussion is that it combines aspects of both Pillar I (the positive psychological states of efficacy, optimism and resilience) with Pillar II (hope, termed by many, and I agree, to signify strength of character). Fortunately, to date, there has been significant interest in the study of character by scholars from positive psychology and their counterparts in the positive organizational behavior and scholarship movements.

Distinguishable from values (Wright and Quick, 2011), personality (Wright and Lauer, 2013), image norms (Hurley-Hanson and Giannantonio, 2007) and themes (Buckingham and Clifton, 2001), character is shaped by one's convictions and is best evidenced by the ability to persist in those convictions in the face of temptation or challenge (Hunter, 2000; Wright and Wefald, 2012). However considered, traditional conceptualizations of character at their core are consistently composed of a moral dimension(s). To that end, Hunter (2000) identified three such character components: moral discipline, moral attachment, and moral autonomy. Perhaps William James (1920) best expressed this strong sense of commitment in the face of adversity and temptation in noting that character involves those mental and moral attributes that leave us most deeply and intensely vibrant and alive. For James, this special, even transcendent moment is best personified by one's inner self signifying that "*This* is the real me!" (p. 199). Influenced by James and the three moral dimensions, the current chapter's author has previously defined character as "those interpenetrable and habitual qualities within individuals, and applicable to organizations that both constrain and lead them to desire and pursue personal and societal good" (Wright and Goodstein, 2007, p. 932).

Perhaps the most widely known and used classification framework (with data from literally millions of respondents) is Peterson and Seligman's (2004) self-report 240-item

Values-in-Action–Inventory of Strengths (VIA-IS). In an impressive investigation, these researchers and their colleagues (Peterson, Park, Hall and Seligman, 2009; Peterson and Seligman, 2004) identified six core virtues (with the strengths of character common to each virtue listed in parentheses): wisdom and knowledge (creativity, curiosity, critical-thinking, love of learning, perspective); courage (bravery, integrity, perseverance, zest); humanity (kindness, capacity to love and be loved, social intelligence); justice (fairness, leadership, citizenship); temperance (forgiveness, modesty, prudence, self-control); and transcendence (appreciation of beauty, gratitude, hope, humor, spirituality) that Peterson and Seligman (2004) suggest transcend both time and culture (for a further discussion, see Wright, 2015).

"Good" character has long been considered as a central and defining feature of positive psychology's Pillar I focus on various aspects of individual health and well-being, the pleasant life (Gavin, Quick, Cooper, and Quick, 2003). For example, the well-being benefits of being industrious and persistent have been established for cancer survivors (Ferrell, Smith, Cullinane, and Melancon, 2003), those afflicted with arthritis (Lambert, Lambert, Klipple, and Mewshaw, 1989), and HIV/AIDS patients (Goodman, Chesney, and Tipton, 1995). Singh and Jha (2008) established that perseverance was positively related to both happiness and life satisfaction, while Mino and Kanemitsu (2005) found a relation with job satisfaction. Fredrickson and Joiner (2002) found evidence that self-regulation is positively related with psychological well-being, while Wright and Walton (2003) investigated the relation between creativity and psychological well-being. Finally, having a spouse high on integrity is important to a marriage as it fosters relationship trust and is potentially central in partner well-being and satisfaction (Yeh, Lorenz, Wickrama, Conger, and Elder, 2006). Considered together, research to date has achieved some measure of success in establishing that an association exists between various strengths of character and individual well-being (for additional discussions of this topic, see Wright, 2014; 2015).

It should be noted, however, that additional scholarly research on the VIA-IS is now needed to determine if each of the 24 subscales (cf., kindness, gratitude, capacity to love and be loved, critical-thinking, social intelligence, etc.) have adequate internal consistency (Cronbach alpha coefficients >0.70), content and construct validity (Wright, 2015). Unfortunately, at present, the extant body of research has failed to confirm the model proposed by Peterson and Seligman (2004). In a sample of adult respondents from the United States, Shryack, Steger, Kruger, and Kallie (2010) failed to find support for the hypothesized six-dimensional model. Instead, they found support for a three- or four-dimensional model as a best fit for their data. Likewise, incorporating a sample of Australian college students, Macdonald, Bore, and Munro (2008) also failed to establish a clean pattern of findings, while obtaining a large number of cross-factor loadings with a four-dimensional model. Finally, based on a sample of Croatian university students, Brdar and Kashdan (2010) suggest a four-dimensional model (Interpersonal Strengths, Fortitude, Vitality, and Cautiousness). However, it is interesting to note that the first dimension, Interpersonal Strengths, explained almost half (47.17%) of the model variance. As a final word of caution, while each of the VIA's strengths of character can certainly be considered as positive traits, talents or attributes, all do not fulfill the moral component criterion. For example, Wright (2015) noted that the strengths of social intelligence, humor, curiosity, and zest are each lacking in a moral dimension as traditionally understood. Future research is needed to more adequately address these issues. Building upon the Pillar II framework of positive character, the discussion now turns to positive psychology's Pillar III, the positive or virtuous institution.

Positive Psychology Meets Positive Organizational Research: Pillar III

> He who exercises government by means of his virtue may be compared to the north pole star, which keeps its place and all the stars turn towards it.
>
> Confucius, *The Confucian Analects*, Book 2:1

A number of social commentators, including scholars in the positive psychology, positive organizational behavior and positive organizational scholarship movements (Hunter, 2000; Sennett, 1998; Wright, 2011; Wright and Goodstein, 2007) have suggested that the widely discussed crises in both private sector and government-based leadership are clearly associated with the perceived decline in the formation of individual character and institutional virtue. Hunter (2000) has gone so far as to suggest that character as traditionally considered is "dead" in today's society. This is highly distressing for many as character certainly does play an instrumental role in a wide variety of human activities and endeavors (Wright and Goodstein, 2007; Wright and Huang, 2012). For example, a growing number of scholars and practitioners have suggested that the paramount need facing our society today is the development of citizens with demonstrated strengths of character (Brooks, 2015; Wright and Lauer, 2013).

This approach may provide additional benefit in assisting scholars to develop viable linkages between Pillar II, individual character, and Pillar III, organizational and societal-level virtue. Wright and Goodstein (2007) suggested that one important avenue in this pursuit would be "to give more attention to the connection between organizational virtue and character with conduct" (p. 947). To that point, long ago, Selznick (1957; 1992, p. 35) strongly argued for increased scholarly attention to better understanding the relationship between character and conduct in noting, "Conduct is an expression of character, character is manifested in patterns of conduct." More specifically, Selznick (1992) posed the following question: "What kind of person, institution, or community will result from following a particular course of conduct or from adopting a given rule or policy?" (p. 35). The work on the "profiles in character" concept by this chapter's author and his colleagues is one attempt to address Selznick's question.

Building on Peterson and Seligman's (2004) character taxonomy and incorporating a group focus approach, Wright and his colleagues (Wright, 2011; Wright, 2015; Wright and Quick, 2011) have developed a number of "top-5" signature strength profiles for success in such work occupations as entrepreneur, nurse, athletic coach, accountant, engineer, even college president! As one example, the top-5 signature strength profile for an entrepreneur provides an informative example of the possible value of this approach. Wright and Quick (2011) defined entrepreneurs as "individuals who acquire or exhibit habitual traits, abilities and strengths of character utilized to effectively recognize opportunities, assume risks in a start-up venture, and overcome obstacles" (p. 977). Signature strength profiles for entrepreneurs include the following character strengths: hope, curiosity, zest, industry, and self-regulation. While work in this area is still exploratory, preliminary results indicate that a number of occupation-specific profiles may be related to various measures of individual betterment and organizational effectiveness (Wright, 2015).

Concluding Thoughts

Starting with significant fanfare and flourish, and in the words of Clint Eastwood, the positive psychology movement has experienced its share of the "good, the bad, and the ugly."

Building upon the work of such early organizational research notables as Anderson (1929), Hersey (1930), Hoppock (1935), Houser (1927) and Mayo (1924), research on the Pillar I framework involving positive emotions has consistently reinforced the role of positive employee attitudes in employee betterment and efficiency. Perhaps Hersey (1929) best summed up this early "good" awareness of the role of positive emotions in noting that "it would seem impossible to escape the conclusion that in the long run at least [wo]men are more productive in a positive emotional state than in a negative [one]" (p. 289). Of course, the widely publicized problems surrounding the positivity ratio have had a far-reaching "bad" and "ugly" effect on the movement. As just one example of the continued widespread use of the positivity ratio, consider the well-known Hawn Foundation. Established by the popular actress Goldie Hawn, this well-meaning organization continues (as I write this chapter) to use the framework of the 3-to-1 positivity ratio as one of their core learning tools to assist in the further development of student optimism and an enhanced self-concept. However, the "good" will eventually succeed in the positive movements. In fact, and far from them being "dead" (cf. Hunter, 2000), the author remains confident that intervention strategies devoted to developing individual character and organizational virtue will ultimately prove successful.

References

Anderson, V. V. (1929). *Psychiatry in Industry*. New York: Harper.

Avey, J., Reichard, R., Luthans, F., and Mhatre, K. (2011). Meta-analysis of the impact of positive psychological capital on employee attitudes, behavior, and performance. *Human Resource Development Quarterly, 22*, 127–152.

Bales, R. F. (1950). *Interaction Process Analysis: A Method for the Study of Small Groups*. Cambridge, MA: Addison-Wesley.

Berkman, P. L. (1971). Life stress and psychological well-being: A replication of Langer's analysis in the midtown Manhattan study. *Journal of Health and Social Behavior, 12*, 35–45.

Bradburn, N. M. (1969). *The Structure of Psychological Well-Being*. Chicago, IL: Aldine.

Brdar, I., and Kashdan, T. B. (2010). Character strengths and well-being in Croatia: An empirical investigation of structure and correlates. *Journal of Research in Personality, 44*, 151–154.

Brief, A. P. (1998). *Attitudes In and Around Organizations*. Thousand Oaks, CA: Sage.

Brooks, D. (2015). *The Road to Character*. New York: Random House.

Brown, N. J. L., Sokal, A. D., and Friedman, H. L. (2013). The complex dynamics of wishful thinking: The critical positivity ratio. *American Psychologist, 68*, 801–813.

Brown, N. J. L., Sokal, A. D., and Friedman, H. L. (2014). Positive psychology and romantic scientism. *American Psychologist, 69*, 636–637.

Buckingham, M., and Clifton, D. O. (2001). *Now, Discover Your Strengths*. New York: Free Press.

Cameron, K. S., Dutton, J. E., and Quinn, R. E. (Eds.) (2003). *Positive Organizational Scholarship: Foundations of a New Discipline*. San Francisco: Berrett-Koehler.

Cooper, C. L., Dewe, P. J., and O'Driscoll, M. P. (2001). *Organizational Stress: A Review and Critique of Theory, Research, and Applications*. Thousand Oaks, CA: Sage.

Csikszentmihalyi, M. (1991). *Flow*. New York: Harper.

Csikszentmihalyi, M. (1997). *Finding Flow*. New York: Basic Books.

Diener, E. (2000). Subjective well-being: The science of happiness and a proposal for a national index. *American Psychologist, 55*, 34–43.

Ferrell, B., Smith, S. L., Cullinane, C. A., and Melancon, C. (2003). Psychological well-being and quality of life in ovarian cancer survivors. *Cancer, 98*, 1061–1071.

Fredrickson, B. L. (1998). What good are positive emotions? *Review of General Psychology, 2*, 300–319.

Fredrickson, B. L. (2000). Cultivating positive emotions to optimize health and well-being. *Prevention and Treatment, 3*(1).

Fredrickson, B. L. (2001). The role of positive emotions in positive psychology: The broaden-and-build theory of positive emotions. *American Psychologist, 56*, 219–226.

Fredrickson, B. L. (2003). Positive emotions and upward spirals in organizations. In K. S. Cameron, J. E. Dutton, and R. E. Quinn (Eds.), *Positive Organizational Scholarship: Foundations of a New Discipline* (pp. 163–175). San Francisco: Berrett-Koehler.

Fredrickson, B. L. (2009). *Positivity*. New York: Crown.

Fredrickson, B. L. (2013). Updated thinking on positivity ratios. *American Psychologist, 68,* 814–822.

Fredrickson, B. L., and Branigan, C. A. (2001). Positive emotions. In T. J. Mayne and G. A. Bonnano (Eds.), *Emotion: Current Issues and Future Directions* (pp. 123–151). New York: Guilford Press.

Fredrickson, B. L., and Joiner, T. (2002). Positive emotions trigger upward spirals toward emotional well-being. *Psychological Science, 13,* 172–175.

Fredrickson, B. L., and Levenson, R. W. (1998). Positive emotions speed recovery from the cardiovascular sequelae of negative emotions. *Cognition and Emotion, 12,* 191–220.

Fredrickson, B. L., and Losada, M. F. (2005). Positive affect and the complex dynamics of human flourishing. *American Psychologist, 60,* 678–686.

Fredrickson, B. L., and Losada, M. F. (2013). Correction to Fredrickson and Losada (2005). *American Psychologist, 68,* 822.

Gavin, J. H., Quick, J. C., Cooper, C. L., and Quick, J. D. (2003). A spirit of personal integrity: The role of character in executive health. *Organizational Dynamics, 32,* 165–179.

Goodman, E., Chesney, M. A., and Tipton, A. C. (1995). Relationship of optimism, knowledge, attitudes, and beliefs to use of HIV antibody testing by at-risk female adolescents. *Psychosomatic Medicine, 57,* 542–546.

Hersey, R. B. (1929). Periodic emotional changes in male workers. *Personnel Journal, 7,* 459–464.

Hersey, R. B. (1930). A monotonous job in an emotional crisis. *Personnel Journal, 9,* 290–296.

Hersey, R. B. (1932). *Workers' Emotions in Shop and Home: A Study of Industrial Workers from the Psychological and Physiological Standpoint*. Philadelphia: University of Pennsylvania Press.

Hobfoll, S. E. (1998). *Stress, Culture, and Community: The Psychology and Philosophy of Stress*. New York: Plenum Press.

Hoppock, R. (1935). *Job Satisfaction*. New York: Harper.

Houser, J. D. (1927). *What the Employee Thinks*. Cambridge, MA: Harvard University Press.

Hunter, J. W. (2000). *The Death of Character: Moral Education in an Age without Good or Evil*. New York: Basic Books.

Hurley-Hanson, A. E., and Giannantonio, C. M. (2007). Image norms: A model of formation and operation. *Journal of Business and Management, 13,* 155–165.

James, W. (1920). *The Letters of William James*, vol. 1, ed. H. James. Boston: Atlantic Monthly Press.

Judge, T. A., Thoresen, C. J., Bono, J. E., and Patton, G. K. (2001). The job satisfaction–job performance relationship: A qualitative and quantitative review. *Psychological Bulletin, 127,* 376–407.

Kornhauser, A. (1933). The technique for measuring employee attitudes. *Personnel Journal, 9,* 99–107.

Kornhauser, A., and Sharp, A. 1932. Employee attitudes: Suggestions from a study in a factory. *Personnel Journal, 10,* 393–401.

Lambert, V. A., Lambert, C. E., Klipple, G. L., and Mewshaw, E. A. (1989). Social support, hardiness and psychological well-being in women and arthritis. *Journal of Nursing Scholarship, 21,* 128–131.

Lorenz, E. N. (1963). Deterministic nonperiodic flow. *Journal of the Atmospheric Sciences, 20,* 130–141.

Lorenz, E. N. (1993). *The Essence of Chaos*. Seattle: University of Washington Press.

Luthans, F. (2002a). Positive psychological behavior: Developing and managing psychological strengths. *Academy of Management Executive, 16,* 57–72.

Luthans, F. (2002b). The need for and meaning of positive organizational behavior. *Journal of Organizational Behavior, 23,* 695–706.

Luthans, F., Avolio, B., Avey, J., and Norman, S. (2007a). Positive psychological capital: Measurement and relationship with performance and satisfaction. *Personnel Psychology, 60,* 541–572.

Luthans, F., and Youssef, C. M. (2007). Emerging positive organizational behavior. *Journal of Management, 33,* 321–349.

Luthans, F., Youssef, C. M., and Avolio, B. (2007b). *Psychological Capital: Developing the Human Competitive Edge*. New York: Oxford University Press.

Macdonald, C., Bore, M., and Munro, D. (2008). Values in action scale and the Big 5: An empirical indication of structure. *Journal of Research in Personality, 42,* 787–799.

Macik-Frey, M., Quick, J. C., and Nelson, D. L. (2007). Advances in occupational health: From a stressful beginning to a positive future. *Journal of Management, 33,* 809–840.

Mayo, E. (1924). Revery and industrial fatigue. *Journal of Personnel Research*, 3, 273–281.

Mino, S., and Kanemitsu, Y. (2005). Cognitive appraisal and situation-appropriate coping flexibility as related to clerical workers' job satisfaction in stressful situations. *Japanese Journal of Health Psychology*, 18, 34–44.

Nelson, D. L., and Cooper, C. L. (2007). *Positive Organizational Behavior*. Thousand Oaks, CA: Sage.

Nickerson, C. A. (2014). No empirical evidence for critical positivity ratios. *American Psychologist*, 69, 626–628.

Pennock, G. A. (1930). Industrial research at Hawthorne: An experimental investigation of rest periods, working conditions and other conditions. *Personnel Journal*, 8, 296–313.

Peterson, C., Park, N., Hall, N., and Seligman, M. E. P. (2009). Zest and work. *Journal of Organizational Behavior*, 30, 161–172.

Peterson, C., and Seligman, M. E. P. (2004). *Character Strengths and Virtues: A Handbook and Classification*. Washington, DC: American Psychological Association.

Pratt, M. G., and Ashforth, B. E. (2003). Fostering positive meaningfulness in work. In K. S. Cameron, J. E. Dutton, and R. E. Quinn (Eds.), *Positive Organizational Scholarship: Foundations of a New Discipline* (pp. 309–327). Berrett-Koehler.

Putnam, M. L. (1930). Improving employee relations: A plan which uses data obtained from employees. *Personnel Journal*, 8, 314–325.

Quick, J. C., Wright, T. A., Adkins, J. A., Nelson, D. L., and Quick, J. D. (2013). *Preventive Stress Management in Organizations*, 2nd edn. Washington, DC: American Psychological Association.

Roethlisberger, F. J., and Dickson, W. J. (1939). *Management and the Worker*. Cambridge, MA: Harvard University Press.

Seligman, M. E.P. (2002). *Authentic Happiness: Using the New Positive Psychology to Realize Your Potential for Lasting Fulfillment*. New York: Free Press.

Seligman, M. E.P., and Csikszentmihalyi, M. (2000). Positive psychology: An introduction. *American Psychologist*, 55, 5–14.

Selznick, P. (1957). *Leadership in Administration*. Berkeley: University of California Press.

Selznick, P. (1992). *The Moral Commonwealth*. Berkeley: University of California Press.

Sennett, R. (1998). *The Corrosion of Character*. New York: W.W. Norton.

Shryack, L., Steger, M. F., Krueger, R. F., and Kallie, C. S. (2010). The structure of virtue: An empirical investigation of the dimensionality of the virtues in action inventory of strengths. *Personality and Individual Differences*, 48, 714–719.

Singh, K., and Jha, S. D. (2008). Positive and negative affect, and grit as predictors of happiness and life satisfaction. *Journal of the Indian Academy of Applied Psychology*, 34, 40–45.

Snow, A. J. (1923). Labor turnover and mental alertness test scores. *Journal of Applied Psychology*, 7, 285–290.

Wright, T. A. (2003). Positive organizational behavior: An idea whose time has truly come. *Journal of Organizational Behavior*, 24, 437–442.

Wright, T. A. (2005). The role of "happiness" in organizational research: Past, present and future directions. In P. L. Perrewé and D. C. Ganster (Eds.), *Research in Occupational Stress and Well Being*, vol. 4 (pp. 221–264). Amsterdam: Elsevier.

Wright, T. A. (2006). The emergence of job satisfaction in organizational research: A historical overview of the dawn of job attitude research. *Journal of Management History*, 12, 262–277.

Wright, T. A. (2011). Character assessment in business ethics education. In D. G. Fisher and D. L. Swanson (Eds.), *Toward Assessing Business Ethics Education* (pp. 361–380). Charlotte, NC: Information Age.

Wright, T. A. (2014). When character and entrepreneurship meet: A view from the world of sport. *Journal of Business and Management*, 20, 5–23.

Wright, T. A. (2015). Distinguished Scholar Invited Essay: Reflections on the role of character in business education and student leadership development. *Journal of Leadership and Organizational Studies*, 22, 253–264.

Wright, T. A., and Bonett, D. G. (2007). Job satisfaction and psychological well-being as nonadditive predictors of workplace turnover. *Journal of Management*, 33, 141–160.

Wright, T. A., and Cropanzano, R. (2000). Psychological well-being and job satisfaction as predictors of job performance. *Journal of Occupational Health Psychology*, 5, 84–94.

Wright, T. A., Cropanzano, R., and Bonett, D. G. (2007). The moderating role of employee positive well-being on the relation between job satisfaction and job performance. *Journal of Occupational Health Psychology*, 12, 93–104.

Wright, T. A., and Doherty, E.M. (1998). Organizational behavior "rediscovers" the role of emotional well-being. *Journal of Organizational Behavior*, 19, 481–485.

Wright, T. A., and Goodstein, J. (2007). Character is not "dead" in management research: A review of individual character and organizational-level virtue. *Journal of Management, 33*, 928–958.

Wright, T. A., and Hobfoll, S. E. (2004). Commitment, psychological well-being and job performance: An examination of conservation of resources (COR) theory and job burnout. *Journal of Business and Management, 9*, 389–406.

Wright, T. A., and Huang, C.-C. (2012). The many benefits of employee well-being in organizational research. *Journal of Organizational Behavior, 33*, 1188–1192.

Wright, T. A., and Lauer, T. (2013). What is character and why it really does matter. *Organizational Dynamics, 42*, 25–34.

Wright, T. A., and Quick, J. C. (2009a). The emerging positive agenda in organizations: Greater than a trickle, but not yet a deluge. *Journal of Organizational Behavior, 30*, 147–159.

Wright, T. A., and Quick, J. C. (2009b). The role of positive-based research in building the science of organizational behavior. *Journal of Organizational Behavior, 30*, 329–336.

Wright, T. A., and Quick, J. C. (2011). The role of character in ethical leadership research. *Leadership Quarterly, 22*, 975–978.

Wright, T. A., and Walton, A. P. (2003). Affect, psychological well-being and creativity: Results of a field study. *Journal of Business and Management, 9*, 21–32.

Wright, T. A., and Wefald, A. J. (2012). Leadership in an academic setting: A view from the top. *Journal of Management Inquiry, 21*, 180–186.

Wright, T. A., and Wright, V. P. (2002). Organizational researcher values, ethical responsibility, and the committed-to-participant research perspective. *Journal of Management Inquiry, 11*, 173–185.

Wrzesniewski, A. (2003). Finding positive meaning in work. In K. S. Cameron, J. E. Dutton, and R. E. Quinn (Eds.), *Positive Organizational Scholarship: Foundations of a New Discipline* (pp. 296–308). San Francisco: Berrett-Koehler.

Yeh, H. C., Lorenz, F. O., Wickrama, K. A. S., Conger, R. D., and Elder, G. H. (2006). Relationships among sexual satisfaction, marital quality, and marital instability at midlife. *Journal of Family Psychology, 20*, 339–343.

26

Demand, Resources, and Their Relationship with Coping

Developments, Issues, and Future Directions

Philip Dewe

Introduction

The sheer volume of research that has helped to increase our understanding of how people cope with work stress has not just been described as "awesome" (Lazarus, 1999, p. 118) but has pointed to the complexity of the topic (Snyder, 2001), the difficulties of researching it (Aldwin, 2000) and the controversies and debate that surround it (Dewe and Cooper, 2012). Nevertheless there is still, as Somerfield and McCrae (2000, p. 620) suggest, a "boundless enthusiasm for researching" coping, tempered somewhat by the continuing debate as to how much progress, despite this "dramatic proliferation" (Folkman and Moskowitz, 2004, p. 745) of coping research particularly over the last three decades, has actually been made (Coyne and Racioppo, 2000). It would not be difficult to draw similar conclusions when thinking in terms of work stress theories, their evolution, and the emphasis giving to the role of coping (Dewe, O'Driscoll, and Cooper, 2010). While theories of work stress have advanced and developed with our state of knowledge, they have also been profoundly influenced by the economic, social and organizational context that surrounds them. These advances have not necessarily followed a simple linear pattern, but it is possible to identify two, not mutually exclusive, themes which seem to accompany much of our theoretical development: the idea of balance (Meurs and Perrewé, 2011), and the role played by demands and resources (Bakker and Demerouti, 2007). How recent advances in demands–resources theories of work stress have influenced our understanding of coping, the issues and challenges that surround such theories, and the direction they offer is the focus of this chapter.

The Handbook of Stress and Health: A Guide to Research and Practice, First Edition.
Edited by Cary L. Cooper and James Campbell Quick.
© 2017 John Wiley & Sons, Ltd. Published 2017 by John Wiley & Sons, Ltd.

Work Stress Theories

While it is possible to argue that all theories of work stress contain elements of demands and resources, when describing the structural, personal and organizational relationships that lead to stress a number of theorists place demands and resources at the core of their theories. They argue that it is this lens and this focal point that provide the context for understanding not just the nature of work stress and its consequences, but coping as well. It is always a perilous business either to try to categorize theories, or select those to discuss. Some authors, depending on their aims, acknowledge but do not refer to those that have been "widely discussed," focusing on the more "newly defined" theories (Brough, O'Driscoll, Kalliath, Cooper, and Poelmans (2009, p. 59), or select on the basis of their impact (Mackey and Perrewé, 2014) their prominence (Meurs and Perrewé, 2011), or their contribution to the demands–resources debate (Bakker and Demerouti, 2007).

To pursue our aim of exploring the contribution that demands–resources models of work stress have made to our understanding of coping, we follow the same course as many of those authors have done. However, to explore the role of coping within the context of a demands–resources framework, and in order to capture a sense of evolution and development, we cover some of the more prominent general stress models. We use the transactional framework offered by Lazarus (1999) as a comparator and as a means of evaluating advances and developments, before moving more to the issues and challenges facing coping researchers more generally. Similarly we use the conservation of resources (COR) model (Hobfoll, 1989) to point to the significant role given to resources and to the ideas of resource loss and resource gain. With this work in mind, we then turn to the job demands–control model of Karasek (1979), its extension to a job demand–control–support model (Johnson and Hall, 1988), and the job demands–resources model (Demerouti, Bakker, Nachreiner, and Schaufeli, 2001). The overriding aim is to use the Lazarus and Hobfoll theories as a context for exploring how coping has been investigated and the role it has played in demands–control–resources models.

Lazarus and the Transactional Theory of Stress

While Lazarus's work reflects a more general stress theory, the authority of his approach and its significance for work and for understanding coping (1966; 1990; 1999; 2001) stems from his transactional, process-oriented framework and the significant role given to the cognitive appraisal processes through which the individual and the environment are linked. The "primacy" of the appraisal process (Meurs and Perrewé, 2011, p. 1046) sits at the heart of Lazarus's model. Lazarus identified two different types of appraisal, pointing to the complexity of their relationship, with each being dependent on the other. Thus, despite their description, both help shape responses to a particular encounter, with any difference between the two a matter of their content rather than timing (Lazarus 1999). The first – primary appraisal – is where the individual appraises an encounter, gives meaning to it, and recognizes that something is at stake. Lazarus discusses such appraisals in terms of harm/loss, threat or challenge to well-being, adding later the idea of benefit in the sense of individual growth (Lazarus, 2001). The secondary appraisal process is where the individual appraises what can be done about it. It is where the individual explores the options and resources available to cope with the encounter. This causal pathway flowing through the appraisal processes implies a sense of imbalance: the appraised demands being greater "than resources to cope with these demands produces strain" (Meurs and Perrewé, 2011, p. 1046).

While it is not free from debate, Lazarus (1999) defines coping as "the constantly chang-ing cognitive and behavioral effort a person makes to manage specific external and/or inter-nal demands that are appraised as taxing or exceeding the resources of the person" (p. 110). Lazarus (1993) did indicate – although, as he argued, "with some loss of information" – that his definition could simply read as "coping consists of cognitive and behavioral efforts to man-age psychological stress" (p. 237). Critics of this definition suggest that it limits the idea of coping, failing to consider ordinary, everyday adaptations, routines, and behaviors (Aldwin, 2000; Costa, Somerfield, and McCrae, 1996; Coyne and Gottlieb 1996), although coping is perhaps more often than not thought of in terms of being a particular type of adaptation (Costa et al., 1996). Nevertheless, Lazarus's definition, while not always generally agreed, is fre-quently quoted; it embraces through the process of appraisal the manner in which demands and resources are construed, contextualized and understood; identifies coping as what people are thinking and doing; establishes at least two major functions of coping, problem-focused and emotion-focused; and sets a benchmark against which other theories can be compared.

Conservation of Resources Theory

Hobfoll's conservation of resources theory was a new attempt at conceptualizing stress. Hobfoll (1989) argued that the proposed model "comprehensively explains behavior during stressful circumstances … while still encompassing the relative importance and complexity of cognitions" (p. 516). The power of Hobfoll's theory (1989; 2001; 2011), its relevance to the work context, and what he argues distinguishes his theory from other stress theories stems from the pivotal role it gives to both resource loss *and* resource gain. At the center of the model is the principle that individuals will strive to maintain, preserve, cultivate, defend, and build those resources that they value, and "that what is threatening to them is the potential or actual loss of these valued resources" (1989, p. 516). Understanding resources, Hobfoll argues, is critical to understanding stress. Resources are defined in terms of those "personal characteris-tics, conditions or energies" that are valued for their own sake or valued because they offer a mechanism for maintaining or achieving valued resources (Hobfoll, 1989, p. 516). Resources represent the primary component of the stress process, and stress occurs when resources are threatened with loss, are actually lost, or where there is a failure to sufficiently invest in or gain resources (Hobfoll, 2001, pp. 341–342). Understanding the potency of resource loss - the way it increases individual vulnerability to further loss and reduces individual capacity to gain resources – and how investing in resources reduces vulnerability and increases capacity to gain further resources reflects, argues Hobfoll, an approach to stress that is active where individuals are "striving to fulfil important roles, achieve important goals and offset a sense of despair" (2011, p. 133).

Hobfoll (1989) argues that what separates his theory from other theories of stress is that it "inherently states what individuals do when confronted with stress and when not confronted with stress; they strive to minimize net loss of resources," as this is the goal of coping (p. 517). Others would agree, describing coping strategies as being at the heart of resources (Ito and Brotheridge, 2003), or as an actual or potential way to attain goals (Freund and Riediger, 2001). While the idea of resources has a "beguiling simplicity and catchiness" (Thompson and Cooper, 2001, p. 411), the nature and types of resources have been well outlined by Hobfoll (1989; 2001; 2011). Research has also explored resources and their relationship with coping strategies (Halbesleben, 2006; Ito and Brotheridge, 2003); the fit between the choice of a coping strategy, a person's reservoir of resources, and the demands of the situation (Hobfoll

1989; Ito and Brotheridge, 2003); the distinction between "what I have" and "what I do," capturing how efficiently resources are used and how from a developmental point of view resource gains may be as important as the loss of resources (Freund and Riediger, 2001, p. 378); and the importance of resource losses and gains for health promotion and stress intervention (Quick and Gavin, 2001). This has all helped to elaborate the resource and coping process.

There is, running through Hobfoll's (2002) work, a growth-related theme and a proactive element where the building up of resources suggests a "forward time perspective" (Schwarzer, 2001). Hobfoll discusses the linking of resources in terms of enriching individual reservoirs, how those with resources are better able to resolve issues, how, as resources may "travel in resource caravans," they facilitate the development and use of other resources, how individuals learn from experiences and grow as a result of feedback, and how "resources fit people's tendencies to be adaptive and find a path" (2002, pp. 318, 320). Turning to the process of appraisal, Hobfoll (2001) argued that this "subjective component of stress" had been given too great an emphasis, and that since, in the conservation of resources model, resources are defined in objective terms (objective resources, conditions, personal characteristics and energies), there is no immediate need or demand to emphasize the primacy of the appraisals in the stress process (p. 359). This led to an exchange of views with Lazarus (2001) about the role and importance of appraising and the nature of objectivity. Searching for a need to find an "accommodation between appraisals and resource based conceptions of the stress process" (Thompson and Cooper, 2001, p. 417), it is clear that Hobfoll (2001) does point to individuals seeing the world as "innately threatening" (p. 341), considers the question of whether there is an equivalency when resources are examined objectively or via appraisals (Hobfoll, 2002), and describes the conditions when, in his model, appraisals will be of "greater importance" and, in contrast, when the objective nature of encounters will "be of greater moment" (2001, p. 359), suggesting that since each lies on a continuum neither can be ignored.

Hobfoll (2002) is correct in his prediction that "in the coming years" resources will remain significant and fundamental to our understanding of stress (p. 320). His model offers a heuristic that acknowledges the explanatory potential of resources, places them at the heart of the stress process, adds value to our understanding of coping, and has established its presence and stamped its authority on the field of stress research through theoretical critique, debate and empirical analysis. There is, as Hobfoll suggests, work still to be done to continue to advance our understanding and explore how exactly and with what efficiency resources are used, the way they are linked together, the nature of those linkages and the constitution and potency of "resource caravans," and the energizing power of "resource spirals" and their role in developing and designing intervention strategies (Dewe and Cooper, 2012).

Job Demands, Control (and Support) Model

Using these two general stress models as a context, we turn first to Karasek (1979) and his job demands–job control model; a model that has been described as playing "a dominant role in shaping the research agenda in the field of work stress and health" (Meurs and Perrewé, 2011, p. 1046). Other authors agree, describing Karasek's model as having had a significant impact (Mackey and Perrewé, 2014), as dominating work-health research (van der Doef and Maes, 1999), as capturing the attention of researchers (de Jonge, Dollard, Dormann, Le Blanc, and Houtman, 2000) and as representing perhaps the most influential model of stress at work (Mark and Smith, 2008). Karasek's (1979) aim was to guide research away from viewing all job characteristics as demanding, and stress as emerging from job stressors alone, to a more systematic, contextualized and analytically correct discussion where stress resulted from the joint effects of work demands and "the range of decision making freedom (discretion) available to the worker facing those demands" (p. 287); hence the job demands–job control (decision latitude) model.

Broadly stated, a combination of high job demands and low job control described high-strain jobs, whereas low job demands and high job control described low-strain jobs. Karasek (1979) went on to describe "active jobs," when both job demands and job control are high, which "leads to development of new behavior patterns on and off the job" (p. 288), and "passive jobs" (low demands–low control) that "induce a decline in overall activity and a reduction in general of problem-solving activity" (p. 288). Johnson and Hall (1988) refined the Karasek model by adding work-related social support, leading into decades of research around the idea of a demands, control, support model. This intervention was, as Johnson and Hall suggest, to shift the emphasis from what was an individual link between the person and the job to a context that included issues around relationships between individuals, since social support may influence the process of control.

The job demand–control–support model has attracted considerable empirical attention. While the findings have been mixed (de Lange, Taris, Kompier, Houtman, and Bongers, 2003), the model itself is not without support, with reviewers confirming the importance of the model by pointing to the need for more research that captures some of the complexity that surrounds the different constructs and their relationship (Rodriguez, Bravo, Peiro, and Schaufeli, 2001) and to counter the model's limitations by engaging in research that captures the "complexities of the stress process" (Mark and Smith, 2008, p. 118). Van der Doef and Maes (1999) pointed, among other new directions for future research, to the need to engage in a more comprehensive review that advances and develops our understanding of the nature of demands, control and support, not just to avoid conceptual overlap but to get at the specifics of the relationship, as only in this way, they add, will it be possible to evaluate the "practical value" of the model (p. 110).

Other reviewers, along with listing methodological, longitudinal and causal pathway issues for attention, have identified similar future requirements and called for measures of work control to be more refined so as to distinguish "control as a resource from responsibility as a demand" (Johnson and Hall, 1988, p. 1341); to consider "what causes control beliefs" (Fox, Dwyer and Ganster, 1993, p. 314); to explore demands in terms of whether they are a challenge or a hindrance, and support in terms of its instrumental role versus its role as an emotional support (Luchman and Gonzalez-Morales, 2013, pp. 46, 47); and to consider "more focused and multifaceted measures of both job demands and job control" (de Jonge et al., 2000, p. 279), more specific and objective outcomes (de Lange et al., 2003), more importance given to personality characteristics (de Jonge, Janssen, and Van Breukelen, 1996), and the need for a greater match in terms of "domains of human psychological functioning" between stressors, resources and strains (de Jonge and Dormann, 2006, p. 1369).

Coping through Enacting Control and Support

Karasek (1979) did, of course, point to the idea that having control and support resourced the individual with "feelings of efficacy and ability to cope with the environment" (p. 303). If the call by many researchers is to refine the job demands, control, support model by exploring the complexity that surrounds the different constructs and their relationship, then what emphasis have researchers given to investigating the role of coping? At least two approaches can be identified. The first, associated with the work of Daniels and his colleagues (Daniels, Beesley, Cheyne, and Wimalasiri, 2008; Daniels, Beesley, Wimalasiri, and Cheyne, 2013; Daniels and Guppy, 1994; Daniels and Harris, 2005), explores the idea that "exercising control" and "eliciting support" improves well-being by fostering problem-focused coping (Daniels and Harris, 2005, p. 221). The second approach follows from the "active job/learning" idea embedded in Karasek's (1979) work where learning facilitates and "may help the person to cope" (p. 288) (Daniels, Boocock, Glover, Hartley, and Holland, 2009; Taris, Kompier, de Lange, Schaufeli, and Schreurs, 2003, p. 2). In the first of a series of papers with colleagues, Daniels found, among complex interactions, general support for their approach; tempered by perceptions of control, support and autonomy provide at times different aspects of control in the workplace, are associated with a stress-buffering effect on well-being, and reflect the determinants of, and the effective use of problem-focused coping (Daniels and Guppy, 1994). Offering problem-focused coping as a context for understanding the role of control and support points to explanatory potential, Daniels and Guppy argue, when such variables are considered within a transactional framework.

Wishing to engage in a "more precise examination" of the expectation that coping with job demands provides one of the more important psychological processes that link control and support to well-being, Daniels and Harris (2005) extended their investigation to a range of coping strategies and expanded the types of well-being measured (pp. 221, 222). The implied role of problem-focused coping as the mechanism through which control and support improve well-being was supported. The authors do, however, point to the way problem-focused coping is enacted: whether this occurs through control or support depends on the type of well-being, with control being enacted associated with the reaching of personal goals, and support being enacted associated with better ratings of affect. Other forms of coping (emotion-focused, avoidance) can also improve well-being and should "not necessarily be discouraged" (p. 235). Beneficial effects were found when avoidance coping was enacted through control and when emotion-focused coping was enacted through support. Three issues become clear from this work (Daniels and Harris, 2005, p. 234): that individuals have the authority as to how control and support are used; that enacting control and support via coping depends on the nature of well-being; and that research should be expanded across a range of coping strategies and to how control and support are used to express affect (see Daniels, Glover, and Mellor, 2014).

Daniels and his colleagues (2008), using an experienced sampling design, continued their work on the job demands, control, support model by exploring the impact on well-being of a range of coping strategies, enacted through control and support in relation to problem-solving demands. Their results confirmed the benefits that accrue to different aspects of well-being through "the consistent" (p. 864) use of problem-focused coping enacted via control and support and, notwithstanding the mixed results, the importance of continuing to explore the enactment of control and support through other types of coping, in this case with an emotion focus and an emotion approach focus. This research support from earlier work confirms the need to continue to give theoretical and empirical attention to investigating the purpose of the enacting of job characteristics, as this remains crucial to understanding their influence; to the importance of linking control and support (coping behaviors) to specific coping functions (problem and emotion focused) to gain insights into what distinguishes one coping type from another;

and to exploring the benefits of more collaborative forms of enacting job characteristics. It is clear that training leading to greater job knowledge and management, and better problem-solving skills, is fundamental to improving job control and supportive interactions (Daniels et al., 2008, pp. 868–869; Daniels et al., 2013).

Coping and the Learning Hypothesis

As mentioned, Karasek (1979) drew attention to what he described as active and passive jobs where learning was either enhanced (active jobs) or inhibited (passive jobs) depending on the levels of control and demands. In jobs with high demands and high control, the argument was that individuals would have the opportunity to engage and learn new behaviors, effectively manage demands, and protect themselves from strain. With high control, the individual makes a "choice" as to how best to cope with a stressor, and that new behavior response, if effective, will be incorporated into the individual's repertoire of coping strategies (i.e., "it will be learned") (Karasek, 1998, p. 34.7). On the other hand, jobs with low demands and low control (passive) "induce a decline in overall activity and a reduction in general problem solving activity" (Karasek, 1979, p. 288), what Karasek (1998) describes as "a very 'unmotivating' job setting which leads to negative learning or gradual loss of previously acquired skills" (p. 34.7). The idea of motivation would seem to embrace both performance motivation as well as the motivation to learn and engage in new behavior.

Karasek's (1998) model also implies that learning will increase as job characteristics change or individuals transition toward jobs that are more active in character (Taris et al., 2003), and that active jobs produce "desirable stress" leading to "increased motivation and learning opportunities" (Theorell and Karasek, 1996, p. 10). It acknowledges that while demands may be both positive and negative in the same way as stress may be, the emphasis firmly remains on demands being concrete and objective (Karasek, 1998). Karasek's (1979; 1998) model predicts both learning and strain built around different combinations of demands and control. Relationships determining the learning hypothesis are not "simply mathematically additive" (Karasek, 1998, p. 34.7); each plays a different role, with control predicted to reduce strain and increase learning, whereas demands are predicted to increase both strain and learning. This points to a level of dependence between the two, suggesting a need to better understand how each (strain and learning) relate to one another (Taris et al., 2003).

Despite the authority and profile of the demands, control, support model, with its focus on both strain and learning, there has, understandably perhaps, "been a failure" by researchers to give the same attention to learning-directed outcomes (Parker and Sprigg, 1999, p. 934). Parker and Sprigg, among others, explore the idea that as proactive individuals would be more likely to take the opportunity to make use of high control, then those in "active" jobs would experience a greater sense of mastery. While these authors found support for the general proposition that relating demands, control to learning outcomes was "reasonably appropriate" for proactive individuals, the "one anomaly" they found was that greater perceived mastery was linked not to high demand, high control, as predicted, but to low demands, high control jobs (Parker and Sprigg, 1999, pp. 935, 936). Even for passive individuals (low proactivity), the better set of learning outcomes stemmed from low demands, high control jobs, leaving Parker and Sprigg to question whether, set against these findings, the term active best described high demand, high control jobs. While suggesting that other outcomes may better capture learning than "having a sense of total mastery over job demands" (1999, p. 936), their results affirmed the influence that demands and control can have over learning, and confirmed that in that interaction proactive personality has an important moderating role to play.

Other researchers, contrary to Karasek's model, have also failed to find the predicted relationships between demands, control and learning outcomes (Holman and Wall 2002; Taris et al., 2003; Taris, Kompier, Geurts, Houtman, and van den Heuvel, 2010). However, what emerges from their research is a consistent finding that supports the view that greater control offers opportunities to engage in and develop skills and behaviors that enable individuals to better cope with the demands of the job. Moreover, while control is seen as "core to the promotion of learning" (Holman and Wall, 2002, p. 299), with high control "indeed conducive to feelings of professional efficacy" (Taris et al., 2010, p. 467), investigations suggest that there is a more complex relationship because demands and control appear differentially related to learning and strain; that more research on how learning and strain "mutually influence" each other is clearly needed; and that a closer examination of the mechanisms that underlie this influence requires more longitudinal analysis and a greater blending of cognitive, behavioral and affective perspectives (e.g., Taris et al., 2003, pp. 17–18; Taris et al., 2010, pp. 470–471). The complexity of this relationship is also illustrated by the way individuals use control and support in association with learning and affective well-being to respond to problem-solving demands (Daniels et al., 2009).

This brief overview of the two approaches to placing coping in the Karasek model, either through how job characteristics are enacted or the learning hypothesis, does not capture the richness, rigor, comprehensiveness, or complexity of design used by the different research studies cited. However, their contributions clearly point to what is needed by the next generation of research. This would include greater attention to developing more "focused and multifaceted measures of both job demands and job control" (Daniels and Harris, 2005; de Jonge et al., 2000, p. 272), as well as active learning (Taris et al., 2003), coping (Daniels et al., 2008) and the issue of exploring and measuring more processes suggested by the transactional theories (Daniels and Guppy, 1994). Then there is the nature of the relationship being investigated, the shared influence and differentiating effects of demands, control and support, what is expected from such relationships, the mechanisms that underpin it and the specifics of what sort of learning or skill acquisition emerges, how strain and learning are linked, the need for more longitudinal design that captures the impact of time (Daniels and Guppy, 1994; de Lange et al., 2003; Holman and Wall, 2002; Parker and Sprigg, 1999; Taris et al., 2003; 2010), the nature of coping, the dynamics between coping strategies and how the different coping strategies are used (Daniels and Harris 2005), the need more generally to explore both positive and negative outcomes (Taris et al., 2010), and whether a model that primarily emphasizes the reduction of stress rather than the encouraging of learning would, if reframed, "explain how one learns from stressful encounters" and whether this would "propose [different] constructs and relationships" (Meurs and Perrewé, 2011, p. 1047).

Job Demands–Resources Model

The history, origins and rational for the job demands–resources model has been well outlined by those associated with its development (Schaufeli and Taris, 2014). Reflecting back on earlier approaches to job design and job stress, Bakker and Demerouti (2007) make the point that, while making a significant contribution to our knowledge, job design theories generally missed out the demands of role stressors, with job stress theories generally overlooking the motivational potential of job resources. By bringing together these two research traditions of job design and job stress into one model, embracing the ideas of demands and resources and the issues of stress and motivation explains why the job demands–resources model, as first outlined by Demerouti and colleagues (2001), has "gained high popularity among researchers" (Schaufeli and Taris, 2014, p. 43). It extended its influence beyond just burnout to significantly advance our understanding of job stress (Brough et al., 2009), gained acceptance because of its utility across all occupations (Demerouti and Bakker, 2011), offered a sense of balance between "positive (resources) and negative (demands) job characteristics" (Schaufeli and Taris, 2014, p. 44), and provided a fruitful context for an ever expanding body of research that supports the model's theoretical and empirical robustness, and its importance to practice and to the well-being of individuals (Bakker and Demerouti, 2014; Nahrgang, Morgeson, and Hofmann, 2011).

The model, as those involved in its development are quick to acknowledge, "fell on fertile ground" (Bakker and Demerouti, 2014; Bakker and Demerouti, 2007; Bakker, van Veldhoven, and Xanthopoulou, 2010; Schaufeli and Taris, 2014). It wasn't just that job stress and motivation research operated primarily in parallel with little reference by one to the other, but that the mixed results stemming from the job demands, control and support model (Karasek, 1979) also provided "an important starting point" (Bakker et al., 2010, p. 4). Why? Because one of its strengths – its simplicity – was also seen as a weakness, both because it failed to capture the complexity of the workplace, particularly at a time when fundamental changes were occurring in the nature and meaning of work, and because of an apparent lack of clarity as to why control was viewed as the only important resource – although researchers, as Karasek himself acknowledged, soon were to add other resources (Bakker and Demerouti, 2007; Bakker et al., 2010; Schaufeli and Taris, 2014). Hobfoll's (1989; 2001) view that resources are important in their own right, in addition to the role they may have in dealing with job demands, also reinforced, in the minds of researchers, the less than complete treatment they had been given, the explanatory power that resided in them, and the richness that exploring them in such a context would provide (Bakker and Demerouti, 2007; Demerouti and Bakker, 2011; Xanthopoulou, Bakker, Demerouti, and Schaufeli, 2009). In short, the job demands, resources model "*complements, encompasses, and integrates* rather than *replaces* older theory" (Schaufeli and Taris, 2014, p. 60).

The job demands, resources model builds from the premise that while occupations may have their specific job characteristics, these can be classified into two general categories – job demands and job resources, giving a model that can be applied across organizations "*irrespective* of the particular demands or resources involved" (Demerouti and Bakker, 2011, p. 2) and offering a utility and flexibility over earlier models (Schaufeli and Taris, 2014). Underlying job demands and job resources are two relatively independent psychological processes. The first is a health impairment or energies process where demanding jobs come with costs that exhaust or deplete energy and are associated with health problems. Job resources, on the other hand, are presumed to have motivational potential leading to positive outcomes (Bakker and Demerouti, 2007; Bakker and Demerouti, 2014; Bakker et al., 2010; Demerouti et al., 2001). Research (see Bakker and Demerouti, 2014) supported the proposition that job demands and job resources trigger two different "psychological processes," which ultimately affect significant organizational outcomes. Building on the idea that job resources are not just needed to manage job demands but are also important in their own right, the motivational process of job resources was refined to include an *intrinsic* role that encouraged "employee growth, learning and development" and an *extrinsic* role where they were "instrumental in achieving work goals" (e.g., Bakker and Demerouti, 2007, p. 313; Bakker et al., 2010; Schaufeli and Taris, 2014).

Not only do job demands and resources have a unique role, the former as predictors of job stress and the latter as predictors of learning and other growth-related outcomes (Bakker et al., 2010), but they also interact. What differentiates the job demands–resources model from earlier models is that it takes a more expanded view, proposing that "*different* types of job demands and job resources may interact in predicting job strain" (Demerouti and Bakker, 2011, p. 3), and that in addition to their role as predictors of motivational processes, job resources generally function as a buffer in interactions with strain (Bakker et al., 2010). Specifically, and in line with the Karasek's (1979) approach, the model proposes that high demands and low resources lead to strain whereas high demands, high resources lead to greater motivation. It is the latter proposal that represents the coping hypothesis (Demerouti and Bakker, 2011). Resources, it is suggested, become more significant and express their motivational potential in the context of challenging demands, and it is under these conditions that resources are more likely to be used as a coping strategy (Bakker and Demerouti, 2007; Bakker et al., 2010; Demerouti and Bakker, 2011).

Demands–Resources Appraisal and Coping

Examining and reviewing the evidence around the motivational and coping role that resources play led Bakker and Demerouti (2007) to consider the proposition that high job resources may bring high levels of motivation irrespective of the level of demands. This was a finding, they add, that requires further examination and perhaps a revision in the nature of predictions, suggesting that personal resources are significant predictors of motivation, reinforcing the need to explore how best to integrate them and personal vulnerabilities into the model (Bakker and Demerouti, 2014; Bakker and Demerouti, 2007; Schaufeli and Taris, 2014; Xanthopoulou et al., 2009); that providing interventions that play to the ability of individuals to use their strengths may help develop their personal resources (Bakker and Demerouti, 2014); that the relationship between demands and resources may, over time, be mutually influencing, requiring further examination of the dynamics of the relationship and of how such relationships develop, including how this informs practice and interventions (Bakker and Demerouti, 2007; Schaufeli and Taris, 2014); and that, as the two processes of health impairment and motivation may not be independent, understanding how each influences the other will require further investigation (Schaufeli and Taris, 2014).

Schaufeli and Taris (2014) describe the job demands–resources model as descriptive in the sense that it specifies "what kinds" of job demands and job resources may, by definition, lead to "what kinds" of outcomes (p. 55), rather than why they do or what mechanisms link them together. The clarity of the model, its utility and flexibility, its balanced approach and the pragmatic and interventional advantages it offers, represent its power and authority. Nevertheless, the importance of developing insights into such mechanisms and processes has not escaped the attention of researchers, particularly when it comes to differentiating qualitatively between the nature of demands, how they are valued (negatively or positively), and whether in that sense all demands can or should be treated equally (Crawford, LePine, and Rich, 2010; Schaufeli and Taris, 2014; Van den Broeck, de Cuyper, De Witte, and Vansteenkiste, 2010). The same can, of course, be said for resources (Schaufeli and Taris, 2014), reflecting perhaps the transactional approach of Lazarus (1999; 2001) and the importance of understanding how demands and resources are appraised.

The idea that "not all jobs demands are necessarily negative," and that their negativity or the way in which they are valued depends more on the relationship between energy expended and recovery time has long found expression in how they have been defined (Bakker and Demerouti, 2007, p. 312; Schaufeli and Taris, 2014). Coupling this with the unexpected finding that some types of job demand are positively related to job engagement (Schaufeli, Bakker, and van Rhenen, 2009; Xanthopoulou et al., 2009) led researchers to the view that perhaps a more subtle way to explain this relationship would be through qualitatively differentiating between job demands (Crawford et al., 2010; Van den Broeck et al., 2010). Working from the assumption that not all job demands are equal and integrating into the job demands–resources model the distinction between challenge and hindrance demands (Cavanaugh, Boswell, Roehling, and Boudreau, 2000), Crawford and his colleagues (2010) found that demands appraised as a challenge were positively related to job engagement, supporting the more general belief that outcomes depend on the nature of the demand and helping to clarify and explain the ambiguity that surrounded the demands–engagement relationship.

Similarly, Van den Broeck and colleagues (2010), differentiating job demands in terms of challenge or hindrance, also found that challenging jobs were related to vigor, the principal component of engagement. They concluded that differentiating demands in this way was both informative and a requirement in order to enhance our understanding of the demands–well-being relationship. Both studies are important because they support and refine the job demands–resources model both empirically and practically, offer an alternative to the traditional and somewhat dominant quantitative/quadratic approach (Van den Broeck et al., 2010), and point to why understanding how demands and for that matter resources are appraised adds to, and enriches, our understanding of the nature of the strain–well-being relationships. Does this mean that it is now time to integrate more formally into the job demands–resources model the transactional notion of appraisal? The answer seems to be not just yet.

Both sets of authors acknowledge the transactional approach (Lazarus, 1999; 2001) and the role of appraisals in providing meaning in terms of challenges, benefits, threats, and loss. However, while noting Lazarus's (1999; 2001) view of appraisals as an intra-individual process, both sets of authors argue that the work context provides a sense of consistency in the way all individuals give meaning to and appraise job demands to the extent that some job demands are "more likely" to be appraised as challenges and others as hindrances (Crawford et al., 2010, p. 837; Van den Broeck et al., 2010, p. 740). Nevertheless, building a level of appraising in the job demands–resources model is a significant step. It draws attention to an alternative approach to understanding the demands–resources relationship and offers a more fertile and innovative pathway than continually working within the boundaries of the more traditional quantitative/quadratic approach (Taris, 2006; Van den Broeck et al., 2010). Appraisal may also provide the context for exploring how, when, and in what way resources can be separated in terms of their coping and motivational roles, a distinction frequently made in the different models. How significant is this distinction, what actually is the core issue that separates one resource from the other, how does one influence the other and are they both part of what we now call proactive coping, and should we be giving more attention to what actually motivates the use of a coping strategy (Folkman and Moskowitz, 2004; Schwarzer, 2001; 2004; Schwarzer and Taubert, 2002). Nevertheless, the empirical robustness of the job demands–resources model, its importance for practice, the intervention strategies that flow from it, and its popularity reflect the creativity and methodological attention given by those associated with its development.

Demands–Resources and Future Directions

Future directions that embrace job crafting (Bakker and Demerouti, 2014); the attention given to personal resources and the ideas of individual flourishing and thriving (Bakker et al., 2010; Demerouti and Bakker, 2011; Schaufeli and Taris, 2014; Xanthopoulou et al., 2009); the nature and architecture of demands and resources, their relational qualities, their meanings, and their mutually influencing relationship (Schaufeli and Taris 2014); the need for more longitudinal work, more alternative qualitative methods (Demerouti and Bakker 2011), more specific and targeted work on the match between resources and coping strategies (Daniels and de Jonge, 2010), and a continuing emphasis on its practical application, its use as an intervention strategy and the addition of objective health indicators (Bakker and Demerouti 2007; Demerouti and Bakker 2011) – all these capture the more contemporary mood. It is one that embraces positivity, creativity, and the questioning of where current methodologies are taking us, what alternative methods can provide, and the obligations we owe to practice and to those whose working lives we study, and it will help to ensure the continued importance of this model, its continued role as one of the leading work stress models, its flexibility and utility, and the undoubted potential it has to aid our understanding.

Nevertheless, resources have always been central to the coping process and are embedded in the transactional model (Lazarus 1999; 2001) through the process of secondary appraisal ("what can I do about it?"). Accepting the dictum that clearly the job demands–resources model "can accommodate many different ideas and findings" (Schaufeli and Taris, 2014, p. 63), then researchers, when considering the nature of resources, may wish to explore in greater detail how such resources are being used, what specific coping strategies are connected with them, what motivational process they provide, and how effectively they are being deployed. To try to understand the coping properties of resources without actually exploring what those specific thoughts and actions may be seems to ignore the explanatory potential that resides in such an approach, and marginalizes coping and the rich meaning it can provide to an inference that requires little further analysis.

Conclusions

Across these models, similar themes as to the direction future research should take ensure that coping is on the agenda, in one form or another, although more often than not it plays more of an indirect explanatory role, offering a way in which findings should be understood. While researchers have made explicit use of different coping strategies, it is to be hoped that applying a more qualitative approach, where the functions and role of resources are differentiated one from the other, would elevate coping to a more central role. Of course this depends on the direction future research takes, the questions that need answering, how priorities are set, and just how far, and how necessary, it is to understand the nature of demands and resources in order to release and understand their explanatory power. Coping research comes with its own set of issues. There is, as mentioned earlier, debate as to whether by defining coping as occurring within the context of a stressful encounter we necessarily limit our understanding of what constitutes coping and where the boundaries lie between coping and everyday adaptation (Dewe and Cooper, 2012). Coping research has always been accompanied by, at various times, an undercurrent of concern, and at other times critical debate surrounding its measurement, the overreliance on questionnaires (Coyne and Gottlieb, 1996; Coyne and Racioppo, 2000), the need for a more acute sensitivity as to when they should be used (Lazarus, 1995), the need for more ecologically sensitive and creative measures (Snyder, 1999), and the recognition that questionnaires are only as good as our motivation to improve them (Folkman, 1992).

Accompanying these operational issues are interpretive challenges (Dewe and Cooper, 2012). Operational issues cannot, of course, be separated from interpretive issues, and again, depending on the methods used to collect the data, they include the classifying of coping strategies, as it is one thing to name a particular strategy but another to understand how it is being used in a stressful encounter; the construction and interpretation of mean scores, because while two people may have identical scores they may cope completely differently; the need to distinguish between the use of a strategy and not just its effectiveness but what we actually mean by coping effectively; and the acknowledgment that coping will ultimately be judged in terms of the context within which it occurs, so understanding contextual issues gives a more complete understanding of coping and the relationship between different coping strategies, the patterns they form, and their functions within that pattern (Dewe and Cooper, 2012).

Coping researchers are, of course, confronting these issues, developing creative approaches to capture the essence of coping, and continuing to advance our knowledge notwithstanding the complexity that surrounds the subject. Those researching job demands and resources are ideally place to contribute to our understanding of coping. While work will continue to focus on the quantitative/quadratic approach to understanding how the different constructs relate, it is the qualitative approach that offers a way forward. Resources are essential to our understanding of coping and provide insights into the secondary appraisal process, where individuals make decisions as to what they can do about the encounter. Understanding more about what resources are called upon, how they are used, how they express coping strategies, how effectively they are being deployed, the cost and benefits of using them, replenishing them and developing then, and the context within which all of this takes place will only help to reinforce and establish the central role they play in the coping process. Much of the research has, quite correctly, focused on resources in the context of secondary appraisal, yet the meanings individuals give to events (primary appraisal) will also be tempered by the nature and availability of resources, both personal and organizational, and research should not overlook the role they play in constructing meaning and determining "what is at stake."

Research is undoubtedly moving in that direction but, rather than using coping merely as a tool for explaining what may be happening, the knowledge and creativity exist to begin to further unravel the nature of resources through the lens of coping, giving the role of resources the attention it deserves and acknowledging its significance in enhancing our understanding of the coping process. It is clear from this review that researchers have already exhibited in their work so far a capacity for thoroughness, a detailed understanding of their field, a willingness to adopt creative and innovative methods, and an ability to execute their way through complexity. It is now time to apply these attributes to unlocking the explanatory potential and the understanding that comes from a more detailed examination of the coping function of resources.

References

Aldwin, C. M. (2000). *Stress, Coping, and Development: An Integrative Perspective*. New York: Guilford Press.

Bakker, A. B., and Demerouti, E. (2007). The job demands–resources model: State of the art. *Journal of Managerial Psychology*, 22, 309–328.

Bakker, A. B., and Demerouti, E. (2014). Job demands–resources theory. In P. Y. Chen and C. Cooper (Eds.), *Work and Wellbeing, vol. 3 of Wellbeing: A Complete Reference Guide* (pp. 37–64). Chichester, UK: Wiley Blackwell.

Bakker, A. B., van Veldhoven, M., and Xanthopoulou, D. (2010). Beyond the demand–control model: Thriving on high job demands and resources. *Journal of Personnel Psychology, 9*, 3–16.

Brough, P., O'Driscoll, M., Kalliath, T., Cooper, C. L., and Poelmans, S. A. Y. (Eds.) (2009). *Workplace Psychological Health: Current Research and Practice*. Cheltenham, UK: Edward Elgar.

Cavanaugh, M. A., Boswell, W. R., Roehling, M. V., and Boudreau, J. W. (2000). An empirical examination of self-report work stress among US managers. *Journal of Applied Psychology, 85*, 65–74.

Costa, P. T., Somerfield, M. R., and McCrae, R. R. (1996). Personality and coping: A reconceptualization. In M. Zeidner and N. M. Endler (Eds.), *Handbook of Coping: Theory, Research, Applications* (pp. 44–61). New York: John Wiley.

Coyne, J. C., and Gottlieb, B. H. (1996). The mismeasure of coping by checklist. *Journal of Personality, 64*, 959–991.

Coyne, J. C., and Racioppo, M. W. (2000). Never the twain shall meet? Closing the gap between coping research and clinical intervention research. *American Psychologist, 55*, 655–664.

Crawford, E. R., LePine, J. A., and Rich, B. L. (2010). Linking job demands and resources to employee engagement and burnout: A theoretical extension and meta-analytic test. *Journal of Applied Psychology, 95*, 834–848.

Daniels, K., Beesley, N., Cheyne, A., and Wimalasiri, V. (2008). Coping processes linking the demands–control–support model, affect and risky decisions at work. *Human Relations, 61*, 845–874.

Daniels, K., Beesley, N., Wimalasiri, V., and Cheyne, A. (2013). Problem solving and well-being: Exploring the instrumental role of job control and social support. *Journal of Management, 39*, 1016–1043.

Daniels, K., Boocock, G., Glover, J., Hartley, R., and Holland, J. (2009). An experience sampling study of learning, affect and the demands control support model. *Journal of Applied Psychology, 94*, 1003–1017.

Daniels, K., and de Jonge, J. (2010). Match making and match breaking: The nature of match within and around job design. *Journal of Occupational and Organizational Psychology, 83*, 1–16.

Daniels, K., Glover, J., and Mellor, N. (2014). An experience sampling study of expressing affect, daily affective well-being, relationship quality and perceived performance. *Journal of Occupational and Organizational Psychology, 87*, 781–805.

Daniels, K., and Guppy, A. (1994). Occupational stress, social support, job control, and psychological well-being. *Human Relations, 47*, 1523–1544.

Daniels, K., and Harris, C. (2005). A daily diary study of coping in the context of the job demands-control-support model. *Journal of Vocational Behavior, 66*, 219–237.

de Jonge, J., Dollard, M. F., Dormann, C., le Blanc, P. M., and Houtman, I., L., D. (2000). The demand–control model: Specific demands, specific control and well-defined groups. *International Journal of Stress Management, 7*, 269–287.

de Jonge, J., and Dormann, C. (2006). Stressors, resources, and strain at work: A longitudinal test of the triple-match principle. *Journal of Applied Psychology, 91*, 1359–1374.

de Jonge, J., Janssen, P. P. M., and Van Breukelen, G. J. P. (1996). Testing the demand–control–support model among health-care professionals: A structural equation model. *Work and Stress, 10*, 209–224.

de Lange, A. H., Taris, T. W., Kompier, M. A. J., Houtman, I. L. D., and Bongers, P. M. (2003). "The very best of the millennium": Longitudinal research and the demand–control (support) model. *Journal of Occupational Health Psychology, 8*, 282–305.

Demerouti, E., and Bakker, A. B. (2011). The job demands–resources model: Challenges for future research. *SA Journal of Industrial Psychology, 37*, 1–9.

Demerouti, E., Bakker, A. B., Nachreiner, F., and Schaufeli, W. B. (2001). The job demands–resources model of burnout. *Journal of Applied Psychology, 86*, 499–512.

Dewe, P., and Cooper, C. (2012). *Well-being and Work: Towards a Balanced Agenda*. Basingstoke, UK: Palgrave Macmillan.

Dewe, P., O'Driscoll, M., and Cooper, C. (2010). *Coping with Work Stress: A Review and Critique*. Chichester, UK: Wiley-Blackwell.

Folkman, S. (1992). Improving coping assessment: Reply to Stone and Kennedy-Moore. In H. S. Friedman (Ed.), *Hostility, Coping and Health* (pp. 215–223). Washington, DC: American Psychological Association.

Folkman, S., and Moskowitz, J. T. (2004). Coping: Pitfalls and promise. *Annual Review of Psychology, 55*, 745–774.

Fox, M. L., Dwyer, D. J., and Ganster, D. C. (1993). Effects of stressful job demands and control on physiological and attitudinal outcomes in a hospital setting. *Academy of Management Journal, 38*, 289–318.

Freund, A. M., and Riediger, M. (2001). What I have and what I do: The role of resource loss and gain throughout life. *Applied Psychology: An International Review, 50*, 370–380.

Halbesleben, J. R. B. (2006). Sources of social support and burnout: A meta-analytic test of the conservation of resources model. *Journal of Applied Psychology, 91*, 1134–1145.

Hobfoll, S. E. (1989). Conservation of resources: A new attempt at conceptualizing stress. *American Psychologist, 44*, 513–524.

Hobfoll, S. E. (2001). The influence of culture, community, and the nested-self in the stress process: Advancing conservation of resources theory. *Applied Psychology: An International Review, 50*, 337–421.

Hobfoll, S. (2002). Social and psychological resources and adaptation. *Review of General Psychology, 6*, 307-324.

Hobfoll, S. E. (2011). Conservation of resources theory: Its implications for stress, health, and resilience. In S. Folkman (Ed.), *The Oxford Handbook of Stress, Health, and Coping* (pp. 127–147). Oxford: Oxford University Press.

Holman, D. J., and Wall, T. W. (2002). Work characteristics, learning-related outcomes, and strain: A test of competing direct effects, mediated, and moderated models. *Journal of Occupational Health Psychology, 7*, 283–301.

Ito, J. K., and Brotheridge, C. M. (2003). Resources, coping strategies, and emotional exhaustion: A conservation of resources perspective. *Journal of Vocational Behavior, 63*, 490–509.

Johnson, J. V., and Hall, E. M. (1988). Job strain, work place social support, and cardiovascular disease: A cross-sectional study of a random sample of the Swedish population. *American Journal of Public Health, 78*, 1336–1342.

Karasek, R. A. (1979). Job demands, job decision latitude, and mental strain: Implications for job redesign. *Administrative Science Quarterly, 24*, 285–308.

Karasek, R. A. (1998).Demand/control model: A social, emotional, and physiological approach to stress risk and active behaviour development. In S. M. Stellman (Gen. Ed.), *Encyclopaedia of Occupational Health and Safety*, 4th edn. (pp. 34.6–34.14). Geneva: International Labour Organization.

Lazarus, R. S. (1966). *Psychological Stress and the Coping Process*. New York: McGraw-Hill.

Lazarus, R. S. (1990). Theory based stress measurement. *Psychological Inquiry, 1*, 3–12.

Lazarus, R. S. (1993). Coping theory and research: Past, present and future. *Psychosomatic Medicine, 55*, 234–247.

Lazarus, R., S. (1995). Vexing research problems inherent in cognitive-mediational theories of emotion – and some solutions. *Psychological Inquiry, 6*, 183–196.

Lazarus, R. S (1999). *Stress and Emotion: A New Synthesis*. London: Free Association.

Lazarus, R. S. (2001). Relational meaning and discrete emotions. In K. R. Scherer, A. Schorr, and T. Johnstone (Eds.), *Appraisal Processes in Emotion: Theory, Methods, Research* (pp. 37–67). New York: Oxford University Press.

Luchman, J. N., and Gonzalez-Morales, M. G. (2013). Demands, control and support: A meta-analytic review of work characteristics interrelationships. *Journal of Occupational Health Psychology, 18*, 37–52.

Mackey, J. D., and Perrewé, P. L. (2014). The AAA (appraisals, attributions, adaptation) model of job stress: The critical role of self-regulation. *Organizational Psychology Review, 4*, 258–278.

Mark, G. M., and Smith, A. P. (2008). Stress models: A review and suggested new direction. In J. Houdmont and S. Leka (Eds.), *Occupational Health Psychology* (pp. 111–144). Nottingham: Nottingham University Press.

Meurs, J. A., and Perrewé, P. L. (2011). Cognitive activation theory of stress: An integrative theoretical approach to work stress. *Journal of Management, 37*, 1043–1068.

Nahrgang, J. D., Morgeson, F. P., and Hofmann, D. A. (2011). Safety at work: A meta-analytic investigation of the link between job demands, job resources, burnout, engagement and safety outcomes. *Journal of Applied Psychology, 96*, 71–94.

Parker, S. K., and Sprigg, C. A. (1999).Minimizing strain and maximizing learning: The role of job demands, job control and proactive personality. *Journal of Applied Psychology, 84*, 925–939.

Quick, J. C., and Gavin, J. H. (2001). Four perspectives on conservation of resources theory: A commentary. *Applied Psychology: An International Review, 50*, 392–400.

Rodriguez, I., Bravo, M. J., Peiro, J. M., and Schaufeli, W. (2001). The demands–control–support model, locus of control and job dissatisfaction: A longitudinal study. *Work and Stress, 15*, 97–114.

Schaufeli, W. B., Bakker, A. B., and Van Rhenen, W. (2009). How changes in job demands and resources predict burnout, work engagement and sickness absenteeism. *Journal of Organizational Behavior, 30*, 893–917.

Schaufeli, W. B., and Taris, T. W. (2014). A critical review of the job demands–resources model: Implications for improving work and health. In G. F. Bauer and O. Hammig (Eds.), *Bridging Occupational, Organizational and Public Health: A Transdisciplinary Approach* (pp. 43–68). Dordrecht: Springer.

Schwarzer, R. (2001). Stress, resources and proactive coping. *Applied Psychology: An International Review, 50*, 400–407.

Schwarzer R. (2004). Manage stress at work through preventive and proactive coping. In E. A. Locke (Ed.), *The Blackwell Handbook of Principles of Organizational Behaviour* (pp. 342–355). Oxford: Blackwell.

Schwarzer, R., and Taubert, S. (2002). Tenacious goal pursuits and strivings: Toward personal growth. In E. Frydenberg (Ed.), *Beyond Coping: Meeting Goals, Visions, and Challenges* (pp. 19–35). Oxford: Oxford University Press.

Synder, C. (1999). *Coping: The Psychology of What Works.* New York: Oxford University Press.

Snyder, C. R. (Ed.). (2001). *Coping with Stress: Effective People and Processes.* Oxford: Oxford University Press.

Somerfield, M., and McCrae, R. (2000). Stress and coping research: Methodological challenges, theoretical advances. *American Psychologist, 55*, 620–625.

Taris, T. W. (2006). Bricks without clay: On urban myths in occupational health psychology. *Work and Stress, 20*, 99–104.

Taris, T. W., Kompier, M. A. J., de Lange, A. H., Schaufeli, W. B., and Schreurs, P. J. G. (2003). Learning new behaviour patterns: A longitudinal test of Karasek's active learning hypothesis among Dutch teachers. *Work and Stress, 17*, 1–20.

Taris, T. W., Kompier, M. A. J., Geurts, S. A. E., Houtman, I. L. D., and van den Heuvel, F. F. M. (2010). Professional efficacy, exhaustion, and work characteristics among police officers: A longitudinal test of the learning-related predictions of the demand–control model. *Journal of Occupational and Organizational Psychology, 83*, 455–474.

Theorell, T., and Karasek, R. A. (1996). Current issues relating to psychosocial job strain and cardiovascular disease research. *Journal of Occupational Health Psychology, 1*, 9–26.

Thompson, M. S., and Cooper, C. L. (2001). A rose by any other name …: A commentary on Hobfoll's conservation of resources theory. *Applied Psychology: An International Review, 50*, 408–418.

Van den Broeck, A., de Cuyper, N., De Witte, H., and Vansteenkiste, M. (2010). Not all job demands are equal: Differentiating job hindrances and job challenges in the job demands–resources model. *European Journal of Work and Organizational Psychology, 19*, 735–759.

Van der Doef, M., and Maes, S. (1999). The job demand–control (–support) model and psychological well-being: A review of 20 years of empirical research. *Work and Stress, 13*, 87–114.

Xanthopoulou, D., Bakker, A. B., Demerouti, E., and Schaufeli, W. B. (2009). Reciprocal relationships between job resources, personal resources, and work engagement. *Journal of Vocational Behavior, 74*, 235–244.

27

Conservation of Resources Theory

Resource Caravans and Passageways in Health Contexts

Lucie Holmgreen, Vanessa Tirone, James Gerhart, and Stevan E. Hobfoll

Since 1988, conservation of resources (COR) theory (Hobfoll, 1988; 1989) has provided a framework within which to understand the processes involved in experiencing, coping with, and becoming resilient to chronic and traumatic stress. Its basic premises have been supported by empirical work in areas ranging from natural disaster recovery (e.g., Blaze and Shwalb, 2009) to occupational burnout (Gorgievski and Hobfoll, 2008). COR theory acknowledges that some circumstances – namely, those that threaten or deplete resources – are objectively stressful. It is an ecological and multileveled theory that seeks to understand individuals nested within their families, communities, and cultures (Hobfoll, 2001). This chapter outlines the tenets of COR theory and explains the role of resources therein. Principles and corollaries of the theory are delineated, and highlights of empirical support are provided for each. The chapter next reviews how COR theory has been used to study health, and finally explores the implications of the theory for health in both clinical and research contexts.

COR theory begins with the basic tenet that people are motivated to acquire, protect, and foster the acquisition of those things which they value – their resources (Hobfoll, 1988; 1998). Stress occurs as a response to any set of circumstances that results in the threatened or actual depletion of resources. The stress response, then, comprises an attempt primarily to limit losses and secondarily to maximize gains, with the loss aspect of the equation disproportionately dominant. As such, behaviors exhibited in stressful contexts may vary markedly in form, yet serve the common function of resource conservation. COR theory therefore emphasizes the objective nature of stress and stress responding over the individual appraisal process emphasized by Lazarus and Folkman (1984). Simultaneously, it focuses on the shared cultural dimensions of stress and resources, positing that although most resources are universally valued, their relative worth is likely to vary cross-culturally (Hobfoll, 2001).

The Handbook of Stress and Health: A Guide to Research and Practice, First Edition.
Edited by Cary L. Cooper and James Campbell Quick.
© 2017 John Wiley & Sons, Ltd. Published 2017 by John Wiley & Sons, Ltd.

The idea that resource loss is the crucial determinant of stress has been supported by a great deal of research. In particular, resource loss is the strongest predictor (or among the strongest predictors) of the severity and duration of psychological distress in the wake of natural disasters (e.g., Blaze and Shwalb, 2009; Freedy, Saladin, Kilpatrick, Resnick, and Saunders, 1994; Paul et al., 2014; Smith and Freedy, 2000). Similarly, resource loss robustly predicts psychological distress – above and beyond trauma exposure – in the context of interpersonal disasters such as ongoing armed conflict (e.g., Hobfoll, Hall, and Canetti, 2012). It has also been shown to predict psychological distress following more isolated incidents of extreme violence, even after controlling for other variables such as prior trauma exposure (e.g., Hobfoll, Tracy, and Galea, 2006). Finally, it is a crucial determinant of occupational burnout (Hobfoll and Shirom, 2000; Shirom, Toker, Melamed, Berliner, and Shapira, 2013).

Resources

COR theory begins with the assumption that much of human behavior and culture is organized around the acquisition and preservation of valued resources. The value of any given resource is determined by the interplay of both phylogenic and ontogenic contingencies. As a result, some resources are essential for survival and are inherently reinforcing across humans, while others are shaped through cultural and personal experiences and so vary cross-culturally, as well as between and within individuals over time. Resources are characterized by their external or internal locus relative to the individual. For example, vigor, hope, and self-efficacy are located within the individual and are key as they provide the energy and motivation to seek and maintain external resources such as stable employment and supportive relationships.

The value of a resource can be explained on a basic level by its necessity for survival. Other resources are less related to survival itself but to the protection of the individual and their status. Hobfoll and Lilly (1993) identified 74 resources in the Conservation of Resources Evaluation (COR-E). Primary resources such as food, health, housing, and clothing are directly related to survival and are valued cross-culturally. Secondary resources such as social support, employment, and community environment gain their reinforcing value through their associations with primary resources such as food and housing. Tertiary resources, such as accomplishment, financial credit, and social status, are culturally constructed and provide access to primary and secondary resources (Hobfoll and Lilly, 1993).

Resource Caravans

Resources tend to be highly correlated and nested within individuals, families, communities, and cultures. Observed correlations across distinct resources are referred to as *resource caravans* because resources tend to be accumulated by individuals and groups and carried across the life span (Hobfoll, 2001). The plausible sociocultural mechanisms that explain and facilitate the nesting of resources are referred to as *resource caravan passageways*. Whereas resource caravans and passageways explain the accumulation and preservation of resources, *risk factor caravans* refer to the constellations of hazards nested within individuals and communities which preclude and drain resources (e.g., Layne et al., 2009). The positive association between social support (external) and self-efficacy (internal) is an example of a resource caravan. Plausible resource caravan passageways that explain this association include the environmental conditioning of adaptive self-talk, modeled social problem solving, and emotion regulation within family, school, and peer groups.

Resource caravans and passageways are evident across levels of social interactions, including the individual, family, and community. The family is a particularly salient nexus where cultural, economic, and public policy processes meet to create resource and risk factor caravans. Socioeconomic status is related to income and linked to an array of health outcomes (Adler and Newman, 2002), and much wealth is nested within families. Families collect and conserve financial resources and share these resources through several mechanisms (Bowles, Gintes, and Groves, 2005). Factors such as intelligence, thought to be highly heritable, only explain a portion of variance in the transmission of wealth, and a multitude of factors may bridge wealth across generations, including better schooling, healthy environments, and financial inheritances (Bowles et al., 2005). In addition to these financial inheritances, families also collect and conserve resources through *inter vivos* transfers in the form of socialization and networking. Through the transmission of favors and the shaping of skills and traits, families provide crucial access to economic opportunities (Corak, 2013). Still, many resources are finite and economies are competitive, and so the same passageways that benefit some families may convey risk to others by consolidating wealth and opportunities among the few.

Risk factor caravans also occur at the level of the family unit in the form of intergenerational violence and trauma. Contextual theories of violence posit that some individuals exposed to childhood abuse may be at risk of engaging in subsequent violent behavior within the family system via behavioral modeling, potentiation of anger, substance abuse, and verbal rules that support aggressive behaviors (Bell and Naugle, 2008; Gardner and Moore, 2008). In turn, physical violence may co-occur with other aggressive characteristics, including hostility, criticism, and emotional volatility, that lead to escalating cycles of conflict and violence (Langhinrichsen-Rohling, Hankla, and Stormberg, 2004).

The community neighborhood is another nexus where cultural, economic, and public policy processes meet to create caravans and passageways. Whereas disparities in wealth and socioeconomic status may exist between families in the same neighborhood, social welfare benefits and other forms of public assistance may reduce disparities by providing equal opportunities in the form of education, effective policing, public sanitation, and equal health-care access. However, disparities are also observed across neighborhoods, school districts, and police precincts due to variability in the local tax base. Some low-income urban neighborhoods are marked by limited opportunities and resources, thus decreasing the probability that community members will obtain ample education and profitable careers that will support the local tax base. Through processes of modeling, chronic stress, and coercion these neighborhoods may also become saturated with interpersonal violence and vicarious exposure to trauma that substantially drain coping resources (Espino et al., 2015; Hobfoll et al., 2013). Escaping these risk factor caravans can be a tremendous task for an individual as obstacles are encountered at personal, family, and community levels.

COR Theory Principles and Corollaries

Principle 1

From the central tenet of COR theory (i.e., that humans are motivated to accrue and conserve resources), several principles and corollaries follow. Principle 1 states that "resource loss is

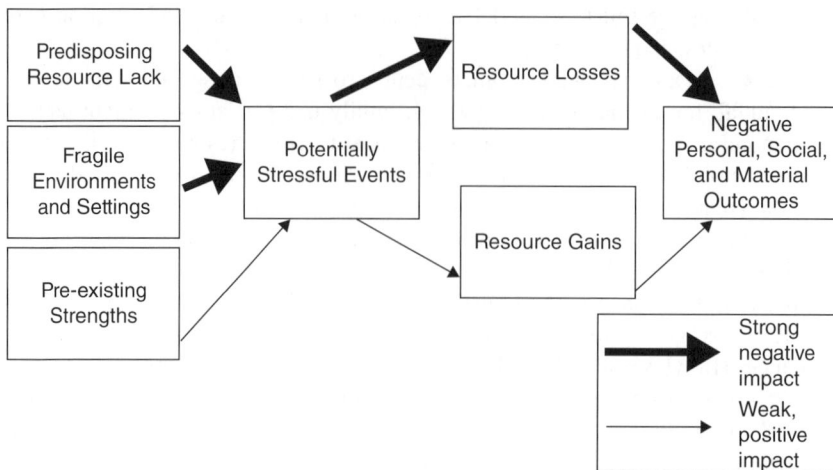

Figure 27.1   Disproportionate impact of lack and loss.

disproportionately more salient than is resource gain" (Hobfoll, 1998, p. 62), "in both degree and speed of impact" (Hobfoll, 2011, p. 128). Thus, loss of a given resource will have a greater psychological impact than will gain of the same resource (see Figure 27.1). This idea echoes the work of Kahneman and Tversky (1979), whose prospect theory posits a cognitive bias in favor of preventing loss as opposed to promoting an equal amount of gain. Principle 1 is supported by research demonstrating that stress responses are most consistently generated by major life events involving significant loss and not by those involving gain or mere transition (see Thoits, 1983, for a review; Hobfoll, 1988; 1989; 1991). In COR theory, a life event creates stress to the extent that it entails or threatens a cascade of resource loss.

This first principle has received a great deal of empirical support. Hobfoll and Lilly (1993) followed groups of individuals over time and found that psychological distress was predicted by resource loss and that resource gain was only important in predicting psychological distress in the context of resource loss. That is, gain by itself was not predictive of lower distress, but it became important in predicting distress level in those individuals who also experienced a significant amount of loss. The same holds for pregnant women, in whom resource loss is associated with psychological distress, and resource gains predict psychological distress only in the context of resource loss (Wells, Hobfoll, and Lavin, 1999). Similarly, psychological distress – including both probable posttraumatic stress disorder (PTSD) and probable depression – was predicted by resource loss but not by resource gain in New Yorkers following the terrorist attacks of September 11, 2001 (Hobfoll et al., 2006).

Principle 2

The second principle of COR theory states that "people must invest resources to protect against resource loss, recover from losses, and gain resources" (Hobfoll, 1998, p. 73). Principle 2 illustrates how the complex relationships among resource loss, gain, and distress impact a wide variety of health behaviors. People invest resources in protecting against health resource loss every time they promote healthy immune functioning by getting a good night's sleep or eating a balanced meal. They invest resources to recover from health resource loss when they take time off of work to recover from an illness or spend money to visit the doctor. Finally, they invest resources to gain further health resources when they spend time and money on exercising to improve their cardiovascular health.

Empirical support for this second principle encompasses everything from studies on self-regulation to the large body of work examining how we use social support and self-efficacy to cope with stress. Consider the example of resource loss and distress in pregnant women. Principles 1 and 2 suggest that a woman balancing multiple roles (e.g., expectant mother and full-time employee) is investing more resources and therefore expecting greater returns than is a woman in only one of these roles. To the extent that such gains do not materialize – that is, to the extent that a resource loss occurs – the employed expectant mother will be more vulnerable to experiencing psychological distress than will the other woman. In fact, Wells, Hobfoll, and Lavin (1997) found exactly that. This is key given the detrimental health impacts of psychological distress during pregnancy on mothers and babies (e.g., Schetter and Tanner, 2012). Other studies have found even more direct evidence of the negative health effects of low reward in the context of high resource investment. Specifically, Siegrist, Peter, Motz, and Strauer (1992) found that such conditions, studied within an occupational framework, predict heart attack and stroke as reliably as do the objective biomarkers of hypertension and left ventricular hypertrophy.

Corollary 1

> Several corollaries follow from COR theory's basic principles The first states that those with greater resources are less vulnerable to resource loss and more capable of orchestrating resource gain. Conversely, those with fewer resources are more vulnerable to resource loss and less capable of achieving resource gain … Moreover, those who lack resources are more likely to experience extreme consequences. (Hobfoll, 1998, p. 80)

This first corollary is intricately connected with the ideas of resource caravans and caravan passageways as one must have available either a personal cache of resources or access to shared resources in order to offset losses or potential losses. Crucially, lack of access creates vulnerability to further loss under stress. Corollary 1 predicts that those with lower social support, less access to health care, longer working hours, and less time and money to prepare healthy meals or exercise will be more vulnerable to the losses entailed by chronic diseases such as diabetes.

This corollary also suggests that individuals who have more resources to begin with, including cultural capital (e.g., Miller and McNamee, 1998) and privileged social status (white race, male sex, greater income) are less vulnerable to psychological distress following chronic or traumatic stress. Paul and colleagues (2014) recently found that not only did resource loss predict greater psychological distress in a sample of hurricane survivors, but that so did female sex and racial minority status. Similarly, among survivors of Hurricane Katrina, predictors of psychological distress included not only resource loss but also being black, being female, and being elderly (e.g., Adeola, 2009). This corollary also affects important medical outcomes. For example, storm-exposed black women were 1.45 times more likely than were white women to give birth to infants in hypoxic distress following Hurricane Andrew (Zahran, Snodgrass, Peek, and Weiler, 2010).

Consistent findings have emerged in populations exposed to ongoing or isolated mass violence. Among Palestinians exposed to ongoing sociopolitical violence, psychosocial resource loss more strongly predicted levels of psychological distress than did trauma exposure, benefit finding, or demographic variables (Heath, Hall, Canetti, and Hobfoll, 2013). Additionally, however, being a woman or an older and less educated man was associated with greater distress, which in turn led to greater domestic violence among men (Heath et al., 2013). Similarly, experiencing less resource loss, being of majority status (Jewish), being male, and having greater income and social support predicted psychological resistance or resilience trajectories in a nationally representative sample of Israelis during a particularly violent period (Hobfoll et al., 2009).

COR theory also predicts distress following traumatic events not involving heavy physical loss. Littleton, Grills-Taquechel, and Axsom (2009) studied Virginia Tech students shortly prior to the mass campus shooting that took place there in 2007, following up with them twice following the event. Students incurring more post-event loss of psychosocial resources (e.g., feeling successful, counting on loyalty from friends) reported greater psychological distress. Those who reported greater social resources *prior* to the shooting were less likely to incur psychosocial resource loss in its aftermath, thus protecting them to some extent from psychological distress.

Corollaries 2 and 3

The second and third corollaries of COR theory are closely linked and state that "those who lack resources are not only more vulnerable to resource loss, but that initial loss begets future loss" (Hobfoll, 1998, p. 81) and "initial resource gain begets further gain" (Hobfoll, 1998, p. 82), respectively. The best illustrations of the third corollary in COR theory are the resource caravan and caravan passageway concepts explored above. Loss spirals, though, given their crucial implications for physical and mental health, are explored in more detail here.

Loss spirals occur because stressors require coping in the form of resource investment. When resources are insufficient to begin with, resource investment may be enough to put a person over the edge, resulting in further losses (see Figure 27.2). Not surprisingly, loss spirals have been observed in populations experiencing ongoing sociopolitical conflict. Heath, Hall, Russ, Canetti and Hobfoll (2012) conducted a four-time-point, 18-month longitudinal study of Palestinians exposed to ongoing violence and conflict. They found that not only did resource loss predict psychological distress over time, but that psychological distress predicted resource loss over time, suggesting that a transactional process took place, with ongoing loss and distress perpetuating one another.

Traumatic events need not be ongoing to produce loss spirals, however; they have also been observed following single-incident traumatic events, including the mass shooting at Virginia Tech (Littleton et al., 2009). In particular, many students reported psychosocial resource losses two months after the event in the form of decrements in intrapersonal resources (e.g., optimism, feelings of pride) as well as interpersonal resources (e.g., companionship). These losses predicted not only posttraumatic symptomology four months later but also further psychosocial resource loss, resulting in a subset of students who appeared "stuck" in a loss spiral (Littleton et al., 2009). The inclusion of resource loss at two and six months after the trauma (along with pre-trauma distress and support) yielded a model accounting for a full 55 percent of the variance in posttraumatic symptomology at six months, illustrating ongoing psychosocial resource loss as a powerful predictor of posttraumatic distress.

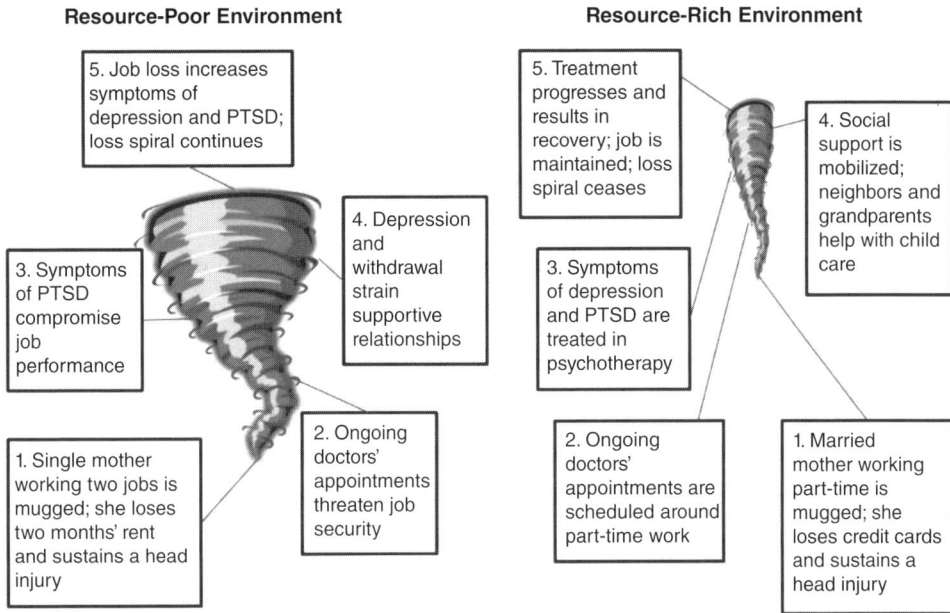

Resource-Poor Environment

5. Job loss increases symptoms of depression and PTSD; loss spiral continues

4. Depression and withdrawal strain supportive relationships

3. Symptoms of PTSD compromise job performance

2. Ongoing doctors' appointments threaten job security

1. Single mother working two jobs is mugged; she loses two months' rent and sustains a head injury

Resource-Rich Environment

5. Treatment progresses and results in recovery; job is maintained; loss spiral ceases

4. Social support is mobilized; neighbors and grandparents help with child care

3. Symptoms of depression and PTSD are treated in psychotherapy

2. Ongoing doctors' appointments are scheduled around part-time work

1. Married mother working part-time is mugged; she loses credit cards and sustains a head injury

Figure 27.2   Loss spirals in resource-poor and resource-rich environments.

Corollary 4

The fourth and final corollary suggested by COR theory is that "those who lack resources are likely to adopt a defensive posture to guard their resources" (Hobfoll, 1998, p. 83). Individuals with few psychological resources may adopt a denial coping strategy (Breznitz, 1983) to preserve their limited resources, despite this strategy's appearing inefficient or irrational. The long-term risk of defensive and avoidant coping is that while these behaviors are reinforced by limiting loss, they also decrease engagement with the broader environmental context, including potential access to other valued resources (Hayes, Luoma, Bond, Masuda, and Lillis, 2006). Thus, after a man receives a diagnosis of cancer, engaging in protective and avoidant strategies (e.g., denial coping) may be beneficial in the short term (e.g., by reducing emotional distress). In the long term, however, emotional distress may persist because his disengagement prevents him from perceiving that environmental contingencies have changed or may change (e.g., treatment options may prolong life and alleviate pain and suffering; Gerhart et al., 2015). In situations such as these, graded exposure can be introduced to increase the odds that the individual will engage in adaptive coping, accrue resources, and obtain a sense of mastery (Hayes et al., 2006).

Research Findings on COR Theory and Health

Stress and Medical Outcomes

Traumatic stress   Two major lines of research have explored the effects of resources on medical outcomes. The first focuses on the intersection between traumatic stress and health. Traumatic stress can be seen as a particularly rapid loss of highly valued resources (Hobfoll,

1991) and is associated with high levels of psychological distress, including PTSD. To the extent that trauma entails resource loss, traumatic events and PTSD are likely to carry with them crucial downstream physical health risks (Hobfoll, Vinokur, Pierce, and Lewandowski-Romps, 2012), an idea borne up by research (e.g., Pacella, Hruska, and Delahanty, 2013). Cook, Aten, Moore, Hook, and Davis (2013) studied university students affected by Hurricane Katrina and found that resource loss predicted psychological distress and poorer self-reported physical health. Similarly, flood victims reported greater psychological distress as well as physical symptoms (e.g., headaches, indigestion) to the extent that they experienced loss of psychosocial resources, such as time with loved ones and optimism (Smith and Freedy, 2000).

Perhaps most striking are studies employing specific biomarkers of health, illness, or immune functioning. Ironson and colleagues (2014) studied survivors of Hurricane Andrew, finding that resource loss (including damage to property) predicted both psychological distress and poorer immune function as measured by objective biomarkers. Pregnant women exposed to the same hurricane in their second or third trimester were 20–26 percent more likely to give birth to infants with hypoxic distress than were nonexposed women (Zahran et al., 2010). Similar observations have been made in populations exposed to sudden bereavement; Cankaya, Chapman, Talbot, Moynihan, and Duberstein (2009) studied female primary care patients and found that those who had experienced the sudden and unexpected loss of a loved one carried biomarkers of inflammatory immune responses.

Occupational burnout   Another body of work has examined the effect of resources on medical outcomes in an occupational context. A number of longitudinal studies have focused on burnout, a result of chronic stress characterized by diminished resources in the form of emotional exhaustion, physical fatigue, and cognitive weariness (e.g., Shirom, Westman, Shamai, and Carel, 1997). For example, increases in employees' burnout are marginally associated with increased risk for hyperlipidemia, and increases in vigor (i.e., a stronghold of emotional, physical, and cognitive energy) are associated with decreased risk (Shirom et al., 2013). Burnout is also associated with elevated risk for the development of type 2 diabetes and coronary heart disease (Melamed, Shirom, Toker, and Shapira, 2006; Toker, Melamed, Berliner, Zeltser, and Shapira, 2012). In a study of 3,368 employed individuals in Finland, burnout was associated with both prevalence and severity of cardiovascular disease among men and musculoskeletal problems among women as assessed by physicians (Honkonen et al., 2006). In a one-year longitudinal study of Swedish women, burnout predicted the presence of musculoskeletal pain and related disability, controlling for other physical health, psychological health, and work-related factors (Grossi, Thomtén, Fandiño-Losada, Soares, and Sundin, 2009).

Researchers have also examined the stress-buffering effect of resources on medical outcomes in an occupational context. In a 20-year follow-up study of healthy employees, vigor was associated with significantly decreased risk of mortality and diabetes (Shirom, Toker, Jacobson, and Balicer, 2010). Having a stimulating and engaging work environment is negatively associated with employees' waist circumference over time (Fried et al., 2013). In a ten-year follow-up study of first-year law students, optimism and social resources prospectively predicted better physical health (Segerstrom, 2007). Thus, jobs which chronically drain internal resources create vulnerability to disease and mortality. Meanwhile, the extent to which people are able to feel energized and stimulated in their occupation appears to have a protective effect on physical health.

Although having a demanding job can erode health, lacking employment can also be damaging. In a population-based study, recent and current unemployment was positively associated with anxiety, depression, and somatic concerns, and negatively associated with self-reported physical health (Kessler, Turner, and House, 1988). In the same study, internal resources, receipt of public assistance, and social support were negatively associated with deleterious outcomes of unemployment. Stressors had a stronger negative impact on physical and mental health outcomes for unemployed people than for employed people. Consistent with COR theory, the major stressor of losing a job most profoundly impacts people who initially lack resources and diminishes individuals' health functioning in the face of future stressors.

Psychological Functioning in Medical Populations and Health Risk Behaviors

COR theory has also been applied to biopsychosocial functioning in medical populations. Loss spirals and resource caravans in particular have been observed to play critical roles in areas of health functioning as diverse as postpartum transition, chronic illness management, and health risk behavior. For example, resource loss predicts increases in anger and depression as women transition from pregnancy to the postpartum period (Wells et al., 1999). The interrelatedness of resources and their loss was further illustrated in a qualitative study of stroke survivors and their families. Egbert, Koch, Coeling, and Ayers (2006) found that loss of mobility led to difficulties for stroke survivors in performing activities of daily life, including driving, which led to social isolation. In this study, the social support networks of patients served as conduits for community integration (Egbert et al., 2006), illustrating the ameliorating role of resource caravans.

Lane and Hobfoll (1992) studied patients with chronic obstructive pulmonary disease and found that losses incurred as a result of their chronic illness led to anger, which in turn led to anger in their partners. This pattern is highly suggestive of a continuing loss spiral whereby increasing loss may jeopardize supportive relationships, thus leading to further loss. Additionally, among women with chronic fatigue syndrome, resource loss and gain predict quality of life whereas fatigue and symptom severity do not (Taylor, Kulkarni, and Shiraishi, 2006). Resource loss is also associated with anxiety and depression among rheumatoid arthritis patients (Dirik and Karanci, 2010).

Resource loss also has important implications for obstetric populations. Pregnant women who have fewer material and psychosocial resources to begin with (less education, income, optimism, self-esteem, etc.) experience more psychological distress, which predicts lower birth weights and shorter gestational periods (Rini, Dunkel-Schetter, Wadhwa, and Sandman, 1999), likely leading to further cascades of resource loss for the mothers.

COR theory also has implications for health risk behaviors. For example, individuals who are experiencing resource loss may try to distract or distance themselves from stress by engaging in poor health behaviors, which can contribute to ongoing loss (Hobfoll and Shirom, 2000). Additionally, COR theory suggests that, in order for interventions with at-risk populations to be successful, they must be perceived as strengthening existing resources and building new resources. In fact, an AIDS prevention intervention based on this framework increased HIV-related knowledge and safe-sex behaviors among single, pregnant, inner-city women (Hobfoll, Jackson, Lavin, Britton, and Shepherd, 1994).

Health-Care Systems

As noted, COR theory explains how individuals nested within larger social networks experience stress when resources are lost or threatened. Thus, in addition to explaining individual patterns of health-related risk and resilience, COR theory can be applied to the health-care systems that serve individuals. Given the long hours and high stakes of loss within medical care, it is not surprising that physicians are at increased risk of burnout compared to the general population (Shanafelt et al., 2012).

COR theory also provides a framework for understanding research utilization by health-care systems, which bear the burden of balancing cost-effectiveness with the need to integrate new scientific findings into patient care practices. A recent study (Alvaro et al., 2010) found support for three key COR-consistent themes in the utilization of research in health-care settings by conducting interviews with research team members, government decision-makers, and health practitioners. First, organizational resources (e.g., availability of incentives to use research evidence, training in how to use research evidence) are required for adaptation and change. Second, the threat of loss leads to the protection of assets (e.g., fear of burnout contributes to practitioners' reluctance to commit time to research projects). Third, resources must be optimized for adaptation (e.g., ongoing education and training after research funding ends creates sustainable change). These findings speak to the importance of considering the resources in supporting research initiatives and providing state of the art patient care.

Implications

Research

We suggest several potentially fruitful lines of inquiry which use COR theory to enrich our understanding of health-related processes. First, further investigation is needed into the multileveled impacts of loss and trauma on both mental and physical health. For example, the important observed risk factor caravan of multiple physical and mental health comorbidities, may have its roots in the passageway (i.e., causal mechanism) of traumatic stress exposure and subsequent inflammatory processes and immune dysregulation (Canetti, Russ, Luborsky, Gerhart, and Hobfoll, 2014). Additionally, COR theory and its principles of loss spirals make explicit that stressors and stress responses can serve as both causes and effects of loss. Conceptualizing serious medical events (e.g., diagnosis of terminal illness, coping with chronic conditions, and acute incidents) as not only a result but also a cause of stress and loss can help researchers delineate the ways in which interventions can more efficiently interrupt these chains of events.

Another timely avenue of research involves understanding the impact of access to health care on physical and mental health outcomes. Research conducted in the state of Massachusetts, where state-supported universal health care was implemented before similar legislation was introduced on a federal level, suggests that accessible health-care coverage reduced all-cause mortality rates by 2.9 percent (Sommers, Long, and Baicker, 2014). Large-scale analysis of the impact of widespread availability of health-care resources on the United States population remains to be done.

Ongoing advancements in statistical analysis have provided many opportunities to explore complex data structures nested within individuals over time. Multilevel structural equation models will enable the testing of bottom-up or emergent effects such as the impact of individual trauma on higher-level constructs (Preacher, Zyphur, and Zhang, 2010). These may include applications of COR theory to understanding how trauma faced by individuals emerges at the community level to impact communal coping, school safety, neighborhood health-care utilization, and regional political climate.

Practice

Extant research suggests practical uses of COR theory to impact health-related outcomes. Trauma experts recommend that sense of safety, calming, senses of self- and community-efficacy, and hope are key resources to foster in primary, secondary, and tertiary interventions aimed at promoting positive psychological outcomes in the face of trauma (Hobfoll et al., 2007). These are likely also prime targets for interventions seeking to promote psychological and physical well-being in medical populations. Importantly, attempts to deliver these ingredients to medical patients using traditional mental health paradigms (e.g., a psychologist delivering individual outpatient psychotherapy) may be ineffective or inaccessible as the intervention is not delivered in the medical context. Rather, these resources can be taught and bolstered by other components of health-care organizations. This design provides natural cues to evoke coping strategies when they are needed most, leading to more effective reinforcement of behavior (Hobfoll et al., 2013).

For example, Stevens, Hobfoll, Anaya, and Finigan (2014) recently piloted a multilevel intervention for pregnant women with posttraumatic stress symptoms. Psychologists delivered brief coping-based psychotherapy to patients and trained obstetricians to deliver trauma-sensitive medical care to the same patients. The intervention led to moderate-to-large reductions in women's posttraumatic stress and depression symptoms postpartum. The dual-delivery nature of the intervention harnesses women's repeated visits with obstetricians as opportunities to boost resources (self-esteem, coping abilities) while simultaneously minimizing further resource depletion due to ongoing anxiety and avoidance of medical care. In this way, treatment interrupts the loss cycle that trauma history and PTSD would otherwise perpetuate. Patients with diverse medical needs will likely benefit from similar psychosocial integration of care.

Conclusions

COR theory offers a multileveled framework within which to understand responses to both chronic and traumatic stress. In particular, it suggests that stress results from any set of circumstances involving threatened or actual loss of valued resources. Furthermore, it is the desire to defend, conserve, and promote acquisition of these valued resources which motivates human behavior in the face of stress. Resources encompass both survival-promoting commodities and objects or conditions with shared cultural value. They do not tend to occur in isolation but rather cluster together, creating resource caravans. According to COR theory, loss is more salient than gain, and loss begets loss.

The theory has received a great deal of empirical support from a wide variety of research domains and designs and has proven particularly helpful in understanding the relationships between stress and physical health. In particular, it offers insights which have guided research on areas such as coping with chronic illness, medical consequences of natural disasters, and the long-term effects of occupational burnout. COR theory principles have implications not only for intervention in disasters entailing rapid and massive loss of personal and community resources but also for improving medical care – especially for those with histories of traumatic stress exposure. COR theory may prove especially useful in informing future research expanding our understanding of health-related resource caravan passageways – that is, the mechanisms by which risk and resilience factors cluster together and impact health.

References

Adeola, F. O. (2009). Mental health and psychosocial distress sequelae of Katrina: An empirical study of survivors. *Research in Human Ecology, 16*(2), 195–210.

Adler, N. E., and Newman, K. (2002). Socioeconomic disparities in health: Pathways and policies. *Health Affairs, 21*, 60–76. doi:10.1377/hlthaff.21.2.60

Alvaro, C., Lyons, R. F., Warner, G., Hobfoll, S. E., Martens, P. J., Labonté, R., and Brown, R. E. (2010). Conservation of resources theory and research use in health systems. *Implementation Science, 5*(79), 1–20. doi:10.1186/1748-5908-5-79

Bell, K. M., and Naugle, A. E. (2008). Intimate partner violence theoretical considerations: Moving towards a contextual framework. *Clinical Psychology Review, 28*, 1096–1107. doi:10.1016/j.cpr.2008.03.003

Blaze, J. T., and Shwalb, D. W. (2009). Resource loss and relocation: A follow-up study of adolescents two years after Hurricane Katrina. *Psychological Trauma: Theory, Research, Practice, and Policy, 1*, 312–322. doi:10.1037/a0017834

Bowles, S., Gintes, H., and Groves, M. O. (2005). *Unequal Changes: Family Background and Economic Success.* Princeton: Princeton University Press.

Breznitz, S. (1983). *The Denial of Stress.* Madison, CT: International Universities Press.

Canetti, D., Russ, E., Luborsky, J., Gerhart, J. I., and Hobfoll, S. E. (2014). Inflamed by the flames? The impact of terrorism and war on immunity. *Journal of Traumatic Stress, 27*, 345–352. doi:10.1002/jts.21920

Cankaya, B., Chapman, B. P., Talbot, N. L., Moynihan, J., and Duberstein, P. R. (2009). History of sudden unexpected loss is associated with elevated interleukin-6 and decreased insulin-like growth factor-1 in women in an urban primary care setting. *Psychosomatic Medicine, 71*, 914–919. doi:10.1097/psy.0b013e3181be7aa8

Cook, S. W., Aten, J. D., Moore, M., Hook, J. N., and Davis, D. E. (2013). Resource loss, religiousness, health, and posttraumatic growth following Hurricane Katrina. *Mental Health, Religion and Culture, 16*, 352–366. doi:10.1037/e700912007-001

Corak, M. (2013). Income inequality, equality of opportunity, and intergenerational mobility. *Journal of Economic Perspectives, 27*, 79–102. doi:10.1257/jep.27.3.79

Dirik, G., and Karanci, A. N. (2010). Psychological distress in rheumatoid arthritis patients: An evaluation within the conservation of resources theory. *Psychology and Health, 25*, 617–632. doi:10.1080/08870440902721818

Egbert, N., Koch, L., Coeling, H., and Ayers, D. (2006). The role of social support in the family and community integration of right-hemisphere stroke survivors. *Health Communication, 20*, 45–55. doi:10.1207/s15327027hc2001_5

Espino, S. R., Fletcher, J., Gonzalez, M., Precht, A., Xavier, J., and Matoff-Stepp, S. (2015). Violence screening and viral load suppression among HIV-positive women of color. *AIDS Patient Care and STDs, 29*(S1), S36–S41. doi:doi:10.1089/apc.2014.0275

Freedy, J. R., Saladin, M. E., Kilpatrick, D. G., Resnick, H. S., and Saunders, B. E. (1994). Understanding acute psychological distress following natural disaster. *Journal of Traumatic Stress, 7*, 257–273. doi:10.1007/bf02102947

Fried, Y., Laurence, G. A., Shirom, A., Melamed, S., Toker, S., Berliner, S., and Shapira, I. (2013). The relationship between job enrichment and abdominal obesity: A longitudinal field study of apparently healthy individuals. *Journal of Occupational Health Psychology, 18*, 458–468. doi:10.1037/a0033730

Gardner, F. L., and Moore, Z. E. (2008). Understanding clinical anger and violence: The anger avoidance model. *Behavior Modification, 32*, 897–912. doi:10.1177/0145445508319282

Gerhart, J., Asvat, Y., Lattie, E., O'Mahony, S., Duberstein, P., and Hoerger, M. (2015). Distress, delay of gratification and preference for palliative care in men with prostate cancer. *Psycho-Oncology.* Epub ahead of print. doi:10.1002/pon.3822

Gorgievski, M. J., and Hobfoll, S. E. (2008). Work can burn us out or fire us up: Conservation of resources in burnout and engagement. In J. R. B. Halbsleben (Ed.), *Handbook of Stress and Burnout in Health Care*, 3rd edn. (pp. 7–22). Hauppauge, NY: Nova Science.

Grossi, G., Thomtén, J., Fandiño-Losada, A., Soares, J. J., and Sundin, Ö. (2009). Does burnout predict changes in pain experiences among women living in Sweden? A longitudinal study. *Stress and Health*, 25, 297–311. doi:10.1002/smi.1281

Hayes, S. C., Luoma, J. B., Bond, F. W., Masuda, A., and Lillis, J. (2006). Acceptance and commitment therapy: Model, processes and outcomes. *Behaviour Research and Therapy*, 44, 1–25. doi:10.1016/j.brat.2005.06.006

Heath, N. M., Hall, B. J., Canetti, D., and Hobfoll, S. E. (2013). Exposure to political violence, psychological distress, resource loss, and benefit finding as predictors of domestic violence among Palestinians. *Psychological Trauma: Theory, Research, Practice, and Policy*, 5, 366–376. doi:10.1037/a0028367

Heath, N. M., Hall, B. J., Russ, E. U., Canetti, D., and Hobfoll, S. E. (2012). Reciprocal relationships between resource loss and psychological distress following exposure to political violence: An empirical investigation of COR theory's loss spirals. *Anxiety, Stress and Coping*, 25, 679–695. doi:10.1080/10615806.2011.628988

Hobfoll, S. E. (1988). *The Ecology of Stress*. Washington, DC: Hemisphere.

Hobfoll, S. E. (1989). Conservation of resources: A new attempt at conceptualizing stress. *American Psychologist*, 44, 513–524. doi:10.1037/0003-066x.44.3.513

Hobfoll, S. E. (1991). Traumatic stress: A theory based on rapid loss of resources. *Anxiety Research*, 4, 187–197. doi:10.1080/08917779108248773

Hobfoll, S. E. (1998). *Stress, Culture, and Community: The Psychology and Physiology of Stress*. New York: Plenum Press.

Hobfoll, S. E. (2001). The influence of culture, community, and the nested-self in the stress process: Advancing conservation of resources theory. *Applied Psychology*, 50, 337–421. doi:10.1111/1464-0597.00062

Hobfoll, S. E. (2011). Conservation of resources theory: Its implication for stress, health, and resilience. In S. Folkman (Ed.), *The Oxford Handbook of Stress, Health, And Coping* (pp. 127–147). New York: Oxford University Press.

Hobfoll, S. E., Hall, B. J., and Canetti, D. (2012). Political violence, psychological distress, and perceived health: A longitudinal investigation in the Palestinian authority. *Psychological Trauma: Theory, Research, Practice, and Policy*, 4, 9–21. doi:10.1037/a0018743

Hobfoll, S. E., Jackson, A. P., Lavin, J., Britton, P. J., and Shepherd, J. B. (1994). Reducing inner-city women's AIDS risk activities: A study of single, pregnant women. *Health Psychology*, 13, 397–403. doi:10.1037/0735-7028.38.5.518

Hobfoll, S. E., and Lilly, R. S. (1993). Resource conservation as a strategy for community psychology. *Journal of Community Psychology*, 21, 128–148. doi:10.1002/1520-6629(199304)21:2<128::AID-JCOP2290210206>3.0.CO;2-5

Hobfoll, S. E., Palmieri, P. A., Johnson, R. J., Canetti-Nisim, D., Hall, B. J., and Galea, S. (2009). Trajectories of resilience, resistance, and distress during ongoing terrorism: The case of Jews and Arabs in Israel. *Journal of Consulting and Clinical Psychology*, 77, 138–148. doi:10.1037/a0014360

Hobfoll, S. E., and Shirom, A. (2000). Conservation of resources theory: Applications to stress and management in the workplace. In R.T. Golembiewski (Ed.), *Handbook of Organization Behavior*, 2nd rev. edn. (pp. 57–81). New York: Dekker.

Hobfoll S. E., Stevens N. R., Gerhart J. I., Clift, A. T., Vechiu, C. V., Verela, V., … Fung, H. (2013). Traumatic stress, health, and strategies for multi-level bio-psycho-social interventions. In K. Moore, K. Kaniasty, P. Buchwald, and A. Sesé (Eds.), *Stress and Anxiety: Applications to Health and Well-Being, Work Stressors, and Assessment* (pp. 7–16). Berlin: Logos.

Hobfoll, S. E., Tracy, M., and Galea, S. (2006). The impact of resource loss and traumatic growth on probable PTSD and depression following terrorist attacks. *Journal of Traumatic Stress*, 19, 867–878. doi:10.1002/jts.20166

Hobfoll, S. E., Vinokur, A. D., Pierce, P. F., and Lewandowski-Romps, L. (2012). The combined stress of family life, work, and war in Air Force men and women: A test of conservation of resources theory. *International Journal of Stress Management*, 19, 217–237. doi:10.1037/a0029247

Hobfoll, S. E., Watson, P., Bell, C. C., Bryant, R. A., Brymer, M. J., Friedman, M. J., … Ursano, R. J. (2007). Five essential elements of immediate and mid–term mass trauma intervention: Empirical evidence. *Psychiatry*, 70, 283–315. doi:10.1521/psyc.2007.70.4.283

Honkonen, T., Ahola, K., Pertovaara, M., Isometsä, E., Kalimo, R., Nykyri, E., … Lönnqvist, J. (2006). The association between burnout and physical illness in the general population: Results from the Finnish Health 2000 study. *Journal of Psychosomatic Research*, 61, 59–66. doi:10.1016/j.jpsychores.2005.10.002

Ironson, G., Kumar, M., Greenwood, D., Schneiderman, N., Cruess, D., Kelsch, C. B., … Baum, A. (2014). Post-traumatic stress symptoms, intrusive thoughts, and disruption are longitudinally related to elevated cortisol and catecholamines following a major hurricane. *Journal of Applied Biobehavioral Research*, 19, 24–52. doi:10.1111/jabr.12014

Kahneman D., and Tversky A. (1979). Prospect theory: An analysis of decision under risk. *Econometrica, 47*, 263–291. doi:10.2307/1914185

Kessler, R. C., Turner, J. B., and House, J. S. (1988). Effects of unemployment on health in a community survey: Main, modifying, and mediating effects. *Journal of Social Issues, 44*(4), 69–85. doi:10.1111/j.1540-4560.1988.tb02092.x

Lane, C., and Hobfoll, S. E. (1992). How loss affects anger and alienates potential supporters. *Journal of Consulting and Clinical Psychology, 60*, 935–942. doi:10.1037/0022-006x.60.6.935

Langhinrichsen-Rohling, J., Hankla, M., and Stormberg, C. D. (2004). The relationship behavior networks of young adults: A test of the intergenerational transmission of violence hypothesis. *Journal of Family Violence, 19*, 139–151. doi:10.1023/b:jofv.0000028074.35688.4f

Layne, C. M., Beck, C., Rimmasch, H., Southwick, J., Moreno, M., and Hobfoll, S. (2009). Promoting "resilient" posttraumatic adjustment in childhood and beyond. In D. Brom, R. Pat-Horenczyk, and J. Ford (Eds.), *Treating Traumatized Children: Risk, Resilience, and Recovery* (pp. 13–47). London: Routledge.

Lazarus, R. S., and Folkman, S. (1984). *Stress, Appraisal, and Coping*. New York: Springer.

Littleton, H., Grills-Taquechel, A., and Axsom, D. (2009). Impaired and incapacitated rape victims: Assault characteristics and post-assault experiences. *Violence and Victims, 24*, 439–457. doi:10.1891/0886-6708.24.4.439

Melamed, S., Shirom, A., Toker, S., and Shapira, I. (2006). Burnout and risk of type 2 diabetes: A prospective study of apparently healthy employed persons. *Psychosomatic Medicine, 68*, 863–869. doi:10.1097/01.psy.0000242860.24009.f0

Miller, R. K., and McNamee, S. J. (1998). *Inheritance and Wealth in America*. New York: Springer.

Pacella, M. L., Hruska, B., and Delahanty, D. L. (2013). The physical health consequences of PTSD and PTSD symptoms: A meta-analytic review. *Journal of Anxiety Disorders, 27*, 33–46. doi:10.1016/j.janxdis.2012.08.004

Paul, L. A., Price, M., Gros, D. F., Gros, K. S., McCauley, J. L., Resnick, H. S., … Ruggiero, K. J. (2014). The associations between loss and posttraumatic stress and depressive symptoms following Hurricane Ike. *Journal of Clinical Psychology, 70*, 322–332. doi:10.1002/jclp.22026

Preacher, K. J., Zyphur, M. J., and Zhang, Z. (2010). A general multilevel SEM framework for assessing multilevel mediation. *Psychological Methods, 15*, 209–233. doi:10.1037/a0020141

Rini, C. K., Dunkel-Schetter, C., Wadhwa, P. D., and Sandman, C. A. (1999). Psychological adaptation and birth outcomes: The role of personal resources, stress, and sociocultural context in pregnancy. *Health Psychology, 18*, 333–345. doi:10.1037/0278-6133.18.4.333

Schetter, C. D., and Tanner, L. (2012). Anxiety, depression and stress in pregnancy: Implications for mothers, children, research, and practice. *Current Opinion in Psychiatry, 25*, 141–148. doi:10.1097/yco.0b013e3283503680

Segerstrom, S. C. (2007). Optimism and resources: Effects on each other and on health over 10 years. *Journal of Research in Personality, 41*, 772–786. doi:10.1016/j.jrp.2006.09.004

Shanafelt, T. D., Boone, S., Tan, L., Dyrbye, L. N., Sotile, W., Satele, D., … Oreskovich, M. R. (2012). Burnout and satisfaction with work–life balance among US physicians relative to the general US population. *Archives of Internal Medicine, 172*, 1377–1385. doi:10.1001/archinternmed.2012.3199

Shirom, A., Toker, S., Jacobson, O., and Balicer, R. D. (2010). Feeling vigorous and the risks of all-cause mortality, ischemic heart disease, and diabetes: A 20-year follow-up of healthy employees. *Psychosomatic Medicine, 72*, 727–733. doi:10.1097/psy.0b013e3181eeb643

Shirom, A., Toker, S., Melamed, S., Berliner, S., and Shapira, I. (2013). Burnout and vigor as predictors of the incidence of hyperlipidemia among healthy employees. *Applied Psychology: Health and Well-Being, 5*, 79–98. doi:10.1111/j.1758-0854.2012.01071.x

Shirom, A., Westman, M., Shamai, O., and Carel, R. S. (1997). Effects of work overload and burnout on cholesterol and triglycerides levels: The moderating effects of emotional reactivity among male and female employees. *Journal of Occupational Health Psychology, 2*, 275–288. doi:10.1037/1076-8998.2.4.275

Siegrist, J., Peter, R., Motz, W., and Strauer, B. E. (1992). The role of hypertension, left ventricular hypertrophy and psychosocial risks in cardiovascular disease: Prospective evidence from blue-collar men. *European Heart Journal, 13*(suppl. D), 89–95. doi:10.1093/eurheartj/13.suppl_d.89

Smith, B. W., and Freedy, J. R. (2000). Psychosocial resource loss as a mediator of the effects of flood exposure on psychological distress and physical symptoms. *Journal of Traumatic Stress, 13*(2), 349–357. doi:10.1023/a:1007745920466

Sommers, B. D., Long, S. K., and Baicker, K. (2014). Changes in mortality after Massachusetts health care reform: A quasi-experimental study. *Annals of Internal Medicine, 160*, 585–593. doi:10.7326/m13-2275

Stevens, N. R., Hobfoll, S. E., Anaya, H. A., and Finigan, M. (2014). Improving pregnancy outcomes for survivors of abuse using trauma-sensitive obstetric care. Symposium conducted at the annual meeting of the International Society for Traumatic Stress Studies, Miami, Nov.

Taylor, R. R., Kulkarni, S., and Shiraishi, Y. (2006). Conservation of resources and quality of life in individuals with chronic fatigue syndrome. *Journal of Chronic Fatigue Syndrome, 13*(4), 3–15. doi:10.1300/j092v13n04_02

Thoits, P. A. (1983). Multiple identities and psychological well-being: A reformulation and test of the social isolation hypothesis. *American Sociological Review, 48*, 174–187. doi:10.2307/2095103

Toker, S., Melamed, S., Berliner, S., Zeltser, D., and Shapira, I. (2012). Burnout and risk of coronary heart disease: A prospective study of 8,838 employees. *Psychosomatic Medicine, 74*, 840–847. doi:10.1097/psy.0b013e31826c3174

Wells, J. D., Hobfoll, S. E., and Lavin, J. (1997). Resource loss, resource gain, and communal coping during pregnancy among women with multiple roles. *Psychology of Women Quarterly, 21*, 645–662. doi:10.1111/j.1471-6402.1997.tb00136.x

Wells, J. D., Hobfoll, S. E., and Lavin, J. (1999). When it rains, it pours: The greater impact of resource loss compared to gain on psychological distress. *Personality and Social Psychology Bulletin, 25*, 1172–1182. doi:10.1177/01461672992512010

Zahran, S., Snodgrass, J. G., Peek, L., and Weiler, S. (2010). Maternal hurricane exposure and fetal distress risk. *Risk Analysis, 30*, 1590–1601. doi:10.1111/j.1539-6924.2010.01453.x

Part Five

Enhancing Individual Well-Being

28

Enhancing Mental Well-Being

Wayne Martin, Brian Jamel Dixon, and Helen Thomas

> To exist in the fleet joy of becoming, to be a channel for life as it flashes by in its gaiety and courage, cool water glistening in the sunlight – in a world of sloth, anxiety, and aggression. To exist for the future of others without being suffocated by their present.
>
> Dag Hammarskjold, *Markings*

How to enhance mental well-being in the current human condition? How to experience the "fleet joy of becoming, to be a channel for life" (Hammarskjold, 1964)? How does one be as "cool water glistening in the sunlight" (Hammarskjold, 1964) in a world of apathy, anguish, and violence without being stifled and discouraged by the state of affairs now? How, in other words, to achieve Hammarskjold's articulation of mental well-being or, for that matter, any other articulation?

The Healthy People 2020 initiative offers a useful definition of mental well-being:

> *Mental well-being* includes being satisfied with one's life; balancing positive and negative emotions; accepting one's self; finding purpose and meaning in one's life; seeking personal growth, autonomy, and competence; believing one's life and circumstances are under one's control; and generally experiencing optimism. (ODPHP, 2016)

We will use this definition of mental well-being as our working one, recognizing that attaining it is beyond most people's skill sets at this time. We also recognize that psychological functioning may be viewed on a spectrum, as framed in the DSM-5 (American Psychiatric Association, 2013). However, mental well-being extends in a positive direction beyond the DSM-5's endpoint of adequate functioning. It could in fact stretch to include exceptional functioning on multilevels; thus, Mohandas K. Gandhi could say, at the height of his strenuous and life-risking activities to liberate India from the British Empire: "I am always on vacation" (Easwaran, 2013).

The Handbook of Stress and Health: A Guide to Research and Practice, First Edition.
Edited by Cary L. Cooper and James Campbell Quick.
© 2017 John Wiley & Sons, Ltd. Published 2017 by John Wiley & Sons, Ltd.

The above definition does not obviate the stresses of life. Rather, it suggests having an arsenal of coping skills at the ready that will result in life's problems being transmogrified into moderate and beneficial challenges. Selye emphasized, "Stress is not what happens to you, but how you react to it" (as cited in Szabo, Tache, and Somogyi, 2012, p. 477). An endocrinologist, Selye had coined the term "biologic stress response" to describe a general biological alarm system observed in rats, but he also coined the term "eustress" to describe what Levi (1971) had discovered: some stress is activated by positive emotions and promotes achievement and optimal performance (Selye, 1974; 1977; Szabo et al., 2012).

We cannot live utterly stress-free lives. Mental well-being depends upon being able to interpret and transform our distress by finding tools for growth. Mental well-being intertwines with spiritual and physical well-being. Likewise, many of the approaches to mental well-being interact synergistically. Hence a constellation of approaches support and activate mental well-being. This chapter will explore some of the more relevant.

Before we get to the metaphysical aspects of mental well-being, let us acknowledge that mental well-being is difficult to attain without a certain base level of physical well-being. Maximizing a pragmatic approach to enhance mental well-being includes accepting biochemical laws before adding plausibly attainable mental skills (aka realistic goals).

Enhancing mental well-being starts with grounded, objective physical well-being defined as parameters that can be quantified and physically measured. The established guidelines for sleep, diet/caloric intake, water consumption, and exercise are thoroughly researched and depend on age, size, and gender. Accessing the appropriate individualized health resources (e.g., licensed health professionals, trusted websites) is critical in maximizing all aspects of well-being.

Sleep

Good sleep is absolutely critical to mental well-being. Decrements in sleep impair performance (Cohen et al., 2010). We now understand that sleep restores psychological functioning. For example, during sleep channels open within the brain to facilitate the removal of toxic waste substances (Xie et al., 2013). Electroencephalography (EEG) employed in longitudinal studies has shown that a history of insomnia increases the likelihood that the subject will also develop depression (Ford and Kamerow, 1989; Breslau, Roth, Rosenthal, and Andreski, 1996) and is also associated with anxiety (Harvey, 2000; 2002; Harvey and Greenhall, 2003).

Many factors may enhance sleep, but medications do not appear to be one of them. In a research study report in the *British Medical Journal*, researchers found that once the placebo effect is accounted for, the efficacy of drugs on sleeplessness is negligible. About 20 percent of medication users also experience side effects (Huedo-Medina, Kirsch, Middlemass, Klonizakis, and Siriwardena, 2012).

Psychological factors such as allostatic load or acute worries also may limit sleep; thus mindfulness helps practitioners improve sleep, perhaps through stress reduction (Black, O'Reilly, Olmstead, Breen, and Irwin, 2015). Habits can support sleep. Stimulus control protocols, a behavioral process whereby the individual learns to associate being in bed with falling asleep and maintaining sleep, have proven efficacy (Morin, Culbert, and Schwartz, 1994). Artificial light impairs the natural production of melatonin and disrupts natural circadian rhythms (Czeisler, 2013) so the environment of light may need to be addressed to maximize sleep.

Diet

A balanced diet is critical to objective well-being and provides a foundation for subjective well-being. The process starts at birth in the form of acquiring "good gut" bacteria. Studies show that infants delivered by Caesarean section have fewer of these healthy microbes compared to their vaginal delivery counterparts (Jakobsson et al., 2013).

From that moment on, what we consume builds a profile of microflora that affects our body functions, immune systems, and our thoughts. The brain and gut communicate through bidirectional use of the same neurotransmitter, serotonin (O'Mahony, Clarke, Borre, Dinan, and Cryan, 2015); dysregulation of serotonin has been long implicated in diagnoses of multiple mental illnesses, including depression and anxiety (Wang and Kasper, 2014).

Our eating habits are an amalgam of biopsychosocial influences. Making mindful decisions regarding diet should include a personal and thoughtful review of "needs" (the scientifically established biological requirements) versus "wants" (psychological and social pressures encouraging overconsumption). Though an ideal mix of proteins, fats, and carbohydrates is reasonably well known, the modern consumer often overlooks the science and instead consumes what "feels" best. While there is a psychosocial benefit from certain delicious foods, keeping in mind basic biochemistry is best.

The goal of a great diet is balanced biochemistry that provides optimal energy efficiency for a specific body and situation. Newer data suggest controlled intermittent fasting may also be beneficial for brain health (van Praag, Fleshner, Schwartz, and Mattson, 2014). A careful review of diet and conscientious consumption empowers individuals and leads to enhanced mental well-being. The use of supplements like vitamins, minerals, and botanicals to maximize nutrient intake is unnecessary with a balanced diet (National Institute of Health, 2013).

Because the word "diet" has negative cultural connotations and typically only encompasses items holding caloric value, thinking in terms of "consumption" is a less judgmental and mentally helpful approach. Consumption of quality calories is important as it provides the energy that fuels the body to engage in constructive, affirming activities.

Water

Consumption of appropriate amounts of water increases fluidity of body functions, and improves interactions between systems. Water is made up of a polar molecule, one side negatively charged, the other positively charged. As a result, this ingredient is constantly moving, much like the human condition over the course of a lifetime. Water, in many ways, is life.

Adequate water must be ingested because metabolized food does not supply enough water to fulfill bodily needs. Water carries needed minerals and nutrients to the body. Water complements a good diet for maximal objective well-being; even mild dehydration can impair cognitive performance. Although in the past a water deficit of 2 percent in the body was thought to impair cognitive performance, it is now believed that a body water deficit of a mere 1 percent may impede cognitive performance (Riebl and Davy, 2013).

Many people do not drink enough water on a daily basis. Exploring the environmental (e.g., availability of sources, cost, quality) and psychosocial influences (e.g., busy schedules, sedentary lifestyles, social pressures) on water intake helps individuals take control of their health and identify ways to improve their personal hydration status.

It must be recognized that food and drink are powerful social tools. A balanced meal combines mindful consumption with positive psychosocial elements. Therefore, mindful consumption of helpful food and adequate water in a personally meaningful environment can lead to enhanced well-being.

Exercise

Well-being is enhanced through physical and mental activity. Thinking of mind and body as a spectrum rather than as two distinct entities means that personally meaningful activity can occur within both realms. Each type of activity has its place on the spectrum; valuing one over the other leads to guilt and decreased well-being.

Physical activity, defined by the World Health Organization as "any bodily movement produced by skeletal muscles that requires energy expenditure" (WHO, 2016) injects energy into cellular systems. That energy promotes movement of water, breaks down fats and carbohydrates, and builds protein. Physical exercise elevates the mood, promotes physical health, and sharpens cognitive function. When done consistently, physical exercise helps insulate a person against stress, both in the amount of distress one can endure without negative consequences and the ability to bounce back resiliently when negative consequences occur (van Praag et al., 2014).

Mental exercise is just as important. Mental activity uses glucose to fuel thinking and emotions and provides context and meaning for our lives. Both types of activity perpetuate a sense of forward momentum, building excitement and optimism, two strongly positive human feelings.

The key lies in finding activities which are meaningful to the individual performing them while actively combating boredom and avoiding hyperarousal (an equally disturbing state). In fact, a Johns Hopkins University study found that even dementia patients decrease in agitation when they are engaged in personally meaningful activities such as pursuing hobbies, making or listening to music, art work, playing cards, and so on (Brooks, 2013). Given that an individual's emotional and physical states change frequently, combining a range of low energy exercises (e.g., tai chi, meditation, walking, reading) with high energy exercises (aerobics, trivia, competitions) combats boredom. Varying the type of personalized meaningful exercise, both physical and mental, directly enhances well-being by combating boredom (Martin, Sadlo, and Stew, 2006).

At the nexus of physical and mental well-being are feedback loops.

Feedback Loops

Csikszentmihalyi (1997) promotes the importance of feedback loops in facilitating the "flow" state of mind. Although feedback loops abound in life, next we examine feedback loops intentionally constructed to cultivate mental well-being: biofeedback, neurofeedback, and games.

Biofeedback and neurofeedback use sophisticated equipment to measure physiology and then feed that information back to the subject (Peek, 2003). This feedback loop provides an opportunity for the subject to engage with their own physiology as though they were looking in a high-tech mirror. The individual may then make adjustments to their physiology. Biofeedback refers to when the source physiology falls under management of the peripheral nervous system; neurofeedback entails the measurement and feedback of the central nervous system.

As with other biobehavioral interventions, the bulk of research and clinical attention has focused on biofeedback and neurofeedback for the treatment of health problems. Nevertheless, some promising psychophysiological work has been directed to mental well-being. Feedback loops may serve as a bridge between physical and mental well-being.

Clinical biofeedback often promotes self-regulation by training the subject to attain calm and positive states of mind consistent with mental well-being. For example, heart rate variability biofeedback (HRVB) provides real-time information about cardiac dynamics and ongoing changes in pulse rate as it reflects breathing, responses to stress, and internal states (Lehrer and Gevirtz, 2014). This can be used to increase a person's capacity to attune to positive states like relaxation and calm, as well as to recognize and understand stress. McCraty, Atkinson, Tiller, Rein, and Watkins (1995) noted that HRVB signals alter significantly in response to positive versus negative internal states and hence they may be employed to train subjects to access and utilize positive states consistent with mental well-being. The Heartmath approach advocated by McCraty emphasizes the deliberate cultivation of these positive mental states.

EEG-neurofeedback, which utilizes brain wave activity in the feedback loop, has been employed to facilitate improved mental states and performance. While this form of feedback utilizes as its base the EEG signal, a wide range of targeted bandwidths and protocols have emerged within clinical practice and research. While a thorough review of findings is beyond the scope of this work, Gruzelier (2014a) reviewed protocols for optimizing cognition and affect, as well as creativity and the performing arts (Gruzelier, 2014b). Outcomes include improved well-being, attention, cognitive skills, memory, mood, and creative performance.

Jane McGonigal (2011) maintains that electronic games create a reality in which human needs may be satisfied, with the accompanying gratification and sense of well-being. She notes that there are over 600 million gamers worldwide because virtual reality is more satisfying of some of our needs than is reality, which is in her framing "broken." McGonigal says:

> Today many of us are suffering from a vast and primal hunger. But it is not a hunger for food – it is a hunger for more and better engagement from the world around us … many gamers have already figured out how to use the immersive power of play to distract themselves from their hunger: a hunger for more satisfying work, for a stronger sense of community, and for a more engaging and meaningful life. (p. 6)

Games, McGonigal claims, deliver intrinsic rewards. Achieving a new level in a game also triggers norepinephrine, epinephrine, and dopamine, a "potent cocktail" that leaves us feeling "satisfied, proud, and highly aroused" (p. 47).

Games are intrinsically and neurologically rewarding in much the same way humor is. Dopamine, a neurotransmitter that is related to pleasure and reward, is also triggered by making someone laugh or smile or by being made to laugh ourselves. We are, in fact, rewarded with a jolt of dopamine when we solve the puzzle of a riddle or joke or discover incongruity, the basis of humor (Berns, 2004). Metcalf and Felible (1992) bemoan "terminal professionalism" which deadens the workplace, increases everyone's stress, and makes life joyless (p. 15). Even in stressful situations, if one cultivates humor, they say, one has "the ability to see the absurdity in difficult situations, the ability to take yourself lightly while taking your work seriously, and a disciplined sense of joy in being alive" (p. 15).

Mindfulness

It is worth noting that biofeedback and neurofeedback can have a certain experiential overlap with the practice of meditation, accessing similar mind states, albeit by very different means.

According to Herbert Benson (2000), practices of contemplation (meditation among others) bring about a "Relaxation Response" which is incompatible with stress responses and thus contributes to well-being. For example, in the Relaxation Response, heart rate, respiration, and blood lactate decrease, among other measures of restfulness and enhanced well-being. Thus meditation and other reflection practices that still the mind contribute to states of higher well-being.

Kabat-Zinn's mindfulness meditation interventions and mindfulness based stress reduction (MBSR) were framed as a nonsectarian version of the mindfulness incorporated within the Buddhist tradition and have demonstrated efficacy with numerous health and mental health problems (Kabat-Zinn, 2005). As with other approaches discussed in this chapter, mindfulness applications have largely been applied to remedying health and mental health problems, and this body of research reveals ways that mindfulness strengthens mental well-being.

Kabat-Zinn (2005) defines mindfulness as being focused in the present moment, acknowledging and accepting the thoughts, emotions, and physical sensations experienced in that moment without judgment. Formal mindfulness practice may be performed for 45 or more minutes daily, and shorter informal practices are designed to be incorporated into daily life.

Research has demonstrated robust effects of mindfulness interventions in support of increased mental well-being. Chiesa and Serretti (2009) found that mindfulness interventions had a strong impact on stress. It may ease negative emotions such as anxiety (Green and Bieling, 2012) and depression (Strauss, Cavanagh., Oliver, and Pettman, 2014). Others have documented favorable responses to mindfulness (Foureur, Besley, Burton, Yu, and Crisp, 2013). Quality of life has also been shown to improve with mindfulness interventions (Kuyken et al., 2008; Godfrin and van Heeringen, 2010; Hassed, de Lisle, Sullivan, and Pier, 2009).

Intrapersonal and Interpersonal Mental Well-Being

Intrapersonal well-being can be affected by choice and effort, although circumstances and one's genetic happiness "set point" play roles (Lyubomirsky, Sheldon, and Schkade, 2005). Intrapersonal mental well-being is evident in individuals who are able to engage in intentional activities on the cognitive, behavioral, and volitional levels (Lyubomirsky et al., 2005). The intentional activities may be chosen in a subjective way or they may be chosen on the basis of universals that have been shown to contribute to well-being: for example, a sense of belonging, self-efficacy, positive reframing of circumstances (Lyubomirsky et al., 2005). Then the intentional activities must be initiated, which requires self-regulatory effort and will, and sustenance. Examples of such intentional activities are acts of kindness, which Lyubomirsky, King, and Diener (2004) found enhanced people's subjective rating of their own happiness.

Mental well-being also depends on our connectivity with others – one's interpersonal life. Relationships with the persons with whom one lives and one's community are crucial to interpersonal mental well-being. The desire for humans to feel at home, to know and be known is universal. Our anthropological beginnings insist on humans living in groups for protection, food, and nurturing. Eric Weiner, who studied happiness on a global level in his bestselling book *The Geography of Bliss* (2008), said, "Our happiness is completely and utterly intertwined with other people: family and friends and neighbors … Happiness is not a noun or a verb. It's a conjunction. Connective tissue" (p. 325).

The work environment is part of one's interpersonal universe. Resource-building makes us happy as we enhance ourselves with skills, knowledge, and abilities. To enhance mental well-being at work, both intrinsic and extrinsic rewards are necessary. Intrinsic rewards include a sense of competence and autonomy (Gagné and Deci, 2005). Combining these with a sense of relatedness or connectivity with others, Deci et al. (2001) found direct positive relations between the satisfaction of these needs and being engaged and experiencing well-being at work. Thus, a positive and nurturing work environment can be an extension to the sense of belonging and feeling of "home." However, a work environment full of distrust, boredom, bullying, and overall poor treatment would have a detrimental effect on mental well-being.

In a perfect world, everyone would have a job that brought meaningful purpose; however, many jobs will need intrapersonal reframing to support mental well-being. Workers may be provided with a meaningful rationale in order to internalize the goal of getting work done and achieve the autonomy and sense of choice that make even uninteresting work more palatable (Deci, Eghrari, Patrick, and Leone, 1994).

Enhancing mental well-being, then, is a participatory, self-directed task that takes place through cognitive, behavioral, and volitional means. Some of the major enhancers of mental well-being are forgiveness, gratitude, altruism, and experiencing nature.

Forgiveness

Forgiveness is indisputably related to psychological adjustment. Studies have shown that forgiveness is positively associated with mental well-being (Berry and Worthington, 2001). Vengefulness, on the other hand, is positively related to negative affectivity/neuroticism. It is also negatively related to agreeableness and satisfaction with life, and has negative implications for interpersonal relationships (McCullough, Bellah, Kilpatrick, and Johnson, 2001). Orth, Berking, Walker, Meier, and Znoj (2008) speculate that forgiveness may help with closure, reduce anger, and increase well-being because it enhances close relationships.

Being unforgiving may make a person perceive himself or herself as being a victim, being weak, being doomed to suffering and misfortune. Being forgiving is negatively associated with depression (Berry, Worthington, O'Connor, Parrott and Wade, 2005) and anxiety (Orcutt, 2006).

Gratitude

Researchers Emmons and McCullough (2003) characterize gratitude as being inherently focused upon something outside the self: "Although a variety of life experiences can elicit feelings of gratitude, prototypically gratitude stems from the perception of a positive personal outcome, not necessarily deserved or earned, that is due to the actions of another person" (p. 377). They also note that gratitude can be directed to a nonhuman – that is, to an animal or to God, or, in modern parlance, we might speak of "the universe" or "the cosmos."

Bertocci and Millard (1963) said that gratitude is "the willingness to recognize the unearned increments of value in one's experience" (p. 369). Counting up these increments is beneficial to subjective well-being. Emmons and McCullough (2003) say: "There are reasons to believe that experiences of gratitude might be associated – perhaps even in a causal fashion – with happiness and well-being" (p. 378). Bono and McCullough (2006) found that gratitude is incompatible with negative emotions and pathological conditions and that it may even offer protection against psychiatric disorders.

In the Emmons and McCullough (2003) study, experimental subjects who listed things they were grateful for exhibited marked positive affect and more general life satisfaction than subjects who listed hassles in their lives and than a control group. What was more, significant others in their lives noted that the subjects seemed happier. The subjects slept better at night and were also more inclined toward affirming prosocial activities after they had counted their own blessings.

Both forgiveness and gratitude are crucial for creating and maintaining healthy social relationships. Coupled together, these are powerful psychological tools to alleviate suffering and enhance well-being. Committing to access these positive characteristics produces opportunities to address and resolve deeper personal schemas (self-doubt, self-image, selfishness, etc.) that threaten well-being.

Nature

Maller, Townsend, Pryor, Brown, and St. Leger (2006) speak of the human health benefits of interacting with plants and animals as well as observing natural scenes through windows. Their review notes that access to nature, even viewed through a window, reduces both physical and mental stress, helps patients recover more quickly and with fewer complications, and calms prisoners and improves their behavior. The authors say: "Natural areas can be seen as one of our most vital health resources. In the context of the growing worldwide mental illness burden of disease, contact with nature may offer an affordable, accessible and equitable choice in tackling the imminent epidemic, within both preventative and restorative public health strategies."

Humans quite naturally turn to nature when seeking well-being. They turn to a beloved pet, to gardening, or they yearningly seek the sky or the moon. We send flowers to funerals to bring nature into the picture and remind ourselves that all life is ephemeral – and yet ever-renewing.

The Future of Mental Well-Being

With increases in environmental stimuli such as constant news updates in 24-hour news cycles, social media, and convenience devices (smartphones, tablets), well-being could wither. Information overload threatens daily practices that improve well-being; the constant push to succeed creates expectations of exhausting one's life in a panic rather than living in the moment.

Booth Tarkington noted in his 1918 Pulitzer Prize winning novel, *The Magnificent Ambersons*, that technology alters the human soul in unpredictable ways. Tarkington has a character reflect on automobiles:

> With all their speed forward they may be step backward in civilization – that is, in spiritual civilization. It may be that they will not add to the beauty of the world, nor to the life of men's souls. I am not sure ... But you can't have the immense outward changes that they will cause without some inward ones, and it may be that ... the spiritual alteration will be bad for us. (Tarkington, 1994, p. 173)

It will be up to us to counteract the impact of technology with increased attention to well-being, making technology serve us rather than the other way around. Future applications of well-being are developing in the burgeoning fields of positive psychology, mindfulness, and solution-focused therapies; these types of insightful approaches emphasize personal accountability and responsibility to "live your best life." The success of these programs will rest on their ability to bring balance to subjective and objective personal well-being, for well-being is both art and science.

Ideally, practical techniques to enhance daily well-being will be promoted through individualized self-introspective assessments and the application of the post-postmodern science idea that there are also universal tenets (such as the efficacy of forgiveness, gratitude, kindness, humor, autonomous work, and experiences with nature) to serve as a foundation from which to launch into meaningful directions toward greater well-being.

References

American Psychiatric Association (2013). *Diagnostic and Statistical Manual of Mental Disorders*, 5th edn. Arlington, VA: American Psychiatric Association.

Benson, H. (2000). *The Relaxation Response*, updated edn. New York: Harper Torch. Originally published 1975.

Berns, G. S. (2004). Something funny happened to reward. *Trends in Cognitive Science*, 8(5), 193–194.

Berry, J. W., and Worthington, E. L. (2001). Forgivingness, relationship quality, stress while imagining relationship events, and physical and mental health. *Journal of Counseling Psychology*, 48, 447–455.

Berry, J. W., Worthington, E. L., O'Connor, L. E., Parrott, L., and Wade, N. G. (2005). Forgivingness, vengeful rumination, and affective traits. *Journal of Personality*, 73, 183–225.

Bertocci, P. A., and Millard, R. M. (1963). *Personality and the Good: Psychological and Ethical Perspectives*. New York: McKay.

Black, D. S., O'Reilly, G. A., Olmstead, R., Breen, E. C., and Irwin, M. R. (2015). Mindfulness meditation and improvement in sleep quality and daytime impairment among older adults with sleep disturbances: A randomized clinical trial. *Journal of the American Medical Association, Internal Medicine*, 175(4), 494–501. doi:10.1001/jamainternmed.2014.8081

Bono, G., and McCullough, M. E. (2006). Positive responses to benefit and harm: Bringing forgiveness and gratitude into cognitive psychotherapy. *Journal of Cognitive Psychotherapy*, 20(2), 2147–2158.

Breslau, N., Roth, T., Rosenthal, L., and Andreski, P. (1996). Sleep disturbance and psychiatric disorders: A longitudinal epidemiological study of young adults. *Biological Psychiatry*, 39(6), 411–418.

Brooks, K. (2013). New program reduces agitation in dementia patients. *Johns Hopkins Magazine (Winter)*. At http://hub.jhu.edu/magazine/2013/winter/dementia-agitation-activities-program (accessed July 2016).

Chiesa, A., and Serretti, A. (2009). Mindfulness-based stress reduction for stress management in healthy people: A review and meta-analysis. *Journal of Alternative and Complementary Medicine*, 15(5), 593–600.

Cohen, D., Wang, W., Wyatt, J., Kronauer, R., Dijk, D., Czeisler, C., and Klerman, E. (2010). Uncovering residual effects of chronic sleep loss on human performance. *Science Translational Medicine*, 2(14), 14ra3.

Csikszentmihalyi, M. (1997). *Finding Flow: The Psychology of Engagement with Everyday Life*. New York: Basic Books.

Czeisler, C. (2013). Perspective: Casting light on sleep deficiency. *Nature*, 497(7450), S13.

Deci, E. L., Eghrari, H., Patrick, B. C., and Leone, D. R. (1994). Facilitating internalization: The self-determination theory perspective. *Journal of Personality*, 62, 119–142.

Deci, E. L., Ryan, R. M., Gagné, M., Leone, D. R., Usunov, J., and Kornazheva, B. P. (2001). Need satisfaction, motivation, and well-being in the work organizations of a former Eastern bloc country. *Personality and Social Psychology Bulletin*, 27, 930–942.

Easwaran, E. (2013). The yoga of work: Love your job, love your life. Yoga International, May 24. At https://yoga international.com/article/view/the-yoga-of-work-love-your-job-love-your-life (accessed July 2016).

Emmons, R. A., and McCullough, M. E. (2003). Counting blessings versus burdens: An experimental investigation of gratitude and subjective well-being in daily life. *Journal of Personality and Social Psychology*, 84(2), 377–389. doi:10.1037/0022-3514.84.2.377

Ford, D. E., and Kamerow, D. B. (1989). Epidemiologic study of sleep disturbances and psychiatric disorders: An opportunity for prevention? *Journal of the American Medical Association, 262*(11), 1479–1484.

Foureur, M., Besley, K., Burton, G., Yu, N., and Crisp, J. (2013). Enhancing the resilience of nurses and midwives: Pilot of a mindfulness based program for increased health, sense of coherence and decreased depression, anxiety and stress. *Contemporary Nurse, 45*(1), 3547–3575.

Gagné, M., and Deci, E. L. (2005). Self-determination theory and work motivation. *Journal of Organizational Behavior, 26*, 331–362. doi:10.1002/job.322

Godfrin, K. A., and van Heeringen, C. (2010). The effects of mindfulness-based cognitive therapy on recurrence of depressive episodes, mental health and quality of life: A randomized controlled study. *Behaviour Research and Therapy, 48*(8), 738–746.

Green, S., and Bieling, P. (2012). Expanding the scope of mindfulness-based cognitive therapy: Evidence for effectiveness in a heterogeneous psychiatric sample. *Cognitive and Behavioral Practice, 19*(1), 174–180.

Gruzelier, J. (2014a). EEG-neurofeedback for optimising performance, I: A review of cognitive and affective outcome in healthy participants. *Neuroscience and Behavioral Reviews, 44*, 124–141. doi:10.1016/j.neubiorev.2013.09.015

Gruzelier, J. (2014b). EEG-neurofeedback for optimising performance, II: Creativity, the performing arts, and ecological validity. *Neuroscience and Behavioral Reviews, 44*, 142–158.

Hammarskjold, D. (1964). *Markings*, trans. Leif Sjoberg and W. H. Auden. London: Faber & Faber.

Harvey, A. G. (2000). Pre-sleep cognitive activity: A comparison of sleep-onset insomniacs and good sleepers. *British Journal of Clinical Psychology, 39*(3), 275–286.

Harvey, A. G. (2002). A cognitive model of insomnia. *Behavioral Research and Therapy, 40*(8), 869–893.

Harvey, A. G., and Greenhall, E. (2003). Catastrophic worry in primary insomnia. *Journal of Behavior Therapy and Experimental Psychiatry, 34*(1)1, 11–23.

Hassed, C., de Lisle, S., Sullivan, G., and Pier, C. (2009). Enhancing the health of medical students: Outcomes of an integrated mindfulness and lifestyle program. *Advances in Health Sciences Education, 14*(3), 387–398. DOI:10.1007/s10459-008-9125-3

Huedo-Medina, T. B., Kirsch, I., Middlemass, J., Klonizakis, M., and Siriwardena, A. N. (2012). Effectiveness of non-benzodiazepine hypnotics in treatment of adult insomnia: Meta-analysis of data submitted to the Food and Drug Administration. *BMJ, 345*, e8343. doi:10.1136/bmj.e8343

Jakobsson, H. E., Abrahamsson, T. R., Jenmalm, M. C., Harris, K., Quince, C., Jernberg, C., … Andersson, A. F. (2013). Decreased gut microbiota diversity, delayed Bacteroidetes colonisation and reduced Th1 responses in infants delivered by Caesarean section. *Gut, 63*(4), 559–566. doi:10.1136/gutjnl-2012-303249

Kabat-Zinn, J. (2005). *Wherever You Go, There You Are*. New York: Hyperion. Originally published 1994.

Kuyken, W., Byford, S., Taylor, R. S., Watkins, E., Holden, E., White, K., … Teasdale, J. D. (2008). Mindfulness-based cognitive therapy to prevent relapse in recurrent depression. *Journal of Consulting and Clinical Psychology, 76*(6), 966–978. doi:10.1037/a0013786

Lehrer, P. M., and Gevirtz, R. (2014). Heart rate variability biofeedback: How and why does it work? *Frontiers in Psychology, 5*, 756. doi:10.3389/fpsyg.2014.00756

Levi, L. (Ed.) (1971). *The Psychosocial Environment and Psychosomatic Diseases, vol. 1 of Society, Stress and Disease*. London: Oxford University Press.

Lyubomirsky, S., King, L. A. and Diener, E. (2004). Is happiness a strength? An examination of the benefits and costs of frequent positive affect. *MS*.

Lyubomirsky, S., Sheldon, K. M., and Schkade, D. (2005). Pursuing happiness: The architecture of sustainable change. *Review of General Psychology, 9*(2). At http://escholarship.org/uc/item/4v03h9gv (accessed July 2016).

Maller, C., Townsend, M., Pryor, A., Brown, P., and St. Leger, L. (2006). Healthy nature, healthy people: "Contact with nature" as an upstream health promotion intervention for populations. *Health Promotion International, 21*(1), 45–54. At http://heapro.oxfordjournals.org/content/21/1/45.long (accessed July 2016).

Martin, M., Sadlo, G., and Stew, G. (2006). The phenomenon of boredom. *Qualitative Research in Psychology, 3*(3), 193–211. doi:10.1191/1478088706qrp066oa

McCraty, R., Atkinson, M., Tiller, W. A., Rein, G., and Watkins, A. D. (1995). The effects of emotions on short-term power spectrum analysis of heart rate variability. *American Journal of Cardiology, 76*(14), 1089–1093.

McCullough, M. E., Bellah, C. G., Kilpatrick, S. D., and Johnson, J. L. (2001). Vengefulness: Relationships with forgiveness, rumination, well-being, and the Big Five. *Personality and Social Psychology Bulletin, 27*, 601–610.

McGonigal, J. (2011). *Reality Is Broken: Why Games Make Us Better and How They Can Change the World*. New York: Penguin.

Metcalf, C. W., and Felible, R. (1992). Humor: An antidote for terminal professionalism. *Industry Week*, *241*(14), 14–19.

Morin, C. M., Culbert, J. P., and Schwartz, S. M. (1994). Nonpharmacological interventions for insomnia: A meta-analysis of treatment efficacy. *American Journal of Psychiatry*, *151*, 1172–1180.

National Institutes of Health (2013). Should you take dietary supplements? *News in Health* (Aug.). At https://newsinhealth.nih.gov/issue/Aug2013/Feature1 (accessed July 2016).

ODPHP (Office of Disease Prevention and Health Promotion) (2016). Health-related quality of life and well-being. ODPHP, Rockville, MD. At http://www.healthypeople.gov/2020/topics-objectives/topic/health-related-quality-of-life-well-being (accessed July 2016).

O'Mahony, S. M., Clarke, G., Borre, Y. E., Dinan, T. G., and Cryan, J. F. (2014). Serotonin, tryptophan metabolism and the brain-gut-microbiome axis. *Behavioral Brain Research*, *277*, 32–48. Epub ahead of print. doi:10.1016/j.bbr.2014.07.027

Orcutt, H. K. (2006). The prospective relationship of interpersonal forgiveness and psychological distress symptoms among college women. *Journal of Counseling Psychology*, *53*, 350–336.

Orth, U., Berking, M., Walker, N., Meier, L. L., and Znoj, H. (2008). Forgiveness and psychological adjustment following interpersonal transgressions: A longitudinal analysis. *Journal of Research in Personality*, *42*, 365–385.

Peek, C. (2003). A primer of biofeedback instrumentation. In *Biofeedback: A Practitioner's Guide*, 3rd edn. New York: The Guilford Press.

Riebl, S. K., and Davy, B. M. (2013). The hydration equation: Update on water balance and cognitive performance. *ACSM's Health and Fitness Journal*, *17*(6), 21–28. doi:10.1249/FIT.0b013e3182a9570f

Selye, H. (1974). *Stress without Distress*. Philadelphia: J. B. Lippincott.

Selye, H. (1977). *The Stress of My Life: A Scientist's Memoirs*. Toronto: McClelland & Stewart.

Strauss, C., Cavanagh, K., Oliver, A., and Pettman, D. (2014). Mindfulness-based interventions for people diagnosed with a current episode of an anxiety or depressive disorder: A meta-analysis of randomised controlled trials. *PLoS One 9*(4), e96110. doi:10.1371/journal.pone.0096110

Szabo, S., Tache, Y., and Somogyi, A. (2012). The legacy of Hans Selye and the origins of stress research: A retrospective 75 years after his landmark brief "letter" to the editor of Nature. *Stress*, *15*(5), 472–478. doi:10.3109/10253890. 2012.710919

Tarkington, B. (1994). *The Magnificent Ambersons*. New York: Bantam Books. Originally published 1918.

van Praag, H., Fleshner, M., Schwartz, M. W., and Mattson, M. P. (2014). Exercise, energy intake, glucose homeostasis, and the brain. *Journal of Neuroscience*, *34*(46), 15139–15149. doi:10.1523/JNEUROSCI.2814-14.2014

Wang, Y., and Kasper, L. H. (2014). The role of microbiome in central nervous system disorders. *Brain, Behavior, and Immunity*, *38*, 1–12. doi:10.1016/j.bbi.2013.12.015

Weiner, E. (2008). *The Geography of Bliss*. New York: Twelve.

WHO (World Health Organization) (2016). Physical activity. At http://www.who.int/topics/physical_activity/en/ (accessed July 2016).

Xie, L., Kang, H., Xu, Q., Chen, M. J., Liao, Y., Thiyagarajan, M., … Nedergaard, M. (2013). Sleep drives metabolite clearance from the adult brain. *Science*, *342*(6156), 373–377.

29

Cancer Survivorship, Cancer-Related PTSD, and Positive Change

A Narrative Overview

Tom Cox, Gianina-Ioana Postavaru, Fehmidah Munir, Juliet Hassard, and Sara MacLennan

Was I deceived, or did a sable cloud
Turn forth her silver lining on the night?

John Milton, *Comus* (1634)

"Keep a good heart Alannan: I've often tould ye there's a silver lining to every cloud."
From the novel *Marian* by Anna Maria Fielding (1840)

Introduction

There has been a growing acceptance over relatively recent years that "having and being treated for cancer" can be experienced as stressful, sometimes severely so, and can be associated with psychological reactions such as depression and anxiety (for example, van't Spijker, Trijsburg, and Duivenvoorden, 1997). In some, having and being treated for cancer may become associated with the occurrence of post traumatic stress disorder (PTSD): cancer-related PTSD (Kangas, Henry, and Bryant, 2002). There has been the steady development of a research literature on this aspect of cancer survivorship despite some initial skepticism about its veracity (for example, Tomich and Helgeson, 2004; Coyne and Tennen, 2010). The possibility that psychological ill-health conditions may be sequelae of the more direct challenges of having cancer

The Handbook of Stress and Health: A Guide to Research and Practice, First Edition.
Edited by Cary L. Cooper and James Campbell Quick.
© 2017 John Wiley & Sons, Ltd. Published 2017 by John Wiley & Sons, Ltd.

and its treatment forces a consideration of psychological interventions to protect the person's health, quality of life, and also ability to work. The importance of dealing with cancer-related PTSD and other psychological health issues increases as a public health risk with the continuing improvements in cancer survival rates. This article focuses on cancer-related PTSD and considers the nature of this challenge in those diagnosed with cancer, its prevalence, and the value of psychological interventions in dealing with it. The later is, in part, considered through the lens of the possibility of something positive emerging from the reality and stress of having cancer.

Cancer, Cancer-Related PTSD, Post Traumatic Growth and Positive Change

PTSD, formally recognized as a psychiatric disorder, has been included in the *Diagnostic and Statistical Manual of Mental Disorders* (*DSM*) since 1980 (DSM-III). The evidence strongly suggests that exposure to severely stressful experiences can be a trigger for, if not the root cause of PTSD. Examples are easily provided not only in relation to natural disasters, for example the Mexico floods (Norris, Murphy, Baker, and Perilla, 2004), the Sichuan earthquake in 2008 (Wang et al., 2009; Zang, Hunt, and Cox, 2011) and Hurricane Katrina (DeSalvo et al., 2007; Davis, Tarcza, and Munson, 2009), but also in relation to those disasters that are man-made. These may have been caused by accident or negligence – rail crashes (Andersen, Christensen, and Petersen, 1991; Hagström, 1995) and the crush at the Hillsborough football stadium (Wright, Binney, and Kunkler, 1994; Sims and Sims, 1998) – or by conflict and war, such as the Northern Irish troubles (Curran and Miller, 2001), Bosnia (Thulesius and Håkansson, 1999; Allwood, Bell-Doran, and Husain, 2002) and Iraq (Johnson and Thompson, 2008). However, until 1994 (and DSM-IV), life-threatening illnesses, such as cancer, were excluded from the diagnosis of PTSD as stressors that could precipitate that condition. They are now included.

The English language, as most others, is replete with observations and sayings, drawn from earlier shared experiences of life. "Every cloud has a silver lining" is one such saying. True or not, it implies that out of stressful experiences and adversity might emerge something positive. This idea has received support from those who have studied or worked with people who have experienced and survived serious and potentially life-threatening illness, not least those who have survived cancer. In 2010, Stanton wrote: "it seems impossible to interact intensively with individuals affected by cancer without becoming aware of the benefits some extract as they struggle with the demands of the experience."

A literature has now developed around the possibility that some positive changes in a person might emerge from their experience of having and coping with cancer. If true and not simply collective wishful thinking (Coyne and Tennen, 2010), such positive change might represent the proverbial *silver lining*. This area of interest is characterized by a cluster of overlapping but slightly different constructs and has attracted a variety of descriptors, usually incorporating the notion of growth or positive change following adversity. These include benefit finding (Helgeson, Reynolds, and Tomich, 2006; Stanton, 2010), a fighting spirit (Greer, Morris, and Pettingale, 1979; Antoni and Lutgendorf, 2007), positive growth (Elliott, Kurylo, and Rivera, 2002) or positive change (Linley and Joseph, 2004), post traumatic growth (Calhoun and Tedeschi, 2006; Tedeschi and Calhoun, 1996; 2004), and stress-related growth (Park and Fenster, 2004). Here, the focus is on *positive change*. This is deliberate both as an economy of terminology and also because it embraces both those who have experienced cancer-related PTSD and those who have not. The article therefore considers post traumatic growth in its discussion of positive change. In some ways, cancer-related PTSD and positive change may represent the extremes of the psychological sequelae of having and being treated for cancer.

Cancer and Cancer-related PTSD

Is being diagnosed with and treated for cancer associated with the experience of PTSD? There have been a number of empirical studies and associated papers published in answer to this question. These have covered samples with a variety of cancer types, those with specific cancer types, particularly breast cancer, as well as specific populations or those at particular points in the patient journey. Three reviews and two empirical studies are discussed here.

Reviews by Kangas and her colleagues (Kangas et al., 2002; Andrykowski and Kangas, 2010) appear to answer this question in the affirmative. In their 2002 review, Kangas and her colleagues examined 13 studies that had assessed the incidence of PTSD in adult cancer patients. The majority of these studies (10/13) concerned women with breast cancer. Five focused on women with early stage disease, four studies included mixed stage patients, and the remaining study explicitly included women with middle to late stage disease. Most of the study designs were cross-sectional and the assessment of PTSD was made using standard instruments somewhere between two months and 12 years following treatment. The designs used may have influenced the incidence rates recorded. For example, Kangas and colleagues (2002) reported that incidence rates varied with the assessment instrument used. Notwithstanding these cautions, most of the available incidence data fell within the range 0–19 percent.

The available literature was later revisited and commented on by Andrykowski and Kangas (2010). They included 18 published studies, although three of them used the same data set, leaving a total of 16 studies that provided new data. The majority concerned cancer patients and survivors diagnosed during adulthood. Half of the studies focused on women with breast cancer and the remainder included patients with a variety of different cancers. Sample sizes varied between 27 and 251. Mean prevalence rate from the eight studies of women with breast cancer was reported as 3.3 percent. Mean prevalence rate from the remaining studies (mixed cancer types) was reported as 10.6 percent. Five of the studies on women with breast cancer reported lifetime prevalence rates with the mean being 12.6 percent. Four of the other remainder studies also reported lifetime prevalence rates with the mean being 18.3 percent.

A more recent review by Abbey, Thompson, Hickish, and Heathcote (2015) compared studies on cancer survivors that used different validated clinical interviews and questionnaires to assess the prevalence of cancer-related PTSD. Prevalence estimates were calculated for each assessment method using random-effects meta-analysis. Studies using the PTSD Checklist – Civilian Version yielded lower prevalence rates using the cut-off method (7.3%) than those using symptom cluster methods (11.2%). Studies using the Structured Clinical Interview for DSM-IV (SCID) also yielded lower prevalence rates (5.1%). Similar findings were commented on by Kangas et al. (2002). As with other reviews, Abbey et al. (2015) found that between-study heterogeneity was substantial.

An empirical study by Guglietti and her colleagues (2010) focused on Canadian women undergoing investigation for ovarian cancer. These women were given a prediagnosis assessment covering PTSD and also pain, stress and depression. One month later, after diagnosis, the women were reassessed on these measures. No clinical cases of PTSD were detected, although 13.6 percent of participants were identified with subsyndromal PTSD. Interestingly, those women diagnosed with ovarian cancer who had higher initial depression scores and then shorter wait times for treatment were more likely to have shown an increase in symptoms of PTSD across the two assessments.

A later empirical study by Kwak and colleagues (2013) looked at prevalence of symptoms of post traumatic stress in 151 adolescent and young adult cancer survivors in the United States aged from 15 to 39 years. A number of different cancer types and treatments were involved in this study. Symptom severity was estimated at 6 and 12 months post diagnosis. The authors report that at 6 and 12 months, respectively, 39 percent and 44 percent of participants reported moderate to severe symptom levels suggestive of PTSD. There was no significant difference between the rates at 6 and 12 months.

The available data suggest that somewhere between 1 in 30 and 1 in 5 of those diagnosed with a cancer show symptoms indicative of clinical PTSD, and possibly more show symptoms suggestive of PTSD. It is not sensible to say whether such rates are high or not. However, they do represent a substantive number of those with cancer who have also to deal with PTSD. Notwithstanding this, the majority of those with cancer do not experience PTSD.

The evidence suggests that risk factors for PTSD in cancer patients may include, in addition to disease and treatment variables, prior exposure to life stressors, a history of psychological disturbance, and the tendency to elevated psychological distress following diagnosis. Poor social support and social functioning, and high emotional reactivity are also risk factors. The "at risk" groups appear to be women, the young, and those of low socioeconomic status and a lower educational level.

Andrykowski and Cordova (1998), for example, explored the factors predicting PTSD symptoms in 82 breast cancer survivors. In addition to PTSD symptoms, physical comorbidity, social support, depression history, and precancer traumatic stressors were assessed through structured telephone interviews. The data indicated that physical comorbidity, education, disease stage, cancer treatment, depression history, and social support accounted for 39 percent of variance in reported PTSD symptoms. In addition to time since treatment completion, precancer traumatic stressors, age at diagnosis, and tamoxifen usage accounted for an additional 16 percent of variance. More severe levels of PTSD symptoms were associated with less social support, greater precancer trauma history, less time since treatment completion, and more advanced disease.

There were hints at the possible role of psychosocial factors in cancer survivorship in the early years of the modern literature on psychosocial oncology (see Cox and Mackay, 1982; Cox, 1984). Cox and Mackay (1982) in their review concluded that the person's reaction to a diagnosis of cancer, along with their early experiences, might be a factor in determining their subsequent condition and quality of life. They noted five possible risk factors. The first three were an inability to express emotion, particularly in relation to anger, the experience of stressful life events involving significant others, and depressive reactions. The remaining two were psychosexual disturbance, and early and unresolved problems with parents. The authors also noted that the evidence *then* related more strongly to the first factor than to the others: the inability to express emotion. This lack might have been a direct reflection of (unrecognized) cancer-related PTSD or, in the family context, a protective buffering as a coping strategy.

One might conclude that the risk factors for cancer-related PTSD appear to be as much about the person and their psychological and social contexts as about their disease.

The symptoms of PTSD reported by those with cancer generally fit those that have been described elsewhere following the experience of other severely stressful and traumatic events (Breslau, 2002). They can be both distressing (for example, Luutonen et al., 2011) and disabling (for example, Kärki, Simonen, Mälkiä, and Selfe, 2005).

According to DSM-IV, and in addition to exposure to a severely stressful event, the symptoms of PTSD are drawn from three clusters: re-experiencing the trauma in nightmares, intrusive memories or flashbacks; numbing of affect and avoidance of thoughts, acts, and situations that symbolize the trauma; and symptoms of excessive arousal. The diagnosis requires the persistence of symptoms for at least one month and the manifestation of clinically significant distress or impairment. For cancer patients, intrusive thoughts and avoidance behavior appear the strongest of these symptoms (Bleicker et al., 2000; Kangas et al., 2002). Andrykowski and Kangas (2010) report that cancer patients and survivors experience feeling very frightened and helpless, and having intrusive and reoccurring recollections, dreams and dissociative flashbacks around the cancer experience. These symptoms appear to be triggered by internal or external cues and by reminders of cancer. At the same time, there have been reports of strong avoidance behavior, both cognitively and behaviorally, associated with memory lapses around cancer-related events (for example, Brezden, Phillips, Abdolell, and Bunston, 2000), including treatment. In addition, there may be emotional numbing, feelings of alienation, and a decline in emotional affectivity often related to intimacy, tenderness and sexuality.

The symptoms clustered around intrusion and avoidance may appear particularly obvious within the first month of diagnosis (Kangas et al., 2002). They may then decline substantively after the first three months following diagnosis or after treatment completion. However, the data also suggest that symptoms of PTSD can fluctuate over the course of the patient's journey, often as a result of treatment.

Cancer-Related PTSD and Positive Change: The Silver Lining?

It is apparent that the person's reactions to having cancer can go beyond what might be thought to be reasonable and be of clinical significance. This can be one of the clouds that gather around the person with cancer. Can there be a silver lining to any of them? The question has been asked whether any positive changes in people can be seen following a diagnosis of cancer. Skepticism has been sensibly expressed. Do the notions of positive change and post traumatic growth refer to a real phenomenon or are they possible products of poor science, exaggerated claims and wishful thinking (Tomich and Helgeson, 2004; Coyne and Tennen, 2010)?

There appear to be a number of explanations of positive change following cancer diagnosis. First, if experienced, any recovery in cancer-related PTSD might be interpreted by the person with cancer as a positive change and reported as such. Thus the experience of post traumatic growth might be little more than relief from the symptoms of PTSD and, significant as that would be, it might not involve any sort of developmental process beyond that. The relationships here might be somewhat circular, in that benefit finding, as an aspect of positive change, might also act as a buffer against PTSD, as suggested by Siegel and Schrimshaw (2007) in relation to living with HIV/AIDS.

Second, positive change might reflect the recognition of the apparently good things that may result from or contextualize the treatment and care given to the person with cancer. These might take the form of increased or more supportive contact with others, who, through the nature of their behavior, may appear to be caring. Nothing in this particular argument devalues the perception of positive change by the person with cancer or the improvement in their *situation* that it signals.

Third, positive change may represent a real and dynamic engagement on the person's part with their journey, resulting in fundamental psychological changes occurring as a result of their experience of cancer and of managing and coping with it. Such change might involve significant cognitive restructuring and result from one or more processes relating to the need to make sense of and attribute meaning to that experience, or seek some form of benefit from it. The basic thesis here is that people need to make sense of their experiences and naturally seek meaning (for example, Heine, Proulx, and Vohs, 2006) and do so in a wide variety of situations, including work (see, for example, Collison and Mackenzie, 1999; Gordon, 2001). Such behavior may be an expression of optimism (Tallman, Altmaier, and Garcia, 2007), but also help reduce uncertainty and possibly improve the sense of well-being, if not mental health (for example, Mascaro and Rosen, 2005). Benefits found and sustained over a period of time might support long-term adjustment (Schwarzer et al., 2006). Sense making may be made manifest cognitively, behaviorally and socially in an attempt to develop an explanatory narrative around severely stressful experiences and better cope with them. The desired output is an appropriate story: the processes involved sequentially may be seeking meaning, sense making, and the construction of a narrative to support coping. Such processes may determine, in part, the person's *adjustment* to cancer, the quality of their life and, possibly, the duration of their survival. The greater the positive change, it might be argued, the better the person's prognosis.

Logically, there is no reason why these three explanations of positive change could not all be true and operate alongside each other. The literature is equivocal and leaves this more complex option open. This complex model suggests that positive change and post traumatic growth might involve or reflect all three processes. One thing that could be common to these is the reduction in the experience of stress.

Stanton (2010) offered a not dissimilar explanatory scheme for positive change also based on three processes. The first of Stanton's processes relates to some people's natural propensity to maintain and report a positive self-view and tendency to be optimistic in the face of adversity. Positive change may be part of this "putting on a brave face." It may function as a coping strategy through a number of cognitive devices such as playing down one's precancer status (Widows, Jacobsen, Booth-Jones, and Fields, 2005) or comparing oneself with others worse off (Stanton, 2010). The second of her three processes relates specifically to benefit seeking as an intentional coping strategy: coping through positive appraisal (Carver, Scheier, and Weintraub,1989). The third process is that positive change is more simply the reporting of benefits that have already accrued through the experience of cancer, its treatment and associated care (Tennen and Affleck, 2002). These suggestions are easily accommodated in the set of explanations outlined above by the authors here.

Stanton (2010) argues that it is possible to differentiate between coping and reporting benefit on the basis of the available evidence. Studies suggest that active coping, through positive appraisal, predicts positive change 12 months later, while the passive reporting of benefits does not. However, she does also suggest that reporting might serve some adaptive purpose and implies that it is not necessarily to be dismissed.

The main difference between the two explanatory models mentioned above appears to lie in relation to the *cognitive restructuring*, which in the first model is the fundamental psychological change, and Stanton's (2010) stronger emphasis on more direct *coping*. The value of both models lies not only in their current explanatory power but also in the way in which the insight offered might be used for the design of effective intervention strategies.

In summary, it has been suggested that many diagnosed with cancer report things that might be interpreted as aspects of positive change and post traumatic growth (Stanton, Bower and Low, 2006). There is evidence to suggest that such reports strengthen from about four months until, at least, 18 months after diagnosis (Manne et al., 2004).

Significance of Positive Change

For many, one of the most important questions is whether or not positive change or post traumatic growth reported following cancer diagnosis and treatment is of any clinical significance. There is some evidence to suggest that it might be, although some are strongly skeptical (Coyne and Tennen, 2010), especially in relation to length of survival following diagnosis. Smedslund and Ringdal (2004) provided an early overview of the effects of psychological interventions on survival time in cancer patients. They considered 13 studies published between 1989 and 2003 reporting data from 14 controlled intervention studies (involving a total of 2,626 participants). Neither randomized studies nor nonrandomized studies showed any overall treatment effect. However, while interventions using group treatment were shown to be ineffective, those using individual treatments were shown to have an effect. They concluded that it was premature to judge such interventions on the then available data.

Length of survival following diagnosis is not the only outcome of merit for patients, their families, and health care. Quality of life is another, as is ability to maintain or return to work. One focus of attention in relation to positive change and post traumatic growth has been effects on mood and on the occurrence of depressive symptoms. Here, it is likely that, even if low mood and depressive symptoms are not precursors of clinical depression, they are major threats to the quality of survivors' lives. Bower and colleagues (2005) reported that perceived positive meaning in the cancer experience, 1–5 years after diagnosis, predicted an increase in positive affect five years later in a sample of 6,763 women with breast cancer. Carver and Antoni (2004) somewhat similarly reported that finding benefit in the year after surgery predicted lower distress and depressive symptoms 4–7 years later in another sample of women diagnosed with breast cancer. However, the review by Stanton et al. (2006) revealed mixed evidence that benefit finding is associated with lower distress or more positive mood, and those authors suggested that this relationship might be moderated by individual differences, especially in relation to motivation and the timing of measurement in relation to the diagnosis of cancer. The meta-analysis by Helgeson and her colleagues (2006), however, showed that, among other things, benefit finding was related significantly to lower depressive symptoms and more positive well-being. Interestingly, it did not appear related to anxiety, global distress, or the quality of life as assessed. However, there was significant variability in effect size across the studies included and, furthermore, relationships varied as a function of the duration of the benefit finding, its measurement, and the racial composition of the sample.

Psychological Interventions: Cognitive Behavioral Change

Much of literature on *psychological* interventions is clinical in nature and, in turn, draws from a variety of different theoretical perspectives from the psychotherapeutic through to the more contemporary theories. Prominent among the different types of intervention reported in the literature are those focused on cognitive behavioral change and narrative theory. Many are designed to either enable emotional expression, such as narrative based therapies, or to reduce the experience of stress. These are briefly discussed here.

In relation to the use of narrative therapy, Stanton and colleagues (2002) have reported a randomized control trial with women who had completed primary treatment for breast cancer. The women were randomly assigned to one of three groups and asked over four sessions to write about their experience with breast cancer. The control group was asked to write about the facts of that experience. Women in the first intervention groups were asked to write about their deepest thoughts and feelings about the experience, and women in the second intervention group were asked to write about the positive aspects of that experience. Both intervention groups reported significantly fewer medical appointments for cancer-related morbidities and reported fewer physical symptoms. Interestingly, neither intervention showed reduced psychological symptoms. The fact that the women involved in the trial had completed primary treatment may be significant. A caution may be necessary. Stanton (2010) argues that writing about the positive aspects of the experience of cancer is not the same as an insistence on positive thinking. She warns that a sole focus on positive thinking, if accompanied by the suppression of negative thoughts and feelings, may be clinically contra-indicated and place an unnecessary burden on those with cancer (for example, Rittenberg, 1995; Gross, 2002).

Later, Graves (2003) published a meta-analysis of 38 randomized studies which had employed components of social cognitive theory (SCT) in interventions with adult cancer patients with the aim of improving their quality of life. She concluded that interventions with more SCT components had significantly larger effect sizes for quality of life outcomes than those with fewer or no such components, both overall and in terms of most of the quality of life subscales. The exceptions were subjective physical and functional outcomes.

In the same year, Rehse and Pukrop (2003) reported another meta-analysis which summarized the results of 37 published, controlled studies investigating the effectiveness of psychosocial interventions on quality of life in adult cancer patients. The overall effect size of psychosocial interventions and the effect of potential moderating variables were examined. These included type and duration of intervention; sociodemographic and clinical parameters; characteristics of quality of life measurement; and the methodological quality of the selected studies. The overall effect size was judged to be moderate. The most important moderating variable was duration of psychosocial intervention, with durations of more than 12 weeks being significantly more effective than interventions of shorter duration. Educational programs were found to be more effective than the other three types covered in the study. They were also ranked higher in regard to active patient involvement. There were no significant differences between the effects of social support, coping skills training, and psychotherapy.

Psychophysiological Mechanisms

The psychophysiological mechanisms through which positive changes might promote a more positive prognosis in relation to cancer need to be explored further. The evidence presented here is drawn from intervention studies using cognitive behavioral stress management (CBSM).

Dunigan, Carr, and Steel (2007) found that positive change as post traumatic growth was associated with longer survival for those with hepato-cellular carcinoma and suggested that it promotes biological homeostasis through hypothalamic modulation of glucocorticoids. This suggestion appears consistent with the findings of Cruess et al. (2000). They reported a study that examined the effects of a CBSM group intervention on serum cortisol levels in women being treated for stage I or II breast cancer. The women were randomly assigned to undergo either a ten-week intervention ($n = 24$) within eight weeks after surgery or were placed on a waiting list ($n = 10$). Cortisol was assessed by means of a radioimmunoassay of blood samples collected at the same time of day just before the start of the intervention and immediately after its completion. The women also reported the degree to which breast cancer had made positive contributions to their lives. Those receiving CBSM reported increased benefit finding and showed reduced serum cortisol levels. Control subjects showed neither change. The researchers report that path analysis suggested that the effect of CBSM on cortisol was mediated by increases in benefit finding.

There are other suggestions that benefit finding might be associated with altered immune system function (Bower, Kemeny, Taylor, and Fahey, 1998; McGregor et al., 2004). These findings and suggested mechanisms are consistent with those suggested much earlier by Cox (1984).

In 2004, McGregor and her colleagues reported a study of the effects of a CBSM intervention on benefit finding and immune function among women in the months following surgery for early-stage breast cancer. Twenty-nine women were randomly assigned to receive either a ten-week CBSM intervention ($n = 18$) or a comparison experience ($n = 11$). The primary psychological outcome measure was benefit finding. The primary immune function outcome measure was in vitro lymphocyte proliferative response to anti CD3. Women in the CBSM intervention reported greater perceptions of benefit associated with the experience of breast cancer compared to the women in the comparison group. At three-month follow-up, women in the CBSM group also had improved lymphocyte proliferation. Finally, increases in benefit finding after the ten-week intervention predicted increases in lymphocyte proliferation at the three-month follow-up. The researchers concluded that the CBSM intervention for women with early-stage breast cancer facilitated positive change in relation to their breast cancer experience, benefit finding, in parallel with later improvement in cellular immune function.

Later, Phillips and her colleagues (2008) reported a study examining the effects of CBSM on late afternoon serum cortisol and relaxation indicators in women who were undergoing treatment for nonmetastatic breast cancer. The CBSM was composed of relaxation, cognitive restructuring, and coping skills training, with 128 patients randomly assigned to receive either a ten-week CBSM group intervention or a one-day psycho-education seminar. Serum cortisol was collected and ability to relax was assessed at study entry and again at 6-month and 12-month follow-up visits. Data were analyzed using latent growth curve modeling. The researchers report that there was a significant effect of the CBSM intervention on change across time for both cortisol and perceived ability to relax. Women receiving CBSM showed significantly greater reductions in cortisol levels across the 12 months compared with those in the control group, who showed no appreciable decline. Women who received CBSM reported greater increases in ability to relax than controls across time. Perceived ability to relax did not statistically mediate CBSM-related reductions in cortisol. The women who participated in the ten-week CBSM intervention during treatment for breast cancer showed decreases in physiological stress in parallel with increases in perceived relaxation skills.

It might be tentatively concluded, on the basis of studies such as these, that CBSM might be associated with reduction in cortisol levels and strengthened immune system function in, at least, women with breast cancer.

Conclusion

Looking back over the evidence sampled and presented here, it is obvious to the authors that this area of scientific concern has not yet reached maturity. While skepticism is warranted and healthy, the evidence has to be judged by "developmental rules" rather than those of a well-defined and established area of science. An aspect of this is keeping an open mind to the possibilities under examination and weighing the risks associated with action on incomplete evidence against those of inaction.

Where do we go from here? An obvious answer to this question is "more and better research," with an emphasis on methodological considerations: a case of motherhood and apple pie. However, such things are more easily demanded than delivered and such activities will continue to take both time and other resources. Furthermore, more thought must be given to the nature of future research in terms of the model of understanding applied and interventions indicated.

We can go beyond "more and better research and reviews." There appears to be broad agreement that psychological and social factors could be at work in determining the quality of life of those with cancer, even if not in influencing the duration of their survival. There is evidence that some types of intervention, for example CBSM and narrative expressive therapy, can alter the psychophysiological function of those with cancer and elevate mood. At least some people with cancer also attempt to make sense of their experiences, find meaning in them and generally cope with those experiences. There is sufficient evidence to start the translation of research knowledge into practice and that is something that many have attempted. The scientific purist might argue that the data are still of insufficient quality and quantity to take action securely and that the area is driven by wishful thinking, as cautioned by Coyne and Tennen (2010). Arguably we should once again apply "developmental rules" and balance the risks associated with proceeding on incomplete evidence against the potential benefits of doing so and the risks of not doing so.

References

Abbey, G., Thompson, S. B., Hickish, T., and Heathcote, D. (2015). A meta-analysis of prevalence rates and moderating factors for cancer-related post-traumatic stress disorder. *Psycho-Oncology, 24,* 371–381.

Allwood, M. A., Bell-Doran, D., and Husain, S. A. (2002). Children's trauma and adjustment reactions to violent and non violent war experiences. *Journal of the American Academy of Child and Adolescent Psychiatry, 41,* 450–457.

Andersen, H. S., Christensen, A. K., and Petersen, G. O. (1991). Post-traumatic stress reactions among rescue workers after a major rail accident. *Anxiety Research, 4,* 245–251

Andrykowski, M. A., and Cordova, M. J. (1998). Factors associated with PTSD symptoms following treatment for breast cancer: Test of the Andersen model. *Journal of Traumatic Stress, 11,* 189–203.

Andrykowski, M. A., and Kangas, M. (2010). Posttraumatic stress disorder associated with cancer diagnosis and treatment. In J. C. Holland et al. (Eds.), *Psycho-Oncology.* Oxford: Oxford University Press.

Antoni, M. H., and Lutgendorf, S. (2007). Psychosocial factors and disease progression in cancer. *Current Directions in Psychological Science, 16,* 42–46.

Bleicker, E. M. A., Pouwer, F., van der Ploeg, H. M., Leer, J. H., and Ader, J. H. (2000). Psychological distress two years after diagnosis of breast cancer: Frequency and prediction. *Patient Education and Counselling, 40,* 209–217.

Bower, J. E., Kemeny, M. E., Taylor, S. E., and Fahey, J. L. (1998). Cognitive processing, discovery of meaning, CD4 decline, and AIDS-related mortality among bereaved HIV-seropositive men. *Journal of Consulting and Clinical Psychology, 66,* 979–986.

Bower, J. E., Meyerowitz, B. E., Desmond, K. A., Bernaards, C. A., Rowland, J. H., and Ganz, P. A. (2005). Perceptions of positive meaning and vulnerability following breast cancer: Predictors and outcomes among long-term breast cancer survivors. *Annals of Behavioral Medicine, 29*, 236–245.

Breslau, N. (2002). Epidemiologic studies of trauma, posttraumatic stress disorder, and other psychiatric disorders. *Canadian Journal of Psychiatry, 47*, 923–929

Brezden, C. B., Phillips, K. A., Abdolell, M., and Bunston, T. I. (2000). Cognitive function in breast cancer patients receiving adjuvant chemotherapy. *Journal of Clinical Oncology, 18*, 2695–2701.

Calhoun, L. G., and Tedeschi, R. G. (2006). *Handbook of Posttraumatic Growth: Research and Practice*. Mahwah, NJ: Lawrence Erlbaum.

Carver, C. S., and Antoni, M. H. (2004). Finding benefit in breast cancer during the year after diagnosis predicts better adjustment 5 to 8 years after diagnosis. *Health Psychology, 23*, 595.

Carver, C. S., Scheier, M. F., and Weintraub, J. K. (1989). Assessing coping strategies: A theoretically based approach. *Journal of Personality and Social Psychology, 56*, 267.

Collison, C., and Mackenzie, A. (1999). The power of story in organizations. *Journal of Workplace Learning, 11*, 38–40.

Cox, T. (1984). Stress: A psychophysiological approach to cancer. In C. Cooper (Ed.), *Psychosocial Stress and Cancer*. Chichester, UK: Wiley.

Cox, T., and Mackay, C. (1982). Psychosocial factors and psychophysiological mechanisms in the aetiology and development of cancers. *Social Science and Medicine, 16*, 381–396.

Coyne, J. C., and Tennen, H. (2010). Positive psychology in cancer care: Bad science, exaggerated claims and unproven medicine. *Annals of Behavioral Medicine, 39*, 16–26.

Cruess, D. G., Antoni, M. H., McGregor, B. A., Kilbourn, K. M., Boyers, A. E., Alferi, S. M., … Kumar, M. (2000). Cognitive-behavioral stress management reduces serum cortisol by enhancing benefit finding among women being treated for early stage breast cancer. *Psychosomatic Medicine, 62*, 304–308.

Curran, P. S., and Miller, P. W (2001). Psychiatric implications of chronic civilian strife or war: Northern Ireland. *Advances in Psychiatric Treatment, 7*, 73–80.

Davis, T. E., Tarcza, E. V., and Munson, M. S. (2009). The psychological impact of hurricanes and storms on adults. In K. E. Cherry (Ed.), *Lifespan Perspective on Natural Disasters*. Heidelberg: Springer.

DeSalvo, K. B., Hyre, A. D., Ompad, D. C., Menke, A., Tynes, L. L., and Muntner, P. (2007). Symptoms of post traumatic stress disorder in a New Orleans workforce following Hurricane Katrina. *Journal of Urban Health, 84*, 142–152

Dunigan, J. T., Carr, B. I., and Steel, J. L. (2007). Posttraumatic growth, immunity and survival in patients with hepatoma. *Digestive Diseases and Sciences, 52*, 2452–2459.

Elliott, T. R, Kurylo, M., and Rivera, P. (2002). Positive growth following acquired physical disability. In C. R. Snyder and S. J. Lopez (Eds.), *Handbook of Positive Psychology*. New York: Oxford University Press.

Gordon, R. D. (2001). Is the sense we take equal to the sense we make? A discussion on sensemaking and power in organisations. *Journal of Management and Organization, 7*, 41–49.

Graves, K. (2003). Social cognitive theory and cancer patients' quality of life: A meta-analysis of psychosocial intervention components. *Health Psychology, 22*, 210–219.

Greer, S., Morris, T., and Pettingale, K. W. (1979). Psychological responses to breast cancer: Effect on outcome. *Lancet, 2(8146)*, 785–787.

Gross, J. J. (2002). Emotion regulation: Affective, cognitive, and social consequences. *Psychophysiology, 39*, 281–291.

Guglietti, C. L., Rosen, B., Murphy, K. J., Laframboise, S., Dodge, J., Ferguson, S., … Ritvo, P. (2010). Prevalence and predictors of PTSD in women undergoing an ovarian cancer investigation. *Psychological Services, 7*, 266–274.

Hagström, R. (1995). The acute psychological impact on survivors following a train accident. *Journal of Traumatic Stress, 8*, 391–402.

Heine, S. J., Proulx, T., and Vohs, K. D. (2006). The meaning maintenance model: On the coherence of social motivations. *Personality and Social Psychology Review, 10*, 88–110.

Helgeson, V. S., Reynolds, K. A., and Tomich, P. L. (2006). A meta-analytic review of benefit finding and growth. *Journal of Consulting and Clinical Psychology, 74*, 797–816

Johnson, H., and Thompson, A. (2008). The development and maintenance of post-traumatic stress disorder (PTSD) in civilian adult survivors of war trauma and torture: A review. *Clinical Psychology Review, 28*, 36–47.

Kangas, M., Henry, J. L., and Bryant, R. A. (2002). Posttraumatic stress disorder following cancer. A conceptual and empirical review. *Clinical Psychology Review, 22*, 499–524.

Kärki, A., Simonen, R., Mälkiä, E., and Selfe, J. (2005). Impairments, activity limitations and participation restrictions 6 and 12 months after breast cancer operation. *Journal of Rehabilitation Medicine*, *37*, 180–188.

Kwak, M., Zebrack, B. J., Meeske, K. A., Embry, L., Aguilar, C., Block, ... Cole, S. (2013). Prevalence and predictors of post-traumatic stress symptoms in adolescent and young adult cancer survivors: A 1-year follow-up study. *Psycho-Oncology*, *22*, 1798–1806.

Linley, P. A., and Joseph, S. (2004). Positive change following trauma and adversity: A review. *Journal of Traumatic Stress*, *17*, 11–21.

Luutonen, S., Vahlberg, T., Eloranta, S., Hyväri, H., and Salminen, E. (2011). Breast cancer patients receiving postoperative radiotherapy: Distress, depressive symptoms and unmet needs of psychosocial support. *Radiotherapy and Oncology*, *100*, 299–303.

Manne, S., Ostroff, J., Winkel, G., Goldstein, L., Fox, K., and Grana, G. (2004). Posttraumatic growth after breast cancer: Patient, partner, and couple perspectives. *Psychosomatic Medicine*, *66*, 442–454.

Mascaro, N., and Rosen, D. H. (2005). Existential meaning's role in the enhancement of hope and prevention of depressive symptoms. *Journal of Personality*, *73*, 985–1014.

McGregor, B., Antoni, M. H., Boyers, A., Alferi, S. M., Blomberg, B. B., and Carver, C. S. (2004). Cognitive-behavioral stress management increases benefit finding and immune function among women with early-stage breast cancer. *Journal of Psychosomatic Research*, *56*, 1–8.

Norris, F. H., Murphy, A. D., Baker, C. K., and Perilla, J. L. (2004). Post disaster PTSD over four waves of a panel study of Mexico's 1999 flood. *Journal of Traumatic Stress*, *17*, 283–292.

Park, C. L., and Fenster, J. R. (2004). Stress-related growth: Predictors of occurrence and correlates with psychological adjustment. *Journal of Social and Clinical Psychology*, *23*, 195–215.

Phillips, K. M., Antoni, M. H., Lechner, S. C., Blomberg, B. B., Llabre, M. M., Avisar, E., ... Carver, C. S. (2008). Stress management intervention reduces serum cortisol and increases relaxation during treatment for nonmetastatic breast cancer. *Psychosomatic Medicine*, *70*,1044–1049.

Rehse, B., and Pukrop, R. (2003). Effects of psychosocial interventions on quality of life in adult cancer patients: Meta-analysis of 37 published controlled outcome studies. *Patient Education and Counseling*, *50*, 179–186.

Rittenberg, C. N. (1995). Positive thinking: An unfair burden for cancer patients? *Supportive Care in Cancer*, *3*, 37–39.

Schwarzer, R., Luszczynska, A., Boehmer, S., Taubert, S., and Knoll, N. (2006). Changes in finding benefit after cancer surgery and the prediction of well-being one year later. *Social Science and Medicine*, *63*, 1614–1624.

Siegel, K., and Schrimshaw, E. W. (2007). The stress moderating role of benefit finding on psychological distress and well-being among women living with HIV/AIDS. *AIDS Behavior*, 11, 421–433.

Sims, A., and Sims, D. (1998). The phenomenology of post-traumatic stress disorder: A symptomatic study of 70 victims of psychological trauma. *Psychopathology*, 31, 96–112

Smedslund, G., and Ringdal, G. I. (2004). Meta-analysis of the effects of psychosocial interventions on survival time in cancer patients. *Journal of Psychosomatic Research*, 57, 123–131.

Stanton, A. (2010). Positive consequences of the experience of cancer: Perceptions of growth and meaning. In J. C. Holland et al. (Eds), *Psycho-Oncology*. Oxford: Oxford University Press.

Stanton, A. L., Bower, J. E., and Low, C. A. (2006). Posttraumatic growth after cancer. In L. G. Calhoun and R. G. Tedeschi (Eds.), *Handbook of Posttraumatic Growth: Research and Practice*. Mahwah, NJ: Lawrence Erlbaum.

Stanton, A. L., Danoff-Burg, S., Sworowski, L. A., Collins, C. A., Branstetter, A. D., Rodriguez-Hanley, A., ... Austenfeld, J. L. (2002). Randomized, controlled trial of written emotional expression and benefit finding in breast cancer patients. *Journal of Clinical Oncology*, *20*, 4160–4168.

Tallman, B. A., Altmaier, E., and Garcia, C. (2007). Finding benefit from cancer. *Journal of Counseling Psychology*, *54*, 481.

Tedeschi, R. G., and Calhoun, L. G. (1996). The Posttraumatic Growth Inventory: Measuring the positive legacy of trauma. *Journal of Traumatic Stress*, *9*, 455–471.

Tedeschi, R. G., and Calhoun, L. G. (2004). Posttraumatic growth: Conceptual foundations and empirical evidence. *Psychological Inquiry*, *15*, 1–18.

Tennen, H., and Affleck, G. (2002). Benefit-finding and benefit-reminding. In C. R. Snyder (Ed.), *Handbook of Positive Psychology*. New York: Oxford University Press.

Thulesius, H., and Håkansson, A. (1999). Screening for post traumatic stress disorder symptoms among Bosnian refugees. *Journal of Traumatic Stress*, *12*, 167–174.

Tomich, P. L., and Helgeson, V. S. (2004). Is finding something good in the bad always good? Benefit finding among women with breast cancer. *Health Psychology*, *23*, 16–23.

van't Spijker, A., Trijsburg, R. W, and Duivenvoorden, H. J. (1997). Psychological sequelae of cancer diagnosis: A meta-analytical review of 59 studies after 1980. *Psychosomatic Medicine, 59,* 583–593.

Wang, L., Zhang, Y., Wang, W., Shi, Z., Shen, J., Li, M., and Yong Xin, Y. (2009). Symptoms of posttraumatic stress disorder among adult survivors three months after the Sichuan earthquake in China. *Journal of Traumatic Stress, 22,* 444–450.

Widows, M. R., Jacobsen, P. B., Booth-Jones, M., and Fields, K. K. (2005). Predictors of posttraumatic growth following bone marrow transplantation for cancer. *Health Psychology, 24,* 266.

Wright, J. C., Binney, V., and Kunkler, J. (1994). Psychological distress in the local Hillsborough or "host" community following the Hillsborough football stadium disaster. *Journal of Community and Applied Social Psychology, 4,* 77–89.

Zang, Y. Y., Hunt, N., and Cox, T. (2011). Guided Narrative Technique: Examining its effect among children traumatised by the earthquake. In O. Bray and P. Bray (Eds.), *Voicing Trauma and Truth: Narratives of Disruption and Transformation.* Oxford: Inter-Disciplinary Press.

30

Sleep, Work, and Well-Being

Erica Carleton and Julian Barling

Introduction

Well-being is of the utmost importance to individuals, deeply affecting the quality of all aspects of their lives. Indeed, the effects of well-being go further than individuals themselves, and organizations should care about the well-being of their employees because of the negative consequences that poor health and well-being have on organizational functioning (e.g., Danna and Griffin, 1999).

If well-being is so important, it behooves us to understand not just its consequences, but its causes as well. Two essential determinants of individuals' well-being are sleep and work (e.g., Kuoppala, Lamminpää, and Husman, 2008; Strine and Chapman, 2005), and not by chance, these are also the two activities that together absorb most of adults' lives (Basner et al., 2007; Barnes, Wagner, and Ghumman, 2012). Despite their importance to well-being, sleep and work are incompatible, as time spent working takes away from the time available for sleep, and vice versa. For example, for full-time employees, as the time spent working has increased over the past 30 years, the amount of time spent sleeping has decreased (Knutson, Van Cauter, Rathouz, DeLeire, and Lauderdale, 2010). Barnes et al. (2012) go further, showing in two separate samples that this relationship is nonlinear: the effects on sleep loss occur disproportionately for those who work the longest hours. This is of the utmost importance, because as time spent working increases and time spent sleeping decreases, well-being and health are negatively impacted (e.g., Shields, 1999), highlighting the need to understand the interrelationship between sleep and work, and how their separate and combined effects influence employee well-being.

The remainder of this chapter focuses on how the two most time-consuming activities in adult life (sleep and work) affect well-being. We begin by establishing the direct effects of both work and sleep on well-being. We then move to consider how work impacts sleep and well-being, with special attention to shift work and work stress, and this is followed by an examination of how sleep impacts work and well-being. Finally, we will consider implications

The Handbook of Stress and Health: A Guide to Research and Practice, First Edition.
Edited by Cary L. Cooper and James Campbell Quick.
© 2017 John Wiley & Sons, Ltd. Published 2017 by John Wiley & Sons, Ltd.

for organizations, and how individuals and organizations can improve the health and well-being of workers.

We acknowledge that there are many definitions and proposed dimensions of well-being. It is not our intention, however, to engage in this conceptual debate. Instead, our goal in this chapter is to understand how sleep and work together impact well-being, and we pay special attention to individuals' psychological and physical functioning.

Work Stress and Well-Being

Research on work stress and its impact on health has a long history (e.g., Ganster and Schaubroeck, 1991; Kornhauser, 1965). Work stress has been linked consistently with a variety of employee outcomes, including negative physical and psychological well-being (e.g. Beehr, 1995; Beehr and Glazer, 2005; Jex and Crossley, 2005). Specific physical health effects of excess work stress include increased incidence of cardiovascular disease (Johnson and Hall, 1988), type 2 diabetes and pre-diabetic metabolic syndrome (Agardh et al., 2003; Chandola, Brunner, and Marmot, 2006), and musculoskeletal disorders (Houtman, Bongers, Smulders, and Kompier, 1994). Fried et al.'s (2013) recent study is indicative of the specificity with which both work stress and well-being are examined: Using longitudinal data and a large sample, inadequate levels of job enrichment (too low or too high) contributed to abdominal obesity.

The psychological consequences of work stress include burnout (Maslach, Schaufeli, and Leiter, 2001), anxiety, depression, and job and life dissatisfaction (Van der Doef and Maes, 1999). Research also demonstrates how low control at work predicts depression and psychiatric symptoms (Mausner-Dorsch and Eaton, 2000) and neurotic disorders (Cropley, Steptoe, and Joekes, 1999). The debate as to whether work stress affects well-being is long over.

Sleep and Well-Being

Medical research has clearly established that sleep impacts health. People who consistently fail to get enough sleep are at an increased risk of chronic disease (e.g., Hublin, Partinen, Koskenvuo, and Kaprio, 2007). For example, being at risk for or having a sleep disorder (e.g., sleep apnea, insomnia) predicts an increased risk for cardiovascular disease (e.g., hypertension, myocardial infarction, arrhythmia, heart failure) and type 2 diabetes (Newman et al., 2000; Public Health Agency of Canada, 2009). In addition, poor sleep quality predicts less severe health issues such as muscle pain, headaches, and gastrointestinal problems (Kuppermann et al., 1995; Schwartz et al., 1999), and obesity and metabolic disturbance (Spiegel, Leproult, and Van Cauter, 1999; Wolk and Somers, 2007).

In terms of the psychological outcomes, poor sleep leads to hostility and frustration (Kahn-Greene, Lipizzi, Conrad, Kamimori, and Killgore, 2006), anxiety and paranoia (Kahn-Greene, Killgore, Kamimori, Balkin, and Killgore, 2007) and depression (Riemann, Berger, and Voderholzer, 2001). Although these all involved subclinical symptoms, research from the field of sleep medicine also shows a high comorbidity between sleep disorders and psychiatric illnesses, especially mood and anxiety disorders (Ohayon, 2002). Similarly, insomnia is a risk factor for mental illness in epidemiologic studies over the past two decades (e.g., Breslau, Roth, Rosenthal, and Andreski, 1996; Ford and Kamerow, 1989). More recently, baseline insomnia was a significant risk factor for incident depression and anxiety 12 months later in a sample of

2,000 United Kingdom residents (Morphy, Dunn, Lewis, Boardman, and Croft, 2007). Taken together, these studies show that different aspects of sleep problems affect well-being.

Work Affecting Sleep

Having established that sleep and work influence well-being, we turn our attention to how sleep and work are interrelated, and how they together affect well-being, and focus on two of the most frequently studied ways in which work impacts sleep, namely shift work and work stress.

Shift Work

There has been a wealth of research on shift work impacts on sleep (e.g., Folkard and Monk, 1985). This should not be surprising given that shift work is ubiquitous. In contrast, sleep is a new research focus in organizational psychology (e.g. Barnes, 2012; Mullins, Cortina, Drake, and Dalal, 2014). Shift work reflects any work schedule that deviates from the traditional day-shift (typically starting between 7 a.m. and 10 a.m.), such as night, early morning, and late afternoon/evening shifts, or rotating shifts. Large deviations from the traditional work schedule, such as working during the dark hours of night, require shift workers to work when they are programmed to sleep, and to try to sleep during times that are biologically more appropriate for wakefulness (Cheng and Drake, 2016). This disrupts the normal sleep/wake cycles.

Sleep/wake cycles include two physiological systems that regulate sleep, sleep/wake home-ostasis and the circadian biological clock (National Sleep Foundation, 2015). The sleep/wake homeostasis clock reflects the drive to sleep, leaving individuals more tired as the day progresses, and ensuring that by night time, they are ready to sleep. The circadian biological clock regulates the timing of periods of sleepiness and wakefulness throughout the day and night (National Sleep Foundation, 2015) so that the drive to sleep is the strongest in the middle of the night (e.g., between 2 and 4 a.m.) and in the early afternoon (e.g. between 1 and 3 p.m.). Any reversal of typical sleep and wake schedules due to shift work is at odds with normal sleep/wake cycles and while some individuals are able to adapt, many shift workers experience functional impairments (Drake et al., 2015). This condition is termed *shift work disorder* and has major consequences on sleep and performance, and importantly on health and well-being at work.

Consequences of shift work for sleep and well-being

The most common complaint of shift workers is lack of sleep (e.g., Parkes, 1999). Shift workers sleep an average of 30 to 60 minutes less per day than day workers (e.g., Park, Matsumoto, Seo, Cho, and Noh, 2000; Pilcher, Lambert, and Huffcutt, 2000). In addition, they experience other difficulties such as in falling and staying asleep. Thus, shift work may trigger sleep difficulties, or exacerbate preexisting insomnia symptoms (Cheng and Drake, 2016). For example, in a large epidemiological study, 18.5 percent of shift workers reported clinically significant sleep difficulties, twice the rate of day workers (Drake, Roehrs, Richardson, Walsh, and Roth, 2004).

Shift work is also associated with poor health. Based on a large-scale long-term study, shift work increased the risk of being diagnosed with chronic conditions, including cardiovascular disease and gastrointestinal disorders (Shields, 2002). In a review of 17 studies, 13 of which were longitudinal, Bøggild and Knutsson (1999) concluded that shift workers had a 40 percent increased risk for cardiovascular disease compared with day workers. Shift work has been associated with reproductive health problems and breast cancer among female employees (Shields, 2002). In addition, Figà-Talamanca's (2006) review of 14 studies examining irregular work hours found that shiftwork was associated with a slight increase in the risk of spontaneous abortion and reduced fertility.

The bulk of research on shift work and well-being has focused on physical outcomes. While mental health outcomes have received less research attention, shiftwork is associated with greater psychological distress, depression, anxiety, and burnout (e.g., Bohle and Tilley, 1989; Healy, Minors, and Waterhouse, 1993; Jamal, 2004).

Consequences of shift work for work-related well-being

In general most outcomes of shift work are a function of the excessive sleepiness caused by insufficient and disrupted sleep (Cheng and Drake, 2016). Thus, one major outcome of sleepiness at work is involuntary sleeping on the job, which can have significant negative effects on work-related well-being (e.g., safety) and the quality of job performance.

One study found that a third of nurses working different shifts reported unintentionally falling asleep (Gold et al., 1992). Aside from preventing any work being done, this increases the risk for injuries, especially when driving. Not surprisingly, night and morning shift workers are at increased risk for motor vehicle accidents (Cheng and Drake, 2016). In one study using a driving simulator, workers driving after a night shift experienced substantially increased sleepiness and decreased driving performance (Åkerstedt, Peters, Anund, and Kecklund, 2005). This effect may be most pronounced for drivers involved in heavy-duty transportation, who have a disproportionately higher number of fatigue-related collisions (Clarke, Ward, Bartle, and Truman, 2009). Indeed, transportation remains one of the deadliest sectors per capita across different counties (e.g., WSIB, 2014), with approximately 40 percent of transportation incidents involving someone driving a commercial vehicle while sleepy or sleeping (TUC, 2013). Acknowledging the consequences for the public at large, who are inadvertently put at risk, gives greater meaning to the effects of shift work.

Even when shift workers do remain awake, but sleepy, reduced cognitive functioning can put the public at risk in other ways. Research in medical settings shows that interns engaged in shift work are more likely to make serious diagnostic and medication errors (e.g., in ordering or administering medication, intravenous fluids, or blood products), even resulting in increased rates of patient death (Barger et al., 2006; Landrigan et al., 2004). Similarly, nurses involved in rotating shifts were twice as prone to work-related accidents or errors, and 2.5 times more likely to experience a near-miss (Gold et al., 1992). One reason for this is that shift work disorder affects psychomotor control, which can impact any work requiring manual dexterity or complex psychomotor tasks, such as surgery or driving (Cheng and Drake, 2016). Thus, medical interns are also at higher risk of self-injury from used needles during the night shifts (Ayas et al., 2006).

In conclusion, shift work increases sleepiness through sleep loss, thereby increasing risk for injuries and accidents at work. In addition, shift work reduces sleep and is linked to both physical and mental disorders. Having examined shift work (which is ubiquitous but visible) and sleep, we now consider a more insidious or invisible work-related factor that impacts both sleep and well-being, namely work stress.

Work Stress

Work stress is an all too prevalent outcome of work, experienced at one time or another by most employees, and it can affect both sleep and well-being. Broadly speaking, work stress is a concept that reflects reactions to objective conditions in the job environment (i.e., job stressors), the subjective experience of the conditions and the cognitive, affective, and physiological reactions to the subjective experiences (i.e., strain; Kahn and Byosiere, 1992; Pratt and Barling, 1988). Different work conditions can constitute stressors (e.g., task-related stressors, role stressors, social stressors, and physical stressors; Sonnentag and Frese, 2012), all of which can be experienced chronically (i.e., enduring across time), as acute stressors, or as short-term events (Pratt and Barling, 1988).[1]

Within this perspective, work stress is a process, and this explains why most employees would experience work stressors, but not all would be negatively affected. Some individuals will experience (objective) work stressors negatively, but others might not. Those who do not would not experience any strain. Of the people who do experience subjective work stress, some might be affected negatively (e.g., poor health), but others might not, thereby not suffering any strain. Sleep problems are a frequent manifestation of strain (e.g., Nixon, Mazzola, Bauer, Krueger, and Spector, 2011) and work-related stress is one the most frequently reported causes of sleep problems (Ertel, Koenen, and Berkman, 2008).

Consequences of work stress for sleep and work-related well-being

The sheer volume of research on this topic enables us to discuss studies separately, depending on whether the data were cross-sectional, longitudinal, or daily.

Cross-sectional studies   Most the research in this area has been cross-sectional, and has examined a wide array of work-related stressors (e.g., task-related stressors, role stressors, social stressors). In general, work stress (e.g., task-related stressors, workload, time pressure) is consistently associated with sleep problems (e.g., Berset, Elfering, Lüthy, Lüthi, and Semmer, 2011; Stenfors, Magnusson Hanson, Oxenstierna, Theorell, and Nilsson, 2013; Winwood and Lushington, 2006). As one example, Barber and Santuzzi (2015) examined telepressure (i.e., preoccupation with and perceived necessity to respond immediately to electronic messages), and found that telepressure predicted poor sleep quality. Social stressors (e.g., interpersonal conflicts; Winwood and Lushington, 2006) and the experience of injustice (Hietapakka et al., 2013) are also associated with poor sleep. Meta-analytical evidence suggests that interpersonal stress has a larger effect on sleep than task-related, role, and time related stressors (see Nixon et al., 2011).

Longitudinal studies   Studies using longitudinal designs are important because they begin to enable causal inferences about the role of work stress. In a review of 16 longitudinal studies on work stress and sleep, Van Laethem, Beckers, Kompier, Dijksterhuis, and Geurts (2013) reported that job demands consistently predicted sleep quality over time. As well, Linton et al.'s (2015) review of 24 studies showed again that high job demands predicted future sleep disturbances.

Along with job demands, social stressors also affect sleep. For example, breach of the psychological contract, or the unwritten set of expectations of the employment relationship as distinct from the formal, codified employment contract, predicted insomnia across time; and in some cases, participants' insomnia symptoms were present eight months later (Ng and Feldman, 2013).

Extending this, researchers examined the longitudinal effects of subjective stress symptoms that result from work stressors on sleep problems. Armon, Shirom, Shapira, and Melamed (2008) showed, after controlling for baseline insomnia, baseline depression, and other relevant variables in a sample of healthy employees, that burnout at baseline predicted insomnia 18 months later.

Daily studies   Researchers have also investigated the same-day effects of work stress on sleep. Studies such as this are important, as they enable an understanding of experiences as they unfold (Iida, Shrout, Laurenceau, and Bolger, 2012). This research has shown that stressful days are followed by impaired sleep (Dahlgren, Kecklund, and Åkerstedt, 2005; Jones and Fletcher, 1996). As one example, sleep was more fragmented (i.e., a higher number of awakenings) the same night that employees experienced social exclusion (Pereira, Meier, and Elfering, 2013). In a separate study, Pereira, Semmer and Elfering (2014) showed that tasks that employees perceive as unreasonable or unnecessary predicted increased sleep fragmentation and problems falling asleep the same night.

Researchers have also shown that during weeks in which employees experienced a high level of stress at work, total sleep time decreased (Dahlgren et al., 2005). Similarly, Syrek and Antoni (2014) showed that over a period of five weeks, the stress associated with unfinished tasks predicted self-reported sleep disturbances over the weekend. Finally, employed students reported poor sleep quality during weeks in which they experienced high levels of work–school conflict (Park and Sprung, 2014).

Taken together, across cross-sectional, longitudinal and daily/weekly studies, work stressors and work stress influence sleep. In the next section, we examine research investigating whether sleep affects work and well-being, and examine potential reciprocal relationships between work stress and sleep. First we will review the impact of sleep on performance, job related attitudes, affect, and behaviors.

Sleep Affecting Work

So we have seen that shift work and work stress affect sleep, but might sleep affect the experience of work? Research on the effects of sleep physiology on human functioning is by no means new (see Harrison and Horne, 2000; Lim and Dinges, 2010). Although more limited, research within organizational psychology now shows that sleep also affects several work-related outcomes. For example, sleep deprivation predicts poor task performance (Kessler et al., 2011; Pilcher and Huffcutt, 1996) and decreased organizational citizenship behavior (Barnes, Ghumman, and Scott, 2013). As well, low sleep quantity predicts decreased job satisfaction (Scott and Judge, 2006). Poor sleep also leads to a host of negative organizational outcomes, including workplace deviance (Christian and Ellis, 2011), cyberloafing (Wagner, Barnes, Lim, and Ferris, 2012), and unethical behavior (Barnes, Schaubroeck, Huth, and Ghumman, 2011).

Self-regulation has emerged as the dominant theoretical framework for understanding the effects of sleep at work (Christian and Ellis, 2011). Baumeister, Heatherton, and Tice (1994) first suggested that self-control depended on a limited energy resource. They proposed an energy theory of self-control, in which self-control is a limited resource that becomes depleted through use (e.g., Baumeister et al., 1994; Baumeister, Bratslavsky, Muraven, and Tice, 1998; Muraven and Baumeister, 2000). Specifically, all acts of self-control draw from a common resource that controls thoughts, emotions and behaviors (Baumeister et al., 1998). The depletion of self-regulatory resources involves a temporary reduction in the capacity to engage in volitional action (Baumeister, Muraven, and Tice, 2000; Christian and Ellis, 2011). In the face of this depletion, at least two courses of action are possible. Replenishment can take place, and sleep is one essential activity through which this can occur (Baumeister et al., 2000). However, if replenishment does not take place, depletion can spiral downwards, negatively affecting several work-related outcomes (Barnes, 2012). Along with the negative effects of sleep on organizational outcomes, sleep is also related to employees' well-being at work. Some of these affective outcomes are examined below.

Affect

Research has long shown that sleep influences affect and emotions (e.g., Pilcher and Huffcutt, 1996). Importantly, sleep interferes with specific aspects of affect that might have important consequences in the workplace. For example, sleep deficits increase negative affect (e.g., hostility) and decrease positive affect (e.g., cheerfulness or joviality; Scott and Judge, 2006; Sonnentag, Binnewies, and Mojza, 2008). Sleep disturbances also interfere with the ability to regulate emotions, particularly negatively valenced emotions (Yoo, Gujar, Hu, Jolesz, and Walker, 2007). In the same vein, sleep loss amplifies the negative emotional consequences of disruptive daytime experiences, and inhibits positive benefit associated with rewarding or goal-enhancing activities (Zohar, Tzischinsky, Epstein, and Lavie, 2005). The effects of sleep deprivation go further, by selectively impairing accurate judgment of facial emotions, especially threat relevant (anger) and reward relevant (happy) categories (Van der Helm, Gujar, and Walker, 2010). Not surprisingly, sleep deprivation is associated with lower emotional intelligence and intrapersonal functioning (Killgore et al., 2008), and individuals who were at risk for a sleep disorder were more likely to report mood impairments, boredom and avoiding interactions with coworkers (Swanson et al., 2011), all of which can negatively influence work-related well-being.

Perceptions of Work

Intriguingly, sleep does not only affect our work per se, it also affects how we perceive our work, and our work stress, because insufficient or poor quality sleep affects how employees evaluate information (Barber and Budnick, 2015), causing them to perceive their work environment as more negative (de Lange, Taris, Kompier, Houtman, and Bongers, 2005). For example, sleep-deprived individuals are more reactive to negative or aversive events than those who are not (Anderson and Platten, 2011; Franzen, Buysse, Dahl, Thompson, and Siegle, 2009). This phenomenon is echoed in research showing that poor sleepers perceive workplace events as more distressing than better sleepers, even when the amount of daily stressors is the same (Morin, Rodrigue, and Ivers, 2003; Zohar et al., 2005). Barber and Budnick (2015) showed across three studies that this phenomenon may be especially likely in the presence of social threats, such as an unfair workplace. These results are important, as they suggest that sleep impacts individuals' perceptions of work and work stress, as a result of which there is a reciprocal relationship between work stress and sleep.

However, findings from studies examining whether this reciprocal relationship exists have been mixed. First, de Lange et al. (2009) replicated the predicted effects from stress to sleep, specifically, that high-strain work environments (characterized by high job demands and low job control) predicted sleep-related complaints (sleep quality, fatigue); however sleep did not influence work stress across their four year, four-wave study. When Magnusson Hanson et al. (2011) extended de Lange et al.'s (2009) study by including lack of social support as a potential job stressor, there was a reciprocal relationship between social support and sleep. However more research is needed to understand sleep's influence on perceptions of work stress.

Workplace Injuries and Accidents

Moving beyond the potential psychological outcomes of sleep to physical well-being, we turn our attention to work-related injuries and accidents, a critical outcome of sleep problems. Importantly, people do not need to fall asleep on the job for an accident to occur. Merely being sleepy at work is associated with increases in risk-taking behavior (Roehrs, Greenwald, and Roth, 2004), because sleep is related to reduced alertness, concentration, vigilance, and attentiveness (e.g., Banks and Dinges, 2007; Drake et al., 2001; Mullins et al., 2014), explaining why there is an increased risk of safety incidents, errors and injuries when people are sleep-deprived at work (e.g., Dinges, 1995).

In an intriguing study, Barnes and Wagner (2009) used Daylight Saving Time to examine the effects of sleep loss on injuries. Their analyses showed that one hour of lost sleep predicted a significant increase in workplace injuries, and in injuries of greater severity. More importantly, they also showed in a follow-up study that 40 minutes of lost sleep was sufficient to result in an increase in injuries. The effects of sleep loss on workplace safety has been documented in different countries, such as Canada (Kling, McLeod, and Koehoorn, 2010) and Finland (Salminen et al., 2010). Additionally, self-reported disturbed sleep, which contributes to daytime sleepiness, predicts accidental death at work (Åkerstedt, Fredlund, Gillberg, and Jansson, 2002). These negative effects that lost sleep has on work-related injuries and accidents really demonstrates the critical importance of sleep to an individual's health and well-being.

Health and Work Withdrawal

Sleep problems also influence work indirectly, through their effects on health. As previously noted, there is a well-established relationship between sleep and health (e.g., Spiegel et al., 1999; Wolk and Somers, 2007); in turn, poor health affects work, and work withdrawal behaviors specifically. Both sleep and health problems result in absenteeism. One study showed that daytime sleepiness predicted taking more days off work for health reasons (Philip, Taillard, Niedhammer, Guilleminault, and Bioulac, 2001). Similarly, disturbed sleep and sleepiness both predicted long-term sickness absence in a national sample in Sweden (Åkerstedt, Kecklund, Alfredsson, and Selen, 2007).

Further evidence for indirect effects of sleep on work withdrawal comes from research showing that poor sleep quality among Japanese white-collar employees predicted poor physical and psychological health, and sickness absence (Minowa and Tango, 2003). Importantly from the organization's perspective, disturbed sleep predicts long-term (90 days or more) and intermediate length (14–89 days) sickness leave (Åkerstedt et al., 2007), as well as medically certified sickness absence from work (Westerlund et al., 2008). Similarly, mediocre or poor sleep predicted long-term work disability (Eriksen, Natvig, and Bruusgaard, 2001). Last, more evidence for indirect effects of sleep on work withdrawal derives from research showing that sleep apnea combined with daytime sleepiness was strongly associated with sick leave (Sivertsen, Björnsdóttir, Øverland, Bjorvatn, and Salo, 2013).

As this review suggests, not only does work affects sleep, but sleep also has important effects on both psychological and physical well-being at work. In the next section we will examine some potential avenues for further research on this important topic, and then review the practical implications of these findings.

Moving Forward

One of the delights in writing a chapter of this nature is the opportunity to read and think deeply about the topic. In doing so, the need for further research investigating how work and sleep influence each other, and in turn influence well-being, becomes even more apparent. What follows are three different areas for investigation that we think would further our understanding of sleep, work and well-being.

First, as already suggested, more research is needed examining the reciprocal relationship between work stress and sleep, and how sleep problems may influence the way in which people perceive work stressors. Some support for the plausibility of this idea emerges from research showing a robust reciprocal relationship between mental health and work stress (e.g. Akashiba et al., 2002; Ford and Kamerow, 1989; de Lange, Taris, Kompier, Houtman, and Bongers, 2004). To explain the reciprocal relationship between mental health and work stress, de Lange et al. suggest that mental health influences work stress by changing the way in which people evaluate their work environment, such that employees experiencing mental health issues might perceive their work environment more negatively. Similar arguments prevail for the effects of sleep problems. Previous research demonstrates that sleep deprivation changes individuals' perceptions of work-related phenomena (Barber and Budnick, 2015). Zapf, Dormann, and Frese (1996) labeled this effect as the "true strain–stressor process", because in this case, stressors (i.e., job stressors) may sometimes be affected by strain (i.e., sleep problems). Although work is beginning in this area (e.g., Barber and Budnick, 2015), more research is needed.

Second, sleep does not only affect physical withdrawal from the workplace (i.e., absenteeism); it also potentially affects psychological and cognitive withdrawal while at work. This can be understood by examining cognitive distraction. For example, sleepiness decreases attentional capacity through hyper-reaction to novel stimuli (Gumenyuk et al., 2010) or through lapses in attention (Drake et al., 2001; Lim and Dinges, 2010). In terms of hyper-reaction to stimuli, Anderson and Horne (2006) demonstrated that sleepiness enhanced participant distraction during the completion of a monotonous cognitive task. In terms of lapses in attention, a meta-analysis conducted by Lim and Dinges (2010) examined the effects of short-term sleep deprivation on cognitive variables, including simple and complex attention, processing speed, working memory, short-term memory, and reasoning and crystalized intelligence. They found that sleep deprivation produced significant differences in most cognitive domains; however, the largest effects were seen in tests of simple, sustained attention. Decreased attentional capabilities resulting from sleepiness therefore likely lead to cognitive distraction at work. Therefore, researchers should examine the impact that sleep has on withdrawal both at work and from work.

Third, one salient feature of the research on the interdependence of sleep and work is that, with a few exceptions (e.g., Guglielmi, Jurado-Gámez, Gude, and Buela-Casal, 2014; Sivertsen et al., 2013; Sjösten et al., 2009; Ulfberg, Carter, and Edling, 2000), it has been based almost exclusively on nonclinical populations, or healthy individuals who do not manifest clinically diagnosed sleep problems. This might be a significant omission: The *International Classification of Sleep Disorders* (American Sleep Disorders Association, 2001) distinguishes more than 80 different sleep disorders and problems, with falling asleep or daytime sleepiness affecting 35–40 percent of the US adult population (Hossain and Shapiro, 2002). Not only might the clinical sleep problems interfere directly with work, but because they have a powerful influence on health (e.g., hypertension, heart disease, irregular heartbeat, heart failure, cerebrovascular disease, depression, and type 2 diabetes; Public Health Agency of Canada, 2009), there is the possibility of indirect effects on work, magnifying the importance of sleep for work.

Thus, it becomes important to understand how individuals with diagnosed sleep disorders cope with their work. Research suggests that obstructive sleep apnea impacts a number of work-related outcomes, including increased stress and burnout (Guglielmi et al., 2014), workplace accidents (Ulfberg et al., 2000), absenteeism (Sivertsen et al., 2008; 2013) and reduced productivity and performance (Mulgrew et al., 2007; Ulfberg, Carter, Talback, and Edling, 1996), and even subsequent sick leave and permanent work disability (Sivertsen et al., 2008; Sivertsen et al., 2013). Future research could also contrast the work-related outcomes of different sleep disorders such as sleep apnea, insomnia and narcolepsy. Last, by nature diagnosed sleep disorders are likely to be ongoing and chronic and therefore might result in unique work outcomes, making it important to contrast the effects of clinically diagnosed vs. everyday sleep problems.

Practical Implications

Our review suggests that two different types of interventions might be available to organizations. First, organizations may directly address job stressors (i.e., job demands and social relationships at work), and the scheduling of shift work (i.e., ensuring that rotating shifts are stable, rotate forward and are longer term) to improve sleep, and thereby health-related outcomes. Organizations could also examine how work-related cultural beliefs about sleep influence employees' sleep and well-being. For example, organizations could help to ensure that employees can recover from demanding work by not expecting emails to be answered at night or on the weekends (e.g. Barber and Santuzzi, 2015).

Another way in which organizations might be able to intervene is suggested by research on nurses' experience with what is referred to as "underpayment inequity" (Greenberg, 2006). A change in pay policy led to a reduction in pay for nurses in two hospitals but no pay reduction in two other hospitals. Not surprisingly, nurses who had experienced pay reductions not only reported feelings of pay unfairness, they also experienced greater insomnia. Supervisors of these nurses then received four hours of leadership training that focused on interactional justice; and this significantly reduced both the nurses' insomnia and feelings of being treated unfairly. These findings are of considerable significance from a practical perspective: The fact that both insomnia and feelings of injustice were reduced by only four hours of training, conducted in group sessions, means that organizations have a relatively inexpensive opportunity to enhance employees' sleep and well-being, and reduce their work stress.

Conclusion

We have shown how sleep and work are reciprocally related, and how both influence employees' psychological and physical well-being. In one way, this knowledge provides a unique challenge to organizations: These findings remind us how work affects well-being outside of the workplace, but they also show that a major cause of work stress and lack of work-related well-being lies outside of the organization. While organizations have traditionally been reluctant to engage in any interventions that might be seen as "meddling" in their employees' non-work, or private lives, minimal organizational interventions exist that can reduce work stress, and enhance employees' sleep and well-being (Greenberg, 2006; Kelloway and Barling, 2010). Given the stakes involved both for employees and their organizations, this is an opportunity not to be missed.

Note

1. For the purpose of this discussion, we consider work stressors together; more finite considerations about the effects of different forms of types of work stressors appear elsewhere (e.g., Barling, Kelloway, and Frone, 2005; Jex and Yankelevich, 2008).

References

Agardh, E. E., Ahlbom, A., Andersson, T., Efendic, S., Grill, V., Hallqvist, J., … Ostenson, C. G. (2003). Work stress and low sense of coherence is associated with type 2 diabetes in middle-aged Swedish women. *Diabetes Care, 26,* 719–724.

Akashiba, T., Kawahara, S., Akahoshi, T., Omori, C., Saito, O., Majima, T., and Horie, T. (2002). Relationship between quality of life and mood or depression in patients with severe obstructive sleep apnea syndrome. *Chest, 122,* 861–865.

Åkerstedt, T., Fredlund, P., Gillberg, M., and Jansson, B. (2002). Work load and work hours in relation to disturbed sleep and fatigue in a large representative sample. *Journal of Psychosomatic Research, 53,* 585–588.

Åkerstedt, T., Kecklund, G., Alfredsson, L., and Selen, J. (2007). Predicting long-term sickness absence from sleep and fatigue. *Journal of Sleep Research, 16,* 341–345.

Åkerstedt, T., Peters, B., Anund, A., and Kecklund, G. (2005). Impaired alertness and performance driving home from the night shift: A driving simulator study. *Journal of Sleep Research, 14,* 17–20.

American Sleep Disorders Association (1997). *International Classification of Sleep Disorders, Revised: Diagnostic and Coding Manual.* Rochester, MN: American Sleep Disorders Association.

Anderson, C., and Horne, J. A. (2006). Sleepiness enhances distraction during a monotonous task. *Sleep, 29,* 573–576.

Anderson, C., and Platten, C. R. (2011). Sleep deprivation lowers inhibition and enhances impulsivity to negative stimuli. *Behavioural Brain Research, 217,* 463–466.

Armon, G., Shirom, A., Shapira, I., and Melamed, S. (2008). On the nature of burnout–insomnia relationships: A prospective study of employed adults. *Journal of Psychosomatic Research, 65,* 5–12.

Ayas, N., Barger, B., Cade, B., Hashimoto, D., Rosner, B., Cronin, J. W., … Czeisler, C. A. (2006). Extended work duration and the risk of self-reported percutaneous injuries in interns. *Journal of the American Medical Association, 296,* 1055–1062.

Banks, S., and Dinges, D. (2007). Behavioral and physiological consequences of sleep restriction. *Journal of Clinical Sleep Medicine, 3,* 519–528.

Barber, L. K., and Budnick, C. J. (2015). Turning molehills into mountains: Sleepiness increases workplace interpretive bias. *Journal of Organizational Behavior, 36,* 360–381.

Barber, L. K., and Santuzzi, A. M. (2015). Please respond ASAP: Workplace telepressure and employee recovery. *Journal of Occupational Health Psychology, 20,* 172–189.

Barger, L. K., Ayas, N. T., Cade, B. E., Cronin, J. W., Rosner, B., Speizer, F. E., and Czeisler, C. A. (2006). Impact of extended-duration shifts on medical errors, adverse events, and attentional failures. *PLoS Medicine, 3,* 2440–2448.

Barling, J., Kelloway, E. K., and Frone, M. R. (Eds.) (2005). *Handbook of Work Stress*. Thousand Oaks, CA: Sage.

Barnes, C. M. (2012). Working in our sleep: Sleep and self-regulation in organizations. *Organizational Psychology Review*, 2, 234–257.

Barnes, C. M., Ghumman, S., and Scott, B. A. (2013). Sleep and organizational citizenship behavior: The mediating role of job satisfaction. *Journal of Occupational Health Psychology*, 18, 16–26.

Barnes, C. M., Schaubroeck, J. M., Huth, M., and Ghumman, S. (2011). Lack of sleep and unethical behavior. *Organizational Behavior and Human Decision Processes*, 115, 169–180.

Barnes, C. M., and Wagner, D. T. (2009). Changing to daylight saving time cuts into sleep and increases workplace injuries. *Journal of Applied Psychology*, 94, 1305–1317.

Barnes, C. M., Wagner, D. T., and Ghumman, S. (2012). Borrowing from sleep to pay work and family: Expanding time-based conflict to the broader non-work domain. *Personnel Psychology* 65, 789–819.

Basner, M., Fomberstein, K., Razavi, F., Banks, S., William, J., Rosa, R., and Dinges, D. (2007). American Time Use Survey: Sleep time and its relationship to waking activities. *Sleep*, 30, 1085–1095.

Baumeister, R. F., Bratslavsky, E., Muraven, M., and Tice, D. M. (1998). Ego depletion: Is the active self a limited resource? *Journal of Personality and Social Psychology*, 74, 1252–1265.

Baumeister, R. F., Heatherton, T. F., and Tice, D. M. (1994). *Losing Control: How and Why People Fail at Self-Regulation*. Waltham, MA: Academic Press.

Baumeister, R. F., Muraven, M., and Tice, D. M. (2000). Ego depletion: A resource model of volition, self-regulation, and controlled processing. *Social Cognition*, 18, 130–150.

Beehr, T. A. (1995). *Psychological Stress in the Workplace*. London: Routledge.

Beehr, T. A., and Glazer, S. (2005). Organizational role stress. In J. Barling, E. K. Kelloway, and M. R. Frone (Eds.), *Handbook of Work Stress* (pp. 7–33). Thousand Oaks, CA: Sage.

Berset, M., Elfering, A., Lüthy, S., Lüthi, S., and Semmer, N. K. (2011). Work stressors and impaired sleep: Rumination as a mediator. *Stress and Health*, 27, e71–e82.

Bøggild, H., and Knutsson, A. (1999). Shift work, risk factors and cardiovascular disease. *Scandinavian Journal of Work, Environment and Health*, 25, 85–99.

Bohle, P., and Tilley, A. J. (1989). The impact of night work on psychological well-being. *Ergonomics*, 32, 1089–1099.

Breslau, N., Roth, T., Rosenthal, L., and Andreski, P. (1996). Sleep disturbance and psychiatric disorders: A longitudinal epidemiological study of young adults. *Biological Psychiatry*, 39, 411–418.

Chandola, T., Brunner, E., and Marmot, M. (2006). Chronic stress at work and the metabolic syndrome: Prospective study. *British Medical Journal*, 332, 521–525.

Cheng, P., and Drake, C. (2016). Shift work and work performance. In J. Barling, C. M. Barnes, E. L. Carleton, and D. T. Wagner (Eds.), *Work and Sleep: Research Insights for the Workplace* (pp. 11–30). New York: Oxford University Press.

Christian, M. S., and Ellis, A. P. (2011). Examining the effects of sleep deprivation on workplace deviance: A self-regulatory perspective. *Academy of Management Journal*, 54, 913–934.

Clarke, D. D., Ward, P., Bartle, C., and Truman, W. (2009). Work-related road traffic collisions in the UK. *Accident Analysis and Prevention*, 41, 345–351.

Cropley, M., Steptoe, A., and Joekes, K. (1999). Job strain and psychiatric morbidity. *Psychological Medicine*, 29, 1411–1416.

Dahlgren, A., Kecklund, G., and Åkerstedt, T. (2005). Different levels of work-related stress and the effects of sleep, fatigue and cortisol. *Scandinavian Journal of Work, Environment and Health*, 31, 277–285.

Danna, K., and Griffin, R. W. (1999). Health and well-being in the workplace: A review and synthesis of the literature. *Journal of Management*, 25, 357–384.

de Lange, A. H., Kompier, M. A., Taris, T. W., Geurts, S. A., Beckers, D. G., Houtman, I. L., and Bongers, P. M. (2009). A hard day's night: A longitudinal study on the relationships among job demands and job control, sleep quality and fatigue. *Journal of Sleep Research*, 18, 374–383.

de Lange, A. H., Taris, T. W., Kompier, M. A., Houtman, I. L., and Bongers, P. M. (2004). The relationships between work characteristics and mental health: Examining normal, reversed and reciprocal relationships in a 4-wave study. *Work and Stress*, 18, 149–166.

de Lange, A. H., Taris, T. W., Kompier, M. A., Houtman, I. L., and Bongers, P. M. (2005). Different mechanisms to explain the reversed effects of mental health on work characteristics. *Scandinavian Journal of Work, Environment and Health*, 31, 3–14.

Dinges, D. F. (1995). An overview of sleepiness and accidents. *Journal of Sleep Research*, 4(S2), 4–14.

Drake, C., Belcher, R., Howard, R., Roth, T., Levin, A. M., and Gumenyuk, V. (2015). Length polymorphism in the Period 3 gene is associated with sleepiness and maladaptive circadian phase in night-shift workers. *Journal of Sleep Research*, *24*, 254–261.

Drake, C. L., Roehrs, T. A., Burduvali, E., Bonahoom, A., Rosekind, M., and Roth, T. (2001). Effects of rapid versus slow accumulation of eight hours of sleep loss. *Psychophysiology*, *38*, 979–987.

Drake, C., Roehrs, T., Richardson, G., Walsh, J. K., and Roth, T. (2004). Shift work sleep disorder: Prevalence and consequences beyond that of symptomatic day workers. *Sleep*, *27*, 1453–1462.

Eriksen, W., Natvig, B., and Bruusgaard, D. (2001). Sleep problems: A predictor of long-term work disability? A four-year prospective study. *Scandinavian Journal of Public Health*, *29*, 23–31.

Ertel, K. A., Koenen, K. C., and Berkman, L. F. (2008). Incorporating home demands into models of job strain: Findings from the work, family and health network. *Journal of Occupational and Environmental Medicine/American College of Occupational and Environmental Medicine*, *50*, 1244–1252.

Figà-Talamanca, I. (2006). Occupational risk factors and reproductive health of women. *Occupational Medicine*, *56*, 521–531.

Folkard, S., and Monk, T. H. (Eds.) (1985). *Hours of Work: Temporal Factors in Work-Scheduling*. Hoboken, NJ: John Wiley & Sons.

Ford, D. E., and Kamerow, D. B. (1989). Epidemiologic study of sleep disturbances and psychiatric disorders: An opportunity for prevention? *Journal of the American Medical Association*, *262*, 1479–1484.

Franzen, P. L., Buysse, D. J., Dahl, R. E., Thompson, W., and Siegle, G. J. (2009). Sleep deprivation alters pupillary reactivity to emotional stimuli in healthy young adults. *Biological Psychology*, *80*, 300–305.

Fried, Y., Laurence, G. A., Shirom, A., Melamed, S., Toker, S., Berliner, S., and Shapira, I. (2013). The relationship between job enrichment and abdominal obesity: A longitudinal field study of apparently healthy individuals. *Journal of Occupational Health Psychology*, *18*, 458–468.

Ganster, D. C., and Schaubroeck, J. (1991). Work stress and employee health. *Journal of Management*, *17*, 235–271.

Gold, D. R., Rogacz, S., Bock, N., Tosteson, T. D., Baum, T. M., Speizer, F. E., and Czeisler, C. A. (1992). Rotating shift work, sleep, and accidents related to sleepiness in hospital nurses. *American Journal of Public Health*, *82*, 1011–1014.

Guglielmi, O., Jurado-Gámez, B., Gude, F., and Buela-Casal, G. (2014). Job stress, burnout, and job satisfaction in sleep apnea patients. *Sleep Medicine*, *15*, 1025–1030.

Gumenyuk, V., Roth, T., Korzyukov, O., Jefferson, C., Kick, A., Spear, L., … Drake, C. L. (2010). Shift work sleep disorder is associated with an attenuated brain response of sensory memory and an increased brain response to novelty: An ERP study. *Sleep*, *33*, 703–713.

Greenberg, J. (2006). Losing sleep over organizational injustice: Attenuating insomniac reactions to underpayment inequity with supervisory training in interactional justice. *Journal of Applied Psychology*, *91*, 58–69.

Harrison, Y., and Horne, J. A. (2000). The impact of sleep deprivation on decision making: A review. *Journal of Experimental Psychology: Applied*, *6*, 236–249.

Healy, D., Minors, D. S., and Waterhouse, J. M. (1993). Shiftwork, helplessness and depression. *Journal of Affective Disorders*, *29*, 17–25.

Hietapakka, L., Elovainio, M., Heponiemi, T., Presseau, J., Eccles, M., and Aalto, A.-M. (2013). Do nurses who work in a fair organization sleep and perform better and why? Testing potential psychosocial mediators of organizational justice. *Journal of Occupational Health Psychology*, *18*, 481–491.

Hossain, J. L., and Shapiro, C. M. (2002). The prevalence, cost implications, and management of sleep disorders: An overview. *Sleep and Breathing*, *6*, 85–102.

Houtman, I. L., Bongers, P. M., Smulders, P. G., and Kompier, M. A. (1994). Psychosocial stressors at work and musculoskeletal problems. *Scandinavian Journal of Work, Environment and Health*, *20*, 139–145.

Hublin, C., Partinen, M., Koskenvuo, M., and Kaprio, J. (2007). Sleep and mortality: A population-based 22-year follow-up study. *Sleep*, *30*, 1245–1253.

Iida, M., Shrout, P. E., Laurenceau, J. P., and Bolger, N. (2012). Using diary methods in psychological research. In H. Cooper (Gen. Ed.), *APA Handbook of Research Methods in Psychology, vol. 1: Foundations, Planning, Measures, and Psychometrics* (pp. 277–305). Washington, DC: American Psychological Association.

Jamal, M. (2004). Burnout, stress and health of employees on non-standard work schedules: A study of Canadian workers. *Stress and Health*, *20*, 113–119.

Jex, S. M., and Crossley C. D. (2005). Organizational consequences. In J. Barling, E. K. Kelloway, and M. R. Frone (Eds.), *Handbook of Work Stress* (pp. 575–600). Thousand Oaks, CA: Sage.

Jex, S. M., and Yankelevich, M. (2008). Work stress. In J. Barling and C. L. Cooper (Eds.), *The SAGE Handbook of Organizational Behavior, vol. 1: Micro Perspectives* (pp. 499–518). Thousand Oaks, CA: Sage.

Johnson, J. V., and Hall, E. M. (1988). Job strain, work place social support, and cardiovascular disease: A cross-sectional study of a random sample of the Swedish working population. *American Journal of Public Health, 78,* 1336–1342.

Jones, F., and Fletcher, B. (1996). Taking work home: A study of daily fluctuations in work stressors, effects on moods and impacts on marital partners. *Journal of Occupational and Organizational Psychology, 69,* 89–106.

Kahn, R. L., and Byosiere, P. (1992). Stress in organizations. In M. D. Dunnette and L. M. Hough (Eds.), *Handbook of Industrial and Organizational Psychology,* 2nd edn., vol. 3 (pp. 571–650). Palo Alto, CA: Consulting Psychologists Press.

Kahn-Greene, E. T., Killgore, D. B., Kamimori, G. H., Balkin, T. J., and Killgore, W. D. S. (2007). The effects of sleep deprivation on symptoms of psychopathology in healthy adults. *Sleep Medicine, 8,* 215–221.

Kahn-Greene, E. T., Lipizzi, E. L., Conrad, A. K., Kamimori, G. H., and Killgore, W. D. (2006). Sleep deprivation adversely affects interpersonal responses to frustration. *Personality and Individual Differences, 41,* 1433–1443.

Kelloway, E. K., and Barling, J. (2010). Leadership development as an intervention in occupational health psychology. *Work and Stress, 24,* 260–279.

Kessler, R. C., Berglund, P. A., Coulouvrat, C., Hajak, G., Roth, T., Shahly, V., and Walsh, J. K. (2011). Insomnia and the performance of US workers: Results from the America Insomnia Survey. *Sleep, 34,* 1161–1171.

Killgore, W. D. S., Kahn-Greene, E. T., Lipizzi, E. L., Newman, R. A., Kamimori, G. H., and Balkin, T. J. (2008). Sleep deprivation reduces perceived emotional intelligence and constructive thinking skills. *Sleep Medicine, 9,* 517–526.

Kling, R. N., McLeod, C. B., and Koehoorn, M. (2010). Sleep problems and workplace injuries in Canada. *Sleep, 33,* 611–618.

Knutson, K. L., Van Cauter, E., Rathouz, P. J., DeLeire, T., and Lauderdale, D. S. (2010). Trends in the prevalence of short sleepers in the USA: 1975–2006. *Sleep, 33,* 37–45.

Kornhauser, A. (1965). *Mental Health of the Industrial Worker.* New York: Wiley

Kuoppala, J., Lamminpää, A., and Husman, P. (2008). Work health promotion, job well-being, and sickness absences: A systematic review and meta-analysis. *Journal of Occupational and Environmental Medicine, 50,* 1216–1227.

Kuppermann, M., Lubeck, D. P., Mazonson, P. D., Patrick, D. L., Stewart, A. L., Buesching, D. P., and Filer, S. K. (1995). Sleep problems and their correlates in a working population. *Journal of General Internal Medicine, 10,* 25–32.

Landrigan, C. P., Rothschild, J. M., Cronin, J. W., Kaushal, R., Burdick, E., Katz, J. T., … Czeisler, C. A. (2004). Effect of reducing interns' work hours on serious medical errors in intensive care units. *New England Journal of Medicine, 351,* 1838–1848.

Lim, J., and Dinges, D. F. (2010). A meta-analysis of the impact of short-term sleep deprivation on cognitive variables. *Psychological Bulletin, 136,* 375–389.

Linton, S. J., Kecklund, G., Franklin, K. A., Leissner, L. C., Sivertsen, B., and Lindberg, E. (2015). The effect of the work environment on future sleep disturbances: A systematic review. *Sleep Medicine Reviews, 23,* 10–19.

Magnusson Hanson, L. L. M., Åkerstedt, T., Näswall, K., Leineweber, C., Theorell, T., and Westerlund, H. (2011). Cross-lagged relationships between workplace demands, control, support, and sleep problems. *Sleep, 34,* 1403–1410.

Maslach, C., Schaufeli, W. B., and Leiter, M. P. (2001). Job burnout. *Annual Review of Psychology, 52,* 397–422.

Mausner-Dorsch, H., and Eaton, W. W. (2000). Psychosocial work environment and depression: Epidemiologic assessment of the demand–control model. *American Journal of Public Health, 90,* 1765–1770.

Minowa, M., and Tango, T. (2003). Impact and correlates of poor sleep quality in Japanese white-collar employees. *Sleep, 26,* 467–471.

Morin, C. M., Rodrigue, S., and Ivers, H. (2003). Role of stress, arousal, and coping skills in primary insomnia. *Psychosomatic Medicine, 65,* 259–267.

Morphy, H., Dunn, K. M., Lewis, M., Boardman, H. F., and Croft, P. R. (2007). Epidemiology of insomnia: A longitudinal study in a UK population. *Sleep, 30,* 274–280.

Mulgrew, A. T., Ryan, C. F., Fleetham, J. A., Cheema, R., Fox, N., Koehoorn, M., … Ayas, N. T. (2007). The impact of obstructive sleep apnea and daytime sleepiness on work limitation. *Sleep Medicine, 9,* 42–53.

Mullins, H. M., Cortina, J. M., Drake, C. L., and Dalal, R. S. (2014). Sleepiness at work: A review and framework of how the physiology of sleepiness impacts the workplace. *Journal of Applied Psychology, 99,* 1096–1112.

Muraven, M., and Baumeister, R. F. (2000). Self-regulation and depletion of limited resources: Does self-control resemble a muscle? *Psychological Bulletin*, *126*, 247–259.

National Sleep Foundation (2015). Sleep drive and your body clock. At http://sleepfoundation.org/sleep-topics/sleep-drive-and-your-body-clock (accessed July 2016).

Newman, A. B., Spiekerman, C. F., Enright, P., Lefkowitz, D., Manolio, T., Reynolds, C. F., and Robbins, J. (2000). Daytime sleepiness predicts mortality and cardiovascular disease in older adults. *Journal of the American Geriatrics Society*, *48*, 115–123.

Ng, T. W. H., and Feldman, D. C. (2013). The effects of organisational embeddedness on insomnia. *Applied Psychology*, *62*, 330–357.

Nixon, A. E., Mazzola, J. J., Bauer, J., Krueger, J. R., and Spector, P. E. (2011). Can work make you sick? A meta-analysis of the relationships between job stressors and physical symptoms. *Work and Stress*, *25*, 1–22.

Ohayon, M. M. (2002). Epidemiology of insomnia: What we know and what we still need to learn. *Sleep Medicine Reviews*, *6*, 97–111.

Park, Y. M., Matsumoto, K., Seo, Y. J., Cho, Y. R., and Noh, T. J. (2000). Sleep–wake behavior of shift workers using wrist actigraph. *Psychiatry and Clinical Neurosciences*, *54*, 359–360.

Park, Y., and Sprung, J. M. (2014). Weekly work–school conflict, sleep quality, and fatigue: Recovery self-efficacy as a cross-level moderator. *Journal of Organizational Behavior*, *36*, 112–127.

Parkes, K. R. (1999). Shiftwork, job type, and the work environment as joint predictors of health-related outcomes. *Journal of Occupational Health Psychology*, *4*, 256–68

Pereira, D., Meier, L. L., and Elfering, A. (2013). Short-term effects of social exclusion at work and worries on sleep. *Stress and Health*, *29*, 240–252.

Pereira, D., Semmer, N. K., and Elfering, A. (2014). Illegitimate tasks and sleep quality: An ambulatory study. *Stress and Health*, *30*, 209–221.

Philip, P., Taillard, J., Niedhammer, I., Guilleminault, C., and Bioulac, B. (2001). Is there a link between subjective daytime somnolence and sickness absenteeism? A study in a working population. *Journal of Sleep Research*, *10*, 111–115.

Pilcher, J. J., and Huffcutt, A. J. (1996). Effects of sleep deprivation on performance: A meta-analysis. *Sleep*, *19*, 318–326.

Pilcher, J. J., Lambert, B. J., and Huffcutt, A. I. (2000). Differential effects of permanent and rotating shifts on self-report sleep length: A meta-analytic review. *Sleep*, *23*, 155–163.

Pratt, L., and Barling, J. (1988). Differentiating daily hassles, acute and chronic stressors: A framework and its implications. In J. R. Hurrell, L. R. Murphy, S. L. Sauter and C. L. Cooper (Eds.), *Occupational Stress: Issues and Developments in Research* (pp. 41–53). London: Taylor & Francis.

Public Health Agency of Canada (2009). *What Is the Impact of Sleep Apnea on Canadians?* Ottawa, ON: Government of Canada.

Riemann, D., Berger, M., and Voderholzer, U. (2001). Sleep and depression – results from psychobiological studies: An overview. *Biological Psychology*, *57*, 67–103.

Roehrs, T., Greenwald, M., and Roth, T. (2004). Risk-taking behavior: Effects of ethanol, caffeine, and basal sleepiness. *Sleep*, *27*, 887–894.

Salminen, S., Oksanen, T., Vahtera, J., Sallinen, M., Harma, M., Salo, P., ... Kivimäki, M. (2010). Sleep disturbances as a predictor of occupational injuries among public sector workers. *Journal of Sleep Research*, *19*, 207–213.

Schwartz, S., Anderson, W. M., Cole, S. R., Cornoni-Huntley, J., Hays, J. C., and Blazer, D. (1999). Insomnia and heart disease: A review of epidemiologic studies. *Journal of Psychosomatic Research*, *47*, 313–333.

Scott, B. A., and Judge, T. A. (2006). Insomnia, emotions, and job satisfaction: A multilevel study. *Journal of Management*, *32*, 622–645.

Shields, M. (1999). Long working hours and health. *Health Reports*, *11*, 33–48.

Shields, M. (2002). Shift work and health. *Health Reports*, *13*, 11–33.

Sivertsen, B., Björnsdóttir, E., Øverland, S., Bjorvatn, B., and Salo, P. (2013). The joint contribution of insomnia and obstructive sleep apnoea on sickness absence. *Journal of Sleep Research*, *22*, 223–230.

Sivertsen, B., Øverland, S., Glozier, N., Bjorvatn, B., Mæland, J. G., and Mykletun, A. (2008). The effect of OSAS on sick leave and work disability. *European Respiratory Journal*, *32*, 1497–1503.

Sjösten, N., Vahtera, J., Salo, P., Oksanen, T., Saaresranta, T., Virtanen, M., ... and Kivimäki, M. (2009). Increased risk of lost workdays prior to the diagnosis of sleep apnea. *Chest*, *136*, 130–136.

Sonnentag, S., Binnewies, C., and Mojza, E. J. (2008). "Did you have a nice evening?" A day-level study on recovery experiences, sleep, and affect. *Journal of Applied Psychology*, *93*, 674–684.

Sonnentag, S., and Frese, M. (2012). Stress in organizations. In N. W. Schmitt and S. Highhouse (Eds.), *Handbook of Psychology, vol. 12: Industrial and Organizational Psychology*, 2nd edn. (pp. 560–592). Hoboken, NJ: Wiley.

Spiegel, K., Leproult, R., and Van Cauter, E. (1999). Impact of sleep debt on metabolic and endocrine function. *Lancet, 354*, 1435–1439.

Stenfors, C. U. D., Magnusson Hanson, L., Oxenstierna, G., Theorell, R., and Nilsson, L.-G. (2013). Psychosocial working conditions and cognitive complaints among Swedish employees. *PLoS ONE, 8*, e60637.

Strine, T. W., and Chapman, D. P. (2005). Associations of frequent sleep insufficiency with health-related quality of life and health behaviors. *Sleep Medicine, 6*, 23–27.

Swanson, L. M., Arnedt, J., Rosekind, M. R., Belenky, G., Balkin, T. J., and Drake, C. (2011). Sleep disorders and work performance: Findings from the 2008 National Sleep Foundation Sleep in America poll. *Journal of Sleep Research, 20*, 487–494.

Syrek, C., and Antoni, C. H. (2014). Unfinished tasks foster rumination and impair sleeping – particularly if leaders have high performance expectations. *Journal of Occupational Health Psychology, 19*, 490–499.

TUC (Trades Union Congress) (2013). Transport and work related road safety. In *Hazards at Work*. London: Trades Union Congress.

Ulfberg, J., Carter, N., and Edling, C. (2000). Sleep-disordered breathing and occupational accidents. *Scandinavian Journal of Work, Environment and Health, 26*, 237–242.

Ulfberg, J., Carter, N., Talback, M., and Edling, C. (1996). Excessive daytime sleepiness at work and subjective work performance in the general population and among heavy snorers and patients with obstructive sleep apnea. *Chest, 110*, 659–663.

Van der Doef, M., and Maes, S. (1999). The job demand–control (–support) model and psychological well-being: A review of 20 years of empirical research. *Work and Stress, 13*, 87–114.

van der Helm, E., Gujar, N., and Walker, M. P. (2010). Sleep deprivation impairs the accurate recognition of human emotions. *Sleep, 33*, 335–342.

Van Laethem, M., Beckers, D. G. J., Kompier, M. A. J., Dijksterhuis, A., and Geurts, S. A. E. (2013). Psychosocial work characteristics and sleep quality: A systematic review of longitudinal and intervention research. *Scandinavian Journal of Work, Environment and Health, 39*, 535–549.

Wagner, D. T., Barnes, C. M., Lim, V. K. G., and Ferris, D. L. (2012). Lost sleep and cyberloafing: Evidence from the laboratory and a daylight saving time quasi-experiment. *Journal of Applied Psychology, 97*, 1068–1076.

Westerlund, H., Alexanderson, K., Åkerstedt, T., Hanson, L. M., Theorell, T., and Kivimäki, M. (2008). Work-related sleep disturbances and sickness absence in the Swedish working population, 1993–1999. *Sleep, 8*, 1169–1177.

Winwood, P. C., and Lushington, K. (2006). Disentangling the effects of psychological and physical work demands on sleep, recovery and maladaptive chronic stress within a large sample of Australian nurses. *Journal of Advanced Nursing, 56*, 679–689.

Wolk, R., and Somers, V. K. (2007). Sleep and metabolic syndrome. *Experimental Physiology, 92*, 67–78.

WSIB (Workplace Safety and Insurance Board) (2014). *By The Numbers: 2013 WSIB Statistical Report*. Toronto: Workplace Safety and Insurance Board.

Yoo, S. S., Gujar, N., Hu, P., Jolesz, F. A., and Walker, M. P. (2007). The human emotional brain without sleep – a prefrontal amygdala disconnect. *Current Biology, 17*, R877–R878.

Zapf, D., Dormann, C., and Frese, M. (1996). Longitudinal studies in organizational stress research: A review of the literature with reference to methodological issues. *Journal of Occupational Health Psychology, 1*, 145–169.

Zohar, D., Tzischinsky, O., Epstein, R., and Lavie, P. (2005). The effects of sleep loss on medical residents' emotional reactions to work events: A cognitive-energy model. *Sleep, 28*, 47–54.

31

Sleep, Cognitive and Mood Symptoms in Myalgic Encephalomyelitis/Chronic Fatigue Syndrome

Examining the Role of the Gut–Brain Axis

Amy Wallis, Melinda L. Jackson, Michelle Ball, Donald P. Lewis, and Dorothy Bruck

A multisystemic neuroimmune condition, myalgic encephalomyelitis/chronic fatigue syndrome (ME/CFS) is a severe, sometimes life-threatening, and chronically disabling condition with persistent and excessive fatigue that leads to considerable functional impairment (Jason et al., 2011). This clinical population presents with a reduced capacity for physical and mental activity and experiences the core symptom of postexertional malaise, combined with neurological (i.e., pain, sleep dysfunction, neurocognitive, neurosensory and/or perceptual), immune, gastrointestinal and energy production impairments (i.e., cardiovascular, respiratory or orthostatic intolerance; Carruthers et al., 2011). With prevalence rates from 0.4 to 1 percent, this heterogeneous population has diverse symptomatology and high comorbidity with psychiatric conditions, particularly anxiety and depressive symptoms (Carruthers et al., 2011; Jason et al., 2012).

Over the past three decades, the emergence of pathophysiological markers and consequential etiological underpinnings has resulted in the development of the ME International Consensus Criteria (ICC; Carruthers et al., 2011). This stringent set of criteria for ME allows "encephalomyelitis" to appropriately reflect underlying neurological pathology, that is, inflammation of the central nervous system (CNS; Carruthers et al., 2011). The term CFS is still used interchangeably with ME and there is continued debate over terminology. In the United States, the Institute of Medicine (2015) most recently proposed the new diagnostic label of *systemic exertion intolerance disease* (SEID) to reflect the core postexertional fatigue after mild physical and cognitive effort. As this proposed label is not yet broadly accepted, this chapter will refer to the condition as ME/CFS, and will focus on the adult presentation of the disorder.

A history of skepticism, blame and symptom minimization has hindered progress within ME/CFS research and clinical fields (Jason et al., 1997). Proponents of psychosocial frameworks of ME/CFS have traditionally explained idiopathic symptoms as resultant from and maintained by maladaptive coping and personality factors (see Harvey and Wesseley, 2009; Vercoulen et al., 1998). Conversely, the bio(psychosocial) medical model focuses on dysfunction of the CNS, neuroimmune, inflammatory and gastrointestinal systems as primarily responsible for symptom manifestation, while recognizing personality and psychosocial factors as secondary (Maes and Twisk, 2010). Robust support for this model has recently been shown by findings of distinct alteration in activated immune markers in ME/CFS compared to healthy controls (Hornig et al., 2015). Figure 31.1 presents the pathophysiological basis of the condition by demonstrating dysregulation in multiple biological systems. Emerging results suggest genetic variations that are likely to predispose ME/CFS onset and development (e.g., Saiki et al., 2008). The gut–brain axis provides one possible explanation of pathways that can influence expression of neurological symptoms in ME/CFS.

Sleep disturbances, neurocognitive impairments and frequently comorbid depressive symptoms are neurological symptoms that are particularly relevant to clinicians from psychology,

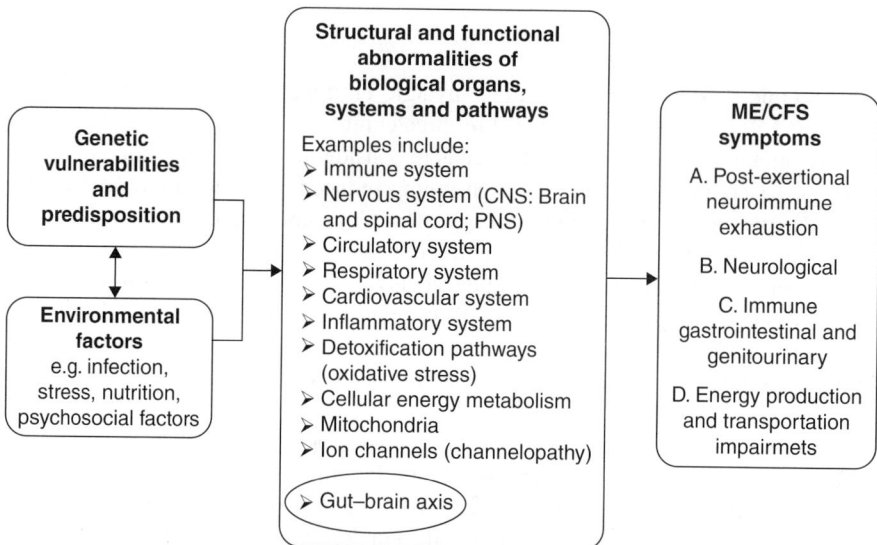

This figure shows the interaction between a genetic predisposition and environmental triggers that precipitate dysfunction within biological organs, systems and/or pathways. The gut–brain axis is highlighted as one of the possible areas of pathophysiological dysfunction that may be involved in ME/CFS symptom expression, as broadly delineated by the International Consensus Criteria (Carruthers et al., 2011).

Figure 31.1   Etiology of ME/CFS.

psychiatry, neurology and general medical disciplines. These symptoms can also have a profound impact on patients' quality of life and general well-being. Rather than isolating each symptom, there is merit in exploring potential overlapping etiology and similar biochemical mechanisms that may precipitate these neurological symptoms. For example, the presence of gastrointestinal symptoms in ME/CFS supports exploration of sleep, cognitive and depressive symptoms within the context of brain–gut interactions.

Brain–Gut Axis

Historically, Western scientific investigation has pursued a top-down approach to understanding physiological functioning, with the brain recognized as the ultimate control system influencing physiology and behavior (Cannon, 1929; Mayer, 2000). Extensive evidence has revealed complex interactions between the brain and the gut through multiple modes of communication, both within and between the enteric nervous system (ENS) and CNS (Rhee, Pothoulakis, and Mayer, 2009). The ENS connects to the intestines, the organ with the largest surface area in the human body (Furness, 2006). The intestinal lumen and gut wall (comprising mucosa, submucosa and enteric muscle layers) houses the largest population of commensal microbiota; contains 70–80 percent of the body's immune cells and regulates enteroendocrine cell production (see Mayer, 2011 and Figure 31.2A). Hence, this has led to growing interest in examining the gut's role in regulating homeostasis of the host in a range of CNS, neuroimmune, and mental health disorders, as well as the more obvious functional gastrointestinal disorders (e.g., irritable bowel syndrome (IBS)). The essential bidirectional communication between the

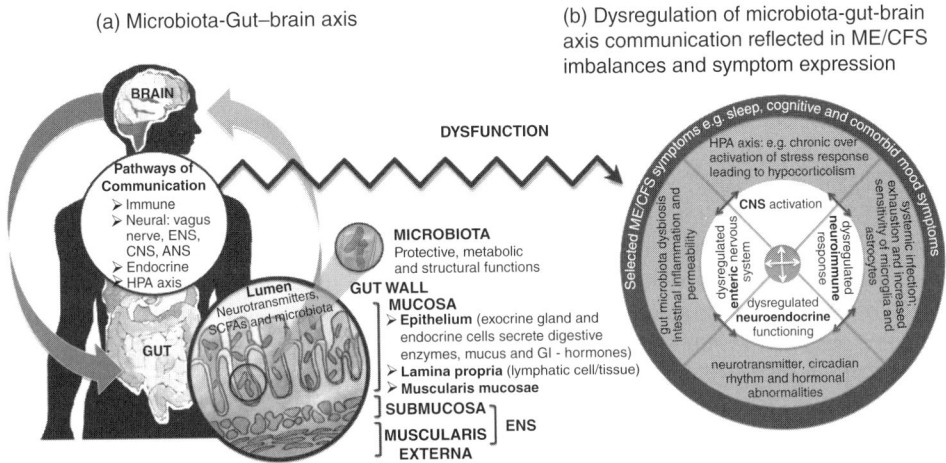

(a) The bidirectional communication between the brain and the gastrointestinal system and the trillions of microorganisms (microbiota) that occupy the lumen and lining of the gut wall. The direct and indirect pathways of communication can be through the immune, endocrine, neural (via the vagus nerve, enteric nervous system (ENS), autonomic nervous system (ANS) and/or central nervous system (CNS)) and the hypothalamic-pituitary-adrenal (HPA) axis. SCFAs: short chain fatty acids. (Adapted from Grenharm, Clarke, Cryan, and Dinan, 2011; Leung, 2014.) (b) Dysfunction within the pathways of communication may provide a possible explanation for the CNS, gastrointestinal, neuroimmune and neuroendocrine imbalances and/or dysregulation observed within ME/CFS. These abnormalities may underlie selected ME/CFS symptoms including specific neurological symptoms (i.e., sleep, cognitive and comorbid mood symptoms).

Figure 31.2   Pathways of communication in the microbiota-gut-brain axis and dysregulation observed in ME/CFS.

brain and the gut occurs through neural, hormonal, immune and microbial pathways (Cryan and Dinan, 2012).

Microbiota-Gut-Brain Axis and Its Role in ME/CFS

Technological advances parallel our growing knowledge of the estimated 100 trillion intestinal microbiota that reside within the intestinal lumen of the human gastrointestinal tract (i.e., commensal intestinal/gut microbiota; Gill et al., 2006). The balance of commensal and pathogenic microbiota can be attributed to healthy or disease states (see Sekirov, Russell, Antunes, and Finlay, 2010). Greater diversity of commensal bacteria is related to optimal health (see Moloney, Desbonnet, Clarke, Dinan, and Cryan, 2014). Some illnesses have been associated with both an overgrowth of pathogenic microbiota and an imbalance in commensal microbiota (i.e., gut dysbiosis; Moloney et al., 2014).

As shown in Figure 31.2A, the microbiota-gut-brain axis incorporates multiple bidirectional pathways of communication through the CNS, autonomic nervous system (ANS), neuroendocrine and neuroimmune, ENS and intestinal microbiota (Cryan and Dinan, 2012; Rhee et al., 2009; Mayer, 2011). The microbiota-gut-brain framework acknowledges the brain's role in signaling gastrointestinal functioning and the converse role that the gut and microbiome can exert on brain functioning (Dinan and Cryan, 2012) as well as providing a possible explanatory pathway for multiple physical, behavioral and affective symptoms (Bested, Logan, and Selhub, 2013; Sekirov et al., 2010). Within ME/CFS, dysfunction of the microbiota-gut-brain axis is a mechanism that may underlie some ME/CFS symptoms, including the sleep, mood and cognitive symptoms examined in this chapter (see Figure 31.2B). It is therefore argued that insights from the fields of microbiology, physiology, neuroscience, immunology, endocrinology, psychiatry and psychology may converge to advance understanding of ME/CFS etiology.

Within ME/CFS populations there is evidence of gut dysbiosis (Fremont, Coomans, Massart, and De Meirleir, 2013; Sheedy et al., 2009) and increased intestinal permeability, that is, aberrations in the mucosal lining of the gastrointestinal tract (Maes and Leunis, 2008; Maes et al., 2012). These results, combined with recent microbiota-gut-brain research (see Moloney et al., 2014), suggests that the gastrointestinal system and microbiome may be instrumental in the pathogenesis and maintenance of ME/CFS (Lakhan and Kirchgessner, 2010). One hypothesis is that the bacterial toxicity produced by an imbalance in microbial composition within the enteric system can produce consequential systemic effects and account for the array of symptoms observed within ME/CFS (Borody, Nowak, and Finlayson, 2012). The complexity and diversity of interactions that the gut microbiome may have on the host can be applied to understand a range of neurocognitive and affective symptoms (Cryan and Dinan, 2012). Before exploring these symptoms in more detail, we shall provide an overview of possible dysfunction of the hypothalamic-pituitary-adrenal (HPA) axis that can both precipitate and perpetuate neurological symptoms observed in ME/CFS.

Stress and the HPA Axis

The hypothalamus produces corticotropin-releasing factor (CRF) that regulates the activation of the endocrine system and associated hormones through the pituitary (e.g., adrenocorticotropic hormone (ACTH) and vasopressin) and adrenal glands (e.g., glucocorticoids, including cortisol and adrenaline; Smith and Vale, 2006). Psychological and physical triggers (including infection, injury and trauma) can activate the stress response through the HPA axis (Dinan and Cryan, 2012). Through the central nervous system (CNS) and the associated regulation of both sympathetic (SNS) and parasympathetic (PNS) branches of the autonomic nervous system (ANS), the HPA axis triggers changes in autonomic processes, including increased respiration, cardiac function and restricted digestion (Buijs and Swaab, 2013). This protective survival response becomes deleterious with chronic overstimulation. Persistent SNS activation restricts relaxation and restoration of autonomous bodily functions through the PNS and can lead to consequential immune, digestive and endocrine dysfunction. The hyperarousal theory refers to the chronic activation of the HPA axis and resultant low cortisol levels (referred to as hypocortisolism; Tak et al., 2011) observed in some ME/CFS patients.

Two recent meta-analyses show evidence of hypocortisolism (as measured by the cortisol awakening response (CAR)) in ME/CFS adults (Powell, Liossi, Moss-Morris, and Schlotz, 2013; Tak et al., 2011). This eventual underactivity of the HPA axis can increase pain perception (Fabian et al., 2009), fatigue and stress sensitivity (Fries, Hesse, Hellhammer, and Hellhammer, 2005). Retrospective psychosocial stress and postviral physiological stress are consistently associated with ME/CFS (Carruthers et al., 2003). In a small sample of CFS women, childhood emotional neglect was associated with reduced HPA reactivity as measured by morning cortisol samples; however, significant correlations were not observed for other types of childhood trauma (Kempke et al., 2015). Additionally, in a cross-sectional study of 117 adult CFS patients, greater CAR was associated with better perceived stress management skills and reduced levels of postexertional malaise (Hall et al., 2014). These results implicate dysfunction of the HPA axis in ME/CFS presentation; however, to date, our understanding of precise mechanisms remains rudimentary.

While chronic exposure to psychosocial stress can lead to hypocortisolism, the simplicity of a direct causal pathway is unlikely in such a complex condition. Analyses by Tak and colleagues (2011) showed disparate associations between hypocortisolism and the functional somatic disorders measured (fibromyalgia and IBS), with the authors questioning the extent of hypocortisolism in the etiology of ME/CFS. To date, there is no robust evidence that hypocortisolism causes the multisystemic dysfunction observed in ME/CFS (Powell et al., 2013). Hypocortisolism is likely to exacerbate fatigue and pain symptoms and may be a consequence of sleep disturbance or comorbid depressive disorders (Tak et al., 2011).

Hypocortisolism and the associated biochemical marker of the attenuated CAR may also be a secondary indicator of other underlying dysfunction. The neurotransmitter system (serotonergic and norepinephrine) and immune system (proinflammatory cytokines) mediate the stress response by regulating CRH and vasopressin (Dinan and Cryan, 2012). When present at high levels during the stress response, vasopressin released by the hypothalamus and/or pituitary gland stimulates the kidneys to promote water retention, increases blood pressure, and has also been shown to exert effects on memory and behavior (Beurel and Nemeroff, 2014). Upregulation and/or downregulation of both the neurotransmitter and immune systems can perpetuate HPA-axis dysfunction. Dysfunction of the neurotransmitter system may explain the high comorbidity associated with stress and psychological symptoms (including depression and anxiety) in ME/CFS. Another possible pathway to HPA dysfunction may be explained by our emerging understanding of the diverse impact of enteric microbiota.

The Role of Gut Microbiota in the Stress Response

Gut pathogens can trigger an immune response that can directly and indirectly mediate hypothalamic functioning (Dinan and Cryan, 2012). However, it is relatively novel to consider that commensal bacteria may exert similar effects on the HPA axis. Gut microbiota can influence the development and programming of the HPA axis in early life. A seminal study by Sudo and colleagues (2004) showed an exaggerated stress response (higher levels of corticosterone and ACTH) for male germ free (GF, i.e., absence of enteric microbiota) mice compared with specific pathogen free (SPF, i.e., "normal" enteric microbiota without the presence of pathogenic bacteria) controls. Sequentially, immediate colonization with *Bifidobacterium infantis* resulted in a reversal of the exaggerated stress response, returning to similar levels as controls. Other murine studies have shown distinct changes in the production of neurotransmitters and neurotrophins (proteins that promote the survival, development and function of neurons (brain derived neurotrophin factor; BDNF)) in the cortex and hippocampus of female GF mice (increased production: Neufeld, Kang, Bienenstock, and Foster, 2011; decreased production: Clarke et al., 2013) and male GF mice (decreased production: Sudo et al., 2004). Inherent in these findings is the irrefutable acknowledgment that the presence or absence of gut microbes affects the development of the host's stress response. What remain unclear are the precise mechanisms of this interaction and evidence within human populations.

It is important to consider the bidirectional nature of this microbiota–stress relationship. Psychosocial stress can alter the composition of the microbiota with short-term and long-term consequences observed at different life stages and with acute or prolonged exposure. For example, animal studies using maternal separation as an early life stressor have shown marked alterations in microbiota composition, behavior and the HPA axis (e.g., Bailey and Coe, 1999; Desbonnet et al., 2010; O'Mahony et al., 2009). While behavioral changes were reversible after treatment with *Bifidobacterium infantis* (Desbonnet et al., 2010), there are divergent findings regarding long-term compositional consequences. In monkeys, Bailey and Coe (1999) found a short-term effect on microbial composition with a significant reduction in *Lactobacillus* at day three postseparation that returned to normal on day seven. Alternatively, O'Mahony and colleagues (2009) revealed long-term compositional changes in the microbiome of rats after three hours of maternal separation each day for ten consecutive days. These compositional changes paralleled irreversible changes to the HPA axis. Other mechanisms, including disturbed sleep and circadian rhythms, may also precipitate and/or perpetuate HPA axis dysfunction (Tak et al., 2011).

Sleep Symptoms

It has been argued that the ultimate function of sleep is restoration and recovery to return the host to homeostasis (Benington, 2000). Hence, sleep difficulties can disrupt recovery processes and may initiate, maintain, exacerbate, and be resultant from disease processes. Sleep disturbances are one of the neurological impairments observed in ME/CFS (Carruthers et al., 2011). Many ME/CFS patients experience a nonrestorative quality to sleep, consistent with their reports of feeling unrefreshed upon awakening (Carruthers et al., 2003; Jackson and Bruck, 2012). Clinical disruptions in sleep include altered sleep patterns, insomnia, excessive daytime napping, sleep–wake cycle irregularities, vivid dreams/nightmares, and diminished

---

Box 31.1 Clarifying terminology

While used interchangeably within colloquial language, sleepiness and fatigue represent distinct constructs within research and clinical settings (Pigeon, Sateia, and Ferguson, 2003; Shen, Barbera, and Shapiro, 2006).

Sleepiness   A state that precipitates sleep onset and a consequence of diminished sleep, regulated by internal states (e.g., circadian rhythms; Mairesse et al., 2010) and external factors (behavioral or environmental; Johns, 2002).

Excessive daytime sleepiness   Describes a pathological level of sleepiness that is disproportionate to the expected level of sleep propensity and pressure (Pigeon et al., 2003). Some ME/CFS patients experience excessive daytime sleepiness; however, the level of sleepiness has been shown to be similar across healthy control, primary insomnia and ME/CFS groups (Neu, Mairesse, Verbanck, and Le Bon, 2015).

Fatigue   Describes a feeling experienced after exertion on an activity requiring high mental or physical energy. Unlike sleepiness that requires sleep to recover, fatigue improves with rest (Neu, Mairesse, Verbanck, Linkowski, and Le Bon, 2014). In ME/CFS, patients experience severe and debilitating levels of chronic fatigue that is disproportionate to the expended energy and frequently persists regardless of rest (Carruthers et al., 2011).

---

sleep quality suggested by unrefreshing sleep and excessive daytime sleepiness (Carruthers et al., 2011). Confusion between comorbid conditions, terminology (see Box 31.1) and objective and subjective sleep measurement methods has made it difficult to understand and appropriately treat sleep symptoms in this population.

ME/CFS is a distinct condition with high comorbidity with primary sleep disorders (e.g., primary insomnia or obstructive sleep apnea), psychiatric conditions and pain disorders (fibromyalgia, IBS, migraine) (see reviews by Jackson and Bruck, 2012 and Mariman, 2013). Sleep disturbances can be symptoms of all of the aforementioned disorders and can be causal (Buchwald, Pascualy, Bombardier, and Kith, 1994) or consequential in nature (i.e., resultant from excessive pain or secondary to psychiatric condition: Benca, Obermeyer, Thisted, and Gillin, 1992). However, sleep disorder status should not preclude a diagnosis of ME/CFS because both conditions can coexist, show differential responses to treatment (Libman et al., 2009), and show neurophysiological distinctions (Neu, Mairesse, Verbanck, and Le Bon, 2015).

Quantifying Sleep Disturbances: Objective and Subjective Differences

There is no clear, single distinguishing marker of sleep disturbance in ME/CFS. There are discrepant findings between subjective and objective measurements, as well as within objective measurement techniques. For example, ME/CFS patients consistently report poorer subjective sleep quality and a subgroup experience significantly greater excessive daytime sleepiness as compared to healthy controls (Creti et al., 2010; Stevens, 2014; Neu et al., 2009; Watson et al., 2003). These self-reports are not substantiated consistently by current objective measurements and equivalent levels of pathological sleepiness are shown when comparing patients with healthy controls on Multiple Sleep Latency Tests (Majer et al., 2007; Reeves et al., 2006; Watson, Jacobsen, Goldberg, Kapur, and Buchwald, 2004). Although recent objective evidence of sleep disturbances (including delayed sleep and more frequent night awakenings) in ME/CFS patients has been shown using actigraphy data (Stevens, 2014). Further contradictory findings are evident when measuring both the macrostructure and microstructure of sleep using polysomnography and actigraphy methods (see review by Jackson and Bruck, 2012).

Research examining slow wave activity (SWA; measured by electroencephalogram spectral power in the delta range; Dijk, Brunner, Beersma, and Borbely, 1990) may shed more light on the physiological mechanisms underlying reports of diminished sleep quality and unrefreshing sleep. SWA during non-rapid eye movement (NREM) sleep reflects sleep homeostasis (Mairesse et al., 2010). Evidence supports impairment in the homeostatic quality of sleep in ME/CFS. Armitage and colleagues (2007) observed that ME/CFS adults had significantly reduced SWA power in the first NREM period after a four-hour sleep delay in comparison to their non-ME/CFS monozygotic twin. There is also evidence of a power exchange pattern in ME/CFS with higher frequencies observed across NREM sleep stages 1–3 (Neu, Mairesse, Verbanck, Linkowski, and Le Bon, 2014). Excess SWS duration was also recorded for this sample and has been interpreted as a compensatory mechanism due to a deficiency in power (Neu et al., 2015). In combination, these results indicate homeostatic dysfunction that may explain the unrefreshing quality of sleep experienced by ME/CFS patients. The reduced SWA power may reflect an upregulated HPA axis (i.e., hyperarousal), prolonged immune activation and/or, as postulated below, disturbances of the gastrointestinal system.

Sleep Symptoms and the Brain–Gut Axis

The homeostatic quality of sleep may be reflected in and/or be reflected by the homeostasis of the host's gastrointestinal system. There is clear evidence that disturbed sleep patterns negatively impact metabolic processes (Bron and Furness, 2009). Less robust but indicative results showing how circadian rhythms regulate the enteric immune response and the effect of proinflammatory cytokines (immune cell proteins) on altering the biological clock also provide insights into the possible bidirectional relationship between sleep symptoms and the gut (Bron and Furness, 2009).

The burgeoning field of gut microbial research is only beginning to examine the associations between the human microbiome and sleep quality and structure. Preclinical evidence suggests that shifts in sleep patterns and the associated intestinal dysbiosis may be modulated by diet (Voigt et al., 2014). Within ME/CFS, gut dysbiosis may also precipitate or perpetuate sleep abnormalities. One study noted that higher levels of commensal *Clostridium* species in the colon of females with ME/CFS were significantly associated with increased likelihood of reporting problematic sleep symptoms (Wallis, Butt, Ball, Lewis, and Bruck, 2016). More research is required to understand the role of intestinal microbiota in regulating sleep.

Neurocognitive Functioning

The ME International Consensus Criteria stipulates two categories of neurocognitive impairments related to (a) information processing (i.e., slowed cognition and associated speech;

impaired attention and concentration difficulties), and (b) short-term memory (including prob-lems with working memory, word retrieval and immediate recall; Carruthers et al., 2011). Patients experience confusion and brain "fog" associated with excessive mental fatigue (Carruthers et al., 2003, p.17). Historically, the method of assessing neurocognitive distur-bances in ME/CFS has relied on self-report and standardized cognitive testing, with a plethora of conflicting findings (see Cockshell and Mathias, 2010; Ocon, 2013). One consistent result is patients' subjective reports of increased mental fatigue and mental effort required to perform at the same level as healthy controls (Cockshell and Mathias, 2014). A recent meta-analysis of objective neuropsychological assessments substantiates deficits in attention, memory and reac-tion time in ME/CFS compared with healthy controls (Cockshell and Mathias, 2010). Other evidence also points to difficulties with executive functioning, including planning, cognitive inhibition and complex information processing (Ocon, 2013).

Discrepant results may be best explained by the inability of neuropsychological tests to ade-quately measure mental effort. Similar performance for healthy controls and ME/CFS patients on standardized test procedures contrasts the increased level of cognitive fatigue reported by ME/CFS patients after testing. This experience of cognitive fatigue has been explained by increased neural involvement of other brain regions required to perform equivalent cognitive tasks. When examining auditory information processing, Lange and colleagues (2005) pro-vided evidence that while ME/CFS patients can process information equally as accurately as healthy controls, they engage larger neural networks within the verbal working memory system to perform the same task. Hence, this corresponds with the subjective perception of increased mental effort.

Within magnetic resonance imaging (MRI) studies, there are contradictory findings. Some evidence for brain abnormalities in ME/CFS (Lange et al., 2001; Lange et al., 1999) opposes other studies that indicate neither differences in the neuroanatomy of patients with ME/CFS (Cope and David, 1996; Cope, Pernet, Kendall, and David, 1995), nor evidence of long-term degradation (Perrin, Embleton, Pentreath, and Jackson, 2010). Different findings may reflect methodological limitations, such as small samples, group homogeneity, assessment methods and the statistical procedures utilized. These studies have used a conventional, categorical comparison of ME/CFS compared with healthy controls. More recent investigations that have used regression analyses have been able to highlight specific regional brain abnormalities in ME/CFS (Barnden, Crouch, Kwiatek, Burnet, and Del Fante, 2015).

Extending earlier studies that have shown brainstem and prefrontal changes in ME/CFS (Costa, Tannock, and Brostoff, 1995; Lange, Wang, DeLuca, and Natelson, 1998; Siessmeier et al., 2003; Tirelli et al., 1998), recent neuroimaging studies implicate the etiological role of the midbrain. Reduced white matter volume (Barnden et al., 2011), signs of neuroinflammation (Nakatomi et al., 2014), and increased plasticity in prefrontal circuits that is distinct from anxiety and depression (Barnden et al., 2015), indicate impairment in nerve conduction within the midbrain of patients with ME/CFS.

Impairment in midbrain regions is conceptually consistent with manifested ME/CFS symp-tomatology. The reticular activation system (RAS) of the midbrain is responsible for regulat-ing sleep–wake transitions, including transition from restful wakefulness to increased attention and alertness (Nolte and Sundsten, 2009). The reticular formation in the RAS is involved in the synthesis of serotonin and involves cholinergic and adrenergic pathways. Additionally, the midbrain's role in regulating homeostasis of the hypothalamus may reflect the altered HPA axis activity observed in ME/CFS. Hence, abnormalities within this region may partially explain the cognitive, sleep and autonomic impairments observed in patients with ME/CFS (Barnden et al., 2015).

Possible Role of Gut Microbiota in Cognitive Dysfunction

No experimental studies have specifically investigated the interaction between gut microbiota and cognition in ME/CFS. However, associations between microbiota and neurocognitive skills (i.e., learning and memory) have been shown in animal models (Foster and McVey Neufeld, 2013). In an experimental murine trial, Li, Dowd, Scurlock, Acosta-Martinez, and Lyte (2009) compared the effect of two diets (50 percent beef versus normal) on microbial composition, memory and learning. Mice fed the beef diet had greater diversity of gut flora and enhanced memory on behavioral testing tasks. Subsequent studies by Gareau et al. (2011) suggest that the formation of memories can be altered by intestinal microbiota. Impaired memory was observed in both GF mice and mice exposed to acute stress, followed by bacterial infection. Memory dysfunction was reversed during daily treatment with probiotics. The postinfection effect on memory, when triggered by acute stress, may parallel the symptom progression in ME/CFS populations.

The neurotoxic effects of specific bacteria and excess D-lactic acid provide alternate pathways that may explain the neurocognitive deficits observed in ME/CFS. The neurotoxic and enterotoxic effects of many species including *Clostridium botulinum* and *Clostridium difficile* have been well documented (Hatheway, 1990). While the commensal properties of *Clostridium* species have been recognized within experimental and clinical research (e.g., Atarashi et al., 2011), recent associations between commensal *Clostridium spp.* and increased self-reported neurocognitive symptoms in females with ME/CFS highlight the potential role of dysbiosis in symptomatic expression (Wallis et al., 2016). In males, higher levels of *Lactobacillus* and *Streptococcus*, both bacteria that produce excess D-lactic acid, were associated with greater neurocognitive impairments (Wallis et al., 2016). Although the reason for sex differences and causation has not been determined, the function and composition of intestinal microbiota may provide new understandings about ME/CFS neurocognitive symptoms.

Depression

There is a marked overlap in symptom presentation between Major Depressive Disorder (MDD) and ME/CFS. Many symptoms of MDD (including change in weight, hypersomnia/insomnia, fatigue and concentration difficulties; American Psychiatric Association, 2013) are primary symptoms in ME/CFS. The symptomatic requirement of a depressed mood and decreased interest in pleasurable activities are key discriminating features for MDD (American Psychiatric Association, 2013). Diagnosis of ME/CFS does not preclude a diagnosis of MDD and there is high comorbidity between these conditions (Ciccone and Natelson, 2003). Between 50 and 80 percent of adult patients with ME/CFS have comorbid depressive symptoms, although the clinical presentation may be different from MDD (Taillefer, Kirmayer, Robbins, and Lasry, 2003).

There are notable similarities between depression and ME/CFS etiology. In both ME/CFS and depression, dysfunction of the HPA axis is observed (Barden, 2004). Biochemically, markers of inflammation, immune activation and dysregulation of the tryptophan catabolite (TRYCAT) pathway are associated with manifested symptoms of both depression and ME/CFS

(Anderson, Berk, and Maes, 2014). Additionally, reduced antioxidant status, mitochondrial abnormalities and bacterial translocation have been observed in both conditions (see Maes, 2011; Gardner and Boles, 2011 for reviews).

While there is compelling evidence that shows an overlap between these conditions, evidence also supports their distinction. Using self-report data, ME/CFS and depression can be discriminated with 100 percent accuracy when using ratings of fatigue duration, postexertional fatigue, unrefreshing sleep, shortness of breath, confusion and self-blame (Hawk, Jason, and Torres-Harding, 2006). Pathophysiological evidence suggests that depression is associated with more neurodegeneration than ME/CFS, which is associated more with dysfunction in an innate immunity pathway involved in defense against viral infections (Maes, 2011). From this biomedical perspective, the conceptual understanding of the similarities between depression and ME/CFS may be better explained by a "co-occurrence due to shared pathways" rather than high "comorbidity" rates (Maes, 2011, p. 791). The shared etiology provides an explanation of symptom overlap and evidence reviewed here supports a clear distinction between depression and ME/CFS as separate conditions.

Depression as a Precipitating (Psychosocial) Factor

In contrast to the bio(psychosocial) medical model, the psychodynamic perspective highlights the role of personality factors that may precipitate and perpetuate the dysfunctional stress response (either overactive or underactive dependent on the illness duration) observed in ME/CFS (Luyten et al., 2011). Psychodynamic theorists explain ME/CFS as developing from self-critical perfectionism involving high personal expectations/goals, negative self-appraisal and associated with high parental demands (Blatt and Luyten, 2009). Luyten and colleagues (2011) propose that this self-critical perfectionism in ME/CFS manifests in overactivity and overachievement that can lead to neglecting physical health needs. Within a sample of ME/CFS adults, higher levels of depression were predicted by increased self-critical perfectionism and the associated increase in the perception of daily hassles (Luyten et al., 2011). Positive correlations between stress sensitivity, self-critical perfectionism and depression were also observed.

Conversely, in a longitudinal study, personality factors were not associated with the development of ME/CFS in adults (Harvey, Wessely, Hotopf, and Wadsworth, 2008). This study indicated that psychiatric illness (not personality) between the ages of 15 and 36 years increased the chance of developing ME/CFS at a later stage. The results suggest that depressive and anxiety symptoms can precipitate the onset of ME/CFS. The authors proposed a causal role for psychiatric illnesses for a subset of ME/CFS patients. If one applies the more recent pathophysiological framework (Maes and Twisk, 2010), the observed relationship between psychiatric illness and ME/CFS may be due to a similar underlying pathophysiology that is a predisposing risk factor for some patients and is a consequential factor for others. The bidirectional nature of this interaction is evident. Depressive symptoms can also be considered consequential to the experience of living with a chronic, ill-defined and unexplained illness.

Depression as a Psychosocial Consequence

Depressive symptoms may be a reaction to the impaired functioning and severity of the chronic illness experience (Dancey and Friend, 2008) or a consequence of the underlying pathophysiology (i.e., immune dysregulation; Attree, Arroll, Dancey, Griffith, and Bansal, 2014). The unknown origin, unclear treatment pathways, unsupportive relationships and lack of recognition/validation of the severity and reality of their experience from medical professionals have been shown to exacerbate distress, anxiety and depression scores within this clinical population compared with other chronic disorders with clear pathophysiology (e.g. autoimmune disorders including systemic lupus erythematosus, multiple sclerosis and rheumatoid arthritis; McInnis, Matheson, and Anisman, 2014). Dancey and Friend (2008) showed that there is an indirect relationship between illness intrusiveness associated with reduced quality of life and an inability to engage in occupational and interest activities that mediate depressive symptoms. While inconclusive due to the cross-sectional design, their results support the development of depressive symptoms as a consequence of ME/CFS and are substantiated by the aforementioned research suggesting biomarkers for ME/CFS and pathophysiological differences with MDD.

Depressive Symptoms and the Microbiota-Gut-Brain Axis

The shared dysregulation of the HPA axis and associated depressive symptoms observed in both depression (Barden, 2004) and ME/CFS (Powell et al., 2013) may be driven by gut microbiota. Preclinical studies showing the role of bacteria in producing neurotransmitters (e.g., gamma-amino butyric acid (GABA) and serotonin) and altering neurotransmitter receptors (see Foster and McVey Neufeld, 2013) have relevance for understanding both the stress response and depressive symptoms. Combined with preclinical animal evidence of the reversal of depressive symptoms after treatment with the probiotic *Bifidobacterium infantis* (Desbonnet, Garrett, Clarke, Bienenstock and Dinan, 2008), these results suggest that the changes in gut microbiota composition may modulate depressive symptoms. Evidence within human populations is reviewed below while considering treatment alternatives.

Treatment

The complexity and heterogeneity of this patient group provide a challenge for both clinicians and patients in navigating the available treatment options. In the absence of a known cure, an individualized management plan is best clinical practice to target the primary and secondary symptoms and hypothesized causal mechanisms for each patient while considering that many patients are hypersensitive to medications and can frequently experience adverse side-effects (Carruthers et al., 2003). Treatment options have been proposed that target different aspects of the disease. For simplicity, these are separated into three categories, where the treatment targets (a) maintaining factors and symptom management, (b) biological systems, and (c) the microbiome, genetic and environmental factors.

Maintaining Factors and Symptom Management

When considering the surface level of ME/CFS presentation, psychosocial treatments have been designed to target maintaining, perpetuating and exacerbating factors and specific symptoms independently. Cognitive behavioral therapy (CBT) and graded exercise therapy (GET) are the two most frequently used therapeutic approaches aimed at correcting faulty cognitions and increasing exercise tolerance respectively. A recent systematic review indicated that CBT and GET have equivalent effectiveness for global health improvements, increasing daily functioning, and reducing fatigue and sleep symptoms (Larun, Brurberg, Odgaard-Jensen, and Price, 2015). It must be noted that results from the largest trial (White et al., 2011) included in this review paper have since been criticised for inappropriate inclusion criteria, outcome measures and inaccurate conclusions (Twisk, 2016). Despite some evidence of treatment effectiveness for certain individuals, CBT and/or GET should be considered adjunctive, potentially advantageous or detrimental at different stages of the condition. Disparity between subjective and objective outcomes suggest that neither CBT nor GET address underlying pathophysiological abnormalities.

Cognitive behavioral therapy   CBT focuses on addressing catastrophizing and fear avoidant beliefs thought to contribute to ME/CFS vulnerability (Flo and Chalder, 2014). Therapists need to be aware that patient avoidance of behaviors that exacerbate symptoms may be a necessary and adaptive response to ME/CFS. Some CBT strategies can help address consequential loss, grief and anxiety related to living with a chronic illness. More targeted CBT strategies attempt to address sleep, cognitive and mood symptoms separately. Managing sleep symptoms may include a combination of cognitive-behavioral and relaxation strategies to treat selected primary sleep disorders, sleep hygiene and related behaviors (Carruthers et al., 2003). For cognitive symptoms, cognitive retraining, mindfulness meditation and mental exercises have been suggested (Carruthers et al., 2003). Symptomatic improvements have been shown for some individuals, with follow-up data suggesting approximately 20 percent of patients make a full recovery (Flo and Chalder, 2014; White et al., 2011). Some subgroups seem to be less responsive to CBT, including patients with hypocorticolism (Roberts et al., 2010) and higher levels of depression at pretreatment (Flo and Chalder, 2014).

Graded exercise therapy   There is some evidence to support the use of GET as a treatment option for ME/CFS (Larun et al., 2015; White et al., 2011). The majority of supportive evidence relies on self-report data rather than physiological measurement of exercise capacity (e.g. VO2 max, aerobic thresholds) or biomarkers of disease improvement. Few GET studies have measured the effect on cognitive functioning, with one study showing a significantly greater reduction in mental fatigue for participants receiving GET compared to the control condition (Moss-Morris, Sharon, Tobin, and Baldi, 2005). There remains limited quality evidence to support the efficacy of GET on depressive symptoms (Larun et al., 2015).

GET has been described as "potentially harmful for the majority of CFS patients" (Twisk and Maes, 2009, p. 287). In a small study, ME/CFS patients who performed a moderate exercise task experienced significantly exacerbated pain and increased physical and mental fatigue (Light, White, Hughen and Light, 2009). Additionally, this exercise task induced increased expression of metabolites that are markers for specific immune and sympathetic nervous system genes between 30 minutes to 48 hours after the exercise task compared to baseline. These changes in genetic expression were not observed in the control group. Evidence that moderate and strenuous exercise can have immune-suppressive consequences and increase activation of inflammatory pathways (increased proinflammatory cytokines, e.g. IL-6, IL-8, TNF-a; associated with genetic markers) suggest that exercise therapy could be deleterious to ME/CFS patients (e.g., increase muscle pain, fatigue and muscle damage), particularly the subgroup of patients with increased immune activation in a resting state (Twisk and Maes, 2009).

Targeting Dysfunction of Biological Systems

Numerous treatment options have been proposed to address ME/CFS pathophysiology. It is beyond the scope of this chapter to review all these in detail. The most common treatments focus on treating immune dysfunction (i.e., immune stimulators or modulators); disturbed inflammation pathways (i.e., natural anti-inflammatory and anti-oxidative substances); HPA axis abnormalities; CNS/Autonomic disturbances; orthostatic intolerance; channelopathy; and targeting the postviral (e.g., antiviral treatment) or bacterial infection (e.g. antibiotic treatment) believed to have triggered disease onset (see Carruthers et al., 2003; Chambers, Bagnall, Hempel, and Forbes, 2006; Maes, 2009).

Antidepressants are commonly prescribed (e.g., 40 percent from 641 patients in a large randomized controlled trial, RCT; White et al., 2011). Benzodiazepines and selective serotonin reuptake inhibitors (SSRIs) are thought to address neuroendocrine dysregulation and consequently used for symptomatic relief of sleep, depression and anxiety symptoms (Carruthers et al., 2003). Melatonin can be used to regulate circadian rhythm disruptions and improve sleep and vitality ratings (Williams, Waterhouse, Mugarza, Minors, and Hayden, 2002). Other pharmaceutical agents (including CNS stimulants and calcium channel-blockers) may be beneficial, dependent on the patient's CNS and cellular functioning (Carruthers et al., 2003).

Nutritional supplementation (specifically magnesium, l-carnitine and S-adenosylmethionine) is a potentially beneficial therapeutic modality requiring further investigation (Porter, Jason, Boulton, Bothne, and Coleman, 2010). Vermeulen and Scholte (2004) showed reduced mental fatigue and improved attention and concentration after supplementation with Acetyl-L-carnitine and propionyl-L-carnitine. Colabamin (B_{12}) injections are frequently used in this population and are proposed to exert effects by reducing oxidative stress (Pall, 2001). Additionally, oral nicotinamide adenine dinucleotide (NADH; Forsyth et al., 1999) and intramuscular magnesium sulphate (Cox and Campbell, 1991) have shown promise to relieve depressive symptoms in clinical trials. Clinical experts recommend magnesium supplementation to aid sleep symptoms (Carruthers et al., 2003). In a recent murine model, reduced intake of magnesium was associated with greater depressive symptoms and reflected changes in microbial composition (Winther et al., 2015). Further research is required to determine the effectiveness of nutritional supplementation, including their potential to exert therapeutic effects on restoring intestinal dysbiosis.

Targeting the Microbiome and the Interplay between Genetic and Environmental Factors

The microbiome is intricately intertwined with genetic expression, nutrition, pathogens, environmental toxins, seasonal shifts and individual characteristics (i.e., ethnicity, age and sex; Human Microbiome Project Consortium, 2012). Hence, the interplay between the microbiome, genetic and environmental factors are considered simultaneously for restoration of intestinal homeostasis in ME/CFS.

Restoring gut balance   Traditionally, antibiotics have shown efficacy for controlling acute infections; however, recent advances suggest wider application for chronic illness, including depression (Miyaoka et al., 2012) and ME/CFS (Nicolson et al., 2000). The evidence of sudden or gradual onset of ME/CFS symptoms postinfection (Hickie et al., 2006) has prompted treatment aimed at viral (e.g., Montoya et al., 2013) and bacterial toxic overload (Nicolson et al., 2000). These treatments are aimed at systemic bacterial infection, while other antibiotic treatments can provide an effective treatment for suppressing overgrowth of commensal bacteria in the gastrointestinal tract (Preidis and Versalovic, 2009). A small pilot study targeting *Streptococcus* overgrowth in the colon of ME/CFS patients has shown initial promise for improving mood, total sleep time, speed of sleep onset and sleep efficiency in patients who responded to six-day treatment with the antibiotic Erythromycin (Jackson, Butt, Ball, Lewis, and Bruck, 2015).

Probiotics are live bacteria that are consumed to encourage colonization of nonpathogenic species in the gastrointestinal tract with desirable health consequences for the host (Altenhoefer et al., 2004). In clinical trials, the use of probiotics shows promising results for emotional regulation. For studies with healthy human participants, probiotic supplementation improved depression scores for individuals with lower scores at baseline (Benton, Williams, and Brown, 2007); was associated with less emotional reactivity to visual stimuli on functional MRI (Tillisch et al., 2013); and reduced subjective mood (anger, depression, anxiety and stress) and urinary cortisol levels (Messaoudi et al., 2011). Rao et al. (2009) investigated the effect of eight-week probiotic supplementation of *Lactobacillus casei* strain on emotional symptoms in 39 ME/CFS patients. Results from this double-blind RCT showed a significant decrease in anxiety symptoms for treatment compared to control but no significant change on subjective reports of depression. Robust clinical trials are required to examine treatment efficacy and the appropriateness for patient subgroups.

Cross-sectional observations within a clinical sample indicate sex interactions between microbial composition and symptom expression (Wallis et al., 2016). Higher *Clostridium* levels were associated with increased self-reported ME/CFS symptoms (including fatigue, neurocognitive, sleep, pain, neurosensory, immunity, gastrointestinal and food/chemical sensitivity symptoms) in females. For males, higher *Lactobacillus* was associated with increased chance of reporting neurocognitive, neurosensory, pain, food/chemical sensitivity and mood symptoms, while increased *Streptococcus* was associated with the tendency for patients to report greater pain and total symptom scores (Wallis et al., 2016). The current authors are conducting a clinical trial for patients with *Streptococcus* overgrowth in the colon to examine possible sex differences in the effect of combined antibiotic and probiotic therapy on sleep, cognition and mood symptoms.

Other treatment modalities, including fecal transplants, dietary modifications, nutritional supplementation and potential consequential effects of psychosocial treatments can influence microbial composition and thus have the potential to restore gut dysbiosis. Fecal transplants show promise in ME/CFS, particularly the subgroup with combined IBS, with initial treatment effectiveness for 70 percent of patients and maintenance for 58 percent (Borody et al., 2012). The intake of dietary fibers, prebiotic or fermented foods and the Mediterranean Diet have been shown to promote a balanced microbial composition and promote optimal physical and mental health outcomes in both healthy and clinical populations (see Dash, Clarke, Berk, and Jacka, 2015). While the emerging evidence is positive for diverse groups, more research is required to examine the utility of these interventions for patients with ME/CFS.

Future Possibilities

Advances in genomic profiling are starting to clarify the role of genetic vulnerabilities in metabolic, detoxification or immune pathways that may precipitate the development of ME/CFS (e.g., Saiki et al., 2008). When combined with our rapidly developing knowledge of the microbiome, there is great potential to appropriately tailor treatment that best fits an individual patient's needs.

Conclusions

The pathophysiology of ME/CFS exerts pervasive effects on sleep, cognitive and depressive symptoms observed in ME/CFS. Symptomatic relief is highly desirable in acute illness periods. However, the body of literature reviewed here shows the interaction and overlap between symptoms and strengthens the case for the pursuit of treatments targeting underlying dysfunction. One possible avenue is through the microbiota-gut-brain axis. Emerging evidence implicates the etiological and therapeutic role of the composition of enteric microbiota. While there is limited evidence to date within the ME/CFS field, it is clear that the gut microbiome can exert effects on the stress response and affective symptoms. More research is needed to ascertain the impact on sleep and neurocognitive symptoms. Etiological conceptualizations and treatment opportunities will parallel advances in understanding metagenomic and host microbiota. To optimize physical and mental health and manage the onslaught of chronic illnesses, the human condition requires integrated conceptual understandings from multidisciplinary fields. As organisms that coexist in an interdependent relationship with other microorganisms, we must not underestimate the intricate, symbiotic dynamic between the host and the microbiome. This relationship may be one part of the jigsaw involved in advancing understanding and therapeutic opportunities in a multisystemic disorder such as ME/CFS.

Note

We thank H. Butt for critically reviewing this manuscript. Bioscreen (Aust.) Pty Ltd. and Victoria University provided postgraduate scholarship funding to A.W. without restriction on publication. M.J., M.B., D.P.L., and D.B declare no competing financial interests.

References

Altenhoefer, A., Oswald, S., Sonnenborn, U., Enders, C., Schulze, J., Hacker, J., and Oelschlaeger, T. A. (2004). The probiotic Escherichia coli strain Nissle 1917 interferes with invasion of human intestinal epithelial cells by different enteroinvasive bacterial pathogens. *FEMS Immunology and Medical Microbiology, 40*, 223–229. doi:10.1016/S0928-8244(03)00368-7

American Psychiatric Association (2013). *Diagnostic and Statistical Manual of Mental Disorders*, 5th edn. Arlington, VA: American Psychiatric Association.

Anderson, G., Berk, M., and Maes, M. (2014). Biological phenotypes underpin the physio-somatic symptoms of somatization, depression, and chronic fatigue syndrome. *Acta Psychiatrica Scandinavica, 129*(2), 83–97. doi:10.1111/acps.12182

Armitage, R., Landis, C., Hoffmann, R., Lentz, M., Watson, N. F., Goldberg, J., and Buchwald, D. (2007). The impact of a 4-hour sleep delay on slow wave activity in twins discordant for chronic fatigue syndrome. *Sleep, 30*, 657–662.

Atarashi, K., Tanoue, T., Taniguchi, T., Honda, K., Shima, T., Imaoka, A., ... Ivanov, I. I. (2011). Induction of colonic regulatory T cells by indigenous Clostridium species. *Science, 331*(6015), 337–341. doi:10.1126/science.1198469

Attree, E. A., Arroll, M. A., Dancey, C. P., Griffith, C., and Bansal, A. S. (2014). Psychosocial factors involved in memory and cognitive failures in people with myalgic encephalomyelitis/chronic fatigue syndrome. *Psychology Research and Behavior Management, 7*, 67–76. doi:10.2147/PRBM.S50645

Bailey, M. T., and Coe, C. L. (1999). Maternal separation disrupts the integrity of the intestinal microflora in infant rhesus monkeys. *Developmental Psychobiology, 35*(2), 146–155. doi:10.1002/(SICI)1098-2302(199909)35:2<146::AID-DEV7>3.0.CO;2-G

Barden, N. (2004). Implication of the hypothalamic-pituitary-adrenal axis in the physiopathology of depression. *Journal of Psychiatry and Neuroscience, 29*(3), 185–193.

Barnden, L. R., Crouch, B., Kwiatek, R., Burnet, R., and Del Fante, P. (2015). Evidence in chronic fatigue syndrome for severity-dependent upregulation of prefrontal myelination that is independent of anxiety and depression. *NMR in Biomedicine, 28*(3), 404–413. doi:10.1002/nbm.3261

Barnden, L. R., Crouch, B., Mernone, A., Kwiatek, R., Burnet, R., Chryssidis, S., ... del Fante, P. (2011). A brain MRI study of chronic fatigue syndrome: Evidence of brainstem dysfunction and altered homeostasis. *NMR in Biomedicine, 24*(10), 1302–1312. doi:10.1002/nbm.1692

Benca, R. M., Obermeyer, W. H., Thisted, R. A., and Gillin, J. C. (1992). Sleep and psychiatric disorders: A meta-analysis. *Archives of General Psychiatry, 49*(8), 651–668. doi:10.1001/archpsyc.1992.01820080059010

Benington, J. H. (2000). Sleep homeostasis and the function of sleep. *Sleep, 23*(7), 959–966.

Benton, D., Williams, C., and Brown, A. (2007). Impact of consuming a milk drink containing a probiotic on mood and cognition. *European Journal of Clinical Nutrition, 61*(3), 355–361. doi:10.1038/sj.ejcn.1602546

Bested, A. C., Logan, A. C., and Selhub, E. M. (2013). Intestinal microbiota, probiotics and mental health: From Metchnikoff to modern advances: Part II – contemporary contextual research. *Gut Pathogens, 5*(3), 1–14.

Beurel, E., and Nemeroff, C. (2014). Interaction of stress, corticotropin-releasing factor, arginine vasopressin and behaviour. *Current Topics in Behavioral Neurosciences, 18*, 67–80. doi:10.1007/7854_2014_306

Blatt, S. J., and Luyten, P. (2009). A structural-developmental psychodynamic approach to psychopathology: Two polarities of experience across the life span. *Development Psychopatholy, 21*, 793–814. doi:10.1017/S0954579409000431

Borody, T. J., Nowak, A., and Finlayson, S. (2012). The GI microbiome and its role in chronic fatigue syndrome: A summary of bacteriotherapy. *Journal of the Australasian College of Nutritional and Environmental Medicine, 31*(3), 3.

Bron, R., and Furness, J. B. (2009). Rhythm of digestion: Keeping time in the gastrointestinal tract. *Clinical and Experimental Pharmacology and Physiology, 36*(10), 1041–1048.

Buchwald, D., Pascualy, R., Bombardier, C., and Kith, P. (1994). Sleep disorders in patients with chronic fatigue. *Clinical Infectious Diseases, 18*(suppl. 1), S68–S72.

Buijs, R. M., and Swaab, D. F. (2013). Differential responses of components of the autonomic nervous system. In R. M. Buijs and D. Swaab (Eds.), *Autonomic Nervous System Handbook of Clinical Neurology: Handbook of Clinical Neurology*, vol. 117 (pp. 13–22): Burlington : Elsevier Science.

Cannon, W. B. (1929). Organisation for physiological homeostasis. *Physiological Reviews, 9*(3), 399–431.

Carruthers, B. M., Jain, A. K., DeMeirleir, K. L., Peterson, D. L., Klimas, N. G., Lerner, A. M., ... van de Sande, M. I. (2003). Myalgic encephalomyelitis/chronic fatigue syndrome: Clinical working case definition, diagnostic and treatment protocols. *Journal of Chronic Fatigue Syndrome, 11*(1), 7–116.

Carruthers, B. M., van de Sande, M. I., De Meirleir, K. L., Klimas, N. G., Broderick, G., Mitchell, T., ... Stevens, S. (2011). Myalgic encephalomyelitis: International Consensus Criteria. *Journal of Internal Medicine, 270*(4), 327–338. doi:10.1111/j.1365-2796.2011.02428.x

Chambers, D., Bagnall, A. M., Hempel, S., and Forbes, C. (2006). Interventions for the treatment, management and rehabilitation of patients with chronic fatigue syndrome/myalgic encephalomyelitis: An updated systematic review. *Journal of the Royal Society of Medicine, 99*(10), 506–520.

Ciccone, D. S., and Natelson, B. H. (2003). Comorbid illness in women with chronic fatigue syndrome: A test of the single syndrome hypothesis. *Psychosomatic Medicine, 65*(2), 268–275. doi:10.1097/01.PSY.0000033125.08272.A9

Clarke, G., Grenham, S., Scully, P., Fitzgerald, P., Moloney, R. D., Shanahan, F., ... Cryan, J. F. (2013). The microbiome-gut-brain axis during early life regulates the hippocampal serotonergic system in a sex-dependent manner. *Molecular Psychiatry, 18*(6), 666–673. doi:10.1038/mp.2012.77

Cockshell, S. J., and Mathias, J. L. (2010). Cognitive functioning in chronic fatigue syndrome: A meta-analysis. *Psychological Medicine, 40*(8), 1253–1267.

Cockshell, S. J., and Mathias, J. L. (2014). Cognitive functioning in people with chronic fatigue syndrome: A comparison between subjective and objective measures. *Neuropsychology, 28*(3), 394–405. doi:10.1037/neu0000025

Cope, H., and David, A. S. (1996). Neuroimaging in chronic fatigue syndrome. *Journal of Neurology, Neurosurgery, and Psychiatry, 60*(5), 471–473.

Cope, H., Pernet, A., Kendall, B., and David, A. (1995). Cognitive functioning and magnetic resonance imaging in chronic fatigue. *British Journal of Psychiatry, 167*(1), 86–94.

Costa, D. C., Tannock, C., and Brostoff, J. (1995). Brainstem perfusion is impaired in chronic fatigue syndrome. *QJM, 88*(11), 767–773.

Cox, I. M., and Campbell, M. J. (1991). Red blood cell magnesium and chronic fatigue syndrome. *Lancet*, *337*(8744), 757.

Creti, L., Libman, E., Baltzan, M., Rizzo, D., Bailes, S., and Fichten, C.S. (2010). Impaired sleep in chronic fatigue syndrome. *Journal of Health Psychology*, *15*(4), 596–607.

Cryan, J. F., and Dinan, T. G. (2012). Mind-altering microorganisms: The impact of the gut microbiota on brain and behaviour. *Nature Reviews. Neuroscience*, *13*(10), 701–712. doi:10.1038/nrn3346

Dancey, C. P., and Friend, J. (2008). Symptoms, impairment and illness intrusiveness – their relationship with depression in women with CFS/ME. *Psychology and Health*, *23*(8), 983–999.

Dash, S., Clarke, G., Berk, M., and Jacka, F. N. (2015). The gut microbiome and diet in psychiatry: Focus on depression. *Current Opinion in Psychiatry*, *28*(1), 1–6. doi:10.1097/YCO.0000000000000117

Desbonnet, L., Garrett, L., Clarke, G., Bienenstock, J., and Dinan, T. G. (2008). The probiotic Bifidobacteria infantis: An assessment of potential antidepressant properties in the rat. *Journal of Psychiatric Research*, *43*, 164–174. doi:10.1016/j.jpsychires.2008.03.009

Desbonnet, L., Garrett, L., Clarke, G., Kiely, B., Cryan, J. F., and Dinan, T. G. (2010). Cognitive, behavioral, and systems neuroscience: Effects of the probiotic Bifidobacterium infantis in the maternal separation model of depression. *Neuroscience*, *170*, 1179–1188. doi:10.1016/j.neuroscience.2010.08.005

Dijk, D.-J., Brunner, D. P., Beersma, D., and Borbely, A. A. (1990). Electroencephalogram power density and slow wave sleep as a function of prior waking and circadian phase. *Sleep*, *13*(5), 430–440.

Dinan, T. G., and Cryan, J. F. (2012). Regulation of the stress response by the gut microbiota: Implications for psychoneuroendocrinology. *Psychoneuroendocrinology*, *37*(9), 1369–1378. doi:http://dx.doi.org/10.1016/j.psyneuen.2012.03.007

Fabian, L. A., McGuire, L., Page, G. G., Goodin, B. R., Edwards, R. R., and Haythornthwaite, J. (2009). The association of the cortisol awakening response with experimental pain ratings. *Psychoneuroendocrinology*, *34*, 1247–1251.

Flo, E., and Chalder, T. (2014). Prevalence and predictors of recovery from chronic fatigue syndrome in a routine clinical practice. *Behaviour Research and Therapy*, *63*, 1–8. doi:10.1016/j.brat.2014.08.013

Forsyth, L. M., Preuss, H. G., MacDowell, A. L., Chiazze, L., Jr., Birkmayer, G. D., and Bellanti, J. A. (1999). Therapeutic effects of oral NADH on the symptoms of patients with chronic fatigue syndrome. *Annals of Allergy, Asthma and Immunology*, *82*(2), 185–191.

Foster, J. A., and McVey Neufeld, K. (2013). Gut–brain axis: How the microbiome influences anxiety and depression. *Trends in Neurosciences*, *36*(5), 305–312. doi.org/10.1016/j.tins.2013.01.005

Fremont, M., Coomans, D., Massart, S., and De Meirleir, K. (2013). High-throughput 16S rRNA gene sequencing reveals alterations of intestinal microbiota in myalgic encephalomyelitis/chronic fatigue syndrome patients. *Anaerobe*, *22*, 50–56. doi:10.1016/j.anaerobe.2013.06.002

Fries, E., Hesse, J., Hellhammer, J., and Hellhammer, D. H. (2005). A new view on hypocortisolism. *Psychoneuroendocrinology*, *30*, 1010–1016.

Furness, J. B. (2006). *The Enteric Nervous System*. Oxford: Wiley-Blackwell.

Gardner, A., and Boles, R. G. (2011). Beyond the serotonin hypothesis: Mitochondria, inflammation and neurodegeneration in major depression and affective spectrum disorders. *Progress in Neuro-Psychopharmacology and Biological Psychiatry*, *35*(3), 730–743. doi:10.1016/j.pnpbp.2010.07.030

Gareau, M. G., Wine, E., Rodrigues, D. M., Sherman, P. M., Cho, J. H., Philpott, D. J., … MacQueen, G. (2011). Bacterial infection causes stress-induced memory dysfunction in mice. *Gut*, *60*(3), 307–317. doi:10.1136/gut.2009.202515

Gill, S. R., Pop, M., DeBoy, R. T., Eckburg, P. B., Turnbaugh, P. J., Samuel, B. S., … Nelson, K. E. (2006). Metagenomic analysis of the human distal gut microbiome. *Science*, *312*(5778), 1355–1359.

Grenham, S., Clarke, G., Cryan, J. F., and Dinan, T. G. (2011). Brain-gut-microbe communication in health and disease. *Frontiers in Physiology*, *2*, 94. doi:10.3389/fphys.2011.00094

Hall, D. L., Lattie, E. G., Antoni, M. H., Fletcher, M. A., Czaja, S., Perdomo, D., and Klimas, N. G. (2014). Stress management skills, cortisol awakening response, and post-exertional malaise in chronic fatigue syndrome. *Psychoneuroendocrinology*, *49*, 26–31. doi:http://dx.doi.org/10.1016/j.psyneuen.2014.06.021

Harvey, S. B., and Wesseley, S. (2009). Chronic fatigue syndrome: Identifying zebras amongst the horses. *BMC Medicine*, *7*, 58.

Harvey, S. B., Wessely, S., Hotopf, M., and Wadsworth, M. (2008). The relationship between prior psychiatric disorder and chronic fatigue: Evidence from a national birth cohort study. *Psychological Medicine*, *38*(7), 933–940. doi:10.1017/S0033291707001900

Hatheway, C. L. (1990). Toxigenic clostridia. *Clinical Microbiology Reviews*, *3*(1), 66–98.

Hawk, C., Jason, L. A., and Torres-Harding, S. (2006). Differential diagnosis of chronic fatigue syndrome and major depressive disorder. *International Journal of Behavioral Medicine*, *13*(3), 244–251. doi:10.1207/s15327558ijbm1303_8

Hickie, I., Davenport, T., Wakefield, D., Vollmer-Conna, U., Cameron, B., Vernon, S. D., ... Dubbo Infectious Outcomes Study Group. (2006). Post-infective and chronic fatigue syndromes precipitated by viral and non-viral pathogens: Prospective cohort study. *BMJ*, *333*, 575.

Hornig, M., Montoya, J. G., Klimas, N. G., Levine, S., Felsenstein, D., Bateman, L., ... Lipkin, W. I. (2015). Distinct plasma immune signatures in ME/CFS are present early in the course of illness. *Science Advances*, *1*(1), e1400121. doi:10.1126/sciadv.1400121

Human Microbiome Project Consortium (2012). Structure, function and diversity of the healthy human microbiome. *Nature*, *486*(7402), 207–214. doi:10.1038/nature11234

Institute of Medicine (2015). Myalgic encephalomyelitis/chronic fatigue syndrome (ME/CFS): Key facts. National Academy of Sciences. At www.nap.edu/html/19012/MECFS_KeyFacts.pdf (accessed July 2016).

Jackson, M. L., and Bruck, D. (2012). Sleep abnormalities in chronic fatigue syndrome/myalgic encephalomyelitis: A review. *Journal of Clinical Sleep Medicine*, *8*(6), 719–728. doi:10.5664/jcsm.2276

Jackson, M. L., Butt, H., Ball, M., Lewis, D. P., and Bruck, D. (2015). Sleep quality and the treatment of intestinal microbiota imbalance in chronic fatigue syndrome: A pilot study. *Sleep Science*, *8*, 124–133. doi:10.1016/j.slsci.2015.10.001

Jason, L. A., Brown, A., Clyne, E., Bartgis, L., Evans, M., and Brown, M. (2012). Contrasting case definitions for chronic fatigue syndrome, myalgic encephalomyelitis/chronic fatigue syndrome and myalgic encephalomyelitis. *Evaluation and the Health Professions*, *35*(3), 280–304. doi:10.1177/0163278711424281

Jason, L., Brown, M., Evans, M., Anderson, V., Lerch, A., Brown, A., ... Porter, N. (2011). Measuring substantial reductions in functioning in patients with chronic fatigue syndrome. *Disability and Rehabilitation*, *33*(7), 589–598. doi:10.3109/09638288.2010.503256

Jason, L. A., Richman, J. A., Friedberg, F., Wagner, L., Taylor, R., and Jordan, K. M. (1997). Politics, science, and the emergence of a new disease: The case of chronic fatigue syndrome. *American Psychologist*, *52*(9), 973–983.

Johns, M. W. (2002). Sleep propensity varies with behaviour and the situation in which it is measured: The concept of somnificity. *Journal of Sleep Research*, *11*(1), 61–67. doi:10.1046/j.1365-2869.2002.00274.x

Kempke, S., Luyten, P., De Coninck, S., Van Houdenhove, B., Mayes, L. C., and Claes, S. (2015). Effects of early childhood trauma on hypothalamic-pituitary-adrenal (HPA) axis function in patients with chronic fatigue syndrome. *Psychoneuroendocrinology*, *52*, 14–21. doi:10.1016/j.psyneuen.2014.10.027

Lakhan, S. E., and Kirchgessner, A. (2010). Gut inflammation in chronic fatigue syndrome. *Nutrition and Metabolism*, *7*(1), 79.

Lange, G., Holodny, A. I., DeLuca, J., Lee, H. J., Yan, X. H., Steffener, J., and Natelson, B. H. (2001). Quantitative assessment of cerebral ventricular volumes in chronic fatigue syndrome. *Applied Neuropsychology*, *8*(1), 23–30.

Lange, G., Lee, H. J., Deluca, J., Tiersky, L. A., Natelson, B. H., and Maldjian, J. A. (1999). Brain MRI abnormalities exist in a subset of patients with chronic fatigue syndrome. *Journal of the Neurological Sciences*, *171*(1), 3–7. doi:10.1016/S0022-510X(99)00243-9

Lange, G., Steffener, J., Cook, D. B., Bly, B. M., Christodoulou, C., Liu, W. C., ... Natelson, B. H. (2005). Objective evidence of cognitive complaints in chronic fatigue syndrome: A BOLD fMRI study of verbal working memory. *Neuroimage*, *26*(2), 513–524.

Lange, G., Wang, S., DeLuca, J., and Natelson, B. H. (1998). Neuroimaging in chronic fatigue syndrome. *American Journal of Medicine*, *105*(3), 50S–53S.

Larun, L., Brurberg, K. G., Odgaard-Jensen, J., and Price, J. R. (2015). Exercise therapy for chronic fatigue syndrome. *Cochrane Database of Systematic Reviews*, *2*, CD003200. doi:10.1002/14651858.CD003200.pub3

Leung, P. S. (Ed.) (2014). *The Gastrointestinal System: Gastrointestinal, Nutritional and Hepatobiliary Physiology*: Dordrecht: Springer. doi:10.1007/978-94-017-8771-0__1

Li, W., Dowd, S. E., Scurlock, B., Acosta-Martinez, V., and Lyte, M. (2009). Memory and learning behavior in mice is temporally associated with diet-induced alterations in gut bacteria. *Physiology and Behavior*, *96*, 557–567. doi:10.1016/j.physbeh.2008.12.004

Libman, E., Creti, L., Baltzan, M., Rizzo, D., Fichten, C. S., and Bailes, S. (2009). Sleep apnea and psychological functioning in chronic fatigue syndrome. *Journal of Health Psychology*, *14*(8), 1251–1267. doi:10.1177/1359105309344895

Light, A. R., White, A. T., Hughen, R. W., and Light, K. C. (2009). Original report: Moderate exercise increases expression for sensory, adrenergic, and immune genes in chronic fatigue syndrome patients but not in normal subjects. *Journal of Pain*, *10*, 1099–1112. doi:10.1016/j.jpain.2009.06.003

Luyten, P., Kempke, S., Van Wambeke, P., Claes, S., Blatt, S. J., and Van Houdenhove, B. (2011). Self-critical perfectionism, stress generation, and stress sensitivity in patients with chronic fatigue syndrome: Relationship with severity of depression. *Psychiatry: Interpersonal and Biological Processes*, *74*(1), 21–30. doi:10.1521/psyc.2011.74.1.21

Maes, M. (2009). Inflammatory and oxidative and nitrosative stress pathways underpinning chronic fatigue, somatization and psychosomatic symptoms. *Current Opinion in Psychiatry*, *22*, 75–83.

Maes, M. (2011). An intriguing and hitherto unexplained co-occurrence: Depression and chronic fatigue syndrome are manifestations of shared inflammatory, oxidative and nitrosative (IOandNS) pathways. *Progress in Neuropsychopharmacology and Biological Psychiatry*, *35*, 784–794. doi:10.1016/j.pnpbp.2010.06.023

Maes, M., and Leunis, J.C. (2008). Normalization of leaky gut in chronic fatigue syndrome (CFS) is accompanied by a clinical improvement: Effects of age, duration of illness and the translocation of LPS from gram-negative bacteria. *Neuro Endocrinology Letters*, *29*(6), 101–109.

Maes, M., Mihaylova, I., Kubera, M., Leunis, J. C., Twisk, F. N. M., and Geffard, M. (2012). IgM-mediated autoimmune responses directed against anchorage epitopes are greater in myalgic encephalomyelitis/chronic fatigue syndrome (ME/CFS) than in major depression. *Metabolic Brain Disease*, *27*(4), 415–423. doi:10.1007/s11011-012-9316-8

Maes, M., and Twisk, F. N. (2010). Chronic fatigue syndrome: Harvey and Wessely's (bio)psychosocial model versus a bio(psychosocial) model based on inflammatory and oxidative and nitrosative stress pathways. *BMC Medicine*, *8*(1), 35.

Mairesse, O., Hofmans, J., Neu, D., Dinis M., Armando L., Cluydts, R., and Theuns, P. (2010). The algebra of sleepiness: Investigating the interaction of homeostatic (S) and circadian (C) processes in sleepiness using linear metrics. *Psicológica*, *31*(3), 541–559.

Majer, M., Jones, J., Unger, E., Youngblood, L., Decker, M., Gurbaxani, B., … Reeves, W. (2007). Perception versus polysomnographic assessment of sleep in CFS and non-fatigued control subjects: Population-based study. *BMC Neurology*, *7*(1), 40.

Mariman, A. (2013). The role of sleep in the chronic fatigue syndrome. Thesis, Faculty of Medicine and Health Sciences, Ghent University. At https://biblio.ugent.be/publication/4092625/file/4336595.pdf (accessed July 2016).

Mayer, E. (2000). The neurobiology of stress and gastrointestinal disease. *Gut*, *47*(6), 861–869.

Mayer, E. (2011). Gut feelings: The emerging biology of gut–brain communication. *Nature Reviews. Neuroscience*, *12*(8), 453–466. doi:10.1038/nrn3071

McInnis, O. A., Matheson, K., and Anisman, H. (2014). Living with the unexplained: Coping, distress, and depression among women with chronic fatigue syndrome and/or fibromyalgia compared to an autoimmune disorder. *Anxiety, Stress and Coping*, *27*(6), 601–618.

Messaoudi, M., Violle, N., Bisson, J. F., Desor, D., Javelot, H., and Rougeot, C. (2011). Beneficial psychological effects of a probiotic formulation (Lactobacillus helveticus R0052 and Bifidobacterium longum R0175) in healthy human volunteers. *Gut Microbes*, *2*(4), 256–261.

Miyaoka, T., Wake, R., Furuya, M., Liaury, K., Ieda, M., Kawakami, K., … Horiguchi, J. (2012). Minocycline as adjunctive therapy for patients with unipolar psychotic depression: An open-label study. *Progress in Neuro-Psychopharmacology and Biological Psychiatry*, *37*(2), 222–226. doi:10.1016/j.pnpbp.2012.02.002

Moloney, R. D., Desbonnet, L., Clarke, G., Dinan, T. G., and Cryan, J. F. (2014). The microbiome: Stress, health and disease. *Mammalian Genome*, *25*(1–2), 49–74. doi:10.1007/s00335-013-9488-5

Montoya, J. G., Kogelnik, A. M., Bhangoo, M. S., Lunn, M. R., Flamand, L., Merrihew, L. E., … Desai, M. (2013). Randomized clinical trial to evaluate the efficacy and safety of valganciclovir in a subset of patients with chronic fatigue syndrome. *Journal of Medical Virology*, *85*(12), 2101–2109. doi:10.1002/jmv.23713

Moss-Morris, R., Sharon, C., Tobin, R., and Baldi, J. C. (2005). A randomized controlled graded exercise trial for chronic fatigue syndrome: Outcomes and mechanisms of change. *Journal of Health Psychology*, *10*(2), 245–259. doi:10.1177/1359105305049774

Nakatomi, Y., Inaba, M., Mizuno, K., Ishii, A., Wada, Y., Tanaka, M., … Shiomi, S. (2014). Neuroinflammation in patients with chronic fatigue syndrome/myalgic encephalomyelitis: An [11]C-(R)-PK11195 PET study. *Journal of Nuclear Medicine*, *55*(6), 945–950. doi:10.2967/jnumed.113.131045

Neu, D., Cappeliez, B., Hoffmann, G., Verbanck, P., Linkowski, P., and Le Bon, O. (2009). High slow-wave sleep and low-light sleep: Chronic fatigue syndrome is not likely to be a primary sleep disorder. *Journal of Clinical Neurophysiology*, *26*(3), 207–212. doi:10.1097/WNP.0b013e3181a1841b

Neu, D., Mairesse, O., Verbanck, P., and Le Bon, O. (2015). Slow wave sleep in the chronically fatigued: Power spectra distribution patterns in chronic fatigue syndrome and primary insomnia. *Clinical Neurophysiology, 126*(10), 1926–1933.

Neu, D., Mairesse, O., Verbanck, P., Linkowski, P., and Le Bon, O. (2014). Non-REM sleep EEG power distribution in fatigue and sleepiness. *Journal of Psychosomatic Research, 76,* 286–291. doi:10.1016/j.jpsychores.2014.02.002

Neufeld, K. M., Kang, N., Bienenstock, J., and Foster, J. A. (2011). Reduced anxiety-like behavior and central neurochemical change in germ-free mice. *Neurogastroenterology and Motility, 23*(3), 255. doi:10.1111/j.1365-2982.2010.01620.x

Nicolson, G. L., Nasralla, M. Y., Franco, A. R., Nicolson, N. L., Erwin, R., Ngwenya, R., and Berns, P. A. (2000). Diagnosis and integrative treatment of intracellular bacterial infections in chronic fatigue and fibromyalgia syndromes, Gulf War illness, rheumatoid arthritis and other chronic illnesses. *Clinical Practice of Alternative Medicine, 1*(2), 92–102.

Nolte, J., and Sundsten, J. W. (2009). *The Human Brain: An Introduction to Its Functional Anatomy.* 6th edn. Philadelphia: Mosby/Elsevier.

Ocon, A. J. (2013). Caught in the thickness of brain fog: Exploring the cognitive symptoms of chronic fatigue syndrome. *Frontiers in Physiology, 4,* 63. doi:10.3389/fphys.2013.00063

O'Mahony, S. M., Marchesi, J. R., Scully, P., Codling, C., Ceolho, A., Quigley, E. M. M., … Dinan, T. G. (2009). Early life stress alters behavior, immunity, and microbiota in rats: Implications for irritable bowel syndrome and psychiatric illnesses. *Biological Psychiatry, 65,* 263–267. doi:10.1016/j.biopsych.2008.06.026

Pall, M. L. (2001). Cobalamin used in chronic fatigue syndrome therapy is a nitric oxide scavenger. *Journal of Chronic Fatigue Syndrome, 8*(2), 39–44.

Perrin, R., Embleton, K., Pentreath, V. W., and Jackson, A. (2010). Longitudinal MRI shows no cerebral abnormality in chronic fatigue syndrome. *British Journal Of Radiology, 83*(989), 419–423. doi:10.1259/bjr/85621779

Pigeon, W. R., Sateia, M. J., and Ferguson, R. J. (2003). Distinguishing between excessive daytime sleepiness and fatigue: Toward improved detection and treatment. *Journal of Psychosomatic Research, 54*(1), 61–69. doi:10.1016/s0022-3999(02)00542-1

Porter, N. S., Jason, L. A., Boulton, A., Bothne, N., and Coleman, B. (2010). Alternative medical interventions used in the treatment and management of myalgic encephalomyelitis/chronic fatigue syndrome and fibromyalgia. *Journal of Alternative and Complementary Medicine, 16*(3), 235–249. doi:10.1089/acm.2008.0376

Powell, D. J. H., Liossi, C., Moss-Morris, R., and Schlotz, W. (2013). Unstimulated cortisol secretory activity in everyday life and its relationship with fatigue and chronic fatigue syndrome: A systematic review and subset meta-analysis. *Psychoneuroendocrinology, 38*(11), 2405–2422. doi:http://dx.doi.org/10.1016/j.psyneuen.2013.07.004

Preidis, G. A., and Versalovic, J. (2009). Targeting the human microbiome with antibiotics, probiotics, and prebiotics: Gastroenterology enters the metagenomics era. *Gastroenterology, 136*(6), 2015–2031.

Rao, A. V., Bested, A. C., Beaulne, T. M., Katzman, M. A., Iorio, C., Berardi, J. M., and Logan, A. C. (2009). A randomized, double-blind, placebo-controlled pilot study of a probiotic in emotional symptoms of chronic fatigue syndrome. *Gut Pathogens, 1*(1), 6. doi:10.1186/1757-4749-1-6

Reeves, W. C., Heim, C., Maloney, E. M., Youngblood, L. S., Unger, E. R., Decker, M. J., … Rye, D. B. (2006). Sleep characteristics of persons with chronic fatigue syndrome and non-fatigued controls: Results from a population-based study. *BMC Neurology, 6,* 41.

Rhee, S. H., Pothoulakis, C., and Mayer, E. A. (2009). Principles and clinical implications of the brain-gut-enteric microbiota axis. *Nature Reviews. Gastroenterology and Hepatology, 6*(5), 306–314.

Roberts, A. D. L., Wessely, S., Chalder, T., Cleare, A. J., Charler, M. L., and Papadopoulos, A. (2010). Does hypocortisolism predict a poor response to cognitive behavioural therapy in chronic fatigue syndrome? *Psychological Medicine, 40*(3), 515–522. doi:10.1017/S0033291709990390

Saiki, T., Kawai, T., Morita, K., Ohta, M., Saito, T., Rokutan, K., and Ban, N. (2008). Identification of marker genes for differential diagnosis of chronic fatigue syndrome. *Molecular Medicine, 14*(9–10), 599–607. doi:10.2119/2007-00059.Saiki

Sekirov, I., Russell, S. L., Antunes, L. C., and Finlay, B. B. (2010). Gut microbiota in health and disease. *Physiological Reviews, 90*(3), 859–904. doi:10.1152/physrev.00045.2009

Sheedy, J. R., Wettenhall, R. E. H., Ssanlon, D., Gooley, P. R., Lewis, D. P., McGregor, N. R., … De Meirleir, K. L. (2009). Increased D-lactic acid intestinal bacteria in patients with chronic fatigue syndrome. *In Vivo, 23*(4), 621–628.

Shen, J., Barbera, J., and Shapiro, C. M. (2006). Distinguishing sleepiness and fatigue: Focus on definition and measurement. *Sleep Medicine Reviews, 10*(1), 63–76.

Siessmeier, T., Schreckenberger, M., Bartenstein, P., Nix, W. A., Hardt, J., and Egle, U. T. (2003). Observer independent analysis of cerebral glucose metabolism in patients with chronic fatigue syndrome. *Journal of Neurology, Neurosurgery, and Psychiatry*, *74*(7), 922–928. doi:10.1136/jnnp.74.7.922

Smith, S. M., and Vale, W. W. (2006). The role of the hypothalamic-pituitary-adrenal axis in neuroendocrine responses to stress. *Dialogues in Clinical Neuroscience*, *8*(4), 383–395.

Stevens, C. (2014). Investigation of naturalistic sleep/wake behaviour in myalgic encephalomyelitis/chronic fatigue syndrome. At http://vuir.vu.edu.au/26239/1/Catherine%20Stevens.pdf (accessed July 2016).

Sudo, N., Chida, Y., Sonoda, J., Oyama, N., Yu, X. N., Kubo, C., … Koga, Y. (2004). Postnatal microbial colonization programs the hypothalamic-pituitary-adrenal system for stress response in mice. *Journal of Physiology*, *558*(1), 263–275. doi:10.1113/jphysiol.2004.063388

Taillefer, S. S., Kirmayer, L. J., Robbins, J. M., and Lasry, J. (2003). Correlates of illness worry in chronic fatigue syndrome. *Journal of Psychosomatic Research*, *54*, 331–337. doi:10.1016/S0022-3999(02)00332-X

Tak, L. M., Cleare, A. J., Ormel, J., Manoharan, A., Kok, I. C., Wessely, S., and Rosmalen, J. G. M. (2011). Review article: Meta-analysis and meta-regression of hypothalamic-pituitary-adrenal axis activity in functional somatic disorders. *Biological Psychology*, *87*, 183–194. doi:10.1016/j.biopsycho.2011.02.002

Tillisch, K., Labus, J., Kilpatrick, L., Jiang, Z., Stains, J., Ebrat, B., … Mayer, E. A. (2013). Consumption of fermented milk product with probiotic modulates brain activity. *Gastroenterology*, *144*(7), 1394–1401. doi:10.1053/j.gastro.2013.02.043

Tirelli, U., Chierichetti, F., Tavio, M., Simonelli, C., Bianchin, G., Zanco, P., and Ferlin, G. (1998). Brain positron emission tomography (PET) in chronic fatigue syndrome: Preliminary data. *American Journal of Medicine*, *105*(3A), 54S–58S.

Twisk, F. N. M., and Maes, M. (2009). A review on cognitive behavorial therapy (CBT) and graded exercise therapy (GET) in myalgic encephalomyelitis (ME)/chronic fatigue syndrome (CFS): CBT/GET is not only ineffective and not evidence-based, but also potentially harmful for many patients with ME/CFS. *Neuro Endocrinology Letters*, *30*(3), 284–299.

Twisk, F. (2016). PACE: CBT and GET are not rehabilitative therapies. *The Lancet Psychiatry*, *3*, e6. doi:10.1016/S2215-0366(15)00554-4

Vercoulen, J. H. M. M., Swanink, C. M. A., Galama, J. M. D., Fennis, J. F. M., Jongen, P. J. H., Hommes, O., … Bleijenberg, G. (1998). The persistence of fatigue in chronic fatigue syndrome and multiple sclerosis: Development of a model. *Journal of Psychosomatic Research*, *45*, 507–517.

Vermeulen, R. C. W., and Scholte, H. R. (2004). Exploratory open label, randomized study of acetyl- and propionylcarnitine in chronic fatigue syndrome. *Psychosomatic Medicine*, *66*(2), 276–282. doi:10.1097/01.psy.0000116249.60477.e9

Voigt, R. M., Forsyth, C. B., Green, S. J., Mutlu, E., Engen, P., Vitaterna, M. H., … Keshavarzian, A. (2014). Circadian disorganization alters intestinal microbiota. *PLoS One*, *9*(5), 1–17. doi:10.1371/journal.pone.0097500

Wallis, A., Butt, H., Ball, M., Lewis, D. P., and Bruck, D. (2016). Support for the microgenderome: Associations in a human clinical population. *Scientific Reports*, *6*, 19171. doi:10.1038/srep19171

Watson, N. F., Jacobsen, C., Goldberg, J., Kapur, V., and Buchwald, D. (2004). Subjective and objective sleepiness in monozygotic twins discordant for chronic fatigue syndrome. *Sleep*, *27*, 973–977.

Watson, N. F., Kapur, V., Arguelles, L. M., Goldberg, J., Schmidt, D. F., Armitage, R., and Buchwald, D. (2003). Comparison of subjective and objective measures of insomnia in monozygotic twins discordant for chronic fatigue syndrome. *Sleep*, *26*, 324–328.

White, P. D., Decesare, J. C., Baber, H. L., Clark, L. V., Goldsmith, K., Potts, L., … Sharpe, M. (2011). Comparison of adaptive pacing therapy, cognitive behaviour therapy, graded exercise therapy, and specialist medical care for chronic fatigue syndrome (PACE): A randomised trial. *Lancet*, *377*(9768), 823–836. doi:10.1016/S0140-6736(11)60096-2

Williams, G., Waterhouse, J., Mugarza, J., Minors, D., and Hayden, K. (2002). Therapy of circadian rhythm disorders in chronic fatigue syndrome: No symptomatic improvement with melatonin or phototherapy. *European Journal of Clinical Investigation*, *32*(11), 831–837.

Winther, G., Elfving, B., Wegener, G., Pyndt Jørgensen, B. M., Kihl, P., Sørensen, D. B., … Lund, S. (2015). Dietary magnesium deficiency alters gut microbiota and leads to depressive-like behaviour. *Acta Neuropsychiatrica*, *27*(3), 168–176. doi:10.1017/neu.2015.7

32

Funny or Funnier?

A Review of the Benefits (and Detriments) of Humor in the Workplace

Michael Sliter, Morgan Jones, and Dennis Devine

The traditional view of the workplace is that it is a place for serious, important endeavors, and there is no room for "funny business." However, in recent years, many organizations have undergone a humor revolution, with very successful companies, such as Google and Zappos, popularizing cultures of fun, mirth, and merriment. While relatively little "hard" evidence links the use of humor to actual business success and profit (Luby, 2014), considerable effort has been dedicated to understanding how humor can affect the workplace. This chapter is dedicated to summarizing the consequences of workplace humor, both positive and negative. We first define humor, then discuss its benefits at both the individual and group levels, consider the "dark side" of humor, and conclude by offering an integrative model and some potential future directions for readers who are looking for new research projects. You may (or may not) catch us attempting to have a little fun as we go along.

Defining Humor

Martineau (1972) defines humor as any instance of communication which is perceived as amusing by others. Martin (2007; not the same person as Martineau) expands this definition, writing that "humor is a broad term that refers to anything that people say or do that is perceived as funny and tends to make others laugh, as well as the mental processes that go into both creating and perceiving such an amusing stimulus, and also the affective response involved in the enjoyment of it" (p. 5). This nice, short definition implies that humor is a process that can be broken down into four essential components: (1) the social context, (2) a cognitive-perceptual

The Handbook of Stress and Health: A Guide to Research and Practice, First Edition.
Edited by Cary L. Cooper and James Campbell Quick.
© 2017 John Wiley & Sons, Ltd. Published 2017 by John Wiley & Sons, Ltd.

process, (3) an emotional response, and (4) the vocal-behavioral expression of laughter (Martin, 2007).

To elaborate on the components, *social context* implies that humor is a phenomenon arising from the interaction of two or more people. Though a person might laugh when no others are present (e.g., recalling a joke; watching a television show), these instances might be considered pseudo-social in that the person laughing is still reacting to experiences with others, whether they be recalled or mediated by the characters in a television show (Martin, 2007). *The cognitive-perceptual process* involves an interplay between the person doing or saying something funny and the person perceiving that humor. The facilitator (we'll use this term to refer to the person generating humor) has to mentally process ideas in order to generate something that might be perceived by others as funny/humorous. The audience (we'll use this term to refer to the person or people perceiving the humor) has to then appraise the statements generated by the facilitator as humorous, witty, or somehow funny. The *emotional response* component necessitates that humor involve more than just simple cognitive awareness that something witnessed was "funny." Robots could achieve that much. Rather, for something to be humorous, it must elicit a pleasant emotional response (which Martin, 2007, terms "mirth"). No mirth is elicited from a flat joke (Dennis Devine, 1980–2016).

As is evidenced, humor is a relatively complex phenomenon involving multiple people and components. However, it is rarely studied as a complex phenomenon, with researchers (particularly organizational scientists) preferring to investigate a "sense of humor," or an individual's disposition toward humor. This research has shown that humor can be conceptualized best as a multifaceted construct, consisting of numerous, humor-related traits that encompass an overall disposition (a relatively stable way of being made up by various traits; Carver and Scheier, 2000). For instance, some researchers have conceptualized "sense of humor" as a cognitive ability – the ability to generate mirth in others (think of a person who writes comic strips) and the ability to recognize and appreciate funny things that others say and do (recognizing humor, humorous people, and humorous situations; Thorson and Powell, 1993). Other scholars have conceptualized humor as a chronic behavioral pattern (think of the "class clown," the person who is always joking, laughing, and attempting to have fun; Craik, Lampert, and Nelson, 1996). Still others have conceptualized humor as a stable coping mechanism (think of the person who makes jokes at a funeral to cope with the loss of a loved one; Martin and Lefcourt, 1983). These diverse conceptualizations of humor that emphasize its dispositional antecedents have muddied the distinction between having a sense of humor, engaging in humorous communication, and the consequences associated with these events. We do not find this amusing.

Serving as intellectual cavalry riding to the assistance of threatened and confused frontier scholars, Martin, Puhlik-Doris, Larsen, Gray, and Weir (2003) offered a model of dispositional humor styles that has become one of the most well-established frameworks for approaching the subject of humor. According to this model, humor styles can be categorized according to whether a person tends to prefer humor that enhances the self (intrapersonal) or relationships (interpersonal/social), and whether the humor is positive or negative in nature. This creates a 2 × 2 model with the following four humor types: affiliative (interpersonal; positive), self-enhancing (intrapersonal; positive), aggressive (interpersonal; negative), and self-defeating (intrapersonal; negative). You can see this model in Figure 32.1, and we encourage you to have a look.

Affiliative humor is a form of humor used to amuse others, reduce tension, and facilitate relationships. This type of humor typically promotes the well-being of others, where a person would attempt to make others laugh and experience happiness. *Self-enhancing humor*

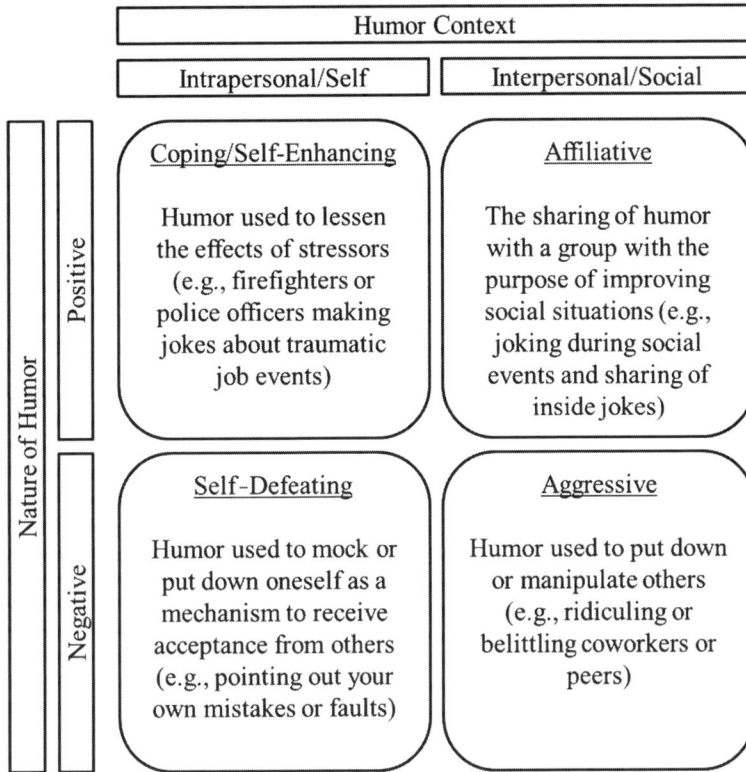

Figure 32.1 Categorization of humor-based nature and context.

refers to taking a humorous outlook on life, regardless of the situation. People high on this dimension will even find humor in negative, incongruous events, and are likely to use humor to cope. *Aggressive humor* is used to tease, ridicule, disparage, and put down others. Often-times, aggressive humor is intended to harm or belittle, such as when a bully makes a joke at the expense of a classmate. Finally, *self-defeating humor* refers to poking fun at oneself to make others laugh or allowing oneself to be disparaged by others for their amusement. This type of humor is linked with low self-esteem and low confidence (Fabrizi and Pollio, 1987; Martin et al., 2003); people using this form of humor typically belittle themselves to gain group acceptance.

The humor styles model (Martin et al., 2003) posits that people have dispositional prefer-ences with regard to using these forms of humor. For example, some individuals may have a strong tendency to use one particular form (e.g., self-enhancing humor), whereas others might tend to use a mix of forms. In essence, usage of the different humor styles is one of *degree* rather than an *absolute*. That is, people – based on their dispositional style and the situation – might use more or less of these different forms. For example, consider Judy. Judy happens to be high in both affiliative humor and aggressive humor – in other words, she generally prefers using humor to make other people feel good about themselves *or* to make them feel not-so-good about themselves. Why Judy is like this is not entirely clear, but that is not the point. If Judy is surrounded by familiar, well-liked colleagues, she might be more likely to engage in lots of affiliative humor and little or no aggressive humor. When surrounded by people she does not know or care about, Judy will likely use lots of aggressive humor and little or no affiliative humor. Those who know Judy may have a hard time predicting whether "nice Judy" or "mean Judy" is going to show up in any given time and place, but that is not the point either. The point is this: The humor form deployed by Judy in any given situation is likely based on an interaction between her dispositional humor-related tendencies and other aspects of the social context.

Benefits of Humor in the Workplace: Individual Level

Humor and Well-Being

Now that we have defined humor as an amusing communicative episode, and discussed how dispositions and situations interact to affect the expression of humor, we will turn to the research that has demonstrated the benefits that humor can have in terms of individual well-being in the context of the workplace. Humor has generally been shown to impact employee well-being outcomes in two ways. First, the experience of humor has a direct impact on employee well-being (e.g., burnout, Abel and Maxwell, 2002; job satisfaction, Booth-Butterfield, Booth-Butterfield, and Wanzer, 2007). Second, humor (particularly coping/self-enhancing humor) has been found to buffer the stressor–strain relationship in employees (e.g., Sliter, Kale, and Yuan, 2014). We will next summarize research that supports these perspectives and ignore any that does not.

Before dipping our intellectual toes into the research itself, it is important to briefly discuss *how* humor can benefit an individual's well-being at work. There are several theories on the source of these benefits, including physiological, cognitive, and behavioral perspectives. Physiologically, people who use humor more frequently are more likely to laugh, and laughter has been found to increase pain tolerance and raise serotonin levels (implicated in positive mood states). Laughter has also been found to reduce symptoms of medical conditions (people exposed to humor are less sensitive to allergens, like dust mites and pollen; we aren't making this up!), and reduce negative physiological reactions to stressful environments (see Wilkins and Eisenbraun, 2009, for a review). From a cognitive perspective, humor can be used to reframe a stressful situation by creating an incongruity between the humor stimulus and the stressful situation (Nerhardt, 1970). In other words, it is hard to feel the pain of running into your office door if you are chuckling at how stupid it must have looked while you did it. More formally, when viewed through a humorous lens, stressors may not be perceived as being as impactful. Additionally, the distraction hypothesis of humor suggests humor might serve to divert individuals from attending to stressors (Lang and Lee, 2010). For instance, the first author of this chapter might not notice his wife nagging him to clean the basement if he is laughing about something on the television (personal communication, Sliter, 2016). Further, from a behavioral perspective, the use of humor can help develop meaningful relationships at work, and these relationships can supply sources of social support in spates of stress (Holmes, 2006). Supportive networks have often been linked with better overall employee well-being (Viswesvaran, Sanchez, and Fisher, 1999), and who doesn't feel good about that?

Probably the best evidence for the direct effect of humor on employee well-being comes from a meta-analysis conducted by Mesmer-Magnus, Glew, and Viswesvaran (2012). These researchers sought to determine the benefits of both employee humor and leader humor on employee health outcomes (e.g., burnout, physical health), employee work-related behaviors and attitudes (e.g., job satisfaction, performance), and leader effectiveness (e.g., leader performance; follower approval). In an exhaustive literature search, Mesmer-Magnus and colleagues (2012) identified 49 independent studies that examined humor in the workplace in relation to at least one of these outcomes of interest. The results were generally consistent with humor having positive consequences. Specifically, trait humor was negatively related to burnout ($\rho = -0.23$), stress ($\rho = -0.25$), and withdrawal ($\rho = -0.16$); it was also positively related to coping effectiveness ($\rho = 0.29$), physical health ($\rho = 0.21$), work performance ($\rho = 0.36$), and satisfaction ($\rho = 0.11$).[1] The major limitation of this paper is that many disparate measures of humor were included in the analysis, with 21 different humor scales based on different definitions of humor used across the 49 studies. Translation: there are too many types of apples and oranges mixed in the fruit salad. Additionally, as the authors noted, the directionality of any causal influence cannot be determined from their analyses. So, it might be that people who are less burnt-out, less stressed, and higher in job performance are more likely to use certain forms of humor that are positive in nature – or vice versa. Nonetheless, these meta-analytic results do suggest a consistent association between sense of humor and individual-level and positive employee outcomes.

Far less research has investigated how humor might buffer the stressor–strain relationship in the workplace. Though the notion that humor is a valuable resource for coping with work stressors is popular, little empirical research has actually tested this assertion, and what has been done has primarily relied on students as opposed to employed adults (e.g., Martin and Lefcourt, 1983; Overholser, 1992). In a recent attempt to test the buffering effect of humor, Sliter and colleagues (2014) examined whether coping humor served as a buffer in the relationship between traumatic workplace stressors and employee outcomes. Specifically, the researchers assessed traumatic stressors in firefighters, such as when firefighters have to deal with injured, dead, or dying victims, or are in danger themselves (e.g., running into a burning building). They found that traumatic stressors lead to posttraumatic stress symptoms, burnout, and absenteeism. In addition, it was observed that firefighters who tended to use coping humor were partially protected from these stressors in terms of posttraumatic stress symptoms and burnout, with the humor–stressor interaction term explaining 6 percent of the variance in each of these outcomes. Now, 6 percent is admittedly not much variance, but it is sufficient to take note of when discussing your own work.

Mesmer-Magnus and colleagues (2013) also examined positive humor (as defined above) as moderators of the stressor–strain relationship in a supplementary analysis. Similar to the findings of Sliter and colleagues (2014), their meta-analytic results showed that positive humor appeared to moderate the workplace stressor-burnout relationship, with interaction terms explaining between 1 and 9 percent of the variance in burnout. Although combining humor types and stressor types into composite measures limits the generalizability of these findings, positive humor does appear to interact with workplace stressors. Given the scarce research on buffering effects of humor in the workplace and the limited generalizability of the meta-analytic results, there is certainly need for more empirical research in this area.

Other Individual-Level Benefits of Humor

Though most research on workplace humor has involved trying to understand its effects on well-being, we would be remiss (as often we are) if we did not touch briefly on some other positive effects of humor. Specifically, we will touch on creativity and job attitudes, like job satisfaction.

Fun people are often thought to be creative. Writing jokes, pointing out incongruities, and making subtle witticisms can be difficult, particularly for second author of this chapter (Morgan Isn't Funny, 2016). It is no surprise, then, that conventional wisdom tells us that humor can be used to spark creativity, and this wisdom has been incorporated into research studies in the workplace. Much of this work has been qualitative in nature. For example, Holmes (2007) recorded everyday workplace interactions – like meetings and phone calls – to examine whether humor relates to beneficial outcomes, including creativity. In many of these interactions, humor was used to foster workplace creativity, such as by helping generate ideas (both humorous and serious ideas) and approaching workplace problems differently. This, and similar studies, provide anecdotal evidence of the relationship between creativity and humor.

More recently, some researchers have made efforts to relate humor to creativity in a quantitative sense. As one recent example, Lang and Lee (2010) examined three distinct types of humor in relation to organizational creativity: liberating humor (humor used to free people from jail; kidding. Humor that facilitates freeing old mindsets and seeing things differently), stress-relieving humor, and controlling humor (humor used to hide commands and reprimands, exerting subtle control over others). Using a sample of employed MBA students and their supervisors, Lang and Lee found that liberating humor was positively related to organizational creativity, and controlling humor (the evil type of humor) was related negative to organizational creativity. Based on this study – one of the first empirically linking workplace humor to creativity – we can surmise that organizations might try to foster certain types of humor (e.g., liberating) in order to facilitate creativity. The cross-sectional nature of this study, of course, precludes causal interpretation; it might be that in creative cultures, employees are just more likely to use jokes. Nonetheless, this is a first step in understanding the humor–creativity relationship at work.

Finally, workplace humor has been shown in a handful of studies to have a beneficial impact on individual attitudes at work. For instance, the use of humor, and positive humor dispositions (e.g., affiliative), have been linked to satisfaction in a variety of occupational groups, including customer service employees (Karl and Peluchette, 2006) and health-care employees (Sala, Krupat, and Roter, 2002), though these findings are not consistent – Atvis and Taber (2006) found a nonsignificant relationship between affiliative humor and job satisfaction in a small sample of newspaper workers. Other attitudes have been linked with humor as well. For instance, in one qualitative study, people reported wanting to stay with an organization (commitment) because of the "fun" culture at work (Meyer, 1999), which implies the use of humor. In another study, self-enhancing and affiliative humor styles were linked with higher levels of work engagement (Van den Broeck, Vander Elst, Dikkers, De Lange, and De Witte, 2012).

Summary

Trait forms of humor – specifically affiliative humor style and coping humor – can be effective in promoting employee work-related well-being and limiting the negative impact of stress. Additionally, certain types of humor (e.g., liberating humor) and trait humor styles have been linked with workplace creativity and positive workplace attitudes. Such findings should be considered preliminary, which means that *we* like them but *you* shouldn't trust them, so we urge researchers to continue to investigate the impact of humor on individual outcomes in the workplace.

Benefits of Humor in the Workplace: Group Level

Although humor is primarily a social phenomenon, most research on the effects of humor has focused on outcomes associated with individuals – creativity, stress reduction, energy, satisfaction, performance, etc. Surprisingly, relatively few studies have addressed the impact of humor on collectives, particularly workgroups. Only a single group-level outcome has received more than passing attention by researchers – cohesiveness, or feelings of connectedness within a workgroup.

Martineau (1972) offered an early model of humor that called attention to its potential benefit with respect to workgroup cohesion. He proposed that humor-related episodes can be either positive or negative in nature (i.e., esteeming or disparaging), initiated by members of the in-group or out-group, and targeted toward group members or those outside the group. His model highlighted the role of humor in promoting social interactions, maintaining relationships, and building strong social bonds – factors that should serve the collective interest by contributing to group norms of open communication.

Empirical Research

Much of the research on humor in workgroups has taken the form of case studies of a single unit or a small team-like organization – these small groups are easier to study, and researchers like easy. In one of the first studies, Coser (1959; 1960) examined the use of humor in 20 meetings of the staff at a psychiatric hospital. Humor served multiple functions in these meetings, including smoothing over conflicts and decreasing the social distance between supervisors and subordinates. In another early study, Lundberg (1969) studied the use of humor in a motor repair shop and found its frequency and impact to depend on status within the group. Jokes were less likely to be viewed as funny if the facilitator was of lower status than the audience, and lower-status targets were less likely to reciprocate with humor. Joking behavior was also more prevalent among equal-status employees (i.e., peers). Traylor (1973) joined a six-person petroleum exploration party working in Alaska for a five-week period. Studious observation and coding revealed a negative relationship between status within the group and the frequency of being the audience of humor. Attraction to the group (a precursor of cohesion) was also inversely correlated with being the target of a humorous act. Collinson (1988) examined the use of humor in an all-male lorry (truck) production factory in England. Humor was employed on the shop-floor for three functional purposes – to resist boredom and efforts by others to control, to elicit conformity with the group's masculine identity, and to control (regulate) the productivity of members. Finally, Vinton (1989) studied different forms of humor in a 13-person family-owned business in the Midwest and found it used to maintain status differentials, ease tension, and socialize younger members. As in Lundberg's study, teasing was generally used by higher-status individuals to encourage lower-status individuals to accomplish their tasks.

More recent studies of humor in organizational settings have continued to rely on qualitative approaches. For instance, Terrion and Ashforth (2002) focused on the use of one type of negative, aggressive humor – putdowns – among Canadian police officers participating in a six-week executive development course. Using a combination of field observation and follow-up interviews, putdown humor was regarded as helping the group become a cohesive unit, with increasing use over time signaling growing trust and solidarity among members. In one of the best examples of the case-study approach, Lynch (2009) conducted a year-long ethnographic study of the kitchen unit in a hotel restaurant. The workgroup was composed of 12 chefs, four cooks, five trainee chefs, and one executive chef. The author, an accomplished chef (so he claimed – we didn't try his food), worked within the unit for the duration of the study. In addition to his own observations, he conducted three rounds of interviews with various kitchen personnel as a check on the veracity of his observations. As in previous work, humor was found to serve multiple positive functions: control the behavior of members, reinforce the identity of the group, passively resist managerial constraints, and ease tensions.

A few studies have examined humor in multiple workgroups using a questionnaire methodology. Duncan (1984; 1985) surveyed the members of small task-focused groups in various organizational settings, including business, health care, and human service organizations. Humor networks were found to exist within these workgroups, with the admission of supervisors (managers) dependent on whether they were viewed as friends. More cohesive workgroups also exhibited different humor-related patterns than less cohesive workgroups. As in other studies, jokes in the form of teasing were also used to regulate the behavior of less motivated members. Avolio, Howell, and Sosik (1999) conducted one of the only studies to examine the impact of humor on workgroup performance: 115 leaders from the top four levels of a large Canadian financial institution were surveyed along with 322 subordinates in their workgroups. Subordinates indicated the frequency with which humor was used by their leader, and the unit of analysis was the workgroup (n = 115). In the structural equations model for unit performance, frequency of humor use by the leader yielded a modest and positive path coefficient ($\beta = 0.13$, $p < 0.05$), suggesting a direct relationship between the frequency of leader use of humor and unit performance. However, humor usage also interacted with leadership style in complex ways, suggesting there is more to maximizing workgroup performance than simply telling more jokes.

Recent Theoretical Models

The scarcity of humor research at the group level of analysis may be in part due to a lack of theoretical guidance in the literature – but this is changing. For instance, Cooper (2008) offered a theoretical model intended to integrate existing individual-level theories of humor and specify the process mechanisms by which humor can affect dyadic (and higher) relationships. Specifically, humor was seen as having the potential to influence relationship quality through four mechanisms: affect-reinforcement, similarity-attraction, self-disclosure and hierarchical salience. With 50 percent less jargon, this translates as humor can create positive affect, highlight interpersonal similarities, promote trust, and reduce the perception of social distance. In addition, Romero and Pescosolido's (2008) model comprehensively addressed the links between humor and workgroup effectiveness. Aligning with Hackman and Walton's (1986) normative theory of group effectiveness, Romero and Pescosolido drew on three well-established theories of humor (incongruity, relief, and superiority) in articulating propositions regarding the beneficial impact of humor on the three primary group-level outcomes specified in Hackman's (1986) model – productivity, learning, and viability. In essence, humor was predicted to influence workgroup productivity via its positive impact on internal communication, leader effectiveness, workgroup culture, and the acceptance of group goals. It was expected to promote group learning by fostering psychological safety, and increase group viability by generating positive affect, contributing to group cohesion, and limiting employee turnover. To summarize for those formally modeling along with us at home, humor = good for groups.

Summary

Despite the ubiquity of humor in the days of our working lives, relatively little empirical attention has been devoted to examining the effects of humor on *workgroups* as opposed to individual members. The paucity of group-level research is explained in part by the difficulty of conducting it, as well as a lack of theoretical guidance. Most extant studies have adopted an ethnographic case-study approach and focused on how humor can benefit workgroups. As a whole, this body of work suggests the use of humor in workgroups serves multiple functions that generally serve to promote group cohesion. Specifically, joking serves to build and maintain group identity, provide an outlet for frustration, ease tensions and smooth over conflicts, and encourage conformity with group norms. Although most research to date has focused on the impact of humor on workgroup cohesiveness, Romero and Pescosolido's (2008) model calls attention to how humor may benefit workgroup productivity and learning as well. Hopefully these new models will inspire more research on these important outcomes.

The Dark Side of Humor

As we have discussed above, humor in the workplace can have a number of beneficial effects on individual and groups. However, in some circumstances, the outcomes associated with humor may not be uniformly positive. Bottom line: workplace humor may have a Darth Vader-style dark side. This is to say that, after the smiles fade, humor also has the potential to harm or alienate coworkers, subordinates, and even superiors. Unfortunately, research on the negative aspects of humor in the workplace is scarce, but we will synthesize what is available.

Although having a good sense of humor and being funny are typically viewed as desirable qualities, not all humor used at work is positive. As noted above, the aggressive and self-defeating forms of humor are negative in nature, essentially representing insults to oneself or others. And as an act of communication that involves a facilitator and an audience, even humor that is intended to be positive in nature might be perceived as negative by the audience. Thus, when humor is used at work, its effect depends on the intent of the sender as well as the perceptions of the audience. This creates ample opportunities for misunderstanding. Ultimately, even if an employee is trying to be funny in a good-natured way, their words might still be perceived negatively by those on the receiving end. Don't just take our word for it – research has our backs. As one example, some people interpret actions that might constitute sexual harassment as benignly amusing, whereas others perceive them as "sexist" incidents that are harmful and worthy of sanction (Bill and Naus, 1992). Indeed, Hemmasi, Graf, and Russ (1994) found that sexual jokes are often perceived as aggressive, and might cause women to feel alienated from co-workers, even if that is not the intention of the person telling the joke. Of course, a clear implication for organizations is that jokes of a sexual nature could create legal issues involving sexual harassment, and should be avoided – unless the joke is really, really funny (like that great one about a penguin and a seal). However, we must limit our specious legal advice to that and note that a full discussion of amusing-but-inappropriate sexual jokes, as well as their legal implications, is beyond the scope of this chapter.

While the perception of humor by the audience is important, the intent of the instigating person also plays a major role in the effect of the humor. As previously noted, one of the primary four humor styles is aggressive, where humor is generated with intent to harm the audience (Martin et al., 2003). Subversive humor is a specific type of aggressive humor viewed as a tool by which subordinates and supervisors can exhibit control or disagreement, generally with little fear of repercussion because of ambiguous intent (e.g. derogatory jokes or witticisms directed at supervisors or managers; Martin, 2007). Holmes and Marra (2002b) identified instances of *subversive humor* in organizations by examining the recorded interactions of actual workgroups and comparing those interactions to the conversations of friends recorded outside of the workplace. The frequency of subversive humor – in the form of quips, mocking, and salutations – was found to be ten times greater within organizations and workgroups than among friends outside of work. Holmes and Marra (2002a) noted that, in fact, 40 percent of the recorded humorous interactions within the workplace meetings were subversive in nature, and generally speaking acted as an agent to isolate individuals from the group by pointing out how they did not fit or conform to the group norms. And not only is this humor frequently used, it might also be harmful to employees. Research has shown a significant positive relationship between occurrences of aggressive humor, job stress, and job dissatisfaction (Avtgis and Taber, 2006) – all of which are broadly related to experiences of burnout and can have negative repercussions for both individuals and organizations (e.g. decreased physical health and turnover; Avtgis and Taber, 2006). This aggressive humor might be so harmful because it can act as a form of workplace mistreatment, such as bullying, supervisor abuse, or ostracism.

Victims of bullying within the workplace have been identified in past research as being the targets of negative social interactions, such as derogatory jokes, and this acts as a social stressor on the targeted individual (Nielsen and Einarsen, 2012). Generally speaking, occurrences of mistreatment in the workplace have negative individual and organizational effects. For example, the victims of social ostracism (at work or otherwise) tend to demonstrate increased negative attitudes and behaviors (e.g., job performance and turnover), specifically those aimed at their antagonist (Hitlan, Kelly, Schepman, Schneider, and Zárate, 2006). Ultimately, victims of bullying experience higher levels of burnout, withdrawal, anxiety, depression, and worse subjective health-related outcomes (Hoel, Sheehan, Cooper, and Einarsen, 2011; Nielsen and Einarsen, 2012). So be nice.

Of additional importance to organizations and leaders is the negative effect of subversive humor at a group and organizational level. For instance, aggressive humor may make employees feel ostracized by the organization as a whole and the audience may experience decreased organizational commitment. As previously discussed, humor can operate at a team level and actually increase group cohesion by creating an "us versus them" mentality, which can be utilized to create a perception that other individuals or workgroups are actually "out groups" (Blanchard, Stewart, Cann, and Follman, 2014). Although group cohesion may be increased, which is typically considered positive (Martineau, 1972), when this mentality exists the potential for negative consequences at an organizational level is also much higher. That is, when humor used to increase group cohesion is negative or subversive, instead of affiliative, it may actually increase the potential for dysfunctional competition between work groups or teams within an organization. For example, a person's affective commitment (emotional attachment to an organization) has the potential to be negatively affected as a result of being the target of subversive humor (Hitlan et al., 2006). Regardless of who the facilitator is (e.g. peer or supervisor) the audience may feel identified as being unlike others within the organization, not just the work team. Additionally, a person's normative commitment (sense of obligation to their organization) may decrease as a result of the humor-based bullying. Furthermore, the audience is more likely to report decreased job satisfaction and productivity at work in comparison to their nontargeted peers (Nielsen and Einarsen, 2012). Finally, individuals exposed to prolonged stress at work tend to report increases in absenteeism intent to leave their organizations (Cole and Bedeian, 2007). What all this means is that harmful humor can be ... harmful to the organizational bottom line. And organizations *hate* when things harm their bottom lines.

Summary

Even though there is great potential for benefit from the use of humor, trying to be funny may also cause real harm to coworkers and the organization as a whole. Negative results can occur because (1) the facilitator really has negative intentions with regard to the target of the humor, or (2) well-intentioned actions may be misinterpreted as hurtful. Subversive humor is one particular subtype of negative humor that may be particularly relevant in organizations precisely because its ambiguous nature makes it difficult to sanction. Indeed, research has shown that subversive humor is more common in the workplace than in friend groups, but this idea begs for further investigation. To conclude, nothing we have said so far supports the following statement but it must be said anyway: The only thing worse than making a joke and falling flat (a common issue with the third author, but never the second) is making a joke and being sued. (In other words, please don't sue us.) As an aside, the first author is hilarious.

Future Directions

One nice thing about a sparse research domain is that it is easy to identify future directions. Most importantly, given the fragmented nature of the literature, we feel workplace humor scholars might benefit from further theoretical guidance. Thus, in this section, we propose an integrative model which we hope will inspire and stimulate further research on workplace humor (see Figure 32.2). In proposing this model, we have three goals: (1) to help researchers

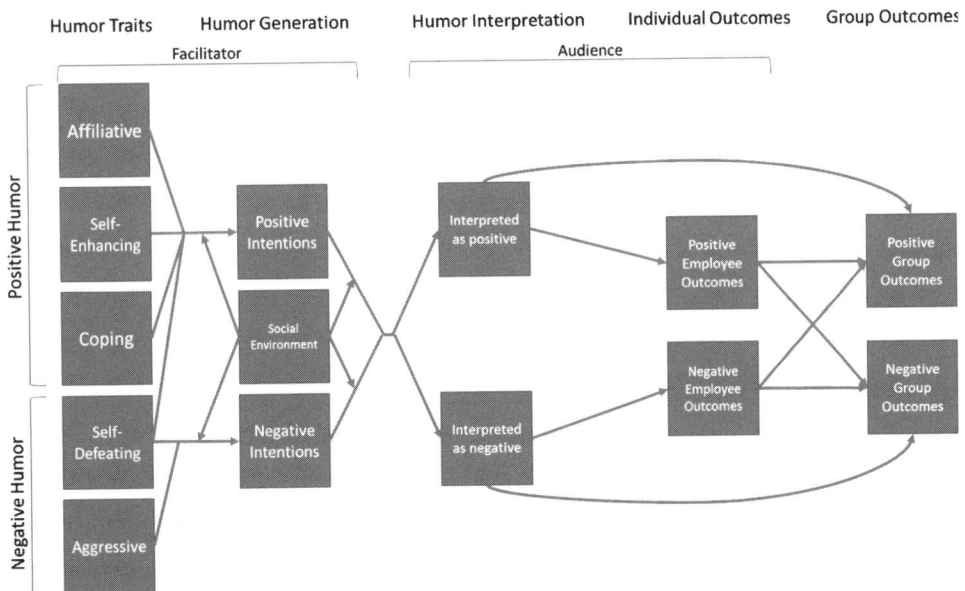

Figure 32.2   Holistic theoretical model on the role of humor in the workplace.

understand the distinction between humor use and humor dispositions (something often confused in the literature), (2) to identify pathways by which humor can positively impact individuals and groups, and (3) to identify pathways by which humor can negatively impact individuals and group, hence illuminating the Dark Side.

Beginning at the left, the integrative model incorporates the notion of dispositional humor styles (traits) that will predispose people to act in certain ways with regard to humor-seeking behavior. In particular, humor styles predispose people to generate certain types of humor with either positive or negative intentions. The consequence of a potentially humorous event will depend largely on the social environment. That is, although "humor-seeking" individuals are likely to engage in activities consistent with their preferred humor style, they might not engage in laughter-seeking behavior if the workplace environment is not supportive of humor. Further, some workplace environments will be more supportive of amusing behavior, and people in those settings might be more likely to attempt being funny than those in less supportive contexts. Regardless of the initiator's intention, the audience still must perceive and interpret any effort to be funny and the result will likely depend on several things: (1) the intention of the humor-seeker, (2) the humor style of the audience, and (3) the work environment. Specifically, in a work environment where humor use is the norm, audiences should be more likely to interpret amusement-seeking behavior positively, whereas in a humorless workplace, such efforts might be interpreted negatively. The interpretation of humor would ultimately (over time) lead to audience outcomes, including positive ones such as higher levels of engagement and satisfaction, and lower negative ones such as burnout and withdrawal. Finally, interpretation by the audience could also promote positive group-level outcomes such as cohesion and helping behaviors, or negative group-level behaviors, like sabotage and undermining.

Though not displayed in the figure, a parallel process could occur in the initiator of the humor. When someone successfully generates humor (evoking a positive interpretation and reaction – laughter – from the audience), the facilitator would experience positive emotions, as well. Over time, the experience of positive emotional interactions would also relate to beneficial outcomes for the facilitator, as well as beneficial group outcomes. Alternately, if the generation of humor fails either through misinterpretation or incompatible styles between the facilitator and the audience, the facilitator might experience negative emotions. Over time, such failure in the generation of humor would lead to (1) a halt in the generation of humor, (2) feelings of misfit, and (3) other negative outcomes.

This model provides a starting point, and we hope that researchers will begin testing it with different methods. Most studies we reviewed on the topic of workplace humor was survey-based, but other methods such as experience sampling or diary studies may prove more effective in capturing the episodic nature of humor use in the workplace. Future studies might also focus on the perspective of the facilitator of humor, as well as the audience – what happens to the facilitator when they succeed or fail in generating humor? Additionally, futuristic research might usefully incorporate constructs at both the individual and group levels of analysis. Specifically, researchers could seek to determine whether humor is a construct that should be aggregated to the group level (is there a climate for humor). Researchers can also investigate whether organizations that are generally supportive of humor are actually more effective? Anecdotal evidence says "yes" (i.e., Google; Zappos), but this should be systematically analyzed and assessed.

Conclusion

Is laughter, in fact, the best medicine? Well, it certainly is cheap and does not require a prescription. Positive forms of humor appear to promote employee satisfaction and health (though this research should be considered to be preliminary). Some research has supported the buffering hypotheses – people who use positive coping humor might be protected from certain workplace stressors. Additionally, humor might help creative cohesive workgroups who may perform better. Like all medicines, though, workplace humor may have negative side effects if not used as directed. In particular, aggressive, or subversive, humor has been shown to harm individuals and organizations through mechanisms similar to bullying and social ostracism. Specifically, the past research on aggressive humor has linked negative experiences to outcomes such as decreased well-being and turnover (Avtgis and Taber, 2006).

Based upon past research that includes both positive and negative aspects of humor, as well as individual and group levels, we conclude there is still much to be learned about workplace humor and many aspects of it yet to be addressed. Clearly the best way to accomplish this would be to use our model of workplace humor and start asking more refined research questions. It has everything that one might desire in a model, including words, boxes, arrows, and feedback loops. It is also probably too complex to be disconfirmed in entirety, so it can also be used confidently. Whether it's our model or one of the better ones reviewed above, by asking more refined questions we can begin to better understand how humor functions in a workplace environment. With that understanding will come our ability to leverage humor to the advantage of the workplace.

Note

1. ρ represents the sample size weighted mean observed correlation corrected for unreliability in both the humor measure and the outcome measure.

References

Abel, M. H., and Maxwell, D. (2002). Humor and affective consequences of a stressful task. *Journal of Social and Clinical Psychology*, *21*, 165–190.

Avolio, B. J., Howell, J. M., and Sosik, J. J. (1999). A funny thing happened on the way to the bottom line: Humor as a moderator of leadership style effects. *Academy of Management Journal*, *42*, 219–227.

Avtgis, T. A., and Taber, K. R. (2006). "I laughed so hard my side hurts, or is that an ulcer?" The influence of work humor on job stress, job satisfaction, and burnout among print media employees. *Communication Research Reports*, *23*, 13–18.

Bill, B., and Naus, P. (1992). The role of humor in the interpretation of sexist incidents. *Sex Roles*, *27*(11–12), 645–664.

Blanchard, A. L., Stewart, O. J., Cann, A., and Follman, L. (2014). Making sense of humor at work. *Psychologist-Manager Journal*, *17*(1), 49–70. doi:10.1037/mgr0000011

Booth-Butterfield, M., Booth-Butterfield, S., and Wanzer, M. (2007). Funny students cope better: Patterns of humor enactment and coping effectiveness. *Communication Quarterly*, *55*, 299–315.

Carver, C. S., and Scheier, M. F. (2000). *Perspectives on Personality*, 4th edn. Needham Heights, MA: Simon & Schuster.

Cole, M. S., and Bedeian, A. G. (2007). Leadership consensus as a cross-level contextual moderator of the emotional exhaustion–work commitment relationship. *Leadership Quarterly*, *18*(5), 447–462.

Collinson, D. L. (1988). Engineering humour: Masculinity, joking and conflict in shop-floor relations. *Organization Studies*, *9*, 181–199.

Cooper, C. (2008). Elucidating the bonds of workplace humor: A relational process model. *Human Relations, 61,* 1087–1115.

Coser, R. L. (1959). Some social functions of laughter: A study of humor in a hospital setting. *Human Relations, 12,* 171–182.

Coser, R. L. (1960). Laughter among colleagues. *Psychiatry, 23,* 81–99.

Craik, K. H., Lampert, M. D., and Nelson, A. J. (1996). Sense of humor and styles of everyday humorous conduct. *Humor: International Journal of Humor Research, 9*(3–4), 273–302.

Duncan, W. J. (1984). Perceived humor and social network patterns in a sample of task oriented groups: A re-examination of prior research. *Human Relations, 11,* 895–907.

Duncan, W. J. (1985). The superiority theory of humor at work: Joking relationships as indicators of formal and informal status patterns in small, task-oriented groups. *Small Group Behavior, 16,* 556–564.

Fabrizi, M. S., and Pollio, H. R. (1987). A naturalistic study of humorous activity in a third, seventh, and eleventh grade classroom. *Merrill-Palmer Quarterly, 33*(1), 107–128.

Hackman, J. R., and Walton, R. E. (1986). Leading groups in organizations. In P. S. Goodman et al., *Designing Effective Work Groups.* San Francisco: Jossey-Bass.

Hemmasi, M., Graf, A., and Russ, G. S. (1994). Gender-related jokes in the workplace: Sexual humor or sexual harassment? *Journal of Applied Social Psychology, 24*(12), 1114–1128.

Hitlan, R. T., Kelly, K. M., Schepman, S., Schneider, K. T., and Zárate, M. A. (2006). Language exclusion and the consequences of perceived ostracism in the workplace. *Group Dynamics: Theory, Research, and Practice, 10*(1), 56–70. doi:10.1037/1089-2699.10.1.56

Hoel, H., Sheehan, M. J., Cooper, C. L., and Einarsen, S. (2011). Organisational effects of workplace bullying. In S. Einarsen, H. Hoel, D. Zapf, and C. L. Cooper (Eds.), *Bullying and Harassment in the Workplace: Developments in Theory, Research, and Practice,* 2nd edn. (pp. 129–148). New York: CRC Press.

Holmes, J. (2006). Sharing a laugh: Pragmatic aspects of humor and gender in the workplace. *Journal of Pragmatics, 38*(1), 26–50.

Holmes, J. (2007). Making humour work: Creativity on the job. *Applied Linguistics, 28*(4), 518–537.

Holmes, J., and Marra, M. (2002a). Having a laugh at work: How humor contributes to workplace culture. *Journal of Pragmatics, 34,* 1683–1710.

Holmes, J., and Marra, M. (2002b). Over the edge? Subversive humor between colleagues and friends. *Humor: International Journal of Humor Research, 15*(1), 65–87. doi:10.1515/humr.2002.006

Karl, K., and Peluchette, J. (2006). How does workplace fun impact employee perceptions of customer service quality? *Journal of Leadership and Organizational Studies, 13*(2), 2–13.

Lang, J. C., and Lee, C. H. (2010). Workplace humor and organizational creativity. *International Journal of Human Resource Management, 21*(1), 46–60.

Lundberg, C.C. (1969). Person-focused joking. Pattern and function. *Human Organization, 28,* 22–28.

Luby, J. (2014). Companies with a sense of humor get it! Profit, that is! Blog. At http://jeannineluby.com/companies-sense-humor-get-profit/ (accessed July 2016).

Lynch, O. H. (2009). Kitchen antics: The importance of humor and maintaining professionalism at work. *Journal of Applied Communication Research, 37,* 444–464.

Martin, R. A. (2007). *The Psychology of Humor: An Integrative Approach.* Amsterdam: Elsevier.

Martin, R. A., and Lefcourt, H. M. (1983). Sense of humor as a moderator of the relation between stressors and moods. *Journal of Personality and Social Psychology, 45*(6), 1313.

Martin, R. A., Puhlik-Doris, P., Larsen, G., Gray, J., and Weir, K. (2003). Individual differences in uses of humor and their relation to psychological well-being: Development of the Humor Styles Questionnaire. *Journal of Research in Personality, 37*(1), 48–75.

Martineau, W. H. (1972). A model of the social functions of humor. In J. Goldstein and P. McGhee (Eds.), *The Psychology of Humor* (pp. 101–125). New York: Academic Press.

Mesmer-Magnus, J., Glew, D. J., and Viswesvaran, C. (2012). A meta-analysis of positive humor in the workplace. *Journal of Managerial Psychology, 27*(2), 155–190.

Meyer, H. (1999). Fun for everyone. *Journal of Business Strategy, 20*(2), 13–17.

Nerhardt, G. (1970). Humor and inclination to laugh: Emotional reactions to stimuli of different divergence from a range of expectancy. *Scandinavian Journal of Psychology, 11*(3), 185–195.

Nielsen, M., and Einarsen, S. (2012). Outcomes of exposure to workplace bullying: A meta-analytic review. *Work and Stress, 26*(4), 309–332.

Overholser, J. C. (1992). Sense of humor when coping with life stress. *Personality and Individual Differences, 13*(7), 799–804.

Romero, E., and Pescosolido, A. (2008). Humor and group effectiveness. *Human Relations, 61*, 395–418.

Sala, F., Krupat, E., and Roter, D. (2002). Satisfaction and the use of humor by physicians and patients. *Psychology and Health, 17*(3), 269–280.

Sliter, M., Kale, A., and Yuan, Z. (2014). Is humor the best medicine? The buffering effect of coping humor on traumatic stressors in firefighters. *Journal of Organizational Behavior, 35*(2), 257–272.

Terrion, J. L., and Ashforth, B. E. (2002). From "I" to "we": The role of putdown humor and identity in the development of a temporary group. *Human Relations, 55*, 55–88.

Thorson, J. A., and Powell, F. C. (1993). Development and validation of a multidimensional sense of humor scale. *Journal of Clinical Psychology, 49*(1), 13–23.

Traylor, G. (1973). Joking in a bush camp. *Human Relations, 26*, 479–486.

Van den Broeck, A., Vander Elst, T., Dikkers, J., De Lange, A., and De Witte, H. (2012). This is funny: On the beneficial role of self-enhancing and affiliative humour in job design. *Psicothema, 24*(1), 87–93.

Vinton, K.L. (1989). Humor in the workplace: It is more than telling jokes. *Small Group Behavior, 20*, 151–166.

Viswesvaran, C., Sanchez, J. I., and Fisher, J. (1999). The role of social support in the process of work stress: A meta-analysis. *Journal of Vocational Behavior, 54*, 314–334.

Wilkins, J., and Eisenbraun, A. J. (2009). Humor theories and the physiological benefits of laughter. *Holistic Nursing Practice, 23*(6), 349–354.

33

Building Positive Psychological Resources

The Effects of Mindfulness, Work Breaks, and Positive Reflection

Elisabeth K. Gilbert, Trevor A. Foulk, and Joyce E. Bono

Throughout the past several decades, employees have experienced a steady increase in work demands, including longer and more irregular work hours, accompanied by more stress and less sleep (Johnson and Lipscomb, 2006). Perhaps in response to these changes in the workplace, there has been a growing research focus on the role resources play in employee well-being and effectiveness. Theories such as Hobfoll's (1989) conservation of resources theory, the job demands–resources model (Demerouti, Bakker, Nachreiner, and Schaufeli, 2001), and ego depletion theory (Baumeister, Bratslavsky, Muraven, and Tice, 1998) build on the notion that individuals possess variable amounts of personal resources, that these resources can be depleted and restored, and that the levels of resources an individual possesses can predict how they will feel, think, or behave. For example, work by Cropanzano, Rupp, and Byrne (2003) links emotional resources to employee effectiveness, providing evidence that when employees were low on emotional resources, their job performance and organizational commitment suffered, and they were less likely to engage in organizational citizenship behaviors. This study, along with many others that take a resource perspective, suggests that resources – and their acquisition and depletion – play an important role in organizations.

One drawback of theory and research in this domain is that they tend to focus on resource depletion. Resource-based theories have primarily been used to answer questions relating to what causes resource depletion, what can be done to prevent it, and what its consequences are. This is not to suggest that building and maintaining resources has been completely ignored in

The Handbook of Stress and Health: A Guide to Research and Practice, First Edition.
Edited by Cary L. Cooper and James Campbell Quick.
© 2017 John Wiley & Sons, Ltd. Published 2017 by John Wiley & Sons, Ltd.

the literature; indeed, recent work suggests that taking breaks from work (Westman and Eden, 1997), expressing gratitude (Emmons and McCullough, 2003), and sharing positive experiences (Burton and King, 2009) can help replenish psychological resources. Yet, it is fair to say that the majority of studies taking a resource perspective are focused on resource depletion, rather than on how resources can be acquired and maintained.

This negative emphasis is unsurprising given that resource losses are more immediately salient than resource gains (Hobfoll, 2001), but another possible reason for the focus on resource depletion may be in the way resources are typically defined. According to Hobfoll (1989), resources are "those objects, personal characteristics, conditions, or energies that are valued by the individual or that serve as a means for attainment of these objects, personal characteristics, conditions, or energies" (p. 516). More recently, Halbesleben, Neveu, Paustian-Underdahl, and Westman (2014) defined a resource as "anything perceived by the individual to help attain his or her goals" (p. 1338). These definitions are so broad that resources exist only in the eyes of the beholder and encompass anything that supports goal attainment. Such broad conceptualizations make it difficult to disentangle resources from their effects. If scholars are to provide clarity on how positive resources can be built – especially via targeted interventions – then a more focused conceptualization of resources would be beneficial.

Many constructs that have been studied as resources, including those in Hobfoll's (2001) index, are distal to employee well-being and performance. Distal resources influence work outcomes, but their effects are indirect, mediated by more proximal resources. For example, proximal psychological resources, such as optimism, mediate the relationship between distal job resources, such as autonomy, and outcomes, such as work engagement (Xanthopoulou, Bakker, Demerouti, and Schaufeli, 2007). We focus on how to build the key psychological and emotional resources that directly promote flourishing and performance in work settings, rather than on their distal antecedents. We define performance broadly to include actions and behaviors of employees that contribute to organizational goals (Rotundo and Sackett, 2002), including task performance as well as citizenship behaviors. Flourishing captures a holistic sense of "doing well" in life, with various related conceptualizations in the literature (Porath, Spreitzer, Gibson, and Garnett, 2012; Keyes, 2007; Diener et al., 2009), some of which blur the distinction between psychological resources (e.g., vigor or mood) and outcomes (e.g., job or life satisfaction).

Because full explication and delineation of psychological resources is beyond the scope of this chapter, we focus our attention on three broad categories of positive psychological resources: *mood*, including positive affect and emotions; *energy*, including vigor and vitality; and *efficacy*, including mastery, resiliency, optimism, purpose, and meaningfulness. A wealth of evidence links these resources to effectiveness and flourishing at work. For example, positive moods and emotions are associated with improved task performance (Miner and Glomb, 2010), creativity (Davis, 2009), and prosocial behavior (George, 1991). Energy, vitality and vigor are related to improved job performance (Carmeli, Ben-Hador, Waldman, and Rupp, 2009), increased organizational citizenship behavior, and decreased deviance (Little, Nelson, Wallace, and Johnson, 2011). Efficacy states such as hope, optimism, self-efficacy, and resiliency predict job performance, organizational commitment, psychological well-being, citizenship, and job satisfaction (Avey, Reichard, Luthans, and Mhatre, 2011).

Numerous factors contribute to the acquisition and maintenance of these positive psychological resources, from job autonomy (Xanthopoulou et al., 2007) to social support from

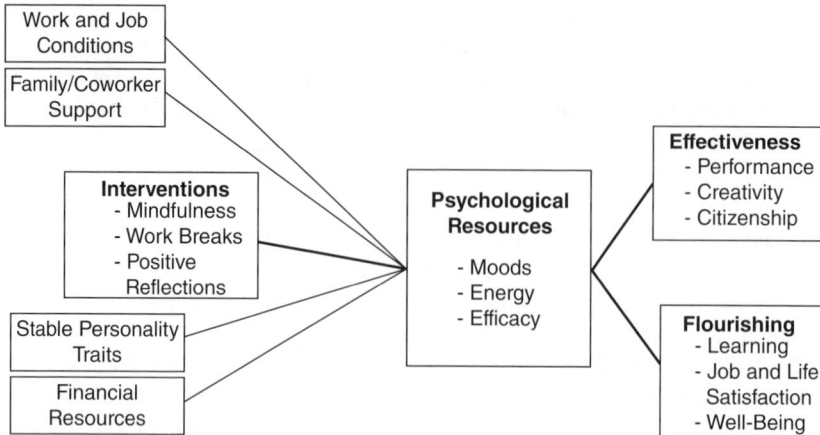

Figure 33.1   Antecedents and consequences of positive psychological resources.

supervisors and coworkers (Halbesleben, 2006), to day-to-day work events such as positive feedback or goal accomplishment (Bono, Glomb, Shen, Kim, and Koch, 2013). Some of these factors represent stable characteristics of individuals or their work environment; others are more variable, but exist outside the control of a work organization. Positive psychological resources can also be deliberately built through the use of targeted interventions. Interventions are defined broadly to include specific actions or techniques that managers and organizations can take to build positive resources, as well as practices that they can encourage employees to engage in. These interventions can be adopted proactively by individuals or assigned by others, though all require active individual participation. We focus on three distinct types of interventions that have been associated with increases in emotional and psychological resources: mindfulness, work breaks, and positive reflection. Figure 33.1 shows the theoretical role of these interventions in predicting positive psychological resources, alongside more distal and well-studied predictors.

Mindfulness

There is a large, rapidly growing, and diverse literature on the resource-building effects of mindfulness and mindfulness-related practices. Glomb, Duffy, Bono, and Yang (2011) defined mindfulness as "a state of consciousness characterized by the receptive attention to and awareness of the present events and experiences, without evaluation, judgment, and cognitive filters" (p. 119). Mindfulness involves a mental focus on what is happening at the present moment (Brown and Ryan, 2003), as an observer of the experience (Bishop et al., 2004). Organizations from food company General Mills, to Google, to the US Army have used mindfulness-based interventions to build and sustain positive emotional and psychological resources among their employees.

Although mindfulness is sometimes treated as a stable individual difference (Brown and Ryan, 2003), there is exhaustive evidence that mindfulness can be learned and that interventions can help individuals achieve heightened states of mindfulness. One of the most widely employed mindfulness programs is Mindfulness-Based Stress Reduction (MBSR; Kabat-Zinn,

1990), which involves eight weeks of intense training. It was originally developed in a medical context, but is also beneficial for healthy individuals (Mackenzie, Poulin, and Seidman-Carlson, 2006). Mindfulness programs can be designed in ways that are appropriate for delivery in organizational settings, and evidence is accruing in support of the effects of even brief training interventions. For example, Poulin, Mackenzie, Soloway, and Karayolas (2008) found that with only four brief mindfulness training sessions, participants who engaged in daily mindfulness practices after training saw increases in well-being. Hülsheger, Alberts, Feinholdt, and Lang (2013) showed that brief daily mindfulness exercises can have positive effects. A broad variety of mindfulness-based practices are taught in these interventions, including both complex tasks such as body scans and focusing meditation (Orsillo and Roemer, 2005) and simple breathing tasks (Arch and Craske, 2006), all of which could be implemented in organizational settings.

There is strong evidence that mindfulness interventions can build emotional and psychological resources. They have been linked to increases in positive mood (Jain et al., 2007; Speca, Carlson, Goodey, and Angen, 2000), as well as decreased reactivity in brain regions associated with response to threats (Desbordes et al., 2012). Mindful individuals react less strongly to negative events, their negative reactions peak more quickly, and they return more quickly to baseline mood states (Davidson, 1998); they are also less subject to negative mood inductions (Arch and Craske, 2006). Mindfulness allows people to view events more objectively (Shapiro, Carlson, Astin, and Freedman, 2006), reducing the emotional toll of negative events. By focusing the mind on current experiences, mindfulness decreases mental chatter and rumination, and leads to feelings of calm (Borders, Earleywine, and Jajodia, 2010).

Mindfulness has also been shown to increase energy and efficacy related resources. For example, mindfulness has been associated with workplace resilience (Aikens et al., 2014; Foureur, Besley, Burton, Yu, and Crisp, 2013; Zwack and Schweitzer, 2013). Foureur et al. (2013) found that an MBSR-based intervention allowed nurses and midwives to become more resilient to stressors in their workplace. Similarly, mindfulness has been shown to increase vigor (Aikens et al., 2014) and energy (Smith et al., 2008). Mindfulness has also been associated with increased compassion (Thomas and Otis, 2010; Tirch, 2010) and empathy (Block-Lerner, Adair, Plumb, Rhatigan, and Orsillo, 2007), positive emotional states that serve as the foundation for good workplace relationships.

Other studies directly link mindfulness to work outcomes. Both state and trait mindfulness (Hülsheger et al., 2013), as well as engagement in self-directed mindfulness activities (Reb, Narayanan, and Chaturvedi, 2014), have been positively associated with job satisfaction. Additionally, mindfulness has been associated with increases in creativity (Ding, Tang, Tang, and Posner, 2014), even after a short intervention. Mindfulness has been associated with increased job performance and decreased turnover intentions (Dane and Brummel, 2013), as well as with indicators of flourishing, such as psychological well-being (Brown and Ryan, 2003) and life satisfaction (Mackenzie et al., 2006).

Research on mindfulness has advanced to the point where the mechanisms by which it affects these outcomes is becoming clearer. Mindfulness affects flourishing and effectiveness, at least in part, by reducing negative and increasing positive emotions, by fostering more effective emotional regulation, by building resilience in the face of threats and stressors, and by enhancing other-directed emotions such as empathy and compassion. Mindfulness-based interventions have been shown to be effective both for individuals under stress and for healthy individuals. Moreover, these interventions are easy to deliver in work settings, and mindfulness practices, such as breathing, mindful eating, and brief focusing meditations, can be practiced unobtrusively throughout the workday and on work breaks.

Work Breaks

Empirical research has clearly established the resource benefits of relaxing during breaks from work, including more positive mood and fewer negative emotions, increased vigor and attentiveness, and reduced fatigue (Fritz, Ellis, Demsky, Lin, and Guros, 2013). However, it is also clear that simply having a break is not sufficient to build resources; time off only promotes recovery when it is used in the right ways. Sonnentag and Fritz (2007) distinguished four types of experiences that allow for resource replenishment during breaks: psychological detachment (setting work-related thoughts aside when away from work), relaxation, mastery (becoming proficient in an activity through positively challenging experiences), and control. Another key point is that break activities should require little effort and should be freely chosen by the individual (Trougakos and Hideg, 2009). Unenjoyable "chore" activities during work breaks are not restorative even if they are not work-related, because they continue to drain psychological and emotional resources (Sonnentag, 2001; Trougakos and Hideg, 2009).

Most of the work on the resource benefits of work breaks has focused on mood and energy, although they may build efficacy resources as well. Brief "micro-breaks" during the workday can increase vitality (Zacher, Brailsford, and Parker, 2014) and positive mood states through such activities as socializing with coworkers (Trougakos and Hideg, 2009) or surfing the internet (Lim and Chen, 2012). Lunch breaks involving activities that are relaxing, or that employees have autonomy in choosing, have been shown to reduce end-of-workday fatigue (Trougakos, Hideg, Cheng, and Beal, 2013), while longer breaks during the workday and between workdays promote the experience of positive emotions (Trougakos, Beal, Green, and Weiss, 2008); recovery after daytime work breaks also leads to increased vigor in the evening (Sanz-Vergel, Demerouti, Moreno-Jiménez, and Mayo, 2010).

Findings are even richer for longer breaks. Psychological detachment from work is associated with improved mood and less fatigue (Sonnentag and Bayer, 2005), while mastery is associated with positive moods and relaxation is linked to feelings of serenity (Sonnentag, Binnewies, and Mojza, 2008). Weekend relaxation has been linked to positive emotions (joviality, self-assurance, and serenity) that last through the following work week; mastery and detachment promote positive moods for a shorter period of time (Fritz, Sonnentag, Spector, and McInroe, 2010). Vacations increase both energy and positive moods (Strauss-Blasche, Reithofer, Schobersberger, Ekmekcioglu, and Marktl, 2005), as well as reducing symptoms of depression (Joudrey and Wallace, 2009).

Many studies have also examined flourishing-related outcomes directly. Weekend experiences characterized by positive work reflection, social activity, and a lack of nonwork hassles were positively related to indicators of flourishing, including a sense of well-being and less burnout after the weekend (Fritz and Sonnentag, 2005). Other benefits of detaching from work and engaging in recovery experiences include increased life satisfaction, decreased emotional exhaustion (e.g., Fritz, Yankelevich, Zarubin, and Barger, 2010), and occupational (Siltaloppi, Kinnunen, and Feldt, 2009) and psychological well-being (Sonnentag and Fritz, 2007). Evidence also shows that the positive benefits of work breaks and detachment from work can spill over to influence life satisfaction of workers' spouses (Hahn and Dormann, 2013; Park and Fritz, 2015). Vacations have similarly been linked to flourishing-related outcomes, including reduced stress and burnout (Westman and Eden, 1997; Etzion, 2003), increased well-being (Fritz and Sonnentag, 2006; De Bloom et al., 2009), and improved life satisfaction (Lounsbury and Hoopes, 1986). Vacation effects fade out in the month following return; however, relaxation during leisure time can delay this effect (Kühnel and Sonnentag, 2011).

Although research exploring the process by which work breaks and detachment impact employees continues, some of these effects stem from the resource-building capacity of work breaks, which increase both positive moods and energy. Work break experiences that promote recovery have also been positively related to task performance (Binnewies, Sonnentag, and Mojza, 2009a; 2009b; 2010), personal initiative and organizational citizenship behavior (Binnewies et al., 2009a; 2010); and work engagement (Sonnentag, 2003; Kühnel, Sonnentag, and Westman, 2009).

Organizations can do many things to create opportunities for resource-building work breaks. They can create physical space for work and lunch breaks that allows for exposure to nature, which evidence suggests promotes well-being (Bowler, Buyung-Ali, Knight, and Pullin, 2010) via positive affect (Hartig, Evans, Jamner, Davis, and Gärling, 2003) and aids stress recovery (Ulrich et al., 1991; Alvarsson, Wiens, and Nilsson, 2010). They can allow employees autonomous choice of activities during breaks. Perhaps most importantly, they can promote psychological detachment during nonwork hours by encouraging employees to limit time spent answering emails or working remotely when away from work. By promoting true recovery and positive resource replenishment during work breaks, organizations have the potential to increase job performance and productivity, along with employee health.

Reflecting on Positive Events

Several independent but related streams of research focus on building emotional and psychological resources via reflection on positive events. In a variety of ways, each of these lines of research builds on the premise that focusing one's attention on positive events in life increases their resource-building capacity.

Reflecting on Good Things

This intervention, often called "three good things," aims at increasing the resource-building effects of positive events by focusing attention on them. Each evening, participants write down three positive events that occurred that day, along with their causes. This practice typically takes place over the course of one to two weeks (Killen and Macaskill, 2015). Bono et al. (2013) identified four potential mechanisms for the effects of this intervention: (a) reflection counteracts the tendency to focus more on negative events than positive ones, (b) reflection combats hedonic adaptation (the tendency for people to quickly return to stable levels of affect), by compelling participants to think deliberately about positive events that might otherwise pass unnoticed, (c) reflection provides an opportunity for participants to relive and share positive events and makes them more accessible in memory, and (d) reflection triggers a cognitive sense-making process that can lead participants to take more notice of available resources around them.

Among the major studies on positive reflections is Seligman, Steen, Park, and Peterson's (2005) comparative test of five positive psychology interventions. For the three good things intervention, they reported significant reductions in depressive symptoms beginning immediately following the intervention period and continuing for a further six months; happiness increased beginning one month after the study period and continued to increase through the end of the six-month observation period. Mongrain and Anselmo-Matthews (2012) replicated the study and found that the same intervention increased happiness at one week, three months, and six months after the intervention period. Killen and Macaskill (2015) directly assessed flourishing in a sample of older adults who kept a nightly three good things diary for two weeks, and found significant increases both immediately after the test and one month later. The fact that resource gains persist and even increase with time suggest that one of the benefits of this intervention may be that it trains participants to notice and savor positive experiences, such that they continue to build resources.

The three good things intervention produces immediate benefits as well. As part of a broader study on building positive resources, Bono et al. (2013) asked participants to complete the intervention at the end of each workday. They found that reflecting on three good things at work was associated with flourishing-related outcomes (e.g., less stress and health complaints, greater detachment from work) in the evening, and these effects were independent of positive events experienced throughout the workday. Although this study did not directly examine psychological resources (e.g., moods, energy, and resilience), their theory posits resources as the mediating process.

Several variations on the three good things paradigm have also produced beneficial results. A three funny things intervention increased happiness and decreased depressive symptoms for up to three months (Gander, Proyer, Ruch, and Wyss, 2013). Four variants incorporating three pleasurable, engaging, or meaningful things each day, or one of each, were all associated with increased well-being (Giannopoulous and Vella-Brodrick, 2011). Another study reported significant increases in positive mood when participants wrote about their own good experiences or the good things experienced by others (Frein and Ponsler, 2014).

Reflecting on good things is an easy practice for organizations or individuals to implement, because it involves a private reflection done by individual workers. Furthermore, it is easy to integrate into individuals' work or personal lives in a number of ways: daily positive reflection interventions have been administered through websites (Seligman et al., 2005; Bono et al., 2013), Facebook (Munson, Lauterbach, Newman, and Resnick, 2010), and university course management platforms (Frein and Ponsler, 2014); participants can also use a private journal. Given that this intervention may work by redirecting attention from negative events to positive ones, it may be particularly beneficial for people in jobs that involve frequent stressful events, such as health care or frontline customer service workers.

Gratitude

A substantial line of research has linked gratitude to positive emotional and psychological resources. Some of this research treats gratitude as a stable trait that differs between individuals, but increasingly research focuses on the resource-building potential of gratitude interventions, in which participants are instructed to think or write about things or people for which they are thankful. Benefits are derived both from experiencing feelings of gratitude and from expressing those feelings, sometimes directly to a specific person.

The form that gratitude interventions take is important. Watkins, Woodward, Stone, and Kolts (2003) tested three types of gratitude interventions (thinking, writing an essay, writing a letter to be delivered to another person) and found that thinking about something one was grateful for was associated with the greatest increase in positive affect, perhaps because participants may feel less efficacious in writing a gratitude letter than in keeping a private gratitude journal (Kaczmarek et al., 2015). Another common approach to gratitude interventions has been asking participants to make a daily or weekly list of up to five things for which they are grateful (Emmons and McCullough, 2003).

Interventions that encourage individuals to experience and express gratitude have primarily been shown to build emotional resources, though one four-week gratitude contemplation intervention was associated with increased efficacy resources as well (self-esteem; Rash, Matsuba, and Prkachin, 2011). Emmons and McCullough (2003) found that a gratitude intervention using lists was associated with increased optimism and positive affect. Using a weekly gratitude-oriented "count your blessings" variation on the three good things intervention discussed above for eight weeks, Chan (2010) asked participants to write up to three things they were thankful for and then reflect on each item with feelings of appreciation and gratitude. Results showed that participants experienced greater positive affect at the end of the intervention, regardless of whether they were high or low in dispositional gratitude.

Other studies, in which participants wrote letters of gratitude to others, produced increased happiness and decreased depressive symptoms. In two of these studies (Seligman et al., 2005; Senf and Liau, 2013), participants wrote a single gratitude letter and delivered it in person. In a third study (Toepfer, Cichy, and Peters, 2012), participants wrote one letter a week for three weeks and all letters were mailed by the researchers only after the conclusion of the study, demonstrating that the benefits of the letter-writing intervention did not result from the recipient's response. Seligman et al.'s (2005) comparison of five online positive psychology interventions found that writing and delivering the gratitude letter produced the largest initial boost in happiness of the five interventions, with effects still in evidence a month later.

Gratitude interventions have also been found to increase outcomes associated with flourishing (Keyes, 2007), such as life satisfaction (Emmons and McCullough, 2003; Chan, 2011; Rash et al., 2011; Toepfer et al., 2012) and well-being (Kaplan et al., 2014). Emmons and Mishra (2011) proposed a variety of mechanisms by which experiencing gratitude might lead to flourishing, including better coping with stress, reduced materialism and negative feelings from social comparisons, and increased development of social resources, but few of these have been explicitly tested. Using our model as a foundation, it seems plausible that the effects of gratitude interventions on flourishing occur via replenishment of emotional resources such as positive mood states, as well as via other psychological resources such as energy, vigor, and self-efficacy.

As with "three good things" and other positive psychology practices, gratitude interventions are easy to implement in a variety of organizational contexts. Given that many gratitude interventions are designed as real letters expressing thankfulness to specific people, they have particular potential for strengthening social networks in teams or organizations, especially ones in which work responsibilities are highly interdependent. Employees could write brief notes expressing gratitude to colleagues as part of a one-time event or an ongoing practice, and doing so offers benefits to both the writer and the receiver.

Capitalization

A third type of positive reflection intervention that may be well suited for building resources within an organizational context is sharing positive experiences, otherwise known as capitalization (Gable and Reis, 2010). The definition of capitalization is "the process of informing another person about the occurrence of a personal event and thereby deriving additional benefit from it" (Gable, Reis, Impett, and Asher, 2004, p. 228).

There are several theoretical reasons to explain why such a simple exercise could help build positive psychological resources. First, evidence suggests that when a person shares a positive event with someone else, the sharer's evaluation of that event becomes more positive, thus increasing positive emotions. Additionally, there is evidence that the process of sharing a positive event with another person makes the event itself more memorable. When people share positive events with others, the event itself may have longer-lasting effects and may continue to build emotional resources over a longer period of time than would an equally positive event not shared with others. Finally, sharing positive events with someone else may act as a means of social verification (Ilies, Keeney, and Scott, 2011), such that sharing a positive event with someone else fundamentally changes the way an individual experiences the positive event; once shared, the event is "no longer subjective, instead it achieves the phenomenological status of objective reality" (Hardin and Higgins, 1996, p. 28). By all three mechanisms, the sharing of the event builds resources beyond the effect of the event itself (Langston, 1994; Gable et al., 2004; Hicks and Diamond, 2008; Lambert, Gwinn, Stillman, and Fincham, 2011).

Interventions that involve sharing positive experiences have been linked directly to psychological resources, including vitality (Lambert et al., 2011), self-esteem (Reis et al., 2010), and feelings of acceptance (Gable and Reis, 2010), but other studies link capitalization to indicators of flourishing, including life satisfaction (Gable et al., 2004), subjective well-being (Gable et al., 2004), and job satisfaction (Ilies et al., 2011). Perhaps the greatest strength of interventions that focus on sharing positive experiences is that implementation is simple and costs little (Ilies et al., 2011). Moreover, organizations that encourage employees to share positive events are asking them to do things they may already do from time to time on a routine basis (Rimé, Philippot, Boca, and Mesquita, 1992).

This intervention shows particular promise for work environments defined by the presence of positive events, particularly positive events that are not typically shared or talked about. For example, in sales organizations, implementing a policy that employees share closings with others might result in a positive spiral whereby the emotional and psychological resources of one person are used to create positive resources for others in the work group. Furthermore, this intervention could be effective in settings defined by both extremely negative as well as extremely positive events, such as medicine, where some patients die and others regain health. Encouraging practices and establishing protocols in which positive patient outcomes are shared with others could magnify the effect of positive outcomes, creating greater resiliency among employees who also need to cope with negative outcomes.

Conclusion

In this chapter, we have identified a subset of emotional and psychological resources, including moods, energy, and efficacy and related constructs that serve as proximal predictors of employee flourishing and effectiveness on the job. We focused on three interventions for which there is a substantial body of literature supporting their resource-building capacities and which can be implemented in an organizational setting. Although these interventions vary in difficulty of implementation – work breaks and positive reflections are easy to implement, but some mindfulness interventions require professional training and regular practice – all involve relatively straightforward and well-tested interventions. Moreover, although our focus here was on building and replenishing emotional and psychological resources, there is also some evidence that each of these interventions may also build and replenish cognitive and physical resources, which represent another path to flourishing and performance that should be more fully explored.

There are many ways in which positive resources might be built in organizations that were not the focus of this chapter. We have not discussed targeted interventions used to manipulate mood directly, such as small gifts (Isen and Levin, 1972; Isen, Daubman, and Nowicki, 1987), humorous movies (Isen et al., 1987), or word association tasks using positively valenced words (Isen, Johnson, Mertz, and Robinson, 1985). Although the efficacy of these manipulations is well established in terms of creating temporary positive mood states, it is not clear from the literature how long these mood states last, nor whether they can be sustained over time. In contrast, the effects of interventions reviewed in this chapter have been shown to persist well after the intervention period ends, from hours or days (work breaks) to weeks or months (reflecting on positive events) to even longer (mindfulness). We have also avoided discussions of supervisory and coworker behaviors that may build positive resources. For example, there is considerable evidence in the literature that having a strong social support network is associated with employee flourishing, in part because high-quality relationships increase psychological safety and learning (Carmeli, Brueller, and Dutton, 2009). There is also increasing evidence that having the opportunity to give to others (Colbert, Bono, and Purvanova, 2015) may aid in the development of positive resources.

Our decision not to focus on factors of the job or work climate that are associated with the acquisition and maintenance of positive emotional and psychological resources is not meant to diminish their importance. Rather, given an already large literature addressing those factors, we chose to focus on easy-to-implement, well-tested and targeted interventions that organizations can use as supplemental means toward building positive resources. Even in the category of easy-to-implement, well-tested interventions, there are other interventions that can be used to build psychological resources. They include physical movement and exercise, goal setting, and positive psychology interventions focused on best possible selves, signature strengths, kindness, or forgiveness. Space considerations limited our review.

This chapter highlights a conceptual challenge in the resource literature: the difficulty of distinguishing between distal and proximal resources and the outcomes associated with their acquisition. We treated psychological resources as the proximal fuel for two primary outcomes, performance and flourishing, but the causal pathways that link various levels and types of resources, and those that link resources with outcomes are not well-defined. One thing is clear: in order to develop targeted interventions aimed at helping employees build and develop positive resources that will ultimately benefit both themselves and organizations, it is critical to focus on the resources most proximal to effectiveness and flourishing.

Although our focus is on psychological resources, there is evidence that the interventions we reviewed here also affect cognitive, neurological, and physical resources in profound ways that may further impact employee effectiveness and flourishing. Thus, organizations with an eye toward conducting interventions that build resources can be encouraged to select those interventions with the broadest resource impact. For example, there is ample evidence that in addition to its effects on emotional and psychological resources, mindfulness also has impressive effects on physical, neurological, and cognitive resources, and especially on self-regulatory abilities (Glomb et al., 2011).

Another intervention with great potential for building psychological, cognitive, and physical resources is sleep. Although we may not typically think of sleep as an organizational intervention, there is no doubt that high-quality sleep is a time when resources are built and replenished and that sleep is associated with effective self-regulation (Barnes, 2012). Moreover, there is emerging evidence that sleep quantity and quality can be affected by work-related behavior, especially the use of technology for work-related tasks during evening hours (Lanaj, Johnson, and Barnes, 2014). Thus, organizations and employees can engage in work-related practices that foster good sleep.

In this chapter, we lay out a small set of interventions useful for building positive psychological resources, but much work remains to be done. An important next step is to develop a comprehensive model of proximal resources that can be built and that benefit individuals and organizations. Only with clarity on the nature of internal positive resources can we turn our attention to building them. The wealth of recent work on resources and interventions that lead to their development and acquisition suggests that the future of the resource-building literature is bright.

References

Aikens, K., Astin, J., Pelletier, K., Levanovich, K., Baase, C., Park, Y. Y., and Bodnar, C. (2014). Mindfulness goes to work: Impact of an online workplace intervention. *Journal of Occupational and Environmental Medicine, 56*(7), 721–731.

Alvarsson, J. J., Wiens, S., and Nilsson, M. E. (2010). Stress recovery during exposure to nature sound and environmental noise. *International Journal of Environmental Research and Public Health, 7*, 1036–1046.

Arch, J., and Craske, J. (2006). Mechanisms of mindfulness: Emotion regulation following a focused breathing induction. *Behaviour Research and Therapy, 44*(12), 1849–1858.

Avey, J. B., Reichard, R. J., Luthans, F., and Mhatre, K. H. (2011). Meta-analysis on the impact of positive psychological capital on employee attitudes, behaviors, and performance. *Human Resource Development Quarterly, 22*(2), 127–152.

Barnes, C. M. (2012). Working in our sleep: Sleep and self-regulation in organizations. *Organizational Psychology Review, 2*, 234–257.

Baumeister, R., Bratslavsky, E., Muraven, M., and Tice, D. (1998). Ego depletion: Is the active self a limited resource? *Journal of Personality and Social Psychology, 74*(5), 1252–1265.

Binnewies, C., Sonnentag, S., and Mojza, E. J. (2009a). Daily performance at work: Feeling recovered in the morning as a predictor of day-level job performance. *Journal of Organizational Behavior, 30*, 67–93.

Binnewies, C., Sonnentag, S., and Mojza, E. J. (2009b). Feeling recovered and thinking about the good sides of one's work. *Journal of Occupational Health Psychology, 14*(3), 243–256.

Binnewies, C., Sonnentag, S., and Mojza, E. J. (2010). Recovery during the weekend and fluctuations in weekly job performance: A week-level study examining intra-individual relationships. *Journal of Occupational and Organizational Psychology, 83*, 419–441.

Bishop, S., Lau, M., Shapiro, S., Carlson, L., Anderson, N., Carmody, J., ... Devins, G. (2004). Mindfulness: A proposed operational definition. *Clinical Psychology: Science and Practice, 11*(3), 230–241.

Block-Lerner, J., Adair, C., Plumb, J., Rhatigan, D., and Orsillo, S. (2007). The case for mindfulness-based approaches in the cultivation of empathy: Does nonjudgmental, present-moment awareness increase capacity for perspective-taking and empathic concern? *Journal of Marital and Family Therapy, 33*(4), 501–516.

Bono, J., Glomb, T., Shen, W., Kim, E., and Koch, A. (2013). Building positive resources: Effects of positive events and positive reflection on work stress and health. *Academy of Management Journal, 56*(6), 1601–1627.

Borders, A., Earleywine, J., and Jajodia, A. (2010). Could mindfulness decrease anger, hostility, and aggression by decreasing rumination? *Aggressive Behavior, 36*(1), 28–44.

Bowler, D. E., Buyung-Ali, L. M., Knight, T. M., and Pullin, A. S. (2010). A systematic review of evidence for the added benefits to health of exposure to natural environments. *BMC Public Health, 10*(456), 1–10.

Brown, K. W., and Ryan, R. M. (2003). The benefits of being present: Mindfulness and its role in psychological well-being. *Journal of Personality and Social Psychology, 84*(4), 822–848.

Burton, C., and King, L. (2009). The health benefits of writing about positive experiences: The role of broadened cognition. *Psychology and Health*, *24*(8), 867–879.

Carmeli, A., Ben-Hador, B., Waldman, D., and Rupp, D. (2009). How leaders cultivate social capital and nurture employee vigor: Implications for job performance. *Journal of Applied Psychology*, *94*(6), 1553–1561.

Carmeli, A., Brueller, D., and Dutton, J. E. (2009). Learning behaviours in the workplace: The role of high-quality interpersonal relationships and psychological safety. *Systems Research and Behavioral Science*, *26*, 81–98.

Chan, D. W. (2010). Gratitude, gratitude intervention and subjective well-being among Chinese school teachers in Hong Kong. *Educational Psychology*, *30*(2), 139–153.

Chan, D. W. (2011). Burnout and life satisfaction: Does gratitude intervention make a difference among Chinese school teachers in Hong Kong? *Educational Psychology*, *31*(7), 809–823.

Colbert, A., Bono, J. E., and Purvanova, R. (2015). Flourishing via workplace relationships: Moving beyond instrumental support. *Academy of Management Journal*, *59*, 1199–1223.

Cropanzano, R., Rupp, D., and Byrne, Z. (2003). The relationship of emotional exhaustion to work attitudes, job performance, and organizational citizenship behaviors. *Journal of Applied Psychology*, *88*(1), 160–189.

Dane, E., and Brummel, B. J. (2013). Examining workplace mindfulness and its relations to job performance and turnover intention. *Human Relations*, *67*(1), 105–128.

Davidson, R. (1998). Anterior electrophysiological asymmetries, emotion, and depression: Conceptual and methodological conundrums. *Psychophysiology*, *35*(5), 607–614.

Davis, M. A. (2009). Understanding the relationship between mood and creativity: A meta-analysis. *Organizational Behavior and Human Decision Processes*, *108*(1), 25–38.

De Bloom, J. D., Kompier, M., Geurts, S., de Weerth, C., Taris, T., and Sonnentag, S. (2009). Do we recover from vacation? Meta-analysis of vacation effects on health and well-being. *Journal of Occupational Health*, *51*(1), 13–25.

Demerouti, E., Bakker, A. B., Nachreiner, F., and Schaufeli, W. B. (2001). The job demands–resources model of burnout. *Journal of Applied Psychology*, *86*(3), 499–512.

Desbordes, G., Negi, L., Pace, T., Wallace, B., Raison, C., and Schwartz, E. (2012). Effects of mindful-attention and compassion meditation training on amygdala response to emotional stimuli in an ordinary, non-meditative state. *Frontiers in Human Neuroscience*, *6*, 292.

Diener, E., Wirtz, D., Tov, W., Kim-Prieto, C., Choi, D-W., Oishi, S., and Biswas-Diener, R. (2009). New well-being measures: Short scales to assess flourishing and positive and negative feelings. *Social Indicators Research*, *97*(2), 143–156.

Ding, X., Tang, Y., Tang, R., and Posner, M. (2014). Improving creativity performance by short-term meditation. *Behavioral and Brain Functions*, *10*(9), 1–8.

Emmons, R., and McCullough, M. (2003). Counting blessings versus burdens: An experimental investigation of gratitude and subjective well-being in daily life. *Journal of Personality and Social Psychology*, *84*(2), 377–389.

Emmons, R., and Mishra, A. (2011). Why gratitude enhances well-being: What we know, what we need to know. In K. M. Sheldon, T. B. Kashdan, and M. F. Steger (Eds.), *Designing Positive Psychology: Taking Stock and Moving Forward* (pp. 248–262). New York: Oxford University Press.

Etzion, D. (2003). Annual vacation: Duration of relief from job stressors and burnout. *Anxiety, Stress, and Coping*, *16*(2), 213–226.

Foureur, M., Besley, K., Burton, G., Yu, N., and Crisp, J. (2013). Enhancing the resilience of nurses and midwives: Pilot of mindfulness based program for increased health, sense of coherence and decreased depression, anxiety, and stress. *Contemporary Nurse*, *45*(1), 114–125.

Frein, S. T., and Ponsler, K. (2014). Increasing positive affect in college students. *Applied Research in Quality of Life*, *9*(1), 1–13.

Fritz, C., Ellis, A., Demsky, C., Lin, B., and Guros, F. (2013). Embracing work breaks: Recovering from work stress. *Organizational Dynamics*, *42*, 274–280.

Fritz, C., and Sonnentag, S. (2005). Recovery, health, and job performance: Effects of weekend experiences. *Journal of Occupational Health Psychology*, *10*(3), 187–1999.

Fritz, C., and Sonnentag, S. (2006). Recovery, well-being, and performance-related outcomes: The role of workload and vacation experiences. *Journal of Applied Psychology*, *91*(4), 936–945.

Fritz, C., Sonnentag, S., Spector, P., and McInroe, J. (2010). The weekend matters: Relationships between stress recovery and affective experiences. *Journal of Organizational Behavior*, *31*(8), 1137–1162.

Fritz, C., Yankelevich, M., Zarubin, A., and Barger, P. (2010). Happy, healthy, and productive: The role of detachment from work during nonwork time. *Journal of Applied Psychology*, *95*(5), 977–983.

Gable, S., and Reis, H. (2010). Good news! Capitalizing on positive events in an interpersonal context. *Advances in Experimental Social Psychology*, *42*, 195–257.

Gable, S., Reis, H., Impett, E., and Asher, R. (2004). What do you do when things go right? The intrapersonal and interpersonal benefits of sharing positive events. *Journal of Personality and Social Psychology, 87*(2), 228–245.

Gander, F., Proyer, R. T., Ruch, W., and Wyss, T. (2013). Strength-based positive interventions: Further evidence for their potential in enhancing well-being and alleviating depression. *Journal of Happiness Studies, 14*(4), 1241–1259.

George, J. M. (1991). State or trait: Effects of positive mood on prosocial behavior at work. *Journal of Applied Psychology, 76*(2), 299–307.

Giannopoulous, V. L., and Vella-Brodrick, D. A. (2011). Effects of positive interventions and orientations to happiness on subjective well-being. *Journal of Positive Psychology, 6*(2), 95–105.

Glomb, T. M., Duffy, M. K., Bono, J. E., and Yang, T. (2011). Mindfulness at work. In J. Martocchio, H. Liao, and A. Joshi (Eds.), *Research in Personnel and Human Resources Management*, vol. 30 (pp. 115–157). Bingley, UK: Emerald.

Hahn, V., and Dormann, C. (2013). The role of partners and children for employees' psychological detachment from work and well-being. *Journal of Applied Psychology, 98*(1), 26–36.

Halbesleben, J. R. B. (2006) Sources of social support and burnout: A meta-analytic test of the conservation of resources model. *Journal of Applied Psychology, 91*, 1134–1135.

Halbesleben, J., Neveu, J., Paustian-Underdahl, S., and Westman, M. (2014). Getting to the "COR": Understanding the role of resources in conservation of resources theory. *Journal of Management, 40*, 1334–1364.

Hardin, C., and Higgins, E. (1996). Shared reality: How social verification makes the subjective objective. In R. M. Sorrentino and E. T. Higgins (Eds.), *Handbook of Motivation and Cognition: The Interpersonal Context*, vol. 31 (pp. 28–84). New York: Guilford Press.

Hartig, T., Evans, G. W., Jamner, L. D., Davis, D. S., and Gärling, T. (2003). Tracking restoration in natural and urban field settings. *Journal of Environmental Psychology, 23*(2), 109–123.

Hicks, A., and Diamond, L. (2008). How was your day? Couples affect when telling and hearing daily events. *Personal Relationships, 15*(2), 205–228.

Hobfoll, S. E. (1989). Conservation of resources: A new attempt at conceptualizing stress. *American Psychologist, 44*(3), 513–524.

Hobfoll, S. E. (2001). The influence of culture, community, and the nested-self in the stress process: Advancing conservation of resources theory. *Applied Psychology, 50*(3), 337–421.

Hülsheger, U. R., Alberts, H. J. E. M., Feinholdt, A., and Lang, J. W. B. (2013). Benefits of mindfulness at work: The role of mindfulness in emotion regulation, emotional exhaustion, and job satisfaction. *Journal of Applied Psychology, 98*(2), 310–325.

Ilies, R., Keeney, J., and Scott, B. (2011). Work–family interpersonal capitalization: Sharing positive work events at home. *Organizational Behavior and Human Decision Processes, 11*(4), 115–126.

Isen, A. M., Daubman, K. A., and Nowicki, G. P. (1987). Positive affect facilitates creative problem solving. *Journal of Personality and Social Psychology, 52*(6), 1122–1131.

Isen, A. M., Johnson, M. M. S., Mertz, E., and Robinson, G. F. (1985). The influence of positive affect on the unusualness of word associations. *Journal of Personality and Social Psychology, 48*(6), 1413–1426.

Isen, A. M., and Levin, P. F. (1972). Effect of feeling good on helping: Cookies and kindness. *Journal of Personality and Social Psychology, 21*(3), 384–388.

Jain, S., Shapiro, S., Swanick, S., Roesch, S., Mills, P., Bell, I., and Schwartz, G. (2007). A randomized controlled trial of mindfulness meditation versus relaxation training: Effects on distress, positive states of mind, rumination, and distraction. *Annals of Behavioral Medicine, 33*(1), 11–21.

Johnson, J. V., and Lipscomb, J. (2006). Long working hours, occupational health and the changing nature of work organization. *American Journal of Industrial Medicine, 49*, 921–929.

Joudrey, A. D., and Wallace, J. E. (2009). Leisure as a coping resource: A test of the job demand–control–support model. *Human Relations, 62*(2), 195–217.

Kabat-Zinn, J. (1990). *Full Catastrophe Living: Using the Wisdom of Your Body and Mind to Face Stress, Pain, And Illness*. New York: Delacorte Press.

Kaczmarek, L. D., Kashdan, T. B., Drążkowski, D., Enko, J., Kosakowski, M., Szäefer, A., and Bujacz, A. (2015). Why do people prefer gratitude journaling over gratitude letters? The influence of individual differences in motivation and personality on web-based interventions. *Personality and Individual Differences, 75*, 1–6.

Kaplan, S., Bradley-Geist, J. C., Ahmad, A., Anderson, A., Hargrove, A. K., and Lindsey, A. (2014). A test of two positive psychology interventions to increase employee well-being. *Journal of Business and Psychology, 29*(3), 367–380.

Keyes, C. L. (2007). Promoting and protecting mental health as flourishing: A complementary strategy for improving national mental health. *American Psychologist*, *62*(2), 95–108.

Killen, A., and Macaskill, A. (2015). Using a gratitude intervention to enhance well-being in older adults. *Journal of Happiness Studies*, *16*, 947–964.

Kühnel, J., and Sonnentag, S. (2011). How long do you benefit from vacation? A closer look at the fade-out of vacation effects. *Journal of Organizational Behavior*, *32*(1), 125–143.

Kühnel, J., Sonnentag, S., and Westman, M. (2009). Does work engagement increase after a short respite? The role of job involvement as a double-edged sword. *Journal of Occupational and Organizational Psychology*, *82*(3), 575–594.

Lambert, N., Gwinn, A., Stillman, T., and Fincham, F. (2011). Feeling tired? How sharing positive experiences can boost vitality. *International Journal of Wellbeing*, *1*(3), 307–314.

Lanaj, K., Johnson, R., and Barnes, C. M. (2014). Beginning the workday yet already depleted? Consequences of late-night smartphone use and sleep. *Organizational Behavior and Human Decision Processes*, *124*, 11–23.

Langston, C. (1994). Capitalizing on and coping with daily-life events: Expressive responses to positive events. *Journal of Personality and Social Psychology*, *67*(6), 1112–1125.

Lim, V. G. K., and Chen, D. J. Q. (2012). Cyberloafing at the workplace: Gain or drain on work? *Behaviour and Information Technology*, *31*(4), 343–353.

Little, L. M., Nelson, D. L., Wallace, J. C., and Johnson, P. D. (2011). Integrating attachment style, vigor at work, and extra-role performance. *Journal of Organizational Behavior*, *32*(3), 464–484.

Lounsbury, J. W., and Hoopes, L. L. (1986). A vacation from work: Changes in work and nonwork outcomes. *Journal of Applied Psychology*, *71*(3), 392.

Mackenzie, C., Poulin, P., and Seidman-Carlson, R. (2006). A brief mindfulness-based stress reduction intervention for nurses and nurse aides. *Applied Nursing Research*, *19*(2), 105–109.

Miner, A. G., and Glomb, T. M. (2010). State mood, task performance, and behavior at work: A within-persons approach. *Organizational Behavior and Human Decision Processes*, *112*, 43–57.

Mongrain, M., and Anselmo-Matthews, T. (2012). Do positive psychology exercises work? A replication of Seligman et al. (2005). *Journal of Clinical Psychology*, *68*(4), 382–389.

Munson, S. A., Lauterbach, D., Newman, M. W., and Resnick, P. (2010). Happier together: Integrating a wellness application into a social network site. In T. Ploug, P Hasle, and H. Oinas-Kukkonen (Eds.), *Persuasive Technology* (pp. 27–39). New York: Springer.

Orsillo, S., and Roemer, L. (2005). *Acceptance and Mindfulness-Based Approaches to Anxiety: Conceptualization and treatment*. New York: Springer.

Park, Y., and Fritz, C. (2015). Spousal recovery support, recovery experiences, and life satisfaction crossover among dual-earner couples. *Journal of Applied Psychology*, *100*, 557–566.

Porath, C., Spreitzer, G., Gibson, C., and Garnett, F. G. (2012). Thriving at work: Toward its measurement, construct validation, and theoretical refinement. *Journal of Organizational Behavior*, *33*, 250–275.

Poulin, P., MacKenzie, S., Soloway, G., and Karayolas, E. (2008). Mindfulness training as an evidenced-based approach to reducing stress and promoting well-being among human service professionals. *International Journal of Health Promotion and Education*, *46*(2), 72–80.

Rash, J., Matsuba, M., and Prkachin, K. (2011). Gratitude and well-being: Who benefits the most from a gratitude intervention? *Applied Psychology: Health and Well-Being*, *3*(3), 350–369.

Reb, J., Narayanan, J., and Chaturvedi, S. (2014). Leading mindfully: Two studies on the influence of supervisor trait mindfulness on employee well-being and performance. *Mindfulness*, *5*(1), 36–45.

Reis, H., Smith, S., Carmichael, C., Caprariello, P., Tsai, F., Rodrigues, A., and Maniaci, M. (2010). Are you happy for me? How sharing positive events with others provides personal and interpersonal benefits. *Journal of Personality and Social Psychology*, *99*(2), 311–329.

Rimé, B., Philippot, P., Boca, S., and Mesquita, B. (1992). Long-lasting cognitive and social consequences of emotion: Social sharing and rumination. *European Review of Social Psychology*, *3*(1), 225–258.

Rotundo, M., and Sackett, P. R. (2002). The relative importance of task, citizenship, and counterproductive performance to global ratings of job performance: A policy-capturing approach. *Journal of Applied Psychology*, *87*(1), 66–80.

Sanz-Vergel, A. I., Demerouti, E., Moreno-Jiménez, B., and Mayo, M. (2010). Work–family balance and energy: A day-level study on recovery conditions. *Journal of Vocational Behavior*, *76*(1), 118–130.

Seligman, M. E. P., Steen, T. A., Park, N., and Peterson, C. (2005). Positive psychology progress: Empirical validation of interventions. *American Psychologist*, *60*(5), 410–421.

Senf, K., and Liau, A. K. (2013). The effects of positive interventions on happiness and depressive symptoms, with an examination of personality as a moderator. *Journal of Happiness Studies*, *14*(2), 591–612.

Shapiro, S. L., Carlson, L. E., Astin, J. A., and Freedman, B. (2006). Mechanisms of mindfulness. *Journal of Clinical Psychology*, *62*(3), 373–386.

Siltaloppi, M., Kinnunen, U., and Feldt, (2009). Recovery experiences as moderators between psychosocial work characteristics and occupational well-being. *Work and Stress*, *23*(4), 330–348.

Smith, B. W., Shelley, B. M., Dalen, J., Wiggins, K., Tooley, E., and Bernard, J. (2008). A pilot study comparing the effects of mindfulness-based and cognitive-behavioral stress reduction. *Journal of Alternative and Complementary Medicine*, *14*(3), 251–258.

Sonnentag, S. (2001). Work, recovery activities, and individual well-being: A diary study. *Journal of Occupational Health Psychology*, *6*(3), 196–210.

Sonnentag, S. (2003). Recovery, work engagement, and proactive behavior: A new look at the interface between nonwork and work. *Journal of Applied Psychology*, *88*, 518–528.

Sonnentag, S., and Bayer, U.-V. (2005). Switching off mentally: Predictors and consequences of psychological detachment from work during off-job time. *Journal of Occupational Health Psychology*, *10*(4), 393–414.

Sonnentag, S., Binnewies, C., and Mojza, E. J. (2008). "Did you have a nice evening?" A day-level study on recovery experiences, sleep, and affect. *Journal of Applied Psychology*, *93*(3), 674–684.

Sonnentag, S., and Fritz, C. (2007). The recovery experience questionnaire: Development and validation of a measure for assessing recuperation and unwinding from work. *Journal of Occupational Health Psychology*, *12*(3), 204–221.

Speca, M., Carlson, L., Goodey, E., and Angen, M. (2000). A randomized, waitlist controlled clinical trial: The effect of a mindfulness-based stress reduction program on mood and symptoms of stress in cancer outpatients. *Psychosomatic Medicine*, *62*, 613–622.

Strauss-Blasche, G., Reithofer, B., Schobersberger, W., Ekmekcioglu, C., and Marktl, W. (2005). Effect of vacation on health: Moderating factors of vacation outcome. *Journal of Travel Medicine*, *12*(2), 94–101.

Thomas, J., and Otis, M. (2010). Intrapsychic correlates of professional quality of life: Mindfulness, empathy, and emotional separation. *Journal of the Society for Social Work and Research*, *1*(2), 83–98.

Tirch, D. (2010). Mindfulness as a context for the cultivation of compassion. *International Journal of Cognitive Therapy*, *3*(2), 113–123.

Toepfer, S., Cichy, K., and Peters, P. (2012). Letters of gratitude: Further evidence for author benefits. *Journal of Happiness Studies*, *13*(1), 187–201.

Trougakos, J. P., Beal, D. J., Green, S. G., and Weiss, H. M. (2008). Making the break count: An episodic examination of recovery activities, emotional experiences, and positive affective displays. *Academy of Management Journal*, *51*(1), 131–146.

Trougakos, J., and Hideg, I. (2009). Momentary work recovery: The role of within-day work breaks. In S. Sonnentag, P. L. Perrewé, and D. C. Ganster (Eds.), *Research in Occupational Stress and Well-Being* (pp. 37–84). Bingley, UK: Emerald.

Trougakos, J., Hideg, I., Cheng, B., and Beal, D. (2013). Lunch breaks unpacked: The role of autonomy as a moderator of recovery during lunch. *Academy of Management Journal*, *57*(2), 405–421.

Ulrich, R., Simons, R., Losito, B., Fiorito, E., Miles, M., and Zelson, M. (1991). Stress recovery during exposure to natural and urban environments. *Journal of Environmental Psychology*, *11*(3), 201–230.

Watkins, P., Woodward, K., Stone, T., and Kolts, R. (2003). Gratitude and happiness: Development of a measure of gratitude, and relationships with subjective well-being. *Social Behavior and Personality*, *31*(5), 431–451.

Westman, M., and Eden, D. (1997). Effects of a respite from work on burnout: Vacation relief and fade-out. *Journal of Applied Psychology*, *82*, 516–527.

Xanthopoulou, D., Bakker, A. B., Demerouti, E., and Schaufeli, W. B. (2007). The role of personal resources in the job demands–resources model. *International Journal of Stress Management*, *14*(2), 121–141.

Zacher, H., Brailsford, H., and Parker, S. (2014). Micro-breaks matter: A diary study on the effects of energy management strategies on occupational well-being. *Journal of Vocational Behavior*, *85*(3), 287–297.

Zwack, J., and Schweitzer, J. (2013). If every fifth physician is affected by burnout, what about the other four? Resilience strategies of experienced physicians. *Academic Medicine*, *88*(3), 382–389.

Part Six

Enhancing Organizational and Community Well-Being

34

Well-Being in Neighborhoods

Current Research and Future Practice

Christopher T. Boyko and Rachel Cooper

Introduction

When purchasing or renting a new dwelling, much consideration is given to the fit between the needs and wants of the people moving in and the amenity features of the dwelling. Consideration also is given to the vicinity in which the dwelling is located, with many people hoping to live in the "right" neighborhood for them. Estate agents employ a lexicon of terms to describe the "right" neighborhood, depending on what a prospective buyer or renter is looking for, or how they wish to promote a particular area: "charming," "community feel," "up and coming area," "sought after," and so forth. Implied by these often-misrepresented descriptions of neighborhoods is that someone will be happy there. More than happy though: their quality of life and well-being will be enhanced, now and in the future. However, there are a host of neighborhood characteristics that will influence people's experiences of their dwelling and that will impact their well-being and ill-being, some of which will not have been known or thought about at the time of moving into a property. This chapter will elucidate some of these characteristics and discuss what today's decision-makers can do to ensure that neighborhoods of the future maximize well-being and minimize ill-being.

This chapter begins by defining relevant terms and outlining a framework for categorizing relationships between the physical environment and well-being, first developed as part of the Foresight Mental Capital and Wellbeing Project in the United Kingdom (Government Office for Science, 2008). The framework will be used in the second section to classify current research on interconnections between neighborhood characteristics and well-being or ill-being. The third section reflects on these relationships and considers what is needed for future interventions in neighborhoods, both in the near and long term. The interventions can take a physical or spatial form, or have a social, psychological or political component. The chapter

The Handbook of Stress and Health: A Guide to Research and Practice, First Edition.
Edited by Cary L. Cooper and James Campbell Quick.
© 2017 John Wiley & Sons, Ltd. Published 2017 by John Wiley & Sons, Ltd.

ends with a discussion about the future of neighborhoods in cities, exploring the development of tools and foresight for well-being that includes a diversity of voices (i.e., not only decision-makers from one profession).

Defining Terms

Well-being   Acknowledging that the term is intangible (Thomas, 2009), socially constructed, contested, and therefore can mean different things to different individuals, groups and organizations, depending on their point of view (Ereaut and Whiting, 2008), the authors use the definition of well-being of the Government Office for Science (2008):

> A dynamic state in which the individual is able to develop their potential, work productively and creatively, build strong and positive relationships with others, and contribute to their community. It is enhanced when an individual is able to fulfil their personal and social goals and achieve a sense of purpose in society. (p. 10)

Although this definition focuses primarily on mental well-being, there is a recognition that individuals also must realize a sense of physical, social and psychological well-being to fulfill their goals and achieve a sense of purpose (Dodge, Daly, Huyton, and Sanders, 2012). Thus, some of the neighborhood characteristics discussed in this section, such as neighborhood walkability, may affect one's well-being beyond just mental well-being (e.g., being physically active as a component of physical well-being).

Ill-being   As described by Headey, Holström, and Wearing (1984; 1985), ill-being "refers to a state of worry, negative affect and somatic complaints that arise from a low sense of personal competence, a lack of control and planning over one's life, and poor socio-economic and family circumstances" (Boyko and Cooper, 2014, p. 71). Individuals experiencing ill-being may feel dissatisfied with their health or standard of living (Headey et al., 1984; 1985; Nyman, 2002), manifesting in states of depression, low self-esteem, pessimism or self-dissatisfaction (Scheff, 1999). Both ill-being and well-being have independent and specific causes and correlations; thus, the two terms are not antonyms (Bradburn, 1969; Bradburn and Caplovitz, 1965; Headey et al., 1984; 1985).

Neighborhood   Employing Galster's (2001) definition, a neighborhood is "the bundle of spatially based attributes associated with clusters of residences, sometimes in conjunction with other land uses" (p. 2112). The spatially based attributes comprise social, cultural, demographic, political, institutional, economic, ecological (Chaskin, 2006; Galster, 2001), emotional, proximity and structural (Galster, 2001) elements.

Trying to define neighborhood can be problematic because, like well-being, it is contingent on who is defining the term and for what reason(s) (Flowerdew, Manley, and Sabel, 2008). For example, a local authority might define neighborhoods through the use of electoral wards in order to obtain meaningful Census data. However, this definition might not fit or might, indeed, overlap with other organizations' understanding of neighborhood (e.g., the National Health Service definition of neighborhood in the UK to help determine Neighborhood Health Centres) or those of residents living in a certain neighborhood who give the area a clear identity for social reasons (e.g., the trendy area of town).

The Framework for Categorizing Relationships between Neighborhood Characteristics and Well-Being

Based on a review of the main physical environment features contributing to mental capital and well-being, Cooper, Boyko, and Codinhoto (2008) created a framework that classified the features into three factors:

- *The quality of the fabric of the physical environment*   Refers to the design and construction of buildings, the spaces between buildings and associated infrastructure as well as the maintenance and regeneration of spaces and places. The quality of the physical environment also can be viewed at different scales, from the site to the city.
- *The quality of the ambient environment*   Refers to related aspects of the physical environment, such as acoustics, lighting, air quality, temperature, color, ventilation, humidity, having views of nature and natural sunlight, and having plants in offices and homes.
- *The psychological impact of the physical and ambient environment*   Refers to perceptions of the environment, and includes density and crowding, sense of safety, fear, wayfinding and access to things (e.g., nature).

We believe this framework could be applied to the myriad studies about neighborhood characteristics and their impact on well-being or ill-being; therefore, the next section breaks down the current research into three subsections according to the framework above.

Current Research

The Quality of the Fabric of the Physical Environment

For people to live comfortably and espouse the well-being benefits of their surroundings, the physical environment must possess minimum quality standards. Many of these standards are overseen by local and national governments as well as various organizations, whereas others are formed out of common sense (e.g., having pavements in neighborhoods gives residents the safety to walk in their area without being hit by vehicles).

Windows   Being able to see windows facing on to a neighborhood street in at least 50 percent of homes led to a much higher propensity of schoolchildren wanting to walk to school (McMillan, 2007).

Light   Being exposed to natural, versus artificial, light throughout the 24-hour day may decrease sleep disorders and agitation at dusk, or "sundowning" (Cooper Marcus, 2009; Keane and Shoesmith, 2005; Torrington and Tregenza, 2007).

Lead paint and other toxins   Living in neighborhoods that have not been renovated to code may result in residents being exposed to lead and other toxic metals, which could impair individuals' cognitive functions throughout their lifetime. Although exposure varies depending on the location of the neighborhood, those living in low socioeconomic areas with a poor built environment appear to suffer the worst exposure (Gilbert and Galea, 2014).

Walkability and pavements   Neighborhoods with high-density housing and employment, plenty of green space for recreational purposes, street intersections (Li, Fisher, Brownson, and Bosworth, 2005), and connectivity as a result of shorter distances between intersections (S. C. Brown and Lombard, 2014) can foster higher levels of walking, particularly among children (Martin and Wood, 2014) and older adults (Li et al., 2005). Moreover, neighborhood walkability and the perception of walkability (as well as social connectedness) among residents may lead to higher levels of physical activity within neighborhoods, including walking for leisure and for transport (Foster, Giles-Corti, and Knuiman, 2011; Kaczynski and Glover, 2012; Saelens, Sallis, Black, and Chen, 2003). Conversely, areas without pavements or with pavements that are poor in quality (Gilbert and Galea, 2014) and with low numbers of street intersections (leading to perceived issues with traffic safety; Li et al., 2005; Mullen, 2003) may decrease walking behavior in residents, especially older residents. Additionally, people with dementia may be deterred from using pavements if they have to share them with cyclists, skateboarders and people using scooters (Alzheimer's Australia NSW, 2011).

Open spaces, green spaces and nature   Proximity (Hartig, 2008; Hartig et al., 1996) and availability (HM Government, 2011a; 2011b) of planting and green spaces may provide many benefits to people (e.g., creating a visual amenity; improving air quality; improving mental health; Knopf, 2001; DfT and DCLG, 2007; see also Gillis and Gatersleben, 2015, for a larger discussion about the well-being benefits of biophilic design). Furthermore, neighborhoods with greater numbers of green spaces, such as parks, report higher levels of perceived efficacy among users (Cohen, Inagami, and Finch, 2008), which can indirectly combat stress (Fan, Das, and Chen, 2011). Parks with higher incidences of social capital among users attract more users and generate more physical activity than parks where social capital is lower (Broyles et al., 2011). Indeed, physical activity in green spaces can enhance self-esteem and mood (Barton and Pretty, 2010). Children who live in neighborhoods with greater quantities of nature exhibit higher levels of physical activity (De Vries, Bakker, van Mechelen, and Hopman-Rock, 2007), are at lower risk for being overweight (Coley, Sullivan, and Kuo, 1997; Liu, Wilson, Qi, and Ying, 2007) and have lower body mass indices (Bell, Wilson, and Liu, 2008). Merely being in contact with, or spending time in, nature within neighborhoods may have a restorative effect on children (Korpela, Kyttä, and Hartig, 2002), help their stress management (Wells and Evans, 2003), enhance overall mental health (Küller and Lindsten, 1992; Milligan and Bingley, 2007), improve emotional responsiveness and approachability (Derr, 2001; Ratanapojnard, 2001), and mitigate attention deficit hyperactivity disorder (Kuo and Taylor, 2004; Taylor, Kuo, and Sullivan, 2001).

Car parking   In high-density, mixed-use neighborhoods in London, lack of parking and parking restrictions were seen as acceptable trade-offs for the benefits of living on the edge of the city center (e.g., increased neighborliness; social cohesion) (Evans, 2014). However, in American mixed-use neighborhoods containing retail-based surface car parks, such parking was seen as detracting from neighborhood sense of community (Wood, Frank, and Giles-Corti, 2010), as they do not promote walkability.

The Quality of the Ambient Environment

The morphology of neighborhoods can indirectly affect the well-being of those living in the area by producing unintended consequences. The three unintended consequences below correlate with ill-being, but there are features of the physical environment that influence well-being (e.g., having views of nature; see Boyko and Cooper, 2014).

Pollution   In the case of air pollution and well-being research, the location of a neighborhood is an important variable in understanding subsequent well-being outcomes. For children, growing up in high-pollution neighborhoods predicted neighborhood-scale juvenile criminal activity as well as schizophrenia in later life (Haynes et al., 2011). Healthy children and dogs living in areas with high air pollution in Mexico City also were found to have lesions and persistent white matter on their brains, which is associated with neuroinflammation (Calderón-Garcidueñas et al., 2008). For older adults, exposure to air pollution in their neighborhoods (along with exposure to noise and dirt) was related to greater feelings of stress, anxiety and tiredness (Day, 2008a; 2008b).

Litter, graffiti, and general neglect   Neighborhood physical neglect in the form of litter, graffiti, vandalism, dilapidation and deterioration of buildings may signal to some that a place is "out of control" (Grabosky, 1995; see also Kelling and Wilson, 1982). This could subsequently impact health and well-being, contributing to an inability to form adequate social ties (Ross and Jang, 2000; Sampson, Raudenbush, and Earls, 1997) or to receive social support (Hill, Burdette, Jokinen-Gordon, and Brailsford, 2013), a decrement in sense of community (Wood and Giles-Corti, 2008), and less likelihood of walking in one's neighborhood (Foster and Giles-Corti, 2008). Moreover, negative perceptions of one's neighborhood in terms of overall quality may stimulate depression (Burdette, Hill, and Hale, 2011; Ellaway and Macintyre., 2009) as well as substance abuse in adults (Burdette et al., 2011). Some environmental problems exert a greater effect than others, however: according to Ellaway and Macintyre (2009), street-scale incivilities, such as litter or graffiti, contribute more to people's depression than do infrastructural problems.

Crime and violence   Neighborhood violence is positively correlated with higher stress levels in children (Karriker-Jaffe, Foshee, and Ennett, 2011). In adolescence, the quality of the neighborhood may influence the start of violent or deviant behavior (as well as substance use and depression) (Galea and Vlahov, 2005), as might the lack of things to do in the neighborhood (Caldwell, Weichold, and Smith, 2006) or the social disorganization experienced within the neighborhood (e.g., social instability) (Calvert, 2002; Wilson et al., 2005). Community crime across all ages also might be higher when there is a prevalence of neighborhood social disorganization (Agnew, 1992; Sampson and Groves, 1989). When social disorganization is low in neighborhoods (i.e., there exists greater social cohesion and collective efficacy), however, there are reduced levels of deviant behavior and depression (Kruger, Reischl, and Gee, 2007; Sampson et al., 1997). Waters, Neale, and Mears (2008) suggest that the overall visual appearance and image of a neighborhood plays an important role in discouraging crime, whereas Evans (2014) believes that the mix of uses in a neighborhood is key (i.e., fewer crimes of the kind that impact residents' well-being are committed in mixed-use areas, but there may be more vehicle and bicycle theft and vandalism).

The Psychological Impact of the Physical and Ambient Environment

The built fabric and surrounding environment within a neighborhood will affect people's emotions, cognitions and behaviors, mainly through their interactions with other people in the area (but also through their memories of the neighborhood) as well as with the area itself. Like the other factors in this framework, there are both positive and negative psychological impacts that contribute to well-being and ill-being.

Density and crowding   In terms of well-being, there is a positive association between high-density living (as well as high density of employment, street intersections and greenspaces) and propensity to walk in one's neighborhood (Li et al., 2005). High-density neighborhoods also have been purported to reduce behavioral and emotional problems in children (Silburn et al., 2006) and strengthen social contacts (Bernard, 1939; Moore, 1986); improve the well-being of older people who live in social, sheltered or retirement housing (Lawton and Nahemow, 1979; Lawton, Nahemow, and Yeh, 1980); and lead to greater cooperation, social ties (Halpern, 1995) and social interaction (Talen, 1999; Young and Willmott, 1957) among neighbors.

Unfortunately, more research demonstrates a relationship between increased density and ill-being. Scholars have demonstrated that living within high-density neighborhoods, particularly in inner cities, is associated with a lower quality of life (i.e., a greater quantity of negative life events) (Cramer, Torgersen, and Kringlen, 2004); psychological stress, especially when both residential and community density is high in a neighborhood (Gómez-Jacinto and Hombrados-Mendieta, 2002); chronic mental fatigue (especially among single parents) (Kuo, 1992); higher admission rates to hospitals for schizophrenia (Faris and Dunham, 1939); psychiatric illness (Duvall and Booth, 1978; Paulus, McCain, and Cox, 1978); psychoses among older people (Gruenberg, 1954); and less social interaction (Dempsey, Smith, and Burton, 2012). This relationship occurs for both adults, particularly in terms of psychological distress (Gabe and Williams, 1993; Ineichen, 1993; Kellett, 1984; Ross and Jang, 2000), and children, particularly in terms of impaired cognitive development (e.g., Booth, 1976; Bradley et al., 1994; Essen, Fogelman, and Head, 1978; Evans, Lepore, Shejwal, and Palsane, 1998; Evans and Saegert, 2000; Gottfried and Gottfried, 1984; Hassan, 1977; Saegert, 1982).

Fear of crime and perceptions of safety   Fear of crime occurs when people perceive their neighborhood to be run-down and neglected (Borst et al., 2008; Carmona, Heath, Oc, and Tiesdell, 2003; Day, 2008a; 2008b; Foster and Giles-Corti, 2008; Foster, Giles-Corti, and Knuiman, 2010; Peace, Holland, and Kellaher, 2006; SDC, 2008; Waters et al., 2008). This physical disorder – especially nonresidential physical disorder – exerts a more powerful influence on fear of crime than does social disorder (e.g., "undesirables" congregating at a park bench) (Perkins and Taylor, 1996). However, when there is a sense of community and attachment in neighborhoods, fear of crime may be reduced (B. Brown, Perkins, and Brown, 2003; Farrell, Aubry, and Coulombe, 2004).

In terms of more general perceptions of safety, research suggests that seeing people outside in a neighborhood begets a sense of community and safety (Wood, Giles-Corti, and Bulsara, 2012), which further creates a feeling of more "eyes on the street" (Evenson, Scott, Cohen, and Vorhees, 2007; Foster et al., 2010). Neighborhoods that are more walkable in design can encourage natural surveillance and may persuade parents to worry less about "stranger danger" (Foster et al., 2015).

Sense of community   Having a strong sense of community may encourage people to walk in their neighborhood, thus contributing to physical well-being (Lund, 2003; Wood et al., 2010). Part of this relationship involves feeling safe to walk in one's neighborhood during the day and night, walking in an area that is perceived to be interesting (Lund, 2002), being in a place that induces positive social interaction (Leyden, 2003; Lund, 2002) and seeing people about – especially children playing at the local school (Wood, Giles-Corti, Zubrick, and Bulsara, 2011; Wood et al., 2012). This relationship also can extend to neighborhoods with a retail presence (Wood et al., 2010). When traffic is both present and heavy, however, perceptions of neighborhood friendliness may be negatively impacted (Mullen, 2003), which could discourage walking and the development of neighborhood social capital.

Furthermore, research suggests that children can help support social capital and sense of community among adults within neighborhoods in a variety of ways (e.g., ask parents or guardians to walk them to and from the local school; have parents participate in school activities; Wood et al., 2011). Having stronger ties to the community, in turn, may have positive repercussions for children, including greater independence to move about their neighborhood (Hüttenmoser, 1995; Prezza, Alparone, Cristallo, and Luigi, 2005), and reducing fears about neighborhood safety (Zubrick et al., 2010).

Much of the above research centers on the positive associations between the built and natural form of neighborhoods and residents' abilities to walk and connect with people, among other things. However, some of the unintended consequences of the form and shape of neighborhoods, such as pollution, and the impacts these consequences have on residents, such as fear of the area at night, need to be highlighted, holistically considered and managed by decision-makers looking to enhance well-being in neighborhoods. The next section posits what future interventions may need to be put in place for the short and long term to assist decision-makers.

Future Interventions for the Near and Long Term, because Infrastructure Needs Long-Term Planning

From the extensive evidence above, there are a number of interventions that can enhance well-being in neighborhoods. First, we must recognize that urban development and improvement can take many years; "place" has cycles of development and neglect. For example, the Devonshire Quarter of Sheffield (the fourth largest urban area in England) is a dense, mixed-use area, quickly developed from agricultural purposes in the beginning of the nineteenth century into small factories and terraced housing, which then were demolished as part of city-wide slum clearance between the 1920s and 1970s. Development was slow, however, until the 1990s and 2000s. A study by Boyko and Cooper (2009), examining 25 years of its renewal, identified five key decisions that helped shape the area:

- Designating Devonshire Green as open space and creating an urban park
- Allowing inner-city housing in the Quarter
- Opening the Forum (small cafe and shops)
- Designing and building West One (property investor who took a small family approach and also was innovative)
- Forming the Devonshire Quarter association with residents, businesses, the voluntary sector, local organizations and students

This successful example illustrates that communities, planners and developers need to consider place-making as a long-term and evolutionary process, whereby they not only understand the needs of the present, but consider the long-term well-being of the place and its community in the future (see Dempsey et al., 2014, on place-keeping).

In order to assess the needs of a neighborhood, there are now numerous tools that evaluate the physical state of a neighborhood: satellite data, GPS and other data collection systems can offer a means of identifying poor infrastructure, lack of green space and poor routes for mobility, such as cycling and walking. Well-being surveys, such as the well-being data of the Office for National Statistics, and local area health data can be assessed against infrastructure analysis to enable decision-makers to understand where improvements should be made and prioritized. Indeed, it would be possible to create neighborhood plans with well-being targets for the community, set local neighborhood agendas for ensuring places are walkable, provide access to green spaces and trees, and so forth.

Furthermore, local regulations can be taken further. For instance, evidence from the previous section suggests that mental well-being in neighborhoods can be affected by one's sense of safety or fear of crime; thus, in terms of crime prevention, it is clear that designing out crime is a way to address this significant problem in neighborhoods (Davey, Wootton, Cooper, and Press, 2005). Implementing such measures as "target hardening" places (i.e., using materials and landscape design to make access to "criminal intent" difficult) can be set as a mandatory aspect of gaining planning permission. In Greater Manchester, for example, the Design for Security consultancy based within Greater Manchester Police (formerly the Architectural Liaison Unit) assesses large developments to ensure they have given sufficient consideration to such measures before planning permission is approved.

The principles of a health and well-being agenda for a neighborhood to ensure its long-term viability should include:

- *Promoting physical activity and healthy diets*   Design streets and neighborhoods with "traffic calming" measures; provide interconnected street layouts and short blocks, especially to provide a buffer zone between pedestrians, cyclists and traffic to promote walking and cycling; ensure good links to nearby facilities and amenities, especially food stores and health centers; encourage local gardening, local produce and sharing.
- *Designing the neighborhood for children*   Provide space that is safe for children to play in, and ensure we can see the children from inside homes, with windows facing the street; provide parks and open spaces, including play areas, especially those comprising natural elements such as trees, water, and rocks which stimulate creativity; provide dedicated spaces in neighborhoods for teenagers to "hang out."
- *Enabling independence in older age*   In neighborhoods, provide a hierarchy of streets from busier, main streets to quieter, residential ones; ensure footways are wide and smooth, and yet signal danger; provide adequate toilet facilities.
- *Reducing stress*   Design homes with good sound insulation and optimize natural daylight; on the street, optimize the amount of greenery, provide quiet, natural spaces that offer opportunities for rest and retreat; in buildings and in city spaces; provide clear signage and wayfinding cues.
- *Promoting positive mood/emotions*   Design homes where people can feel private, including interesting features where possible; incorporate human-scale details, such as flower boxes and balconies; optimize greenery and views of it, and provide space for conviviality and leisure.

- *Facilitating good relationships*   Design neighborhoods that have shared space and community spaces; enable social networking digitally and physically; provide opportunities for "chatting over the fence."
- *Helping make people feel safe from crime*   Design in good natural surveillance of public spaces; provide adequate street lighting; design places and spaces that are easy to maintain.
- *Reducing the sense of crowding*   Design public spaces that enable people to move through with ease; incorporate landmarks and wayfinding cues in buildings and neighborhoods, such as trees, mailboxes, clocks and towers; design a sense of space either horizontally or vertically.
- *Making moving about easy*   Design public transport systems that are flexible, user friendly and easy to understand, accessible, and that do not pollute; encourage walking and cycling.

Implementing such an agenda will not succeed if it is left to local authorities or private investors. Making such decisions must include the community and individuals who live in the neighborhoods and city; together they must take ownership of their future. However, this is easier said than done, and we need to use the new tools of open democracy and community participation to co-design and co-create these future places. For example, in the city of Lancaster in the north of England, a virtually derelict piece of land around its historic castle needed development. The local authority wanted to consult with the community about how the future of this area should look, feel and function. With the help of Lancaster University, researchers designed a program of community events and activities that involved over 700 people in the creation of common aspirations for the future development of that space. Another project in that city, "Active Parks," brought together local residents, Lancaster City Council and health organizations to co-design a health trail that offered a new way of motivating and making physical activity specific to local people in their park. This included different levels of physical activity that fit into a general walk or dog-walking schedule, the use of new technology to link to further information or perhaps the use of augmented reality and games to make physical activity in parks fun and playful.

Approaches to Thinking about the Future: Foresight

The dangers of co-design and co-creation are the tendency to focus on the well-being and neighborhood concerns of today, rather than in the future. To ensure that the design and decision-making processes in relation to our neighborhoods take into consideration the longer-term issues facing us globally, such as climate change, aging and growing populations, lack of natural resources and energy shortages, we also must use techniques to help professional planners, decision-makers and communities to think long-term, to use foresight techniques (Horizon Scanning Programme, 2014). These may include using future scenarios, which are not forecasts or predictions but plausible, challenging and relevant stories about how the future may unfold (Hunt et al., 2012). Many future scenarios have been created and used by organizations to challenge ideas about the future and plans being made today, to ensure they are more robustly considered against alternative future possibilities.

Of course, the potential for modeling change is increasingly available to communities; there is such a plethora of data about population size, health outcomes, mobilities and other lifestyle indicators that modeling trends for a neighborhood also are a potential approach to foresight and "future proofing" ideas for neighborhood development (Lombardi et al., 2012).

Taking these techniques and data into the community can be useful in enabling "community imagination," and helping communities to undertake "thought experiments" that might produce radical solutions to neighborhood problems. For example, a community could work on how to expand the "sharing economy" to a "sharing neighborhood," enabling them to determine how they could share space, time and skills to make a better neighborhood, and indeed designing one that will support well-being not only for themselves but also for future generations.

The evidence in relation to current research is pretty clear on what we need to do to support well-being in neighborhoods. Future practice and research need to apply a multidisciplinary and community lens to the issues, by adopting action research, informed by retrospective evidence, to enhance well-being in neighborhoods and cities of the future.

References

Agnew, R. (1992). Foundation for a general strain theory of crime and delinquency. *Criminology, 30*(1), 47–87.

Alzheimer's Australia NSW (2011). Building dementia and age-friendly neighbourhoods. Discussion Paper 3. North Ryde, Australia: Alzheimer's Australia NSW.

Barton, J., and Pretty, J. (2010). What is the best dose of nature and green exercise for improving mental health? A multi-study analysis. *Environmental Science and Technology, 44*(10), 3947–3955.

Bell, J. F., Wilson, J. S., and Liu, G. C. (2008). Neighborhood greenness and 2-year changes in body mass index of children and youth. *American Journal of Preventive Medicine, 35*(6), 547–553.

Bernard, J. (1939). The neighborhood behavior of school children in relation to age and socioeconomic status. *American Sociological Review, 4*(5), 652–662.

Booth, A. (1976). *Urban Crowding and Its Consequences*. New York: Praeger.

Borst, H., Miedema, H., de Vries, S., Graham, J., and van Dongen, J. (2008). Relationships between street characteristics and perceived attractiveness for walking reported by elderly people. *Journal of Environmental Psychology, 28*(4), 353–361.

Boyko, C., and Cooper, C. (2009). The urban design decision-making process: Case studies. In R. Cooper, G. Evans, and C. Boyko (Eds.), *Designing Sustainable Cities* (pp. 18–41). Chichester, UK: Wiley-Blackwell.

Boyko, C. T., and Cooper, R. (2014). Density and mental wellbeing. In R. Cooper, E. Burton, and C. L. Cooper (Eds.), *Wellbeing and the Environment*, vol. 2 of *Wellbeing: A Complete Reference Guide* (pp. 69–90). Chichester, UK: Wiley Blackwell.

Bradburn, N. M. (1969). *The Structure of Psychological Well-Being*. Chicago: Aldine.

Bradburn, N. M., and Caplovitz, D. (1965). *Reports on Happiness: A Pilot Study of Behavior Related Mental Health*. Chicago: Aldine.

Bradley, R. H., Whiteside, L., Mundfrom, D. J., Casey, P. H., Kelleher, K., and Pope, S. K. (1994). Early indications of resilience and their relation to experiences in the home environments of low birthweight, premature children living in poverty. *Child Development, 65*(2), 346–360.

Brown, B., Perkins, D., and Brown, G. (2003). Place attachment in a revitalizing neighborhood: Individual and block levels of analysis. *Journal of Environmental Psychology, 23*(3), 259–271.

Brown, S. C., and Lombard, J. (2014). Neighborhoods and social interaction. In R. Cooper, E. Burton, and C. L. Cooper (Eds.), *Wellbeing and the Environment*, vol. 2 of *Wellbeing: A Complete Reference Guide* (pp. 91–117). Chichester, UK: Wiley Blackwell.

Broyles, S., Mowen, A., Theall, K., Gustat, J., and Rung, A. (2011). Integrating social capital into a park-use and active-living framework. *American Journal of Preventive Medicine, 40*(5), 522–529.

Burdette, A. M., Hill, T. D., and Hale, L. (2011). Household disrepair and the mental health of low-income urban women. *Journal of Urban Health, 88*(1), 142–153.

Calderón-Garcidueñas, L., Mora-Tiscareño, A., Ontiveros, E., Gómez-Garcia, G., Barragán-Meija, G., Broadway, J., ... Engle, R. W. (2008). Air pollution, cognitive deficits and brain abnormalities: A pilot study with children and dogs. *Brain and Cognition*, 68(2), 117–127.

Caldwell, L. L., Weichold, K., and Smith, E. A. (2006). Peer influence, substance use and leisure: A cross-cultural comparison. *SUCHT/Journal of Addiction Research and Practice*, 52(4), 261–267.

Calvert, W. J. (2002). Neighborhood disorder, individual protective factors, and the risk of adolescent delinquency. *Association of Black Nursing Faculty Journal*, 13(6), 127–135.

Carmona, M., Heath, T., Oc, T., and Tiesdell, S. (2003). *Public Places Urban Spaces. The Dimensions of Urban Design*. Oxford: Architectural Press.

Chaskin, R. (2006). Defining neighborhoods. In M. S. Lewis and W. R. Klein (Eds.), *Planning and Urban Design Standards* (pp. 409). Hoboken, NJ: John Wiley & Sons.

Cohen, D. A., Inagami, S., and Finch, B. (2008). Non-residential neighborhood exposures suppress neighborhood effects on self-rated health. *Social Science and Medicine*, 65(8), 1779–1791.

Coley, R. L., Sullivan, W. C., and Kuo, F. E. (1997). Where does community grow? *Environment and Behavior*, 29(4), 468–494.

Cooper, R., Boyko, C., and Codinhoto, R. (2008). *Mental capital and Wellbeing and the Physical Environment*. London: Government Office for Science.

Cooper Marcus, C. (2009). Landscape design: Patient-specific healing gardens. At http://www.worldhealthdesign. com/patient-specific-healing-gardens.aspx (accessed July 2016).

Cramer, V., Torgersen, S., and Kringlen, E. (2004). Quality of life in a city: The effect of population density. *Social Indicators Research*, 69(1), 103–116.

Davey, C. L., Wootton, A. B., Cooper, R., and Press, M. (2005). Design against crime: Extending the reach of crime prevention through environmental design. *Security Journal*, 18(2), 39–51.

Day, R. (2008a). Local environments and older people's health: Dimensions from a comparative qualitative study in Scotland. *Health and Place*, 14(2), 299–312.

Day, R. (2008b). *Local Urban Environments and the Wellbeing of Older People*. Glasgow: Scottish Centre for Research on Social Justice.

Dempsey, N., Brown, C., and Bramley, G. (2012). The key to sustainable urban development in UK cities? The influence of density on social sustainability. *Progress in Planning*, 77(3), 89–141.

Dempsey, N., Smith, H., and Burton, M. (Eds.) (2014). *Place-Keeping: Open Space Management in Practice*. London: Routledge.

Derr, V. L. (2001). Voices from the mountains: Children's sense of place in three communities of northern New Mexico. Thesis, Yale University.

De Vries, S. I., Bakker, I., van Mechelen, W., and Hopman-Rock, M. (2007). Determinants of activity-friendly neighborhoods for children: Results from the SPACE study. *American Journal of Health Promotion*, 21(4S), 312–316.

DfT and DCLG (2007). *Manual for Streets*. London: Department for Transport and Department for Communities and Local Government.

Dodge, R., Daly, A. P., Huyton, J., and Sanders, L. D. (2012). The challenge of defining wellbeing. *International Journal of Wellbeing*, 2(3), 222–235.

Duvall, D., and Booth, A. (1978). The housing environment and women's health. *Journal of Health and Social Behavior*, 19(4), 410–417.

Ellaway, A., and Macintyre, S. (2009). Are perceived neighbourhood problems associated with the likelihood of smoking? *Journal of Epidemiology and Community Health*, 63(1), 78–80.

Ereaut, G., and Whiting, R. (2008). *What Do We Mean by 'Wellbeing'? And Why Might It Matter?* Research Report No. DCSF-RW073. London: Department for Children, Schools and Families.

Essen, J., Fogelman, K., and Head, J. (1978). Children's housing and their health and physical development. *Child: Care, Health and Development*, 4(6), 357–369.

Evans, G. (2014). Living in the city: Mixed use and quality of life. In R. Cooper, E. Burton, and C. L. Cooper (Eds.), *Wellbeing and the Environment*, vol. 2 of *Wellbeing: A Complete Reference Guide* (pp. 119–146). Chichester, UK: Wiley Blackwell.

Evans, G. W., Lepore, S., Shejwal, B. R., and Palsane, M. N. (1998). Chronic residential crowding and children's well being: An ecological perspective. *Child Development*, 69(6), 1514–1523.

Evans, G. W., and Saegert, S. (2000). Residential crowding in the context of inner city poverty. In S. Wapner, J. Demick, H. Minami, and T. Yamamoto (Eds.), *Theoretical Perspectives in Environment-Behavior Research: Underlying Assumptions, Research Problems, and Methodologies* (pp. 247–268). New York: Plenum.

Evenson, K. R., Scott, M. M., Cohen, D. A., and Vorhees, C. C. (2007). Girls' perception of neighborhood factors on physical activity, sedentary behavior, and BMI. *Obesity*, *15*(2), 430–445.

Fan, Y., Das, K., and Chen, Q. (2011). Neighborhood green, social support, physical activity, and stress: Assessing the cumulative impact. *Health and Place*, *17*(6), 1202–1211.

Faris, R. E. L., and Dunham, H. W. (1939). *Mental Disorders in Urban Areas: An Ecological Study of Schizophrenia and Other Psychoses*. Chicago: University of Chicago Press.

Farrell, S. J., Aubry, T., and Coulombe, D. (2004). Neighborhoods and neighbors: Do they contribute to personal well-being? *Journal of Community Psychology*, *32*(1), 9–25.

Flowerdew, R., Manley, D. J., and Sabel, C. E. (2008). Neighbourhood effects on health: Does it matter where you draw the boundaries? *Social Science and Medicine*, *66*(6), 1241–1255.

Foster, S., and Giles-Corti, B. (2008). The built environment, neighborhood crime and constrained physical activity: An exploration of inconsistent research findings. *Preventive Medicine*, *47*(3), 241–251.

Foster, S., Giles-Corti, B., and Knuiman, M. (2010). Neighbourhood design and fear of crime: A social-ecological examination of the correlates of residents' fear in new suburban housing developments. *Health and Place*, *16*(6), 1156–1165.

Foster, S., Giles-Corti, B., and Knuiman, M. (2011). Creating safe walkable streetscapes: Does house design and upkeep discourage incivilities in suburban neighbourhoods. *Journal of Environmental Psychology*, *31*(1), 79–88.

Foster, S., Wood, L., Francis, J., Knuiman, M., Villanueva, K., and Giles-Corti, B. (2015). Suspicious minds: Can features of the local neighbourhood ease parents' fears about stranger danger. *Journal of Environmental Psychology*, *42*, 48–56. doi:10.1016/j.jenvp.2015.02.001

Gabe, J., and Williams, P. (1993). Women, crowding and mental health. In R. Burridge and D. Ormandy (Eds.), *Unhealthy Housing: Research, Remedies and Reform* (pp. 137–149). London: E. and F. N. Spon.

Galea, S., and Vlahov, D. (2005). Urban health: Evidence, challenges, and directions. *Annual Review of Public Health*, *26*, 341–365.

Galster, G. (2001). On the nature of neighbourhood. *Urban Studies*, *38*(12), 2111–2124.

Gilbert, E., and Galea, S. (2014). Urban neighborhoods and mental health across the life course. In R. Cooper, E. Burton, and C. L. Cooper (Eds.), *Wellbeing and the Environment*, vol. 2 of *Wellbeing: A Complete Reference Guide* (pp. 23–50). Chichester, UK: Wiley Blackwell.

Gillis, K., and Gatersleben, B. (2015). A review of psychological literature on the health and wellbeing benefits of biophilic design. *Buildings*, *5*(3), 948–963.

Gómez-Jacinto, L., and Hombrados-Mendieta, I. (2002). Multiple effects of community and household crowding. *Journal of Environmental Psychology*, *22*(3), 233–246.

Gottfried, A. W., and Gottfried, A. E. (1984). Home environment and cognitive development in young children of middle-socioeconomic-status families. In A. W. Gottfried (Ed.), *Home Environment and Cognitive Development* (pp. 57–115). New York: Academic Press.

Government Office for Science (2008). *Foresight Mental Capital and Wellbeing Project*. London: Government Office for Science.

Grabosky, P. N. (1995). Fear of crime, and fear reduction strategies. *Current Issues in Criminal Justice*, *7*(1), 417–424.

Gruenberg, E. M. (1954). Community conditions and psychoses of the elderly. *American Journal of Psychiatry*, *110*(12), 888–896.

Halpern, D. (1995). *Mental Health and the Environment: More Bricks Than Mortar?* Oxford: Taylor & Francis.

Hartig, T. (2008). Green space, psychological restoration, and health inequality. *Lancet*, *372*(9650), 1614–1615.

Hartig, T., Book, A., Garvill, J., Olsson, T., and Garling, T. (1996). Environmental influences on psychological restoration. *Scandinavian Journal of Psychology*, *37*(4), 378–393.

Hassan, R. (1977). Social and psychological implications of high population density. *Civilisations*, *27*(3/4), 228–244.

Haynes, E. N., Chen, A., Ryan, P., Succop, P., Wright, J., and Dietrich, K. N. (2011). Exposure to airborne metals and particulate matter and risk for youth adjudicated for criminal activity. *Environmental Research*, *111*(8), 1243–1248.

Headey, B., Holström, E., and Wearing, A. (1984). Well-being and ill-being: Different dimensions? *Social Indicators Research*, *14*(2), 115–139.

Headey, B., Holström, E., and Wearing, A. (1985). Models of well-being and ill-being. *Social Indicators Research*, *17*(3), 211–234.

Hill, T. D., Burdette, A. M., Jokinen-Gordon, H. M., and Brailsford, J. M. (2013). Neighborhood disorder, social support, and self-esteem: Evidence from a sample of low-income women living in three cities. *Cities and Community*, *12*(4), 380–395.

HM Government (2011a). *Healthy Lives, Healthy People: Update and Way Forward*. Cm 8134. London: Department of Health.

HM Government (2011b). *Laying the Foundations: A Housing Strategy for England*. London: Department for Communities and Local Government.

Horizon Scanning Programme (2014). *The Futures Toolkit: Tools for Strategic Futures for Policy-Makers and Analysts*. London: HM Government.

Hunt, D. V. L., Lombardi D. L., Atkinson S., Barber, A. R. G., Barnes M., Boyko, C. T., ... Rogers, C. D. F. (2012). Scenario archetypes: Converging rather than diverging themes. *Sustainability*, *4*(4), 740–772.

Hüttenmoser, M. (1995). Children and their living surroundings: Empirical investigation into the significance of living surroundings for the everyday life and development of children. *Children's Environments*, *12*(4), 403–413.

Ineichen, B. (1993). *Homes and Health: How Housing and Health Interact*. London: E. and F. N. Spon.

Kaczynski, A., and Glover, T. (2012). Talking the talk, walking the walk: Examining the effect of neighbourhood walkability and social connectedness on physical activity. *Journal of Public Health*, *34*(3), 382–389.

Karriker-Jaffe, K. J., Foshee, V. A., and Ennett, S. T. (2011). Examining how neighborhood disadvantage influences trajectories of adolescent violence: A look at social bonding and psychological distress. *Journal of School Health*, *81*(12), 764–773.

Keane, W., and Shoesmith, J. (2005). Creating the ideal person-centered program and environment for residential dementia care: Ten steps and ten challenges toward a new culture. *Alzheimer's Care Quarterly*, *6*(4), 316–324.

Kellett, J. M. (1984). Crowding and territoriality: A psychiatric view. In H. Freeman (Ed.), *Mental Health and the Environment* (pp. 71–96). Edinburgh: Churchill Livingstone.

Kelling, G. L., and Wilson, J. Q. (1982). Broken windows: The police and neighborhood safety. *Atlantic Monthly* (Mar.), 29–38.

Knopf, K. (2001). *Stratford-on-Avon District Design Guide*. Issue 1. Stratford-on-Avon, UK: Stratford-on-Avon District Council.

Korpela, K., Kyttä, M., and Hartig, T. (2002). Restorative experience, self-regulation, and children's place preferences. *Journal of Environmental Psychology*, *22*(4), 387–398.

Kruger, D. J., Reischl, T. M., and Gee, G. C. (2007). Neighborhood social conditions mediate the association between physical deterioration and mental health. *American Journal of Community Psychology*, *40*(3–4), 261–271.

Küller, R., and Lindsten, C. (1992). Health and behavior of children in classrooms with and without windows. *Journal of Environmental Psychology*, *12*(4), 305–317.

Kuo, F. E. (1992). Inner cities and chronic mental fatigue. In E. Arias and M. Gross (Eds.), *EDRA 23/1992: Equitable and Sustainable Habitats: Proceedings of the Environmental Design Research Association Annual Conference*. Boulder, CO: Environmental Design Research Association.

Kuo, F. E., and Taylor, A. F. (2004). A potential natural treatment for attention-deficit/hyperactivity disorder: Evidence from a national study. *American Journal of Public Health*, *94*(9), 1580–1586.

Lawton, M. P., and Nahemow, L. (1979). Social areas and the wellbeing of tenants in housing for the elderly. *Multivariate Behavioral Research*, *14*(4), 463–484.

Lawton, M. P., Nahemow, L., and Yeh, T.-M. (1980). Neighborhood environment and the wellbeing of older tenants in planned housing. *International Journal of Aging and Human Development*, *11*(3), 221–227.

Leyden, K. M. (2003). Social capital and the built environment: The importance of walkable neighborhoods. *American Journal of Public Health*, *93*(9), 1546–1551.

Li, F., Fisher, K. J., Brownson, R., and Bosworth, M. (2005) Multilevel modelling of built environment characteristics related to neighbourhood walking activity in older adults. *Journal of Epidemiology and Public Health*, *59*(7), 558–564.

Liu, G. C., Wilson, J. S., Qi, R., and Ying, J. (2007). Green neighborhoods, food retail and childhood overweight: Differences by population density. *American Journal of Health Promotion*, *21*(4S), 317–325.

Lombardi, D. R., Leach, J. M., Rogers, C. D. F., Aston, R., Barber, A., Boyko, C. T ... Whyatt, J. D. (2012). *Designing Resilient Cities. A Guide to Good Practice*. Bracknell, UK: IHS BRE Press.

Lund, H. (2002). Pedestrian environments and sense of community. *Journal of Planning Education and Research*, *21*(3), 301–312.

Lund, H. (2003). Testing the claims of New Urbanism: Local access, pedestrian travel, and neighboring behaviors. *Journal of the American Planning Association*, *69*(4), 414–429.

Martin, K. E., and Wood, L. J. (2014). "We live here too" ... What makes a child-friendly neighborhood? In R. Cooper, E. Burton, and C. L. Cooper (Eds.), *Wellbeing and the Environment*, vol. 2 of *Wellbeing: A Complete Reference Guide* (pp. 147–184). Chichester, UK: Wiley Blackwell.

McMillan, T. E. (2007). The relative influence of urban form on a child's travel mode to school. *Transportation Research Part A: Policy and Practice, 41*(1), 69–79.

Milligan, C., and Bingley, A. (2007). Restorative places or scary spaces? The impact of woodland on the mental well-being of young adults. *Health and Place, 13*(4), 799–811.

Moore, R. C. (1986). *Childhood's Domain: Play and Place in Child Development*. London: Croom Helm.

Mullen, E. (2003). Do you think that your local area is a good place for young people to grow up? The effects of traffic and car parking on young people's views. *Health and Place, 9*(4), 351–360.

Nyman, J. (2002). Does unemployment contribute to ill-being: Results from a panel study among adult Finns, 1989/90 and 1997. Doctoral thesis, University of Helsinki.

Paulus, P. B., McCain, G., and Cox, V. C. (1978). Death rates, psychiatric commitments, blood pressure and perceived crowding as a function of institutional crowding. *Environmental Psychology and Nonverbal Behavior, 3*(2), 107–116.

Peace, S., Holland, C., and Kellaher, L. (2006). *Environment and Identity in Later Life*. Maidenhead: Open University Press.

Perkins, D. D., and Taylor, R. B. (1996). Ecological assessments of community disorder: Their relationship to fear of crime and theoretical implications. *American Journal of Community Psychology, 24*(1), 63–107.

Prezza, M., Alparone, F. R., Cristallo, C., and Luigi, S. (2005). Parental perception of social risk and of positive potentiality of outdoor autonomy for children: The development of two instruments. *Journal of Environmental Psychology, 25*(4), 437–453.

Ratanapojnard, S. (2001). Community oriented biodiversity environmental education: Its effects on knowledge, values, and behavior among rural fifth- and sixth- grade students in northeastern Thailand. Doctoral dissertation, School of Forestry and Environmental Studies, Yale University.

Ross, C., and Jang, S. (2000). Neighborhood disorder, fear, and mistrust: The buffering role of social ties with neighbors. *American Journal of Community Psychology, 20*(4), 401–420.

Saegert, S. (1982). Environment and children's mental health: Residential density and low-income children. In A. Baum, and J. E., Singer (Eds.), *Handbook of Psychology and Health* (pp. 247–271). Hillsdale, NJ: Erlbaum.

Saelens, B. E., Sallis, J. F., Black, J. B., and Chen, D. (2003). Neighborhood-based differences in physical activity: An environment scale evaluation. *American Journal of Public Health, 93*(9), 1552–1558.

Sampson, R. J., and Groves, W. B. (1989). Community structure and crime: Testing social-disorganization theory. *American Journal of Sociology, 94*(4), 774–802.

Sampson, R. J., Raudenbush, S. W., and Earls, F. (1997). Neighborhoods and violent crime: A multilevel study of collective efficacy. *Science, 277*(5328), 918–924.

Scheff, T. J. (1999). *Being Mentally Ill*, 3rd edn. New York: Aldine de Gruyter.

SDC (Sustainable Development Commission) (2008). *Health, Place and Nature: How Outdoor Environments Influence Health and Well-Being: A Knowledge Base*. London: Sustainable Development Commission.

Silburn, S. R., Zubrick, S. R., De Maio, J. A., Shepherd, C., Griffin, J. A., Mitrou, F. G., ... Pearson, G. (2006). *The Western Australian Aboriginal Child Health Survey: Strengthening the Capacity of Aboriginal Children, Families and Communities*. Perth, Australia: Curtin University of Technology and Telethon Institute for Child Health Research.

Talen, E. (1999). Sense of community and neighborhood form: An assessment of the social doctrine of New Urbanism. *Urban Studies, 36*(8), 1361–1379.

Taylor, A. F., Kuo, F. E., and Sullivan, W. C. (2001). Coping with ADD. *Environment and Behavior, 33*(1), 54–77.

Thomas, J. (2009). Current measures and the challenges of measuring children's well-being. Working Paper. Newport, UK: Office for National Statistics.

Torrington, J., and Tregenza, P. (2007). Lighting for people with dementia. *Lighting Research and Technology, 39*(1), 81–97.

Waters, J., Neale, R., and Mears, K. (2008). *Design and Community Regeneration: Older People in Socio-economically Deprived Communities in South Wales*. Reading, UK: Strategic Promotion of Ageing Research Capacity.

Wells, N. M., and Evans, G. W. (2003). Nearby nature: A buffer of life stress among rural children. *Environment and Behavior, 35*(3), 311–330.

Wilson, N., Syme, S. L., Boyce, W. T., Battistitch, V. A., and Selvin, S. (2005). Adolescent alcohol, tobacco, and marijuana use: The influence of neighborhood disorder and hope. *American Journal of Health Promotion, 20*(1), 11–19.

Wood, L., Frank, L., and Giles-Corti, B. (2010). Sense of community and its relationship with walking and neighborhood design. *Social Science and Medicine, 70*(9), 1381–1390.

Wood, L., and Giles-Corti, B. (2008). Is there a place for social capital in the psychology of health and place? *Journal of Environmental Psychology, 28*(2), 154–163.

Wood, L., Giles-Corti, B., and Bulsara, M. (2012). Streets apart: Does social capital vary with neighbourhood design? *Urban Studies Research, 2012,* 1–11.

Wood, L., Giles-Corti, B., Zubrick, S., and Bulsara, M. (2011). "Through the kids … we connected with our community": Children as catalysts of social capital. *Environment and Behavior, 45*(3), 344–368.

Young, M., and Willmott, P. (1957). *Family and Kinship in East London.* London: Routledge & Kegan Paul.

Zubrick, S., Wood, L., Villanueva, K., Wood, G., Giles-Corti, B., and Christian, H. (2010). *Nothing But Fear Itself? Parental Fear as a Determinant Impacting on Child Physical Activity and Independent Mobility.* Melbourne: Victorian Health Promotion Foundation.

35

Creating Workplace Well-Being

Time for Practical Wisdom

Joel B. Bennett, John Weaver, Mim Senft, and Michael Neeper

> Knowledge consists of knowing that a tomato is a fruit, and wisdom consists of not putting it in a fruit salad.
>
> Miles Kington

Growing interest in workplace well-being suggests a potential paradigm shift in how society thinks about and treats worker health. Such interest is prompted, in part, by studies showing that well-being can lead to more engaged and productive workers (Bryson, Forth and Stokes, 2014; Lockwood, 2007; SHRM, 2015). At some intrinsic level, work is by itself health producing. In their best evidence synthesis of dozens of studies, Waddell and Burton (2006) conclude that work is generally good for physical health and mental well-being, worklessness is associated with the opposite, and work can reverse the adverse health effects of unemployment. But many workers aspire to more than just acceptable conditions; well-being can mean more than productivity, job functioning, or job satisfaction (cf. satisficing, Schwartz et al., 2002). By most definitions, well-being goes beyond merely coping and includes optimism, a meaningful life, prosperity and success, thriving and flourishing (Dodge, Daly, Huyton, and Sanders, 2012). Clearly, well-being can manifest at different levels of human functioning, from the basic needs provided by safe employment (Hoffmeister, Gibbons, Schwatka, and Rosecrance, 2015) to the expression of virtues/character strengths (Kaufman, 2015), as well as the self-actualization and fulfillment of a meaningful vocation (Milliman, Czaplewski, and Ferguson, 2003) or integrating spirituality with work (Cunningham, 2014). This chapter examines how workplace conditions help workers grow across these levels, with the goal of helping workplace managers and leaders wisely use existing knowledge (evidence) to create or leverage those conditions.

The Handbook of Stress and Health: A Guide to Research and Practice, First Edition.
Edited by Cary L. Cooper and James Campbell Quick.
© 2017 John Wiley & Sons, Ltd. Published 2017 by John Wiley & Sons, Ltd.

Indeed, studies show certain workplace conditions further optimize or support the health-producing function of work. In particular, experiencing a sense of control, social support, and low job strain predict feelings of well-being (Stansfeld et al., 2013), and well-being can be facilitated by positive work practices and interventions (Czabala and Charzynska, 2014; McDaid and Park, 2014), such that employees may experience higher levels of thriving in the face of positive challenges (Bakker and Demerouti, 2008; Spreitzer and Porath, 2013). Most research on creating workplace well-being suggests that there are certain limiting and facilitative conditions (contextual factors) – within the individual, workplace, economy, and community – that significantly influence (a) the relationship between work and well-being, (b) the effects of working conditions on well-being, and (c) the effectiveness of workplace interventions. This emerging holistic view is critical to understand for anyone who is looking for a panacea or single solution to creating well-being at work (Karanika-Murray and Weyman, 2013).

The field of workplace well-being will stagnate unless workplace decision-makers (those who can use knowledge) have an articulate understanding – or "wisdom" – of these contextual factors (see "Managerial Wisdom" below). If the research is clear about anything, it is that workplace conditions and interventions do not function like a pill or drug that has a singular effect on a targeted disease. Scientific knowledge may be best used to advise employers on *how* to wisely and strategically approach setting up those conditions and interventions rather than *directing them* to a single or "best" solution. Because the target is the workplace or work setting itself, time should be spent on understanding the motives of leaders, enculturation and capacity building (motivating, appealing to values, setting the stage, preparation, engaging stakeholders), rather than on moving too quickly to implement a particular intervention (Trice and Beyer, 1993). Indeed, rapid market growth of workplace interventions to promote health can lead employers to have a commoditized view of programs, with unrealistic expectations of success, and potential unintended consequences (e.g., prematurely abandoning a program) (Goetzel et al., 2014; Mattke et al., 2013).

Thus, while this chapter reviews studies and practices showing that it is possible to create well-being in the workplace, we are careful to place these in a broader context rather than establish a simple box-and-arrow causal model showing "what works." Indeed, reviews point to the effectiveness of diverse well-being programs on diverse populations (e.g., Bolier et al., 2013; Czabala and Charzynska, 2014; Goetzel et al., 2014; Harter, Schmidt, and Keyes, 2003; Mazzucchelli, Kane, and Rees, 2010), but there has been no systematic dissemination, translational research, or advice that can help worksite decision-makers use extant knowledge. By all appearances, researchers have been inordinately busy in accumulating knowledge without much to show in learning how to help worksite leaders apply these insights with wisdom.

Chapter Organization

The chapter is organized in three sections. Section 1 discusses key issues that need to be articulated: agreement on definition of well-being; understanding employer motives for adopting programs; and some understanding of how extant evidence and research is translated into practice and how effective practices can be further researched for refinement. Following this discussion, we offer a guiding framework to help researchers discuss possible approaches to creating well-being with wisdom.

Section 2 reviews three types of evidence for efforts to create workplace well-being: findings from the past ten years of work with the Psychologically Healthy Workplace Program of the American Psychological Association (APA); a review of practices in the use of human resources and benefits management that employers often rely upon to make decisions about programs; and a synthesis of quantitative findings that show which workplace factors are associated with well-being, and what type of programs can be effective. The goal of section 2 is to identify key practices.

Following from these previous sections – our review of disparate issues and information sources – the authors discerned a level of coherence in the field that is often overlooked. One purpose of this chapter is to align these different findings into a coherent framework that can be used in real-world settings. Hence, section 3 takes the information reviewed in the previous sections to deduce and identify key leverage points that can help employers create well-being at work. Importantly, we do not provide a singular list of tips as much as guidance on how to leverage the conditions necessary to make interventions, benefits, human resources, and all possible resources activate or catalyze well-being. Our goal is to make such guidance useful to three primary stakeholders: practitioners of wellness, health promotion, and employee assistance; employers; and the researchers who can help apply studies for optimal benefit.

Managerial Wisdom

The past few decades have seen significant growth in the psychological and management literature (both theoretical and empirical) on the topic of wisdom, too much to review here (e.g., Kessler, and Bailey, 2007; Nonaka, Chia, Holt, and Peltokorpi, 2014; Sternberg, 2003). For purposes of this chapter, we rely on McKenna, Rooney, and Boal's (2009) meta-theoretical model as it provides a careful synthesis of the literature to extract five key principles or propositions about wise leadership. They are summarized here (see original article for detailed wording):

1. Wise leaders use reason and careful observation to establish facts and reach correct conclusions.
2. Wise leaders allow for nonrational and subjective elements when making decisions, including spirituality, vision, insight, and foresight. They may sometimes go with their gut.
3. Wise leaders value humane and virtuous outcomes and produce virtuous and tolerant decisions.
4. Wise leaders and their actions are practical and oriented toward everyday life, including work.
5. Wise leaders are articulate, understand the aesthetic dimension of their work, and seek the intrinsic personal and social rewards of contributing to the good life.

These propositions are summarized here as preparation and contextualization for the following chapter sections. Clearly, decision-makers can review the knowledge in this chapter and correctly conclude that well-being programs work (Principle 1) but may never use programs or ideas, or use them ineffectively because they lack foresight (Principle 2), fail to see the virtue of the effort (Principle 3), or lack practical guidance (Principle 4). Alternatively, some business leaders may be very strong advocates and champions of well-being for its intrinsic value (Principle 5) and widely implement practices, without ever looking at the research

(Principle 1). This latter point is important for researchers to acknowledge; the qualitative evidence below suggests that the majority of real-world decisions around well-being efforts may have more to do with values and nonrational factors than evidence-based deductions. Either way, our hope is that the following sections inspire readers to integrate all five principles in their quest to create well-being in the workplaces that they either lead, study, work in or consult for.

Key Issues

Definitions

A myriad of disciplinary perspectives have offered a definition of well-being: positive psychology researchers (Denier, Suh, Lucas, and Smith, 1999; Seligman, 2011), National Institute for Occupational Safety and Health (Schulte et al., 2015), the Centers for Disease Control (2016), the OECD (2013), the World Health Organization (2016), the Canadian Standards Association (2013) and the New Economics Foundation (Jeffrey, Abdallah, and Michaelson, 2014), to name just a few. A synthesis of these perspectives indicates that well-being is a complex and temporally dynamic mixture of factors across different areas or domains of living.

Well-being factors include the *provision of an adequate environment*, including access to food, shelter, clothing, and financial stability as well as reasonable levels of security from harm. It includes positive physical health, as expressed by more than the absence of disease but also the presence of enough energy and strength to meet environmental demands. It involves *a healthy psychological state* that includes the ability to make flexible psychological adaptations to the external environment, the ability to act with some autonomy and self-direction in life and the opportunity to express talents. An individual experiencing well-being is able to *establish mutually supportive relationships* in which the opportunity to give to others is as essential as the opportunity to receive support. And it includes the ability to *live a purposeful and meaningful life*.

Well-being may not be achieved in a unitary or simultaneous fashion in all domains of an individual's life. In particular, the workplace is only one arena where an individual may attain a state of well-being. A person may voluntarily submit to circumstances that impinge on his or her well-being in one environment (e.g., a highly demanding work load) in an attempt to enhance a sense of well-being in another arena (e.g., time with family). Each individual may experience well-being and the contribution of work to well-being, therefore, in idiosyncratic ways. The complexity of this definition, then, recognizes that well-being may not be equally achieved across the environmental, physical, psychological, social, and spiritual domains of life. Accordingly, well-being includes some determination of what is most valuable in life. It is possible that an individual worker experiences well-being in all of his or her life domains. It is also possible that many workers allocate resources to one or more domains (environmental, physical, psychological, social, and spiritual) *in accord with the most deeply held values* of that individual, even if it results in suboptimal functioning in other domains.

These efforts to achieve well-being include a temporal dimension. The work toward optimal functioning in one or more of these domains may provide the experience of well-being drawn from a sense of making progress toward a hoped-for outcome. In other words, the movement toward optimal functioning may provide the experience of well-being even when optimal functioning is not yet achieved.

Our definition of well-being, then, is distinctly process oriented and one in which the individual is able (i.e., has the *potential*) to achieve or be actively working toward optimal functioning in one or more of the environmental, physical, psychological, social, or spiritual domains of life in accord with his or her deeply held values.

In this definition, the workplace can and often will be a place where the effort to achieve well-being is encountered. The well-being of employees, further, is not antithetical to organizational success. The two are often inextricably intertwined. To the extent that workers who achieve or attempt to achieve optimal functioning foster organizational success (and research suggests as much; e.g., Peterson et al., 2011), the workplace must support the well-being of employees to be able to reach its maximum potential.

Overlapping constructs   In the interest of fostering wisdom, the definition provided here should not be restrictive or semantically rigid. There is a growing body of research on a wide variety of related constructs that correlate with, overlap with, or subserve well-being. This includes mindfulness (Brown and Ryan, 2003), resilience (Fletcher and Sarkar, 2013; Spangler, Koesten, Fox, and Radel, 2012), psychological capital (Avey, Luthans, Smith, and Palmer, 2010), sense of coherence (Nilsson, Andersson, Ejlertsson, and Troein, 2012), hardiness (Abdollahi, Talib, Yaacob, and Ismail, 2014), and self-leadership (Stewart, Courtright, and Manz, 2011). It also includes the relationship between well-being and worker engagement (Shuck and Reio, 2014). When initially advising and consulting with leaders or designers of well-being programs, it is important to not get caught up in semantics or let academic concerns about construct validity get in the way. Better to find those meanings that appeal to wise action; whatever works! At the same time, familiarity with these other constructs can guide well-being designs in ways that might be the best fit for a particular situation.

Employer Motives for Adapting Practices

Employer motives for adopting well-being or prevention practices are complex and influenced by many factors: leader upbringing and personality, leader ability to articulate the employee value proposition, local business and public health needs, industry norms, as well as historical and economic context (cf. HERO, 2015; Partnership for Prevention, 2014; Winkelman Consulting, 2002). This section provides a preliminary understanding by framing motivation within three approaches that often overlap with each other.

The humanitarian approach   The connection between an engaged, resilient workforce and a profitable company is not a new concept. Many enlightened business owners in the early 1900s understood that the benefits of supporting their employees' well-being beyond a salary could positively impact the profitability of their company. One example is John Wanamaker of Wanamaker's department stores, whose flagship store was in Philadelphia. Wanamaker offered employees access to the John Wanamaker Commercial Institute (employee education), free medical care, recreational facilities (Camp Wanamaker), profit-sharing plans, and pensions – long before these types of benefits were considered standard in corporate employment. A review of Wanamaker's biography (Lach, 2000) suggests that he was a man of strong religious faith who earned success from humble beginnings and whose support of employees was significantly motivated by character and virtue: his own faith, upbringing, and resilience.

Fast forward to 2010, when the *Harvard Business Review* (Berry, Mirabito, and Baun, 2010) defined workplace wellness as "an organized, employer-sponsored program that is designed to support employees (and, sometimes, their families) as they adopt and sustain behaviors that reduce health risks, improve quality of life, enhance personal effectiveness, and benefit the organization's bottom line." By this definition, wellness and profit are intertwined. Many executives often need this connection to be very explicit; that is, in terms of return on investment (ROI). A recent survey of executives indicates that workforce health is not rated among the top drivers of productivity or performance, although leaders believe health is a significant contributor (HERO, 2015). ROI is seen as a way of measuring such contribution because it's the standard measurement from a business perspective; for the given use of money, CEOs need to know how much profit or cost saving is realized as a result. In concept, ROI is a driver for most business decisions. Many of the programs put in place by companies to address wellness/well-being for employees and, in some cases, their families, have focused exclusively on ROI. As a result, a variety of wellness ROI calculator tools have been made available to help justify investments (Bennett, 2009).

The return-on-investment approach   Recent increases in health insurance benefits costs is a primary reason companies in the United States have taken an ROI approach. This has led financial executives to focus on reducing health benefit claims costs by targeting workers with the highest claims risk, that is, those with the highest claims costs. The 2008 economic recession further highlighted employer motivation to get employees and their dependents healthier, specifically in order to lower the cost of employee benefits spend. Human resource "Benefits Plan Designs" were created, such as high deductible plans designs, in-network only plan designs, and a reduction in overall benefits available to employees (Rosenbloom, 2011).

These efforts helped lower employer costs in the short term, but with a growing recognition that changing plan design does not necessarily impact employee health. Many wellness programs also focused on health risk assessments and diet and exercise activities, providing measureable incentives for participation and sometimes insurance penalties for nonparticipation. Increased use of incentives and penalties were adopted to drive better ROI of the programs (Volpp, Asch, Galvin, and Loewenstein, 2011). It should be emphasized that a number of research reviews indicated that wellness programs – if designed well – can be effective and produce a significant ROI (e.g., Baicker, Cutler, and Song, 2010; Baxter et al., 2014; Bolnick, Millard, and Dugas, 2013; Chapman, 2012). In a review of this and related literature, a report from the RAND Corporation (Mattke et al., 2013) suggested that while ROI may not always be realized, the report emphasized the critical importance of attending to many contextual factors to enhance success.

The value-on-investment approach   Many of the aforementioned benefits-design efforts either failed to provide the hoped for ROI or the sustainable healthy lifestyles that drove claims costs. This may be due, in large part, to a failure to pay attention to the importance of well-designed, comprehensive, and multicomponent interventions that underlie the ROI studies (Goetzel et al., 2014). Recently, employers have growing recognition of many complex factors that influence workplaces and employee health, leading them to consider a broader approach that subsumes ROI as one of several motives for program adoption (Global Wellness Institute, 2015). Such factors include the need to work with an aging workforce, recognition of mental health issues, the impact of 24/7 work weeks and associated technologies that burden workers, remote workers, and environmental factors. To address these factors holistically, employers are starting to embrace the value of investment (VOI) of their well-being programs (Grossmeier, Terry, and Anderson, 2014).

The concept of VOI was introduced by Gartner, an information technology research and advisory company (Harris, Grey, and Rozwell, 2001). Their definition of VOI is: "intangible assets that contribute heavily to an organization's performance. These intangible assets include knowledge, processes, the organizational structure, and ability to collaborate. Where ROI is the measure of the tangible benefits of a project or activity, VOI is the measure of the intangible benefits of a project or an activity. VOI includes ROI."

These intangibles include a culture that impacts attracting and retaining talent, systems that engage employees, and resources that support employee health beyond benefits. From a VOI perspective, employee engagement may become a more important prerequisite or foundation for participation in well-being efforts (SHRM, 2015). Business leaders are starting to recognize that high-performing employees require support and an environment to work at peak level, no different from a winning athletic team. VOI means more than money. It's the unexpected benefit of investing in the workforce to support employees' sense of purpose, values and inclusion in the goals and vision of the company (Albrecht et al., 2015). Both ROI and VOI are now being seeing in the broader context of the employee value proposition (EVP).

An integrated approach (humanitarian + ROI + VOI)   A synthesis of the above motives in the context of wisdom suggests that an integrated approach is likely the most optimal approach. Some leaders will be motivated more by one approach than another (e.g., "show me the money" vs. "I want to do the right thing"). However, most leaders are motivated by all factors to some degree, wherein some motives come more to the foreground at different times than do others. To make the best use of evidence, knowledge, and information about "what works," leaders should pay attention to their inner motivations. They should be wary if they are just looking to either only achieve ROI, only pursue VOI, or only do it for the virtue of the effort. In the world of business, a requisite balance is needed.

Evidence-Based? A Note on Research to Practice

It is entirely possible that some leaders will make decisions entirely independent of the motives just reviewed. As noted above in the principles of McKenna and colleagues'(2009), "wise leaders … establish facts" and will look for strong evidence that something works. However, despite a significant body of research literature on workplace health, wellness, and well-being practices, it is not often the case that findings lead directly to employer guidelines on practices (Ryan, McPeck, and Chapman, 2011). More often, commercial factors (sales, insurance, cost) or normative factors (professional friendships, industry norms, business association messages, local access) dictate what types of programs or strategies are used. To be concise, the field could benefit from a set of agreed upon guidelines for implementing evidence-based programs in work settings (cf. Aarons, Hurlburt, and Horwitz, 2011; Briner and Walshe, 2015). The purpose of this chapter is not to discuss the challenges associated with the development or adherence to such guidelines, but interested readers might like to view the National Registry of Evidence-Based Prevention Programs and Practices in the United States (SAMHSA, 2016) or the Cochrane Reviews (i.e., Cochrane, 2015).

Using Evidence: The Need of a Guiding Framework

Following from above, there is a vast array of factors that can influence why, when, and how worksites implement well-being initiatives, and these factors will influence the degree to which

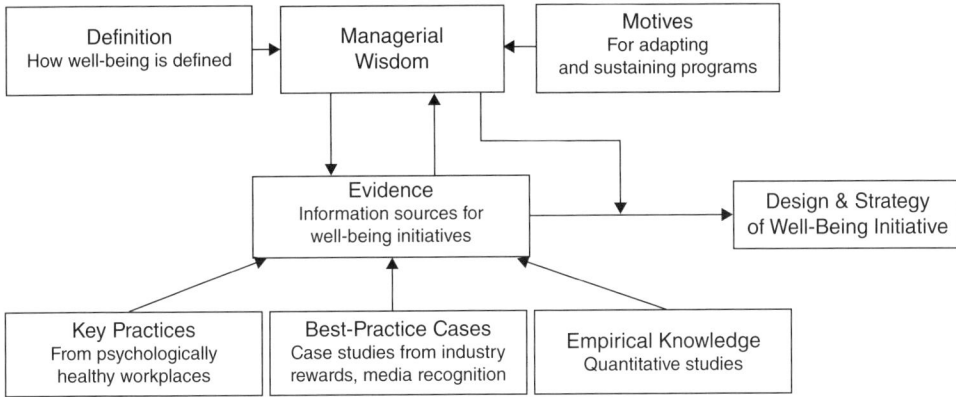

Figure 35.1 Framework for understanding the impact and wise use of evidence on well-being designs.

worksite leaders will utilize existing evidence in their implementation decisions. It should not be assumed that leaders will always follow a rational, reasoned approach or that they have the time, resources, or ability to effectively consider evidence. Even with clear evidence-based guidelines for programs, real-world factors often shape and even override the use of such guidelines. To help frame the information and evidence about effective well-being programs that are reviewed in section 2 of this chapter, we propose a framework to help readers understand the elements associated with *wisely* creating well-being workplace programs as well as the dynamics behind how leaders decide to use evidence. Again, knowledge may only be useful when it is applied with wisdom.

Figure 35.1 summarizes the major sections of this chapter. First, we emphasize that leaders need to approach evidence with wisdom and that such wisdom is influenced by how well-being is defined and the motives for adapting and sustaining programs (top of figure). We propose our process-oriented definition of well-being, one that includes reference to deeply held values, as best fitting a wise approach. Second, in a bidirectional manner, wisdom will influence what types of evidence are used and such evidence can influence wisdom. The evidence itself (center of figure) can inform well-being design and strategy but is significantly influenced (moderated by) managerial wisdom (or the lack thereof). The final section of this chapter discusses how such wisdom draws upon evidence and leverages insights to design and strategize well-being initiatives. Third, we prescriptively suggest that leaders consider three types of information sources that are detailed below in section 2: key practices from the Psychologically Healthy Workplaces, best-practice case studies, and empirical knowledge drawn from quantitative studies.

The Evidence

Well-Being and Positive Mental Health (the APA Psychologically Healthy Workplace Awards)

In 1999, the New Jersey Psychological Association gave out the first Psychologically Healthy Workplace Awards (PHWA). Since that time, 56 state, provincial, and territorial associations across the United States and Canada, with support from the American Psychological

Association, have presented awards to more than 500 organizations. In 2003, the APA launched the Best Practice honors, to recognize outstanding and innovative practices among these award-winning companies. The first annual National Psychologically Healthy Workplace Awards were given in 2006, based on nominations drawn from the pool of previous state-level winners. In 2015, the APA selected its first Organizational Excellence Award, to highlight effective applications of psychology in the workplace.

The APA Psychologically Healthy Workplace Program approach has attempted to explicitly consider the intersection between employee well-being and organizational success (Grawitch and Ballard, 2015) and has pursued a real-world, best practices model to investigate this relationship. Five workplace practices are considered to be key elements of a psychologically healthy workplace in this approach:

- Employee involvement
- Growth and development
- Work–life balance
- Employee recognition
- Health and safety

There has been a focused effort to support research into each of these factors to validate their contribution to the effectiveness of the workplace (Day, Kelloway, and Hurrell, 2014; Grawitch and Ballard, 2015; Grawitch, Gottschalk, and Munz, 2006; Grawitch, Leford, Ballard, and Barber, 2009).

In addition, data has been collected from national award winners since 2006 and compared to representative samples of businesses. Although these data samples are small, based on fewer than ten winning companies each year, the results have been accumulated to look for trends. For example, in 2009, workplaces that won national psychologically healthy workplace awards showed 28% less turnover of employees, 14% fewer employees reporting chronic work stress, 43% more employees who would recommend their workplace as a good place to work, and 24% higher levels of employee satisfaction compared to a nationally representative survey (APA, 2009). These differences have been stable or even more significant year after year. In 2014, national psychologically healthy workplaces had 19% less turnover and 21% higher job satisfaction ratings than the national sample (APA, 2014).

In addition, the APA has collected data on factors related to employee well-being in national surveys and compared the data from psychologically healthy organizations. Employees in APA-recognized psychologically healthy workplaces are 32% more likely to say they feel valued at work, 24% more likely to say they are motivated to do their best, 52% more likely to say their organization supports a healthy lifestyle, 50% more likely to participate regularly in health and wellness programs, 40% more likely to report they have adequate mental health resources, and 39% more likely to say they have adequate stress management resources (APA, 2014).

The APA psychologically healthy workplaces are selected on the basis of the five factors listed above and the model holds that these factors are key practices associated with improved well-being and organizational success. If there are practices that lead to employee well-being that does not support organizational success, or practices that promote company profitability at the expense of the well-being of the workforce, these organizations are not eligible for recognition.

Employee involvement   PHWA winners are 33 percent more likely to report that their organizations value employee involvement than a representative national sample (APA, 2014) – and this has been consistently associated with improved employee attitudes (Vandenberg, Richardson, and Eastman, 1999), higher job satisfaction (Freeman, Kleiner, and Ostroff, 2000) and employee well-being and happiness (Cheng, 2014).

Growth and development   PHWA winners are 29 percent more likely to report that their organization values training and development (APA, 2014) – and this has been linked to employee motivation, increased job satisfaction and lower levels of stress (Salas and Weaver, 2015). Grawitch, Trares, and Kohler (2007) found that there were correlations between opportunities for growth and development and work–life balance, organizational commitment, lower emotional exhaustion, lower turnover intentions and greater well-being.

Work–life balance   PHWA winners are 32 percent more likely to report that their organizations value work–life balance than a representative national sample (APA, 2104) – and this is associated with improved psychological well-being in the workforce (Greenhaus and Powell, 2003), job satisfaction (Allen, 2001), and lowered stress and burnout (Boyar, Maertz, Pearson, and Keough, 2003).

Employee recognition   PHWA winners are 41 percent more likely to report that their organization values recognition than a representative national sample (APA, 2014) – and this has been cited as more important for feeling appreciated and having interesting work than salary (Kowalewski and Phillips, 2012). Indeed the winners were 32 percent more likely to say they were valued at work than the US average.

Health and safety   PHWA winners are 50 percent more likely to regularly participate in a health and wellness program than a nationally representative sample (APA, 2014) – involving both the prevention of injuries and illness as well as the promotion of a healthy and safe work environment. The efforts in the workplace to establish safety, with a primary focus on prevention of injuries, and health, with a primary focus on the promotion of health and well-being, are actually distinct but related practices (Basen-Engquist, Hudmon, Tripp, and Chamberlain, 1998; Mearns, Hope, Ford, and Tetrick, 2010).

Because the number of companies which have been recognized as psychologically healthy by APA is small, and because this endeavor is primarily an effort to recognize best practices rather than a more systematic examination of the contribution of specific workplace practices, the data that have been collected are difficult to generalize. These organizations are self-selected and go through an extensive process at the level of state, province or territory to be recognized prior to entering a second selection process to be considered for a national award. This means that these are not average companies attempting to find a way to be profitable in a competitive environment, but companies that have created or discovered unique ways to foster employee well-being and organizational success.

It is not clear from this process if the best practices that APA has highlighted in its awards are practices that would have wide application across many workplaces. In fact, there has been an often repeated belief that there is no "one-size-fits-all" solution to develop a psychologically healthy workplace (Grawitch and Ballard, 2015).

Still, there is a growing research base that demonstrates that each of the facets considered to be crucial to a psychologically healthy workplace is strongly associated with both organizational success and employee well-being. It assumes that each facet will work synergistically with the others in workplace practices across the entire organization. Even though there are limitations because of the small self-selected sample, there are clear data to demonstrate that these organizations are achieving meaningful outcomes.

Summary

This model has deliberately taken a broader approach to what constitutes well-being in the workplace. It is more than the absence of diagnosable psychiatric disorders. It includes the environmental, physical, psychological, and social dimensions of our definition. The organizations that have been given awards have typically had strong leaders who valued employee well-being and made that an explicit goal within the strategic and long-range goals for organizational success. Employees responded to this by developing high levels of loyalty and alignment with the goals of the organization. While it is unlikely that the Psychologically Healthy Workplace initiative can be copied in a widespread way across the work world, it provides some basic insights into five key practices that can be leveraged to improve well-being in the workplace.

Other Best-Practice Case Vignettes

There are several other initiatives, in addition to the PHWA, that also provide awards or recognition for employer best-practices in wellness, well-being, or health and productivity management (e.g., Goetzel et al., 2007) and there are a number of organizational health "scorecards" used to guide the development of programs (Terry, 2013). These efforts may be seen as providing worksite leaders with a set of qualitative criteria. News releases of best practices may influence leaders looking for examples within their particular industries; and more so than these leaders' understanding of any research white paper or quantitative synthesis. The following vignettes from disparate industries and awards are provided as examples for readers interested in exploring further.

American Cast Iron Pipe Company – manufacturing   American Cast Iron Pipe Company (ACIP) is a recent representative of over 50 work organizations that have won the C. Everett Koop Award since the awards began in 1994 (Health Project, 2016; see Putnam, 2015). Importantly, in 1924 ACIP's original owner, John Eagan, created a trust that transferred ownership of the company to the employees. Eagan was one of the first to provide on-site medical care in 1915, and the medical clinic is still currently on-site. ACIP provides an on-site fitness facility, health coaching, diabetes education and on-site physical therapy. As a result of this dual focus on ownership and health, employees feel cared for and they also have a vested interest in the company's success. Outcomes include minimal turnover and over 80 percent engagement in wellness programs for the past eight years.

National Association of College Stores – retail   The National Association of College Stores (NACS) recently won the American Heart Association's (AHA) "Fit Friendly" Award (see

Cook, 2012). The AHA provides hundreds of awards each year across four categories (Gold, Platinum, Worksite Innovation, and Community Innovation) via an online application form (AHA, 2016). NACS has had wellness programming for more than 20 years, with annual health fairs (e.g., with cooking demonstrations, healthy snack samples, visits from Jazzercise and Zumba instructors), health screenings, an on-site gym, walking paths, and a "Five for Life" program, which encourages staff to get 30 minutes of activity, five days a week, for life.

Steptoe and Johnson – law firm   The *Washington Business Journal* named Steptoe and Johnson LLP to its list of Greater Washington's Healthiest Employers of 2014 (see Burke, 2014). To be considered for the award, companies completed a 75-question application (see Healthiest Employers, 2016) that assesses culture and leadership commitment, foundational components, strategic planning, communication and marketing, programming and interventions, and reporting and analysis. Steptoe's Wellness Program provides preventive care initiatives, an on-site gym and shower facilities, free bicycle storage for bike-commuting employees, free on-site instructor-led fitness classes, Wellness Walks of one to three miles from the office, and incentives for employee participation in charity-driven races and walks in the Washington area.

SAS – software   In 2014, SAS – international software company located in North Carolina – ranked second on the elite Top 25 World's Best Multinational Workplaces list from Great Place to Work® (2016; SAS, 2014). SAS has also been featured 11 straight years in the annual top ten of *Fortune* magazine's list of "100 Best Companies to Work For" in the US. This is due, in part, to their wellness program, built around its Recreation and Fitness Center, which is open to SAS employees, retirees and family members. The wellness program also includes health checks, smoking cessation and rewards for fitness accomplishments, participation in leisure-time activities and completion of the six-month Your Way to Wellness program. The on-site health-care center provides primary health care and preventive services to employees and covered dependents. "In our industry, rapid innovation and extreme customer care are essential," Jim Goodnight, CEO of SAS, says. "The best way to make that happen is by supporting people. We have spent decades perfecting a culture and work environment that encourages creativity by addressing the day-to-day stresses and concerns that employees inevitably bring to work" (SAS, 2014).

Summary

Based on vignettes like these, it appears that companies with the most successful well-being programs understand that such efforts have a direct impact on the financial success of the company, not just on medical claims costs. Senior leadership views well-being as integrated into the overall work culture, versus a standalone program. Though each industry has its own specific needs, well-being is valued as something that meets each company's core values and overall corporate vision. It could be to minimize employee turnover, to create an environment that fosters creativity, foster better customer service, or to be recognized as an employer of choice to attract the best talent. No matter the reason for the focus on well-being, the above cases testify that senior leadership recognizes that the value of these programs, the VOI, gives them a competitive edge.

Key practices discerned across these vignettes include the following (also see Goetzel et al., 2007; Putnam, 2015; Terry, 2013):

- Visible senior leadership
- Developing programs that are integrated into the company culture beyond benefits
- Include tools and resources that meet their specific employees' needs and cultures
- Fostering engaged employee wellness champions committees and networks
- A willingness to grow a program over time
- Actively show that they value their employees

Quantitative Studies

It helps to distinguish a basic level of well-being from gradations of higher levels of well-being (e.g., flow, thriving, joy). In this section, we identify eight factors shown to predict well-being primarily in empirical, quantitative studies. However, because well-being exists at different levels and is itself dynamic, the relationship between these eight factors and well-being also follows four dynamics:

- *Well-being as potential*   First, as defined here, well-being emphasizes human potential and the ability of work, career, and vocation to help bring out this potential ("potentiate," see factor 1).
- *Necessary and sufficient conditions*   Second, in order to reach an a priori or base criterion of well-being, one or more factors may be sufficient for some employees but necessary for other employees. Some employees may be satisfied with a basic sense of well-being through intrinsic work motivation (see factor 2), whereas others may need additional factors.
- *Raising or moving up levels (growth)*   Third, one or more factors may be necessary for employees to achieve, enhance and maintain higher levels of well-being; that is, beyond a base or previous level of functioning.
- *Activation*   Finally, there is a dynamic relationship between human potential (factor 1) and various environmental conditions and resources (factors 7 and 8) that can help activate or bring out that potential. Some employees may reach their highest level of well-being in spite of resource deficiencies and/or only because of the other factors listed (self-efficacy, support, control, meaning, coping skills, i.e., factors 2 through 6). Alternately, some employees may only reach their highest level of well-being because environmental resources (factors 7 and 8) help to activate some other factor.

Following, in proposed sequence, each factor is listed, with a proposition. This proposition is followed by a capsule review of some quantitative studies that highlight the factor. These reviews are not intended to be comprehensive.

Potentiation (includes resilience, hardiness, thriving, transformational coping, psychological capital)

> *Employees have the capacity – by virtue of personality, training, and resources – to transform the challenges of work into positive outcomes for themselves and others.*

By "potentiation" we mean bringing out the positive and life-supporting potential of a factor, as in medicine where the enhancement of one agent by another occurs so that the combined effect is greater than the sum of the effects alone (Bennett, 2014). Several lines of research suggest that, as a function of adversity, challenge, or other work-related issues, individuals may demonstrate a level of skill, competency, or productivity that would not have otherwise come to the fore (cf. Phoolka and Kaur, 2012; Maddi, Kahn, and Maddi, 1998; McGonigle, 2015; Seery, Holman, and Silver, 2010). For example, the relatively new concept of thriving combines the areas of learning and vitality at work (Spreitzer et al., 2005). Using structural equation modeling, Paterson, Luthans, and Jeung (2014) found thriving correlated to several variables that influence employee well-being. Specifically, social support, psychological capital, heedful relating, and task focus all predicted thriving at work, which led to an increase in employee performance. Robertson, Cooper, Sarkar, and Curran (2015) examined the relationship between employee resilience and well-being, and found that training can improve employee resilience, mental health and subjective well-being. Reviews of resilience training suggest that it can improve well-being but that more rigorous studies are warranted (Leppin et al., 2014; Macedo et al., 2014). Leon and Halbesleben (2014) proposed an integrative model of both individual and environmental factors that contribute to employee resilience.

Intrinsic work value/work motivation

Employees, just by virtue of having employment, have a sense of well-being that would not be possible if they were not employed.

Compared to unemployment, employed workers tend to have greater psychological well-being (Flint, Bartley, Shelton, and Sacker, 2013; Knabe, Rätzel, Schöb, and Weimann, 2010; McKee-Ryan, Song, Wanberg, and Kinicki, 2005). While work, by itself, may provide a basis for well-being, there have been significant advances in the science of work motivation to show that many factors impact work motivation and its potential relationship with well-being (Latham and Pinder, 2005; Van den Broeck et al., 2013). In particular, wide empirical support for self-determination theory confirms that human beings need to be considered competent and autonomous and that employment can fulfill these psychological needs (Deci and Ryan, 2014; Gagné and Deci, 2005). It follows that a work environment that supports employee autonomy would lead to greater health. This was found in a study by Nie and colleagues (2015). However, high intrinsic work motivation – enjoying work for work's sake – was more directly related to fewer ill-health symptoms; such intrinsic motivation mediated the relationship between a climate that supports employee autonomy and health symptoms. Also, employees who scored high in autonomous motivation report the highest job satisfaction and work engagement/motivation, as well as the lowest levels of job burnout (Van den Broeck et al., 2013).

Efficacy

Employees experience well-being because they demonstrate a skill or competency and feel a sense of self-efficacy or collective-efficacy by virtue of this behavior.

There is much research on the relationship between self-efficacy and employee well-being. Williams, Wissing, Rothmann, and Temane (2010) demonstrated that general self-efficacy (along with job demands and resources) predicted psychological well-being as well as employee engagement (i.e., vigor and dedication). Hope has a positive effect on general self efficacy, which, in turn, has a positive effect on employee well-being (Duggleby, Cooper, and Penz, 2009). Employees with more self-efficacy (in their professional life) report higher psychosocial well-being (i.e., less burnout and more engagement; Ventura, Salanova, and Llorens, 2015). Intervention research shows that it is possible to improve self-efficacy and positive affect (Ouweneel, Le Blanc, and Schaufeli, 2013; Kaplan et al., 2014). Van den Heuvel, Demerouti, and Peeters (2015) developed a Job Crafting Intervention that enabled employees to proactively develop a sense of self-efficacy while helping build a motivating work environment, both leading to improved affective well-being.

Support (cohesiveness, inclusion, belonging, coworker and supervisor support)

Employees have well-being when they feel supported or a sense of connectedness to the group.

The presence of positive worker relationships appears to have a direct effect on well-being and also serves to protect (buffer) well-being in the face of negative interpersonal factors (e.g., incivility). Meta-analytic evidence suggests that different types of perceived support at work (coworker, supervisor, organizational) predict greater job satisfaction, with organizational support being the strongest predictor (Ng and Sorensen, 2008). Stansfeld et al. (2013), assessing social support and work characteristics in 5,182 civil servants, found that support predicted subjective well-being. While workers who are treated unfairly in the work environment are subject to low job satisfaction and high levels of distress, workers who report a supportive coworker relationship suffer fewer negative effects from mistreatment (Sloan, 2011). Moradi and Cheraghi (2015) found that social support has the ability to increase a worker's psychological well-being as well as decrease depression; this effect, however, indirectly occurred through self-esteem, satisfying the need for relating to other individuals, and the need to feel competent and useful. Linnabery, Stuhlmacher, and Towler (2014) found consistent results with a sample of black women professionals. They also demonstrated that when social support systems are lacking, self-help coping strategies can help overcome those support deficiencies. Cassidy, McLaughlin, and McDowell (2014) found that psychological capital and social support actually mediate the impact that workplace bullying can have on a worker's well-being.

Stress management/coping

Well-being of employees occurs as they effectively navigate job demands, or the environment affords time and resources to reduce demands and recover from them on a regular basis.

Several reviews of the stress literature suggest that well-being is supported when (a) individual-level stress management practices, like proactive or positive coping (Dewe, 2014), positive response to job demands (Simmons, 2014), and cognitive-behavioral approaches (Richardson and Rothstein, 2008), are integrated with (b) organizational-level or more systemic approaches to stress (LaMontagne et al., 2007; Tetrick and Winslow, 2015). Interventions that promote mindfulness and emotional intelligence are also growing in popularity. For example, Bazarko, Cate, Azocar, and Kreitzer (2013) found that mindfulness-based stress reduction decreased reported stress and work burnout, and improved employee well-being in sample of nurses.

Other researchers have affirmed the link between mindfulness-based stress reduction programs and overall employee well-being (e.g., Adams, 2011; Aikens et al. 2014; Foureur et al., 2013; etc.). Zomer (2012) examined the relationship between well-being, emotional intelligence, and stress coping strategies and found that emotional intelligence, as well as several stress coping mechanisms, have significant effects on employee psychological well-being.

Control/meaning

Employees have well-being due to some degree of autonomy, meaningfulness, and/or control in their work; the more they have of each of these, the more likely will they be to have ongoing well-being and it is better to have one than none at all.

In their review of the literature, Eatough and Spector (2014) provide a compelling case that perceived control (in its varied forms of empowerment, autonomy, locus of control, etc.) has a positive impact on well-being. Gagné and Bhave (2011) also reviewed research discussing the importance of work autonomy to employee engagement and well-being. Specific studies also describe various benefits of control. For example, Rousseau, Eddleston, Patel, and Kellermanns (2014) found that control over work correlates with reduced likelihood of workplace bullying and greater well-being. Boxall and Macky (2014) demonstrated that greater autonomy (or control in the work environment) and involvement in decision-making produced positive well-being. Nie et al. (2015) recently found that perceived autonomy support (how much an employee believes they have freedom in their job) from an employee's organization directly predicts job satisfaction, with indirect effects through different variables (i.e., intrinsic motivation, identified regulation, introjected regulation, and external regulation).

Human resources/rewards

Employees have well-being when provided with resources, rewards and benefits to assist them with the above factors and via four general avenues: (a) protective policies/general human resource benefits, (b) health promotion/wellness efforts, (c) employee assistance programs, and (d) training and professional development.

Effective human resource programs that provide health benefits, healthy and safe work conditions, good communication, employee assistance, training, and high performance work systems may create conditions that enhance employee well-being (Gonçalves and Neves, 2012; Chenoweth, 2011; Grawitch et al., 2006; Markey et al., 2008; Marschke and Mujtaba, 2014; Messersmith, Patel, Lapek, and Gould-Williams, 2011). Creed, French, and Hood (2015) discovered that work-based benefits such as enabling resources, rewards, and involvement had a positive statistical relationship with engagement (dedication) and general well-being. This relationship was indirect, with workplace facilitation being their link. Thompson and Prottas (2006) found that several organizational benefits have a positive predictive effect on employees. Specifically, family benefits decreased employee stress, increased employee well-being, life satisfaction, and positive spillover from work to family life, and decreased turnover intention. Also, alternative work schedules increased employee job and life satisfaction. Edmunds, Stephenson, and Clow (2013), assessing health promotion in small and medium-sized enterprises, found that a physical activity intervention decreased employee body mass index, perceived stress, and negative mood states. These changes led to increased employee health and well-being. The employee assistance program (EAP) is an employee benefit that deserves special mention as it provides a variety of resources – psychological training, workshops, counseling, manager consultation and debriefing – that both address stress and promote well-being (Bennett et al., 2015). Recent studies suggest that EAPs are effective in enhancing worker productivity (Attridge, 2013; Sharar and Lennox, 2014; Sharar, Pompe, and Lennox, 2012; Sharar, Lennox, and Burke, 2010). Outcome measures in the latter studies include items on life satisfaction and work engagement (stimulated by and passionate about work). Most recently, a more rigorous quasi-experimental trial showed that employees accessing an EAP had reduced absenteeism and presenteeism issues compared to a matched comparison group (Richmond, Pampel, Wood, and Nunes, 2015).

Environment

Employees have well-being when their work environment is both (a) physically supportive (ergonomics, safety, nontoxic) and (b) psychosocially facilitative (climate and culture).

A sampling of recent publications details a myriad of physical environment factors that can influence employee well-being (e.g., Cooper, Burton, and Cooper, 2014; Lottrup, Grahn, and Stigsdotter, 2013; McGuire and McLaren, 2009; Smith and Pitt, 2009). These factors include work space, chair and table integrity, walkability, visual access to green space, air quality, lighting, noise, greenery, enriched versus lean office design, and other ergonomics. A parallel literature describes the impact of the psychosocial environment (culture and climate) on well-being (Hoebbel, Golaszewski, Swanson, and Dorn, 2012; Lin and Lin, 2014; Lomas, 2015; Putnam, 2015). In addition, employee relationships with managers, supervisors, and coworkers may be categorized under support (see factor 4) but they also play an important role in the work environment (Mellor and Webster, 2013; Steinbrecher and Bennett, 2003; Thompson and Prottas, 2006). As one example, Hamar, Coberley, Pope, and Rula (2015) examined an organization that implemented a well-being improvement strategy that yielded significant increases in well-being and productivity two years after strategy implementation. Also, Rousseau et al. (2014) discussed how workplace environments could either exacerbate or ameliorate workplace bullying. They reported that workplace bullying could be reduced by creating a trusting environment; specifically, employee trust in upper management.

Summary

While the preceding review is not comprehensive, it seems clear that key correlates or predictive factors repeatedly appear in well-being studies. Figure 35.2 provides one way to organize these factors in a coherent model. The figure is not provided to suggest any specific empirical or causal ordering. Rather, the framework helps to summarize the above and also helps to transition to the final section of the chapter. At the center of this framework is the dynamic goal of promoting well-being and its enhancement. Given our definition of well-being, this goal is fundamentally influenced by four dynamics (potential, conditions, levels, and activation), which shape how and when well-being manifests, is drawn out, or activated. From our review of the quantitative literature, there are eight factors that play a role in the creation and enhancement of well-being. *Potentiation* is essential because leaders must recognize that every

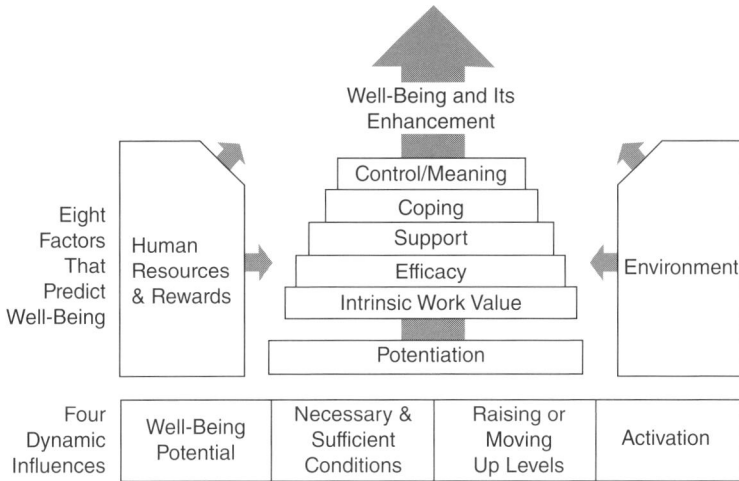

Figure 35.2   Organizing factors that predict well-being: a suggested framework.

worker has – to some degree – the potential to have not only well-being but also the potential to increase well-being and in ways that mutually serve the worker and the business. Leaders and designers of programs can help to bring out this potential through two major "levers" (see next section): their *human resource design/workplace reward systems* and the *work environment*. Third, these two major levers can directly impact well-being and they also can facilitate employee experiences of *intrinsic value*, *efficacy*, *support*, *coping*, and *control/meaning*, all of which have been shown to predict well-being. In the next section, we further elaborate upon and deduce those major levers that wise leaders should attend to when creating well-being programs.

How to Create Well-being at Work: An Integration

Key Levers

The following list of levers was derived from the preceding review as well as from the authors' own work in consulting with businesses. Each of the levers is highly interrelated with the others and should not be treated as independent. Readers will sense some redundancy across these levers. The term "lever" is used to draw focus to the fact that creating well-being requires understanding those facilitative conditions that need to be leveraged. This stands in contrast to the outworn idea of finding, implementing, or designing a particular program that "works." We emphasize that well-being is not a program. It is a way of doing business with wise leadership.

The levers are organized into three categories and the first lever in each category stays true to several insights discussed in McKenna and colleagues' (2009) model of wise leadership. Specifically, wise leaders recognize their own fallibility, that social relationships at work are often messy and complex, and that – accordingly – wise leadership entails social intelligence, cognitive complexity, behavioral complexity and ultimately discernment. Hence, to discern the best actions, wise leaders leverage well-being by always seeking input. They do so at all stages: when getting started, they genuinely look at employees' well-being needs and ideas (lever 1), when transitioning to design, they assess the readiness of the organization (lever 6), and during program design, they select features that fit the discerned needs and readiness levels (lever 10).

Getting started: wise leadership fundamentals

The first five levers pertain to the wisdom attitude of well-being leaders and also those responsible (e.g., HR, Wellness Coordinators) for overseeing how the business seeks to enhance the eight factors that predict well-being (see Figure 35.2) and then craft well-being programs for such enhancement. In some ways, these first levers have more to do with being, perspective, and insight than with doing, taking action, or making hard and fast decisions.

1. *Genuinely seek employee input on their well-being needs and their ideas about program design and then genuinely respond to such input in a timely manner*   Wise leaders produce virtuous decisions and contribute to the social good. At the most fundamental level, this can only happen by seeking to understand the needs of those served by any well-being strategy (Grawitch et al., 2009). An excessive focus on program administration, incentives, or the failure to integrate well-being with other initiatives (see lever 13 below) can cost companies. This occurs when program design fails to meet employees' intrinsic needs and potential strengths (e.g., intrinsic work value, efficacy, support, etc.).
2. *Leadership engagement should be as genuine and discerning as possible (move beyond episodic gestures to more deliberate activities)*   While successful programs can emerge with limited leadership engagement, such engagement is necessary for a culture of well-being. Ultimately, leaders make the best decisions about program investment based on the wisdom principles and motives described above. The best programs often have leaders who share their own personal health stories, visibly participate in programs, and recognize others' success (see Sørensen and Holman, 2014). Conversely, it helps to be vigilant when the C-Suite participates without connecting to overall company goals and values (i.e., knowing "the why"). Such inconsistency hurts the program and is often associated with nonintegrated, episodic efforts (see Vogel, 2015):
   - encouraging people to sign up for a once-a-year company sponsored walk to sponsor a charity, but in a workaholic culture where people are expected sit for long hours;
   - having a registered dietitian come in for a few sessions, but without healthy options in vending machines and cafeterias, or actively advocating for healthier restaurants close to the business;
   - supporting and funding a few stress management courses, but not having an ongoing strategy around mitigating negative stress situations.
   Ideally, efforts at well-being leadership should equate with efforts in new product and sales development (Partners for Prevention, 2014). In reality, most business leaders lack the time for such investment or the propensity for any training in health education. Consequently, a partner or coach from the well-being team can help them integrate well-being into the company culture (see Kilfedder and Litchfield, 2014). Such coaches can help managers foster authenticity, reminding them to (a) seek out and genuinely recognize employees who have made steps toward better well-being, (b) launch any new well-being offering and connecting it (in their own words) to the vision of the company, and (c) work with middle management so they understand program value (VOI), with clear expectations that those

managers will support team well-being. Well-being leadership treats all the levers on this list as an opportunity to first discern and then bring out the potential strengths of the business and its employees (e.g., "If my team works better then my organization is going to be better"). The next three levers elaborate on this point.

3. *View well-being as primarily a dimension of "teamwork"*   Most workplaces are primarily oriented toward "task work." There are products to be made and sold, or services to be offered, that are the lifeblood of a successful business. At the same time, positive teamwork helps create a thriving environment. The process by which products and services come to market require employees to work as a team. Work is essential to individual well-being, but the process of accomplishing tasks can overshadow and interfere with attention to teamwork. Most leaders focus more on tasks (work flow, quality, time frame) but those who are really successful also focus on *how* work is done and discern ways that allow workers to experience team cohesion. Clearly, relationships at work play a significant role in the experience of well-being (Mastroianni and Storberg-Walker, 2014). To leverage well-being, give regular attention to teamwork. For example, in regularly scheduled staff meetings, devote time to discussing the improvement of teamwork in addition to the task work required to meet the business goals.

4. *Emphasize stakeholder priorities (know the "why")*   Leaders need to discern what is most important to all the stakeholders to drive a clear understanding of the value of investment. Though it can be time-consuming, gaining buy-in sustains and drives the program forward over time. Before employers start to discuss the "what" and the "how" of programs, they need to figure out their "why." When the "why" clearly connects to corporate vision and values, employees and the C-Suite can jointly agree on the value of well-being. If the biggest "why" is addressed and clearly communicated, stakeholders will understand the value of the investment (VOI). Stakeholders include, but are not limited to the C-Suite, managers, human resources, benefits, business continuation planning (BCP), recruiting, international office contacts, employee education, safety committees, building operations, and any on-site clinics, on-site gyms, or wellness/health vendors who serve the overall program. Examples of the well-being "why" include employee attraction and retention, better safety, better morale, better communications and engagement in what the company currently offers, or better targeted programs to specific demographics. Once stakeholders agree on why, then designers can move into (a) what they want to do, (b) how they want to roll it out to targeted group or groups, and (c) how the why is going to be measured.

5. *Build well-being into the culture as an integral part of the culture, rather than being seen as an additional program or policy*   The preceding levers (3 and 4) actively serve this lever. Human beings have a limited ability to hold multiple ideas in attention for a long time. If not managed well, excessive focus on task factors can often contradict the factors that predict well-being. This can frustrate those management-focused leaders who expect greater productivity and may then be accused of mistreating workers when their intention is simply to supply a product or service. A well-being culture has value because it enhances teamwork. As such, it may be viewed as a necessary condition for business success. Indeed, this is what appears to be true for those who have won the Psychologically Healthy Workplace Awards as well as the other awards cited in the earlier section (e.g., Koop, *Fortune*'s 100). Leaders need to discern whether stakeholders view well-being efforts as a means of extracting profit out of the workforce or as a way to care for the workers. In the first instance, the program may negatively impact well-being, while in the second instance

the same program may enhance the workforce in a positive way. Leaders and well-being designers need ways to promote the value of the workforce (employee value proposition) as essential to the mission of the organization and to bring about sustainable well-being.

Setting the stage: moving to design

The next four levers are more likely to become important when planning, ramping up, or strategizing on the long-term success of a programmatic effort. This is where the attitude and perspective conveyed through the first five levers start to take shape in the day-to-day practical reality of a well-being strategy. Each lever answers a corresponding question. In order: Are we ready? Are my champions in place and am I committed to them? Does everyone have a clear understanding of the effort or strategy? Do we all know and agree upon the outcomes we expect to see?

6. *Proactively assess the level of organizational readiness* for programs and incrementally build programs and nudge the culture in ways that are sensitive to current readiness but also move the culture to the next level. It is clear that businesses have different levels of readiness for well-being programs (Bennett, 2010; Hannon et al., 2015). Just as leaders seek employee input (lever 1), program designers should proactively think about the overall readiness of the organization – or particular department or work group. This includes assessing projected budget, time afforded to any internal wellness manager or champion (see next lever), level of stakeholder engagement, overall attitude of receptivity, and the general climate of learning and well-being.

7. *Show commitment to wellness or well-being champions (internal health advocates)* who themselves have a genuine interest in well-being for themselves and others. Many wellness programs can succeed with a strong, passionate, and knowledgeable employee – even when leadership buy-in is lacking. These wellness coordinators and champions can use the other levers described; for example, seek input (lever 1), act with authenticity (lever 2), build a team (lever 3) and assess stakeholder priorities (lever 4). Hence, whether or not leaders are engaged, it is important to leverage these champions as leaders. They are likely going to be the ones who will be the front-line actors on all the design levers listed below (cf. Bennett and Simone, 2014; Staywell, 2015). The first author has developed a curriculum to train well-being champions that has been used in a variety of contexts (Bennett and Linde, 2016).

8. *Make programs clear, coherent, and applicable* as early as possible by using seasoned wellness consultants or (second best) assembling resources before program launch. Companies can be overwhelmed with program implementation, asking employees, often with no training in health, to do RFPs (request for proposals) for well-being programs. They have no experience in designing a culturally specific strategy, finding partners to help build a program, or knowing how to get credible information about evidence-based programs. The business world does not expect an inexperienced accountant to create an accurate P&L statement. And yet companies ask these untrained employees to come up with an impactful well-being strategy. At the end of the day, employees need to have a very clear understanding of the resources available, and internal designers or purchasers need detailed information and planning guides to help. They need to know how they can adapt programs to their culture,

appropriate time frames for implementation, realistic numbers around initial engagement, choice architecture and behavioral economics, and key components to an effective marketing and communications strategy. A seasoned wellness professional or consultant can help a program avoid mistakes. Alternately, having various good resources can help these wellness professionals through the specifics of getting them from an RFP, to a pilot, to a launch, to ongoing engagement.

9. *Establish metrics of relevance that stakeholders agree with* – an agreed upon metric or measurement is important to assess program growth and success. Companies want to see participation and engagement, or how engagement impacts employee turnover, workers' compensation claims, performance or productivity. Make sure that any "soft" successes in the program (e.g., improved rates of subjective well-being) are clearly tied back to the agreed upon "why" (see lever 4 above). Over time, it's also important to periodically discuss the reasons for having the program, making sure that changes in company goals align with well-being goals. Programs also have many stakeholders, who may have changing interests in more than one outcome. To establish relevant metrics amidst these various concerns, well-being consultants should have their own clear definition of well-being, ways of measuring program processes and program subcomponents, and ways of connecting these components to positive outcomes for employees (not just employers). Documentation of these practices and periodic data acquisition allow internal champions to measure progress and external consultants to ascertain how programs were conducted, how they succeeded or failed, and modifications needed.

In motion: design details and mechanics

The next four levers are most active when the program is designed, about to be launched, or in full swing. Customizations, communications, environmental supports, and program integrations are the "nuts and bolts" or mechanics of a high-quality, successful well-being program.

10. *Use tailored and personalized interventions (modularize for intrinsic motivation)*   Following from our definition of well-being, it is essential to honor the dynamic and highly personal nature of employee well-being; each employee has their own well-being journey (that includes ups and downs) and well-being means different things to each one of them. A well-being program that focuses its resources on high-quality smoking cessation will not be successful if a potential participant's main concern is a disabled child or adult parent struggling with early signs of dementia. Working within the company's budget, offering diverse resources for different needs helps drive success (e.g., Hartung and Hahlweg, 2010). Following research on wellness programs, a robust approach should help keep the healthy people healthy, help those in the beginning stages of having an issue (physical health, mental health, financial health, purpose, career growth), and help those who are most at risk (e.g,. Edington, 2014). These programs are modular; they recognize that each person participating in the program will have their own intrinsic motivation for committing themselves to a particular goal.

11. *Foster a comprehensive communications strategy at all levels*   No program, no matter how well designed or aligned with company culture, will be successful if the target audience doesn't understand the program, how it can help them, and/or how to sign up

and access it. Because there may be very different needs for different employee groups within a company, deciding who they are and how they need to hear information is important to driving engagement numbers. People have very different preferences and learning styles. They may also have different access to technology. Taking the time to evaluate all communication streams is time well spent. Younger employees might respond better to text messages or social media options. Older employees might prefer emails or education sessions in person. In some cases, telephone messaging can be impactful. It helps to understand how, where, and when people get information. Questions to ask include:

- Do they get their information from an unofficial leader in their group?
- Are there places in the building where people regularly check postings?
- Can you creatively use elevator doors, entryways, staircases and other well-trafficked areas for messaging?
- When do they read messages?
- What types of messages have worked in the past and what style of communication was used (formal/informal/specific company style of writing, etc.)?
- Is it important to get information to dependents at home and what's the best way to do that (email, direct mail, meetings where spouses/partners are invited, websites they can access, information hotline they can access)?
  - Is there an opportunity to build a wellness champions' network to help with better communications?

12. *Move from a "don't neglect" the environment attitude to "intentionally enhance" the physical work environment* The look and feel of an office environment influences performance as well as health and well-being. For example, bad lighting is not only harmful in terms of visual issues and headaches, it can also impact biochemistry (melatonin production). Having plants in the office, and the right kind of plants, can impact air quality. Access to water can impact everything from urinary tract medical claims to impaired cognitive function due to mild dehydration. Chairs and desks that are not properly adjusted can lead to neck and back issues. Understanding the health issues in a newly constructed building can also make a big difference in the overall health and well-being of the workforce going into that building. One example of best practices for environmental design is the "WELL Building Standard" developed by Delos (2016). Its seven concepts include Air, Water, Nourishment, Light, Fitness, Comfort, Mind. In addition, contributing in positive ways to work environment can influence overall environmental sustainability (Stelmack, Foster, and Hindman, 2014), which can impact the well-being of the surrounding community.

13. *Keep your sights on the details of program integration* The above definitions of well-being, wise leadership, and motives – along with the disparate sources of evidence reviewed – all point to one thing: effective well-being programs are integrated into the messaging, benefits, and human resource operational components of the business. The best programs are unified, easily navigated, and aligned with other benefits and programs offered by the company. Of the thirteen levers listed here, this last one requires more in-depth review, especially for large organizational systems (e.g., military, governmental, corporate, or multinational) and may be more relevant for larger businesses. It may help to think of the following five as the "mini-levers" of program integration. The authors, through their consultation with large systems, are aware of the frustrations faced by human resource professionals who have to focus almost all their efforts on the factors below, to

the neglect of the previous levers. Program integration is important but it really "sings" when the other levers are working to support *and* sustain such integration.

13.1 *Benefits and wellness* should collaborate to create a unified message to employees and dependents. Proactive use of metrics can break down organizational silos that influence health (e.g., health and safety; employee assistance and wellness; Hymel et al., 2011; Yandrick, 1996). Take medical claims, for instance. When urinary tract infections signal that workers are not well hydrated, planning can include more water stations and signage/reminders to drink. Musculoskeletal claims suggest the need for work pacing, ergonomics, and possible stretch breaks. Some medical issues can be very expensive (e.g., pregnancy and infertility). Employees don't always have guidance for self-care around such issues. As one example, the retailer Aéropostale addressed rising health-care costs, especially those related to maternity, by targeting its highly female, Gen X and Y, mostly retail workforce (Xerox, 2016). They used social media and the wellness team to create health communications and social support systems that led employees to gain better advice and also maintain some fiscal responsibility. As a result, C-section rates dropped from 44 to 33 percent (below the national average) and first-year savings were estimated at $140,000, with additional improvements to productivity, employee engagement and retention. Some companies are also willing to share aggregate (anonymous) data around claims costs and associated spending. Not all companies are willing to be so transparent, but workers benefit by understanding how health costs impact the company and start to see how well-being programs mutually benefit them and the company. If done well, such messaging conveys the "we" in wellness; such as, "our company wants to maintain success in the marketplace for years to come, continue to provide jobs, and help you stay healthy." Such cultural awareness is maintained through cross-marketing wellness and benefit offerings that support employees and their families.

13.2 *Employee recruiting and wellness* can also be a very good partnership. There is some indication that the millennial population may be particularly receptive to wellness programs (Miller, 2014). Businesses are increasingly concerned with attracting and retaining talent, and a robust program can be a differentiator when potential employees are evaluating benefits. A well-being strategy that supports employees and their families sends a statement about the company culture and how it values employees.

13.3 *Business continuation planning and employee assistance programs* can work together as part of a resilience strategy. Increasingly, companies are actively looking for ways to protect themselves from data or security breaches and also have the tools to survive a catastrophic event (violence, pandemic event, flood, hurricane, etc.). In these efforts, little attention is paid to how to support those specific people tasked with keeping the company running. As any major event will be stressful, well-being programs should include a plan around using EAP services to share with the BCP team. Such planning can make a considerable difference in maintaining operations during a crisis, and bouncing back from it. For example, understanding the value of flu shots to prevent a pandemic can be an important initiative for both BCP and wellness.

13.4 *Training of new managers* can make well-being resources more explicit. Research suggests that employees leave managers more than they leave companies (e.g., Kalemci and Kalemci, 2012). Through employee orientation, often the responsibility of human resources, new managers can learn how to identify and support employees with health and wellness issues. For a workforce to operate at peak performance, managers need to be aware of company resources in terms of employee assistance and well-being tools, resources, and education. They will benefit from understanding the value of having employees who are trained to be resilient, who get support for an issue before it disrupts performance, and who together respect that healthier choices will lead to a stronger organization.

13.5 *Compensation, retirement planning and wellness* play a part. Recall that for many workers, well-being may be primarily a function of having some secure employment. These workers might benefit most from education in financial literacy. When it comes to finance, the main focus of an integrated well-being team often pertains to retirement savings or a college savings fund for dependent children. However, the team can also focus on financial literacy as a path toward well-being (Miller, Reichelstein, Salas, and Zia, 2015; Taft, Hosein, and Mehrizi, 2013). There is a clear correlation between the health of someone's finances and their well-being (e.g., Kim, Garman, and Sorhaindo, 2003). When employees have access to someone who can teach basics like budgeting, walking them through the home-buying process or educating them about life insurance and the specific details of short-term and long-term disability can provide a great integration between general well-being and financial wellness. For example, if a financial counselor recognizes signs of physical stress, that can be an opportunity to provide a counseling referral to the EAP. Some companies that administer a company's 401(k) pension plan have educational resources and webinars that can be incorporated into a corporate well-being program at little or no cost.

Five Steps: A Roadmap to Building Sustainable Well-Being

The authors recognize that the list of factors and levers above may be too long or cumbersome to communicate in the real-world, practical, or urgent contexts of the business environment. We offer the following five steps as a final synthesis that may be more easily conveyed. When these steps are implemented there is a much greater probability that the cultural context will be supportive of well-being in a way that it will be sustainable and will enhance positive outcomes for the organization.

Step one: The executive team begins to develop wise leadership through attitude, perspective, and insight This includes being aware of both factual and theoretical dimensions of their organization and openness to the value of creating and sustaining well-being for the entire workforce. While the task of the organization is to offer products and services, there is a clear recognition of the value of gaining input from the team, the teamwork that leads to a successful outcome, and a commitment to promote the process of enhancing the whole person as a part of the organizational commitment.

Step two: Shift focus to the environment that serves everyone and that contains the 13 levers The workplace must be a well-led, safe, healthy, and encouraging place. The environment should contribute to the opportunities for workers to thrive rather than just survive. There is a recognition that both safety practices and environmental services are fundamentals that need to be established to create a foundation for further well-being.

Step three: Honor the human resources department as essential to well-being through talent acquisition and talent development The HR department must be supported in and view their role as dynamic and constantly adaptive, especially when setting the stage (levers 6 through 9) and implementing programs (levers 10 through 13). They recruit individuals with potential to contribute to the goals of the company, *and* they must take seriously the effort to continually help the workforce grow and develop. This includes setting policy that encourages growth (rather than policy that is reactive and only addresses liability or minimal performance standards). HR must be involved in creating an environment that potentiates the workforce. The HR department bridges the needs of the organization and the needs of the employees and must work diligently to align the goals of each of these dimensions of the organization.

Step four: Establish explicit training in skills that enhance the efficacy and autonomy of the workforce To foster efficacy, autonomy, effective coping, and a sense of control, it is essential to recognize that these are not skills that are learned only once and are then always there, but that they are skills that must be continually exercised to become effective and to be sustainable. The success of the organization involves the ongoing, creative input of workers at all levels of the organization. There is a need to continue to update technical skills in any modern workplace that is attempting to maintain a competitive edge. There is also an need to provide ongoing training in process skills – skills that involve appreciation of the contributions individuals make to the overall mission. This requires a new mindset for (at least some) organizations, involving changes in policy (spearheaded by the HR department) and in management styles (spearheaded by executives) to continually enhance the value of the workers.

Step five: Provide a supportive environment that creates a culture of well-being within the organization This includes all of the factors and levers described in the preceding sections of this chapter. It requires being clear about the value of the work that is done (the VOI) – beyond the goal of making money for the organization (the ROI). It also includes creating an environment in which there is a sense of being a part of a team and effort to create a supportive and caring environment. This can include the wellness programming (within a context of creating well-being rather than within the context of medical cost offset), but is broader than that.

Summary

The goal of this last chapter section was to synthesize evidence and distill practical advice on how to create well-being at work, with an emphasis on doing so with managerial wisdom. Figure 35.3 summarizes the 13 well-being levers and five steps used when applying such wisdom to the creation of well-being. Returning to the first section of this chapter (see Figure 35.1), evidence itself can inform well-being design and strategy but such information is significantly influenced by the application of managerial wisdom (or the lack thereof). Knowing that a tomato is a fruit may not necessarily inhibit someone from cutting it into a fruit salad. Similarly, knowing all the evidence for workplace well-being will not necessarily translate into effective practices. We offer the items listed in Figure 35.3 as ways of leveraging conditions in order to create well-being and as specific steps in a road map to well-being.

Getting Started: Wise Leadership Fundamentals

1. Genuinely seek employee input
2. Make leadership engagement genuine
3. View well-being as "teawork"
4. Emphasize stakeholder priorities
5. Build well-being into the culture

Setting the Stage: Moving to Design

6. Proactively assess organizational readiness
7. Show commitment to champions
8. Make programs clear, coherent, applicable
9. Establish metrics of relevance

In Motion: Design Details and Mechanics

10. Use tailored interventions (modularize)
11. Foster comprehensive communications
12. Intentionally enhance the work environment
13. Keep sight of details of program integration

Five Steps: Road Map to Well-Being

I. Develop wise leadership

II. Shift focus to environment

III. Honour human resources

IV. Train for efficacy and autonomy

V. Provide a supportive culture

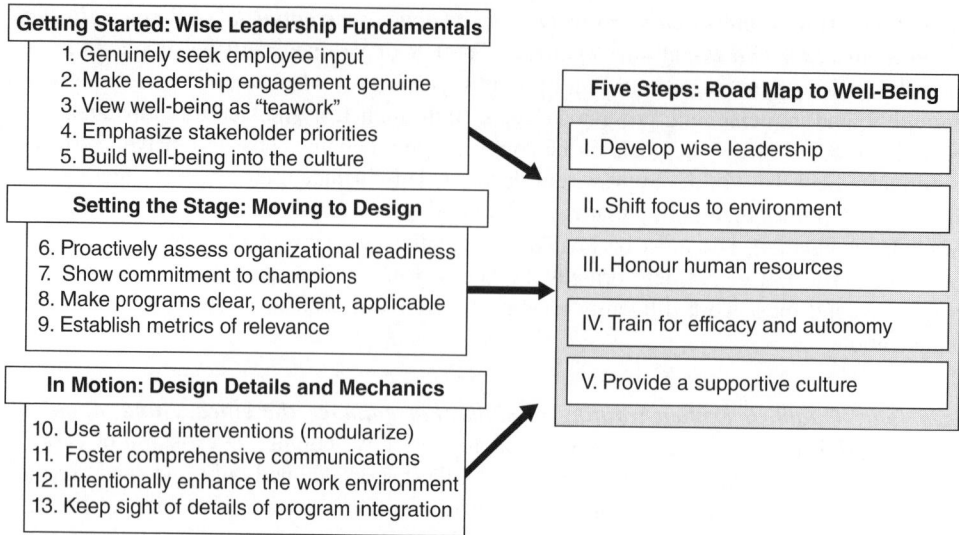

Figure 35.3   Well-being levers and five steps used when applying managerial wisdom.

Next Steps for Practitioners, Researchers, and Worksite Leaders

The identification of optimal methods for the creation of well-being will likely require collaboration from practitioners (in employee assistance, wellness, safety, and human resources) and from researchers who study the practices and services of these practitioners. Ultimately, though, it will require the wise decision-making of those leaders who first, choose one strategy, initiative, or program over another; second, observe the consequences of those choices; and third, ideally consult with the practitioners and researchers as these consequences – whatever they are – are realized.

This chapter is an attempt to provide information that will assist all three of these groups. For practitioners, we hope that we have done a fair job of representing the viewpoints, resources, advantages, and challenges they face as they seek to make wise choices when selling, consulting on, or delivering programs. The next steps for practitioners might be to review the levers and the road map as practical tools they can use. Specifically, we hope that the evidence (quantitative and qualitative) and case studies provided build confidence that these levers and steps could actually work.

For researchers, we recognize that we have built perhaps too broad a framework to have any real utility (see Figure 35.1) or too expedient a summary of the research to be accurate (see Figure 35.2). It remains to be seen whether the eight factors are distinct enough to warrant separate categories or whether they have equally important predictive value. Clearly, more work needs to be done to establish a taxonomy of the leading predictors of employee well-being and how much well-being is, as a construct, distinct from neighboring constructs noted (e.g., mindfulness, sense of coherence). It is also possible that well-being might emerge as a "superordinate" or latent construct that combines key elements of these other important contributions to well-being. The next steps for researchers include testing out these basic questions as well as more applied studies. The latter may include creating and testing interventions – through clinical trials – that test the impact of various levers and steps.

For worksite leaders we hope that the detailed information provided serves as a resource for their own leadership development but also as a persuasive call to work more closely and collaboratively with their key human resource partners, as well as with consultants who can bring evidence-based knowledge to bear on key decisions. Leadership development is a broad and complex topic, with many theories, ideas, practice guidelines, and training curricula. In 2014, United States spending on corporate training grew by 15 percent (the highest growth rate in seven years) to over $70 billion in the US and over $130 billion worldwide (Bersin, 2014), and the largest contributor to this budget (35 percent) was in the area of leadership development. As wellness and well-being programs become more integral as the "way of doing business," we foresee that wisdom (not knowledge) about the predictive factors, levers, and steps will enhance leadership skill and impact. Actually, we believe that such wisdom will be a central key to effective business leadership for many years to come.

References

Aarons, G. A., Hurlburt, M., and Horwitz, S. M. (2011). Advancing a conceptual model of evidence-based practice implementation in public service sectors. *Administration and Policy in Mental Health and Mental Health Services Research*, 38(1), 4–23.

Abdollahi, A., Talib, A. M., Yaacob, S. N., and Ismail, Z. (2014). Hardiness as a mediator between perceived stress and happiness in nurses. *Journal of Psychiatric and Mental Health Nursing*, 21(9), 789–796.

Adams, R. L. (2011). *Examining the Effects of Mindfulness-Based Stress Reduction (MBSR) Training on Working Adults*. Palo Alto, CA: Institute of Transpersonal Psychology.

AHA (American Heart Association) (2016). Fit-friendly worksites recognition. At http://www.heart.org/ HEARTORG/HealthyLiving/WorkplaceHealth/Fit-FriendlyWorksites/Fit-Friendly-Worksites-Recognition_UCM _460612_Article.jsp#.V773zJgrKUk (accessed July 2016).

Aikens, K. A., Astin, J., Pelletier, K. R., Levanovich, K., Baase, C. M., Park, Y. Y., and Bodnar, C. M. (2014). Mindfulness goes to work: Impact of an online workplace intervention. *Journal of Occupational and Environmental Medicine*, 56(7), 721–731.

Albrecht, S. L., Bakker, A. B., Gruman, J. A., Macey, W. H., and Saks, A. M. (2015). Employee engagement, human resource management practices and competitive advantage: An integrated approach. *Journal of Organizational Effectiveness: People and Performance*, 2(1), 7–35.

Allen, T. D. (2001) Family-supportive work environments: The role of organizational perceptions. *Journal of Vocational Behavior*, 58, 414–435.

APA (American Psychological Association) (2009). Psychologically healthy workplaces have lower turnover, less stress, and higher satisfaction. At http://www.apaexcellence.org/assets/general/phwp-chart-2009.pdf (accessed July 2016).

APA (American Psychological Association) (2014). 2014 work and well-being survey. At http://www.apaexcel lence.org/assets/general/2014-work-and-wellbeing-survey-results.pdf (accessed July 2016).

Attridge, M. (2013). The business value of employee assistance: A review of the art and science of ROI [return on investment]. Keynote address at the meeting of the Employee Assistance Professionals Association, Phoenix, AZ. At https://archive.hshsl.umaryland.edu/handle/10713/3905 (accessed July 2016).

Avey, J. B., Luthans, F., Smith, R. M., and Palmer, N. F. (2010). Impact of positive psychological capital on employee well-being over time. *Journal of Occupational Health Psychology*, 15(1), 17.

Baicker, K., Cutler, D., and Song, Z. (2010). Workplace wellness programs can generate savings. *Health Affairs*, 29(2), 304–311.

Bakker, A. B., and Demerouti, E. (2008). Towards a model of work engagement. *Career Development International*, 13(3), 209–223.

Basen-Engquist, K., Hudmon, K. S., Tripp, M., and Chamberlain, R. (1998). Worksite health and safety climate: Scale development and effects of a health promotion intervention. *Preventing Medicine*, 27, 111–119.

Baxter, S., Sanderson, K., Venn, A. J., Blizzard, C. L., and Palmer, A. J. (2014). The relationship between return on investment and quality of study methodology in workplace health promotion programs. *American Journal of Health Promotion*, 28(6), 347–363.

Bazarko, D., Cate, R. A., Azocar, F., and Kreitzer, M. J. (2013). The impact of an innovative mindfulness-based stress reduction program on the health and well-being of nurses employed in a corporate setting. *Journal of Workplace Behavioral Health*, 28(2), 107–133.

Bennett, J. (2009). Why bother waiting? Do it now! ROI [return on investment] estimation versus ROI studies? Presentation, Advanced Worksite Academy, National Wellness Institute. At http://www.slideshare.net/JoelBennett/roi-calculator-presentation-for-nwi-2009 (accessed July 2016).

Bennett, J. (2010). Organizational readiness for prevention. *Wellness Manager* (Aug. 4). At https://wellnessmanager.wordpress.com/2010/08/04/organizational-readiness-for-prevention/ (accessed July 2016).

Bennett, J. B. (2014). *Raw Coping Power: From Stress to Thriving*. Fort Worth: Organizational Wellness and Learning Systems, Inc.

Bennett, J., Bray, J., Hughes, D., Hunter, J., Frey, J. J., Roman, P., and Sharar, D. (2015). Bridging public health with workplace behavioral health services. At http://www.eapassn.org/Portals/11/Docs/Newsbrief/PBRNwhitepaper.pdf (accessed July 2016).

Bennett, J. B., and Linde, B. (2016) *Well-Being Champions: A Competency-Based Guidebook*. Fort Worth: Organizational Wellness & Learning Systems.

Bennett, J., and Simone, l. (2014). Wellness champion competencies. Paper presented at National Wellness Conference, June. At http://www.slideshare.net/JoelBennett2/wellness-champion-competencies-national-wellness-institute2014 (accessed July 2016).

Berry, L., Mirabito, A., and Baun, W. (2010). What's the hard return on employee wellness programs. *Harvard Business Review*, 88(12), pp. 104–112.

Bersin, J. (2014). Spending on corporate training soars: Employee capabilities now a priority. Forbes/Leadership (Feb. 4). At http://www.forbes.com/sites/joshbersin/2014/02/04/the-recovery-arrives-corporate-training-spend-skyrockets/ (accessed July 2016).

Bolier, L., Haverman, M., Westerhof, G. J., Riper, H., Smit, F., and Bohlmeijer, E. (2013). Positive psychology interventions: A meta-analysis of randomized controlled studies. *BMC Public Health*, 13(1), 119.

Bolnick, H., Millard, F., and Dugas, J. P. (2013). Medical care savings from workplace wellness programs: What is a realistic savings potential?. *Journal of Occupational and Environmental Medicine*, 55(1), 4–9.

Boxall, P., and Macky, K. (2014). High-involvement work processes, work intensification and employee well-being. *Work, Employment and Society*, 28(6), 963–984.

Boyar, S. L., Maertz, C., Pearson, A., and Keough, S. (2003). Work–family conflict: A model of linkages between work and family domain variables and turnover intentions. *Journal of Managerial Issues*, 15, 175–190.

Briner, R. B., and Walshe, N. D. (2015). An evidence-based approach to improving the quality of resource-oriented well-being interventions at work. *Journal of Occupational and Organizational Psychology*, 88(3), 563–586.

Brown, K. W., and Ryan, R. M. (2003). The benefits of being present: Mindfulness and its role in psychological well-being. *Journal of Personality and Social Psychology*, 84(4), 822.

Bryson, A., Forth, J., and Stokes, L. (2014). Does worker wellbeing affect workplace performance? Department for Business, Innovation and Skills, UK Government.

Burke, C. (2014). 50 companies named Greater Washington's healthiest employers. *Washington Business Journal* (Aug. 8). At http://www.bizjournals.com/washington/news/2014/08/08/50-companies-named-greater-washingtons-healthiest.html (accessed July 2016).

Canadian Standards Association (2013). *Psychological Health and Safety in the Workplace: Prevention, Promotion, and Guidance to Staged Implementation*. CAN/CSA-Z1003-13/BNQ 9700-803/2013. Toronto: CSA Group.

Cassidy, T., McLaughlin, M., and McDowell, E. (2014). Bullying and health at work: The mediating roles of psychological capital and social support. *Work and Stress*, 28(3), 255–269.

Centers for Disease Control (2016). Well-being concepts. At http://www.cdc.gov/hrqol/wellbeing.htm (accessed July 2016).

Chapman, L. S. (2012). Meta-evaluation of worksite health promotion economic return studies: 2012 update. *American Journal of Health Promotion*, 26(4), TAHP-1.

Cheng, Z. (2014) The effects of employee involvement and participation on subjective well-being: Evidence from China. *Social Indicators Research*, 118, 457–483.

Chenoweth, D. (2011). *Promoting Employee Well-Being: Wellness Strategies to Improve Health, Performance and the Bottom Line*. Alexandria, VA: Society for Human Resource Management.

Cochrane (2015). *2015 Annual Review*. At http://www.cochrane.org/ (accessed July 2016).

Cook, J. (2012). The benefits of workplace wellness programs. *Associations Now* (July). American Society of Association Executives. At https://www.asaecenter.org/Resources/ANowDetail.cfm?ItemNumber=182047 (accessed July 2016).

Cooper, R., Burton, E., and Cooper, C. L. (2014). *Wellbeing and the Environment, vol. 2 of Wellbeing: A Complete Reference Guide*. Chichester, UK: Wiley Blackwell.

Creed, P. A., French, J., and Hood, M. (2015). Working while studying at university: The relationship between work benefits and demands and engagement and well-being. *Journal of Vocational Behavior*, *86*, 48–57.

Cunningham, C. J. (2014). Religion and spirituality as factors that influence occupational stress and well-being. In P. L. Perrewé, C. C. Rosen, and J. R. B. Halbesleben (Eds.), *The Role of Demographics in Occupational Stress and Well-Being* (pp. 135–172). Bingley, UK: Emerald.

Czabala, C., and Charzynska, K. (2014). A systematic review of mental health promotion in the workplace. In F. Huppert, and C. L. Cooper (Eds.), *Interventions and Policies to Enhance Wellbeing, vol. 6 of Wellbeing: A Complete Reference Guide* (pp. 221–276). Chichester, UK: Wiley Blackwell.

Day, A., Kelloway, E. K., and Hurrell, J. J. (2014). *Workplace Well-Being: How to Build Psychologically Healthy Workplaces*. Chichester, UK: Wiley Blackwell

Deci, E., and Ryan, R. (2014). The importance of universal psychological needs for understanding motivation in the workplace. In M. Gagné (Ed.), *The Oxford Handbook of Work Engagement, Motivation, and Self-Determination Theory* (pp. 13–32). Oxford: Oxford University Press.

Delos (2016). WELL Building Standard. At http://delos.com/about/well-building-standard/ (accessed July 2016).

Denier, E., Suh, M., Lucas, E., and Smith, H. (1999) Subjective well-being: Three decades of progress. *Psychological Bulletin*, *125*(2), 276–302.

Dewe, P. (2014). Positive psychology and coping: Towards a better understanding of the relationship. In P. Y. Chen and C. L. Cooper (Eds.), *Work and Wellbeing, vol. 3 of Wellbeing: A Complete Reference Guide* (pp. 65–90). Chichester, UK: Wiley Blackwell.

Dodge, R., Daly, A. P., Huyton, J., and Sanders, L. D. (2012). The challenge of defining wellbeing. *International Journal of Wellbeing*, *2*(3), 222–235.

Duggleby, W., Cooper, D., and Penz, K. (2009). Hope, self-efficacy, spiritual well-being and job satisfaction. *Journal of Advanced Nursing*, *65*(11), 2376–2385.

Eatough, E. M., and Spector, P. E. (2014). The role of workplace control in positive health and wellbeing. In P. Chen and C. L. Cooper (Eds.), *Work and Wellbeing, vol. 3 of Wellbeing: A Complete Reference Guide* (pp. 91–110). Chichester, UK: Wiley Blackwell.

Edington, D. (2014). Helping employees stay healthy is a good investment. Society for Human Resource Management. At https://www.shrm.org/resourcesandtools/hr-topics/benefits/pages/dee-edington.aspx (accessed July 2016).

Edmunds, S., Stephenson, D., and Clow, A. (2013). The effects of a physical activity intervention on employees in small and medium enterprises: A mixed methods study. *Work*, *46*(1), 39–49.

Fletcher, D., and Sarkar, M. (2013). Psychological resilience. *European Psychologist*, *18*(1), 12–23.

Flint, E., Bartley, M., Shelton, N., and Sacker, A. (2013). Do labour market status transitions predict changes in psychological well-being? *Journal of Epidemiology and Community Health*, *67*(9), 796–802.

Foureur, M., Besley, K., Burton, G., Yu, N., and Crisp, J. (2013). Enhancing the resilience of nurses and midwives: Pilot of a mindfulness-based program for increased health, sense of coherence and decreased depression, anxiety and stress. *Contemporary Nurse*, *45*(1), 114–125.

Freeman, R. B., Kleiner, M. M., and Ostroff, C. (2000). *The Anatomy of Employee Involvement and Its Effects on Firms and Workers*. Working Paper No. 8050. Cambridge, MA: National Bureau of Economic Research.

Gagné, M., and Bhave, D. (2011). Autonomy in the workplace: An essential ingredient to employee engagement and well-being in every culture. In V. Chirkov, R. Ryan, and K. M. Sheldon (Eds.), *Human Autonomy in Cross-Cultural Context* (pp. 163–187). New York: Springer.

Gagné, M., and Deci, E. L. (2005). Self-determination theory and work motivation. *Journal of Organizational Behavior*, *26*(4), 331–362.

Global Wellness Institute (2015). *Redefining Workplace Wellness: 2015 Roundtable Report*. At http://www.global wellnessinstitute.org/re-defining-workplace-wellness-roundtable (accessed July 2016).

Goetzel, R. Z., Henke, R. M., Tabrizi, M., Pelletier, K. R., Loeppke, R., Ballard, D. W., … and Metz, R. D. (2014). Do workplace health promotion (wellness) programs work? *Journal of Occupational and Environmental Medicine*, *56*(9), 927–934.

Goetzel, R. Z., Shechter, D., Ozminkowski, R. J., Marmet, P. F., Tabrizi, M. J., and Roemer, E. C. (2007). Promising practices in employer health and productivity management efforts: Findings from a benchmarking study. *Journal of Occupational and Environmental Medicine*, 49(2), 111–130.

Gonçalves, S. P., and Neves, J. (2012). The link between perceptions of human resource management practices and employee well-being at work. *Advances in Psychology Study*, 1(1), 31–38.

Grawitch, M., and Ballard, D. (2015). *The Psychologically Healthy Workplace*. Washington, DC: American Psychological Association

Grawitch, M. J., Gottschalk, M., and Munz, D. C. (2006). The path to a healthy workplace: A critical review linking healthy workplace practices, employee well-being, and organizational improvements. *Consulting Psychology Journal: Practice and Research*, 58(3), 129.

Grawitch, M. J., Leford, J. E., Ballard, D. W., and Barber, L. K. (2009). Leading the healthy workforce: The integral role of employee involvement. *Consulting Psychology Journal: Practice and Research*, 61(2), 122–135.

Grawitch, M. J., Trares, S., and Kohler, J. M. (2007). Healthy workplace practices and employee outcomes. *International Journal of Stress Management*, 14(3), 275–293.

Great Place to Work (2016). The world's best. At http://www.greatplacetowork.net/best-companies/worlds-best-multinationals (accessed July 2016).

Greenhaus, J. H., and Powell, G. N. (2003). When work and family collide: Deciding between competing role demands. *Academy of Management Review*, 31, 72–92.

Grossmeier, J., Terry, P. E., and Anderson, D. R. (2014). Broadening the metrics used to evaluate corporate wellness programs: The case for understanding the total value of the investment. In R. J. Burke and A. M. Richardsen (Eds.), *Corporate Wellness Programs: Linking Employee and Organizational Health* (pp. 297–321). Cheltenham, UK: Edward Elgar.

Hamar, B., Coberley, C., Pope, J. E., and Rula, E. Y. (2015). Well-being improvement in a midsize employer. *Journal of Occupational and Environmental Medicine*, 57(4), 367–373.

Hannon, P. A., Helfrich, C. D., Chan, K. G., Allen, C. L., Hammerback, K., Kohn, M. J., ... and Harris, J. R. (2015). Development and pilot test of the Workplace Readiness Questionnaire, a theory-based instrument to measure small workplaces' readiness to implement wellness programs. *American Journal of Health Promotion*. Epub ahead of print.

Harris, K., Grey, M. C., and Rozwell, C. (2001). Changing the view of ROI to VOI – Value on Investment. Technical Report. At https://www.gartner.com/doc/348953/changing-view-roi-voi- (accessed July 2016).

Harter, J. K., Schmidt, F. L., and Keyes, C. L. (2003). Well-being in the workplace and its relationship to business outcomes: A review of the Gallup studies. *Flourishing: Positive Psychology and the Life Well-Lived*, 2, 205–224.

Hartung, D., and Hahlweg, K. (2010). Strengthening parent well-being at the work–family interface: A German trial on workplace Triple P. *Journal of Community and Applied Social Psychology*, 20(5), 404–418.

Health Project (2016). C. Everett Koop National Health Awards. At http://thehealthproject.com/ (accessed July 2016).

Healthiest Employers (2016). We recognize wellness. At https://healthiestemployers.com/awards/about-wellness-award/ (accessed July 2016).

HERO (Health Enhancement Research Organization) (2015). Exploring the value proposition for workforce health: Business leader attitudes about the role of health as a driver of productivity and performance. At http://hero-health.org/wp-content/uploads/2015/02/HPP-Business-Leader-Survey-Full-Report_FINAL.pdf (accessed July 2016).

Hoebbel, C., Golaszewski, T., Swanson, M., and Dorn, J. (2012). Culture change. *American Journal of Health Promotion*, 26(5), ii–iii.

Hoffmeister, K., Gibbons, A., Schwatka, N., and Rosecrance, J. (2015). Ergonomics climate assessment: A measure of operational performance and employee well-being. *Applied Ergonomics*, 50, 160–169.

Hymel, P. A., Loeppke, R. R., Baase, C. M., Burton, W. N., Hartenbaum, N. P., Hudson, T. W., ... and Larson, P. W. (2011). Workplace health protection and promotion: A new pathway for a healthier – and safer – workforce. *Journal of Occupational and Environmental Medicine*, 53(6), 695–702.

Jeffrey, K., Abdallah, S., and Michaelson, J. (2014). *Wellbeing at Work: A Review of the Literature*. At http://b.3cdn.net/nefoundation/71c1bb59a2ce151df7_8am6bqr2q.pdf (accessed July 2016).

Kalemci, I., and Kalemci, R. (2012). Organizational and supervisory support in relation to employee turnover intentions. *Journal of Managerial Psychology*, 27(5), 518–534.

Kaplan, S., Bradley-Geist, J. C., Ahmad, A., Anderson, A., Hargrove, A. K., and Lindsey, A. (2014). A test of two positive psychology interventions to increase employee well-being. *Journal of Business and Psychology*, 29(3), 367–380.

Karanika-Murray, M., and Weyman, A. K. (2013). Optimising workplace interventions for health and well-being: A commentary on the limitations of the public health perspective within the workplace health arena. *International Journal of Workplace Health Management*, *6*(2), 104–117.

Kaufman, S. (2015). Which character strengths are most predictive of well-being? *Scientific American*, blog, Aug. 2. At http://blogs.scientificamerican.com/beautiful-minds/which-character-strengths-are-most-predictive-of-well-being/ (accessed July 2016).

Kessler, E. H., and Bailey, J. R. (2007). *Handbook of Organizational and Managerial Wisdom*. Thousand Oaks, CA: Sage.

Kilfedder, C., and Litchfield, P. (2014). Wellbeing as a business priority: Experience from the corporate world. In F. Huppert and C. L. Cooper (Eds.), *Interventions and Policies to Enhance Wellbeing, vol. 6 of Wellbeing: A Complete Reference Guide* (pp. 357–386). Chichester, UK: Wiley Blackwell.

Kim, J., Garman, E. T., and Sorhaindo, B. (2003). Relationships among credit counseling clients' financial wellbeing, financial behaviors, financial stressor events, and health. *Journal of Financial Counseling and Planning*, *14*(2).

Knabe, A., Rätzel, S., Schöb, R., and Weimann, J. (2010). Dissatisfied with life but having a good day: Time-use and well-being of the unemployed. *Economic Journal*, *120*(547), 867–889.

Kowalewski, S. J., and Phillips, S. L. (2012). Preferences for performance-based employee rewards: Evidence from small business environments. *International Journal of Management and Marketing Research*, *5*, 65–76.

Lach, E. L. (2000). Wanamaker, John. In *American National Biography Online*. At http://www.anb.org/articles/10/10-01706.html (accessed July 2016).

LaMontagne, A. D., Keegel, T., Louie, A. M., Ostry, A., and Landsbergis, P. A. (2007). A systematic review of the job-stress intervention evaluation literature, 1990–2005. *International Journal of Occupational and Environmental Health*, *13*(3), 268–280.

Latham, G. P., and Pinder, C. C. (2005). Work motivation theory and research at the dawn of the twenty-first century. *Annual Review of Psychology*, *56*, 485–516.

Leon, M. R., and Halbesleben, J. B. (2014). Building resilience to improve employee well-being. In M. Rossi, J. A. Meurs, and P. L. Perrewé (Eds.), *Improving Employee Health and Well-Being* (pp. 65–81). Charlotte, NC: Information Age.

Leppin, A. L., Bora, P. R., Tilburt, J. C., Gionfriddo, M. R., Zeballos-Palacios, C., and Dulohery, M. M. (2014). The efficacy of resiliency training programs: A systematic review and meta-analysis of randomized trials. *PLoS ONE*, *9*(10), e111420.

Lin, Y. W., and Lin, Y. Y. (2014). A multilevel model of organizational health culture and the effectiveness of health promotion. *American Journal of Health Promotion*, *29*(1), e53–e63.

Linnabery, E., Stuhlmacher, A. F., and Towler, A. (2014). From whence cometh their strength: Social support, coping, and well-being of black women professionals. *Cultural Diversity and Ethnic Minority Psychology*, *20*(4), 541–549.

Lockwood, N. R. (2007). Leveraging employee engagement for competitive advantage. *Society for Human Resource Management Research Quarterly*, *1*, 1–12.

Lomas, T. (2015). Positive social psychology: A multilevel inquiry into sociocultural well-being initiatives. *Psychology, Public Policy, and Law*, *21*(3), 338.

Lottrup, L., Grahn, P., and Stigsdotter, U. K. (2013). Workplace greenery and perceived level of stress: Benefits of access to a green outdoor environment at the workplace. *Landscape and Urban Planning*, *110*, 5–11.

Macedo, T., Wilheim, L., Gonçalves, R., Coutinho, E. S., Vilete, L., Figueira, I., and Ventura, P. (2014). Building resilience for future adversity: A systematic review of interventions in non-clinical samples of adults. *BMC Psychiatry*, *14*(1), 227.

Maddi, S. R., Kahn, S., and Maddi, K. L. (1998). The effectiveness of hardiness training. *Consulting Psychology Journal: Practice and Research*, *50*(2), 78.

Markey, R., Lamm, F., Harris, C., Ravenswood, K., Williamson, D., Knudsen, H. L., … and Lind, J. (2008). Improving productivity through enhancing employee wellness and well-being. Paper presented at Third European Congress of the Work and Labour Network, Rome, Italy.

Marschke, E., and Mujtaba, B. G. (2014). Creating a wellness culture through human resources. *Journal of Physical Education*, *1*(1), 61–80.

Mastroianni, K., and Storberg-Walker, J. (2014). Do work relationships matter? Characteristics of workplace interactions that enhance or detract from employee perceptions of well-being and health behaviors. *Health Psychology and Behavioral Medicine*, *2*(1), 798–819.

Mattke, S., Liu, H., Caloyeras, J. P., Huang, C. Y., Van Busum, K. R., Khodyakov, D., and Shier, D. (2013). *Workplace Wellness Programs Study: Final Report*. Santa Monica: RAND Corporation.

Mazzucchelli, T. G., Kane, R. T., and Rees, C. S. (2010). Behavioral activation interventions for well-being: A meta-analysis. *Journal of Positive Psychology*, 5(2), 105–121.

McDaid, D., and Park, A. (2014). Investing in wellbeing in the workplace: More than just a business case. In D. McDaid and C. L. Cooper (Eds.), *The Economics of Wellbeing, vol. 5 of Wellbeing: A Complete Reference Guide* (pp. 215–238). Chichester, UK: Wiley Blackwell.

McGonigle, K. (2015) *The Upside of Stress: Why Stress Is Good for You, and How to Get Good at It*. New York: Avery.

McGuire, D., and McLaren, L. (2009). The impact of physical environment on employee commitment in call centres: The mediating role of employee well-being. *Team Performance Management*, 15(1/2), 35–48.

McKee-Ryan, F., Song, Z., Wanberg, C. R., and Kinicki, A. J. (2005). Psychological and physical well-being during unemployment: A meta-analytic study. *Journal of Applied Psychology*, 90(1), 53.

McKenna, B., Rooney, D., and Boal, K. B. (2009). Wisdom principles as a meta-theoretical basis for evaluating leadership. *Leadership Quarterly*, 20(2), 177–190.

Mearns, K., Hope, L., Ford, M. T., and Tetrick, L. E. (2010). Investment in work-force health: Exploring the implications for workforces safety climate and commitment. *Accident Analysis and Prevention*, 42, 1445–1454.

Mellor, N., and Webster, J. (2013). Enablers and challenges in implementing a comprehensive workplace health and well-being approach. *International Journal of Workplace Health Management*, 6(2), 129–142.

Messersmith, J. G., Patel, P. C., Lepak, D. P., and Gould-Williams, J. S. (2011). Unlocking the black box: Exploring the link between high-performance work systems and performance. *Journal of Applied Psychology*, 96(6), 1105–1118.

Milliman, J., Czaplewski, A. J., and Ferguson, J. (2003). Workplace spirituality and employee work attitudes: An exploratory empirical assessment. *Journal of Organizational Change Management*, 16(4), 426–447.

Miller, S. (2014). Millennials most receptive to wellness outreach. Society for Human Resource Management. At https://www.shrm.org/resourcesandtools/hr-topics/benefits/pages/millennials-wellness.aspx (accessed July 2016).

Miller, M., Reichelstein, J., Salas, C., and Zia, B. (2015). Can you help someone become financially capable? A meta-analysis of the literature. Policy Research Working Paper 6745. World Bank.

Moradi, M., and Cheraghi, A. (2015). The relationship of social supports to psychological well-being and depression: The mediating roles of self-esteem and basic psychological needs. *Journal of Iranian Psychologists*, 11(43), 297–312.

Ng, T. W., and Sorensen, K. L. (2008). Toward a further understanding of the relationships between perceptions of support and work attitudes: A meta-analysis. *Group and Organization Management*, 33(3), 243–268.

Nie, Y. Y., Chua, B. L., Yeung, A. S., Ryan, R. M., and Chan, W. Y. (2015). The importance of autonomy support and the mediating role of work motivation for well-being: Testing self-determination theory in a Chinese work organisation. *International Journal of Psychology*, 50(4), 245–255.

Nilsson, P., Andersson, I. H., Ejlertsson, G., and Troein, M. (2012). Workplace health resources based on sense of coherence theory. *International Journal of Workplace Health Management*, 5(3), 156–167.

Nonaka, I., Chia, R., Holt, R., and Peltokorpi, V. (2014). Wisdom, management and organization. *Management Learning*, 45(4), 365–376.

OECD (Organization for Economic Co-operation and Development) (2013). Economic well-being. In *OECD Framework for Statistics on the Distribution of Household Income, Consumption and Wealth* (pp. 25–38). At http://www.oecd.org/statistics/OECD-ICW-Framework-Chapter2.pdf (accessed July 2016).

Ouweneel, E., Le Blanc, P. M., and Schaufeli, W. B. (2013). Do-it-yourself: An online positive psychology intervention to promote positive emotions, self-efficacy, and engagement at work. *Career Development International*, 18(2), 173–195.

Partnership for Prevention (2014). *Leading by Example: Creating a Corporate Health Strategy: The American Health Strategy Project Early Adopter Experience*. At http://www.prevent.org/initiatives/leading-by-example.aspx (accessed July 2016).

Paterson, T. A., Luthans, F., and Jeung, W. (2014). Thriving at work: Impact of psychological capital and supervisor support. *Journal of Organizational Behavior*, 35(3), 434–446.

Peterson, S. J., Luthans, F., Avolio, B. J., Walumbwa, F. O., and Zhang, Z. (2011). Psychological capital and employee performance: A latent growth modeling approach. *Personnel Psychology*, 64(2), 427–450.

Phoolka, E. S., and Kaur, N. (2012). Adversity quotient: A new paradigm to explore. *Contemporary Business Studies*, 3, 67–78.

Putnam, L. (2015). *Workplace Wellness That Works: 10 Steps to Infuse Well-Being and Vitality into Any Organization*. Hoboken, NJ: Wiley.

Richardson, K. M., and Rothstein, H. R. (2008). Effects of occupational stress management intervention programs: A meta-analysis. *Journal of Occupational Health Psychology*, 13(1), 69.

Richmond, M. K., Pampel, F. C., Wood, R. C., and Nunes, A. P. (2015). The impact of employee assistance services on workplace outcomes: Results of a prospective, quasi-experimental study. *Journal of Occupational Health Psychology*. Epub ahead of print.

Robertson, I. T., Cooper, C. L., Sarkar, M., and Curran, T. (2015). Resilience training in the workplace from 2003 to 2014: A systematic review. *Journal of Occupational and Organizational Psychology*, 88(3), 533–562.

Rosenbloom, J. (2011). *The Handbook of Employee Benefits: Health and Group Benefits*, 7th edn. New York: McGraw Hill Professional.

Rousseau, M. B., Eddleston, K. A., Patel, P. C., and Kellermanns, F. W. (2014). Organizational resources and demands influence on workplace bullying. *Journal of Managerial Issues*, 26(3), 286–313.

Ryan, M., McPeck, W., and Chapman, L. S. (2011). Evidence-based programming: A practitioner's guide. *American Journal of Health Promotion*, 25, TAHP-1.

Salas, E., and Weaver, S. J. (2015) Employee growth and development: Cultivating human capital. In M. Grawitch and D. Ballard (Eds.), *The Psychologically Healthy Workplace*. Washington, DC: American Psychological Association.

SAMHSA (Substance Abuse and Mental Health Services Administration) (2016). NREPP: SAMHSA's National Registry of Evidence-Based Prevention Programs and Practices. At http://www.nrepp.samhsa.gov/ (accessed July 2016).

SAS (2014). SAS ranks no. 2 on 2014 Fortune list of best companies to work for in the US. Press release. At http://www.sas.com/en_us/news/press-releases/2014/january/great-workplace-US-Fortune-2014.html (accessed July 2016).

Schulte, P. A., Guerin, R. J., Schill, A. L., Bhattacharya, A., Cunningham, T. R., Pandalai, S. P., … Stephenson, C. M. (2015). Considerations for incorporating "well-being" in public policy for workers and workplaces. *American Journal of Public Health*, 105(8), e31–e44.

Schwartz, B., Ward, A., Monterosso, J., Lyubomirsky, S., White, K., and Lehman, D. R. (2002). Maximizing versus satisficing: Happiness is a matter of choice. *Journal of Personality and Social Psychology*, 83(5), 1178–1197.

Seery, M. D., Holman, E. A., and Silver, R. C. (2010). Whatever does not kill us: Cumulative lifetime adversity, vulnerability, and resilience. *Journal of Personality and Social Psychology*, 99(6), 1025.

Seligman, M. P. (2011) *Flourish: A New Understanding of Happiness and Well-Being – and How to Achieve Them*. London: Nicholas Brealey.

Sharar, D., and Lennox, R. (2014) The workplace effects of EAP use: "Pooled" results from 20 different EAPs with before and after WOS 5-item data. *EASNA Research Notes*, 4(1), 1–5.

Sharar, D. A., Lennox, R., and Burke, J. (2010). Conducting an EAP evaluation using the workplace outcome suite. *Journal of Employee Assistance*, 40(4), 24–27.

Sharar, D., Pompe, J., and Lennox, R. (2012). Evaluating the workplace effects of EAP counseling. *Journal of Health and Productivity*, 6(2), 5–14.

SHRM (Society for Human Resource Management) (2015). 2015 Employee job satisfaction and engagement report: Optimizing organizational culture for success. At http://www.shrm.org/research/surveyfindings/pages/job-satisfaction-and-engagement-report-optimizing-organizational-culture-for-success.aspx (accessed July 2016).

Shuck, B., and Reio, T. G. (2014). Employee engagement and well-being: A moderation model and implications for practice. *Journal of Leadership and Organizational Studies*, 21(1), 43–58.

Simmons, B. L. (2014). Organizational characteristics of happy organizations. In P. Y. Chen and C. L. Cooper (Eds.), *Work and Wellbeing, vol. 3 of Wellbeing: A Complete Reference Guide* (pp. 139–156). Chichester, UK: Wiley Blackwell.

Sloan, M. M. (2011). Unfair treatment in the workplace and worker well-being: The role of coworker support in a service work environment. *Work and Occupations*, 39(1), 3–34.

Smith, A., and Pitt, M. (2009). Sustainable workplaces: Improving staff health and well-being using plants. *Journal of Corporate Real Estate*, 11(1), 52–63.

Sørensen, O. H., and Holman, D. (2014). A participative intervention to improve employee well-being in knowledge work jobs: A mixed-methods evaluation study. *Work and Stress*, 28(1), 67–86.

Spangler, N. W., Koesten, J., Fox, M. H., and Radel, J. (2012). Employer perceptions of stress and resilience intervention. *Journal of Occupational and Environmental Medicine*, 54(11), 1421–1429.

Spreitzer, G. M., and Porath, C. (2013). Self-determination as a nutriment for thriving: Building an integrative model of human growth at work. In M. Gagné (Ed.), *Oxford Handbook of Work Engagement, Motivation, and Self-Determination Theory* (pp. 245–258). Oxford: Oxford University Press.

Spreitzer, G. M., Sutcliffe, K., Dutton, J., Sonenshein, S., and Grant, A. M. (2005). A socially embedded model of thriving at work. *Organization Science*, 16(5), 537–549.

Stansfeld, S. A., Shipley, M. J., Head, J., Fuhrer, R., and Kivimäki, M. (2013). Work characteristics and personal social support as determinants of subjective well-being. *PLoS ONE*, *8*(11), e81115.

Staywell (2015). StayWell unveils employer guide to developing effective employee wellness champion networks. News release. At http://staywell.com/staywell-unveils-employer-guide-to-developing-effective-employee-wellness-champion-networks/ (accessed July 2016).

Steinbrecher, S., and Bennett, J. B. (2003). *Heart-Centered Leadership: An Invitation to Lead from the Inside Out*. Memphis: Black Pants.

Sternberg, R. J. (2003). *Wisdom, Intelligence and Creativity Synthesized*. Cambridge: Cambridge University Press.

Stelmack, A., Foster, K., and Hindman, D. (2014). *Sustainable Residential Interiors*, 2nd edn. Hoboken, NJ: John Wiley & Sons.

Stewart, G. L., Courtright, S. H., and Manz, C. C. (2011). Self-leadership: A multilevel review. *Journal of Management*, *37*(1), 185–222.

Taft, M. K., Hosein, Z. Z., and Mehrizi, S. M. (2013). The relation between financial literacy, financial wellbeing and financial concerns. *International Journal of Business and Management*, *8*(11), 63.

Terry, P. (2013). Editor's desk: Organizational health scorecards: The art of health promotion ideas for improving health outcomes. *American Journal of Health Promotion*, *27*(5), 1–12.

Tetrick, L. E., and Winslow, C. J. (2015). Workplace stress management interventions and health promotion. *Annual Review of Organizational Psychology and Organizational Behavior*, *2*(1), 583–603.

Thompson, C. A., and Prottas, D. J. (2006). Relationships among organizational family support, job autonomy, perceived control, and employee well-being. *Journal of Occupational Health Psychology*, *11*(1), 100.

Trice, H. M., and Beyer, J. M. (1993). *The Cultures of Work Organizations*. Upper Saddle River, NJ: Prentice Hall.

Vandenberg, R. J., Richardson, H. A., and Eastman, L. J. (1999) The impact of high involvement work processes on organizational effectiveness: A second-order latent variable approach. *Group and Organizational Management, 24*, 300–339.

Van den Broeck, A., Lens, W., De Witte, H., and Van Coillie, H. (2013). Unraveling the importance of the quantity and the quality of workers' motivation for well-being: A person-centered perspective. *Journal of Vocational Behavior*, *82*(1), 69–78.

Van den Heuvel, M., Demerouti, E., and Peeters, M. W. (2015). The job crafting intervention: Effects on job resources, self-efficacy, and affective well-being. *Journal of Occupational and Organizational Psychology*, *88*(3), 511–532.

Ventura, M. S., Salanova, M., and Llorens, S. (2015). Professional self-efficacy as a predictor of burnout and engagement: The role of challenge and hindrance demands. *Journal of Psychology*, *149*(3), 277–302.

Vogel, C. (2015). Conversation with Joel Bennett, Ph.D. *Benefits Magazine*, *52*(6), 10–13. International Foundation of Employee Benefits Plans, Brookfield, WI.

Volpp, K. G., Asch, D. A., Galvin, R., and Loewenstein, G. (2011). Redesigning employee health incentives: Lessons from behavioral economics. *New England Journal of Medicine*, *365*(5), 388–390.

Waddell, G., and Burton, A. K. (2006). *Is Work Good for Your Wellbeing*. London: Stationery Office.

Williams, S., Wissing, M. P., Rothmann, S., and Temane, Q. M. (2010). Self efficacy, work, and psychological outcomes in a public service context. *Journal of Psychology in Africa*, *20*(1), 53–60.

Winkelman Consulting (2002). Benchmark worksite wellness study: Final report. North Dakota Department of Health Division of Health Promotion. At https://www.ndhealth.gov/Publications/CommunityHealth/Benchmark WorksiteWellnessStudy.pdf (accessed July 2016).

World Health Organization (2016). *Mental Health: Strengthening Our Response*. Fact sheet. At http://www.who.int/mediacentre/factsheets/fs220/en/ (accessed July 2016).

Xerox (2016). Improving wellness through social media. At http://www.xerox.com/downloads/usa/en/buck/casestudies/hrc_cs_wellness_through_social_media.pdf (accessed July 2016).

Yandrick, R. (1996). *Behavioral Risk Management: How to Avoid Preventable Losses from Mental Health Problems at Work*. San Francisco: Jossey-Bass.

Zomer, L. (2012). The relationships among emotional intelligence, gender, coping strategies, and well-being in the management of stress in close interpersonal relationships and the workplace. Doctoral dissertation, University of Toronto.

36

Well-Being and Aesthetics

A Social Perspective on the Aged Body in Modern Dance

Stina Johansson and Maria Sjölund

Background

In *The Coming of Age* (1972), Simone de Beauvoir reminds us that old age is our universal human destiny, but that its perceived meaning is specifically related to our historical, cultural and social situation. We all need to deal with age as a complex phenomenon that shifts in meaning over time, with the image of elderly people differing from time to time and from place to place. The understanding of aging in Western culture, as well as in theorizing and research, has a "double meaning," however. We *are* and we *become* human beings in the complex social contexts where we find ourselves. Thus, in a society where age is used to make distinctions between people, young or old, healthy or unhealthy, and where it is used as an objective marker, it is important to explore how (elderly) people experience and negotiate age and aging in relation to their well-being.

Sjölund (2012) found, in her vignette dialogue with a group of amateur dancers aged 65+, that their notions of being and becoming old in society were filled with fears about being dependent and being reduced to an aged person with standardized needs, unable to live a worthy life. The informants felt that society fails to treat old people well in terms of the social support received. It was clear that several of the informants felt that the scope for individuals to decide how to live and what to do is threatened. In this chapter, we will take a closer look at their reflections on aging and well-being, found in their diaries during an intense period of rehearsal for a public dance performance. Independence is an important value in Swedish aging in place ideology (*hemmaboendeideologin*), which means to be cared for at home with support from public services for as long as possible, in contrast to institutional care. This is a value strongly internalized, and sometimes mixed up with the quest for independence, in personal attitudes and behaviors since the 1950s.

The Handbook of Stress and Health: A Guide to Research and Practice, First Edition.
Edited by Cary L. Cooper and James Campbell Quick.
© 2017 John Wiley & Sons, Ltd. Published 2017 by John Wiley & Sons, Ltd.

Söderberg (2012) and Söderberg, Ståhl, and Emilsson (2013) found that when personal independence was threatened due to functional decline, it initiated a process of stigmatization. A
tendency to hide the "stigma" of being dependent set in, with communicative complications
for family members and others in the social network. A feeling of shame was common when
communication failed (Söderberg, 2012). The fears of being a burden on society and fears of
being dependent on other people were also present in Sjölund's (2012) material from amateur
dancers. The most radical voice said he "would prefer to die the same day he stopped being
independent." The amateur dancers expressed the attitude that aging individuals have a great
deal of responsibility to keep themselves active and healthy, and that the day you can no longer
do this, you stop believing you are going to live a meaningful life.

There is a need for more knowledge about what is going on in the minds of aging people and
their networks. Late modernity offers a perspective of old people as subjects. Are older people
able to generate their own "human agency"? In social policy discussions this is combined
with a risk. Are they able to take on the challenge of taking charge of their lives? This is
a discussion about care management, institutional structures and old people as autonomous
consumers of care (Powell and Wahidin 2005). Care, protection and vulnerability are subject to
critical review in social elder-care research. Do researchers and social workers contribute to the
stigmatizing process with their lack of knowledge about tensions between self-defined forms
of well-being and support service assessment? Söderberg (2014) has found evidence that they
do. Care assessments often prioritize risk and particular aspects of physical safety. Isolation
can be such a risk. The elderly are often associated with lack of autonomy, responsibility and
personal authority (Fawcett and Reynolds, 2010).

This chapter is about the tension between social context and old individuals' negotiations
of autonomy, responsibility and personal authority over their aging in relation to their own
well-being.

Active/Productive/Subjective Aging

Active aging in terms of participation in daily activities is often associated with well-being
(Fawcett 2011; 2014). Researchers often refer to social activities, often including a dimension
of altruism, helping others, but also the prevention of disease via physical training, to prolong
the healthy period of life. Volunteering in organizations or care for grandchildren are examples
of such activities. Also staying longer in the workforce could be a sign of being active in
old age. A review of literature (Principi, Chiatti, Lamura, and Frerichs, 2012) showed that
people report that they volunteer in order to maintain their skills, talent and energy, but also
that they were interested in developing new skills. Those who volunteer are characterized
by a high level of educational and socioeconomic status, and they are also healthy. In some
studies volunteering has been found to have health-related outcomes (Principi et al., 2012).
Principi et al. also found that the desire for self-development was reported less frequently.
Ageist practices could also prevent active participation.

In material from the English Longitudinal Study of Ageing, McMunn et al. (2009) found
that people who were in paid work, or volunteering, were less likely to become depressed,
and reported higher mean quality of life and life satisfaction, with the exception of paid work
among those women who did not feel that their efforts were appreciated. In other words, reciprocity in the relationships was very important. Caring was not associated with life satisfaction among women. There are contextual differences, where the United States is identified as a

society where high participation in civil society among older adults is desired and also orga-nized in senior volunteer programs or grandparent programs. European societies, with various traditions, can be characterized by a much less advanced policy debate on the volunteering of older citizens. In addition, the relation between paid work and volunteering differs between the United States and Europe.

Individual capacities for well-being are under discussion. One concept connected to well-being is "wisdom," often described as increasingly complex and dialectic thinking, including awareness of paradoxes and contradictions and the ability to deal with uncertainty, inconsistency, imperfection and compromise. Balance is one of the core components, sometimes described as a search for a compromise between knowledge and doubt. Some definitions include the ability to move beyond the given (for a more detailed analysis of the concept, see Staudinger, 2008).

Images of Age and Aging

Many people consider "being seen as old" and "being treated as old" as negative experiences. Minichiello, Browne, and Kendig (2000) found that active aging can be seen as a positive way of presenting and interpreting oneself as different from "the old group." Many of their informants mentioned negative treatment in terms of poor access to transport and housing, low income or forced retirement. The informants also mentioned that interaction in everyday life involves negative treatment. Others are "keeping watch" for one's vulnerabilities. Instead of accepting ageism, as many do, some people actively negotiate new images of aging for themselves and for a changed image of old people in the future. The concept of *interactive ageism*, how people handle vulnerable situations, was used. There were also older people who experienced positive stereotypes, according to Minichiello et al. (2000). Stereotypes of any kind are problematic to handle, or at least not helpful in situations when notions of well-being and aging are being individually negotiated, as we will be discussing in this chapter.

Well-Being and Social Activity

An engaged lifestyle is an important component of successful aging. Searching for studies that focused on "social and leisure activity and well-being," Adams, Leibbrandt, and Moon (2011) found that domains associated with subjective well-being, health or survival included social, leisure, productive, physical, intellectual, service and solitary activities. Many older adults with high participation in social and leisure activities report positive well-being. Social, leisure and productive activities all have associations and predictive relationships with aspects of well-being. Informal social activity has accumulated the most evidence of an influence on well-being. Well-being includes life satisfaction, happiness, positive affect or quality of life. It could also mean freedom from depression. Activities may affect well-being through their intellectual and physical demands and through the reinforcement of one's self-concept. A Swedish study found that maintaining equilibrium or widening one's range of activities proved to be important in staving off some of the negative psychological effects of functional decline or social losses in later life (Silverstein and Parker, 2002).

The search for meaning could be an important key variable to discover. In any case, as Litwin and Shiovitz-Ezra (2006) found when using data from an Israeli national sample, the qual-ity of social relationships emerged as the most influential variable in the connection between activity and well-being. As Gale, Cooper, Deary, and Sayer (2014) show, also higher levels of psychological well-being reduced the risk of pre-frailty and frailty. Examination of scores for hedonic (pleasure) and eudaimonic (control, autonomy and self-realization) well-being showed that higher scores on both were associated with a decreased risk. Gale et al. (2014) suggest that maintaining a stronger sense of psychological well-being in later life protects against the development of physical frailty.

Participating in meaningful activities as a way of self-actualization is included in what Allardt (1993) defines as a part of *being*, the third pillar of his theory of well-being. His two other pillars of well-being are *having* a material standard of living, and *loving*, which refers to people's social relations. We have chosen to explore the concept of "participating in meaningful activities" as a part of being. Karisto and Haapola (2015) argue that such activities are rewarding in themselves, by being a source of joy and immediate social rewards. They are also beneficial in the long run. There is evidence that cultural activity and participation may decrease morbidity and mortality and may increase well-being in many ways (see, for example, Hyyppä and Mäki, 2001). In this chapter we will primarily focus on the immediate rewards. We are also aware that participating in social activities can involve feelings of shortcomings and that other social complications can be generated when people meet.

Milligan et al. (2016) reviewed papers on gendered social activities to learn about the relation between older men's activities and their health and well-being. They found limited evidence that gendered social activities have impact on the mental health and well-being of older men, but little evidence of impact on their physical health. Successful interventions included range of activities, accessibility, local support and skilled coordination.

There is a risk that social workers prioritize physical rather than emotional aspects. Social work plays a special role in socializing individual strengths, promoting well-being and fostering individual connectedness (Fawcett 2014). Music has been found to provide people with ways of understanding and developing their self-identity or connecting with other people (Hays and Minichiello, 2005). Music can be connected with well-being and it is also a way to experience and express spirituality. Hays and Minichiello found that music promotes quality of life by promoting a positive self-esteem, by helping people feel competent and independent, and by reducing feelings of isolation and loneliness. Feelings of identity and fellowship can be strengthened through communication via dance and music-making. Ronström (1994) observes:

> By dancing and making music together, people can experience a strong feeling of identity and fellowship, without ever needing to be confronted with the question of whether they have anything else in common beyond these experiences. This capacity to store, communicate and create multivalent messages is an important answer to why dancing and music-making has become so important. (p. 6)

There are other leisure activities that have effect on health and survival. Cooper and Thomas (2002) studied social dance in Essex and London and found, among other things, that social dancers aged 60+ can experience the joy of a fit and able body "in both real and mythic senses." Lennartsson and Silverstein (2001) found that activity, not only social, has positive effects on the survival of very old individuals. They suggest that psychological dimensions of activities, such as motivation, inner direction and a sense of purpose, may be mediating factors.

We want to examine how the elderly in the dance project mentioned at the start of the chapter, negotiate their self-esteem and desire to be independent in vulnerable situations. How do they maintain their individuality in the dance group? How do they react to being viewed as old and/or being treated as old? Which situations are seen as a threat to their self-esteem? Which interactive processes take place in the minds of the participants when certain vulnerabilities have to be protected in order to maintain a positive self-esteem?

On a policy level it has also been suggested that cultural aspects such as dancing and singing, leisure and pleasure, could be added to the discussion of prevention and promotion (European Commission, 2010). The SCL/PRB Index of Well-Being in Older Populations, developed by the Stanford Center on Longevity and the Population Reference Bureau, summarizes 12 key indicators of well-being in old age in four domains – material, physical, social, and emotional well-being. To measure emotional well-being, questions are asked about depression, risk of suicide, and satisfaction with current life situation and future prospects (Kaneda, Lee, and Pollard, 2011).

The Dance Project

We have followed a dance project and its artistic focus on age and aging and the movement of the aged body in modern dance from a social scientist's point of view. It was part of the artistic research project "Movement as the Memory of the Body," which assumed that dance holds strong associations and memories. Age and aging was both given new meaning and rephrased in stereotypical terms through the individual's participation in the dance project and later in the dance performance, "Döden, Döden" (Smiling at Death).

To perform modern dance on stage in Western culture is something that is traditionally reserved for younger people. The age of retirement for dancers is low (in Sweden it is currently 41). As dancers are often seen as "old" even before middle age when it comes to their professional career, the dance project as a situation can be seen as negotiating age in a special way. In this context, there was nothing strange about being recruited as an old amateur dancer if one was older than 65, even though most of the informants would not have thought of themselves as old. The context of the dance project made it okay to be an old amateur dancer. The amateur dancers in the project were co-creators in a context (modern dance) challenging the norm of the young and strong body (Schwaiger, 2012). The dance project invited us to reflect on, question and observe age, aging and the older people participating, whose experience we seek to explore in this study.

To participate in the dance project you had to be 65 years of age or over, and in terms of mobility you had to be able to walk up steep and narrow stairs to get to the rehearsal room. There was a total of 17 amateur participants in the dance project, selected by the choreographer at an audition based on artistic criteria.

The project attracted people who were interested in art, music, and literature, and could be classified as "consumers of culture." Normally, this group includes more women than men and the dance project was not an exception. It goes without saying that the competition for a position in the project was greater for women than for men.

The choreographer used old age (65+) as a qualification requirement for participation as an amateur dancer (Lilja, 2006). The preparedness of the group of participants for "being seen as old" in the dance project, based on aesthetic dimensions, was to some extent explicit and clear to the participants from start. In the project description, the choreographer presents how she would like to explore elderly people's movements in a working process that could provide new creative sources for artistic portrayal and, in addition, focus on more aesthetic aspects of aging bodies and their cultural value on the dance stage (Lilja, 2006).

The audition for the dance project was advertised in national newspapers; more than 50 people applied. Forty women and eight men filled in a questionnaire handed out at the audition where they, among other things, explained why they wanted to compete for contribution in the dance project. Nearly every second female applicant (16) at the audition reported that curiosity was the main reason why she wanted to participate in the dance project. One in four female applicants (10) indicated that the project seemed exciting or challenging, and more than half (24) mentioned their need for exercise. A few women indicated that their main motive was a matter of creating new connections and social solidarity. Five of the men indicated curiosity as a reason to approach the dance project. Four of the men indicated their need for exercise as a reason for wanting to participate in the dance project, while only one male applicant found the project exciting and challenging.

Several of the 17 project participants, the women especially, participated regularly in some type of physical activity. Something all the dance project participants had in common was that during their working life they had been in occupations and professions that required higher education, such as lawyer, physiotherapist, author, teacher, psychotherapist, and social worker. Some of them were still professionally active, as employee or self-employed. Their calendars were also filled with social activities. Voluntary work, being a board member or involved in an association, and working as social contact person were mentioned as meaningful in their life at the time of the dance project. Professional background and employment were often mentioned as important to the informants in the interviews. For some of them this meant having expectations of the dance project, which we will get back to later on.

The project gave the dancers a unique chance to reflect on age, aging and old age. The amateur dancers were encouraged by the project leader to write diaries where they reflected on age and aging in relation to their participation and performance in the project. Sjölund (2012), in her analysis of the interview data, reported that the meaning of age was negotiated and that there were tensions between referring to age and aging as resources and referring to them as a problem associated with restrictions.

Some of the informants reflected on how the dance project made them aware of their own stereotypical images of old people. Examples included strategies for avoiding meetings for senior citizens and activities that could be associated with old age. At the beginning of the dance project, some of the informants thought that the other old amateur dancers would quit, or that they might fall down and die during the rehearsals, but no one did. Initial thoughts about the other amateur dancers in the group, as not interesting or capable people to be with, were a theme some informants mentioned spontaneously. Afterwards, some of the informants reflected and realized that they had had a more stereotypical notion about old people than they would like to admit. That it is possible to think of old people as beautiful and capable was a result of the dance project, according to one of the respondents.

Becoming aware of being old is a rather ambivalent situation when it comes to activities. Keeping active but not too active and doing the right kind of activities seemed important. Explicit strategies to keep the body in shape to resist the aging process occurred. Maintaining a balance between activity and inactivity was difficult. As an aged person, other people think one should not work for wages, and those who do may get the question "why are you still working?" However, doing nothing is neither fun nor desirable – it is even worse than being questioned. For the informants, activity was meaningful in itself as well as a strategy to resist the aging process.

Leadership as a Part of the Social Context

As a professional dancer and choreographer and Professor of Choreographic Composition at Stockholm University of the Arts, Efva Lilja was the one who initiated the project "Movement as the Memory of the Body" (*Rörelsen som kroppens minne*). The leadership also included her assistant, Helene, also a dancer, and Aba, one of the professional dancers also participating in the project. He was a good support for the male participants, who could get good advice from a qualified person of their own age.

From the interviews we learned that the project leader, the professional dancer Efva Lilja, "took great responsibility for the group all the time" (8.A.F). (The codes can be found in Table 36.1) 8.A.F describes the sometimes unclear boundaries "between what our problems were and how they should be tackled, and what Efva's responsibility was." Efva's professional background attracted those who wanted to develop "something new" and "challenging" in their lives as retired. "I don't want therapeutic employment, but I am looking for something genuine" (11.A.F). 11.A.F went to a gym "almost obsessively" four or five times a week and that was where she also found information about the dance project. She confesses high initial expectations and describes Efva's style of leadership as both controlling and encouraging:

Yes, but they praised you to the skies and I must say: Efva – absolutely incredible, but God! And she stood by scrutinizing … and so did Helene. They stood by and observed and that did not make any sense, but I know I never felt so seen, not the way I was here. And they said everything I did was so amazing and they made me believe it. (11.A.F)

Table 36.1   Participants in the dance project

Participant no.	Birth date/age code*	Gender	Interview (2006)	Diary (2005)	Informant key
1	1937/A	Male	Yes	Yes	1.A.M
2	1940/A	Male	No	Yes	2.B.M
3	1931/B	Female	Yes	Yes	3.B.F
4	1938/A	Female	Yes	Yes	4.A.F
5	1939/A	Female	Yes	Yes	5.A.F
6	1939/A	Female	No	Yes	6.A.F
7	1927/B	Female	No	Yes	7.B.F
8	1938/A	Female	Yes	Yes	8.A.F
9	1937/A	Male	Yes	No	9.A.M
10	1938/A	Male	Yes	Yes	10.A.M
11	1936/A	Female	Yes	Yes	11.A.F
12	1937/A	Female	No	Yes	12.A.F
13	1938/A	Female	Yes	Yes	13.A.F
14	1915/C	Female	Yes	Yes	14.C.F
15	1932/B	Male	Yes	Yes	15.B.M
16	1920/C	Female	Yes	Yes	16.C.F

*Age code: 65–70 = A; 71–80 = B; 80≤ = C.
Alt. 80+ = C.

11.A.F, who did not find any problems and praised the group atmosphere, finds all the praise incredible, but she also mentions a friend who "thinks it's annoying because she praises everything too much." 8.A.F commented:

> But we followed her directions all the time anyway, and it was good because we were out of imagination. So she was forced to do it. It was just like she said "that is my responsibility" and she really outlined the course. So she made sure that nobody came in too fast or got too much caught. But we were not familiar with the piece, so we didn't understand what she was doing … she was good at controlling.

8.A.F and 11.A.F felt safe and comfortable in the group. 8.A.F pointed out her voluntary participation and mentioned both the pleasure they felt meeting the other participants and the fun they all shared together.

In response to questions about potential conflicts in the group, some examples were included of people who obstructed the work by being late, altering movements without permission, changing the decor, ignoring instructions. Efva saw it all and she was completely respected because of her experience and great knowledge.

The dance project can be described as a meeting between a competent leader and participants with fairly high expectations of the project. Although the leader, Efva, was a trained dancer and dance instructor, it might be that it was the first time she had worked with a group aged 65+, which meant new experiences both for her and the participants.

The background material suggests that as an artistic project this was a complete success. It is likely that the project resulted in improved well-being. But we are looking at the project from a social work perspective, and our research interest is on the individual processes interfering with the artistic development. One can say that there is a disciplinary bias in the focus on processes of inclusion–exclusion, self-reliance, ambivalences, and negotiations. We also searched for actual health status, routines, and coping strategies among the amateur dancers.

Method

We have used a mixed method in order to describe the tension between the experience of external demands and inner efforts to follow your desires. We have searched for important themes in the reflections of the elderly about being elderly and active in the project to deepen our understanding of well-being among the elderly. The mixed method provides the informants with opportunities to reflect on and define the situation via verbal narrative and writing, two methods that demonstrate different individual skills, to convey their experiences. The data collection was spread out over time because of the mixed method. Twelve interviews were conducted with the amateur dancers the year after the most intense period of the dance project (Sjölund, 2012). The interviews were tape recorded and transcribed verbatim.

It is important to know that the diaries were written by the amateur dancers during the dance project, which provided opportunity for immediate reaction and reflection. This is different from providing mature reflections in a later interview. The interviews were performed after one year; what this implies for the reflection will be discussed in the concluding part.

Table 36.2 presents the data collected during the different phases of the dance project. The intensive phase of the dance project lasted for a period of four months during the spring of 2005, including workshop, rehearsal and dance performance. Various post-projects extended

Table 36.2   Overview of the data material

Time	Dance project activity	Data collected	Number of informants
Year 1 (December 2004)	Audition	Mini-survey	48
Year 2 (January 2005)	Workshop	Diaries	15
Year 2 (February–April 2005)	Rehearsal/Dance performance	Diaries	13
Year 3 (February–March 2006)	Post-projects	Interviews	12

up to two years after the original dance project was carried out, and involved several of the project participants. In this paper we are interested in the immediate reactions and have therefore chosen to concentrate on the diaries and used some of the interview material in the background presentation.

The choreographer and leader of the project was not available to discuss and reflect on personal matters during the workshop or the rehearsals. The dancers were instructed to put pen to paper and write their reflections in diaries during the dance project as a way to raise questions and record personal reflections of importance in relation to the project. The reflections could include matters that might be too complicated or time-consuming to talk about in the group, and which focused on the dance. The choreographer and the leaders of the project were the main receivers and readers of the diaries.

The choreographer wanted the participants to answer the questions: (1) What did I do today? (2) What did I think about it? Twelve of the participants in the amateur group and one professional elderly dancer agreed to a personal interview and also gave us access to the diaries they used for reflection during the dance project. Nine women and four men are included in this study. The women were aged between 67 and 91 years, the youngest man was 68 and the oldest was 74 years of age. After the performance we asked each of the amateur dancers for a copy of their diary and all 17 project participants received a letter where we asked for written consent. They could answer yes or no. In addition, two participants who were unable to participate in the interview gave us access to their diaries, and one man who was interviewed did not keep a diary (see Table 36.1). One of the participants never answered phone calls or a letter so his diary, if he did keep one, is not included.

We were inspired by Milligan, Bingley, and Gatrell (2005), who found that diaries could be used effectively in exploring health issues among both older men and older women. They found that diary techniques can offer unique insight into the ongoing health routines and coping strategies of older people and can uncover often hidden aspects of their daily lives and routines. Placing the control over the data in the hands of the participants gives them the opportunity to decide how much or how little they are willing to share with others. As such, the diaries can serve as an important supplement to more conventional methods of data collection. Diary methods are useful for gathering different kinds of sensitive data that could be difficult to collect through other methods.

General Result from the Analysis of the Interviews

The analysis of the interviews in Sjölund's study (2012) showed that the meaning of age was negotiated in that there were tensions between referring to age and aging as resources and referring to them as a problem associated with restrictions. The informants struggled to define the meaning of age and aging as one thing or another, but they were all able to refer to age as both a resource and a problem in different ways. The resources that came forward had to do with increased self-reliance and not being afraid of making a fool of oneself as much as before. Some of the amateur dancers were sure they would not have dared to participate in the dance project when they were younger. Another resource mentioned among the participants in the dance project was an increased ability to consider other elderly people as beautiful and creative individuals. The problems referred to concerned physical changes and the increased risk of disability that could prevent a person from being an active and independent individual in the future. Connected to this, the aging body emerged as a reason for engaging in physical activities, but also as an implicit threat that one might not be able to engage in such activities.

What was also revealed in the interviews (Sjölund, 2012) was the realization that other people seemed to be more preoccupied with their old age in relation to what they did than the amateur dancers were. Other people's interest in their age was at times what made them aware of their own age. Some of the informants also contemplated how the dance project had made them aware of their own stereotypical images of old people. Afterwards some of the informants spontaneously realized that they had had more stereotypical notions about aged people than they would like to admit. We want to take a closer look at the diary material in order to find out how our informants formulated the restrictions, the process of increased self-reliance, their own stereotyping, and so on.

The Diaries

The participants were instructed to write down things that were brought up during the sessions. For many of the participants the diary was where they wrote down instructions to memorize how to perform the often complicated movements. The participants (see Table 36.1) were told that the diary was to be used for reflection, and for some of them the diary was used for more personal comments.

Reading the diaries we were able to define some general and specific themes. The ones we found were the following: search for meaning; being seen as old; keeping watch; being treated as old/interactive ageism; increased self-reliance; feeling of identity and fellowship; and when the body does not cooperate. Having read through the material once more searching for subthemes, we found that in each theme there was an ambivalence that also increased over time. The later in the project, the stronger the ambivalence among the participants and the greater the variety. The quotes have been somewhat edited to increase readability for international readers.

General Result of the Analysis of the Diaries

We want to return to the aim of the project, to create an expression where the memory of movement and the lived body become the core components in the process. In the diaries we found that dancing could bring back memories from events earlier in life. Like Hays and Minichiello (2005), who found that music could relate to certain things in their lives, like childhood, family, romantic memories, our informants write about dance evoking strong memories related to the past. Both unhappy and more positive memories were mentioned in the diaries.

One of the participants had been subjected to incest and other types of violence in her child-hood, and she writes that her body remembered these situations and she had a bad reaction during parts of the rehearsal. We will not go deeper into this, but would like to comment that the trust this person must have felt when mentioning her painful memories and reactions in her diary, open for the leaders and researchers to read, is admirable. However, the main inter-ests in the diaries were often related to their dance performance and remembering movements and instructions. But they were also about connecting personal memories from the past and present everyday life reflections to the dancing and individual meaning. As the dancers' task was to describe a period that for many of them coincided with their present stage in life, the body memory and the role of interpretation also interacted, as it did for 14.C.F, who wrote the following during the workshop:

> I was in a group of three ladies, and our task was to act out fatigue. I became a little worried, that's what I feel daily, from morning until about noon – well, it's how my body tells me that I'm 89 years old and that I should be happy to still be able to dance and be involved in everyday life in the afternoon and evening – but – it turned out all wrong when I recreated my own feeling of tiredness for the other three ladies – however – when the four of us are together and Efva instructs us again and again – we found new ways to express ourselves – in the "final stages" when we performed the various steps in a certain order in a complete sequence, it is as if I have to complete each step before starting the next – then – I felt that this was fatigue. So when 3.B.F and I finally leaned our heads towards each other, I would – standing in the middle of the floor, eyes closed with my head on her shoulder and arms hanging – have been able to fall asleep.

14.C.F's description of her struggle with the steps is a rather representative excerpt from the diaries. Most of them describe difficulties remembering the stages and the steps, and some of them were almost ready to give up as they found participation very demanding. That they decided to stay says something about their feelings of increasing remuneration. This creates something we could call well-being, a feeling of satisfaction at still being able to learn and perform. Their struggle to reach that final stage was filled with resistance as well as being fascinated with the purpose.

Search for Meaning and Solving the Life Puzzle

Silverstein and Parker (2002) found that to participate in activities makes old people evaluate their life situation in positive terms. The addition of new activities could compensate for losses in other domains. This could be true for our informants as well, but the picture they paint in the diaries is that the dance project has to compete with many other activities in an already full calendar, including anything from caring for grandchildren to participating in other cultural events.

In some of the diaries we found reflections on aging and its meaning in their personal lives. In reflections from 15.B.M below, he describes his happiness at being accepted to the project. His reaction to the initial meeting was quite cool, but it seems to have become a feather in his cap, something to communicate in his network. 15.B.M writes about his impressions and his own reactions when attending the dance project: "I was accepted! At my first audition at the age of 72. Dance Professor Efva Lilja searched for amateurs aged 65+ for a dance project. I had no idea what to expect, but how excited I felt!" He describes the introductory session when they introduced themselves and explained why they wanted to participate in the project. They were there for various reasons, but one reason they shared was curiosity. He also describes his impression of one of the participants:

> Most poignant was a very aristocratic woman in her seventies, who told us that she has always been afraid of intimacy, bodily touch and to show emotions, but now, since a few years back, her life had taken a new turn, she sold her belongings and moved into a studio apartment, determined to dare make something of the rest of her life.

Some of the participants were hoping to be selected for the project so strongly that their hearts were beating fast when they checked their email on a daily basis. When they finally received a positive reply, they cheered and jumped around. 15.B.M was cooler about it, but describes it as "great to receive positive news; I called my kids and told friends that I met that I was going to start a new career as a dancer."

The reflections written at the beginning of rehearsals differ from those written at their end. It also became clear that the participants could have additional reasons for being in the project. For some of the women this had to do with physical change, and hoping to improve their physical status. On the last day of workshop, 12.A.F wrote about not being on good terms with her body and that she hoped to lose some weight:

> My belly has become firmer and my butt flatter. Yay! Maybe I'm on the verge of making friends with my body again, as I lose weight I get more respect for my body. Hopefully my reasoning holds. Will try to do these dance steps at home, could combine it with vocal exercises. This was a great idea! Yes, I think I agree!

12.A.F wants to become slimmer and hopes that the dancing will help her. She has not really been happy with the group and the dance during the last workshops, and when they were all invited to have coffee and cake after a workshop she became quite upset, writing that tears burned behind her eyes. She was unable to understand what coffee and cake had to do with dancing (and her weight loss), and she was very offended and upset at the invitation. She wanted to actively prevent physical change and writes to one of the professional dancers: "Dear X, you said that you walk around with a body that you do not recognize anymore [freely quoted]. I've thought about this many times. The desire to reclaim my body. I want to dance. Now I dance. And it is possible to lead the dance too." This is a sign that the group dynamics could sometimes be very intense.

12.A.F communicates her doubts about her capacity and describes the project as "a strange mixture of being good enough as a social individual, dancing muse, neutral body material. No wonder it's confusing at times and hard to concentrate."

(Re)negotiations of Being and Becoming Elderly/Old

When we identified the theme in the interviews the year after the most intense part of the project, we used the term "to be seen as old" to understand situations when individuals were actually under constant negotiation. In the diaries, however, the participants did not write much about what it meant to them "to be seen as old." It seems it is not an important explicit theme for them. Their energy seems to have been used for the learning process. We did, however, find some exceptions when taking a closer look at the diaries. 16.C.F reflected on the contrast between young and old dancers after the performance, having seen another of Efva Liljas's dance performances "Nöd och lust" (For Better, For Worse), where young dancers were dressed in white. She then realized that the old dancers had all been dressed in black. Does what 16.C.F notes in her diary mean that she feels that they have all participated in a partly ageist project? That she had participated in what Minichiello et al. (2000) call "interactive ageism?" which means to participate in jokes and general negative attitudes about growing older. It is certainly one possible interpretation of what she writes in her diary. However, the project aimed to explore old age and aging bodies on stage and opens up that type of reflection. The reflection by 16.C.F was made at the end of the project, and as a contrast to the other performance. Another interpretation is that she really had understood the aim of the dance project as a study of aging and ageism and that she was therefore able to focus on this in her reflections. The context and contrasts seemed to make the reflections obvious to 16.C.F in this particular situation.

There are examples of the project serving as an eye-opener for the participants. Age and aging seem to become important after the performance and when they compare their effort to other people's and comparable phenomena in society, but not when the amateur dancers reflect individually in the diaries on their experiences and thoughts during the dance project. Time was needed to complete their reflections. We have chosen to categorize the eye-openers as signs of a movement toward what Minichiello et al. (2000) call "sageism," which they define as the phenomenon of old people being looked upon as better, wiser or more experienced. In their diaries, some of the participants have started to consider themselves as braver as and more patient than they had considered themselves to be before participating in the project.

16.C.F was sensitive to what Minichiello et al. (2000) have called "the notion of oldness," that the black color signals slowness, decreased vitality and a downward trend compared to the white color.

Minichiello et al. (2000) found situations in their material where informants describe situations where they have been prevented from participating in certain activities or where they withdraw from situations where they have been treated as old or unwanted. The narratives presented are from situations in which old people often participate, such as hospitals, traffic or shops. This could become a vicious circle if people adjust their lives to the negative attitudes toward the elderly. This project aimed to normalize aging by inviting them to an arena that was normally closed to their age group. Those who choose to participate could be expected to want to negotiate new images of aging. What can we find in the diaries about this?

"Are old people not worthy to be on stage?" 3.B.F reflects on the meaning of her participation and also negotiates her participation. 3.B.F is a social worker and was very involved in dance and physical exercise late in life, after she had retired from working life. She was over the moon to be chosen to participate in the dance project as she knows this kind of activity is exclusive and limited in size. But she had a small personal crisis when she realized that she would not be on the stage as much as she would have liked when it came to the performance. In fact, she thought her presence was really insignificant and she writes about herself in her diary as being childish but nonetheless very upset. All the hours invested in training and rehearsals would in fact result in only a few minutes onstage. The childishness was about becoming so frustrated over such a thing – at her age she should not make such a fuss about it, she argues in the diary. But since she realizes it caused her a small personal crisis, she actually uses both a written and a verbal strategy to negotiate and influence her conditions of participation in the dance show.

Here is 3.B.F (middle of rehearsal):

> Today we met the professional elderly dancers and singers who would be participating in the official dance performance. We got a feeling for what it was going to be like. I got really sad and disappointed actually. My presence on stage will be the least of all! Do I really want to sacrifice all the time it takes to be present on stage just a few measly minutes? Am I childish?! Will I take this up for discussion or not?

Then 3.B.F a few days later:

> I phoned one of the project assistants. I told her about my little crisis. She was open-minded and understanding of my opinion and feelings about this. She thought it would be possible to change the program. Wonderful to be met with such empathy. I had such expectations when going to the rehearsal at 5 – and actually, small changes had been made, with movements added for the four of us old ladies. … now I can focus on the performance!

This is a rich example of a successful negotiation about how an old person should be treated.

In the diary of 2.B.M, a recently retired bank clerk, another reflection on the value of an old person's time can be found. He was critical about not being paid for his participation in the dance project. This was never a theme in the group discussions, but something 2.B.M perceived as negative treatment based on age. He continued to participate and kept his criticism to himself in the diary during the length of the project. He wrote in his diary that he became more and more critical during the dance project and he decided not to hand over his original diary; instead he chose to share a reworded diary in the form of a letter addressed to the choreographer and the leaders of the project. This is what 2.B.M wrote in the letter after the performance:

> I truly enjoyed the experience of participating in the dance project. I was never a victim, I've had fun most of the time and I've met many likable people. But I happen to be an inveterate skeptic and it only gets worse with age.
>
> I think that a serious mistake was made already in the project budget/grant application, when it was decided that the group of old amateur dancers was not going to be paid. Even the time of the retired has a value, and we should have been compensated, at least symbolically. Otherwise, all the praise about our valuable participation and engagement seems to ring false. It reveals a patronizing attitude. The low-water-mark was of course when we even had to pay to attend the dance project closing party.

2.B.M never found a good time to talk about this in the group. To write about it in the diary was a way for him to handle the situation. The official code was not to talk about personal reactions in the group. Did anyone share his opinion? 2.B.M thought his critical theme threatened the good atmosphere in the group, a risk he was not willing to take. A written letter instead of a direct protest was the result. In this case, it did not result in any change.

"Keeping Watch"

Minichiello et al. (2000) describe processes where "people observe and monitor older persons for signs of incipient oldness." Does the person still remain healthy, are they still able to participate and engage in social situations? "Keeping watch consists of elements of caring and protecting the elder from harm. It is also a process through which older people reassure themselves that a particular sign or lapse was only temporary and not an indicator that they are now 'old.'" Minichiello et al. argue that elders become observant as to whether they are categorized and treated as aging and old. Maybe 3.B.F's reflection in her diary on the time spent rehearsing compared to the time on stage is a sign of her keeping watch on what it is proper to use old people for.

1.A.M is a 78-year-old professional writer who is used to expressing himself in writing. He was also struggling with serious health issues during the dance project and writes about it in the diary, but never spoke about it to anyone in the dance group. 1.A.M was in a vulnerable situation due to bad hearing and the hidden disability that is Parkinson's Disease (Mr. P), which causes tremors, making it a challenge to dance in a group or as a soloist. His diary workshop reads: "I have obvious difficulties with timing and coordination. I suspect Mr. P. My reflexes work against me, my movements are slow. But I will not reveal Mr. P if I'm not directly asked, if someone discovers my hidden disability. Otherwise, the body will keep up."

Special movements are invented in the group and 1.A.M soon becomes an important person and takes on a position that challenges the latent threat manifested by "Mr. P," which is his name for the disease invading his body. It is like a crime novel, should he reveal "Mr. P" or not? From his diary workshop:

> Today I also had to "dance solo." It was great. Intoxicating. Then I was just a little dazed when we got to talk afterwards, and then at the coffee table, with cake. ... But it's my importunate companion Mr. P. So far, I have kept my mouth shut. If something were to happen, it is possible that I will be forced to explain myself. ...
>
> I have recently pondered Mr. P. Should I mention this to the choreographer or not? What could I gain from this? What would be the reason? ... Perhaps silence is what is best for him. In any case, I am happy that I have kept my mouth shut so far.

His diary at the end of rehearsal reads: "I had to take my anti-retroviral drugs in the open. It is clear this is something the others take note of. Sooner or later, the secret will be revealed, no matter what I do. Can I flat out deny if asked directly?"

1.A.M's. negotiation is evident in his diary: "So now we need to not let this get to our heads, not spoil the good spirit that prevails in this remarkable group of people. Be humble and go out to do this little thing with complete concentration each time. No tripping on stage, thank you!" He chose to hide his dilemma in the dance group, but it was something he talked about in the interview as he knew we had read about this issue in the diary:

> But since I had some health issues, I was a little hesitant. One thing was that I have bad hearing; unfortunately it so happened that both my hearing aids broke down at the same time. So I was really crippled for some sessions – I had difficulties hearing what the choreographer said, for example.
>
> So that was the one, and the other was that I thought quite a long time about if I was going to reveal that I had Parkinson's. I decided to not say anything, and I believe it was for the best, but then when this came up with the real dance show idea, well then I decided to not say anything until it was over, this is of course included in the workbook. So then it became a bit of a challenge anyway, that I was going to be able to go through with this. (1.A.M)

Another way of keeping watch is to refer to working life and ask why the same type of contribution is met differently. We remember 2.B.M who wonders if old people have a lower value as they were not paid for their contribution in the performance. The different expectations about people's willingness to volunteer in unpaid activities, which means that their personal time is used for the pleasure of others, and the situation where different colors reinforced stereotypes are similar to what Minichiello et al. (2000) described as one dimension of ageism in their study. 2.B.M was highly aware of the value of payment and found himself belittled when his effort did not receive monetary compensation.

Increased Self-Reliance

We argue, with reference to Allardt's (1993) concept of "being," that a good level of self-reliance is intertwined with creating well-being. Self-reliance is, as we see it, necessary for self-actualization, which Allardt identifies as a part of "being." But old people's self-reliance is fragile and must be handled with care. Many of them express uncertainty and ambiguity about their chances of fitting in with the project. 6.A.F, for example, initially had high expectations that the dance project was going bring something new into her life, but became frustrated because the expectations on her to develop certain abilities was too high. Her self-reliance was threatened.

6.A.F writes at the workshop stage:

> This project came at just the right time in my life. I'm at a stage where I feel I need something new in life, and I am convinced that this will be something positive and fun for me. I want to meet new people and be able to make something completely new. I felt that the entire group was very positive, and I look forward to the group solidarity that can be provided.

Behind these high expectations and positive experiences, 6.A.F also searched for some sort of recognition. "But I feel a bit dazed and confused – I do not understand why I out of so many applicants was chosen to participate. I also do not understand what Efva can get out of this." Why her and what happens?

6.A.F only participated in the workshop. She argues for her decision in the diary:

> It felt difficult today. The others are so serious. Me, I take it for what it is – something that I wanted to try for fun. But I found preparing the movements harder than I expected. Have worked extensively with a certain sequence, but it is still not right. I felt like an outsider in the group today. Felt no closeness. Began to cry saying farewell to Efva. I should probably not participate in the show. I can't cope with it mentally. Too bad, because it would have been fun to participate. I thank you for this time.

5.A.F was also very anxious and excited to be involved in the project. She describes the past year as having been very difficult on a personal level. She writes that her body needs to rest, but that she was put on the tip, and that she still is a seeker even though it really was the rest that she needed the most. At the first workshop meeting, she expresses her uncertainty in the diary. "And now, if three people independently from one another, think that I fit in here, I must be showing something in this context that I do not see myself." She hands it over to the others to evaluate her achievements and expresses some confidence for the future. "I hope I can learn something more about myself and that could certainly be useful. Will this be the first time of the year I will be included in the restoration of myself?"

She further describes distracted living, with GP visits, a housing project, needing to remember the scheduled massage, and so on. Her life seems to be difficult to coordinate at the moment. She also worries about talking too much when a TV team visited to cover the project, and thinks a lot about how the TV team, journalists and researchers will portray her. Toward the end of the period of the workshops she finds that her interest in participating has decreased. By the end of the workshop period, 5.A.F was writing: "So insanely tired and irritable, overtired – cannot be bothered writing today either. Worry about all the nonsense I have said in front of the TV camera. Not looking forward to going to the workshop – will not go through this 'grief of being fatigue' [*trötthetssorgen*]."

However, she is grateful for all the times she has "dragged herself there," and Efva and staff and all the workshop friends helped her through. She concludes that after all it is a privilege to be part of the project. "I can't enjoy this here and now, but I will of course carry it with me as another treasure in my life."

4.A.F (middle of rehearsal) writes at the final workshop meeting that she is happy to participate and that she would like to continue. She trusts that Efva will tell her if she doubts that 4.A.F will be able to handle the task: "It's amazing, I am in – really – although I can't be that good!!" 4.A.F's feelings are quite ambivalent, she both trusts and distrusts her ability. 4.A.F (middle of rehearsal):

> We have now received the schedule for the rehearsals – really! Now I believe it to be for real, not just my imagination. It will happen. Throughout March my thoughts will be filled with the joy of "working on" a performance! Despite the knowledge that my contribution on stage was fairly marginal, my contribution was, for me anyway, incredibly important! Self-esteem, I'm not that young, I've never set foot on a stage in my life, it will be great fun!

Furthermore 4.A.F wrote in her diary about the premiere and how exciting and nerve-wracking she felt it was to be on stage. "But I think it went well. Xx [a friend] (who originally signed me up) told me that she was very pleased with my effort – it made me so happy. It meant a lot to me to meet them all, professionals and amateurs! Imagine going to the city theater and appearing on stage for real! If this doesn't give you a boost I don't know what could!"

5.A.F was one of those who was able to get all the advantages of the project, and she also took part in a small post-project in Flemingsberg in the late spring. She writes:

> Thank you once again, I had the pleasure and confidence to be part of a very nice experience. To get to preserve life, even unto death, in a meaningful way (even if the body gets old after all the years) is something to pray about! To get a new reason to live, even if there is no future, that is a challenge!

11.A.F is a professional social worker and as such is able to compare professional attitudes and norms. After a few workshops, 11.A.F wrote in her diary: "Work in Efvas project has made me more analytical and attentive to the movements than before, although in my previous work I learnt to pay attention to people's body language to protect myself." She had also come in contact with aging and death in a positive way. She was able to appreciate the elements of humor in "Smiling at Death," which is so "fatally close" in all its transience. The project made her think about death, which can be frightening, but which was so natural in the project that it no longer was. She was reminded that aging can be beautiful. "When I see our old bodies dance/move I was moved by a tremendous warmth and affection to what I saw. I felt a sadness, regret and disappointment in my reactions to what I saw." She could experience the moral philosophical theme in the dance project. "It provokes memories and thoughts of good and evil. The movements symbolize so much for me and sometimes the feeling is so strong the tears are not far away." She was able to recognize the beauty of the dance. "It can be seen in the absolute concentration and quietness that most of us expressed in various performances."

It is interesting to hear 11.A.F's positive experience of the dance performance "For Better, For Worse." In contrast to 16.C.F, 11.A.F found the performance of "Smiling at Death" more beautiful in relation to the dance performed by the young people all dressed in white. "This experience became even stronger when seeing the performance by the young dancers with their young strong bodies that are perfectly tensed springs. How different from us, who are older, and our more thoughtful movements. Strong, strong. Sad, but those of us old also had young strong bodies once!"

Feeling of Identity and Fellowship

Hays and Minichiello (2005) found that music provides a way for people to explore who they are and express themselves to others. It can be a symbolic and meaningful medium for promoting wellness. Ronström (1994) also found that people can experience a strong feeling of identity and fellowship through music. We assume that dance can have the same influence on the individual's ability to understand their emotions and ability to socialize. Could the diaries provide a key to their reflections on social relations in a deeper sense during their participation in the dance project?

We found that reflections on social interaction and experience of solidarity in the group from one day to the next seemed to be a focus for many of the participants. What happened in the group and how they felt being engaged in the dance project was on the agenda. During the rehearsals, the group came together and created connections, mostly friendly. Some of them comment in their diaries on how those relationships were important for creating a feeling of magic.

From 16.C.F (Premiere!): "So the show begins. You feel as if you're a bubble – we belong together – all of us. I'm in a trance. My inner 16.C.F stay awake! It will soon be your turn! So I enter the world of fairy tales called reality. Smiling at Death! So the darkness will fall. Applause. Thank God"

After the performance, skilled and thoughtful technical staff instantly sprang into action. The stage was changed, for "For Better, For Worse" (the performance with the young dancers). Youth stormed onto the stage. Again, 16.C.F was rapt, fascinated. "Think of Smiling at Death! – have tonal effects. Here it is the sound effects. The lighting is magical over the intense vitality of the dancers. I rejoice, I solidify, and I dance in my mind (wasn't this last thing something of a cliché?)."

In the foyer outside the theater an after-party took place. The foyer had a magnificent photo exhibition including video projections. 16.C.F described the atmosphere as happy and relaxed. There were swings in the foyer, she writes. 2.B.M did swing – with a wine glass in his hand.

"Inspired by 2.B.M's swinging, I did it too, with a banana in my hand. It was fun." 16.C.F asks why there are no swings for the elderly in the parks. Swinging – it is such fun, she discovered, even at a so-called respectable age. In addition, it is an excellent example of the movement of the body's memory.

The dance project served as a social resource, but also a source for identification. In the diaries there are examples of how the group dynamics worked in forming friendships and opportunities for identification. 7.B.F (workshop) reflects on the coffee break: "17 complete strangers have met three times, without talking or discussing with each other to any great extent. Here we are now, gathered for a cup of tea/coffee – raisin cookies and talking and laughing like we're old friends who haven't met for a long time and have plenty to talk about …" 7.B.F (after the performance) is still enthusiastic:

> Soon "the curtain falls" – and it will be all over, I will wake up in reality, no, not just yet … 24 hours have passed. What happened? Like a big family, no, an extended family. This natural blend of young and old gathered around the "Last Supper." The young with growing curiosity about what life will offer, "Open Sesame"! I am old, among the old people we're stuck in the last show's magical experience. But what now, it's over, come back to reality, where you were before the dance project!!! In my actions certainly, but I'm still affected by it … 2.B.M expresses feelings of friendship and fellowship …

12.A.F (workshop), who was a professional actress, is perhaps less positive. She feels that she has to control her feelings, and she feels differently compared to the others in the way they interpret the movement tasks:

> When I make a movement that is handed to me, I am filled with emotional imagination. So I control my emotion, my movement, though I move according to my feeling when I dance. In a way, it is like electric current that can be brought in both one and the other direction. No wonder that you become confused and tired when both directions are competing for power.

The project could play a more extensive role for identity building than only to prepare a performance. 12.A.F wants to use the dance project as a chance to start a new life after a down period. She felt disappointed and excluded when they were offered cake, which she did not want, as she was trying to lose weight. She felt that cakes did nothing to help her reach her goal and she felt excluded:

> A reminder of social exclusion again. A bit of "coziness and relaxation" and cake for inspiration – WHY? A glass of juice and something more similar to proper food was the only thing I could think of! Close to tears, overreacting of course. Happy for the little talk with Aba, but I would rather say Jan [his real name]. I really feel at home with these people who continue their lives as themselves. It's as if this workshop 65+ ends as it begins, everyone goes back to their old habits. (12.A.F (after the workshop) on the train)

For 12.A.F it was a new experience to meet men in situations like these. She enjoyed it, but she was still far away mentally from both the women and the men in the project. She felt that it was a completely different world and she compared the strange feeling she felt with a situation where half of the participants came from other cultures. "Exciting to think about.

And the courage to dance this is the same as a great deal of self-absorption, or? I think the questions to Efva lack empathy and rather consist of false female modesty. Or is it real?" 12.A.F wonders if they were just good enough. She doubts that the group was chosen because they had certain skills. "Were we chosen because we are a body material, not to be evaluated if it we are good enough. … But this is a strange mixture of being good enough as a social individual, dancing muse, neutral body material. No wonder it's confusing at times and hard to concentrate."

12.A.F expresses her ambivalence about the project. Is she good enough? Is it possible to meet and understand each other in a project where the participants are so different? And what happens next? Will they all go back to their old lives? It seems as if the project fills an important role in her life and that it will be a loss when the project is over. On an emotional scale the group was extremely heterogeneous, like the society of elderly people in general.

When the Body Does Not Cooperate

Minichiello et al. (2000) discuss how people develop strategies to minimize the impact of ageism in their lives. Nobody wants to be excluded. However, they have to accept that there will be physical changes, and that it can be difficult to foresee how much energy will be needed in relation to the power they can obtain.

A common reflection noted in the diaries was on the difficulties of physical coordination and remembering different dance steps and movements. The men mostly had troubles with concurrency, while one movement at a time was not really a problem for any of them, according to the descriptions in their diaries. The women had no problems with concurrency, but they were more insecure about their performance. All the women had critical comments on their physical ability, both in relation to what they wanted to express and in relation to the group. 4.A.F described her feelings about her uncooperative legs at the second rehearsal: "Good to see them all again. First warm up – easy and comfortable, then the free dance steps that make my legs react as if there were at least 6 of them (not 2 like everyone else) and all (legs) made their own faulty moves. Helen bravely tried to help me – without any greater success."

An insightful reflection on not being able to do what one would like to do is expressed by 14.C.F, making an important point about herself accepting her physical limitations:

Even if Efva tries to help me, I find it so incredibly difficult. My body is not willing to cooperate, no memories are released – but it is really me trembling (it comes with old age), and I have to push myself terribly to do the moves this slowly. I simply can't – fortunately this became clear to me now … all you can do is accept it … I am still very reluctant … (14.C.F on the second day of the workshop)

The acceptance in this case does not mean not participating in the dance project, but under-standing what one can or cannot do. The feeling of frustration about being exhausted is an irrelevant energy drainer for 14.C.F She has to accept the fact that her body is not able to cope with everything she wants to do all the time. The dance project made her discover and reflect on how her own ability varies throughout the day. In the morning and until lunchtime she is always very tired – but in the afternoon her energy seems to come back. Her diary describes her frustration and how she copes with it.

12.A.F, the woman in a troubled social situation, who also wanted to lose weight through the rehearsals, early on in her diary discusses her high expectations combined with a worry that she might fail.

> The method is exciting, I feel some movements are entirely clear, I receive support. … Now, this must be a success! But why do I feel that the environment is so restraining? I'm scared, I had a nightmare last night, and it was about being late. Woke up at 5, fell asleep again. I'm afraid to talk too much, make mistakes, be disruptive, the timing is all wrong for me. I'm looking forward to each session, but my nerves are frayed. (12.A.F (workshop))

Unfortunately, 12.A.F had an accident on the ice and all the soft parts in her arm were injured. After almost two months, the arm still had not healed. She was in pain during the night, and unable to lift her arm or make slow movements when taking things off shelves. To shake hands was painful. But she made progress and after two months she was able to shift gears (in her car) without using both of her hands.

Here is 12.A.F looking back after she had seen the performance in which she did not participate:

> [Middle rehearsal] what happened changed the circumstances, and it helped me to stop this self-torture [participating in the dance performance]. … Oh how I long for the freedom of not being afraid to get hurt … I wonder how come 14.C.F is not able to dance, is she reminded of her pains again? – Sure, we have to dance because it is a natural way to express what happens in the mind and brain. The body must live. Unfortunately, not everyone can have physical contact with another person.

12.A.F did not have the courage to withdraw her participation on her own. She was critical. 12.A.F experienced the atmosphere at the Efva Lilja Dance Company as very controlled, elitist ("I felt the urge to fart and curse so when I passed the door my foot got stuck and I hurt myself"). She felt that the design (esthetics) was prioritized over a friendly, living, natural, non-controlling eye! She enjoyed viewing the materials chosen, tables, stairs, carpets, dressing room. But she shudders when she puts her arm on the long metal table.

12.A.F's exaltation obviously did not last until the end. After the last workshop she wrote that she was bothered by the cameras, but that she was trying to forget that the "eyes" were there. She had "as per usual" difficulties in feeling comfortable in a crowd, and was bothered by the fact that not everyone in the group was able to capture the simple motions Efva had developed for them. She forsakes her personal life: "My social emotional life is, as usual, secondary when I get absorbed in an event in the dance." She wanted to be on good terms with her body again. Having respect for her body she would be able to lose weight, she argues. She hopes that she will succeed, and she will practice the dance steps at home. She could combine it with vocal exercises. Even if she had not been so successful, she thought it was a great idea. "Yes, I think I agree!"

> Dear Conny [one of the professional dancers], you said that you walk around with a body you do not recognize [freely quoted]. I've thought about it many times. The desire to reclaim my body back to life. I will dance, Now I dance, And it is possible to lead the dance too. "Toute seule." Hugs, 12.A.F.

Efva Lilja's esthetic perspective had a downside, which we will discuss in the concluding section.

Discussion

Returning to de Beauvoir's experiences (lived meaning) of aging as related to our historical, cultural and social situation: we all need to deal with age as a complex phenomenon that shifts in meaning over time, as the picture of elderly people differs from time to time and from place to place and with consequences for experiences of well-being. Maybe the old body is not so loaded with conflicting emotions as the young body can be, and therefore, when being visualized, as in the dance project, it is something that has to be explored. The dance project made the bodies visible and the physical sensations possible to define and explore together with others. To get to know oneself by exchanging experiences with others can be empowering. Maybe artists have something to teach us that can serve as guidance in the process of attitude change.

People in Third Age are often consumers of cultural events, and rarely performers. As performers they have to compare themselves with younger people and often professionals. This project also bears traces of this kind of thinking, which some of the participants find frustrating. Elitist, some of them write. A project like this is maybe too hard to copy to be used for most of the elderly, but sometimes a group can act as forerunner and pathfinder.

One thing we can learn is that there is no definite borderline between the healthy and the diseased body. Many of the participants suffered from disease but were able to take part in the project. Their diseases never became an issue in the public discussion between the participants or between the participants and the leaders. People commented on their fear that their disease was going to trouble them or become a problem in the group. Some found it too trying when their bodies did not cooperate, which resulted in frustration, exclusion or discrimination through the attitude that the focus was on the esthetic expression. We will return to this when discussing the implications for social work practices.

To Negotiate New Meanings of Aging

Old people are often considered as a burden, something that would make the participants of the dance project quite upset. We have described situations when they make a choice not to be a burden, even if they sometimes take the risk of being revealed, such as the person with the serious medical condition. 1.A.M chose to hide the stigma of "Mr. P," which he described in his diary, together with his fear of being a burden to the group. We will raise this dilemma when we look at implications for social work practices. It is important to discuss publicly what is normal for a group of the elderly to make more people willing to participate in "risky" projects. Risky could mean the risk of losing face, that somebody might recognize your dependency. It could also mean becoming aware of your limitations. In the material there are examples of both being classified as old by others and reaching limits. We also have examples of the same event being experienced quite differently, like the contrast between the two performances "Smiling at Death" and "For Better, For Worse." 11.A.F appreciated the contrast and found the black costumes completely appropriate, while 16.C.F experienced the contrast as another way to diminish old people. These two people had different references in terms of what could be defined as "normal," which indicates a creative diversity.

The Mixed Method

We have used different methods to collect and analyze data: the survey, the diaries and finally the interviews. By using different materials we can trace the process of maturity starting from the initial expectations, via the rehearsals, the performance and finally the reflections on what really happened. In this article we have mainly concentrated on the diaries, and we can also see that during the period when the diaries were written, there is a process of maturity. We have chosen to explore the process in several stages, the workshop and the rehearsals in three stages: the start, the middle and the end, or the expectations, the progression and the evaluation. One year after the end of the project, the second author conducted the interviews. For us it has been very educational to be able to follow the process.

The participants in the dance project were to a great extent well-prepared and well-informed about what the project was about. Some of them were keen to work with the well-known choreographer Efva Lilja. This makes the project special and difficult to copy. We want to raise a question about the role of forerunners when norm-breaking lifestyles – in this case active and visible – are initiated. The material is rich and tells us that such an individual process contains both satisfaction and anxiety and doubts. Most people were able to complete the project, but for a few of them the difficulties were too great, as we learn from their reflections and reactions.

Implications for Social Work Practices

We received good insight into what was going on in the minds of aging people when taking part in a professional artistic project. From the diaries we have been able to follow old people's subjective meanings. Older people have been found to be able to generate their own "agents of change." In social policy discussion, this is combined with a risk and we can confirm that many of the very competent participants in the project doubted their abilities. They have shown that it is not easy to take on the challenge of taking the lead in norm-breaking activities. What we would like to know is how researchers and social workers can contribute to an anti-stigmatizing process where tensions between social norms prevent well-being. We have found that the dance project opened minds for change. In running the project, Efva Lilja had an exclusively esthetic aim, and in that form it cannot be copied on a large scale. The idea of borrowing inspiration from modern dance to awaken the memory of the body could preferably be used in other forms. Social workers could use therapeutic techniques to support older people's awareness of ageist norms or norms that prevent them from experiencing well-being.

There is a risk that a project aiming to work with people's physical memory in a heterogeneous group of old people may make some of them recall memories that have been repressed. This project demonstrated that in some cases professional therapeutic help may be needed. Efva Lilja made a professional choice to draw a strict line between esthetics and emotions in the group. She was probably aware that emotions of various kinds could emerge, which is why she suggested that the participants should keep diaries. Her professional background did not lend itself to taking care of the emotions in the group. From the diaries we learn that some kind of social or psychological back-up could be needed with a more heterogeneous group. If the idea of this project were to be copied, a piece of good advice would be to think about the ethical consequences and make preparations so as to not hurt anyone physically or psychically.

References

Adams, K. B., Leibbrandt, S., and Moon, H. (2011). A critical review of the literature on social and leisure activity and wellbeing in later life. *Ageing and Society, 31*(4), 683–712.

Allardt, E. (1993). Having, loving, being: An alternative to the Swedish model of welfare research. In M. Nussbaum and A. Sen (Eds.), *The Quality of Life* (pp. 88–94). Oxford: Clarendon Press.

Cooper, L., and H. Thomas (2002). Growing old gracefully: Social dance in the third age. *Ageing and Society*, 22(6), 689–708.

de Beauvoir, S. (1972). *The Coming of Age*, trans. P. O'Brian. New York: W. W. Norton.

European Commission (2010). Mental health and wellbeing in older people – making it happen: Conclusions from the conference. At http://ec.europa.eu/health/mental_health/docs/ev_20100628_report__en.pdf (accessed July 2016).

Fawcett, B. (2011). Day care, older people and carers: An exploratory study of the relationship between day care centre attendance, increased resilience and improved health and psycho-social outcomes. Research report, University of Sydney.

Fawcett, B. (2014). Well-being and older people: The place of day clubs in reconceptualising participation and challenging deficit. *British Journal of Social Work*, 44, 831–848.

Fawcett, B., and Reynolds, J. (2010). Mental health and older women. *British Journal of Social Work*, 40(5), 1488–1502. doi:10.1093/bjsw.bcp042

Gale, C. R., Cooper, C., Deary, I. J., and Sayer, A. (2014). Psychological well-being and incident frailty in men and women: The English Longitudinal Study of Ageing. *Psychological Medicine*, 44(4), 697–706. doi:10.1017/S0033291713001384

Hays, T., and Minichiello, V. (2005). The contribution of music to quality of life in older people: An Australian qualitative study. *Ageing and Society*, 25(2), 261–278.

Hyyppä, M. T., and Mäki, J. (2001). Why do Swedish-speaking Finns have longer active life? An area for social capital research. *Health Promotion International*, 16(1), 55–64.

Kaneda, T., Lee, M., and Pollard, K. (2011). *SCL/PRB Index of Well-Being in Older Populations*. Stanford: Stanford Center on Longevity and Population Reference Bureau.

Karisto, A., and Haapola, I. (2015). Generations in ageing Finland: Finding your place in the demographic structure. In K. Komp and S. Johansson (Eds.), *Population Ageing from a Lifecourse Perspective: Critical and International Approaches*. Bristol, UK: Policy Press.

Lennartsson, C., and Silverstein, M. (2001). Does engagement with life enhance survival of elderly people in Sweden? The role of social and leisure activities. *Journals of Gerontology, Series B: Psychological Sciences and Social Sciences*, 56(6), S335–S342.

Litwin, H., and Shiovitz-Ezra, S. (2006). The association between activity and wellbeing in later life: What really matters. *Ageing and Society*, 26(2), 225–242.

Lilja, E. (Ed.) (2006). *Movement as the Memory of the Body: New Choreographic Work for the Stage*. Stockholm: University College of Dance.

McMunn, A., Nazroo, J., Wahrendorf, M., Breeze, E., and Zaninotto, P. (2009). Participation in socially productive activities, reciprocity and wellbeing in later life: Baseline results in England. *Ageing and Society*, 29(5), 765–782.

Milligan, C., Bingley, A., and Gatrell, A. (2005). Digging deep: Using diary techniques to explore the place of health and well-being amongst older people. *Social Science and Medicine*, 61, 1882–1892.

Milligan, C., Neary, D., Payne, S., Hanratty, B., Irwin, P., and Dowrick, C. (2016). Older men and social activity: A scoping review of Men's Sheds and other gendered interventions. *Ageing and Society*, 36(5), 895–923.

Minichiello, V., Browne, J., and Kendig, H. (2000). Perceptions and consequences of ageism: Views of older people. *Ageing and Society*, 20, 253–278.

Powell, J. L., and Wahidin, A. (2005). Aging in the "risk society." *International Journal of Sociology and Social Policy*, 25(8), 70–99.

Principi, A., Chiatti, C., Lamura, G., and Frerichs, F. (2012). The engagement of older people in civil society organizations. *Educational Gerontology*, 38(2), 83–106.

Ronström, O. (1994). "I'm old and I'm proud!" Dance, music and the formation of cultural identity among pensioners in Sweden. *World of Music*, 36(3), 5–30.

Schwaiger, E. (2012). *Ageing, Gender, Embodiment and Dance: Finding a Balance*. New York: Palgrave Macmillan.

Silverstein, M., and Parker, M. G. (2002). Leisure activities and quality of life among the oldest old in Sweden. *Research on Aging*, 24(5), 528–547.

Sjölund, M. (2012). Levd erfarenhet av ålder [Lived experiences of aging]. Dissertation, Department of Social Work, Umeå University.

Söderberg, M. (2012). Family membersá strategies when their elderly relatives consider relocation to a residential home: Adapting, representing and avoiding. *Journal of Aging Studies*, 26, 495–503.

Söderberg, M. (2014). Hänsynstagandets paradoxer [The paradoxes of consideration]. Dissertation, Department of Social Work, Lund University, Sweden.

Söderberg, M., Ståhl, A., and Emilsson, U. M. (2013). Independence as a stigmatizing value for older people considering relocation to a residential home. *European Journal of Social Work*, *16*(3), 391–406.

Staudinger, U. (2008). A psychology of wisdom: History and recent developments. *Research in Human Development*, *5*(2), 107–120.

37

Social Class, Health, Stress, and Heart Disease

Applying a Prevention Model

Demetria F. Henderson, Debra L. Nelson, and James Campbell Quick

Introduction

The demographics of the United States present a clear picture of the economic divide occurring in our society. Geographically, the Northeast and West have the highest median incomes of $56,775 and $56,181 respectively, followed by the Midwest with a median income of $52,082 and the South trailing with a median income of $48,128 (US Census Bureau, 2014). In addition, there has been an increasing divide between the *haves* and *have nots*. Between 2002 and 2012, the US Census Bureau American Community Survey reports that the national percentage of people living in poverty increased from 12.2 to 15.9 percent. These percentages equate to 48.8 million people living in poverty in 2012, up from 33.3 million people in 2000 (US Census Bureau, 2013). The US median household net worth of the tenth percentile was −$905 in 2000, but by 2011, this number had dramatically decreased to −$6,029. During the same time period, the wealthiest households in the ninetieth percentile saw an increase from $569,375 to $630,754 (US Census Bureau, 2012). The economic disparity between the upper and lower echelons of our society cannot be denied. Issues such as these are at the forefront of research on class.

Some would argue that the US is a classless society. Due to the perception that American society is less divided by class, American sociologists have often given less attention to class and class issues in comparison to their European counterparts (Scott, 1996). In the US, the tendency is to veer away from the term *class* and to refer to social ranking as a social identity or social status group (Scott, 1996). Social identity groups are groups of individuals who share

The Handbook of Stress and Health: A Guide to Research and Practice, First Edition.
Edited by Cary L. Cooper and James Campbell Quick.
© 2017 John Wiley & Sons, Ltd. Published 2017 by John Wiley & Sons, Ltd.

common characteristics that define and set them apart by socially constructed boundaries, such as race, gender, sexual orientation, and class (Brazzel, 2008). Most individuals are at the same time members of dominant groups (groups with power) and subordinated groups (groups without power and privilege) (Brazzel, 2007). As a result, group identification greatly influences self-perception of our social status in relation to our group membership (Brewer and Hewstone, 2004) as well as other-perception of our social status.

According to Diemer and Ali (2009), social class has been an integral part of work experiences, going back as far as ancient Greece and Egypt. Researchers and practitioners alike have focused primarily on the effects of race, gender, and age differences, and in most recent years sexual orientation issues (e.g., Bell, Özbilgin, Beauregard, and Sürgevil, 2011; Ragins and Cornwell, 2001; Trau, 2015), leaving the study of social class in the workplace unattended (Brown, Fukunaga, Umemoto, and Wicker, 1996; Liu et al., 2004a). There has been much research to date that demonstrates the negative outcomes of racial, gender, and age discrimination, particularly on health outcomes. We argue that differences in one's social class can be just as predictive of poor health consequences.

The purpose of this chapter is to explore the link between social class and various health outcomes. We will begin with an exploration of what is social class. Next, we discuss social class as a stigma symbol, which leads to adverse health symptoms. Stress is then discussed in greater detail, followed by a review of the Preventive Stress Management™ (PSM) model. We then offer an intervention plan, framed by the PSM model, that individuals, organizations, and society can apply in coping with stress. We conclude with a recap of our discussion, along with suggestions for future research.

Social Class

Conceptualization of Social Class

A major area of concern regarding the study of social class is the ambiguity of terms associated with it. Liu and his colleagues (2004a) found 448 different words used to describe social class (e.g., social class, social status, socioeconomic status, inequality). As a result, inconsistencies in the theoretical conceptualization and measurement of social class have plagued research on the topic.

Conceptually, a broad variety of definitions for social class have been offered. Perry and Wallace (2013) argue that social class is psychological in nature and define it as the "identification with a particular economic culture that one is exposed to within his/her environment (e.g., family, school, community)" (p. 82). In yet another definition, social class is defined as an individual's economic position based on income, educational level, and occupation (Liu et al., 2004a). A common theme inherent in these two definitions is that social class includes an economic component that distinguishes individuals or groups of individuals from one another. For our purposes, we utilize Rothman's (2002) definition of social class as "a group of individuals or families who occupy a similar position in the economic system of production, distribution, and consumption of goods and services in industrial societies" (p. 6).

In addition to the conceptualization of social class, another issue confounding research on social class is the varied methodologies used by researchers in measuring the construct. Much of the earlier research on social class used objective indicators of socioeconomic status (SES) (Kraus, Piff, and Keltner, 2009), which consists of factors such as educational level, income, and occupation (Bullock, 2004; Liu, Soleck, Hopps, Dunston, and Pickett, 2004b). In utilizing these three indices, an area of concern is how to combine these three indices to yield an accurate measure of social class. Additionally, it is not clear how differences in class can be extrapolated when individuals have similar objective backgrounds (Kraus et al., 2009). As a result, researchers have begun to examine subjective measures of social class and SES in relation to health outcomes using the MacArthur Scale of Subjective SES (e.g., Adler, Epel, Castellazzo, and Ickovics, 2000; Singh-Manoux, Adler, and Marmot, 2003). The scale consists of a picture of a ladder with ten rungs, each rung representing individuals with varying levels of income, education, and occupational status. Subjects are asked to place an 'X' on the rung of the ladder which best describes how they perceive their social status in comparison to others. More recently, subjective measures of social class are being used to investigate how social class is signaled and stigmatizes individuals (Brannon and Markus, 2013; Fiske, 2013; Kraus and Keltner, 2009).

Stigmatization of Class

Although many individuals agree that there are levels of class – upper, middle, and lower – the impact of this stratification in relation to career development and advancement is not well understood (Diemer and Ali, 2009). Similar to race, class is socially constructed (Liu et al., 2004b) and can provide a framework for how certain individuals are expected to behave (Kraus and Stephens, 2012). As such, classism, much like racism and sexism, may result in feelings of low self-worth due to the negative attitudes and behaviors people are subjected to by those of higher power (Lott, 2012).

Lott (2012) contends that there are two types of classism – institutional and interpersonal. Institutional classism refers to the "maintenance and reinforcement of low status by social institutions that present barriers to increase the difficulty of accessing resources" (p. 654); whereas interpersonal classism is characterized by prejudice, discrimination, and the development of negative stereotypes known as stereotype threat. The theory of stereotype threat suggests that individuals of stigmatized social groups may be constantly at risk of underperformance and that these risks may be the result of situational factors in addition to elements such as poverty, parenting style, and socialization (Nguyen and Ryan, 2008; Steele and Aronson, 1995). In a study on class differences and test performance, researchers found that when the low social class background of students was made salient during testing situations, students performed more poorly than both low and high social class students who were not subjected to the same test manipulations (Croizet and Claire, 1998). In another study, Granfield (1991) demonstrated that law students who were raised in working-class families felt stigmatized by their backgrounds and developed coping mechanisms and defenses for dealing with the stigmatization. Thus, we argue that much like racism deals with the discriminatory practices and marginalization of individuals because of their race, classism acts as a discriminatory function of social class and can affect the experiences, lives, and health of individuals on a daily basis (Liu et al., 2004b).

Social Class, Health, and Stress

Individuals from lower classes have been found to have poorer health, lower life expectancy, and more stressful lives (Rossides, 1997). Poor health care, risky lifestyles, bad food choices, and poor health practices have all been offered as explanations for the disparity in health outcomes between lower-class and upper-class individuals (Cohen, Kaplan, and Salonen, 1999). However, when examining health differences between the middle and higher classes, these explanations failed to demonstrate a clear causal relationship.

In an effort to explain the graded relationship between health and all levels of SES, Adler and her colleagues (1994) examined the causal impact of psychosocial and behavioral factors. They argue that physical environment, social environment, socialization and experiences, and health behaviors, in addition to income, education, and occupation, work in concert in the development of an individual's path in life (Adler et al., 1994). The socioeconomic status and health gradient suggests that the stepwise decline of individuals in SES predicts such factors as greater risks of heart disease, psychological issues, and infant mortality (Sapolsky, 2005). Researchers found that subjective social status had a significant relationship with psychological factors (i.e., chronic stress, pessimism, control over life, active coping, and passive coping) and physiological factors (i.e., sleep latency and heart rate) after controlling for objective indicators of social class and negative affect, suggesting that psychological perceptions do indeed contribute to the SES and health gradient (Adler et al., 2000). In research from the anthropology field, it was found that perceptions of rank among primates exhibited a strong association to chronic psychological stress (Sapolsky, 2005). Hence, self-perception of social class may be a powerful predictor of a person's health outcomes. Individuals who perceive themselves as being of high class rank tend to have more control over resources, contributing to a sense of empowerment over their social environment; whereas, individuals with perceptions of low class rank inhibit their behaviors and attitudes and are more constrained by social norms (Keltner, Gruenfeld, and Anderson, 2003).

The Whitehall II study of London-based civil service employees found evidence that there was a relationship between socioeconomic status and health (North et al., 1993; North, Syme, Feeney, Shipley, and Marmot, 1996). Another finding from this study indicated that subjective social status has a strong predictive relationship to five health outcomes (that is, angina, diabetes, respiratory illness, perceived general health, and GHQ (General Health Questionnaire) depression) (Singh-Manoux et al., 2003). In other words, individuals rating themselves as low social status showed higher incidence of angina, diabetes, respiratory illness (men only), poor self-rated health, and depression. Results from studies such as these highlight the importance of social class and why it deserves further exploration by researchers, especially in regards to health-related outcomes. In the next section, we concentrate our discussion of health issues on stress and explore the effects of stress on individuals, organizations, and society.

Stress: Causes, Process, and Consequences

Conceptually, stress is a creatively ambiguous word yet an excellent rubric for examining the causes, process, and consequences of human adaptation and adjustment. Stress is both the spice of life and the kiss of death (Levi, 2000). Stress has been linked to seven of the ten leading causes of death in the developed countries (J. C. Quick and Cooper, 2003), with heart disease accounting for roughly 25 percent of all deaths. The cardiovascular system is centrally involved in the stress response, which is the psychophysiological response that individuals experience to threat, challenge, environmental demands, and self-imposed pressures and expectations (Cannon, 1915). Stress is best understood as a process that is initiated by either environmental or self-imposed causes that trigger the activation of the stress response. The consequences of the stress response and process can be good, as in the euphemism of eustress, or bad, as in the range of forms of medical, behavioral, and psychological distress. These good and bad consequences have collective consequences for organizations, communities, and societies.

Causes of Stress

LePine, Podsakoff, and LePine (2005) developed an important distinction in positive and negative causes of stress when they distinguished challenge stressors from hindrance stressors. Challenge stressors still trigger the stress response in individuals while at the same time offering the individual an opportunity to grow, develop, and achieve greater mastery of self and the environment. In Vaillant's (1977) framework, the successful adaptation to life and stress is what enables us to live and to live well. Hence, challenge stressors are good. Hindrance stressors, on the other hand, are not good and even are bad as causes of stress because they lead to frustration and not to mastery.

While the challenge versus hindrance stressor distinction is both valuable and important, it does not focus as much on the substantive causes of stress. Environmental conditions, technology, occupation, emotional labor, work roles, the volume and pace of work, leadership, and interpersonal relationships are among the key causes of stress for individuals in the workplace (J. C. Quick, Wright, Adkins, Nelson, and Quick, 2013). However, there is significant individual variance in response to specific causes of stress so that what is stressful for one individual may well be almost a nonevent for another individual.

Coupled with the individual variability in response to causes of stress is the issue of self-imposed or internally generated causes of stress within the individual. For example, workaholic behavior is a self-imposed cause of stress that has a range of negative and adverse consequences for the individual, their family, and potentially others in the work environment (J. D. Quick, Henley, and Quick, 2004). Worry, or more specifically pathologic worry, would be another example of a self-imposed cause of stress. A critical distinction here is between ruminating worry that is pathologic and function worry about legitimate problems or stressors that leads to problem-solving actions and positive outcomes.

For both working and nonworking adults, another major cause of stress is work–family conflict (Hammer, Kossek, Anger, Bodner, and Zimmerman, 2011). There can be significant spillover effects of stress from the work environment that impact the employee's family life, and stressors in the family and home environment spill over into the workplace. The cause of stress can be in either life space and have effects beyond it.

The Stress Response Process

Regardless of the cause of stress or its locus of origin, there is a patterned and predictable stress response process that is triggered by the cause of stress. This process is initiated by the perception of an event, circumstance, or person as the cause of stress. This perception initiates the combined action of the sympathetic nervous system and the endocrine system. While Cannon (1935) focused the bulk of his attention on helping us understand the sympathetic nervous system elements of the stress response, Selye (1956) made important contributions to our understanding of the endocrine system elements of the response.

The stress response is highly functional and adaptive for short-term emergency and performance events because of the shunting of blood to the brain and large muscle groups, the lighting up of the reticular activation system in the brain stem for heightened perceptual engagement, the release of glucose and fatty acids into the bloodstream as fueling agents, and the shutting down of the immune system that is not needed in intense activation.

While all of these elements of the stress response process are functional and adaptive in the short run, the long-term consequences of this allostatic load can be very damaging to many parts of the individual's psychophysiology (McEwen, 1998). Allostasis serves a protective function for the individual and promotes adaptation, again in the short run. However, carrying allostatic load for prolonged periods has primary (e.g., anxiety and tension), secondary (e.g., elevated blood pressure and body mass index), and tertiary (e.g., cardiovascular disease, depression, mortality) effects that are damaging and even lethal.

Consequences of Stress

McEwen's (1998) research on allostasis shows that the consequences of stress can be protective, adaptive, and functional, all of which are positive. LePine et al. (2005) offer evidence that challenge stress yields positive consequences and functional gains for the individual. Hence, eustress embodies the positive and functional consequences of stress. Fredrickson's (2009) research in positive psychology points in the direction of balancing the positive with the negative, because bad things do happen and the failure to recognize and cope with bad events is nonadaptive.

However, much of the twentieth-century research on stress focused on the consequences of stress that fall under the heading of distress, with cardiovascular disease (CVD) leading the list. Because the cardiovascular system is centrally involved in the stress response and because heart disease is the leading cause of death for both men and women in developed societies, special attention should be placed on this consequence. While family history has been known for some time as a risk factor for heart disease, CVD is not a single-cause disease. Rather, multiple risk factors that are modifiable, many falling under the stress rubric, have been identified. Chang, Hahn, Teutsch, and Hutwagner (2001) identified eight such risk factors for ischemic heart disease mortality: hypertension, elevated serum cholesterol, diabetes, overweight, current smoking, physical inactivity, depression, and nonuse of replacement hormones. The Centers for Disease Control (CDC, 2005) found racial/ethnic and socioeconomic disparities in these multiple risk factors for heart disease and stroke. Women have been an underrepresented sample in much research on heart disease despite the fact that it is their leading cause of death. Mehta, Wei, and Wenger (2015) bring attention to additional risk factors for women, including mental stress, depression, low SES status, work stress, and marital stress.

Not all bad consequences of stress are lethal, and nor is heart disease always lethal. The American Psychological Association identifies the top five early warning signs and symptoms of stress as:

1. irritability or anger
2. fatigue
3. lack of interest, motivation, or energy
4. feeling nervous or anxious
5. headache

The leading presenting complaints of stress to health-care providers are anxiety and depression (J. C. Quick and Cooper, 2003), while the leading behavioral form of distress and preventable death is tobacco abuse. J. C. Quick et al. (2013) and J. C. Quick (2014) provide extensive reviews of the research on a range of consequences of stress.

Preventive Stress Management™: A Prevention Model

Among theories of stress, Preventive Stress Management™ is unique because of its roots in preventive medicine and public health. PSM's major premise is that effective stress management consists of promoting eustress, the positive, healthy form of stress, and preventing and/or resolving distress, the negative form of stress. Another hallmark of PSM is the underlying philosophy that stress is an inevitable feature of life, but distress can be both managed and prevented. The theory and practice of PSM are guided by the following principles:

1. *Individual health and organizational health are interdependent* An organization's human assets flourish in healthy organizations, and organizations' survival depends on vital, vigorous individuals.
2. *Leaders have a responsibility for individual and organizational health* Because individual and organizational health are interdependent, leaders, as stewards of the organization, are in positions to promote well-being.
3. *Individual distress and organizational distress are not inevitable* While stress is a natural part of life, distress does not have to be. Through positive and responsible prevention, distress can be prevented and managed.
4. *Each individual and organization reacts uniquely to stress* There is no "one size fits all" solution to stress management. Interventions must be tailored to the unique needs of the individuals and organizations being served.
5. *Organizations are ever-changing, dynamic entities* Organizations, comprised of individuals, are open systems that navigate natural life cycles. Acknowledgment of this change process means that interventions must be similarly dynamic and adaptive.

As applied to social class, these principles imply that "organization" is not only business organizations, but also institutions and society as a whole. The extension of the preventive management philosophy to the challenges of social class broadens the macro lens of application of PSM.

With the five principles as a philosophical underpinning, the heart of PSM is the prevention model shown in Figure 37.1. As shown in the model, there are three levels of prevention. Primary prevention focuses on the demands or stressors. These demands may take various forms, and sometimes it may not be possible to alter the stressor itself. What can be altered in these cases is the individual's perception of the demand or stressor. This is the stage of susceptibility, and the emphasis is on eliminating or reducing risk factors.

In secondary prevention, the focus is on the individual and organizational response to stress. Efforts here are intended to develop hardiness and resilience. This stage also involves early detection of disease, and restoration of healthy habits.

Tertiary prevention is therapeutic in that it addresses symptoms or disease. It involves getting professional help for the individual and organizational distress. The aim of the three-stage model is to prevent or halt the progression of stress into full-blown distress. It is always preferable to begin with primary prevention, supplement with secondary prevention, and hopefully tertiary prevention is not necessary, but becomes a safety net should needs arise.

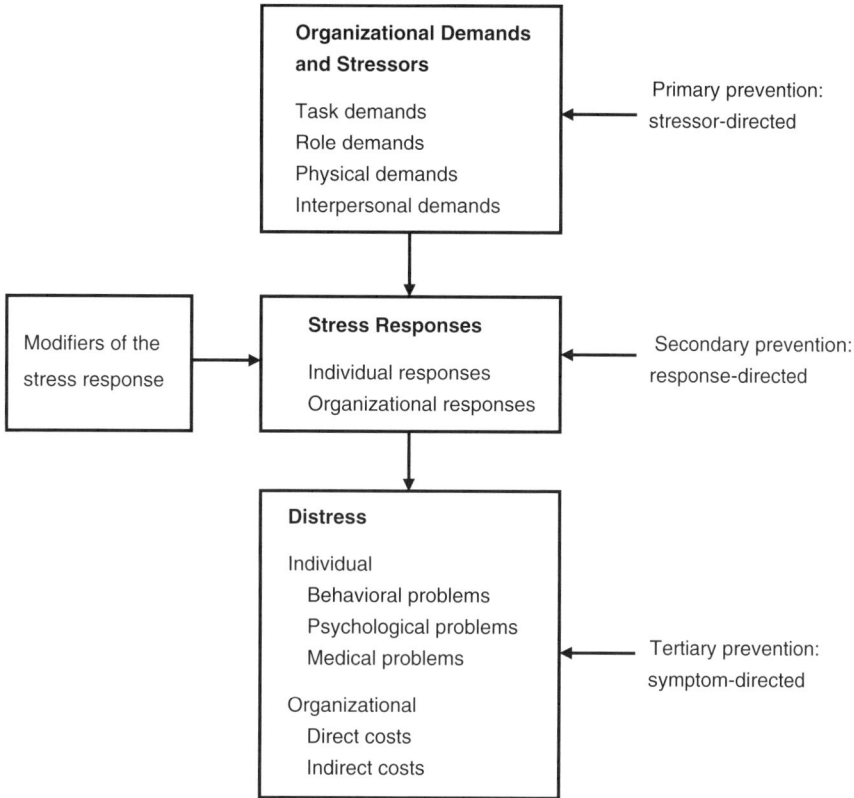

Figure 37.1   The preventive stress management model (from J. C. Quick et al., 2013, p. 24; reprinted with permission from the American Psychological Association).

In addition to preventing and resolving distress, the PSM approach encompasses eustress generation. This means creating conditions in which individuals can experience the positive stress response through engagement and challenge (Nelson and Simmons, 2011; Simmons and Nelson, 2007). Eustress generation creates health and well-being, and is an important complement to distress prevention.

Preventive stress management has contributed to research and practice in multiple arenas, including gender differences, stress in the military services, newcomer socialization, managerial well-being, and executive health. It has also been applied to chronic challenges such as workplace accidents, workplace violence, and sexual harassment (Hargrove, Quick, Nelson, and Quick, 2011). In the next section, we extend the application of PSM to propose interventions directed toward the stress associated with social class.

From a Prevention Model to an Intervention Plan

An intervention consists of planned activities, actions, and/or events intended to help improve performance and effectiveness (Cummings and Worley, 2009). Thus, prior to embarking on any plan of intervention, a thorough diagnosis of the problem or situation must be performed to ascertain the true nature of the issue at hand. We argue that for any intervention plan to be effective several questions must be asked:

1. Is the root cause of the issue at the individual, organizational, or societal level, that is, who is the target of the problem?
2. How well does the plan fit the needs of the target?
3. Is the proposed course of action feasible and able to produce an effective change or outcome?
4. Does the intervention plan support a sustained change? That is, will the target be equipped with the tools and knowledge to maintain the new status quo?

As discussed previously, stress affects not only individuals, but organizations and society at large. Murphy (1996) conducted a critical review of literature that examined the effects of workplace stress management interventions on job-related outcomes as well as health outcomes which included physiological, psychological, and somatic measures. His findings suggest that a combination of intervening stress techniques had a greater impact on coping with stress in comparison to a single intervention technique. We offer an intervention plan utilizing the Preventive Stress Management™ model as a framework for mitigating the deleterious effects of stress across various target levels, as shown in Figure 37.2.

Primary Intervention

At the primary level, the intervention plan is designed to modify or reduce the stressors (J. C. Quick et al., 2013). For individuals, one of the most effective means for coping with stress is to have a strong and supportive social network. The six degrees of separation principle states that our personal contacts are valuable to the extent that they help us reach, in as few connections as possible, the far-off person who has the information we need (Ibarra and Hunter, 2007). Thus, the ability to develop a broad, yet dense, network as a means for increasing one's social network and gaining access to more opportunities is essential for individuals of all classes, particularly lower-class individuals. According to Ibarra, Kilduff, and Tsai (2005), individuals can be taught new schemas and modes of behavior by being exposed to patterns of social relationships that prove advantageous in the structuring of networks.

		Primary intervention	Secondary intervention	Tertiary intervention
Target level	Individual	Social support Mentoring Goal setting	Increasing psychological capital Coaching Mindfulness awareness training	Professional assistance Meditation
	Organizational	Career planning Person–job fit	Leadership skills and style Supervisor support Team building	Organization development intervention
	Societal	Community alliances	Coping groups	Crisis intervention Trauma educational planning

Figure 37.2 Preventive stress model intervention techniques.

Mentoring, a cohesive family unit, and peers are instrumental techniques in building one's network and social support system. Mentoring has been shown to have a significant impact in furthering the career advancement of individuals, as well as their personal growth (Kram and Isabella, 1985; Perna and Lerner, 1995). Higgins and Kram (2001) introduced a typology of developmental networks that integrates social network theory with research on mentoring. Although the study looked at the more formal network of mentoring relationships, components of the typology can be applied to other network relationships since the root of the typology is based on network theory. The typology consists of two key factors: the diversity of an individual's developmental networks, and the strength of the developmental relationships that make up these networks. Hence, as individuals aim to increase the variability in both the sources and strength of their support system, the better equipped they will be in reducing their stressors, as social support has been argued to be one of the strongest protectors against stress. Cohen and Wills (1985) concluded that social support acts as both a main effect and as a buffer against stress which contributes to positive effects of well-being. Research examining the relationship between SES and perceived health found that greater social support, less perceived stress and anger, and better health practices were associated with higher levels of SES and self-reported health for the United States and Finland (Cohen et al., 1999).

Another technique that can be used to decrease stress in individuals is goal setting. Goal-setting intervention plans can also help to circumvent negative effects of ambiguity, which often contributes to increased stress levels. Quick (1979) studied the dyadic nature of goal setting and found that after training, goal behaviors significantly increased while stress significantly decreased.

In addition to not having a clear goal, an unclear vision of one's career path can contribute to stress not only for the individual, but for organizations as well. When employees are stressed, research shows that there are greater instances of job dissatisfaction, which can morph and fester throughout the organization like a cancer creating a climate of discontent. At the organizational level, career path planning and role clarity can help to alleviate stress and the factors that contribute to stress. Ideally, a career path should involve both the employee and the organization as a means of ensuring that the fit between the person and the job is strong and well meshed. Person–job fit has been shown to have a strong positive effect on job satisfaction and organizational commitment, leading to decreased instances of intent to quit and lower levels of strains (Cable and DeRue, 2002; Kristof-Brown, Zimmerman, and Johnson, 2005).

At the societal level, building alliances within the community can also be beneficial. Social networks play a critical role in determining the degree to which individuals will succeed in achieving their goals. Bourdieu (1986) defines social capital as the aggregate of the actual or potential resources that are linked to a network of mutual acquaintances who provide members within the network with the support of the collectively owned capital. Thus, the social relationship itself is important as it allows individuals access to resources possessed by their fellow members. In addition, the amount and quality of the resources are of significance. Building social capital is a key component to building social support systems, which serve as buffering agents against stress. Community interventions can be valuable, particularly to those of lower class, to help foster the building of social capital by increasing an individual's access to varied resources. According to Hobfoll (2001), stress occurs when resources are lost or become threatened. Hence, if a person is able to build a reservoir of resources, they will have the resources at the ready to combat and reduce stress as it occurs.

Secondary Intervention

At the secondary level, the goal of interventions is to change how individuals and organizations respond to stressors (J. C. Quick et al., 2013). Techniques that can be used to help individuals in their response to stressors include: (a) increasing psychological capital, (b) coaching, and (c) mindfulness training. Psychological capital (PsyCap) is a relatively new construct in the domain of organizational behavior that seeks to help organizations achieve a competitive advantage through their people, that is, a human competitive edge (Luthans, Youssef, and Avolio, 2007). From a developmental perspective, PsyCap addresses *who you are* and *who you are becoming* (Avolio and Luthans, 2006; Luthans et al., 2007; Nelson and Cooper, 2007). PsyCap is defined as:

> An individual's positive psychological state of development and is characterized by: (1) having confidence (self-efficacy) to take on and put in the necessary effort to succeed at challenging tasks; (2) making a positive attribution (optimism) about succeeding now and in the future; (3) persevering toward goals and, when necessary, redirecting paths to goals (hope) in order to succeed; and (4) when beset by problems and adversity, sustaining and bouncing back and even beyond (resiliency) to attain success. (Luthans et al., 2007, p. 3)

Although PsyCap is a relatively new construct, it has been shown that individuals who are able to access these positive resources display a significant decrease in perceived symptoms of job stress (Avey, Luthans, and Jensen, 2009). Hence, intervention programs aimed at increasing resiliency, hope, optimism, and self-efficacy can serve as a resource pool that individuals can access when responding to stress and stressful events.

Coaching as an intervention technique presents another approach for responding to stressors. Coaching is "a human development process that involves structured, focused, interaction and the use of appropriate strategies, tools and techniques to promote desirable and sustainable change for the benefit of the coachee and potentially for other stakeholders" (Cox, Bachkirova, and Clutterbuck, 2010, p. 1). Berg and Karlsen (2013) suggest that coaching as a means for increasing management role conflict skills can have a mitigating effect on stress levels as individuals work on developing strong communication skills and improving methods to cope with external work pressures.

At the organizational level, leadership, supervisor support, performance appraisal systems, and team building may all serve as techniques organizations can use in helping them adapt their responses to stress. Coaching as a means for improving leadership skills such as visualization, positive self-talk, and empowerment was shown to be beneficial in coping with stress (Berg and Karlsen, 2013). Darling and Utecht (2010) argue that when leaders take on the responsibility for controlling how they respond to external events and recommit to bringing purpose, passion, and direction to the workplace, organizational life will change significantly. In another study that explored the relationship between leadership and stress, transactional leadership was found to weaken the negative influence of hindrance stressors on job performance, whereas transformational leadership was found to enhance the positive effect of challenge stressors on job performance (Zhang, Lepine, Buckman, and Wei, 2014). In addition, organizational policies that promote team building and supervisor support (Lee and Ashforth, 1996) can buffer employees from the deleterious effects of stress (Avey et al., 2009; Nel and Spies, 2007).

Community intervention programs at all levels of society can be beneficial resources for stress prevention. In a three-month follow-up, community residents in an eight-week mindfulness stress reduction program saw significant reduction in psychological distress and medical symptoms in comparison to residents who received educational materials and were instructed to use community resources for stress management (Williams, Kolar, Reger, and Pearson, 2001). Although community programs can be beneficial, findings such as this highlight the importance of planned intervention programs in coping with stress. For example, coping groups, comprised of 10–12 participants engaged in several sessions over the course of a few weeks, assisted community members in coping with traumatic loss and stress (Macy et al., 2004; Mitchell and Everly, 1996).

Tertiary Prevention

The goal of tertiary prevention is to heal the individual's or organization's symptoms of distress (J. C. Quick et al., 2013). At these times, professional assistance may be necessary to help individuals overcome their stress-induced symptoms. Therapy, counseling sessions, and medical help are tools that individuals can turn to for help during the healing process. In addition, meditation has been shown to be a highly effective intervention technique (Murphy, 1996).

At the organizational level, organizational development intervention and workplace wellness programs may be used as tertiary intervention plans. Thus, when organizations need to engage in a transformative change, leaders must begin with a thorough assessment of the problem in order to determine the most effective course of action. As such, organizations must adhere to communicating clearly with their employees, to allowing participative decision-making, and to exercising empathy and support.

Many traumatic events that people encounter are due to random events that occur without notice (Macy et al., 2004). Crisis interventions which provide emergency psychological care to help victims of trauma return to a functional level have been found to be effective when combating stressors caused by traumatic events (Flannery and Everly, 2000). Macy and his colleagues contend that community-based psychological trauma interventions are probable solutions to assisting communities and their members to resolve and adapt to traumatic episodes. Hence, in addition to communities being prepared for traumatic events, professionals must be armed with the knowledge and skills needed to help community members during these stressful events.

Conclusion

The negative, linear relationship between socioeconomic status and both morbidity and mortality has been known for some decades now. We build from that core set of data to explore the broader relationship between social class, stress, and health by drawing on the public health notions of prevention, especially as translated into and applied in organizations. We have conceived broader application of these prevention ideas beyond organizations, with implications for public policy. Good public policy must address individual needs along with organizational needs and the needs of the larger society. We have aimed to address all of these three levels of analysis, broadening the lens from business organizations to include government agencies and not-for-profit organizations at the institutional level. While stress and health are frequently thought of as individual experiences and concerns, there are more macro forces in operation that operate in the contextual environment of these individuals.

This macro perspective aligns with the public health notions of prevention where primary prevention is always the preferred point of intervention. While we address primary, secondary, and tertiary prevention in our model, primary prevention is always the first place to start. By setting conditions that are healthy and eustressful for all concerned, the burden of suffering in a society is reduced and the demand for secondary and tertiary prevention is moderated.

References

Adler, N. E., Boyce, T., Chesney, M. A., Cohen, S., Folkman, S., Kahn, R. L., and Syme, S. L. (1994). Socioeconomic status and health: The challenge of the gradient. *American Psychologist, 49*(1), 15–24. doi:10.1037/0003-066X.49.1.15

Adler, N. E., Epel, E. S., Castellazzo, G., and Ickovics, J. R. (2000). Relationship of subjective and objective social status with psychological and physiological functioning: Preliminary data in healthy white women. *Health Psychology, 19*(6), 586–592. doi:10.1037/0278-6133.19.6.586

Avey, J. B., Luthans, F., and Jensen, S. M. (2009). Psychological capital: A positive resource for combating employee stress and turnover. *Human Resource Management, 48*(5), 677–693.

Avolio, B. J., and Luthans, F. (2006). *The High Impact Leader: Moments Matter in Accelerating Authentic Leadership Development*. New York: McGraw Hill.

Bell, M. P., Özbilgin, M. F., Beauregard, T. A., and Sürgevil, O. (2011). Voice, silence, and diversity in 21st century organizations: Strategies for inclusion of gay, lesbian, bisexual, and transgender employees. *Human Resource Management, 50*(1), 131–146. doi:10.1002/hrm.20401

Berg, M. E., and Karlsen, J. T. (2013). Managing stress in projects using coaching leadership tools. *Engineering Management Journal, 25*(4), 52–61.

Bourdieu, P. (1986). The forms of capital. In J. G. Richardson (Ed.), *Handbook of Theory and Research for the Sociology of Education* (pp. 241–258). New York: Greenwood.

Brannon, T. N., and Markus, H. R. (2013). Social class and race: Burdens but also some benefits of chronic low rank. *Psychological Inquiry, 24*(2), 97–101. doi:10.1080/1047840X.2013.794102

Brazzel, M. (2007). Diversity and social justice practices for OD [organization development] practitioners. *OD Practitioner, 39*(3), 15–21.

Brazzel, M. (2008). Deep diversity, social justice, and organization development. *OD Seasonings, 5*(2), 10.

Brewer, M. B., and Hewstone, M. (2004). *Self and Social Identity*. Oxford: Blackwell.

Brown, M. T., Fukunaga, C., Umemoto, D., and Wicker, L. (1996). Annual review, 1990–1996: Social class, work, and retirement behavior. *Journal of Vocational Behavior, 49*(2), 159–189.

Bullock, H. E. (2004). Class diversity in the workplace. In M. S. Stockdale and F. J. Crosby (Eds.), *The Psychology and Management of Workplace Diversity* (pp. 224–242). Oxford: Blackwell.

Cable, D. M., and DeRue, D. S. (2002). The convergent and discriminant validity of subjective fit perceptions. *Journal of Applied Psychology, 87*(5), 875–884. doi:10.1037/0021-9010.87.5.875

Cannon, W. B. (1915). *Bodily Changes in Pain, Hunger, Fear And Rage: An Account of Recent Researches into the Function of Emotional Excitement*. New York: Appleton-Century-Crofts.

Cannon, W. B. (1935). Stresses and strains of homeostasis. *American Journal of the Medical Sciences, 189*(1), 13–14.

CDC (Centers for Disease Control) (2005). Racial/ethnic and socioeconomic disparities in multiple risk factors for heart disease and stroke – United States, 2003. *Morbidity and Mortality Weekly Report, 54*(5), 113–117.

Chang, M., Hahn, R. A., Teutsch, S. M., and Hutwagner, L. C. (2001). Multiple risk factors and population attributable risk for ischemic heart disease mortality in the United States, 1971–1992. *Journal of Clinical Epidemiology, 54*(6), 634–644.

Cohen, S., Kaplan, G. A., and Salonen, J. T. (1999). The role of psychological characteristics in the relation between socioeconomic status and perceived health. *Journal of Applied Social Psychology, 29*(3), 445–468. doi:10.1111/j.1559-1816.1999.tb01396.x

Cohen, S., and Wills, T. A. (1985). Stress, social support, and the buffering hypothesis. *Psychological Bulletin, 98*(2), 310–357. doi:10.1037/0033-2909.98.2.310

Cox, E., Bachkirova, T., and Clutterbuck, D. A. (Eds.) (2010). *The Complete Handbook of Coaching*. Thousand Oaks, CA: Sage.

Croizet, J.-C., and Claire, T. (1998). Extending the concept of stereotype and threat to social class: The intellectual underperformance of students from low socioeconomic backgrounds. *Personality and Social Psychology Bulletin, 24*(6), 588–594.

Cummings, T. G., and Worley, C. G. (2009). *Organization Development and Change*, 9th edn. Mason, OH: South-Western.

Darling, J. R., and Utecht, R. L. (2010). Leadership responsiveness to The Key in an era of socioeconomic stress: A focused team-building paradigm. *Organization Development Journal, 28*(3), 45–59.

Diemer, M. A., and Ali, S. R. (2009). Integrating social class into vocational psychology: Theory and practice implications. *Journal of Career Assessment, 17*(3), 247–265.

Fiske, S. T. (2013). What's in a theory of rank? *Psychological Inquiry, 24*(2), 109–111. doi:10.1080/1047840X.2013.792578

Flannery, R. B., and Everly, G. S. (2000). Crisis intervention: A review. *International Journal of Emergency Mental Health, 2*(2), 119–126.

Fredrickson, B. (2009). *Positivity: Groundbreaking Research Reveals How to Embrace the Hidden Strength of Positive Emotions, Overcome Negativity, and Thrive*. New York: Crown.

Granfield, R. (1991). Making it by faking it: Working-class students in an elite academic environment. *Journal of Contemporary Ethnography, 20*(3), 331–351.

Hammer, L. B., Kossek, E. E., Anger, W. K., Bodner, T., and Zimmerman, K. L. (2011). Clarifying work–family intervention processes: The roles of work–family conflict and family-supportive supervisor behaviors. *Journal of Applied Psychology, 96*(1), 134–150. doi:10.1037/a0020927

Hargrove, M. B., Quick, J. C., Nelson, D. L., and Quick, J. D. (2011). The theory of preventive stress management: A 33-year review and evaluation. *Stress and Health: Journal of the International Society for the Investigation of Stress, 27*(3), 182–193.

Higgins, M. C., and Kram, K. E. (2001). Reconceptualizing mentoring at work: A developmental network perspective. *Academy of Management Review, 26*(2), 264–288.

Hobfoll, S. E. (2001). The influence of culture, community, and the nested-self in the stress process: Advancing conservation of resources theory. *Applied Psychology, 50*(3), 337–421. doi:10.1111/1464-0597.00062

Ibarra, H., and Hunter, M. (2007). How leaders create and use networks. *Harvard Business Review, 85*(1), 40–47.

Ibarra, H., Kilduff, M., and Tsai, W. (2005). Zooming in and out: Connecting individuals and collectivities at the frontiers of organizational network research. *Organization Science, 16*(4), 359–371. doi:10.1287/orsc.1050.0129

Keltner, D., Gruenfeld, D. H., and Anderson, C. (2003). Power, approach, and inhibition. *Psychological Review, 110*(2), 265–284. doi:10.1037/0033-295X.110.2.265

Kram, K. E., and Isabella, L. A. (1985). Mentoring alternatives: The role of peer relationships in career development. *Academy of Management Journal, 28*(1), 110–132.

Kraus, M. W., and Keltner, D. (2009). Signs of socioeconomic status: A thin-slicing approach. *Psychological Science, 20*(1), 99–106.

Kraus, M. W., Piff, P. K., and Keltner, D. (2009). Social class, sense of control, and social explanation. *Journal of Personality and Social Psychology, 97*(6), 992–1004. doi:10.1037/a0016357

Kraus, M. W., and Stephens, N. M. (2012). A road map for an emerging psychology of social class. *Social and Personality Psychology Compass, 6*(9), 642–656.

Kristof-Brown, A. L., Zimmerman, R. D., and Johnson, E. C. (2005). Consequences of individual's fit at work: A meta-analysis of person–job, person–organization, person–group, and person–supervisor fit. *Personnel Psychology, 58*(2), 281–342. doi:10.1111/j.1744-6570.2005.00672.x

Lee, R. T., and Ashforth, B. E. (1996). A meta-analytic examination of the correlates of the three dimensions of job burnout. *Journal of Applied Psychology, 81*(2), 123–133.

Lepine, J. A., Podsakoff, N. P., and Lepine, M. A. (2005). A meta-analytic test of the challenge stressor–hindrance stressor framework: An explanation for inconsistent relationships among stressors and performance. *Academy of Management Journal, 48*(5), 764–775. doi:10.5465/AMJ.2005.18803921

Levi, L. (2000). *Guidance on Work-Related Stress: Spice of Life or Kiss of Death?* Luxembourg: Office for Official Publications of the European Communities.

Liu, W. M., Ali, S. R., Soleck, G., Hopps, J., Dunston, K., and Pickett, T., Jr. (2004a). Using social class in counseling psychology research. *Journal of Counseling Psychology, 51*(1), 3–18.

Liu, W. M., Soleck, G., Hopps, J., Dunston, K., and Pickett, T., Jr. (2004b). A new framework to understand social class in counseling: The social class worldview model and modern classism theory. *Journal of Multicultural Counseling and Development, 32*(2), 95–122.

Lott, B. (2012). The social psychology of class and classism. *American Psychologist, 67*(8), 650–658. doi:10.1037/a0029369

Luthans, F., Youssef, C. M., and Avolio, B. J. (2007). *Psychological Capital: Developing the Human Competitive Edge*. New York: Oxford University Press.

Macy, R. D., Behar, L., Paulson, R., Delman, J., Schmid, L., and Smith, S. F. (2004). Community-based, acute post-traumatic stress management: A description and evaluation of a psychosocial-intervention continuum. *Harvard Review of Psychiatry, 12*(4), 217–228.

McEwen, B. S. (1998). Protective and damaging effects of stress mediators. *New England Journal of Medicine, 338*(3), 171–179.

Mehta, P. K., Wei, J., and Wenger, N. K. (2015). Ischemic heart disease in women: A focus on risk factors. *Trends in Cardiovascular Medicine, 25*(2), 140–151. doi.org/10.1016/j.tcm.2014.10.005

Mitchell, J. T., and Everly, G. S. (1996). *Critical Incident Stress Debriefing (CISD): An Operations Manual for the Prevention of Traumatic Stress among Emergency Service and Disaster Workers*. Ellicott City, MD: Chevron.

Murphy, L. R. (1996). Stress management in work settings: A critical review of the health effects. *American Journal of Health Promotion, 11*(2), 112–135. doi:10.4278/0890-1171-11.2.112

Nel, D., and Spies, G. (2007). The use of play therapy mediums in a stress management program with corporate employees. *Journal of Workplace Behavioral Health, 22*(1), 33–51.

Nelson, D. L., and Cooper, C. L. (Eds.) (2007). *Positive Organizational Behavior*. Thousand Oaks, CA: Sage.

Nelson, D. L., and Simmons, B. L. (2011). Savoring eustress while coping with distress: The holistic model of stress. In J. C. Quick and L. E. Tetrick (Eds.), *Handbook of Occupational Health Psychology*, 2nd edn. (pp. 55–74). Washington, DC: American Psychological Association.

Nguyen, H.-H. D., and Ryan, A. M. (2008). Does stereotype threat affect test performance of minorities and women? A meta-analysis of experimental evidence. *Journal of Applied Psychology, 93*(6), 1314–1334.

North, F. M., Syme, S. L., Feeney, A., Head, J., Shipley, M. J., and Marmot, M. G. (1993). Explaining socioeconomic differences in sickness absence: The Whitehall II study. *British Medical Journal, 306*(6874), 361–366.

North, F. M., Syme, S. L., Feeney, A., Shipley, M., and Marmot, M. (1996). Psychosocial work environment and sickness absence among British civil servants: The Whitehall II study. *American Journal of Public Health, 86*(3), 332–340. doi:10.2105/AJPH.86.3.332

Perna, F. M., and Lerner, B. M. (1995). Mentoring and career development among university faculty. *Journal of Education, 177*(2), 31.

Perry, J. C., and Wallace, E. (2013). Career issues and social class. In W. Ming Liu (Ed.), *The Oxford Handbook of Social Class in Counseling* (pp. 81–102). New York: Oxford University Press.

Quick, J. C. (1979). Dyadic goal setting and role stress: A field study. *Academy of Management Journal, 22*(2), 241–252. doi:10.2307/255587

Quick, J. C. (2014). Stress. In *Oxford Bibliographies* (Management). At http://www.oxfordbibliographies.com/obo/page/management (accessed July 2016).

Quick, J. C., and Cooper, C. L. (2003). *Stress and Strain*, 2nd edn. Oxford: Health Press.

Quick, J. C., Wright, T. A., Adkins, J. A., Nelson, D. L., and Quick, J. D. (2013). *Preventive Stress Management in Organizations*, 2nd edn. Washington, DC: American Psychological Association.

Quick, J. D., Henley, A. B., and Quick, J. C. (2004). The balancing act: At work and at home. *Organizational Dynamics, 33*(4), 426–438. doi:10.1016/j.orgdyn.2004.09.008

Ragins, B. R., and Cornwell, J. M. (2001). Pink triangles: Antecedents and consequences of perceived workplace discrimination against gay and lesbian employees. *Journal of Applied Psychology, 86*(6), 1244–1261.

Rossides, D. W. (1997). *Social Stratification: The Interplay of Class, Race, and Gender*, 2nd edn. Upper Saddle River, NJ: Prentice Hall.

Rothman, R. A. (2002). *Inequality and Stratification: Race, Class, and Gender*, 4th edn. Upper Saddle River, NJ: Prentice Hall.

Sapolsky, R. M. (2005). The influence of social hierarchy on primate health. *Science, 308*(5722), 648–652. doi:10.1126/science.1106477

Scott, J. (1996). *Stratification and Power: Structures of Class, Status and Command*. Cambridge, UK: Polity Press.

Selye, H. (1956). *The Stress of Life*. New York: McGraw-Hill.

Simmons, B. L., and Nelson, D. L. (2007). Eustress at work: Extending the holistic stress model. In D. L. Nelson and C. L. Cooper (Eds.), *Positive Organizational Behavior: Accentuating the Positive at Work* (pp. 40–54). Thousand Oaks, CA: Sage.

Singh-Manoux, A., Adler, N. E., and Marmot, M. G. (2003). Subjective social status: Its determinants and its association with measures of ill-health in the Whitehall II study. *Social Science and Medicine, 56*(6), 1321–1333. doi:10.1016/s0277-9536(02)00131-4

Steele, C. M., and Aronson, J. (1995). Stereotype threat and the intellectual test performance of African Americans. *Journal of Personality and Social Psychology, 69*(5), 797–811.

Trau, R. N. C. (2015). The impact of discriminatory climate perceptions on the composition of intraorganizational developmental networks, psychosocial support, and job and career attitudes of employees with an invisible stigma. *Human Resource Management, 54*(2), 345–366. doi:10.1002/hrm.21630

US Census Bureau (2012). Distribution of household wealth in the US: 2000 to 2011. At https://www.census.gov/people/wealth/files/Wealth%20distribution%202000%20to%202011.pdf (accessed July 2016).

US Census Bureau (2013). Poverty: 2000 to 2012. American Community Survey Briefs. At https://www.census.gov/prod/2013pubs/acsbr12-01.pdf (accessed July 2016).

US Census Bureau (2014). Income and poverty in the United States: 2013. Current Population Reports. At https://www.census.gov/content/dam/Census/library/publications/2014/demo/p60-249.pdf (accessed July 2016).

Vaillant, G. E. (1977). *Adaptation to Life*. Boston: Little, Brown.

Williams, K. A., Kolar, M. M., Reger, B. E., and Pearson, J. C. (2001). Evaluation of a wellness-based mindfulness stress reduction intervention: A controlled trial. *American Journal of Health Promotion, 15*(6), 422–432. doi:10.4278/0890-1171-15.6.422

Zhang, Y., Lepine, J. A., Buckman, B. R., and Wei, F. (2014). It's not fair … or is it? The role of justice and leadership in explaining work stressor–job performance relationships. *Academy of Management Journal, 57*(3), 675–697. doi:10.5465/amj.2011.1110

Author Index

Note: Italic *f* and *t* after a page number indicates Figures and Tables respectively.

Subject Index

Note: Italic *b*, *f* and *t* after a page number indicates Boxes, Figures and Tables respectively.

ABP (ambulatory blood pressure) 104–6
absenteeism 49, 111, 151, 285, 366, 368*t*, 376, 381, 419, 527
    abundance of data on 19
    burnout determines 43
    cost to business of 147
    health problems result in 492
    increase in 14
    predicted 176
    productivity loss due to 158*t*, 161*t*
    reduced 586
    sleep and 492, 493
    stress-related 287, 365, 533
absorption 40, 241
    see also self-absorption
abuse 255, 267
    childhood 201, 202, 214, 445
    domestic 214
    emotional 202, 265
    general 198
    psychological 198
    supervisor 532
    tobacco 636
    verbal 214, 269
    see also alcohol abuse; drug abuse; physical abuse; sexual abuse
accidents 255, 473, 625
    leading to disablement or death 262
    nuclear 264
    risk for 488

    serious 67
    see also transport accidents; workplace accidents
Acetyl-L-carnitine 514
ACIP (American Cast Iron Pipe Company) 580
ACTH (adrenocorticotropic hormone) 257, 504
actigraphy 508
addiction 317
    regular and binge use of substances 190
    relapse prevention 270–1
    stress and 252–79
    see also drug addiction
adrenalin 101, 126, 172, 505
    see also HPA
aesthetics 395, 572
    well-being and 605–29
AET (affective events theory) 365, 367, 368*t*, 370, 373, 377
    see also negative affective events
affect 491
    see also NA; PA; PANAS
affect preferences 85–6
affective well-being 59, 66, 70, 246, 434
    degree of social support and 69
    improved 584
    low 58
    positive 245
    predictions for different forms of 64

The Handbook of Stress and Health: A Guide to Research and Practice, First Edition.
Edited by Cary L. Cooper and James Campbell Quick.
© 2017 John Wiley & Sons, Ltd. Published 2017 by John Wiley & Sons, Ltd.